Shakespeare's Tragedies

Shakespeare's
Tragedies

Edited by

David Bevington

The University of Chicago

PEARSON
Longman

New York   San Francisco   Boston
London   Toronto   Sydney   Tokyo   Singapore   Madrid
Mexico City   Munich   Paris   Cape Town   Hong Kong   Montreal

Managing Editor: Erika Berg
Development Editor: Michael Greer
Executive Marketing Manager: Ann Stypuloski
Project Coordination and Electronic Page Makeup: Electronic Publishing Services Inc., NYC
Cover Designer/Manager: Wendy Ann Fredericks
Cover Art: Ophelia wearing garlands, 1842; Redgrave, Richard, 1804–88, English; The Art Archive/Victoria and Albert Museum
    London/Sally Chappell.
Manufacturing Buyer: Lucy Hebard
Printer and Binder: Hamilton Printing Co.
Cover Printer: Lehigh Press, Inc.

About the cover:
Ophelia Weaving Her Garlands, an 1842 oil painting by English painter Richard Redgrave (1804–1888), is often praised for its psychological insight. Now displayed in the Victoria and Albert Museum in London, it was originally exhibited accompanied by these lines from *Hamlet:* "There is a willow grows askannt the brook / That shows his hoar leaves in the glassy stream; / Therewith fantastic garlands did she make / Of crowflowers, nettles, daisies, and long purples" (4.7.167-70).

The Library of Congress has cataloged the single volume, hardcover edition as follows:
Shakespeare, William, 1564–1616.
    [Works. 2003]
    The complete works of Shakespeare / edited by David Bevington.—5th ed.
        p. cm.
    Includes bibliographical references and index.
    ISBN 0-321-09333-X
    I. Bevington, David M. II. Title.
PR2754.B4 2003
822.3'3—dc21   2003045975

Please visit us at http://www.ablongman.com

ISBN 0-321-36628-X

1 2 3 4 5 6 7 8 9 10—HT—09 08 07 06

CONTENTS

Preface   vi

PREFACE

I have had the extraordinary privilege of editing and reediting *The Complete Works of Shakespeare* throughout my career as teacher and scholar, beginning in the early 1970s. The work is now in its fifth edition. Each new edition has, I hope, made advances in thoroughness and accuracy. Now seems a good time to publish that edition in four separate volumes. Shakespeare was such a prolific writer that the single-volume edition is heavy and hard to carry around. At the same time, his work can be conveniently and logically divided into four volumes of more or less equal size: the comedies, the English history plays, the tragedies, and the late romances combined with the poems and sonnets. These units can lend themselves well to classroom use or to general reading: sometimes courses in Shakespeare focus during one term on the comedies and histories, and during another on the tragedies and late romances, whereas more general courses in literary study and appreciation may sometimes choose to study the sonnets, or a few particular plays.

My hope is that this four-volume edition, with each volume separately available, can offer to students and general readers an unusually flexible and accessible anthology for study, for pleasure, and for continued reference.

KEY FEATURES OF THE FOUR-VOLUME PORTABLE EDITION

- **Flexible arrangement in volumes of convenient size,** grouped according to genres of comedy, history, tragedy, and romances and poems.

- **Thoroughly revised and updated notes and glosses** provide contemporary readers the support they need to understand Elizabethan language and idioms in accessible and clear modern language, line by line.
- **A richly illustrated general introduction** provides readers with the historical and cultural background required to understand Shakespeare's works in context.
- **Significantly revised introductory essays on each of the plays and poems** offer new insight into major themes, cultural issues, and critical conflicts.
- **Updated appendices** include the most recent information on sources, textual choices, performance history, dating of the works, and bibliographic resources.

From the start of my editing career I have aimed at explaining difficult passages, not just single words, keeping in mind the questions that readers might ask as to possible meanings. In undertaking the latest revision I was astonished to discover how extensively I have wanted to rewrite the commentary notes. The present edition incorporates many such changes. Some notes I had written seemed to me just plain wrong; many others seemed to me in need of greater clarity and accessibility. I have been both abashed to see how much improvement was necessary and grateful to be able to profit from my own experience with these texts in the classroom.

Issues of post-colonialism, gender relations, ethnic conflict, attitudes toward war and politics, ambiguities of language, the canon, dating, multiple authorship, and textual revision have been on the march since the early 1980s especially. These are heady times in which to attempt to practice literary criticism. Introductory essays need to be open to recent as well as more traditional critical approaches; they should open up issues for examination rather than offer pronouncements. I have listened carefully to reviewers who have occasionally found my introductions to earlier editions too confident of my own reading of the plays and poems. I have attempted to make an important correction in this matter, especially by adding some examples of production history and recent criticism that offer radically different readings of the dramatic texts. A teaching text should ask questions and offer the reader alternative possibilities. Discussion of recent film and stage history can enhance our appreciation of the plays in performance while at the same time enriching possibilities of interpretation.

This edition differs from other currently available editions of the *Complete Works* in being presented from the viewpoint of a single editor. That is at once its strength and no doubt its weakness. The viewpoint is, I would venture to say, a moderate and inclusive one, deeply interested in new critical approaches while also attuned to the kinds of responses that Shakespeare has evoked in past generations. I like the fact that this edition began in the Middle West, in Chicago, and that it serves a host of colleges and universities many of which are also in the great heartland of America. This edition attempts to be middle American, intended for a broad spectrum of educational uses and for private enjoyment as well.

I hope that the potential hubris of a single editorship is significantly ameliorated by the way in which this edition, like its predecessors, has made extensive use of editorial consultants. Each consultant was asked to respond to a particular play or work, including the notes and commentary. Many of the responses have been extraordinary and have sharpened issues I could never have addressed sufficiently on my own. The consultants, listed in the front of the book, are experts not only in Shakespeare studies but in the particular work I asked them to consider. I am deeply grateful for their help. Lois Potter, originally asked to serve as a consultant on performance history, presented so many suggestions that Longman and I asked her to write a new essay on the subject.

A BRIEF GUIDE TO THE EDITORIAL PRACTICES AND STYLE USED IN THIS EDITION

The running title at the top of each page of text gives the Through Line Numbers (TLN) of each play based on the *Norton First Folio of Shakespeare*. That facsimile of the original provides line numberings throughout, one number for each line of type. The advantage of this system is that it is universal, applying to all editions whether new or old. Such editions vary in line numbering depending on how the text is divided into scenes and how prose is numbered in columns of varying width. Because the TLN system is truly universal it is often used by textual scholars.

Line numbers in the text indicate that a gloss is to be found at the foot of the column for some word or phrase in the line in question.

Stage directions in square brackets are editorially added. Those without brackets, or in parentheses, are from the original Folio or Quarto text. The same is true of the numberings of acts and scenes.

The notes indicate the place of each scene. These indications should not be read as meaning that the stage needs to "look" like a particular street or house or room. Shakespeare's plays were acted essentially without scenery, as is often the case today. The indications of place are meant solely to give the reader information on the imagined location, as those locations can shift quite rapidly.

When the scansion of verse requires that vowels are to receive a syllable they would not normally receive, the vowel in question is marked with an accent grave. Thus, "lovèd" is to be pronounced in two syllables, "lov-ed." When the word has no such accented vowel it should receive the normal pronunciation. These markings normally correspond with a similar system in the original Folio and Quarto texts, although in those texts "loved" is normally bisyllabic, whereas "lov'd" is monosyllabic.

In the commentary notes, capitalization and end punctuation of each note is determined by how the paraphrase in the note fits into the Shakespearean text it represents. If the phrase being glossed begins a sentence, the note will begin with a capital letter, and correspondingly with end punctuation. The idea here is to make the paraphrase as smoothly compatible with the text as possible.

Any reader interested in further discussion on modernizing of spelling is invited to consult the Preface of the fourth updated edition.

ACKNOWLEDGMENTS

I am grateful to the reviewers who made numerous suggestions for improvements in this new edition. For their detailed and thoughtful suggestions, I would like to thank the following: Nick Barker, Covenant College, Lookout Mountain, Georgia; Celia A. Easton, SUNY Geneseo; Peter Greenfield, University of Puget Sound; Glenn Hopp, Howard Payne University; George Justice, Louisiana State University; Joseph Tate, University of Washington; Ann Tippett, Monroe Community College; Lewis Walker, University of North Carolina, Wilmington; Robert F. Wilson Jr., University of Missouri, Kansas City; and David Wilson-Okamura, East Carolina University.

A number of faculty were generous enough to respond to a survey we conducted to learn more about the undergraduate Shakespeare course market today. Thanks to the following for providing guidance and information: Mark Aune, North Dakota State University; Douglas A. Brooks, Texas A & M University; Robert Cirasa, Kean University; Bill Dynes, University of Indianapolis; Lisa Freinkel, University of Oregon; John Hagge, Iowa State University; Ritchie D. Kendall, University of North Carolina, Chapel Hill; Robert Levine, Boston University; Allen Michie, Iowa State University; Neil Nakadate, Iowa State University; Bonnie Nelson, Kansas State University; Robert O'Brien, California State University, Chico; Arlene Okerlund, San Jose State University; George Rowe, University of Oregon; Lisa S. Starks, University of South Florida; and Nathaniel Wallace, South Carolina State University.

I want to acknowledge a special debt of gratitude to the editorial advisory board members, who provided detailed suggestions on the plays, commentaries, notes, and appendixes. The names of our editorial consultants are listed facing the title page.

Lois Potter of the University of Delaware went far beyond the call of duty by completely rewriting Appendix 3 on Shakespeare in Performance. That her work was done under intense deadline pressure makes the achievement of her wonderful and learned essay all the more impressive.

SUPPLEMENTS

The following supplements are available free when ordered with this text. Please consult your local Longman representative if you would like to set up a value pack.

Evaluating a Performance, **by Mike Greenwald,** informs students about stage and theatrical performance and helps them to become more critical viewers of dramatic productions (ISBN 0-321-09541-3).

Screening Shakespeare: Using Film to Understand the Plays, **by Michael Greer,** is a brief, practical guide to select feature films of the most commonly taught plays (ISBN 0-321-19479-9).

Shakespeare: Script, Stage, Screen, **by David Bevington, Anne Marie Welsh, and Michael L. Greenwald,** is an edition designed for the teaching of Shakespeare plays most usefully studied in these contexts, with extensive discussions and commentary on stage and screen adaptations (ISBN 0-321-19813-1).

I would be most grateful if you would bring to my attention any errors you find. Such errors can be corrected in a subsequent printing. My e-mail address is bevi@uchicago.edu.

David Bevington

GENERAL INTRODUCTION

THE TRAGEDIES

When Shakespeare's plays were first published in a one-volume complete edition in the so-called First Folio of 1623, seven years after his death, they were grouped by the editors into three categories: comedies, histories, and tragedies. Out of a total of thirty-six plays (*Pericles* was omitted from this collection), eleven are listed as tragedies. Yet what is meant by "tragedies" turns out to be more complicated than one might at first suppose.

No doubt we would all agree that *Hamlet, Othello, King Lear,* and *Macbeth* fill any conventional definition of the term; they are deservedly recognized as Shakespeare's towering achievement in the genre. Nor would most readers quarrel with calling *Titus Andronicus, Julius Caesar, Timon of Athens, Coriolanus,* and *Antony and Cleopatra* tragedies, though we need to acknowledge that these tragedies based on ancient classical history and legend are somehow different in kind from the "great" tragedies listed above. Next, what about *Romeo and Juliet*? As Prince Escalus says at the end of that play, "never was a story of more woe / Than this of Juliet and her Romeo," and yet its first two acts are as wonderfully comic as any comedy Shakespeare ever wrote. And then *Cymbeline* is included by the Folio editors at the end of the section on "tragedies." Today, this play is universally described as one of the late romances or tragicomedies, along with *The Winter's Tale, Pericles,* and *The Tempest*. What is it doing among the tragedies? *Troilus and Cressida* is no less problematic. Printed without regular pagination between the histories and tragedies and not listed in the table of contents, it may perhaps have been regarded also as a tragedy by the Folio editors, because it ends with the deaths of Patroclus and Hector, along with the dismal collapse of the love affair for which the play is named, and is about a famous war that will end in the destruction of Troy. To a significant degree, it can be grouped with the tragedies listed above that deal with ancient classical history and legend, though it is also a bitterly satirical "dark" comedy.

To complicate the question of genre still further, several of Shakespeare's plays on English history deal with tragic events, and are sometimes called tragedies on their title pages: *The Tragedy of King Richard the Third* (Quarto edition of 1597), *The Tragedy of Richard the Second* (Quarto of the same year), *The True Tragedy of Richard Duke of York and the Death of Good King Henry the Sixth* (Octavo version, 1595, of *Henry VI, Part III*). *The Life and Death of King John*, first appearing in the 1623 Folio, ends with the death of that king. In that same Folio volume, *Richard II* and *Richard III* are similarly entitled *The Life and Death of Richard the Second* and *The Life and Death of Richard the Third*. The terms of genre are flexible throughout the Shakespeare canon and require further definition.

Even the unquestionably "great" tragedies at the heart of Shakespeare's achievement in tragedy are of various kinds. *Othello* and *Macbeth* are perhaps good places to begin, because they may best seem to fulfill the classical idea of tragedy embodied in Aristotle's *Poetics.* Each centers on a tragic protagonist who is of noble stature; Othello is descended from kings, and Macbeth is a Scottish nobleman who becomes king. Each has admirable qualities of courage, poetic sensitivity, charisma, and an awareness of the difference between good and evil. Yet each succumbs to an inner weakness: jealousy in Othello's case, ambition in Macbeth's. Each is aware of the immeasurable cost of succumbing to that weakness. Othello knows only too well that his happiness will be destroyed with the loss of Desdemona; Macbeth is painfully aware that the killing of the good King Duncan is a heinous crime that will demand reprisal both in this world and the next. This knowledge does not prevent the tragic fall of these protagonists. Thus, although we must allow for substantial adjustments in the vast cultural differences between Aristotle's Athens and Shakespeare's England, Othello and Macbeth appear to be more or less consistent with Aristotle's famous definition of tragedy. The tragic protagonist, according to Aristotle, should be neither an entirely virtuous person nor a truly wicked person who suffers grievous misfortune; in the first instance we will be repelled by the injustice, whereas in the second instance we will have no reason to experience pity for one who is pitiless or fear of the consequences in the case of one who deserves what he gets. Instead, the tragic protagonist should be "a man who is neither a paragon of virtue and justice nor undergoes the change to misfortune through any real badness or wickedness, but because of some mistake." "Mistake" is here a translation of that much-disputed term, *hamartia*, sometimes rendered as "tragic flaw" but more nearly a failure or mistake. As applied to Othello or Macbeth, one could indeed argue that a "tragic flaw" is at work, because both of these plays analyze the moral choices of the protagonists in a Christian context that defines the failure in terms of good and evil; as Macbeth says of the crime he is about to commit, King Duncan's virtues "Will plead like angels, trumpet-tongued, against / The deep damnation of his taking-off" (1.7.18–20). Classical Greek *hamartia* does not define itself in terms of good and evil, but rather of pollution and shame. Still, Othello and Macbeth are, in an approximate sense, Aristotelian tragic protagonists in that their stories are "imitative of fearful and pitiable happenings" containing the necessary ingredients of *peripety* or reversal of fortune and an accompanying *anagnorisis* or recognition of the meaning of the tragic event, a "shift from ignorance to awareness."

When we look at Shakespeare's other great tragedies, however, we soon realize that he cared little for Aristotle's rules, and that other models of tragedy beg to be recognized. *Hamlet* is often analyzed as though it centers around a "tragic flaw," with *hamartia* used in that distorted sense in order to explain Hamlet's tragedy. If one approaches the play from an Aristotelian perspective, expecting to find a *hamartia* as the fulfillment of the Aristotelian definition, one will of course find something. The usual candidate is Hamlet's purported delay in carrying out the revenge his father's ghost has ordered him to accomplish. Hamlet knows he must kill Claudius, but is held back by his own melancholy or scholarly indecisiveness, or by a psychological reluctance to kill his uncle for doing the very thing he, Hamlet, unconsciously longs to do, that is, to possess the mother for himself; so runs the neo-Aristotelian line of reasoning. But Shakespeare is in no sense bound by Aristotelian definition, and in the play itself Hamlet has very cogent reasons for not proceeding rashly to act on his father's command; the play abounds in instances showing him (and us) that unconsidered rash action (such as the killing of Polonius, or Laertes's plotting to assassinate Hamlet) can lead to unintended and disastrous result. Action is truly problematic in *Hamlet*, and to that important extent Hamlet is better understood as a good man dealing with a world in moral collapse than as someone who is pulled down by an internal flaw. At the very least, one should approach this play with a profound skepticism as to whether Aristotle's ideas about *hamartia* really apply.

King Lear challenges an Aristotelian reading in still other ways. To begin with, it has a richly elaborated double plot, one centering on Lear and his three daughters, the other on the Earl of Gloucester and his two sons. Although Shakespeare often employs double plotting in writing comedy, in tragedy it is strikingly unusual. *King Lear* enables the two plots to speak to each other in truly eloquent ways, as when the madness of Lear is counterpointed by the blinding of Gloucester; and the two plots are expertly interwoven, as in Shakespearean comedy. As a result, what may be the greatest of all Shakespeare's tragedies seems unconcerned with the Aristotelian dictum that "tragedy is an imitation of an action which is complete and whole and has some magnitude . . . 'Whole' is that which has beginning, middle, and end." This definition has been taken to mean that tragedy should have only one plot, as demonstrated in the Greek tragedy that Aristotle regarded as the greatest exemplar of the genre, Sophocles's *Oedipus the King. King Lear* does not subject itself to that classical tragic definition. Furthermore, in both its plots *King Lear* subjects the tragic protagonists to such terrifying injustice as to wipe from the record any sense in which a "tragic flaw" or "mistake" can be seen to account for their tragic falls. True enough, Lear is ungovernably choleric and Gloucester fatally gullible, but that does not help us understand how humanity could be capable of the cruelty that brings these two old men to madness and despair. As Lear justly laments, "I am a man / More sinned against than sinning" (3.2.59–60).

Shakespeare's tragedies based on classical history and legend are no less varied in their self-presentations as tragedy. Shakespeare was a pragmatic man of the theater, who wrote what worked for his audiences. *Titus Andronicus* is a revenge play in the mode of Thomas Kyd's influential *The Spanish Tragedy* (c. 1583–7), full of violent plots and deaths, and to a significant extent anticipating *Hamlet*, which, among its other tragic features, is also a revenge play in an enduringly popular genre on the Elizabethan stage. *Julius Caesar* is sometimes analyzed in Aristotelian terms as the tragedy of Brutus, who does indeed make what one can define as a tragic mistake in pridefully allowing himself to be seduced into become the chief conspirator against Caesar, but such a reading of the play ignores the sense in which it anomalously features dual protagonists in Brutus and Caesar, not to mention Cassius. *Timon of Athens* is perhaps best classified as a moral satire against human greed and ingratitude; though the protagonist is suitably a good man with the amiable weaknesses of excessive generosity and trustingness of his fellow Athenians, his descent into bitter misanthropy is more an indictment of a pervasive moral corruption than a study in *hamartia*. *Coriolanus* is perhaps the most Aristotelian of these classical plays, because its chief figure, Coriolanus himself, is a nobly courageous soldier whose intemperate despising of Rome's plebeians and their tribunes undoes all that his political allies had hoped to accomplish through his leadership, but even here the force of sentiment is more directed against the absurdities of political conflict than against the man who is finally victimized by the impasses that Rome cannot reconcile.

Romeo and Juliet and *Antony and Cleopatra,* one early in Shakespeare's career and one quite late, are love tragedies centered in each instance on a pair of lovers. The result is dual protagonists, not recognizably in the Aristotelian mold. *Romeo and Juliet* defies Aristotelian convention in almost every possible way. Aristotle urges that a tragic protagonist should be "better than average," both morally and socially; Greek tragedy deals with the lives of kings and princes, whereas comedy should be "an imitation of persons who are inferior" in the sense of being on a social level with members of the audience. Romeo and Juliet are perfect for comedy. They come from respectable and even wealthy families, but not from the ruling class; they are interesting to us as young lovers, not as political figures. Their falling in love is much like that of Orlando and Rosalind in *As You Like It*, or Hermia and Lysander in *A Midsummer Night's Dream*, or Claudio and Hero in *Much Ado About Nothing*. As in those plays, falling in love is seen as a delicious kind of madness. The tribulations faced by Romeo and Juliet are those of lovers in romantic comedy generally: parental opposition to what young lovers desire. The world appears to be hostile to young love, in comedy as in *Romeo and Juliet*, and indeed one can think of this love-

ly tragedy as a working out in tragic terms of the very difficulties that young lovers must face everywhere. In comedy, they are rescued from their plight and are joined in marriage at the end; in *Romeo and Juliet*, that happiness is thwarted by a kind of destiny they cannot escape. "Then I defy you, stars!" cries Romeo (5.1.24) as he prepares to find Juliet in her tomb and take his own life rather than be separated from her in death. Romeo does, to be sure, bring on his own misfortune to a significant extent by killing Juliet's cousin Tybalt as a reprisal for the death of Mercutio, but to see *Romeo and Juliet* as an Aristotelian tragedy centered around this event as Romeo's *hamartia* is to lose sight of a larger vision of tragic waste. The lovers die because they are too hasty, of course, especially Romeo, but they also die because social conflicts and insensitivities have made it impossible for them to come together as they wish. They are "Poor sacrifices of our enmity," as Juliet's father Capulet sadly admits (5.3.304). In this sense *Romeo and Juliet* is a tragedy of sacrifice. So is *Hamlet*, in a way, and the idea of sacrifice applies poignantly as well to the deaths of Ophelia, Desdemona, Cordelia, and still others.

If one asks Aristotelian questions of *Antony and Cleopatra,* as many classically trained scholars have done, one is apt to conclude that the play is the tragedy of Antony. He is, in the Aristotelian sense, a great man whose fatal weakness for Cleopatra undoes all that he has accomplished in his lustrous career as soldier and triumvir. Plutarch's estimate of Antony, in the biography of this man that Shakespeare used as his chief source for his play, is of a truly great warrior whose fall into sexual enervation, however understandable, is an object lesson that other men should heed. Cleopatra is an incredibly attractive woman, as Plutarch sees her, but all the more reason for a noble Roman to be wary and true to his calling as a leader. Yet such a reading does serious injustice to Shakespeare's play. If Antony is to be seen as the Aristotelian flawed tragic hero, then the fifth act becomes little more than an afterthought; Antony has killed himself by this time, leaving the scene to Cleopatra. Surely a more balanced reading of the play will restore her to equal billing as dual protagonist. To recognize this necessity is also to see that Cleopatra is an entirely different sort of tragic protagonist, one whose story ends in death but also in a triumph of her personal greatness in calling Octavius Caesar "ass / Unpolicied" (5.2.307–8). Cleopatra suffers a reversal of fortune, but not with the kind of *anagnorisis* or recognition that comes to Antony as to other tragic heroes; Cleopatra is who she is from first to last, and in a crucial sense she beats great Caesar at his own game.

Correspondingly, the play asks us to ponder the impoverishment of the human spirit required if one is determined to become like Caesar, hugely successful in geopolitical terms but something of a failure as a man. He is calculating, shrewd, implacable, and deeply fearful of any impulse toward erotic or sybaritic pleasure. His great dream is to contain Cleopatra and degrade her by taking her captive to Rome. She will not allow that. Her fifth-act vision of what it means to love grandly on the scale that Antony and Cleopatra have attempted is finally so exalted that the sheer poetry of it casts into relative insignificance the military defeat that the lovers have suffered. In these terms, *Antony and Cleopatra* frees itself triumphantly from any classical restrictions of the genre. Its very temporal and geographical scale is equally generous, covering as it does the history of Rome from 41 BC down to the lovers' suicides in 30 BC and moving repeatedly back and forth from Egypt to Rome, southern Italy, Sicily, Athens, and the Middle East. Such is Shakespeare's disregard for the often-repeated neo-Aristotelian formula, not actually enunciated in the *Poetics* but perhaps implied by Aristotle's call for a unified tragic plot, that a play should limit its action to twenty-four hours and to a single location! Similarly, Antony is so ennobled by Cleopatra's loving admiration for him that he becomes much more than Plutarch's Aristotelian protagonist brought low by a tragic mistake or error; he is the immortal partner of Cleopatra, remembered forever in Shakespeare's dramatic poetry as one who transcends human failure.

Shakespeare's conception of tragedy is thus, above all, flexible, changing, not confined by classical definition. It varies its sense of genre to fit each particular story and to suit the purposes of a great dramatist in moving his audiences to pity, fear, and understanding.

Cymbeline is "tragic" to the degree that it deals with a weighty subject and with noble and royal characters. Like some other comedies that introduce the threat of evil, such as *The Merchant of Venice, Much Ado About Nothing,* and especially *Measure for Measure, Cymbeline* contains potentially tragic depictions of human failure and unhappiness, most notably in the tortured soliloquies of Posthumus Leonatus when that young protagonist suffers the unbearable pangs of sexual jealousy and is subsequently convinced that he has ordered the death of his virtuous wife. The killing of the Queen's son, Cloten, by one of Imogen's brothers seems more in keeping with tragedy than comedy, even if Cloten is a thoroughly repulsive character. Yet *Cymbeline* follows a tragicomic story line that ends eventually in forgiveness and a restored happiness. It is grouped today among Shakespeare's late romances, and is accordingly placed in the present edition with *Pericles, The Winter's Tale,* and *The Tempest.*

LIFE IN SHAKESPEARE'S ENGLAND

England during Shakespeare's lifetime (1564–1616) was a proud nation with a strong sense of national identity, but it was also a small nation by modern standards. Probably not more than five million people lived in the whole of England, considerably fewer than now live in London. England's territories in France were no longer extensive, as they had been during the fourteenth century and earlier; in fact, by the end of Queen Elizabeth's reign (1558–1603), England had virtually retired from the territories she had previously controlled on the Continent, especially in France. Wales was a conquered principality. England's overseas empire in America had scarcely begun, with the Virginia settlement established in the 1580s. Scotland was not yet a part of Great Britain; union with Scotland would not take place until 1707, despite the fact that King James VI of Scotland assumed the English throne in 1603 as James I of England. Ireland, although declared a kingdom under English rule in 1541, was more a source of trouble than of economic strength. The last years of Elizabeth's reign, especially from 1597 to 1601, were plagued by the rebellion of the Irish under Hugh O'Neill, Earl of Tyrone. Thus, England of the sixteenth and early seventeenth centuries was both small and isolated.

THE SOCIAL AND ECONOMIC BACKGROUND

By and large, England was a rural land. Much of the kingdom was still wooded, though timber was being used increasingly in manufacturing and shipbuilding. The area of the Midlands, today heavily industrialized, was at that time still a region of great trees, green fields, and clear streams. England's chief means of livelihood was agriculture. This part of the economy was generally in a bad way, however, and people who lived off the land did not share in the prosperity of many Londoners. A problem throughout the sixteenth century was that of "enclosure": the conversion by rich landowners of croplands into pasturage. Farmers and peasants complained bitterly that they were being dispossessed and starved for the benefit of livestock. Rural uprisings and food riots were common, to the dismay of the authorities. Some Oxfordshire peasants arose in 1596, threatening to massacre the gentry and march on London; other riots had occurred in 1586 and 1591. There were thirteen riots in Kent alone during Elizabeth's reign. Unrest continued into the reign of James I, notably the Midlands' rising of 1607. Although the government did what it could to inhibit enclosure, the economic forces at work were too massive and too inadequately understood to be curbed by governmental fiat. The absence of effective bureaucracies or agencies of coercion compounded the difficulty of governmental control. Pasture used large areas with greater efficiency than crop farming, and required far less labor. The wool produced by the pasturing of sheep was needed in ever increasing amounts for the manufacture of cloth.

BY PERMISSION OF THE FOLGER SHAKESPEARE LIBRARY

"Enclosure" was a problem throughout the sixteenth century in England. Crop lands were converted into pasturage. The livelihood of the plowman was threatened by the pasturing of sheep and the growing production of wool.

The wool industry also experienced occasional economic difficulties, to be sure; overexpansion in the early years of the sixteenth century created a glutted market that collapsed disastrously in 1551, producing widespread unemployment. Despite such fluctuations and reversals, however, the wool industry at least provided handsome profits for some landowners and middlemen. Mining and manufacture in coal, iron, tin, copper, and lead, although insignificant by modern standards, also were expanding at a significant rate. Trading companies exploited the rich new resources of the Americas, as well as of eastern Europe and the Orient. Queen Elizabeth aided economic development by keeping England out of war with her continental enemies as long as possible, despite provocations from those powers and despite the eagerness of some of her advisers to retaliate.

Certainly England's economic condition was better than the economic condition of the rest of the Continent; an Italian called England "the land of comforts." Yet although some prosperity did exist, it was not evenly distributed. Especially during Shakespeare's first years in London, in the late 1580s and the 1590s, the gap between rich and poor grew more and more extreme. Elizabeth's efforts at peacemaking were no longer able to prevent years of war with the Catholic powers of the Continent. Taxation grew heavier, and inflation proceeded at an unusually rapid rate during this period. A succession of bad harvests compounded the miseries of those who dwelled on the land. When the hostilities on the Continent ceased for a time in about 1597, a wave of returning

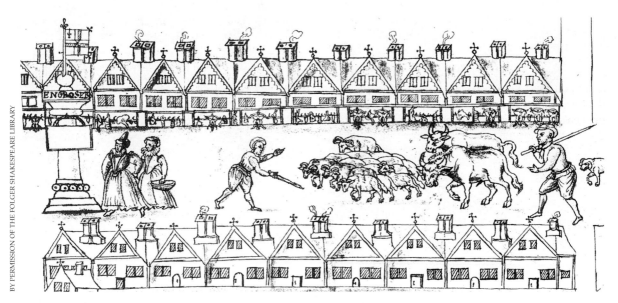

BY PERMISSION OF THE FOLGER SHAKESPEARE LIBRARY

Sixteenth-century London was a city teeming with activity. Pedestrians were often forced to make way for the livestock being driven through the streets.

veterans added to unemployment and crime. The rising prosperity experienced by Shakespeare and other fortunate Londoners was undeniably real, but it was not universal. Nowhere was the contrast between rich and poor more visible than in London.

London

Sixteenth-century London was at once more attractive and less attractive than twenty-first-century London. It was full of trees and gardens; meadows and cultivated lands reached in some places to its very walls. Today we can perhaps imagine the way in which it bordered clear streams and green fields when we approach from a distance some noncommercial provincial city such as Lincoln, York, or Hereford. Partly surrounded by its ancient wall, London was by no means a large metropolis. With

190,000 to 200,000 inhabitants in the city proper and its suburbs, it was nonetheless the largest city of Europe, and its dominance among English cities was even more striking; in 1543–1544, London paid thirty times the subsidy of Norwich, then the second-largest city in the kingdom (15,000 inhabitants). Although London's population had expanded into the surrounding area in all directions, the city proper stretched along the north bank of the Thames River from the old Tower of London on the east to St. Paul's Cathedral and the Fleet Ditch on the west—a distance of little more than a mile. Visitors approaching London from the south bank of the Thames (the Bankside) and crossing London Bridge could see virtually all of this exciting city lying before them. London Bridge itself was one of the major attractions of the city, lined with shops and richly decorated on occasion for the triumphal entry of a king or queen.

Yet London had its grim and ugly side as well. On London Bridge could sometimes be seen the heads of executed traitors. The city's houses were generally small and crowded; its streets were often narrow and filthy. In the absence of sewers, open ditches in the streets served to collect and carry off refuse. Frequent epidemics of the bubonic plague were the inevitable result of unsanitary

This detail from a 1572 map of London shows closely packed buildings intersected with throroughfares, with gardens and open spaces on the outskirts.

COURTESY, GUILDHALL LIBRARY, CORPORATION OF LONDON

London Bridge, lined with shops, houses, and severed heads on poles, provided a colorful route for those traveling between the north and south banks of the Thames. A number of Elizabethan theaters, including the Globe, were located on the south bank.

BY PERMISSION OF THE FOLGER SHAKESPEARE LIBRARY

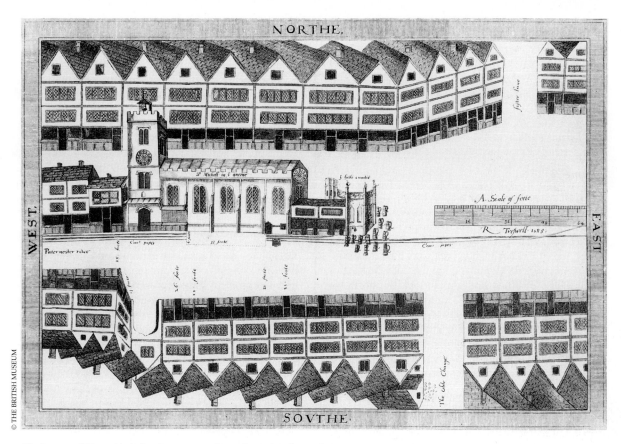

The taverns of Cheapside in London were popular and occasionally rowdy.

conditions and medical ignorance. Lighting of the streets at night was generally nonexistent, and the constabulary was notoriously unreliable. Shakespeare gives us unforgettable satires of night watchmen and bumbling police officials in *Much Ado About Nothing* (Dogberry and the night watch) and *Measure for Measure* (Constable Elbow). Prostitution thrived in the suburbs, conveniently located, although beyond the reach of the London authorities. Again, we are indebted to Shakespeare for a memorable portrayal in *Measure for Measure* of just such a demimonde (Mistress Overdone the bawd, Pompey her pimp, and various customers). Houses of prostitution were often found in the vicinity of the public theaters, since the theaters also took advantage of suburban locations to escape the stringent regulations imposed by London's Lord Mayor and Council of Aldermen. The famous Globe Theatre, for example, was on the south bank of the Thames, a short distance west of London Bridge. Another theatrical building (called simply "The Theatre"), used earlier by Shakespeare and the Lord Chamberlain's players, was located in Finsbury Fields, a short distance across Moorfields from London's northeast corner. The suburbs also housed various con games and illegal operations,

some of them brilliantly illustrated (and no doubt exaggerated) in Ben Jonson's *The Alchemist* (1610).

Roughly half of London's total population, perhaps 100,000 people, lived within its walls, and as many more in the suburbs. The royal palace of Whitehall, Westminster Abbey (then known as the Abbey Church of St. Peter), the Parliament House, and Westminster Hall were well outside London, two miles or so to the west on the Thames River. They remain today in the same location, in Westminster, although the metropolis of London has long since surrounded these official buildings.

Travel

Travel was still extremely painful and slow because of the poor condition of the roads. Highway robbers were a constant threat. (The celebrated highway robbery in Shakespeare's *1 Henry IV* takes place at Gads Hill, on the main road between London and Canterbury.) English inns seem to have been good, however, and certainly much better than the inns of the Continent. Travel on horseback was the most common method of transportation, and probably the most comfortable, since coach building was a new and imperfect art. Coaches of state, some of which we see in prints and pictures of the era, were lumbering affairs, no doubt handsome enough in processions, but springless, unwieldly, and hard to pull. Carts and wagons were used for carrying merchandise, but packsaddles were safer and quicker. Under such difficulties, no metropolitan area such as London could possibly have thrived in the interior. London depended for its commercial greatness upon the Thames River and its access to the North Sea.

Commerce

When Elizabeth came to the English throne in 1558, England's chief foreign trade was with Antwerp, Bruges, and other Belgian cities. Antwerp was an especially important market for England's export of wool cloth. This market was seriously threatened, however, since the Low Countries were under the domination of the Catholic King of Spain, Philip II. When Philip undertook to punish his Protestant subjects in the Low Countries for their religious heresy, many of Elizabeth's counselors and subjects urged her to come to the defense of England's Protestant neighbors and trading allies. Elizabeth held back. Philip's armies attacked Antwerp in 1576 and again in 1585, putting an end to the commercial ascendancy of that great northern European metropolis. Perhaps as many as one-third of Antwerp's merchants and artisans settled in London, bringing with them their expert knowledge of commerce and manufacture. The influx of so many skilled workers and merchants into London produced problems of unemployment and overcrowding but contributed nevertheless to London's emergence as a leading port of trade.

English ships assumed a dominant position in Mediterranean trade, formerly carried on mainly by the Venetians. In the Baltic Sea, England competed successfully in trade that had previously been controlled by the Hanseatic League. Bristol thrived on commerce with Ireland and subsequently on trade with the Western Hemisphere. Boston and Hull increased their business with Scandinavian ports. The Russia Company was founded in 1555; the Levant Company became the famous East India Company in 1600; and the Virginia Company opened up trade with the New World in the Western Hemisphere. Fisheries were developed in the North Sea, in the waters north of Ireland, and off the banks of Newfoundland. Elizabeth and her ministers encouraged this commercial expansion.

The Poor Laws and Apprenticeship

Despite the new prosperity experienced by many Elizabethans, especially in London, unemployment remained a serious problem. The suppresssion of the monasteries in 1536–1539, as part of Henry VIII's reformation of the Catholic Church, had dispossessed a large class of persons who were not easily reemployed. Other causes of unemployment, such as the periodic collapse of the wool trade, dispossession of farm workers by enclosure of land, the sudden influx of skilled artisans from Antwerp, and the return of army veterans, have already been mentioned. Elizabethan parliaments attempted to cope with the problem of unemployment but did so in ways that seem unduly harsh today. Several laws were passed between 1531, when the distinction between those poor needing charity and those unwilling to work first became law, and 1597–1598. The harshest of the laws was that of 1547, providing that vagabonds be branded and enslaved for two years; escape was punishable by death or life enslavement. This act was repealed in 1549, but subsequent acts of 1572 and 1576 designated ten classes of vagrants and required municipal authorities to provide work for the healthy unemployed of each town or parish. This localization of responsibility laid the basis for what has been known historically as the "poor rate" (a local tax levied for the support of the poor) and for that sinister institution, the workhouse. The provisions of this act remained in force for centuries. The most comprehensive laws were those of the Parliament of 1597–1598, which repeated many provisions of earlier acts and added harsh, punitive penalties intended to send vagabonds back to the parishes in which they had been born or had last worked. After 1597, no begging was permitted; the poor were supposed to be provided for by the "poor rate" already established.

Regulations for apprentices were no less strict. An act of Parliament of 1563, known as the Statute of Artificers, gave the craft trades of England—still organized as medieval guilds—virtually complete authority over the young persons apprenticed to a trade. The law severely limited access to apprenticeship to sons of families with

BY PERMISSION OF THE BRITISH LIBRARY

Although some Elizabethans rose to great wealth, poverty and unemployment were widespread.

estates worth at least forty shillings of income. Apprenticeship usually began between the ages of fourteen and seventeen, and lasted for a period of not less than seven years. During this time, the young worker lived with the family of the employer. Without such an extensive apprenticeship, entry into the skilled crafts was virtually impossible. Apprenticeships were not open, however, in all guilds, and the law courts subsequently ruled that apprenticeship rules did not apply to crafts developed after 1563, so that exceptions did exist. All able-bodied workers not bound to crafts were supposed to work in agriculture. Acting companies, such as the company Shakespeare joined, were not technically organized as guilds, though the boys who played women's parts were in some cases at least bound by the terms of apprenticeship; a number of the adult actors belonged to one London guild or another and could use that status to apprentice boys. We do not know whether Shakespeare actually served such an indenture before becoming a full member of his acting company.

Social Change

The opportunities for rapid economic advance in Elizabethan England, though limited almost entirely to those who were already prosperous, did produce social change and a quality of restlessness in English society. "New men" at court were an increasing phenomenon under the Tudor monarchs, especially Henry VII and Henry VIII, who tended to rely on loyal counselors of humble origin rather than on the once-too-powerful nobility. Cardinal Wolsey, for example, rose from obscurity to become the most mighty subject of Henry VIII's realm, with a newly built residence (Hampton Court) rivaling the splendor of the King's own palaces. He was detested as an upstart by old aristocrats, such as the Duke of Norfolk, and his sudden fall was as spectacular as had been his rise to power. The Earl of Leicester, Queen Elizabeth's first favorite, was a descendant of the Edmund Dudley who had risen from unpretentious beginnings to great eminence under Henry VII, Queen Elizabeth's grandfather. Although Queen Elizabeth did not contribute substantially to the new aristocracy—she created only three peers from 1573 onward—new and influential families were numerous throughout the century. Conversely, the ancient families discovered that they were no longer entrusted with positions of highest authority. To be sure, the aristocracy remained at the apex of England's social structure. New aspirants to power emulated the aristocracy by purchasing land and building splendid residences, rather than defining themselves as a rich new "middle class." Bourgeois status was something the new men put behind them as quickly as they could. Moreover, social mobility could work in both directions: upward and downward. Many men were quickly ruined by the costly and competitive business of seeking favor at the Tudor court. The poor, in a vast majority, enjoyed virtually no rights at all. Nonetheless, the Elizabethan era was one of greater opportunity for rapid social and economic advancement among persons of wealth than England had heretofore known.

Increased economic contacts with the outside world inevitably led to the importation of new styles of living. Such new fashions, together with the rapid changes now possible in social position, produced a reaction of dismay from those who feared the destruction of traditional English values. Attitudes toward Italy veered erratically between condemnation and admiration: on the one hand, Italy was the home of the Catholic Church and originator of many supposedly decadent fashions, whereas, on the other hand, Italy was the cradle of humanism and the country famed for Venice's experiment in republican government. To many conservative Englishmen, the word *Italianate* connoted a whole range of villainous practices, including diabolical methods of torture and revenge: poisoned books of devotion that would kill the unsuspecting victims who kissed them, ingeniously contrived chairs that would close upon the person who sat in them, and the like. The revenge plays of Shakespeare's contemporaries, such as *Antonio's Revenge* by John Marston, *The Revenger's Tragedy* probably by Thomas Middleton, and *The White Devil* by John Webster, offer spectacular caricatures of the so-called Italianate style in murder. The name of Italy was also associated with licentiousness, immorality, and outlandish fashions in clothes. France, too, was accused of encouraging such extravagances in dress as ornamented headdresses, stiffly pleated ruffs, padded doublets, puffed or double sleeves, and richly decorated hose. Rapid changes in fashion added to the costliness of being up to date and thereby increased the outcry against vanity in dress. Fencing, dicing, the use of cosmetics, the smoking of tobacco, the drinking of imported wines, and almost every vice known to humanity were attributed by angry moralists to the corrupting influence from abroad.

Not all Englishmen deplored continental fashion, of course. Persons of advanced taste saw the importation of European styles as a culturally liberating process. Fashion thus became a subject of debate between moral traditionalists and those who welcomed the new styles. The controversy was a bitter one, with religious overtones, in which the reformers' angry accusations became increasingly extreme. This attack on changing fashion was, in fact, an integral part of the Puritan movement. It therefore stressed the sinfulness, not only of extravagance in clothing, but also of the costliness in building great houses and other such worldly pursuits. Those whose sympathies were Puritan became more and more disaffected with the cultural values represented by the court, and thus English society drifted further and further toward irreconcilable conflict.

COURTESY, THE FOLGER SHAKESPEARE LIBRARY

This brothel scene, featuring gambling or dicing, illustrates some of the vices that were attributed to the corrupting influence from abroad.

Shakespeare's personal views on this controversy are hard to determine and do not bear importantly on his achievement as an artist. Generally, however, we can observe that his many references to changes in fashion cater neither to the avant-garde nor to reactionary traditionalists. Shakespeare's audience was, after all, a broadly national one. It included many well-informed Londoners who viewed "Italianate" fashion neither with enthusiasm nor with alarm, but with satiric laughter. Such spectators would certainly have seen the point, for example, in Mercutio's witty diatribe at the expense of the new French style in fencing. The object of his scorn is Tybalt, who, according to Mercutio, "fights as you sing prick song" and fancies himself to be "the very butcher of a silk button." "Is not this a lamentable thing," asks Mercutio rhetorically, "that we should be thus afflicted with these strange flies, these fashionmongers, these pardon-me's, who stand so much on the new form that they cannot sit at ease on the old bench?" (*Romeo and Juliet*, 2.4.20–35). In a similar vein, Shakespeare's audience would have appreciated the joking in *The Merchant of Venice* about England's servile imitation of continental styles in clothes. "What say you, then, to Falconbridge, the young baron of England?" asks Nerissa of her mistress Portia concerning one of Portia's many suitors. Portia replies, "How oddly he is suited! I think he bought his doublet in Italy, his round hose in France, his bonnet in Germany, and his behavior everywhere" (1.2.64–74). Court butterflies in Shakespeare's plays who bow and scrape and fondle their plumed headgear, like Le Beau in *As You Like It* and Osric in *Hamlet*, are the objects of ridicule. Hotspur in *1 Henry IV*, proud northern aristocrat that he is, has nothing but contempt for an effeminate courtier, "perfumèd like a milliner," who has come from King Henry to discuss the question of prisoners (1.3.36). Throughout Shakespeare's plays, the use of cosmetics generally has the negative connotation of artificial beauty used to conceal inward corruption, as in Claudius's reference to "the harlot's cheek, beautied with plast'ring art" (*Hamlet*, 3.1.52). Yet Shakespeare's treatment of newness in fashion is never shrill in tone. Nor does he fail in his dramas to give an honorable place to the ceremonial use of wealth and splendid costuming. His plays thus avoid both extremes in the controversy over changing fashions, though they give plentiful evidence as to the liveliness and currency of the topic.

Shakespeare also reflects a contemporary interest in the problem of usury, especially in *The Merchant of Venice*. Although usury was becoming more and more of a necessity, emotional attitudes toward it changed only slowly. The traditional moral view condemned usury as forbidden by Christian teaching; on the other hand, European governments of the sixteenth century found themselves increasingly obliged to borrow large sums of money. The laws against usury were alternatively relaxed and enforced, according to the economic exigencies of the moment. Shakespeare's plays capture the Elizabethan ambivalence of attitude toward this feared but necessary practice (see Introduction to *The Merchant of Venice*). Similarly, most Englishmen had contradictory attitudes toward what we today would call the law of supply and demand in the marketplace. Conservative moralists complained bitterly when merchants exploited the scarcity of some commodity by forcing up prices; the practice was denounced as excessive profit taking and declared to be sinful, like usury. In economic policy, then, as in matters of changing fashion or increased social mobility, many Englishmen were ambivalent about the perennial conflict between the old order and the new.

Elizabethan Houses

Those fortunate Englishmen who grew wealthy in the reign of Elizabeth took special pleasure in building

Tudor mansions were often splendid, with impressive gardens and terraces. Shown here is Little Moreton Hall, in Cheshire, built in 1559.

themselves fine new houses with furnishings to match. Chimneys were increasingly common, so that smoke no longer had to escape through a hole in the roof. Pewter, or even silver dishes, took the place of the wooden spoon and trencher. Beds, and even pillows, became common. Carpets were replacing rushes as covering for the floors; wainscoting, tapestries or hangings, and pictures appeared on the walls; and glass began to be used extensively for windows.

Despite the warnings of those moralists who preached against the vanity of worldly acquisition, domestic comfort made considerable progress in Elizabethan England. Many splendid Tudor mansions stand today, testifying to the important social changes that had taken place between the strife-torn fifteenth century and the era of relative peace under Elizabeth. The battlement, the moat, the fortified gate, and the narrow window used for archery or firearms generally disappeared in favor of handsome gardens and terraces. At the lower end of the social scale, the agricultural laborers who constituted the great mass of the English population were generally poor, malnourished, and uneducated, but they seem to have enjoyed greater physical security than did their ancestors

in the fifteenth century, and no longer needed to bring their cows, pigs, and poultry into their dwellings at night in order to protect them from thieves. City houses, of which many exist today, were often large and imposing structures, three or four stories in height, and framed usually of strong oak with the walls filled in with brick and plaster. Although the frontage on the streets of London was usually narrow, many houses had trees and handsome gardens at the rear. Of course London also had its plentiful share of tenements for the urban poor.

With the finer houses owned by the fortunate elite came features of privacy that had been virtually unknown to previous generations. Life in the household of a medieval lord had generally focused on the great hall, which could serve variously as the kitchen, dining hall, and sitting room for the entire family and its retainers. The men drank in the hall in the evenings and slept there at night. The new dwellings of prosperous Elizabethans, on the other hand, featured private chambers into which the family and the chief guests could retire.

The Elizabethans built well. Not only do we still admire their houses, but also we can see from their oriel windows and stained glass, their broad staircases, their jewels, and their costumes that they treasured the new beauty of their lives made possible by the culture of the Renaissance. Although the graphic and plastic arts did not thrive in England to the same extent as in Italy, France, and the Low Countries, England made lasting achievements in architecture, as well as in music, drama, and all forms of literature.

THE POLITICAL AND RELIGIOUS BACKGROUND

England under the Tudors suffered from almost unceasing religious conflict. The battle over religion affected every aspect of life and none more so than politics. At the very beginning of the Tudor reign, to be sure, England's problem was not religious but dynastic. Henry VII, the first of the Tudor kings, brought an end to the devastating civil wars of the fifteenth century with his overthrow of Richard III at the battle of Bosworth Field in 1485. The civil wars thus ended were the so-called Wars of the Roses, between the Lancastrian House of Henry VI (sym-

bolized by the red rose) and the Yorkist House of Edward IV (symbolized by the white rose). Shakespeare chose these eventful struggles as the subject for his first series of English history plays, from *Henry VI* in three parts to *Richard III*. The House of Lancaster drew its title from John of Gaunt, Duke of Lancaster, father of Henry IV and great-grandfather of Henry VI; the House of York drew its title from Edmund Langley, Duke of York, great-grandfather of Edward IV and Richard III. Because John of Gaunt and Edmund Langley had been brothers, virtually all the noble contestants in this War of the Roses were cousins of one another, caught in a remorseless dynastic struggle for control of the English crown. Many of them lost their lives in the fighting. By 1485, England was exhausted from civil conflict. Although Henry VII's own dynastic claim to the throne was weak, he managed to suppress factional opposition and to give England the respite from war so desperately needed. His son, Henry VIII, inherited a throne in 1509 that was more secure than it had been in nearly a century.

On Sundays crowds gathered to listen to the sermon at St. Paul's Cathedral, the subject of this anonymous painting dated 1616.

Henry VIII's notorious marital difficulties, however, soon brought an end to dynastic security and civil accord. Moreover, religious conflict within the Catholic Church was growing to the extent that a break with Rome appeared inevitable. Henry's marriage troubles precipitated that momentous event. Because he divorced his first wife, Katharine of Aragon, in 1530 without the consent of Rome, he was excommunicated by the pope. His response in 1534 was to have himself proclaimed "Protector and only Supreme Head of the Church and Clergy of England." This decisive act signaled the beginning of the Reformation in England, not many years after Martin Luther's momentous break with the papacy in 1517 and the consequent beginning of Lutheran Protestantism on the Continent. In England, Henry's act of defiance split the Church and the nation. Many persons chose Sir Thomas More's path of martyrdom rather than submit to Henry's new title as supreme head of the English church. Henry's later years did witness a period of retrenchment in religion, after the downfall of Thomas Cromwell in 1540, and indeed Henry's break with Rome had had its origin in political and marital strife as well as in matters of dogma and liturgy. Nevertheless, the establishment of an English church was now an accomplished fact. The accession of Henry's ten-year-old son Edward VI in 1547 gave reformers an opportunity to bring about rapid changes in English Protestantism. Archbishop Cranmer's forty-two articles of religion (1551) and his prayer book laid the basis for the Anglican Church of the sixteenth century.

The death of the sickly Edward VI in 1553 brought with it an intense crisis in religious politics and a temporary reversal of England's religious orientation. The Duke of Northumberland, Protector and virtual ruler of England in Edward's last years, attempted to secure a Protestant succession and his own power by marrying his son to Lady Jane Grey, a granddaughter of Henry VII, whom Edward had named heir to the throne, but the proclamation of Lady Jane as Queen ended in failure. She was executed, as were her husband and father-in-law. For five years, England returned to Catholicism under the rule of Edward's elder sister Mary, daughter of the Catholic Queen Katharine of Aragon. The crisis accompanying such changes of government during this midcentury period was greatly exacerbated by the fact that all three of Henry VIII's living children were considered illegitimate by one faction or another of the English people. In Protestant eyes, Mary was the daughter of the divorced Queen Katharine, whose marriage to Henry had never been valid because she had previously been the spouse of Henry VIII's older brother Arthur. This Arthur had died at a young age, in 1502, shortly after his state marriage to the Spanish princess. If, as the Protestants insisted, Arthur had consummated the marriage, then Katharine's subsequent union with her deceased husband's brother was invalid, and Henry was free, instead, to marry Anne Boleyn—the mother-to-be of Elizabeth. In Catholic eyes, however, both Elizabeth and her brother Edward VI (son of Jane Seymour, Henry VIII's third wife) were the bastard issue of Henry's bigamous marriages; Henry's one and only true marriage in the Catholic faith was that to Katharine of Aragon. Edward and Elizabeth were regarded by many Catholics, at home and abroad, not only as illegitimate children, but also as illegitimate rulers, to be disobeyed and even overthrown by force. Thus, dynastic and marital conflicts became matters of grave political consequence.

Because of these struggles, Elizabeth's accession to the throne in 1558 remained an uncertainty until the last moment. Once she actually became ruler, England returned once more to the Protestant faith. Even then, tact and moderation were required to prevent open religious war. Elizabeth's genius at compromise prompted her to seek a middle position for her church, one that combined an episcopal form of church government (owing no allegiance to the pope) with an essentially traditional form of liturgy and dogma. As much as was practicable, she left matters up to individual conscience; she drew the line, however, where matters of conscience tended to "exceed their bounds and grow to be matter of faction." In practice, this meant that she did not tolerate avowed Catholics on the religious right or Protestant sects who denied the doctrine of the Trinity on the religious left. The foundation for this so-called Elizabethan compromise was the thirty-nine articles, adopted in 1563 and based in many respects upon Cranmer's forty-two articles of 1551. The compromise did not please everyone, of course, but it did achieve a remarkable degree of consensus during Elizabeth's long reign.

Queen Elizabeth and Tudor Absolutism

Elizabeth had to cope with a religiously divided nation and with extremists of both the right and the left who wished her downfall. She was a woman, in an age openly skeptical of women's ability or right to rule. Her success in dealing with such formidable odds was in large measure the result of her personal style as a monarch. Her combination of imperious will and femininity and her brilliant handling of her many contending male admirers have become legendary. She remained unmarried throughout her life, in part, at least, because marriage would have upset the delicate balance she maintained among rival groups, both foreign and domestic. Marriage would have committed her irretrievably to either one foreign nation or to one constituency at home. She chose instead to bestow her favor on certain courtiers, notably Robert Dudley (whom she elevated to be the Earl of Leicester) and, after Leicester's death in 1588, Robert

The Knights of the Garter belonged to the highest order of knighthood; many were influential courtiers and favorites of Queen Elizabeth. A masterful politician, Elizabeth remained unmarried throughout her life. A marriage would have upset the political balance and would have committed her to one foreign nation or to one constituency at home.

Devereux, second Earl of Essex. Her relationship with these men, despite her partiality to them, was marked by her outbursts of tempestuous jealousy. In addition, she relied on the staid counsel of her hard-working ministers: Lord Burghley, Sir Francis Walsingham, Burghley's son Robert Cecil, and a few others.

In her personal style as monarch, Elizabeth availed herself of the theory of absolute supremacy. Under all the Tudors, England was nominally at least an absolute monarchy in an age when many of England's greatest rivals—France, Spain, the Holy Roman Empire—were also under absolutist rule. "Absolutism" meant that the monarch served for life, could not legally be removed from office, and was normally succeeded by his eldest son—all of this bolstered by claims of divine sanction, though the claims were frequently contested. The rise of absolutism throughout Renaissance Europe was the result of an increase of centralized national power and a corresponding decrease in autonomous baronial influence. Henry VII's strong assertion of his royal authority at the expense of the feudal lords corresponded roughly in time with the ascendancy of Francis I of France (1515) and Charles V of the Holy Roman Empire (1519). Yet England had long enjoyed a tradition of rule by consensus. When Elizabeth came to the throne, England was already

in some ways a "limited" monarchy. Parliament, and especially the members of the House of Commons, claimed prerogatives of their own and were steadily gaining in both experience and power. In the mid-1560s, for example, the Commons made repeated attempts to use parliamentary tax-levying authority as a means of obliging Elizabeth to name a Protestant successor to the throne. The attempt, despite its failure to achieve its immediate goal, was significant; the Commons had shown that they were a force to be reckoned with. Even though Elizabeth made skillful rhetorical use of the theory of absolutism, portraying herself as God's appointed deputy on earth, her idea of absolutism should not be confused with despotism. To be sure, Elizabeth learned to avoid parliamentary interference in her affairs whenever possible; there were only thirteen sessions of Parliament in her forty-five years of rule. Still, Parliament claimed the right to establish law and to levy taxes on which the monarchy had to depend. Elizabeth needed all her considerable diplomatic skills in dealing with her parliaments and with the English people, who were self-reliant and proud of their reputation for independence. Elizabeth had more direct authority over her Privy Council, since she could appoint its members herself, yet even here she consulted faithfully with them on virtually everything she did. Nor

were her closest advisers reluctant to offer her advice. Many vocal leaders in her government, including Walsingham and Leicester, urged the Queen during the 1570s and 1580s to undertake a more active military role on the Continent against the Catholic powers. So did her later favorite, the Earl of Essex. With remarkable tact, she managed to retain the loyalty of her militant and sometimes exasperated counselors, and yet to keep England out of war with Spain until that country actually launched an invasion attempt in 1588 (the Great Armada).

Catholic Opposition

During her early years, Elizabeth sought through her religious compromise to ease the divisions of her kingdom and attempted to placate her enemies abroad (notably Philip of Spain) rather than involve England in a costly war. For about twelve years, while England's economy gained much-needed strength, this policy of temporizing succeeded. Yet Elizabeth's more extreme Catholic opponents at home and abroad could never be reconciled to the daughter of that Protestant "whore," Anne Boleyn. England's period of relative accommodation came to an end in 1569 and 1570, with Catholic uprisings in the north and with papal excommunication of the English Queen.

As a declared heretic, Elizabeth's very life was in danger; her Catholic subjects were encouraged by Rome to disobey her and to seek means for her violent overthrow. Conspirators did, in fact, make attempts on the Queen's life, notably in the so-called Babington conspiracy of 1586, named for one of the chief participants. This plot, brought to light by Secretary of State Walsingham, sought to place Mary, Queen of Scots on the English throne in Elizabeth's stead. Mary was Elizabeth's kinswoman; Mary's grandmother, sister to Henry VIII, had been married to James IV of Scotland. So long as Elizabeth remained childless, Mary was a prominent heir to the English throne. Catholics pinned their hopes on her succession, by force if necessary; Protestant leaders urged Elizabeth to marry and give birth to a Protestant heir or at least to name a Protestant successor. Mary had abdicated the Scottish throne in 1567 after the sensational murder of her Catholic counselor David Rizzio, the murder of Mary's husband, the Earl of Darnley (in which Mary was widely suspected to have taken part), and her subsequent marriage to Darnley's slayer, the Earl of Bothwell. Taking refuge in England, Mary remained a political prisoner and the inevitable focus of Catholic plotting against Elizabeth for approximately two decades. She, in fact, assented in writing to Babington's

Along with the defeat of the Spanish Armada in 1588, the 1587 beheading of Mary, Queen of Scots, shown holding a crucifix and surrounded by official witnesses in this contemporary illustration, virtually ended any serious Catholic challenge to Elizabeth's throne.

plot against Elizabeth. All that long while Elizabeth resisted demands from her Protestant advisers that she execute her kinswoman and thereby end a constant threat to the throne; Elizabeth was reluctant to kill a fellow monarch and agreed fully with Mary's son James that "anointing by God cannot be defiled by man." Nonetheless, Mary's clear involvement in the Babington conspiracy led to the so-called Bond of Association, in which thousands of Englishmen pledged to prevent the succession of any person plotting Elizabeth's death, and then at last to Mary's execution in 1587. By that time, Spain was mounting an invasion against England, the Great Armada of 1588, and Elizabeth's temporizing tactics were no longer feasible. The long years of peace had done their work, however, and England was considerably stronger and more resolute than thirty years before. With Elizabeth's tacit approval, Sir Francis Drake and other naval commanders carried the fighting to Spain's very shore and to her American colonies. The war with Spain continued from 1588 until about 1597.

Elizabeth's great compromise dealt not only with the political dangers of opposition but also with the more central theological issues. England was sorely divided, as was much of Europe, on such matters as whether Christ's body was transubstantially present in the Mass, as Catholic faith maintained; whether good works were effi-

cacious in salvation or whether people could be saved by God's grace alone, as the Reformers insisted; whether a portion of humankind was predeterminately damned, as the Calvinists believed; and the like. During the turbulent years of the Reformation, many people died for their faith. In general, the Elizabethan compromise insisted on allegiance to the English throne, church, and ecclesiastical hierarchy but allowed some latitude in matters of faith. The degree of elaboration in vestments and ritual was also an explosive issue on which the English church attempted to steer a central and pragmatic course, although conflicts inevitably arose within the church itself.

Protestant Opposition

The threat from the Protestant left was no less worrisome than that from the Catholic right. Protestant reformers had experienced their first taste of power at the time of Henry VIII's break with Rome in 1534. Under Thomas Cromwell, Cardinal Wolsey's successor as the King's chief minister, the monasteries were suppressed and William Tyndale's English Bible was authorized. The execution of Cromwell introduced a period of conservative retrenchment, but the accession of Edward VI in 1547 brought reform once more into prominence. Thereafter, Mary's Catholic reign drove most of the reformers into exile on the Continent. When they returned after 1558, many had been made more radical by their continental experience.

To be sure, reform covered a wide spectrum, from moderation to radicalism. Some preferred to work within the existing hierarchical structure of church and state, whereas others were religious separatists. Only the more radical groups, such as the Brownists and Anabaptists, endorsed ideas of equality and communal living. The abusive epithet "Puritan," applied indiscriminately to all reformers, tended to obscure the wide range of difference in the reform movement. The reformers were, to some extent, united by a dislike for formal ritual and ecclesiastical garments, by a preference for a simple and pious manner of living, and by a belief in the literal word of the Bible rather than the traditional teachings of the church fathers. They stressed personal responsibility in religion and were Calvinist in their emphasis on human depravity and the need for grace through election. Yet at first only the more radical were involved in a movement to separate entirely from the established English church.

The radicals on the religious left, even if they represented at first only a minority of the reformers, posed a serious threat to Elizabeth's government. Their program bore an ironic resemblance to that of the Catholic opposition on the religious right. In their theoretical writings, the extreme reformers justified overthrow of what they considered to be tyrannical rule, just as Catholic spokesmen had absolved Elizabeth's subjects of obedience to her on the grounds that she was illegitimate. Both extremes appealed to disobedience in the name of a higher religious law, as enunciated in Romans 13:1–2: "For there is no power but of God." Among the reforming theoreticians was John Ponet, whose *Short Treatise of Politic Power* (1556) argued that a monarch is subject to a social contract and must rule according to laws that are equally subscribed to by Parliament, the clergy, and the people.

The Doctrine of Passive Obedience

Elizabeth's government countered such assaults on its authority, from both the right and the left, with many arguments, of which perhaps the most central was that of passive obedience. This doctrine condemned rebellion under virtually all circumstances. Its basic assumption was that the king or queen is God's appointed deputy on earth. To depose such a monarch must therefore be an act of disobedience against God's will. Since God is all-wise and all-powerful, his placing of an evil ruler in power must proceed from some divine intention, such as the punishment of a wayward people. Rebellion against God's "scourge" merely displays further disobedience to God's will. A people suffering under a tyrant must wait patiently for God to remove the burden, which he will surely do when the proper time arrives.

This doctrine was included in the official book of homilies of the Church of England and was read from the pulpit at regular intervals. The best-known such homily, entitled *Against Disobedience and Willful Rebellion,* had been preceded by such tracts as William Tyndale's *Obedience of a Christian Man* (1528); a book of homilies, published in 1547, including an "Exhortation Concerning Good Order and Obedience"; Thomas Cranmer's *Notes for a Sermon on the Rebellion of 1549;* and Hugh Latimer's *Sermon on the Lord's Prayer* (1552). Shakespeare heard such homilies often, and he expresses their ideas through several of his characters, such as John of Gaunt and the Bishop of Carlisle in *Richard II* (1.2.37–41, 4.1.115–50). This is not to say that he endorses such ideas, for he sets them in dramatic opposition to other and more heterodox concepts. We can say, nevertheless, that Shakespeare's audience would have recognized in Gaunt's speeches a clear expression of a familiar and officially correct position.

The Political Ideas of Machiavelli

The orthodoxies of the Elizabethan establishment were under attack, not only from the Catholic right and the Protestant left, but also from a new and revolutionary point of view that set aside all criteria of religious morality. Tudor defense of order was based, as we have seen, on the assumption that the monarch rules in accord with a divine plan, a higher Law of Nature to which every just ruler is attuned. Political morality must be at one with religious morality. Catholic and Protestant critiques of the Tudor establishment made similar assumptions, even though they appealed to revolution in the name of that religious morality. To Niccolò Machiavelli, on the other hand, politics was a manipulative science best governed by the dictates of social expediency. His philosophy did not, as many accusingly charged, lead necessarily to the cynical promotion of mere self-interest. Nevertheless, he did argue, in his *Discourses* and *The Prince,* that survival and political stability are the first obligations of any ruler. Machiavelli regarded religion as a tool of the enlightened ruler rather than as a morally absolute guide. He extolled in his ideal leader the quality of *virtù*—a mixture of cunning and forcefulness. He saw history as a subject offering practical lessons in the kind of pragmatic statecraft he proposed.

Machiavelli was a hated name in England, and most of his works were never available in an English printed edition during Shakespeare's lifetime. (The *Florentine History* was translated in 1595; *The Prince* was not translated until 1640.) Nevertheless, his writings were available in Italian, French, and Latin editions, and in manuscript English translations. His ideas certainly had a profound impact on the England of the 1590s. Marlowe caricatures the Italian writer in his *The Jew of Malta,* but he clearly was fascinated by what Machiavelli had to say. Shakespeare, too, reveals a complex awareness. However much he may lampoon the Machiavellian type of conscienceless villain in *Richard III*, he shows us more plausible pragmatists in *Richard II* and *1 Henry IV*. Conservative theories of the divine right of kings are set in debate with the more heterodox ambitions of Henry Bolingbroke (who then adopts the most orthodox of political vocabularies once he is king). Bolingbroke is not a very attractive figure, but he does succeed politically where Richard has failed.

Shakespeare thus reveals himself as less a defender of the established order than as a great dramatist able to give sympathetic expression to the aspirations of all sides in a tense political struggle. His history plays have been variously interpreted either as defenses of monarchy or as subtle pleas for rebellion, but the consensus today is that the plays use political conflict as a way of probing the motivations of social behavior. To be sure, the plays do stress the painful consequences of disorder and present, on the whole, an admiring view of monarchy (especially in *Henry V*), despite the manifest limitations of that institution. Certainly, we can sense that Shakespeare's history plays were written for a generation of Englishmen who had experienced political crisis and who could perceive issues of statecraft in Shakespeare's plays that were relevant to England's struggles in the 1580s and the 1590s. The play of *King John*, for example, deals with a king whose uncertain claim to the throne is challenged by France and the papacy in the name of John's nephew, Arthur; Elizabeth faced a similar situation in her dilemma over her kinswoman, Mary, Queen of Scots. Elizabeth also bitterly acknowledged the cogency of a popular analogy comparing her reign with that of King Richard II, and, when Shakespeare's play about Bolingbroke's overthrow of Richard was apparently revived for political purposes shortly before the Earl of Essex's abortive rebellion against Elizabeth in 1601, Shakespeare's acting company had some explaining to do to the authorities (see Introduction to *Richard II*). Nevertheless, Shakespeare's attitudes toward the issues of his own day are ultimately unknowable and unimportant, since his main concern seems to have been with the dramatization of political conflict rather than with the urging of a polemical position.

Shakespeare on Religion

Our impressions of Shakespeare's personal sympathies in religion are similarly obscured by his refusal to use his art for polemical purposes. To be sure, members of his mother's family in Warwickshire seem to have remained loyal to Catholicism, and his father John Shakespeare may conceivably have undergone financial and other difficulties in Stratford for reasons of faith. (See "Shakespeare's Family" below, in the section on Shakespeare's Life and Work.) Certainly Shakespeare himself displays a familiarity with some Catholic practices and theology,

as when the Ghost of Hamlet's father speaks of being "Unhousled, disappointed, unaneled" (i.e., not having received last rites) at the time of his murder (*Hamlet*, 1.5.78). Nonetheless, we see in his plays a spectrum of religious attitudes portrayed with an extraordinary range of insight. In matters of doctrine, his characters are at various times acquainted with Catholic theology or with the controversy concerning salvation by faith or good works (see *Measure for Measure*, 1.2.24–5), and yet a consistent polemical bias is absent. Some Catholic prelates are schemers, like Pandulph in *King John*. Ordinarily, however, Shakespeare's satirical digs at ecclesiastical pomposity and hypocrisy have little to do with the Catholic question. Cardinal Beaufort in *1 Henry VI* is a political maneuverer, but so are many of his secular rivals. Cardinal Wolsey in *Henry VIII* is motivated by personal ambition, rather than by any sinister conspiracy of the international church. Many of Shakespeare's nominally Catholic clerics, such as Friar Laurence in *Romeo and Juliet* or Friar Francis in *Much Ado About Nothing*, are gentle and well-intentioned people, even if occasionally bumbling. We can certainly say that Shakespeare consistently avoids the chauvinistic anti-Catholic baiting so often found in the plays of his contemporaries.

The same avoidance of extremes can be seen in his portrayal of Protestant reformers, though the instances in this case are few. Malvolio in *Twelfth Night* is fleetingly compared with a "puritan" (2.3.139–46), although Shakespeare insists that no extensive analogy can be made. Angelo in *Measure for Measure* is sometimes thought to be a critical portrait of the Puritan temperament. Even if this were so, Shakespeare's satire is extremely indirect compared with the lampoons written by his contemporaries Ben Jonson and Thomas Dekker.

Stuart Absolutism

Queen Elizabeth's successor, James I of the Scottish house of Stuarts, reigned from 1603 to 1625. Even more than Elizabeth, he was a strong believer in the divinely appointed authority of kings; whereas she had insisted on divine sanction, James and his successor Charles called it a divine right. Although James succeeded easily to the throne in 1603, since he was Protestant with a legitimate claim of descent from Henry VIII, the English people did not take to this foreigner from the north. James was eccentric in his personal habits, and the English were always inclined to be suspicious of the Scots in any case. As a result, James was less successful in dealing with the heterogeneous and antagonistic forces that Elizabeth had kept in precarious balance. At the Hampton Court Conference of 1604, relations quickly broke down between James and the Puritan wing of the church, so that even its more moderate adherents joined forces with the separatists. James had similar difficulties with an increasingly radical group in the House of Commons. In the widening rift between the absolutists and those who defended the supremacy of Parliament, James's court moved toward the right. Catholic sympathies at court became common. Civil war was still a long way off and by no means inevitable; the beheading of King Charles I (James's son) would not occur until 1649. Still, throughout James's reign, the estrangement between the right and the left was becoming more and more uncomfortable. The infamous Gunpowder Plot of 1605, in which Guy Fawkes and other Catholic conspirators were accused of having plotted to blow up the houses of Parliament, raised hysteria to a new intensity. Penal laws against papists were harshly enforced. The Parliament of 1614 included in its membership John Pym, Thomas Wentworth, and John Eliot—men who were to become turbulent spokesmen against taxes imposed without parliamentary grant, imprisonment without the stating of specific criminal charges, and other purported abuses of royal power. The polarization of English society naturally affected the London theaters. Popular London audiences (generally sympathetic with religious reform) eventually grew disaffected with the stage, while even the popular acting companies came under the increasing domination of the court. Shakespeare's late plays reflect the increasing influence of a courtly audience.

THE INTELLECTUAL BACKGROUND

Renaissance Cosmology

In learning, as in politics and religion, Shakespeare's England was a time of conflict and excitement. Medieval ideas of a hierarchical and ordered creation were under attack but were still widely prevalent, and were used to justify a hierarchical order in society itself. According to the so-called Ptolemaic system of the universe, formulated by Ptolemy of Alexandria in the second century A.D., the earth stood at the center of creation. Around it moved, in nine concentric spheres, the heavenly bodies of the visible universe, in order as follows (from the earth outward): the moon, Mercury, Venus, the sun, Mars, Jupiter, Saturn, the fixed stars on a single plane, and lastly the *primum mobile,* imparting motion to the whole system. (See the accompanying illustration.) Some commentators proposed alternate arrangements or speculated as to the existence of one or two additional spheres, in particular a "crystalline sphere" between the fixed stars and the *primum mobile.* These additional spheres were needed to cope with matters not adequately explained in Ptolemaic astronomy, such as the precession of the equinoxes. More troublesomely, the seemingly erratic retrograde motion of the planets—that is, the refusal of Mars and other planets to move around the earth in steady orbit—

called forth increasingly ingenious theories, such as Tycho Brahe's scheme of epicycles. Still, the conservative appeal of the earth-centered cosmos remained very strong. How could one suppose that the earth was not at the center of the universe?

The *primum mobile* was thought to turn the entire universe around the earth once every twenty-four hours. Simultaneously, the individual heavenly bodies moved more slowly around the earth on their individual spheres, constantly changing position with respect to the fixed stars. The moon, being the only heavenly body that seemed subject to change in its monthly waxing and waning, was thought to represent the boundary between the unchanging universe and the incessantly changing world. Beneath the moon, in the "sublunary" sphere, all creation was subject to death as a result of Adam's fall from grace; beyond the moon lay perfection. Hell was imagined to exist deep within the earth, as in Dante's *Inferno,* or else outside the *primum mobile* and far below the created universe in the realm of chaos, as in Milton's *Paradise Lost.*

Heaven or the Empyrean stood, according to most Ptolemaic systems, at the top of the universe. Between heaven and earth dwelled the nine angelic orders, each associated with one of the nine concentric spheres. According to a work attributed to Dionysius the Areopagite, *On the Heavenly Hierarchy* (fifth century A.D.), the nine angelic orders consisted of three hierarchies. Closest to God were the contemplative orders of Seraphim, Cherubim, and Thrones; next, the intermediate orders of Dominions, Powers, and Virtues; and finally the active orders of Principalities, Archangels, and Angels. These last served as God's messengers and intervened from time to time in the affairs of mortals. Ordered life among humans, although manifestly imperfect when compared with the eternal bliss of the angelic orders, still modeled itself on that platonic idea of perfect harmony. Thus the state, the church, and the family all resembled one another because they resembled (however distantly) the kingdom of God. Richard Hooker, in his *Of the Laws of Ecclesiastical Polity* (1594–1597), defends the established Church of England in terms that emanate from a comparable idea of a divine, creative, and ordering law of nature "Whose seat is the bosom of God, whose voice the harmony of the world."

The devils of hell were fallen angels, with Satan as their leader. Such evil spirits might assume any number of shapes, such as demons, goblins, wizards, or witches. Believers in evil spirits generally made no distinction between orthodox Christian explanations of evil and the more primitive folklore of witchcraft. Belief in witchcraft was widespread indeed; King James I took the matter very seriously. So did Reginald Scot's *The Discovery of Witchcraft* (1584), though its author also attempted to confute what he regarded as ignorant superstition and charlatanism.

Ptolemy's earth-centered system of the universe (top) was challenged by the sun-centered system of Copernicus (bottom) with the publishing of De revolutionibus orbium coelestium *in 1543. Shakespeare, like other major poets of the English Renaissance, poetically represents the universe in cosmic terms as described by Ptolemy, but also reflects uncertainties generated by the new cosmology.*

Throughout Shakespeare's lifetime, belief and skepticism about such matters existed side by side.

A similar ambiguity pertained to belief in the Ptolemaic universe itself. All major poets of the Renaissance, including Shakespeare, Spenser, and Milton (who completed *Paradise Lost* after 1660), represented the universe in cosmic terms essentially as described by Ptolemy. Yet Nicolaus Copernicus's revolutionary theory of a sun-centered solar system (*De revolutionibus orbium coelestium,* published on the Continent in 1543) and the discovery of a new star in Cassiopeia in 1572 stimulated much new thought. Galileo Galilei, born in the same year as Shakespeare (1564), published in 1610 the results of his telescopic examinations of the moon, thereby further confirming Copernicus's hypothesis. Although the news of Galileo's astounding discovery came too late to affect any but the latest of Shakespeare's plays, a sense of excitement and dislocation was apparent throughout most of the years of his writing career. Thomas Nashe, in 1595, referred familiarly to Copernicus as the author "who held that the sun remains immobile in the center of the world, and that the earth is moved about the sun" (Nashe, *Works,* ed. R. B. McKerrow, 1904–1910, 3.94). John Donne lamented in 1611–1612 that the "new philosophy" (i.e., the new science) "calls all in doubt." Skeptical uncertainty about the cosmos was on the rise. The poetic affirmations in Renaissance art of traditional ideas of the cosmos can best be understood as a response to uncertainty—a statement of faith in an age of increasing skepticism.

Alchemy and Medicine

In all areas of Renaissance learning, the new and the old science were juxtaposed. Alchemy, for example, made important contributions to learning, despite its superstitious character. Its chief goal was the transformation of base metals into gold, on the assumption that all metals were ranked on a hierarchical scale and could be raised from lower to higher positions on that scale by means of certain alchemical techniques. Other aims of alchemy included the discovery of a universal cure for diseases and of a means for preserving life indefinitely. Such aims encouraged quackery and prompted various exposés, such as Chaucer's "The Canon's Yeoman's Tale" (late fourteenth century) and Jonson's *The Alchemist* (1610). Yet many of the procedures used in alchemy were essentially chemical procedures, and the science of chemistry received a valuable impetus from constant experimentation. Queen Elizabeth was seriously interested in alchemy throughout her life.

In physics, medicine, and psychology, as well, older concepts vied with new. Traditional learning apportioned all physical matter into four elements: earth, air, fire, and water. Each of these was thought to be a different combination of the four "qualities" of the universe: hot, cold,

Gedruckt zu Franckfurt am Mayn/durch Johan Feyerabendt. 1 5 9 8.

Alchemists employed relatively sophisticated equipment in their futile search for the "philosopher's stone," a reputed substance supposed to possess the property of changing other metals into gold and silver.

hand (*Othello*, 3.4.39); those of age were "a moist eye, a dry hand, a yellow cheek, a white beard, a decreasing leg, an increasing belly" (*2 Henry IV*, 1.2.179–81). A common remedy for illness was to let blood and thereby purge the body of unwanted humors.

The name traditionally associated with such theories was that of Galen, the most celebrated of ancient writers on medicine (c. 130 A.D.). A more revolutionary name was that of Paracelsus, a famous German physician (c. 1493–1541) who attacked the traditional medical learning of his time and urged a more unfettered pragmatic research into pharmacy and medicine. Such experimentalism bore fruit in the anatomical research of Vesalius (1514–1564) and in William Harvey's investigations of the circulation of the blood (c. 1616). Nevertheless, the practice of medicine in Renaissance times remained under the influence of the "humors" theory until quite late, and its ideas are found throughout Shakespeare's writings.

moist, and dry. Earth combined cold and dry; air, hot and moist; fire, hot and dry; and water, cold and moist. Earth and water were the baser or lower elements, confined to the physical world; fire and air were aspiring elements, tending upward. Humans, as a microcosm of the larger universe, contained in themselves the four elements. The individual's temperament, or "humor" or "complexion," depended on which "humor" predominated in that person. The four humors in humans corresponded to the four elements of physical matter. The blood was hot and moist, like air; yellow bile or choler was hot and dry, like fire; phlegm was cold and moist, like water; and black bile was cold and dry, like earth. A predominance of blood in an individual created a sanguine or cheerful temperament (or humor), yellow bile produced a choleric or irascible temperament, phlegm produced a phlegmatic or stolid temperament, and black bile produced a melancholic temperament. Diet could affect the balance among these humors, since an excess of a particular food would stimulate overproduction of one humor. The stomach and the liver, which converted food into humors, were regarded as the seat of human passions. The spleen was thought to be the seat of laughter, sudden impulse, or caprice, and also melancholy. (Hotspur, in *1 Henry IV*, is said to be "governed by a spleen," 5.2.19.) Strong emotional reactions could be explained in terms of the physiology of the humors: in anger, the blood rushed to the head and thereby produced a flush of red color and staring eyes; in fear, the blood migrated to the heart and thus left the face and liver pale, and so on. Sighs supposedly cost the heart a drop of blood, while wine could refortify it (as Falstaff insists in *2 Henry IV*, 4.3.90–123). The signs of youth were warmth and moisture, as in Desdemona's "hot and moist"

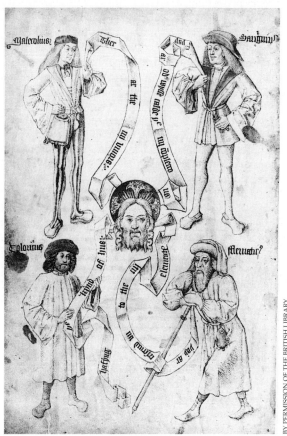

The four humors of black bile, blood, yellow bile or choler, and phlegm, as shown in this illustration from an illuminated manuscript, were believed to govern the human personality by producing a disposition toward melancholic, sanguine, choleric, or phlegmatic temperaments.

Learning

In learning generally, and in theories of education, new ideas conflicted with old. The curriculum of schools and colleges in the Renaissance was inherited largely from the Middle Ages and displayed many traditional characteristics. The curriculum consisted of the seven Liberal Arts: a lower division, called the trivium, comprised of grammar, rhetoric, and logic; and an upper division, called the quadrivium, comprised of arithmetic, geometry, astronomy, and music. In addition, there were the philosophical studies associated chiefly with Aristotle: natural philosophy, ethics, and metaphysics.

Aristotle's name had a towering influence in medieval times and remained important to the Renaissance as well. Even among his Renaissance admirers, however, Aristotle proved more compelling in practical matters than in the abstract scholastic reasoning associated with his name in the Middle Ages. The Italian Aristotelians whose work made its way into England were interested primarily in the science of human behavior. Aristotelian ethics was for them a practical subject, telling people how to live usefully and well and how to govern themselves politically. Rhetoric was the science of persuasion, enabling people to use eloquence for socially useful goals. Poetry was a kind of rhetoric, a language of persuasion which dramatists, too, might use for morally pragmatic ends.

At the same time, new thinkers were daring to attack Aristotle by name as a symbol of traditional medieval thought. The attack was not always fair to Aristotle himself, whose work had been bent to the *a priori* purposes of much medieval scholasticism. Nevertheless, his name had assumed such symbolic importance that he had to be confronted directly. The Huguenot logician Petrus Ramus (1515–1572), defiantly proclaiming that "everything that Aristotle taught is false," argued for rules of logic as derived from observation. He urged, for example, that his students learn about rhetoric from observing in detail Cicero's effect on his listeners, rather than by the rote practice of syllogism. Actually, Ramus's thought was less revolutionary in its concepts of logic than in the tremendous ferment of opinion caused by his iconoclastic teaching.

A basic issue at stake in the anti-Aristotelian movement was that of traditional authority versus independent observation. How do people best acquire true knowledge—through the teachings of their predecessors or through their own discovery? The issue had profound implications for religious truth as well: should individuals heed the collective wisdom of the earthly church or read the Bible with their individual perceptions as their guide? Is "reason" an accretive wisdom handed down by authority or a quality of the individual soul? Obviously, a middle ground exists between the two extremes, and no new thinker of the Renaissance professed to abandon entirely the use of ancient author-

ity. For men like Henricus Agrippa (1486–1535) and Sir Francis Bacon (1561–1626), however, scholastic tradition had exerted its oppressive influence far too long. Authority needed to be examined critically and scientifically. Bacon, in his *The Advancement of Learning* (1605), fought against the blind acceptance of ancient wisdom and argued that "knowledge derived from Aristotle, and exempted from liberty of examination, will not rise again higher than the knowledge of Aristotle." Sir Walter Ralegh and others joined in the excited new search for what human "reason" could discover when set free from scholastic restraint. Such belief in the perfectibility of human reason owed some of its inspiration to Italian Neoplatonic humanists like Giovanni Pico della Mirandola (1463–1494), who, in his *Oration on the Dignity of Man*, celebrated a human race "constrained by no limits" in accordance with the potential of its own free will. The new learning did not seem to trouble these men in their religious faith, although a tension between scientific observation and faith in miracles was to become plentifully evident in the seventeenth century.

The Nature of Humankind

Medieval thought generally assigned to humankind a uniquely superior place in the order of creation on earth. That assumption of superiority rested on biblical and patristic teachings about the hierarchy of creation, in which humanity stood at the apex of physical creation nearest God and the angels. Humankind was thus supreme on earth in the so-called chain of being. Human reason, though subject to error because of sinfulness, enabled humans to aspire toward divinity. Humans were, in the view of medieval philosophers, the great amphibians, as well as the microcosm of the universe, part bestial and part immortal, doomed by Adam's fall to misery and death in this life but promised eternal salvation through Christ's atonement. Right reason, properly employed, could lead to the truths of revealed Christianity and thus give humankind a glimpse of the heavenly perfection one day to be ours. Renaissance Neoplatonism, as expounded, for example, in the writings of Marsilio Ficino, Pico della Mirandola, and Baldassare Castiglione (in *The Courtier*, translated by Sir Thomas Hoby in 1561), offered humanity a vision of a platonic ladder, extending from the perception of physical beauty to contemplation of the platonic idea of beauty and finally to the experiencing of God's transcendent love.

Protestant thought of the Renaissance did not wholly disagree with this formulation, but it did place a major new emphasis on human reprobation. The idea was not new, for Saint Augustine (354–430) had insisted on human depravity and our total dependence on God's inscrutable grace, but, in the years of the Reformation, this theology took on a new urgency. Martin Luther

(1483–1540), by rejecting veneration of the Virgin Mary and the saints, and by taking away the sacraments of confession and penance, by which individual Christians could seek the institutional comforts of the Catholic Church, exposed the individual sinner to agonies of conscience that could result in a sense of alienation and loss. The rewards were great for those who found new faith in God's infinite goodness, but the hazards of predestinate damnation were fearsome to those who were less sure of their spiritual welfare. Luther's God was inscrutable, majestic, and infallible. Luther's God decreed salvation for the elect and damnation for all others, and His will could not be challenged or questioned. The individual was to blame for sin, even though God hardened the hearts of the reprobate. John Calvin (1509–1564) placed even greater stress on predestinate good and evil and insisted that the grace of salvation was founded on God's freely given mercy that humans could not possibly deserve. Salvation was God's to give or withhold as He wished; humans might not repine that in His incomprehensible wisdom God has "barred the door of life to those whom He has given over to damnation." Faced with such a view of human spiritual destiny, the

individual Christian's lot was one of potential tragedy. The human soul was a battleground of good and evil.

Michel de Montaigne (1533–1592), Shakespeare's great French contemporary, provided a very different and heterodox way of thinking about human imperfection. In his "Apology for Raymond Sebond" and other of his essays, Montaigne questioned the assumption of humanity's superiority to the animal kingdom, and in doing so gave Shakespeare a fundamentally different way to consider the nature of humankind—a way that reflects itself, for example, in Hamlet's observations on humans as "quintessence of dust." Montaigne stressed humans' arrogance, vanity, and frailty. He was unconvinced of humanity's purported moral superiority to the animals and argued that animals are no less endowed with a soul. Montaigne undermined, in other words, the hierarchy in which the human race was the unquestioned master of the physical world, just as Copernican science overturned the earth-centered cosmos and Machiavelli's political system dismissed as an improbable fiction the divinely constituted hierarchy of the state. Montaigne's very choice of the essay as his favorite literary form bespeaks his commitment to attempts and explorations, rather than to definite solu-

This guide, graphically setting forth the ideals to which every English gentlewoman and gentleman should aspire, illustrates the Renaissance concept that outward deportment and accomplishments should correctly and invariably mirror a person's inner nature.

tions; etymologically, the very word "essay" signifies an exploration or inquiry. Montaigne was not alone in his skepticism about human nature; his ideas had much in common with Bernardino Telesio's *De Rerum Natura* and with the writings of the Italian Giordano Bruno. Montaigne was followed in the seventeenth century by that overpowering iconoclast, Thomas Hobbes, who extended the concept of mechanical laws governing human society and human psychology. Hobbes postdates Shakespeare, to be sure, but one has only to consider Iago's philosophy of the assertive individual will (in *Othello*) or Edmund's contempt for his father Gloucester's astrological pieties (in *King Lear*) to see the enormous impact on Shakespeare of the new heterodoxies of his age. Shakespeare makes us aware that skeptical thought can be used by dangerous men like Iago, Edmund, and Richard III to promote their own villainies in a world no longer held together by the certitudes of traditional faith, but he also shows us the gullibility of some traditionalists and the abuses of power that can be perpetrated in the name of ancient and divine privilege by a king like Richard II. Above all, Shakespeare delights in the play of mind among competing ideas, inviting us to wonder, for example, if Caliban in *The Tempest* is not invested with natural qualities that Prospero, his Christian colonizer, does not sufficiently understand, and whether some of the other supposedly civilized Europeans who come to Caliban's island do not have a great deal to learn from its uncivilized beauty.

LONDON THEATERS AND DRAMATIC COMPANIES

Throughout Shakespeare's life, the propriety of acting any plays at all was a matter of bitter controversy. Indeed, when one considers the power and earnestness of the opposition, one is surprised that such a wealth of dramatic excellence could come into being and that Shakespeare's plays should reflect so little the anger and hostility generated by this continuing conflict.

Religious and Moral Opposition to the Theater

From the 1570s onward, and even earlier, the city fathers of London revealed an ever-increasing distrust of the public performance of plays. They fretted about the dangers of plague and of riotous assembly. They objected to the fact that apprentices idly wasted their time instead of working in their shops. And always the municipal authorities suspected immorality. Thus, by an order of the Common Council of London, dated December 6, 1574, the players were put under severe restrictions.

The order cites the reasons. The players, it was charged, had been acting in the innyards of the city, which

in consequence were haunted by great multitudes of people, especially youths. These gatherings had been the occasions of frays and quarrels, "evil practices of incontinency in great inns"; the players published "uncomely and unshamefast speeches and doings," withdrew the Queen's subjects from divine service on Sundays and holidays, wasted the money of "poor and fond persons," gave opportunity to pick pockets, uttered "busy and seditious matters," and injured and maimed people by the falling of their scaffolds and by weapons and powder used in plays. The order goes on to state the Common Council's fear that if the plays, which had been forbidden on account of the plague, should be resumed, God's wrath would manifest itself by an increase of the infection. Therefore, no innkeeper, tavernkeeper, or other person might cause or suffer to be openly played "any play, interlude, comedy, tragedy, matter, or show" which had not been first licensed by the mayor and the Court of Aldermen.

The mayor and aldermen did not always state their case plainly, because Queen Elizabeth was a patron of the players, and because the players had friends and patrons in the Privy Council and among the nobility; sometimes, however, they did so quite boldly. One sees the case against plays stated syllogistically in the following words of Thomas White, a preacher at Paul's Cross in 1577:

Look but upon the common plays of London, and see the multitude that flocketh to them and followeth them! Behold the sumptuous theater houses, a continual monument of London prodigality and folly! But I understand they are now forbidden because of the plague. I like the policy well if it hold still, for a disease is but botched and patched up that is not cured in the cause, and the cause of plagues is sin, if you look to it well, and the cause of sin are plays. Therefore the cause of plagues are plays. (From *A Sermon preached at Paul's Cross . . . in the Time of the Plague,* 1578.)

Moved, no doubt, by the prohibition of the Common Council, James Burbage, with a company of actors under the patronage of the Earl of Leicester, leased a site in Shoreditch, a London suburb in Middlesex, beyond the immediate jurisdiction of the official enemies in the Common Council, whose authority extended only to the city limits. By 1576, he had completed the Theatre. Perhaps he called it "the Theatre" because it had no competitor (other than the Red Lion, established in 1567 and used seemingly as a playing place for feasts and festival days in the performance style of Corpus Christi and saints' plays). Burbage erected what may have been England's first permanent commercial theatrical building. In general, the building combined features of the innyard and the animal-baiting house, having a central and probably paved courtyard open to the sky (like an innyard) and surrounding galleries on all sides (like an animal-baiting house). Burbage erected a stage at one side of the circular arena and put dressing rooms behind it to form the "tir-

The George Inn of Southwark, England, London's only surviving galleried inn, was destroyed by fire in 1676 but rebuilt the following year with two galleries instead of the original three. Despite these changes, the George Inn gives us the best picture we have of the kind of space in which traveling companies could mount their plays on bare platform stages.

ing house" or backstage area for the actors; the facade of this "tiring house" served as a visible backdrop to the stage itself. Burbage's Theatre became the model for other public playhouses, such as the Curtain, the Swan, and the Globe, which were constructed later.

By building his playhouse in Shoreditch, Burbage gained immunity from the London authorities. The city fathers could not suppress plays or control them with perfect success if they were performed in Middlesex, or in the "liberty" of Blackfriars and similar districts exempted by charters from London's civic authority (see "London's Private Theaters," below), or (in the case of later playhouses) on the Bankside across the Thames in Surrey. In order to get at them in these suburban regions, the city authorities had to petition the Queen's Privy Council to give orders to the magistrates and officers of the law in these counties. The Queen's Privy Council, although always on the most polite terms with the Lord Mayor and his brethren of the city and always open to the argument that the assemblage of crowds caused the spread of the plague, was to a much less degree in sympathy with the moral scruples of the city. Current arguments for the plays, derived from the works of scholars, poets, and playwrights, were numerous and often heard: namely, that classical antiquity gave precedent for dramatic spectacles; that by drawing a true picture of both the bad and the good in life, plays enabled people to choose the good; that people should have wholesome amusement; and that plays provided livelihood for loyal subjects of the Queen.

Of these arguments, to be sure, the Privy Council made little use, resting the case for plays instead on what was, no doubt, an unanswerable argument: that since the players were to appear before Her Majesty, especially during the Christmas/Shrovetide period, the players needed practice in order to prepare themselves to please the royal taste. A good deal of politic fencing ensued, and, so far as orders, complaints, and denunciations were concerned, the reforming opposition had much the better of it. The preachers thundered against plays. Pamphleteers denounced all matters pertaining to the stage: Stephen Gosson in *The School of Abuse, Containing a Pleasant Invective Against Poets, Pipers, Players, Jesters and Suchlike Caterpillars of a Commonwealth* (1579) and other works; Philip Stubbes in *The Anatomy of Abuses* (1583); and finally and most furiously of all, William Prynne in *Histrio-Mastix: The Players' Scourge or Actor's Tragedy* (1633). Gosson spoke of plays as "the inventions of the devil, the offerings of idolatry, the pomp of worldlings, the blossoms of vanity, the root of apostacy, food of iniquity, riot and adultery." "Detest them," he warned. "Players are masters of vice, teachers of wantonness, spurs to impurity, the sons of idleness."

At first, such diatribes represented an extreme reforming opinion obviously not shared by a majority of London viewers. They kept coming to plays, and the flourishing public theaters attracted the talents of the age's leading dramatists. An ominous note of polarization was sounded, however, early in the reign of James I (1603–1625) when the rift between the Puritans and the court broke into open antagonism. After about 1604, when James alienated the Puritans at the Hampton Court Conference, the split between popular audiences and the best drama of the age became increasingly evident. Shakespeare's company, now the King's men, gravitated, whether through choice or necessity, toward the precinct of the court. Although the public theater, with its capacity for large audiences, continued to serve as a lively center of theatrical activity, Puritan opposition to the stage gathered momentum. Many dramatists, in turn, grew more satirical of London customs and more attuned to courtly tastes. Eventually, Puritan hostility to the theater was at least part of the motive behind Parliament's order to close the theaters in 1642.

The Public Theaters

A year or more after Burbage built the Theatre in 1576, the Curtain was put up near it by Philip Henslowe, or possibly by Henry Laneman, or Lanman. About ten years later, Philip Henslowe built the Rose, the first playhouse on the Bankside (the southern bank of the Thames River). In 1599, James Burbage's sons Richard and Cuthbert dismantled the Theatre because of trouble about the lease of the land and rebuilt it as the Globe on the Bankside. This Globe playhouse burned on June 29, 1613, from the discharge of cannon backstage during a performance of *All Is True*, a play thought to be identical with Shakespeare's *Henry VIII*. The Globe was rebuilt, probably in its original polygonal form, that is, essentially round with a large number of sides. In 1600, Henslowe built the Fortune as a theater for the Lord Admiral's men, who were chief rivals to the Lord Chamberlain's men. The companies were differently organized, in that the Lord Chamberlain's men were joint sharers in their own enterprise and owners of their own theatrical building, whereas Henslowe owned the Fortune (and the Rose before it) and served as landlord to the Admiral's men—no doubt profiting handsomely from their activities.

Various records of these theatrical buildings have survived. One such record is the Fortune contract, preserved at Dulwich College among other invaluable papers of Philip Henslowe, theatrical entrepreneur and father-in-law of the famous Edward Alleyn of the Lord Admiral's men. The contract for building the Fortune was let to the same contractor who had built the new Globe, and, since the specifications required that the Fortune should be like the Globe in all its main features, except that it was to be square instead of polygonal, we may gain from these specifications an idea of the Globe. A second documentary record is a drawing of the Swan, a Bankside theater, accompanying a description of the playhouse by Johannes De Witt, who visited London in 1596. The drawing, which was discovered in the University Library at Utrecht, is the work of one Van Buchell and may be based on drawings by De Witt himself. Besides the Fortune contract and the Swan drawing, we have two or three little pictures of the Elizabethan public stage on the title pages of published plays, the most important being that on the title page of William Alabaster's *Roxana* (1632). Just recently, in 1989, the discovery and excavation of the foundations of the Rose playhouse and partial excavation of the Globe playhouse foundations in Southwark, together with the construction of a modern replica of the Globe playhouse near the site of these two theaters, have added invaluable archeological information about the dimensions of that acting arena.

The London Public Stage

From these documents and pictures and from scattered references to the theaters, as well as from extended studies of stage directions and scenic conditions in plays themselves, we have a fairly clear idea of the public stage in London. Its features are these: a pit about seventy feet in diameter, usually circular and open to the sky; surrounding this, galleries in three tiers, containing the most expensive seats; and a rectangular stage, about forty-three by twenty-seven feet, wider than it was deep, raised about five and one-half feet above the surface of the yard, sometimes built on trestles so that it could be removed if the house was also customarily used for bearbaiting and bullbaiting. The flat, open stage usually contained one trapdoor. Part of the stage was afforded some protection from the weather by a brightly decorated wooden roof supported by posts, constituting the "heavens." Above this roof was a "hut," perhaps containing suspension gear for ascents and descents. (The Rose appears originally to have been generally smaller than what is described here, with a stage that tapered toward the front to a width of only twenty-five feet or so. The building was somewhat expanded in 1592 but was still small compared with other theaters. The original building shows no certain evidence of a roof over the stage supported by pillars, but the later building appears to have had roof pillars at the front of the stage.)

BY PERMISSION OF THE FOLGER SHAKESPEARE LIBRARY

This drawing of an Elizabethan public stage appeared on the title page of the published version of William Alabaster's play Roxana *(1632).*

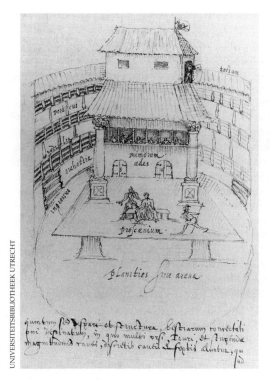

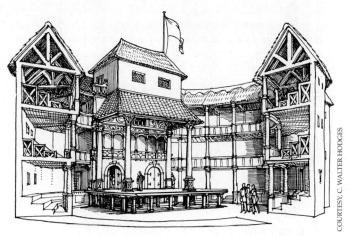

This diagram of the Swan Theatre (left) by Van Buchell (c. 1596), based on the observations of Johannes De Witt, shows features of the public playhouse shared by James Burbage's Theatre and the Globe. A modern sketch of the Swan Theatre (right) shows the open, encircling roof and a full view of the tiring house. Like the Globe and other open theaters, the design of the Swan seems to resemble the Elizabethan innyard with an added stage.

At the back of the stage was a partition wall, the "tiring-house facade," with at least two doors in it connecting the stage with the actors' dressing rooms or "tiring house." In the Rose, the tiring-house facade seems to have curved with the polygonal shape of the theater building, but in the DeWitt drawing the Swan facade looks perfectly straight across. Some theaters appear to have had no more than two doors, left and right, as shown in the Swan drawing; other theaters may have had a third door in the center. The arrangement of the Globe playhouse in this important matter cannot be finally determined, although some particular scenes from Shakespeare's plays seem to demand a third door. In any case, the so-called inner stage, long supposed to have stood at the rear of the Elizabeth stage, almost certainly did not exist. A more modest "discovery space" could be provided at one of the curtained doors when needed, as for example in *The Tempest* when Ferdinand and Miranda are suddenly "discovered" at their game of chess by Prospero. Such scenes never called for extensive action within the discovery space, however, and, indeed, the number of such discoveries in Elizabethan plays is very few. Well-to-do spectators who may have been seated in the gallery above the rear of the stage could not see into the discovery space. Accordingly, it was used sparingly and only for brief visual effects. Otherwise, the actors performed virtually all their scenes on the open stage. Sometimes curtains were hung over the tiring-house facade between the doors to facilitate scenes of concealment, as when Polonius and Claudius eavesdrop on Hamlet and Ophelia.

An upper station was sometimes used as an acting space, but not nearly so often as was once supposed. The gallery seats above the stage, sometimes known as the "Lord's room," were normally sold to well-to-do spectators. (We can see such spectators in the Swan drawing and in Alabaster's *Roxana*.) Occasionally, these box seats could be used by the actors, as when Juliet appears at her window (it is never called a balcony). In military sequences, as in the *Henry VI* plays, the tiring-house facade could represent the walls of a besieged city, with the city's defenders appearing "on the walls" (i.e., in the gallery above the stage) in order to parley with the besieging enemy standing below on the main stage. Such scenes were relatively infrequent, however, and usually required only a small number of persons to be aloft. A music room, when needed, could be located in one of the gallery boxes over the stage, but public theaters did not emulate the private stages with music rooms and music between the acts until some time around 1609.

The use of scenery was almost wholly unknown on the Elizabethan public stage, although we do find occasional

Elizabethan dancers, shown above, perform on a stage below a gallery of musicians. Imported stage designs from Italy made more use of perspective scenery than did the commercial theaters.

Rose playhouse foundations suggest an audience there of around 2,000.) For the most part, the audience was affluent, consisting chiefly of the gentry and of London's substantial mercantile citizenry who paid two to three pence or more for gallery seats or the "Lord's room," but the ample pit or yard also provided room for small shopkeepers and artisans who stood for a penny. The spectators were lively, demanding, and intelligent. Although Shakespeare does allow Hamlet to refer disparagingly on one occasion to the "groundlings" who "for the most part are capable of nothing but inexplicable dumbshows and noise" (*Hamlet*, 3.2.11–12), Shakespeare appealed to the keenest understanding of his whole audience, thereby achieving a breadth of vision seldom found in continental courtly drama of the same period. The vitality and financial success of the Elizabethan public theater is without parallel in English history. The city of London itself, in 1600 or so, had only about 100,000 inhabitants, yet throughout Shakespeare's career several companies were competing simultaneously for this audience and constantly producing new plays. Most new plays ran for only a few performances, so that the acting companies were always in rehearsal with new shows. The actors needed phenomenal memories and a gift of improvisation as well. Their acting seems to have been of a high caliber, despite the speed with which they worked. Among other things, many of them were expert fencers and singers.

The London public stage inherited many of its practices from native and medieval traditions. The fluid, open stage, with spectators on four sides, recalled the arena staging of many early Corpus Christi cycles, saints' plays, and morality plays. The adult professional companies were, as we have seen, descended from the itinerant troupes that had acted their plays throughout England in guildhalls, private residences, monastic houses and schools, and perhaps occasionally outdoors on booth stages (though the evidence for this last possible venue is scarce). The Elizabethan tiring-house facade and platform stage may have owed much to the kinds of theatrical space that touring actors had known, and perhaps to the arrangement of a booth stage and a trestle platform set up against one wall of an innyard where the guests of the inn could enjoy a performance, along with standing spectators in the yard. When the itinerant actors had set up their plays in noblemen's banqueting halls or at court, at any rate, they encountered another space that had an important influence on their concept of a theater: the Tudor hall. We must next examine the significance of this indoor theatrical setting.

hints of the use of labels to designate a certain door or area as a fixed location (as, perhaps, in *The Comedy of Errors*). For the most part, the scene was unlimited and the concept of space was fluid. No proscenium arch or curtain stood between the actors and the audience, and so the action could not be easily interrupted. Only belatedly did the public companies adopt the private-theater practice of entr'acte music, as we have seen. Most popular Elizabethan plays were written to be performed nonstop. Five-act structure had little currency, especially at first, and the occasional act divisions in the published versions of Shakespeare's plays may be nonauthorial. Acting tempo was brisk. The Prologue of *Romeo and Juliet* speaks of "the two hours' traffic of our stage." Plays were performed in the afternoons and had to be completed by dark in order to allow the audience to return safely to London. During the winter season, playing time was severely restricted. Outbreaks of plague often occasioned the closing of the theaters, especially in warm weather.

A capacity audience for the popular theaters came to about 2,000 to 3,000 persons. (The recently excavated

The Tudor Hall

The Tudor banqueting hall played a major part in the staging of much early Tudor drama. Medwall's *Fulgens and Lucrece*, one of the earliest such plays, was written to be performed during the intervals of a state banquet. The patrician guests were seated at tables, while servingmen bustled to and fro or stood crowded together at the doors in the hall "screen." This screen or partition traversed the lower end of the rectangular hall, providing a passageway to the kitchens and to the outside. Its doors—often two, sometimes three—were normally curtained to prevent drafts. This arrangement of the doors bears an interesting resemblance to that of many playhouses in late Elizabethan England, both public and private. Moreover, hall screens and passageways were normally surmounted by a gallery, where musicians could play—an architectural feature markedly resembling the upper galleries of late Elizabethan theaters. Could the Tudor hall screen provide a natural facade for dramatic action? Perhaps it did, although records from Shakespeare's era only rarely document an actual performance in front of the screen, whereas performances were common at the upper end of the hall in front of the dais or in the midst of the hall, where the persons of highest social rank sitting on the dais would have had the best view. The actors of *Fulgens and Lucrece* clearly made use of the doorways in the hall screen, sometimes joking with the servingmen as the actors pushed their way into the hall, but they probably acted in the center, among the spectators' tables. John Heywood's *Play of the Weather* calls for a similar *mise en scène*. Although this ready-made "stage" sufficed for most Tudor plays, the actors sometimes provided additional stage structures; *Weather,* for example, calls for a throne room into which Jupiter can retire without leaving the hall. Similar structures could represent a shop, an orchard, a mountain, or what have you.

Guild and town halls, where players on tour performed before the mayor and council (and sometimes a wider public), provided a similar physical environment except that we cannot be sure that such spaces had galleries in the sixteenth century. Since the gallery is not necessary for many Tudor plays, the players may well have gained experience in halls of this kind that influenced their techniques of staging once they had gravitated to London.

Although both medieval and continental drama offered traditions of multiple staging, in which a series of simultaneously visible and adjacent structures would represent as fixed locations all the playing areas needed for the performance of a play, Tudor indoor staging seems to have made less use of this method than was once supposed. Nor did the various indoor theaters of Tudor England make extensive use of neoclassical staging from Italy, with its street scene in perspective created by means of lath-and-canvas stage "houses." Italian scenery of this sort came into use sooner in the court masque than in regular drama. Nevertheless, we do find in the Tudor indoor theater a neoclassical tendency toward a fixed locale, in preference to the unlimited open stage. *Gammer Gurton's Needle*, for example, acted probably in a university hall, seems to have used one stage structure, or possibly one door, to represent Gammer's house throughout the action, and another to represent Dame Chat's house. Shakespeare may have been influenced by this kind of fixed-locale staging in *The Comedy of Errors*. (Alan Nelson's *Early Cambridge Theaters*, 1994, is an important resource for school staging.)

The Tudor banqueting hall provided a place to "stage" much early Tudor drama. The actors performed on the floor among the tables of the guests. The Middle Temple Hall, shown here, later served as the location for a performance of Shakespeare's Twelfth Night *on February 2, 1602. The Middle Temple is one of the Inns of Court, where young men studied law and occasionally relaxed by staging dramatic entertainments.*

The Private Stage

Despite such influences on the public stage, the most significant contribution of the Tudor hall and its hall screen was to the so-called private stage of the late Elizabethan period—"private" in the sense of being intended for a more select and courtly audience than that which frequented the "public" theaters. In the 1570s, choir boys began performing professionally to courtly and intellectual audiences in London. The choir boys had long performed plays for the royal and noble households to which they were attached, but in the 1570s they were, in effect, organized into professional acting companies. Sebastian Westcote and the Children of Paul's may have originated this enterprise. Their theater was apparently some indoor hall in the vicinity of St. Paul's in London, outfitted much like the typical domestic Tudor hall to which the boys had grown accustomed. Comparable indoor "private" theaters soon followed at Blackfriars and Whitefriars.

At some point, a low stage was constructed in front of the hall screen, and seats were provided for all the spectators. Many of these seats were in the "pit," or what we would call the "orchestra," facing toward the stage at one end of the rectangular room. Other seats were in galleries along both sides of the room; these were quite elaborate in the so-called Second Blackfriars of 1596 and provided two or three tiers of seats. Elegant box seats stood at either side of the stage itself. The Second Blackfriars had a permanently built tiring house to the rear of the stage, with probably three doors. Above it was a gallery used vari-

ously as a lord's room, a music room, and an upper station for occasional acting.

The private theater flourished during the 1580s and again after 1598–1599, having been closed down during most of the 1590s because of its satirical activities. Although it was a commercial theater, it was "private" in its clientele, because its high price of admission (sixpence) excluded those who could stand in the yards of the "public" theaters for a penny (roughly the equivalent of an hour's wage for a skilled worker). Plays written for the more select audiences of the "private" theaters tended to be more satirical and oriented to courtly values than those written for the "public" theaters, although the distinction is by no means absolute.

London Private Theaters

The important private theaters of Shakespeare's London were two in the precinct, or "liberty," of Blackfriars, an early one in Whitefriars about which little is known, a later one there, and a theater at Paul's, the exact location and nature of which is not known. In the thirteenth century, the mother house of the Dominican friars, or Blackfriars, was established on the sloping ground between St. Paul's Cathedral and the river. It was a sizable institution, ultimately covering about five acres of ground. It stood on the very border of the city and, after the custom of the time, was made a liberty; that is to say, it had its own local government and was removed from the immediate jurisdiction of the city of London. After the suppression of the friary and the confiscation of its lands, the jealousy existing between the Privy Council, representing the crown, and the mayor and aldermen, representing the city and probably also the rights of property holders, prevented the district of the Blackfriars from losing its political independence of the municipality. It was still a liberty and therefore attractive to players and other persons wishing to avoid the London authorities. At the same time, aristocrats residing in the area required protection, and the crown had certain rights still in its control.

From 1576 to 1584, the Children of the Queen's Chapel, one of the two most important companies of boy actors, had used a hall in the precinct of Blackfriars in which to act their plays. Here were acted at least some of John Lyly's plays. In 1596, James Burbage purchased property in this precinct and seems to have spent a good deal of money in its adaptation for use as an indoor theater (the so-called Second Blackfriars). He probably appreciated its advantages over Cripplegate or the Bankside of greater proximity to London and of protection against the elements, particularly for use in winter. But the aristocratic residents of the Blackfriars by petition to the Privy Council prevented him from making use of his theater. Plays within the city proper had only recently been finally and successfully prohibited, and the petitioners no doubt

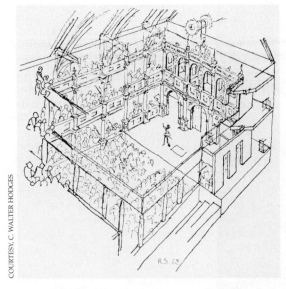

COURTESY: C. WALTER HODGES

A reconstruction of the Second Blackfriars, featuring a rectangular stage, a tiring house with three doors, and a gallery.

objected to their intrusion into Blackfriars on the grounds that the plays and their crowds were a nuisance.

Burbage's new indoor theater may have lain idle from the time of its preparation until 1600; but, in any case, in that year it became the scene of many plays. It was let by lease for the use of the Children of the Chapel, who in 1604 became the Children of the Queen's Revels. Their theater managers brought into their service a number of new dramatists—Ben Jonson, John Marston, George Chapman, and later John Webster. The vogue of the plays acted by the Children of the Chapel was so great as to damage the patronage of the established companies and to compel them to go on the road. Out of this rivalry between the children and the adult actors arose that open competition alluded to in *Hamlet* (2.2.328–362) and sometimes referred to today as the "War of the Theaters." The skirmishes were relatively brief, arising in part from a clash of personalities among Jonson, Marston, and Thomas Dekker, but the debate between public and private acting companies was significant as an indication of whether London drama would continue to play to large popular audiences or would increasingly turn to a more courtly clientele. In 1608, the Burbage interests secured the evacuation of the lease, so that the theater in Blackfriars became the winter playhouse of Shakespeare's company from that time forward.

System of Patronage

In 1572, common players of interludes, along with minstrels, bearwards, and fencers, were included within the hard terms of the act for the punishment of vagabonds, provided that such common players were not enrolled as the servants of a baron of the realm or of some honorable person of greater degree. The result was a system of patronage of theatrical companies in Elizabethan and Jacobean times, according to which players became the "servants" of some nobleman or of some member of the royal family.

By the time Shakespeare came to London in the late 1580s, many of these companies were already in existence, some of which long antedated the passage of the act of 1572. Provincial records of the visits of players, to be sure, sometimes failed to distinguish actors from acrobats or other public performers who were similarly organized. Nonetheless, we have evidence that various companies of players performed in London and elsewhere in the late 1580s under the patronage of the Queen, the Earl of Worcester, the Earl of Leicester, the Earl of Oxford, the Earl of Sussex, the Lord Admiral, and Charles, Lord Howard of Effingham. These companies were eventually much reduced in number; usually only three adult companies acted at any given time in London during Shakespeare's prime. In addition, the children's companies, privately controlled, acted intermittently but at times very successfully. The most important of these were the Children of the Chapel and Queen's Revels and the Children of Paul's, but there were also boy players of Windsor, Eton College, the Merchant Taylors, Westminster, and other schools.

Shakespeare and the London Theatrical Companies

We know that by 1592 Shakespeare had arrived in London and had achieved sufficient notice as a young playwright to arouse the resentment of a rival dramatist, Robert Greene. In that year, shortly before he died, Greene—or possibly his editor after Greene's death—lashed out at an "upstart crow, beautified with our feathers," who had had the audacity to fancy himself "the only Shake-scene in a country" (*Groats-worth of Wit*). This petulant outburst was plainly directed at Shakespeare, since Greene included in his remarks a parody of some lines from *3 Henry VI*. As a university man and an established dramatist, Greene seems to have resented the intrusion into his profession of a mere player who was not university trained. This "upstart crow" was achieving a very real success on the London stage. Shakespeare had probably already written *The Comedy of Errors, Love's Labor's Lost, The Two Gentlemen of Verona*, the *Henry VI* plays, and *Titus Andronicus*, and perhaps also *Richard III* and *The Taming of the Shrew*.

For which acting company or companies had he written these plays, however? By 1594, we know that Shakespeare was an established member of the Lord Chamberlain's company, important enough, in fact, to have been named, along with Will Kempe and Richard Burbage, as payee for court performances on December 26 and 28 of 1594. But when had he joined the Chamberlain's men, and for whom had he written and acted previously? These are the problems of the so-called dark years, during which Shakespeare came to London (perhaps around 1587) and got started on his career.

One prestigious acting company he could have joined was the Earl of Leicester's company, led by James Burbage, father of Shakespeare's later colleague, Richard Burbage. Leicester was a favorite minister of Queen Elizabeth until his death in 1588, and his company of actors received from the Queen in 1574 an extraordinary patent to perform plays anywhere in England, despite all local prohibitions, provided that the plays were approved beforehand by the master of the Queen's Revels. Since an act of 1572 had outlawed all unlicensed troupes, Leicester's men and similar companies attached to important noblemen were given a virtual monopoly over public acting. In 1576, Burbage built the Theatre for his company in the northeast suburbs of London. This group also toured the provinces: Leicester's company visited Stratford-upon-Avon in 1587. Conceivably, Shakespeare served an apprenticeship in this company, though no evidence exists to prove a connection. Leicester's company had lost some of its prominence in 1583, when several of its best men joined the newly formed Queen's men, with Richard Tarlton as its most famous actor. The remaining members of Leicester's company disbanded in 1588 upon the death of the Earl, and many of its principal actors ultimately became part of Lord Strange's company. These probably included George Bryan, Will Kempe, and Thomas Pope, all of whom subsequently went on to become Lord Chamberlain's men.

Lord Strange's (The Earl of Derby's) Men

The Queen's men gained an extraordinary prominence in the 1580s, as Scott McMillin and Sally-Beth MacLean have shown in the *Queen's Men and Their Plays* (1998). This acting group was assembled under royal sponsorship as an instrument of furthering the Protestant Reformation through its performances of plays, and did so with notable success, although it then declined rapidly in the early 1590s chiefly because as a touring company it was unprepared to compete with the new companies that learned how to succeed in the metropolis by staging a wide variety of plays in a fixed London theater. Prominent among the acting companies to which Shakespeare could have belonged when he came to London, probably in the late 1580s, were Lord Strange's men, the Lord Admiral's men, the Earl of Pembroke's men, and the Earl of Sussex's men. Scholars have long speculated that Shakespeare may have joined the company of Ferdinando Stanley, Lord Strange (who in 1593 became the Earl of Derby). The names of George Bryan, Will Kempe, and Thomas Pope appear on a roster of Strange's company in 1593, along with those of John Heminges and Augustine Phillips. All of these men later became part of the Lord Chamberlain's company, most of them when it was first formed in 1594. Shakespeare's name does not appear on the 1593 Lord Strange's list (which was a license for touring in the provinces), but he may possibly have stayed in London to attend to his writing while the company toured. Certainly, an important number of his later associates belonged to this group.

During the years from 1590 to 1594, some of Lord Strange's men appear to have joined forces on occasion with Edward Alleyn and others of the Admiral's men. This impressive combination of talents enjoyed a successful season in 1591–1592, with six performances at court. Alleyn's father-in-law, Philip Henslowe, recorded in his *Diary* the performances of the combined players in early 1592, probably at the Rose Theatre. Their repertory included a *Harey the vj* and a *Titus & Vespacia.* The latter play is, however, no longer thought to have any connection with Shakespeare's *Titus Andronicus;* and the *Harey the vj* may or may not have been Shakespeare's, since *3 Henry VI* was (according to its 1595 title page) acted by Pembroke's men, rather than Lord Strange's men. If Shakespeare was a member of the Strange-Admiral's combination in 1591–1592, we are at a loss to explain why

Clowns were enormously popular on the Elizabethan stage. Of the many Elizabethan clowns whose names are known to us, Richard Tarlton is one of the most famous. (Will Kempe, in Shakespeare's company, the Lord Chamberlain's men, is another; see pp. lxviii-lxix.) Tarlton is shown here inside an elaborate letter T, dancing a jig with his pipe and tabor. Such jigs were often used at the conclusion of a play.

BY PERMISSION OF THE BRITISH LIBRARY

Henslowe's 1592 list records so many performances of plays by Marlowe, Greene, Kyd, and others, but none that are certainly by Shakespeare. On the other hand, the *Harey the vj* may be his, and the title page of the 1594 Quarto of *Titus Andronicus* does list the Earl of Derby's men as performers of the play, in addition to the Earl of Pembroke's and the Earl of Sussex's men. (Lord Strange's men became officially known as the Earl of Derby's men when Lord Strange was made an earl in September 1593.) At any rate, the company disbanded when the Earl died in April 1594, leaving them without a patron. The connection with the Admiral's men was discontinued, with Alleyn returning to the Admiral's men and the rest of the group forming a new company under the patronage of Henry Carey, first Lord Hunsdon, the Lord Chamberlain.

The Earl of Pembroke's Men

The other company to which Shakespeare is most likely to have belonged prior to 1594 is the Earl of Pembroke's company. This group came to grief in 1593–1594, evidently as a result of virulent outbursts of the plague, which had kept the theaters closed during most of 1592 and 1593. Pembroke's men were forced to tour the provinces and then to sell a number of their best plays to the booksellers. Henslowe wrote to Alleyn in September

1593 of the extreme financial plight of Pembroke's company: "As for my lord of Pembroke's [men], which you desire to know where they be, they are all at home and has been this five or six weeks, for they cannot save their charges [expenses] with travel, as I hear, and were fain to pawn their parell [apparel] for their charge." Soon thereafter this company disbanded.

Pembroke's men were associated with a significant number of Shakespeare's early plays. Among the playbooks they evidently sold in 1593–1594 were *The Taming of a Shrew* and *The True Tragedy of Richard Duke of York*. The first of these was published in 1594 with the assertion that it had been "sundry times acted by the Right Honorable the Earle of Pembroke his Servants." Although the text of this quarto is not Shakespeare's play as we know it but, instead, an anonymous version, most scholars now feel certain that it was an imitation of Shakespeare's play and that the work performed by Pembroke's men was, in fact, Shakespeare's. The same conclusion pertains to a performance in 1594 of "*the Tamynge of a Shrowe*" at Newington Butts, a playhouse south of London Bridge. Henslowe's *Diary* informs us that the actors on this occasion were either the Lord Chamberlain's or the Lord Admiral's men. The probability, then, is that Shakespeare's *The Taming of the Shrew* passed from Pembroke's men to the Chamberlain's men when Pembroke's company collapsed in 1593–1594.

The True Tragedy of Richard Duke of York, published in 1595, was a seemingly unauthorized quarto of Shakespeare's *3 Henry VI*. Its title page declared that it had been "sundry times acted by the Right Honorable the Earl of Pembroke his Servants." Probably they acted *2 Henry VI* as well, to which part three was a sequel. In addition, the 1594 Quarto of *Titus Andronicus* mentions on its title page the Earl of Pembroke's servants, although the Earl of Derby's and the Earl of Sussex's men are named there as well. Thus, Pembroke's men performed as many as four of Shakespeare's early plays—more than we can assign to any other known company. Nevertheless, their claim to Shakespeare remains uncertain. We simply do not know who acted several of Shakespeare's earliest plays, such as *The Comedy of Errors, Love's Labor's Lost,* and *The Two Gentlemen of Verona.* Lord Strange's (Derby's) men, as we have seen, did act something called *Harey the vj* and are named on the 1594 title page of *Titus Andronicus.* Sussex's men may conceivably have owned for a time some early Shakespearean plays that later went to the Lord Chamberlain's men, such as *Titus Andronicus.* The Queen's men, although associated with no known Shakespeare play, other than the old *King Lear* (acted jointly with Sussex's men in 1593), were a leading company during the years in question. All we can say for sure is that the difficulties of 1592–1593 with the plague and the death of the Earl of Derby in 1594 led to a major reshuffling of the London acting companies. From this reshuffling emerged in 1594 the Lord Chamberlain's company, with Shakespeare and Richard Burbage (whose earlier history is also difficult to trace) as two of its earliest and most prominent members.

SHAKESPEARE'S LIFE AND WORK

THE EARLY YEARS, 1564–C. 1594

Stratford-upon-Avon

About Shakespeare's place of birth, Stratford-upon-Avon, there is no doubt. He spent his childhood there and returned periodically throughout his life. During most or all of his long professional career in London, his wife and children lived in Stratford. He acquired property and took some interest in local affairs. He retired to Stratford and chose to be buried there. Its Warwickshire surroundings lived in his poetic imagination.

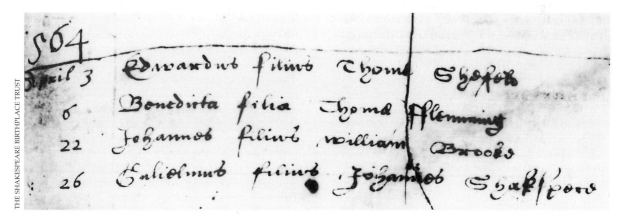

The earliest written reference to William Shakespeare is this record of his christening in the register of Holy Trinity Church at Stratford, April 26, 1564. The entry reads, "Gulielmus filius Johannes Shakspere."

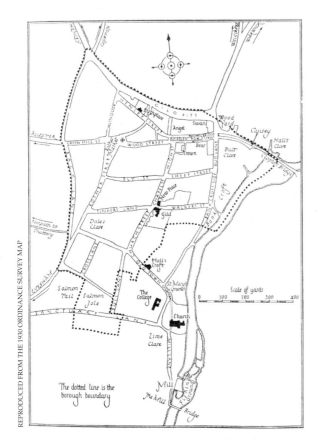

The town of Stratford-upon-Avon as Shakespeare knew it. The house in which he is considered to have been born is on Henley Street; the larger house he purchased in 1597, New Place, is on Chapel Street.

The Stratford of Shakespeare's day was a "handsome small market town" (as described by William Camden) of perhaps 1,500 inhabitants, with fairly broad streets and half-timbered houses roofed with thatch. It could boast of a long history and an attractive setting on the river Avon. A bridge of fourteen arches, built in 1496 by Sir Hugh Clopton, Lord Mayor of London, spanned the river. Beside the Avon stood Trinity Church, built on the site of a Saxon monastery. The chapel of the Guild of the Holy Trinity, dating from the thirteenth century, and an old King Edward VI grammar school were buildings of note. Stratford had maintained a grammar school at least since 1424 and probably long before that. It was a town without the domination of clergy, aristocracy, or great wealth. It lay in a rich agricultural region, in the county of Warwickshire. To the north of Stratford lay the Forest of Arden.

Shakespeare's Family

The family that bore the name of Shakespeare was well distributed throughout England, but was especially numerous in Warwickshire. A name "Saquespee," in various spellings, is found in Normandy at an early date. It means, according to J. Q. Adams, "to draw out the sword quickly." That name, in the form "Sakspee," with many variants, is found in England; also the name "Saksper," varying gradually to the form "Shakespeare." It may have been wrought into that form by the obvious military meaning of "one who shakes the spear."

Our first substantial records of the family begin with Richard Shakespeare, who was, in all probability, Shakespeare's grandfather, a farmer living in the village of Snitterfield four miles from Stratford. He was a tenant on the property of Robert Arden of Wilmcote, a wealthy man with the social status of gentleman. Richard Shakespeare died about 1561, possessed of an estate valued at the very respectable sum of thirty-eight pounds and seventeen shillings.

His son John made a great step forward in the world by his marriage with Mary Arden, daughter of his father's landlord. John Shakespeare had some property of his own and through his wife acquired a good deal more. He moved from Snitterfield to Stratford at some date before 1552. He rose to great local importance in Stratford and bought several houses, among which was the one on Henley Street traditionally identified as Shakespeare's birthplace. William Shakespeare was born in 1564 and was baptized on April 26. The exact date of his birth is not known, but traditionally we celebrate it on April 23, the feast day of St. George, England's patron saint. (The date is at least plausible in view of the practice of baptizing infants shortly after birth.) The house in which Shakespeare was probably born, though almost entirely rebuilt and changed in various and unknown ways during the years that have intervened since Shakespeare's birth, still stands. It is of considerable size, having four rooms on the ground floor, and must, therefore, have been an important business house in the Stratford of those days. John Shakespeare's occupation seems to have been that of a tanner and glover; that is, he cured skins, made gloves and some other leather goods, and sold them in his shop. He was also a dealer in wool, grain, malt, and other farm produce.

The long story, beginning in 1552, of John Shakespeare's success and misfortunes in Stratford is attested to by many borough records. He held various city offices. He was ale taster (inspector of bread and malt), burgess (petty constable), affeeror (assessor of fines), city chamberlain (treasurer), alderman, and high bailiff of the town—the highest municipal office in Stratford. At some time around 1576, he applied to the Herald's office for the right to bear arms and style himself a gentleman. This petition was later to be renewed and successfully carried through to completion by his famous son. In 1577 or 1578, however, when William was as yet only thirteen or fourteen years old, John Shakespeare's fortunes began

This house on Henley Street in Stratford is considered to have been the birthplace of Shakespeare. Its considerable size shows what must have been an important house of business. Shakespeare's father dealt chiefly in leather goods, though he also traded in wool, grain, and other farm produce.

a sudden and mysterious decline. He absented himself from council meetings. He had to mortgage his wife's property and showed other signs of being in financial difficulty. He became involved in serious litigation and was assessed heavy fines. Although he kept his position on the corporation council until 1586 or 1587, he was finally replaced as alderman because of his failure to attend. Conceivably, John Shakespeare's sudden difficulties were the result of persecution for his Catholic faith, since John's wife's family had remained loyal to Catholicism, and the old faith was being attacked with new vigor in the Warwickshire region in 1577 and afterwards. This hypothesis is unsubstantial, however, especially in view of the fact that some Catholics and Puritans seemed to have held posts of trust and to have remained prosperous in Stratford during this period. In the last analysis, we have little evidence as to John Shakespeare's religious faith or as to the reasons for his sudden reversal of fortune.

The family of Shakespeare's mother could trace its ancestry back to the time of William the Conqueror, and Shakespeare's father, in spite of his troubles, was a citizen of importance. John Shakespeare made his mark, instead of writing his name, but so did other men of the time who we know could read and write. His offices, particularly that of chamberlain, and the various public functions he discharged indicate that he must have had some education.

Shakespeare in School

Nicholas Rowe, who published in 1709 the first extensive biographical account of Shakespeare, reports the tradition that Shakespeare studied "for some time at a Free-School." Although the list of students who actually attended the King's New School at Stratford-upon-Avon in the late sixteenth century has not survived, we cannot doubt that Rowe is reporting accurately. Shakespeare's father, as a leading citizen of Stratford, would scarcely have spurned the benefits of one of Stratford's most prized institutions. The town had had a free school since the thirteenth century, at first under the auspices of the Church. During the reign of King Edward VI (1547–1553), the Church lands were expropriated by the crown and the town of Stratford was granted a corporate charter. At this time, the school was reorganized as the King's New School, named in honor of the reigning monarch. It prospered. Its teachers, or "masters," regularly held degrees from Oxford during Shakespeare's childhood and received salaries that were superior to those of most comparable schools.

Much has been learned about the curriculum of such a school. A child would first learn the rudiments of reading and writing English by spending two or three years in a "petty" or elementary school. The child learned to read from a "hornbook," a single sheet of paper mounted on a board and protected by a thin transparent layer

The interior of the Stratford grammar school: a late and not very reliable tradition claims that Shakespeare's desk was third from the front on the left-hand side.

of horn, on which was usually printed the alphabet in small and capital letters and the Lord's Prayer. The child would also practice an ABC book with catechism. When the child had demonstrated the ability to read satisfactorily, the child was admitted, at about the age of seven, to the grammar school proper. Here the day was a rigorous one, usually extending from 6 A.M. in the summer or 7 A.M. in the winter until 5 P.M. Intervals for food or brief recreation came at midmorning, noon, and midafternoon. Holidays occurred at Christmas, Easter, and Whitsuntide (usually late May and June), comprising perhaps forty days in all through the year. Discipline was strict, and physical punishment was common.

Latin formed the basis of the grammar school curriculum. The scholars studied grammar, read ancient writers, recited, and learned to write in Latin. A standard text was the *Grammatica Latina* by William Lilly or Lyly, grandfather of the later Elizabethan dramatist John Lyly. The scholars also became familiar with the *Disticha de Moribus* (moral proverbs) attributed to Cato, *Aesop's Fables,* the *Eclogues* of

Baptista Spagnuoli Mantuanus or Mantuan (alluded to in *Love's Labor's Lost*), the *Eclogues* and *Aeneid* of Virgil, the comedies of Plautus or Terence (sometimes performed in Latin by the children), Ovid's *Metamorphoses* and other of his works, and possibly some Horace and Seneca.

Shakespeare plentifully reveals in his dramatic writings an awareness of many of these authors, especially Plautus (in *The Comedy of Errors*), Ovid (in *A Midsummer Night's Dream* and elsewhere), and Seneca (in *Titus Andronicus*). Although he often consulted translations of these authors, he seems to have known the originals as well. He had, in Ben Jonson's learned estimation, "small Latin and less Greek"; the tone is condescending, but the statement does concede that Shakespeare had some of both. He would have acquired some Greek in the last years of his grammar schooling. By twentieth-century standards, Shakespeare had a fairly comprehensive amount of training in the ancient classics, certainly enough to account for the general, if unscholarly, references we find in the plays.

Shakespeare's Marriage

When Shakespeare was eighteen years old, he married Anne Hathaway, a woman eight years his senior. (The inscription on her grave states that she was sixty-seven when she died in August 1623.) The bishop's register of Worcester, the central city of the diocese, shows for November 27, 1582, the issue of a bishop's license for the marriage of William Shakespeare and Anne "Whately"; the bond of sureties issued next day refers to her as "Hathaway." She has been identified with all reasonable probability as Agnes (or Anne) Hathaway, daughter of the then recently deceased Richard Hathaway of the hamlet of Shottery, a short distance from Stratford.

The obtaining of a license was not normally required for a marriage. William Shakespeare and Anne Hathaway seem to have applied for a license on this occasion because they wished to be married after only one reading of the banns rather than the usual three. (The reading of the banns, or announcement in church of a forthcoming marriage, usually on three successive Sundays, enabled any party to object to the marriage if he or she knew of any legal impediment.) Since the reading of all banns was suspended for long periods during Advent (before Christmas) and Lent (before Easter), a couple intending to marry shortly before Christmas might have had to wait until April before the banns could be read thrice. Accordingly, the bishop not uncommonly granted a license permitting couples to marry during the winter season with only one reading of the banns. To obtain such a license, two friends of the bride's family had to sign a bond obligating themselves to pay the bishop up to forty pounds, should any impediment to the marriage result in a legal action against the bishop for having issued the license.

The actual record of the marriage in a parish register has not survived, but presumably the couple were married shortly after obtaining the license. They may have been married in Temple Grafton, where Anne had relatives. The couple took up residence in Stratford. Anne was already pregnant at the time of the marriage, for she gave birth to a daughter, Susanna, on May 26, 1583. The birth of a child six months after the wedding may explain the need for haste the previous November. These circumstances, and Anne's considerable seniority in age to William, have given rise to much speculation about matters that can never be satisfactorily resolved. We do know that a formal betrothal in the presence of witnesses could legally validate a binding relationship, enabling a couple to consummate their love without social stigma. We know also that Shakespeare dramatized the issue of premarital contract and pregnancy in *Measure for Measure*. Whether Shakespeare entered into such a formal relationship with Anne is, however, undiscoverable.

On February 2, 1585, Shakespeare's only other children, the twins Hamnet and Judith, were baptized in

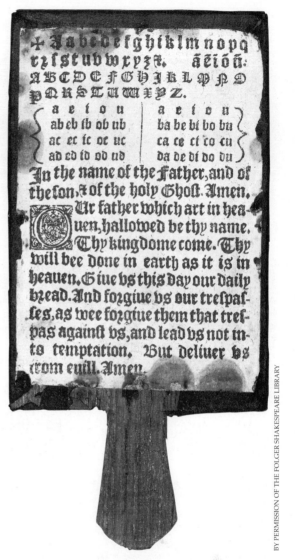

The hornbook pictured here—showing the alphabet and the Lord's Prayer—was part of a child's education in Shakespeare's time.

Stratford Church. The twins seem to have been named after Shakespeare's friends and neighbors, Hamnet Sadler, a baker, and his wife, Judith.

The Seven "Dark" Years

From 1585, the year in which his twins were baptized, until 1592, when he was first referred to as an actor and dramatist of growing importance in London, Shakespeare's activities are wholly unknown. Presumably, at some time during this period he made his way to London and entered its theatrical world, but otherwise we can only record traditions and guesses as to what he did between the ages of 21 and 28.

A schoolroom in Tudor England.

One of the oldest and most intriguing suggestions comes from John Aubrey, who, in collecting information in the late seventeenth century about actors and dramatists for his "Minutes of Lives," sought the help of one William Beeston. John Dryden believed Beeston to be "the chronicle of the stage," and Aubrey seems also to have had a high opinion of Beeston's theatrical knowledge. In his manuscript, Aubrey made a note to himself:

The substantial farmhouse owned by the Hathaways of Shottery, originally known as "Hewland" but now almost universally famous as Anne Hathaway's Cottage.

"W. Shakespeare—quaere [i.e., inquire of] Mr. Beeston, who knows most of him." Aubrey then cites Beeston as his authority for this tradition about Shakespeare:

Though, as Ben Jonson says of him, that he had but little Latin and less Greek, he understood Latin pretty well, for he had been in his younger years a schoolmaster in the country.

Beeston had been a theatrical manager all his life. He was the son of the actor Christopher Beeston, who had been a member of Shakespeare's company, probably from 1596 until 1602, and who therefore had occasion to know Shakespeare well.

Shakespeare's own grammar school education would not have qualified him to be the master of a school, but he could have served as "usher" or assistant to the master. The idea that Shakespeare may have taught in this way is not unattractive. Although, as we have seen, he had some acquaintance with Plautus, Ovid, and other classical writers through his own grammar school reading, a stint as schoolmaster would have made these authors more familiar and readily accessible to him when he began writing his plays and nondramatic poems. His earliest works—*The Comedy of Errors, Love's Labor's Lost, Titus Andronicus, Venus and Adonis, The Rape of Lucrece*—show most steadily and directly the effect of his classical reading. Schoolteaching experience might have encouraged his ambitions to be a writer, like Marlowe or Greene, who went to London not to be actors but to try their hands at poetry and playwriting. All in all, however, it seems more probable that Shakespeare became a young actor rather than a schoolteacher.

Another tradition about the years from 1585 to 1592 asserts that Shakespeare served part of an apprenticeship in Stratford. This suggestion comes to us from one John Dowdall, who, traveling through Warwickshire in 1693, heard the story from an old parish clerk who was showing him around the town of Stratford. According to this parish clerk, Shakespeare had been bound as apprentice to a butcher but ran away from his master to London where he was received into a playhouse as "servitor." John Aubrey records a similar tradition: "When he [Shakespeare] was a boy he exercised his father's trade." Aubrey believed this trade to have been that of a butcher. Moreover, says Aubrey, "When he killed a calf, he would do it in a high style, and make a speech." No other evidence confirms, however, that Shakespeare was a runaway apprentice. The allusion to "killing a calf" may, instead, refer to an ancient rural amusement in which the slaughter of a calf was staged behind a curtain for the entertainment of visitors at county fairs. Conceivably, Shakespeare's participation in such a game during his youth may have given rise to the tradition that he had been a butcher's apprentice.

Another legend, that of Shakespeare's deer stealing, has enjoyed wide currency. We are indebted for this story to the Reverend Richard Davies, who, some time between 1688 and 1709, jotted down some gossipy interpolations in the manuscripts of the Reverend William Fulman. (Fulman himself was an antiquarian who had collected a number of notes about Shakespeare and Stratford.) According to Davies, Shakespeare was "much given to all unluckiness in stealing venison and rabbits, particularly from Sir ——— Lucy, who had him oft whipped and sometimes imprisoned and at last made him fly his native country, to his great advancement." This tradition has led to speculation by Nicholas Rowe that Justice Shallow of *2 Henry IV* and *The Merry Wives of Windsor* is a satirical portrait of Sir Thomas Lucy of Charlecote Hall and that Shakespeare even composed an irreverent ballad about Lucy that added to the urgency of Shakespeare's departure for London. In fact, however, there is no compelling reason to believe that Shallow is based on Lucy, on Justice William Gardiner of Surrey (as Leslie Hotson insists), or on any live Elizabethan. We don't know that Shakespeare ever drew contemporary portraits in his plays, as is sometimes alleged; is Polonius in *Hamlet* Lord Burghley, for example, or is he Shakespeare's original portrait of a minister of state who is also a busybody? Nor do we know if the deer-slaying incident took place at all. It makes interesting fiction but unreliable biography.

Shakespeare's Arrival in London

Because of the total absence of reliable information concerning the seven years from 1585 to 1592, we do not know how Shakespeare got his start in the theatrical world. He may have joined one of the touring companies that came to Stratford and then accompanied the players to London. Edmund Malone offered the unsupported statement (in 1780) that Shakespeare's "first office in the theater was that of prompter's attendant." Presumably, a young man from the country would have had to begin at the bottom. Shakespeare's later work certainly reveals an intimate and practical acquaintance with technical matters of stagecraft. In any case, his rise to eminence as an actor and a writer seems to have been rapid. He was fortunate also in having at least one prosperous acquaintance in London, Richard Field, formerly of Stratford and the son of an associate of Shakespeare's father. Field was a printer, and in 1593 and 1594 he published two handsome editions of Shakespeare's first serious poems, *Venus and Adonis* and *The Rape of Lucrece.*

"The Only Shake-scene in a Country"

The first allusion to Shakespeare after his Stratford days is a vitriolic attack on him. It occurs in *Greene's Groatsworth of Wit Bought with a Million of Repentance,* written by Robert Greene during the last months of his wretched existence (he died in poverty in September

1592). A famous passage in this work lashes out at the actors of the public theaters for having deserted Greene and for bestowing their favor instead on a certain upstart dramatist. The passage warns three fellow dramatists and University Wits, Christopher Marlowe, Thomas Nashe, and George Peele, to abandon the writing of plays before they fall prey to a similar ingratitude. The diatribe runs as follows:

> . . . Base minded men all three of you, if by my misery you be not warned. For unto none of you (like me) sought those burs to cleave—those puppets, I mean, that spake from our mouths, those antics garnished in our colors. Is it not strange that I, to whom they all have been beholding, is it not like that you, to whom they all have been beholding, shall (were ye in that case as I am now) be both at once of them forsaken? Yes, trust them not. For there is an upstart crow, beautified with our feathers, that with his "Tiger's heart wrapped in a player's hide" supposes he is as well able to bombast out a blank verse as the best of you, and, being an absolute *Johannes Factotum*, is in his own conceit the only Shake-scene in a country.

The "burs" here referred to are the actors who have forsaken Greene in his poverty for the rival playwright "Shake-scene"—an obvious hit at Shakespeare. The sneer at a *"Johannes Factotum"* suggests another dig at Shakespeare for being a jack-of-all-trades—actor, playwright, poet, and theatrical handyman in the directing and producing of plays. The most unmistakable reference to Shakespeare, however, is to be found in the burlesque line, "Tiger's heart wrapped in a player's hide," modeled after "Oh, tiger's heart wrapped in a woman's hide!" from *3 Henry VI* (1.4.137). Shakespeare's success as a dramatist had led to an envious outburst from an older, disappointed rival. (Did Shakespeare possibly have this attack in mind some years later when he has Polonius object, in *Hamlet*, 2.2.111–12, "'beautified' is a vile phrase"?)

Soon after Greene's death, Henry Chettle, who had seen the manuscript through the press (and who today some believe to have written the attack himself), issued an apology in his *Kind-Heart's Dream* that may refer to Shakespeare. The apology begins with a disclaimer of all personal responsibility for the incident and with Chettle's insistence that he has neither known nor wishes to know Marlowe (whom Greene's pamphlet had accused of atheism). Toward another unidentified playwright, on the other hand, Chettle expresses genuine concern and regret that Chettle had not done more to soften the acerbity of Greene's vitriol:

> The other, whom at that time I did not so much spare as since I wish I had, for that, as I have moderated the heat of living writers and might have used my own discretion (especially in such a case, the author being dead), that I did not I am as sorry as if the original fault had been my fault; because myself have seen his demeanor no less civil than he excellent in the quality

he professes. Besides, divers of worship have reported his uprightness of dealing, which argues his honesty and his facetious grace in writing that approves his art.

If the unnamed person here is to be understood as Shakespeare, it represents him in a most attractive light. Chettle freely admits to having been impressed by this person's civility. He praises the dramatist as "excellent in the quality he professes," that is, excellent as an actor. Chettle notes with approval that the man he is describing enjoys the favor of certain persons of importance, some of whom have borne witness to his uprightness in dealing. *Greene's Groatsworth of Wit,* then, with its rancorous attack on Shakespeare, has paradoxically led to the plausible inference (though not certain in its identification) that in 1592 Shakespeare was regarded as a man of pleasant demeanor, honest reputation, and acknowledged skill as an actor and writer.

Dramatic Apprenticeship

By the end of the year 1594, when after the long plague the theatrical companies were again permitted to act before London audiences, we find Shakespeare as a member of the Lord Chamberlain's company. Probably he had already written *The Comedy of Errors, Love's Labor's Lost, The Two Gentlemen of Verona*, the *Henry VI* plays, and *Titus Andronicus*. (A *Love's Labor's Won*, mentioned by Francis Meres in 1598, is possibly either a lost play or an alternate title for one of the extant comedies.) He may also have completed *The Taming of the Shrew, A Midsummer Night's Dream, Richard III, King John,* and *Romeo and Juliet*. Although some scholars still question his authorship in part or all of *Titus* and the *Henry VI* plays, no one questions that they are from the period around 1590.

Shakespeare's early development is hard to follow because of difficulties in exact dating of the early plays and because some of the texts (such as *Love's Labor's Lost*) may have been later revised. As a learner making rapid progress in the skill of his art, Shakespeare was also subjected to outside influences that can only partly be determined. Among these influences, we may be sure, were the plays of his contemporary dramatists. If we could define these influences and form an idea of the kinds of plays acceptable on the stage during Shakespeare's early period, we could better understand the milieu in which he began his work.

Fortunately, we know a fair amount concerning the dramatic repertory in London during Shakespeare's early years. Henslowe's *Diary*, for example, records the daily performances of plays by the Lord Strange's men, in conjunction with the Admiral's men, from February 19, 1592 to June 22, 1592. Many of their plays unfortunately are lost, but enough of them are preserved to indicate the sorts of drama then in vogue. The Strange-Admiral's repertory included Christopher Marlowe's *The Jew of Malta,* Robert Greene's *Orlando Furioso* and *Friar Bacon and Friar Bungay,* Robert Greene and Thomas Lodge's *A Looking Glass for London and England,* Thomas Kyd's *The Spanish Tragedy,* the anonymous *A Knack to Know a Knave,* and possibly George Peele's *The Battle of Alcazar,* and Shakespeare's *1 Henry VI.* We find, in other words, a tragedy with a villain as hero, a romantic comedy masquerading as a heroic play, a love comedy featuring a lot of magic, a biblical moral, England's first great revenge tragedy, a popular satiric comedy aimed at dissolute courtiers and usurers, a history play about Portugal's African empire, and an English history play. The titles of other works now lost suggest a similar amalgam of widely differing genres.

Comparatively few plays may have been written during the period when plays were forbidden because of the long plague of 1592–1594. When the Lord Chamberlain's men and the Lord Admiral's men acted under Henslowe's management at the suburban theater of Newington Butts from June 3–13, 1594, their repertories seem to have consisted largely of old plays. In this brief period, they are thought to have acted *Titus Andronicus, Hamlet* (the pre-Shakespearean version), *The Taming of a Shrew* (quite possibly Shakespeare's version), *The Jew of Malta,* a lost play called *Hester and Ahasuerus,* and others.

The Lord Admiral's men probably moved soon afterwards in 1594 to the Rose on the Bankside, across the river Thames from the city of London, where they continued to play under Henslowe's management until 1603. During the years 1594–1597, Henslowe kept in his *Diary* a careful record of their plays and of the sums of money taken in. This circumstance enables us to know a great deal more about the repertory of Shakespeare's rival company than we can ever know about his own. When the Lord Admiral's men began again in 1594, they had five of Marlowe's plays. They seem also to have had Peele's *Edward I,* Kyd's *The Spanish Tragedy,* and a Henry V play. They may also have had plays by both Greene and Peele (Henslowe's chaotic spelling makes it hard to determine), although some of the principal dramas of these two authors had probably ceased to be acted.

We do not know as much about the repertory of the Lord Chamberlain's company as we do about that of the Lord Admiral's men. We know enough, however, to be sure that in 1594 both companies were acting the same sorts of plays that had been on the boards in 1592. We have, therefore, grounds for assuming that, in spite of the loss of many plays (some of which may have been important), the chief contemporary influences upon Shakespeare during his early period were those of Marlowe, Greene, Peele, and Kyd. As an actor possibly in Lord Strange's company or the Earl of Pembroke's company, he would have been familiar with their plays.

Shakespeare learned also from Lyly, though perhaps more from reading Lyly's plays than from actually seeing or performing in them. The boy actors for whom Lyly wrote were forced by the authorities to suspend acting in about 1591 because of their tendency toward controversial satire, and a number of Lyly's plays were printed at that time. As a theatrical figure, therefore, Lyly belonged really to the previous decade.

The Early Plays

Although Shakespeare's genius manifests itself in his early work, his indebtedness to contemporary dramatists and to classical writers is also more plainly evident than in his later writings. His first tragedy, *Titus Andronicus* (c. 1589–1592), is more laden with quotations and classical references than any other tragedy he wrote. Its genre owes much to the revenge play that had been made so popular by Thomas Kyd. Like Kyd, Shakespeare turns to Seneca but also reveals on stage a considerable amount of sensational violence in a manner that is distinctly not classical. For his first villain, Aaron the Moor, Shakespeare borrows some motifs from the morality play and its gleefully sinister tempter, the Vice. Shakespeare may also have had in mind the boastful antics of Marlowe's Vicelike Barabas, in *The Jew of Malta.* Certainly, Shakespeare reveals an extensive debt in his early works to Ovid and to the vogue of Ovidian narrative poetry in the early 1590s, as, for example, in his repeated allusions to the story of Philomela and Tereus (in *Titus Andronicus*) and in his Ovidian poems, *Venus and Adonis* and *The Rape of Lucrece* (1593, 1594).

Shakespeare was still questing for a suitable mode in tragedy and was discovering that the English drama of the 1590s offered no single, clear model. His only other early tragedy, *Romeo and Juliet* (c. 1594–1596), proved to be as different a tragedy from *Titus Andronicus* as could be imagined. Revenge is still prominent in *Romeo and Juliet* but is ultimately far less compelling a theme than the brevity of love and the sacrifice the lovers make of themselves to one another. Shakespeare's source is not the revenge drama of Seneca or Kyd, but a romantic love narrative derived from the fiction of Renaissance Italy. Elements of comedy so predominate in the play's first half that one senses a closer affinity to *A Midsummer Night's Dream* than to *The Spanish Tragedy.*

Shakespeare discovered his true bent more quickly in comedy than in tragedy. Again, however, he experimented with a wide range of models and genres. *The Comedy of Errors* (c. 1589–1594) brings together elements of two plots from the Latin drama of Plautus. The character types and situations are partly derivative, but Shakespeare still reveals an impressive skill in plot construction. *Love's Labor's Lost* (c. 1588–1597) is Shakespeare's most Lylyan early comedy, with its witty debates and its amicable, if brittle, war between the sexes. The play also features an array of humorous characters, including a clownish bumpkin, a country slut, a fantastic courtier, a pedant, a country

A contemporary illustration of Titus Andronicus, *the earliest of Shakespeare's tragedies. Shakespeare's early plays demonstrated that he was more than a slavish imitator of predecessors such as Kyd and Marlowe.*

THE GREAT POND AT ELVETHAM
arranged for the Second Day's Entertainment.

A. Her Majestie's presence seate and traine.   B. Nereus and his followers.   C. The pinnace of Neæra and her musicke.   D. The Ship-ile.
E. A boate with musicke, attending on the pinnace of Neæra.   F. The Fort-mount.   G. The Snaile-mount.   H. The Roome of Estate.
I. Her Majestie's Court.   K. Her Majestie's Wardrop.   L. The place whence Silvanus and his companie issued.

An entertainment presented by the Earl of Hertford to Queen Elizabeth during her visit to Elvetham in 1591 is seemingly referred to by Shakespeare in A Midsummer Night's Dream, *2.1.157–64. The scene shows an elaborate water pageant in honor of the Queen, who appears enthroned at the left of the picture.*

curate, and the like, whose mannerisms and wordplay add to the rich feast of language in a play that centers its attention on proper and improper styles. *The Two Gentlemen of Verona* (c. 1590–1594) and *The Taming of the Shrew* (c. 1590–1593) are derived from Italianate romantic fiction and comedy. In both, Shakespeare skillfully combines simultaneous plots that offer contrasting views on love and friendship. (*The Taming of the Shrew* makes effective use of a "frame" plot involving a group of characters who serve as audience for the rest of the play.) *A Midsummer Night's Dream* (c. 1595), with its four brilliantly interwoven actions involving court figures, lovers, fairies, and Athenian tradesmen, shows us Shakespeare already at the height of his powers in play construction, even though the comic emphasis on love's irrationality in this play is still in keeping with Shakespeare's early style. The early comedies do

not ignore conflict and danger, as we see in the threatened execution of Egeon in *The Comedy of Errors* and the failure of courtships in *Love's Labor's Lost*, but these plays do not as yet fully explore the social dilemmas of *The Merchant of Venice*, the narrowly averted catastrophe of *Much Ado About Nothing*, or the melancholy vein of *As You Like It* and *Twelfth Night*. On stage, early comedies such as *The Comedy of Errors* and *The Taming of the Shrew* are as hilariously funny as anything Shakespeare ever wrote.

Shakespeare's early history plays show a marked affinity with those of Marlowe, Peele, and Greene. Yet today Shakespeare is given more credit for pioneering in the genre of the English history play than he once was. If all the *Henry VI* plays (c. 1589–1592) are basically his, as scholars now often allow, he had more imitators in this genre than predecessors. He scored a huge early success with the heroic character of Lord Talbot in *1 Henry VI*, and by the time Richard Duke of Gloucester had emerged from the *Henry VI* plays to become King Richard III, Shakespeare's fame as a dramatist was assured. He had, of course, learned much from Marlowe's "mighty line" in *Tamburlaine* (1587–1588) and perhaps from Peele's *The Battle of Alcazar* (1588–1589). The anonymous *Famous Victories of Henry V* (1583–1588) must have preceded and influenced his work. Even so, Shakespeare had done much more than simply "beautify" himself with the "feathers" of earlier dramatists, as Greene (or Chettle) enviously charged. Even in his earliest work, Shakespeare already displayed an extraordinary ability to transcend the models from which he learned.

SHAKESPEARE IN THE THEATER, C. 1594–1601

By the year 1594, Shakespeare had already achieved a considerable reputation as a poet and dramatist. We should not be surprised that many of his contemporaries thought of his nondramatic writing as his most significant literary achievement. Throughout his lifetime, in fact, his contemporary fame rested, to a remarkable degree, on his nondramatic poems, *Venus and Adonis*, *The Rape of Lucrece*, and the *Sonnets* (which were circulated in manuscript prior to their unauthorized publication in 1609). One of the earliest tributes suggesting the importance of the poems is found in an anonymous commendatory verse prefixed to Henry Willobie's *Willobie His Avisa* (1594). It summarizes the plot and theme of *The Rape of Lucrece*:

> Though *Collatine* have dearly bought,
> To high renown, a lasting life,
> And found—that most in vain have sought—
> To have a fair and constant wife,
>   Yet Tarquin plucked his glittering grape,
>   And Shakespeare paints poor Lucrece' rape.

Richard Barnfield, in his *Poems in Divers Humors* (1598), praised the "honey-flowing vein" of Shakespeare's *Venus and Adonis* and *The Rape of Lucrece*.

Yet Shakespeare's plays were also highly regarded by his contemporaries, even if those plays were accorded a literary status below that given to the narrative and lyrical poems. Francis Meres insisted, in 1598, that Shakespeare deserved to be compared not only with Ovid for his verse but also with Plautus and Seneca for his comedies and tragedies:

> As the soul of Euphorbus was thought to live in Pythagoras, so the sweet, witty soul of Ovid lives in mellifluous and honey-tongued Shakespeare: witness his *Venus and Adonis*, his *Lucrece*, his sugared sonnets among his private friends, etc.
>
> As Plautus and Seneca are accounted the best for comedy and tragedy among the Latins, so Shakespeare among the English is the most excellent in both kinds for the stage: for

comedy, witness his *Gentlemen of Verona*, his *Errors*, his *Love's Labor's Lost*, his *Love's Labor's Won*, his *Midsummer Night's Dream*, and his *Merchant of Venice;* for tragedy, his *Richard the II*, *Richard the III*, *Henry the IV*, *King John*, *Titus Andronicus*, and his *Romeo and Juliet*.

Comedy and tragedy were, after all, literary forms sanctioned by classical precept. By calling some of Shakespeare's English history plays "tragedies," Meres endowed them with the respectability of an ancient literary tradition, recognizing, too, that many of Shakespeare's historical plays culminate in the death of an English king.

John Weever, too, in his epigram *Ad Gulielmum Shakespeare* in *Epigrams in the Oldest Cut and Newest Fashion* (1599), mentioned not only the ever-popular narrative poems but also *Romeo and Juliet* and a history play about one of the Richards:

> Honey-tongued Shakespeare! When I saw thine issue,
> I swore Apollo got them and none other:
> Their rosy-tainted features clothed in tissue,
> Some heaven-born goddess said to be their mother;
> Rose-cheeked Adonis, with his amber tresses,
> Fair fire-hot Venus, charming him to love her;
> Chaste Lucretia virgin-like her dresses,
> Proud lust-stung Tarquin seeking still to prove her;
> *Romeo, Richard*—more whose names I know not.
> Their sugared tongues and power-attractive beauty
> Say they are saints, although that saints they show not,
> For thousands vows to them subjective duty;
> They burn in love thy children. Shakespeare het them.
> Go, woo thy muse more nymphish brood beget them.

Even Gabriel Harvey, an esteemed classical scholar and friend of Edmund Spenser, considered Shakespeare's play *Hamlet* to be worthy of no less praise than the best of the Ovidian poems. Harvey's comments are to be found in a marginal note to a copy of Speght's *Chaucer*, written down some time between 1598 and 1601:

> The younger sort takes much delight in Shakespeare's *Venus and Adonis*, but his *Lucrece* and his tragedy of *Hamlet, Prince of Denmark* have it in them to please the wiser sort.

Shakespeare's growing fame was even such that his dramatic characters began to enter into the intellectual life of the time. The name of Falstaff became a byword almost as soon as he made his appearance on the stage. The references were not always friendly. A play written to be performed by the rival Admiral's company in answer to *1 Henry IV*, called *Sir John Oldcastle* (1599), took Falstaff to task for being a "pampered glutton" and an "aged counsellor to youthful sin." Evidently, the authors of this attack were offended by the fact that Falstaff had been named "Oldcastle" in an early version of *1 Henry IV*, thereby dishonoring the name of one whom many Puritans regarded as a martyr to their cause (see the Introduction to *1 Henry IV*). Generally, however, the references

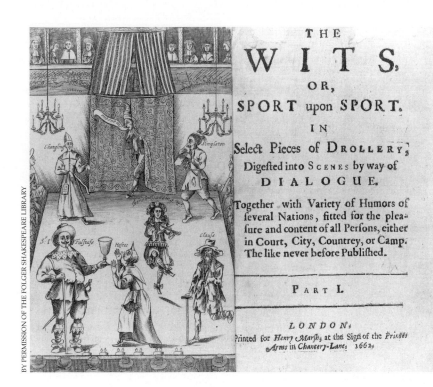

Falstaff and Mistress Quickly are shown here in a composite theatrical illustration of about 1662. The engraving, used as the frontispiece to Francis Kirkman's The Wits, or Sport upon Sport, *also shows other theatrical types. Visible are candelabras and footlights for stage lighting and a curtained area used perhaps for "discoveries." Spectators are visible in the gallery above, as they are also in the De Witt drawing of the Swan Theatre on p. xlvi and in Alabaster's* Roxana *on p. xlv.*

during this period to Falstaff and his cronies were fond. In a letter to a friend in London, for example, Sir Charles Percy fretted jocosely that his prolonged stay in the country among his rustic neighbors might cause him to "be taken for Justice Silence or Justice Shallow" (1600). In another letter, from the Countess of Southampton to her husband (written seemingly in 1599), Falstaff's name had become so familiar that it was used apparently as a privately understood substitute for the name of some real person in an item of court gossip:

All the news I can send you, that I think will make you merry, is that I read in a letter from London that Sir John Falstaff is by his Mistress Dame Pintpot made father of a godly miller's thumb, a boy that's all head and very little body; but this is a secret.

Shakespeare's immense popularity as a dramatist was bound to invite some resentment. One irreverent reaction is found in the so-called *Parnassus* trilogy (1598–1603). The three plays in this series consist of *The Pilgrimage to Parnassus* and *The Return from Parnassus,* in two parts, all of which were acted by the students of St. John's College, Cambridge.

These *Parnassus* plays take a mordantly satirical view of English life around 1600, from the point of view of university graduates attempting to find gainful employment. The graduates discover, to their vocal dismay, that they must seek the patronage of fashion-mongering courtiers, complacent justices of the peace, professional acting com-

panies who offer them pitifully small wages, and the like. One especially foolish patron, to whom the witty Ingenioso applies for a position, is a poetaster named Gullio. This courtly fop aspires to be a fashionable poet himself, and agrees to hire Ingenioso if the latter will help him with his verse writing. In fact, however, as Ingenioso scornfully observes in a series of asides, Gullio's verses are "nothing but pure Shakespeare and shreds of poetry that he hath gathered at the theaters." Most of all, Gullio loves to plagiarize from *Venus and Adonis* and *Romeo and Juliet.* With unparalleled presumption, he actually requests Ingenioso to compose poems "in two or three divers veins, in Chaucer's, Gower's and Spenser's and Mr. Shakespeare's," which Gullio will then pass off as his own inspiration. When Ingenioso does so extempore, producing, among other things, a fine parody of *Venus and Adonis,* Gullio is as delighted as a child. Although he admires Spenser, Chaucer, and Gower, Gullio confesses that Shakespeare is his favorite; he longs to hang Shakespeare's portrait "in my study at the court" and vows he will sleep with *Venus and Adonis* under his pillow (*The Return from Parnassus,* Part I, 1009–1217). Later on (lines 1875–1880), some university graduates trying out as actors in Shakespeare's company are requested to recite a few famous lines from the beginning of *Richard III*—lines that, in the satirical context of this play, sound both stereotyped and bombastic. Shakespeare's fame made him an easy target for university "wits" who regarded the theater of London

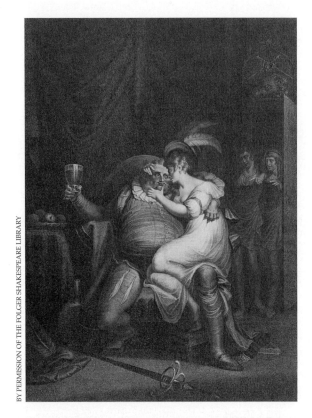

Henry Fuseli's nineteenth-century interpretation of Falstaff shows him in the tavern in Eastcheap with Doll Tearsheet on his lap while Prince Hal and Poins, disguised as tapsters, enter from behind. Falstaff is perhaps saying, "Peace, good Doll, do not speak like a death's-head" (2 Henry IV, 2.4.232–3).

as lowbrow. Still, the portrait throughout is more satirical of those who plagiarize and idolize Shakespeare than of the dramatist's own work. In their backhanded tribute, the *Parnassus* authors make plain that Shakespeare was a household name even at the universities.

Shakespeare's Career and Private Life

During the years from 1594 to 1601, Shakespeare seems to have prospered as an actor and writer for the Lord Chamberlain's men. Whether he had previously belonged to Lord Strange's company or to the Earl of Pembroke's company, or possibly to some other group, is uncertain, but we know that he took part in 1594 in the general reorganization of the companies, out of which emerged the Lord Chamberlain's company. In 1595, his name appeared, for the first time, in the accounts of the Treasurer of the Royal Chamber as a member of the Chamberlain's company of players, which had presented two comedies before Queen Elizabeth at Greenwich in the Christmas season of 1594. This company usually performed at the Theatre, northeast of London, from 1594

until 1599, when they moved to the Globe playhouse south of the Thames. They seem to have been the victors in the intense economic rivalry between themselves and the Lord Admiral's company at the Rose playhouse under Philip Henslowe's management. Fortunately for all the adult companies, the boys' private theatrical companies were shut down during most of the 1590s. Shakespeare's company enjoyed a phenomenal success, and in short time it became the most successful theatrical organization in England.

The nucleus of the Chamberlain's company in 1594 was the family of Burbage. James Burbage, the father, was owner of the Theatre, Cuthbert Burbage was a manager, and Richard Burbage became the principal actor of the troupe. Together the Burbages owned five "shares" in the company, entitling them to half the profits. Shakespeare and four other principal actors—John Heminges, Thomas Pope, Augustine Phillips, and Will Kempe—owned one share each. Not only was Shakespeare a full sharing actor, but also he was the principal playwright of the company. He was named as a chief actor in the 1616 edition of Ben Jonson's *Every Man in His Humor,* performed by the Chamberlain's company in 1598. Later tradition reports, with questionable reliability, that Shakespeare specialized in "kingly parts" or in the roles of older men, such as Adam in *As You Like It* and the Ghost in *Hamlet.* Shakespeare was more celebrated as a playwright than as an actor, and his acting responsibilities may well have diminished as his writing reputation grew. The last occasion on which he is known to have acted was in Jonson's *Sejanus* in 1603.

His prosperity appears in the first record of his residence in London. The tax returns, or Subsidy Rolls, of a parliamentary subsidy granted to Queen Elizabeth for the year 1596 show that Shakespeare was a resident in the parish of St. Helen's, Bishopsgate, near the Theatre, and was assessed at the respectable sum of five pounds. By the next year, Shakespeare had evidently moved to Southwark, near the Bear Garden, for the returns from

First among the actors in Shakespeare's company was Richard Burbage (1567–1619). He played Hamlet, Othello, King Lear, and presumably other major roles including Macbeth, Antony, Coriolanus, and Prospero.

Bishopsgate show his taxes delinquent. He was later located and the taxes paid.

In 1596, Shakespeare suffered a serious personal loss: the death of his only son Hamnet, at the age of eleven. Hamnet was buried at Stratford in August.

Shakespeare acquired property in Stratford during these years, as well as in London. In 1597 he purchased New Place, a house of importance and one of the two largest in the town. Shakespeare's family entered the house as residents shortly after the purchase and continued to live there until long after Shakespeare's death. The last of his family, his granddaughter, Lady Bernard, died in 1670, and New Place was sold.

Shakespeare was also interested in the purchase of land at Shottery in 1598. He was listed among the chief holders of corn and malt in Stratford that same year and sold a load of stone to the Stratford corporation in 1599.

No less suggestive of Shakespeare's rapid rise in the world is his acquisition of the right to bear arms, or, in other words, his establishment in the rank and title of gentleman. The Herald's College in London preserves two drafts of a grant of arms to Shakespeare's father, devised by one William Dethick and dated October 20, 1596. Although we may certainly believe that the application was put forward by William Shakespeare, John Shakespeare was still living, and the grant was drawn up in the father's name. The device for Shakespeare's coat of arms makes a somewhat easy use of the meaning of his name:

Gold on a bend sables, a spear of the first steeled argent. And for his crest of cognizance a falcon, his wings displayed argent, standing on a wreath of his colors, supporting a spear, gold

steeled as aforesaid, set upon a helmet with mantles and tassels, as hath been accustomed and doth more plainly appear depicted on this margent.

According to one of the documents in the grant, John Shakespeare, at the height of his prosperity as a Stratford burgher, had applied twenty years before to the Herald's College for authority to bear arms. The family may not have been able to meet the expense of seeing the application through, however, until William Shakespeare had made his fortune. The grant of heraldic honors to John Shakespeare was confirmed in 1599.

A lawsuit during this period gives us a rather baffling glimpse into Shakespeare's life in the theater. From a writ discovered by Leslie Hotson (*Shakespeare Versus Shallow,* 1931) in the records of the Court of the Queen's Bench, Michaelmas term 1596, we learn that a person named William Wayte sought "for fear of death" to have William Shakespeare, Francis Langley, and two unknown women bound over to keep the peace. Earlier in the same term, moreover, Francis Langley had sworn out a similar writ against this same William Wayte and his stepfather William Gardiner, a justice of the peace in Surrey. Langley was owner of the Swan playhouse on the bankside, near the later-built Globe. His quarrel with Gardiner and Wayte appears to have jeopardized all the acting companies that performed plays south of the Thames, for William Gardiner's jurisdiction included the Bankside theater district. Gardiner and Wayte vengefully tried to drive the theaters out of the area. Possibly Shakespeare's company acted occasionally at the Swan in 1596. Hotson speculates that Shakespeare retaliated by immortalizing

This recreation of what New Place purportedly looked like during Shakespeare's ownership suggests that it must have indeed been an imposing structure. It was warmed by ten fireplaces and had surrounding grounds that included two gardens and two barns.

Gardiner and Wayte as Shallow and Slender in *The Merry Wives of Windsor*. The date of 1596 is too early for that play, and we do not know that Shakespeare drew contemporary portraits in his drama, but we can wonder if lawsuits of this sort gave him no very high opinion of the law's delay and the insolence of office.

During this period Shakespeare's plays began to appear occasionally in print. His name was becoming such a drawing card that it appeared on the title pages of the Second and Third Quartos of *Richard II* (1598), the Second Quarto of *Richard III* (1598), *Love's Labor's Lost* (1598), and the Second Quarto of *1 Henry IV* (1599).

In 1599, the printer William Jaggard sought to capitalize unscrupulously on Shakespeare's growing reputation by bringing out a slender volume of twenty or twenty-one poems called *The Passionate Pilgrim*, attributed to Shakespeare. In fact, only five of the poems were assuredly his, and none of them was newly composed for the occasion. Three came from *Love's Labor's Lost* (published in 1598) and two from Shakespeare's as yet unpublished sonnet sequence.

Contemporary Drama

Shakespeare was without doubt the leading dramatist of the period from 1594 to 1601, not only in our view, but also in that of his contemporaries. The earlier group of dramatists from whom he had learned so much—Lyly, Greene, Marlowe, Peele, Kyd, Nashe—were either dead or no longer writing plays. The group of dramatists who were to rival him in the 1600s and eventually surpass him in contemporary popularity had not yet become well known.

Ben Jonson's early career is obscure. He may have written an early version of his *A Tale of a Tub* in 1596 and *The Case Is Altered* in 1597, though both were later revised. Unquestionably, his first major play was *Every Man in His Humor* (1598), in which Shakespeare acted. This comedy did much to establish the new vogue of comedy of humors, a realistic and satirical kind of drama featuring "humors" characters whose personalities are dominated by some exaggerated trait. We are invited to laugh at the country simpleton, the jealous husband, the overly careful father, the cowardly braggart soldier, the poetaster, and the like. Shakespeare responded to the vogue of humors comedy in his *Henry IV* plays and *The Merry Wives*. Jonson followed his great success with *Every Man Out of His Humor* (1599), an even more biting vision of human folly. George Chapman also deserves important credit for the establishment of humors comedy, with his *The Blind Beggar of Alexandria* (1596) and *An Humorous Day's Mirth* (1597).

Despite the emergence of humors comedy, however, with its important anticipations of Jacobean and even Restoration comedy of manners, the prevailing comedy to be seen on the London stage between 1595 and 1601 was romantic comedy. William Haughton wrote *Englishmen for My Money* in 1598. Thomas Dekker's *Old Fortunatus*, the dramatization of a German folktale, appeared in 1599. Dekker's *The Shoemaker's Holiday* (1599), despite its seemingly realistic touches of life among the apprentices of London, is a thoroughly romanticized saga of rags to riches. A young aristocrat disguises himself as a shoemaker to woo a mayor's daughter; love conquers social rank, and the King himself sentimentally blesses the union. Thomas Heywood wrote heroical romances and comedies, perhaps including *Godfrey of Boulogne* (1594), although most of his early works have disappeared. The boys' private theaters were closed during most of the 1590s, until 1598–1599, and thus the child actors could not perform the satirical comedies at which they were so adept.

Patriotic history drama also continued to flourish on the public stage during those years when Shakespeare wrote his best history plays. Heywood wrote the two parts of *Edward IV* between 1592 and 1599. The anonymous *Edward III* appeared in 1595 or earlier, enough in the vein of Shakespeare's histories that it is sometimes attributed (albeit on uncertain and impressionistic grounds) to him. *Sir Thomas More,* by Munday, Dekker, Chettle, and perhaps Heywood, was written sometime in the later 1590s and very probably revised by Shakespeare himself. Chettle and Munday wrote a trilogy of plays about *Robert, Earl of Huntingdon,* or Robin Hood (1598–1599), on themes that remind us of Shakespeare's *As You Like It*. These plays were performed by the Admiral's men, who also produced the two parts of *Sir John Oldcastle* (1599–1600) by Drayton, Hathway, Munday, and others, in rivalry with Shakespeare's *Henry IV* plays.

Shakespeare's Work

Shakespeare thus wrote his greatest history plays for an audience that knew the genre well. The history play had first become popular just at the start of Shakespeare's career, during the patriotic aftermath of the defeat of the Spanish Armada (1588). Shakespeare himself did much to establish the genre. He wrote first his four-play series dealing with the Lancastrian wars of the fifteenth century, and then went backwards in historical time to King John's reign and to the famous reigns of Henry IV and Henry V.

His romantic comedies were also written for audiences that knew what to expect from the genre. From the comedies of Greene, Peele, Munday, and the rest, as well as Shakespeare himself, Elizabethan audiences were thoroughly familiar with such conventions as fairy charms, improbable adventures in forests, heroines disguised as young men, shipwrecks, love overcoming differences in social rank, and the like. Yet the conventions also demanded more than mere horseplay or foolish antics. Plays of this sort customarily affirmed "wholesome" moral values and appealed to generosity and decency. They were written, like the history plays, for a socially diversified, though generally intelligent and well-to-do, audience.

Several critical terms have been used to suggest the special quality of Shakespeare's comedies during this period of the later 1590s. "Romantic comedy" implies first of all a story in which the main action is about love, but it can also imply elements of the improbable and the miraculous. (The difference between the "romantic comedies" of the later 1590s and the "romances" of Shakespeare's last years, 1606–1613, is that, in part at least, romantic comedy seeks to "make wonder familiar," whereas the romances seek to make the familiar wonderful.) "Philosophical comedy" emphasizes the moral and sometimes Christian idealism underlying many of these comedies of the 1590s: the quest for deep and honest understanding between men and women in *Much Ado About Nothing*, the awareness of an eternal and spiritual dimension to love in *The Merchant of Venice*, and the theme of love as a mysterious force able to regenerate a corrupted social world from which it has been banished in *As You Like It*. "Love-game comedy" pays particular attention to the witty battle of the sexes that we find in several of these plays. "Festive comedy" urges the celebratory nature of comedy, especially in *Twelfth Night* and the *Henry IV* plays, in which Saturnalian revelry must contend against grim and disapproving forces of sobriety. "Comedy of forgiveness," although applicable to only a limited number of plays of this period (especially *Much Ado*), stresses the unexpected second chance that the world of comedy extends to even the most undeserving of heroes; Claudio is forgiven his ill treatment of Hero, although the play's villain, Don John, is not.

SHAKESPEARE IN THE THEATER, C.1601–1608

When the Globe, the most famous of the London public playhouses, was built in 1599, one-half interest in the property was assigned to the Burbage family, especially to the brothers Cuthbert and Richard Burbage. The other half was divided among five actor-sharers: Shakespeare, Will Kempe, Thomas Pope, Augustine Phillips, and John Heminges. Kempe left the company, however, in 1599 and subsequently became a member of the Earl of Worcester's men. His place as leading comic actor was taken by Robert Armin, an experienced man of the theater and occasional author, whose comic specialty was the role of the wise fool. We can observe in Shakespeare's plays the effects of Kempe's departure and of Armin's arrival. Kempe had apparently specialized in clownish and rustic parts, such as those of Dogberry in *Much Ado*, Lancelot Gobbo in *The Merchant of Venice*, and Bottom in *A Midsummer Night's Dream*. (We know that he played Dogberry because his name appears in the early Quarto, derived from the play manuscript; similar evidence links his name to the role of Peter in *Romeo and Juliet*.) For Armin, on the other hand, Shakespeare evidently created such roles as Touchstone in *As You Like It*, Feste in *Twelfth Night*, Lavatch in *All's Well That Ends Well*, and the Fool in *King Lear*.

Other shifts in personnel can sometimes be traced in Shakespeare's plays, especially changes in the number and ability of the boy actors (whose voices would suddenly start to crack at puberty). Shakespeare makes an amusing point about the relative size of two boy actors, for example, in *A Midsummer Night's Dream* and in *As You Like It*; this option may have been available to him only at certain times. On the other hand, not all changes in the company roster can be related meaningfully to

Among the members of Shakespeare's acting company were John Lowin, William Sly, and Nathaniel Field.

Will Kempe (above), for whom Shakespeare created several clownish roles, was a member of the Lord Chamberlain's men and a noted Elizabethan comic. Kempe left the company in 1599 and was replaced by Robert Armin (right), an accomplished actor who specialized in fool's roles.

Shakespeare's dramatic development. Augustine Phillips, who died in 1605, was a full actor-sharer of long standing in the company, but his "type" of role was probably not sharply differentiated from that of several of his associates. Shakespeare's plays, after all, involve many important supporting roles, and versatility in the undertaking of such parts must have been more common than specialization. (Phillips is remembered also for his last will and testament: he left a bequest of "a thirty shillings piece in gold" to "my fellow, William Shakespeare," and similar bequests to other members of the troupe.)

With the reopening of the boys' acting companies in 1598–1599, a serious economic rivalry sprang up between them and the adult companies. The Children of the Chapel Royal occupied the theater in Blackfriars, and the Children of Paul's probably acted in their own singing school in St. Paul's churchyard. Their plays exploited a new vogue for satire. The satiric laughter was often directed at the city of London and its bourgeois inhabitants: socially ambitious tradesmen's wives, Puritan zealots, and the like. Other favorite targets included parvenu knights at court, would-be poets, and hysterical governmental officials. The price of admission at the private theaters was considerably higher than at the Globe or Rose, so the clientele tended to be more fashionable. Sophisticated authors like Ben Jonson, George Chapman, and John Marston tended to find writing for the boy actors more rewarding literarily than writing for the adult players.

One manifestation of the rivalry between public and private theaters was the so-called War of the Theaters, or Poetomachia. In part, this was a personal quarrel between Jonson on one side and Marston and Thomas Dekker on the other. Underlying this quarrel, however, was a serious hostility between a public theater and one that catered more to the elite. Dekker, with Marston's encouragement, attacked Jonson as a literary dictator and snob—one who subverted public decency. Jonson replied with a fervent defense of the artist's right to criticize everything that the artist sees wrong. The major plays in the exchange (1600–1601) were Jonson's *Cynthia's Revels,* Dekker and Marston's *Satiromastix,* and Jonson's *The Poetaster.*

Shakespeare allows Hamlet to comment on the theatrical rivalry (2.2.330–62), with seeming regret for the fact that the boys have been overly successful and that many adult troupes have been obliged to tour the provinces. Most of all, though, Hamlet's remarks deplore the needless bitterness on both sides. The tone of kindly remonstrance makes it seem unlikely that Shakespeare took an active part in the fracas. To be sure, in the Cambridge play *2 Return from Parnassus* (1601–1603), the character called Will Kempe does assert that his fellow actor, Shakespeare, had put down the famous Ben Jonson:

Why, here's our fellow Shakespeare puts them all down, ay, and Ben Jonson, too. O, that Ben Jonson is a pestilent fellow! And he brought up Horace giving the poets a pill, but our fellow Shakespeare hath given him a purge that made him bewray his credit (lines 1809–1813).

Nevertheless, no play exists in which Shakespeare did put down Jonson, and the reference may be instead to *Satiromastix,* which was performed by Shakespeare's company. Or perhaps "put down" means simply "surpassed." In fact, Shakespeare and Jonson remained on cordial terms, despite their differences in artistic outlook.

Upon the death of Queen Elizabeth in 1603 and the accession to the throne of King James I, Shakespeare's company added an important new success to their already great prosperity. According to a document of instruction from King James to his Keeper of the Privy Seal, dated May 19, 1603, and endorsed as "The Players' Privilege," the acting company that had formerly been the Lord Chamberlain's men now became the King's company. The document names Shakespeare, Richard Burbage, Augustine Phillips, John Heminges, Henry Condell, Will Sly, Robert Armin, Richard Cowley, and Lawrence Fletcher—the last, an actor who had played before the King and the Scottish court in 1599 and 1601. These players are accorded the usual privileges of exercising their art anywhere within the kingdom and are henceforth to be known as the King's company. The principal members of the troupe also were appointed to the honorary rank of Grooms of the Royal Chamber. We therefore find them duly recorded in the Accounts of the Master of the Wardrobe on March 15, 1604, as recipients of the customary grants of red cloth, so that they, dressed in the royal livery, might take part in the approaching coronation procession of King James. The same men are mentioned in these grants as in the Players' Privilege. Shakespeare's name stands second in the former document and first in the latter. In a somewhat similar manner, the King's players, as Grooms of the Royal Chamber, were called in attendance on the Spanish ambassador at Somerset House in August 1604.

The Revels Accounts of performances at court during the winter season of 1604–1605 contain an unusually full entry, listing several of Shakespeare's plays. The list includes *Othello, The Merry Wives of Windsor, Measure for Measure,* "The play of Errors," *Love's Labor's Lost, Henry V,* and *The Merchant of Venice.* The last play was "again commanded by the King's majesty," and so was performed a second time. This list also sporadically notes the names of "the poets which made the plays," ascribing three of these works to "Shaxberd." (Probably the final *d* is an error for *e,* since the two characters are easily confused in Elizabethan handwriting; the word represents "Shaxbere" or "Shaxpere.") The entire entry was once called into question as a possible forgery but is now generally regarded as authentic.

A number of records during this period show us glimpses of Shakespeare as a man of property. On May 1, 1602, John and William Combe conveyed to Shakespeare one hundred and seven acres of arable land, plus twenty acres of pasture in the parish of Old Stratford, for the sizable payment of three hundred and twenty pounds. The deed was delivered to Shakespeare's brother Gilbert and not to the poet, who was probably at that time occupied in London. On September 28 of the same year, Shakespeare acquired the title to "one cottage and one garden by estimation a quarter of an acre," located opposite his home (New Place) in Stratford.

Shakespeare made still other real-estate investments in his home town. In 1605 he purchased an interest in the tithes of Stratford and adjacent villages from one Ralph Hubaud for the considerable sum of four hundred and forty pounds. The purchasing of tithes was a common financial transaction in Shakespeare's time, though unknown today. Tithes were originally intended for the support of the Church but had, in many cases, become privately owned and hence negotiable. The owners of tithes paid a fixed rental sum for the right to collect as many of these taxes as they could, up to the total amount due under the law. Shakespeare seems, on this occasion in 1605, to have bought from Ralph Hubaud a one-half interest, or "moiety," in certain tithes of Stratford and vicinity. Later, probably in 1609, Shakespeare was one of those who brought a bill of complaint before the Lord Chancellor, requesting that certain other titheholders be required to come into the High Court of Chancery and make answer to the complaints alleged, namely, that they had not paid their proportional part of an annual rental of twenty-seven pounds, thirteen shillings, and four pence on the whole property in the tithes to one Henry Barker. This Barker had the theoretical right to foreclose on the entire property if any one of the forty-two titheholders failed to contribute his share of the annual fee. The suit was, in effect, a friendly one, designed to ensure that all those who were supposed to contribute did so on an equitable and businesslike basis.

We learn from the Stratford Registers of baptism, marriage, and burial of the changes in Shakespeare's family during this period. His father died in 1601, his brother Edmund in 1607, and his mother in 1608. On June 5, 1607, his daughter Susanna was married to Dr. John Hall in Holy Trinity Church, Stratford. Their first child, and Shakespeare's first grandchild, Elizabeth, was christened in the same church on February 21, 1608.

Shakespeare's Reputation, 1601–1608

Allusions to Shakespeare are frequent during this period of his life. One amusing reference is not literary but professes to tell about Shakespeare's prowess as a lover and rival of his good friend and theatrical colleague, Richard Burbage. Perhaps the joke was just a good bawdy story and should not be taken too seriously, but it is nonetheless one of the few anecdotes that date from Shakespeare's lifetime. Our informant is John Manningham, a young law student, who notes in his commonplace book in 1602 the following:

13 March 1601 [1602] . . . Upon a time, when Burbage played Richard III there was a citizen grew so far in liking with him

that, before she went to the play, she appointed him to come that night unto her by the name of Richard the Third. Shakespeare, overhearing their conclusion, went before, and was entertained and at his game ere Burbage came. Then message being brought that Richard the Third was at the door, Shakespeare caused return to be made that William the Conqueror was before Richard the Third. Shakespeare's name William.

Other allusions of the time are more literary. Shakespeare's greatness is, by this time, taken for granted. Anthony Scoloker, for example, in his epistle prefatory to *Diaphantus, or the Passions of Love* (1604), attempts to describe an excellent literary work in this way:

It should be like the never-too-well read Arcadia . . . or to come home to the vulgar's element, like friendly Shakespeare's tragedies, where the comedian rides, when the tragedian stands on tip-toe. Faith, it should please all, like Prince Hamlet.

The antiquarian William Camden includes Shakespeare's name among his list of England's greatest writers in his *Remains of a Greater Work Concerning Britain* (1605):

These may suffice for some poetical descriptions of our ancient poets. If I would come to our time, what a world could I present to you out of Sir Philip Sidney, Edmund Spenser, Samuel Daniel, Hugh Holland, Ben Jonson, Thomas Campion, Michael Drayton, George Chapman, John Marston, William Shakespeare, and other most pregnant wits of these our times, whom succeeding ages may justly admire.

An attempt to use one of Shakespeare's plays for political purposes had some potentially serious repercussions. Two days before the abortive rebellion of the Earl of Essex on February 7, 1601, Shakespeare's company was commissioned to perform a well-known play in its repertory about King Richard II. This play must almost surely have been Shakespeare's. Evidently, the purpose of this extraordinary performance was to awaken public sympathy for Essex by suggesting that Queen Elizabeth was another Richard II, surrounded by corrupt favorites and deaf to the pleas of her subjects. Essex's avowed intention was to remove from positions of influence those men whom he considered his political enemies. Fortunately, Shakespeare's company was later exonerated of any blame in the affair (see the Introduction to *Richard II*).

Perhaps no other allusion to Shakespeare during this period can suggest so well as the following quotation the extent to which Shakespeare's plays had become familiar to English citizens everywhere. The quotation is taken from the notes of a certain Captain Keeling, commander of the East India Company's ship *Dragon*, off Sierra Leone, in the years 1607 and 1608:

1607, Sept. 5. I sent the interpreter, according to his desire, aboard the *Hector*, where he broke fast, and after came aboard me, where we gave the tragedy of *Hamlet*.

30. Captain Hawkins dined with me, where my companions acted *King Richard the Second*.

[March 31.] I invited Captain Hawkins to a fish dinner and had *Hamlet* acted aboard me, which I permit to keep my people from idleness and unlawful games or sleep.

Other Drama of the Period

Even without Shakespeare, the early Jacobean drama in England would rank as one of the most creative periods in the history of all theater. (The word *Jacobean* is derived from *Jacobus,* the Latin form of the name of King James I.) Shakespeare's earlier contemporaries—Lyly, Greene, Marlowe, Peele, Kyd—were dead or silent, but another generation of playwrights was at hand. George Chapman, John Marston, and Ben Jonson all began writing plays shortly before 1600. So did Thomas Dekker and Thomas Heywood, whose dramatic output, often in collaboration, would prove to be considerable. Francis Beaumont, John Fletcher, Cyril Tourneur, and Thomas Middleton emerged into prominence in about 1606 or 1607. John Webster collaborated with Dekker and others in such plays as *Westward Ho* and *Sir Thomas Wyatt* around 1604, although he did not write his great tragedies until 1609–1614. Lesser talents, such as Henry Chettle, Anthony Munday, Henry Porter, John Day, and William Haughton, continued to pour forth an abundant supply of workmanlike plays. As Shakespeare's career developed, therefore, he enjoyed the fellowship and, no doubt, the rivalry of a remarkably gifted and diverse group of practicing dramatists.

Early Jacobean drama is, on the whole, characteristically different from the late Elizabethan drama that had preceded it. Other dramatists besides Shakespeare mirror his shift of focus from romantic comedies and patriotic histories to "problem" plays and tragedies. The boys' companies, reopening in 1598–1599 after virtually a decade of silence, did much to set the new tone. They avoided almost entirely the English history play, with its muscularly heroic style, so unsuited for the acting capabilities of boys. Besides, sophisticated audiences were sated with jingoistic fare, and even in the public theaters the genre had pretty well run its course. The fashion of the moment turned instead to revenge tragedy and satiric comedy.

The Jacobean revenge play owed much of its original inspiration to Thomas Kyd's *The Spanish Tragedy* (c. 1587), with its influential conventions: the intervention of supernatural forces, the feigned madness of the avenger, his difficulty in ascertaining the true facts of the murder, his morbid awareness of the conflict between human injustice and divine justice, his devising of a play within the play, and his invention of ingenious methods of slaughter in the play's gory ending. Kyd may also have written an early version of *Hamlet* featuring similar motifs. Shakespeare confronted cosmic issues of justice and human depravity in his revenge tragedy, *Hamlet* (c. 1599–1601), as indeed Kyd had done, but most followers of Kyd preferred to revel in the sensationalism of the genre. Some private-theater dramatists, such as Marston, subjected the conventions of the genre to caricature. Marston's revenge plays, written chiefly for Paul's boys and (after 1604) for the Children of the Queen's Revels, include *Antonio's Revenge* (1599–1601) and *The Malcontent* (1600–1604). These dramas are marked by flamboyantly overstated cynicism and are, in many ways, as close to satire as they are to tragedy. Marston had, in fact, made his first reputation as a nondramatic satirist, with *The Metamorphosis of Pygmalion's Image* and *The Scourge of Villainy* in 1598. His plays represent a continuation in dramatic form of the techniques of the Roman satirist. The typical Marstonian avenger, such as Malevole in *The Malcontent,* is an exaggeratedly unattractive authorial spokesman, pouring forth venomous hatred upon the loathsome and degenerate court in which he finds himself.

Similar in their exaggerated pursuit of the grotesque and the morbid are Cyril Tourneur's *The Atheist's Tragedy* (1607–1611) and a play formerly attributed to Tourneur but probably by Thomas Middleton, *The Revenger's Tragedy* (1606–1607). These plays are brilliant in the plotting of impossible situations and in the invention of cunning Italianate forms of torture and murder. Any sympathetic identification with the characters of these plays is sacrificed in the interests of technical virtuosity. As a result, the plays are more ironic than cathartic in their effect; we are overwhelmed by life's dark absurdities rather than ennobled by a vision of humanity's tragic grandeur. *The Tragedy of Hoffman, or A Revenge for a Father* by Henry Chettle (Admiral's men, 1602) is similarly grotesque and lacking in sympathy for its revenger hero. To be sure, George Chapman's *Bussy D'Ambois* (1600–1604) and its sequel, *The Revenge of Bussy D'Ambois* (1607–1612), are thoughtful plays about human aspiration, in the vein of Marlowe's *Tamburlaine,* but even these plays employ a good deal of Senecan bloody melodrama.

The revenge play enjoyed a great popularity on the public stage and (in a caricatured form) on the private stage. The public theater did, however, cater also to its Puritan-leaning audiences with more pious and moral tragedy. *Arden of Feversham* (c. 1591) is a good early example of what has come to be called domestic or homiletic tragedy. In the studiously plain style of a broadside ballad, it sets forth the facts of an actual murder that had occurred in 1551 and had been reported in Holinshed's *Chronicles.* The play interprets those events earnestly and providentially. The most famous play in the genre of domestic tragedy is Thomas Heywood's *A Woman Killed with Kindness* (1603). It tells, not of a murder, but of an adultery, for which the goodhearted but offending wife must be perpetually banished by her grieving husband. The play succeeds in elevating the private sorrows of its ordinary characters to tragic stature. The moral stances appear to be

unambiguous: adultery is a heinous offense but can be transcended by Christian forgiveness; dueling is evil. Still, a mix of sympathies is perhaps reflective of shifting public attitudes toward the role of women in marriage. Other plays in the vein of domestic tragedy include *A Yorkshire Tragedy* (1605–1608), *The Miseries of Enforced Marriage* (1605–1606), and *Two Lamentable Tragedies* (c. 1594–1598).

In comedy, the greatest writer of the period besides Shakespeare was Ben Jonson. His predilection was toward the private theater, though he continued to write occasionally for the public stage as well. To an ever-increasing extent, he fixed his satirical gaze on those values and institutions which Thomas Heywood cherished: the city of London, its bourgeois citizens, its traditional approach to morality, and its religious zeal. *Every Man Out of His Humor* (1599), written for the Chamberlain's men, features a foolish uxorious citizen, his socially aspiring wife, and her fashionmongering lover—humors types that were to appear again and again in the genre of satirical comedy known as "city comedy." (See Brian Gibbons, *Jacobean City Comedy,* 1968.) *Volpone* (1605–1606), though technically not a London city comedy, since it purportedly takes place in Venice, castigates greed among lawyers, businessmen, and other professional types. *The Alchemist* (1610) ridicules the affectations of petty shopkeepers, lawyers' clerks, Puritan divines, and others. *Bartholomew Fair* (1614) and *The Alchemist* give us Jonson's most memorable indictment of the Puritans.

Numerous other writers contributed to humors comedy and city comedy. George Chapman probably deserves more credit than he usually receives for having helped determine the shape of humors comedy in his *The Blind Beggar of Alexandria* (1596), *An Humorous Day's Mirth* (1597), *All Fools* (1599–1604), *May-Day* (1601–1609), *The Gentleman Usher* (1602–1604), and others. Francis Beaumont, assisted perhaps by John Fletcher, ridicules London grocers and apprentices for their naive tastes in romantic chivalry in *The Knight of the Burning Pestle* (1607–1610). Some satire in this vein, to be sure, is reasonably good-humored. *Eastward Ho* (1605), by Chapman, Jonson, and Marston, is genially sympathetic toward the lifestyle of the small shopkeeper, even though the play contains a good deal of satire directed at social climbing and sharp business practices. Thomas Dekker's collaboration with Thomas Middleton on *The Honest Whore* (Part I, 1604) gives us an amused and yet warm portrayal of a linen draper who succeeds in business by insisting that the customer is always right. Dekker often shows a wry but generous appreciation of bourgeois ethics, as in *The Shoemaker's Holiday* (1599). Yet even he turns against the Puritans in *If This Be Not a Good Play, the Devil Is in It* (1611–1612).

Marston shows his talent for city comedy in *The Dutch Courtesan* (1603–1605). Perhaps the most ingratiating and truly funny of the writers of city comedy, however, is Middleton. His *A Trick to Catch the Old One* (1604–1607) illustrates the tendency of Jacobean comedy to move away both from Shakespeare's romantic vein and Jonson's morally satirical vein toward a more lighthearted comedy of manners, anticipating the style of Restoration comedy. One of Middleton's most hilarious and philosophically unpretentious plays, though plotted with great ingenuity of situation, is *A Mad World, My Masters* (1604–1607). *Michaelmas Term*, written about the same time, exposes the sharp practices of usurers and lawyers. All these Middleton plays were written for Paul's boys.

Romantic comedy, though overshadowed by humors and city comedy during the 1600s, still held forth at the public theaters. A leading exponent was Thomas Heywood, in such plays as *The Fair Maid of the West*, or *A Girl Worth Gold* (1597–1610). Heywood also wrote English history plays designed to prove the sturdiness and historical importance of the London citizenry he so loved, as in *Edward IV* (1597–1599), *The Four Prentices of London* (c. 1600), and *If You Know Not Me You Know Nobody* (1605). Classical tragedy also continued to be written, despite the vogue of revenge tragedy. Ben Jonson rather dogmatically illustrated his classical theories of tragedy in *Sejanus* (1603) and *Catiline* (1611). Samuel Daniel wrote *Philotas* in 1604 and a revision of his *Cleopatra* in 1607. Heywood's *The Rape of Lucrece* appeared in 1606–1608. These are not, however, the immortal tragedies for which the Jacobean period is remembered.

Shakespeare's Work, 1601–1608

Shakespeare's plays of this period are characteristically Jacobean in their fascination with the dark complexities of sexual jealousy, betrayal, revenge, and social conflict.

The comedies are few in number and lack the joyous affirmation we associate with *Twelfth Night* and earlier plays. *Measure for Measure*, for example, is not about young men and women happily in love, but about premarital sex and the insoluble problems that arise when vice-prone men attempt to legislate morality for their fellow mortals. Angelo, self-hating and out of emotional control, is a tragic hero providentially rescued from his own worst self. The Duke and Isabella must use ethically dubious means—the bed trick—to effect their virtuous aims. Comedy in the play deals darkly in terms of prostitution, slander, and police inefficiency.

All's Well That Ends Well, though less grim than *Measure for Measure* in its confrontation of human degeneracy, does apply a similar bed trick as its central plot device. Just as important, the obstacles to love are internal and psychological, rather than external; that is, the happy union of Bertram and Helena is delayed, not by parental objections or by accident (as in *Romeo and Juliet* and *A Midsummer Night's Dream*), but by Bertram's unreadiness for the demands of a mature marital relationship. *Troilus and Cressida* is a play in which love is paralyzed by a combination of external and internal forces. Troilus must hand Cressida over to the Greeks because his code of honor bids him put his country's cause before his own, and yet that code of "honor" is based on Paris's rape of Helen. Cressida simply gives herself up to Diomedes, knowing she is not strong enough to stand alone in a moral wilderness. The combatants in the greatest war in all history turn out to be petty bickerers who play nasty games on one another and sulk when their reputations are impugned. The cause for which both sides fight is squalid and senseless.

Raphael Holinshed's Chronicles of England, Scotland, and Ireland, *which was published (1577, 2nd edition in 1587) before Shakespeare's career began, served as principal historic source for many plays, including* Macbeth, King Lear, *and* Cymbeline, *as well as the history plays. Here, in a woodcut from the* Chronicles, *Macbeth and Banquo are shown encountering the three weird sisters.*

In *Hamlet*, Shakespeare explores similar dilemmas posed by human carnality. Women, in Hamlet's misogynistic angst, are too often frail; men are too often importunate and brutal. How is a thoughtful person to justify his or her own existence? Should one struggle actively against injustice and personal wrong? How can one know what is really true or foresee the complex results of action? How, in *Othello*, can the protagonist resist temptation and inner weakness, prompting him to destroy the very thing on which his happiness depends? Is Macbeth tempted to sin by the weird sisters and his wife, or is the choice to murder Duncan ultimately his? To what extent is humanity responsible for its tragic fate? Most of all, in *King Lear*, are the heavens themselves indifferent to human bestiality? Must Cordelia die? Yet, despite these overwhelmingly pessimistic questions, and the tragic consequences they imply for all human life, Shakespeare's "great" tragedies affirm at least the nobility of humanity's striving to know itself, and the redeeming fact that human goodness does exist (in Desdemona, Duncan, Cordelia), even if those who practice goodness are often slaughtered.

The Roman or classical tragedies are something apart from the "great" tragedies. They are more ironic in tone, more dispiriting, though they, too, affirm an essential nobility in humanity. Brutus misguidedly leads a revolution against Caesar but dies loyal to his great principles. Timon of Athens proves the appalling ingratitude of his fellow creature and resolutely cuts himself off from all human contact. Coriolanus proclaims himself an enemy of the Roman people and seeks to destroy them for their ingratitude, though he is compromised and destroyed at last by his promptings of human feeling. Antony, too, is pulled apart by an irreconcilable conflict. Yet, in this play at least, Shakespeare achieves, partly through the greatness of Cleopatra, a triumph over defeat that seems to offer a new resolution of humanity's tragic dilemma.

THE LATE YEARS: 1608–1616

In the summer of 1608, Shakespeare's acting company signed a twenty-one-year lease for the use of the Blackfriars playhouse, an indoor and rather intimate, artificially lighted theater inside the city of London, close to the site of St. Paul's cathedral. A private theater had existed on this spot since 1576, when the Children of the Chapel and then Paul's boys began acting their courtly plays for paying spectators in a building that had once belonged to the Dominicans, or Black Friars. James Burbage had begun construction in 1596 of the so-called Second Blackfriars theater in the same building. Although James encountered opposition from the residents of the area and died before he could complete the work, James's son Richard did succeed in opening the new theater in 1600. At first, he leased it (for twenty-one

years) to a children's company, but when that company was suppressed in 1608 for offending the French ambassador in a play by George Chapman, Burbage seized the opportunity to take back the unexpired lease and to set up Blackfriars as the winter playhouse for his adult company, the King's men. By this time, the adult troupes could plainly see that they needed to cater more directly to courtly audiences than they once had done. Their popular audiences were becoming increasingly disenchanted with the drama. Puritan fulminations against the stage gained in effect, especially when many playwrights refused to disguise their satirical hostility toward Puritans and the London bourgeoisie.

Several of Shakespeare's late plays may have been acted both at the Globe and at Blackfriars. The plays he wrote after 1608–1609—*Cymbeline, The Winter's Tale*, and *The Tempest*—all show the distinct influence of the dramaturgy of the private theaters. Also, we know that an increasing number of Shakespeare's plays were acted at the court of King James. *Othello, King Lear*, and *The Tempest* are named in court revels accounts, and *Macbeth* dramatizes Scottish history with a seemingly explicit reference to King James as the descendant of Banquo who bears the "twofold balls and treble scepters" (4.1.121); James had received a double coronation as King of England and Scotland, and took seriously his assumed title as King of Great Britain, France, and Ireland. On the other hand, Shakespeare's plays certainly continued to be acted at the Globe to the very end of his career. The 1609 Quarto of *Pericles* advertises that it was acted "by his Majesty's Servants, at the Globe on the Bankside." The 1608 Quarto of *King Lear* mentions a performance at court and assigns the play to "his Majesty's servants playing usually at the Globe on the Bankside." Simon Forman saw *Macbeth, Cymbeline*, and *The Winter's Tale* at the Globe. Finally, a performance of *Henry VIII* on June 29, 1613, resulted in the burning of the Globe to the ground, though afterwards it soon was rebuilt.

Shakespeare's last plays, written with a view to Blackfriars and the court, as well as to the Globe, are now usually called "romances" or "tragicomedies," or sometimes both. Although they were not known by these terms in Shakespeare's day—they were grouped with the comedies in the First Folio of 1623, except for *Cymbeline*, which was placed among the tragedies—the very ambiguity about the genre in this arrangement is suggestive of an uncertainty as to whether they were seen as predominantly comic or tragic. The term "romance" suggests a return to the kind of story Robert Greene had derived from Greek romance: tales of adventure, long separation, and tearful reunion, involving shipwreck, capture by pirates, riddling prophecies, children set adrift in boats or abandoned on foreign shores, the illusion of death and subsequent restoration to life, the revelation of the identity of long-lost children by birthmarks, and the like. The term "tragicomedy" suggests

COURTESY, GUILDHALL LIBRARY, CORPORATION OF LONDON

This section of Wenceslaus Hollar's "Long View" of London dates from 1647, some years after Shakespeare's death, but gives nonetheless a fine view of two theater buildings on the south bank of the Thames River, across from the city. The two labels of "The Globe" and "Beere bayting" should in fact be reversed; the Globe (rebuilt in 1613) appears to the left and below the bearbaiting arena.

a play in which the protagonist commits a seemingly fatal error or crime, or (as in *Pericles*) suffers an extraordinarily adverse fortune to test his patience; in either event, he must experience agonies of contrition and bereavement until he is providentially delivered from his tribulations. The tone is deeply melancholic and resigned, although suffused also with a sense of gratitude for the harmonies that are mysteriously restored.

The appropriateness of such plays to the elegant atmosphere of Blackfriars and the court is subtle but real. Although one might suppose at first that old-fashioned naiveté would seem out of place in a sophisticated milieu, the naiveté is only superficial. Tragicomedy and pastoral romance were, in the period from 1606 to 1610, beginning to enjoy a fashionable courtly revival. The leading practitioners of the new genre were Beaumont and Fletcher, though Shakespeare made a highly significant contribution. Perhaps sophisticated audiences responded to pastoral and romantic drama as the nostalgic evocation of an idealized past, a chivalric "golden world" fleetingly recovered through an artistic journey back to naiveté and

innocence. The evocation of such a world demands the kind of studied but informal artifice we find in many tragicomic plays of the period: the elaborate masques and allegorical shows, the descents of enthroned gods from the heavens (as in *Cymbeline*), the use of quaint Chorus figures like Old Gower or Time (in *Pericles* and *The Winter's Tale*), and the quasi-operatic blend of music and spectacle. At their best, such plays powerfully compel belief in the artistic world thus artificially created. The very improbability of the story becomes, paradoxically, part of the means by which an audience must "awake its faith" in a mysterious truth.

Shakespeare did not merely ape the new fashion in tragicomedy and romance. In fact, he may have done much to establish it. His *Pericles*, written seemingly in about 1606–1608 for the public stage before Shakespeare's company acquired Blackfriars, anticipated many important features, not only of Shakespeare's own later romances, but also of Beaumont and Fletcher's *The Maid's Tragedy* and *Philaster* (c. 1608–1611). Still, Shakespeare was on the verge of retirement, and the future belonged to Beaumont and Fletcher. Gradually, Shakespeare disengaged himself, spending more and more time in Stratford. His last-known stint as an actor was in Jonson's *Sejanus* in 1603. Some time in 1611 or 1612, he probably gave up his lodgings in London, though he still may have returned for such occasions as the opening performance of *Henry VIII* in 1613. He continued to be one of the proprietors of the newly rebuilt Globe, but his involvement in its day-to-day operations dwindled.

Shakespeare's Reputation, 1608–1616

Shakespeare's reputation among his contemporaries was undiminished in his late years, even though Beaumont and Fletcher were the new rage at the Globe and Blackfriars. Among those who apostrophized Shakespeare was John Davies of Hereford in *The Scourge of Folly* (entered in the Stationers' Register in 1610):

> To our English Terence, Mr. Will Shakespeare.
>
> Some say, good Will, which I, in sport, do sing:
> Hadst thou not played some kingly parts in sport,
> Thou hadst been a companion for a king,
> And been a king among the meaner sort.
> Some others rail. But, rail as they think fit,
> Thou hast no railing, but a reigning, wit.
> And honesty thou sow'st, which they do reap,
> So to increase their stock which they do keep.

The following sonnet is from *Run and a Great Cast* (1614) by Thomas Freeman:

> To Master W. Shakespeare.
>
> Shakespeare, that nimble Mercury thy brain

Lulls many hundred Argus-eyes asleep,
So fit, for all thou fashionest thy vein,
At th' horse-foot fountain thou hast drunk full deep.
Virtue's or vice's theme to thee all one is.
Who loves chaste life, there's *Lucrece* for a teacher;
Who list read lust, there's *Venus and Adonis,*
True model of a most lascivious lecher.
Besides, in plays thy wit winds like Meander,
Whence needy new composers borrow more
Than Terence doth from Plautus or Menander.
But to praise thee aright, I want thy store.
   Then let thine own works thine own worth upraise,
   And help t' adorn thee with deservèd bays.

Ben Jonson took a more critical view, though he also admired Shakespeare greatly. In the Induction to his *Bartholomew Fair* (1631 edition), Jonson compared the imaginary world he presented in his play with the more improbable fantasies of romantic drama:

If there be never a servant-monster i' the fair, who can help it? He [the author, Jonson] says; nor a nest of antics? He is loath to make Nature afraid in his plays, like those that beget tales, Tempests, and suchlike drolleries to mix his head with other men's heels.

From this, one judges that Jonson had in mind not only *The Tempest* but also Shakespeare's other late romances. He similarly protested in the Prologue to his 1616 edition of *Every Man in His Humor* that his own playwriting was free of the usual romantic claptrap:

Where neither Chrous wafts you o'er the seas,
Nor creaking throne comes down the boys to please,
Nor nimble squib is seen to make afeard
The gentlewomen, nor rolled bullet heard
To say it thunders, nor tempestuous drum
Rumbles to tell you when the storm doth come.

Still, Shakespeare's reputation was assured. John Webster paid due homage, in his note To the Reader accompanying *The White Devil* (1612), to "the right happy and copious industry of M. *Shakespeare,* M. *Dekker,* & M. *Heywood,*" along with Chapman, Jonson, Beaumont, and Fletcher.

Records of the Late Years

Shakespeare's last recorded investment in real estate was the purchase of a house in Blackfriars, London, in 1613. There is no indication he lived there, for he had retired to Stratford. He did not pay the full purchase price of one hundred and forty pounds, and the mortgage deed executed for the unpaid balance furnishes one of the six unquestioned examples of his signature.

John Combe, a wealthy bachelor of Stratford and Shakespeare's friend, left him a legacy of five pounds in his will at the time of Combe's death in 1613. At about the same time, John's kinsman William Combe began a controversial attempt to enclose Welcombe Common, that is, to convert narrow strips of arable land to pasture. Presumably, Combe was interested in a more efficient means of using the land. Enclosure was, however, an explosive issue, since many people feared they would lose the right to farm the land and would be evicted to make room for cattle and sheep. Combe attempted to guarantee Shakespeare and other titheholders that they would lose no money. He offered similar assurances to the Stratford Council, but the townspeople were adamantly opposed. Shakespeare was consulted by letter as a leading titheholder. The letter is lost, but, presumably, it set forth the Council's reasons for objecting to enclosure. Shakespeare's views on the controversy remain unknown. Eventually, the case went to the Privy Council, where Combe was ordered to restore the land to its original use.

One of the most interesting documents from these years consists of the records of a lawsuit entered into in 1612 by Stephen Belott against his father-in-law, Christopher Mountjoy, a Huguenot maker of women's ornamental headdresses who resided on Silver Street, St. Olave's parish, London. Belott sought to secure the payment of a dower promised him at the time of his marriage to Mountjoy's daughter. In this suit, Shakespeare was summoned as a witness and made deposition on five interrogatories. From this document we learn that Shakespeare was a lodger in Mountjoy's house at the time of the marriage in 1604 and probably for some time before that, since he states in his testimony that he had known Mountjoy for more than ten years. Shakespeare admitted that, at the solicitation of Mountjoy's wife, he had acted as an intermediary in the arrangement of the marriage between Belott and Mountjoy's daughter. Shakespeare declared himself unable, however, to recall the exact amount of the portion or the date on which it was to have been paid. Shakespeare's signature to his deposition is authentic and one of the best samples of his handwriting that we have.

In January of 1615 or 1616, Shakespeare drew up his last will and testament with the assistance of his lawyer Francis Collins, who had aided him earlier in some of his transactions in real estate. On March 25, 1616, Shakespeare revised his will in order to provide for the marriage of his daughter Judith and Thomas Quiney in that same year. Shakespeare's three quavering signatures, one on each page of this document, suggest that he was in failing health. The cause of his death on April 23 is not known. An intriguing bit of Stratford gossip is reported by John Ward, vicar of Holy Trinity in Stratford from 1662 to 1689, in his diary: "Shakespeare, Drayton, and Ben Jonson had a merry meeting, and it seems drank too hard, for Shakespeare died of a fever there contracted." The report comes fifty years after Shakespeare's death, however, and is hardly an expert medical opinion.

The will disposes of all the property of which Shakespeare is known to have died possessing, the greater share of it going to his daughter Susanna. His recently married daughter Judith received a dowry, a provision for any children that might be born of her marriage, and other gifts. Ten pounds went to the poor of Stratford; Shakespeare's sword went to Mr. Thomas Combe; twenty-six shillings and eight pence apiece went to Shakespeare's fellow actors Heminges, Burbage, and Condell to buy them mourning rings; and other small bequests went to various other friends and relatives.

An interlineation contains the bequest of Shakespeare's "second best bed with the furniture," that is, the hangings, to his wife. Anne's name appears nowhere else in the will. Some scholars, beginning with Edmund Malone, have taken this reference as proof of an unhappy marriage, confirming earlier indications, such as the hasty wedding to a woman who was William's senior by eight years and his prolonged residence in London for twenty years or more seemingly without his family. The evidence is inconclusive, however. Shakespeare certainly supported his family handsomely, acquired much property in Stratford, and retired there when he might have remained still in London. Although he showed no great solicitude for Anne's well-being in the will, her rights were protected by law; a third of her husband's estate went to her without having to be mentioned in the will. New Place was to be the home of Shakespeare's favorite daughter Susanna, wife of the distinguished Dr. John Hall. Anne Shakespeare would make her home with her daughter and, with her dower rights secured by law, would be quite as wealthy as she would need to be.

The date of Shakespeare's death (April 23, 1616) and his age (his fifty-third year) are inscribed on his monument. This elaborate structure, still standing in the chancel of Trinity Church, Stratford, was erected some time before 1623 by the London stonecutting firm of Gheerart Janssen and his sons. Janssen's shop was in Southwark, near the Globe, and may have been familiar to the actors. The bust of Shakespeare is a conventional sort of statuary for its time. Still, it is one of the only two contemporary likenesses we have. The other is the Droeshout engraving of Shakespeare in the Folio of 1623.

The epitaph on the monument reads as follows:

Iudicio Phylium, genio Socratem, arte Maronem;
Terra tegit, populus maeret, Olympus habet.
Stay passenger. Why goest thou by so fast?

As with so many other things in his life, the curious terms of Shakespeare's will have led to endless and provocative conjecture.

MR. WILLIAM
SHAKESPEARES
COMEDIES,
HISTORIES, &
TRAGEDIES.

Published according to the True Originall Copies.

LONDON
Printed by Isaac Iaggard, and Ed. Blount. 1623.

Martin Droeshout's engraving on the title page of the First Folio is one of only two authentic likenesses of Shakespeare in existence.

Read, if thou canst, whom envious Death hath placed
Within this monument: Shakespeare, with whom
Quick Nature died, whose name doth deck this tomb
Far more than cost, sith all that he hath writ
Leaves living art but page to serve his wit.

Obiit anno domini 1616,
Aetatis 53, die 23 April.

These lines, of which the beginning Latin couplet compares Shakespeare with Nestor (King of Pylos) for wise judgment, Socrates for genius, and Virgil (Maro) for poetic art, and avers that the earth covers him, people grieve for him, and Mount Olympus (that is, heaven) has him, indicate the high reputation he enjoyed at the time of his death. More widely known, perhaps, are the four lines inscribed over Shakespeare's grave near the north wall of the chancel. A local tradition assigns them to Shakespeare himself and implies that he wrote them "to suit the capacity of clerks and sextons," whom he wished apparently to frighten out of the idea of opening the grave to make room for a new occupant:

Good friend, for Jesus' sake forbear
To dig the dust enclosèd here.
Blest be the man that spares these stones,
And curst be he that moves my bones.

Whether Shakespeare actually wrote these lines cannot, however, be determined.

Other Dramatists

The most significant new development in the drama of the period from about 1608 to 1616, apart from Shakespeare's new interest in romance and tragicomedy, was the emergence of the famous literary partners Francis Beaumont and John Fletcher. Beaumont, the son of a distinguished lawyer, studied for a while at Oxford and then at the Inner Temple before drifting into a literary career. In 1613, he married an heiress and retired almost completely from the theater. John Fletcher was the son of Richard Fletcher, Queen Elizabeth's chaplain and later Bishop of London. The young man probably studied at Cambridge. The father died in 1596 heavily in debt, leaving the young Fletcher to support a family of eight children. Fletcher became a professional writer, earning his living as chief dramatist for the King's men. He was Shakespeare's successor. Fletcher's cousins, Giles and Phineas Fletcher, gained some reputation as poets. Beaumont and Fletcher, who were close friends, regarded themselves also as poets and as members of the "tribe of Ben"—the disciples of the great Ben Jonson who often gathered together at the Mermaid Tavern for an evening of witty literary conversation.

What things have we seen
Done at the Mermaid! heard words that have been
So nimble, and so full of subtle flame,

As if that every one from whence they came
Had meant to put his whole wit in a jest,
And had resolved to live a fool the rest
Of his dull life!

(Master Francis Beaumont's Letter to Ben Jonson)

Beaumont and Fletcher actually collaborated on only about seven plays: *The Woman Hater,* a comedy (1606); *The Maid's Tragedy,* a tragedy (1608–1611); *Philaster,* a tragicomedy (1608–1610); *Cupid's Revenge,* a tragedy (c. 1607–1612); *The Coxcomb,* a comedy (1608–1610); *A King and No King,* a tragicomedy (1611); *The Scornful Lady,* a tragicomedy (1613–1616); and perhaps one or two others. They may have collaborated on *The Knight of the Burning Pestle* (c. 1607–1610), though it was chiefly Beaumont's. Beaumont also wrote *Mask of the Inner Temple and Gray's Inn* (1613). Fletcher unassisted wrote *The Faithful Shepherdess* (1608–1609), *The Night Walker* (c. 1611), *Bonduca* (1611–1614), *Valentinian* (1610–1614), and others. He also collaborated with several other writers, including Massinger, Middleton, Field, and Rowley. Importantly, he seems to have collaborated with Shakespeare on *The Two Noble Kinsmen* (1613–1616) and, probably, on *Henry VIII.* Eventually, most of these various dramatic enterprises were gathered together in 1647 as the works of Beaumont and Fletcher. They have remained known as such ever since, partly because the original collaboration of these two men did so much to set a new style in coterie drama.

The plays they wrote together, such as *The Maid's Tragedy* and *Philaster,* offer an interesting comparison with Shakespeare's contemporary writing in a similar genre. Beaumont and Fletcher often employ exotic settings, like Rhodes or Sicily. In such an environment, refined aristocratic characters are caught in dynastic struggles or in a rarified conflict between love and honor. They must cope with stereotyped villains, such as tyrants or shamelessly lustful courtiers. The sentiments are lofty, the rhetoric is mannered; elaborately contrived situations are offered with no pretense of verisimilitude. The characters live according to lofty chivalric codes and despise ill breeding above all else. In the plotting of the tragicomic reversal, the audience is sometimes deliberately deceived into believing something that is not true, so that the sudden happy outcome arrives as a theatrically contrived surprise. Disguising and masking are common motifs. The audience is deliberately made aware throughout of the play's theatrical artifice, statuesque scene building, and titillating sensationalism.

Although Shakespeare wrote no tragedies after *Coriolanus,* great tragedy did continue to appear on the Jacobean stage. John Webster wrote his two most splendid plays, *The White Devil* and *The Duchess of Malfi,* between 1609 and 1614. Both contain elements of the still-popular revenge tradition. They also manage to achieve a vision of triumphant human dignity in defeat that merits comparison with Shakespeare's greatest tragic achievement. Still to come were *The Changeling* (1622) by Thomas Middleton and William Rowley, *Women Beware Women* (c. 1620–1627) by Middleton, *'Tis Pity She's a Whore* (1629?–1633) by John Ford, and others. Although these tragedies are more concerned with the grotesque than are Shakespeare's great tragedies, and more obsessed with abnormal human psychology (incest, werewolfism, and the like), they are nonetheless sublime achievements in art. The genius of the age for tragedy did not die with Shakespeare. During Shakespeare's last years, George Chapman was also writing his best tragedies, including *Charles Duke of Byron* in 1608, *The Revenge of Bussy D'Ambois* in about 1610, and *Chabot, Admiral of France* between 1611 and 1622. Ben Jonson's *Catiline His Conspiracy*, a classical tragedy, appeared in 1611; Marston's *The Insatiate Countess*, in about 1610.

The Anti-Stratfordian Movement

What we know of Shakespeare's life is really quite considerable. The information we have is just the kind one would expect. It hangs together and refers to one man and one career. Though lacking in the personal details we should like to have, it is both adequate and plausible. Yet the past hundred years or so have seen the growth of a tendency to doubt Shakespeare's authorship of the plays and poems ascribed to him. The phenomenon is sometimes called the "anti-Stratfordian" movement, since its attack is leveled at the literary credentials of the man who was born in Stratford and later became an actor in London. Although based on no reliable evidence, the movement has persisted long enough to become a kind of myth. It also has the appeal of a mystery thriller: who really wrote Shakespeare's plays? A brief account must be made here of the origins of the anti-Stratfordian movement.

Beginning in the late eighteenth century, and especially in the mid nineteenth century, a few admirers of Shakespeare began to be troubled by the scantiness of information about England's greatest author. As we have already seen, good reasons exist for the scarcity: the great London fire of 1666 that destroyed many records, the relatively low social esteem accorded to popular dramatists during the Elizabethan period, and the like. Also, we do actually know more about Shakespeare than about most of his contemporaries in the theater, despite the difficulties imposed by the passage of time. Still, some nineteenth-century readers saw only that they knew far less about Shakespeare than about many authors of more recent date.

Moreover, the impressions of the man did not seem to square with his unparalleled literary greatness. William Shakespeare had been brought up in a small country town; were his parents cultured folk or even literate? No record of his schooling has been preserved; was Shakespeare himself able to read and write, much less write immortal plays and poems? The anti-Stratfordians did not deny the existence of a man called Shakespeare from Stratford-upon-Avon, but they found it incredible that such a person should be connected with the works ascribed to him. Mark Twain, himself an anti-Stratfordian, was fond of joking that the plays were not by Shakespeare but by another person of the same name. Beneath the humor in this remark lies a deep-seated mistrust: how could a country boy have written so knowledgeably and eloquently about the lives of kings and queens? Where could such a person have learned so much about the law, about medicine, about the art of war, about heraldry? The puzzle seemed a genuine one, even though no one until the late eighteenth century had thought to question Shakespeare's authorship of the plays—least of all his colleagues and friends, such as Ben Jonson, who admitted that Shakespeare's classical learning was "small" but insisted that Shakespeare was an incomparable genius.

The first candidate put forward in the anti-Stratfordian cause as the "real" author of the plays was Sir Francis Bacon, a reputable Elizabethan writer with connections at court and considerable cultural attainments. Yet the ascription of the plays to Bacon was based on no documentary evidence. It relied, instead, on the essentially snobbish argument that Bacon was better born and purportedly better educated than Shakespeare—an argument that appealed strongly to the nineteenth century in which a university education was becoming more and more a distinctive mark of the cultivated person. The assertion of Bacon's authorship was also based on a conspiratorial theory of history; that is, its believers had to assume the existence of a mammoth conspiracy in Elizabethan times in which Shakespeare would allow his name to be used by Bacon as a *nom de plume* and in which Shakespeare's friends, such as Ben Jonson, would take part. (Jonson knew Shakespeare too well, after all, to have been duped for a period of almost twenty years.) The motive for such an arrangement, presumably, was that Bacon did not deign to lend his dignified name to the writing of popular plays (since they were considered subliterary) and so chose a common actor named Shakespeare to serve as his alter ego. This theory of an elaborate hoax involving England's greatest literary giant has proved powerfully attractive to modern writers like Mark Twain who have sometimes referred to themselves as rebels against the cultural "Establishment" of their own times.

The claim that Bacon wrote Shakespeare's works was soon challenged in the name of other prominent Elizabethans: the Earl of Oxford, the Earl of Southampton, Anthony Bacon, the Earl of Rutland, the Earl of Devonshire, Christopher Marlowe, and others. Since documentary claims as to Bacon's authorship of the Shakespearen canon were nonexistent, other Elizabethans could be proposed to fill his role just as satisfactorily as Bacon himself. The anti-Stratfordian movement gained momentum and came to include several prominent persons, including Delia Bacon and Sigmund Freud, as well as Mark Twain. One of the appeals of the anti-Stratfordian movement in recent years has proved to be a kind of amateur sleuthing or scholarship, carried on by professional lawyers, doctors, and the like, who have explored Shakespeare's interest in law and medicine as a hobby and have convinced themselves that Shakespeare's wisdom in these subjects entitles him to claim a better birth than that of a glover's son from Stratford. Ingenious efforts at "deciphering" hidden meanings in the works have been adduced to prove one authorship claim or another. The academic "Establishments" of modern universities have been accused of perpetuating Shakespeare's name out of mere vested self-interest: Shakespeare scholarship is an industry, and its busy workers need to preserve their source of income.

We must ask in all seriousness, however, whether such assertions are not offering answers to nonexistent questions. Responsible scholarship has admirably dispelled the seeming mystery of Shakespeare's humble beginnings. T. W. Baldwin, for example, in *William Shakespeare's Petty School* (1943) and *William Shakspere's Small Latine and Lesse Greeke* (1944), has shown just what sort of classical training Shakespeare almost surely received in the free grammar school of Stratford. It is precisely the sort of training that would have enabled him to use classical authors as he does, with the familiarity of one who likes to read. His Latin and Greek were passable but not strong; he often consulted modern translations, as well as classical originals. Just as importantly, Shakespeare's social background was, in fact, typical of many of the greatest writers of the English Renaissance. He earned his living by his writing, and thus had one of the strongest of motives for success. So did his contemporaries Marlowe (who came from a shoemaker's family) and Jonson (whose stepfather was a brickmason). Greene, Peele, Nashe, and many others sold plays and other writings for a livelihood. Although a few wellborn persons, such as Bacon and Sir Philip Sidney, also made exceptional contributions to literature, and although a number of courtiers emulated Henry VIII and Elizabeth as gifted amateurs in the arts, the court was not the direct or major source of England's literary greatness. Most courtiers were not, like Shakespeare, professional writers. A man like Bacon lacked Shakespeare's connection with a commercial acting company. Surely the theater was a more relevant "university" for Shakespeare than Oxford or Cambridge, where most of his studies would have been in ancient languages and in divinity.

SHAKESPEARE'S LANGUAGE: HIS DEVELOPMENT AS POET AND DRAMATIST

LANGUAGE AND ARTISTIC DEVELOPMENT

One indication of Shakespeare's greatness is his extraordinary development. As he worked through his writing career of more than twenty years, he constantly explored new themes, perfected genres and moved on to new ones, and saw ever more deeply into the human condition. Many of the works that have made him immortal were not written until he was nearly forty years old or more. The study of his development is, in itself, an interesting and complex subject. It is one that requires an accurate dating of his plays and poems.

The First Folio, published in 1623 as the first "complete edition" of Shakespeare's plays in the large and handsome folio format for which the printed sheet was folded only once, gives no help in determining the order of composition of Shakespeare's plays. They are arranged in three groups—comedies, histories, and tragedies—without regard for dates of composition. The first comedy in the Folio is *The Tempest,* known to be one of Shakespeare's latest plays; the second is *The Two Gentlemen of Verona,* one of the earliest. The histories are arranged in order of the English kings whose reigns they treat, although Shakespeare clearly did not write them in that order. The tragedies show no discernible arrangement by date. Information about dating can partially be recovered from the fact that eighteen of the thirty-six plays in the First Folio had previously been published in single quarto volumes at various times, with dates on their title pages. *Pericles,* which was not included in the First Folio, appeared in quarto format in 1609. (The quarto format required that the printed sheet be folded twice, resulting in a smaller page than that of a folio volume.) All the quarto editions, except *Romeo and Juliet* and *Love's Labor's Lost,* were entered in the Register of the Stationers' Company of London; two other plays, *As You Like It* (entered in the Stationers' Register in 1600) and *Antony and Cleopatra* (S.R. 1608), although not printed in quarto, were entered in the Stationers' Register possibly in order to forestall publication by printers who had no right to them. The date of entry of a play in the register indicates that, at least by that time, the play was in existence. The quarto editions also have certain information on their title pages regarding date, author, and publisher, and sometimes tell what theatrical company acted the play. Other kinds of external evidence of date include references to Shakespeare's plays in diaries, journals, or accounts of the period, and quotations from his plays in the literary works of Elizabethan and Jacobean writers. Allusions in Shakespeare's plays themselves to contemporary events, although difficult to prove beyond dispute, can sometimes be helpful. See Appendix 1, at the end of this volume, for a detailed discussion on "Canon, Dates, and Early Texts" of each of Shakespeare's plays.

Once Shakespeare's plays have been arranged in approximate chronological order on the basis of the kinds of external evidence already described, we can perceive that his style underwent a continuous development from his earliest work to the end of his career as a dramatist. Matters of style are not easy to talk about precisely, and we can hardly expect to be able to date a particular passage as having been written in 1604, say, as distinguished from 1602. Overall, on the other hand, the early and late Shakespeare are strikingly distinguishable. Take, for example, the following two passages. One is from the Duke of Clarence's description of his dream in *Richard III* (1.4.21–33), written in about 1591–1594, near the start of Shakespeare's career:

> Oh, Lord, methought what pain it was to drown!
> What dreadful noise of waters in my ears!
> What sights of ugly death within my eyes!
> Methoughts I saw a thousand fearful wracks;
> Ten thousand men that fishes gnawed upon;
> Wedges of gold, great anchors, heaps of pearl,
> Inestimable stones, unvalued jewels,
> All scattered in the bottom of the sea.
> Some lay in dead men's skulls, and in the holes
> Where eyes did once inhabit there were crept,
> As 'twere in scorn of eyes, reflecting gems,
> That wooed the slimy bottom of the deep
> And mocked the dead bones that lay scattered by.

The second is Prospero's description of his magic in *The Tempest* (5.1.33–50), from about 1610–1611 when Shakespeare was on the verge of retirement:

> Ye elves of hills, brooks, standing lakes, and groves,
> And ye that on the sands with printless foot
> Do chase the ebbing Neptune, and do fly him
> When he comes back; you demi-puppets that
> By moonshine do the green sour ringlets make,
> Whereof the ewe not bites; and you whose pastime
> Is to make midnight mushrooms, that rejoice
> To hear the solemn curfew; by whose aid,
> Weak masters though ye be, I have bedimmed
> The noontide sun, called forth the mutinous winds,
> And twixt the green sea and the azured vault
> Set roaring war; to the dread rattling thunder
> Have I given fire, and rifted Jove's stout oak
> With his own bolt; the strong-based promontory
> Have I made shake, and by the spurs plucked up
> The pine and cedar; graves at my command
> Have waked their sleepers, oped, and let 'em forth
> By my so potent art.

These two passages have been chosen for comparison, in part because they are both set speeches in blank verse, rich in formal characteristics. Put side by side, they reveal a stylistic shift that we can observe in other less formal poetry and even in prose. The shift is away from rhetorical balance toward a freedom from verse restraint, a deliberate syncopation of blank verse rhythms, and a complication of syntax.

Completely regular blank verse, invariably consisting of ten syllables to each unrhymed line, with an accent falling on every other syllable, soon becomes monotonous. The iambic pattern can, however, be varied by a number of subtle changes. Extra syllables, accented and unaccented, can be added to the line, or a line may occasionally be short by one or more syllables. The regular alternation of accented and unaccented syllables, producing the effect of five iambic "feet" in each line (each foot consisting of an accented and an unaccented syllable), can be interrupted by the occasional inversion of a foot. Pauses, or caesuras, may occur at several points in the line. Most importantly, the line can be "end-stopped"—with a strong pause at the end of the line—or "run on" without interruption into the next line. Variations of this sort can transform blank verse from a formal and rhetorical vehicle into one that is highly conversational and supple.

Shakespeare increasingly abandons formal end-stopped verse for a fluid and more conversational style. In the preceding two passages, the first introduces a grammatical stop at the end of every line, except the ninth, whereas the second passage tends to run on past the end of the line; it does so in all but the fifth and tenth lines. Similarly, the passage from *The Tempest* is more apt to introduce a grammatical pause in the middle of a verse line, whereas the passage from *Richard III* stops between clauses in midline only in line 9. Shakespeare's later style is freer in its use of so-called feminine ends at the ends of lines, that is, endings with an unstressed syllable added on to the final stress of the iambic pattern; "fly him," "pastime," and "thunder" are good examples of this. A corollary of Shakespeare's increased use of feminine line endings and nonstopped blank verse is that the lines of his later verse are more apt to end in conjunctions, prepositions, auxiliary verbs, possessive pronouns, and other lightly stressed words. The *Richard III* passage generally ends in strong verbs and nouns, such as "drown," "ears," "eyes," and so on, whereas the *Tempest* passage makes use of "that," "up," and "forth."

Stylistic traits such as these can be quantified to demonstrate a fairly steady course of progression from the early to later plays. Early plays have low percentages of run-on lines in relation to the total number of lines: *1 Henry VI* has 10.4 percent, *2 Henry VI* 11.4 percent, *3 Henry VI* 9.5 percent, *The Comedy of Errors* 12.9 percent, and *The Two Gentlement of Verona* 12.4 percent, whereas *Cymbeline* has 46.0 percent, *The Winter's Tale* 37.5 percent, *The Tempest* 41.5 percent, and *Henry VIII* 46.3 percent. Feminine

A CATALOGVE

of the feuerall Comedies, Hiſtories, and Tragedies contained in this Volume.

COMEDIES.

He Tempeſt.	Folio 1.
The two Gentlemen of Verona.	20
The Merry Wiues of Windſor.	38
Meaſure for Meaſure.	61
The Comedy of Errours.	85
Much adoo about Nothing.	101
Loues Labour loſt.	122
Midſommer Nights Dreame.	145
The Merchant of Venice.	163
As you Like it.	185
The Taming of the Shrew.	208
All is well, that Ends well.	230
Twelfe=Night, or what you will.	255
The Winters Tale.	304

HISTORIES.

The Life and Death of King John.	Fol. 1.
The Life & death of Richard the ſecond.	23

The Firſt part of King Henry the fourth.	46
The Second part of K.Henry the fourth.	74
The Life of King Henry the Fift.	69
The Firſt part of King Henry the Sixt.	96
The Second part of King Hen. the Sixt.	120
The Third part of King Henry the Sixt.	147
The Life & Death of Richard the Third.	173
The Life of King Henry the Eight.	205

TRAGEDIES.

The Tragedy of Coriolanus.	Fol.1.
Titus Andronicus.	31
Romeo and Juliet.	53
Timon of Athens.	80
The Life and death of Julius Cæſar.	109
The Tragedy of Macbeth.	131
The Tragedy of Hamlet.	152
King Lear.	283
Othello,the Moore of Venice.	310
Anthony and Cleopater.	346
Cymbeline King of Britaine.	369

John Heminges and Henry Condell, Shakespeare's fellow actors, gathered contents for the First Folio, published in 1623. They collected thirty-six plays in the volume, omitting Pericles *and* The Two Noble Kinsmen. Troilus and Cressida *is included in most copies of the First Folio but is not listed here in the contents.*

or "double" endings run from a total of 9 in *Love's Labor's Lost* and 29 in *A Midsummer Night's Dream* to 708 in *Coriolanus*, 726 in *Cymbeline*, and 1,195 in *Henry VIII*. The actual number of light or weak endings increases from none in *The Comedy of Errors* and *The Two Gentlemen of Verona* to 104 in *Coriolanus*, 130 in *Cymbeline*, and 100 in *The Tempest*.

Other stylistic characteristics, though not discernible in the two examples from *Richard III* and *The Tempest*, spell out a similar development toward flexibility. For example, Shakespeare increasingly divides a verse line between two or more speakers. *The Comedy of Errors* and *1 Henry VI* do so hardly at all, whereas in *Cymbeline* the figures rise to a remarkable 85 percent of all instances in which one speaker stops speaking and another begins; *The Winter's Tale* does so in 87.6 percent of such instances, and *The Tempest*, in 84.5 percent.

Shakespeare's use of prose in his plays depends, to a significant extent, on genre, especially in his early work. At the start of his career, Shakespeare seldom uses prose, except in the speeches of clowns, servants, and rustics, whereas blank verse is his common vehicle of expression in speeches of heightened oratory or dramatic seriousness. *1 Henry VI* and *3 Henry VI*, *King John*, and *Richard II* are essentially written throughout in verse—usually blank verse. Prose is more common in the early comedies because of the presence of the Dromios, Christopher Sly, and Bottom the Weaver, but the love scenes are generally in verse. Poetry is important to the lyric plays of the mid-1590s, such as *The Merchant of Venice, A Midsummer Night's Dream*, and *Romeo and Juliet*. Prose assumes a major function, on the other hand, in plays of comic wit in the later 1590s, including *1 Henry IV* (45 percent), *2 Henry IV* (54 percent), *Much Ado About Nothing* (74 percent), and *The Merry Wives of Windsor* (81 percent), and here we see that comedy is used not for wisecracking servants so much as for Falstaff, Beatrice, and Benedick. Thereafter, prose is essential to Shakespeare's comic world. It also takes on a major function in *Hamlet* (31 percent), as, for instance, when Hamlet converses with his onetime friends Rosencrantz and Guildenstern, when he plagues Polonius with his satirical wit, or when he philosophizes with Horatio, though verse is, of course, appropriate for the soliloquies and the moments of confrontation with Claudius. In the other great tragedies as well, prose has become for Shakespeare an instrument of limitless flexibility. Although the mixture of prose and blank verse is thus hard to quantify in any steady progression of percentages, the pattern of increased versatility is undeniable. Many of the late plays make less use of prose because of their choice of subject, but all excel in prose comic scenes for Autolycus, Caliban, and many others.

In his use of rhyme, as well, Shakespeare's practice changes from the early to late plays. Early plays and those of the lyric period, such as *A Midsummer Night's Dream* and *Romeo and Juliet*, use a great deal of rhyme, whereas late plays, such as *The Tempest*, use practically none. The commonest form of rhyme is the iambic pentameter measure rhymed in couplet, as when Phoebe, quoting Marlowe's *Hero and Leander,* says in *As You Like It* (3.5.81–2):

> Dead shepherd, now I find thy saw of might,
> "Who ever loved that loved not at first sight?"

Shakespeare does not limit his use of rhyme to the couplet, however. *Romeo and Juliet* and *Love's Labor's Lost* each contains a number of complete sonnets, as well as rhymed sequences made up of a quatrain followed by a couplet, and a good deal of alternate rhyme. Doggerel lines of verse appear in some of the early plays.

One quite formal use of the rhymed couplet does not conform to the statistical pattern that we observe generally in the use of rhyme. Because the Elizabethan theater lacked a front curtain to mark a pause between scenes in a play, Elizabethan dramatists often gave emphasis to a scene ending by means of a rhymed couplet. Possibly the device served also as a cue to those actors backstage who were waiting to begin the next scene. At any rate, the use of scene-ending couplets is common in some plays that otherwise make little use of rhyme. For example, Act 1, scene 5 of *Hamlet* virtually ends with the following concluding statement by the protagonist:

> The time is out of joint. O cursèd spite,
> That ever I was born to set it right!

Apart from this convention, however, use of rhyme in Shakespeare is normally indicative of early style. His lovers in the early plays often speak in rhyme; later, they tend to use prose.

Impossible to quantify, but no less significant in any study of the evolution of Shakespeare's art, is his use of imagery. Images are key to his poetic imagination, and, in part, they can be appreciated out of chronological context, because Shakespeare's mind dwells incessantly on certain image clusters: the family as a metaphor for the state, the garden as an image of social order and disorder, images of medicine and healing applied to the ills of the individual and the commonwealth, images of sexual desire and activity, images of hunting and of other sports, biblical images (Eden, Cain and Abel, Christ's ministry, his Passion, the Last Judgment, etc.), mythological allusions (Danae, Actaeon, Phaethon, Noah, Niobe), and many others. Patterns of imagery have been well studied by Caroline Spurgeon in her *Shakespeare's Imagery and What It Tells Us* (1935), Maurice Charney in *The Function of Imagery in the Drama* (1961), and others. In addition, we can see throughout Shakespeare's career the evolution of an imagistic style, as convincingly demonstrated by Wolfgang Clemen in *The Development of Shakespeare's Imagery* (1951). The early Shakespeare uses figures of speech for decoration and amplification, and learns only gradually to integrate these figures into a presentation of theme, subject, and individual character. In Shakespeare's later work, simile is often transformed into metaphor and assumes an organic function in relation to the entire play. By the end of his career, virtually every aspect of his style has been transformed from one of formal and rhetorical regularity to one of vast flexibility and range.

SHAKESPEARE'S ENGLISH

Pronunciation

How would Shakespeare's plays have sounded to our ears? The distance between Shakespearean and modern English is clearly not as great as in the case of Chaucer, and yet significant differences remain. Spoken English, especially in the pronunciation of vowel sounds, has undergone many striking changes since the early seventeenth century. We can assume that however much Shakespeare's own speech may have been colored by his Warwickshire boyhood, his acting company as a whole was most heavily influenced by London dialect. This form of English had become notably more dominant than in Chaucer's day, though it also included an admixture of northern, eastern, and southern forms because of the cosmopolitan character of the city. Shakespeare often pokes fun at regional dialects in his plays, especially at Welsh, Scottish, and Irish, and at the accents of Frenchmen or other foreigners attempting to speak English (see, for example, *Henry V* and *The Merry Wives of Windsor*).

Reconstructing how early modern English would have sounded is, to be sure, not always easy, since dialect did vary substantially from region to region, and since the ascertaining of pronunciations is often based on rhymes when we cannot be sure how either word in a rhyming pair was pronounced and cannot safely assume that rhymes were exact. Nevertheless, here, in summary form, are some approximate suggestions for pronouncing words in Shakespeare that are not similarly pronounced today. These examples can be applied to similar words: for example, *way* and *say* have the same vowel sound as *day; night,* the same vowel sound as *wide.*

> *folk* (sound the *l*)
> *gnaw* (sound the *g*)
> *knife* (sound the *k; i* as in *wide,* below)
> *brush* (rhymes with *push; r* somewhat trilled)
> *dull* (rhymes with *pull*)
> *seam* (pronounced *same,* with open *a*)
> *old* (pronounced *auld*)
> *now* (pronounced *noo*)
> *house* (pronounced *hoos*)
> *soul* (pronounced *saul*)
> *know* (pronounced *knaw,* with sounded *k*)
> *own* (pronounced *awn*)

> *tune* (pronounced *tiwn*)
> *rule* (pronounced *riwl; r* somewhat trilled)
> *day* (pronounced *die*)
> *time* (pronounced *toime*)
> *wide* (pronounced *woide*)
> *join* (rhymes with *line*)
> *creeping* (pronounced *craypin,* with open *a*)
> *dissention* (in four syllables, without *sh* sound)
> *persuasion* (in four syllables, without *zh* sound)

A matter of more practical importance than phonetic changes is that of differences in Shakespeare's English and ours in the accentuation of syllables. Many cases of variable stress can be found in which he seems to have been at liberty to accent the word in two different ways; in other cases, words were customarily accented on a different syllable from that in current speech. For example, the following accentuations are either usual or frequent: *aspect´, charac´ter, com´mendable, com´plete, con´cealed, con´fessor, consort´* (as a noun), *contract´* (noun), *de´testable, dis´tinct, envy´, for´lorn, hu´mane, instinct´, ob´scure, persev´er, pi´oner, ple´beians, portents´, pur´sue, record´* (noun), *reven´ue, se´cure, sinis´ter, welcome´.*

Not only are *-tion* and *-sion* regularly pronounced as two syllables, but the same situation causes other words in which *e* or *i* stand before vowels to be uttered in Shakespeare's language with one more syllable than in ours; for example, *oce-an, courti-er, marri-age.* We may even have *cre-ature, tre-asure,* and *venge-ance.* Nasals and liquids are frequently pronounced as if an extra vowel were introduced between them and a preceding letter. Accordingly, we have *wrest(e)ler, Eng(e)land, assemb(e)ly,* and *ent(e)rance,* as well as *de-ar, you(e)r,* and *mo-re.* Final *-er* often has a greater syllabic importance than it has in later poetry. Final *-(e)s* in the genitive singular and the plural of nouns not ending in an *-s* sound may constitute a separate syllable; for example, "To show his teeth as white as whale's bone" (*Love's Labor's Lost,* 5.2.333).

The study of metrics is fraught with peril. Knowledge of syllabification can often be circular in that it has to assume a kind of metrical regularity in the line of a verse. Even so, in scanning of Shakespeare's verse it helps to ascertain as accurately as we can how many syllables he intended a given word to have. As compared to modern-day English, a Shakespearean word may have (1) an additional syllable, or (2) one fewer syllables, or (3) two adjoining syllables in adjoining words that coalesce or elide. Spelling may not always indicate these differences to a modern reader.

1. The following lines give us extra-syllable words in *moon's, juggler, entrance,* and *complexion:*

> I do wander everywhere,
> Swifter than the moon's sphere.
> (*A Midsummer Night's Dream,* 2.1.6–7)

O me! You juggler! You cankerblossom!
(*A Midsummer Night's Dream*, 3.2.282)

After the prompter, for our entrance.
(*Romeo and Juliet*, 1.4.8)

Mislike me not for my complexion.
(*The Merchant of Venice*, 2.1.1)

Similarly, the words *captain, monstrous, esperance, this* (this is), *George* (*Richard III*, 5.5.9), *valiant, villain,* and *jealous* sometimes have extra syllables in pronunciation.

2. In the following line, *marry* is elided into one syllable:

Good mother, do not *marry* me to yond fool.
(*The Merry Wives of Windsor*, 3.4.83)

Similarly, the words *lineal, journeying, carrion, celestial, herald, royal, malice, absolute, perjury, madame, needle, taken, heaven, spirit, devil, gentleman, unpeople, forward, gather, innocent, violet, Africa, eagle, listen,* and *venomous* have usually one fewer syllables than in current English.

3. The following examples are of elision between the syllables of adjoining words:

Why should I joy in *an abortive* birth?
(*Love's Labor's Lost*, 1.1.104)

The *lover, all* as frantic,
(*A Midsummer Night's Dream*, 5.1.10)

Romans, *do me* right.
(*Titus Andronicus*, 1.1.204)

Differences in accentuation and lengthening or shortening of words thus have great importance in the reading and scanning of Shakespeare's verse. Shortening of words by elision or by slurring is common in Shakespeare, but at least in this matter modern practice forms a good guide. Syllables ending in vowels are not infrequently elided before words beginning with a vowel, as in "How cáme /*we* ashóre" (*The Tempest*, 1.2.159) and "too hárd / a knót / for mé / t' un*tie*" (*Twelfth Night*, 2.2.41). Syncopation, or the omission of a syllable, often occurs in words with *r*, as in "I wár-rant / it wíll" (*Hamlet*, 1.2.248); and in final -*er, -el,* and -*le,* as in "Trável you / farre ón" (*The Taming of the Shrew*, 4.2.74). The following words and other similar ones may be treated as monosyllabic in Shakespeare's verse: *whether, ever, hither, other, father, evil, having.* Almost any unaccented syllable of a polysyllabic word (especially if it contains an *i*) may be softened and ignored. This syncopation is frequent in polysyllabic words and proper names: "Thoughts spécu / latíve" (*Macbeth*, 5.4.19) and "Did sláy / this Fórtinbras; / who by / a seáled /compáct" (*Hamlet*, 1.1.90). Other occasions for slurring, as listed by Abbott in his *Shakespearian Grammar,* are light vowels pre-

ceded by heavy vowels, as in *power, dying,* and so on; plurals and possessives of nouns ending in an *s* sound, as in *empress'* and *Mars';* final -*ed* following *d* or *t,* as in "you háve / exceéded / all prómise" (*As You Like It,* 1.2.234); and the -*est* of superlatives (pronounced -*st*) after dentals and liquids, as "the stérn'st / good-níght" (*Macbeth,* 2.2.4) and "thy éldest / son's són" (*King John,* 2.1.177).

Grammar and Rhetoric

Shakespeare's grammar presents but few differences in forms from the grammar of current modern English. The -*eth* ending in the third person singular of the present tense, indicative mood, was very commonly used, especially in serious prose. Shakespeare frequently uses this older form, especially *hath, doth,* and *saith,* but seems to prefer the form in -*s* or -*es.* In a few cases, he also seems to use the old northern plural in -*s* or -*es* in the third person of the present indicative, as " . . . at those springs, / On chaliced flowers that *lies*" (*Cymbeline,* 2.3.22–3). He does not always agree with modern usage in the forms of the past tenses and the perfect participles of the verbs that he employs. He retains some lost forms of the strong verbs, sometimes ignores distinctions we make between the past tense and the perfect participle, and treats some verbs as weak (or regular) which are now strong (or irregular). For example, he uses *arose* for *arisen, swam* for *swum, foughten* for *fought, gave* for *given, took* for *taken, sprung* for *sprang, writ* for *wrote, blowed* for *blew, weaved* for *wove,* and *shaked* for *shaken.* Forms like *degenerate* for *degenerated* and *exhaust* for *exhausted* are especially common. A few instances are to be found of the archaic *y-* with the past participle, as in *yclad.* For the possessive case of the neuter personal pronoun *it,* Shakespeare normally uses the regular form at that time, *his;* but he also uses the possessive form *it,* and in his plays first published in the First Folio in 1623 we find several occurrences of the new form *its.* Shakespeare uses the old form *moe,* as well as *more,* and *enow* as the plural of *enough,* though these forms have been modernized in this edition because they are used so inconsistently. He uses *near* and *next* along with *nearer* and *nearest,* as the comparative and superlative of *nigh.* These are the most obvious of the formal differences between Shakespeare's grammar and our own.

The functional differences are more considerable. Elizabethan language exercised an extraordinary freedom, even for English, in the use of one part of speech for another. Shakespeare uses verbs, adjectives, adverbs, and pronouns as nouns. He makes verbs out of nouns and adjectives and, of course, uses nouns as adjectives, for this is a distinguishing characteristic of English speech, but he also uses adverbs, verbs, and prepositional phrases as adjectives, as in "Looks he as freshly as he did . . . ?" (*As You Like It,* 3.2.227). Almost any adjective may be freely used as an adverb, as in "And in my house you shall be friendly lodged" (*The Taming of the Shrew*, 4.2.109). He makes active words—both adjectives and verbs—discharge a passive function, as in "the sightless [invisible] couriers of the air" (*Macbeth*, 1.7.23) and "this aspect of mine / Hath feared the valiant," that is, caused the valiant to be afraid (*The Merchant of Venice*, 2.1.8–9). He makes wider use of the infinitive as a verbal noun or as a gerundive participle than do we: "This to be true / I do engage my life" (*As You Like It*, 5.4.164–5), "My operant powers their functions leave to do" (*Hamlet*, 3.2.172), "Nor do I now make moan to be abridged" (*The Merchant of Venice*, 1.1.126), and "You might have saved me my pains, to have taken [by having taken] it away yourself" (*Twelfth Night*, 2.2.5–7). The functions of prepositions in Elizabethan English were so various that one can only refer the student to the notes to the text or to a dictionary.

In certain other features, however, as, for example, in the use of modal auxiliaries, Shakespeare's language is as restricted and conventional as ours is at formal levels, or even more so. *Shall* is regularly used in Shakespeare to express something inevitable in future time and is, therefore, the usual future tense for all persons. *Will*, which originally expressed intention, determination, or willingness, was, to be sure, beginning to encroach on *shall* for the expression of futurity in the second and third persons, but its use usually still retains in Shakespeare a consciousness of its original meaning. *Should* and *would* had their original senses of obligation and volition, respectively, and had other peculiarities, then as now, of considerable difficulty. The subjunctive mood was vital to Shakespeare as a means of expressing condition, doubt, concession, command, wish, or desire, and, in dependent clauses, indefinitiveness, purpose, or sometimes simple futurity. Note the following examples:

But if my father *had* not scanted me . . .
Yourself, renownèd prince, then *stood* as fair.
(*The Merchant of Venice*, 2.1.17, 20)

Live a thousand years,
I *shall* not find myself so apt to die.
(*Julius Caesar*, 3.1.161–2)

Lest your retirement do *amaze* your friends.
(*1 Henry IV*, 5.4.6)

'*Twere* best he speak no harm of Brutus here.
(*Julius Caesar*, 3.2.70)

Melt Egypt into Nile, and kindly creatures
Turn all to serpents!
(*Antony and Cleopatra*, 2.5.79–80)

Yet were it true
To say this boy *were* like me.
(*The Winter's Tale*, 1.2.134–5)

And may direct his course as *please* himself.
(*Richard III*, 2.2.129)

Some other features of Shakespeare's grammar are as follows: he often omits the relative pronoun; he often uses the nominative case of the pronoun for the accusative case, and vice versa; he uses *him, her, me,* and *them* as true reflexives to mean *himself, herself, myself,* and *themselves;* he employs double negatives and double comparatives and superlatives; he shows a consciousness in the use of *thee* and *thou* of their application to intimates and inferiors and of their insulting quality when addressed to strangers (e.g., "If thou 'thou'-est him some thrice, it shall not be amiss," *Twelfth Night*, 3.2.43–4); he employs *which* to refer to both persons and things; and he does not discriminate closely between *ye*, nominative, and *you*, objective. He makes frequent use of the dative constructions, that is, the objective forms of the pronouns, *me, thee, you, him, her,* and so on, without prepositions where the meaning is "by me," "for me," "with me," "to me," "of me," and the like. For example:

I am appointed *him* [by him] to murder you.
(*The Winter's Tale*, 1.2.411)

She looks *us* [to us] like
A thing made more of malice than of duty.
(*Cymbeline*, 3.5.32–3)

One prominent feature of Shakespeare's grammar is his use of the ethical dative, a construction in which the pronoun is generally used to indicate the person interested in the statement. In *King John* (3.4.146), the phrase "John lays you plots," means something like "John lays plots which you may profit by." In the following, *me* means "to my detriment" or "to my disadvantage":

See how this river comes *me* cranking in
And cuts *me* from the best of all my land
A huge half-moon.
(*1 Henry IV*, 3.1.95–7)

"Whip *me* such honest knaves" (*Othello*, 1.1.51) means "In my judgment such knaves should be whipped." In Quickly's description of Mistress Page, the dative *you* is equivalent to "mark you," "take notice":

. . . a civil modest wife, and one, I tell you, that will not miss *you* morning nor evening prayer, as any is in Windsor.
(*The Merry Wives of Windsor*, 2.2.92–4)

At times, however, the ethical dative is idiomatic and virtually without equivalent meaning in modern English; the sense of the passage is best obtained by omitting the pronoun.

Shakespeare, like other Renaissance poets, makes extensive use of the forms and figures of rhetoric. He is fond, for example, of using the abstract for the concrete, as in the words addressed by Surrey to Cardinal Wolsey: "Thou scarlet sin" (*Henry VIII*, 3.2.255). Transpositions are numerous, as are inversions, ellipses, and broken or confused constructions, as in the following examples:

> That thing you speak of,
> I took it for a man. (*Absolute construction.*)
>> (*King Lear*, 4.6.77–8)

> Souls and bodies hath he divorced three. (*Transposition of adjective.*)
>> (*Twelfth Night*, 3 4 238–9)

> A happy gentleman in blood and lineaments. (*Transposition of adjectival phrase.*)
>> (*Richard II*, 3.1.9)

> Your state of fortune and your due of birth. (*Transposition of pronoun.*)
>> (*Richard III*, 3.7.120)

> She calls me proud, and [says] that she could not love me. (*Ellipsis.*)
>> (*As You Like It*, 4.3.17)

> Returning were as tedious as [to] go o'er. (*Ellipsis.*)
>> (*Macbeth*, 3.4.139)

> They call him Doricles, and boasts himself
> To have a worthy feeding. (*Ellipsis of nominative.*)
>> (*The Winter's Tale*, 4.4.168–9)

> Of all men else I have avoided thee. (*Confusion of two constructions.*)
>> (*Macbeth*, 5.8.4)

> The venom of such looks, we fairly hope,
> Have lost their quality. (*Confusion of number arising from proximity.*)
>> (*Henry V*, 5.2.18–19)

> Rather proclaim it, Westmorland, through my host
> That he which hath no stomach to this fight,
> Let him depart. (*Construction changed by change of thought.*)
>> (*Henry V*, 4.3.34–6)

> For always I am Caesar. (*Inversion of adverb.*)
>> (*Julius Caesar*, 1.2.212)

Shakespeare often uses rhetorical figures for symmetrical effects, especially in the early, ornamental style of *Richard III* and the nondramatic poems. Following are definitions of some of the most popular figures he uses, with illustrations from *Venus and Adonis*:

1. *Parison.* The symmetrical repetition of words in grammatically parallel phrases: "How love makes young men thrall, and old men dote" (line 837).

2. *Isocolon.* The symmetrical repetition of sounds and words in phrases of equal length, as in the previous example, and in this: "Or as the wolf doth grin before he barketh, /Or as the berry breaks before it staineth" (lines 459–60). Parison and isocolon are frequently combined.

3. *Anaphora.* The symmetrical repetition of a word at the beginning of a sequence of clauses or sentences, often at the beginning of lines. Anaphora is frequently combined with parison and isocolon, as in the second example already given, and in this: " 'Give me my hand,' saith he. 'Why dost thou feel it?' / 'Give me my heart,' saith she, 'and thou shalt have it' " (lines 373–4).

4. *Antimetabole.* The symmetrical repetition of words in inverted order: "She clepes him king of graves and grave for kings" (line 995).

5. *Anadiplosis.* The beginning of a phrase with the final words of the previous phrase: "O, thou didst kill me; kill me once again!" (line 499).

6. *Epanalepsis.* The symmetrical repetition of a word or words at the beginning and ending of a line: "He sees his love, and nothing else he sees" (line 287).

7. *Ploce.* The insistent repetition of a word within the same line or phrase: "Then why not lips on lips, since eyes in eyes?" (line 120).

8. *Epizeuxis.* An intensified form of ploce, repeating the word without another intervening word: " 'Ay me!' she cries, and twenty times, 'Woe, woe!' / And twenty echoes twenty times cry so" (lines 833–4).

9. *Antanaclasis.* The shifting of a repeated word from one meaning to another: "My love to love is love but to disgrace it," or " 'Where did I leave?' 'No matter where,' quoth he, / 'Leave me' " (lines 412, 715–6).

For other figures and illustrations, see Sister Miriam Joseph, *Shakespeare's Use of the Arts of Language* (1947) and Brian Vickers, "Shakespeare's Use of Rhetoric," in *A New Companion to Shakespeare Studies*, edited by Kenneth Muir and S. Schoenbaum (1971).

Vocabulary

Renaissance English was hospitable to foreign importation. Many words taken directly from Latin became a permanent part of the language, serving to enrich its power to express thought and its rhythmical capabilities; others were ultimately discarded. The principal borrowings were in the realm of learning and culture. Such words usually retained a vital sense of their original Latin meaning. Sometimes such words have not replaced native words of the same meaning, so that we have such pairs of synonyms as *acknowledge* and *confess*, just as Shakespeare had *wonder* and *admiration*. Because of this Latin heritage, even a slight knowledge of Latin is a great advantage in the correct understanding of Elizabethan writers, since many Latin borrowings have taken on since the sixteenth century a different shade of meaning from that in which they were borrowed. The Latin sense of *aggravate* ("to add weight to") still struggles for recognition; but *apparent* no longer means primarily "visible to sight," and *intention* does not convey the idea of "intentness." The *Oxford English Dictionary* (*OED*) provides a wealth of information about derivations and changes in meaning.

Latin words were often taken over in their Latin forms, as *objectum* and *subjectum, statua* and *aristocratia,* and later were made to conform to English spelling and stress, though a few, such as *decorum,* still have a Latin form. French continued to be drawn upon and sometimes caused a new Latin borrowing to be adopted in a French form, just as, on the other hand, such words as *adventure* were supplied with a *d* to make them conform to Latin spelling. This principle is illustrated in the pedantry of Holofernes when he objects (*Love's Labor's Lost,* 5.1.20) to "det" as the pronunciation of "debt." Spanish, Italian, and Dutch also supplied many terms. Spanish gave words having to do with commerce, religion, and the New World, such as *mosquito, alligator, ambuscado,* and *grandee.* From Italian came terms of art, learning, and dueling: *bandetto, portico, canto, stoccato.* The Dutch contributed many nautical and oriental words.

These foreign borrowings were a part of what might be called the linguistic ambition of the age, a desire for forcible expression. Language was in a plastic state, so that it had an unparalleled freedom in both vocabulary and form. With this freedom, to be sure, came some confusion, since the Elizabethan era saw few efforts at grammatical precision. Such efforts were later to be made by the age of Dryden and the Royal Society, and by learned men ever since, prompted by an awareness that English was too vague and irregular for use as a means of scientific expression. Still, we readily perceive that English profited from its Renaissance expansion and its subsequent absorption with Shakespeare and the English Bible. It gained, for example, an increased facility in making compounds. Shakespeare, with his *cloud-capped towers* and his *home-keeping wits,* was a genius at this. Also from Shakespeare's time came the English adaptability in the use of prefixes, such as *dis-, re-,* and *en-,* and of suffixes, such as *-ful, -less, -ness,* and *-hood.*

SHAKESPEARE CRITICISM

In his own time, Shakespeare achieved a reputation for immortal greatness that is astonishing when we consider the low regard in which playwrights were then generally held. Francis Meres compared him to Ovid, Plautus, and Seneca, and proclaimed Shakespeare to be England's most excellent writer in both comedy and tragedy. John Weever spoke of "honey-tongued Shakespeare." The number of such praising allusions is high. Even Ben Jonson, a learned writer strongly influenced by the classical tradition, lauded Shakespeare as "a monument without a tomb," England's best poet, exceeding Chaucer, Spenser, Beaumont, Kyd, and Marlowe. In tragedy, Jonson compared Shakespeare with Aeschylus, Euripides, and Sophocles; in comedy, he insisted Shakespeare had no rival even in "insolent Greece or haughty Rome." This tribute appeared in Jonson's commendatory poem written for the Shakespeare First Folio of 1623.

To be sure, Jonson had more critical things to say about Shakespeare. Even in the Folio commendatory poem, Jonson could not resist a dig at Shakespeare's "small Latin, and less Greek." To William Drummond of Hawthornden, he objected that Shakespeare "wanted art" because in a play (*The Winter's Tale*) he "brought in a number of men saying they had suffered shipwreck in Bohemia, where there is no sea near by some hundred miles." In *Timber,* or *Discoveries,* Jonson chided Shakespeare for his unrestrained facility in writing. "The players have often mentioned it as an honor to Shakespeare, that in his writing, whatsoever he penned he never blotted out [a] line. My answer hath been, would he had blotted a thousand." In a preface to his own play, *Every Man in His Humor* (1616 edition), Jonson satirized English history plays (such as Shakespeare's) that "with three rusty swords, / And help of some few foot-and-half-foot words, / Fight over York and Lancaster's long jars, / And in the tiring-house bring wounds to scars." He also jeered at plays lacking unity of time in which children grow to the age of sixty or older and at nonsensical romantic plays featuring fireworks, thunder, and a chorus that "wafts you o'er the seas."

These criticisms are all of a piece. As a classicist himself, Jonson held in high regard the classical unities. He deplored much English popular drama, including some of Shakespeare's plays, for their undisciplined mixture of comedy and tragedy. Measured against his cherished ideals of classical decorum and refinement of language, Shakespeare's histories and the late romances—*Pericles, Cymbeline, The Winter's Tale,* and *The Tempest*—seemed irritatingly naive and loose-jointed. Yet Jonson knew that Shakespeare had an incomparable genius, superior even to his own. Jonson's affection and respect for Shakespeare seem to have been quite unforced. In the midst of his critical remarks in *Timber,* he freely conceded that "I loved the man, and do honor his memory (on this side idolatry) as much as any. He was indeed honest, and of an open and free nature, had an excellent fantasy, brave notions, and gentle expressions."

The Age of Dryden and Pope

Jonson's attitude toward Shakespeare lived on into the Restoration period of the late seventeenth century. A commonplace of that age held it proper to "admire" Ben Jonson but to "love" Shakespeare. Jonson was the more correct poet, the better model for imitation. Shakespeare often had to be rewritten according to the sophisticated tastes of the Restoration (see Appendix 3 for an account of Restoration stage adaptations of Shakespeare), but he was also regarded as a natural genius. Dryden reflected this view in his *Essay of Dramatic Poesy* (1668) and his *Essay on the Dramatic Poetry of the Last Age* (1672). Dryden condemned *The Winter's Tale, Pericles,* and several other late romances for "the lameness of their plots" and for their "ridiculous incoherent story" which is usually "grounded on impossibilities." Not only Shakespeare, he charged, but several of his contemporaries "neither understood correct plotting nor that which they call *the decorum of the stage.*" Had Shakespeare lived in the Restoration, Dryden believed, he would doubtless have written "more correctly" under the influence of a language that had become more "courtly" and a wit that had grown more "refined." Shakespeare, he thought, had limitless "fancy" but sometimes lacked "judgment." Dryden regretted that Shakespeare had been forced to write in "ignorant" times and for audiences who "knew no better." Like Jonson, nevertheless, Dryden had the magnanimity to perceive that Shakespeare transcended his limitations. Shakespeare, said Dryden, was "the man who of all modern and perhaps ancient poets had the largest and most comprehensive soul." From a classical writer, this was high praise indeed.

Alexander Pope's edition of Shakespeare (1725) was based upon a similar estimate of Shakespeare as an untutored genius. Pope freely "improved" Shakespeare's language, rewriting lines and excising those parts he considered vulgar, in order to rescue Shakespeare from the barbaric circumstances of his Elizabethan milieu. Other critics of the Restoration and early eighteenth century who stressed Shakespeare's "natural" genius and imaginative powers were John Dennis, Joseph Addison, and the editors Nicholas Rowe and Lewis Theobald.

The Age of Johnson

Shakespeare was not without his detractors during the late seventeenth and early eighteenth centuries; after all, classical criticism tended to distrust imagination and fancy. Notable among the harsher critics of the Restoration period was Thomas Rymer, whose *Short View of Tragedy* (1692) included a famous attack on *Othello* for making too much out of Desdemona's handkerchief. In the eighteenth century, Voltaire spoke out sharply against Shakespeare's violation of the classical unities, though Voltaire also had some admiring things to say.

The most considered answer to such criticism in the later eighteenth century was that of Dr. Samuel Johnson, in his edition of Shakespeare's plays and its great preface (1765). Shakespeare, said Johnson, is the poet of nature who "holds up to his readers a faithful mirror of manners and of life. His characters are not modified by the customs of particular places, unpracticed by the rest of the world. . . . In the writings of other poets a character is too often an individual; in those of Shakespeare it is commonly a species." Johnson's attitudes were essentially classical in that he praised Shakespeare for being universal, for having provided a "just representation of general nature," and for having stood the test of time. Yet Johnson also magnanimously praised Shakespeare for having transcended the classical rules. Johnson triumphantly vindicated the mixture of comedy and tragedy in Shakespeare's plays and the supposed indecorum of his characters.

Of course, Johnson did not praise everything he saw. He objected to Shakespeare's loose construction of plot, careless huddling together of the ends of his plays, licentious humor, and, above all, the punning wordplay. He deplored Shakespeare's failure to satisfy the demands of poetic justice, especially in *King Lear,* and he regretted that Shakespeare seemed more anxious to please than to instruct. Still, Johnson did much to free Shakespeare from the constraint of an overly restrictive classical approach to criticism.

The Age of Coleridge

With the beginning of the Romantic period, in England and on the Continent, Shakespeare criticism increasingly turned away from classical precept in favor of a more spontaneous and enthusiastic approach to Shakespeare's creative genius. The new Shakespeare became indeed a rallying cry for those who now deplored such "regular" dramatic poets as Racine and Corneille. Shakespeare became a seer, a bard with mystic powers of insight into the human condition. Goethe, in *Wilhelm Meister* (1796), conceived of Hamlet as the archetypal "Romantic" poet: melancholic, delicate, and unable to act.

Critical trends in England moved toward similar conclusions. Maurice Morgann, in his *Essay on the Dramatic Character of Sir John Falstaff* (1777), glorified Falstaff into a rare individual of courage, dignity, and—yes—honor. To do so, Morgann had to suppress much evidence as to Falstaff's overall function in the *Henry IV* plays. Dramatic structure, in fact, did not interest him; his passion was "character," and his study of Falstaff reflected a new Romantic preoccupation with character analysis. Like other character critics who followed him, Morgann tended to move away from the play itself and into a world where the dramatic personage being considered might lead an independent existence. What would it have been like to know Falstaff as a real person? How would he have behaved on occasions other than those reported by Shakespeare? Such questions fascinated Morgann and others because they led into grand speculations about human psychology and philosophy. Shakespeare's incomparably penetrating insights into character prompted further investigations of the human psyche.

Other late eighteenth-century works devoted to the study of character included Lord Kames's *Elements of Criticism* (1762), Thomas Whately's *Remarks on Some of the Characters of Shakespeare* (1785), William Richardson's *Philosophical Analysis and Illustration of Some of Shakespeare's Remarkable Characters* (1774), and William Jackson's *Thirty Letters on Various Subjects* (1782). Morgann spoke for this school of critics when he insisted, "It may be fit to consider them [Shakespeare's characters] rather as historic than dramatic beings; and, when occasion requires, to account for their conduct from the whole of character, from general principles, from latent motives, and from policies not avowed."

Samuel Taylor Coleridge, the greatest of the English Romantic critics, was profoundly influenced by character criticism, both English and continental. He himself made important contributions to the study of character. His conception of Hamlet, derived in part from Goethe and Hegel, as one who "vacillates from sensibility, and procrastinates from thought, and loses the power of action in the energy of resolve," was to dominate nineteenth-century interpretations of Hamlet. His insight into Iago's evil nature—"the motive-hunting of a motiveless malignity"— was also influential.

Nevertheless, Coleridge did not succumb to the temptation, as did so many character critics, of ignoring the unity of an entire play. Quite to the contrary, he affirmed in Shakespeare an "organic form" or "innate" sense of shape, developed from within, that gave new meaning to Shakespeare's fusion of comedy and tragedy, his seeming anachronisms, his improbable fictions, and his supposedly rambling plots. Coleridge heaped scorn on the eighteenth-century idea of Shakespeare as a "natural" but untaught genius. He praised Shakespeare not for having mirrored life, as Dr. Johnson had said, but for having created an imaginative world attuned to its own internal harmonies. He saw Shakespeare as an inspired but deliberate artist who fitted together the parts of his imaginative world with consummate skill. "The judgment of Shakespeare is commensurate with his genius."

In all this, Coleridge was remarkably close to his German contemporary and rival, August Wilhelm Schlegel, who insisted that Shakespeare was "a profound artist, and not a blind and wildly luxuriant genius." In Shakespeare's plays, said Schlegel, "The fancy lays claim to be considered as an independent mental power governed according to its own laws." Between them, Coleridge and Schlegel utterly inverted the critical values of the previous age, substituting "sublimity" and "imagination" for universality and trueness to nature.

Other Romantic critics included William Hazlitt (*Characters of Shakespear's Plays,* 1817), Charles Lamb (*On the Tragedies of Shakespeare,* 1811), and Thomas De Quincey (*On the Knocking at the Gate in Macbeth,* 1823). Hazlitt reveals a political liberalism characteristic of a number of Romantic writers in his skeptical view of Henry V's absolutism and his imperialist war against the French. John Keats has some penetrating things to say in his letters about Shakespeare's "negative capability," or his ability to see into characters' lives with an extraordinary self-effacing sympathy. As a whole, the Romantics were enthusiasts of Shakespeare, and sometimes even idolaters. Yet they consistently refused to recognize him as a man of the theater. Lamb wrote, "It may seem a paradox, but I cannot help being of opinion that the plays of Shakespeare are less calculated for performance on a stage than those of almost any other dramatist whatever." Hazlitt similarly observed: "We do not like to see our author's plays acted, and least of all, *Hamlet.* There is no play that suffers so much in being transferred to the stage." These hostile attitudes toward the theater reflected, in part, the condition of the stage in nineteenth-century England. In part, however, these attitudes were the inevitable result of character criticism, or what Lamb called the desire "to know the internal workings and movements of a great mind, of an Othello or a Hamlet for instance, the *when* and the *why* and the *how far* they should be moved." This fascination with character swept everything before it during the Romantic period.

A. C. Bradley and the Turn of the Century

The tendency of nineteenth-century criticism, then, was to exalt Shakespeare as a poet and a philosopher rather than as a playwright, and as a creator of immortal characters whose "lives" might be studied as though existing independent of a dramatic text. Not infrequently, this critical approach led to a biographical interpretation of Shakespeare through his plays, on the assumption that what he wrote was his own spiritual autobiography and a key to his own fascinating character. Perhaps the most famous critical study in this line was Edward Dowden's *Shakspere: A Critical Study of His Mind and Art* (1875), in which he traced a progression from Shakespeare's early exuberance and passionate involvement through brooding pessimism to a final philosophical calm.

At the same time, the nineteenth century also saw the rise of a more factual and methodological scholarship, especially in the German universities. Dowden, in fact, reflected this trend as well, for one of the achievements of philological study was to establish with some accuracy the dating of Shakespeare's plays and thus make possible an analysis of his artistic development. Hermann Ulrici's *Über Shakespeares dramatische Kunst* (1839) and Gottfried Gervinus's edition of 1849 were among the earliest studies to interest themselves in Shakespeare's chronological development.

The critic who best summed up the achievement of nineteenth-century Shakespeare criticism was A. C. Bradley, in his *Shakespearean Tragedy* (1904) and other studies. *Shakespearean Tragedy* dealt with the four "great" tragedies: *Hamlet, Othello, King Lear,* and *Macbeth.* Bradley revealed his Romantic tendencies in his focus on psychological analysis of character, but he also brought to his work a scholarly awareness of the text that had been missing in some earlier character critics. His work continues to have considerable influence today, despite modern tendencies to rebel against nineteenth-century idealism. To Bradley, Shakespeare's tragic world was ultimately explicable and profoundly moral. Despite the overwhelming impression of tragic waste in *King Lear*, he argued, we as audience experience a sense of compensation and completion that implies an ultimate pattern in human life. "Good, in the widest sense, seems thus to be the principle of life and health in the world; evil, at least in these worst forms, to be a poison. The world reacts against it violently, and, in the struggle to expel it, is driven to devastate itself." Humanity must suffer because of its fatal tendency to pursue some extreme passion, but humanity learns through suffering about itself and the nature of its world. We as audience are reconciled to our existence through purgative release; we smile through our tears. Cordelia is wantonly destroyed, but the fact of her transcendent goodness is eternal. Although in one sense she fails, said Bradley, she is "in another sense superior to the world in which [she] appears; is, in some way which we do not seek to define, untouched by the doom that overtakes [her]; and is rather set free from life than deprived of it."

Historical Criticism

The first major twentieth-century reaction against character criticism was that of the so-called historical critics. (On the later critical movement known as the New Historicism, see below, following "Jan Kott and the Theater of the Absurd.") These critics insisted on a more hardheaded and skeptical appraisal of Shakespeare through better understanding of his historical milieu: his theater, his audience, and his political and social environment. In good part, this movement was the result of a new professionalism of Shakespearean studies in the twentieth century. Whereas earlier critics—Dryden, Pope, Johnson, and Coleridge—had generally been literary amateurs in the best sense, early twentieth-century criticism became increasingly the province of those who taught in universities. Historical research became a professional activity. Bradley himself was Professor of English Literature at Liverpool and Oxford, and did much to legitimize the incorporation of Shakespeare into the humanities curriculum. German scholarship produced the first regular periodical devoted to Shakespeare studies, *Shakespeare-Jahrbuch,* to be followed in due course in England and

America by *Shakespeare Survey* (beginning in 1948), *Shakespeare Quarterly* (1950), and *Shakespeare Studies* (1965).

From the start, historical criticism took a new look at Shakespeare as a man of the theater. Sir Walter Raleigh (Professor of English Literature at Oxford, not to be confused with his Elizabethan namesake) rejected the Romantic absorption in psychology and turned his attention instead to the artistic methods by which plays affect theater-going spectators. The poet Robert Bridges insisted that Shakespeare had often sacrificed consistency and logic for primitive theatrical effects designed to please his vulgar audience. Bridges's objections were often based on serious lack of information about Shakespeare's stage, but they had a healthy iconoclastic effect nonetheless on the scholarship of his time. In Germany, Levin Schücking pursued a similar line of reasoning in his *Character Problems in Shakespeare's Plays* (1917, translated into English in 1922). Schücking argued that Shakespeare had disregarded coherent structure and had striven instead for vivid dramatic effect ("episodic intensification") in his particular scenes. Schücking's *The Meaning of Hamlet* (1937) explained the strange contradictions of that play as resulting from primitive and brutal Germanic source materials which Shakespeare had not fully assimilated.

A keynote for historical critics of the early twentieth century was the concept of artifice or convention in the construction of a play. Perhaps the leading spokesman for this approach was E. E. Stoll, a student of G. L. Kittredge of Harvard University, himself a leading force in historical scholarship in America. Stoll vigorously insisted, in such works as *Othello: An Historical and Comparative Study* (1915), *Hamlet: An Historical and Comparative Study* (1919), and *Art and Artifice in Shakespeare* (1933), that a critic must never be sidetracked by moral, psychological, or biographical interpretations. A play, he argued, is an artifice arising out of its historical milieu. Its conventions are implicit agreements between playwright and spectator. They alter with time, and a modern reader who is ignorant of Elizabethan conventions is all too apt to be misled by his own post-Romantic preconceptions. For example, a calumniator like Iago in *Othello* is conventionally supposed to be believed by the other characters on stage. We do not need to speculate about the "realities" of Othello's being duped, and, in fact, we are likely to be led astray by such Romantic speculations. Stoll went so far as to affirm, in fact, that Shakespearean drama intentionally distorts reality through its theatrical conventions in order to fulfill its own existence as artifice. *Hamlet* is not a play about delay but a revenge story of a certain length, containing many conventional revenge motifs, such as the ghost and the "mousetrap" scheme used to test the villain, and deriving many of its circumstances from Shakespeare's sources; delay is a conventional device needed to continue the story to its conclusion.

Stoll's zeal led to excessive claims for historical criticism, as one might expect in the early years of a pioneering movement. At its extreme, historical criticism came close to implying that Shakespeare was a mere product of his environment. Indeed, the movement owed many of its evolutionist assumptions to the supposedly scientific "social Darwinism" of Thomas Huxley and other late nineteenth-century social philosophers. In more recent years, however, the crusading spirit has given way to a more moderate historical criticism that continues to be an important part of Shakespearean scholarship.

Alfred Harbage, for example, in *As They Liked It* (1947) and *Shakespeare and the Rival Traditions* (1952), has analyzed the audience for which Shakespeare wrote and the rivalry between popular and elite theaters in the London of his day. Harbage sees Shakespeare as a popular dramatist writing for a highly intelligent, enthusiastic, and socially diversified audience. More recently, in *The Privileged Playgoers of Shakespeare's London, 1576–1642* (1981), Ann Jennalie Cook has qualified Harbage's view, arguing that Shakespeare's audience was, for the most part, affluent and well connected. G. E. Bentley has amassed an invaluable storehouse of information about *The Jacobean and Caroline Stage* (1941–1968), just as E. K. Chambers earlier had collected documents and data on *The Elizabethan Stage* (1923). Other studies by these historical scholars include Chambers's *William Shakespeare: A Study of Facts and Problems* (1930), and Bentley's *Shakespeare and His Theatre* (1964) and *The Profession of Dramatist in Shakespeare's Time* (1971). T. W. Baldwin exemplifies the historical scholar who, like Stoll, claims too much for the method; nevertheless, much information on Shakespeare's schooling, reading, and professional theatrical life is available in such works as *William Shakspere's Small Latine and Lesse Greeke* (1944) and *The Organization and Personnel of the Shakespearean Company* (1927). Hardin Craig uses historical method in *An Interpretation of Shakespeare* (1948).

Historical criticism has contributed greatly to our knowledge of the staging of Shakespeare's plays. George Pierce Baker, in *The Development of Shakespeare as a Dramatist* (1907), continued the line of investigation begun by Walter Raleigh. Harley Granville-Barker brought to his *Prefaces to Shakespeare* (1930, 1946) a wealth of professional theatrical experience of his own. Ever since his time, the new theatrical method of interpreting Shakespeare has been based to an ever increasing extent on a genuine revival of interest in Shakespearean production. John Dover Wilson shows an awareness of the stage in *What Happens in Hamlet* (1935) and *The Fortunes of Falstaff* (1943). At its best, as in John Russell Brown's *Shakespeare's Plays in Performance* (1966), in John Styan's *Shakespeare's Stagecraft* (1967), in Michael Goldman's *Shakespeare and the Energies of Drama* (1972), and in Alan Dessen's *Elizabethan Drama and the Viewer's Eye* (1977) and his *Recovering Shakespeare's Theatrical Vocabulary* (1995), this critical method

reveals many insights into the text that are hard to obtain without an awareness of theatrical technique.

Supporting this theatrical criticism, historical research has learned a great deal about the physical nature of Shakespeare's stage. J. C. Adams's well-known model of the Globe Playhouse, as presented in Irwin Smith's *Shakespeare's Globe Playhouse: A Modern Reconstruction* (1956), is now generally discredited in favor of a simpler building, as reconstructed by C. Walter Hodges (*The Globe Restored*, 1953, 2nd edition, 1968), Bernard Beckerman (*Shakespeare at the Globe*, 1962, 2nd edition, 1967), Richard Hosley ("The Playhouses and the Stage" in *A New Companion to Shakespeare Studies*, edited by K. Muir and S. Schoenbaum, 1971, and several other good essays), T. J. King (*Shakespearean Staging, 1599–1642*, 1971), and others. Information on the private theaters, such as the Blackfriars, where Shakespeare's plays were also performed, appears in William Armstrong, *The Elizabethan Private Theatres* (1958); Richard Hosley, "A Reconstruction of the Second Blackfriars" (*The Elizabethan Theatre*, 1969); Glynne Wickham, *Early English Stages* (1959–1972); and others. For further information on innyard theaters and on courtly or private theaters, see the contributions of Herbert Berry, D. F. Rowan, W. Reavley Gair, and others cited in the bibliography at the end of this volume.

A related pursuit of historical criticism has been the better understanding of Shakespeare through his dramatic predecessors and contemporaries. Willard Farnham, in *The Medieval Heritage of Elizabethan Tragedy* (1936), traces the evolution of native English tragedy through the morality plays of the early Tudor period. J. M. R. Margeson's *The Origins of English Tragedy* (1967) broadens the pattern to include still other sources for Elizabethan ideas on dramatic tragedy. Bernard Spivack, in *Shakespeare and the Allegory of Evil* (1958), sees Iago, Edmund, Richard III, and other boasting villains in Shakespeare as descendants of the morality Vice. In *Shakespeare and the Idea of the Play* (1962), Anne Righter (Barton) traces the device of the play-within-the-play and the metaphor of the world as a stage back to medieval and classical ideas of dramatic illusion. Irving Ribner's *The English History Play in the Age of Shakespeare* (1959, revised 1965) examines Shakespeare's plays on English history in the context of the popular Elizabethan genre to which they belonged. Robert Weimann's *Shakespeare and the Popular Tradition in the Theatre* (translated from the German in 1978) is a Marxist study in the social dimension of dramatic form and function. Many other studies of this sort could be cited, including Glynne Wickham's *Shakespeare's Dramatic Heritage* (1969), Oscar J. Campbell's *Shakespeare's Satire* (1943), M. C. Bradbrook's *Themes and Conventions of Elizabethan Tragedy* (1935), and S. L. Bethell's *Shakespeare and the Popular Dramatic Tradition* (1944).

Another important concern of historical criticism has been the relationship between Shakespeare and the ideas of his age—cosmological, philosophical, and political. Among the first scholars to study Elizabethan cosmology were Hardin Craig in *The Enchanted Glass* (1936) and A. O. Lovejoy in *The Great Chain of Being* (1936). As their successor, E. M. W. Tillyard provided in *The Elizabethan World Picture* (1943) a definitive view of the conservative and hierarchical values that Elizabethans were supposed to have espoused. In *Shakespeare's History Plays* (1944), Tillyard extended his essentially conservative view of Shakespeare's philosophical outlook to the histories, arguing that they embody a "Tudor myth" and thereby lend support to the Tudor state. Increasingly, however, critics have disputed the extent to which Shakespeare in fact endorsed the "establishment" values of the Elizabethan world picture. Theodore Spencer, in *Shakespeare and the Nature of Man* (1942), discusses the impact on Shakespeare of radical new thinkers like Machiavelli, Montaigne, and Copernicus. In political matters, Henry A. Kelly's *Divine Providence in the England of Shakespeare's Histories* (1970) has challenged the existence of a single "Tudor myth" and has argued that Shakespeare's history plays reflect contrasting political philosophies set dramatically in conflict with one another. M. M. Reese's *The Cease of Majesty* (1961) also offers a graceful corrective to Tillyard's lucid but occasionally one-sided interpretations. Revisions in this direction continue in the work of the so-called new historicists and cultural materialists, to be discussed below.

Historical criticism has also yielded many profitable specialized studies, in which Shakespeare is illuminated by a better understanding of various sciences of his day. Lily Bess Campbell approaches Shakespearean tragedy through Renaissance psychology in *Shakespeare's Tragic Heroes: Slaves of Passion* (1930). Paul Jorgensen uses Elizabethan documents on the arts of war and generalship in his study *Shakespeare's Military World* (1956). Many similar studies examine Shakespeare in relation to law, medicine, and other professions.

"New" Criticism

As we have seen, historical criticism is still an important part of Shakespeare criticism; for better or worse, it is the stuff of some research-oriented universities and their Ph.D. programs. Since its beginning, however, historical criticism has had to face a critical reaction, generated, in part, by its own utilitarian and fact-gathering tendencies. The suggestions urged by Stoll and others that Shakespeare was the product of his cultural and theatrical environment tended to obscure his achievement as a poet. Amassing of information about Shakespeare's reading or his theatrical company often seemed to inhibit the scholar from responding to the power of words and images.

Such at any rate was the rallying cry of the *Scrutiny* group in England, centered on F. R. Leavis, L. C. Knights,

and Derek Traversi, and the "new" critics in America, such as Cleanth Brooks. The new critics demanded close attention to the poetry without the encumbrance of historical research. Especially at first, the new critics were openly hostile to any criticism distracting readers from the text. The satirical force of the movement can perhaps best be savored in L. C. Knights's "How Many Children Had Lady Macbeth?" (1933), prompted by the learned appendices in Bradley's *Shakespearean Tragedy*: "When was the murder of Duncan first plotted? Did Lady Macbeth really faint? Duration of the action in *Macbeth*. Macbeth's age. 'He has no children.'"

In part, the new critical movement was (and still is) a pedagogical movement, a protest against the potential dryness of historical footnoting and an insistence that classroom study of Shakespeare ought to focus on a response to his language. Cleanth Brooks's "The Naked Babe and the Cloak of Manliness" (in *The Well Wrought Urn*, 1947) offers to the teacher a model of close reading that focuses on imagery and yet attempts to see a whole vision of the play through its language. G. Wilson Knight concentrates on imagery and verbal texture, sometimes to the exclusion of the play as a whole, in his *The Wheel of Fire* (1930), *The Imperial Theme* (1931), *The Shakespearian Tempest* (1932), *The Crown of Life* (1947), and others. William Empson is best known for his *Seven Types of Ambiguity* (1930) and *Some Versions of Pastoral* (1935). Derek Traversi's works include *An Approach to Shakespeare* (1938), *Shakespeare: The Last Phase* (1954), *Shakespeare: From Richard II to Henry V* (1957), and *Shakespeare: The Roman Plays* (1963). Perhaps the greatest critic of this school has been L. C. Knights, whose books include *Explorations* (1946), *Some Shakespearean Themes* (1959), *An Approach to Hamlet* (1960), and *Further Explorations* (1965). T. S. Eliot's perceptive and controversial observations have also had an important influence on critics of this school. Other studies making good use of the new critical method include Robert Heilman's *This Great Stage* (1948) and *Magic in the Web* (1956). Many of these critics are concerned not only with language but also with the larger moral and structural implications of Shakespeare's plays as discovered through a sensitive reading of the text.

More specialized studies of Shakespearean imagery and language include Caroline Spurgeon's *Shakespeare's Imagery and What It Tells Us* (1935). Its classifications are now recognized to be overly statistical and restricted in definition, but the work has nonetheless prompted valuable further study. Among later works are Sister Miriam Joseph's *Shakespeare's Use of the Arts of Language* (1947, partly reprinted in *Rhetoric in Shakespeare's Time*, 1962), Wolfgang Clemen's *The Development of Shakespeare's Imagery* (1951), and M. M. Mahood's *Shakespeare's Wordplay* (1957). The study of prose has not received as much attention as that of poetry, although Brian Vickers's *The Artistry of Shakespeare's Prose* (1968) and Milton Crane's

Shakespeare's Prose (1951) make significant contributions. See also Edward Armstrong's *Shakespeare's Imagination* (1963) and Kirby Farrell's *Shakespeare's Creation: The Language of Magic and Play* (1975).

A more recent development in studies of Shakespeare's imagery has led to the examination of visual images in the theater as part of Shakespeare's art. Reginald Foakes ("Suggestions for a New Approach to Shakespeare's Imagery," *Shakespeare Survey,* 5, 1952, 81–92) and Maurice Charney (*Shakespeare's Roman Plays: The Function of Imagery in the Drama,* 1961) were among the first to notice that Caroline Spurgeon and other "new" critics usually excluded stage picture in their focus on verbal image patterns. Yet Shakespeare's extensive involvement with the practicalities of theatrical production might well lead one to suspect that he arranges his stage with care and that the plays are full of hints as to how he communicates through visual means. Costume, properties, the theater building, the blocking of actors in visual patterns onstage, expression, movement—all of these contribute to the play's artistic whole. Francis Fergusson analyzes the way in which the Elizabethan theatrical building provides *Hamlet* with an eloquently expressive idea of order and hierarchy, against which are ironically juxtaposed Claudius's acts of killing a king and marrying his widow (*The Idea of a Theater,* 1949). Other studies of stage imagery include Ann Pasternak Slater's *Shakespeare the Director* (1982) and David Bevington's *Action Is Eloquence: Shakespeare's Language of Gesture* (1984).

Another call for expansion of the occasionally narrow limits of "new" criticism comes from the so-called Chicago school of criticism, centered on R. S. Crane, Richard McKeon, Elder Olson, Bernard Weinberg, and others, who, in the 1950s and 1960s, espoused a formal or structural approach to criticism, using Aristotle as its point of departure. Crane was reacting to the new critics who, in his view, restricted the kinds of answers they could obtain by limiting themselves to one methodology. Critics hostile to the Chicago school have responded, to be sure, that Crane's own approach tends to produce its own dogmatism. Formalist analyses of Shakespeare plays are to be found, for example, in the work of W. R. Keast, Wayne Booth, and Norman Maclean; see *Critics and Criticism,* edited by R. S. Crane (1952) and the bibliography at the back of this book.

Psychological Criticism

In a sense, Freudian and other psychological criticism continues the "character" criticism of the nineteenth century. Freudian critics sometimes follow a character into a world outside the text, analyzing Hamlet (for instance) as though he were a real person whose childhood traumas can be inferred from the symptoms he displays. The most famous work in this vein is *Hamlet and Oedipus* (1910,

revised 1949), by Freud's disciple, Ernest Jones. According to Jones, Hamlet's delay is caused by an oedipal trauma. Hamlet's uncle, Claudius, has done exactly what Hamlet himself incestuously and subconsciously wished to do: kill his father and marry his mother. Because he cannot articulate these forbidden impulses to himself, Hamlet is paralyzed into inactivity. Jones's critical analysis thus assumes, as did such Romantic critics as Coleridge, that the central problem of *Hamlet* is one of character and motivation: why does Hamlet delay? (Many modern critics would deny that this is a problem or would insist, at least, that by setting such a problem, Jones has limited the number of possible answers. Avi Erlich proposes an entirely different psychological reading of the play in *Hamlet's Absent Father,* 1972.) Psychological criticism sometimes also reveals its affinities with nineteenth-century character criticism in its attempt to analyze Shakespeare's personality through his plays, as though the works constituted a spiritual autobiography. The terminology of psychological criticism is suspect to some readers because it is at least superficially anachronistic when dealing with a Renaissance writer. The terminology is also sometimes overburdened with technical jargon.

Nonetheless, psychological criticism has afforded many insights into Shakespeare not readily available through other modes of perception. Jones's book makes clear the intensity of Hamlet's revulsion toward women as a result of his mother's inconstancy. At a mythic level, Hamlet's story certainly resembles that of Oedipus, and Freudian criticism is often at its best when it shows us this universal aspect of the human psyche. Freudian terminology need not be anachronistic when it deals with timeless truths. Psychological criticism can reveal to us Shakespeare's preoccupation with certain types of women in his plays, such as the domineering and threatening masculine type (Joan of Arc, Margaret of Anjou) or, conversely, the long-suffering and patient heroine (Helena in *All's Well,* Hermione in *The Winter's Tale*). Psychological criticism is perhaps most useful in studying family relationships in Shakespeare. It also has much to say about the psychic or sexual connotations of symbols. Influential books include Norman O. Brown's *Life Against Death: The Psychoanalytical Meaning of History* (1959) and Norman Holland's *Psychoanalysis and Shakespeare* (1966) and *The Shakespearean Imagination* (1964).

Richard Wheeler's *Turn and Counter-Turn: Shakespeare's Development and the Problem Comedies* (1981) applies psychoanalytic method to a study of Shakespeare's development, in which, as Wheeler sees it, the sonnets and the problem plays are pivotal as Shakespeare turns from the safely contained worlds of romantic comedy (with non-threatening heroines) and the English history play (in which women are generally denied anything more than a marginal role in state affairs) to the tragedies, in which sexual conflict is shown in all its potentially terrifying destructiveness. Wheeler's completion of C. L. Barber's *The Whole Journey: Shakespeare's Power of Development* (1986) continues the study of Shakespeare's development in the late plays. The dichotomies of gender and genre urged in these studies and continued by Linda Bamber (*Comic Women, Tragic Men: A Study of Gender and Genre in Shakespeare*, 1982), among others, have been challenged by Jonathan Goldberg in his essay, "Shakespearean Inscriptions: The Voicing of Power," in *Shakespeare and the Question of Theory* (edited by Patricia Parker and Geoffrey Hartman, 1985). A collection of essays under the editorship of Murray Schwartz and Coppélia Kahn, *Representing Shakespeare* (1980), affords a sample of work by Janet Adelman, David Willbern, Meredith Skura, David Sundelson, Madelon Gohlke Sprengnether, Joel Fineman, and others.

Much psychoanalytic criticism of the 1980s has sought to displace Freud's emphasis upon the relation of son and father in the oedipal triangle in favor of attention to the mother and child preoedipal relation; a model here is the work of Karen Horney (e.g., *Neurosis and Human Growth: The Struggle Toward Self-Realization*, 1950). Jacques Lacan (*Écrits*, translated by Alan Sheridan, 1977) and Erik Erikson (*Childhood and Selfhood*, 1978) are also prominent theorists in the post-Freudian era. Despite such changes, the psychoanalytic critic still attempts to discover in the language of the play the means by which he or she can reconstruct an early stage in the development of one or more of the dramatic characters.

Mythological Criticism

Related to psychological criticism is the search for archetypal myth in literature, as an expression of the "collective unconscious" of the human race. Behind such an approach lie the anthropological and psychological assumptions of Jung and his followers. One of the earliest studies of this sort was Gilbert Murray's *Hamlet and Orestes* (1914), analyzing the archetype of revenge for a murdered father. Clearly this custom goes far back into tribal prehistory and emerges in varying but interrelated forms in many different societies. This anthropological universality enables us to look at Hamlet as the heightened manifestation of an incredibly basic story. *Hamlet* gives shape to urgings that are a part of our innermost social being. The struggle between the civilized and the primitive goes on in us as in the play *Hamlet*.

The vast interdisciplinary character of mythological criticism leaves it vulnerable to charges of speculativeness and glib theorizing. At its best, however, mythological criticism can illuminate the nature of our responses as audience to a work of art. Northrop Frye argues, in *A Natural Perspective* (1965), that we respond to mythic patterns by imagining ourselves participating in them communally. The Greek drama emerged, after all, from Dionysiac ritual. All drama celebrates in one form or another the primal myths of vegetation, from the death of the year to the renewal or resurrection of life. In his most influential book, *Anatomy of Criticism* (1957), Frye argues that mythic criticism presents a universal scheme for the investigation of all literature, or all art, since art is itself the ordering of our most primal stirrings. Frye sees in drama (as in other literature) a fourfold correspondence to the cyclical pattern of the year: comedy is associated with spring, romance with summer, tragedy with autumn, and satire with winter. Historically, civilization moves through a recurrent cycle from newness to decadence and decay; this cycle expresses itself culturally in a progression from epic and romance to tragedy, to social realism, and, finally, to irony and satire before the cycle renews itself. Thus, according to Frye, the genres of dramatic literature (and of other literary forms as well) have an absolute and timeless relationship to myth and cultural history. That is why we as audience respond so deeply to form and meaning as contained in genre. C. L. Barber, in *Shakespeare's Festive Comedy* (1959), makes a similar argument: our enjoyment of comedy arises from our intuitive appreciation of such "primitive" social customs as Saturnalian revels, May games, and fertility rites. John Holloway offers an anthropological study of Shakespeare's tragedies in *The Story of the Night* (1961).

Frye's critical system has not been without its detractors. For example, Frederick Crews (*Psychoanalysis and Literary Process*, 1970) argues that Frye's system is too self-contained in its ivory tower and too much an abstract artifact of the critical mind to be "relevant" to the social purposes of art. Nevertheless, Frye continues to be one of the most influential critics of the late twentieth century.

Typological Criticism

Another controversy of the later twentieth century has to do with the Christian interpretation of Shakespeare. Do the images and allusions of Shakespeare's plays show him to be deeply immersed in a Christian culture inherited from the Middle Ages? Does he reveal a typological cast of mind, so common in medieval literature, whereby a story can suggest through analogy a universal religious archetype? For example, does the mysterious Duke in *Measure for Measure* suggest to us a God figure, hovering unseen throughout the play to test human will and then to present humanity with an omniscient but merciful judgment? Is the wanton slaughter of the good Cordelia in *King Lear* reminiscent of the Passion of Christ? Can Portia in *The Merchant of Venice* be seen as an angelic figure descending from Belmont into the fallen human world of Venice? Often the operative question we must ask is: "How far should such analogy be pursued?" Richard II unquestionably likens himself to Christ betrayed by the disciples, and at times the play evokes images of Adam banished from Paradise, but do these allusions coalesce into a sustained analogy?

Among the most enthusiastic searchers after Christian meaning are J. A. Bryant, in *Hippolyta's View* (1961); Roy Battenhouse, in *Shakespearean Tragedy: Its Art and Christian Premises* (1969); and R. Chris Hassel, in *Renaissance Drama and the English Church* (1979) and *Faith and Folly in Shakespeare: Romantic Comedies* (1980). Their efforts have encountered stern opposition, however. One notable dissenter is Roland M. Frye, whose *Shakespeare and Christian Doctrine* (1963) argues that Shakespeare cannot be shown to have known much Renaissance theology and that, in any case, his plays are concerned with human drama rather than with otherworldly questions of damnation or salvation. Frye's argument stresses the incompatibility of Christianity and tragedy, as do also D. G. James's *The Dream of Learning* (1951) and Clifford Leech's *Shakespeare's Tragedies and Other Studies in Seventeenth-Century Drama* (1950). Virgil Whitaker's *The Mirror Up to Nature* (1965) sees religion as an essential element in Shakespeare's plays but argues that Shakespeare uses the religious knowledge of his audience as a shortcut to characterization and meaning, rather than as an ideological weapon. The controversy will doubtless long continue, even though the typological critics have had to assume a defensive posture.

Jan Kott and the Theater of the Absurd

At an opposite extreme from the Christian idealism of most typological critics is the iconoclasm of those who have been disillusioned by recent events in history. One who brilliantly epitomizes political disillusionment in the aftermath of World War II, especially in Eastern Europe, is Jan Kott. The evocative debunking of romantic idealism set forth in his *Shakespeare Our Contemporary* (1964, translated from the Polish) has enjoyed enormous influence since the 1960s, especially in the theater. Kott sees Shakespeare as a dramatist of the absurd and the grotesque. In this view, Shakespearean plays are often close to "black" comedy or comedy of the absurd, as defined by Antonin Artaud (*The Theatre and Its Double,* 1958) and Jerzy Grotowski (*Towards a Poor Theatre,* 1968). Indeed, Kott has inspired productions that expose traditional values to skepticism and ridicule. Portia and Bassanio in *The Merchant of Venice* become scheming adventurers; Henry V becomes a priggish warmonger. History is for Kott a nightmare associated with his country's experience in World War II, and Shakespeare's modernity can be seen in his sardonic portrayal of political opportunism and violence. Even *A Midsummer Night's Dream* is a play of disturbingly erotic brutality, Kott argues. Here is an interpretation of Shakespeare that was bound to have an enormous appeal in a world confronted by the assassinations of the Kennedys and Martin Luther King, Jr.; by incessant war in the Middle East, Southeast Asia, and much of the third world; by the threat of nuclear annihilation and ecological disaster; and by political leadership generally perceived as interested only in the public-relations techniques of self-preservation. An essentially ironic view of politics and, more broadly, of human nature has informed a good deal of criticism since Kott's day and has led to the dethronement of E. M. W. Tillyard and his essentially positive view of English patriotism and heroism in the history plays.

New Historicism and Cultural Materialism

A more recent way of investigating Shakespeare through the demystifying perspective of modern experience—the so-called new historicism— has focused on the themes of political self-fashioning and role playing in terms of power and subversion. This critical school has paid close attention to historians and cultural anthropologists like Lawrence Stone (*The Crisis of the Aristocracy, 1558–1641,* 1965) and Clifford Geertz (*Negara: The Theatre State in Nineteenth-Century Bali,* 1980), who explore new ways of looking at the relationship between historical change and the myths generated to bring it about or to retain power. Geertz analyzes the way in which the ceremonies and myths of political rule can, in effect, become a self-fulfilling reality; kings and other leaders, acting out their roles in ceremonials designed to encapsulate the myth of their greatness and divine origin, essentially become what they have created in their impersonations of power. Such a view of political authority is an inherently skeptical one, seeing government as a process of manipulating illusions. When Shakespeare's English history plays—or indeed any plays dealing with conflicts of authority—are analyzed in these terms, subversion and containment become important issues. Do the plays of Shakespeare and other Renaissance dramatists celebrate the power of the Tudor monarchs, or do they question and undermine assumptions of hierarchy? Did Elizabethan drama serve to increase skepticism and pressure for change, or was it, conversely, a way of easing that pressure so that the power structure could remain in force?

The "new historicism" is a name applied to a kind of literary criticism practiced in America, prominently by Stephen Greenblatt. Especially influential have been his *Renaissance Self-Fashioning* (1980), *Shakespearean Negotiations* (1988), and his editing of the journal *Representations.* Those who pursue similar concerns, including Louis Montrose, Stephen Orgel, Richard Helgerson, Don E. Wayne, Frank Whigham, Richard Strier, Jonathan Goldberg, David Scott Kastan, and Steven Mullaney, share Greenblatt's goals to a greater or lesser extent and think of themselves only with important reservations as "new historicists"; the term is misleadingly categorical, and Greenblatt, among others, is eager to enlarge the parameters of the method rather than to allow it to harden into an orthodoxy. (Greenblatt, in fact, prefers the term "poetics of culture" to "new historicism," even though the latter phrase remains better known.) Still, these critics do generally share a number of common concerns. Among the ways in which new historicists seek to separate themselves from earlier historical critics is by denying that the work of art is a unified and self-contained product of an independent creator in masterful control of the meaning of the work. Instead, the new historicists represent the work as shot through with the multiple and contradictory discourses of its time. New historicists also deny the notion that art merely "reflects" its historical milieu; instead, they argue that art is caught up in, and contributes to, the social practices of its time. Although the boundary between new and old historical criticism is often hard to draw, in general the new historicists are apt to be skeptical of the accepted canon of literary texts and are drawn to a markedly politicized reading of Renaissance plays. One finds everywhere in the new historicism a deep ambivalence toward political authority.

Mikhail Bakhtin's provocative ideas on carnival (*L'Oeuvre de François Rabelais et la Culture Populaire du Moyen Age*, 1970) have had an important influence in new historical circles, as reflected, for example, in the work of Michael Bristol (*Carnival and Theatre: Plebeian Culture and the Structure of Authority in Renaissance England*, 1985), Peter Stallybrass, Gail Paster, and others. Like new historicism, this critical approach looks at so-called high cultural entertainment, including Shakespeare, in relation to the practices of popular culture, thereby breaking down the distinction between "high" and "popular." Literary and nonliterary texts are subjected to the same kind of serious scrutiny. Popular origins of the theater receive new attention, as in Robert Weimann's *Shakespeare and the Popular Tradition in the Theater: Studies in the Social Dimension of Dramatic Form and Function* (published in German in 1967 and in English translation in 1978).

Cultural materialism, in Britain, takes an analogous approach to the dethroning of canonical texts and the emphasis on art as deeply implicated in the social practices of its time but differs from American new historicism on the issue of change. New historicism is sometimes criticized for its lack of a model for change and for its reluctant belief, instead (in Greenblatt's formulation especially), that all attempts at subversion through art are destined to be contained by power structures in society; art permits the expression of heterodox points of view, but only as a way of letting off steam, as it were, and thereby easing the pressures for actual radical change. British cultural materialism, in contrast, is more avowedly committed not only to radical political interpretation but also to rapid political change, partly in response to what are perceived to be more deeply rooted class differences than are found in America. Jonathan Dollimore's *Radical Tragedy* (1984) and

Political Shakespeare (1985), edited by Dollimore and Alan Sinfield, enlist the dramatist on the side of class struggle. So do *Alternative Shakespeares,* edited by John Drakakis (1985), and Terry Eagleton's *Shakespeare and Society* (1967) and *William Shakespeare* (1986). Raymond Williams, not himself a Shakespearean critic, is an acknowledged godfather of the movement.

Feminist Criticism

Feminist criticism is such an important and diverse field that it has necessarily and productively reached into a number of related disciplines, such as cultural anthropology and its wealth of information about family structures. In his *The Elementary Structures of Kinship* (1949, translated 1969) and other books, Claude Lévi-Strauss analyzes the way in which men, as fathers and as husbands, control the transfer of women from one family to another in an "exogamous" marital system designed to strengthen commercial and other ties among men. Recent feminist criticism has had a lot to say about patriarchal structures in the plays and poems of Shakespeare, some of it building upon Lévi-Strauss's analysis of patriarchy; see, for example, Karen Newman, "Portia's Ring: Unruly Women and Structures of Exchange in *The Merchant of Venice*," *Shakespeare Quarterly*, 38 (1987), 10–33, and Lynda Boose, "The Father and the Bride in Shakespeare," *PMLA*, 97 (1982), 325–47. Coppélia Kahn has examined the ideology of rape in *The Rape of Lucrece,* showing how the raped woman is devalued by the shame that attaches to her husband, even though she is innocent (*Shakespeare Studies*, 9, 1976, 45–72).

Another important source of insight for feminist criticism is the anthropological work on rites of passage by Arnold Van Gennep (*The Rites of Passage,* translated by M. B. Vizedom and G. L. Caffee, 1960) and Victor Turner (*The Ritual Process,* 1969), among others. The focus here is on the dangers of transition at times of birth, puberty, marriage, death, and other turning points of human life. Feminist criticism, in dealing with such crises of transition, concerns itself not only with women's roles but also, more broadly, with gender relations, with family structures, and with the problems that males encounter in their quest for mature sexual identity. Coppélia Kahn's *Man's Estate; Masculine Identity in Shakespeare* (1981) looks particularly at the difficulty of the male in confronting the hazards of maturity. Robert Watson's *Shakespeare and the Hazards of Ambition* (1984) also looks at the male in the political context of career and self-fashioning. Marjorie Garber's *Coming of Age in Shakespeare* (1981) takes a broad look at maturation.

As these titles suggest, the models are often psychological, as well as anthropological. One focus of feminist criticism is the role of women in love and marriage. Feminist critics disagree among themselves as to whether the portrait painted by Shakespeare and other Elizabethan dramatists is a hopeful one, as argued, for example, by Juliet Dusinberre in *Shakespeare and the Nature of Women* (1975, 1996), or repressive, as argued by Lisa Jardine in *Still Harping on Daughters: Women and Drama in the Age of Shakespeare* (1983). Recent historians add an important perspective, especially Lawrence Stone in his *The Family, Sex, and Marriage in England, 1500–1800* (1977). Did the Protestant emphasis on marriage as a morally elevated and reciprocal relationship have the paradoxical effect of arousing in men an increased hostility and wariness toward women and a resulting increase in repression and violence? Or, as David Underdown suggests, should we look to economic explanations of hostility and wariness toward women in the Renaissance? His studies indicate that repression of women is greatest in regions of the country where their place in the economy offers the possibility of their having some control over family finances. (See *Revel, Riot, and Rebellion: Popular Culture in England, 1603–1660*, 1985, pp. 73–105, especially p. 99.)

Certainly, recent criticism has paid a lot of attention to male anxieties about women in Shakespeare's plays, as various male protagonists resolve to teach women a lesson (*The Taming of the Shrew*), succumb to dark fantasies of female unfaithfulness (*Much Ado About Nothing, Othello*), or are overwhelmed by misogynistic revulsion (*Hamlet, King Lear*). It is as though Shakespeare, in his plays and poems, works through the problems that men experience throughout their lives in their relationships with women, from the insecurities of courtship to the desire for possession and control in marriage, and from jealous fears of betrayal to the longing for escape into middle-age sexual adventure (as in *Antony and Cleopatra*). The late plays show us the preoccupation of the aging male with the marriages of his daughters (another form of betrayal) and with the approach of death.

Recently, feminist criticism has begun to increase its historical consciousness. Critics such as Gail Paster, Jean Howard, Phyllis Rackin, Dympna Callaghan, Lorraine Helms, Jyotsna Singh, Alison Findlay, Lisa Jardine, and Karen Newman focus on the construction of gender in early modern England in terms of social and material conditions, abandoning the nonhistorical psychological model of earlier feminist criticism. See the bibliography at the end of this book for feminist studies by these and other feminist critics, including Catherine Belsey, Carol Neely, Peter Erickson, Meredith Skura, Marianne Novy, Margo Hendricks, Kim Hall, Philippa Berry, Frances Dolan, Mary Beth Rose, Valerie Traub, Susan Zimmerman, Lynda Boose, and Ania Loomba. Gender studies concerned with issues of same-sex relationships have made important contributions in recent years, in the work of Bruce Smith, Laurie Shannon, Jonathan Goldberg, Stephen Orgel, Leonard Barkan, Mario DiGangi, and others.

Poststructuralism and Deconstruction

A major influence today in Shakespeare criticism, as in virtually all literary criticism of recent date, is the school of analysis known as poststructuralism or deconstruction; the terms, though not identical, significantly overlap. This school derives its inspiration originally from the work of certain French philosophers and critics, chief among whom are Ferdinand de Saussure, a specialist in linguistics, Michel Foucault, a historian of systems of discourse, and Jacques Derrida, perhaps the most highly visible exponent and practitioner of deconstruction. The ideas of these men were first introduced into American literary criticism by scholars at Yale such as Geoffrey Hartman, J. Hillis Miller, and Paul de Man. The ideas are controversial and difficult.

Poststructuralism and deconstruction begin with an insistence that language is a system of difference—one in which the signifiers (such as words and gestures) are essentially arbitrary to the extent that "meaning" and "authorial intention" are virtually impossible to fix precisely; that is, language enjoys a potentially infinite subjectivity. To an extent, this approach to the subjectivity of meaning in a work of art resembles "new" criticism in its mistrust of "message" in literature, but the new method goes further. It resists all attempts at paraphrase, for example, insisting that the words of a text cannot be translated into other words without altering something vital; indeed, there is no way of knowing if an author's words will strike any two readers or listeners in the same way. The very concept of an author has been challenged by Michel Foucault ("What Is an Author?" in *Language, Counter-Memory, Practice,* edited by Donald F. Bouchard, 1977). Deconstruction proclaims that there is no single identifiable author in the traditional sense; instead of a single text, we have a potentially infinite number of texts.

Both the theory and practice of deconstruction remain highly controversial. Although poststructuralism and deconstruction owe a debt to the general philosophical theory of signs and symbols known as semiotics, in which the function of linguistic signs is perceived to be artificially constructed, the new method also calls into question the very distinctions on which the discipline of semiotics is based. Derrida builds upon the work of Saussure and yet goes well beyond him in an insistence that words (signifiers) be left in play rather than attached to their alleged meaning (signifieds). Frank Lentricchia (*After the New Criticism,* 1980) takes the Yale school critics to task for interpreting Derrida in too formalist and apolitical a sense. Despite disagreements among theorists, nevertheless, the approach has deeply influenced Shakespeare criticism as a whole by urging critics to consider the suppleness with which signifiers (words) in the Shakespearean text are converted by listeners and readers into some approximation of meaning.

The ramifications of poststructuralism and deconstruction are increasingly felt in other forms of criticism, even those at least nominally at odds with poststructuralist assumptions. Some radical textual critics, for example, are fascinated by the unsettling prospects of the deconstructed text. What does one edit and how does one go about editing when words are to be left in play, to the infinite regress of meaning? The problems are acutely examined in a collection of essays called *The Division of the Kingdom,* edited by Gary Taylor and Michael Warren, on the two early and divergent texts of *King Lear* (1983). The method of linguistic analysis known as "speech-act theory," developed by the philosopher J. L. Austin as a way of exploring how we perform certain linguistic acts when we swear oaths or make asseverations and the like, is sharply at variance with deconstruction in its premises about a correlation between speech and intended meaning, and yet it, too, can help us understand the instability of spoken or written language in Shakespeare. Joseph Porter's *The Drama of Speech Acts* (1979), for example, looks at ways in which Shakespeare's characters in the plays about Henry IV and Henry V reveal, through their language of oath making and oath breaking, asseveration, and the like, their linguistic adaptability or lack of adaptability to historical change. Richard II resists historical change in the very way he speaks; Prince Hal embraces it. A third related field of analysis that is interested in the instability of meaning in Shakespeare's texts is metadramatic criticism, where the focus is on ways in which dramatic texts essentially talk about the drama itself, about artistic expression, and about the artist's quest for immortality in art. James Calderwood's *Shakespearean Metadrama* (1971) is an influential example.

At its extreme, then, deconstructive criticism comes close to undermining all kinds of "meaningfulness" in artistic utterance and to being thus at war with other methods of interpretation. Still, deconstruction continues to remain influential, because it also usefully challenges complacent formulations of meaning and because it promotes such a subtle view of linguistic complexity.

At its best, late twentieth-century criticism transcends the splintering effect of a heterogeneous critical tradition to achieve a synthesis that is at once unified and multiform in its vision. The pluralistic approach aims at overall balance and a reinforcement of one critical approach through the methodology of another. Many of the works already cited in this introduction refuse to be constricted by methodological boundaries. The best historical criticism makes use of close explication of the text where appropriate; image patterns can certainly reinforce mythological patterns; typological interpretation, when sensibly applied, serves the cause of image study. Some fine books are so eclectic in their method that one hesitates to apply the label of any one critical school. Among such works are Maynard Mack's *King Lear in Our Time* (1965), David Young's *Something of Great Constancy: The Art of A Midsummer Night's Dream* (1966), R. G. Hunter's *Shakespeare and the Comedy of Forgiveness* (1965), Janet Adelman's *The Common Liar: An Essay on "Antony and Cleopatra"* (1973), Stanley Cavell's "The Avoidance of Love: A Reading of King Lear," in *Must We Mean What We Say?* (1969, reprinted in *Disowning Knowledge in Six Plays of Shakespeare,* 1987), and Paul Jorgensen's *Our Naked Frailties: Sensational Art and Meaning in Macbeth* (1971).

Into the Twenty-First Century

The sense of where we are in the twenty-first century in Shakespeare criticism reflects the uncertainties and guardedly hopeful expectations of the academic profession as a whole. The period of the 1970s and 1980s, described previously, was one of extraordinary ferment, brought on by a host of developments: the Vietnam War and its aftermath, the assassinations of the Kennedys and Martin Luther King, the impact of French linguistic and philosophical thought on American intellectual writing, the frustrations of many academics with Reaganomics and their consequent fascination with British Marxism, emerging demands on behalf of minorities and women, a revolution in social and sexual mores accompanied by a backlash in the name of "family values," conflict over American foreign policy in the Middle East (Israel, Iraq), and much more. The result was what must be regarded as a genuine revolution in methods of critical analysis and reading. The literary text became multivalent, ambiguous, deconstructed, dethroned as a unique artifact, and was seen, instead, as a product of and contributing to its social and intellectual environment. The author became a construction of criticism and of a new kind of literary history.

Shakespeare studies have taken a lead in all of this new exploration. Although one of the postmodern demands has been for a recanonizing of literature in favor of newer literature, works by women and minorities, and works from countries other than Britain and the United States instead of the traditional canon of dead white European males, Shakespeare not only has survived this recanonization but also has become more prominent than ever. Other Renaissance writers such as Ben Jonson, John Webster, Thomas Dekker, Thomas Nashe, John Lyly, Edmund Spenser, and even Christopher Marlowe, John Milton, and John Donne have been the victims of declining enrollments in classes generally, but Shakespeare triumphs. Why?

One compelling answer is that Shakespeare is simply indispensable to postmodern critical inquiry. His texts are so extraordinarily responsive that new questions put to them—about the changing role of women, about cynicism in the political process, about the protean near-indeterminacy of meaning in language— evoke insights that are hard to duplicate in other literary texts. Shakespeare does not seem out of date. The very impulse of so much recent criticism to claim Shakespeare as "our contemporary," attuned to our own skepticisms and disillusionment and even despair (as in the writings of Jan Kott, for example), attests to his unparalleled engagement with the issues about which we care so deeply. Even those who argue that Shakespeare exhibits the male hang-ups of a patriarchal society and that he is a social snob who glorifies aristocracy and warfare do not see Shakespeare as a writer who is out of touch with the values of our contemporary society but, rather, as one who gives eloquent testimonial to structures that were alive in our cultural past and with which we sense a continuum today even if outward circumstances have changed. The best scholarship does not condemn Shakespeare for believing in kingship or for sometimes showing men as victorious in the battle of the sexes; instead, that criticism is interested in the whole process of the literary text's participation in the creation of culture. Even when recent scholarship is concerned with examining class and gender issues to clarify some of the systematic oppressiveness of early modern culture, it does so generally in an attempt to negotiate the relationship of the present to the past, rather than assuming a superiority in our modern world's approaches to issues of class, gender, and ethnicity.

To be sure, a number of Shakespeare's plays are in trouble today because they make us uncomfortable about these issues. *The Merchant of Venice* is, in the eyes of many, almost unproduceable, because the anti-Semitic emotions it explores are so distasteful. It is less often assigned now in classrooms than it once was, even though, when it is taught or produced onstage, it can lead to extraordinarily searching discussions of painful but real issues. The same is true of *The Taming of the Shrew*, which is being taken from the shelves of more than a few libraries because of its apparent flaunting of sexist behavior toward women. *Othello* offends some readers and viewers because of its racist language and, in the view of some, racial stereotypes. Yet, the power of Shakespeare's language continues to exert its spell despite, and in part because of, these troubling conflicts over the role of dramatic art in modern society.

The world of Shakespeare criticism today, after two decades or so of revolution, is seemingly one of consolidation. At a March 1995 meeting of the Shakespeare Association of America in Chicago, many conferees wondered: Where is the profession going? What are the hot new issues? Who are the new critics that no one wants to miss? And, in fact, there seemed to be little dramatic excitement of this sort, little agreement as to any discernible new trend. To some, this is frustrating. Where does one turn for real creativity after a thoroughgoing revolution such as we have experienced?

To others, a time of stocktaking is potentially healthy. There seems to be relatively little interest in turning the clock back; postmodernism and indeterminacy have changed the critical landscape for better and for worse. Now that this new landscape begins to seem familiar, however, new members of the profession seem less anxious to resolve their own identity crises in terms of affiliating with some critical school or other. The critical challenges are there, not so stridently new as they were ten years ago, and adaptable to various uses.

The result is increasing variety in the kinds of critical work being done. Some of it is recognizably traditional, dealing with stage history and conditions of performance during Shakespeare's lifetime, as, for example, in T. J. King, *Casting Shakespeare's Plays: London Actors and Their Roles* (1992); William Ingram, *The Business of Playing: The Beginnings of the Adult Professional Theater in Elizabethan London* (1992); David Bradley, *From Text to Performance in the Elizabethan Theatre: Preparing the Play for the Stage* (1992); David Mann, *The Elizabethan Player: Contemporary Stage Representation* (1991); John H. Astington, ed., *The Development of Shakespeare's Theater* (1992); Andrew Gurr, *Playgoing in Shakespeare's London* (1987, 2nd edition, 1996) and *The Shakespearian Playing Companies* (1996); and Roslyn Lander Knutson, *The Repertory of Shakespeare's Company, 1594–1613* (1991). Background and historical studies of the conditions that helped produce Shakespeare's theater can sometimes be informatively revisionist in the sense of toppling cherished older notions without at the same time being postmodern in approach. Examples here might include Richard Dutton, *Mastering the Revels: The Regulation and Censorship of English Renaissance Drama* (1991); Scott McMillin and Sally-Beth MacLean, *The Queen's Men and Their Plays* (1998); and Leeds Barroll, *Politics, Plague, and Shakespeare's Theater: The Stuart Years* (1991).

Other studies are more openly revisionist in a postmodern vein, sometimes in dealing with hypotheses about bibliography and textual studies, as in Margreta de Grazia, *Shakespeare Verbatim: The Reproduction of Authenticity and the 1790 Apparatus* (1991) and Grace Ioppolo, *Revising Shakespeare* (1991). The New Folger Library Shakespeare, edited by Barbara Mowat and Paul Werstine (1992—), gives a more measured approach. The Arden Shakespeare is currently bringing out new critical editions of all the plays in individual volumes (Arden 3), as are the New Cambridge Shakespeare and the Oxford Shakespeare. Occasionally a conservative counterblast is heard, as in Brian Vickers's entertaining, learned, and feisty polemic, *Appropriating Shakespeare: Contemporary Critical Quarrels* (1993). A forum of essays edited by Ivo Kamps, called *Shakespeare Left and Right*, gives us a chance to weigh arguments from various sides.

What the contemporary critical scene does best is to free critics to be who they are and to write without paying dues to any particular affiliation. The results are refreshingly diverse. Among the books that show this spread of critical approaches are Karen Newman, *Fashioning Femininity and the English Renaissance Drama* (1991); Bruce R. Smith, *Homosexual Desire in Shakespeare's England* (1991); Janet Adelman, *Suffocating Mothers: Fantasies of Maternal Origin in Shakespeare's Plays, "Hamlet" to "The Tempest"* (1992); Alan Sinfield, *Faultlines: Cultural Materialism and the Politics of Dissident Reading* (1992); Valerie Traub, *Desire and Anxiety: Circulations of Sexuality in Shakespearean Drama* (1992); Richard Burt, *Licensed by Authority: Ben Jonson and the Discourses of Censorship* (1993); Linda Charnes, *Notorious Identity: Materializing the Subject in Shakespeare* (1993); Lars Engle, *Shakespearean Pragmatism: Market of His Time* (1993); Gail Kern Paster, *The Body Embarrassed: Drama and the Disciplines of Shame in Early Modern England* (1993); Meredith Anne Skura, *Shakespeare the Actor and the Purposes of Playing* (1993); Frances E. Dolan, *Dangerous Familiars: Representations of Domestic Crime in England, 1550–1700* (1994); Kim F. Hall, *Things of Darkness: Economies of Race and Gender in Early Modern England* (1994); Jean Howard, *The Stage and Social Struggle in Early Modern England* (1994); Robert Watson, *The Rest Is Silence: Death as Annihilation in the English Renaissance* (1994); Katharine Eisaman Maus, *Inwardness and Theatre in the English Renaissance Drama* (1995); Louis Montrose, *The Purpose of Playing: Shakespeare and the Cultural Politics of the Elizabethan Theatre* (1996); Patricia Parker, *Shakespeare from the Margins: Language, Culture, Context* (1996); Jean E. Howard and Phyllis Rackin, *Engendering a Nation: A Feminist Account of Shakespeare's English Histories* (1997); Anthony B. Dawson and Paul Yachnin, *The Culture of Playgoing in Shakespeare's England* (2001); David Scott Kastan, *Shakespeare and the Book* (2001); Mary Beth Rose, *Gender and Heroism in Early Modern English Literature* (2002); and Stephen Orgel, *The Authentic Shakespeare* (2002). For other suggestions, see recent entries in the bibliography at the back of this volume.

The Tragedies

Titus Andronicus

Although *Titus Andronicus* has been singled out by some critics as unworthy of Shakespeare's genius—T. S. Eliot called it "one of the stupidest and most uninspired plays ever written"—recent performance history has shown that *Titus* can succeed brilliantly before audiences. In his memorable production at Stratford-upon-Avon in 1959, Peter Brook chose to stage the entrance of the ravished and mutilated Lavinia (Vivien Leigh) with scarlet ribbons trailing from her wrists and mouth, in a visual stylizing that gave to the violence an emotional seriousness even while it avoided gory realism. The long ribbons translated the text into visual symbols. Titus (Laurence Olivier) was a battered veteran from the start of the play, war-wearied, Lear-like in his suffering and agonies of disillusionment. Deborah Warner's more realistic production, at the Swan Theatre, Stratford-upon-Avon in 1987 with Sonia Ritter as Lavinia, stressed the horror of rape and its painful relevance to a late-twentieth-century world deeply concerned with human rights and especially the victimization of women. Interpretations of Tamora in this and other productions have variously seen her as exotic, sexually magnetic, cunning, playful, and deeply sadistic. Most recently, an innovative film version by Julie Taymor, with Anthony Hopkins as Titus, has intrigued a larger audience with this relatively little-known play about wanton violence. Hopkins shows how grim black humor can ironize the effects of gross cruelty and turn our laughter into an attempt to comprehend humanity's apparently fathomless penchant for inhumanity. Recent criticism, too, has taken *Titus* seriously as a study in violence that is painfully relevant to our modern experience.

Titus Andronicus is unmistakably an early play. First published in quarto in 1594 "as it was played by the Right Honorable the Earl of Derby, Earl of Pembroke, and Earl of Sussex Their Servants," it could have been written as early as 1590–1591 or even before. The allusion in theater owner and manager Philip Henslowe's *Diary* for January 24, 1594, to a new production by Sussex's men of "Titus & Ondronicus" could refer to a new play or one newly revised or newly acquired by the company. Shakespeare's *Titus Andronicus* was thus widely separated in time from the great tragedies; *Romeo and Juliet* is the only other tragedy (excluding the English history plays) of the decade preceding 1599. Moreover, the play may not be entirely Shakespeare's. The first three scenes (Act 1 together with scenes 1 and 2 of Act 2) and the first scene of Act 4 have been plausibly attributed to George Peele. The two dramatists seem to have worked on their separate stints independently, with some resulting discrepancies. Shakespeare was apparently responsible for the play's overall design. Even so, *Titus Andronicus* was thus widely separated in time and in collaborative authorship from the great tragedies that Shakespeare would produce, most of them a decade or more later. How are we to respond to and appraise an apprenticeship in tragedy that is so isolated in terms of artistic career from the mature tragedies that we reckon among his greatest achievements?

Titus Andronicus is studded with bookish references to classical authors—another likely indication of an early date. No other tragedy, and perhaps no other Shakespearean play, reveals such direct evidence of youthful learning. Some of its many untranslated Latin phrases are school children's favorites, such as the *"Integer vitae"* of Horace that is immediately recognized by Chiron. "I read it in the grammar long ago," he says (4.2.23). Classical allusions compare the chief characters of the play with Aeneas and Dido, Queen of Carthage; Hector, King Priam, and Queen Hecuba of Troy; Ajax and Odysseus among the Greeks; Hercules, Prometheus, Orpheus, Coriolanus, Semiramis the siren Queen of Assyria, Pyramus, Cornelia the mother of the Gracchi, Actaeon; and others. Yet these learned references are far from being a mere display of youthful learning; through a controlled and self-conscious artistry, they enable us to explore a tragic world whose moral dimensions are defined in terms of classical literary models. Especially significant are the references to victims of rape and vengeance: Virginia the Roman, killed by her father Virginius to save her from rape; the chaste Lucrece, ravished by Tarquin; Philomel, raped and deprived of her tongue by Tereus, whose name she then reveals by weaving the information into a tapestry; and Procne, her sister and the wife of Tereus, who avenges Philomel by serving Tereus's son ltys to him in a meal.

Titus Andronicus does not record actual historical events. Shakespeare, assisted by Peele, seems to have put it together from a medley of sources, none of which provided a complete narrative model. An eighteenth-century chapbook called *The History of Titus Andronicus*, once thought to give a reliable version of an original to which the dramatists has access, has now been shown to be an expansion of the story based on a ballad of 1594 which in turn was modeled on the extant play, so that this play stands first in the line of succession. The dramatists drew from varied materials. Ovid's *Metamorphoses* gave them a number of legends, especially that of Tereus, Philomel, and Procne. Seneca's *Thyestes* offered in dramatic form a similar tale of vengeance, in which two sons are slain and served to their parent in a grisly banquet. One or even two plays about Titus may have existed prior to the text we have. Even if Shakespeare used such prose and dramatic sources in writing his major portion of the play, however, some scholars believe that one or even two plays about Titus may have existed prior to Shakespeare's and that we can deduce their contributions to his work by examining two later continental plays derived from them: *Tragaedia van Tito Andronico* (German, 1620) and *Aran en Titus* (Dutch, 1641). Possibly one of these earlier plays was the "Titus & Vespacia" entered in Henslowe's *Diary* for April 11, 1592, as acted by Lord Strange's men. Even if the dramatists used such prose and dramatic sources, however, they also knew well the Ovidian and Senecan originals that had inspired them. Elizabethan revenge tragedy, containing some Senecan influences (though those Senecan elements should not be over-stressed), was a strongly formative influence, especially Kyd's *The Spanish Tragedy* (c. 1587). The phenomenal recent stage successes of Marlowe had left their mark: Titus's killing of his son Mutius recalls *Tamburlaine Part II*, and Aaron's Vice-like boasting of wanton villainy recalls *The Jew of Malta*. The dramatists' reading of Virgil is evident not only in repeated references to the tragic love story of Dido and Aeneas but also in the choice of the name Lavinia (*The Aeneid*, Book 7 ff.)

As this sizable list of influences suggests, *Titus Andronicus* remains close to its models, however original it may be in its narrative outline. Although the play anticipates several motifs in Shakespeare's later tragedies—the ingratitude of Rome toward its honored general as in *Coriolanus*, Roman political factionalism as in *Julius Caesar*, infirm old age confronted by human bestiality as in *King Lear*—*Titus Andronicus* is the kind of revenge play one might expect of a gifted young playwright and collaborator in the early 1590s. The successful models for tragic writing in those years were Kyd and Marlowe; Greene, Peele, and others paid these two the flattery of imitation. So, to an extent, did Shakespeare. We can best understand *Titus Andronicus* if we view it as a revenge play in the sensational vein of Shakespeare's immediate predecessors, with substantial assistance by Peele and with generous additions of Ovidian pathos. We should not look to *Titus Andronicus* for that poetic density and complexity of vision we find in later Shakespearean tragedy; as a revenge play, *Titus Andronicus* focuses on violence and horror, and its mood is one of revulsion. The style, too, requires some adjustment in our expectations. Owing much to Kyd, Marlowe, and Ovid, it is replete with rhetorical figures and classical allusions in the manner of Shakespeare's Ovidian poems from the early 1590s, *Venus and Adonis* and *The Rape of Lucrece*. Even if its "early" features are manifest, the style works to good dramatic effect in highly wrought scenes, as when Titus pleads for justice to the unresponsive senators (3.1.1–47) or lays a trap for Tamora and her sons under the guise of his supposed madness (5.2). The seeming incongruity of violent action and elaborately refined metaphor, as in Titus's florid lament for Lavinia's mutilation (3.1.65 ff.), is not, as Eugene Waith has shown (*Shakespeare Survey*, 1957, 39–49), without its purpose, for it evokes pathos on behalf of gruesome suffering in a deliberately Ovidian manner, abstracting and generalizing human torment. As in Ovid, the interest is not in moralizing lessons but in the "transforming power of intense states of emotion."

Violence is an enduring feature of *Titus Andronicus*, and its function must be understood if the play is not to be dismissed as merely hyperbolical in its bloodshed. We are constantly aware of ritual human sacrifice, murder, and maiming, as in Titus's sentencing of Tamora's son Alarbus and his slaying of his own son Mutius, the massacre by Tamora's sons of Bassianus and their ravishing of Lavinia, the subsequent execution of two of Titus's sons wrongfully accused of Bassianus's murder, the cutting off of Titus's hand, the feeding to Tamora of her sons' bodies ground into a fine paste, and still more. Savage mutilation is characteristic of many of these atrocities, especially in the lopping off of hands and tongue. The play's climax is, in the manner of revenge tragedy, a spectacle of blood, with the deaths in rapid succession of Lavinia, Tamora, Titus, and Saturninus. These multiple slaughters cause revulsion in some viewers, such as T. S. Eliot, but to others the violence reveals a pattern and offers its own ethical stance on vengeance. Although we do not sense in this early play the same controlled perspective on human evil as in *Hamlet*, for example, we see that Shakespeare is intensely aware of the conflict between order and disorder. In the final scenes, Aaron the Moor is caught and sentenced to execution, Tamora and Saturninus are slain, Titus's brother Marcus appeals to Roman justice for vindication on the grounds that his family had no alternative, and Titus's last remaining son Lucius vows as the new emperor to "heal Rome's harms and wipe away her woe" (5.3.148). Even if this resolution does not fully satisfy the ethical dilemmas with which the play began, it reveals Shakespeare's disinclination to allow the fulfillment of private vengeance to be the play's ultimate concern. Shakespeare is interested throughout in the ethical problems generated by revenge, and the play's relentless horror may be a commentary on the self-defeating nature of a revenge code. Violence is also integral to the theatrical design of the play; its pattern of vengeance and counter-vengeance seems strikingly modern to us, attuned as we are to the twentieth-century "theater of cruelty" championed by Antonin Artaud.

The first part of *Titus Andronicus* functions to give the avenger a motive for his bloody course of action. Ironically, Titus is himself responsible for setting in motion the events that will overwhelm him. His family, the Andronici, are the first to practice vengeance, a fact that diminishes the sympathy they might later have been able to enjoy as victims and exiles. In fact, it is Lucius, ultimately to become the restorer of political stability, who first demands the ritual slaying of a captive Goth, Tamora's son Alarbus, to appease the spirits of the Andronici slain in battle. Such a demand is understandable in terms of family honor, but it is also vengeful and pagan. Despite the Romans' claim to be superior to the barbarians they fight (see 1.1.379, for example), their acts too often do not justify that claim to moral superiority. This irony is complete when the Gothic Queen Tamora and her sons become the spokespersons for godlike mercy. As Tamora's son Chiron bitterly observes, "Was never Scythia half so barbarous" (1.1.131).

Equally violent and unnatural is Titus's slaying of his own son Mutius for assisting in the abduction of Titus's daughter, Lavinia. This tragic error stems, like the first, from Titus's narrow sense of family honor. Titus has unwisely refused the imperial crown, bestowing it instead on the treacherous Saturninus, and has promised Lavinia as bride to the new emperor, despite her prior betrothal to Saturninus's virtuous rival and brother, Bassianus. Titus's reasons for these actions are never satisfactorily explained, but presumably arise from a misguided if honorable impulse to let others exercise political power while he, the valiant defender of Rome, plays the role of senior statesman. He is also, like King Lear, imperious and paternalistic in his own family, insisting on having his way. When Titus's sons and Bassianus are driven to the expedient of abducting the lady, Titus cannot endure the shame of his violated promise and so kills Mutius in the ensuing melee. Yet, for this sacrifice on

behalf of the Emperor, Titus receives only ingratitude and hostility. Moreover, he has taught Tamora and her sons to seek vengeance.

Once the Andronici become the victims of Tamora and her supporters, they gain in sympathy. They suffer unspeakable atrocities. Hunted down by jeering sadists who amuse themselves through rape and mutilation, the Andronici band together in mutual tribulation and selflessly attempt to ease one another's agony. They discover Rome to be a "wilderness of tigers" (3.1.54) in which the law blindly condemns Titus's innocent sons for the murder of Bassianus. Still, Titus has committed the first barbarism and turns increasingly to barbarism in his desire for vengeance. Because the Andronici are too much like their enemies, the prevailing mood, as in most revenge plays, is more ironic than tragic. There is no strong sense (despite the capture of Aaron) that moral order is restored along with political order. The Andronici are vindicated, and they have gained some wisdom through suffering, but they are still the avengers who gave the first offense.

Equally unsettling is the play's depiction of gender relations. Titus is a patriarchal figure who responds with violence toward his own son when that son challenges his authority to give away his daughter Lavinia to Saturninus. In the play's bloody conclusion, Titus is the slayer of his own daughter as well, lest she "survive her shame" and by her presence continually remind Titus of the disgrace he has suffered by her rape (5.3.41–2). The archaic code of male domination insists that a father's honor is paramount and that his daughter's death is preferable to shameful life even if, as in Lavinia's case, she is wholly innocent and victimized in losing her chastity. (In *The Rape of Lucrece*, an innocent wife must pay the same terrible price to vindicate her husband's honor.) At the opposite end of the spectrum, Tamora personifies a masculine fantasy of the fearsome transgressing female. Because she is both wanton and domineering, her sexuality is intolerable to most noble Romans; she captivates Saturninus and Aaron with her sensual beauty, but ultimately in this play such a dangerous woman must be tricked into the gruesomely appropriate crime of eating her own sons. Roman order is reestablished at last. Even so, its patriarchal ascendancy has been responsible for the carnage to no less an extent than has the more overtly erotic violence of the non-Roman "barbarians" like Tamora, her sons, and Aaron.

Titus Andronicus displays many conventions of the revenge play found earlier in *The Spanish Tragedy*. The avenger, Titus, is a man of high position conscientiously serving the state, like Kyd's Hieronimo, who discovers that the state itself is too corrupt to give him justice for the wrongs done to his family. The evildoers are members of the Emperor's family, protected by their royal connection. Private and public interests clash, and public welfare is the loser. The avenger has difficulty proving the identity of the villains but finds an ingenious way at last (through Lavinia's writing in the sand). Once he becomes the avenger, like Hieronimo, Titus grows as remorseless and canny as his enemies. He becomes a menace to public order, uttering enigmatic threats and blazoning forth the injustices of the state. Verging on true madness, he also employs madness as a cloak for his Machiavellian intrigues. His plotting succeeds in duping Queen Tamora into allowing him to arrange his gruesome banquet. The drama ends, like *The Spanish Tragedy*, in a kind of play-within-the-play, as Tamora's two sons take the roles of Rape and Murder, Tamora, Revenge, and Titus the cook. Playacting turns deadly earnest with a rapid succession of slaughters. Titus and Lavinia, like Hieronimo and Bel-Imperia, do not outlive their act of vengeance.

This conventional pattern accepts revenge as inevitable and consistent according to its own code. As in *The Spanish Tragedy*, where the choric Revenge controls the action for his own sinister purposes and welcomes the suffering of innocents or the collapse of governments as grist for his mill, *Titus Andronicus* portrays a world in which the avenger can act seemingly only through violence. Even Lavinia and Titus's young grandson endorse plotting and murder. Titus practices cunning toward his enemies, vowing to "o'erreach them in their own devices" (5.2.143). Our attention is increasingly drawn to the artistry of the "devices" on both sides. The machinations of Aaron and Tamora demand ingenuity in return. An eye must pay for an eye; the punishment must fit the crime. To be sure, Titus and his family do struggle to understand the moral nature of their universe. "If any power pities wretched tears, / To that I call," prays Titus, lifting his mangled hand toward heaven and imploring divine assistance (3.1.208–9). Repeatedly, the Andronici ask if a divine justice exists, if it cares about savagery among humans, and if that justice will assist the defenseless. "O heavens," asks Marcus, "can you hear a good man groan / And not relent, or not compassion him?" (4.1.124–5). Why should such terrible evils afflict the human race "Unless the gods delight in tragedies?" (line 61). Marcus seeks the identities of his niece's ravishers, hoping that Lavinia will be able to "display at last / What God will have discovered for revenge" (lines 74–5). Is revenge to be God's or humanity's? In part, at least, Marcus sees himself and his family as agents of divine justice, like Hamlet, though Titus's own errors will also require his own destruction. Yet even these questionings about the cosmos are a part of the revenge tradition, for Hieronimo in *The Spanish Tragedy* implores the gods in similar terms. Titus, for all his pleas to the heavens, is ultimately the avenger in a revenge play. He does not, like Hamlet, submit himself to what he takes to be the will of Providence and wait for whatever opportunity heaven will provide. Titus swears an oath of revenge and proceeds with the most gruesome acts imaginable. In his death there is no talk of reconcili-

ation between divine and human will. As the moment of climax approaches, revenge is seen to be a force from hell, from the "infernal kingdom," while true justice is employed "with Jove in heaven" (5.2.30; 4.3.40). Titus is a protagonist suited to a play in which revenge proceeds by its own pitiless rules, in which brutality is the dominant fact of life, and in which violence is the only apparent means of redress. Divine ideas of justice mock humanity's blind attempts at self-governance without offering reassurance and direction.

Titus Andronicus illuminates the nature of evil more than it attempts to transcend evil through human nobility, as in the later tragedies. This distinctive quality is made especially manifest by the play's outward resemblance to *King Lear*. Titus is old, infirm of judgment, and victimized by his own decision to relinquish power to a person whose villainy he does not comprehend. He is, as Lear says of himself, certainly more sinned against than sinning. Titus approaches madness and generalizes in his grief about the omnipresence of murder and ingratitude in nature (3.2.52–78). His reflections on human injustice suggest the immense difficulty of distinguishing illusion from true substance ("Grief has so wrought on him / He takes false shadows for true substances," lines 79–80), a motif of illusion that reappears in the allegorical play-within-the-play. Queen Tamora reveals an innate viciousness and sexual depravity like that of Goneril and Regan. Aaron the Moor, perhaps the first of Shakespeare's gloating Vice-like villains, resembles Edmund in *King Lear* as well as Richard III, Don John (in *Much Ado About Nothing*), and Iago (in *Othello*). *Titus Andronicus* shows us, in embryonic form and close to their sources, many of Shakespeare's later tragic themes and methods.

Aaron the Moor is the most vital character in this early play. Like the Vice of the morality play or like Marlowe's stage Machiavel, Aaron takes delight in pure evil and displays his cunning for the admiration of the audience. Evil to him is "sport," "wit," "stratagem," and, above all, "policy" (5.1.96; 2.3.1; 2.1.104). His malice encompasses all humanity and proceeds from no motive other than the sinister pleasure he takes in devising plots. When he is finally captured, Aaron boasts triumphantly of the extent and variety of his cruel accomplishments:

> Even now I curse the day—and yet, I think,
> Few come within the compass of my curse—
> Wherein I did not some notorious ill,
> As kill a man, or else devise his death,
> Ravish a maid, or plot the way to do it,
> Accuse some innocent and forswear myself,
> Set deadly enmity between two friends,
> Make poor men's cattle break their necks,
> Set fire on barns and haystacks in the night
> And bid the owners quench them with their tears.
> Oft have I digged up dead men from their graves
> And set them upright at their dear friends' door,
> Even when their sorrows almost was forgot. (5.1.125–37)

Through its depiction of evil as both comic and diabolical, this portrait gives us a vivid insight into the origins of a particular type of remorseless, gloating villain that Shakespeare was to develop in his later history plays and tragedies.

The seemingly attractive side to Aaron, his fiercely protective instincts toward his bastard son born of Tamora, is part of the central evil of this play: pride of family turning to violent revenge. Aaron and his son in their blackness of complexion are equated with barbarism, pagan atheism (Aaron scoffs at those who believe in God), and diabolism. Racial issues are thus as painfully explicit as those of gender in this play: Rome claims superiority over black peoples as over the Scythians, and yet the play sees Rome as fatally violent in its patriarchal, sexist, and racist assumptions. Aaron and Tamora are not the moral opposites of Saturninus and his Roman subjects but are, instead, symbolic of the inner darkness and carnality shared by all sorts of people.

As a revenge play, *Titus Andronicus* is theatrically effective. To be appreciated properly, it should be seen or read in these terms, rather than with the expectations we bring to *King Lear*. Shakespeare here presents barbarism and civilization as polar opposites, but he refuses to equate Rome with civilization, and he allows Titus at last no escape from the barbarism that he himself sets in motion. No tragic self-awareness grows out of Titus's humiliation, as it does in *King Lear*, no regret other than for having relinquished power to Saturninus. Instead of tragic self-awareness, we are left with an overpowering impression of the human potential for brutality. This vision is unameliorated. The constant reminder of a better world of justice and compassion merely serves to heighten the play's ironic and futile sense of wasted goodness.

Titus Andronicus

[Dramatis Personae

SATURNINUS, *son of the late Emperor of Rome, and afterward declared Emperor*
BASSIANUS, *his brother*

TITUS ANDRONICUS, *a noble Roman, general against the Goths*
LUCIUS,
QUINTUS,
MARTIUS, } *his sons*
MUTIUS,
LAVINIA, *his daughter*
YOUNG LUCIUS, *a BOY, Lucius's son*
MARCUS ANDRONICUS, *tribune of the people, and Titus's brother*
PUBLIUS, *Marcus's son*
SEMPRONIUS,
CAIUS, } *Titus's kinsmen*
VALENTINE,

TAMORA, *Queen of the Goths, afterward Empress of Rome*
ALARBUS,
DEMETRIUS, } *her sons*
CHIRON,
AARON, *a Moor, her lover*
NURSE

A Roman CAPTAIN
MESSENGER *to Titus*
CLOWN
AEMILIUS, *a noble Roman*
GOTHS
A Roman LORD
A ROMAN

Senators, Tribunes, Judges, Goths, Soldiers, Attendants, a Child of Aaron and Tamora

SCENE: *Rome, and the country near it*]

[1.1]

*[Flourish.] Enter the tribunes and senators
aloft; and then enter [below] Saturninus and his
followers at one door, and Bassianus and his followers [at the other,] with drums and trumpets.*

SATURNINUS

Noble patricians, patrons of my right,
Defend the justice of my cause with arms;
And, countrymen, my loving followers,
Plead my successive title with your swords.   4
I am his firstborn son that was the last   5
That ware the imperial diadem of Rome.   6
Then let my father's honors live in me,
Nor wrong mine age with this indignity.   8

BASSIANUS

Romans, friends, followers, favorers of my right,
If ever Bassianus, Caesar's son,
Were gracious in the eyes of royal Rome,   11
Keep then this passage to the Capitol,   12
And suffer not dishonor to approach
The imperial seat, to virtue consecrate,   14
To justice, continence, and nobility;   15
But let desert in pure election shine,   16
And, Romans, fight for freedom in your choice.

[Enter] Marcus Andronicus, with the crown.

MARCUS

Princes, that strive by factions and by friends
Ambitiously for rule and empery,   19
Know that the people of Rome, for whom we stand
A special party, have by common voice   21
In election for the Roman empery
Chosen Andronicus, surnamèd Pius   23
For many good and great deserts to Rome.
A nobler man, a braver warrior,
Lives not this day within the city walls.
He by the Senate is accited home   27
From weary wars against the barbarous Goths,

That with his sons, a terror to our foes,   29
Hath yoked a nation strong, trained up in arms.   30
Ten years are spent since first he undertook
This cause of Rome, and chastisèd with arms
Our enemies' pride. Five times he hath returned
Bleeding to Rome, bearing his valiant sons
In coffins from the field.   35
And now at last, laden with honor's spoils,
Returns the good Andronicus to Rome,
Renownèd Titus, flourishing in arms.   38
Let us entreat, by honor of his name   39
Whom worthily you would have now succeed,   40
And in the Capitol and Senate's right,
Whom you pretend to honor and adore,   42
That you withdraw you and abate your strength,
Dismiss your followers, and, as suitors should,
Plead your deserts in peace and humbleness.

SATURNINUS

How fair the tribune speaks to calm my thoughts!   46

BASSIANUS

Marcus Andronicus, so I do affy   47
In thy uprightness and integrity,
And so I love and honor thee and thine,
Thy noble brother Titus and his sons,
And her to whom my thoughts are humbled all,   51
Gracious Lavinia, Rome's rich ornament,
That I will here dismiss my loving friends,
And to my fortunes and the people's favor
Commit my cause in balance to be weighed.

Exeunt soldiers [of Bassianus].

SATURNINUS

Friends that have been thus forward in my right,
I thank you all and here dismiss you all,
And to the love and favor of my country
Commit myself, my person, and the cause.

[Exeunt the soldiers of Saturninus.]

Rome, be as just and gracious unto me
As I am confident and kind to thee.   61
Open the gates and let me in.

BASSIANUS

Tribunes, and me, a poor competitor.   63

*[Flourish.] They [Saturninus and Bassianus]
go up into the Senate House.*

Enter a Captain.

**1.1. Location: Rome. Before the Capitol. The tomb of the
Andronici is provided onstage, possibly as a large property
backstage or at a trapdoor.**
0.1 *Flourish* trumpet call.   **0.2** *aloft* i.e., probably in the gallery,
rearstage above the tiring-house, looking down on the main stage.
0.3 *followers* (including soldiers; see *Exeunt soldiers* at lines 55.1 and
59.1)   **0.4** *drums and trumpets* drummers and trumpeters.   **4 successive title** hereditary title to the succession   **5 his . . . that** the firstborn
son of him who   **6 ware** wore   **8 age** seniority.   **this indignity** i.e.,
the challenge of my right by a younger brother.   **11 Were gracious**
found favor and acceptance   **12 Keep** guard, defend   **14 consecrate**
consecrated   **15 continence** self-restraint   **16 pure election** free
choice, i.e., of the Roman citizens. (Bassianus urges the Romans to let
merit, or *desert*, prevail, rather than inherited right.)   **17.1** *[Enter] . . .
crown* (In the Folio text, Marcus enters aloft, but the Quarto version,
which makes no mention of this, may have been staged differently.
When Marcus awards to Titus a white cloak at lines 185–6 below, the
action is more suited to Marcus's being on the main stage, and he
could well stay there throughout.)   **19 empery** rule (as emperor)
21 A special party i.e., a representative group specially chosen. (As a
tribune, Marcus Andronicus has been elected by the *people of Rome*,
line 20, the plebeians, to represent their rights.)   **23 Chosen** i.e., nom-
inated.   **surnamèd** given the honorary epithet of.   **Pius** dutiful,
patriotic   **27 accited** summoned

29 That who, i.e., Titus   **30 yoked** subdued   **35 field** (The Quarto
follows with three and one-half lines deleted from the Second and
Third Quartos and the Folio because they are inconsistent with lines
96–147 below and probably represent a canceled first draft that the
printer of the Quarto mistakenly included: "and at this day / To the
monument of the Andronici, / Done sacrifice of expiation, / And
slain the noblest prisoner of the Goths.")   **38 flourishing** eminent
39–40 by . . . succeed i.e., by the honorable name of him you choose
as worthy candidate   **42 Whom** i.e., which (referring to the right of
the Capitol and Senate).   **pretend** assert, profess   **46 fair** courteously, gently   **47 affy** trust   **51 all** entirely   **61 confident** without
suspicion   **63 poor competitor** rival of lower rank. (Bassianus is
younger brother and thus not in the direct line of inheritance.)
63.2 *go up* (The *gates* mentioned in line 62 are presumably a door in
the facade of the tiring-house, rearstage, below the gallery. Saturninus
and Bassianus presumably exit through this door and ascend inside
the tiring-house to the gallery or Senate House, where they reappear
with the tribunes and senators.)

CAPTAIN

Romans, make way! The good Andronicus,
Patron of virtue, Rome's best champion,   65
Successful in the battles that he fights,
With honor and with fortune is returned
From where he circumscribèd with his sword   68
And brought to yoke the enemies of Rome.   69

Sound drums and trumpets, and then enter two
of Titus' sons, [Martius and Mutius]; and then
two men bearing a coffin covered with black;
then two other sons [Lucius and Quintus]; then
Titus Andronicus; and then Tamora, the Queen
of Goths, and her three sons [Alarbus,] Chiron,
and Demetrius, with Aaron the Moor, and oth-
ers as many as can be. Then set down the coffin,
and Titus speaks.

TITUS

Hail, Rome, victorious in thy mourning weeds!   70
Lo, as the bark that hath discharged his freight   71
Returns with precious lading to the bay
From whence at first she weighed her anchorage,   73
Cometh Andronicus, bound with laurel boughs,
To re-salute his country with his tears,
Tears of true joy for his return to Rome.
Thou great defender of this Capitol,   77
Stand gracious to the rites that we intend!
Romans, of five-and-twenty valiant sons,
Half of the number that King Priam had,   80
Behold the poor remains, alive and dead.
These that survive let Rome reward with love;
These that I bring unto their latest home,   83
With burial amongst their ancestors.   84
Here Goths have given me leave to sheathe my sword.   85
Titus, unkind and careless of thine own,   86
Why suffer'st thou thy sons, unburied yet,
To hover on the dreadful shore of Styx?   88
Make way to lay them by their brethren.

                               They open the tomb.

There greet in silence, as the dead are wont,
And sleep in peace, slain in your country's wars!
O sacred receptacle of my joys,
Sweet cell of virtue and nobility,
How many sons hast thou of mine in store
That thou wilt never render to me more!   95

LUCIUS

Give us the proudest prisoner of the Goths,
That we may hew his limbs, and on a pile
Ad manes fratrum sacrifice his flesh   98
Before this earthy prison of their bones,

That so the shadows be not unappeased,   100
Nor we disturbed with prodigies on earth.   101

TITUS

I give him you, the noblest that survives,
The eldest son of this distressèd queen.

TAMORA [*kneeling*]

Stay, Roman brethren! Gracious conqueror,   104
Victorious Titus, rue the tears I shed,
A mother's tears in passion for her son;   106
And if thy sons were ever dear to thee,
Oh, think my son to be as dear to me!
Sufficeth not that we are brought to Rome   109
To beautify thy triumphs, and return   110
Captive to thee and to thy Roman yoke,
But must my sons be slaughtered in the streets
For valiant doings in their country's cause?
Oh, if to fight for king and commonweal
Were piety in thine, it is in these.
Andronicus, stain not thy tomb with blood!   116
Wilt thou draw near the nature of the gods?
Draw near them then in being merciful.
Sweet mercy is nobility's true badge.
Thrice noble Titus, spare my firstborn son.

TITUS [*raising her*]

Patient yourself, madam, and pardon me.   121
These are their brethren, whom your Goths beheld   122
Alive and dead, and for their brethren slain
Religiously they ask a sacrifice.
To this your son is marked, and die he must
T'appease their groaning shadows that are gone.

LUCIUS

Away with him! And make a fire straight,   127
And with our swords, upon a pile of wood,
Let's hew his limbs till they be clean consumed.   129

                       Exeunt Titus' sons with Alarbus.

TAMORA

Oh, cruel, irreligious piety!

CHIRON

Was never Scythia half so barbarous.   131

DEMETRIUS

Oppose not Scythia to ambitious Rome.   132
Alarbus goes to rest, and we survive
To tremble under Titus' threat'ning look.
Then, madam, stand resolved, but hope withal   135
The selfsame gods that armed the Queen of Troy   136
With opportunity of sharp revenge
Upon the Thracian tyrant in his tent
May favor Tamora, the Queen of Goths—

100 **shadows** shades, ghosts   101 **prodigies** omens, portents of ill
104 **s.d. *kneeling*** (In a drawing of Act 1 of *Titus*, done in about 1595
by Henry Peacham, Tamora's sons are also shown kneeling.)
106 **passion** grief   109 **Sufficeth not** Doesn't it suffice   110 **triumphs**
(1) successes (2) entry procession in honor of victory.   **return** i.e.,
accompany your return   116 **tomb** family tomb   121 **Patient** Calm
122 **their brethren** i.e., the brothers of those who have been slain
127 **straight** at once   129 **clean** wholly   131 **Scythia** a region north
of the Black Sea; its people were notorious for their savagery
132 **Oppose** Contrast   135 **withal** besides   136 **Queen of Troy**
Hecuba, wife of Priam, who after the fall of Troy was carried to
Greece as a slave; there she found occasion to avenge the death of her
son Polydorus by killing the two sons of the murderer, Polymnestor,
King of Thrace

---

65 **Patron** sponsor and pattern   68 **circumscribèd** restrained, confined
69.5 *Titus Andronicus* (Titus may enter drawn in a chariot; he refers to
his chariot in line 250.)   70 **weeds** garments.   71 **bark** sailing vessel.
his its   73 **anchorage** anchors   77 **Thou** i.e., Jupiter Capitolinus
80 **King Priam** King of Troy at the time of its fall; he had fifty sons
83 **latest** final   84 **With** i.e., let Rome reward with   85 **Here . . . sword**
i.e., The defeated Goths have been so good as to let me put up my
weapon. (Said ironically; the Goths had no choice.)   86 **unkind** deficient in natural feeling   88 **Styx** river surrounding Hades across which
souls might not cross until they had received proper burial.   95 **more**
again.   98 ***Ad manes fratrum*** to the departed spirits of (our) brothers

When Goths were Goths and Tamora was queen—
To quit the bloody wrongs upon her foes.   141

Enter the sons of Andronicus again [with their swords bloody].

LUCIUS
See, lord and father, how we have performed
Our Roman rites. Alarbus' limbs are lopped,
And entrails feed the sacrificing fire,
Whose smoke, like incense, doth perfume the sky.
Remaineth naught but to inter our brethren
And with loud 'larums welcome them to Rome.   147
TITUS
Let it be so, and let Andronicus
Make this his latest farewell to their souls.   149

Sound trumpets, and lay the coffin in the tomb.

In peace and honor rest you here, my sons;
Rome's readiest champions, repose you here in rest,
Secure from worldly chances and mishaps!
Here lurks no treason, here no envy swells,
Here grow no damnèd drugs; here are no storms,   154
No noise, but silence and eternal sleep.
In peace and honor rest you here, my sons!

Enter Lavinia.

LAVINIA
In peace and honor live Lord Titus long;
My noble lord and father, live in fame!
Lo, at this tomb my tributary tears   159
I render for my brethren's obsequies,   160
And at thy feet I kneel, with tears of joy   [*kneeling*]
Shed on this earth for thy return to Rome.
Oh, bless me here with thy victorious hand,
Whose fortunes Rome's best citizens applaud!
TITUS
Kind Rome, that hast thus lovingly reserved
The cordial of mine age to glad my heart!   166
Lavinia, live; outlive thy father's days
And fame's eternal date, for virtue's praise!   168
                                             [*She rises.*]
MARCUS
Long live Lord Titus, my belovèd brother,   169
Gracious triumpher in the eyes of Rome!
TITUS
Thanks, gentle tribune, noble brother Marcus.
MARCUS
And welcome, nephews, from successful wars,
You that survive, and you that sleep in fame!
Fair lords, your fortunes are alike in all,   174

That in your country's service drew your swords;
But safer triumph is this funeral pomp
That hath aspired to Solon's happiness,   177
And triumphs over chance in honor's bed.   178
Titus Andronicus, the people of Rome,
Whose friend in justice thou hast ever been,
Send thee by me, their tribune and their trust,   181
This palliament of white and spotless hue,   182
And name thee in election for the empire   183
With these our late-deceasèd emperor's sons.
Be *candidatus* then, and put it on,   185
And help to set a head on headless Rome.
                                   [*He offers Titus a white robe.*]
TITUS
A better head her glorious body fits
Than his that shakes for age and feebleness.
What, should I don this robe and trouble you?
Be chosen with proclamations today,
Tomorrow yield up rule, resign my life,
And set abroad new business for you all?   192
Rome, I have been thy soldier forty years,
And led my country's strength successfully,
And buried one-and-twenty valiant sons,
Knighted in field, slain manfully in arms,
In right and service of their noble country.   197
Give me a staff of honor for mine age,
But not a scepter to control the world.
Upright he held it, lords, that held it last.
MARCUS
Titus, thou shalt obtain and ask the empery.   201
SATURNINUS
Proud and ambitious tribune, canst thou tell?   202
TITUS   Patience, Prince Saturninus.
SATURNINUS   Romans, do me right.
Patricians, draw your swords, and sheathe them not
Till Saturninus be Rome's emperor.
Andronicus, would thou were shipped to hell
Rather than rob me of the people's hearts!
LUCIUS
Proud Saturnine, interrupter of the good
That noble-minded Titus means to thee!
TITUS [*to Saturninus*]
Content thee, prince. I will restore to thee
The people's hearts, and wean them from
    themselves.   212
BASSIANUS
Andronicus, I do not flatter thee,
But honor thee, and will do till I die.
My faction if thou strengthen with thy friends,
I will most thankful be; and thanks to men
Of noble minds is honorable meed.   217

---

141 quit requite   **147 'larums** trumpet calls   **149.1 *the coffin***
(Although there is presumably more than one dead son, the staging
may have relied on one coffin for the sake of economy.)   **154 drugs**
poisonous plants   **159 tributary** paid in tribute   **160 obsequies** acts
performed in honor of the dead   **166 cordial** restorative; or comfort,
pleasure   **168 And . . . praise!** and, as a tribute to your virtue, may
you outlive fame itself!   **169 MARCUS** (Many editors have Marcus
speak from above, since the Folio stage direction earlier at line 17.1–2
specifies that he is to enter *"aloft,"* but the Quarto version makes no
mention of this. The present edition keeps him on the main stage
throughout.)   **174 Fair . . . all** You noble lords who have survived,
you share a common good fortune in having been victorious

177 Solon's happiness i.e., the happiness defined by Solon (a Greek
sage and lawgiver): that no man may be called happy until after his
death   **178 And . . . bed** and triumphs over the vicissitudes of fortune in an honorable grave.   **181 trust** trusted representative
182 palliament candidate's gown or cloak   **183 in election** i.e., as a
candidate   **185 *candidatus*** a candidate. (Literally, one clad in white.)
192 abroad i.e., on foot   **197 In . . . of** serving the just cause of
201 obtain and ask obtain simply by asking   **202 canst thou tell?** i.e.,
that's what you think.   **212 from themselves** i.e., from their present
intention.   **217 meed** reward.

TITUS
    People of Rome, and people's tribunes here,
    I ask your voices and your suffrages.   219
    Will ye bestow them friendly on Andronicus?
TRIBUNES
    To gratify the good Andronicus
    And gratulate his safe return to Rome,   222
    The people will accept whom he admits.
TITUS
    Tribunes, I thank you, and this suit I make:
    That you create our emperor's eldest son,   225
    Lord Saturnine, whose virtues will, I hope,
    Reflect on Rome as Titan's rays on earth,   227
    And ripen justice in this commonweal.
    Then, if you will elect by my advice,
    Crown him and say, "Long live our emperor!"
MARCUS
    With voices and applause of every sort,
    Patricians and plebeians, we create
    Lord Saturninus Rome's great emperor,
    And say, "Long live our Emperor Saturnine!"   234
            [Saturninus is crowned. A long flourish till they
                                        come down.]
SATURNINUS
    Titus Andronicus, for thy favors done
    To us in our election this day,
    I give thee thanks in part of thy deserts,   237
    And will with deeds requite thy gentleness.   238
    And, for an onset, Titus, to advance   239
    Thy name and honorable family,
    Lavinia will I make my empress,
    Rome's royal mistress, mistress of my heart,
    And in the sacred Pantheon her espouse.   243
    Tell me, Andronicus, doth this motion please thee?   244
TITUS
    It doth, my worthy lord, and in this match
    I hold me highly honored of Your Grace.   246
    And here in sight of Rome to Saturnine,
    King and commander of our commonweal,
    The wide world's emperor, do I consecrate
    My sword, my chariot, and my prisoners,
    Presents well worthy Rome's imperious lord.   251
    Receive them, then, the tribute that I owe,
    Mine honor's ensigns humbled at thy feet.   253
            [A tribute is laid at Saturninus' feet.]
SATURNINUS
    Thanks, noble Titus, father of my life!
    How proud I am of thee and of thy gifts
    Rome shall record, and when I do forget
    The least of these unspeakable deserts,   257
    Romans, forget your fealty to me.

TITUS [to Tamora]
    Now, madam, are you prisoner to an emperor,
    To him that for your honor and your state
    Will use you nobly and your followers.
SATURNINUS [aside]
    A goodly lady, trust me, of the hue
    That I would choose, were I to choose anew.—
    Clear up, fair queen, that cloudy countenance.
    Though chance of war hath wrought this change of
        cheer,   265
    Thou com'st not to be made a scorn in Rome.
    Princely shall be thy usage every way.
    Rest on my word, and let not discontent   268
    Daunt all your hopes. Madam, he comforts you
    Can make you greater than the Queen of Goths.   270
    Lavinia, you are not displeased with this?
LAVINIA
    Not I, my lord, sith true nobility   272
    Warrants these words in princely courtesy.   273
SATURNINUS
    Thanks, sweet Lavinia.—Romans, let us go.
    Ransomless here we set our prisoners free.
    Proclaim our honors, lords, with trump and drum.
            [Tamora, Chiron, Demetrius, and Aaron are
        released. Sound drums and trumpets. Saturninus
                                    starts to leave, attended.]
BASSIANUS [seizing Lavinia]
    Lord Titus, by your leave, this maid is mine.
TITUS
    How, sir? Are you in earnest then, my lord?
BASSIANUS
    Ay, noble Titus, and resolved withal
    To do myself this reason and this right.
MARCUS
    Suum cuique is our Roman justice.   281
    This prince in justice seizeth but his own.
LUCIUS [joining Bassianus]
    And that he will and shall, if Lucius live.
TITUS
    Traitors, avaunt! Where is the Emperor's guard?   284
    Treason, my lord! Lavinia is surprised!   285
SATURNINUS
    Surprised? By whom?
BASSIANUS   By him that justly may
    Bear his betrothed from all the world away.
MUTIUS
    Brothers, help to convey her hence away,
    And with my sword I'll keep this door safe.
            [Exeunt Bassianus, Marcus, Lucius, Quintus,
                                and Martius, with Lavinia.]
TITUS [to Saturninus]
    Follow, my lord, and I'll soon bring her back.

---

219 voices votes. suffrages votes. 222 gratulate salute, rejoice in 225 create i.e., elect 227 Titan's (Helios, the sun god, was a descendant of the Titans.) 234.2 come down (This stage direction is in the Folio.) 237 in as 238 gentleness nobleness. 239 onset beginning 243 Pantheon Roman temple dedicated to all the gods 244 motion proposal 246 hold me consider myself. of by 251 imperious imperial 253 ensigns tokens 257 unspeakable inexpressible

265 cheer countenance 268 Rest Rely 270 Can who can 272 sith since 273 Warrants justifies 281 Suum cuique To each his own 284–5 Traitors . . . surprised! (Evidently, Saturninus, starting to leave, has not quite realized what has happened, and his guard, accompanying him, has been caught napping. Surprised means "taken, seized.")

MUTIUS [*guarding the door*]
My lord, you pass not here.
TITUS   What, villain boy?
Barr'st me my way in Rome?   [*He stabs Mutius.*]
MUTIUS   Help, Lucius, help!   292
[*He dies.*]
[*During the fray, exeunt Saturninus, Tamora,*
Demetrius, Chiron, and Aaron.]

[*Enter Lucius.*]

LUCIUS [*to Titus*]
My lord, you are unjust; and more than so,
In wrongful quarrel you have slain your son.
TITUS
Nor thou nor he are any sons of mine.   295
My sons would never so dishonor me.
Traitor, restore Lavinia to the Emperor.
LUCIUS
Dead, if you will, but not to be his wife
That is another's lawful promised love.   [*Exit.*] 299

Enter aloft the Emperor [*Saturninus*] *with*
Tamora and her two sons and Aaron the Moor.

SATURNINUS
No, Titus, no. The Emperor needs her not,
Nor her, nor thee, nor any of thy stock.
I'll trust by leisure him that mocks me once;   302
Thee never, nor thy traitorous haughty sons,
Confederates all thus to dishonor me.
Was none in Rome to make a stale   305
But Saturnine? Full well, Andronicus,
Agree these deeds with that proud brag of thine
That said'st I begged the empire at thy hands.
TITUS
Oh, monstrous! What reproachful words are these?
SATURNINUS
But go thy ways; go, give that changing piece   310
To him that flourished for her with his sword.   311
A valiant son-in-law thou shalt enjoy,
One fit to bandy with thy lawless sons,   313
To ruffle in the commonwealth of Rome.   314
TITUS
These words are razors to my wounded heart.
SATURNINUS
And therefore, lovely Tamora, Queen of Goths,
That like the stately Phoebe 'mongst her nymphs 317
Dost overshine the gallant'st dames of Rome,

If thou be pleased with this my sudden choice,
Behold, I choose thee, Tamora, for my bride,
And will create thee Empress of Rome.
Speak, Queen of Goths, dost thou applaud my choice?
And here I swear by all the Roman gods,
Sith priest and holy water are so near,
And tapers burn so bright, and everything
In readiness for Hymenaeus stand,   326
I will not re-salute the streets of Rome,
Or climb my palace, till from forth this place   328
I lead espoused my bride along with me.
TAMORA
And here in sight of heaven to Rome I swear,
If Saturnine advance the Queen of Goths,
She will a handmaid be to his desires,
A loving nurse, a mother to his youth.
SATURNINUS
Ascend, fair queen, Pantheon. Lords, accompany
Your noble emperor and his lovely bride,
Sent by the heavens for Prince Saturnine,
Whose wisdom hath her fortune conquerèd.   337
There shall we consummate our spousal rites.   338
Exeunt omnes [*except Titus*].
TITUS
I am not bid to wait upon this bride.   339
Titus, when wert thou wont to walk alone,
Dishonored thus and challengèd of wrongs?   341

Enter Marcus and Titus' sons [*Lucius,*
Quintus, and Martius].

MARCUS
Oh, Titus, see, oh, see what thou hast done!
In a bad quarrel slain a virtuous son.
TITUS
No, foolish tribune, no; no son of mine,
Nor thou, nor these, confederates in the deed
That hath dishonored all our family—
Unworthy brother and unworthy sons!
LUCIUS
But let us give him burial as becomes;   348
Give Mutius burial with our brethren.
TITUS
Traitors, away! He rests not in this tomb.
This monument five hundred years hath stood,
Which I have sumptuously re-edified.   352
Here none but soldiers and Rome's servitors   353
Repose in fame, none basely slain in brawls.
Bury him where you can, he comes not here.
MARCUS
My lord, this is impiety in you.
My nephew Mutius' deeds do plead for him;
He must be buried with his brethren.

292.2–3 *During . . . Aaron* (Evidently Saturninus, realizing he has been
dishonored by the seizure of Lavinia and having decided in any case
that he prefers Tamora, lines 262–3, decides to ascend to the Capitol
and proclaim forthwith his choice of Tamora and repudiation of
Lavinia.)   295 **Nor** Neither. (Also in line 301.)   299 s.d. *Exit* (Lucius
may take Mutius's body with him and return with it at line 341, but
the presence of the dead body onstage from lines 299 to 341 would not
be an inappropriate horror.)   302 **by leisure** not any time soon, barely
305 **Was . . . stale** Was there no one in Rome to be made a laughing-
stock   310 **changing piece** fickle wench   311 **flourished . . . sword**
brandished his sword to obtain her.   313 **bandy** brawl   314 **ruffle**
swagger   317 **Phoebe** Diana, goddess of the hunt and of chastity,
and associated with the moon. The irony of linking chastity with
Tamora soon becomes apparent in the play.

326 **Hymenaeus** Roman god of marriage   328 **climb** ascend the
stairs to   337 **Whose . . . conquerèd** i.e., whose wise choice to be my
queen has overcome her ill fortune of being conquered in battle.
338.1 *omnes* all.   339 **bid** invited   341 **challengèd** accused
348 **becomes** is fitting   352 **re-edified** rebuilt.   353 **servitors** armed
defenders

MARTIUS
And shall.

QUINTUS   Or him we will accompany.

TITUS
"And shall"? What villain was it spake that word?

MARTIUS
He that would vouch it in any place but here.   361

TITUS
What, would you bury him in my despite?

MARCUS
No, noble Titus, but entreat of thee
To pardon Mutius and to bury him.

TITUS
Marcus, even thou hast struck upon my crest,   365
And, with these boys, mine honor thou hast wounded.
My foes I do repute you every one.
So trouble me no more, but get you gone.

QUINTUS
He is not with himself. Let us withdraw.   369

MARTIUS
Not I, till Mutius' bones be buried.
          The brother [Marcus] and the sons kneel.

MARCUS
Brother, for in that name doth nature plead—

MARTIUS
Father, and in that name doth nature speak—

TITUS
Speak thou no more, if all the rest will speed.   373

MARCUS
Renownèd Titus, more than half my soul—

LUCIUS
Dear father, soul and substance of us all—

MARCUS
Suffer thy brother Marcus to inter   376
His noble nephew here in virtue's nest,
That died in honor and Lavinia's cause.
Thou art a Roman; be not barbarous.
The Greeks upon advice did bury Ajax,   380
That slew himself, and wise Laertes' son
Did graciously plead for his funerals.   382
Let not young Mutius, then, that was thy joy,
Be barred his entrance here.

TITUS   Rise, Marcus, rise.
          [They rise.]
The dismal'st day is this that e'er I saw,
To be dishonored by my sons in Rome!
Well, bury him, and bury me the next.
          They put him [Mutius] in the tomb.

LUCIUS
There lie thy bones, sweet Mutius, with thy friends,
Till we with trophies do adorn thy tomb.   389
          They all kneel.

ALL
No man shed tears for noble Mutius;
He lives in fame that died in virtue's cause.   391
          [They rise.] Exeunt all but Marcus and Titus.

MARCUS
My lord, to step out of these dreary dumps,   392
How comes it that the subtle Queen of Goths
Is of a sudden thus advanced in Rome?

TITUS
I know not, Marcus, but I know it is—
Whether by device or no, the heavens can tell.   396
Is she not then beholding to the man   397
That brought her for this high good turn so far?

MARCUS
Yes, and will nobly him remunerate.   399

          [Flourish.] Enter the Emperor [Saturninus],
          Tamora, and her two sons, with [Aaron] the
          Moor, at one door. Enter at the other door
          Bassianus and Lavinia, with others, [Lucius,
          Martius, and Quintus].

SATURNINUS
So, Bassianus, you have played your prize.   400
God give you joy, sir, of your gallant bride!

BASSIANUS
And you of yours, my lord! I say no more,
Nor wish no less; and so I take my leave.

SATURNINUS
Traitor, if Rome have law or we have power,   404
Thou and thy faction shall repent this rape.   405

BASSIANUS
"Rape" call you it, my lord, to seize my own,
My true-betrothèd love and now my wife?
But let the laws of Rome determine all;
Meanwhile am I possessed of that is mine.   409

SATURNINUS
'Tis good, sir. You are very short with us,
But if we live we'll be as sharp with you.

BASSIANUS
My lord, what I have done, as best I may
Answer I must, and shall do with my life.
Only thus much I give Your Grace to know:
By all the duties that I owe to Rome,
This noble gentleman, Lord Titus here,
Is in opinion and in honor wronged,   417

---

361 vouch . . . here maintain what I said anywhere but in this sacred place.   **365 my crest** the crest of my helmet (symbolizing the honor of my name)   **369 not with himself** distracted.   **373 if . . . speed** if all is to succeed, or, possibly, if you remaining sons do not wish to be slain like Mutius.   **376 Suffer** Permit   **380 advice** deliberation. **Ajax** Greek hero of the Trojan War who went mad because the armor of Achilles was awarded to Odysseus, slew a flock of sheep deludedly thinking them Greeks, and later committed suicide in shame; he was refused burial until *Laertes' son*, line 381, Odysseus, successfully pleaded for his funeral rites   **382 funerals** funeral obsequies. (Compare French *funerailles*.)

389 trophies memorials   **389.1 *They all kneel*** (Some editors think it unlikely that Titus joins his sons in kneeling or in saying lines 390–1, but Titus has relented and is not without feeling for the son he has slain.)   **391.1 *Exeunt*** (Perhaps the sons go off in order to accompany Bassianus' entry at line 399, or they may simply stand aside.) **392 dumps** melancholy   **396 device** scheming   **397 beholding** beholden   **399 Yes . . . remunerate** (Said sarcastically; Tamora will show her gratitude in physical ways.)   **400 played your prize** played and won your bout (as in fencing).   **404 we** I. (The royal plural; also at lines 410–11, etc.)   **405 rape** forcible seizure.   **409 that** that which **417 opinion** reputation

That, in the rescue of Lavinia,
With his own hand did slay his youngest son
In zeal to you, and highly moved to wrath
To be controlled in that he frankly gave.   421
Receive him, then, to favor, Saturnine,
That hath expressed himself in all his deeds
A father and a friend to thee and Rome.

TITUS
Prince Bassianus, leave to plead my deeds.   425
'Tis thou, and those, that have dishonored me.   426
Rome and the righteous heavens be my judge
How I have loved and honored Saturnine!
                                    [He kneels.]

TAMORA [to Saturninus]
My worthy lord, if ever Tamora
Were gracious in those princely eyes of thine,
Then hear me speak indifferently for all;   431
And at my suit, sweet, pardon what is past.

SATURNINUS
What, madam? Be dishonored openly,
And basely put it up without revenge?   434

TAMORA
Not so, my lord. The gods of Rome forfend   435
I should be author to dishonor you!   436
But on mine honor dare I undertake   437
For good Lord Titus' innocence in all,
Whose fury not dissembled speaks his griefs.   439
Then at my suit look graciously on him;
Lose not so noble a friend on vain suppose,   441
Nor with sour looks afflict his gentle heart.
[Aside to Saturninus] My lord, be ruled by me, be won
    at last;
Dissemble all your griefs and discontents.
You are but newly planted in your throne;
Lest then the people, and patricians too,
Upon a just survey take Titus' part   447
And so supplant you for ingratitude,
Which Rome reputes to be a heinous sin,
Yield at entreats; and then let me alone.   450
I'll find a day to massacre them all
And raze their faction and their family,
The cruel father and his traitorous sons
To whom I suèd for my dear son's life,
And make them know what 'tis to let a queen
Kneel in the streets and beg for grace in vain.—
[Aloud] Come, come, sweet Emperor; come,
    Andronicus;
Take up this good old man, and cheer the heart   458
That dies in tempest of thy angry frown.

SATURNINUS
Rise, Titus, rise. My empress hath prevailed.

TITUS [rising]
I thank Your Majesty and her, my lord.
These words, these looks, infuse new life in me.

TAMORA
Titus, I am incorporate in Rome,   463
A Roman now adopted happily,   464
And must advise the Emperor for his good.
This day all quarrels die, Andronicus.   466
And let it be mine honor, good my lord,
That I have reconciled your friends and you.
For you, Prince Bassianus, I have passed
My word and promise to the Emperor
That you will be more mild and tractable.
And fear not, lords, and you, Lavinia:
By my advice, all humbled on your knees,
You shall ask pardon of His Majesty.   474
        [Lucius, Martius, Quintus, and Lavinia kneel.]

LUCIUS
We do, and vow to heaven and to His Highness
That what we did was mildly as we might,   476
Tend'ring our sister's honor and our own.   477

MARCUS [kneeling]
That, on mine honor, here do I protest.   478

SATURNINUS [turning away]
Away, and talk not! Trouble us no more.

TAMORA
Nay, nay, sweet Emperor, we must all be friends.
The tribune and his nephews kneel for grace;
I will not be denied. Sweetheart, look back.

SATURNINUS
Marcus, for thy sake and thy brother's here,
And at my lovely Tamora's entreats,
I do remit these young men's heinous faults.
Stand up.   [The Andronici rise.]
Lavinia, though you left me like a churl,
I found a friend, and sure as death I swore
I would not part a bachelor from the priest.
Come; if the Emperor's court can feast two brides,
You are my guest, Lavinia, and your friends.
This day shall be a love-day, Tamora.   492

TITUS
Tomorrow, an it please Your Majesty   493
To hunt the panther and the hart with me,
With horn and hound we'll give Your Grace bonjour.   495

SATURNINUS
Be it so, Titus, and gramercy too.   496
        Exeunt. Sound trumpets. Manet [Aaron the] Moor.

♣

421 To . . . gave i.e., to be restrained from freely bestowing Lavinia on you, Saturninus.   425 leave to plead cease pleading on behalf of   426 those those sons of mine   431 indifferently impartially   434 put it up put up with it   435 forfend forbid   436 be author propose a way   437 undertake assert, vouch   439 Whose . . . griefs whose unconcealed anger gives testimonial to his grievances.   441 vain suppose idle supposition   447 survey examination   450 at entreats to entreaty.   let me alone leave it to me.   458 Take up raise from kneeling

463 am incorporate in have been admitted to the fellowship of   464 happily (1) fortunately (2) opportunely   466 all let all   474.1 Lucius . . . kneel (Perhaps Bassianus kneels also, though his pardon seems to have been assured at line 469.)   476–7 was mildly . . . Tend'ring was done as mildly as we could manage, taking into account the need to defend   478 That . . . protest I acted on the same honorable impulse.   492 love-day (1) day appointed to settle disputes (2) day for love   493 an if   495 bonjour good day.   496 gramercy great thanks.   496.1 Manet He remains onstage. (The Folio has Aaron exiting with the rest and reentering. The tomb of Act 1 is possibly concealed by a curtain backstage.)

[2.1]

AARON
Now climbeth Tamora Olympus' top,   1
Safe out of fortune's shot, and sits aloft,
Secure of thunder's crack or lightning flash,   3
Advanced above pale envy's threatening reach.
As when the golden sun salutes the morn
And, having gilt the ocean with his beams,
Gallops the zodiac in his glistering coach   7
And overlooks the highest-peering hills,   8
So Tamora.
Upon her wit doth earthly honor wait,   10
And virtue stoops and trembles at her frown.   11
Then, Aaron, arm thy heart and fit thy thoughts
To mount aloft with thy imperial mistress,
And mount her pitch whom thou in triumph long   14
Hast prisoner held, fettered in amorous chains
And faster bound to Aaron's charming eyes   16
Than is Prometheus tied to Caucasus.   17
Away with slavish weeds and servile thoughts!   18
I will be bright, and shine in pearl and gold,
To wait upon this new-made empress.
To wait, said I? To wanton with this queen,
This goddess, this Semiramis, this nymph,   22
This siren that will charm Rome's Saturnine
And see his shipwreck and his commonweal's.
Holla! What storm is this?   25

Enter Chiron and Demetrius, braving.

DEMETRIUS
Chiron, thy years wants wit, thy wits wants edge   26
And manners, to intrude where I am graced   27
And may, for aught thou knowest, affected be.   28
CHIRON
Demetrius, thou dost overween in all,   29
And so in this, to bear me down with braves.   30
'Tis not the difference of a year or two
Makes me less gracious or thee more fortunate;
I am as able and as fit as thou
To serve, and to deserve my mistress' grace,
And that my sword upon thee shall approve,   35
And plead my passions for Lavinia's love.
AARON [*aside*]
Clubs, clubs! These lovers will not keep the peace.   37

2.1. Location: Scene continues. Aaron remains onstage.
1 Olympus home of the Greek gods   **3 of** from   **7 Gallops** gallops through   **8 overlooks** looks down on from on high   **10 wit** intelligence.   **wait** attend   **11 virtue . . . frown** her displeasure makes even virtue (or, the virtuous) afraid.   **14 pitch** height to which a falcon soars before descending on its prey. (The image of *mounting* has sexual connotations also.)   **16 charming** exerting a magic spell   **17 Prometheus** Titan who stole fire from the chariot of the sun and gave it to humanity; as punishment, Zeus fastened him to a mountain in the Caucasus and sent a vulture to feast on his liver   **18 weeds** garments   **22 Semiramis** mythical Queen of Assyria, famous for her cruelty and lust   **25.1** *braving* defying (each other).   **26 wants** lack.   **edge** sharpness, incisiveness   **27 graced** favored   **28 affected** loved   **29 overween** arrogantly presume   **30 braves** threats.   **35 approve** prove   **37 Clubs, clubs!** (A cry summoning the apprentices of London to join in or to suppress a riot or rebellion.)

DEMETRIUS
Why, boy, although our mother, unadvised,   38
Gave you a dancing-rapier by your side,   39
Are you so desperate grown to threat your friends?   40
Go to! Have your lath glued within your sheath   41
Till you know better how to handle it.
CHIRON
Meanwhile, sir, with the little skill I have,
Full well shalt thou perceive how much I dare. ·
DEMETRIUS
Ay, boy, grow ye so brave?   *They draw.*
AARON [*coming forward*]   Why, how now, lords?
So near the Emperor's palace dare ye draw   46
And maintain such a quarrel openly?
Full well I wot the ground of all this grudge.   48
I would not for a million of gold
The cause were known to them it most concerns,
Nor would your noble mother for much more
Be so dishonored in the court of Rome.
For shame, put up.
DEMETRIUS   Not I, till I have sheathed   53
My rapier in his bosom, and withal   54
Thrust those reproachful speeches down his throat
That he hath breathed in my dishonor here.
CHIRON
For that I am prepared and full resolved,
Foul-spoken coward, that thund'rest with thy tongue
And with thy weapon nothing dar'st perform!
AARON   Away, I say!
Now, by the gods that warlike Goths adore,
This petty brabble will undo us all.   62
Why, lords, and think you not how dangerous
It is to jet upon a prince's right?   64
What, is Lavinia then become so loose,
Or Bassianus so degenerate,
That for her love such quarrels may be broached   67
Without controlment, justice, or revenge?   68
Young lords, beware! And should the Empress know
This discord's ground, the music would not please.   70
CHIRON
I care not, I, knew she and all the world.   71
I love Lavinia more than all the world.
DEMETRIUS
Youngling, learn thou to make some meaner choice.   73
Lavinia is thine elder brother's hope.
AARON
Why, are ye mad? Or know ye not in Rome
How furious and impatient they be,
And cannot brook competitors in love?   77

---

38 unadvised ill-advisedly   **39 a dancing-rapier** an ornamental weapon worn in dancing   **40 to** as to   **41 Go to** (An expression of impatience.)   **lath** counterfeit stage weapon of wood   **46 So . . . palace** (It was usually against the law to draw a sword in the presence of the King or near his royal residence. See also line 64.)   **48 wot** know   **53 put up** sheathe your swords.   **54 withal** besides   **62 brabble** quarrel, brawl   **64 jet** encroach   **67 broached** begun, set flowing   **68 controlment** restraint   **70 ground** basis. (With a pun on the musical meaning "bass upon which a melody is constructed.")   **71 knew she** if she knew   **73 meaner** of lower degree   **77 brook** endure

I tell you, lords, you do but plot your deaths
By this device.
CHIRON   Aaron, a thousand deaths
Would I propose to achieve her whom I love.   80
AARON
To achieve her? How?
DEMETRIUS   Why makes thou it so strange?   81
She is a woman, therefore may be wooed;
She is a woman, therefore may be won;
She is Lavinia, therefore must be loved.
What, man, more water glideth by the mill
Than wots the miller of, and easy it is   86
Of a cut loaf to steal a shive, we know.   87
Though Bassianus be the Emperor's brother,
Better than he have worn Vulcan's badge.   89
AARON [aside]
Ay, and as good as Saturninus may.
DEMETRIUS
Then why should he despair that knows to court it   91
With words, fair looks, and liberality?
What, hast not thou full often struck a doe
And borne her cleanly by the keeper's nose?   94
AARON
Why then, it seems some certain snatch or so   95
Would serve your turns.
CHIRON   Ay, so the turn were served.   96
DEMETRIUS
Aaron, thou hast hit it.
AARON   Would you had hit it too!   97
Then should not we be tired with this ado.
Why, hark ye, hark ye, and are you such fools
To square for this? Would it offend you then   100
That both should speed?   101
CHIRON
Faith, not me.
DEMETRIUS   Nor me, so I were one.   102
AARON
For shame, be friends, and join for that you jar.   103
'Tis policy and stratagem must do   104
That you affect, and so must you resolve   105
That what you cannot as you would achieve,   106
You must perforce accomplish as you may.   107
Take this of me: Lucrece was not more chaste   108
Than this Lavinia, Bassianus' love.
A speedier course than lingering languishment   110

Must we pursue, and I have found the path.
My lords, a solemn hunting is in hand;   112
There will the lovely Roman ladies troop.
The forest walks are wide and spacious,
And many unfrequented plots there are,   115
Fitted by kind for rape and villainy.   116
Single you thither then this dainty doe,   117
And strike her home by force, if not by words;   118
This way, or not at all, stand you in hope.
Come, come, our empress, with her sacred wit   120
To villainy and vengeance consecrate,   121
Will we acquaint withal what we intend;   122
And she shall file our engines with advice   123
That will not suffer you to square yourselves,   124
But to your wishes' height advance you both.
The Emperor's court is like the house of Fame,   126
The palace full of tongues, of eyes, and ears;
The woods are ruthless, dreadful, deaf, and dull.
There speak and strike, brave boys, and take your turns;
There serve your lust, shadowed from heaven's eye,
And revel in Lavinia's treasury.
CHIRON
Thy counsel, lad, smells of no cowardice.
DEMETRIUS
Sit fas aut nefas, till I find the stream   133
To cool this heat, a charm to calm these fits,
Per Stygia, per manes vehor.   Exeunt. 135

❧

[2.2]

*Enter Titus Andronicus and his three sons [and
Marcus], making a noise with hounds and horns.*

TITUS
The hunt is up, the morn is bright and gray,   1
The fields are fragrant, and the woods are green.
Uncouple here, and let us make a bay   3
And wake the Emperor and his lovely bride,
And rouse the Prince, and ring a hunter's peal,   5
That all the court may echo with the noise.
Sons, let it be your charge, as it is ours,   7
To attend the Emperor's person carefully.

---

80 propose be ready to meet   81 Why . . . strange? Why do you act
so surprised?   86 wots knows   87 shive slice   89 Vulcan's badge
i.e., cuckold's horns, alluding to the public shame to which Vulcan
was exposed by his wife Venus's affair with Mars.   91 knows to
court it knows how to play the wooer   94 cleanly by clean past,
without being observed   95 snatch sudden or quick catch. (With a
bawdy pun: "a quickie.")   96 serve your turns answer your purposes. (With sexual suggestion of a turn in the bed that is underscored in Chiron's reply.)   97 hit it . . . hit it hit the nail on the head
. . . scored sexually   100 square quarrel   101 speed succeed.   102 so
so long as   103 join . . . jar conspire to obtain what you're quarreling
over.   104 policy contrivance, craft   105 That you affect that which
you desire   106–7 That . . . may that if you can't do this in the way
you'd prefer, you must necessarily accomplish it as best you can, by
whatever means.   108 Lucrece a chaste Roman lady ravished by Tarquin, as told in Shakespeare's poem *The Rape of Lucrece*   110 languishment love distress

112 solemn ceremonial   115 plots i.e., plots of ground   116 by kind
by nature   117 Single Single out (as in hunting)   118 home effectually, thoroughly, to the desired place. (With sexual suggestion.)
120 sacred i.e., consecrated (to villainy)   121 consecrate dedicated
122 withal with   123 file our engines sharpen our devices
124 That . . . yourselves that will make it possible for you not to quarrel with each other over this   126 house of Fame residence of rumor.
(Described in Ovid's *Metamorphoses*, Book 12, and in Chaucer's *Hous
of Fame*; see also Virgil, *Aeneid*, 4.179–90.)   133 Sit fas aut nefas Be it
right or wrong   135 Per . . . vehor I am carried through the Stygian
regions, through the realm of the shades. (Adapted from Seneca's
Hippolytus, line 1180.)
2.2. Location: The grounds of the Emperor's palace.
1 gray cold, sunless light of early morning   3 Uncouple . . . bay
Unleash the hounds, and incite them to keep up a deep, prolonged
barking   5 ring a hunter's peal blow a peal on the hunting horns (to
set the dogs going)   7 ours mine

I have been troubled in my sleep this night,
But dawning day new comfort hath inspired.   10

Here a cry of hounds, and wind horns in a peal.
Then enter Saturninus, Tamora, Bassianus,
Lavinia, Chiron, Demetrius, and their attendants.

Many good morrows to Your Majesty;
Madam, to you as many and as good.
I promisèd Your Grace a hunter's peal.

SATURNINUS
And you have rung it lustily, my lords—   14
Somewhat too early for new-married ladies.

BASSIANUS
Lavinia, how say you?

LAVINIA   I say no;
I have been broad awake two hours and more.

SATURNINUS
Come on, then, horse and chariots let us have,
And to our sport. [*To Tamora*] Madam, now shall ye see
Our Roman hunting.

MARCUS   I have dogs, my lord,
Will rouse the proudest panther in the chase   21
And climb the highest promontory top.

TITUS
And I have horse will follow where the game   23
Makes way and run like swallows o'er the plain.   24

DEMETRIUS [*aside to Chiron*]
Chiron, we hunt not, we, with horse nor hound,
But hope to pluck a dainty doe to ground.   *Exeunt.*

[2.3]

Enter Aaron alone [with a bag of gold].

AARON
He that had wit would think that I had none,
To bury so much gold under a tree
And never after to inherit it.   3
Let him that thinks of me so abjectly
Know that this gold must coin a stratagem   5
Which, cunningly effected, will beget
A very excellent piece of villainy.
And so repose, sweet gold, for their unrest   8
That have their alms out of the Empress' chest.   9
                          [*He hides the gold.*]

Enter Tamora alone to the Moor.

TAMORA
My lovely Aaron, wherefore look'st thou sad,
When everything doth make a gleeful boast?   11
The birds chant melody on every bush,
The snake lies rollèd in the cheerful sun,   13
The green leaves quiver with the cooling wind
And make a checkered shadow on the ground.
Under their sweet shade, Aaron, let us sit,
And whilst the babbling echo mocks the hounds,
Replying shrilly to the well-tuned horns,
As if a double hunt were heard at once,
Let us sit down and mark their yellowing noise;   20
And after conflict such as was supposed
The wand'ring prince and Dido once enjoyed   22
When with a happy storm they were surprised   23
And curtained with a counsel-keeping cave,   24
We may, each wreathèd in the other's arms,
Our pastimes done, possess a golden slumber,
Whiles hounds and horns and sweet melodious birds
Be unto us as is a nurse's song
Of lullaby to bring her babe asleep.

AARON
Madam, though Venus govern your desires,
Saturn is dominator over mine.   31
What signifies my deadly-standing eye,   32
My silence, and my cloudy melancholy,   33
My fleece of woolly hair that now uncurls
Even as an adder when she doth unroll
To do some fatal execution?
No, madam, these are no venereal signs.   37
Vengeance is in my heart, death in my hand,
Blood and revenge are hammering in my head.
Hark, Tamora, the empress of my soul,
Which never hopes more heaven than rests in thee,   41
This is the day of doom for Bassianus:
His Philomel must lose her tongue today,   43
Thy sons make pillage of her chastity
And wash their hands in Bassianus' blood.
See'st thou this letter? Take it up, I pray thee,   46
                          [*giving her a letter*]
And give the King this fatal-plotted scroll.
Now question me no more; we are espied.
Here comes a parcel of our hopeful booty,   49
Which dreads not yet their lives' destruction.

Enter Bassianus and Lavinia.

TAMORA
Ah, my sweet Moor, sweeter to me than life!

---

11 boast display.   **13 rollèd** coiled   **20 yellowing** yelling, baying
22 prince i.e., Aeneas, who, taking shelter from a storm with Dido in a
cave during a hunt, made love to her   **23 happy** fortuitous   **24 And . . .**
cave and were concealed by a secret-keeping cave   **31 Saturn . . . mine**
i.e., Saturn, as the dominant planet in my horoscope, governs my temperament and makes it cold and sullen (unlike Venus's effect, which is
amorous).   **32 deadly-standing** fixed with a death-dealing stare
33 cloudy gloomy   **37 venereal** erotic, Venus-like   **41 Which . . .**
thee which hopes for no greater bliss than may be found in you
43 Philomel (An allusion to the story in Ovid's *Metamorphoses* of
Philomela, raped by her brother-in-law, Tereus; compare with 2.4.26
below. He cut out her tongue so that she could not disclose his villainy. She succeeded in weaving the account of her misfortune in a
tapestry.)   **46 Take it up** Take it   **49 parcel** part.   **hopeful** hoped-for

---

10.1 cry deep barking.   *wind* blow   **14 lustily** heartily   **21 Will** that
will.   **chase** royal hunting ground   **23 horse will** horses that will
24 run (The First Quarto's "runnes" is possible, in parallel to *Makes,*
but the verb probably applies to the *horse* rather than to the *game.*)
2.3. Location: A forest near Rome. A pit is provided in the stage,
presumably at a trapdoor, and near it some representation of an
elder tree.
3 inherit possess   **5 coin** fabricate. (With a pun on the literal meaning.)
8–9 for . . . chest i.e., to discomfit those who will find this gold taken
from Tamora's treasure chest.

AARON

No more, great Empress. Bassianus comes.
Be cross with him, and I'll go fetch thy sons   53
To back thy quarrels, whatsoe'er they be.   [*Exit.*]

BASSIANUS

Who have we here? Rome's royal empress,
Unfurnished of her well-beseeming troop?   56
Or is it Dian, habited like her,   57
Who hath abandonèd her holy groves
To see the general hunting in this forest?

TAMORA

Saucy controller of my private steps!   60
Had I the power that some say Dian had,
Thy temples should be planted presently   62
With horns, as was Actaeon's, and the hounds   63
Should drive upon thy new-transformèd limbs,   64
Unmannerly intruder as thou art!

LAVINIA

Under your patience, gentle Empress,   66
'Tis thought you have a goodly gift in horning,   67
And to be doubted that your Moor and you   68
Are singled forth to try experiments.   69
Jove shield your husband from his hounds today!
'Tis pity they should take him for a stag.

BASSIANUS

Believe me, Queen, your swart Cimmerian   72
Doth make your honor of his body's hue,
Spotted, detested, and abominable.
Why are you sequestered from all your train,
Dismounted from your snow-white goodly steed,
And wandered hither to an obscure plot,
Accompanied but with a barbarous Moor,
If foul desire had not conducted you?

LAVINIA

And, being intercepted in your sport,
Great reason that my noble lord be rated   81
For sauciness. [*To Bassianus*] I pray you, let us hence,
And let her joy her raven-colored love;   83
This valley fits the purpose passing well.   84

BASSIANUS

The King my brother shall have note of this.

LAVINIA

Ay, for these slips have made him noted long.   86
Good king, to be so mightily abused!   87

TAMORA

Why have I patience to endure all this?

Enter Chiron and Demetrius.

DEMETRIUS

How now, dear sovereign, and our gracious mother,
Why doth Your Highness look so pale and wan?

TAMORA

Have I not reason, think you, to look pale?
These two have 'ticed me hither to this place.   92
A barren detested vale you see it is;
The trees, though summer, yet forlorn and lean,
Overcome with moss and baleful mistletoe;   95
Here never shines the sun; here nothing breeds,
Unless the nightly owl or fatal raven.   97
And when they showed me this abhorrèd pit,
They told me here at dead time of the night
A thousand fiends, a thousand hissing snakes,
Ten thousand swelling toads, as many urchins,   101
Would make such fearful and confusèd cries
As any mortal body hearing it
Should straight fall mad or else die suddenly.
No sooner had they told this hellish tale
But straight they told me they would bind me here
Unto the body of a dismal yew
And leave me to this miserable death.
And then they called me foul adulteress,
Lascivious Goth, and all the bitterest terms   110
That ever ear did hear to such effect;
And had you not by wondrous fortune come,
This vengeance on me had they executed.
Revenge it, as you love your mother's life,
Or be ye not henceforth called my children.

DEMETRIUS

This is a witness that I am thy son.
                                   Stab him [*Bassianus*].

CHIRON

And this for me, struck home to show my strength.
                    [*He also stabs Bassianus, who dies.*]

LAVINIA

Ay, come, Semiramis, nay, barbarous Tamora,   118
For no name fits thy nature but thy own!

TAMORA [*to Chiron*]

Give me the poniard. You shall know, my boys,   120
Your mother's hand shall right your mother's wrong.

DEMETRIUS

Stay, madam, here is more belongs to her.   122
First thresh the corn, then after burn the straw.   123
This minion stood upon her chastity,   124
Upon her nuptial vow, her loyalty,
And with that painted hope braves your mightiness;   126
And shall she carry this unto her grave?

CHIRON

An if she do, I would I were an eunuch.   128
Drag hence her husband to some secret hole
And make his dead trunk pillow to our lust.

---

53 Be cross Pick a quarrel **56 Unfurnished . . . troop** unprovided with a suitable escort. **57 Dian** Diana, huntress and goddess of chastity. (Here used sarcastically.) **habited** dressed **60 Saucy controller** Impudent critic, censurer **62 presently** immediately **63 Actaeon's** (An allusion to the story of Actaeon, who was transformed into a stag by Diana and killed by his own hounds as punishment for having watched her and her nymphs at their bath. The horns here signify cuckoldry.) **64 drive** rush **66 Under . . . Empress** If you will allow my saying so, noble and kind Empress. (Said with ironic politeness.) **67 horning** cuckolding **68 doubted** suspected, feared **69 Are . . . experiments** i.e., are alone together to experiment with each other. **72 Cimmerian** i.e., of black complexion. (The Cimmerii in the *Odyssey* live in perpetual darkness.) **81 my noble lord** i.e., Bassianus. **rated** berated **83 joy** enjoy **84 passing** surpassingly **86 slips** offenses. **noted** notorious, stigmatized **87 abused** deceived.

92 'ticed enticed **95 Overcome** overgrown. **baleful** i.e., parasitic **97 fatal** ominous **101 urchins** (1) hedgehogs (2) goblins, elves **110 Goth** (A quibble; pronounced somewhat like "goat," symbolic of lechery.) **118 Semiramis** (See the note to 2.1.22.) **120 poniard** dagger. **122 belongs to her** that is to be her portion. **123 First . . . straw** (The proverbial phrase "to thrash in a woman's barn" means to have sex with her. *Corn* is grain.) **124 minion** hussy, wench **126 painted** specious, unreal **128 An if** If

TAMORA
  But when ye have the honey ye desire,
  Let not this wasp outlive, us both to sting.   132
CHIRON
  I warrant you, madam, we will make that sure.—
  Come, mistress, now perforce we will enjoy
  That nice-preservèd honesty of yours.   135
LAVINIA
  O Tamora! Thou bearest a woman's face—
TAMORA
  I will not hear her speak. Away with her!
LAVINIA
  Sweet lords, entreat her hear me but a word.
DEMETRIUS [to Tamora]
  Listen, fair madam. Let it be your glory
  To see her tears, but be your heart to them
  As unrelenting flint to drops of rain.
LAVINIA
  When did the tiger's young ones teach the dam?
  Oh, do not learn her wrath; she taught it thee!   143
  The milk thou suck'st from her did turn to marble;   144
  Even at thy teat thou hadst thy tyranny.   145
  Yet every mother breeds not sons alike;
  [To Chiron]   Do thou entreat her show a woman's pity.
CHIRON
  What, wouldst thou have me prove myself a bastard?   148
LAVINIA
  'Tis true, the raven doth not hatch a lark.
  Yet have I heard—Oh, could I find it now!—   150
  The lion, moved with pity, did endure   151
  To have his princely paws pared all away.   152
  Some say that ravens foster forlorn children   153
  The whilst their own birds famish in their nests.   154
  Oh, be to me, though thy hard heart say no,
  Nothing so kind, but something pitiful!   156
TAMORA
  I know not what it means.—Away with her!   157
LAVINIA
  Oh, let me teach thee! For my father's sake,
  That gave thee life when well he might have slain thee,
  Be not obdurate; open thy deaf ears.
TAMORA
  Hadst thou in person ne'er offended me,
  Even for his sake am I pitiless.
  Remember, boys, I poured forth tears in vain
  To save your brother from the sacrifice,
  But fierce Andronicus would not relent.
  Therefore away with her, and use her as you will—
  The worse to her, the better loved of me.
LAVINIA
  O Tamora, be called a gentle queen,
  And with thine own hands kill me in this place!

For 'tis not life that I have begged so long;
  Poor I was slain when Bassianus died.
                          [She clutches Tamora imploringly.]
TAMORA
  What beg'st thou, then? Fond woman, let me go.   172
LAVINIA
  'Tis present death I beg, and one thing more   173
  That womanhood denies my tongue to tell: 174
  Oh, keep me from their worse-than-killing lust,
  And tumble me into some loathsome pit,
  Where never man's eye may behold my body!
  Do this, and be a charitable murderer.
TAMORA
  So should I rob my sweet sons of their fee.
  No, let them satisfy their lust on thee.
DEMETRIUS [to Lavinia]
  Away! For thou hast stayed us here too long.
LAVINIA
  No grace, no womanhood? Ah, beastly creature!
  The blot and enemy to our general name!   183
  Confusion fall—   184
CHIRON
  Nay, then I'll stop your mouth. [To Demetrius] Bring
    thou her husband.
  This is the hole where Aaron bid us hide him.
         [Demetrius and Chiron throw the body of Bassianus
                 into the pit, then exeunt, dragging off Lavinia.]
TAMORA
  Farewell, my sons. See that you make her sure.   187
  Ne'er let my heart know merry cheer indeed
  Till all the Andronici be made away.   189
  Now will I hence to seek my lovely Moor,
  And let my spleenful sons this trull deflower.   [Exit.] 191

         Enter Aaron, with two of Titus' sons [Quintus
         and Martius].

AARON
  Come on, my lords, the better foot before.   192
  Straight will I bring you to the loathsome pit
  Where I espied the panther fast asleep.
QUINTUS
  My sight is very dull, whate'er it bodes.
MARTIUS
  And mine, I promise you. Were it not for shame,
  Well could I leave our sport to sleep awhile.
                          [He falls into the pit.]
QUINTUS
  What, art thou fallen? What subtle hole is this,
  Whose mouth is covered with rude-growing briers
  Upon whose leaves are drops of new-shed blood
  As fresh as morning dew distilled on flowers?
  A very fatal place it seems to me.
  Speak, brother. Hast thou hurt thee with the fall?

---

132 **outlive** live longer   135 **nice-preservèd honesty** fastidiously preserved chastity   143 **learn** teach   144 **thou suck'st** that you sucked
145 **hadst thy tyranny** gained your cruelty.   148 **a bastard** i.e., false to
my parentage, an unnatural son.   150 **find it** find it true   151–2 **The
lion . . . away** (In their unnatural cruelty, Tamora and her sons stand out
in contrast to the grateful lion of proverbial lore that refuses to attack
the person who once removed a thorn from its paw.)   153 **forlorn** abandoned (by other birds)   154 **birds** chicks   156 **Nothing . . . pitiful!** if
not as kind as the raven, do show at least some pity!   157 **it** i.e., pity

172 **Fond** Foolish   173 **present** immediate   174 **denies** forbids   183 **our
general name** i.e., women's reputation.   184 **Confusion** Destruction
187 **sure** safe, incapable of revenge.   189 **made away** murdered.
191 **spleenful** lustful.   **trull** whore, slut   192 **better foot before** best
foot forward.

MARTIUS
    Oh, brother, with the dismal'st object hurt   204
    That ever eye with sight made heart lament!   205
AARON [aside]
    Now will I fetch the King to find them here,
    That he thereby may have a likely guess
    How these were they that made away his brother.
                                                    Exit.
MARTIUS
    Why dost not comfort me and help me out
    From this unhallowed and bloodstainèd hole?
QUINTUS
    I am surprisèd with an uncouth fear.   211
    A chilling sweat o'erruns my trembling joints;
    My heart suspects more than mine eye can see.
MARTIUS
    To prove thou hast a true-divining heart,
    Aaron and thou look down into this den
    And see a fearful sight of blood and death.
QUINTUS
    Aaron is gone, and my compassionate heart
    Will not permit mine eyes once to behold
    The thing whereat it trembles by surmise.   219
    Oh, tell me who it is! For ne'er till now
    Was I a child to fear I know not what.
MARTIUS
    Lord Bassianus lies berayed in blood,   222
    All on a heap, like to a slaughtered lamb,
    In this detested, dark, blood-drinking pit.
QUINTUS
    If it be dark, how dost thou know 'tis he?
MARTIUS
    Upon his bloody finger he doth wear
    A precious ring that lightens all this hole,   227
    Which like a taper in some monument   228
    Doth shine upon the dead man's earthy cheeks   229
    And shows the ragged entrails of this pit.   230
    So pale did shine the moon on Pyramus   231
    When he by night lay bathed in maiden blood.   232
    Oh, brother, help me with thy fainting hand—
    If fear hath made thee faint, as me it hath—
    Out of this fell devouring receptacle,   235
    As hateful as Cocytus' misty mouth.   236
QUINTUS [offering to help]
    Reach me thy hand, that I may help thee out,
    Or, wanting strength to do thee so much good,   238
    I may be plucked into the swallowing womb
    Of this deep pit, poor Bassianus' grave.
    I have no strength to pluck thee to the brink.

MARTIUS
    Nor I no strength to climb without thy help.
QUINTUS
    Thy hand once more; I will not loose again
    Till thou art here aloft or I below.
    Thou canst not come to me—I come to thee.
                                    [He falls in.]

    Enter the Emperor [Saturninus, with atten-
    dants], and Aaron the Moor.

SATURNINUS
    Along with me! I'll see what hole is here,   246
    And what he is that now is leapt into it.
                            [He speaks into the pit.]
    Say, who art thou that lately didst descend
    Into this gaping hollow of the earth?
MARTIUS [from within the pit]
    The unhappy sons of old Andronicus,
    Brought hither in a most unlucky hour
    To find thy brother Bassianus dead.
SATURNINUS
    My brother dead! I know thou dost but jest.
    He and his lady both are at the lodge
    Upon the north side of this pleasant chase;   255
    'Tis not an hour since I left them there.
MARTIUS
    We know not where you left them all alive,
    But, out alas! Here have we found him dead.   258

    Enter Tamora, [Titus] Andronicus, and Lucius.

TAMORA   Where is my lord the King?
SATURNINUS
    Here, Tamora, though gripped with killing grief.
TAMORA
    Where is thy brother Bassianus?
SATURNINUS
    Now to the bottom dost thou search my wound: 262
    Poor Bassianus here lies murderèd.
TAMORA
    Then all too late I bring this fatal writ,
    The complot of this timeless tragedy,   265
    And wonder greatly that man's face can fold   266
    In pleasing smiles such murderous tyranny.
                        She giveth Saturnine a letter.
SATURNINUS (reads the letter)
    "An if we miss to meet him handsomely,   268
    Sweet huntsman—Bassianus 'tis we mean—
    Do thou so much as dig the grave for him.   270
    Thou know'st our meaning. Look for thy reward
    Among the nettles at the elder tree   272
    Which overshades the mouth of that same pit
    Where we decreed to bury Bassianus.   274
    Do this, and purchase us thy lasting friends."   275

204–5 with . . . lament! I am hurt with the most dismal sight that ever made the heart lament!   **211 surprisèd** overcome.   **uncouth** strange **219 by surmise** even to imagine.   **222 berayed in** defiled by **227 ring** (Presumably the carbuncle, which was believed to emit light.)   **228 monument** tomb   **229 earthy** clay-colored, pale **230 ragged entrails** rough interior   **231 Pyramus** the lover of Thisbe, who killed himself in the mistaken supposition that she was dead. (See *A Midsummer Night's Dream*, 1.2, 3.1, and 5.1.)   **232 maiden blood** (Although Pyramus dies first, Thisbe then plunges his sword into her bosom, so that they are bathed in the blood of both.) **235 fell** savage   **236 Cocytus' misty mouth** i.e., the mouth of hell. *Cocytus* is the river of lamentations in Hades.   **238 wanting** lacking

246 Along Come along   **255 chase** hunting ground   **258 out alas!** alas! (*Out* intensifies the interjection.)   **262 search** probe   **265 complot** plot, conspiracy.   **timeless** untimely   **266 fold** hide, enfold   **268 An if** If. **handsomely** conveniently   **270 Do . . . as** be so good as to. (Said with mock ceremoniousness.)   **272 elder tree** (An ominous sign; tradition-ally, Judas hanged himself from an elder tree after having betrayed Jesus.)   **274 decreed** decided   **275 purchase** win

Oh, Tamora, was ever heard the like?
This is the pit, and this the elder tree.
Look, sirs, if you can find the huntsman out
That should have murdered Bassianus here.   279

AARON [*finding the gold*]
My gracious lord, here is the bag of gold.

SATURNINUS [*to Titus*]
Two of thy whelps, fell curs of bloody kind,   281
Have here bereft my brother of his life.—
Sirs, drag them from the pit unto the prison!
There let them bide until we have devised
Some never-heard-of torturing pain for them.
　　　　　[*Martius and Quintus are dragged out of the pit,
　　　　　　　　　and Bassianus's body is raised.*]

TAMORA
What, are they in this pit? Oh, wondrous thing!
How easily murder is discoverèd!

TITUS [*kneeling*]
High Emperor, upon my feeble knee
I beg this boon, with tears not lightly shed,
That this fell fault of my accursèd sons—
Accursèd if the fault be proved in them—

SATURNINUS
If it be proved? You see it is apparent.   292
Who found this letter? Tamora, was it you?

TAMORA
Andronicus himself did take it up.   294

TITUS
I did, my lord, yet let me be their bail.
For, by my fathers' reverend tomb, I vow   296
They shall be ready at Your Highness' will
To answer their suspicion with their lives.   298

SATURNINUS
Thou shalt not bail them. See thou follow me.
Some bring the murdered body, some the murderers.
Let them not speak a word. The guilt is plain;
For, by my soul, were there worse end than death,
That end upon them should be executed.

TAMORA
Andronicus, I will entreat the King.
Fear not thy sons; they shall do well enough.   305

TITUS [*rising*]
Come, Lucius, come. Stay not to talk with them.   306
　　　　　[*Exeunt bearing the dead body of Bassianus;
　　　　　　　　　Martius and Quintus under guard.*]

❖

[2.4]

*Enter the Empress' sons with Lavinia, her hands
cut off, and her tongue cut out, and ravished.*

DEMETRIUS
So, now go tell, an if thy tongue can speak,
Who 'twas that cut thy tongue and ravished thee.

CHIRON
Write down thy mind, bewray thy meaning so,   3
An if thy stumps will let thee play the scribe.

DEMETRIUS
See how with signs and tokens she can scrawl.   5

CHIRON [to *Lavinia*]
Go home, call for sweet water, wash thy hands.   6

DEMETRIUS
She hath no tongue to call, nor hands to wash;
And so let's leave her to her silent walks.

CHIRON
An 'twere my cause, I should go hang myself.   9

DEMETRIUS
If thou hadst hands to help thee knit the cord.   10
　　　　　　　　Exeunt [*Chiron and Demetrius*].

　　[Wind horns.] Enter Marcus from hunting.
　　[Lavinia flees from him.]

MARCUS
Who is this? My niece, that flies away so fast?
Cousin, a word. Where is your husband?   12
　　　　　　　　　[*He see her injuries.*]
If I do dream, would all my wealth would wake me!   13
If I do wake, some planet strike me down,   14
That I may slumber an eternal sleep!
Speak, gentle niece, what stern ungentle hands   16
Hath lopped and hewed and made thy body bare
Of her two branches, those sweet ornaments
Whose circling shadows kings have sought to sleep in,   19
And might not gain so great a happiness   20
As half thy love? Why dost not speak to me?   21
Alas, a crimson river of warm blood,
Like to a bubbling fountain stirred with wind,
Doth rise and fall between thy rosèd lips,
Coming and going with thy honey breath.
But, sure, some Tereus hath deflowered thee   26
And, lest thou shouldst detect him, cut thy tongue.   27
Ah, now thou turn'st away thy face for shame!
And notwithstanding all this loss of blood,
As from a conduit with three issuing spouts,
Yet do thy cheeks look red as Titan's face   31
Blushing to be encountered with a cloud.   32
Shall I speak for thee? Shall I say 'tis so?
Oh, that I knew thy heart, and knew the beast,
That I might rail at him to ease my mind!
Sorrow concealèd, like an oven stopped,   36
Doth burn the heart to cinders where it is.
Fair Philomela, why, she but lost her tongue,

---

279 **should** was to　281 **fell** cruel, fierce.　**kind** nature　292 **apparent** evident.　294 **take** pick　296 **fathers'** forefathers'　298 **their suspicion** the suspicion they are under　305 **Fear not** Fear not for　306 **them** i.e., Martius and Quintus.
2.4. Location: The forest still.

3 **bewray** reveal　5 **scrawl** gesticulate. (But also anticipating her writing in 4.1.70-9.)　6 **sweet** perfumed　9 **cause** case　10 **knit** tie the knot in
10.2 *Wind horns* Blow hunting horns (offstage. The stage direction is from the Folio.)　12 **Cousin** Kinswoman　13 **would . . . me** I would give all my wealth to have this be only a bad dream.　14 **strike me down** exert its baleful influence on me　16 **stern** cruel　19 **shadows** i.e., protection, shelter　20–1 **And . . . thy love** and could find nowhere any happiness half so great as having your love.　26 **Tereus** i.e., the ravisher of Philomela; see the note to 2.3.43　27 **detect** expose
31 **Titan's** the sun god's　32 **Blushing . . . cloud** (The sun blushes for shame at being covered by a cloud, as if in concealment of some secret sorrow or shame; see lines 36–7.)　36 **stopped** closed too long, plugged up

And in a tedious sampler sewed her mind;   39
But, lovely niece, that mean is cut from thee.
A craftier Tereus, cousin, hast thou met,
And he hath cut those pretty fingers off
That could have better sewed than Philomel.
Oh, had the monster seen those lily hands
Tremble like aspen leaves upon a lute
And make the silken strings delight to kiss them,
He would not then have touched them for his life!   47
Or had he heard the heavenly harmony
Which that sweet tongue hath made,
He would have dropped his knife and fell asleep,
As Cerberus at the Thracian poet's feet.   51
Come, let us go and make thy father blind,
For such a sight will blind a father's eye.
One hour's storm will drown the fragrant meads;   54
What will whole months of tears thy father's eyes?
Do not draw back, for we will mourn with thee.
Oh, could our mourning ease thy misery!   *Exeunt.*

❖

[3.1]

*Enter the judges and senators [and tribunes]
with Titus' two sons bound, passing over the
stage to the place of execution, and Titus going
before, pleading.*

TITUS
Hear me, grave fathers! Noble tribunes, stay!
For pity of mine age, whose youth was spent
In dangerous wars whilst you securely slept;
For all my blood in Rome's great quarrel shed,   4
For all the frosty nights that I have watched,   5
And for these bitter tears which now you see
Filling the agèd wrinkles in my cheeks,
Be pitiful to my condemnèd sons,
Whose souls is not corrupted as 'tis thought.
For two-and-twenty sons I never wept,   10
Because they died in honor's lofty bed.
     [*Titus*] *Andronicus lieth down and the judges
             pass by him.* [*Titus weeps.*]
For these, tribunes, in the dust I write
My heart's deep languor and my soul's sad tears.
Let my tears stanch the earth's dry appetite;   14
My sons' sweet blood will make it shame and blush.   15
                 [*Exeunt all but Titus.*]
O earth, I will befriend thee more with rain
That shall distill from these two ancient urns   17

Than youthful April shall with all his showers.
In summer's drought I'll drop upon thee still;   19
In winter with warm tears I'll melt the snow,
And keep eternal springtime on thy face,
So thou refuse to drink my dear sons' blood.   22

     Enter Lucius, with his weapon drawn.

O reverend tribunes! O gentle, agèd men!
Unbind my sons, reverse the doom of death,   24
And let me say, that never wept before,
My tears are now prevailing orators.
LUCIUS
O noble father, you lament in vain.
The tribunes hear you not. No man is by,
And you recount your sorrows to a stone.
TITUS
Ah, Lucius, for thy brothers let me plead.—
Grave tribunes, once more I entreat of you—
LUCIUS
My gracious lord, no tribune hears you speak.
TITUS
Why, 'tis no matter, man. If they did hear,
They would not mark me; if they did mark,
They would not pity me; yet plead I must,
And bootless unto them.   36
Therefore I tell my sorrows to the stones,
Who, though they cannot answer my distress,
Yet in some sort they are better than the tribunes,
For that they will not intercept my tale.   40
When I do weep, they humbly at my feet
Receive my tears and seem to weep with me;
And, were they but attirèd in grave weeds,   43
Rome could afford no tribunes like to these.   44
A stone is soft as wax, tribunes more hard than stones;
A stone is silent and offendeth not,
And tribunes with their tongues doom men to death.
                       [*He rises.*]
But wherefore stand'st thou with thy weapon drawn?
LUCIUS
To rescue my two brothers from their death,
For which attempt the judges have pronounced
My everlasting doom of banishment.
TITUS
O happy man! They have befriended thee.
Why, foolish Lucius, dost thou not perceive
That Rome is but a wilderness of tigers?
Tigers must prey, and Rome affords no prey
But me and mine. How happy art thou then
From these devourers to be banishèd!
But who comes with our brother Marcus here?

     Enter Marcus with Lavinia.

MARCUS
Titus, prepare thy agèd eyes to weep,
Or if not so, thy noble heart to break.
I bring consuming sorrow to thine age.

---

39 tedious sampler laboriously contrived embroidered cloth or tapestry. (See the note to 2.3.43.)   **sewed her mind** put her story down in embroidery   **47 for his life** to save his life.   **51 Cerberus . . . feet** (According to legend, Orpheus's sweet singing charmed even Cerberus, the three-headed dog guarding the entrance to Hades.) **54 meads** meadows
3.1. Location: Rome. A street.
4 my i.e., my and my sons'   **5 watched** stayed awake   **10 two-and-twenty** (At 1.1.79 and 195, we are told that twenty-one of Titus's twenty-five sons died fighting. Mutius is the twenty-second to die, though scarcely "in honor's lofty bed," as Titus sees it.)   **14 stanch** satisfy   **15 shame** be ashamed   **17 urns** i.e., tear-filled eyes

19 still continually   **22 So** on condition that   **24 doom** sentence
36 bootless in vain   **40 For that** in that.   **intercept** interrupt
43 grave weeds sober garments   **44 afford** provide

TITUS
    Will it consume me? Let me see it, then.
MARCUS
    This was thy daughter.
TITUS   Why, Marcus, so she is.
LUCIUS   Ay me, this object kills me!   64
TITUS
    Fainthearted boy, arise, and look upon her.   65
    Speak, Lavinia, what accursèd hand
    Hath made thee handless in thy father's sight?
    What fool hath added water to the sea,
    Or brought a faggot to bright-burning Troy?
    My grief was at the height before thou cam'st,
    And now, like Nilus, it disdaineth bounds.   71
    Give me a sword, I'll chop off my hands too,
    For they have fought for Rome, and all in vain;
    And they have nursed this woe in feeding life;   74
    In bootless prayer have they been held up,
    And they have served me to effectless use.   76
    Now all the service I require of them
    Is that the one will help to cut the other.
    'Tis well, Lavinia, that thou hast no hands,
    For hands to do Rome service is but vain.
LUCIUS
    Speak, gentle sister, who hath martyred thee?   81
MARCUS
    Oh, that delightful engine of her thoughts,   82
    That blabbed them with such pleasing eloquence,   83
    Is torn from forth that pretty hollow cage
    Where, like a sweet melodious bird, it sung
    Sweet varied notes, enchanting every ear.
LUCIUS
    Oh, say thou for her: who hath done this deed?
MARCUS
    Oh, thus I found her, straying in the park,
    Seeking to hide herself, as doth the deer
    That hath received some unrecuring wound.   90
TITUS
    It was my dear, and he that wounded her   91
    Hath hurt me more than had he killed me dead;
    For now I stand as one upon a rock
    Environed with a wilderness of sea,
    Who marks the waxing tide grow wave by wave,
    Expecting ever when some envious surge   96
    Will in his brinish bowels swallow him.   97
    This way to death my wretched sons are gone;
    Here stands my other son, a banished man,
    And here my brother, weeping at my woes;
    But that which gives my soul the greatest spurn   101
    Is dear Lavinia, dearer than my soul.

    Had I but seen thy picture in this plight,
    It would have madded me; what shall I do
    Now I behold thy lively body so?   105
    Thou hast no hands to wipe away thy tears,
    Nor tongue to tell me who hath martyred thee.
    Thy husband he is dead, and for his death   108
    Thy brothers are condemned, and dead by this.   109
    Look, Marcus! Ah, son Lucius, look on her!
    When I did name her brothers, then fresh tears
    Stood on her cheeks, as doth the honey-dew   112
    Upon a gathered lily almost withered.
MARCUS
    Perchance she weeps because they killed her husband;
    Perchance because she knows them innocent.
TITUS
    If they did kill thy husband, then be joyful,
    Because the law hath ta'en revenge on them.
    No, no, they would not do so foul a deed;
    Witness the sorrow that their sister makes.
    Gentle Lavinia, let me kiss thy lips;
    Or make some sign how I may do thee ease.
    Shall thy good uncle, and thy brother Lucius,
    And thou, and I, sit round about some fountain,   123
    Looking all downwards to behold our cheeks
    How they are stained, like meadows yet not dry
    With miry slime left on them by a flood?
    And in the fountain shall we gaze so long
    Till the fresh taste be taken from that clearness,
    And made a brine pit with our bitter tears?
    Or shall we cut away our hands, like thine?
    Or shall we bite our tongues, and in dumb shows   131
    Pass the remainder of our hateful days?
    What shall we do? Let us that have our tongues
    Plot some device of further misery,   134
    To make us wondered at in time to come.
LUCIUS
    Sweet father, cease your tears, for at your grief
    See how my wretched sister sobs and weeps.
MARCUS
    Patience, dear niece. Good Titus, dry thine eyes.
TITUS
    Ah, Marcus, Marcus! Brother, well I wot   139
    Thy napkin cannot drink a tear of mine,   140
    For thou, poor man, hast drowned it with thine own.
LUCIUS
    Ah, my Lavinia, I will wipe thy cheeks.
TITUS
    Mark, Marcus, mark! I understand her signs.
    Had she a tongue to speak, now would she say
    That to her brother which I said to thee.
    His napkin, with his true tears all bewet,

---

64 object object of sight   **65 arise** (Evidently, Lucius has collapsed or fallen to his knees in grief.)   **71 Nilus** the Nile   **74 they . . . life** i.e., in sustaining Rome, my hands have merely prolonged the misery of the Andronici   **76 effectless** fruitless   **81 martyred** mutilated **82 engine** instrument   **83 blabbed** uttered   **90 unrecuring** incurable **91 dear** (With a familiar pun on *deer*, line 89.)   **96 Expecting ever when** continually awaiting the moment when.   **envious** spiteful **97 his** its   **101 spurn** stroke, kick

105 lively living, actual (as contrasted with her picture)   **108 husband he** husband   **109 by this** by this time.   **112 honey-dew** sweet dew-like substance, or the dew itself   **123 fountain** spring   **131 bite** bite out.   **dumb shows** mute pageants   **134 device** (1) strategy (2) dramatic representation   **139 wot** know   **140 napkin** handkerchief

Can do no service on her sorrowful cheeks.
Oh, what a sympathy of woe is this,
As far from help as Limbo is from bliss!   149

Enter Aaron the Moor alone.

AARON
Titus Andronicus, my lord the Emperor
Sends thee this word: that if thou love thy sons,
Let Marcus, Lucius, or thyself, old Titus,
Or any one of you, chop off your hand
And send it to the King. He for the same
Will send thee hither both thy sons alive,   155
And that shall be the ransom for their fault.   156

TITUS
O gracious Emperor! O gentle Aaron!
Did ever raven sing so like a lark,
That gives sweet tidings of the sun's uprise?
With all my heart I'll send the Emperor my hand.
Good Aaron, wilt thou help to chop it off?

LUCIUS
Stay, father, for that noble hand of thine,
That hath thrown down so many enemies,
Shall not be sent. My hand will serve the turn.
My youth can better spare my blood than you,
And therefore mine shall save my brothers' lives.

MARCUS
Which of your hands hath not defended Rome
And reared aloft the bloody battle-ax,
Writing destruction on the enemy's castle?
Oh, none of both but are of high desert.
My hand hath been but idle; let it serve
To ransom my two nephews from their death.
Then have I kept it to a worthy end.

AARON
Nay, come, agree whose hand shall go along,
For fear they die before their pardon come.

MARCUS
My hand shall go.

LUCIUS   By heaven, it shall not go!

TITUS
Sirs, strive no more. Such withered herbs as these
Are meet for plucking up, and therefore mine.   178

LUCIUS
Sweet father, if I shall be thought thy son,
Let me redeem my brothers both from death.

MARCUS
And for our father's sake and mother's care,
Now let me show a brother's love to thee.

TITUS
Agree between you. I will spare my hand.   183

LUCIUS   Then I'll go fetch an ax.
MARCUS   But I will use the ax.
                                      Exeunt [Lucius and Marcus].
TITUS
Come hither, Aaron. I'll deceive them both.
Lend me thy hand, and I will give thee mine.   187
AARON [*aside*]
If that be called deceit, I will be honest,
And never whilst I live deceive men so;
But I'll deceive you in another sort,
And that you'll say, ere half an hour pass.
                                      He cuts off Titus' hand.

Enter Lucius and Marcus again.

TITUS
Now stay your strife. What shall be is dispatched.
Good Aaron, give His Majesty my hand.
Tell him it was a hand that warded him   194
From thousand dangers. Bid him bury it.
More hath it merited; that let it have.   196
As for my sons, say I account of them
As jewels purchased at an easy price,
And yet dear too, because I bought mine own.   199
AARON
I go, Andronicus, and for thy hand
Look by and by to have thy sons with thee.   201
[*Aside*] Their heads, I mean. Oh, how this villainy
Doth fat me with the very thoughts of it!   203
Let fools do good, and fair men call for grace;   204
Aaron will have his soul black like his face.   *Exit.*
TITUS [*kneeling*]
Oh, here I lift this one hand up to heaven
And bow this feeble ruin to the earth.
If any power pities wretched tears,
To that I call! [*To Lavinia, who kneels*] What, wouldst
    thou kneel with me?
Do, then, dear heart, for heaven shall hear our prayers,
Or with our sighs we'll breathe the welkin dim   211
And stain the sun with fog, as sometime clouds
When they do hug him in their melting bosoms.   213
MARCUS
O brother, speak with possibility,   214
And do not break into these deep extremes.
TITUS
Is not my sorrow deep, having no bottom?
Then be my passions bottomless with them.   217
MARCUS
But yet let reason govern thy lament.
TITUS
If there were reason for these miseries,   219
Then into limits could I bind my woes.

---

149 Limbo region bordering hell, where were confined the souls of those barred from heaven through no fault of their own, such as good persons who lived before the Christian era or who died unbaptized **155 Will . . . alive** (Aaron's secret double meaning may be, "will send to you here, you being alive, both your sons.") **156 that** (Secretly, *that* may refer to the sons being sent here—dead.) **178 meet** fit **183 spare** (In a virtuous deception, Titus uses a double meaning for *spare;* ostensibly he means "save from being cut off," but secretly he means "do without.")

187 Lend . . . mine (Another pun, on *hand:* "Give me your assistance, and I'll give you my hand.") **194 warded** guarded   **196 that** i.e., burial   **199 dear** (1) expensive (2) precious. **because . . . own** because I am buying back what was mine to begin with, my own dear sons.   **201 Look** expect   **203 fat** fatten, feed   **204 fair** (1) fair-complexioned (2) fair-minded.   **grace** virtue   **211 Or . . . dim** or make cloudy the sky with our sighs   **213 melting** i.e., dissolving into teardroplike rain   **214 with** within the bounds of   **217 Then . . . them** Then let my passionate outbursts be ceaseless (*bottomless*), like my sorrows.   **219 reason** explanation. (Playing on *reason,* rational behavior, in line 218.)

When heaven doth weep, doth not the earth o'erflow? 221
If the winds rage, doth not the sea wax mad,
Threat'ning the welkin with his big-swoll'n face?
And wilt thou have a reason for this coil? 224
I am the sea. Hark how her sighs doth blow! 225
She is the weeping welkin, I the earth.
Then must my sea be movèd with her sighs,
Then must my earth with her continual tears
Become a deluge overflowed and drowned,
Forwhy my bowels cannot hide her woes, 230
But like a drunkard must I vomit them. 231
Then give me leave, for losers will have leave
To ease their stomachs with their bitter tongues. 233

Enter a Messenger, with two heads and a hand.

MESSENGER
Worthy Andronicus, ill art thou repaid
For that good hand thou sent'st the Emperor.
Here are the heads of thy two noble sons,
And here's thy hand in scorn to thee sent back—
Thy grief their sports, thy resolution mocked, 238
That woe is me to think upon thy woes 239
More than remembrance of my father's death.
    [He sets down the heads and hand, and exit.]
MARCUS
Now let hot Etna cool in Sicily, 241
And be my heart an ever-burning hell!
These miseries are more than may be borne.
To weep with them that weep doth ease somedeal, 244
But sorrow flouted at is double death. 245
LUCIUS
Ah, that this sight should make so deep a wound,
And yet detested life not shrink thereat! 247
That ever death should let life bear his name, 248
Where life hath no more interest but to breathe! 249
    [Lavinia kisses Titus.]
MARCUS
Alas, poor heart, that kiss is comfortless
As frozen water to a starvèd snake. 251
TITUS
When will this fearful slumber have an end? 252
MARCUS
Now, farewell, flatt'ry! Die, Andronicus. 253
Thou dost not slumber. See thy two sons' heads,

Thy warlike hand, thy mangled daughter here,
Thy other banished son with this dear sight 256
Struck pale and bloodless, and thy brother, I,
Even like a stony image, cold and numb.
Ah, now no more will I control thy griefs! 259
Rend off thy silver hair, thy other hand
Gnawing with thy teeth, and be this dismal sight
The closing up of our most wretched eyes. 262
Now is a time to storm. Why art thou still?
TITUS   Ha, ha, ha!
MARCUS
Why dost thou laugh? It fits not with this hour.
TITUS
Why, I have not another tear to shed.
Besides, this sorrow is an enemy,
And would usurp upon my wat'ry eyes
And make them blind with tributary tears. 269
Then which way shall I find Revenge's cave?
For these two heads do seem to speak to me
And threat me I shall never come to bliss
Till all these mischiefs be returned again 273
Even in their throats that hath committed them.
Come, let me see what task I have to do.
You heavy people, circle me about, 276
That I may turn me to each one of you
And swear unto my soul to right your wrongs.
    [They form a circle about Titus,
    and he pledges each.]
The vow is made. Come, brother, take a head,
And in this hand the other will I bear.
    [They pick up the two heads, and give the hand
    to Lavinia.]
And, Lavinia, thou shalt be employed:
Bear thou my hand, sweet wench, between thy teeth.
As for thee, boy, *[to Lucius]* go get thee from my sight;
Thou art an exile, and thou must not stay.
Hie to the Goths and raise an army there.
And if ye love me, as I think you do,
Let's kiss and part, for we have much to do.
    [They kiss.] Exeunt [Titus, Marcus, and Lavinia].
LUCIUS
Farewell, Andronicus, my noble father,
The woefull'st man that ever lived in Rome.
Farewell, proud Rome, till Lucius come again!
He loves his pledges dearer than his life. 291
Farewell, Lavinia, my noble sister.
Oh, would thou wert as thou tofore hast been! 293
But now nor Lucius nor Lavinia lives 294
But in oblivion and hateful griefs.
If Lucius live, he will requite your wrongs
And make proud Saturnine and his empress

---

221 weep i.e., rain (as though in tears).   **o'erflow** become flooded.
224 coil noise, fuss.   **225 her** i.e., Lavinia's, personifying the winds'
rage   **230 Forwhy** because.   **bowels** (Supposed to be the seat of
compassion; also, the bowels of the earth.)   **231 vomit** (The double
image is of vomiting and of volcanic eruption. Grief is like a conflict
of the four elements of fire, air, water, and earth—anger, sighs, tears,
and bowels.)   **233 ease their stomachs** relieve their resentments.
(With a play on *vomit*.)   **238 sports** entertainment   **239 That . . . me**
so that I am woeful   **241 Etna** volcanic mountain on the island of
Sicily (which will, compared to Marcus's burning heart, seem cool.
Compare with the note to line 231.)   **244 doth ease somedeal** eases
the heart somewhat   **245 But . . . death** i.e., but to mock and deny
sorrow is to experience it again and again.   **247 shrink** wither away
248 bear his name i.e., still be called life   **249 Where . . . breathe** i.e.,
where virtually nothing remains of life except the drawing of breath.
251 starvèd benumbed with cold   **252 fearful slumber** dreadful
nightmare   **253 flatt'ry** comforting deception.

256 dear grievous   **259 control** try to restrain   **262 closing up** closing
in death   **269 tributary tears** tears paid as tribute (to sorrow, the
usurping enemy).   **273 mischiefs** evils, injuries   **276 heavy** sorrowing
291 He . . . life His vows are more important to him than his life; or,
he loves his family, left behind in Rome as hostages to fortune, more
than his life.   **293 tofore** heretofore, formerly   **294 nor Lucius** neither Lucius

Beg at the gates, like Tarquin and his queen.   298
Now will I to the Goths and raise a power   299
To be revenged on Rome and Saturnine.   *Exit Lucius.*

❧

[3.2]

A banquet [set out]. Enter [Titus] Andronicus,
Marcus, Lavinia, and the boy [young Lucius].

TITUS
So, so. Now sit, and look you eat no more
Than will preserve just so much strength in us
As will revenge these bitter woes of ours.
Marcus, unknit that sorrow-wreathen knot.   4
Thy niece and I, poor creatures, want our hands   5
And cannot passionate our tenfold grief   6
With folded arms. This poor right hand of mine
Is left to tyrannize upon my breast,   8
Who, when my heart, all mad with misery,   9
Beats in this hollow prison of my flesh,
Then thus I thump it down.   [*He beats his breast.*]
[*To Lavinia*] Thou map of woe, that thus dost talk in
    signs,   12
When thy poor heart beats with outrageous beating,
Thou canst not strike it thus to make it still.
Wound it with sighing, girl, kill it with groans;   15
Or get some little knife between thy teeth
And just against thy heart make thou a hole,
That all the tears that thy poor eyes let fall
May run into that sink and, soaking in,   19
Drown the lamenting fool in sea-salt tears.   20
MARCUS
Fie, brother, fie! Teach her not thus to lay
Such violent hands upon her tender life.
TITUS
How now, has sorrow made thee dote already?   23
Why, Marcus, no man should be mad but I.
What violent hands can she lay on her life?
Ah, wherefore dost thou urge the name of hands,
To bid Aeneas tell the tale twice o'er   27
How Troy was burnt and he made miserable?
Oh, handle not the theme, to talk of hands,
Lest we remember still that we have none.   30
Fie, fie, how franticly I square my talk,   31
As if we should forget we had no hands
If Marcus did not name the word of hands!
Come, let's fall to; and, gentle girl, eat this.
Here is no drink! Hark, Marcus, what she says;

I can interpret all her martyred signs.
She says she drinks no other drink but tears,
Brewed with her sorrow, mashed upon her cheeks.   38
Speechless complainer, I will learn thy thought;
In thy dumb action will I be as perfect   40
As begging hermits in their holy prayers.
Thou shalt not sigh, nor hold thy stumps to heaven,
Nor wink, nor nod, nor kneel, nor make a sign,
But I of these will wrest an alphabet
And by still practice learn to know thy meaning.   45
BOY [*weeping*]
Good grandsire, leave these bitter deep laments!
Make my aunt merry with some pleasing tale.
MARCUS
Alas, the tender boy, in passion moved,   48
Doth weep to see his grandsire's heaviness.
TITUS
Peace, tender sapling! Thou art made of tears,
And tears will quickly melt thy life away.
                    Marcus strikes the dish with a knife.
What dost thou strike at, Marcus, with thy knife?
MARCUS
At that that I have killed, my lord: a fly.
TITUS
Out on thee, murderer! Thou kill'st my heart.
Mine eyes are cloyed with view of tyranny.
A deed of death done on the innocent
Becomes not Titus' brother. Get thee gone!
I see thou art not for my company.
MARCUS
Alas, my lord, I have but killed a fly.
TITUS
"But"? How if that fly had a father and mother?
How would he hang his slender gilded wings   61
And buzz lamenting doings in the air!   62
Poor harmless fly,
That, with his pretty buzzing melody,
Came here to make us merry! And thou hast killed
    him.
MARCUS
Pardon me, sir. It was a black ill-favored fly,   66
Like to the Empress' Moor. Therefore I killed him.
TITUS   Oh, oh, oh!
Then pardon me for reprehending thee,
For thou hast done a charitable deed.
Give me thy knife. I will insult on him,   71
Flattering myself as if it were the Moor   72
Come hither purposely to poison me.—
There's for thyself, and that's for Tamora!
                    [*He takes the knife and strikes.*]
Ah, sirrah!   75
Yet I think we are not brought so low   76

298 Tarquin Tarquinius Superbus, seventh king of Rome, who, because his son had raped a Roman lady, Lucretia, was banished and his kingdom overthrown; a republic was then established   **299 power** army **3.2. Location: Rome. Titus's house.**
0.1 banquet (A table with chairs and dishes is brought on.)   **4 sorrow-wreathen knot** arms folded in a conventional expression of grief. **5 want** lack   **6 passionate** express passionately   **8 tyrannize** i.e., by beating   **9 Who** which   **12 map** picture   **15 Wound it with sighing** (Each sigh was believed to cost the heart a drop of blood.)   **19 sink** receptacle   **20 fool** (Here a term of pity or endearment.)   **23 dote** be deranged   **27 Aeneas** (Aeneas tells of the fall of Troy in Book 2 of Virgil's *Aeneid*.)   **30 still** continually   **31 square** shape, regulate

38 mashed mixed with hot water in a mash, as for brewing   **40 action** gesture.   **perfect** thoroughly acquainted   **45 still** continual   **48 passion** sorrow   **61 he** i.e., the father   **62 And . . . air** i.e., and tell sad stories, expressing his sorrow by buzzing about.   **66 ill-favored** ugly **71 insult on** exult over   **72 Flattering . . . if** deluding myself into believing   **75 sirrah** (Ordinary term of address to inferiors.)   **76 Yet . . . not** I do not think we are yet

But that between us we can kill a fly
That comes in likeness of a coal black Moor.

MARCUS
Alas, poor man! Grief has so wrought on him
He takes false shadows for true substances.

TITUS
Come, take away. Lavinia, go with me.   81
I'll to thy closet and go read with thee   82
Sad stories chancèd in the times of old.   83
Come, boy, and go with me. Thy sight is young,
And thou shalt read when mine begin to dazzle.   85

Exeunt.

[4.1]

*Enter Lucius's son, and Lavinia running after
him, and the boy flies from her, with his books
under his arm. Enter Titus and Marcus.*

BOY
Help, grandsire, help! My aunt Lavinia
Follows me everywhere, I know not why.
Good uncle Marcus, see how swift she comes.
Alas, sweet aunt, I know not what you mean.
                                    [*He drops his books.*]

MARCUS
Stand by me, Lucius. Do not fear thine aunt.

TITUS
She loves thee, boy, too well to do thee harm.

BOY
Ay, when my father was in Rome she did.   7

MARCUS
What means my niece Lavinia by these signs?

TITUS
Fear her not, Lucius. Somewhat doth she mean.   9

MARCUS
See, Lucius, see how much she makes of thee;
Somewhither would she have thee go with her.
Ah, boy, Cornelia never with more care   12
Read to her sons than she hath read to thee   13
Sweet poetry and Tully's *Orator*.   14
Canst thou not guess wherefore she plies thee thus?   15

BOY
My lord, I know not, I, nor can I guess,
Unless some fit or frenzy do possess her;
For I have heard my grandsire say full oft,
Extremity of griefs would make men mad,
And I have read that Hecuba of Troy   20
Ran mad for sorrow. That made me to fear,
Although, my lord, I know my noble aunt

Loves me as dear as e'er my mother did,
And would not but in fury fright my youth—   24
Which made me down to throw my books and fly,
Causeless, perhaps. But pardon me, sweet aunt,
And, madam, if my uncle Marcus go,   27
I will most willingly attend Your Ladyship.

MARCUS   Lucius, I will.   29
        [*Lavinia turns over with her stumps the book
                    that young Lucius has let fall.*]

TITUS
How now, Lavinia? Marcus, what means this?
Some book there is that she desires to see.
Which is it, girl, of these?—Open them, boy.
[*To Lavinia*] But thou art deeper read and better skilled;
Come and take choice of all my library,
And so beguile thy sorrow till the heavens
Reveal the damned contriver of this deed.—
Why lifts she up her arms in sequence thus?   37

MARCUS
I think she means that there were more than one
Confederate in the fact. Ay, more there was;   39
Or else to heaven she heaves them for revenge.

TITUS
Lucius, what book is that she tosseth so?   41

BOY
Grandsire, 'tis Ovid's *Metamorphoses*.
My mother gave it me.

MARCUS   For love of her that's gone,
Perhaps, she culled it from among the rest.

TITUS
Soft, so busily she turns the leaves!   (*Help her.*)
What would she find? Lavinia, shall I read?
This is the tragic tale of Philomel,   48
And treats of Tereus' treason and his rape;   49
And rape, I fear, was root of thy annoy.   50

MARCUS
See, brother, see! Note how she quotes the leaves.   51

TITUS
Lavinia, wert thou thus surprised, sweet girl,
Ravished and wronged as Philomela was,
Forced in the ruthless, vast, and gloomy woods?   54
See, see!
Ay, such a place there is, where we did hunt—
Oh, had we never, never hunted there!—
Patterned by that the poet here describes,
By nature made for murders and for rapes.

MARCUS
Oh, why should nature build so foul a den,
Unless the gods delight in tragedies?

TITUS
Give signs, sweet girl—for here are none but friends—
What Roman lord it was durst do the deed.
Or slunk not Saturnine, as Tarquin erst,   64

---

81 **take away** clear the table. (The "banquet" and furniture are
removed from the stage as the scene ends.)   82 **closet** private room
83 **chancèd** that occurred   85 **dazzle** become dazzled, unable to see.
4.1. Location: Rome. Titus's garden.
7 **Ay . . . did** i.e., Yes, she loved me back in those happy days when my
father was still here, before our troubles began.   9 **Somewhat** Something   12 **Cornelia** the mother of the Gracchi brothers, the two most
famous tribunes in Roman history. (Her success in educating her sons
was highly regarded.)   13 **Read** gave instruction   14 **Tully's *Orator*** a
treatise on rhetoric by Cicero, either *De Oratore* or *ad M. Brutum Orator*.
15 **plies** importunes   20 **Hecuba** (See 1.1.136 and note.)

24 **but in fury** except in madness   27 **go** i.e., come with us. (See line
11.) The boy doesn't want to be alone with his mad aunt.   29 **Lucius**
young Lucius, the boy   37 **in sequence** one after the other   39 **fact**
deed, crime.   41 **tosseth** turns the pages of   48–9 **Philomel, Tereus**
(Compare with the note for 2.3.43.)   50 **annoy** injury.   51 **quotes**
examines   54 **vast** desolate   64 **Or . . . erst** Or was it Saturnine who
slunk, like Tarquin of old. (See 3.1.298 and note.)

That left the camp to sin in Lucrece' bed?

MARCUS
Sit down, sweet niece. Brother, sit down by me.
                                        [*They sit.*]
Apollo, Pallas, Jove, or Mercury   67
Inspire me, that I may this treason find!
My lord, look here. Look here, Lavinia.
         He writes his name with his staff, and guides it
                          with feet and mouth.
This sandy plot is plain; guide, if thou canst,   70
This after me. I have writ my name
Without the help of any hand at all.
Cursed be that heart that forced us to this shift!   73
Write thou, good niece, and here display at last
What God will have discovered for revenge.   75
Heaven guide thy pen to print thy sorrows plain,
That we may know the traitors and the truth!
         She takes the staff in her mouth, and guides
                  it with her stumps, and writes.
Oh, do ye read, my lord, what she hath writ?

TITUS   "*Stuprum.* Chiron. Demetrius."   79

MARCUS
What, what! The lustful sons of Tamora
Performers of this heinous, bloody deed?

TITUS
Magni Dominator poli,   82
Tam lentus audis scelera, tam lentus vides?   83

MARCUS
Oh, calm thee, gentle lord, although I know
There is enough written upon this earth
To stir a mutiny in the mildest thoughts
And arm the minds of infants to exclaims.   87
My lord, kneel down with me; Lavinia, kneel;
And kneel, sweet boy, the Roman Hector's hope.   89
                                        [*All kneel.*]
And swear with me—as, with the woeful fere   90
And father of that chaste dishonored dame,   91
Lord Junius Brutus sware for Lucrece' rape—   92
That we will prosecute by good advice   93
Mortal revenge upon these traitorous Goths,
And see their blood or die with this reproach.
                                        [*They rise.*]

TITUS
'Tis sure enough, an you knew how.   96
But if you hunt these bear whelps, then beware:
The dam will wake an if she wind ye once.   98
She's with the lion deeply still in league,   99

And lulls him whilst she playeth on her back,   100
And when he sleeps will she do what she list.   101
You are a young huntsman, Marcus. Let alone,   102
And come, I will go get a leaf of brass,   103
And with a gad of steel will write these words,   104
And lay it by. The angry northern wind   105
Will blow these sands like Sibyl's leaves abroad,   106
And where's our lesson then? Boy, what say you?   107

BOY
I say, my lord, that if I were a man,
Their mother's bedchamber should not be safe   109
For these base bondmen to the yoke of Rome.   110

MARCUS
Ay, that's my boy! Thy father hath full oft
For his ungrateful country done the like.   112

BOY
And, uncle, so will I, an if I live.

TITUS
Come, go with me into mine armory.
Lucius, I'll fit thee, and withal my boy   115
Shall carry from me to the Empress' sons
Presents that I intend to send them both.
Come, come. Thou'lt do my message, wilt thou not?

BOY
Ay, with my dagger in their bosoms, grandsire.

TITUS
No, boy, not so. I'll teach thee another course.
Lavinia, come. Marcus, look to my house.
Lucius and I'll go brave it at the court.   122
Ay, marry, will we, sir, and we'll be waited on.   123
         Exeunt [*Titus, Lavinia, and young Lucius*].

MARCUS
O heavens, can you hear a good man groan
And not relent, or not compassion him?   125
Marcus, attend him in his ecstasy,   126
That hath more scars of sorrow in his heart   127
Than foemen's marks upon his battered shield,
But yet so just that he will not revenge.
Revenge the heavens for old Andronicus!   *Exit.* 130

❖

67 Pallas Pallas Athene, Minerva   **70 plain** level, smooth   **73 shift** expedient.   **75 will have discovered** wishes to have uncovered   **79 *Stuprum* Rape.   82–3 *Magni* . . . *vides?*** Ruler of the mighty heavens, are you so slow to hear crimes, so slow to see? (Derived from Seneca, *Hippolytus*, 671–2, and the *Moral Epistles*, 107.)   **87 exclaims** exclamations, outcries.   **89 the Roman . . . hope** i.e., you who are the hope of your father, just as Astyanax was the hope of the great Hector of Troy.   **90–2 as . . . rape** just as both Lucius Junius Brutus, the woeful husband (*fere*, spouse), and the father of that chaste dishonored lady, Lucrece, swore to avenge her rape. (See 2.1.108 and note.)   **93 prosecute . . . advice** pursue by well-considered means   **96 an if** if   **98 dam** mother. **wind** scent   **99 the lion** the royal beast, i.e., Saturninus.   **still** always

100 playeth on her back (1) sports playfully like a wild animal (2) provides sex to Saturninus   **101 list** choose, please. (With a suggestion of sexual infidelity.)   **102–5 You . . . by** i.e., You are inexperienced in dealing with such cunning enemies, Marcus. Leave off your useless oaths vowing frontal attack, and I will devise something that will give permanence to our outcries, like words etched on a sheet of brass with a steel stylus, by means of which I will store our vengeance up (*lay it by*) until the time is ripe.   **105–7 The angry . . . then?** Your oaths are like sands too easily scattered (like the prophecies of the Cumaean Sibyl, posted at the windswept entrance to her cave), and where will we be then with what we intend?
109–10 Their . . . Rome no place of hiding would be spared in my seeking to destroy these slaves who, rightly considered (i.e., setting aside their having been freed by Saturninus), are captives of Rome.   **112 done the like** i.e., fought against tyranny   **115 fit thee** provide you with arms.   **withal** in addition   **122 brave it** put on a good show, cut a bold figure   **123 marry** (A mild interjection, equivalent to "Indeed!"; originally an oath, "by the Virgin Mary.")   **be waited on** i.e., demand attention.   **125 compassion** have compassion for   **126 ecstasy** madness   **127 That** he who   **130 Revenge the heavens** May the heavens take revenge (since Andronicus will not)

[4.2]

Enter Aaron, Chiron, and Demetrius, at one door, and at the other door young Lucius and another, with a bundle of weapons and verses writ upon them.

CHIRON

Demetrius, here's the son of Lucius.
He hath some message to deliver us.

AARON

Ay, some mad message from his mad grandfather.

BOY

My lords, with all the humbleness I may,
I greet your honors from Andronicus—
[*Aside*] And pray the Roman gods confound you both!   6

DEMETRIUS

Gramercy, lovely Lucius. What's the news?   7

BOY [*aside*]

That you are both deciphered, that's the news,   8
For villains marked with rape.—May it please you,
My grandsire, well advised, hath sent by me   10
The goodliest weapons of his armory
To gratify your honorable youth,   12
The hope of Rome; for so he bid me say.
And so I do, and with his gifts present
Your Lordships, that, whenever you have need,
You may be armèd and appointed well.   16
        [*His attendant presents the bundle.*]
And so I leave you both—[*aside*] like bloody villains.
                    Exit [*with attendant*].

DEMETRIUS

What's here? A scroll, and written round about?   19
Let's see:
[*He reads.*] "*Integer vitae, scelerisque purus,*   20
        Non eget Mauri iaculis, nec arcu."   21

CHIRON

Oh, 'tis a verse in Horace; I know it well.
I read it in the grammar long ago.   23

AARON

Ay, just; a verse in Horace; right, you have it.   24
[*Aside*] Now, what a thing it is to be an ass!
Here's no sound jest! The old man hath found their
    guilt,   26
And sends them weapons wrapped about with lines
That wound, beyond their feeling, to the quick.   28
But were our witty empress well afoot,   29
She would applaud Andronicus' conceit.   30

4.2. Location: Rome. The Emperor's palace.
0.3 *another* (Presumably an attendant of Lucius, bearing the weapons and verses; see line 16.1.)   6 confound destroy   7 Gramercy Many thanks   8 deciphered detected   10 well advised having considered carefully   12 gratify grace, please   16 appointed equipped   19 round about all around.   20–1 *Integer . . . arcu* (The opening lines of perhaps the best known of the Odes of Horace, 1, 22: "He who is spotless in life and free of crime needs not the Moorish javelin or bow.")   23 grammar i.e., Latin grammar book. (William Lilly's grammar book, containing this passage, was widely used in Elizabethan England.)   24 just precisely   26 Here's no sound jest! (Said ironically to mean its opposite: Here's a splendid joke indeed!)   28 beyond . . . quick i.e., far beyond the capacity of Demetrius and Chiron to be sensitive to the injury, yet to the very heart of the matter.   29 witty clever.   afoot up and about, i.e., not in childbed (as we soon learn she is)   30 conceit design.

But let her rest in her unrest awhile.—   31
And now, young lords, was 't not a happy star   32
Led us to Rome, strangers, and, more than so,
Captives, to be advancèd to this height?
It did me good, before the palace gate
To brave the tribune in his brother's hearing.   36

DEMETRIUS

But me more good to see so great a lord
Basely insinuate and send us gifts.   38

AARON

Had he not reason, Lord Demetrius?
Did you not use his daughter very friendly?

DEMETRIUS

I would we had a thousand Roman dames
At such a bay, by turn to serve our lust.   42

CHIRON

A charitable wish, and full of love!

AARON

Here lacks but your mother for to say amen.

CHIRON

And that would she, for twenty thousand more.   45

DEMETRIUS

Come, let us go and pray to all the gods
For our belovèd mother in her pains.   47

AARON

Pray to the devils. The gods have given us over.
                    Trumpets sound [*within*].

DEMETRIUS

Why do the Emperor's trumpets flourish thus?

CHIRON

Belike for joy the Emperor hath a son.   50

DEMETRIUS

Soft, who comes here?

        Enter Nurse, with a blackamoor child
        [*in her arms*].

NURSE   Good morrow, lords.   51
Oh, tell me, did you see Aaron the Moor?

AARON

Well, more or less, or ne'er a whit at all,   53
Here Aaron is; and what with Aaron now?   54

NURSE

O gentle Aaron, we are all undone.
Now help, or woe betide thee evermore!

AARON

Why, what a caterwauling dost thou keep!   57
What dost thou wrap and fumble in thy arms?

NURSE

Oh, that which I would hide from heaven's eye,
Our empress' shame and stately Rome's disgrace!
She is delivered, lords, she is delivered.

---

31 her unrest i.e., her labor of delivery   32 happy fortunate   36 To . . . hearing i.e., to taunt Marcus in Titus's presence.   38 insinuate ingratiate himself by flattery   42 At such a bay cornered thus (as in hunting).   by turn (1) one after the other (2) doing a sexual "turn"   45 more more such occasions.   47 pains labor pains. (Tamora is being delivered of a child sired by Aaron; see lines 29–31 above.)   50 Belike Probably   51 Soft i.e., Wait a minute   53 more (Punning on *Moor*.)   54 what what's your business   57 keep keep up.

AARON   To whom?   62
NURSE   I mean she is brought abed.
AARON
Well, God give her good rest. What hath he sent her?   64
NURSE   A devil.
AARON
Why, then she is the devil's dam. A joyful issue!   66
NURSE
A joyless, dismal, black, and sorrowful issue!   67
Here is the babe, as loathsome as a toad
Amongst the fair-faced breeders of our clime.
The Empress sends it thee, thy stamp, thy seal,   70
And bids thee christen it with thy dagger's point.
AARON
Zounds, ye whore, is black so base a hue?   72
[To the child] Sweet blowze, you are a beauteous
    blossom, sure.   73
DEMETRIUS   Villain, what hast thou done?
AARON   That which thou canst not undo.
CHIRON   Thou hast undone our mother.
AARON   Villain, I have done thy mother.   77
DEMETRIUS
And therein, hellish dog, thou hast undone her.
Woe to her chance, and damned her loathèd choice!   79
Accurst the offspring of so foul a fiend!   80
CHIRON   It shall not live.
AARON   It shall not die.
NURSE
Aaron, it must. The mother wills it so.
AARON
What, must it, Nurse? Then let no man but I
Do execution on my flesh and blood.
DEMETRIUS
I'll broach the tadpole on my rapier's point.   86
Nurse, give it me. My sword shall soon dispatch it.
AARON   [taking the child and drawing his sword]
Sooner this sword shall plow thy bowels up.
Stay, murderous villains, will you kill your brother?
Now, by the burning tapers of the sky
That shone so brightly when this boy was got,   91
He dies upon my scimitar's sharp point
That touches this my firstborn son and heir!
I tell you, younglings, not Enceladus   94
With all his threat'ning band of Typhon's brood,   95
Nor great Alcides, nor the god of war   96
Shall seize this prey out of his father's hands.

What, what, ye sanguine, shallow-hearted boys!   98
Ye white-limed walls! Ye alehouse painted signs!   99
Coal black is better than another hue
In that it scorns to bear another hue;
For all the water in the ocean
Can never turn the swan's black legs to white,
Although she lave them hourly in the flood.   104
Tell the Empress from me, I am of age
To keep mine own, excuse it how she can.   106
DEMETRIUS
Wilt thou betray thy noble mistress thus?
AARON
My mistress is my mistress, this myself,   108
The vigor and the picture of my youth.
This before all the world do I prefer;
This maugre all the world will I keep safe,   111
Or some of you shall smoke for it in Rome.   112
DEMETRIUS
By this our mother is forever shamed.
CHIRON
Rome will despise her for this foul escape.   114
NURSE
The Emperor in his rage will doom her death.
CHIRON
I blush to think upon this ignomy.   116
AARON
Why, there's the privilege your beauty bears.   117
Fie, treacherous hue, that will betray with blushing
The close enacts and counsels of thy heart!   119
Here's a young lad framed of another leer.   120
Look how the black slave smiles upon the father,
As who should say, "Old lad, I am thine own."   122
He is your brother, lords, sensibly fed   123
Of that self blood that first gave life to you,   124
And from that womb where you imprisoned were
He is enfranchisèd and come to light.
Nay, he is your brother by the surer side,   127
Although my seal be stampèd in his face.   128
NURSE
Aaron, what shall I say unto the Empress?
DEMETRIUS
Advise thee, Aaron, what is to be done,   130
And we will all subscribe to thy advice.   131
Save thou the child, so we may all be safe.   132

---

62 To whom (Aaron plays on *delivered,* line 61, in the sense of
"handed over or transferred to another person," though he, of course,
knows that the Nurse means "delivered of a child.")   **64 God . . . rest**
(Again, Aaron jestingly pretends to misinterpret *brought abed,* line 63,
in its literal sense.)   **66 dam** mother.   **issue** result.   **67 issue** offspring.   **70 thy stamp, thy seal** i.e., bearing your imprint
72 Zounds By His (Christ's) wounds   **73 blowze** red-cheeked one.
(Usually addressed to a wench or slattern; here, an affectionately abusive term for the child.)   **77 done** i.e., had sexual intercourse with.
(Playing on *undone* in the previous line.)   **79 chance** luck.   **damned**
damned be   **80 Accurst** Accursed be   **86 broach** impale   **91 got** begotten   **94 Enceladus** one of the giants who rose against the gods and
were defeated by them; Enceladus was buried under Mount Etna in
Sicily   **95 Typhon** a terrible giant-monster who attacked the gods and
was flung into Tartarus   **96 Alcides** Hercules, a descendant of Alcaeus

98 sanguine red-cheeked (as distinguished from black-complex-
ioned).   **shallow-hearted** cowardly   **99 white-limed** whitewashed.
(The image is of a fair exterior hiding darkness within.)   **alehouse
painted signs** i.e., cheap painted imitations of men.   **104 lave** wash.
flood stream.   **106 excuse . . . can** let her explain her situation as well
as she can.   **108 this myself** i.e., this child is a part of myself
111 maugre in spite of   **112 smoke** i.e., suffer. (The metaphor is from
burning at the stake.)   **114 escape** escapade, outrageous transgression.   **116 ignomy** ignominy, shame.   **117 Why . . . bears** i.e., Blushing is one of the benefits of your fair complexion. (Said ironically;
Aaron prefers a hue that cannot incriminate itself.)   **119 close enacts**
secret purposes   **120 framed** made.   **leer** countenance, complexion.
122 As . . . say as if saying, as if one might say   **123–4 sensibly . . .
blood** given corporeal sustenance by that same blood   **127 surer** i.e.,
mother's   **128 seal be stampèd** (See line 70 above; the child bears the
imprint of the father in his looks.)   **130 Advise thee** Consider
131 subscribe agree   **132 so** so long as

AARON
    Then sit we down, and let us all consult.
    My son and I will have the wind of you;   134
    Keep there. Now talk at pleasure of your safety.
                              [They sit.]

DEMETRIUS [*to the Nurse*]
    How many women saw this child of his?

AARON
    Why, so, brave lords! When we join in league,
    I am a lamb; but if you brave the Moor,   138
    The chafèd boar, the mountain lioness,   139
    The ocean swells not so as Aaron storms.
    [*To the Nurse*] But say again, how many saw the child?

NURSE
    Cornelia the midwife and myself,
    And no one else but the delivered Empress.

AARON
    The Empress, the midwife, and yourself.
    Two may keep counsel when the third's away.
    Go to the Empress, tell her this I said.   *He kills her.*
    Wheak, wheak!—   147
    So cries a pig preparèd to the spit.   148
                          [They all stand up.]

DEMETRIUS
    What mean'st thou, Aaron? Wherefore didst thou
      this?

AARON
    Oh, Lord, sir, 'tis a deed of policy.   150
    Shall she live to betray this guilt of ours,
    A long-tongued, babbling gossip? No, lords, no.
    And now be it known to you my full intent.
    Not far, one Muly lives, my countryman:
    His wife but yesternight was brought to bed;
    His child is like to her, fair as you are.
    Go pack with him, and give the mother gold,   157
    And tell them both the circumstance of all,
    And how by this their child shall be advanced
    And be receivèd for the Emperor's heir,
    And substituted in the place of mine,
    To calm this tempest whirling in the court;
    And let the Emperor dandle him for his own.
    Hark ye, lords, you see I have given her physic,   164
                       [pointing to the Nurse]
    And you must needs bestow her funeral.   165
    The fields are near, and you are gallant grooms.   166
    This done, see that you take no longer days,   167
    But send the midwife presently to me.   168
    The midwife and the nurse well made away,
    Then let the ladies tattle what they please.

CHIRON
    Aaron, I see thou wilt not trust the air
    With secrets.

DEMETRIUS   For this care of Tamora,
    Herself and hers are highly bound to thee.
            Exeunt [Demetrius and Chiron,
             bearing off the Nurse's body].

AARON
    Now to the Goths, as swift as swallow flies,
    There to dispose this treasure in mine arms   175
    And secretly to greet the Empress' friends.   176
    Come on, you thick-lipped slave, I'll bear you hence,
    For it is you that puts us to our shifts.   178
    I'll make you feed on berries and on roots,
    And feed on curds and whey, and suck the goat,
    And cabin in a cave, and bring you up   181
    To be a warrior and command a camp.
                    Exit [with the child].

❖

[4.3]

Enter Titus, old Marcus, [his son Publius,]
young Lucius, and other gentlemen
[Sempronius, Caius], with bows; and Titus
bears the arrows with letters on the ends of
them.

TITUS
    Come, Marcus, come. Kinsmen, this is the way.
    Sir boy, let me see your archery.
    Look ye draw home enough, and 'tis there straight.   3
    Terras Astraea reliquit;   4
    Be you remembered, Marcus, she's gone, she's fled.   5
    Sirs, take you to your tools. You, cousins, shall
    Go sound the ocean, and cast your nets;
    Happily you may catch her in the sea;   8
    Yet there's as little justice as at land.
    No; Publius and Sempronius, you must do it;
    'Tis you must dig with mattock and with spade,
    And pierce the inmost center of the earth.
    Then, when you come to Pluto's region,   13
    I pray you, deliver him this petition.
    Tell him it is for justice and for aid,
    And that it comes from old Andronicus,
    Shaken with sorrows in ungrateful Rome.
    Ah, Rome! Well, well, I made thee miserable
    What time I threw the people's suffrages   19
    On him that thus doth tyrannize o'er me.
    Go, get you gone, and pray be careful all,
    And leave you not a man-of-war unsearched.

---

134 **have . . . you** take the position of advantage (as in hunting, where to be downwind is to be where one will not be scented by the game) 138 **brave** taunt, defy. (Playing on *brave*, gallant, well-dressed, in line 137.)   139 **chafèd** enraged 147 **Wheak** (Aaron mimics her dying cry.) 148 **preparèd to the spit** being spitted for roasting. 150 **policy** prudent action. 157 **pack** make a deal 164 **physic** medicine 165 **bestow** provide, furnish 166 **grooms** fellows. 167 **days** time 168 **presently** at once

175 **dispose** dispose of 176 **greet . . . friends** i.e., join forces with the Goths, who presumably will defend Tamora's interests in Rome. 178 **shifts** stratagems, tricks. 181 **cabin** lodge **4.3. Location: Rome. A public place.**
3 **home** to the full extent (of the bow). **'tis there straight** it will reach the point aimed at forthwith. 4 *Terras Astraea reliquit* Astraea (the goddess of justice) has abandoned the earth. (From Ovid, *Metamorphoses*, 1.150.) 5 **Be you remembered** remember. **she's** Justice is 8 **Happily** haply, perhaps 13 **Pluto's region** the underworld, ruled over by Pluto 19 **What time** when. **suffrages** assent, votes

This wicked emperor may have shipped her hence,   23
And, kinsmen, then we may go pipe for justice.   24

MARCUS
Oh, Publius, is not this a heavy case,   25
To see thy noble uncle thus distract?   26

PUBLIUS
Therefore, my lords, it highly us concerns
By day and night t'attend him carefully,
And feed his humor kindly as we may,   29
Till time beget some careful remedy.   30

MARCUS
Kinsmen, his sorrows are past remedy.   31
Join with the Goths and with revengeful war
Take wreak on Rome for this ingratitude,   33
And vengeance on the traitor Saturnine.

TITUS
Publius, how now? How now, my masters?   35
What, have you met with her?   36

PUBLIUS
No, my good lord, but Pluto sends you word,
If you will have Revenge from hell, you shall.
Marry, for Justice, she is so employed,   39
He thinks, with Jove in heaven, or somewhere else,
So that perforce you must needs stay a time.   41

TITUS
He doth me wrong to feed me with delays.
I'll dive into the burning lake below   43
And pull her out of Acheron by the heels.   44
Marcus, we are but shrubs, no cedars we,
No big-boned men framed of the Cyclops' size,   46
But metal, Marcus, steel to the very back,
Yet wrung with wrongs more than our backs can bear.
And sith there's no justice in earth nor hell,   49
We will solicit heaven and move the gods
To send down Justice for to wreak our wrongs.   51
Come, to this gear. You are a good archer, Marcus.   52
                               He gives them the arrows.
"Ad Jovem," that's for you; here, "Ad Apollinem";   53
"Ad Martem," that's for myself;   54
Here, boy, "to Pallas"; here, "to Mercury";   55
"To Saturn," Caius—not "to Saturnine"!
You were as good to shoot against the wind.   57
To it, boy! Marcus, loose when I bid.   58
Of my word, I have written to effect;   59
There's not a god left unsolicited.

MARCUS
Kinsmen, shoot all your shafts into the court.
We will afflict the Emperor in his pride.

TITUS
Now, masters, draw. [*They shoot.*] Oh, well said,
   Lucius!   63
Good boy, in Virgo's lap! Give it Pallas.   64

MARCUS
My lord, I aim a mile beyond the moon;   65
Your letter is with Jupiter by this.

TITUS   Ha, ha!
Publius, Publius, what hast thou done?
See, see, thou hast shot off one of Taurus' horns.   69

MARCUS
This was the sport, my lord: when Publius shot,
The Bull, being galled, gave Aries such a knock   71
That down fell both the Ram's horns in the court;   72
And who should find them but the Empress' villain?   73
She laughed, and told the Moor he should not choose   74
But give them to his master for a present.   75

TITUS
Why, there it goes. God give His Lordship joy!   76

      *Enter the Clown, with a basket, and two
      pigeons in it.*

News, news from heaven! Marcus, the post is come.—
Sirrah, what tidings? Have you any letters?
Shall I have justice? What says Jupiter?

CLOWN   Ho, the gibbet maker? He says that he hath   80
taken them down again, for the man must not be   81
hanged till the next week.

TITUS   But what says Jupiter, I ask thee?

CLOWN   Alas, sir, I know not Jupiter. I never drank
with him in all my life.

TITUS   Why, villain, art not thou the carrier?   86

CLOWN   Ay, of my pigeons, sir; nothing else.

TITUS   Why, didst thou not come from heaven?

CLOWN   From heaven! Alas, sir, I never came there.
God forbid I should be so bold to press to heaven in
my young days. Why, I am going with my pigeons to
the tribunal plebs, to take up a matter of brawl betwixt   92
my uncle and one of the Emperal's men.   93

MARCUS   [*to Titus*]   Why, sir, that is as fit as can be to
serve for your oration; and let him deliver the
pigeons to the Emperor from you.

---

23 **her** i.e., Justice, the goddess Astraea. (In his madness, Titus imagines that Saturninus may ship Astraea out of the country in an armed naval vessel, a *man-of-war*.)   24 **pipe** whistle, i.e., look in vain   25 **heavy case** sad situation   26 **distract** distracted, crazed.   29 **feed his humor** humor him   30 **careful** showing and requiring care   31 **remedy** (In the Quarto, this word is followed by a catchword *But* at the foot of the page that is not repeated in the first line of the next page, possibly suggesting an omission in the text, something like "But let us live in hope that Lucius will.")   33 **wreak** vengeance   35 **masters** good sirs. 36 **her** i.e., Justice.   39 **for** as for   41 **stay a time** wait awhile. 43 **burning lake** i.e., Phlegethon, the burning river of the underworld 44 **Acheron** a river in the underworld   46 **Cyclops** one-eyed giants in Homer's *Odyssey* (9)   49 **sith** since   51 **for to wreak** to avenge 52 **gear** business.   53–4 *Ad Jovem, Ad Apollinem, Ad Martem* to Jove, to Apollo, to Mars   55 **Pallas** Pallas Athene   57 **You . . . wind** You might as well shoot against the wind (as appeal to Saturninus). 58 **loose** let fly   59 **Of** On

63 **well said** well done   64 **in Virgo's lap** in the constellation of the Virgin (the zodiacal sign representing Astraea, having fled from earth).   **Give it Pallas** i.e., Shoot the arrow labeled "Pallas" there.   65 **a mile . . . moon** (Marcus' literal meaning is intended to humor Titus' madness, but his expression also means "wild conjecture, far wide of the mark," thus commenting on the madness of their proceedings.)   69 **Taurus** the Bull; a zodiacal sign   71 **galled** slightly wounded.   **Ares** the horned Ram; a zodiacal sign   72 **horns** i.e., signs of being a cuckold, bestowed by Aaron on the Emperor 73 **villain** i.e., Aaron, both servant and villain in the modern sense. 74–5 **should . . . But** must   76 **there it goes** (A hunting cry of encouragement.)   76.1 *Clown* rustic   80 **gibbet maker** (The Clown seems to have heard "Jupiter" as "gibbeter.")   81 **them** i.e., the gallows. **must not be** is not to be   86 **carrier** postman. (But the Clown answers in the sense of "one who carries things.")   92 **tribunal plebs** i.e., *tribuni plebs*, tribunes charged to look after the interests of the plebeians   93 **Emperal's** (Malapropism for "Emperor's.")

TITUS [*to Clown*]
Sirrah, come hither. Make no more ado,   97
But give your pigeons to the Emperor.
By me thou shalt have justice at his hands.
Hold, hold; meanwhile here's money for thy charges. 100
                                        [*He gives money.*]
Give me pen and ink.
Sirrah, can you with a grace deliver up a supplication?
CLOWN   Ay, sir.
TITUS [*writing and handing him a supplication*]   Then
here is a supplication for you. And when you come to
him, at the first approach you must kneel, then kiss
his foot, then deliver up your pigeons, and then look
for your reward. I'll be at hand, sir; see you do it
bravely.   109
CLOWN   I warrant you, sir. Let me alone.   110
TITUS
Sirrah, hast thou a knife? Come let me see it.
              [*He takes the knife and gives it to Marcus.*]
Here, Marcus, fold it in the oration;
[*To the Clown*] For thou must hold it like an humble
supplant.—
And when thou hast given it to the Emperor,
Knock at my door and tell me what he says.
CLOWN   God be with you, sir. I will.   *Exit.*
TITUS   Come, Marcus, let us go. Publius, follow me.
                                                 Exeunt.

❧

[4.4]

*Enter Emperor [Saturninus] and Empress
[Tamora] and her two sons [and others, including guards]. The Emperor brings the arrows in
his hand that Titus shot at him. [The Emperor
and Empress sit.]*

SATURNINUS
Why, lords, what wrongs are these! Was ever seen
An emperor in Rome thus overborne,   2
Troubled, confronted thus, and, for the extent   3
Of equal justice, used in such contempt?   4
My lords, you know, as know the mightful gods,
However these disturbers of our peace
Buzz in the people's ears, there naught hath passed
But even with law against the willful sons   8
Of old Andronicus. And what an if
His sorrows have so overwhelmed his wits?
Shall we be thus afflicted in his wreaks,   11
His fits, his frenzy, and his bitterness?
And now he writes to heaven for his redress.
See, here's "to Jove," and this "to Mercury,"
This "to Apollo," this to the god of war—

Sweet scrolls to fly about the streets of Rome!
What's this but libeling against the Senate
And blazoning our unjustice everywhere?   18
A goodly humor, is it not, my lords?   19
As who would say, in Rome no justice were.
But if I live, his feignèd ecstasies   21
Shall be no shelter to these outrages;
But he and his shall know that justice lives   23
In Saturninus' health, whom, if he sleep,   24
He'll so awake as he in fury shall   25
Cut off the proud'st conspirator that lives.   26
TAMORA
My gracious lord, my lovely Saturnine,
Lord of my life, commander of my thoughts,
Calm thee, and bear the faults of Titus' age,
Th'effects of sorrow for his valiant sons,
Whose loss hath pierced him deep and scarred his
    heart;
And rather comfort his distressèd plight
Than prosecute the meanest or the best   33
For these contempts. [*Aside*] Why, thus it shall become
High-witted Tamora to gloze withal.   35
But, Titus, I have touched thee to the quick;
Thy lifeblood out, if Aaron now be wise,   37
Then is all safe, the anchor in the port.

              Enter Clown.

How now, good fellow, wouldst thou speak with us?
CLOWN   Yea, forsooth, an your mistress-ship be emperial.
TAMORA   Empress I am, but yonder sits the Emperor.
CLOWN   'Tis he. [*He kneels.*] God and Saint Stephen give
you good e'en. I have brought you a letter and a   43
couple of pigeons here.
              He [Saturninus] reads the letter.
SATURNINUS
Go, take him away, and hang him presently.   45
CLOWN   How much money must I have?   46
TAMORA   Come, sirrah, you must be hanged.
CLOWN   Hanged! By'r Lady, then I have brought up a   48
neck to a fair end.   *Exit [guarded].*
SATURNINUS
Despiteful and intolerable wrongs!
Shall I endure this monstrous villainy?
I know from whence this same device proceeds.
May this be borne?—as if his traitorous sons,
That died by law for murder of our brother,
Have by my means been butchered wrongfully!
Go, drag the villain hither by the hair.
Nor age nor honor shall shape privilege.   57

97 Sirrah (In the early texts, this line is preceded by four lines that
appear to be a first draft of lines 102–3: "TITUS Tell me, can you deliver
an oration to the Emperor with a grace? CLOWN Nay, truly, sir, I could
never say grace in all my life.")   **100 charges** expenses.   **109 bravely**
handsomely, stylishly.   **110 Let me alone** Leave it to me.
4.4. Location: Rome. Before or in the palace.
2 overborne oppressed   **3 for the extent** as his reward for the exercising   **4 equal** evenhanded   **8 even** conformable   **11 wreaks**
revengeful acts

18 blazoning proclaiming   **19 humor** whim, caprice   **21 ecstasies** fits
of madness   **23–6 But . . . lives** but Titus and the Andronici will learn
(to their sorrow) that justice is alive and well in me, Saturninus, whose
fury, once awakened, will punish even the proudest of conspirators.
(Some editors emend "he" in lines 24 and 25 to "she," supposing that
the reference is to the goddess of Justice.)   **33 the meanest or the best**
those of low or high station   **35 High-witted** clever.   **to gloze withal**
to deceive in this way.   **37 Thy lifeblood out** once your lifeblood is
spilled.   **wise** i.e., wise enough to keep silent about the baby
43 good e'en good afternoon or evening   **45 presently** at once.
46 must I am I to   **48 By'r Lady** By Our Lady, the Virgin Mary
57 Nor neither.   **shape privilege** make for exemption.

For this proud mock I'll be thy slaughterman,
Sly frantic wretch, that holp'st to make me great   59
In hope thyself should govern Rome and me.   60

Enter nuntius, Aemilius.

What news with thee, Aemilius?
AEMILIUS
Arm, my lords! Rome never had more cause.
The Goths have gathered head, and with a power   63
Of high-resolvèd men bent to the spoil   64
They hither march amain under conduct   65
Of Lucius, son to old Andronicus,
Who threats in course of this revenge to do
As much as ever Coriolanus did.   68
SATURNINUS
Is warlike Lucius general of the Goths?
These tidings nip me, and I hang the head
As flowers with frost or grass beat down with storms.
Ay, now begins our sorrows to approach.
'Tis he the common people love so much;
Myself hath often heard them say,
When I have walkèd like a private man,   75
That Lucius' banishment was wrongfully,   76
And they have wished that Lucius were their emperor.
TAMORA
Why should you fear? Is not your city strong?
SATURNINUS
Ay, but the citizens favor Lucius
And will revolt from me to succor him.
TAMORA
King, be thy thoughts imperious, like thy name.   81
Is the sun dimmed, that gnats do fly in it?   82
The eagle suffers little birds to sing
And is not careful what they mean thereby,   84
Knowing that with the shadow of his wings
He can at pleasure stint their melody;   86
Even so mayst thou the giddy men of Rome.   87
Then cheer thy spirit, for know, thou Emperor,
I will enchant the old Andronicus
With words more sweet and yet more dangerous
Than baits to fish or honey-stalks to sheep,   91
Whenas the one is wounded with the bait,   92
The other rotted with delicious feed.   93
SATURNINUS
But he will not entreat his son for us.   94
TAMORA
If Tamora entreat him, then he will;
For I can smooth and fill his agèd ears   96
With golden promises, that were his heart

Almost impregnable, his old ears deaf,
Yet should both ear and heart obey my tongue.
[*To Aemilius*] Go thou before to be our ambassador.
Say that the Emperor requests a parley
Of warlike Lucius, and appoint the meeting   102
Even at his father's house, the old Andronicus.
SATURNINUS
Aemilius, do this message honorably,
And if he stand on hostage for his safety,   105
Bid him demand what pledge will please him best.   106
AEMILIUS
Your bidding shall I do effectually.   *Exit.*
TAMORA
Now will I to that old Andronicus
And temper him with all the art I have   109
To pluck proud Lucius from the warlike Goths.
And now, sweet Emperor, be blithe again
And bury all thy fear in my devices.
SATURNINUS
Then go successantly, and plead to him.   *Exeunt.* 113

❖

[5.1]

*[Flourish.] Enter Lucius with an army
of Goths, with drums and soldiers.*

LUCIUS
Approvèd warriors and my faithful friends,   1
I have receivèd letters from great Rome   2
Which signifies what hate they bear their emperor
And how desirous of our sight they are.
Therefore, great lords, be as your titles witness,   5
Imperious, and impatient of your wrongs,
And wherein Rome hath done you any scath   7
Let him make treble satisfaction.   8
A GOTH
Brave slip, sprung from the great Andronicus,   9
Whose name was once our terror, now our comfort,
Whose high exploits and honorable deeds
Ingrateful Rome requites with foul contempt,
Be bold in us. We'll follow where thou lead'st,   13
Like stinging bees in hottest summer's day
Led by their master to the flowered fields,   15
And be avenged on cursèd Tamora.
ALL THE GOTHS
And as he saith, so say we all with him.
LUCIUS
I humbly thank him, and I thank you all.
But who comes here, led by a lusty Goth?   19

*Enter a Goth, leading of Aaron with his child in
his arms.*

---

59 **holp'st** helped   60.1 *nuntius* messenger   63 **gathered head** raised
an army.   **power** armed force   64 **bent to the spoil** intent on plunder
65 **amain** forcefully, swiftly.   **conduct** command   68 **Coriolanus** an
early Roman hero turned enemy of Rome, about whom Shakespeare
wrote one of his later tragedies   75 **walkèd . . . man** i.e., gone in disguise among the commoners, like Henry V or the Duke in *Measure for
Measure*   76 **wrongfully** wrongfully imposed   81 **imperious** imperial   82 **that** merely because   84 **careful** full of concern   86 **stint** stop
87 **giddy** changeable in opinion and allegiance   91 **honey-stalks**
clover. (Too much clover can make sheep ill.)   92 **Whenas** when
93 **rotted** afflicted by the rot, a liver disease in sheep   94 **entreat his
son** i.e., entreat Lucius not to attack Rome   96 **smooth** flatter

102 **Of** with   105 **stand** insist   106 **demand** request   109 **temper**
work upon   113 **successantly** at once
5.1. Location: Near Rome.
0.2 *drums* drummers   1 **Approvèd** Put to proof, tried   2 **letters** a
letter   5 **be . . . witness** live up to the greatness your noble titles
proclaim   7 **scath** injury   8 **him** Saturninus (who is to pay for all
the wrongs Rome has done the Goths)   9 **slip** offspring, scion
13 **bold** confident   15 **their master** (Bees were thought to be led by
a king bee.)   19 **lusty** valiant

ANOTHER GOTH
    Renownèd Lucius, from our troops I strayed
    To gaze upon a ruinous monastery,   21
    And as I earnestly did fix mine eye
    Upon the wasted building, suddenly   23
    I heard a child cry underneath a wall.
    I made unto the noise, when soon I heard   25
    The crying babe controlled with this discourse: 26
    "Peace, tawny slave, half me and half thy dam! 27
    Did not thy hue bewray whose brat thou art,   28
    Had nature lent thee but thy mother's look,
    Villain, thou mightst have been an emperor.
    But where the bull and cow are both milk white,
    They never do beget a coal black calf.
    Peace, villain, peace!"—even thus he rates the babe— 33
    "For I must bear thee to a trusty Goth,
    Who, when he knows thou art the Empress' babe,
    Will hold thee dearly for thy mother's sake."
    With this, my weapon drawn, I rushed upon him,
    Surprised him suddenly, and brought him hither
    To use as you think needful of the man.   39
LUCIUS
    O worthy Goth, this is the incarnate devil
    That robbed Andronicus of his good hand!
    This is the pearl that pleased your empress' eye,
    And here's the base fruit of her burning lust.— 43
    Say, walleyed slave, whither wouldst thou convey 44
    This growing image of thy fiendlike face?   45
    Why dost not speak? What, deaf? Not a word?—
    A halter, soldiers! Hang him on this tree,
    And by his side his fruit of bastardy.
AARON
    Touch not the boy. He is of royal blood.
LUCIUS
    Too like the sire for ever being good.   50
    First hang the child, that he may see it sprawl— 51
    A sight to vex the father's soul withal.
    Get me a ladder.
                [*A ladder is brought, which Aaron*
                                is made to ascend.]
AARON   Lucius, save the child,
    And bear it from me to the Empress.
    If thou do this, I'll show thee wondrous things
    That highly may advantage thee to hear.
    If thou wilt not, befall what may befall,
    I'll speak no more but "Vengeance rot you all!"
LUCIUS
    Say on. An if it please me which thou speak'st, 59
    Thy child shall live, and I will see it nourished. 60
AARON
    An if it please thee! Why, assure thee, Lucius,
    'Twill vex thy soul to hear what I shall speak;
    For I must talk of murders, rapes, and massacres,

    Acts of black night, abominable deeds,
    Complots of mischief, treason, villainies,   65
    Ruthful to hear, yet piteously performed.   66
    And this shall all be buried in my death,
    Unless thou swear to me my child shall live.
LUCIUS
    Tell on thy mind. I say thy child shall live.
AARON
    Swear that he shall, and then I will begin.
LUCIUS
    Who should I swear by? Thou believest no god.
    That granted, how canst thou believe an oath?
AARON
    What if I do not? As, indeed, I do not.
    Yet, for I know thou art religious   74
    And hast a thing within thee callèd conscience,
    With twenty popish tricks and ceremonies
    Which I have seen thee careful to observe,
    Therefore I urge thy oath. For that I know   78
    An idiot holds his bauble for a god   79
    And keeps the oath which by that god he swears,
    To that I'll urge him. Therefore thou shalt vow
    By that same god, what god soe'er it be
    That thou adorest and hast in reverence,
    To save my boy, to nourish and bring him up,
    Or else I will discover naught to thee.
LUCIUS
    Even by my god I swear to thee I will.
AARON
    First know thou, I begot him on the Empress.
LUCIUS
    O most insatiate and luxurious woman!   88
AARON
    Tut, Lucius, this was but a deed of charity
    To that which thou shalt hear of me anon.   90
    'Twas her two sons that murdered Bassianus;
    They cut thy sister's tongue, and ravished her,
    And cut her hands, and trimmed her as thou sawest. 93
LUCIUS
    O detestable villain! Call'st thou that trimming?
AARON
    Why, she was washed and cut and trimmed, and 'twas
    Trim sport for them which had the doing of it. 96
LUCIUS
    O barbarous, beastly villains, like thyself!
AARON
    Indeed, I was their tutor to instruct them.
    That codding spirit had they from their mother, 99
    As sure a card as ever won the set;   100
    That bloody mind I think they learned of me,
    As true a dog as ever fought at head.   102
    Well, let my deeds be witness of my worth.
    I trained thy brethren to that guileful hole 104

---

21 ruinous decayed   **23 wasted** ruined   **25 made unto** approached
26 controlled calmed   **27 slave** (Used affectionately, as also in *brat*, line 28, and *villain*, lines 30 and 33.) **dam** mother.   **28 bewray** reveal
33 rates chides   **39 use . . . man** deal with the man as you think fit.
43 fruit i.e., the baby   **44 walleyed** glaring   **45 image** likeness
50 for ever being ever to be   **51 sprawl** twitch convulsively in the death agony   **59 An if** If   **60 nourished** cared for.

65 Complots conspiracies   **66 Ruthful** lamentable, pitiable. **piteously** in a way to excite pity   **74 for** because   **78 urge** insist on. **For that** Because   **79 bauble** fool's stick   **88 luxurious** lecherous
90 To compared to   **93 trimmed** (1) decked out, made ready (2) cut off the excrescences (3) ravished **96 Trim** fine. (With a play on *trimmed*, lines 93–5.) **99 codding** lustful **100 set** game **102 as . . . head** as ever went for the bear's head (in bearbaiting). **104 trained** lured

Where the dead corpse of Bassianus lay;
I wrote the letter that thy father found,
And hid the gold within that letter mentioned,
Confederate with the Queen and her two sons;
And what not done, that thou hast cause to rue,
Wherein I had no stroke of mischief in it?
I played the cheater for thy father's hand,   111
And when I had it, drew myself apart
And almost broke my heart with extreme laughter.
I pried me through the crevice of a wall   114
When, for his hand, he had his two sons' heads,
Beheld his tears, and laughed so heartily
That both mine eyes were rainy like to his;
And when I told the Empress of this sport,
She swoonèd almost at my pleasing tale,
And for my tidings gave me twenty kisses.

A GOTH
What, canst thou say all this and never blush?

AARON
Ay, like a black dog, as the saying is.   122

LUCIUS
Art thou not sorry for these heinous deeds?

AARON
Ay, that I had not done a thousand more.
Even now I curse the day—and yet, I think,
Few come within the compass of my curse—
Wherein I did not some notorious ill,
As kill a man, or else devise his death,
Ravish a maid, or plot the way to do it,
Accuse some innocent and forswear myself,
Set deadly enmity between two friends,
Make poor men's cattle break their necks,
Set fire on barns and haystacks in the night
And bid the owners quench them with their tears.
Oft have I digged up dead men from their graves
And set them upright at their dear friends' door,
Even when their sorrows almost was forgot,
And on their skins, as on the bark of trees,
Have with my knife carvèd in Roman letters,
"Let not your sorrow die, though I am dead."
But I have done a thousand dreadful things   141
As willingly as one would kill a fly,
And nothing grieves me heartily indeed
But that I cannot do ten thousand more.

LUCIUS [to his soldiers]
Bring down the devil, for he must not die
So sweet a death as hanging presently.   146
                        [Aaron is brought down.]

AARON
If there be devils, would I were a devil,
To live and burn in everlasting fire,

So I might have your company in hell
But to torment you with my bitter tongue!

LUCIUS
Sirs, stop his mouth, and let him speak no more.
                        [Aaron is gagged.]

                Enter Aemilius.

A GOTH
My lord, there is a messenger from Rome
Desires to be admitted to your presence.   153

LUCIUS   Let him come near.
Welcome, Aemilius. What's the news from Rome?

AEMILIUS
Lord Lucius, and you princes of the Goths,
The Roman Emperor greets you all by me;
And, for he understands you are in arms,   158
He craves a parley at your father's house,
Willing you to demand your hostages,
And they shall be immediately delivered.

A GOTH   What says our general?

LUCIUS
Aemilius, let the Emperor give his pledges   163
Unto my father and my uncle Marcus,
And we will come. March away.   [Flourish. Exeunt.]

                        ❧

[5.2]

        Enter Tamora and her two sons, disguised.

TAMORA
Thus, in this strange and sad habiliment,   1
I will encounter with Andronicus
And say I am Revenge, sent from below
To join with him and right his heinous wrongs.
Knock at his study, where they say he keeps   5
To ruminate strange plots of dire revenge.
Tell him Revenge is come to join with him
And work confusion on his enemies.   8

        They knock, and Titus [above] opens his
        study door.

TITUS
Who doth molest my contemplation?
Is it your trick to make me ope the door,
That so my sad decrees may fly away   11
And all my study be to no effect?
You are deceived, for what I mean to do,
See here, in bloody lines I have set down,
And what is written shall be executed.
                        [He shows a paper.]

TAMORA
Titus, I am come to talk with thee.

---

111 **cheater** (1) deceiver (2) escheater, one designated to take care of property forfeited to the crown   114 **pried me** peered. (*Me* is used colloquially.)   122 **like a black dog** ("To blush like a black dog" is a proverb with ironic meaning, as here; at 4.2.117–19, Aaron is proud that, being black, he cannot blush.)   141 **But** i.e., But why go on with this recital. (Sometimes emended to *Tut*, as in the Second Quarto.)   146 **presently** immediately.

153 **Desires** who desires   158 **for** since   163 **pledges** hostages. (Both sides to the parley are to send hostages to the opposite camp while the talks continue, to ensure against any treacherous dealing.)   **5.2. Location: Rome. The court of Titus' house.**
1 **sad habiliment** somber garments   5 **keeps** keeps himself
8 **confusion** destruction   11 **sad decrees** solemn resolutions

TITUS
No, not a word. How can I grace my talk,
Wanting a hand to give it action?   18
Thou hast the odds of me; therefore no more.   19
TAMORA
If thou didst know me, thou wouldst talk with me.
TITUS
I am not mad; I know thee well enough.
Witness this wretched stump, witness these crimson
    lines,   22
Witness these trenches made by grief and care,   23
Witness the tiring day and heavy night,
Witness all sorrow, that I know thee well
For our proud empress, mighty Tamora.
Is not thy coming for my other hand?
TAMORA
Know, thou sad man, I am not Tamora;
She is thy enemy, and I thy friend.
I am Revenge, sent from th'infernal kingdom
To ease the gnawing vulture of thy mind
By working wreakful vengeance on thy foes.   32
Come down and welcome me to this world's light;
Confer with me of murder and of death.
There's not a hollow cave or lurking-place,
No vast obscurity or misty vale   36
Where bloody murder or detested rape
Can couch for fear, but I will find them out,   38
And in their ears tell them my dreadful name,
Revenge, which makes the foul offender quake.
TITUS
Art thou Revenge? And art thou sent to me
To be a torment to mine enemies?
TAMORA
I am. Therefore come down and welcome me.
TITUS
Do me some service ere I come to thee.
Lo, by thy side where Rape and Murder stands.
Now give some surance that thou art Revenge: 46
Stab them, or tear them on thy chariot wheels,
And then I'll come and be thy wagoner,
And whirl along with thee about the globe.
Provide thee two proper palfreys, black as jet,   50
To hale thy vengeful wagon swift away   51
And find out murderers in their guilty caves;
And when thy car is loaden with their heads,   53
I will dismount, and by thy wagon wheel
Trot like a servile footman all day long,
Even from Hyperion's rising in the east   56
Until his very downfall in the sea;
And day by day I'll do this heavy task,
So thou destroy Rapine and Murder there.   59
TAMORA
These are my ministers, and come with me.

TITUS
Are they thy ministers? What are they called?
TAMORA
Rape and Murder, therefore callèd so
'Cause they take vengeance of such kind of men.   63
TITUS
Good Lord, how like the Empress' sons they are,
And you the Empress! But we worldly men   65
Have miserable, mad, mistaking eyes.
O sweet Revenge, now do I come to thee,
And if one arm's embracement will content thee,
I will embrace thee in it by and by.   [Exit above.]
TAMORA
This closing with him fits his lunacy.   70
Whate'er I forge to feed his brainsick humors   71
Do you uphold and maintain in your speeches,
For now he firmly takes me for Revenge;
And being credulous in this mad thought,
I'll make him send for Lucius his son,
And whilst I at a banquet hold him sure,   76
I'll find some cunning practice out of hand   77
To scatter and disperse the giddy Goths
Or at the least make them his enemies.
See, here he comes, and I must ply my theme.   80

          [Enter Titus below.]

TITUS
Long have I been forlorn, and all for thee.
Welcome, dread Fury, to my woeful house.   82
Rapine and Murder, you are welcome too.
How like the Empress and her sons you are!
Well are you fitted, had you but a Moor.   85
Could not all hell afford you such a devil?
For well I wot the Empress never wags   87
But in her company there is a Moor;
And, would you represent our queen aright,
It were convenient you had such a devil.   90
But welcome as you are. What shall we do?
TAMORA
What wouldst thou have us do, Andronicus?
DEMETRIUS
Show me a murderer, I'll deal with him.
CHIRON
Show me a villain that hath done a rape,
And I am sent to be revenged on him.
TAMORA
Show me a thousand that hath done thee wrong,
And I will be revengèd on them all.
TITUS [to Demetrius]
Look round about the wicked streets of Rome,
And when thou find'st a man that's like thyself,
Good Murder, stab him; he's a murderer.

18 Wanting . . . action lacking a hand to provide suitable gesture by
way of support.   19 odds of advantage over   22 crimson i.e., bloody
(as in line 14)   23 trenches i.e., wrinkles   32 wreakful vengeful
36 obscurity place of darkness and desolation   38 couch lie hidden
46 surance assurance   50 proper excellent, handsome.   palfreys
horses   51 hale pull   53 car chariot   56 Hyperion's the sun god's
59 So provided that

63 of . . . men i.e., upon rapists and murderers.   65 worldly mortal
70 closing agreeing   71 forge invent.   humors moods, whims
76 hold him sure detain Lucius where he can do no harm   77 practice
plot.   out of hand on the spur of the moment   80 ply my theme
apply myself to my plan.   82 Fury (The Furies were primeval beings
devoted to avenging certain crimes, especially against the ties of kinship.)   85 fitted i.e., fitted out to resemble the Empress   87 wags
moves about   90 were convenient would be fitting

[*To Chiron*] Go thou with him, and when it is thy hap   101
To find another that is like to thee,
Good Rapine, stab him; he is a ravisher.
[*To Tamora*] Go thou with them, and in the Emperor's
    court
There is a queen, attended by a Moor;
Well shalt thou know her by thine own proportion,
For up and down she doth resemble thee.   107
I pray thee, do on them some violent death;
They have been violent to me and mine.

TAMORA
Well hast thou lessoned us; this shall we do.
But would it please thee, good Andronicus,
To send for Lucius, thy thrice-valiant son,
Who leads towards Rome a band of warlike Goths,
And bid him come and banquet at thy house,
When he is here, even at thy solemn feast,   115
I will bring in the Empress and her sons,
The Emperor himself, and all thy foes,
And at thy mercy shall they stoop and kneel,
And on them shalt thou ease thy angry heart.
What says Andronicus to this device?

TITUS [*calling*]
Marcus, my brother! 'Tis sad Titus calls.

Enter Marcus.

Go, gentle Marcus, to thy nephew Lucius;
Thou shalt inquire him out among the Goths.
Bid him repair to me and bring with him   124
Some of the chiefest princes of the Goths.
Bid him encamp his soldiers where they are.
Tell him the Emperor and the Empress too
Feast at my house, and he shall feast with them.
This do thou for my love; and so let him,
As he regards his agèd father's life.

MARCUS
This will I do, and soon return again.   [*Exit.*]

TAMORA
Now will I hence about thy business
And take my ministers along with me.

TITUS
Nay, nay, let Rape and Murder stay with me,
Or else I'll call my brother back again
And cleave to no revenge but Lucius.   136

TAMORA [*aside to her sons*]
What say you, boys? Will you abide with him
Whiles I go tell my lord the Emperor
How I have governed our determined jest?   139
Yield to his humor, smooth and speak him fair,   140
And tarry with him till I turn again.   141

TITUS [*aside*]
I knew them all, though they supposed me mad,
And will o'erreach them in their own devices—
A pair of cursèd hellhounds and their dam!

DEMETRIUS
Madam, depart at pleasure. Leave us here.

TAMORA
Farewell, Andronicus. Revenge now goes
To lay a complot to betray thy foes.   147

TITUS
I know thou dost; and, sweet Revenge, farewell.
    [*Exit Tamora.*]

CHIRON
Tell us, old man, how shall we be employed?

TITUS
Tut, I have work enough for you to do.   [*He calls.*]
    Publius, come hither! Caius, and Valentine!

[*Enter Publius, Caius, and Valentine.*]

PUBLIUS   What is your will?
TITUS   Know you these two?

PUBLIUS
The Empress' sons, I take them: Chiron, Demetrius.   154

TITUS
Fie, Publius, fie! Thou art too much deceived.
The one is Murder, and Rape is the other's name;
And therefore bind them, gentle Publius.
Caius and Valentine, lay hands on them.
Oft have you heard me wish for such an hour,
And now I find it. Therefore bind them sure,   160
And stop their mouths if they begin to cry.   [*Exit.*]   161
    [*Publius, Caius, and Valentine lay hold
                on Chiron and Demetrius.*]

CHIRON
Villains, forbear! We are the Empress' sons.

PUBLIUS
And therefore do we what we are commanded.—   163
Stop close their mouths; let them not speak a word.
    [*They gag and bind the two sons.*]
Is he sure bound? Look that you bind them fast.

*Enter Titus Andronicus with a knife,
and Lavinia with a basin.*

TITUS
Come, come, Lavinia. Look, thy foes are bound.—
Sirs, stop their mouths. Let them not speak to me,
But let them hear what fearful words I utter.—
O villains, Chiron and Demetrius!
Here stands the spring whom you have stained with
    mud,   170
This goodly summer with your winter mixed.
You killed her husband, and for that vile fault
Two of her brothers were condemned to death,
My hand cut off and made a merry jest;
Both her sweet hands, her tongue, and that more dear
Than hands or tongue, her spotless chastity,
Inhuman traitors, you constrained and forced.
What would you say if I should let you speak?
Villains, for shame you could not beg for grace.   179

---

101 **hap** chance   107 **up and down** from top to toe   115 **solemn**
stately   124 **repair** come   136 **but Lucius** i.e., but that which Lucius
and his army can provide.   139 **governed . . . jest** managed the
exploit we determined on.   140 **smooth . . . fair** flatter and humor
him   141 **turn** return

147 **complot** conspiracy   154 **take them** take them to be   160 **sure**
securely   161 **cry** cry out.   163 **therefore** for that very reason
170 **spring** i.e., Lavinia   179 **for shame . . . grace** i.e., your colossal
shame would not let you beg for mercy, would choke your plea.

Hark, wretches, how I mean to martyr you.   180
This one hand yet is left to cut your throats,
Whiles that Lavinia 'tween her stumps doth hold   182
The basin that receives your guilty blood.
You know your mother means to feast with me,
And calls herself Revenge, and thinks me mad.
Hark, villains, I will grind your bones to dust,
And with your blood and it I'll make a paste,   187
And of the paste a coffin I will rear,   188
And make two pasties of your shameful heads,   189
And bid that strumpet, your unhallowed dam,
Like to the earth swallow her own increase.   191
This is the feast that I have bid her to,
And this the banquet she shall surfeit on;
For worse than Philomel you used my daughter,
And worse than Procne I will be revenged.   195
And now prepare your throats. Lavinia, come.
                He cuts their throats.
Receive the blood, and when that they are dead,
Let me go grind their bones to powder small,
And with this hateful liquor temper it,   199
And in that paste let their vile heads be baked.
Come, come, be everyone officious   201
To make this banquet, which I wish may prove
More stern and bloody than the Centaurs' feast.   203
So, now bring them in, for I'll play the cook
And see them ready against their mother comes.   205
           Exeunt [bearing the dead bodies].

[5.3]

Enter Lucius, Marcus, and the Goths [with Aaron prisoner, and an attendant bearing his child].

LUCIUS
Uncle Marcus, since 'tis my father's mind
That I repair to Rome, I am content.   2
A GOTH
And ours with thine, befall what fortune will.   3
LUCIUS
Good uncle, take you in this barbarous Moor,
This ravenous tiger, this accursed devil.   4
Let him receive no sust'nance. Fetter him

Till he be brought unto the Empress' face   7
For testimony of her foul proceedings.   8
And see the ambush of our friends be strong;   9
I fear the Emperor means no good to us.
AARON
Some devil whisper curses in my ear
And prompt me that my tongue may utter forth
The venomous malice of my swelling heart!
LUCIUS
Away, inhuman dog, unhallowed slave!
Sirs, help our uncle to convey him in.
          [Exeunt Goths, with Aaron.]
            Sound trumpets [within].
The trumpets show the Emperor is at hand.

Enter Emperor [Saturninus] and Empress [Tamora], with [Aemilius,] tribunes, [senators], and others.

SATURNINUS
What, hath the firmament more suns than one?   17
LUCIUS
What boots it thee to call thyself a sun?   18
MARCUS
Rome's emperor, and nephew, break the parle.   19
These quarrels must be quietly debated.
The feast is ready which the careful Titus   21
Hath ordained to an honorable end,
For peace, for love, for league, and good to Rome.
Please you therefore draw nigh and take your places.
SATURNINUS   Marcus, we will.
       [A table is brought in. The company sit down.]

Trumpets sounding, enter Titus like a cook, placing the dishes, and Lavinia with a veil over her face, [young Lucius, and others].

TITUS
Welcome, my gracious lord; welcome, dread Queen;
Welcome, ye warlike Goths; welcome, Lucius;
And welcome, all. Although the cheer be poor,   28
'Twill fill your stomachs. Please you eat of it.
SATURNINUS
Why art thou thus attired, Andronicus?
TITUS
Because I would be sure to have all well
To entertain Your Highness and your empress.
TAMORA
We are beholding to you, good Andronicus.   33
TITUS
An if Your Highness knew my heart, you were.—   34
My lord the Emperor, resolve me this: 35
Was it well done of rash Virginius   36

180 martyr torture, kill cruelly   **182 Whiles that** while   **187 paste** dough   **188 coffin** pie crust. (Also suggesting the container in which they will be buried.)   **189 pasties** meat pies   **191 Like . . . increase** swallow her offspring, just as the earth devours all her children when they have died.   **195 worse than Procne** (An allusion to Procne's revenge on Tereus for raping her sister Philomel; compare with the note for 2.3.43. She killed her son Itys and served his flesh to Tereus, his father. In Seneca's *Thyestes,* Atreus similarly sets before Thyestes a dish of his own children's flesh.)   **199 temper** moisten, mix   **201 officious** busy   **203 Centaurs' feast** i.e., the wedding feast of Pirithous and Hippodamia to which the Lapithae invited the Centaurs, fabulous creatures, half-men and half-horses. (The Centaurs attempted to carry off the women but were slaughtered by their hosts.)   **205 against** by the time that
5.3. Location: The scene appears to take place in a court in Titus's house; in the opening lines, Lucius speaks as if he and his soldiers have just arrived in Rome.
2 repair return   **3 ours with thine** i.e., our intentions are in agreement with yours   **4 in** i.e., into Titus's house; see line 123

7 unto before   **8 For testimony of** to testify regarding   **9 ambush** forces lying in wait to attack   **17 What . . . than one** i.e., Two suns cannot occupy the same heavenly sphere, and Rome cannot have two kings at once.   **18 boots** avails   **19 break the parle** cease the dispute.   **21 careful** (1) full of sorrows (2) assiduous   **28 cheer** fare   **33 beholding** beholden   **34 were** would be.   **35 resolve** answer   **36 Virginius** (According to Livy, the Roman centurion Virginius killed his daughter to prevent her from being raped. Shakespeare chooses, instead, an alternate version that was also current in the Renaissance: Virginius kills his daughter after her rape to preserve her honor. This version is closer to the action of Shakespeare's play.)

To slay his daughter with his own right hand
Because she was enforced, stained, and deflowered?

SATURNINUS   It was, Andronicus.

TITUS   Your reason, mighty lord?

SATURNINUS
Because the girl should not survive her shame,   41
And by her presence still renew his sorrows.   42

TITUS
A reason mighty, strong, and effectual;
A pattern, precedent, and lively warrant
For me, most wretched, to perform the like.
Die, die, Lavinia, and thy shame with thee,
And with thy shame thy father's sorrow die!
                                        [*He kills Lavinia.*]

SATURNINUS
What hast thou done, unnatural and unkind?   48

TITUS
Killed her for whom my tears have made me blind.
I am as woeful as Virginius was,
And have a thousand times more cause than he
To do this outrage, and it now is done.

SATURNINUS
What, was she ravished? Tell who did the deed.

TITUS
Will't please you eat? Will't please Your Highness
   feed?

TAMORA
Why hast thou slain thine only daughter thus?

TITUS
Not I; 'twas Chiron and Demetrius.
They ravished her and cut away her tongue,
And they, 'twas they that did her all this wrong.

SATURNINUS
Go fetch them hither to us presently.   59

TITUS
Why, there they are, both bakèd in this pie,
Whereof their mother daintily hath fed,
Eating the flesh that she herself hath bred.
'Tis true, 'tis true; witness my knife's sharp point.
                                    He stabs the Empress.

SATURNINUS
Die, frantic wretch, for this accursèd deed!
                                        [*He kills Titus.*]

LUCIUS
Can the son's eye behold his father bleed?
There's meed for meed, death for a deadly deed!   66
            [*He kills Saturninus. A great tumult, during
             which Marcus, Lucius, and others go aloft.*]

MARCUS
You sad-faced men, people and sons of Rome,
By uproars severed, as a flight of fowl   68
Scattered by winds and high tempestuous gusts,
Oh, let me teach you how to knit again
This scattered corn into one mutual sheaf,   71
These broken limbs again into one body.

A ROMAN LORD
Let Rome herself be bane unto herself,   73
And she whom mighty kingdoms curtsy to,   74
Like a forlorn and desperate castaway   75
Do shameful execution on herself!   76
But if my frosty signs and chaps of age,   77
Grave witnesses of true experience,
Cannot induce you to attend my words,   79
[*To Lucius*] Speak, Rome's dear friend, as erst our
   ancestor,   80
When with his solemn tongue he did discourse
To lovesick Dido's sad-attending ear   82
The story of that baleful burning night
When subtle Greeks surprised King Priam's Troy.
Tell us what Sinon hath bewitched our ears,   85
Or who hath brought the fatal engine in
That gives our Troy, our Rome, the civil wound.   87
My heart is not compact of flint nor steel,   88
Nor can I utter all our bitter grief,
But floods of tears will drown my oratory
And break my utt'rance, even in the time
When it should move ye to attend me most
And force you to commiseration.
Here's Rome's young captain. Let him tell the tale,
While I stand by and weep to hear him speak.

LUCIUS
Then, gracious auditory, be it known to you
That Chiron and the damned Demetrius
Were they that murderèd our emperor's brother,
And they it were that ravishèd our sister.
For their fell faults our brothers were beheaded,   100
Our father's tears despised and basely cozened   101
Of that true hand that fought Rome's quarrel out   102
And sent her enemies unto the grave;
Lastly, myself unkindly banishèd,   104
The gates shut on me, and turned weeping out
To beg relief among Rome's enemies,
Who drowned their enmity in my true tears
And oped their arms to embrace me as a friend.
I am the turned-forth, be it known to you,   109
That have preserved her welfare in my blood   110
And from her bosom took the enemy's point,   111
Sheathing the steel in my adventurous body.   112
Alas, you know I am no vaunter, I;
My scars can witness, dumb although they are,   114
That my report is just and full of truth.

41 **Because** In order that   42 **still** continually   48 **unkind** (1) unnatural
(2) cruel.   59 **presently** at once.   66 **meed for meed** measure for measure.   66.1–2 *A great . . . aloft* (In lines 130–4, Marcus and Lucius offer
to throw themselves down from where they are speaking.)   68 **severed**
disunited   71 **corn** grain

73–6 **Let . . . herself!** (This Roman lord's first reaction to the horror he
has witnessed is to foresee apocalyptically a downfall of the Roman
Empire and of civilization itself. Both Emperor Saturninus and Rome's
great general, Titus, lie dead, along with other casualties. *Bane* is poison.
The speaker may be Aemilius, but not necessarily so.)   77 **if . . . age** if
my white hairs and wrinkles   79 **attend** listen to   80 **as . . . ancestor**
just as formerly our founder, Aeneas, spoke   82 **sad-attending** seriously listening   85 **Sinon** the crafty Greek who persuaded the Trojans
to take the wooden horse (the *fatal engine*) into their city   87 **civil**
incurred in civil strife   88 **compact** composed   100 **For . . . faults** For
the savage deeds of Chiron and Demetrius   101 **cozened** cheated
102 **fought . . . out** fought to the finish on behalf of Rome   104
unkindly unnaturally   109 **turned-forth** exile   110 **in** by   111 **from . . .
point** took in my own bosom the sword's point aimed at her, Rome's,
bosom   112 **adventurous** willing to incur risk   114 **dumb . . . are** (The
scars are dumb mouths, giving mute testimony.)

But soft, methinks I do digress too much,
Citing my worthless praise. Oh, pardon me,
For when no friends are by, men praise themselves.

MARCUS
Now is my turn to speak. Behold the child:
    [pointing to the child in the arms of an attendant]
Of this was Tamora deliverèd,
The issue of an irreligious Moor,
Chief architect and plotter of these woes.
The villain is alive in Titus' house,
And as he is to witness, this is true.
Now judge what cause had Titus to revenge
These wrongs unspeakable, past patience,
Or more than any living man could bear.
Now have you heard the truth. What say you,
    Romans?
Have we done aught amiss, show us wherein,   129
And from the place where you behold us pleading,
The poor remainder of Andronici
Will hand in hand all headlong hurl ourselves
And on the ragged stones beat forth our souls
And make a mutual closure of our house.   134
Speak, Romans, speak, and if you say we shall,
Lo, hand in hand, Lucius and I will fall.

AEMILIUS
Come, come, thou reverend man of Rome,
And bring our emperor gently in thy hand,
Lucius our emperor; for well I know
The common voice do cry it shall be so.

ALL
Lucius, all hail, Rome's royal emperor!

MARCUS [to attendants]
Go, go into old Titus' sorrowful house
And hither hale that misbelieving Moor
To be adjudged some direful slaughtering death
As punishment for his most wicked life.
    [Exeunt attendants. Marcus, Lucius,
    and the others come down.]

ALL
Lucius, all hail, Rome's gracious governor!

LUCIUS
Thanks, gentle Romans. May I govern so
To heal Rome's harms and wipe away her woe!
But, gentle people, give me aim awhile,   149
For nature puts me to a heavy task.
Stand all aloof, but, uncle, draw you near
To shed obsequious tears upon this trunk.—   152
Oh, take this warm kiss on thy pale cold lips,
    [kissing Titus]
These sorrowful drops upon thy bloodstained face,
The last true duties of thy noble son!

MARCUS [kissing Titus]
Tear for tear, and loving kiss for kiss,
Thy brother Marcus tenders on thy lips.
Oh, were the sum of these that I should pay
Countless and infinite, yet would I pay them!

LUCIUS [to young Lucius]
Come hither, boy. Come, come, and learn of us
To melt in showers. Thy grandsire loved thee well.
Many a time he danced thee on his knee,
Sung thee asleep, his loving breast thy pillow;
Many a story hath he told to thee,
And bid thee bear his pretty tales in mind
And talk of them when he was dead and gone.

MARCUS
How many thousand times hath these poor lips,
When they were living, warmed themselves on thine!
Oh, now, sweet boy, give them their latest kiss.   169
Bid him farewell; commit him to the grave.
Do them that kindness, and take leave of them.   171

BOY [kissing Titus]
Oh, grandsire, grandsire! Ev'n with all my heart
Would I were dead, so you did live again!
Oh, Lord, I cannot speak to him for weeping.
My tears will choke me if I ope my mouth.

    [Enter attendants with Aaron.]

A ROMAN
You sad Andronici, have done with woes.   176
Give sentence on this execrable wretch
That hath been breeder of these dire events.

LUCIUS
Set him breast-deep in earth and famish him;
There let him stand and rave and cry for food.
If anyone relieves or pities him,
For the offense he dies. This is our doom.   182
Some stay to see him fastened in the earth.

AARON
Ah, why should wrath be mute and fury dumb?
I am no baby, I, that with base prayers
I should repent the evils I have done.
Ten thousand worse than ever yet I did
Would I perform, if I might have my will.
If one good deed in all my life I did,
I do repent it from my very soul.

LUCIUS
Some loving friends convey the Emperor hence,
And give him burial in his fathers' grave.   192
My father and Lavinia shall forthwith
Be closèd in our household's monument.
As for that ravenous tiger, Tamora,
No funeral rite, nor man in mourning weed,
No mournful bell shall ring her burial;
But throw her forth to beasts and birds to prey.   198
Her life was beastly and devoid of pity,
And being dead, let birds on her take pity.   200
    Exeunt, [bearing the dead bodies].

---

169 latest last   **171 them** i.e., the lips.   **176 A ROMAN** (The speech is sometimes assigned to Aemilius.)   **182 doom** judgment.
192 fathers' (The original text's "fathers" could signify singular or plural. Probably Lucius means the ancestral tomb.)   **198 prey** prey upon.   **200 pity** (The First Quarto text closes the play with this line. The Second Quarto and subsequent texts add the following four lines: "See justice done on Aaron, that damned Moor, By whom our heavy haps had their beginning. Then, afterwards, to order well the state, That like events may ne'er it ruinate.")

129 Have we If we have   **134 closure** conclusion, death   **149 give me aim** bear with me, give me encouragement. (An archery metaphor: to give aim is to stand near the target and help direct the shooter's aim by observing the results.)   **152 obsequious** dutiful, mourning

Romeo and Juliet

Though a tragedy, *Romeo and Juliet* is, in some ways, more closely comparable to Shakespeare's romantic comedies and early writings than to his later tragedies. Stylistically belonging to the years 1594–1596, it is in the lyric vein of the sonnets, *A Midsummer Night's Dream, The Merchant of Venice*, and *Richard II*, all of which are from the mid 1590s. Like them, it uses a variety of rhyme schemes (couplets, quatrains, octets, and even sonnets) and revels in punning, metaphor, and wit combat. It is separated in tone and in time from the earliest of the great tragedies, *Julius Caesar* and *Hamlet*, by almost half a decade, and, except for the experimental *Titus Andronicus*, it is the only tragedy (that is not also a history) that Shakespeare wrote in the first decade of his career—a period devoted otherwise to romantic comedy and English history.

Like many comedies, *Romeo and Juliet* is a love story, celebrating the exquisite, brief joy of youthful passion. Even its tragic ending stresses the poignancy of that brief beauty, not the bitter futility of love, as in *Troilus and Cressida* or *Othello*. The tragic ending of *Romeo and Juliet* underscores the observation made by a vexed lover in *A Midsummer Night's Dream* that "The course of true love never did run smooth" (1.1.134). True love in *Romeo and Juliet*, as in *A Midsummer Night's Dream*, is destined to be crossed by differences in blood or family background, differences in age, arbitrary choices of family or friends, or uncontrollable catastrophes, such as war, death, and sickness. Love is thus, as in *A Midsummer Night's Dream*, "momentary as a sound, / Swift as a shadow, short as any dream," swallowed up by darkness; "So quick bright things come to confusion" (1.1.143–9). A dominant pattern of imagery in *Romeo and Juliet* evokes a corresponding sense of suddenness and violence: fire, gunpowder, hot blood, lightning, the inconstant wind, the storm-tossed or shipwrecked vessel. The beauty of a love that is so threatened and so fragile is intensified by the brevity of the experience. A tragic outcome therefore affirms the uniqueness and pristine quality of youthful ecstasy. The flowering and fading of a joy "too rich for use, for earth too dear" (1.5.48), does not so much condemn the unfeeling world as welcome the martyrdom of literally dying for love.

As protagonists, Romeo and Juliet lack tragic stature by any classical definition or in terms of the medieval convention of the Fall of Princes. The lovers are not extraordinary except in their passionate attachment to one another. They belong to prominent merchant families rather than to the nobility. They (especially Juliet) are very young, more so than any other of Shakespeare's tragic protagonists, and are indeed younger than most couples marrying in England at the time the play was written; Juliet is not yet fourteen (1.2.9, 1.3.13). Romeo and Juliet's dilemma of parental opposition is of the domestic sort often found in comedy. In fact, several characters in the play partly resemble the conventional character types of the Latin comic playwright Plautus or of Italian neoclassical comedy: the domineering father who insists that his daughter marry according to his choice, the unwelcome rival wooer, the garrulous and bawdy nurse, and, of course, the lovers. The Italian *novella*, to which Shakespeare often turned for his plots, made use of these same types and paid little attention to the classical precept that protagonists in a tragic story ought to be persons of high rank who are humbled through some inner flaw, or hamartia.

The story of Romeo and Juliet goes back ultimately to the fifth-century A.D. Greek romance of *Ephesiaca*, in which we find the motif of the sleeping potion as a means of escaping an unwelcome marriage. Masuccio of Salerno, in his *Il Novellino*, in 1476, combined the narrative of the heroine's deathlike trance and seeming burial alive with that of the hero's tragic failure to receive news from the friar that she is still alive. Luigi da Porto, in his *novella* (c. 1530), set the scene at Verona, provided the names of Romeo and Giulietta for the hero and heroine, added the account of their feuding families, the Montecchi and Cappelletti, introduced the killing of Tybalt (Theobaldo), and provided other important details. Luigi's version was followed by Matteo Bandello's famous *Novelle* of 1554, which was translated into French by Pierre Boaistuau (1559). The French version became the source for Arthur Brooke's long narrative poem in English, *The Tragical History of Romeus and Juliet* (1562). Brooke mentions having seen a play on the subject, but it is doubtful that Shakespeare knew this old play or, if he did know it, made use of it. Brooke's poem was his chief and probably only source. Shakespeare has condensed Brooke's action from nine months to less than a week, has greatly expanded the role of Mercutio, and has given to the Nurse a warmth and humorous richness not found in the usual Italian duenna, or *balia*. He has also tidied up the Friar's immorality and deleted the antipapal tone. Inheriting from Brooke a cautionary narrative against unruly yielding to sexual passion, in the homiletic vein of Puritan preachers, Shakespeare instead sympathizes with the perils of young lovers whose desires are unappreciated by an unfeeling world. Throughout all these changes, Shakespeare retains Brooke's romantic (rather than classically tragic) conception of love overwhelmed by external obstacles.

Like the romantic comedies, *Romeo and Juliet* is often funny and bawdy. Samson and Gregory in the first scene are slapstick cowards, hiding behind the law and daring to quarrel only when reinforcements arrive. The Nurse delights us with her earthy recollections of the day she weaned Juliet: the child tasting "the wormwood on the nipple / Of my dug" (1.3.31–2), the warm Italian sun, an earthquake, the Nurse's husband telling his lame but often-repeated bawdy joke about women falling on their backs. Mercutio employs his inventive and sardonic humor to twit Romeo for lovesickness and the Nurse for her pomposity. She, in turn, scolds Peter and plagues Juliet (who is breathlessly awaiting news from Romeo) with a history of her back ailments. Mercutio and the Nurse are among Shakespeare's bawdiest characters. Their wry and salacious view of love contrasts with the nobly innocent and yet physically passionate love of Romeo and Juliet. Mercutio and the Nurse cannot take part in the play's denouement; one dies, misinterpreting Romeo's appeasement of Tybalt, and the other proves insensitive to Juliet's depth of feeling. Yet the disappearance of these engaging companions takes from the play some of its vitality and most of its funniness. The death of Tybalt turns the play from comedy to tragedy.

The lovers, too, are at first well suited to Shakespearean romantic comedy. When we meet Romeo, he is not in love with Juliet at all, despite the play's title, but is mooning over a "hardhearted wench" (in Mercutio's words) named Rosaline. This "goddess" appropriately never appears in the play; she is almost a disembodied idea in Romeo's mind, a scornful beauty like Phoebe in *As You Like It*. Romeo's love for her is tedious and self-pitying, like that of the conventional wooer in a sonnet sequence by Francesco Petrarch or one of his imitators. Juliet, although not yet fourteen, must change all this by teaching Romeo the nature of true love. She will have none of his shopworn clichés learned in the service of Rosaline, his flowery protestations and swearing by the moon, lest they prove to be love's perjuries. With her innocent candor, she insists (like many heroines of the romantic comedies) on dispelling the mask of pretense that lovers too often show one another. "Capulet" and "Montague" are mere labels, not the inner self. Although Juliet would have been more coy, she confesses, had she known that Romeo was overhearing her, she will now "prove more true / Than those that have more cunning to be strange" (2.2.100–1). She is more practical than he in assessing danger and making plans. Later she also proves herself remarkably able to bear misfortune.

The comedy of the play's first half is, to be sure, overshadowed by the certainty of disaster. The opening chorus plainly warns us that the lovers will die. They are "star-crossed," and they speak of themselves as such. Romeo fears "Some consequence yet hanging in the stars" when he reluctantly goes to the Capulets' feast (1.4.107); after he has slain Tybalt, he cries "Oh, I am fortune's fool!" (3.1.135); and, at the news of Juliet's supposed death, he proclaims "Then I defy you, stars!" (5.1.24). Yet in what sense are Romeo and Juliet "star-crossed"? The concept is deliberately broad in this play, encompassing many factors, such as hatred, bumbling, bad luck, and simple lack of awareness.

The first scene presents feuding as a major cause in the tragedy. The quarrel between the two families is so ancient that the original motives are no longer even discussed. Inspired by the "fiery" Tybalt, factionalism pursues its mindless course, despite the efforts of the Prince to end it. Although the elders of both families talk of peace, they call for their swords quickly enough when a fray begins. Still, this senseless hatred does not lead to tragedy until its effects are fatally complicated through misunderstanding. With poignant irony, good intentions are repeatedly undermined by lack of knowledge. We can see why Juliet does not tell her family of her secret marriage with a presumably hated Montague, but, in fact, Capulet has accepted Romeo as a guest in his house under the terms of chivalric hospitality, praising him as a "virtuous and well governed youth" (1.5.69). For all his dictatorial ways, and the manifest advantages he may see in marrying his daughter to an aristocrat like Paris, Capulet would, of course, never propose the match if he knew his daughter to be married already. Not knowing of Juliet's marriage, he and his wife can only interpret her refusal to marry Paris as caprice. Count Paris himself is victim of this tragedy of unawareness. He is an eminently suitable wooer for Juliet, rich and nobly born, considerate, peace-loving, and deeply fond of Juliet (as he shows by his private and sincere grief at her tomb). Certainly, he would never intentionally woo a married woman. Not knowing, he plays the unattractive role of the rival wooer and dies for it. Similarly, Mercutio cannot understand Romeo's seemingly craven behavior toward Tybalt and so begins the duel that leads to Romeo's banishment. The final scene, with Friar Laurence's retelling of the story, allows us to see the survivors confronted with what they have all unknowingly done.

Chance, or accident, plays a role of importance equal to that of hatred and unawareness. An outbreak of the plague prevents Friar John from conveying Friar Laurence's letter to Romeo at Mantua. Friar Laurence, going hurriedly to the Capulets' tomb, arrives in time for Juliet's awakening but some minutes after Romeo has killed Paris and taken poison. Juliet awakens only moments later. The Watch comes just too late to prevent her suicide. Friar Laurence expresses well the sense of frustration at plans gone awry by such narrow margins: "what an unkind hour / Is guilty of this lamentable chance!" (5.3.145–6). Earlier, Capulet's decision to move the wedding date up one day has crucially affected the timing. Human miscalculation contributes also to the catastrophe: Mercutio is killed under Romeo's arm, and Friar Laurence wonders unhappily if any of his complicated plans "Miscarried by my fault" (5.3.267). Character and human decision play a part in this tragedy, for Romeo should not have dueled with Tybalt, no matter what the provocation. In choosing to kill Tybalt, he has deliberately cast aside as "effeminate" the gentle and forgiving qualities he has learned from his love of Juliet (3.1.113) and thus is guilty of a rash and self-destructive action. To ascribe the cause of the tragedy in Aristotelian fashion to his and Juliet's impulsiveness is, however, to ignore much of the rest of the play.

Instead, the ending of the play brings a pattern out of the seeming welter of mistakes and animosities. "A greater power than we can contradict / Hath thwarted our intents," says Friar Laurence, suggesting that the seeming bad luck of the delayed letter was, in fact, the intent of a mysterious higher intelligence (5.3.153–4). Prince Escalus, too, finds a necessary meaning in the tragic event. "See what a scourge is laid upon your hate," he admonishes the Montagues and Capulets, "That heaven finds means to kill your joys with love." Romeo and Juliet are "Poor sacrifices of our enmity" (lines 292–304). As the Prologue had foretold, their deaths will "bury their parents' strife"; the families' feud is a stub-

born evil force "Which, but their children's end, naught could remove." Order is preciously restored; the price is great, but the sacrifice nonetheless confirms a sense of a larger intention in what had appeared to be simply hatred and misfortune. Throughout the play, love and hate are interrelated opposites, yoked through the rhetorical device of oxymoron, or inherent contradiction. Romeo apostrophizes "O brawling love, O loving hate" (1.1.176), and Juliet later echoes his words: "My only love sprung from my only hate" (1.5.139). This paradox expresses a conflict in humankind, as in the universe itself. "Two such opposèd kings encamp them still / In man as well as herbs," says Friar Laurence, "grace and rude will" (2.3.27–8). Hatred is a condition of our corrupted wills, of our fall from grace, and it attempts to destroy what is gracious in human beings. In this cosmic strife, love must pay the sacrifice, as Romeo and Juliet do with their lives, but, because their deaths are finally perceived as the cost of so much hatred, the two families come to terms with their collective guilt and resolve henceforth to be worthy of the sacrifice.

Structurally, *Romeo and Juliet* gives considerable prominence to the feuding of the two families. Public scenes occur at key points—at beginning, middle, and end (1.1, 3.1, and 5.3)—and each such scene concerns violence and its consequences. The play begins with a brawl. Tybalt is a baleful presence in 1.1 and 3.1, implacably bent on vengeance. The three public scenes are alike, too, in that they bring into confrontation the entire families of Capulets and Montagues, who call for swords and demand reprisal from the state for what they themselves have set in motion. Prince Escalus dominates these three public scenes. He must offer judgment in each, giving the families fair warning, then exiling Romeo for Tybalt's death, and finally counseling the families on the meaning of their collective tragedy. He is a spokesman for public order and security ("Mercy but murders, pardoning those that kill," 3.1.196), even though he is also unable to prevent the tragedy. He stands above the conflict and yet is affected by it; his own kinsman, Mercutio, is one of the casualties. For all his dignity and impartiality, Escalus's official function is somehow tangential to the central emotional experience of the play. The law does not provide a remedy. Still, it can preside and arbitrate. To Escalus is given the final speech promising both punishment and pardon, and it is he who sums up the paradoxical interdependence of love and hate. Although the morning after the catastrophe brings with it sorrow, it also brings peace, however "glooming." Escalus is master of ceremonies for a restored order through which the families and we are reconciled to what has occurred.

In good part, the public scenes of the play serve to frame the love plot and the increasing isolation of the separated lovers, but these public scenes have a function of their own to the extent that the tragedy has touched and altered everyone. The final tableau is not the kiss of the dying lovers but the handclasp of the reconciled fathers. The long, last public ceremonial is important because, although the private catastrophe of the lovers is unalterably complete, recognition occurs only when the Friar recounts at great length to all the community the story we already know. As we watch the bereaved families responding with shock to the story of Romeo and Juliet's tragedy, we understand the reason for its length: only when it is too late do the families begin to comprehend their own complicity in the disaster that has occurred. This recognition is not that of the protagonists, as in the Aristotelian conception of recognition, nor does it accompany a reversal in the love tragedy; that reversal already has taken place in Romeo's banishment and the lovers' deaths. This lack of correspondence with an Aristotelian definition of tragedy is not, however, a structural flaw; rather, it is a manifestation of the dual focus of the tragedy on the lovers and on all Verona. The city itself is a kind of protagonist, suffering through its own violence and coming at last to the sad comfort that wisdom brings.

The timeless nature of a tragic story about young lovers has resulted in its being an irresistible vehicle for modern updatings in the theater and in film, many of them highly successful in bringing the play into the lives of modern and young audiences. Productions in this vein have raised important questions about the protagonists' attitudes toward love and the nature of the social environment in which their tragedy occurs. The play's vivid bawdry invites an atmosphere of hedonism that can be understood, implicitly at least, in terms of the sexual revolution of the 1960s and afterwards. The boy actor who originally played Juliet on Shakespeare's stage has been replaced by Olivia Hussey, for example, in Franco Zeffirelli's popular film of 1968; Hussey is so gorgeously appealing in her first long night-time conversation with Romeo that his insistent "Oh, wilt thou leave me so unsatisfied?" takes on new urgency. Subsequently, the film briefly shows the lovers in bed,

unclothed. Mercutio is sometimes portrayed as homosexual: mutedly so in the Zeffirelli film, aggressively so in Terry Hands's 1973 production at Stratford-upon-Avon, and flamboyantly so in Baz Luhrmann's immensely successful film, *Romeo + Juliet*, of 1996. In this last version, Mercutio is an African American drag queen, while Friar Laurence is a New Age priest. Juliet's mother in this same film is hilarious as a pill-popping, chain-smoking, and hard-drinking society dame slithering her ectomorphically slim body into a Cleopatra outfit for the huge masked ball that she and her nouveau riche husband are putting on in their tastelessly expensive block-long mansion—just the sort of parents whom one can count on not to understand their daughter. Luhrmann's Nurse is an Hispanic woman bellowing "Huliet! Huliet!" to remind us that the film is set in a southern United States city like Los Angeles or Miami. (It was actually filmed in Mexico City.) The street violence is also Hispanic, with rival gangs setting fire to gas stations and shooting automatic weapons during high-speed car chases. This updating of the violence with which the play begins owes some of its inspiration, presumably, to Leonard Bernstein's *West Side Story* (1957), set in Spanish Harlem.

Such innovations are at their best when they point to the play's insistent dramatization of violence and love in conflict. What responsibility does society bear for youthful tragedy when the models for behavior available to young people are what they are in today's world? How can a young man like Romeo escape the peer pressures of gang loyalties and macho stereotypes? Romeo struggles against these pressures in his crucial moment of decision; knowing that Juliet has taught him a better way, he yet succumbs to the mores of his tribe and to his own need to revenge on Tybalt the death of Mercutio. In these modern productions, as in the play itself, the violent response is too believable. As Friar Laurence says, "grace and rude will" do battle within the human psyche, too often with tragic outcome, and young love must pay the price.

Romeo and Juliet

The Prologue

[*Enter Chorus.*]

CHORUS
Two households, both alike in dignity,   1
  In fair Verona, where we lay our scene,
From ancient grudge break to new mutiny,   3
  Where civil blood makes civil hands unclean.   4
From forth the fatal loins of these two foes.
  A pair of star-crossed lovers take their life; 6
Whose misadventured piteous overthrows   7
Doth with their death bury their parents' strife.
The fearful passage of their death-marked love,   9
  And the continuance of their parents' rage,
Which, but their children's end, naught could remove,
  Is now the two hours' traffic of our stage;   12
The which if you with patient ears attend,
What here shall miss, our toil shall strive to mend.   14
                                    [*Exit.*]

❦

Prologue.
1–14 (The Prologue is in the form of a sonnet.)
1 dignity rank, status   **3 mutiny** strife, discord   **4 Where . . . unclean** where citizens' hands uncivilly are stained in civil strife with their fellow citizens' blood.   **6 star-crossed** thwarted by destiny, by adverse stars   **7 misadventured** unlucky

9 passage progress   **12 two hours' traffic** A conventional way of referring to the length of stage performances in the early modern period, not to be taken too literally, but indicative of a brisk pace   **14 What . . . mend** what is defective or inadequate in the short summary I have given you here, the actors' efforts in the following two hours will amply and fully make clear.

[1.1]

*Enter Samson and Gregory, with swords
and bucklers, of the house of Capulet.*

SAMSON   Gregory, on my word, we'll not carry coals.   1
GREGORY   No, for then we should be colliers.   2
SAMSON   I mean, an we be in choler, we'll draw.   3
GREGORY   Ay, while you live, draw your neck out of   4
collar.   5
SAMSON   I strike quickly, being moved.   6
GREGORY   But thou art not quickly moved to strike.
SAMSON   A dog of the house of Montague moves me.   8
GREGORY   To move is to stir, and to be valiant is to
stand. Therefore, if thou art moved, thou run'st away.   10
SAMSON   A dog of that house shall move me to stand. I
will take the wall of any man or maid of Montague's.   12
GREGORY   That shows thee a weak slave, for the   13
weakest goes to the wall.   14
SAMSON   'Tis true, and therefore women, being the
weaker vessels, are ever thrust to the wall. Therefore I   16
will push Montague's men from the wall and thrust
his maids to the wall.
GREGORY   The quarrel is between our masters and us   19
their men.   20
SAMSON   'Tis all one. I will show myself a tyrant: when   21
I have fought with the men, I will be civil with the
maids—I will cut off their heads.
GREGORY   The heads of the maids?
SAMSON   Ay, the heads of the maids, or their maiden-
heads. Take it in what sense thou wilt.   26
GREGORY   They must take it in sense that feel it.   27
SAMSON   Me they shall feel while I am able to stand,   28
and 'tis known I am a pretty piece of flesh.   29
GREGORY   'Tis well thou art not fish; if thou hadst, thou   30
hadst been Poor John. Draw thy tool. Here comes of   31
the house of Montagues.

*Enter two other Servingmen
[Abraham and another].*

SAMSON   My naked weapon is out. Quarrel, I will back
thee.
GREGORY   How, turn thy back and run?
SAMSON   Fear me not.   36
GREGORY   No, marry. I fear thee!   37
SAMSON   Let us take the law of our side. Let them   38
begin.
GREGORY   I will frown as I pass by, and let them take it
as they list.   41
SAMSON   Nay, as they dare. I will bite my thumb at   42
them, which is disgrace to them if they bear it.
          [*Samson makes taunting gestures.*]
ABRAHAM   Do you bite your thumb at us, sir?
SAMSON   I do bite my thumb, sir.
ABRAHAM   Do you bite your thumb at us, sir?
SAMSON   [*aside to Gregory*]   Is the law of our side if I
say ay?
GREGORY   [*aside to Samson*]   No.
SAMSON   [*to Abraham*]   No, sir, I do not bite my thumb
at you, sir, but I bite my thumb, sir.
GREGORY   Do you quarrel, sir?
ABRAHAM   Quarrel, sir? No, sir.
SAMSON   But if you do, sir, I am for you. I serve as good
a man as you.
ABRAHAM   No better.
SAMSON   Well, sir.

Enter Benvolio.

GREGORY   [*to Samson*]   Say "better." Here comes one of   58
my master's kinsmen.   59
SAMSON   [*to Abraham*]   Yes, better, sir.
ABRAHAM   You lie.
SAMSON   Draw, if you be men. Gregory, remember thy
washing blow.   *They fight.*   63
BENVOLIO   Part, fools!
Put up your swords. You know not what you do.

Enter Tybalt [with sword drawn].

TYBALT
What, art thou drawn among these heartless hinds?   66
Turn thee, Benvolio. Look upon thy death.
BENVOLIO
I do but keep the peace. Put up thy sword,
Or manage it to part these men with me.   69
TYBALT
What, drawn and talk of peace? I hate the word
As I hate hell, all Montagues, and thee.
Have at thee, coward!   [*They fight.*]   72

*Enter three or four Citizens with clubs
or partisans.*

1.1. Location: Verona. A public place.
0.2 *bucklers* small shields   **1 carry coals** i.e., endure insults.   **2 colliers**
(Coal carriers were regarded as dirty and of evil repute.)   **3 an** if.
choler anger (produced by one of the four humors).   **draw** draw
swords.   **5 collar** i.e., hangman's noose. (With pun on *colliers* and
choler.)   **6 moved** i.e., to anger. (With pun in next line.)   **8 moves**
incites   **10 stand** i.e., stand one's ground.   **12 take the wall** take the
cleaner side of the walk nearest the wall, thus forcing others out into
the gutter   **13–14 the weakest . . . wall** (A proverb expressing the
idea that the weakest are always forced to give way.)   **16 weaker
vessels** (Saint Paul bids husbands give honor to their wives "as unto
the weaker vessel," 1 Peter 3:7.)   **thrust to the wall** (With suggestion
of amorous assault.)   **19–20 between . . . men** i.e., between the males
of one household and the males of the other household; we have no
quarrel with the women.   **21 one** the same.   **26 what sense** whatever meaning   **27 They . . . feel it** i.e., It is the maids who must
receive by way of physical sensation (*sense*) what I have to offer,
because they are the ones who can feel it.   **28 stand** (With suggestion
of "have an erection," continued in the next few lines in *draw thy tool*
and *my naked weapon is out*.)   **29–30 flesh . . . fish** (Refers to the
proverbial phrase, "neither fish nor flesh.")   **31 Poor John** hake
salted and dried—a poor Lenten kind of food. (Probably with a
bawdy suggestion of sexual insufficiency.).   **comes of** i.e., come
members of

36 Fear Mistrust. (But Gregory deliberately misunderstands in the
next line, saying, in effect, "No indeed, do you think I'd be afraid of
you?")   **37 marry** i.e., indeed. (Originally an oath, "by the Virgin
Mary.")   **38 take the law of** have the law on   **41 list** please.   **42 bite
my thumb** i.e., make an insulting and probably obscene gesture
58–9 one . . . kinsmen i.e., Tybalt, who is approaching. (Not Benvolio,
who has just entered unobserved by the servingmen.)   **63 washing**
slashing with great force   **66 heartless hinds** cowardly menials.
69 manage use   **72 Have at thee** i.e., On guard, here I come
72.2 *partisans* long-handled spears.

CITIZENS
Clubs, bills, and partisans! Strike! Beat them down!   73
Down with the Capulets! Down with the Montagues!   74

Enter old Capulet in his gown, and his Wife.

CAPULET
What noise is this? Give me my long sword, ho!   75
CAPULET'S WIFE
A crutch, a crutch! Why call you for a sword?
CAPULET
My sword, I say! Old Montague is come
And flourishes his blade in spite of me.   78

Enter old Montague and his Wife.

MONTAGUE
Thou villain Capulet!—Hold me not; let me go.
MONTAGUE'S WIFE
Thou shalt not stir one foot to seek a foe.   80

Enter Prince Escalus, with his train.

PRINCE
Rebellious subjects, enemies to peace,
Profaners of this neighbor-stainèd steel—   82
Will they not hear? What, ho! You men, you beasts,
That quench the fire of your pernicious rage
With purple fountains issuing from your veins,   85
On pain of torture, from those bloody hands
Throw your mistempered weapons to the ground   87
And hear the sentence of your movèd prince.   88
Three civil brawls, bred of an airy word,   89
By thee, old Capulet, and Montague,
Have thrice disturbed the quiet of our streets
And made Verona's ancient citizens
Cast by their grave-beseeming ornaments   93
To wield old partisans in hands as old,
Cankered with peace, to part your cankered hate.   95
If ever you disturb our streets again
Your lives shall pay the forfeit of the peace.   97
For this time all the rest depart away.
You, Capulet, shall go along with me,
And Montague, come you this afternoon,
To know our farther pleasure in this case,
To old Freetown, our common judgment-place.   102
Once more, on pain of death, all men depart.

Exeunt [all but Montague, Montague's Wife,
and Benvolio].

MONTAGUE
Who set this ancient quarrel new abroach?   104
Speak, nephew, were you by when it began?   105
BENVOLIO
Here were the servants of your adversary,
And yours, close fighting ere I did approach.
I drew to part them. In the instant came
The fiery Tybalt with his sword prepared,   109
Which, as he breathed defiance to my ears,
He swung about his head and cut the winds
Who, nothing hurt withal, hissed him in scorn.   112
While we were interchanging thrusts and blows,
Came more and more, and fought on part and part   114
Till the Prince came, who parted either part.   115
MONTAGUE'S WIFE
Oh, where is Romeo? Saw you him today?
Right glad I am he was not at this fray.
BENVOLIO
Madam, an hour before the worshiped sun
Peered forth the golden window of the east,   119
A troubled mind drave me to walk abroad,   120
Where, underneath the grove of sycamore
That westward rooteth from this city side,   122
So early walking did I see your son.
Towards him I made, but he was ware of me   124
And stole into the covert of the wood.   125
I, measuring his affections by my own,   126
Which then most sought where most might not be
found,   127
Being one too many by my weary self,
Pursued my humor, not pursuing his,   129
And gladly shunned who gladly fled from me.   130
MONTAGUE
Many a morning hath he there been seen,
With tears augmenting the fresh morning's dew,
Adding to clouds more clouds with his deep sighs;
But all so soon as the all-cheering sun
Should in the farthest east begin to draw
The shady curtains from Aurora's bed,   136
Away from light steals home my heavy son   137
And private in his chamber pens himself,
Shuts up his windows, locks fair daylight out,
And makes himself an artificial night.
Black and portentous must this humor prove
Unless good counsel may the cause remove.
BENVOLIO
My noble uncle, do you know the cause?
MONTAGUE
I neither know it nor can learn of him.

---

73 **Clubs** rallying cry, summoning apprentices with their clubs.
bills long-handled spears with hooked blades   74.1 *gown* nightgown, dressing gown   75 **long sword** heavy, old-fashioned sword
78 **spite** defiance, despite   80.1 *train* retinue.   82 **Profaners . . . steel**
you who profane your weapons by staining them with neighbors'
blood   85 **purple** bloody, dark red   87 **mistempered** (1) having been
tempered, or hardened, in hot blood rather than cold water (2) malignant, ill-tempered   88 **movèd** angry   89 **airy** flippant, saucy
93 **grave-beseeming ornaments** i.e., staffs and other appurtenances
suited to wise old age   95 **Cankered . . . cankered** corroded (from
disuse) . . . malignant   97 **Your . . . peace** death will be the penalty for
breaking the peace.   102 **Freetown** (Brooke's translation, in his poem
Romeus and Juliet, of Villa Franca, as found in the Italian story.)
common public

104 **set . . . abroach** reopened this old quarrel, set it flowing.   105 **by**
near   109 **prepared** drawn, ready   112 **Who . . . withal** which winds,
not at all injured thereby   114 **on part and part** on one side and the
other   115 **either part** both parties.   119 **forth** from forth   120 **drave
. . . abroad** drove me to take a walk   122 **That . . . side** that grows on
the west side of this city   124 **made** moved.   **ware** wary, aware
125 **covert** cover, hiding place   126 **affections** wishes, inclination
127 **Which . . . found** which then chiefly desired a place where I
might be alone   129 **humor** mood   130 **who** him who   136 **Aurora**
goddess of dawn   137 **heavy** (1) sad (2) the opposite of *light*.   **son**
(punning on *sun*, line 134)

BENVOLIO

Have you importuned him by any means?   145

MONTAGUE

Both by myself and many other friends.
But he, his own affections' counselor,
Is to himself—I will not say how true,   148
But to himself so secret and so close,   149
So far from sounding and discovery,   150
As is the bud bit with an envious worm   151
Ere he can spread his sweet leaves to the air
Or dedicate his beauty to the sun.
Could we but learn from whence his sorrows grow,
We would as willingly give cure as know.

Enter Romeo.

BENVOLIO

See where he comes. So please you, step aside.   156
I'll know his grievance or be much denied.

MONTAGUE

I would thou wert so happy by thy stay   158
To hear true shrift.—Come, madam, let's away.   159

Exeunt [Montague and his Wife].

BENVOLIO

Good morrow, cousin.

ROMEO   Is the day so young?   160

BENVOLIO

But new struck nine.

ROMEO   Ay me! Sad hours seem long.
Was that my father that went hence so fast?

BENVOLIO

It was. What sadness lengthens Romeo's hours?

ROMEO

Not having that which, having, makes them short.

BENVOLIO   In love?

ROMEO   Out—

BENVOLIO   Of love?

ROMEO

Out of her favor where I am in love.

BENVOLIO

Alas, that Love, so gentle in his view,   169
Should be so tyrannous and rough in proof!   170

ROMEO

Alas, that Love, whose view is muffled still,   171
Should without eyes see pathways to his will!   172
Where shall we dine?—Oh, me! What fray was here?
Yet tell me not, for I have heard it all.
Here's much to do with hate, but more with love.
Why, then, O brawling love, O loving hate,
O anything of nothing first create,   177
O heavy lightness, serious vanity,
Misshapen chaos of well-seeming forms,
Feather of lead, bright smoke, cold fire, sick health,

Still-waking sleep, that is not what it is!   181
This love feel I, that feel no love in this.
Dost thou not laugh?

BENVOLIO   No, coz, I rather weep.   183

ROMEO

Good heart, at what?

BENVOLIO   At thy good heart's oppression.

ROMEO

Why, such is love's transgression.
Griefs of mine own lie heavy in my breast,
Which thou wilt propagate, to have it pressed   187
With more of thine. This love that thou hast shown   188
Doth add more grief to too much of mine own.
Love is a smoke made with the fume of sighs;
Being purged, a fire sparkling in lovers' eyes;   191
Being vexed, a sea nourished with lovers' tears.
What is it else? A madness most discreet,   193
A choking gall, and a preserving sweet.
Farewell, my coz.

BENVOLIO   Soft! I will go along.   195
An if you leave me so, you do me wrong.   196

ROMEO

Tut, I have lost myself. I am not here.
This is not Romeo; he's some other where.

BENVOLIO

Tell me in sadness, who is that you love?   199

ROMEO   What, shall I groan and tell thee?

BENVOLIO

Groan? Why, no, but sadly tell me who.   201

ROMEO

Bid a sick man in sadness make his will—
A word ill urged to one that is so ill!   203
In sadness, cousin, I do love a woman.

BENVOLIO

I aimed so near when I supposed you loved.

ROMEO

A right good markman! And she's fair I love.   206

BENVOLIO

A right fair mark, fair coz, is soonest hit.   207

ROMEO

Well, in that hit you miss. She'll not be hit
With Cupid's arrow. She hath Dian's wit,   209
And, in strong proof of chastity well armed,   210
From Love's weak childish bow she lives unharmed.
She will not stay the siege of loving terms,   212
Nor bide th'encounter of assailing eyes,   213
Nor ope her lap to saint-seducing gold.
Oh, she is rich in beauty, only poor
That when she dies, with beauty dies her store.   216

181 Still-waking continually awake   **183 coz** cousin, kinsman
187–8 propagate . . . thine increase by having it, i.e., my own grief,
oppressed or made still heavier with your grief on my account.
(The image of propagating and pressing is appropriately sexual.)
191 purged i.e., of smoke   **193 discreet** judicious, prudent   **195 Soft!**
i.e., Wait a moment!   **196 An if** If   **199 sadness** seriousness.   **is that**
is it that   **201 sadly** seriously. (But Romeo plays on the word, and
on *in sadness*, in the sense of "sorrowfully.")   **203 A word** i.e., *sadly*
or *in sadness*—too sad a word, says Romeo, for a melancholy lover
206 fair beautiful   **207 fair mark** clear, distinct target   **209 Dian**
Diana, huntress and goddess of chastity   **210 proof** armor   **212 stay**
submit to   **213 bide** abide, endure   **216 store** wealth. (She will die
without children, and therefore her beauty will die with her.)

145 any means every means possible.   **148 true** i.e., wise in counseling himself   **149 close** secretive   **150 sounding** being fathomed (to
discover deep or inner secrets)   **151 envious** malicious   **156 So
please you** If you please   **158 happy** fortunate, successful   **159 To** as
to.   **shrift** confession.   **160 cousin** kinsman.   **169 Love** Cupid.
view appearance   **170 in proof** in reality, in experience.   **171 view . . .
still** sight is blindfolded always. (Love is blind.)   **172 to his will** to
what he wants.   **177 create** created

BENVOLIO
Then she hath sworn that she will still live chaste? 217
ROMEO
She hath, and in that sparing makes huge waste, 218
For beauty starved with her severity 219
Cuts beauty off from all posterity.
She is too fair, too wise, wisely too fair,
To merit bliss by making me despair. 222
She hath forsworn to love, and in that vow 223
Do I live dead, that live to tell it now.
BENVOLIO
Be ruled by me. Forget to think of her.
ROMEO
Oh, teach me how I should forget to think!
BENVOLIO
By giving liberty unto thine eyes:
Examine other beauties.
ROMEO   'Tis the way
To call hers, exquisite, in question more. 229
These happy masks that kiss fair ladies' brows,
Being black, puts us in mind they hide the fair.
He that is strucken blind cannot forget
The precious treasure of his eyesight lost.
Show me a mistress that is passing fair: 234
What doth her beauty serve but as a note
Where I may read who passed that passing fair? 236
Farewell. Thou canst not teach me to forget.
BENVOLIO
I'll pay that doctrine, or else die in debt.   *Exeunt.* 238

❖

[1.2]

Enter Capulet, County Paris, and the Clown
[*a Servingman*].

CAPULET
But Montague is bound as well as I, 1
In penalty alike, and 'tis not hard, I think,
For men so old as we to keep the peace.
PARIS
Of honorable reckoning are you both, 4
And pity 'tis you lived at odds so long.
But now, my lord, what say you to my suit?
CAPULET
But saying o'er what I have said before: 7
My child is yet a stranger in the world;
She hath not seen the change of fourteen years.
Let two more summers wither in their pride
Ere we may think her ripe to be a bride.

PARIS
Younger than she are happy mothers made.
CAPULET
And too soon marred are those so early made.
The earth hath swallowed all my hopes but she;
She is the hopeful lady of my earth. 15
But woo her, gentle Paris, get her heart;
My will to her consent is but a part;
And, she agreed, within her scope of choice 18
Lies my consent and fair-according voice. 19
This night I hold an old accustomed feast, 20
Whereto I have invited many a guest
Such as I love; and you among the store, 22
One more, most welcome, makes my number more.
At my poor house look to behold this night
Earth-treading stars that make dark heaven light.
Such comfort as do lusty young men feel 26
When well-appareled April on the heel 27
Of limping winter treads, even such delight
Among fresh fennel buds shall you this night 29
Inherit at my house. Hear all, all see, 30
And like her most whose merit most shall be;
Which on more view of many, mine, being one, 32
May stand in number, though in reck'ning none. 33
Come, go with me. [*To the Servingman, giving a paper*]
  Go, sirrah, trudge about 34
Through fair Verona; find those persons out
Whose names are written there, and to them say,
My house and welcome on their pleasure stay. 37
                Exit [*with Paris*].
SERVINGMAN   Find them out whose names are written
here! It is written that the shoemaker should meddle 39
with his yard and the tailor with his last, the fisher 40
with his pencil, and the painter with his nets; but I am 41
sent to find those persons whose names are here writ, 42
and can never find what names the writing person 43
hath here writ. I must to the learned.—In good time! 44

Enter Benvolio and Romeo.

---

217 **still** always   218 **sparing** miserliness   219 **starved with** killed by
222 **To . . . despair** to achieve her own salvation through chaste living
while driving me to the spiritually dangerous state of despair.
223 **forsworn to** renounced, repudiated   229 **in question more** even
more keenly to mind, into consideration.   234 **mistress** i.e., eligible
young woman. **passing** surpassingly   236 **passed** surpassed
238 **I'll . . . debt** i.e., I'll fulfill my obligation to do that, or feel I have
failed as a friend.
1.2. Location: Verona.
0.1 *County* Count   1 **bound** legally obligated (to keep the peace)
4 **reckoning** estimation, repute   7 **o'er** again

15 **the hopeful . . . earth** i.e., my heir and hope for posterity. (*Earth*
includes property and lands.)   18 **she** if she be   19 **according** agreeing   20 **old accustomed** traditional   22 **store** group   26 **lusty** lively
27 **well-appareled** newly clothed in green   29 **fennel** flowering herb
thought to have the power of awakening passion   30 **Inherit** possess
32–3 **Which . . . none** i.e., when you have looked over many ladies,
my daughter, being one of them, may be numerically counted among
the lot, but you will not think her worth your notice. (Capulet refers
to the proverbial saying, "one is no number.")   34 **sirrah** (Customary
form of address to servants.)   37 **on . . . stay** wait to serve their pleasure.   39–41 **It is . . . nets** i.e., If a shoemaker cannot be expected to
have any skill with a *yard* (a tailor's yardstick) and conversely a tailor
with a *last* (a shoemaker's form), and similarly with a painter's *pencil*
(a paintbrush) in a fisherman's hands or a net in a painter's hands,
why should I, an illiterate servant, be expected to be able to read a
written note of invitation? (*Meddle, yard,* and *pencil* are often slang
expressions for sexual activity and the male sexual organ, but since
last and *nets* don't seem to convey sexual meaning here, the humor is
more directed at comic inappropriateness.)   42 **find** locate   43 **find**
figure out   44 **In good time** i.e., Here comes help.

BENVOLIO
  Tut, man, one fire burns out another's burning,
  One pain is lessened by another's anguish;   46
  Turn giddy, and be holp by backward turning;   47
  One desperate grief cures with another's languish.   48
  Take thou some new infection to thy eye,
  And the rank poison of the old will die.   50
ROMEO
  Your plaintain leaf is excellent for that.   51
BENVOLIO
  For what, I pray thee?
ROMEO   For your broken shin.
BENVOLIO   Why, Romeo, art thou mad?
ROMEO
  Not mad, but bound more than a madman is;   54
  Shut up in prison, kept without my food,
  Whipped and tormented and—Good e'en, good
    fellow.   56
SERVINGMAN   God gi' good e'en. I pray, sir, can you read?   57
ROMEO
  Ay, mine own fortune in my misery.
SERVINGMAN   Perhaps you have learned it without   59
  book. But, I pray, can you read anything you see?   60
ROMEO
  Ay, if I know the letters and the language.
SERVINGMAN   Ye say honestly. Rest you merry!   62
                                            [Going.]
ROMEO   Stay, fellow, I can read.   He reads the letter.
  "Signor Martino and his wife and daughters,
  County Anselme and his beauteous sisters,
  The lady widow of Vitruvio,
  Signor Placentio and his lovely nieces,
  Mercutio and his brother Valentine,
  Mine uncle Capulet, his wife, and daughters,
  My fair niece Rosaline, and Livia,
  Signor Valentio and his cousin Tybalt,
  Lucio and the lively Helena."
  A fair assembly. Whither should they come?
SERVINGMAN   Up.
ROMEO   Whither? To supper?
SERVINGMAN   To our house.
ROMEO   Whose house?
SERVINGMAN   My master's.
ROMEO
  Indeed, I should have asked thee that before.
SERVINGMAN   Now I'll tell you without asking. My
  master is the great rich Capulet; and if you be not of
  the house of Montagues, I pray, come and crush a cup   82
  of wine. Rest you merry!   [Exit.]

BENVOLIO
  At this same ancient feast of Capulet's   84
  Sups the fair Rosaline whom thou so loves,
  With all the admirèd beauties of Verona.
  Go thither, and with unattainted eye   87
  Compare her face with some that I shall show,
  And I will make thee think thy swan a crow.
ROMEO
  When the devout religion of mine eye   90
    Maintains such falsehood, then turn tears to fires;   91
  And these who, often drowned, could never die,   92
    Transparent heretics, be burnt for liars!   93
  One fairer than my love? The all-seeing sun
  Ne'er saw her match since first the world begun.
BENVOLIO
  Tut, you saw her fair, none else being by,
  Herself poised with herself in either eye;   97
  But in that crystal scales let there be weighed   98
  Your lady's love against some other maid
  That I will show you shining at this feast,
  And she shall scant show well that now seems best.   101
ROMEO
  I'll go along, no such sight to be shown,
  But to rejoice in splendor of mine own.   [Exeunt.] 103

                            ❖

[1.3]

        Enter Capulet's Wife and Nurse.

WIFE
  Nurse, where's my daughter? Call her forth to me.
NURSE
  Now, by my maidenhead at twelve year old,
  I bade her come. What, lamb! What, ladybird!   3
  God forbid, where's this girl? What, Juliet!   4

              Enter Juliet.

JULIET   How now? Who calls?
NURSE   Your mother.
JULIET
  Madam, I am here. What is your will?
WIFE
  This is the matter.—Nurse, give leave awhile,   8
  We must talk in secret.—Nurse, come back again;
  I have remembered me, thou's hear our counsel.   10
  Thou knowest my daughter's of a pretty age.

46 another's anguish the anguish of another pain   47 holp . . . turning helped by turning in the reverse direction   48 cures . . . languish
is cured by the suffering of a second *grief* or pain.   50 rank foul
51 Your . . . that i.e., (sardonically) Your proverbial nostrums are
about as useful in curing my real grief as is a folk remedy for minor
abrasions such as a *broken shin* (line 52) or surface wound on the leg—
that is, no use at all.   54 bound (The usual treatment for madness.)
56 Good e'en Good evening. (Used after noon.)   57 gi' give you
59–60 Perhaps . . . book (1) Perhaps that's some sort of book that
you've committed to memory (2) Misery is something one can learn
without knowing how to read.   62 Rest you merry i.e., Farewell.
(The servingman can see he is getting nowhere.)   82 crush i.e., drink

84 ancient customary   87 unattainted unbiased   90–3 When . . .
liars! (Romeo, recalling that persons suspected of witchcraft were
sometimes thrown into water to see if they would drown or float, and
that those who did not drown were declared witches and burned at
the stake, protests that whenever he is a heretic in love by looking at
some woman other than Rosaline he should be similarly burned by
having his own tears turn into flames, since he will have shown that
his flood of tears could not drown him, i.e., was insufficient.
Transparent means "manifest," "clear.")   97 poised weighed, balanced   98 crystal scales i.e., Romeo's eyes   101 scant scarcely
103 mine own i.e., the sight of my own Rosaline.
1.3. Location: Verona. Capulet's house.
3 ladybird (A term of affection.)   4 God forbid (A mild oath.)
8 give leave leave us   10 thou's thou shalt

NURSE
Faith, I can tell her age unto an hour.

WIFE
She's not fourteen.

NURSE   I'll lay fourteen of my teeth—
And yet, to my teen be it spoken, I have but four—   14
She's not fourteen. How long is it now
To Lammastide?

WIFE   A fortnight and odd days.   16

NURSE
Even or odd, of all days in the year,
Come Lammas Eve at night shall she be fourteen.
Susan and she—God rest all Christian souls!—   19
Were of an age. Well, Susan is with God;
She was too good for me. But, as I said,
On Lammas Eve at night shall she be fourteen,
That shall she, marry, I remember it well.   23
'Tis since the earthquake now eleven years,
And she was weaned—I never shall forget it—
Of all the days of the year, upon that day;
For I had then laid wormwood to my dug,   27
Sitting in the sun under the dovehouse wall.
My lord and you were then at Mantua—
Nay, I do bear a brain! But, as I said,   30
When it did taste the wormwood on the nipple
Of my dug and felt it bitter, pretty fool,   32
To see it tetchy and fall out wi'th' dug!   33
"Shake" quoth the dovehouse. 'Twas no need, I trow,   34
To bid me trudge!   35
And since that time it is eleven years,
For then she could stand high-lone; nay, by the rood,   37
She could have run and waddled all about.
For even the day before, she broke her brow,   39
And then my husband—God be with his soul!
'A was a merry man—took up the child.   41
"Yea," quoth he, "dost thou fall upon thy face?
Thou wilt fall backward when thou hast more wit,   43
Wilt thou not, Jule?" and, by my halidom,   44
The pretty wretch left crying and said "Ay."
To see now how a jest shall come about!   46
I warrant, an I should live a thousand years,
I never should forget it. "Wilt thou not, Jule?" quoth
  he,
And, pretty fool, it stinted and said "Ay."   49

WIFE
Enough of this. I pray thee, hold thy peace.

NURSE
Yes, madam. Yet I cannot choose but laugh
To think it should leave crying and say "Ay."
And yet, I warrant, it had upon it brow   53
A bump as big as a young cockerel's stone—   54
A perilous knock—and it cried bitterly.
"Yea," quoth my husband, "fall'st upon thy face?
Thou wilt fall backward when thou comest to age,
Wilt thou not, Jule?" It stinted and said "Ay."

JULIET
And stint thou too, I pray thee, Nurse, say I.   59

NURSE
Peace, I have done. God mark thee to his grace!
Thou wast the prettiest babe that e'er I nursed.
An I might live to see thee married once,   62
I have my wish.

WIFE
Marry, that "marry" is the very theme
I came to talk of. Tell me, daughter Juliet,
How stands your disposition to be married?   66

JULIET
It is an honor that I dream not of.

NURSE
An honor? Were not I thine only nurse,
I would say thou hadst sucked wisdom from thy teat.   69

WIFE
Well, think of marriage now. Younger than you
Here in Verona, ladies of esteem,
Are made already mothers. By my count
I was your mother much upon these years   73
That you are now a maid. Thus then in brief:
The valiant Paris seeks you for his love.

NURSE
A man, young lady! Lady, such a man
As all the world—why, he's a man of wax.   77

WIFE
Verona's summer hath not such a flower.

NURSE
Nay, he's a flower, in faith, a very flower.   79

WIFE
What say you? Can you love the gentleman?
This night you shall behold him at our feast.
Read o'er the volume of young Paris' face,
And find delight writ there with beauty's pen;
Examine every married lineament   84
And see how one another lends content;   85
And what obscured in this fair volume lies   86
Find written in the margent of his eyes.   87
This precious book of love, this unbound lover,   88

---

14 teen sorrow. (Playing on *teen* and *four* in *fourteen*.)   **16 Lammas-tide** the days near August 1.   **19 Susan** the Nurse's own child, who has evidently died   **23 marry** i.e., by the Virgin Mary. (A mild oath.)   **27 wormwood** (A bitter-tasting plant used to wean the child from the *dug* or "teat.")   **30 bear a brain** maintain a keen memory.   **32 fool** (A term of endearment here.)   **33 tetchy** peevish, irritable   **34 "Shake" . . . dovehouse** i.e., The dovehouse shook.   **trow** believe, assure you   **35 trudge** be off quickly.   **37 high-lone** on her feet, without help.   **rood** cross   **39 broke her brow** bruised her forehead (by falling)   **41 'A** He   **43 wit** understanding   **44 by my halidom** (A mild oath: "by all things holy," but popularly confused with "by my Holy Dame.")   **46 come about** come true.   **49 stinted** ceased

53 it its   **54 cockerel's stone** young rooster's testicle   **59 say I** (With a pun on *said "Ay"* of previous line.)   **62 An** If.   **once** someday   **66 disposition** inclination   **69 thy teat** the teat that nourished you.   **73 much . . . years** at much the same age   **77 a man of wax** as handsome as a figure modeled in wax.   **79 Nay** Indeed   **84 married lineament** harmonized feature   **85 And . . . content** and see how his handsome features enhance one another   **86–7 And what . . . eyes** and whatever you don't fully grasp by seeing his handsome features, find explained in his eyes, as though they were a kind of marginal gloss or commentary found in books.   **88 unbound** i.e., because not bound in marriage. (With a double meaning in the continuing metaphor of an unbound book.)

To beautify him, only lacks a cover. 89
The fish lives in the sea, and 'tis much pride 90
For fair without the fair within to hide. 91
That book in many's eyes doth share the glory, 92
That in gold clasps locks in the golden story; 93
So shall you share all that he doth possess
By having him, making yourself no less.

NURSE
No less? Nay, bigger. Women grow by men. 96

WIFE
Speak briefly, can you like of Paris' love? 97

JULIET
I'll look to like, if looking liking move; 98
But no more deep will I endart mine eye
Than your consent gives strength to make it fly.

Enter Servingman.

SERVINGMAN   Madam, the guests are come, supper
served up, you called, my young lady asked for, the
Nurse cursed in the pantry, and everything in extremity. I must hence to wait. I beseech you, follow straight. 104
WIFE   We follow thee.   [*Exit Servingman.*]
                              Juliet, the County stays. 105

NURSE
Go, girl, seek happy nights to happy days.   *Exeunt.*

❖

[1.4]

*Enter Romeo, Mercutio, Benvolio, with five or
six other masquers; torchbearers.*

ROMEO
What, shall this speech be spoke for our excuse? 1
Or shall we on without apology? 2

BENVOLIO
The date is out of such prolixity. 3
We'll have no Cupid hoodwinked with a scarf, 4
Bearing a Tartar's painted bow of lath, 5
Scaring the ladies like a crowkeeper, 6
Nor no without-book prologue, faintly spoke
After the prompter, for our entrance;
But let them measure us by what they will, 9
We'll measure them a measure, and be gone. 10

ROMEO
Give me a torch. I am not for this ambling.
Being but heavy, I will bear the light. 12

MERCUTIO
Nay, gentle Romeo, we must have you dance.

ROMEO
Not I, believe me. You have dancing shoes
With nimble soles; I have a soul of lead 15
So stakes me to the ground I cannot move.

MERCUTIO
You are a lover; borrow Cupid's wings,
And soar with them above a common bound. 18

ROMEO
I am too sore enpiercèd with his shaft 19
To soar with his light feathers, and so bound
I cannot bound a pitch above dull woe. 21
Under love's heavy burden do I sink.

MERCUTIO
And, to sink in it, should you burden love— 23
Too great oppression for a tender thing.

ROMEO
Is love a tender thing? It is too rough,
Too rude, too boisterous, and it pricks like thorn.

MERCUTIO
If love be rough with you, be rough with love;
Prick love for pricking, and you beat love down. 28
Give me a case to put my visage in. 29
                              [*He puts on a mask.*]
A visor for a visor! What care I 30
What curious eye doth quote deformities? 31
Here are the beetle brows shall blush for me.

BENVOLIO
Come, knock and enter, and no sooner in
But every man betake him to his legs. 34

ROMEO
A torch for me. Let wantons light of heart
Tickle the senseless rushes with their heels, 36
For I am proverbed with a grandsire phrase: 37
I'll be a candle-holder and look on. 38
The game was ne'er so fair, and I am done. 39

---

89 a cover i.e., marriage, an embracing wife.   **90–1 The fish . . . hide**
i.e., The fish has its own suitable environment, and similarly in marriage the fair Juliet (here imagined as a beautiful book cover "binding" Paris) would suitably enhance Paris's worth.   **92–3 That book
. . . story** i.e., In many persons' eyes, a good story is all the more
admirable for being handsomely bound. (*Clasps* means [1] book fas-
tenings [2] embraces.)   **96 bigger** i.e., by pregnancy.   **97 like of** be
pleased with   **98 liking move** may provoke affection   **104 straight**
at once.   **105 County stays** Count (Paris) waits for you.
1.4. Location: Verona. A street.
1 speech (Masquers were customarily preceded by a messenger or
"presenter" with a set speech of compliment.)   **2 on** go on, approach
3 The date . . . prolixity Such windy rhetoric is out of fashion.
4 Cupid i.e., messenger or "presenter," probably a boy, disguised as
Cupid.   **hoodwinked** blindfolded   **5 Tartar's . . . bow** (Tartars'
bows, shorter and more curved than the English longbow, were
thought to have resembled the old Roman bow with which Cupid
was pictured.)   **lath** flimsy wood   **6 crowkeeper** scarecrow
7 without-book memorized   **9 measure** judge   **10 measure . . .
measure** tread a dance for them

12 heavy (1) sad (2) the opposite of *light* (as at 1.1.137)   **15 soul** (Punning on *sole.*)   **18 common bound** (1) ordinary limit (2) normal
dance leap.   **19 sore** sorely. (With pun on *soar.*)   **21 bound** leap.
(With wordplay on *bound*, "confined," in the previous line.)   **pitch**
height. (A term from falconry for the highest point of a hawk's flight.)
23 And . . . love i.e., You wouldn't just sink *under* love's heavy burden, you'd sink *into* it and burden it. (Suggesting sexual penetration.)
28 Prick . . . down i.e., If love gets rough, fight back. (But with bawdy
suggestion of *pricking* as a way to satisfy desire and cause detumescence.)   **29 case** mask   **30 A visor . . . visor** i.e., A mask for an ugly
masklike face.   **31 quote** take notice of   **34 to his legs** to dancing.
36 senseless rushes reeds used as floor covering, or insensate green
rushes   **37 proverbed . . . phrase** furnished with an old proverb
38 candle-holder i.e., bystander. (Referring to the proverbial idea that
one who lacks ability himself can hold the candle and thus provide
light for one who is able to act.)   **39 The game . . . done** (Another
proverbial truism, that it is best to quit when one is ahead.)

MERCUTIO
Tut, dun's the mouse, the constable's own word.   40
If thou art dun, we'll draw thee from the mire   41
Of—save your reverence—love, wherein thou stickest   42
Up to the ears. Come, we burn daylight, ho!   43
ROMEO
Nay, that's not so.
MERCUTIO   I mean, sir, in delay
We waste our lights in vain, like lamps by day.
Take our good meaning, for our judgment sits   46
Five times in that ere once in our five wits.   47
ROMEO
And we mean well in going to this masque,
But 'tis no wit to go.
MERCUTIO   Why, may one ask?   49
ROMEO
I dreamt a dream tonight.
MERCUTIO   And so did I.   50
ROMEO
Well, what was yours?
MERCUTIO   That dreamers often lie.   51
ROMEO
In bed asleep, while they do dream things true.
MERCUTIO
Oh, then, I see Queen Mab hath been with you.   53
She is the fairies' midwife, and she comes
In shape no bigger than an agate stone   55
On the forefinger of an alderman,   56
Drawn with a team of little atomi   57
Over men's noses as they lie asleep.
Her chariot is an empty hazelnut,
Made by the joiner squirrel or old grub,   60
Time out o' mind the fairies' coachmakers.
Her wagon spokes made of long spinners' legs,   62
The cover of the wings of grasshoppers,
Her traces of the smallest spider web,
Her collars of the moonshine's wat'ry beams,
Her whip of cricket's bone, the lash of film,   66
Her wagoner a small gray-coated gnat,   67

Not half so big as a round little worm   68
Pricked from the lazy finger of a maid.   69
And in this state she gallops night by night
Through lovers' brains, and then they dream of love;
O'er courtiers' knees, that dream on curtsies straight;   72
O'er lawyers' fingers, who straight dream on fees;
O'er ladies' lips, who straight on kisses dream,
Which oft the angry Mab with blisters plagues
Because their breaths with sweetmeats tainted are.   76
Sometime she gallops o'er a courtier's nose,
And then dreams he of smelling out a suit.   78
And sometime comes she with a tithe-pig's tail   79
Tickling a parson's nose as 'a lies asleep;
Then dreams he of another benefice.   81
Sometime she driveth o'er a soldier's neck,
And then dreams he of cutting foreign throats,
Of breaches, ambuscadoes, Spanish blades,   84
Of healths five fathom deep, and then anon   85
Drums in his ear, at which he starts and wakes,
And being thus frighted swears a prayer or two
And sleeps again. This is that very Mab
That plats the manes of horses in the night,   89
And bakes the elflocks in foul sluttish hairs,   90
Which once untangled much misfortune bodes.   91
This is the hag, when maids lie on their backs,
That presses them and learns them first to bear,   93
Making them women of good carriage.   94
This is she—
ROMEO   Peace, peace, Mercutio, peace!
Thou talk'st of nothing.
MERCUTIO   True, I talk of dreams,
Which are the children of an idle brain,
Begot of nothing but vain fantasy,   98
Which is as thin of substance as the air,
And more inconstant than the wind, who woos
Even now the frozen bosom of the north,
And being angered, puffs away from thence,
Turning his side to the dew-dropping south.
BENVOLIO
This wind you talk of blows us from ourselves.   104
Supper is done, and we shall come too late.
ROMEO
I fear, too early; for my mind misgives   106
Some consequence yet hanging in the stars

---

40 dun's . . . word i.e., "keep still"—just the sort of thing a constable might say. (Matching proverb with proverb, Mercutio answers Romeo's "I am done" by twitting him for being mousy. Constables were much laughed at for inappropriately pompous speech.)
41–3 If . . . ears (To Mercutio, Romeo's love melancholy recalls the Christmas game called "Dun is in the mire," in which a heavy log, representing a horse named Dun, was hauled out of an imaginary mire by the players. *Save your reverence* is Mercutio's mock apology for speaking of so improper an expression as being mired up to the ears in love.)   43 burn daylight i.e., waste time. (But Romeo quibbles, protesting that it is not literally daytime.)   46–7 Take . . . wits Try to understand what I am trying to say (rather than quibbling with phrases like "burn daylight"), for wise judgment is five times more pleased with good meaning than with the ingenious wit of our frail senses.   49 wit wisdom (playing on *wits* in line 47; *mean* in line 48 plays on *meaning* in line 46)   50 tonight last night.   51 lie tell falsehoods. (But Mercutio answers in the sense of "lie down in bed.")
53 Queen Mab (Possibly a name of Celtic origin for the Fairy Queen.)
55 agate stone (Precious stone often carved with diminutive figures and set in a ring.)   56 alderman member of the municipal council
57 atomi tiny creatures (atoms)   60 joiner furniture maker.   grub insect larva (which bores holes in nuts)   62 spinners' spiders'
66 film gossamer thread   67 wagoner chariot driver

68–9 a round . . . maid (Worms proverbially breed in the fingers of the idle.)   72 curtsies bows, obeisances.   straight immediately
76 sweetmeats candies or candied preserves   78 smelling . . . suit i.e., finding a petitioner who will pay for the use of his influence at court.   79 tithe-pig pig given to the parson in lieu of money as the parishioner's tithing, or granting of a tenth   81 benefice ecclesiastical living.   84 Of breaches . . . blades of opening up gaps in fortifications, of ambushes, of swords from Toledo in Spain, where the best swords were made   85 Of healths . . . deep of toasts drunk deep
89 That plats . . . night (According to popular superstition, the tangles that persistently turn up in the manes of horses were "witches' stirrups," i.e., footholds for witches as they rode.)   90–1 And bakes . . . bodes (*Elflocks* or clumps of matted hair were so named because they were imagined to be the work of elves, who would torment anyone so presumptuous as to untangle the elflocks.)   93 learns teaches
94 good carriage (1) commendable deportment (2) skill in bearing the weight of men in sexual intercourse (3) able subsequently to carry a child.   98 vain fantasy delusive imagination   104 from ourselves from our plans.   106 misgives fears

Shall bitterly begin his fearful date   108
With this night's revels, and expire the term   109
Of a despisèd life closed in my breast
By some vile forfeit of untimely death.
But He that hath the steerage of my course
Direct my suit! On, lusty gentlemen.   113
BENVOLIO   Strike, drum.   *They march about the stage,*   114
                                    and [retire to one side].

❧

[1.5]

Servingmen come forth with napkins.

FIRST SERVINGMAN   Where's Potpan, that he helps not
to take away? He shift a trencher? He scrape a trencher?   2
SECOND SERVINGMAN   When good manners shall lie all
in one or two men's hands, and they unwashed too,
'tis a foul thing.
FIRST SERVINGMAN   Away with the joint stools, remove   6
the court cupboard, look to the plate. Good thou, save   7
me a piece of marchpane, and, as thou loves me, let   8
the porter let in Susan Grindstone and Nell.
                              [Exit Second Servingman.]
    Anthony and Potpan!

        [Enter two more Servingmen.]

THIRD SERVINGMAN   Ay, boy, ready.
FIRST SERVINGMAN   You are looked for and called for,
asked for and sought for, in the great chamber.
FOURTH SERVINGMAN   We cannot be here and there
too. Cheerly, boys! Be brisk awhile, and the longest   15
liver take all.   *Exeunt.*   16

        Enter [Capulet and family and] all the guests
        and gentlewomen to the masquers.

CAPULET *[to the masquers]*
Welcome, gentlemen! Ladies that have their toes
Unplagued with corns will walk a bout with you.   18
Ah, my mistresses, which of you all
Will now deny to dance? She that makes dainty,   20
She, I'll swear, hath corns. Am I come near ye now?   21
Welcome, gentlemen! I have seen the day
That I have worn a visor and could tell
A whispering tale in a fair lady's ear
Such as would please. 'Tis gone, 'tis gone, 'tis gone.
You are welcome, gentlemen! Come, musicians, play.
                            Music plays, and they dance.

A hall, a hall! Give room! And foot, it, girls.   27
[To Servingmen]   More light, you knaves, and turn the
    tables up,   28
And quench the fire; the room is grown too hot.
[To his cousin]   Ah, sirrah, this unlooked-for sport
    comes well.   30
Nay, sit, nay, sit, good cousin Capulet,   31
For you and I are past our dancing days.
How long is't now since last yourself and I
Were in a mask?
SECOND CAPULET   By'r Lady, thirty years.
CAPULET
What, man? 'Tis not so much, 'tis not so much;
'Tis since the nuptial of Lucentio,
Come Pentecost as quickly as it will,   37
Some five-and-twenty years, and then we masked.
SECOND CAPULET
'Tis more, 'tis more. His son is elder, sir;
His son is thirty.
CAPULET   Will you tell me that?
His son was but a ward two years ago.   41
ROMEO *[to a Servingman]*
What lady's that which doth enrich the hand
Of yonder knight?
SERVINGMAN   I know not, sir.
ROMEO
Oh, she doth teach the torches to burn bright!
It seems she hangs upon the cheek of night
As a rich jewel in an Ethiop's ear—
Beauty too rich for use, for earth too dear!   48
So shows a snowy dove trooping with crows   49
As yonder lady o'er her fellows shows.
The measure done, I'll watch her place of stand,   51
And, touching hers, make blessèd my rude hand.   52
Did my heart love till now? Forswear it, sight!   53
For I ne'er saw true beauty till this night.
TYBALT
This, by his voice, should be a Montague.
Fetch me my rapier, boy. What dares the slave   56
Come hither, covered with an antic face,   57
To fleer and scorn at our solemnity?   58
Now, by the stock and honor of my kin,
To strike him dead I hold it not a sin.
CAPULET
Why, how now, kinsman? Wherefore storm you so?

---

27 A hall i.e., Clear the hall for dancing   **28 turn . . . up** move the tables out of the way for the dancing (by taking up the boards and then removing the supporting trestles)   **30 sirrah** (Normally used in addressing social inferiors. Perhaps Capulet uses a jesting tone toward his kinsman or possibly addresses himself.)   **unlooked-for sport** i.e., arrival of the masquers, providing more men for the dancing   **31 cousin** (Cousin often means "kinsman"; at 1.2.69, "Mine uncle Capulet" is named on the invitation list.)   **37 Pentecost** seventh Sunday after Easter (and never as late as mid-July, two weeks before Lammas or August 1, when according to 1.3.16, the play takes place; a seeming inconsistency).   **41 a ward** a minor under guardianship   **48 dear** precious.   **49 shows** appears   **51 The measure done** When this dance is over.   **her place of stand** where she stands   **52 hers** her hand.   **rude** rough   **53 Forswear it** Deny any previous oath   **56 What** How   **57 antic face** grotesque mask   **58 fleer** jeer. **solemnity** time-honored festivity.

---

108 date appointed time   **109 expire** bring to an end   **113 lusty** lively   **114 drum** drummer.
1.5. Location: The action, continuous from the previous scene, is now imaginatively transferred to a hall in Capulet's house.
2 take away clear the table.   **trencher** wooden dish or plate.   **6 joint stools** stools of which the parts are fitted by a joiner or furniture maker   **7 court cupboard** sideboard.   **plate** silverware.   **8 marchpane** cake made from sugar and almonds, marzipan   **15–16 the longest . . . all** (A proverb in defense of merriment.)   **18 walk a bout** dance a turn   **20 makes dainty** seems coyly reluctant (to dance)   **21 Am . . . now?** Have I hit a sensitive point, struck home?

TYBALT
  Uncle, this is a Montague, our foe,
  A villain that is hither come in spite   63
  To scorn at our solemnity this night.
CAPULET
  Young Romeo is it?
TYBALT   'Tis he, that villain Romeo.
CAPULET
  Content thee, gentle coz, let him alone.
  'A bears him like a portly gentleman,   67
  And, to say truth, Verona brags of him
  To be a virtuous and well governed youth.
  I would not for the wealth of all this town
  Here in my house do him disparagement.
  Therefore be patient; take no note of him.
  It is my will, the which if thou respect,
  Show a fair presence and put off these frowns,   74
  An ill-beseeming semblance for a feast.   75
TYBALT
  It fits when such a villain is a guest.
  I'll not endure him.
CAPULET   He shall be endured.
  What, goodman boy? I say he shall. Go to!   78
  Am I the master here, or you? Go to.
  You'll not endure him! God shall mend my soul,
  You'll make a mutiny among my guests!   81
  You will set cock-a-hoop! You'll be the man! 82
TYBALT
  Why, uncle, 'tis a shame.
CAPULET   Go to, go to,
  You are a saucy boy. Is't so, indeed?
  This trick may chance to scathe you. I know what, 85
  You must contrary me. Marry, 'tis time.—   86
  Well said, my hearts!—You are a princox, go.   87
  Be quiet, or—More light, more light!—For shame!
  I'll make you quiet.—What, cheerly, my hearts!
TYBALT
  Patience perforce with willful choler meeting 90
  Makes my flesh tremble in their different greeting. 91
  I will withdraw. But this intrusion shall,
  Now seeming sweet, convert to bitt'rest gall.   Exit.
ROMEO [to Juliet]
  If I profane with my unworthiest hand   94
    This holy shrine, the gentle sin is this: 95
  My lips, two blushing pilgrims, ready stand
    To smooth that rough touch with a tender kiss.
JULIET
  Good pilgrim, you do wrong your hand too much,

  Which mannerly devotion shows in this;
  For saints have hands that pilgrims' hands do touch, 100
    And palm to palm is holy palmers' kiss.   101
ROMEO
  Have not saints lips, and holy palmers too?
JULIET
  Ay, pilgrim, lips that they must use in prayer.
ROMEO
  Oh, then, dear saint, let lips do what hands do. 104
    They pray; grant thou, lest faith turn to despair.
JULIET
  Saints do not move, though grant for prayers' sake. 106
ROMEO
  Then move not, while my prayer's effect I take. 107
                       [He kisses her.]
  Thus from my lips, by thine, my sin is purged.
JULIET
  Then have my lips the sin that they have took.
ROMEO
  Sin from my lips? Oh, trespass sweetly urged!
    Give me my sin again.   [He kisses her.]
JULIET   You kiss by th' book.   111
NURSE [approaching]
  Madam, your mother craves a word with you.
                     [Juliet retires.]
ROMEO
  What is her mother?
NURSE   Marry, bachelor,   113
  Her mother is the lady of the house,
  And a good lady, and a wise and virtuous.
  I nursed her daughter that you talked withal. 116
  I tell you, he that can lay hold of her
  Shall have the chinks.
ROMEO [aside]   Is she a Capulet?   118
  Oh, dear account! My life is my foe's debt.   119
BENVOLIO [approaching]
  Away, begone! The sport is at the best.   120
ROMEO
  Ay, so I fear; the more is my unrest.
              [The masquers prepare to leave.]
CAPULET
  Nay, gentlemen, prepare not to be gone.
  We have a trifling foolish banquet towards.   123
            [One whispers in his ear.]
  Is it e'en so? Why, then, I thank you all.
  I thank you, honest gentlemen. Good night.   125

63 **spite** malice 67 **portly** of good deportment 74 **presence** demeanor 75 **semblance** facial expression 78 **goodman boy** (A belittling term for Tybalt; *Goodman* applied to one below the rank of gentleman but still of some substance, like a wealthy farmer.) **Go to** (An expression of irritation.) 81 **mutiny** disturbance 82 **You . . . man!** i.e., You'll set mischief abroach (literally, turn the tap and let the liquor flow)! You'll be the big shot! 85 **scathe** harm 86 **contrary** oppose, thwart. **'tis time** i.e., it's time you were taught a lesson. 87 **Well said** Well done. (Said to the dancers.) **princox** saucy boy 90–1 **Patience . . . greeting** The attempt to be patient under duress when I am so angry causes me to tremble at the contrary meeting of these two opposite impulses. 94–107 (These lines are in the form of a Shakespearean sonnet; they are followed by a quatrain.) 95 **shrine** i.e., Juliet's hand

100 **saints** i.e., images of saints that are venerated by pilgrims 101 **palmers** pilgrims who have been to the Holy Land and have brought back a palm. (With a pun on the palm of the hand.) 104 **let . . . do** let lips touch, just as hands touch. 106 **Saints . . . sake** Venerated images and statues of saints remain motionless but nonetheless intercede on behalf of praying pilgrims. 107 **move** (Romeo quibbles on Juliet's metaphorical use of the word *move* to urge that she remain motionless while he kisses her.) 111 **by th' book** by the rules, like an expert. 113 **What** Who 116 **withal** with. 118 **the chinks** plenty of coins, money. (A slang expression.) 119 **dear account** heavy reckoning. **my foe's debt** due to my foe, at his mercy. 120 **The sport . . . best** i.e., It is time to leave. (Refers to the proverb, "When play is at the best, it is time to leave"; compare at 1.4.39.) 123 **foolish banquet towards** insignificant light refreshment just ready. 125 **honest** honorable

More torches here! Come on then, let's to bed. 126
[*To his cousin*] Ah, sirrah, by my fay, it waxes late. 127
I'll to my rest.
　　　　　[*All proceed to leave but Juliet and the Nurse.*]

JULIET
Come hither, Nurse. What is yond gentleman?

NURSE
The son and heir of old Tiberio.

JULIET
What's he that now is going out of door?

NURSE
Marry, that, I think, be young Petruchio.

JULIET
What's he that follows here, that would not dance?

NURSE　I know not.

JULIET
Go ask his name. [*The Nurse goes.*] If he be marrièd,
My grave is like to be my wedding bed. 136

NURSE　[*returning*]
His name is Romeo, and a Montague,
The only son of your great enemy.

JULIET
My only love sprung from my only hate!
Too early seen unknown, and known too late!
Prodigious birth of love it is to me 141
That I must love a loathèd enemy.

NURSE
What's tis? What's tis?

JULIET　　　　　A rhyme I learned even now 143
Of one I danced withal.　　*One calls within* "Juliet."

NURSE　　　　　Anon, anon! 144
Come, let's away. The strangers all are gone.　*Exeunt.*

❧

[2.0]

[*Enter*] Chorus.

CHORUS
Now old desire doth in his deathbed lie, 1
　And young affection gapes to be his heir; 2
That fair for which love groaned for and would die, 3
　With tender Juliet matched, is now not fair. 4
Now Romeo is beloved and loves again,
　Alike bewitchèd by the charm of looks; 6
But to his foe supposed he must complain, 7
　And she steal love's sweet bait from fearful hooks. 8
Being held a foe, he may not have access
　To breathe such vows as lovers use to swear; 10
And she as much in love, her means much less
　To meet her new-belovèd anywhere.

But passion lends them power, time means, to meet, 13
Temp'ring extremities with extreme sweet.　　[*Exit.*] 14

❧

[2.1]

Enter Romeo alone.

ROMEO
Can I go forward when my heart is here? 1
Turn back, dull earth, and find thy center out. 2
　　　　　　　　　[*Romeo retires.*]

Enter Benvolio with Mercutio.

BENVOLIO
Romeo! My cousin Romeo! Romeo!

MERCUTIO　He is wise
And, on my life, hath stol'n him home to bed.

BENVOLIO
He ran this way and leapt this orchard wall.
Call, good Mercutio.

MERCUTIO　　　　　Nay, I'll conjure too. 7
Romeo! Humors! Madman! Passion! Lover! 8
Appear thou in the likeness of a sigh.
Speak but one rhyme, and I am satisfied;
Cry but "Ay me!" Pronounce but "love" and "dove."
Speak to my gossip Venus one fair word, 12
One nickname for her purblind son and heir, 13
Young Abraham Cupid, he that shot so trim 14
When King Cophetua loved the beggar maid.— 15
He heareth not, he stirreth not, he moveth not;
The ape is dead, and I must conjure him.— 17
I conjure thee by Rosaline's bright eyes,
By her high forehead and her scarlet lip,
By her fine foot, straight leg, and quivering thigh,
And the demesnes that there adjacent lie, 21
That in thy likeness thou appear to us.

BENVOLIO
An if he hear thee, thou wilt anger him. 23

MERCUTIO
This cannot anger him. 'Twould anger him
To raise a spirit in his mistress' circle 25
Of some strange nature, letting it there stand 26

---

126 torches i.e., to light the guests as they leave　**127 fay** faith
136 like likely　**141 Prodigious** Ominous　**143 tis** this. (Dialect pronunciation.)　**144 Anon** i.e., We're coming
2.0. Chorus.
1–14 (This chorus is a sonnet.)　**2 gapes** waits open-mouthed　**3 fair** beauty, i.e., Rosaline　**4 matched** compared　**6 Alike** i.e., equally with Juliet　**7 foe supposed** i.e., Juliet, a Capulet; also, his opposite number in the war of love.　**complain** offer his love plaint　**8 And she . . . hooks** and she must steal moments of happy love from frightening circumstances designed to catch her unawares.　**10 use** are accustomed

13 time means time lends them means　**14 Temp'ring extremities** mitigating the hardships.　**sweet** sweetness, pleasure.
2.1. Location: Verona. Outside of Capulet's walled orchard.
1 forward i.e., away　**2 Turn . . . out** (Romeo bids his own earth-bound body find out its *center*, its soul or heart (i.e., Juliet), much as in the Ptolemaic system all earthly things seek out their center, the earth, standing at the center of the universe. His body is *dull* in that, like earth, it is the lowest and heaviest of the four elements, associated with melancholy.)　**7 conjure** raise him with magical incantation　**8 Humors** Moods.　**12 gossip** crony　**13 purblind** dim-sighted　**14 Young Abraham** i.e., one who is young and yet, like the Biblical Abraham, old; Cupid was paradoxically the youngest and the oldest of the gods　**15 King Cophetua** (In an old ballad, the King falls in love with a beggar maid and makes her his queen.)　**17 ape** (Used as a term of endearment.)　**21 demesnes** regions. (With bawdy suggestion as to what is adjacent to the thighs; bawdy puns on terms of conjuration continue in *raise, spirit,* i.e., "phallus" or "semen," *circle, stand, laid it, raise up.*)　**23 An if** If　**25 circle** (1) conjuring circle (2) vagina　**26 strange** belonging to another person. (With suggestion of a rival possessing Rosaline sexually.)

Till she had laid it and conjured it down;   27
That were some spite. My invocation   28
Is fair and honest; in his mistress' name
I conjure only but to raise up him.

BENVOLIO
Come, he hath hid himself among these trees
To be consorted with the humorous night.   32
Blind is his love, and best befits the dark.

MERCUTIO
If love be blind, love cannot hit the mark.
Now will he sit under a medlar tree   35
And wish his mistress were that kind of fruit
As maids call medlars when they laugh alone.
Oh, Romeo, that she were, oh, that she were
An open-arse, and thou a pop'ring pear!   39
Romeo, good night. I'll to my truckle bed;   40
This field bed is too cold for me to sleep.   41
Come, shall we go?

BENVOLIO   Go, then, for 'tis in vain
To seek him here that means not to be found.
                                    Exit [*with Mercutio*].

[2.2]

ROMEO [*coming forward*]
He jests at scars that never felt a wound.   1
          [*A light appears above, as at Juliet's window.*]
But soft, what light through yonder window breaks?
It is the east, and Juliet is the sun.
Arise, fair sun, and kill the envious moon,
Who is already sick and pale with grief
That thou her maid art far more fair than she.   6
Be not her maid, since she is envious;   7
Her vestal livery is but sick and green   8
And none but fools do wear it. Cast it off.
          [*Juliet appears aloft as at her window.*]
It is my lady, oh, it is my love.
Oh, that she knew she were!
She speaks, yet she says nothing. What of that?

Her eye discourses. I will answer it.
I am too bold. 'Tis not to me she speaks.
Two of the fairest stars in all the heaven,
Having some business, do entreat her eyes
To twinkle in their spheres till they return.   17
What if her eyes were there, they in her head?   18
The brightness of her cheek would shame those stars
As daylight doth a lamp; her eyes in heaven
Would through the airy region stream so bright   21
That birds would sing and think it were not night.
See how she leans her cheek upon her hand!
Oh, that I were a glove upon that hand,
That I might touch that cheek!

JULIET   Ay me!
ROMEO [*aside*]   She speaks.
Oh, speak again, bright angel, for thou art
As glorious to this night, being o'er my head,
As is a wingèd messenger of heaven
Unto the white-upturnèd wond'ring eyes   29
Of mortals that fall back to gaze on him
When he bestrides the lazy puffing clouds
And sails upon the bosom of the air.

JULIET [*to herself*]
Oh, Romeo, Romeo, wherefore art thou Romeo?   33
Deny thy father and refuse thy name!
Or, if thou wilt not, be but sworn my love,
And I'll no longer be a Capulet.

ROMEO [*aside*]
Shall I hear more, or shall I speak at this?

JULIET
'Tis but thy name that is my enemy;
Thou art thyself, though not a Montague.   39
What's Montague? It is nor hand, nor foot,   40
Nor arm, nor face, nor any other part
Belonging to a man. Oh, be some other name!
What's in a name? That which we call a rose
By any other word would smell as sweet;
So Romeo would, were he not Romeo called,
Retain that dear perfection which he owes   46
Without that title. Romeo, doff thy name,   47
And for thy name, which is no part of thee,   48
Take all myself.

ROMEO   I take thee at thy word!
Call me but love, and I'll be new baptized;
Henceforth I never will be Romeo.

JULIET
What man art thou that, thus bescreened in night,   52
So stumblest on my counsel?

ROMEO   By a name   53
I know not how to tell thee who I am.
My name, dear saint, is hateful to myself,
Because it is an enemy to thee;
Had I it written, I would tear the word.

---

27 laid it (1) laid the spirit to rest (2) provided sexual satisfaction leading to detumescence   **28 were some spite** would be vexing.   **32 consorted** associated.   **humorous** (1) moist, damp (2) well suited to the *humor* of melancholy   **35 medlar** a fruit that was edible only when partly decayed, used as a slang term for women's sexual organs   **39 open-arse** (Another name for the *medlar*, making explicit the sexual metaphor.)   **pop'ring pear** poppering pear (named after Poperinghe in Flanders). A fruit with phallic associations because of its shape and its suggestive name ("pop 'er in").   **40 truckle bed** a bed on casters to be rolled under a standing bed when not in use   **41 field bed** i.e., the ground
2.2. Location: The action, continuous from the previous scene, is now imaginatively transferred to inside Capulet's orchard. A rhymed couplet links the two scenes. Romeo has been hiding from his friends as though concealed by the orchard wall. He speaks at once and then turns to observe Juliet's window, which is probably in the gallery above, rearstage.
1.1 *A light appears* (Some editors assume that Juliet is visible at line 1.)   **6 maid** i.e., votary of Diana, goddess of the moon and patroness of virgins   **7 her** the moon's, Diana's, as the goddess of chastity. (Addressed to Juliet as the sun; Romeo hopes that she will not be a devotee of chastity.)   **8 Her vestal livery** the uniform of Diana's chaste votaries. **sick and green** (Suggesting the pallor of moonlight, as well as anemia or *greensickness* [see 3.5.156], to which teenage girls were susceptible.)

17 spheres transparent concentric shells supposed to carry the heavenly bodies with them in their revolution around the earth   **18 there** i.e., in the spheres   **21 stream** shine   **29 white-upturnèd** looking upward so that the whites of the eyes are visible   **33 wherefore** why   **39 though not** (1) even if you were not (2) though not in anything essential   **40 nor hand** neither hand   **46 owes** owns   **47 doff** cast off   **48 for** in exchange for   **52 bescreened** concealed   **53 counsel** secret thought.

JULIET

My ears have yet not drunk a hundred words
Of thy tongue's uttering, yet I know the sound:
Art thou not Romeo and a Montague?

ROMEO

Neither, fair maid, if either thee dislike.   61

JULIET

How camest thou hither, tell me, and wherefore?
The orchard walls are high and hard to climb,
And the place death, considering who thou art,
If any of my kinsmen find thee here.

ROMEO

With love's light wings did I o'erperch these walls,   66
For stony limits cannot hold love out,
And what love can do, that dares love attempt;
Therefore thy kinsmen are no stop to me.

JULIET

If they do see thee, they will murder thee.

ROMEO

Alack, there lies more peril in thine eye
Than twenty of their swords. Look thou but sweet,
And I am proof against their enmity.   73

JULIET

I would not for the world they saw thee here.

ROMEO

I have night's cloak to hide me from their eyes;
And but thou love me, let them find me here.   76
My life were better ended by their hate
Than death proroguèd, wanting of thy love.   78

JULIET

By whose direction found'st thou out this place?

ROMEO

By love, that first did prompt me to inquire.
He lent me counsel, and I lent him eyes.
I am no pilot; yet, wert thou as far
As that vast shore washed with the farthest sea,
I should adventure for such merchandise.

JULIET

Thou knowest the mask of night is on my face,
Else would a maiden blush bepaint my cheek
For that which thou hast heard me speak tonight.
Fain would I dwell on form—fain, fain deny   88
What I have spoke; but farewell compliment!   89
Dost thou love me? I know thou wilt say "Ay,"
And I will take thy word. Yet if thou swear'st
Thou mayst prove false. At lovers' perjuries,
They say, Jove laughs. O gentle Romeo,
If thou dost love, pronounce it faithfully.
Or if thou thinkest I am too quickly won,
I'll frown and be perverse and say thee nay,
So thou wilt woo, but else not for the world.
In truth, fair Montague, I am too fond,   98
And therefore thou mayst think my havior light.   99
But trust me, gentleman, I'll prove more true
Than those that have more cunning to be strange.   101

I should have been more strange, I must confess,
But that thou overheard'st, ere I was ware,   103
My true-love passion. Therefore pardon me,
And not impute this yielding to light love,
Which the dark night hath so discoverèd.   106

ROMEO

Lady, by yonder blessèd moon I vow,
That tips with silver all these fruit-tree tops—

JULIET

Oh, swear not by the moon, th'inconstant moon,
That monthly changes in her circled orb,   110
Lest that thy love prove likewise variable.

ROMEO

What shall I swear by?

JULIET   Do not swear at all;
Or, if thou wilt, swear by thy gracious self,
Which is the god of my idolatry,
And I'll believe thee.

ROMEO   If my heart's dear love—

JULIET

Well, do not swear. Although I joy in thee,
I have no joy of this contract tonight.   117
It is too rash, too unadvised, too sudden,   118
Too like the lightning, which doth cease to be
Ere one can say it lightens. Sweet, good night!
This bud of love, by summer's ripening breath,
May prove a beauteous flower when next we meet.
Good night, good night! As sweet repose and rest   123
Come to thy heart as that within my breast!

ROMEO

Oh, wilt thou leave me so unsatisfied?

JULIET

What satisfaction canst thou have tonight?

ROMEO

Th'exchange of thy love's faithful vow for mine.

JULIET

I gave thee mine before thou didst request it;
And yet I would it were to give again.

ROMEO

Wouldst thou withdraw it? For what purpose, love?

JULIET

But to be frank and give it thee again.   131
And yet I wish but for the thing I have.
My bounty is as boundless as the sea,
My love as deep; the more I give to thee,
The more I have, for both are infinite.
                              [*The Nurse calls within.*]
I hear some noise within. Dear love, adieu!—
Anon, good Nurse!—Sweet Montague, be true.
Stay but a little; I will come again.   [*Exit, above.*]

ROMEO

Oh, blessèd, blessèd night! I am afeard,
Being in night, all this is but a dream,
Too flattering-sweet to be substantial.

                    [*Enter Juliet, above.*]

61 thee dislike displeases you.   **66 o'erperch** fly over   **73 proof** protected   **76 but** unless   **78 proroguèd** postponed.   **wanting of** lacking   **88 Fain** Gladly.   **dwell on form** preserve the proper formalities   **89 compliment** etiquette, convention.   **98 fond** infatuated   **99 havior light** behavior frivolous.   **101 strange** reserved, aloof, modest.

103 ware aware   **106 Which** i.e., which yielding.   **discoverèd** revealed.   **110 orb** orbit, sphere   **117 contract** exchanging of vows   **118 unadvised** unconsidered   **123 As** May just as   **131 frank** liberal, bounteous

JULIET
    Three words, dear Romeo, and good night indeed.
    If that thy bent of love be honorable,   143
    Thy purpose marriage, send me word tomorrow,
    By one that I'll procure to come to thee,
    Where and what time thou wilt perform the rite,
    And all my fortunes at thy foot I'll lay
    And follow thee my lord throughout the world.
NURSE [*within*]   Madam!
JULIET
    I come, anon.—But if thou meanest not well,
    I do beseech thee—
NURSE [*within*]   Madam!
JULIET   By and by, I come—   151
    To cease thy strife and leave me to my grief.   152
    Tomorrow will I send.
ROMEO   So thrive my soul—
JULIET   A thousand times good night!   [*Exit, above.*]
ROMEO
    A thousand times the worse, to want thy light.
    Love goes toward love as schoolboys from their
      books,
    But love from love, toward school with heavy looks.
                         [*He starts to leave.*]

           Enter Juliet [*above*] *again.*

JULIET
    Hist! Romeo, hist! Oh, for a falconer's voice,
    To lure this tassel-gentle back again!   160
    Bondage is hoarse and may not speak aloud,   161
    Else would I tear the cave where Echo lies   162
    And make her airy tongue more hoarse than mine
    With repetition of "My Romeo!"
ROMEO
    It is my soul that calls upon my name.
    How silver-sweet sound lovers' tongues by night,
    Like softest music to attending ears!
JULIET
    Romeo!
ROMEO   My nyas?
JULIET   What o'clock tomorrow   168
    Shall I send to thee?
ROMEO   By the hour of nine.
JULIET
    I will not fail. 'Tis twenty year till then.—
    I have forgot why I did call thee back.
ROMEO
    Let me stand here till thou remember it.
JULIET
    I shall forget, to have thee still stand there,   173
    Remembering how I love thy company.

ROMEO
    And I'll still stay, to have thee still forget,
    Forgetting any other home but this.
JULIET
    'Tis almost morning. I would have thee gone—
    And yet no farther than a wanton's bird,   178
    That lets it hop a little from his hand,
    Like a poor prisoner in his twisted gyves,   180
    And with a silken thread plucks it back again,
    So loving-jealous of his liberty.   182
ROMEO
    I would I were thy bird.
JULIET   Sweet, so would I.
    Yet I should kill thee with much cherishing.
    Good night, good night! Parting is such sweet sorrow
    That I shall say good night till it be morrow.
                         [*Exit, above.*]
ROMEO
    Sleep dwell upon thine eyes, peace in thy breast!
    Would I were sleep and peace, so sweet to rest!
    Hence will I to my ghostly friar's close cell,   189
    His help to crave, and my dear hap to tell.   *Exit.* 190

                           ♣

[2.3]

      Enter Friar [*Laurence*] *alone, with a basket.*

FRIAR LAURENCE
    The gray-eyed morn smiles on the frowning night,
    Check'ring the eastern clouds with streaks of light,
    And fleckled darkness like a drunkard reels   3
    From forth day's path and Titan's fiery wheels.   4
    Now, ere the sun advance his burning eye,   5
    The day to cheer and night's dank dew to dry,
    I must up-fill this osier cage of ours   7
    With baleful weeds and precious-juicèd flowers.   8
    The earth that's nature's mother is her tomb;
    What is her burying grave, that is her womb;
    And from her womb children of divers kind
    We sucking on her natural bosom find,
    Many for many virtues excellent,
    None but for some, and yet all different.   14
    Oh, mickle is the powerful grace that lies   15
    In plants, herbs, stones, and their true qualities.   16
    For naught so vile that on the earth doth live   17
    But to the earth some special good doth give;
    Nor aught so good but, strained from that fair use,   19
    Revolts from true birth, stumbling on abuse.
    Virtue itself turns vice, being misapplied,
    And vice sometime by action dignified.

      Enter Romeo.

---

143 **bent** purpose, inclination   151 **By and by** Immediately
152 **strife** striving   160 **tassel-gentle** tercel gentle, the male of the
goshawk   161 **Bondage is hoarse** i.e., In confinement one can speak
only in a loud whisper   162 **tear** pierce (with noise).   **Echo** (In Book
3 of Ovid's *Metamorphoses*, Echo, rejected by Narcissus, pines away in
lonely caves until only her voice is left.)   168 **nyas** eyas, fledgling
173 **still** always

178 **wanton's** spoiled child's   180 **gyves** fetters   182 **his** its
189 **ghostly** spiritual.   **close** narrow   190 **dear hap** good fortune
2.3. Location: Verona. Friar Laurence's monastery garden.
3 **fleckled** dappled   4 **From forth** out of the way of.   **Titan's** (Helios,
the sun god, was a descendant of the race of Titans.)   5 **advance** raise
7 **osier cage** willow basket   8 **baleful** harmful   14 **None but for some**
there are none that are not useful for something   15 **mickle** great.
grace beneficent virtue   16 **true** proper, inherent   17 **For naught so**
vile For there is nothing so vile   19 **strained** forced, perverted

Within the infant rind of this weak flower
Poison hath residence and medicine power:
For this, being smelt, with that part cheers each part;   25
Being tasted, stays all senses with the heart.   26
Two such opposèd kings encamp them still   27
In man as well as herbs—grace and rude will;
And where the worser is predominant,
Full soon the canker death eats up that plant.   30

ROMEO
Good morrow, Father.

FRIAR LAURENCE   Benedicite!   31
What early tongue so sweet saluteth me?
Young son, it argues a distempered head   33
So soon to bid good morrow to thy bed.
Care keeps his watch in every old man's eye,
And where care lodges sleep will never lie;
But where unbruisèd youth with unstuffed brain   37
Doth couch his limbs, there golden sleep doth reign.
Therefore thy earliness doth me assure
Thou art uproused with some distemp'rature;
Or if not so, then here I hit it right:
Our Romeo hath not been in bed tonight.

ROMEO
That last is true. The sweeter rest was mine.

FRIAR LAURENCE
God pardon sin! Wast thou with Rosaline?

ROMEO
With Rosaline, my ghostly father? No.
I have forgot that name, and that name's woe.

FRIAR LAURENCE
That's my good son. But where hast thou been, then?

ROMEO
I'll tell thee ere thou ask it me again.
I have been feasting with mine enemy,
Where on a sudden one hath wounded me
That's by me wounded. Both our remedies   51
Within thy help and holy physic lies.   52
I bear no hatred, blessèd man, for, lo,
My intercession likewise steads my foe.   54

FRIAR LAURENCE
Be plain, good son, and homely in thy drift.   55
Riddling confession finds but riddling shrift.   56

ROMEO
Then plainly know my heart's dear love is set
On the fair daughter of rich Capulet.
As mine on hers, so hers is set on mine,
And all combined, save what thou must combine
By holy marriage. When and where and how
We met, we wooed, and made exchange of vow
I'll tell thee as we pass; but this I pray,
That thou consent to marry us today.

FRIAR LAURENCE
Holy Saint Francis, what a change is here!
Is Rosaline, that thou didst love so dear,

So soon forsaken? Young men's love then lies
Not truly in their hearts, but in their eyes.
Jesu Maria, what a deal of brine
Hath washed thy sallow cheeks for Rosaline!
How much salt water thrown away in waste
To season love, that of it doth not taste!
The sun not yet thy sighs from heaven clears,
Thy old groans yet ringing in mine ancient ears.
Lo, here upon thy cheek the stain doth sit
Of an old tear that is not washed off yet.
If e'er thou wast thyself and these woes thine,   77
Thou and these woes were all for Rosaline.
And art thou changed? Pronounce this sentence then: 79
Women may fall, when there's no strength in men.

ROMEO
Thou chid'st me oft for loving Rosaline.

FRIAR LAURENCE
For doting, not for loving, pupil mine.

ROMEO
And bad'st me bury love.

FRIAR LAURENCE   Not in a grave
To lay one in, another out to have.

ROMEO
I pray thee, chide not. She whom I love now
Doth grace for grace and love for love allow.   86
The other did not so.

FRIAR LAURENCE   Oh, she knew well
Thy love did read by rote, that could not spell.   88
But come, young waverer, come, go with me,
In one respect I'll thy assistant be;   90
For this alliance may so happy prove
To turn your households' rancor to pure love.   92

ROMEO
Oh, let us hence! I stand on sudden haste.   93

FRIAR LAURENCE
Wisely and slow. They stumble that run fast.

Exeunt.

❖

[2.4]

Enter Benvolio and Mercutio.

MERCUTIO
Where the devil should this Romeo be?   1
Came he not home tonight?   2

BENVOLIO
Not to his father's. I spoke with his man.

MERCUTIO
Why, that same pale hardhearted wench, that
    Rosaline,
Torments him so that he will sure run mad.

BENVOLIO
Tybalt, the kinsman to old Capulet,
Hath sent a letter to his father's house.

---

25 **that part** i.e., the odor   26 **stays** halts.   **with** together with   27 **them still** themselves always   30 **canker** cankerworm   31 **Benedicite!** A blessing on you!   33 **argues** demonstrates, provides evidence of.   **distempered** disturbed, disordered   37 **unstuffed** not overcharged, carefree   51 **Both our remedies** The remedy for both of us   52 **physic** medicine, healing property   54 **intercession** petition.   **steads** helps   55 **homely** simple   56 **shrift** absolution.

77 **If . . . thine** If ever you had any proper sense of self and understanding of your love sorrows   79 **sentence** maxim   86 **grace** favor.   88 **did read . . . spell** i.e., was like a schoolboy's exercise, repeating words without understanding.   90 **In one respect** for one reason (at least)   92 **To** as to   93 **stand on** am in need of, insist on
2.4. **Location:** Verona. A street.
1 **should** can   2 **tonight** last night.

MERCUTIO   A challenge, on my life.

BENVOLIO   Romeo will answer it.   9

MERCUTIO   Any man that can write may answer a letter.

BENVOLIO   Nay, he will answer the letter's master, how he dares, being dared.

MERCUTIO   Alas poor Romeo! He is already dead, stabbed with a white wench's black eye, run through the ear with a love song, the very pin of his heart cleft 15 with the blind bow-boy's butt shaft. And is he a man 16 to encounter Tybalt?

BENVOLIO   Why, what is Tybalt?

MERCUTIO   More than prince of cats. Oh, he's the 19 courageous captain of compliments. He fights as you 20 sing prick song, keeps time, distance, and proportion; 21 he rests his minim rests, one, two, and the third in 22 your bosom. The very butcher of a silk button, a 23 duellist, a duellist, a gentleman of the very first house, 24 of the first and second cause. Ah, the immortal 25 *passado!* The *punto reverso!* The *hay!*   26

BENVOLIO   The what?

MERCUTIO   The pox of such antic, lisping, affecting phan- 28 tasimes, these new tuners of accent! "By Jesu, a very 29 good blade! A very tall man! A very good whore!" 30 Why, is not this a lamentable thing, grandsire, that we 31 should be thus afflicted with these strange flies, these 32 fashionmongers, these pardon-me's, who stand so 33 much on the new form that they cannot sit at ease on 34 the old bench? Oh, their bones, their bones!   35

Enter Romeo.

BENVOLIO   Here comes Romeo, here comes Romeo.

MERCUTIO   Without his roe, like a dried herring. Oh, 37 flesh, flesh, how art thou fishified! Now is he for the numbers that Petrarch flowed in. Laura to his lady 39 was but a kitchen wench—marry, she had a better

love to berhyme her—Dido a dowdy, Cleopatra a 41 gypsy, Helen and Hero hildings and harlots, Thisbe a 42 gray eye or so, but not to the purpose. Signor Romeo, 43 *bonjour!* There's a French salutation to your French 44 slop. You gave us the counterfeit fairly last night.   45

ROMEO   Good morrow to you both. What counterfeit did I give you?

MERCUTIO   The slip, sir, the slip. Can you not conceive? 48

ROMEO   Pardon, good Mercutio. My business was great, and in such a case as mine a man may strain courtesy.

MERCUTIO   That's as much as to say, such a case as yours 51 constrains a man to bow in the hams.   52

ROMEO   Meaning, to curtsy.   53

MERCUTIO   Thou hast most kindly hit it.   54

ROMEO   A most courteous exposition.

MERCUTIO   Nay, I am the very pink of courtesy.   56

ROMEO   Pink for flower.

MERCUTIO   Right.

ROMEO   Why then is my pump well flowered.   59

MERCUTIO   Sure wit, follow me this jest now till thou hast worn out thy pump, that when the single sole of it is worn, the jest may remain, after the wearing, solely singular.   63

ROMEO   Oh, single-soled jest, solely singular for the 64 singleness!   65

MERCUTIO   Come between us, good Benvolio. My wits faints.

ROMEO   Switch and spurs, switch and spurs! Or I'll cry 68 a match.   69

MERCUTIO   Nay, if our wits run the wild-goose chase, I 70 am done, for thou hast more of the wild goose in one of thy wits than, I am sure, I have in my whole five. Was I with you there for the goose?   73

ROMEO   Thou wast never with me for anything when thou wast not there for the goose.   75

MERCUTIO   I will bite thee by the ear for that jest.   76

ROMEO   Nay, good goose, bite not.

MERCUTIO   Thy wit is a very bitter sweeting; it is a most 78 sharp sauce.   79

ROMEO   And is it not, then, well served in to a sweet goose?

---

9 answer it accept the challenge. (But Mercutio replies in the sense of "write in reply.")   **15 pin** peg in the center of a target   **16 butt shaft** unbarbed arrow, allotted to children and thus to Cupid.   **19 prince of cats** (The name of the king of cats in *Reynard the Fox* was Tybalt or Tybert.)   **20 captain of compliments** master of ceremony and dueling etiquette.   **21 prick song** music written out.   **proportion** rhythm   **22 minim rests** short rests in musical notation   **23 butcher ... button** i.e., one able to strike a specific button on his adversary's person   **24 first house** best school of fencing   **25 first and second cause** causes according to the code of dueling that would oblige one to seek the satisfaction of one's honor.   **26 passado** forward thrust. *punto reverso* backhanded stroke. *hay* thrust through. (From the Italian *hai*, meaning "you have [it].")   **28 The pox of** Plague take. **antic** grotesque   **28–9 phantasimes** coxcombs, fantastically dressed or mannered   **29 new tuners of accent** those who introduce new foreign words and slang phrases into their speech.   **30 tall** valiant   **31 grandsire** i.e., one who disapproves of the new fashion and prefers old custom   **32 flies** parasites   **33 pardon-me's** i.e., those who affect overly polite manners. (Other romantic heroines are **stand** (1) insist (2) the opposite of *sit*, line 34   **34–5 form ... bench** (*Form* means both "fashion" or "code of manners" and "bench.")   **35 bones** French *bon*, "good" (with play on English *bone*)   **37 Without his roe** i.e., Looking thin and emaciated, sexually spent. (With a pun on the first syllable of Romeo's name; the remaining syllables, *me-oh*, sound like the expression of a melancholy lover. *Roe* also suggests a female deer or "dear.")   **39 numbers** verses. **Laura** the lady to whom the Italian Renaissance poet Petrarch addressed his love poems. (Other romantic heroines are named in the following passage: Dido, Queen of Carthage; Cleopatra; Helen of Troy; Hero, beloved of Leander; and Thisbe, beloved of Pyramus.)   **to** in comparison with

41 dowdy homely woman   **42 gypsy** Egyptian; whore. **hildings** good-for-nothings   **43 not** i.e., that is not   **44 to** to match   **44–5 French slop** loose trousers of French fashion.   **45 fairly** handsomely, effectively   **48 slip** (Counterfeit coins were called "slips.")   **conceive** i.e., get the joke.   **51 case** (1) situation (2) physical condition. (Mercutio also bawdily suggests that Romeo has been in a *case*, i.e., the female genitalia.)   **52 bow in the hams** (1) make a low bow (2) show the effects of venereal disease.   **53 curtsy** bow, make obeisance.   **54 kindly** graciously. (But also suggesting natural and physical explanations.)   **56 pink** embodied perfection. (But suggesting also the flower called *pink*, the color, and *pinking*; see next note.)   **59 pump well flowered** i.e., shoe expertly pinked or perforated in ornamental figures suggesting flowers.   **63 solely singular** unique.   **64 single-soled** i.e., thin, contemptible   **65 singleness** feebleness.   **68 Switch and spurs** i.e., Keep up the rapid pace of the hunt (in the game of wits)   **68–9 cry a match** claim the victory.   **70 wild-goose chase** a horse race in which the leading rider dares his competitors to follow him wherever he goes   **73 Was ... goose?** Did I score a point in calling you a goose?   **75 for the goose** (1) behaving like a goose (2) looking for a prostitute.   **76 bite ... ear** i.e., give you an affectionate nibble on the ear. (Said ironically, however, and Romeo parries.)   **78 sweeting** sweet-flavored variety of apple   **79 sharp sauce** (1) "biting" retort (2) tart sauce, of the sort that should be served with cooked goose (as Romeo points out).

MERCUTIO   Oh, here's a wit of cheveril, that stretches 82
from an inch narrow to an ell broad! 83

ROMEO   I stretch it out for that word "broad," which,
added to the goose, proves thee far and wide a broad 85
goose.

MERCUTIO   Why, is not this better now than groaning for
love? Now art thou sociable, now art thou Romeo;
now art thou what thou art, by art as well as by nature.
For this driveling love is like a great natural that runs 90
lolling up and down to hide his bauble in a hole. 91

BENVOLIO   Stop there, stop there.

MERCUTIO   Thou desirest me to stop in my tale against 93
the hair. 94

BENVOLIO   Thou wouldst else have made thy tale large.

MERCUTIO   Oh, thou art deceived; I would have made it
short, for I was come to the whole depth of my tale
and meant indeed to occupy the argument no longer.

ROMEO   Here's goodly gear! 99

Enter Nurse and her man [Peter].

A sail, a sail! 100

MERCUTIO   Two, two: a shirt and a smock. 101

NURSE   Peter!

PETER   Anon!

NURSE   My fan, Peter.

MERCUTIO   Good Peter, to hide her face, for her fan's
the fairer face.

NURSE   God gi' good morrow, gentlemen.

MERCUTIO   God gi' good e'en, fair gentlewoman.

NURSE   Is it good e'en? 109

MERCUTIO   'Tis no less, I tell ye, for the bawdy hand of
the dial is now upon the prick of noon. 111

NURSE   Out upon you! What a man are you? 112

ROMEO   One, gentlewoman, that God hath made for
himself to mar. 114

NURSE   By my troth, it is well said. "For himself to mar," 115
quoth 'a? Gentlemen, can any of you tell me where I 116
may find the young Romeo?

ROMEO   I can tell you; but young Romeo will be older
when you have found him than he was when you
sought him. I am the youngest of that name, for fault 120
of a worse.

NURSE   You say well.

MERCUTIO   Yea, is the worst well? Very well took, i'faith, 123
wisely, wisely.

NURSE   If you be he, sir, I desire some confidence with 125
you.

BENVOLIO   She will indite him to some supper. 127

MERCUTIO   A bawd, a bawd, a bawd! So ho! 128

ROMEO   What hast thou found?

MERCUTIO   No hare, sir, unless a hare, sir, in a lenten 130
pie, that is something stale and hoar ere it be spent. 131

[He sings.]

An old hare hoar,
And an old hare hoar,
Is very good meat in Lent.
But a hare that is hoar
Is too much for a score, 136
When it hoars ere it be spent.

Romeo, will you come to your father's? We'll to dinner thither.

ROMEO   I will follow you.

MERCUTIO   Farewell, ancient lady. Farewell, *[singing]*
"Lady, lady, lady."   *Exeunt [Mercutio and Benvolio].* 142

NURSE   I pray you, sir, what saucy merchant was this 143
that was so full of his ropery? 144

ROMEO   A gentleman, Nurse, that loves to hear himself
talk, and will speak more in a minute than he will
stand to in a month. 147

NURSE   An 'a speak anything against me, I'll take him 148
down, an 'a were lustier than he is, and twenty such 149
Jacks; and if I cannot, I'll find those that shall. Scurvy 150
knave! I am none of his flirt-gills. I am none of his 151
skains-mates. *[To Peter]* And thou must stand by, too, 152
and suffer every knave to use me at his pleasure!

PETER   I saw no man use you at his pleasure. If I had,
my weapon should quickly have been out; I warrant 155
you, I dare draw as soon as another man, if I see
occasion in a good quarrel, and the law on my side.

NURSE   Now, afore God, I am so vexed that every part 158
about me quivers. Scurvy knave! Pray you, sir, a 159
word; and as I told you, my young lady bid me
inquire you out. What she bid me say, I will keep to
myself. But first let me tell ye, if ye should lead her
in a fool's paradise, as they say, it were a very gross
kind of behavior, as they say. For the gentlewoman
is young; and therefore if you should deal double

---

82 **cheveril** kid leather, easily stretched   83 **ell** (forty-five inches)
85 **broad** large, complete; perhaps also wanton   90 **natural** idiot
91 **lolling** with his tongue (or bauble) hanging out.   **bauble** (1) jester's
wand (2) phallus   93 **stop in my tale** (1) stop short in my story (2) stuff
in my penis   93–4 **against the hair** against the grain, against my wish.
(With bawdy suggestion of pubic hair. The sexual punning continues
in *large* [erect], *short* [detumescent], *come to the depth of my tale, occupy,*
etc.)   99 **goodly gear** matter for mockery. (With suggestion of "ample
sexual apparatus.")   100 **A sail** (To Romeo, the Nurse is an imposing
galleon in full sail.)   101 **a shirt and a smock** i.e., a man and a woman.
109 **Is it good e'en?** Is it afternoon already?   111 **prick** point on the
dial of a clock. (With bawdy suggestion.)   112 **Out upon you** (Expression of indignation.)   **What** What kind of   114 **mar** i.e., disfigure
morally through sin. (Humankind, made in God's image, mars that
image sinfully.)   115 **troth** faith   116 **quoth 'a** said he. (A sarcastic
interjection, meaning "forsooth" or "indeed.")   120 **fault** lack

123 **took** understood   125 **confidence** (The Nurse's mistake for "conference.")   127 **indite** (Benvolio's deliberate malapropism for
"invite.")   128 **So ho** (Cry of hunter sighting game.)   130 **hare**
(Slang word for "prostitute"; similarly, with *stale* and *meat* in the following lines.)   130–1 **a lenten pie** a pie that should contain no meat,
in observance of Lent   131 **hoar** moldy. (With pun on "whore"; *stale*
also can mean "whore.")   **spent** consumed.   136 **for a score** for a
reckoning, to pay good money for   142 **"Lady, lady, lady"** (Refrain
from the ballad *Chaste Susanna.*)   143 **merchant** i.e., fellow   144 **ropery** vulgar humor, knavery.   147 **stand to** carry out, stand in support
of   148 **An 'a** If he   148–9 **take him down** cut him down to size.
(With unintended bawdy suggestion.)   150 **Jacks** knaves   151 **flirt-
gills** loose women.   152 **skains-mates** (Perhaps daggermates, outlaws, or gangster molls.)   155 **weapon** (With bawdy suggestion,
perhaps unrecognized by the speaker, as also in *at his pleasure.*)
158–9 **every part . . . quivers** (More bawdy suggestion, unrecognized
by the Nurse.)

with her, truly it were an ill thing to be offered to any
gentlewoman, and very weak dealing.   167

ROMEO   Nurse, commend me to thy lady and mistress.
I protest unto thee—   169

NURSE   Good heart, and i'faith I will tell her as much.
Lord, Lord, she will be a joyful woman.

ROMEO   What wilt thou tell her, Nurse? Thou dost not
mark me.   173

NURSE   I will tell her, sir, that you do protest, which, as
I take it, is a gentlemanlike offer.

ROMEO   Bid her devise
Some means to come to shrift this afternoon,   177
And there she shall at Friar Laurence' cell
Be shrived and married. Here is for thy pains.   179
                                        [*He offers money.*]

NURSE   No, truly, sir, not a penny.

ROMEO   Go to, I say you shall.

NURSE
This afternoon, sir? Well, she shall be there.

ROMEO
And stay, good Nurse, behind the abbey wall.
Within this hour my man shall be with thee
And bring thee cords made like a tackled stair,   185
Which to the high topgallant of my joy   186
Must be my convoy in the secret night.   187
Farewell. Be trusty, and I'll quit thy pains.   188
Farewell. Commend me to thy mistress.
                                   [*Romeo starts to leave.*]

NURSE
Now God in heaven bless thee! Hark you, sir.

ROMEO   What say'st thou, my dear Nurse?

NURSE
Is your man secret? Did you ne'er hear say,   192
"Two may keep counsel, putting one away"?   193

ROMEO
'Warrant thee, my man's as true as steel.

NURSE   Well, sir, my mistress is the sweetest lady—
Lord, Lord! When 'twas a little prating thing—Oh,
there is a nobleman in town, one Paris, that would
fain lay knife aboard; but she, good soul, had as lief   198
see a toad, a very toad, as see him. I anger her
sometimes and tell her that Paris is the properer man,   200
but I'll warrant you, when I say so, she looks as pale
as any clout in the versal world. Doth not rosemary   202
and Romeo begin both with a letter?   203

ROMEO   Ay, Nurse, what of that? Both with an R.

NURSE   Ah, mocker! That's the dog's name; R is for   205
the—No; I know it begins with some other letter; and   206
she hath the prettiest sententious of it, of you and   207
rosemary, that it would do you good to hear it.

ROMEO   Commend me to thy lady.

NURSE   Ay, a thousand times.   [*Exit Romeo.*]
Peter!

PETER   Anon!

NURSE   Before, and apace.   *Exeunt.*   212

                              ❧

[2.5]

Enter Juliet.

JULIET
The clock struck nine when I did send the Nurse;
In half an hour she promised to return.
Perchance she cannot meet him. That's not so.
Oh, she is lame! Love's heralds should be thoughts,
Which ten times faster glides than the sun's beams
Driving back shadows over louring hills.   6
Therefore do nimble-pinioned doves draw Love,   7
And therefore hath the wind-swift Cupid wings.
Now is the sun upon the highmost hill
Of this day's journey, and from nine till twelve
Is three long hours, yet she is not come.
Had she affections and warm youthful blood,   12
She would be as swift in motion as a ball;
My words would bandy her to my sweet love,   14
And his to me.
But old folks, many feign as they were dead—   16
Unwieldy, slow, heavy, and pale as lead.

        Enter Nurse [and Peter].

Oh, God, she comes!—O honey Nurse, what news?
Hast thou met with him? Send thy man away.

NURSE   Peter, stay at the gate.   [*Exit Peter.*]

JULIET
Now, good sweet Nurse—Oh, Lord, why lookest thou
sad?
Though news be sad, yet tell them merrily;
If good, thou shamest the music of sweet news
By playing it to me with so sour a face.

NURSE
I am aweary. Give me leave awhile.   25
Fie, how my bones ache! What a jaunce have I had!   26

JULIET
I would thou hadst my bones and I thy news.
Nay, come, I pray thee, speak. Good, good Nurse,
speak.

---

167 weak contemptible   **169 protest** vow. (Romeo may intend only
to protest his good intentions, but the Nurse seemingly takes the
word to mean "propose," as if Romeo is making a *gentlemanlike offer*
[line 175] of marriage that would ensure against Juliet's being led into
a *fool's paradise* [line 163]—i.e., being seduced.)   **173 mark** attend to
177 shrift confession and absolution   **179 shrived** absolved
185 tackled stair rope ladder   **186 topgallant** highest mast and sail of
a ship, the summit   **187 convoy** conveyance, means of passage
188 quit reward, requite   **192 secret** trustworthy.   **193 keep counsel**
keep a secret   **198 fain lay knife aboard** like to assert his claim (just
as a guest at an inn did by bringing his knife to the dinner table; with
sexual suggestion also).   **lief** willingly   **200 properer** handsomer
202 clout faded rag.   **versal** universal.   **rosemary** (Associated with
weddings and funerals.)   **203 a letter** one and the same letter.

205 the dog's name (The letter *R* was thought to resemble the dog's
growl.)   **205–6 R is for ... letter** (Perhaps the Nurse is about to say
"arse," but has a notion that it begins with some other letter. In any case,
she decides against saying such an indelicate word.)   **207 sententious**
(The Nurse probably means "sentences," maxims.)   **212 Before, and
apace** Go before me quickly.
2.5. Location: Verona. Outside Capulet's house, perhaps in the
orchard or garden.
6 louring dark, threatening   **7 Love** i.e., Venus, whose chariot was
drawn by swift-winged doves   **12 affections** desires   **14 bandy** toss
to and fro, as in tennis   **16 feign as** act as though   **25 Give me leave**
Let me alone   **26 jaunce** jouncing, jolting

NURSE
  Jesu, what haste! Can you not stay awhile?   29
  Do you not see that I am out of breath?
JULIET
  How art thou out of breath, when thou hast breath
  To say to me that thou art out of breath?
  The excuse that thou dost make in this delay
  Is longer than the tale thou dost excuse.   34
  Is thy news good or bad? Answer to that;
  Say either, and I'll stay the circumstance.   36
  Let me be satisfied: is't good or bad?
NURSE   Well, you have made a simple choice. You know   38
  not how to choose a man. Romeo? No, not he. Though
  his face be better than any man's, yet his leg excels all
  men's; and for a hand, and a foot, and a body, though
  they be not to be talked on, yet they are past compare.   42
  He is not the flower of courtesy, but, I'll warrant him,
  as gentle as a lamb. Go thy ways, wench. Serve God.
  What, have you dined at home?
JULIET
  No, no; but all this did I know before.
  What says he of our marriage? What of that?
NURSE
  Lord, how my head aches! What a head have I!
  It beats as it would fall in twenty pieces.
  My back o' t'other side—ah, my back, my back!   50
  Beshrew your heart for sending me about   51
  To catch my death with jauncing up and down!
JULIET
  I'faith, I am sorry that thou art not well.
  Sweet, sweet, sweet Nurse, tell me, what says my
      love?
NURSE
  Your love says, like an honest gentleman,
  And a courteous, and a kind, and a handsome,
  And, I warrant, a virtuous—Where is your mother?
JULIET
  Where is my mother? Why, she is within,
  Where should she be? How oddly thou repliest!
  "Your love says, like an honest gentleman,   60
  'Where is your mother?' "
NURSE   O God's Lady dear!
  Are you so hot? Marry, come up, I trow.   62
  Is this the poultice for my aching bones?
  Henceforward do your messages yourself.
JULIET
  Here's such a coil! Come, what says Romeo?   65
NURSE
  Have you got leave to go to shrift today?
JULIET   I have.
NURSE
  Then hie you hence to Friar Laurence' cell;   68
  There stays a husband to make you a wife.

---

29 **stay** wait   34 **excuse** excuse yourself from telling.   36 **stay the circumstance** wait patiently for the details.   38 **simple** foolish   42 **be
not to be talked on** are beneath mention (especially in refined ladylike company)   50 **o' t'other** on the other   51 **Beshrew** A curse on.
(Used as a mild oath.)   60 **honest** honorable   62 **hot** impatient.
Marry, come up (An expression of impatient reproof.)   65 **coil** turmoil, fuss.   68 **hie** hasten

---

  Now comes the wanton blood up in your cheeks;
  They'll be in scarlet straight at any news.   71
  Hie you to church. I must another way,
  To fetch a ladder, by the which your love
  Must climb a bird's nest soon when it is dark.   74
  I am the drudge, and toil in your delight,
  But you shall bear the burden soon at night.
  Go. I'll to dinner. Hie you to the cell.
JULIET
  Hie to high fortune! Honest Nurse, farewell.

                          Exeunt [separately].

[2.6]

          Enter Friar [Laurence] and Romeo.

FRIAR LAURENCE
  So smile the heavens upon this holy act   1
  That after-hours with sorrow chide us not!
ROMEO
  Amen, amen! But come what sorrow can,
  It cannot countervail the exchange of joy   4
  That one short minute gives me in her sight.
  Do thou but close our hands with holy words,   6
  Then love-devouring death do what he dare;
  It is enough I may but call her mine.
FRIAR LAURENCE
  These violent delights have violent ends
  And in their triumph die, like fire and powder,   10
  Which as they kiss consume. The sweetest honey
  Is loathsome in his own deliciousness,   12
  And in the taste confounds the appetite.   13
  Therefore love moderately. Long love doth so;
  Too swift arrives as tardy as too slow.

                Enter Juliet.

  Here comes the lady. Oh, so light a foot
  Will ne'er wear out the everlasting flint.
  A lover may bestride the gossamers   18
  That idles in the wanton summer air,   19
  And yet not fall, so light is vanity.   20
JULIET
  Good even to my ghostly confessor.   21
FRIAR LAURENCE
  Romeo shall thank thee, daughter, for us both.   22
JULIET
  As much to him, else is his thanks too much.   23

---

71 **in scarlet straight** i.e., blushing immediately   74 **bird's nest** i.e.,
Juliet's room. (Continues the association of Juliet as a bird, as at 1.3.3,
2.2.168–82, with erotic suggestion. The bawdry is continued in *bear
the burden* two lines later.)
2.6. Location: Verona. Friar Laurence's cell.
1 **So . . . heavens** May the heavens so smile   4 **countervail** outweigh,
counterbalance   6 **close** join   10 **powder** gunpowder   12 **his** its
13 **confounds** destroys   18 **gossamers** filmy cobwebs   19 **wanton**
playful   20 **vanity** transitory human joy.   21 **ghostly** spiritual
22 **thank thee** i.e., give a kiss in thanks for your greeting   23 **As . . .
too much** either (1) Then I must repay him with a kiss, lest I be over-
paid, or (2) My greeting is to Romeo as much as to you; otherwise, his
greeting would exceed mine.

ROMEO
    Ah, Juliet, if the measure of thy joy
    Be heaped like mine, and that thy skill be more   25
    To blazon it, then sweeten with thy breath   26
    This neighbor air, and let rich music's tongue
    Unfold the imagined happiness that both   28
    Receive in either by this dear encounter.   29

JULIET
    Conceit, more rich in matter than in words,   30
    Brags of his substance, not of ornament.   31
    They are but beggars that can count their worth.
    But my true love is grown to such excess
    I cannot sum up sum of half my wealth.   34

FRIAR LAURENCE
    Come, come with me, and we will make short work;
    For, by your leaves, you shall not stay alone
    Till Holy Church incorporate two in one.   *[Exeunt.]*

❖

[3.1]

Enter Mercutio, Benvolio, and men.

BENVOLIO
    I pray thee, good Mercutio, let's retire.
    The day is hot, the Capels are abroad,   2
    And if we meet we shall not scape a brawl,
    For now, these hot days, is the mad blood stirring.

MERCUTIO   Thou art like one of these fellows that when
he enters the confines of a tavern, claps me his sword   6
upon the table and says, "God send me no need of
thee!" and by the operation of the second cup draws   8
him on the drawer, when indeed there is no need.   9

BENVOLIO   Am I like such a fellow?

MERCUTIO   Come, come, thou art as hot a Jack in thy   11
mood as any in Italy, and as soon moved to be moody,   12
and as soon moody to be moved.   13

BENVOLIO   And what to?

MERCUTIO   Nay, an there were two such, we should   15
have none shortly, for one would kill the other. Thou!
Why, thou wilt quarrel with a man that hath a hair
more or a hair less in his beard than thou hast. Thou
wilt quarrel with a man for cracking nuts, having no
other reason but because thou hast hazel eyes. What
eye but such an eye would spy out such a quarrel? Thy
head is as full of quarrels as an egg is full of meat, and   22
yet thy head hath been beaten as addle as an egg for   23
quarreling. Thou hast quarreled with a man for cough-
ing in the street, because he hath wakened thy dog that

hath lain asleep in the sun. Didst thou not fall out
with a tailor for wearing his new doublet before   27
Easter? With another, for tying his new shoes with old
ribbon? And yet thou wilt tutor me from quarreling!

BENVOLIO   An I were so apt to quarrel as thou art, any
man should buy the fee simple of my life for an hour   31
and a quarter.   32

MERCUTIO   The fee simple! Oh, simple!   33

Enter Tybalt, Petruchio, and others.

BENVOLIO   By my head, here comes the Capulets.

MERCUTIO   By my heel, I care not.

TYBALT   *[to his companions]*
    Follow me close, for I will speak to them.—
    Gentlemen, good e'en. A word with one of you.

MERCUTIO   And but one word with one of us? Couple it
with something: make it a word and a blow.

TYBALT   You shall find me apt enough to that, sir, an
you will give me occasion.

MERCUTIO   Could you not take some occasion without
giving?

TYBALT   Mercutio, thou consortest with Romeo.   44

MERCUTIO   "Consort"? What, dost thou make us minstrels? An thou make minstrels of us, look to hear
nothing but discords. Here's my fiddlestick; here's   47
that shall make you dance. Zounds, "consort"!   48

BENVOLIO
    We talk here in the public haunt of men.
    Either withdraw unto some private place,
    Or reason coldly of your grievances,   51
    Or else depart; here all eyes gaze on us.   52

MERCUTIO
    Men's eyes were made to look, and let them gaze.
    I will not budge for no man's pleasure, I.

Enter Romeo.

TYBALT
    Well, peace be with you, sir. Here comes my man.

MERCUTIO
    But I'll be hanged, sir, if he wear your livery.   56
    Marry, go before to field, he'll be your follower;   57
    Your Worship in that sense may call him "man."   58

TYBALT
    Romeo, the love I bear thee can afford
    No better term than this: thou art a villain.

ROMEO
    Tybalt, the reason that I have to love thee
    Doth much excuse the appertaining rage   62
    To such a greeting. Villain am I none.

---

25 that if   **26 blazon** describe, set forth. (A heraldic term.)
28 Unfold make known.   **imagined** i.e., unexpressed   **29 in either**
from each other   **30–1 Conceit . . . ornament** True understanding,
more enriched by the actual reality (of love) than by mere words, finds
more worth in the substance of that reality than in outward show.
34 sum up sum add up the total
3.1. Location: Verona. A public place.
2 Capels Capulets   **6 claps me** claps. (*Me* is a now-archaic dative of
reference, used colloquially.)   **8–9 draws . . . drawer** draws his sword
against the tapster or waiter   **9 there is no need** i.e., of his sword.
11 as hot a Jack as hot-tempered a fellow   **12 moody** angry   **13 to be
moved** at being provoked.   **15 an** if   **22 meat** i.e., edible matter
23 addle addled, confused

27 doublet man's jacket   **31 fee simple** outright possession   **31–2 an
hour . . . quarter** i.e., my life would last no longer in such circumstances.
33 Oh, simple! Oh, how stupid!   **44 consortest** keep company with.
(But Mercutio quibbles on its musical sense of "accompany" or "play
together.")   **47 fiddlestick** (Mercutio means his sword.)   **48 that** that
which.   **Zounds** By God's (Christ's) wounds   **51 coldly** calmly
52 depart go away separately   **56 livery** servant's uniform. (Mercutio
deliberately mistakes Tybalt's phrase *my man* to mean "my servant.")
57 field field where a duel might occur   **58 Your Worship** (A title of
honor used here with mock politeness.)   **62 the appertaining rage** the
rage that would ordinarily be appropriate to

Therefore, farewell. I see thou knowest me not.

TYBALT
Boy, this shall not excuse the injuries   65
That thou hast done me. Therefore turn and draw.

ROMEO
I do protest I never injured thee,
But love thee better than thou canst devise   68
Till thou shalt know the reason of my love.
And so, good Capulet—which name I tender   70
As dearly as mine own—be satisfied.

MERCUTIO
Oh, calm, dishonorable, vile submission!
Alla stoccata carries it away.   [*He draws.*]   73
Tybalt, you ratcatcher, will you walk?   74

TYBALT   What wouldst thou have with me?

MERCUTIO   Good king of cats, nothing but one of your
nine lives, that I mean to make bold withal, and, as   77
you shall use me hereafter, dry-beat the rest of the   78
eight. Will you pluck your sword out of his pilcher by   79
the ears? Make haste, lest mine be about your ears ere   80
it be out.

TYBALT   I am for you.   [*He draws.*]

ROMEO
Gentle Mercutio, put thy rapier up.

MERCUTIO   Come, sir, your *passado*.   [*They fight.*] 84

ROMEO
Draw, Benvolio, beat down their weapons.
Gentlemen, for shame, forbear this outrage!
Tybalt, Mercutio, the Prince expressly hath
Forbid this bandying in Verona streets.
Hold, Tybalt! Good Mercutio!
    [*Tybalt under Romeo's arm stabs Mercutio.*] *Away*
                Tybalt [*with his followers*].

MERCUTIO   I am hurt.   89
A plague o' both your houses! I am sped.   90
Is he gone, and hath nothing?

BENVOLIO   What, art thou hurt?

MERCUTIO
Ay, ay, a scratch, a scratch; marry, 'tis enough.
Where is my page? Go, villain, fetch a surgeon.
                                        [*Exit Page.*]

ROMEO
Courage, man, the hurt cannot be much.

MERCUTIO   No, 'tis not so deep as a well, nor so wide as
a church door, but 'tis enough, 'twill serve. Ask for me
tomorrow, and you shall find me a grave man. I am   97
peppered, I warrant, for this world. A plague o' both   98
your houses! Zounds, a dog, a rat, a mouse, a cat, to
scratch a man to death! A braggart, a rogue, a villain,
that fights by the book of arithmetic! Why the devil   101
came you between us? I was hurt under your arm.

ROMEO   I thought all for the best.

MERCUTIO
Help me into some house, Benvolio,
Or I shall faint. A plague o' both your houses!
They have made worm's meat of me. I have it,
And soundly too. Your houses!
                Exit [*supported by Benvolio*].

ROMEO
This gentleman, the Prince's near ally,   108
My very friend, hath got this mortal hurt   109
In my behalf; my reputation stained
With Tybalt's slander—Tybalt, that an hour
Hath been my cousin! O sweet Juliet,   112
Thy beauty hath made me effeminate,   113
And in my temper softened valor's steel.   114

        Enter Benvolio.

BENVOLIO
O Romeo, Romeo, brave Mercutio is dead!
That gallant spirit hath aspired the clouds,   116
Which too untimely here did scorn the earth.

ROMEO
This day's black fate on more days doth depend;   118
This but begins the woe others must end.   119

        [*Enter Tybalt.*]

BENVOLIO
Here comes the furious Tybalt back again.

ROMEO
Alive in triumph, and Mercutio slain!
Away to heaven, respective lenity,   122
And fire-eyed fury be my conduct now!   123
Now, Tybalt, take the "villain" back again
That late thou gavest me, for Mercutio's soul
Is but a little way above our heads,
Staying for thine to keep him company.
Either thou or I, or both, must go with him.

TYBALT
Thou, wretched boy, that didst consort him here,
Shalt with him hence.

ROMEO   This shall determine that.
                They fight. Tybalt falls.

BENVOLIO   Romeo, away, begone!
The citizens are up, and Tybalt slain.

65 Boy (A deliberate and grave insult when addressed to a grown man. Tybalt's use of *thee* and *thou* in lines 59–60 and following is similarly insulting; Romeo's use of this personal form in lines 61–4 and 67–9, on the other hand, is appropriate to a close family tie that he privately acknowledges but is of course misunderstood by Tybalt and the bystanders.) **68 devise** imagine **70 tender** value **73 *Alla stoccata* . . . away** i.e. (scornfully), This elegant Italian way of fencing, and the fancy terminology to go with it, will win the day, I suppose. (*Alla stoccata* means "at the thrust.") **74 ratcatcher** (An allusion to Tybalt as king of cats; see 2.4.19.) **77 make bold withal** make free with **78 dry-beat** beat soundly (without drawing blood) **79–80 out . . . ears** out of its scabbard by the handle or hilt. **84 passado** forward thrust. (Another fancy Italian fencing term of the sort Mercutio despises.) **89 s.d. *Away Tybalt*** (Because the phrase is unusual for an exit stage direction, some editors plausibly assign this as a speech to Petruchio, who enters at line 33.1 and is otherwise silent.) **90 sped** done for.

97 grave (Mercutio thus puns with his last breath.) **98 peppered** finished, done for **101 by . . . arithmetic** by the numbers, as in a textbook on fencing (as at 2.4.20–3). **108 ally** kinsman **109 very** true **112 cousin** kinsman. **113 effeminate** weak **114 temper** disposition. (But with a play on the tempering of a steel sword.) **116 aspired** ascended to **118 This day's . . . depend** This day hangs threateningly over the time to come **119 others** other days to come **122 respective lenity** considerate gentleness **123 conduct** guide

Stand not amazed. The Prince will doom thee death   133
If thou art taken. Hence, begone, away!

ROMEO
Oh, I am fortune's fool!

BENVOLIO   Why dost thou stay?   135

Exit Romeo.

Enter Citizens.

FIRST CITIZEN
Which way ran he that killed Mercutio?
Tybalt, that murderer, which way ran he?

BENVOLIO
There lies that Tybalt.

FIRST CITIZEN   Up, sir, go with me.
I charge thee in the Prince's name, obey.

*Enter Prince [attended], old Montague,
Capulet, their Wives, and all.*

PRINCE
Where are the vile beginners of this fray?

BENVOLIO
O noble Prince, I can discover all   141
The unlucky manage of this fatal brawl.   142
There lies the man, slain by young Romeo,
That slew thy kinsman, brave Mercutio.

CAPULET'S WIFE
Tybalt, my cousin! O my brother's child!
O Prince! O cousin! Husband! Oh, the blood is spilled
Of my dear kinsman! Prince, as thou art true,
For blood of ours shed blood of Montague.
O cousin, cousin!

PRINCE
Benvolio, who began this bloody fray?

BENVOLIO
Tybalt, here slain, whom Romeo's hand did slay.
Romeo, that spoke him fair, bid him bethink   152
How nice the quarrel was, and urged withal   153
Your high displeasure. All this—utterèd
With gentle breath, calm look, knees humbly bowed—
Could not take truce with the unruly spleen   156
Of Tybalt deaf to peace, but that he tilts
With piercing steel at bold Mercutio's breast,
Who, all as hot, turns deadly point to point,
And, with a martial scorn, with one hand beats
Cold death aside and with the other sends
It back to Tybalt, whose dexterity
Retorts it. Romeo he cries aloud,   163
"Hold, friends! Friends, part!" and swifter than his
    tongue
His agile arm beats down their fatal points,
And twixt them rushes; underneath whose arm
An envious thrust from Tybalt hit the life   167
Of stout Mercutio, and then Tybalt fled;   168
But by and by comes back to Romeo,
Who had but newly entertained revenge,   170

And to't they go like lightning, for, ere I
Could draw to part them was stout Tybalt slain,
And, as he fell, did Romeo turn and fly.
This is the truth, or let Benvolio die.

CAPULET'S WIFE
He is a kinsman to the Montague.
Affection makes him false; he speaks not true.   176
Some twenty of them fought in this black strife,
And all those twenty could but kill one life.
I beg for justice, which thou, Prince, must give.
Romeo slew Tybalt; Romeo must not live.

PRINCE
Romeo slew him, he slew Mercutio.
Who now the price of his dear blood doth owe?

MONTAGUE
Not Romeo, Prince, he was Mercutio's friend;
His fault concludes but what the law should end,   184
The life of Tybalt.

PRINCE   And for that offense
Immediately we do exile him hence.
I have an interest in your hate's proceeding;
My blood for your rude brawls doth lie a-bleeding;   188
But I'll amerce you with so strong a fine   189
That you shall all repent the loss of mine.
I will be deaf to pleading and excuses;
Nor tears nor prayers shall purchase out abuses.   192
Therefore use none. Let Romeo hence in haste,   193
Else, when he is found, that hour is his last.   194
Bear hence this body and attend our will.   195
Mercy but murders, pardoning those that kill.   196

Exeunt, [some carrying Tybalt's body].

❧

[3.2]

Enter Juliet alone.

JULIET
Gallop apace, you fiery-footed steeds,   1
Towards Phoebus' lodging! Such a wagoner   2
As Phaëthon would whip you to the west   3
And bring in cloudy night immediately.   4
Spread thy close curtain, love-performing night,   5

133 **amazed** dazed.   **doom thee death** sentence you to death
135 **fool** dupe.   141 **discover** reveal   142 **manage** conduct   152 **fair**
civilly.   **bethink** consider   153 **nice** trivial.   **withal** besides
156 **take truce** make peace   163 **Retorts** returns   167 **envious** malicious   168 **stout** brave   170 **entertained** harbored thoughts of

176 **Affection** Partiality   184 **concludes but** only finishes   188 **My
blood** i.e., blood of my kinsman. (Here we learn that Mercutio is kin
to the Prince.)   189 **amerce** penalize   192 **Nor** neither.   **purchase
out abuses** redeem misdeeds.   193 **hence** depart   194 **Else** Otherwise   195 **attend our will** be on hand to hear further judgment.
196 **but murders** merely encourages murder by excessive leniency
3.2. Location: Verona. Capulet's house.
1 **apace** quickly.   **steeds** i.e., the horses of the sun god's chariot
2 **Phoebus** (Often equated with Helios, the sun god.)   **lodging** i.e., in
the west, below the horizon.   **2–4 Such . . . immediately** i.e., One
who is impetuously young, as we are, would understand the need to
make the day as short as possible and would quickly bring it to an
end. (The mythical allusion is sadly ironic, for Phaëthon drove the
chariot of the sun so badly that he had to be destroyed by Zeus.)
5 **close** enclosing

That runaways' eyes may wink, and Romeo   6
Leap to these arms, untalked of and unseen.   7
Lovers can see to do their amorous rites
By their own beauties; or, if love be blind,
It best agrees with night. Come, civil night,   10
Thou sober-suited matron all in black,
And learn me how to lose a winning match   12
Played for a pair of stainless maidenhoods.
Hood my unmanned blood, bating in my cheeks,   14
With thy black mantle till strange love grown bold   15
Think true love acted simple modesty.
Come, night. Come, Romeo. Come, thou day in night;
For thou wilt lie upon the wings of night
Whiter than new snow upon a raven's back.
Come, gentle night, come, loving, black-browed night,
Give me my Romeo, and when I shall die   21
Take him and cut him out in little stars,
And he will make the face of heaven so fine
That all the world will be in love with night
And pay no worship to the garish sun.   25
Oh, I have bought the mansion of a love
But not possessed it, and though I am sold,
Not yet enjoyed. So tedious is this day
As is the night before some festival
To an impatient child that hath new robes
And may not wear them. Oh, here comes my nurse,   31

> *Enter Nurse, with cords.*

And she brings news, and every tongue that speaks
But Romeo's name speaks heavenly eloquence.
Now, Nurse, what news? What hast thou there? The
  cords
That Romeo bid thee fetch?
NURSE   Ay, ay, the cords.
                                   [*She throws them down.*]
JULIET
Ay me, what news? Why dost thou wring thy hands?
NURSE
Ah, weraday! He's dead, he's dead, he's dead!   37
We are undone, lady, we are undone!
Alack the day, he's gone, he's killed, he's dead!
JULIET
Can heaven be so envious?
NURSE   Romeo can,   40
Though heaven cannot. Oh, Romeo, Romeo!
Who ever would have thought it? Romeo!

JULIET
What devil art thou that dost torment me thus?
This torture should be roared in dismal hell.
Hath Romeo slain himself? Say thou but "Ay,"
And that bare vowel "I" shall poison more   46
Than the death-darting eye of cockatrice.   47
I am not I, if there be such an "Ay,"
Or those eyes shut, that makes thee answer "Ay."   49
If he be slain, say "Ay," or if not, "No."
Brief sounds determine of my weal or woe.   51
NURSE
I saw the wound. I saw it with mine eyes—
God save the mark!—here on his manly breast.   53
A piteous corpse, a bloody piteous corpse;
Pale, pale as ashes, all bedaubed in blood,
All in gore-blood. I swoonèd at the sight.   56
JULIET
Oh, break, my heart! Poor bankrupt, break at once!
To prison, eyes; ne'er look on liberty!
Vile earth, to earth resign; end motion here,   59
And thou and Romeo press one heavy bier!   60
NURSE
O Tybalt, Tybalt, the best friend I had!
O courteous Tybalt! Honest gentleman!   62
That ever I should live to see thee dead!
JULIET
What storm is this that blows so contrary?
Is Romeo slaughtered, and is Tybalt dead?
My dearest cousin, and my dearer lord?
Then, dreadful trumpet, sound the general doom!   67
For who is living, if those two are gone?
NURSE
Tybalt is gone, and Romeo banishèd;
Romeo that killed him, he is banishèd.
JULIET
Oh, God! Did Romeo's hand shed Tybalt's blood?
NURSE
It did, it did. Alas the day it did!
JULIET
O serpent heart, hid with a flow'ring face!   73
Did ever dragon keep so fair a cave?   74
Beautiful tyrant! Fiend angelical!
Dove-feathered raven! Wolvish-ravening lamb!
Despisèd substance of divinest show!   77
Just opposite to what thou justly seem'st,
A damnèd saint, an honorable villain!
O nature, what hadst thou to do in hell
When thou didst bower the spirit of a fiend   81
In mortal paradise of such sweet flesh?
Was ever book containing such vile matter

6–7 That runaways' . . . unseen (Perhaps Juliet is thinking of the elopement that will surely be necessary once she and Romeo secretly marry; they will embrace in the dark of *love-performing night,* untalked of and unseen by others and by each other. A difficult passage that is sometimes interpreted, uncertainly, as referring to the sun's horses as the *runaways. Wink* means "close, be shut.")   **10 civil** circumspect, somberly attired   **12 learn** teach   **14 Hood** Cover. (A term in falconry; the hawk's eyes were covered so that it would not *bate* or beat its wings.)   **unmanned** untamed (in falconry; with a pun on "not yet sexually possessed")   **15 strange** diffident   **21 I** (Often emended to *he,* following the Fourth Quarto, but Juliet may mean that when she is dead she will share Romeo's beauty with the world. Dying may also hint at sexual climax.)   **25 garish** dazzling   **31.1 cords** ropes (for the ladder).   **37 weraday!** welladay, alas!   **40 envious** malicious.

46 "I" (Pronounced identically with "Ay.")   **47 cockatrice** basilisk, a mythical serpent that could kill by its look.   **49 those eyes shut** if Romeo's eyes are shut (in death)   **51 weal** welfare, happiness   **53 God . . . mark** (An oath registering shock and horror.)   **56 gore-blood** clotted blood.   **59 Vile . . . here** May my vile body resign itself to burial, ending life itself   **60 press** weigh down.   **bier** litter for carrying corpses.   **62 Honest** Honorable   **67 trumpet** i.e., the last trumpet.   **general doom** Day of Judgment.   **73 hid . . . face** concealed beneath a beautiful face.   **74 keep** occupy, guard.   **cave** i.e., one with treasure in it.   **77 show** appearance.   **81 bower** give lodging to

So fairly bound? Oh, that deceit should dwell
In such a gorgeous palace!
NURSE   There's no trust,
No faith, no honesty in men; all perjured,
All forsworn, all naught, all dissemblers.   87
Ah, where's my man? Give me some aqua vitae.   88
These griefs, these woes, these sorrows make me old.
Shame come to Romeo!
JULIET   Blistered be thy tongue
For such a wish! He was not born to shame.
Upon his brow shame is ashamed to sit,
For 'tis a throne where honor may be crowned
Sole monarch of the universal earth.
Oh, what a beast was I to chide at him!
NURSE
Will you speak well of him that killed your cousin?
JULIET
Shall I speak ill of him that is my husband?
Ah, poor my lord, what tongue shall smooth thy name   98
When I, thy three-hours wife, have mangled it?
But wherefore, villain, didst thou kill my cousin?
That villain cousin would have killed my husband.
Back, foolish tears, back to your native spring!
Your tributary drops belong to woe,   103
Which you, mistaking, offer up to joy.
My husband lives, that Tybalt would have slain,   105
And Tybalt's dead, that would have slain my
    husband.
All this is comfort. Wherefore weep I then?
Some word there was, worser than Tybalt's death,
That murdered me. I would forget it fain,   109
But oh, it presses to my memory
Like damnèd guilty deeds to sinners' minds!
"Tybalt is dead, and Romeo—banishèd."
That "banishèd," that one word "banishèd"
Hath slain ten thousand Tybalts. Tybalt's death
Was woe enough, if it had ended there;
Or, if sour woe delights in fellowship
And needly will be ranked with other griefs,   117
Why followed not, when she said "Tybalt's dead,"
"Thy father," or "thy mother," nay, or both,
Which modern lamentation might have moved?   120
But with a rearward following Tybalt's death,   121
"Romeo is banishèd"—to speak that word
Is father, mother, Tybalt, Romeo, Juliet,
All slain, all dead. "Romeo is banishèd!"
There is no end, no limit, measure, bound,
In that word's death; no words can that woe sound.   126
Where is my father and my mother, Nurse?
NURSE
Weeping and wailing over Tybalt's corpse.
Will you go to them? I will bring you thither.

JULIET
Wash they his wounds with tears? Mine shall be spent,
When theirs are dry, for Romeo's banishment.
Take up those cords.—Poor ropes, you are beguiled,
Both you and I, for Romeo is exiled.
He made you for a highway to my bed,
But I, a maid, die maiden-widowèd.
Come, cords, come, Nurse. I'll to my wedding bed,
And death, not Romeo, take my maidenhead.
NURSE [taking up the cords]
Hie to your chamber. I'll find Romeo
To comfort you. I wot well where he is.   139
Hark ye, your Romeo will be here at night.
I'll to him. He is hid at Laurence' cell.
JULIET [giving a ring]
Oh, find him! Give this ring to my true knight,
And bid him come to take his last farewell.
                                    Exeunt [separately].

[3.3]

Enter Friar [Laurence].

FRIAR LAURENCE
Romeo, come forth; come forth, thou fearful man.   1
Affliction is enamored of thy parts,   2
And thou art wedded to calamity.

        [Enter] Romeo.

ROMEO
Father, what news? What is the Prince's doom?   4
What sorrow craves acquaintance at my hand
That I yet know not?
FRIAR LAURENCE   Too familiar
Is my dear son with such sour company.
I bring thee tidings of the Prince's doom.
ROMEO
What less than doomsday is the Prince's doom?   9
FRIAR LAURENCE
A gentler judgment vanished from his lips: 10
Not body's death, but body's banishment.
ROMEO
Ha, banishment? Be merciful, say "death";
For exile hath more terror in his look,
Much more than death. Do not say "banishment."
FRIAR LAURENCE
Here from Verona art thou banishèd.
Be patient, for the world is broad and wide.
ROMEO
There is no world without Verona walls   17
But purgatory, torture, hell itself.
Hence "banishèd" is banished from the world,
And world's exile is death. Then "banishèd,"   20
Is death mistermed. Calling death "banishèd,"

---

87 **naught** worthless, evil   **88 man** servant.   **aqua vitae** alcoholic
spirits.   **98 poor my lord** my poor lord.   **smooth thy name** speak
your name kindly   **103 Your . . . woe** You should be shed, offered as
a tribute, on some occasion of real woe   **105 that** whom   **109 fain**
gladly   **117 needly** of necessity.   **ranked with** accompanied by
120 Which . . . moved which might have prompted a normal grief-
stricken response.   **121 rearward** rearguard, following afterward
126 sound (1) fathom (2) express.

139 wot know
3.3. Location: Verona. Friar Laurence's cell.
1 fearful full of fear   **2 parts** qualities   **4 doom** judgment.
9 doomsday the Day of judgment, i.e., end of the world
10 vanished issued (into air)   **17 without** outside of   **20 world's
exile** exile from the world

Thou cut'st my head off with a golden ax
And smilest upon the stroke that murders me.
FRIAR LAURENCE
Oh, deadly sin! Oh, rude unthankfulness!
Thy fault our law calls death, but the kind Prince, 25
Taking thy part, hath rushed aside the law 26
And turned that black word "death" to "banishment."
This is dear mercy, and thou see'st it not.
ROMEO
'Tis torture, and not mercy. Heaven is here
Where Juliet lives, and every cat and dog
And little mouse, every unworthy thing,
Live here in heaven and may look on her,
But Romeo may not. More validity, 33
More honorable state, more courtship lives 34
In carrion flies than Romeo. They may seize
On the white wonder of dear Juliet's hand
And steal immortal blessing from her lips,
Who even in pure and vestal modesty 38
Still blush, as thinking their own kisses sin; 39
But Romeo may not, he is banishèd.
Flies may do this, but I from this must fly.
They are free men, but I am banishèd.
And sayest thou yet that exile is not death?
Hadst thou no poison mixed, no sharp-ground knife,
No sudden mean of death, though ne'er so mean, 45
But "banishèd" to kill me? "Banishèd"?
Oh, Friar, the damnèd use that word in hell;
Howling attends it. How hast thou the heart,
Being a divine, a ghostly confessor,
A sin absolver, and my friend professed,
To mangle me with that word "banishèd"?
FRIAR LAURENCE
Thou fond mad man, hear me a little speak. 52
ROMEO
Oh, thou wilt speak again of banishment.
FRIAR LAURENCE
I'll give thee armor to keep off that word,
Adversity's sweet milk, philosophy,
To comfort thee, though thou art banishèd.
ROMEO
Yet "banishèd"? Hang up philosophy! 57
Unless philosophy can make a Juliet,
Displant a town, reverse a prince's doom, 59
It helps not, it prevails not. Talk no more.
FRIAR LAURENCE
Oh, then I see that madmen have no ears.
ROMEO
How should they, when that wise men have no eyes?
FRIAR LAURENCE
Let me dispute with thee of thy estate. 63

ROMEO
Thou canst not speak of that thou dost not feel. 64
Wert thou as young as I, Juliet thy love,
An hour but married, Tybalt murderèd,
Doting like me, and like me banishèd,
Then mightst thou speak, then mightst thou tear thy
hair,
And fall upon the ground, as I do now,
Taking the measure of an unmade grave.
[He falls upon the ground.] Knock [within].
FRIAR LAURENCE
Arise. One knocks. Good Romeo, hide thyself.
ROMEO
Not I, unless the breath of heartsick groans,
Mistlike, infold me from the search of eyes. Knock.
FRIAR LAURENCE
Hark, how they knock!—Who's there?—Romeo, arise.
Thou wilt be taken.—Stay awhile!—Stand up.
Knock.
Run to my study.—By and by!—God's will,
What simpleness is this?—I come, I come! Knock. 77
Who knocks so hard? Whence come you? What's your
will? [Going to the door.]
NURSE [within]
Let me come in, and you shall know my errand.
I come from Lady Juliet.
FRIAR LAURENCE Welcome, then.
[He opens the door.]

Enter Nurse.

NURSE
O holy Friar, oh, tell me, holy Friar,
Where's my lady's lord, where's Romeo?
FRIAR LAURENCE
There on the ground, with his own tears made drunk.
NURSE
Oh, he is even in my mistress' case, 84
Just in her case! Oh, woeful sympathy! 85
Piteous predicament! Even so lies she,
Blubb'ring and weeping, weeping and blubb'ring.—
Stand up, stand up! Stand, an you be a man.
For Juliet's sake, for her sake, rise and stand!
Why should you fall into so deep an O? 90
ROMEO Nurse! [He rises.]
NURSE
Ah sir, ah sir! Death's the end of all.
ROMEO
Spakest thou of Juliet? How is it with her?
Doth not she think me an old murderer, 94
Now I have stained the childhood of our joy
With blood removed but little from her own?
Where is she? And how doth she? And what says
My concealed lady to our canceled love? 98

---

25 **Thy fault . . . death** For your crime, the law demands a death sentence 26 **rushed** thrust 33 **validity** true worth 34 **courtship** (1) courtliness (2) occasion for wooing 38 **vestal** maidenly 39 **Still . . . sin** continually look red, as though blushing to think that their touching each other is sin 45 **mean . . . mean** means . . . base 52 **fond** foolish, frantic 57 **Yet** Still 59 **Displant** uproot 63 **dispute** reason. **estate** situation.

64 **that** that which 77 **simpleness** foolishness 84 **even** exactly. **case** situation 85 **woeful sympathy** mutuality of grief. 90 **an O** a fit of groaning. (A sexual meaning, unrecognized by the speaker, is suggested by *rise and stand* in the previous line.) 94 **old** hardened 98 **concealed** secret. **canceled** nullified (by the impending exile)

NURSE
   Oh, she says nothing, sir, but weeps and weeps,
   And now falls on her bed, and then starts up,
   And "Tybalt" calls, and then on Romeo cries,
   And then down falls again.
ROMEO   As if that name,
   Shot from the deadly level of a gun,   103
   Did murder her, as that name's cursèd hand
   Murdered her kinsman. Oh, tell me, Friar, tell me,
   In what vile part of this anatomy
   Doth my name lodge? Tell me, that I may sack   107
   The hateful mansion.
                [He draws a weapon, but is restrained.]
FRIAR LAURENCE   Hold thy desperate hand!
   Art thou a man? Thy form cries out thou art;
   Thy tears are womanish, thy wild acts denote
   The unreasonable fury of a beast.
   Unseemly woman in a seeming man,
   And ill-beseeming beast in seeming both!
   Thou hast amazed me. By my holy order,
   I thought thy disposition better tempered.   115
   Hast thou slain Tybalt? Wilt thou slay thyself,
   And slay thy lady, that in thy life lives,
   By doing damnèd hate upon thyself?
   Why railest thou on thy birth, the heaven, and earth,
   Since birth, and heaven, and earth, all three do meet 120
   In thee at once, which thou at once wouldst lose?
   Fie, fie, thou shamest thy shape, thy love, thy wit,   122
   Which, like a usurer, abound'st in all,   123
   And usest none in that true use indeed   124
   Which should bedeck thy shape, thy love, thy wit. 125
   Thy noble shape is but a form of wax,   126
   Digressing from the valor of a man;
   Thy dear love sworn but hollow perjury,
   Killing that love which thou hast vowed to cherish;
   Thy wit, that ornament to shape and love,
   Misshapen in the conduct of them both,   131
   Like powder in a skilless soldier's flask   132
   Is set afire by thine own ignorance,
   And thou dismembered with thine own defense. 134
   What, rouse thee, man! Thy Juliet is alive,
   For whose dear sake thou wast but lately dead;   136
   There art thou happy. Tybalt would kill thee,   137
   But thou slewest Tybalt; there art thou happy.
   The law that threatened death becomes thy friend
   And turns it to exile; there art thou happy.
   A pack of blessings light upon thy back,
   Happiness courts thee in her best array,
   But like a mishavèd and sullen wench   143
   Thou pout'st upon thy fortune and thy love.

103 **level** aim   107 **sack** destroy   115 **tempered** harmonized, balanced.   120 **birth . . . earth** life, soul, and body   122–5 **thou shamest . . . wit** you shame your physical form, love, and mind (corresponding to life, soul, and body), all of which you have in abundance but which you misuse as a usurer misuses wealth, using improperly the treasure that you should put to proper use.   126 **form of wax** waxwork, mere outer form   131 **conduct** guidance   132 **powder** gunpowder.   **flask** powder horn   134 **dismembered . . . defense** blown to pieces by that which should defend you, i.e., your *wit*, or intellect.   136 **wast . . . dead** i.e., only recently were wishing yourself dead. (See line 70.)   137 **happy** fortunate.   143 **mishavèd** misbehaved

   Take heed, take heed, for such die miserable.
   Go, get thee to thy love, as was decreed.   146
   Ascend her chamber; hence and comfort her.
   But look thou stay not till the watch be set,   148
   For then thou canst not pass to Mantua,
   Where thou shalt live till we can find a time
   To blaze your marriage, reconcile your friends,   151
   Beg pardon of the Prince, and call thee back
   With twenty hundred thousand times more joy
   Than thou went'st forth in lamentation.
   Go before, Nurse. Commend me to thy lady,
   And bid her hasten all the house to bed,
   Which heavy sorrow makes them apt unto.
   Romeo is coming.
NURSE
   Oh, Lord, I could have stayed here all the night
   To hear good counsel. Oh, what learning is!—
   My lord, I'll tell my lady you will come.
ROMEO
   Do so, and bid my sweet prepare to chide.
NURSE [*giving a ring*]
   Here, sir, a ring she bid me give you, sir.
   Hie you, make haste, for it grows very late.   [*Exit.*]
ROMEO
   How well my comfort is revived by this!
FRIAR LAURENCE
   Go hence. Good night. And here stands all your state: 166
   Either be gone before the watch be set,
   Or by the break of day disguised from hence.
   Sojourn in Mantua. I'll find out your man,
   And he shall signify from time to time
   Every good hap to you that chances here.   171
   Give me thy hand. 'Tis late. Farewell, good night.
ROMEO
   But that a joy past joy calls out on me,
   It were a grief so brief to part with thee.   174
   Farewell.   *Exeunt [separately].*

[3.4]

Enter old Capulet, his Wife, and Paris.

CAPULET
   Things have fall'n out, sir, so unluckily,   1
   That we have had no time to move our daughter. 2
   Look you, she loved her kinsman Tybalt dearly,
   And so did I. Well, we were born to die.
   'Tis very late. She'll not come down tonight.
   I promise you, but for your company   6
   I would have been abed an hour ago.
PARIS
   These times of woe afford no times to woo.
   Madam, good night. Commend me to your daughter.

146 **decreed** (1) arranged earlier (2) decreed by heaven for those who have married.   148 **the watch be set** guards are posted (at the city gates)   151 **blaze** publish, divulge.   **friends** relations   166 **here . . . state** your fortune depends on what follows   171 **good hap** fortunate event   174 **brief** quickly
3.4. Location: Verona. Capulet's house.
1 **fall'n out** happened   2 **move** persuade   6 **promise** assure

WIFE
> I will, and know her mind early tomorrow.
> Tonight she's mewed up to her heaviness.   11

CAPULET
> Sir Paris, I will make a desperate tender   12
> Of my child's love. I think she will be ruled
> In all respects by me; nay, more, I doubt it not.
> Wife, go you to her ere you go to bed.
> Acquaint her here of my son Paris' love,
> And bid her, mark you me, on Wednesday next—   17
> But soft, what day is this?

PARIS   Monday, my lord.   18

CAPULET
> Monday! Ha, ha! Well, Wednesday is too soon;
> O' Thursday let it be. O'Thursday, tell her,
> She shall be married to this noble earl.
> Will you be ready? Do you like this haste?
> We'll keep no great ado—a friend or two;
> For hark you, Tybalt being slain so late,   24
> It may be thought we held him carelessly,   25
> Being our kinsman, if we revel much.
> Therefore we'll have some half a dozen friends,
> And there an end. But what say you to Thursday?

PARIS
> My lord, I would that Thursday were tomorrow.

CAPULET
> Well, get you gone. O' Thursday be it, then.
> [*To his Wife*] Go you to Juliet ere you go to bed;
> Prepare her, wife, against this wedding day.—   32
> Farewell, my lord.—Light to my chamber, ho!—
> Afore me, it is so very late   34
> That we may call it early by and by.
> Good night.   *Exeunt.*

❧

[3.5]

Enter Romeo and Juliet aloft [at the window].

JULIET
> Wilt thou be gone? It is not yet near day.
> It was the nightingale, and not the lark,
> That pierced the fearful hollow of thine ear;   3
> Nightly she sings on yond pomegranate tree.
> Believe me, love, it was the nightingale.

ROMEO
> It was the lark, the herald of the morn,
> No nightingale. Look, love, what envious streaks
> Do lace the severing clouds in yonder east.   8
> Night's candles are burnt out, and jocund day   9
> Stands tiptoe on the misty mountain tops.
> I must be gone and live, or stay and die.

JULIET
> Yond light is not daylight, I know it, I.
> It is some meteor that the sun exhaled   13
> To be to thee this night a torchbearer
> And light thee on thy way to Mantua.
> Therefore stay yet. Thou need'st not to be gone.

ROMEO
> Let me be ta'en; let me be put to death.
> I am content, so thou wilt have it so.   18
> I'll say yon gray is not the morning's eye;
> 'Tis but the pale reflex of Cynthia's brow.   20
> Nor that is not the lark whose notes do beat
> The vaulty heaven so high above our heads.
> I have more care to stay than will to go.   23
> Come, death, and welcome! Juliet wills it so.
> How is't, my soul? Let's talk. It is not day.

JULIET
> It is, it is. Hie hence, begone, away!   26
> It is the lark that sings so out of tune,
> Straining harsh discords and unpleasing sharps.   28
> Some say the lark makes sweet division;   29
> This doth not so, for she divideth us.
> Some say the lark and loathèd toad changed eyes;   31
> Oh, now I would they had changed voices too,
> Since arm from arm that voice doth us affray,   33
> Hunting thee hence with hunt's-up to the day.   34
> Oh, now begone! More light and light it grows.

ROMEO
> More light and light, more dark and dark our woes!

Enter Nurse [hastily].

NURSE   Madam!
JULIET   Nurse?
NURSE
> Your lady mother is coming to your chamber.
> The day is broke; be wary, look about.   [*Exit.*]

JULIET
> Then window, let day in, and let life out.

ROMEO
> Farewell, farewell! One kiss, and I'll descend.
>   [*They kiss. He climbs down from the window.*]

JULIET
> Art thou gone so? Love, lord, ay, husband, friend!   43
> I must hear from thee every day in the hour,
> For in a minute there are many days.
> Oh, by this count I shall be much in years   46
> Ere I again behold my Romeo!

ROMEO [*from below her window*]   Farewell!

---

11 mewed up cooped up with. (A term from falconry, reminiscent of 2.2.159–68.) **heaviness** sorrow. **12 desperate tender** bold offer **17 mark you me** listen to this **18 soft** wait a minute **24 late** recently **25 held him carelessly** did not regard him highly **32 against** in anticipation of **34 Afore me** i.e., By my life. (A mild oath.)
3.5. Location: Verona. Capulet's orchard with Juliet's chamber window above, and, at lines 68 ff., the interior of Juliet's chamber. **3 fearful** apprehensive, anxious **8 severing** separating **9 jocund** cheerful

13 exhaled i.e., has drawn out of the ground. (Meteors were thought to be vapors of luminous gas drawn up by the sun.) **18 so** as long as, since **20 reflex** reflection. **Cynthia's** the moon's **23 care** desire, concern **26 Hie hence** Hasten away **28 sharps** notes relatively high in pitch and hence discordant. **29 division** variations on a melody, made by dividing each note into notes of briefer duration **31 changed** exchanged. (A popular saying, to account for the observation that the lark has very ordinary eyes and the toad remarkable ones.) **33 arm from arm** from one another's arms. **affray** frighten **34 hunt's-up** a song or tune originally designed to awaken huntsmen; later, used also to serenade a newly married couple **43 friend** lover. **46 much in years** much older

   I will omit no opportunity
   That may convey my greetings, love, to thee.
JULIET
   Oh, think'st thou we shall ever meet again?
ROMEO
   I doubt it not, and all these woes shall serve
   For sweet discourses in our times to come.
JULIET
   Oh, God, I have an ill-divining soul!   54
   Methinks I see thee, now thou art so low,
   As one dead in the bottom of a tomb.
   Either my eyesight fails or thou lookest pale.
ROMEO
   And trust me, love, in my eye so do you.
   Dry sorrow drinks our blood. Adieu, adieu!   *Exit.* 59
JULIET
   O Fortune, Fortune! All men call thee fickle.
   If thou art fickle, what dost thou with him
   That is renowned for faith? Be fickle, Fortune.
   For then, I hope, thou wilt not keep him long,
   But send him back.

               Enter Mother [Capulet's Wife].

WIFE   Ho, daughter, are you up?
JULIET
   Who is't that calls? It is my lady mother.
   Is she not down so late, or up so early?   66
   What unaccustomed cause procures her hither?   67
             [She goeth down from the window.]
WIFE
   Why, how now, Juliet?
JULIET   Madam, I am not well.
WIFE
   Evermore weeping for your cousin's death?
   What, wilt thou wash him from his grave with tears?
   An if thou couldst, thou couldst not make him live;
   Therefore, have done. Some grief shows much of love, 72
   But much of grief shows still some want of wit.   73
JULIET
   Yet let me weep for such a feeling loss.   74
WIFE
   So shall you feel the loss, but not the friend
   Which you weep for.
JULIET   Feeling so the loss,
   I cannot choose but ever weep the friend.   77
WIFE
   Well, girl, thou weep'st not so much for his death
   As that the villain lives which slaughtered him.

JULIET
   What villain, madam?
WIFE   That same villain, Romeo.
JULIET *[aside]*
   Villain and he be many miles asunder.—
   God pardon him! I do, with all my heart;
   And yet no man like he doth grieve my heart.   83
WIFE
   That is because the traitor murderer lives.
JULIET
   Ay, madam, from the reach of these my hands.
   Would none but I might venge my cousin's death!
WIFE
   We will have vengeance for it, fear thou not.
   Then weep no more. I'll send to one in Mantua,
   Where that same banished runagate doth live,   89
   Shall give him such an unaccustomed dram   90
   That he shall soon keep Tybalt company.
   And then, I hope, thou wilt be satisfied.
JULIET
   Indeed, I never shall be satisfied
   With Romeo till I behold him—dead—
   Is my poor heart so for a kinsman vexed.
   Madam, if you could find out but a man
   To bear a poison, I would temper it,   97
   That Romeo should, upon receipt thereof,
   Soon sleep in quiet. Oh, how my heart abhors
   To hear him named, and cannot come to him
   To wreak the love I bore my cousin   101
   Upon his body that hath slaughtered him!   102
WIFE
   Find thou the means, and I'll find such a man.
   But now I'll tell thee joyful tidings, girl.
JULIET
   And joy comes well in such a needy time.
   What are they, beseech Your Ladyship?
WIFE
   Well, well, thou hast a careful father, child,   107
   One who, to put thee from thy heaviness,   108
   Hath sorted out a sudden day of joy   109
   That thou expects not, nor I looked not for.
JULIET
   Madam, in happy time, what day is that?
WIFE
   Marry, my child, early next Thursday morn,   112
   The gallant, young, and noble gentleman,
   The County Paris, at Saint Peter's Church
   Shall happily make thee there a joyful bride.
JULIET
   Now, by Saint Peter's Church, and Peter too,
   He shall not make me there a joyful bride!

---

54 ill-divining prophesying of evil   **59 Dry sorrow** (The heat of the body in sorrow and despair was thought to descend into the bowels and dry up the blood.)   **66 down** in bed   **67 procures** induces to come.   **67.1** (As indicated by the bracketed stage direction, which is from the First Quarto, Juliet, who has appeared until now at her "window" above the stage, evidently descends quickly to the main stage and joins her mother for the remainder of the scene. The stage, which before was to have been imagined as Capulet's orchard, is now Juliet's chamber. Juliet's mother has entered onto the main stage four lines earlier.)   **72 have done** cease.   **73 want of wit** lack of intelligence.   **74 feeling** deeply felt   **77 the friend** (Juliet secretly means "my lover," as at line 43, but, of course, her mother hears it as "Tybalt.")

83 no man like he no man so much as he.   **grieve** (1) anger (2) grieve with longing. (Juliet speaks to her mother throughout in intentional ambiguities, at lines 85, 86, 99, 100–2, etc.)   **89 runagate** renegade, fugitive   **90 Shall** who will.   **dram** dose. (Literally, one-eighth of a fluid ounce.)   **97 temper** (1) mix, concoct (2) alloy, dilute. (In her intended double meanings about Romeo dead, poisoned, and sleeping in quiet, Juliet is, of course, unaware of an ironic anticipation of how these things will be fulfilled.)   **101 wreak** (1) avenge (2) bestow   **102 his body that** the body of him who   **107 careful** full of care (for you)   **108 heaviness** sorrow   **109 sorted** chosen   **112 Marry** i.e., By the Virgin Mary

I wonder at this haste, that I must wed
Ere he that should be husband comes to woo.
I pray you, tell my lord and father, madam,
I will not marry yet, and when I do I swear
It shall be Romeo, whom you know I hate,
Rather than Paris. These are news indeed!

WIFE
Here comes your father. Tell him so yourself,
And see how he will take it at your hands.

Enter Capulet and Nurse.

CAPULET
When the sun sets, the earth doth drizzle dew,
But for the sunset of my brother's son
It rains downright.—
How now, a conduit, girl? What, still in tears?   129
Evermore show'ring? In one little body
Thou counterfeits a bark, a sea, a wind;   131
For still thy eyes, which I may call the sea,
Do ebb and flow with tears; the bark thy body is,
Sailing in this salt flood; the winds, thy sighs,
Who, raging with thy tears, and they with them,
Without a sudden calm, will overset   136
Thy tempest-tossèd body.—How now, wife?
Have you delivered to her our decree?

WIFE
Ay, sir, but she will none, she gives you thanks.   139
I would the fool were married to her grave!

CAPULET
Soft, take me with you, take me with you, wife.   141
How? Will she none? Doth she not give us thanks?
Is she not proud? Doth she not count her blest,   143
Unworthy as she is, that we have wrought   144
So worthy a gentleman to be her bride?   145

JULIET
Not proud you have, but thankful that you have.
Proud can I never be of what I hate,
But thankful even for hate that is meant love.   148

CAPULET
How, how, how, how, chopped logic? What is this?
"Proud," and "I thank you," and "I thank you not,"
And yet "not proud"? Mistress minion, you,   151
Thank me no thankings, nor proud me no prouds,
But fettle your fine joints 'gainst Thursday next   153
To go with Paris to Saint Peter's Church,
Or I will drag thee on a hurdle thither.   155
Out, you greensickness carrion! Out, you baggage!   156
You tallow-face!

WIFE [*to Capulet*] Fie, fie! What, are you mad?   157

JULIET [*kneeling*]
Good father, I beseech you on my knees,
Hear me with patience but to speak a word.

CAPULET
Hang thee, young baggage, disobedient wretch!
I tell thee what: get thee to church o' Thursday
Or never after look me in the face.
Speak not, reply not, do not answer me!
My fingers itch. Wife, we scarce thought us blest
That God had lent us but this only child;
But now I see this one is one too much,
And that we have a curse in having her.
Out on her, hilding!

NURSE   God in heaven bless her!   168
You are to blame, my lord, to rate her so.   169

CAPULET
And why, my Lady Wisdom? Hold your tongue,
Good Prudence. Smatter with your gossips, go.   171

NURSE
I speak no treason.

CAPULET   Oh, God-i'-good-e'en!   172

NURSE
May not one speak?

CAPULET   Peace, you mumbling fool!
Utter your gravity o'er a gossip's bowl,   174
For here we need it not.

WIFE   You are too hot.

CAPULET   God's bread, it makes me mad!   176
Day, night, hour, tide, time, work, play,   177
Alone, in company, still my care hath been
To have her matched. And having now provided
A gentleman of noble parentage,
Of fair demesnes, youthful, and nobly liened,   181
Stuffed, as they say, with honorable parts,   182
Proportioned as one's thought would wish a man—
And then to have a wretched puling fool,   184
A whining mammet, in her fortune's tender,   185
To answer, "I'll not wed, I cannot love,
I am too young; I pray you, pardon me."
But, an you will not wed, I'll pardon you.   188
Graze where you will, you shall not house with me.
Look to't, think on't. I do not use to jest.   190
Thursday is near. Lay hand on heart; advise.   191
An you be mine, I'll give you to my friend;
An you be not, hang, beg, starve, die in the streets,
For, by my soul, I'll ne'er acknowledge thee,
Nor what is mine shall never do thee good.
Trust to't, bethink you. I'll not be forsworn.   *Exit.* 196

JULIET
Is there no pity sitting in the clouds
That sees into the bottom of my grief?

---

129 conduit water pipe, fountain **131 bark** sailing vessel **136 Without** unless there is **139 will . . . thanks** says "no thank you," she'll have no part of it. **141 take . . . you** let me understand you **143 count her** consider herself **144 wrought** arranged for **145 bride** bridegroom. **148 hate . . . love** that which is hateful but which was meant lovingly. **151 minion** spoiled darling, minx **153 fettle** make ready. **'gainst** in anticipation of **155 a hurdle** a conveyance on which criminals were dragged to execution **156 greensickness** (An anemic ailment of young unmarried women; it suggests Juliet's paleness.) **baggage** hussy. **157 tallow-face** paleface.

168 hilding jade, baggage. **169 rate** berate, scold **171 Smatter** Chatter. **gossips** gossiping women friends **172 God-i'-good-e'en** i.e., For God's sake. (Literally, God give you good evening.) **174 gravity** wisdom. (Said contemptuously.) **176 God's bread** i.e., By God's (Christ's) Sacrament **177 tide** season **181 demesnes** estates. **liened** descended **182 parts** qualities **184 puling** whining **185 mammet** doll. **in . . . tender** when an offer of good fortune is made to her **188 pardon you** i.e., allow you to depart. (Said caustically.) **190 do not use** am not accustomed **191 advise** consider carefully. **196 be forsworn** i.e., go back on my word.

O sweet my mother, cast me not away!
Delay this marriage for a month, a week;
Or if you do not, make the bridal bed
In that dim monument where Tybalt lies.
WIFE
Talk not to me, for I'll not speak a word.
Do as thou wilt, for I have done with thee.   *Exit.*
JULIET [*rising*]
Oh, God!—O Nurse, how shall this be prevented?
My husband is on earth, my faith in heaven.   206
How shall that faith return again to earth,   207
Unless that husband send it me from heaven   208
By leaving earth? Comfort me, counsel me.   209
Alack, alack, that heaven should practice stratagems
Upon so soft a subject as myself!
What say'st thou? Hast thou not a word of joy?
Some comfort, Nurse.
NURSE   Faith, here it is.
Romeo is banished, and all the world to nothing   214
That he dares ne'er come back to challenge you,   215
Or if he do, it needs must be by stealth.
Then, since the case so stands as now it doth,
I think it best you married with the County.
Oh, he's a lovely gentleman!
Romeo's a dishclout to him. An eagle, madam,   220
Hath not so green, so quick, so fair an eye
As Paris hath. Beshrew my very heart,   222
I think you are happy in this second match,
For it excels your first; or if it did not,
Your first is dead—or 'twere as good he were,
As living here and you no use of him.
JULIET   Speak'st thou from thy heart?
NURSE
And from my soul too. Else beshrew them both.
JULIET   Amen!   229
NURSE   What?
JULIET
Well, thou hast comforted me marvelous much.
Go in, and tell my lady I am gone,
Having displeased my father, to Laurence' cell
To make confession and to be absolved.
NURSE
Marry, I will; and this is wisely done.   [*Exit.*]
JULIET
Ancient damnation! Oh, most wicked fiend!   236
Is it more sin to wish me thus forsworn,   237
Or to dispraise my lord with that same tongue
Which she hath praised him with above compare
So many thousand times? Go, counselor,
Thou and my bosom henceforth shall be twain.   241

I'll to the Friar to know his remedy.
If all else fail, myself have power to die.   *Exit.*

❖

[4.1]

Enter Friar [Laurence] and County Paris.

FRIAR LAURENCE
On Thursday, sir? The time is very short.
PARIS
My father Capulet will have it so,
And I am nothing slow to slack his haste.   3
FRIAR LAURENCE
You say you do not know the lady's mind?
Uneven is the course. I like it not.
PARIS
Immoderately she weeps for Tybalt's death,
And therefore have I little talked of love,
For Venus smiles not in a house of tears.   8
Now, sir, her father counts it dangerous
That she do give her sorrow so much sway,
And in his wisdom hastes our marriage
To stop the inundation of her tears,
Which, too much minded by herself alone,   13
May be put from her by society.   14
Now do you know the reason of this haste.
FRIAR LAURENCE [*aside*]
I would I knew not why it should be slowed.—
Look, sir, here comes the lady toward my cell.

Enter Juliet.

PARIS
Happily met, my lady and my wife!
JULIET
That may be, sir, when I may be a wife.
PARIS
That "may be" must be, love, on Thursday next.
JULIET
What must be shall be.
FRIAR LAURENCE   That's a certain text.
PARIS
Come you to make confession to this father?
JULIET
To answer that, I should confess to you.
PARIS
Do not deny to him that you love me.
JULIET
I will confess to you that I love him.
PARIS
So will ye, I am sure, that you love me.
JULIET
If I do so, it will be of more price,   27
Being spoke behind your back, than to your face.

---

206 **my faith in heaven** i.e., I am married to Romeo in the sight of
heaven.   **207–9 How . . . leaving earth?** i.e., How can I remarry while
Romeo is still alive?   **214 all . . . nothing** the odds are overwhelming
215 challenge lay claim to   **220 dishclout** dishrag   **222 Beshrew** (A
mild oath. Also in line 228.)   **229 Amen** (Juliet says "Amen" as
though to answer the Nurse's prayer that her heart and soul be
cursed. The Nurse does not get the point.)   **236 Ancient damnation!**
Damnable old woman!   **237 forsworn** i.e., false to my marriage vows
241 bosom secret thoughts.   **twain** separated.

4.1. Location: Verona. Friar Laurence's cell.
3 nothing . . . haste not at all reluctant to lessen his haste, i.e., willing to
speed matters along.   **8 Venus . . . tears** (1) amorousness is not appropriate in a house of mourning (2) the planet Venus does not exert a
favorable influence when it is in an inauspicious *house* or constellation
of the zodiac.   **13 too . . . alone** too mind-consuming when she is alone
14 society companionship.   **27 more price** greater worth

PARIS

Poor soul, thy face is much abused with tears.

JULIET

The tears have got small victory by that,
For it was bad enough before their spite. 31

PARIS

Thou wrong'st it more than tears with that report. 32

JULIET

That is no slander, sir, which is a truth;
And what I spake, I spake it to my face. 34

PARIS

Thy face is mine, and thou hast slandered it.

JULIET

It may be so, for it is not mine own.— 36
Are you at leisure, holy Father, now,
Or shall I come to you at evening Mass?

FRIAR LAURENCE

My leisure serves me, pensive daughter, now.— 39
My lord, we must entreat the time alone. 40

PARIS

God shield I should disturb devotion! 41
Juliet, on Thursday early will I rouse ye.
Till then, adieu, and keep this holy kiss. *Exit.*

JULIET

Oh, shut the door! And when thou hast done so,
Come weep with me—past hope, past cure, past help!

FRIAR LAURENCE

Ah, Juliet, I already know thy grief;
It strains me past the compass of my wits. 47
I hear thou must, and nothing may prorogue it, 48
On Thursday next be married to this county.

JULIET

Tell me not, Friar, that thou hearest of this,
Unless thou tell me how I may prevent it.
If in thy wisdom thou canst give no help,
Do thou but call my resolution wise
And with this knife I'll help it presently. 54
                              [*She shows a knife.*]
God joined my heart and Romeo's, thou our hands;
And ere this hand, by thee to Romeo sealed,
Shall be the label to another deed, 57
Or my true heart with treacherous revolt
Turn to another, this shall slay them both. 59
Therefore, out of thy long-experienced time, 60
Give me some present counsel, or, behold,
Twixt my extremes and me this bloody knife 62
Shall play the umpire, arbitrating that
Which the commission of thy years and art 64
Could to no issue of true honor bring.
Be not so long to speak; I long to die 66
If what thou speak'st speak not of remedy.

FRIAR LAURENCE

Hold, daughter. I do spy a kind of hope,
Which craves as desperate an execution
As that is desperate which we would prevent.
If, rather than to marry County Paris,
Thou hast the strength of will to slay thyself,
Then is it likely thou wilt undertake
A thing like death to chide away this shame,
That cop'st with Death himself to scape from it; 75
And if thou darest, I'll give thee remedy.

JULIET

Oh, bid me leap, rather than marry Paris,
From off the battlements of any tower,
Or walk in thievish ways, or bid me lurk 79
Where serpents are; chain me with roaring bears,
Or hide me nightly in a charnel house, 81
O'ercovered quite with dead men's rattling bones,
With reeky shanks and yellow chopless skulls; 83
Or bid me go into a new-made grave
And hide me with a dead man in his tomb—
Things that, to hear them told, have made me
    tremble—
And I will do it without fear or doubt,
To live an unstained wife to my sweet love.

FRIAR LAURENCE

Hold, then. Go home, be merry, give consent
To marry Paris. Wednesday is tomorrow.
Tomorrow night look that thou lie alone;
Let not the Nurse lie with thee in thy chamber.
Take thou this vial, being then in bed,
                          [*showing her a vial*]
And this distilling liquor drink thou off, 94
When presently through all thy veins shall run
A cold and drowsy humor; for no pulse 96
Shall keep his native progress, but surcease; 97
No warmth, no breath shall testify thou livest;
The roses in thy lips and cheeks shall fade
To wanny ashes, thy eyes' windows fall 100
Like death when he shuts up the day of life;
Each part, deprived of supple government, 102
Shall, stiff and stark and cold, appear like death.
And in this borrowed likeness of shrunk death
Thou shalt continue two-and-forty hours,
And then awake as from a pleasant sleep.
Now, when the bridegroom in the morning comes
To rouse thee from thy bed, there art thou dead.
Then, as the manner of our country is,
In thy best robes uncovered on the bier
Thou shalt be borne to that same ancient vault
Where all the kindred of the Capulets lie.
In the meantime, against thou shalt awake, 113
Shall Romeo by my letters know our drift, 114

---

31 spite malice.   **32 Thou . . . report** Your apology for your face slanders it more than your tears do.   **34 to my face** (1) openly (2) about my face.   **36 is not mine own** (1) is beyond my control, does not reveal me truly (2) belongs to Romeo.   **39 pensive** sorrowful   **40 entreat . . . alone** ask you to leave us alone.   **41 God shield** God forbid **47 compass** bounds   **48 prorogue** delay   **54 presently** at once. **57 label** strip attached to a deed to carry the seal; hence, confirmation, seal   **59 both** i.e., hand and heart.   **60 time** age   **62 extremes** extreme difficulties   **64 commission** authority.   **art** skill   **66 so long** so slow. (With wordplay on *long*, "yearn," later in this same line.)

75 That . . . himself either (1) you who are willing to encounter Death by killing yourself, or (2) that simulates Death itself.   **it** this shame **79 thievish ways** roads frequented by thieves   **81 charnel house** vault for human bones   **83 reeky** reeking, malodorous.   **chopless** without the lower jaw   **94 distilling** infusing the body, or distilled **96 humor** fluid   **97 his native** its natural.   **surcease** cease **100 wanny** wan, pale   **102 supple government** control of motion **113 against** anticipating when   **114 drift** plan

And hither shall he come; and he and I
Will watch thy waking, and that very night   116
Shall Romeo bear thee hence to Mantua.
And this shall free thee from this present shame,
If no inconstant toy nor womanish fear   119
Abate thy valor in the acting it.

JULIET [*taking the vial*]
Give me, give me! Oh, tell not me of fear!

FRIAR LAURENCE
Hold, get you gone. Be strong and prosperous   122
In this resolve. I'll send a friar with speed
To Mantua, with my letters to thy lord.

JULIET
Love give me strength, and strength shall help afford. 125
Farewell, dear Father!   *Exeunt [separately].*

❖

[4.2]

*Enter Father Capulet, Mother [Capulet's Wife],
Nurse, and Servingmen, two or three.*

CAPULET
So many guests invite as here are writ.
          [*Exit one or two servingmen.*]
Sirrah, go hire me twenty cunning cooks.   2

SERVINGMAN   You shall have none ill, sir, for I'll try if   3
they can lick their fingers.

CAPULET   How canst thou try them so?

SERVINGMAN   Marry, sir, 'tis an ill cook that cannot lick
his own fingers; therefore he that cannot lick his
fingers goes not with me.

CAPULET   Go, begone.   [*Exit Servingman.*]
We shall be much unfurnished for this time.   10
What, is my daughter gone to Friar Laurence?

NURSE   Ay, forsooth.

CAPULET
Well, he may chance to do some good on her.
A peevish self-willed harlotry it is.   14

Enter Juliet.

NURSE
See where she comes from shrift with merry look.

CAPULET
How now, my headstrong, where have you been
          gadding?

JULIET
Where I have learned me to repent the sin
Of disobedient opposition
To you and your behests, and am enjoined   19
By holy Laurence to fall prostrate here,   [*kneeling*]
To beg your pardon. Pardon, I beseech you!
Henceforward I am ever ruled by you.

CAPULET
Send for the County! Go tell him of this.
I'll have this knot knit up tomorrow morning.

JULIET
I met the youthful lord at Laurence' cell
And gave him what becomèd love I might,   26
Not stepping o'er the bounds of modesty.

CAPULET
Why, I am glad on't. This is well. Stand up.
          [*Juliet rises.*]
This is as 't should be. Let me see the County;
Ay, marry, go, I say, and fetch him hither.
Now, afore God, this reverend holy friar,
All our whole city is much bound to him.   32

JULIET
Nurse, will you go with me into my closet   33
To help me sort such needful ornaments   34
As you think fit to furnish me tomorrow?

WIFE
No, not till Thursday. There is time enough.

CAPULET
Go, Nurse, go with her. We'll to church tomorrow.
          Exeunt [Juliet and Nurse].

WIFE
We shall be short in our provision.
'Tis now near night.

CAPULET   Tush, I will stir about,
And all things shall be well, I warrant thee, wife.
Go thou to Juliet, help to deck up her.
I'll not to bed tonight. Let me alone.   42
I'll play the huswife for this once.—What, ho!—   43
They are all forth. Well, I will walk myself
To County Paris, to prepare up him
Against tomorrow. My heart is wondrous light,
Since this same wayward girl is so reclaimed.
          Exeunt.

❖

[4.3]

Enter Juliet and Nurse.

JULIET
Ay, those attires are best. But, gentle Nurse,
I pray thee, leave me to myself tonight;
For I have need of many orisons   3
To move the heavens to smile upon my state,
Which, well thou knowest, is cross and full of sin. 5

Enter Mother [Capulet's Wife].

WIFE
What, are you busy, ho? Need you my help?

JULIET
No, madam, we have culled such necessaries   7
As are behooveful for our state tomorrow.   8
So please you, let me now be left alone,
And let the Nurse this night sit up with you,

---

116 **watch** keep a watch over, be on hand for   119 **toy** idle fancy
122 **prosperous** successful   125 **help afford** provide help.
4.2. Location: Verona. Capulet's house.
2 **cunning** skilled   3 **none ill** no bad ones.   **try** test   10 **unfurnished** unprovided   14 **A peevish . . . is** i.e., She's a silly good-for-nothing.   19 **behests** commands

26 **becomèd** befitting   32 **bound** indebted   33 **closet** chamber
34 **sort** choose   42 **Let me alone** Leave things to me.   43 **huswife** housewife
4.3. Location: Verona. Capulet's house; Juliet's bed, enclosed by bedcurtains, is set up in the discovery space.
3 **orisons** prayers   5 **cross** perverse   7 **culled** picked out
8 **behooveful** needful.   **state** ceremony

For I am sure you have your hands full all
In this so sudden business.
WIFE   Good night.
Get thee to bed and rest, for thou hast need.
                        Exeunt [*Capulet's Wife and Nurse*].
JULIET
Farewell! God knows when we shall meet again.
I have a faint cold fear thrills through my veins   15
That almost freezes up the heat of life.
I'll call them back again to comfort me.—
Nurse!—What should she do here?
My dismal scene I needs must act alone.
Come, vial.   [*She takes out the vial.*]
What if this mixture do not work at all?
Shall I be married then tomorrow morning?
No, no, this shall forbid it. Lie thou there.
                    [*She lays down a dagger.*]
What if it be a poison, which the Friar
Subtly hath ministered to have me dead,
Lest in this marriage he should be dishonored
Because he married me before to Romeo?
I fear it is; and yet methinks it should not,
For he hath still been tried a holy man.   29
How if, when I am laid into the tomb,
I wake before the time that Romeo
Come to redeem me? There's a fearful point!
Shall I not then be stifled in the vault,
To whose foul mouth no healthsome air breathes in,
And there die strangled ere my Romeo comes?
Or, if I live, is it not very like   36
The horrible conceit of death and night,   37
Together with the terror of the place—
As in a vault, an ancient receptacle,   39
Where for this many hundred years the bones
Of all my buried ancestors are packed;
Where bloody Tybalt, yet but green in earth,   42
Lies fest'ring in his shroud; where, as they say,
At some hours in the night spirits resort—
Alack, alack, is it not like that I,
So early waking, what with loathsome smells,
And shrieks like mandrakes torn out of the earth,   47
That living mortals, hearing them, run mad—   48
Oh, if I wake, shall I not be distraught,
Environèd with all these hideous fears,   50
And madly play with my forefathers' joints,
And pluck the mangled Tybalt from his shroud,
And in this rage, with some great kinsman's bone   53
As with a club dash out my desp'rate brains?
Oh, look! Methinks I see my cousin's ghost
Seeking out Romeo, that did spit his body   56

Upon a rapier's point. Stay, Tybalt, stay!   57
Romeo, Romeo, Romeo! Here's drink—I drink to thee.
            [*She drinks and falls upon her bed,
                    within the curtains.*]

[4.4]

Enter Lady of the House [*Capulet's Wife*]
and Nurse.

WIFE
Hold, take these keys, and fetch more spices, Nurse.
NURSE
They call for dates and quinces in the pastry.   2

Enter old Capulet.

CAPULET
Come, stir, stir, stir! The second cock hath crowed.
The curfew bell hath rung; 'tis three o'clock.
Look to the baked meats, good Angelica.   5
Spare not for cost.
NURSE   Go, you cotquean, go,   6
Get you to bed. Faith, you'll be sick tomorrow
For this night's watching.   8
CAPULET
No, not a whit. What, I have watched ere now
All night for lesser cause, and ne'er been sick.
WIFE
Ay, you have been a mouse-hunt in your time,   11
But I will watch you from such watching now.   12
                    Exeunt Lady and Nurse.
CAPULET   A jealous hood, a jealous hood!   13

Enter three or four [*Servingmen*] *with spits and
logs, and baskets.*

Now, fellow, what is there?
FIRST SERVINGMAN
Things for the cook, sir, but I know not what.
CAPULET   Make haste, make haste. [*Exit First Servingman.*]
[*To Second Servingman*]   Sirrah, fetch drier logs.
Call Peter. He will show thee where they are.
SECOND SERVINGMAN
I have a head, sir, that will find out logs   18
And never trouble Peter for the matter.
CAPULET
Mass, and well said. A merry whoreson, ha!   20

15 **faint** producing faintness.   **thrills** that pierces, shivers   **29 still
been tried** always been tried and proven to be   **36 like** likely. (Also
at line 45.)   **37 conceit** idea   **39 As** namely   **42 green** new, freshly
47 mandrakes (The root of the mandragora or mandrake resembled
the human form; the plant was fabled to utter a shriek when torn
from the ground.)   **48 That** so that   **50 fears** objects of fear   **53 rage**
madness.   **great** i.e., of an earlier generation, as in *great*-grandfather
56 spit impale

57 Stay Stop, wait
4.4. Location: Scene continues. Juliet's bed remains visible.
2 pastry room in which pastry was made.   **5 baked meats** pies, pastry   **6 cotquean** i.e., a man who acts the housewife. (Literally, a cottage housewife.)   **8 watching** being awake.   **11 mouse-hunt** i.e.,
hunter of women. (Literally, a weasel.)   **12 watch . . . watching** i.e.,
keep an eye on you to prevent such nighttime activity. (Playing on
watching in line 8.)   **13 A jealous hood** i.e., You wear the cap of jealousy   **18 I . . . logs** i.e., (1) I have a good head for finding things (2)
My wooden head knows all about logs   **20 Mass** By the Mass.
whoreson i.e., fellow. (An abusive term used familiarly.)

Thou shalt be loggerhead.   [*Exit Servingman.*]
                              Good faith, 'tis day.   21
The County will be here with music straight,   22
For so he said he would.   *Play music* [*within*].
                    I hear him near.
Nurse! Wife! What, ho! What, Nurse, I say!

    Enter Nurse.

Go waken Juliet, go and trim her up.
I'll go and chat with Paris. Hie, make haste,
Make haste. The bridegroom he is come already.
Make haste, I say.   [*Exit Capulet.*]

           ❖

[4.5]

    [*The Nurse goes to the bed.*]

NURSE
Mistress! What, mistress! Juliet!—Fast, I warrant her,
   she.   1
Why, lamb, why, lady! Fie, you slugabed!
Why, love, I say! Madam! Sweetheart! Why, bride!
What, not a word? You take your pennyworths now.   4
Sleep for a week; for the next night, I warrant,
The County Paris hath set up his rest   6
That you shall rest but little. God forgive me,   7
Marry, and amen! How sound is she asleep!   8
I needs must wake her.—Madam, madam, madam!
Ay, let the County take you in your bed;   10
He'll fright you up, i'faith.—Will it not be?
                    [*She opens the bedcurtains.*]
What, dressed, and in your clothes, and down again?
I must needs wake you. Lady, lady, lady!
Alas, alas! Help, help! My lady's dead!
Oh, weraday, that ever I was born!   15
Some aqua vitae, ho! My lord! My lady!   16

    [*Enter Capulet's Wife.*]

WIFE
What noise is here?
NURSE   Oh, lamentable day!
WIFE
What is the matter?
NURSE   Look, look! Oh, heavy day!   18
WIFE
Oh, me, oh, me! My child, my only life!
Revive, look up, or I will die with thee!
Help, help! Call help.

    Enter Father [*Capulet*].

CAPULET
For shame, bring Juliet forth. Her lord is come.

NURSE
She's dead, deceased. She's dead, alack the day!
WIFE
Alack the day, she's dead, she's dead, she's dead!
CAPULET
Ha! Let me see her. Out, alas! She's cold.
Her blood is settled, and her joints are stiff;   26
Life and these lips have long been separated.
Death lies on her like an untimely frost
Upon the sweetest flower of all the field.
NURSE
Oh, lamentable day!
WIFE   Oh, woeful time!
CAPULET
Death, that hath ta'en her hence to make me wail,
Ties up my tongue and will not let me speak.

    Enter Friar [*Laurence*] *and the County* [*Paris,*
    with Musicians].

FRIAR LAURENCE
Come, is the bride ready to go to church?
CAPULET
Ready to go, but never to return.
Oh, son, the night before thy wedding day
Hath Death lain with thy wife. There she lies,
Flower as she was, deflowered by him.
Death is my son-in-law, Death is my heir;
My daughter he hath wedded. I will die,
And leave him all; life, living, all is Death's.   40
PARIS
Have I thought long to see this morning's face,   41
And doth it give me such a sight as this?
WIFE
Accurst, unhappy, wretched, hateful day!
Most miserable hour that e'er time saw
In lasting labor of his pilgrimage!   45
But one, poor one, one poor and loving child,
But one thing to rejoice and solace in,
And cruel Death hath catched it from my sight!
NURSE
O woe! O woeful, woeful, woeful day!
Most lamentable day, most woeful day
That ever, ever I did yet behold!
O day, O day, O day! O hateful day!
Never was seen so black a day as this.
O woeful day, O woeful day!
PARIS
Beguiled, divorcèd, wrongèd, spited, slain!
Most detestable Death, by thee beguiled,
By cruel, cruel thee quite overthrown!
O love! O life! Not life, but love in death!
CAPULET
Despised, distressèd, hated, martyred, killed!
Uncomfortable time, why cam'st thou now   60

---

21 **loggerhead** (1) put in charge of getting logs (2) a blockhead.
22 **straight** straightway, immediately
4.5. Location: Scene continues. Juliet's bed remains visible.
1 **Fast** Fast asleep   4 **pennyworths** small portions (of sleep)   6 **set . . .**
rest staked his all, resolved to play all out. (From the card game of
primero, here with obviously bawdy meaning.)   7–8 **God . . . amen!**
(The Nurse apologizes amiably for her bawdy talk.)   10 **take . . . bed**
(1) find you still abed (2) possess you sexually   15 **weraday** wellaway,
alas   16 **aqua vitae** strong alcoholic spirits   18 **heavy** sorrowful

26 **settled** congealed   40 **living** means of living, property
41–64 **Have . . . burièd** (A stage direction in the First Quarto, "*All at
once cry out and wring their hands*," may suggest that the four mourners are to speak simultaneously, a possibility since all have six lines of
text.)   45 **lasting** unceasing   60 **Uncomfortable** Comfortless

To murder, murder our solemnity? 61
O child! O child! My soul, and not my child!
Dead art thou! Alack, my child is dead,
And with my child my joys are burièd. 64

FRIAR LAURENCE
Peace, ho, for shame! Confusion's cure lives not 65
In these confusions. Heaven and yourself
Had part in this fair maid; now heaven hath all,
And all the better is it for the maid.
Your part in her you could not keep from death, 69
But heaven keeps his part in eternal life.
The most you sought was her promotion, 71
For 'twas your heaven she should be advanced; 72
And weep ye now, seeing she is advanced
Above the clouds, as high as heaven itself?
Oh, in this love you love your child so ill
That you run mad, seeing that she is well.
She's not well married that lives married long,
But she's best married that dies married young.
Dry up your tears, and stick your rosemary 79
On this fair corpse, and, as the custom is,
And in her best array, bear her to church;
For though fond nature bids us all lament, 82
Yet nature's tears are reason's merriment. 83

CAPULET
All things that we ordainèd festival 84
Turn from their office to black funeral: 85
Our instruments to melancholy bells,
Our wedding cheer to a sad burial feast,
Our solemn hymns to sullen dirges change, 88
Our bridal flowers serve for a buried corpse,
And all things change them to the contrary. 90

FRIAR LAURENCE
Sir, go you in, and, madam, go with him,
And go, Sir Paris. Everyone prepare
To follow this fair corpse unto her grave.
The heavens do lour upon you for some ill; 94
Move them no more by crossing their high will. 95
Exeunt. Manet [Nurse with Musicians].

FIRST MUSICIAN
Faith, we may put up our pipes and be gone.

NURSE
Honest good fellows, ah, put up, put up!
For well you know this is a pitiful case.   [*Exit.*]

FIRST MUSICIAN
Ay, by my troth, the case may be amended. 99

Enter Peter.

PETER   Musicians, oh, musicians, "Heart's ease," 100
"Heart's ease." Oh, an you will have me live, play
"Heart's ease."
FIRST MUSICIAN   Why "Heart's ease"?
PETER   Oh, musicians, because my heart itself plays "My
heart is full." Oh, play me some merry dump to 105
comfort me.
FIRST MUSICIAN   Not a dump we! 'Tis no time to play
now.
PETER   You will not, then?
FIRST MUSICIAN   No.
PETER   I will then give it you soundly.
FIRST MUSICIAN   What will you give us?
PETER   No money, on my faith, but the gleek; I will give 113
you the minstrel. 114
FIRST MUSICIAN   Then will I give you the serving- 115
creature. 116
PETER   Then will I lay the serving-creature's dagger on 117
your pate. I will carry no crotchets. I'll re you, I'll fa 118
you. Do you note me? 119
FIRST MUSICIAN   An you re us and fa us, you note us.
SECOND MUSICIAN   Pray you, put up your dagger and 121
put out your wit. 122
PETER   Then have at you with my wit! I will dry-beat 123
you with an iron wit, and put up my iron dagger.
Answer me like men:
"When griping griefs the heart doth wound, 126
And doleful dumps the mind oppress,
Then music with her silver sound—" 128
Why "silver sound"? Why "music with her silver
sound"? What say you, Simon Catling? 130
FIRST MUSICIAN   Marry, sir, because silver hath a sweet
sound.
PETER   Pretty! What say you, Hugh Rebeck? 133
SECOND MUSICIAN   I say "silver sound" because musi-
cians sound for silver. 135
PETER   Pretty too! What say you, James Soundpost? 136
THIRD MUSICIAN   Faith, I know not what to say.

---

61 **solemnity** ceremony, festivity.   65 **Confusion's** Calamity's   69 **Your part** i.e., The mortal part you begot   71 **promotion** social advancement   72 **your heaven** i.e., your idea of the greatest good   79 **rosemary** symbol of immortality and enduring love; therefore used at both funerals and weddings   82 **fond nature** foolish human nature   83 **nature's . . . merriment** that which causes human nature to weep is an occasion of joy to reason.   84 **ordainèd festival** intended to be festive   85 **office** function   88 **sullen** mournful   90 **them** themselves   94 **lour . . . ill** frown upon you because of some sinfulness   95 **Move** anger.   95.1 *Manet* She remains onstage   99 **the case . . . amended** things generally could be much better. (With a punning suggestion of an instrument case that is in need of repair.)   99.1 *Peter* (The Second Quarto has *Enter Will Kemp*, the actor for whom Shakespeare or perhaps the bookkeeper intended this role.)

100 **"Heart's ease"** (A popular ballad; so too with "My heart is full" in lines 104–5.)   105 **dump** mournful tune or dance   113 **gleek** scornful rebuke   113–14 **I will . . . minstrel** I will insult you by calling you what you are, a minstrel. (Minstrels were widely regarded as vagabonds.)   115–16 **Then . . . serving-creature** Then I'll insult you right back by calling you what you are, a servant.   117–18 **Then . . . crotchets** Then I'll knock you about the head with my dagger. I'll not put up with your whims. (*Crotchets* are also quarter notes, appropriate to the musicians' trade.)   118–19 **I'll re . . . me?** i.e., I'll give you a thrashing, do you hear? (Again using musical terms: *re* and *fa* are the names of notes, and *note* can mean "set to music.")   121–2 **put up . . . wit** sheathe your dagger and stop being a smart aleck. (But *put up* and *put out* can also mean "display." Peter chooses to answer to this meaning.)   123 **have at you** i.e., here I come.   **dry-beat** thrash (without drawing blood)   126–8 **"When . . . sound"** (From Richard Edwards's song, "In Commendation of Music," published in *The Paradise of Dainty Devices*, 1576.)   130 **Catling** (A catling was a small lute-string made of catgut.)   133 **Rebeck** (A rebeck was a fiddle with three strings.)   135 **sound** make music   136 **Soundpost** (A soundpost is the pillar or peg that supports the sounding board of a stringed instrument.)

PETER   Oh, I cry you mercy, you are the singer. I will say   138
for you. It is "music with her silver sound" because
musicians have no gold for sounding: 140
　　　"Then music with her silver sound
　　　　With speedy help doth lend redress."   *Exit.*
FIRST MUSICIAN   What a pestilent knave is this same!
SECOND MUSICIAN   Hang him, Jack! Come, we'll in here,
tarry for the mourners, and stay dinner.   *Exeunt.* 145

❖

[5.1]

Enter Romeo.

ROMEO
If I may trust the flattering truth of sleep,   1
My dreams presage some joyful news at hand.
My bosom's lord sits lightly in his throne,   3
And all this day an unaccustomed spirit
Lifts me above the ground with cheerful thoughts.
I dreamt my lady came and found me dead—
Strange dream, that gives a dead man leave to
　　think!—
And breathed such life with kisses in my lips
That I revived and was an emperor.
Ah me, how sweet is love itself possessed   10
When but love's shadows are so rich in joy!   11

Enter Romeo's man [Balthasar, booted].

News from Verona! How now, Balthasar,
Dost thou not bring me letters from the Friar?
How doth my lady? Is my father well?
How fares my Juliet? That I ask again,
For nothing can be ill if she be well.
BALTHASAR
Then she is well, and nothing can be ill.
Her body sleeps in Capels' monument,
And her immortal part with angels lives.
I saw her laid low in her kindred's vault,
And presently took post to tell it you.   21
Oh, pardon me for bringing these ill news,
Since you did leave it for my office, sir.   23
ROMEO
Is it e'en so? Then I defy you, stars!—
Thou knowest my lodging. Get me ink and paper,
And hire post-horses. I will hence tonight.
BALTHASAR
I do beseech you, sir, have patience.
Your looks are pale and wild, and do import   28
Some misadventure.
ROMEO　　　　　　　　Tush, thou art deceived.
Leave me, and do the thing I bid thee do.
Hast thou no letters to me from the Friar?

BALTHASAR
No, my good lord.
ROMEO　　　　　　　　No matter. Get thee gone,
And hire those horses. I'll be with thee straight.
　　　　　　　　　　　　　Exit [Balthasar].
Well, Juliet, I will lie with thee tonight.
Let's see for means. O mischief, thou art swift   35
To enter in the thoughts of desperate men!
I do remember an apothecary—   37
And hereabouts 'a dwells—which late I noted   38
In tattered weeds, with overwhelming brows,   39
Culling of simples. Meager were his looks;   40
Sharp misery had worn him to the bones;
And in his needy shop a tortoise hung,
An alligator stuffed, and other skins
Of ill-shaped fishes; and about his shelves
A beggarly account of empty boxes,   45
Green earthen pots, bladders, and musty seeds,
Remnants of packthread, and old cakes of roses   47
Were thinly scattered to make up a show.
Noting this penury, to myself I said,
"An if a man did need a poison now,   50
Whose sale is present death in Mantua,   51
Here lives a caitiff wretch would sell it him."   52
Oh, this same thought did but forerun my need,
And this same needy man must sell it me.
As I remember, this should be the house.
Being holiday, the beggar's shop is shut.—
What, ho! Apothecary!

[Enter Apothecary.]

APOTHECARY　　　　　　　Who calls so loud?
ROMEO
Come hither, man. I see that thou art poor.
Hold, there is forty ducats. [*He shows gold.*] Let me
　　have   59
A dram of poison, such soon-speeding gear   60
As will disperse itself through all the veins
That the life-weary taker may fall dead,
And that the trunk may be discharged of breath   63
As violently as hasty powder fired
Doth hurry from the fatal cannon's womb.
APOTHECARY
Such mortal drugs I have, but Mantua's law   66
Is death to any he that utters them.   67
ROMEO
Art thou so bare and full of wretchedness,
And fearest to die? Famine is in thy cheeks,

---

138 cry you mercy beg your pardon   **140 have . . . sounding** i.e., (1)
are paid only silver for playing (2) have no gold to jingle in their
pockets   **145 stay** await
5.1. Location: Mantua. A street.
1 flattering i.e., telling me what I want to believe   **3 bosom's lord**
i.e., heart   **10 itself possessed** actually enjoyed   **11 love's shadows**
dreams of love   **11.1 booted** wearing riding boots—a conventional
stage sign of traveling   **21 presently took post** at once started off
with post-horses   **23 for my office** as my duty   **28 import** denote

35 for means by what means.   **37 apothecary** druggist   **38 which . . .
noted** whom lately I noticed   **39 weeds** garments.   **overwhelming
brows** forehead and eyebrows jutting out over his eyes   **40 simples**
medicinal herbs.   **Meager** Impoverished   **45 beggarly account** poor
array   **47 cakes of roses** petals pressed into cakes to be used as perfume   **50 An if** If   **51 present** immediate   **52 caitiff** miserable.
would who would   **59 ducats** gold coins.   **60 soon-speeding gear**
quickly effective stuff   **63 trunk** body   **66 mortal** deadly   **67 any he**
anyone.   **utters** issues, sells

Need and oppression starveth in thy eyes,   70
Contempt and beggary hangs upon thy back.
The world is not thy friend, nor the world's law;
The world affords no law to make thee rich.
Then be not poor, but break it, and take this.

APOTHECARY
My poverty but not my will consents.

ROMEO
I pay thy poverty and not thy will.

APOTHECARY [*giving poison*]
Put this in any liquid thing you will
And drink it off, and if you had the strength
Of twenty men it would dispatch you straight.

ROMEO [*giving gold*]
There is thy gold—worse poison to men's souls,
Doing more murder in this loathsome world
Than these poor compounds that thou mayst not sell.
I sell thee poison; thou hast sold me none.
Farewell. Buy food, and get thyself in flesh.
                                        [*Exit Apothecary.*]
Come, cordial and not poison, go with me   85
To Juliet's grave, for there must I use thee.   *Exit.*

❧

[5.2]

Enter Friar John to Friar Laurence.

FRIAR JOHN
Holy Franciscan friar! Brother, ho!

Enter [Friar] Laurence.

FRIAR LAURENCE
This same should be the voice of Friar John.
Welcome from Mantua! What says Romeo?
Or if his mind be writ, give me his letter.

FRIAR JOHN
Going to find a barefoot brother out—
One of our order—to associate me   6
Here in this city visiting the sick,
And finding him, the searchers of the town,   8
Suspecting that we both were in a house
Where the infectious pestilence did reign,
Sealed up the doors and would not let us forth,
So that my speed to Mantua there was stayed.   12

FRIAR LAURENCE
Who bare my letter, then, to Romeo?

FRIAR JOHN
I could not send it—here it is again—
Nor get a messenger to bring it thee,
So fearful were they of infection.   [*He gives a letter.*]

FRIAR LAURENCE
Unhappy fortune! By my brotherhood,
The letter was not nice but full of charge,   18
Of dear import, and the neglecting it   19
May do much danger. Friar John, go hence.
Get me an iron crow and bring it straight   21
Unto my cell.

FRIAR JOHN   Brother, I'll go and bring it thee.   *Exit.*

FRIAR LAURENCE
Now must I to the monument alone.
Within this three hours will fair Juliet wake.
She will beshrew me much that Romeo   26
Hath had no notice of these accidents;   27
But I will write again to Mantua,
And keep her at my cell till Romeo come—
Poor living corpse, closed in a dead man's tomb!
                                            Exit.

❧

[5.3]

*Enter Paris, and his Page [bearing flowers, per-
fumed water, and a torch. Juliet, lying in seeming death atop her bier and perhaps concealed at
first from the audience's view, is understood to
be in the Capulets' burial vault, with Tybalt's
body also there.]*

PARIS
Give me thy torch, boy. Hence, and stand aloof.   1
Yet put it out, for I would not be seen.
Under yond yew trees lay thee all along,   3
Holding thy ear close to the hollow ground.
So shall no foot upon the churchyard tread,
Being loose, unfirm, with digging up of graves,   6
But thou shalt hear it. Whistle then to me
As signal that thou hearest something approach.
Give me those flowers. Do as I bid thee. Go.

PAGE [*aside*]
I am almost afraid to stand alone   10
Here in the churchyard, yet I will adventure.
                                        [*He retires.*]

PARIS [*strewing flowers and perfumed water*]
Sweet flower, with flowers thy bridal bed I strew—   12
    Oh, woe! Thy canopy is dust and stones—   13
Which with sweet water nightly I will dew,   14
    Or wanting that, with tears distilled by moans.   15
The obsequies that I for thee will keep   16
Nightly shall be to strew thy grave and weep.
                                    Whistle Boy.
The boy gives warning something doth approach.
What cursèd foot wanders this way tonight

---

18 nice trivial.   **charge** importance   **19 dear** precious, urgent   **21 crow**
crowbar   **26 beshrew** i.e., reprove   **27 accidents** events
**5.3. Location: Verona. A churchyard and the vault or tomb belong-
ing to the Capulets. Juliet's bier may be thrust onstage from the
"discovery" space or may be concealed until the tomb is "opened"
by Romeo at 83.1, perhaps by the drawing back of curtains.
1 aloof** to one side, at a distance.   **3 all along** at full length   **6 Being**
i.e., the soil being   **10 stand** stay   **12 Sweet flower** i.e., Juliet
13 canopy covering   **14 sweet** perfumed.   **dew** moisten   **15 wanting** lacking   **16 obsequies** ceremonies in memory of the dead

---

70 starveth are revealed by the starving look   **85 cordial** restorative
for the heart
5.2. Location: Verona. Friar Laurence's cell.
6 associate accompany   **8 searchers of the town** town officials charged
with public health (and especially concerned about the *pestilence* or
plague)   **12 speed** successful journey, progress.   **stayed** stopped.

To cross my obsequies and true love's rite?   20
What, with a torch? Muffle me, night, awhile.   21
                                        [*He retires.*]

Enter Romeo and Balthasar, [*with a torch, a
mattock, and a crowbar*].

ROMEO
Give me that mattock and the wrenching iron.   22
                                        [*He takes the tools.*]
Hold, take this letter. Early in the morning
See thou deliver it to my lord and father.
                                        [*He gives a letter and takes a torch.*]
Give me the light. Upon thy life I charge thee,
Whate'er thou hearest or see'st, stand all aloof
And do not interrupt me in my course.   27
Why I descend into this bed of death
Is partly to behold my lady's face,
But chiefly to take thence from her dead finger
A precious ring—a ring that I must use
In dear employment. Therefore hence, begone.   32
But if thou, jealous, dost return to pry   33
In what I farther shall intend to do,
By heaven, I will tear thee joint by joint
And strew this hungry churchyard with thy limbs.   36
The time and my intents are savage-wild,
More fierce and more inexorable far
Than empty tigers or the roaring sea.   39
BALTHASAR
I will be gone, sir, and not trouble ye.
ROMEO
So shalt thou show me friendship. Take thou that.
                                        [*He gives him money.*]
Live, and be prosperous; and farewell, good fellow.
BALTHASAR [*aside*]
For all this same, I'll hide me hereabout.   43
His looks I fear, and his intents I doubt.   [*He retires.*]   44
ROMEO
Thou detestable maw, thou womb of death,   45
Gorged with the dearest morsel of the earth,
Thus I enforce thy rotten jaws to open,
And in despite I'll cram thee with more food.   48
                                        [*He begins to open the tomb.*]
PARIS
This is that banished haughty Montague
That murdered my love's cousin, with which grief
It is supposèd the fair creature died,
And here is come to do some villainous shame
To the dead bodies. I will apprehend him.
                                        [*He comes forward.*]
Stop thy unhallowed toil, vile Montague!
Can vengeance be pursued further than death?

Condemnèd villain, I do apprehend thee.
Obey and go with me, for thou must die.
ROMEO
I must indeed, and therefore came I hither.
Good gentle youth, tempt not a desperate man.
Fly hence and leave me. Think upon these gone;   60
Let them affright thee. I beseech thee, youth,
Put not another sin upon my head
By urging me to fury. Oh, begone!
By heaven, I love thee better than myself,
For I come hither armed against myself.
Stay not, begone. Live, and hereafter say
A madman's mercy bid thee run away.
PARIS
I do defy thy conjuration,   68
And apprehend thee for a felon here.
ROMEO
Wilt thou provoke me? Then have at thee, boy!
                                        [*They fight.*]
PAGE
Oh, Lord, they fight! I will go call the watch.   [*Exit.*]
PARIS
Oh, I am slain! [*He falls.*] If thou be merciful,
Open the tomb, lay me with Juliet.   [*He dies.*]
ROMEO
In faith, I will. Let me peruse this face.
Mercutio's kinsman, noble County Paris!
What said my man when my betossèd soul
Did not attend him as we rode? I think
He told me Paris should have married Juliet.   78
Said he not so? Or did I dream it so?
Or am I mad, hearing him talk of Juliet,
To think it was so? Oh, give me thy hand,
One writ with me in sour misfortune's book.
I'll bury thee in a triumphant grave.
                                        [*He opens the tomb.*]
A grave? Oh, no! A lantern, slaughtered youth,   84
For here lies Juliet, and her beauty makes
This vault a feasting presence full of light.   86
Death, lie thou there, by a dead man interred.
                                        [*He lays Paris in the tomb.*]
How oft when men are at the point of death
Have they been merry, which their keepers call   89
A lightening before death! Oh, how may I   90
Call this a lightening? O my love, my wife!
Death, that hath sucked the honey of thy breath,
Hath had no power yet upon thy beauty.
Thou art not conquered; beauty's ensign yet   94
Is crimson in thy lips and in thy cheeks,
And death's pale flag is not advancèd there.   96
Tybalt, liest thou there in thy bloody sheet?   97
Oh, what more favor can I do to thee
Than with that hand that cut thy youth in twain
To sunder his that was thine enemy?   100

---

20 cross interrupt   **21 Muffle** Conceal.   **22 wrenching iron** crowbar.
27 course intended action.   **32 dear employment** important business.
33 jealous suspicious   **36 hungry** hungry for corpses   **39 empty**
hungry   **43 For all this same** All the same   **44 fear** distrust.   **doubt**
suspect.   **45 womb** belly   **48 in despite** defiantly   **48.1 He . . . tomb**
Whether the tomb is represented by a bier thrust onstage or by a curtained recess (see indication of scene location above at the start of
5.3), Romeo may mime the action here and at line 83.1 of using tools
to open it.

60 gone dead   **68 conjuration** solemn entreaty   **78 should have** was
to have   **84 lantern** turret room full of windows   **86 feasting presence** reception chamber for feasting   **89 keepers** attendants, jailers
90 lightening exhilaration (supposed to occur just before death)
94 ensign banner   **96 advancèd** raised   **97 sheet** shroud.   **100 his**
i.e., my (Romeo's) own

Forgive me, cousin!—Ah, dear Juliet,
Why art thou yet so fair? Shall I believe
That unsubstantial Death is amorous,   103
And that the lean abhorrèd monster keeps
Thee here in dark to be his paramour?
For fear of that I still will stay with thee   106
And never from this palace of dim night
Depart again. Here, here will I remain
With worms that are thy chambermaids. Oh, here
Will I set up my everlasting rest   110
And shake the yoke of inauspicious stars
From this world-wearièd flesh. Eyes, look your last!
Arms, take your last embrace! And lips, O you
The doors of breath, seal with a righteous kiss
A dateless bargain to engrossing death!   115
                        [_He kisses Juliet._]
Come, bitter conduct, come, unsavory guide,   116
Thou desperate pilot, now at once run on   117
The dashing rocks thy seasick weary bark!
Here's to my love. [_He drinks._] O true apothecary!
Thy drugs are quick. Thus with a kiss I die. [_He dies._]

        Enter Friar [_Laurence_] _with lantern, crow,
        and spade._

FRIAR LAURENCE
Saint Francis be my speed! How oft tonight   121
Have my old feet stumbled at graves! Who's there?
BALTHASAR
Here's one, a friend, and one that knows you well.
FRIAR LAURENCE
Bliss be upon you. Tell me, good my friend,
What torch is yond that vainly lends his light   125
To grubs and eyeless skulls? As I discern,   126
It burneth in the Capels' monument.
BALTHASAR
It doth so, holy sir, and there's my master,
One that you love.
FRIAR LAURENCE   Who is it?
BALTHASAR   Romeo.
FRIAR LAURENCE
How long hath he been there?
BALTHASAR   Full half an hour.
FRIAR LAURENCE
Go with me to the vault.
BALTHASAR   I dare not, sir.
My master knows not but I am gone hence,
And fearfully did menace me with death
If I did stay to look on his intents.
FRIAR LAURENCE
Stay, then, I'll go alone. Fear comes upon me.
Oh, much I fear some ill unthrifty thing.   136

BALTHASAR
As I did sleep under this yew tree here
I dreamt my master and another fought,
And that my master slew him.
FRIAR LAURENCE [_advancing to the tomb_]   Romeo!
Alack, alack, what blood is this which stains
The stony entrance of this sepulcher?
What mean these masterless and gory swords
To lie discolored by this place of peace?   143
                        [_He looks in the tomb._]
Romeo! Oh, pale! Who else? What, Paris too?
And steeped in blood? Ah, what an unkind hour   145
Is guilty of this lamentable chance!
The lady stirs.   [_Juliet wakes._]
JULIET
O comfortable Friar, where is my lord?   148
I do remember well where I should be,
And there I am. Where is my Romeo?
                        [_A noise within._]
FRIAR LAURENCE
I hear some noise. Lady, come from that nest
Of death, contagion, and unnatural sleep.
A greater power than we can contradict
Hath thwarted our intents. Come, come away.
Thy husband in thy bosom there lies dead,
And Paris, too. Come, I'll dispose of thee
Among a sisterhood of holy nuns.
Stay not to question, for the watch is coming.
Come, go, good Juliet. [_A noise again._] I dare no longer
        stay.   _Exit_ [_Friar Laurence_].
JULIET
Go, get thee hence, for I will not away.
What's here? A cup, closed in my true love's hand?
Poison, I see, hath been his timeless end.   162
O churl, drunk all, and left no friendly drop   163
To help me after? I will kiss thy lips;
Haply some poison yet doth hang on them,   165
To make me die with a restorative.   [_She kisses him._]
Thy lips are warm.

        Enter [_Paris's_] _Boy and Watch._

FIRST WATCH   Lead, boy. Which way?
JULIET
Yea, noise? Then I'll be brief. O happy dagger!   169
                        [_She takes Romeo's dagger._]
This is thy sheath. There rust, and let me die.
                        [_She stabs herself and dies._]
PAGE
This is the place, there where the torch doth burn.
FIRST WATCH
The ground is bloody. Search about the churchyard.
Go, some of you, whoe'er you find attach.   173
                        [_Exeunt some._]

Pitiful sight! Here lies the County slain,

---

103 **unsubstantial** lacking material existence   106 **still** always
110 **set . . . rest** (See 4.5.6. The meaning is, "make my final determination," with allusion to the idea of repose.)   115 **dateless bargain**
everlasting contract.   **engrossing** monopolizing, taking all; also,
drawing up the contract   116 **conduct** guide (i.e., the poison)
117 **desperate** reckless, despairing   121 **be my speed** prosper me and
let me arrive in time.   125 **vainly** uselessly   126 **grubs** insect larvae
136 **unthrifty** unfortunate.

143.1 _He looks . . . tomb_ Whether the Friar is to enter the tomb
depends on staging arrangements.   145 **unkind** unnatural
148 **comfortable** comforting   162 **timeless** (1) untimely (2) everlasting   163 **churl** miser   165 **Haply** perhaps   169 **happy** opportune
173 **attach** arrest, detain.

And Juliet bleeding, warm, and newly dead,
Who here hath lain these two days buried.
Go tell the Prince. Run to the Capulets.
Raise up the Montagues. Some others search.
                              [*Exeunt others.*]
We see the ground whereon these woes do lie,
But the true ground of all these piteous woes   180
We cannot without circumstance descry.   181

     Enter [some of the Watch, with] Romeo's
     man [Balthasar].

SECOND WATCH
Here's Romeo's man. We found him in the
   churchyard.
FIRST WATCH
Hold him in safety till the Prince come hither.   183

     Enter Friar [Laurence], and another Watchman
     [with tools].

THIRD WATCH
Here is a friar, that trembles, sighs, and weeps.
We took this mattock and this spade from him
As he was coming from this churchyard's side.
FIRST WATCH
A great suspicion. Stay the Friar, too.   187

     Enter the Prince [and attendants].

PRINCE
What misadventure is so early up
That calls our person from our morning rest?   189

     Enter Capels [Capulet and his Wife].

CAPULET
What should it be that is so shrieked abroad?
CAPULET'S WIFE
Oh, the people in the street cry "Romeo,"
Some "Juliet," and some "Paris," and all run
With open outcry toward our monument.
PRINCE
What fear is this which startles in our ears?   194
FIRST WATCH
Sovereign, here lies the County Paris slain,
And Romeo dead, and Juliet, dead before,
Warm and new killed.
PRINCE
Search, seek, and know how this foul murder comes. 198
FIRST WATCH
Here is a friar, and slaughtered Romeo's man,
With instruments upon them fit to open   200
These dead men's tombs.
CAPULET
O heavens! O wife, look how our daughter bleeds!
This dagger hath mista'en, for lo, his house   203
Is empty on the back of Montague,
And it mis-sheathèd in my daughter's bosom!

CAPULET'S WIFE
Oh, me! This sight of death is as a bell
That warns my old age to a sepulcher.

     Enter Montague.

PRINCE
Come, Montague, for thou art early up
To see thy son and heir more early down.
MONTAGUE
Alas, my liege, my wife is dead tonight;
Grief of my son's exile hath stopped her breath.
What further woe conspires against mine age?
PRINCE   Look, and thou shalt see.
MONTAGUE *[seeing Romeo's body]*
O thou untaught! What manners is in this,   214
To press before thy father to a grave?   215
PRINCE
Seal up the mouth of outrage for a while,   216
Till we can clear these ambiguities
And know their spring, their head, their true descent; 218
And then will I be general of your woes   219
And lead you even to death. Meantime, forbear,   220
And let mischance be slave to patience.   221
Bring forth the parties of suspicion.   222
FRIAR LAURENCE
I am the greatest, able to do least,
Yet most suspected, as the time and place
Doth make against me, of this direful murder;   225
And here I stand, both to impeach and purge   226
Myself condemnèd and myself excused.   227
PRINCE
Then say at once what thou dost know in this.
FRIAR LAURENCE
I will be brief, for my short date of breath   229
Is not so long as is a tedious tale.
Romeo, there dead, was husband to that Juliet,
And she, there dead, that Romeo's faithful wife.
I married them, and their stol'n marriage day
Was Tybalt's doomsday, whose untimely death
Banished the new-made bridegroom from this city,
For whom, and not for Tybalt, Juliet pined.
You, to remove that siege of grief from her,
Betrothed and would have married her perforce   238
To County Paris. Then comes she to me,
And with wild looks bid me devise some means
To rid her from this second marriage,
Or in my cell there would she kill herself.
Then gave I her—so tutored by my art—
A sleeping potion, which so took effect
As I intended, for it wrought on her   245
The form of death. Meantime I writ to Romeo   246

---

214 **untaught** ill-mannered youth. (Said with affectionate irony.)
215 **press** hasten, go   216 **mouth of outrage** (1) popular outcry (2)
entrance to the tomb   218 **spring, head** (Both words mean "source.")
219 **be . . . woes** be leader in lamentation   220 **even to death** in
lamentation for the dead.   221 **let . . . patience** i.e., let us bear our
misfortune patiently.   222 **of** under   225 **make** conspire, tell
226–7 **to . . . excused** to accuse myself of what is to be condemned in
me and to exonerate myself where I ought to be excused.   229 **date
of breath** time left to live   238 **perforce** by compulsion   245 **wrought**
fashioned   246 **form** appearance

---

180 **ground** basis. (Playing on the meaning "earth" in line 179.)   **181
circumstance** details   **183 in safety** under guard   **187 Stay** Detain
189 our person (The royal "we.")   **194 startles** cries alarmingly
198 know learn   **200 instruments** tools   **203 his house** its scabbard

That he should hither come as this dire night   247
To help to take her from her borrowed grave,
Being the time the potion's force should cease.
But he which bore my letter, Friar John,
Was stayed by accident, and yesternight   251
Returned my letter back. Then all alone
At the prefixèd hour of her waking
Came I to take her from her kindred's vault,
Meaning to keep her closely at my cell   255
Till I conveniently could send to Romeo.
But when I came, some minute ere the time
Of her awakening, here untimely lay
The noble Paris and true Romeo dead.
She wakes, and I entreated her come forth
And bear this work of heaven with patience.
But then a noise did scare me from the tomb,
And she, too desperate, would not go with me,
But, as it seems, did violence on herself.
All this I know, and to the marriage
Her nurse is privy; and if aught in this   266
Miscarried by my fault, let my old life
Be sacrificed some hour before his time   268
Unto the rigor of severest law.

PRINCE
We still have known thee for a holy man.   270
Where's Romeo's man? What can he say to this?

BALTHASAR
I brought my master news of Juliet's death,
And then in post he came from Mantua   273
To this same place, to this same monument.
This letter he early bid me give his father,   275
                          [*showing a letter*]
And threatened me with death, going in the vault,
If I departed not and left him there.

PRINCE [*taking the letter*]
Give me the letter. I will look on it.
Where is the County's page, that raised the watch?
Sirrah, what made your master in this place?   280

PAGE
He came with flowers to strew his lady's grave,
And bid me stand aloof, and so I did.
Anon comes one with light to ope the tomb,
And by and by my master drew on him,
And then I ran away to call the watch.

PRINCE
This letter doth make good the Friar's words,
Their course of love, the tidings of her death;
And here he writes that he did buy a poison
Of a poor 'pothecary, and therewithal   289
Came to this vault to die, and lie with Juliet.
Where be these enemies? Capulet, Montague,
See what a scourge is laid upon your hate,
That heaven finds means to kill your joys with love.   293
And I, for winking at your discords, too   294
Have lost a brace of kinsmen. All are punished.   295

CAPULET
O brother Montague, give me thy hand.
This is my daughter's jointure, for no more   297
Can I demand.

MONTAGUE   But I can give thee more,
For I will raise her statue in pure gold,   299
That whiles Verona by that name is known
There shall no figure at such rate be set   301
As that of true and faithful Juliet.

CAPULET
As rich shall Romeo's by his lady's lie;
Poor sacrifices of our enmity!

PRINCE
A glooming peace this morning with it brings;
     The sun, for sorrow, will not show his head.
Go hence to have more talk of these sad things.
     Some shall be pardoned, and some punishèd;
For never was a story of more woe
Than this of Juliet and her Romeo.   [*Exeunt.*]

247 **as this** this very   251 **stayed** stopped   255 **closely** secretly
266 **privy** in on the secret   268 **his** its   270 **still** always   273 **post**
haste   275 **This . . . father** He bade me give this letter to his father
early in the morning (5.3.23–4)   280 **made** did

289 **therewithal** with the poison   293 **kill your joys** (1) destroy your
happiness (2) kill your children.   **with** by means of   294 **winking at**
shutting my eyes to   295 **a brace** of two   297 **jointure** marriage
settlement   299 **raise** (The Second Quarto reading, "raie," is defended
by some editors in the sense of "array," make ready.)   301 **rate** value

Julius Caesar

Julius Caesar stands midway in Shakespeare's dramatic career, at a critical juncture. In some ways, it is an epilogue to his English history plays of the 1590s; in other ways, it introduces the period of the great tragedies. The play evidently was first performed at the new Globe playhouse in the fall of 1599, shortly after *Henry V* (the last of Shakespeare's history plays about medieval England) and around the time of *As You Like It* (one of the last of Shakespeare's happy romantic comedies). It shortly preceded *Hamlet.* It is placed among the tragedies in the Folio of 1623, where it was first published, and is entitled *The Tragedy of Julius Caesar,* but in the table of contents it is listed as *The Life and Death of Julius Caesar* as though it were a history.

Julius Caesar shares with Shakespeare's history plays an absorption in the problems of civil war and popular unrest. Rome, like England, suffers an internal division that is reflected in the perturbed state of the heavens themselves. The commoners, or plebeians, are easily swayed by demagogues. Opportunists prosper in this atmosphere of crisis, although fittingly even they are sometimes undone by their own scheming. Politics seems to require a morality quite apart from that of personal life, posing a tragic dilemma for Brutus, as it did for Richard II or Henry VI. The blending of history and tragedy in *Julius Caesar,* then, is not unlike that found in several English history plays. Rome was a natural subject to which Shakespeare might turn in his continuing depiction of political behavior. Roman culture had recently been elevated to new importance by the classical orientation of the Renaissance. As a model of political organization, it loomed larger in Elizabethan consciousness than it does in ours, because so few other models were available and because Greek culture was less accessible in language and tradition. According to a widely accepted mythology, Elizabethans considered themselves descended from the Romans through another Brutus, the great-grandson of Aeneas.

Yet the differences between Roman and English history are as important as the similarities. Rome's choice during her civil wars lay between a senatorial republican form of government and a strong single ruler. Although the monarchical English might be inclined to be suspicious of republicanism, they had no experience to compare with it—certainly not their various peasants' revolts, such as Jack Cade's rebellion (in *2 Henry VI*). On the other hand, Roman one-man rule as it flourished under Octavius Caesar lacked the English sanctions of divine right. Rome was, after all, a pagan culture, and Shakespeare carefully preserves this non-Christian frame of reference. The gods are frequently invoked and appear to respond with prophetic dreams and auguries, but their ultimate intentions are baffling. Human beings strive blindly; the will of the gods is inscrutable. The outcome of *Julius Caesar* is far different from the restoration of providentially ordained order at the end of *Richard III*. Calm is restored and political authority reestablished, but we are by no means sure that a divine morality has been served. Roman history for Shakespeare is history divested of its divine imperatives and located in a distant political setting, making dispassionate appraisal less difficult.

In Plutarch's *Lives of the Noble Grecians and Romans*, as translated by Sir Thomas North, Shakespeare discovered a rich opportunity for pursuing the ironies of political life to which he had been increasingly attracted in the English histories. In fact, he was drawn throughout his career to Plutarch: to the portrait of Portia in "The Life of Marcus Brutus," not only for Portia in *Julius Caesar*, but also for Lucrece in *The Rape of Lucrece*, Kate in *1 Henry IV*, and Portia in *The Merchant of Venice*; to "The Life of Theseus" for the Duke of *A Midsummer Night's Dream*; and to various lives for *Julius Caesar, Coriolanus, Antony and Cleopatra*, and *Timon of Athens*. Freed from the orthodoxies of the Elizabethan world view, Shakespeare turned in the Roman or classical plays toward irony or outright satire (as in *Troilus and Cressida*) and toward the personal tragedy of political dilemma (as in *Coriolanus* and *Julius Caesar*). These are to be the dominant motifs of the Roman or classical plays, as distinguished from both the English histories and the great tragedies of evil, in which politics plays a lesser part (*Hamlet, Othello, King Lear, Macbeth*).

Julius Caesar is an ambivalent study of civil conflict. As in *Richard II,* the play is structured around two protagonists rather than one. Caesar and Brutus, men of extraordinary abilities and debilitating weaknesses, are more like one another than either would care to admit. This antithetical balance reflects a dual tradition: the medieval view of Dante and of Geoffrey Chaucer, condemning Brutus and Cassius as conspirators, and the Renaissance view of Sir Philip Sidney and Ben Jonson, condemning Caesar as a tyrant. These opposing views still live on in various twentieth-century productions that seek to enlist the play on the side of conservatism or liberalism. In one famous production by Orson Welles for the Mercury Theatre in 1937, Caesar was made out to resemble Benito Mussolini, Italy's fascist dictator, with reference also to Franco's fascists in Spain when that civil war was at its peak. Welles's subtitle for his production, "Death of a Dictator," left no doubt as to the intended statement. The film version of 1953 by John Houseman and Joseph Maniewicz dyed its khaki military uniforms green to suggest the German Wehrmacht; the music adopted for the production deliberately aped the music that accompanied Nazi marching columns in newsreels in the 1930s. Trevor Nunn, at Stratford-upon-Avon in 1972, similarly drew overt parallels to German fascism. At Stratford, Connecticut, in 1979, director Gerald Freedman presented Caesar as a Latin American dictator; at Ashland, Oregon, in 1982, Jerry Turner likened Caesar to Che Guevara. Such interpretations reflect what the conspirators themselves believe, as they cry "Liberty! Freedom! Tyranny is dead!" but the play itself invites widely varying interpretations. Caesar has sometimes appeared as a great leader and a man of great natural authority despite his manifest weaknesses, involved in a struggle to the death with conspirators whose motives and personalities are as complex as his. Anthony Quayle and Michael Langham sought such a balance in their 1950 production at Stratford-upon-Avon; so did Glen Byam Shaw in 1957. The film version of 1953 by John Houseman and Joseph Maniewicz achieved a kind of balance, despite its antifascist leanings, by evenly distributing its major roles among various well-known actors and actresses—John Gielgud as Cassius, Marlon Brando as Antony, James Mason as Brutus, Louis Calhern as Caesar, Greer Garson as Calpurnia, Deborah Kerr as Portia—instead of allowing one actor to dominate the play. Most recent criticism similarly has abandoned the fruitless debate as to whether Brutus or Caesar is the tragic protagonist, and whether one or the other of them is to be seen as morally superior, in favor of a multiple perspective.

Caesar is a study in paradox. He is unquestionably a great general, astute in politics, decisive in his judgments, and sharp in his evaluation of men, as, for example, in his distrust of Cassius with his "lean and hungry look" (1.2.194). Yet this mightiest of men, who in Cassius's phrase bestrides the narrow world "like a Colossus" (line 136), is also deaf in one ear, prone to fevers and epilepsy, unable to compete with Cassius by swimming the Tiber fully armed, and afflicted with a sterile marriage. Physical limitations of this sort are common enough, but in Caesar they are constantly juxtaposed with his aspirations to be above mortal weakness. He dies boasting that he is like the "northern star," constant, unique, "Unshaked of motion" (3.1.61–71). He professes to fear nothing and yet is notoriously superstitious. He calmly reflects that "death, a necessary end, / Will come when it will come," and then arrogantly boasts in the next moment that "Danger knows full well / That Caesar is more dangerous than he" (2.2.36–45). As his wife puts it, Caesar's "wisdom is consumed in confidence" (line 49). He willfully betrays his own best instincts and ignores plain warnings through self-deception. He stops a procession to hear a soothsayer and then dismisses the man as "a dreamer" (1.2.24). He commissions his augurers to determine whether he should stay at home on the ides of March and then persuades himself that acting on their advice would be a sign of weakness. Most fatally, he thinks himself above flattery and so is especially vulnerable to it. So wise and powerful a man as this cannot stop the process of his own fate, because his fate and character are interwoven: he is the victim of his own hubris. His insatiable desire for the crown overbalances his judgment; no warnings of the gods can save him. Even his virtues conspire against him, for he regards himself as one who puts public interest ahead of personal affairs, and so he brushes aside the letter of Artemidorus that would have told him of the conspiracy.

Brutus, for all his opposition to Caesar, is also a paradoxical figure. His strengths are quite unlike those of Caesar, but his weaknesses are surprisingly similar. Brutus is a noble Roman from an ancient family whose glory it has been to defend the personal liberties of Rome, the republican tradition. Brutus's virtues are personal virtues. He enjoys an admirable rapport with his courageous and intelligent wife, and is genuinely kind to his servants. In friendship he is trustworthy. He deplores oaths in the conspiracy because his word is his bond. He finds Caesar's ambition for power distasteful and vulgar; his opposition to Caesar is both idealistic and patrician. Brutus's hubris is a pride of family, and on this score he is vulnerable to flattery. As Cassius reminds him, alluding to Brutus's ancestor Lucius Junius Brutus, who founded the Roman Republic in 509 B.C.: "There was a Brutus once that would have brooked / Th'eternal devil to keep his state in Rome / As easily as a king" (1.2.159–61). Should not Marcus Brutus be the savior of his country from a return to tyranny? Is not he a more fit leader for Rome than Caesar? " 'Brutus' and 'Caesar.' What should be in that 'Caesar'? / Why should that name be sounded more than yours?" (lines 142–3). Cassius's strategy is to present to Brutus numerous testimonials "all tending to the great opinion / That Rome holds of his name" (lines 318–19). Cassius plays the role of tempter here, but the notion he suggests is not new to Brutus.

The parallelism of Brutus's pride and Caesar's ambition is strongly underscored by the way in which these great figures appear to us in two adjoining scenes: 2.1 and 2.2. In these two scenes, the protagonists enter alone during the troubled night, call for a servant, receive the conspirators, and dispute the wise caution of their wives. Both men are predisposed to the temptations that are placed before them. Brutus has often thought of himself as the indispensable man for the preservation of Rome's liberties. Despite his good breeding and coolly rational manner, he is as dominating a personality as Caesar and as hard to move once his mind is made up. Indeed, the conspiracy founders on Brutus's repeated insistence on having his own way. He allows no oaths among the conspirators and will not kill Antony along with Caesar. He permits Antony to speak after him at Caesar's funeral. He vetoes Cicero as a fellow conspirator. In each instance, the other conspirators are unanimously opposed to Brutus's choice but yield to him. Brutus cuts off Cassius's objections before hearing them fully, being accustomed to having his way without dispute. His motives are in part noble and idealistic: Brutus wishes to have the conspirators behave generously and openly, as heroes rather than as henchmen. Yet there is something loftily patrician in his desire to have the fruits of conspiracy without any of the dirty work. His willingness to have Antony speak after him betrays a vain confidence in his own oratory and an unjustified faith in the plebeian mob. Moreover, when Brutus overrides Cassius once more in the decision to fight at Philippi and is proved wrong by the event, no idealistic motive can excuse Brutus's insistence on being obeyed; Cassius is the more experienced soldier. Still, Brutus's fatal limitations as leader of a coup d'état are inseparable from his virtues as a private man. The truth is that such a noble man is, by his very nature, unsuited for the stern exigencies of assassination and civil war. Brutus is strong-minded about his ideals, but he cannot be ruthless. The means and the end of revolution drift further and further apart. He cannot supply his troops at Philippi because he will not forage among the peasants of the countryside and will not countenance among his allies the routine corruptions of an army in time of war, though at the same time that he upbraids Cassius for not sending him gold he does not stop to ask where the gold would come from. Even suicide is distasteful for Brutus, obliging him to embarrass his friends by asking their help. Brutus is too high-minded and genteel a man for the troubled times in which he lives.

The times indeed seem to demand ruthless action of the sort Antony and Octavius are all too ready to provide. The greatest irony of Brutus's fall is that the coup he undertakes for Roman liberty yields only further diminutions of that liberty. The plebeians are not ready for the commonwealth Brutus envisages. From the first, they are portrayed as amiable but "saucy" (even in the opinion of their tribunes, Flavius and Marullus). They adulate Caesar at the expense of their previous idol, Pompey. When Brutus successfully appeals for a moment to their changeable loyalties, they cry "Let him be Caesar," and "Caesar's better parts / Shall be crowned in Brutus" (3.2.51–2). If Brutus were not swayed by this hero-worship, he would have good cause to be disillusioned. To his credit, he is not the demogogue the plebeians take him for and so cannot continue to bend them to his will. Cassius, too, for all his villainlike role as tempter to Brutus, his envious motive, and his Epicurean skepticism, reveals a finer nature as the play progresses. Inspired perhaps by Brutus's philosophic idealism, Cassius turns philosopher also and accepts defeat in a noble but ineffectual cause. Yet even his death is futile; Cassius is misinformed about the fate of his friend Titinius and so stabs himself just when the battle is going well for the conspirators.

The ultimate victors are Antony and Octavius. Antony, whatever finer nature he may possess, becomes under the stress of circumstance a cunning bargainer with the conspirators and a masterful rhetorician who characterizes himself to the plebeians as a "plain blunt man" (3.2.219). In sardonic soliloquy at the end of his funeral oration, he observes, "Now let it work. Mischief, thou art afoot. / Take thou what course thou wilt" (lines 261–2). He is, to be sure, stirred by loyalty to Caesar's memory, but to the end of avenging Caesar's death he is prepared to unleash violence at whatever risk to the state. He regards Lepidus contemptuously as a mere creature under his command. Antony is older than Octavius and teaches the younger man about political realities, but an Elizabethan audience would probably savor the irony that Octavius will subsequently beat Antony at his own game. At Philippi, Octavius's refusal to accept Antony's directions in the battle (5.1.16–20) gives us a glimpse of the peremptory manner for which he is to become famous, like his predecessor. Antony and Octavius together are, in any case, a fearsome pair, matter-of-factly noting down the names of those who must die, including their own kinsmen. They cut off the bequests left to the populace in Caesar's will, by which Antony had won the hearts of the plebeians (4.1). Many innocent persons are sacrificed in the new reign of terror, including Cicero and the poet unluckily named Cinna. In such deaths, art and civilization yield to expediency. Rationality gives way to frenzied rhetoric and to a struggle for power in which

Rome's republican tradition is buried forever. Such is the achievement of Brutus's noble revolution.

Appropriately for such a depiction of ambivalent political strife, *Julius Caesar* is written chiefly in the oratorical mode. It resembles its near contemporary, *Henry V,* in devoting so much attention to speeches of public persuasion. The famous orations following Caesar's assassination—one by Brutus in the so-called Laconic style (that is, concise and sententious) and one by Antony in the Asiatic style (that is, more florid, anecdotal, and literary)—are only the most prominent of many public utterances. In the first scene, Marullus rebukes the plebeians for their disloyalty to Pompey and for the moment dissuades them from idolizing Caesar. Decius Brutus changes Caesar's presumably unalterable mind about staying home on the ides of March (2.2). Caesar lectures the Senate on the virtues of constancy. Before Philippi, the contending armies clash with verbal taunts. Antony and Octavius end the play with tributes to the dead Brutus. In less public scenes as well, oratory serves to win Brutus over to the conspirators, to urge unavailingly that Brutus confide in his wife, or to warn the unheeding Caesar of his danger. The decline of the conspirators' cause shows in their descent from rational discourse to private bickering (4.3). The play gives us a range of rhetorical styles, from the deliberative (having to do with careful consideration of choices) to the forensic (analogous to pleading at law, maintaining one side or the other of a given question), to the epideictic (for display, as in set orations). The imagery, suitably public and rhetorical in its function, is of a fixed star in the firmament, a Colossus bestriding the petty world of humans, a tide of fortune in the affairs of humankind, a statue spouting fountains of blood. The city of Rome is a vivid presence in the play, conveyed at times through Elizabethan anachronisms, such as striking clocks, sweaty nightcaps, "towers and windows, yea, . . . chimney tops" (1.1.39), but in an eclectic fusion of native and classical traditions wherein anachronisms become functionally purposeful. Style affords us one more way of considering *Julius Caesar* as a Janus play, looking back to Shakespeare's history plays and forward to his tragedies.

Women are marginalized in *Julius Caesar,* much as in Shakespeare's English history plays. Portia and Calpurnia are alike, not only in their concern for their husbands' welfare, but also in their inability to do anything to ensure their husbands' safety and prosperity. Fittingly in such an unremittingly patriarchal play, Portia and Calpurnia are noble Roman matrons of the type we also see earlier in *The Rape of Lucrece* or *Titus Andronicus* and later in Octavia (*Antony and Cleopatra*) and Volumnia *(Coriolanus):* unassailably virtuous, descended from patrician stock, and submissive to the essentially male values of unflinching duty and stoical reserve. Portia, daughter of the great Cato of Utica who committed suicide rather than submit to Caesar's tyranny, emulates her father's example by taking her own life rather than outlive her husband's shame in defeat. Calpurnia expounds her prophetic dream of Caesar's bleeding statue (2.2.76–9) only to be rebuked for womanly cowardice. These women do what they can to offer their men an alternative perspective on political ambition—one in which caution and attentiveness to family values stand in opposition to the competitive mores of the male-dominated world—but the women are doomed, like Cassandra and Andromache (in *Troilus and Cressida*), to see their quiet wisdom ignored or misinterpreted. Most touching of all is the scene of marital mutuality between Portia and Brutus (2.1.234–310), in which we realize that Portia's concern and sympathy for her husband cannot save Brutus from himself.

A structural pattern to be found in *Julius Caesar,* as noted by John Velz (see bibliography), is the replicating action of rise and fall by which the great men of ancient Rome succeed one another. The process antedates the play itself, for Pompey's faded glory mentioned in Act 1 is a reminder—or should be a reminder—that good fortune lasts but a day. We behold Caesar at the point of his greatest triumph and his imminent decline to death. "O mighty Caesar! Dost thou lie so low?" asks Antony when he sees the prostrate body of the once most powerful man alive. "Are all thy conquests, glories, triumphs, spoils, / Shrunk to this little measure?" (3.1.150–2). Brutus and Cassius step forward into prominence only to be supplanted by Antony and Octavius. Antony is unaware, though presumably the audience is aware, that Antony is to fall at the hands of Octavius. The process of incessant change, reinforced by such metaphors as the tide in the affairs of humans (already noted), offering its mocking comment on Caesar's self-comparison to the fixed northern star, is not simply a meaningless descent on the grand staircase of history, for Octavius's *Pax Romana* lies at the end of the cycle from republic to empire. Still, that resting place is beyond the conclusion of this open-ended play. What we see here again and again is a human blindness to history, through which a succession of protagonists repeat one another's errors without intending to do so. Cassius, like Caesar, goes to his death in the face of unpropitious omens that he now partly believes to be true. The eagles that accompanied Cassius and his army to Philippi desert him as the moment of battle approaches. These omens suggest a balance between character and fate, for, though the leaders of Rome have one by one fallen through their own acts and choices, they have also, it seems, fulfilled a prearranged destiny. Brutus, confronted by the Ghost of Caesar and assured that he will see this spirit of Caesar at Philippi, answers resolutely, "Why, I will see thee at Philippi, then" (4.3.288). Defeated in battle, as he sensed he would be, Brutus takes his own life. Cassius dies on his birthday. *Sic transit gloria mundi.*

Julius Caesar

[*Dramatis Personae*

JULIUS CAESAR
CALPURNIA, *Caesar's wife*
MARK ANTONY,
OCTAVIUS CAESAR, } *triumvirs after Caesar's death*
LEPIDUS,

MARCUS BRUTUS
PORTIA, *Brutus's wife*
CAIUS CASSIUS,
CASCA,
DECIUS BRUTUS,
CINNA, } *conspirators with Brutus*
METELLUS CIMBER,
TREBONIUS,
CAIUS LIGARIUS,

CICERO,
PUBLIUS, } *senators*
POPILIUS LENA,
FLAVIUS,
MARULLUS, } *tribunes of the people*

SOOTHSAYER
ARTEMIDORUS, *a teacher of rhetoric*
CINNA, *a poet*
Another POET

LUCILIUS,
TITINIUS,
MESSALA,
YOUNG CATO,
VOLUMNIUS,
VARRO, } *officers and soldiers in the army of Brutus and Cassius*
CLAUDIUS,
CLITUS,
DARDANIUS,
LABEO,
FLAVIUS,

PINDARUS, *Cassius's servant*
LUCIUS,
STRATO, } *Brutus's servants*
Caesar's SERVANT
Antony's SERVANT
Octavius's SERVANT

CARPENTER
COBBLER
Five PLEBEIANS
Three SOLDIERS *in Brutus' army*
Two SOLDIERS *in Antony's army*
MESSENGER

GHOST *of Caesar*

Senators, Plebeians, Officers, Soldiers, and Attendants

SCENE: *Rome; the neighborhood of Sardis; the neighborhood of Philippi*]

1.1

Enter Flavius, Marullus, and certain commoners over the stage.

FLAVIUS
Hence! Home, you idle creatures, get you home!

Is this a holiday? What, know you not,
Being mechanical, you ought not walk   3
Upon a laboring day without the sign   4
Of your profession?—Speak, what trade art thou?
CARPENTER   Why, sir, a carpenter.
MARULLUS
Where is thy leather apron and thy rule?

1.1 Location: Rome. A street.

3 **mechanical** of the artisan class   4 **sign** garb and implements

1055

What dost thou with thy best apparel on?—
You, sir, what trade are you?
COBBLER   Truly, sir, in respect of a fine workman, I am   10
but, as you would say, a cobbler.   11
MARULLUS
But what trade art thou? Answer me directly.
COBBLER   A trade, sir, that I hope I may use with a safe
conscience, which is indeed, sir, a mender of bad soles.   14
FLAVIUS
What trade, thou knave? Thou naughty knave, what
trade?   15
COBBLER   Nay, I beseech you, sir, be not out with me.   16
Yet if you be out, sir, I can mend you.   17
FLAVIUS
What mean'st thou by that? Mend me, thou saucy
fellow?
COBBLER   Why, sir, cobble you.   19
FLAVIUS   Thou art a cobbler, art thou?
COBBLER   Truly, sir, all that I live by is with the awl. I 21
meddle with no tradesman's matters nor women's   22
matters, but withal I am indeed, sir, a surgeon to old   23
shoes. When they are in great danger, I recover them.   24
As proper men as ever trod upon neat's leather have   25
gone upon my handiwork.
FLAVIUS
But wherefore art not in thy shop today?
Why dost thou lead these men about the streets?
COBBLER   Truly, sir, to wear out their shoes, to get myself
into more work. But indeed, sir, we make holiday
to see Caesar and to rejoice in his triumph.   31
MARULLUS
Wherefore rejoice? What conquest brings he home?
What tributaries follow him to Rome   33
To grace in captive bonds his chariot wheels?
You blocks, you stones, you worse than senseless
things!   35
O you hard hearts, you cruel men of Rome,
Knew you not Pompey? Many a time and oft   37
Have you climbed up to walls and battlements,   38
To towers and windows, yea, to chimney tops,   39
Your infants in your arms, and there have sat
The livelong day, with patient expectation,

To see great Pompey pass the streets of Rome.   42
And when you saw his chariot but appear,
Have you not made an universal shout,
That Tiber trembled underneath her banks   45
To hear the replication of your sounds   46
Made in her concave shores?   47
And do you now put on your best attire?
And do you now cull out a holiday?   49
And do you now strew flowers in his way
That comes in triumph over Pompey's blood?   51
Begone!
Run to your houses, fall upon your knees,
Pray to the gods to intermit the plague   54
That needs must light on this ingratitude.   55
FLAVIUS
Go, go, good countrymen, and for this fault
Assemble all the poor men of your sort;   57
Draw them to Tiber banks, and weep your tears
Into the channel, till the lowest stream   59
Do kiss the most exalted shores of all.   60
                          Exeunt all the commoners.
See whe'er their basest mettle be not moved.   61
They vanish tongue-tied in their guiltiness.
Go you down that way towards the Capitol;
This way will I. Disrobe the images   64
If you do find them decked with ceremonies.   65
MARULLUS   May we do so?
You know it is the Feast of Lupercal.   67
FLAVIUS
It is no matter. Let no images
Be hung with Caesar's trophies. I'll about   69
And drive away the vulgar from the streets;   70
So do you too, where you perceive them thick.
These growing feathers plucked from Caesar's wing
Will make him fly an ordinary pitch,   73
Who else would soar above the view of men   74
And keep us all in servile fearfulness.   *Exeunt.*

10 **in . . . workman** (1) as far as skilled work is concerned (2) compared with a skilled worker   **11 cobbler** (1) one who works with shoes (2) bungler.   **14 soles** (With pun on "souls.")   **15 naughty** good-for-nothing   **16 out** out of temper   **17 out** having worn-out shoes.   **mend you** (1) cure your bad temper (2) repair your shoes. **19 cobble you** mend your shoes. (The meaning "to pelt with stones" also suggests itself here, though perhaps it was not in general use until later in the seventeenth century.)   **21 awl** (Punning on *all*.) **22 meddle with** (1) have to do with (2) have sexual intercourse with **23 withal** yet. (With pun on *with awl*.)   **24 recover** (1) resole (2) cure **25 proper** fine, handsome.   **as . . . leather** (Proverbial. *Neat's leather* is cowhide.)   **31 triumph** triumphal procession. (Caesar had overthrown the sons of Pompey the Great in Spain at the Battle of Munda, March 17, 45 B.C. The triumph was held that October.)   **33 tributaries** captives who will pay ransom (tribute)   **35 senseless** insensible like stone (hence, unfeeling)   **37 Pompey** (Caesar had overthrown the great soldier and onetime triumvir at the Battle of Pharsalus in 48 B.C. Pompey fled to Egypt, where he was murdered.)   **38–9 battlements . . . chimney tops** (The details are appropriate to an Elizabethan cityscape.)

42 **great** (Alludes to Pompey's epithet, *Magnus*, "great.")   **pass** pass through   **45 Tiber** the Tiber River   **46 replication** echo   **47 concave** hollowed out, overhanging   **49 cull** pick   **51 Pompey's blood** (1) Pompey's offspring (2) the blood of the Pompeys.   **54 intermit** suspend   **55 needs must** must necessarily   **57 sort** rank   **59–60 till . . . all** until even at its lowest reach the river is filled to the brim.   **61 See . . . moved** See how even their ignoble natures can be appealed to. (*Mettle* and *metal* are interchangeable, meaning both "temperament" and the natural substance. A base *metal* is one that is easily changed or *moved*, unlike gold; compare 1.2.308–10.)   **64 images** statues (of Caesar in royal regalia, set up by his followers)   **65 ceremonies** ceremonial trappings.   **67 Feast of Lupercal** a feast of purification (*Februa*, whence *February*) in honor of Pan, celebrated from ancient times in Rome on February 15 of each year. (Historically, this celebration came some months after Caesar's triumph in October of 45 B.C. The celebrants, called *Luperci*, raced around the Palatine Hill and the Circus carrying thongs of goatskin, with which they lightly struck those who came in their way. Women so touched were suppposed to be cured of barrenness; hence Caesar's wish that Antony would strike Calpurnia, 1.2.6–9.)   **69 trophies** spoils of war hung up as memorials of victory.   **about** go around the other way   **70 vulgar** commoners, plebeians   **73 pitch** highest point in flight. (A term from falconry.)   **74 else** otherwise

[1.2]

*Enter Caesar, Antony for the course, Calpurnia,
Portia, Decius, Cicero, Brutus, Cassius, Casca, a
Soothsayer; after them, Marullus and Flavius;
[citizens following].*

CAESAR
Calpurnia!
CASCA   Peace, ho! Caesar speaks.
CAESAR   Calpurnia!
CALPURNIA   Here, my lord.
CAESAR
Stand you directly in Antonio's way   3
When he doth run his course. Antonio!
ANTONY   Caesar, my lord?
CAESAR
Forget not, in your speed, Antonio,
To touch Calpurnia; for our elders say
The barren, touchèd in this holy chase,
Shake off their sterile curse.
ANTONY   I shall remember.   9
When Caesar says "Do this," it is performed.
CAESAR
Set on, and leave no ceremony out.   [*Flourish.*]   11
SOOTHSAYER   Caesar!
CAESAR   Ha? Who calls?
CASCA
Bid every noise be still. Peace yet again!
                              [*The music ceases.*]
CAESAR
Who is it in the press that calls on me?   15
I hear a tongue shriller than all the music
Cry "Caesar!" Speak. Caesar is turned to hear.
SOOTHSAYER
Beware the ides of March.
CAESAR   What man is that?   18
BRUTUS
A soothsayer bids you beware the ides of March.
CAESAR
Set him before me. Let me see his face.
CASSIUS
Fellow, come from the throng. [*The Soothsayer comes
          forward.*] Look upon Caesar.
CAESAR
What say'st thou to me now? Speak once again.
SOOTHSAYER   Beware the ides of March.
CAESAR
He is a dreamer. Let us leave him. Pass.   24
          Sennet. Exeunt. Manent Brutus and Cassius.
CASSIUS
Will you go see the order of the course?   25

BRUTUS   Not I.
CASSIUS   I pray you, do.
BRUTUS
I am not gamesome. I do lack some part   28
Of that quick spirit that is in Antony.
Let me not hinder, Cassius, your desires;
I'll leave you.
CASSIUS
Brutus, I do observe you now of late.
I have not from your eyes that gentleness
And show of love as I was wont to have.   34
You bear too stubborn and too strange a hand   35
Over your friend that loves you.
BRUTUS   Cassius,
Be not deceived. If I have veiled my look,   37
I turn the trouble of my countenance
Merely upon myself. Vexèd I am   39
Of late with passions of some difference,   40
Conceptions only proper to myself,   41
Which give some soil, perhaps, to my behaviors.   42
But let not therefore my good friends be grieved—
Among which number, Cassius, be you one—
Nor construe any further my neglect
Than that poor Brutus, with himself at war,
Forgets the shows of love to other men.
CASSIUS
Then, Brutus, I have much mistook your passion,
By means whereof this breast of mine hath buried   49
Thoughts of great value, worthy cogitations.   50
Tell me, good Brutus, can you see your face?
BRUTUS
No, Cassius, for the eye sees not itself
But by reflection, by some other things.
CASSIUS   'Tis just.   54
And it is very much lamented, Brutus,
That you have no such mirrors as will turn
Your hidden worthiness into your eye,
That you might see your shadow. I have heard   58
Where many of the best respect in Rome,   59
Except immortal Caesar, speaking of Brutus
And groaning underneath this age's yoke,
Have wished that noble Brutus had his eyes.   62
BRUTUS
Into what dangers would you lead me, Cassius,
That you would have me seek into myself
For that which is not in me?
CASSIUS
Therefore, good Brutus, be prepared to hear;
And since you know you cannot see yourself

**1.2. Location: A public place or street, perhaps as in the previous
scene.**
0.1 *for the course* i.e., stripped for the race, carrying a goatskin thong
3 Antonio (Here and occasionally elsewhere Shakespeare employs
Italian forms of Latin proper names, perhaps for metrical reasons.)
9 sterile curse curse of barrenness.   **11 Set on** Proceed   **15 press**
throng   **18 ides of March** March 15.   **24.1** *Sennet* trumpet call signaling the arrival or departure of a dignitary.   *Manent* They remain
onstage   **25 order of the course** ritual and progress of the race.

28 gamesome fond of sports, merry.   **34 wont** accustomed   **35 You
. . . hand** You behave too stubbornly and in too unfriendly a manner.
(The metaphor is from horsemanship.)   **37 veiled my look** i.e., been
introverted, seemed less friendly   **39 Merely** entirely   **40 passions
of some difference** conflicting emotions   **41 only proper to** relating
only to   **42 soil** blemish   **49–50 By . . . value** because of which misunderstanding (my assuming you were displeased with me) I have
kept to myself important thoughts   **54 just** true.   **58 shadow** image,
reflection.   **59 best respect** highest repute and station   **62 had his
eyes** (1) could see things from the perspective of Caesar's critics, or
(2) could see better with his own eyes.

So well as by reflection, I, your glass,   68
Will modestly discover to yourself   69
That of yourself which you yet know not of.
And be not jealous on me, gentle Brutus.   71
Were I a common laughter, or did use   72
To stale with ordinary oaths my love   73
To every new protester; if you know   74
That I do fawn on men and hug them hard
And after scandal them, or if you know   76
That I profess myself in banqueting   77
To all the rout, then hold me dangerous.   78

Flourish, and shout.

BRUTUS
What means this shouting? I do fear the people
Choose Caesar for their king.

CASSIUS   Ay, do you fear it?
Then must I think you would not have it so.

BRUTUS
I would not, Cassius, yet I love him well.
But wherefore do you hold me here so long?
What is it that you would impart to me?
If it be aught toward the general good,
Set honor in one eye and death i'th'other
And I will look on both indifferently;   87
For let the gods so speed me as I love   88
The name of honor more than I fear death.

CASSIUS
I know that virtue to be in you, Brutus,
As well as I do know your outward favor.   91
Well, honor is the subject of my story.
I cannot tell what you and other men
Think of this life; but, for my single self,
I had as lief not be as live to be   95
In awe of such a thing as I myself.   96
I was born free as Caesar, so were you;
We both have fed as well, and we can both
Endure the winter's cold as well as he.
For once, upon a raw and gusty day,
The troubled Tiber chafing with her shores,
Caesar said to me, "Dar'st thou, Cassius, now
Leap in with me into this angry flood
And swim to yonder point?" Upon the word,
Accoutred as I was, I plungèd in   105
And bade him follow; so indeed he did.
The torrent roared, and we did buffet it
With lusty sinews, throwing it aside   108
And stemming it with hearts of controversy.   109

But ere we could arrive the point proposed,
Caesar cried, "Help me, Cassius, or I sink!"
Ay, as Aeneas, our great ancestor,   112
Did from the flames of Troy upon his shoulder
The old Anchises bear, so from the waves of Tiber
Did I the tirèd Caesar. And this man
Is now become a god, and Cassius is
A wretched creature and must bend his body   117
If Caesar carelessly but nod on him.
He had a fever when he was in Spain,
And when the fit was on him I did mark
How he did shake. 'Tis true, this god did shake.
His coward lips did from their color fly,   122
And that same eye whose bend doth awe the world   123
Did lose his luster. I did hear him groan.   124
Ay, and that tongue of his that bade the Romans
Mark him and write his speeches in their books,
Alas, it cried, "Give me some drink, Titinius,"
As a sick girl. Ye gods, it doth amaze me
A man of such a feeble temper should   129
So get the start of the majestic world   130
And bear the palm alone.   *Shout. Flourish.* 131

BRUTUS   Another general shout!
I do believe that these applauses are
For some new honors that are heaped on Caesar.

CASSIUS
Why, man, he doth bestride the narrow world
Like a Colossus, and we petty men   136
Walk under his huge legs and peep about
To find ourselves dishonorable graves.
Men at some time are masters of their fates.
The fault, dear Brutus, is not in our stars,
But in ourselves, that we are underlings.
"Brutus" and "Caesar." What should be in that
    "Caesar"?
Why should that name be sounded more than yours? 143
Write them together, yours is as fair a name;
Sound them, it doth become the mouth as well;
Weigh them, it is as heavy; conjure with 'em,
"Brutus" will start a spirit as soon as "Caesar."   147
Now, in the names of all the gods at once,
Upon what meat doth this our Caesar feed
That he is grown so great? Age, thou art shamed!
Rome, thou hast lost the breed of noble bloods!   151
When went there by an age since the great flood   152

---

68 **glass** mirror   69 **modestly discover** reveal without exaggeration
71 **jealous on** suspicious of.   **gentle** noble   72 **laughter** laughing-
stock, as at 4.3.114; or perhaps *laugher*, a shallow fellow who laughs at
every jest.   **did use** were accustomed   73 **stale** cheapen, make common.   **ordinary** (1) commonplace (2) customary (3) tavern   74 **protester** one who protests or declares friendship   76 **after scandal**
afterwards slander   77 **profess myself** make declarations of friendship   78 **rout** mob   78.1 *Flourish* Fanfare for a dignitary   87 **indifferently** impartially   88 **speed me** make me prosper   91 **favor**
appearance.   95 **as lief not be** just as soon not exist   96 **such . . .
myself** i.e., a fellow mortal.   105 **Accoutred** fully dressed in armor
108 **lusty sinews** vigorous might. (Literally, tendons.)   109 **stemming** making headway against.   **hearts of controversy** hearts fired
up by rivalry.

112 **Aeneas** hero of Virgil's *Aeneid*, the legendary founder of Rome
(hence *our great ancestor*), who bore his aged father Anchises out of
burning Troy as it was falling to the Greeks   117 **bend his body** bow
122 **color** (1) i.e., normal healthy hue (2) military colors, flag. (The lips
are personified as deserters.)   123 **bend** glance, gaze   124 **his** its
129 **temper** constitution   130 **get . . . of** gain ascendancy over
131 **palm** victor's prize   136 **Colossus** (A 100-foot-high bronze statue
of Helios, the sun god, one of the seven wonders of the ancient
world, was commonly supposed to have stood astride the entrance to
the harbor of Rhodes.)   143 **be sounded** (1) be spoken and celebrated
(2) resound   147 **start** raise. (Perhaps the crowd is heard to shout a
third time at this point, or somewhere else in this conversation. At
line 226 below, we are told that "They shouted thrice.")   151 **the
breed . . . bloods** the bloodline of men of noble stock and valiant
spirit.   152 **flood** i.e., the classical analogue of Noah's flood, in which
all humanity was destroyed except for Deucalion and his wife Pyrrha

But it was famed with more than with one man?   153
When could they say, till now, that talked of Rome,
That her wide walks encompassed but one man?
Now is it Rome indeed, and room enough,   156
When there is in it but one only man.
Oh, you and I have heard our fathers say
There was a Brutus once that would have brooked   159
Th'eternal devil to keep his state in Rome   160
As easily as a king.   161

BRUTUS
That you do love me, I am nothing jealous.   162
What you would work me to, I have some aim.   163
How I have thought of this and of these times
I shall recount hereafter. For this present,
I would not, so with love I might entreat you,   166
Be any further moved. What you have said   167
I will consider; what you have to say
I will with patience hear and find a time
Both meet to hear and answer such high things.   170
Till then, my noble friend, chew upon this:
Brutus had rather be a villager
Than to repute himself a son of Rome
Under these hard conditions as this time
Is like to lay upon us.   175

CASSIUS   I am glad that my weak words
Have struck but thus much show of fire from Brutus.   177

Enter Caesar and his train. [Brutus and
Cassius continue to confer privately.]

BRUTUS
The games are done, and Caesar is returning.

CASSIUS
As they pass by, pluck Casca by the sleeve,
And he will, after his sour fashion, tell you
What hath proceeded worthy note today.

BRUTUS
I will do so. But look you, Cassius,
The angry spot doth glow on Caesar's brow,
And all the rest look like a chidden train.   184
Calpurnia's cheek is pale, and Cicero
Looks with such ferret and such fiery eyes   186
As we have seen him in the Capitol,
Being crossed in conference by some senators.   188

CASSIUS
Casca will tell us what the matter is.

CAESAR   Antonio!

ANTONY   Caesar?

CAESAR
Let me have men about me that are fat,

Sleek-headed men, and such as sleep o' nights.
Yond Cassius has a lean and hungry look.
He thinks too much. Such men are dangerous.

ANTONY
Fear him not, Caesar, he's not dangerous.
He is a noble Roman, and well given.   197

CAESAR
Would he were fatter! But I fear him not.
Yet if my name were liable to fear,
I do not know the man I should avoid
So soon as that spare Cassius. He reads much,
He is a great observer, and he looks
Quite through the deeds of men. He loves no plays,   203
As thou dost, Antony; he hears no music.   204
Seldom he smiles, and smiles in such a sort   205
As if he mocked himself and scorned his spirit
That could be moved to smile at anything.
Such men as he be never at heart's ease
Whiles they behold a greater than themselves,
And therefore are they very dangerous.
I rather tell thee what is to be feared
Than what I fear, for always I am Caesar.
Come on my right hand, for this ear is deaf,
And tell me truly what thou think'st of him.
        Sennet. Exeunt Caesar and his train. [Casca remains
                               with Brutus and Cassius.]

CASCA   You pulled me by the cloak. Would you speak 215
with me?

BRUTUS
Ay, Casca. Tell us what hath chanced today,   217
That Caesar looks so sad.   218

CASCA   Why, you were with him, were you not?

BRUTUS
I should not then ask Casca what had chanced.

CASCA   Why, there was a crown offered him; and, being
offered him, he put it by with the back of his hand,
thus, and then the people fell a-shouting.

BRUTUS   What was the second noise for?

CASCA   Why, for that too.

CASSIUS
They shouted thrice. What was the last cry for?   226

CASCA   Why, for that too.

BRUTUS   Was the crown offered him thrice?

CASCA   Ay, marry, was't, and he put it by thrice, every 229
time gentler than other, and at every putting-by mine
honest neighbors shouted.   231

CASSIUS   Who offered him the crown?

CASCA   Why, Antony.

BRUTUS
Tell us the manner of it, gentle Casca.   234

CASCA   I can as well be hanged as tell the manner of it.
It was mere foolery; I did not mark it. I saw Mark An-

---

153 **famed with** famous for   156 **Rome, room** (Pronounced alike.)
159 **Brutus** i.e., Lucius Junius Brutus, who expelled the Tarquins and
founded the Roman republic (c. 509 B.C.).   **brooked** tolerated
160 **keep his state** set himself up in majesty   161 **As . . . king** as readily as he would tolerate a king.   162 **nothing jealous** not at all doubtful.   163 **work** persuade.   **aim** inkling.   166 **so . . . you** if I might
entreat you in the name of friendship   167 **moved** urged.   170 **meet**
fitting   175 **like** likely   177.1 *train* retinue. (See 1.2.0.1–4 for the
names of those in the procession.)   184 **a chidden train** scolded followers.   186 **ferret** ferretlike, i.e., small and red   188 **crossed in conference** opposed in debate

---

197 **given** disposed.   203 **through** i.e., into the motives of   204 **hears
no music** (Regarded as a sign of a morose and treacherous character.)
205 **sort** manner   215 **cloak** (Elizabethan costume; see also *sleeve,* line
179, and *doublet,* line 265. The Roman toga was sleeveless.)
217 **chanced** happened   218 **sad** serious.   226 **thrice** (See note at
1.2.147.)   229 **marry** i.e., indeed. (Originally, "by the Virgin Mary.")
231 **honest** worthy. (Said contemptuously.)   234 **gentle** noble

tony offer him a crown—yet 'twas not a crown neither, 'twas one of these coronets—and, as I told you, 238 he put it by once; but for all that, to my thinking, he would fain have had it. Then he offered it to him again; 240 then he put it by again; but to my thinking he was very loath to lay his fingers off it. And then he offered it the third time. He put it the third time by, and still 243 as he refused it the rabblement hooted and clapped 244 their chapped hands, and threw up their sweaty night- 245 caps, and uttered such a deal of stinking breath be- 246 cause Caesar refused the crown that it had almost choked Caesar, for he swooned and fell down at it. And for mine own part I durst not laugh for fear of opening my lips and receiving the bad air.

CASSIUS
But soft, I pray you. What, did Caesar swoon? 251

CASCA He fell down in the marketplace, and foamed at mouth, and was speechless.

BRUTUS
'Tis very like. He hath the falling sickness. 254

CASSIUS
No, Caesar hath it not, but you and I,
And honest Casca, we have the falling sickness.

CASCA I know not what you mean by that, but I am sure Caesar fell down. If the tag-rag people did not 258 clap him and hiss him, according as he pleased and displeased them, as they use to do the players in the 260 theater, I am no true man. 261

BRUTUS
What said he when he came unto himself?

CASCA Marry, before he fell down, when he perceived the common herd was glad he refused the crown, he plucked me ope his doublet and offered them his throat 265 to cut. An I had been a man of any occupation, if I 266 would not have taken him at a word, I would I might go to hell among the rogues. And so he fell. When he came to himself again, he said if he had done or said anything amiss, he desired Their Worships to think it was his infirmity. Three or four wenches where I stood cried, "Alas, good soul!" and forgave him with all their hearts. But there's no heed to be taken of them; if Caesar had stabbed their mothers they would have done no less.

BRUTUS
And after that, he came thus sad away? 276

CASCA Ay.

CASSIUS Did Cicero say anything?

CASCA Ay, he spoke Greek.

CASSIUS To what effect?

CASCA Nay, an I tell you that, I'll ne'er look you i'th' face again. But those that understood him smiled at one another and shook their heads; but, for mine own part, it was Greek to me. I could tell you more news too. Marullus and Flavius, for pulling scarves off Cae- 285 sar's images, are put to silence. Fare you well. There 286 was more foolery yet, if I could remember it.

CASSIUS Will you sup with me tonight, Casca?

CASCA No, I am promised forth. 289

CASSIUS Will you dine with me tomorrow?

CASCA Ay, if I be alive, and your mind hold, and your dinner worth the eating.

CASSIUS Good. I will expect you.

CASCA Do so. Farewell both. *Exit.*

BRUTUS
What a blunt fellow is this grown to be!
He was quick mettle when he went to school. 296

CASSIUS
So is he now in execution
Of any bold or noble enterprise,
However he puts on this tardy form. 299
This rudeness is a sauce to his good wit, 300
Which gives men stomach to digest his words 301
With better appetite.

BRUTUS
And so it is. For this time I will leave you.
Tomorrow, if you please to speak with me,
I will come home to you; or, if you will,
Come home to me, and I will wait for you.

CASSIUS
I will do so. Till then, think of the world. 307
Exit Brutus.

Well, Brutus, thou art noble. Yet I see
Thy honorable mettle may be wrought 309
From that it is disposed. Therefore it is meet 310
That noble minds keep ever with their likes;
For who so firm that cannot be seduced?
Caesar doth bear me hard, but he loves Brutus. 313
If I were Brutus now, and he were Cassius,
He should not humor me. I will this night 315
In several hands in at his windows throw, 316
As if they came from several citizens,
Writings, all tending to the great opinion

---

285 **scarves** decorations, festoons 286 **put to silence** dismissed from office. (So reported in Plutarch. Shakespeare's wording ominously suggests that they were executed.) 289 **promised forth** engaged to dine out. 296 **quick mettle** of a lively temperament 299 **However** however much. **tardy form** air of ennui and disengagement. 300 **rudeness** rough manner. **wit** intellect 301 **stomach** appetite, inclination 307 **the world** i.e., the state of the world. 309 **mettle** (As often, the word combines the senses of *mettle*, "temperament," and *metal*, "substance." The latter meaning continues here in the chemical metaphor of metal that is *wrought* or transmuted. As *honorable mettle* [or noble metal], gold cannot be transmuted into base substances, and yet Cassius proposes to do just that with Brutus. Compare this with 1.1.61.) 309–10 **wrought . . . disposed** turned away from its natural disposition. 310 **meet** fitting 313 **doth . . . hard** bears me a grudge and keeps me on a short rein 315 **He . . . humor me** i.e., I wouldn't put up with being cajoled or humored. (*He* could refer to Caesar or Brutus.) 316 **several hands** different handwritings

---

238 **coronets** chaplets, garlands 240 **fain** gladly 243–4 **still as** whenever 245–6 **nightcaps** (Scornful allusion to the *pilleus*, a felt cap worn by the plebeians on festival days.) 251 **soft** i.e., wait a minute 254 **like** likely. **falling sickness** epilepsy. (But Cassius takes it to mean "falling into servitude.") 258 **tag-rag** ragtag, riffraff 260 **use** are accustomed 261 **true** honest 265 **plucked me ope** pulled open. (*Me* is used colloquially.) **doublet** Elizabethan upper garment, like a jacket 266 **An** If. **man . . . occupation** (1) working man (2) man of action 276 **sad** somberly

That Rome holds of his name, wherein obscurely
Caesar's ambition shall be glancèd at.   320
And after this let Caesar seat him sure,   321
For we will shake him, or worse days endure.   *Exit.*

[1.3]

Thunder and lightning. Enter, [meeting,] Casca
[with his sword drawn] and Cicero.

CICERO
Good even, Casca. Brought you Caesar home?   1
Why are you breathless? And why stare you so?
CASCA
Are not you moved, when all the sway of earth   3
Shakes like a thing unfirm? Oh, Cicero,
I have seen tempests when the scolding winds
Have rived the knotty oaks, and I have seen   6
Th'ambitious ocean swell and rage and foam
To be exalted with the threat'ning clouds;   8
But never till tonight, never till now,
Did I go through a tempest dropping fire.
Either there is a civil strife in heaven,
Or else the world, too saucy with the gods,   12
Incenses them to send destruction.
CICERO
Why, saw you anything more wonderful?   14
CASCA
A common slave—you know him well by sight—
Held up his left hand, which did flame and burn
Like twenty torches joined, and yet his hand,
Not sensible of fire, remained unscorched.   18
Besides—I ha' not since put up my sword—   19
Against the Capitol I met a lion,   20
Who glazed upon me and went surly by   21
Without annoying me. And there were drawn   22
Upon a heap a hundred ghastly women,   23
Transformèd with their fear, who swore they saw
Men all in fire walk up and down the streets.
And yesterday the bird of night did sit   26
Even at noonday upon the marketplace,
Hooting and shrieking. When these prodigies   28
Do so conjointly meet, let not men say,   29
"These are their reasons, they are natural,"
For I believe they are portentous things
Unto the climate that they point upon.   32
CICERO
Indeed, it is a strange-disposèd time.
But men may construe things after their fashion,   34

Clean from the purpose of the things themselves.   35
Comes Caesar to the Capitol tomorrow?
CASCA
He doth; for he did bid Antonio
Send word to you he would be there tomorrow.
CICERO
Good night then, Casca. This disturbèd sky
Is not to walk in.
CASCA   Farewell, Cicero.   *Exit Cicero.*

Enter Cassius.

CASSIUS
Who's there?
CASCA   A Roman.
CASSIUS   Casca, by your voice.
CASCA
Your ear is good. Cassius, what night is this!   42
CASSIUS
A very pleasing night to honest men.
CASCA
Who ever knew the heavens menace so?
CASSIUS
Those that have known the earth so full of faults.
For my part, I have walked about the streets,
Submitting me unto the perilous night,
And thus unbracèd, Casca, as you see,   48
Have bared my bosom to the thunder-stone;   49
And when the cross blue lightning seemed to open   50
The breast of heaven, I did present myself
Even in the aim and very flash of it.
CASCA
But wherefore did you so much tempt the heavens?
It is the part of men to fear and tremble   54
When the most mighty gods by tokens send   55
Such dreadful heralds to astonish us.   56
CASSIUS
You are dull, Casca, and those sparks of life
That should be in a Roman you do want,   58
Or else you use not. You look pale, and gaze,
And put on fear, and cast yourself in wonder,   60
To see the strange impatience of the heavens.
But if you would consider the true cause
Why all these fires, why all these gliding ghosts,
Why birds and beasts from quality and kind,   64
Why old men, fools, and children calculate,   65
Why all these things change from their ordinance,   66
Their natures, and preformèd faculties,   67
To monstrous quality—why, you shall find   68
That heaven hath infused them with these spirits
To make them instruments of fear and warning
Unto some monstrous state.   71

320 **glancèd** hinted   321 **seat him sure** seat himself securely in
power (i.e., watch out)
1.3 Location: A street.
1 **Brought** Escorted   3 **sway** established order   6 **rived** split
8 **exalted with** raised to the level of   12 **saucy** insolent   14 **more**
wonderful else that was wondrous.   18 **Not sensible of** not feeling
19 **put up** sheathed   20 **Against** in front of, opposite   21 **glazed**
stared glassily   22 **annoying** harming   22–3 **drawn . . . heap** hud-
dled together   23 **ghastly** pallid   26 **bird of night** owl, a bird of evil
omen   28 **prodigies** abnormalities, wonders   29 **conjointly meet**
coincide   32 **climate** region   34 **construe** interpret.   **after their**
fashion in their own way

35 **Clean . . . purpose** contrary to the actual import or meaning
42 **what night** what a night   48 **unbracèd** with doublet unfastened
49 **thunder-stone** thunderbolt   50 **cross** forked, jagged   54 **part**
appropriate role   55 **tokens** signs   56 **astonish** stun, terrify
58 **want** lack   60 **put on** adopt, show signs of.   **in wonder** into a
state of wonder   64 **from . . . kind** (behaving) contrary to their true
nature   65 **calculate** reckon, prophesy   66 **ordinance** established
nature   67 **preformèd** innate, congenital   68 **monstrous** unnatural
71 **Unto . . . state** pointing to some disorder in the commonwealth or
state of affairs.

Now could I, Casca, name to thee a man
Most like this dreadful night,
That thunders, lightens, opens graves, and roars
As doth the lion in the Capitol—
A man no mightier than thyself or me
In personal action, yet prodigious grown 77
And fearful, as these strange eruptions are. 78

CASCA
'Tis Caesar that you mean, is it not, Cassius?

CASSIUS
Let it be who it is. For Romans now
Have thews and limbs like to their ancestors'; 81
But, woe the while, our fathers' minds are dead, 82
And we are governed with our mothers' spirits.
Our yoke and sufferance show us womanish. 84

CASCA
Indeed, they say the senators tomorrow
Mean to establish Caesar as a king,
And he shall wear his crown by sea and land
In every place save here in Italy.

CASSIUS
I know where I will wear this dagger then;
Cassius from bondage will deliver Cassius.
Therein, ye gods, you make the weak most strong; 91
Therein, ye gods, you tyrants do defeat.
Nor stony tower, nor walls of beaten brass, 93
Nor airless dungeon, nor strong links of iron,
Can be retentive to the strength of spirit; 95
But life, being weary of these worldly bars, 96
Never lacks power to dismiss itself.
If I know this, know all the world besides, 98
That part of tyranny that I do bear
I can shake off at pleasure.   *Thunder still.*

CASCA   So can I. 100
So every bondman in his own hand bears
The power to cancel his captivity.

CASSIUS
And why should Caesar be a tyrant then?
Poor man, I know he would not be a wolf
But that he sees the Romans are but sheep;
He were no lion, were not Romans hinds. 106
Those that with haste will make a mighty fire
Begin it with weak straws. What trash is Rome,
What rubbish and what offal, when it serves 109
For the base matter to illuminate 110
So vile a thing as Caesar! But, O grief,
Where hast thou led me? I perhaps speak this
Before a willing bondman; then I know
My answer must be made. But I am armed, 114
And dangers are to me indifferent. 115

CASCA
You speak to Casca, and to such a man
That is no fleering telltale. Hold. My hand. 117
Be factious for redress of all these griefs, 118
And I will set this foot of mine as far
As who goes farthest.   [*They shake hands.*]

CASSIUS   There's a bargain made. 120
Now know you, Casca, I have moved already 121
Some certain of the noblest-minded Romans
To undergo with me an enterprise
Of honorable dangerous consequence;
And I do know by this they stay for me 125
In Pompey's porch. For now, this fearful night, 126
There is no stir or walking in the streets,
And the complexion of the element 128
In favor 's like the work we have in hand, 129
Most bloody, fiery, and most terrible.

        Enter Cinna.

CASCA
Stand close awhile, for here comes one in haste. 131

CASSIUS
'Tis Cinna; I do know him by his gait.
He is a friend.—Cinna, where haste you so?

CINNA
To find out you. Who's that? Metellus Cimber?

CASSIUS
No, it is Casca, one incorporate 135
To our attempts. Am I not stayed for, Cinna?

CINNA
I am glad on't. What a fearful night is this! 137
There's two or three of us have seen strange sights.

CASSIUS Am I not stayed for? Tell me.

CINNA
Yes, you are. Oh, Cassius, if you could
But win the noble Brutus to our party—

CASSIUS
Be you content. Good Cinna, take this paper, 142
                  [*giving papers*]
And look you lay it in the praetor's chair, 143
Where Brutus may but find it. And throw this 144
In at his window. Set this up with wax
Upon old Brutus' statue. All this done, 146
Repair to Pompey's porch, where you shall find us. 147
Is Decius Brutus and Trebonius there?

CINNA
All but Metellus Cimber, and he's gone

---

77 **prodigious** ominous   78 **fearful** inspiring fear   81 **thews** sinews, muscles   82 **woe the while** alas for the age   84 **yoke and sufferance** patience under the yoke   91 **Therein** i.e., In the ability to commit suicide   93 **Nor** Neither   95 **Can . . . spirit** can confine a resolute spirit   96 **bars** (1) prison bars (2) burdens (such as tyranny)   98 **know . . . besides** let the rest of the world know   100 s.d. *Thunder still* Continuous thunder.   106 **were** would be.   **hinds** (1) female of the red deer (2) servants, menials.   109 **offal** refuse, wood shavings   110 **matter** i.e., fuel   114 **My answer . . . made** I will have to answer (to Caesar) for what I have said.   **armed** (1) provided with weapons (2) morally fortified   115 **indifferent** unimportant.

117 **fleering** fawning; scornful.   **Hold. My hand** Enough; here is my hand.   118 **factious** active as a partisan.   **griefs** grievances   120 **who** whoever   121 **moved** urged   125 **by this** by this time.   **stay** wait   126 **Pompey's porch** the colonnade of Pompey's great open theater, dedicated in 55 B.C. (Caesar was assassinated there, though Shakespeare has the assassination take place in the Capitol [i.e., the Senate chamber].)   128 **element** sky   129 **favor 's** appearance is   131 **close** concealed, still   135 **incorporate** admitted as a member   137 **on't** of it.   142 **Be you content** Set your mind at rest.   143 **praetor's chair** official seat of a praetor, Roman magistrate ranking next below the consul. (Brutus was praetor, one of sixteen.)   144 **Where . . . it** where Brutus cannot help finding it.   146 **old Brutus** (Lucius Junius Brutus; Brutus was reputed to be his descendant.)   147 **Repair** proceed. (Also in line 152.)

To seek you at your house. Well, I will hie,   150
And so bestow these papers as you bade me.

CASSIUS
That done, repair to Pompey's theater.   *Exit Cinna.*
Come, Casca, you and I will yet ere day
See Brutus at his house. Three parts of him   154
Is ours already, and the man entire
Upon the next encounter yields him ours.

CASCA
Oh, he sits high in all the people's hearts;
And that which would appear offense in us,   158
His countenance, like richest alchemy,   159
Will change to virtue and to worthiness.   160

CASSIUS
Him and his worth, and our great need of him,
You have right well conceited. Let us go,   162
For it is after midnight, and ere day
We will awake him and be sure of him.   *Exeunt.*

❖

2.1

Enter Brutus in his orchard.

BRUTUS   What, Lucius, ho!—
I cannot by the progress of the stars
Give guess how near to day.—Lucius, I say!—
I would it were my fault to sleep so soundly.—
When, Lucius, when? Awake, I say! What, Lucius!   5

Enter Lucius.

LUCIUS   Called you, my lord?
BRUTUS
Get me a taper in my study, Lucius.   7
When it is lighted, come and call me here.
LUCIUS   I will, my lord.   *Exit.*
BRUTUS
It must be by his death. And for my part
I know no personal cause to spurn at him,   11
But for the general. He would be crowned.   12
How that might change his nature, there's the
        question.
It is the bright day that brings forth the adder,
And that craves wary walking. Crown him—that—   15
And then I grant we put a sting in him
That at his will he may do danger with.
Th'abuse of greatness is when it disjoins
Remorse from power. And to speak truth of Caesar,   19

I have not known when his affections swayed   20
More than his reason. But 'tis a common proof   21
That lowliness is young ambition's ladder,   22
Whereto the climber-upward turns his face;
But when he once attains the upmost round   24
He then unto the ladder turns his back,
Looks in the clouds, scorning the base degrees   26
By which he did ascend. So Caesar may.
Then, lest he may, prevent. And since the quarrel
Will bear no color for the thing he is,   29
Fashion it thus: that what he is, augmented,   30
Would run to these and these extremities;
And therefore think him as a serpent's egg
Which, hatched, would, as his kind, grow
        mischievous;   33
And kill him in the shell.

Enter Lucius.

LUCIUS
The taper burneth in your closet, sir.   35
Searching the window for a flint, I found
This paper, thus sealed up, and I am sure
It did not lie there when I went to bed.
        Gives him the letter.
BRUTUS
Get you to bed again. It is not day.
Is not tomorrow, boy, the ides of March?   40
LUCIUS   I know not, sir.
BRUTUS
Look in the calendar and bring me word.
LUCIUS   I will, sir.   *Exit.*
BRUTUS
The exhalations whizzing in the air   44
Give so much light that I may read by them.
        Opens the letter and reads.
"Brutus, thou sleep'st. Awake, and see thyself!
Shall Rome, etc. Speak, strike, redress!"
"Brutus, thou sleep'st. Awake!"
Such instigations have been often dropped
Where I have took them up.
"Shall Rome, etc." Thus must I piece it out:
Shall Rome stand under one man's awe? What, Rome?
My ancestors did from the streets of Rome
The Tarquin drive, when he was called a king.
"Speak, strike, redress!" Am I entreated
To speak and strike? O Rome, I make thee promise,
If the redress will follow, thou receivest   57
Thy full petition at the hand of Brutus.   58

Enter Lucius.

LUCIUS   Sir, March is wasted fifteen days.
        Knock within.

150 **hie** go quickly   154 **parts** i.e., quarters   158–60 **that which . . . worthiness** his endorsement and honorable name will convert into virtue and worthiness those things in our conspiracy that would otherwise seem offensive, just as alchemy is supposed to transform base metals into richest gold.   162 **conceited** (1) conceived, grasped (2) expressed in a figure.
2.1. Location: Rome. Brutus' orchard, or garden.
5 **When** (An exclamation of impatience.)   7 **Get . . . taper** Put a candle for me   11 **spurn** kick   12 **general** general cause, common good.
15 **craves** requires.   **that** that is the issue   19 **Remorse** scruple, compassion

20 **affections swayed** passions ruled   21 **proof** experience   22 **lowliness** pretended humbleness   24 **round** rung   26 **base degrees** (1) lower rungs (2) persons of lower social station   29 **Will . . . is** can carry no appearance of justice so far as his conduct to date is concerned   30 **Fashion it** put the matter   33 **as his kind** according to its nature.   **mischievous** harmful   35 **closet** private chamber, study   40 **ides** fifteenth day   44 **exhalations** meteors   57 **If . . . follow** i.e., if striking Caesar will lead to the reform of grievances   58 **at** from

BRUTUS
    'Tis good. Go to the gate; somebody knocks.
                                                 [Exit Lucius.]
    Since Cassius first did whet me against Caesar,
    I have not slept.
    Between the acting of a dreadful thing
    And the first motion, all the interim is   64
    Like a phantasma or a hideous dream.   65
    The genius and the mortal instruments   66
    Are then in council; and the state of man,   67
    Like to a little kingdom, suffers then
    The nature of an insurrection.   69

              Enter Lucius.

LUCIUS
    Sir, 'tis your brother Cassius at the door,   70
    Who doth desire to see you.
BRUTUS   Is he alone?
LUCIUS
    No, sir. There are more with him.
BRUTUS   Do you know them?
LUCIUS
    No, sir. Their hats are plucked about their ears,
    And half their faces buried in their cloaks,
    That by no means I may discover them   75
    By any mark of favor.
BRUTUS   Let 'em enter.   *[Exit Lucius.]* 76
    They are the faction. O conspiracy,
    Sham'st thou to show thy dangerous brow by night,
    When evils are most free? Oh, then, by day   79
    Where wilt thou find a cavern dark enough
    To mask thy monstrous visage? Seek none,
        conspiracy!
    Hide it in smiles and affability;
    For if thou put thy native semblance on,
    Not Erebus itself were dim enough   84
    To hide thee from prevention.   85

        Enter the conspirators, Cassius, Casca, Decius,
        Cinna, Metellus [Cimber] , and Trebonius.

CASSIUS
    I think we are too bold upon your rest.   86
    Good morrow, Brutus. Do we trouble you?
BRUTUS
    I have been up this hour, awake all night.
    Know I these men that come along with you?
CASSIUS
    Yes, every man of them, and no man here
    But honors you; and every one doth wish
    You had but that opinion of yourself

    Which every noble Roman bears of you.
    This is Trebonius.
BRUTUS   He is welcome hither.
CASSIUS
    This, Decius Brutus.
BRUTUS   He is welcome too.
CASSIUS
    This, Casca; this, Cinna; and this, Metellus Cimber.
BRUTUS   They are all welcome.
    What watchful cares do interpose themselves   98
    Betwixt your eyes and night?
CASSIUS   Shall I entreat a word?
              They [Brutus and Cassius] whisper.
DECIUS
    Here lies the east. Doth not the day break here? 101
CASCA   No.
CINNA
    Oh, pardon, sir, it doth; and yon gray lines
    That fret the clouds are messengers of day.   104
CASCA
    You shall confess that you are both deceived.   105
    Here, as I point my sword, the sun arises,
    Which is a great way growing on the south,   107
    Weighing the youthful season of the year.   108
    Some two months hence, up higher toward the north
    He first presents his fire; and the high east   110
    Stands, as the Capitol, directly here.
BRUTUS *[coming forward]*
    Give me your hands all over, one by one.   112
CASSIUS
    And let us swear our resolution.
BRUTUS
    No, not an oath. If not the face of men,   114
    The sufferance of our souls, the time's abuse— 115
    If these be motives weak, break off betimes, 116
    And every man hence to his idle bed;   117
    So let high-sighted tyranny range on   118
    Till each man drop by lottery. But if these, 119
    As I am sure they do, bear fire enough
    To kindle cowards and to steel with valor   121
    The melting spirits of women, then, countrymen,
    What need we any spur but our own cause
    To prick us to redress? What other bond   124
    Than secret Romans that have spoke the word 125
    And will not palter? And what other oath   126
    Than honesty to honesty engaged   127
    That this shall be or we will fall for it?

---

64 **motion** proposal or impulse   65 **phantasma** hallucination
66–7 The genius . . . council The tutelary god or attendant spirit allotted to every person at birth is then intensely at debate with the person's physical faculties and passionate nature   69 **The nature of an** a kind of   70 **brother** i.e., brother-in-law. (Cassius had married a sister of Brutus.)   75 **discover** identify   76 **favor** appearance.   79 **free** free to roam at will.   84 **Erebus** primeval Darkness (sprung, according to Hesiod, from Chaos and his sister Night)   85 **prevention** detection and being forestalled.   86 **upon** in intruding upon

98 **watchful cares** sleep-preventing worries   101 **Here** (Decius points eastward.)   104 **fret** mark with interlacing lines   105 **deceived** mistaken.   107 **growing** encroaching   108 **Weighing** considering, in consequence of   110 **high** due   112 **all over** one and all   114–16 **If . . . betimes** If the gravely serious faces of Romans, the suffering we feel, the corruptions of the present day are insufficient to move us, we should break off at once   117 **idle** (1) unused (2) in which men are idle   118 **high-sighted** upward-gazing (compare with 2.1.26); or haughty, looking down from on high   119 **by lottery** i.e., as the capricious tyrant chances to pick on him. **these** i.e., these injustices just cited   121 **cowards** even cowards. **steel** harden   124 **prick** spur   125 **Than . . . word** than the word of Romans who, having given their word of honor, will remain secret   126 **palter** shift position evasively.   127 **honesty** personal honor

Swear priests and cowards and men cautelous,   129
Old feeble carrions, and such suffering souls   130
That welcome wrongs; unto bad causes swear   131
Such creatures as men doubt. But do not stain   132
The even virtue of our enterprise,   133
Nor th'insuppressive mettle of our spirits,   134
To think that or our cause or our performance   135
Did need an oath, when every drop of blood
That every Roman bears—and nobly bears—
Is guilty of a several bastardy   138
If he do break the smallest particle
Of any promise that hath passed from him.

CASSIUS
But what of Cicero? Shall we sound him?   141
I think he will stand very strong with us.

CASCA
Let us not leave him out.

CINNA   No, by no means.

METELLUS
Oh, let us have him, for his silver hairs
Will purchase us a good opinion   145
And buy men's voices to commend our deeds.
It shall be said his judgment ruled our hands;
Our youths and wildness shall no whit appear,
But all be buried in his gravity.

BRUTUS
Oh, name him not. Let us not break with him,   150
For he will never follow anything
That other men begin.

CASSIUS   Then leave him out.

CASCA   Indeed he is not fit.

DECIUS
Shall no man else be touched but only Caesar?

CASSIUS
Decius, well urged. I think it is not meet   156
Mark Antony, so well beloved of Caesar,
Should outlive Caesar. We shall find of him   158
A shrewd contriver; and you know his means,   159
If he improve them, may well stretch so far   160
As to annoy us all. Which to prevent,   161
Let Antony and Caesar fall together.

BRUTUS
Our course will seem too bloody, Caius Cassius,
To cut the head off and then hack the limbs,
Like wrath in death and envy afterwards;   165
For Antony is but a limb of Caesar.
Let's be sacrificers, but not butchers, Caius.
We all stand up against the spirit of Caesar,
And in the spirit of men there is no blood.

Oh, that we then could come by Caesar's spirit
And not dismember Caesar! But, alas,
Caesar must bleed for it. And, gentle friends,   172
Let's kill him boldly, but not wrathfully;
Let's carve him as a dish fit for the gods,
Not hew him as a carcass fit for hounds.
And let our hearts, as subtle masters do,
Stir up their servants to an act of rage   177
And after seem to chide 'em. This shall make
Our purpose necessary, and not envious;   179
Which so appearing to the common eyes,
We shall be called purgers, not murderers.   181
And for Mark Antony, think not of him;   182
For he can do no more than Caesar's arm
When Caesar's head is off.

CASSIUS   Yet I fear him,
For in the engrafted love he bears to Caesar—   185

BRUTUS
Alas, good Cassius, do not think of him.
If he love Caesar, all that he can do
Is to himself—take thought and die for Caesar.   188
And that were much he should, for he is given   189
To sports, to wildness, and much company.

TREBONIUS
There is no fear in him. Let him not die,   191
For he will live, and laugh at this hereafter.   192
                                                        Clock strikes.

BRUTUS
Peace! Count the clock.

CASSIUS   The clock hath stricken three.

TREBONIUS
'Tis time to part.

CASSIUS   But it is doubtful yet
Whether Caesar will come forth today or no;
For he is superstitious grown of late,
Quite from the main opinion he held once
Of fantasy, of dreams, and ceremonies.   198
It may be these apparent prodigies,   199
The unaccustomed terror of this night,
And the persuasion of his augurers   201
May hold him from the Capitol today.

DECIUS
Never fear that. If he be so resolved,
I can o'ersway him; for he loves to hear
That unicorns may be betrayed with trees,   205
And bears with glasses, elephants with holes,   206
Lions with toils, and men with flatterers;   207

129–32 **Swear . . . doubt** Let priests and cowards and shifty old men tottering on the brink of the grave swear oaths, and long-suffering souls that submit supinely to wrongs; it is contemptible, untrustworthy persons like these who swear oaths to bad causes.   133 **even** steadfast, consistent   134 **insuppressive** indomitable   135 **or . . . or** either . . . or   138 **a several bastardy** an individual act unworthy of his parentage   141 **sound him** sound him out.   145 **purchase** procure. (Playing on the financial sense of *silver,* line 144.)   150 **break with** confide in   156 **meet** fitting   158 **of** in   159 **shrewd** malicious; artful   160 **improve** exploit, make good use of   161 **annoy** injure   165 **envy** malice

172 **gentle** noble   177 **their servants** i.e., our hands   179 **envious** malicious   181 **purgers** those who heal by bleeding the patient   182 **for** as for   185 **engrafted** firmly implanted   188 **take thought** give way to melancholy   189 **much he should** more than is to be expected of him, hence unlikely; or, eminently desirable   191 **no fear** nothing to fear   192.1 *Clock strikes* (An anachronism much commented upon; the mechanical clock was not invented until c. 1300.)   198 **fantasy** imaginings.   **ceremonies** omens drawn from the performance of some rite.   199 **apparent** manifest, both visible and obvious   201 **augurers** augurs, official interpreters of omens   205 **unicorns . . . trees** i.e., by having the unicorn imprison itself by driving its horn into a tree as it charges at the hunter   206 **glasses** mirrors (enabling the hunter to approach the bear while it dazzles itself in the mirror).   **holes** pitfalls   207 **toils** nets, snares

But when I tell him he hates flatterers,
He says he does, being then most flattered.
Let me work;
For I can give his humor the true bent,   211
And I will bring him to the Capitol.
CASSIUS
Nay, we will all of us be there to fetch him.
BRUTUS
By the eighth hour. Is that the uttermost?   214
CINNA
Be that the uttermost, and fail not then.
METELLUS
Caius Ligarius doth bear Caesar hard,   216
Who rated him for speaking well of Pompey.   217
I wonder none of you have thought of him.
BRUTUS
Now, good Metellus, go along by him.   219
He loves me well, and I have given him reasons;
Send him but hither, and I'll fashion him.   221
CASSIUS
The morning comes upon 's. We'll leave you, Brutus.
And, friends, disperse yourselves; but all remember
What you have said, and show yourselves true
      Romans.
BRUTUS
Good gentlemen, look fresh and merrily;
Let not our looks put on our purposes,   226
But bear it as our Roman actors do,
With untired spirits and formal constancy.   228
And so good morrow to you every one.   229
                          Exeunt. Manet Brutus.
Boy! Lucius!—Fast asleep? It is no matter.   230
Enjoy the honey-heavy dew of slumber.
Thou hast no figures nor no fantasies   232
Which busy care draws in the brains of men;   233
Therefore thou sleep'st so sound.

            Enter Portia.

PORTIA   Brutus, my lord!
BRUTUS
Portia, what mean you? Wherefore rise you now?
It is not for your health thus to commit
Your weak condition to the raw cold morning.
PORTIA
Nor for yours neither. You've ungently, Brutus,   238
Stole from my bed. And yesternight, at supper,
You suddenly arose, and walked about
Musing and sighing, with your arms across,   241

And when I asked you what the matter was,
You stared upon me with ungentle looks.
I urged you further; then you scratched your head
And too impatiently stamped with your foot.
Yet I insisted, yet you answered not,   246
But with an angry wafture of your hand   247
Gave sign for me to leave you. So I did,
Fearing to strengthen that impatience
Which seemed too much enkindled, and withal   250
Hoping it was but an effect of humor,   251
Which sometime hath his hour with every man.   252
It will not let you eat, nor talk, nor sleep,
And could it work so much upon your shape
As it hath much prevailed on your condition,   255
I should not know you Brutus. Dear my lord,   256
Make me acquainted with your cause of grief.
BRUTUS
I am not well in health, and that is all.
PORTIA
Brutus is wise, and were he not in health
He would embrace the means to come by it.
BRUTUS
Why, so I do. Good Portia, go to bed.   261
PORTIA
Is Brutus sick? And is it physical   262
To walk unbracèd and suck up the humors   263
Of the dank morning? What, is Brutus sick,
And will he steal out of his wholesome bed
To dare the vile contagion of the night,
And tempt the rheumy and unpurgèd air   267
To add unto his sickness? No, my Brutus,
You have some sick offense within your mind,
Which by the right and virtue of my place
I ought to know of. [*She kneels.*] And upon my knees
I charm you, by my once-commended beauty,   272
By all your vows of love, and that great vow
Which did incorporate and make us one,
That you unfold to me, your self, your half,
Why you are heavy, and what men tonight   276
Have had resort to you; for here have been
Some six or seven, who did hide their faces
Even from darkness.
BRUTUS   Kneel not, gentle Portia.
                                     [*He raises her.*]
PORTIA
I should not need if you were gentle Brutus.
Within the bond of marriage, tell me, Brutus,
Is it excepted I should know no secrets   282
That appertain to you? Am I your self
But as it were in sort or limitation,   284

---

211 humor disposition **214 the eighth hour** i.e., 8 A.M. (The Elizabethan way of reckoning time. By Roman reckoning, the day began at
6 A.M., so that *the eighth hour* would be 2 P.M.) **uttermost** latest.
216 bear Caesar hard bear a grudge toward Caesar. (See 1.2.313n.)
217 rated rebuked **219 by him** by way of his house. **221 fashion**
shape (to our purposes) **226 put on** display, wear in open view
228 formal constancy steadfast appearance, decorum. **229.1** *Manet*
He remains onstage **230 Lucius** (Brutus calls to his servant, who is
evidently within, asleep, after having admitted the conspirators at
line 85; later, at line 310, he is still within when Brutus calls to him.)
232 figures imaginings **233 care** anxiety **238 ungently** discourte-
ously, unkindly **241 across** folded. (A sign of melancholy.)

246 Yet . . . yet Still . . . still **247 wafture** waving **250 withal** moreover **251 humor** imbalance of temperament **252 his** its **255 condition** inner state of mind **256 know you** recognize you as **261 so I
do** (Said with a double meaning not perceived by Portia: I seek
through Caesar's death the means to better the health of the state.)
262 physical healthful **263 unbracèd** with loosened clothing.
humors damps, mists **267 rheumy and unpurgèd** conducive to illness and not cleansed of its impurities (which night air was thought to
contain) **272 charm** conjure, entreat **276 heavy** sad **282 excepted**
made an exception that **284 in . . . limitation** only up to a point. (A
legal phrase.)

To keep with you at meals, comfort your bed,   285
And talk to you sometimes? Dwell I but in the suburbs 286
Of your good pleasure? If it be no more,
Portia is Brutus' harlot, not his wife.

BRUTUS
You are my true and honorable wife,
As dear to me as are the ruddy drops
That visit my sad heart.

PORTIA
If this were true, then should I know this secret.
I grant I am a woman, but withal   293
A woman that Lord Brutus took to wife.
I grant I am a woman, but withal
A woman well reputed, Cato's daughter.   296
Think you I am no stronger than my sex,
Being so fathered and so husbanded?
Tell me your counsels, I will not disclose 'em.   299
I have made strong proof of my constancy,
Giving myself a voluntary wound
Here, in the thigh. Can I bear that with patience,
And not my husband's secrets?

BRUTUS   O ye gods,
Render me worthy of this noble wife!

Knock [within].

Hark, hark, one knocks. Portia, go in awhile,
And by and by thy bosom shall partake
The secrets of my heart.
All my engagements I will construe to thee,   308
All the charactery of my sad brows.   309
Leave me with haste.   *Exit Portia.*
    [*Calling*]   Lucius, who's that knocks?

Enter Lucius and [Caius] Ligarius [wearing a kerchief].

LUCIUS
Here is a sick man that would speak with you.   311

BRUTUS
Caius Ligarius, that Metellus spake of.
Boy, stand aside.   [*Exit Lucius.*]
        Caius Ligarius, how?   313

LIGARIUS
Vouchsafe good morrow from a feeble tongue.   314

BRUTUS
Oh, what a time have you chose out, brave Caius,   315
To wear a kerchief! Would you were not sick!

LIGARIUS
I am not sick, if Brutus have in hand
Any exploit worthy the name of honor.

BRUTUS
Such an exploit have I in hand, Ligarius,

---

285 **keep** stay, be   286 **suburbs** periphery. (In Elizabethan London, prostitutes frequented the suburbs.)   293 **withal** in addition 296 **Cato's daughter** (Cato the Younger of Utica was famous for his integrity; he sided with Pompey against Caesar in 48 B.C. and later killed himself rather than submit to Caesar's tyranny. He was Brutus's uncle as well as his father-in-law.)   299 **counsels** secrets   308 **construe** explain fully   309 **charactery** handwriting, i.e., what is figured there 311 **sick man** (In Elizabethan medicine, a poultice was often applied to the forehead of a patient and wrapped in a handkerchief; hence the kerchief in line 316.)   313 **how?** i.e., how are you?   314 **Vouchsafe** Deign (to accept)   315 **brave** noble

---

Had you a healthful ear to hear of it.

LIGARIUS
By all the gods that Romans bow before,
I here discard my sickness! [*He throws off his kerchief.*]
            Soul of Rome!
Brave son, derived from honorable loins!
Thou like an exorcist hast conjured up
My mortifièd spirit. Now bid me run,   325
And I will strive with things impossible,
Yea, get the better of them. What's to do?

BRUTUS
A piece of work that will make sick men whole.   328

LIGARIUS
But are not some whole that we must make sick?

BRUTUS
That must we also. What it is, my Caius,
I shall unfold to thee as we are going
To whom it must be done.

LIGARIUS   Set on your foot,   332
And with a heart new-fired I follow you
To do I know not what; but it sufficeth
That Brutus leads me on.   *Thunder.*

BRUTUS   Follow me, then.   *Exeunt.*

❖

[2.2]

Thunder and lightning. Enter Julius Caesar, in his nightgown.

CAESAR
Nor heaven nor earth have been at peace tonight.   1
Thrice hath Calpurnia in her sleep cried out,
"Help, ho, they murder Caesar!"—Who's within?

Enter a Servant.

SERVANT   My lord?

CAESAR
Go bid the priests do present sacrifice   5
And bring me their opinions of success.   6

SERVANT   I will, my lord.   *Exit.*

Enter Calpurnia.

CALPURNIA
What mean you, Caesar? Think you to walk forth?
You shall not stir out of your house today.

CAESAR
Caesar shall forth. The things that threatened me
Ne'er looked but on my back. When they shall see
The face of Caesar, they are vanishèd.

CALPURNIA
Caesar, I never stood on ceremonies,   13

---

325 **mortifièd** deadened   328 **whole** healthy, i.e., free of the disease of tyranny.   332 **To whom** i.e., to him to whom
2.2 Location: Caesar's house.
0.2 **nightgown** housecoat.   1 **Nor** Neither   5 **present sacrifice** immediate examination of the entrails of sacrificed animals for omens
6 **success** the result, what will follow.   13 **stood on ceremonies** attached importance to omens

Yet now they fright me. There is one within,
Besides the things that we have heard and seen,
Recounts most horrid sights seen by the watch. 16
A lioness hath whelpèd in the streets, 17
And graves have yawned and yielded up their dead. 18
Fierce fiery warriors fight upon the clouds
In ranks and squadrons and right form of war, 20
Which drizzled blood upon the Capitol.
The noise of battle hurtled in the air; 22
Horses did neigh, and dying men did groan,
And ghosts did shriek and squeal about the streets.
Oh, Caesar, these things are beyond all use, 25
And I do fear them.

CAESAR   What can be avoided
Whose end is purposed by the mighty gods?
Yet Caesar shall go forth; for these predictions
Are to the world in general as to Caesar.

CALPURNIA
When beggars die there are no comets seen;
The heavens themselves blaze forth the death of
      princes. 31

CAESAR
Cowards die many times before their deaths;
The valiant never taste of death but once.
Of all the wonders that I yet have heard,
It seems to me most strange that men should fear,
Seeing that death, a necessary end,
Will come when it will come.

Enter a Servant.

                     What say the augurers?

SERVANT
They would not have you to stir forth today.
Plucking the entrails of an offering forth,
They could not find a heart within the beast.

CAESAR
The gods do this in shame of cowardice.
Caesar should be a beast without a heart
If he should stay at home today for fear.
No, Caesar shall not. Danger knows full well
That Caesar is more dangerous than he.
We are two lions littered in one day,
And I the elder and more terrible;
And Caesar shall go forth.

CALPURNIA   Alas, my lord,
Your wisdom is consumed in confidence. 49
Do not go forth today! Call it my fear
That keeps you in the house, and not your own.
We'll send Mark Antony to the Senate House,
And he shall say you are not well today.
Let me, upon my knee, prevail in this.   [*She kneels.*]

CAESAR
Mark Antony shall say I am not well,

And for thy humor I will stay at home. 56

                     [*He raises her.*]

      Enter Decius.

Here's Decius Brutus. He shall tell them so.
DECIUS
Caesar, all hail! Good morrow, worthy Caesar.
I come to fetch you to the Senate House.
CAESAR
And you are come in very happy time 60
To bear my greeting to the senators
And tell them that I will not come today.
Cannot is false, and that I dare not, falser;
I will not come today. Tell them so, Decius.
CALPURNIA
Say he is sick.
CAESAR   Shall Caesar send a lie?
Have I in conquest stretched mine arm so far
To be afeard to tell graybeards the truth?
Decius, go tell them Caesar will not come.
DECIUS
Most mighty Caesar, let me know some cause,
Lest I be laughed at when I tell them so.
CAESAR
The cause is in my will: I will not come.
That is enough to satisfy the Senate.
But for your private satisfaction,
Because I love you, I will let you know.
Calpurnia here, my wife, stays me at home. 75
She dreamt tonight she saw my statue, 76
Which like a fountain with an hundred spouts
Did run pure blood; and many lusty Romans 78
Came smiling and did bathe their hands in it.
And these does she apply for warnings and portents 80
Of evils imminent, and on her knee
Hath begged that I will stay at home today.
DECIUS
This dream is all amiss interpreted;
It was a vision fair and fortunate.
Your statue spouting blood in many pipes,
In which so many smiling Romans bathed,
Signifies that from you great Rome shall suck
Reviving blood, and that great men shall press 88
For tinctures, stains, relics, and cognizance. 89
This by Calpurnia's dream is signified.
CAESAR
And this way have you well expounded it.
DECIUS
I have, when you have heard what I can say;
And know it now. The Senate have concluded
To give this day a crown to mighty Caesar.
If you shall send them word you will not come,

---

16 **watch** (An anachronism, since there was no *watch*, or "body of night watchmen," in Caesar's Rome.)   17 **whelpèd** given birth
18 **yawned** gaped   20 **right form** regular formation   22 **hurtled** clashed   25 **use** normal experience   31 **blaze forth** proclaim (in a blaze of light)   49 **consumed in confidence** destroyed by over-confidence.

56 **humor** whim   60 **happy** opportune   75 **stays** detains
76 **tonight** last night   78 **lusty** lively, merry   80 **apply for** interpret as   88 **press** crowd around   89 **tinctures** handkerchiefs dipped in the blood of martyrs, with healing powers; or colors in a coat of arms. (*Tinctures, stains,* and *relics* are all venerated properties, as though Caesar were a saint.)   **cognizance** heraldic emblems worn by a nobleman's followers.

Their minds may change. Besides, it were a mock   96
Apt to be rendered for someone to say   97
"Break up the Senate till another time
When Caesar's wife shall meet with better dreams."
If Caesar hide himself, shall they not whisper
"Lo, Caesar is afraid"?
Pardon me, Caesar, for my dear dear love
To your proceeding bids me tell you this,   103
And reason to my love is liable.   104

CAESAR
How foolish do your fears seem now, Calpurnia!
I am ashamèd I did yield to them.
Give me my robe, for I will go.

Enter Brutus, Ligarius, Metellus, Casca,
Trebonius, Cinna, and Publius.

And look where Publius is come to fetch me.
PUBLIUS
Good morrow, Caesar.
CAESAR   Welcome, Publius.
What, Brutus, are you stirred so early too?
Good morrow, Casca. Caius Ligarius,
Caesar was ne'er so much your enemy
As that same ague which hath made you lean.   113
What is't o'clock?
BRUTUS   Caesar, 'tis strucken eight.   114
CAESAR
I thank you for your pains and courtesy.

Enter Antony.

See, Antony, that revels long o' nights,
Is notwithstanding up. Good morrow, Antony.
ANTONY   So to most noble Caesar.
CAESAR [*to a Servant*]   Bid them prepare within.   119
                              [*Exit Servant.*]
I am to blame to be thus waited for.
Now, Cinna. Now, Metellus. What, Trebonius,
I have an hour's talk in store for you;
Remember that you call on me today.
Be near me, that I may remember you.
TREBONIUS
Caesar, I will. [*Aside*] And so near will I be
That your best friends shall wish I had been further.
CAESAR
Good friends, go in and taste some wine with me,
And we, like friends, will straightway go together.
BRUTUS [*aside*]
That every like is not the same, O Caesar,   129
The heart of Brutus earns to think upon!   *Exeunt.* 130

❧

96–7 mock . . . rendered sarcastic remark apt to be made   103 proceeding advantage   104 reason . . . liable my reasoning is swayed by
my affection.   113 ague fever   114 eight 8 A.M. (See 2.1.214n on
Roman time.)   119 prepare within i.e., set out wine in the other room
and prepare to leave. (Perhaps addressed to the servant who entered
at line 37, or to Calpurnia.) The ritual drinking of wine is a pledge of
friendship that should preclude violence; see lines 127–8.
129 That . . . same i.e., That not all those who behave "like friends"
(line 128) are actually so. (Proverbial.)   130 earns grieves

[2.3]

Enter Artemidorus [reading a paper].

ARTEMIDORUS   "Caesar, beware of Brutus; take heed of
Cassius; come not near Casca; have an eye to Cinna;
trust not Trebonius; mark well Metellus Cimber; De-
cius Brutus loves thee not; thou hast wronged Caius
Ligarius. There is but one mind in all these men, and
it is bent against Caesar. If thou be'st not immortal,
look about you. Security gives way to conspiracy. The   7
mighty gods defend thee! Thy lover,   8
                              Artemidorus."
Here will I stand till Caesar pass along,
And as a suitor will I give him this.
My heart laments that virtue cannot live
Out of the teeth of emulation.   13
If thou read this, O Caesar, thou mayest live;
If not, the Fates with traitors do contrive.   *Exit.* 15

❧

[2.4]

Enter Portia and Lucius.

PORTIA
I prithee, boy, run to the Senate House.
Stay not to answer me, but get thee gone.—
Why dost thou stay?
LUCIUS   To know my errand, madam.
PORTIA
I would have had thee there and here again
Ere I can tell thee what thou shouldst do there.
[*Aside*] O constancy, be strong upon my side;   6
Set a huge mountain 'tween my heart and tongue!
I have a man's mind, but a woman's might.
How hard it is for women to keep counsel!—   9
Art thou here yet?
LUCIUS   Madam, what should I do?
Run to the Capitol, and nothing else?
And so return to you, and nothing else?
PORTIA
Yes, bring me word, boy, if thy lord look well,
For he went sickly forth; and take good note
What Caesar doth, what suitors press to him.
Hark, boy, what noise is that?
LUCIUS   I hear none, madam.
PORTIA   Prithee, listen well.
I heard a bustling rumor, like a fray,   19
And the wind brings it from the Capitol.
LUCIUS   Sooth, madam, I hear nothing.   21

Enter the Soothsayer.

2.3 Location: A street near the Capitol.
7 Security gives way Overconfidence opens a path   8 lover friend
13 Out . . . emulation beyond the bite of grudging envy.   15 contrive
conspire.
2.4 Location: Before the house of Brutus.
6 constancy resolution   9 counsel a secret.   19 bustling rumor confused sound.   fray fight   21 Sooth Truly

PORTIA
Come hither, fellow. Which way hast thou been?
SOOTHSAYER   At mine own house, good lady.
PORTIA
What is't o'clock?
SOOTHSAYER   About the ninth hour, lady.   24
PORTIA
Is Caesar yet gone to the Capitol?
SOOTHSAYER
Madam, not yet. I go to take my stand,
To see him pass on to the Capitol.
PORTIA
Thou hast some suit to Caesar, hast thou not?
SOOTHSAYER
That I have, lady, if it will please Caesar
To be so good to Caesar as to hear me:
I shall beseech him to befriend himself.
PORTIA
Why, know'st thou any harm 's intended towards him?
SOOTHSAYER
None that I know will be, much that I fear may chance.
Good morrow to you. Here the street is narrow.
The throng that follows Caesar at the heels,
Of senators, of praetors, common suitors,   36
Will crowd a feeble man almost to death.
I'll get me to a place more void, and there   38
Speak to great Caesar as he comes along.   *Exit.*
PORTIA
I must go in. Ay me, how weak a thing
The heart of woman is! O Brutus,
The heavens speed thee in thine enterprise!—
Sure, the boy heard me.—Brutus hath a suit
That Caesar will not grant.—Oh, I grow faint.—
Run, Lucius, and commend me to my lord;
Say I am merry. Come to me again   46
And bring me word what he doth say to thee.
                                  Exeunt [separately].

❖

3.1

Flourish. Enter Caesar, Brutus, Cassius, Casca,
Decius, Metellus [Cimber], Trebonius, Cinna,
Antony, Lepidus, Artemidorus, Publius, [Popilius
Lena], and the Soothsayer; [others following].

CAESAR [*to the Soothsayer*]   The ides of March are come.
SOOTHSAYER   Ay, Caesar, but not gone.
ARTEMIDORUS   Hail, Caesar! Read this schedule.   3
DECIUS
Trebonius doth desire you to o'erread,

At your best leisure, this his humble suit.
ARTEMIDORUS
O Caesar, read mine first, for mine's a suit
That touches Caesar nearer. Read it, great Caesar.
CAESAR
What touches us ourself shall be last served.
ARTEMIDORUS
Delay not, Caesar, read it instantly.
CAESAR
What, is the fellow mad?
PUBLIUS   Sirrah, give place.   10
CASSIUS
What, urge you your petitions in the street?
Come to the Capitol.

     [*Caesar goes to the Capitol and takes his place, the*
     rest following.]

POPILIUS [*to Cassius*]
I wish your enterprise today may thrive.
CASSIUS   What enterprise, Popilius?
POPILIUS [*to Cassius*]   Fare you well.
                              [*He advances to Caesar.*]
BRUTUS   What said Popilius Lena?
CASSIUS
He wished today our enterprise might thrive.
I fear our purpose is discoverèd.
BRUTUS
Look how he makes to Caesar. Mark him.   19
                    [*Popilius speaks apart to Caesar.*]
CASSIUS
Casca, be sudden, for we fear prevention.
Brutus, what shall be done? If this be known,
Cassius or Caesar never shall turn back,   22
For I will slay myself.
BRUTUS   Cassius, be constant.   23
Popilius Lena speaks not of our purposes;
For look, he smiles, and Caesar doth not change.   25
CASSIUS
Trebonius knows his time, for look you, Brutus,
He draws Mark Antony out of the way.
                          [*Exit Trebonius with Antony.*]
DECIUS
Where is Metellus Cimber? Let him go
And presently prefer his suit to Caesar.   29
BRUTUS
He is addressed. Press near and second him.   30
CINNA
Casca, you are the first that rears your hand.
                              [*They press near Caesar.*]
CAESAR
Are we all ready? What is now amiss
That Caesar and his Senate must redress?

---

24 the ninth hour i.e., 9 A.M. (In Roman reckoning, the ninth hour
would be 3 P.M.)   **36 praetors** judges   **38 void** empty, uncrowded
46 merry cheerful. (Not "mirthful.")
3.1 Location: Before the Capitol, and, following line 12, within the
Capitol.
0.4 *others following* (Citizens may be present, though not certainly
so; see lines 83 and 93–4.)   **3 schedule** document.

10 Sirrah Fellow. (A form of address to a social inferior.)   **place** way.
19 makes to advances toward   **22–3 Cassius . . . myself** Either Cassius or Caesar will never return from the Capitol alive, for I will commit suicide if this attempt fails.   **23 be constant** hold steady.
25 change change expression.   **29 presently prefer** immediately urge
30 addressed ready.

METELLUS [*kneeling*]
   Most high, most mighty, and most puissant Caesar,   34
   Metellus Cimber throws before thy seat
   An humble heart—
CAESAR   I must prevent thee, Cimber.   36
   These couchings and these lowly courtesies   37
   Might fire the blood of ordinary men,   38
   And turn preordinance and first decree   39
   Into the law of children. Be not fond   40
   To think that Caesar bears such rebel blood   41
   That will be thawed from the true quality   42
   With that which melteth fools—I mean, sweet words,
   Low-crookèd curtsies, and base spaniel fawning.   44
   Thy brother by decree is banishèd.
   If thou dost bend and pray and fawn for him,   46
   I spurn thee like a cur out of my way.   47
   Know, Caesar doth not wrong, nor without cause
   Will he be satisfied.
METELLUS
   Is there no voice more worthy than my own
   To sound more sweetly in great Caesar's ear
   For the repealing of my banished brother?   52
BRUTUS [*kneeling*]
   I kiss thy hand, but not in flattery, Caesar,
   Desiring thee that Publius Cimber may
   Have an immediate freedom of repeal.   55
CAESAR
   What, Brutus?
CASSIUS [*kneeling*]   Pardon, Caesar! Caesar, pardon!
   As low as to thy foot doth Cassius fall,
   To beg enfranchisement for Publius Cimber.   58
CAESAR
   I could be well moved, if I were as you;
   If I could pray to move, prayers would move me.   60
   But I am constant as the northern star,   61
   Of whose true-fixed and resting quality   62
   There is no fellow in the firmament.   63
   The skies are painted with unnumbered sparks;
   They are all fire and every one doth shine;
   But there's but one in all doth hold his place.
   So in the world: 'tis furnished well with men,
   And men are flesh and blood, and apprehensive;   68
   Yet in the number I do know but one
   That unassailable holds on his rank,   70
   Unshaked of motion. And that I am he,   71
   Let me a little show it even in this:

   That I was constant Cimber should be banished,
   And constant do remain to keep him so.
CINNA [*kneeling*]
   O Caesar—
CAESAR   Hence! Wilt thou lift up Olympus?   75
DECIUS [*kneeling*]
   Great Caesar—
CAESAR   Doth not Brutus bootless kneel?   76
CASCA   Speak hands for me!
       They stab Caesar, [Casca first, Brutus last].
CAESAR   *Et tu, Brutè?* Then fall, Caesar!   *Dies.*   78
CINNA
   Liberty! Freedom! Tyranny is dead!
   Run hence, proclaim, cry it about the streets.
CASSIUS
   Some to the common pulpits, and cry out   81
   "Liberty, freedom, and enfranchisement!"   82
BRUTUS
   People and senators, be not affrighted.
   Fly not; stand still. Ambition's debt is paid.   84
CASCA
   Go to the pulpit, Brutus.
DECIUS   And Cassius too.
BRUTUS   Where's Publius?   86
CINNA
   Here, quite confounded with this mutiny.   87
METELLUS
   Stand fast together, lest some friend of Caesar's
   Should chance—
BRUTUS
   Talk not of standing. Publius, good cheer.   90
   There is no harm intended to your person,
   Nor to no Roman else. So tell them, Publius.
CASSIUS
   And leave us, Publius, lest that the people,
   Rushing on us, should do your age some mischief.
BRUTUS
   Do so, and let no man abide this deed   95
   But we the doers.   *[Exeunt all but the conspirators.]*

       Enter Trebonius.

CASSIUS
   Where is Antony?
TREBONIUS   Fled to his house amazed.   97
   Men, wives, and children stare, cry out, and run
   As it were doomsday.
BRUTUS   Fates, we will know your pleasures.   99
   That we shall die, we know; 'tis but the time,   100
   And drawing days out, that men stand upon.   101

---

34 puissant powerful   **36 prevent** forestall   **37 couchings . . . courtesies** kneelings and submissive bows   **38 fire the blood of** incite **39–40 And turn . . . children** and turn preordained law into the kinds of childish and flexible rules that children use in their games. **40 fond** so foolish as   **41 rebel** rebellious against reason   **42 true quality** proper firmness and stability. (The metaphor is from alchemy.)   **44 Low-crookèd curtsies** obsequious bows   **46 bend** bow **47 spurn** kick   **52 repealing** recall   **55 freedom of repeal** permission to return.   **58 enfranchisement** i.e., restoration of citizenship **60 pray to move** make petition (as you do)   **61 northern star** polestar **62 resting** remaining stationary   **63 fellow** equal   **68 apprehensive** capable of perception   **70 rank** place in line or file, position **71 Unshaked of motion** (1) unswayed by petitions (2) with perfect steadiness.

75 Olympus mountain dwelling of the Greek gods   **76 bootless** in vain   **78 Et tu, Brutè?** You too, Brutus? (Literally, "Even thou.") **81 common pulpits** public platforms or rostra   **82 enfranchisement** restoration of civil rights. (Cf. line 58 above.)   **84 Ambition's debt** What Caesar's ambition deserved   **86 Publius** (An old senator, too confused to flee.)   **87 mutiny** uprising, discord.   **90 standing** making a stand.   **95 abide** (1) suffer the consequences of (2) remain here with   **97 amazed** stupified.   **99 As** as if   **100–1 'tis . . . upon** i.e., it is only the time of our deaths, and how long we have to live, that we are uncertain about, make a question of.

CASCA
    Why, he that cuts off twenty years of life
    Cuts off so many years of fearing death.
BRUTUS
    Grant that, and then is death a benefit.
    So are we Caesar's friends, that have abridged
    His time of fearing death. Stoop, Romans, stoop,
    And let us bathe our hands in Caesar's blood
    Up to the elbows and besmear our swords.
    Then walk we forth even to the marketplace,   109
    And, waving our red weapons o'er our heads,
    Let's all cry "Peace, freedom, and liberty!"
CASSIUS
    Stoop, then, and wash. [*They bathe their hands and
        weapons.*] How many ages hence
    Shall this our lofty scene be acted over
    In states unborn and accents yet unknown!   114
BRUTUS
    How many times shall Caesar bleed in sport,   115
    That now on Pompey's basis lies along   116
    No worthier than the dust!
CASSIUS   So oft as that shall be,
    So often shall the knot of us be called   119
    The men that gave their country liberty.
DECIUS
    What, shall we forth?
CASSIUS   Ay, every man away.
    Brutus shall lead, and we will grace his heels   122
    With the most boldest and best hearts of Rome.

        Enter a Servant.

BRUTUS
    Soft, who comes here? A friend of Antony's.
SERVANT [*kneeling*]
    Thus, Brutus, did my master bid me kneel;
    Thus did Mark Antony bid me fall down,
    And, being prostrate, thus he bade me say:
    "Brutus is noble, wise, valiant, and honest;   128
    Caesar was mighty, bold, royal, and loving.
    Say I love Brutus and I honor him;
    Say I feared Caesar, honored him, and loved him.
    If Brutus will vouchsafe that Antony
    May safely come to him and be resolved   133
    How Caesar hath deserved to lie in death,
    Mark Antony shall not love Caesar dead
    So well as Brutus living, but will follow
    The fortunes and affairs of noble Brutus
    Thorough the hazards of this untrod state   138
    With all true faith." So says my master Antony.
BRUTUS
    Thy master is a wise and valiant Roman;
    I never thought him worse.

    Tell him, so please him come unto this place,   142
    He shall be satisfied and, by my honor,
    Depart untouched.
SERVANT   I'll fetch him presently.   144
                        Exit Servant.
BRUTUS
    I know that we shall have him well to friend.   145
CASSIUS
    I wish we may. But yet have I a mind
    That fears him much, and my misgiving still   147
    Falls shrewdly to the purpose.   148

        Enter Antony.

BRUTUS
    But here comes Antony.—Welcome, Mark Antony.
ANTONY
    O mighty Caesar! Dost thou lie so low?
    Are all thy conquests, glories, triumphs, spoils,
    Shrunk to this little measure? Fare thee well.—
    I know not, gentlemen, what you intend,
    Who else must be let blood, who else is rank;   154
    If I myself, there is no hour so fit
    As Caesar's death's hour, nor no instrument
    Of half that worth as those your swords, made rich
    With the most noble blood of all this world.
    I do beseech ye, if you bear me hard,   159
    Now, whilst your purpled hands do reek and smoke, 160
    Fulfill your pleasure. Live a thousand years,   161
    I shall not find myself so apt to die;   162
    No place will please me so, no mean of death,
    As here by Caesar, and by you cut off,
    The choice and master spirits of this age.
BRUTUS
    Oh, Antony, beg not your death of us.
    Though now we must appear bloody and cruel,
    As by our hands and this our present act
    You see we do, yet see you but our hands
    And this the bleeding business they have done.
    Our hearts you see not. They are pitiful;   171
    And pity to the general wrong of Rome—
    As fire drives out fire, so pity pity—   173
    Hath done this deed on Caesar. For your part,
    To you our swords have leaden points, Mark Antony. 175
    Our arms in strength of malice, and our hearts   176
    Of brothers' temper, do receive you in   177
    With all kind love, good thoughts, and reverence.
CASSIUS
    Your voice shall be as strong as any man's   179
    In the disposing of new dignities.   180

109 the marketplace i.e., the Forum   **114 accents** languages   **115 in sport** for entertainment   **116 on Pompey's . . . along** lies prostrate on the pedestal of Pompey's statue   **119 knot** group   **122 grace his heels** follow him close at heels (in a triumphal procession; cf. 1.1.34)   **128 honest** honorable   **133 be resolved** receive an explanation   **138 Thorough** through.   **untrod state** still unexplored state of affairs

142 so if it should   **144 presently** immediately.   **145 to friend** for a friend.   **147 fears** distrusts   **148 Falls . . . purpose** is intensely to the point.   **154 let blood** bled (a medical term), i.e., killed.   **rank** swollen, diseased (and hence in need of bleeding)   **159 bear me hard** bear ill will to me   **160 purpled** bloody.   **reek** steam   **161 Live** If I should live   **162 apt** ready   **171 pitiful** full of pity   **173 pity pity** i.e., pity for the general wrong of Rome has driven out pity for Caesar   **175 leaden** blunt   **176–7 Our . . . temper** i.e., Both our arms, though seeming strong in enmity, and our hearts, full of brotherly feeling   **179 voice** vote, authority   **180 dignities** offices of state.

BRUTUS
Only be patient till we have appeased
The multitude, beside themselves with fear,
And then we will deliver you the cause   183
Why I, that did love Caesar when I struck him,
Have thus proceeded.

ANTONY   I doubt not of your wisdom.
Let each man render me his bloody hand.
          [*He shakes hands with the conspirators.*]
First, Marcus Brutus, will I shake with you;
Next, Caius Cassius, do I take your hand;
Now, Decius Brutus, yours; now yours, Metellus;
Yours, Cinna; and, my valiant Casca, yours;
Though last, not least in love, yours, good Trebonius.
Gentlemen all—alas, what shall I say?
My credit now stands on such slippery ground   193
That one of two bad ways you must conceit me,   194
Either a coward or a flatterer.
That I did love thee, Caesar, oh, 'tis true!
If then thy spirit look upon us now,
Shall it not grieve thee dearer than thy death   198
To see thy Antony making his peace,
Shaking the bloody fingers of thy foes—
Most noble—in the presence of thy corpse?
Had I as many eyes as thou hast wounds,
Weeping as fast as they stream forth thy blood,
It would become me better than to close   204
In terms of friendship with thine enemies.
Pardon me, Julius! Here wast thou bayed, brave hart,   206
Here didst thou fall, and here thy hunters stand,
Signed in thy spoil and crimsoned in thy lethe.   208
O world, thou wast the forest to this hart,
And this indeed, O world, the heart of thee!
How like a deer, strucken by many princes,
Dost thou here lie!

CASSIUS
Mark Antony—

ANTONY   Pardon me, Caius Cassius.
The enemies of Caesar shall say this;   214
Then in a friend it is cold modesty.   215

CASSIUS
I blame you not for praising Caesar so,
But what compact mean you to have with us?
Will you be pricked in number of our friends,   218
Or shall we on and not depend on you?

ANTONY
Therefore I took your hands, but was indeed
Swayed from the point by looking down on Caesar.
Friends am I with you all, and love you all,

Upon this hope, that you shall give me reasons
Why and wherein Caesar was dangerous.

BRUTUS
Or else were this a savage spectacle.   225
Our reasons are so full of good regard   226
That were you, Antony, the son of Caesar,
You should be satisfied.

ANTONY   That's all I seek,
And am moreover suitor that I may
Produce his body to the marketplace,   230
And in the pulpit, as becomes a friend,   231
Speak in the order of his funeral.   232

BRUTUS
You shall, Mark Antony.

CASSIUS   Brutus, a word with you.
    [*Aside to Brutus*] You know not what you do. Do not
      consent
That Antony speak in his funeral.
Know you how much the people may be moved
By that which he will utter?

BRUTUS [*aside to Cassius*]   By your pardon:
I will myself into the pulpit first
And show the reason of our Caesar's death.
What Antony shall speak, I will protest   240
He speaks by leave and by permission,
And that we are contented Caesar shall
Have all true rites and lawful ceremonies.
It shall advantage more than do us wrong.

CASSIUS [*aside to Brutus*]
I know not what may fall. I like it not.   245

BRUTUS
Mark Antony, here, take you Caesar's body.
You shall not in your funeral speech blame us,
But speak all good you can devise of Caesar,
And say you do't by our permission.
Else shall you not have any hand at all
About his funeral. And you shall speak
In the same pulpit whereto I am going,
After my speech is ended.

ANTONY   Be it so.
I do desire no more.

BRUTUS
Prepare the body then, and follow us.   255
                        Exeunt. Manet Antony.

ANTONY
Oh, pardon me, thou bleeding piece of earth,
That I am meek and gentle with these butchers!
Thou art the ruins of the noblest man
That ever livèd in the tide of times.   259
Woe to the hand that shed this costly blood!   260
Over thy wounds now do I prophesy—
Which, like dumb mouths, do ope their ruby lips

---

183 **deliver** report to   193 **credit** credibility   194 **conceit** think, judge
198 **dearer** more deeply   204 **close** come to an agreement
206 **bayed** brought to bay.   **hart** stag. (With pun on *heart*.)
208 **Signed . . . spoil** marked with the tokens of your slaughter.
(The *spoil* in hunting is the cutting up of the quarry and distribution
of reward to the hounds.)   **lethe** river of oblivion in the underworld,
here associated with death and blood. (Perhaps fused with Cocytus,
river of blood in the underworld.)   214 **The enemies** Even the
enemies   215 **cold modesty** sober moderation.   218 **pricked** marked
down

225 **else were this** otherwise this would be   226 **regard** account, consideration   230 **Produce** bring forth.   **marketplace** Forum
231 **pulpit** public platform   232 **order** ceremony   240 **protest**
announce, insist   245 **fall** befall, happen.   255.1 *Manet* He remains
onstage   259 **tide of times** course of all history.   260 **costly** (1) valuable (2) fraught with dire consequences

To beg the voice and utterance of my tongue—
A curse shall light upon the limbs of men;
Domestic fury and fierce civil strife
Shall cumber all the parts of Italy;   266
Blood and destruction shall be so in use
And dreadful objects so familiar   268
That mothers shall but smile when they behold
Their infants quartered with the hands of war,   270
All pity choked with custom of fell deeds;   271
And Caesar's spirit, ranging for revenge,   272
With Ate by his side come hot from hell,   273
Shall in these confines with a monarch's voice   274
Cry havoc and let slip the dogs of war,   275
That this foul deed shall smell above the earth
With carrion men, groaning for burial.

        Enter Octavius' Servant.

You serve Octavius Caesar, do you not?
SERVANT I do, Mark Antony.
ANTONY
Caesar did write for him to come to Rome.
SERVANT
He did receive his letters, and is coming,   281
And bid me say to you by word of mouth—
O Caesar!—   [*Seeing the body.*]
ANTONY
Thy heart is big. Get thee apart and weep.
Passion, I see, is catching, for mine eyes,   285
Seeing those beads of sorrow stand in thine,
Began to water. Is thy master coming?
SERVANT
He lies tonight within seven leagues of Rome.   288
ANTONY
Post back with speed and tell him what hath chanced. 289
Here is a mourning Rome, a dangerous Rome,
No Rome of safety for Octavius yet;   291
Hie hence and tell him so. Yet stay awhile;
Thou shalt not back till I have borne this corpse
Into the marketplace. There shall I try,   294
In my oration, how the people take
The cruel issue of these bloody men,   296
According to the which thou shalt discourse   297
To young Octavius of the state of things.   298
Lend me your hand.   *Exeunt* [*with Caesar's body*].

[3.2]

    Enter Brutus and [*presently*] *goes into the pulpit,
and Cassius, with the Plebeians.*

PLEBEIANS
We will be satisfied! Let us be satisfied!   1
BRUTUS
Then follow me, and give me audience, friends.—
Cassius, go you into the other street
And part the numbers.   4
Those that will hear me speak, let 'em stay here;
Those that will follow Cassius, go with him;
And public reasons shall be renderèd
Of Caesar's death.
FIRST PLEBEIAN   I will hear Brutus speak.
SECOND PLEBEIAN
I will hear Cassius, and compare their reasons
When severally we hear them renderèd.   10
      [*Exit Cassius, with some of the Plebeians.*]
THIRD PLEBEIAN
The noble Brutus is ascended. Silence!
BRUTUS Be patient till the last.
Romans, countrymen, and lovers, hear me for my   13
cause, and be silent that you may hear. Believe me for
mine honor, and have respect to mine honor, that you
may believe. Censure me in your wisdom, and awake   16
your senses, that you may the better judge. If there be   17
any in this assembly, any dear friend of Caesar's, to
him I say that Brutus' love to Caesar was no less than
his. If then that friend demand why Brutus rose
against Caesar, this is my answer: not that I loved Caesar less, but that I loved Rome more. Had you rather
Caesar were living and die all slaves, than that Caesar
were dead, to live all free men? As Caesar loved me, I
weep for him; as he was fortunate, I rejoice at it; as he
was valiant, I honor him; but, as he was ambitious, I
slew him. There is tears for his love; joy for his fortune;
honor for his valor; and death for his ambition.
Who is here so base that would be a bondman? If any,
speak, for him have I offended. Who is here so rude   30
that would not be a Roman? If any, speak, for him
have I offended. Who is here so vile that will not love
his country? If any, speak, for him have I offended. I
pause for a reply.
ALL None, Brutus, none!
BRUTUS Then none have I offended. I have done no
more to Caesar than you shall do to Brutus. The ques-   37
tion of his death is enrolled in the Capitol, his glory   38
not extenuated wherein he was worthy, nor his   39

---

266 **cumber** overwhelm; entangle, burden 268 **objects** sights
270 **quartered** cut to pieces 271 **custom . . . deeds** the familiarity of
cruel deeds 272 **ranging** roaming up and down in search of prey
273 **Ate** goddess of discord and moral chaos 274 **confines** regions.
monarch's i.e., authoritative 275 **Cry havoc** give the signal for sack,
pillage, and slaughter, taking no prisoners. **let slip** unleash
281 **letters** (Not necessarily plural. The Latin word for letter, *litterae*,
has a plural form.) 285 **Passion** Sorrow 288 **lies** lodges. **seven
leagues** about twenty miles 289 **Post** Ride. **chanced** happened.
291 **Rome** (With pun on "room," as at 1.2.156.) 294 **try** test
296 **cruel issue** outcome of the cruelty 297 **the which** the outcome of which 298 **young Octavius** (He was eighteen in March
of 44 B.C.)

3.2 Location: The Forum.
1 **be satisfied** have an explanation. 4 **part** divide 10 **severally** separately 13 **lovers** friends. (This speech by Brutus is in what Plutarch
calls the Lacedemonian or Spartan style, brief and sententious. Its
content is original with Shakespeare.) 16 **Censure** Judge 17 **senses**
intellectual powers 30 **rude** barbarous 37 **than . . . Brutus** (In lines
45–7 below, Brutus offers to die for Rome if his country should ask.)
37–8 **The question . . . enrolled** The considerations that necessitated
his death are recorded 39 **extenuated** minimized

offenses enforced for which he suffered death.   40

*Enter Mark Antony [and others] with Caesar's
body.*

Here comes his body, mourned by Mark Antony, who,
though he had no hand in his death, shall receive the
benefit of his dying, a place in the commonwealth, as
which of you shall not? With this I depart, that, as I
slew my best lover for the good of Rome, I have the   45
same dagger for myself when it shall please my country to need my death.

ALL   Live, Brutus, live, live!   [*Brutus comes down.*]

FIRST PLEBEIAN
Bring him with triumph home unto his house.

SECOND PLEBEIAN
Give him a statue with his ancestors.   50

THIRD PLEBEIAN
Let him be Caesar.

FOURTH PLEBEIAN   Caesar's better parts
Shall be crowned in Brutus.

FIRST PLEBEIAN
We'll bring him to his house with shouts and clamors.

BRUTUS
My countrymen—

SECOND PLEBEIAN   Peace, silence! Brutus speaks.

FIRST PLEBEIAN   Peace, ho!

BRUTUS
Good countrymen, let me depart alone,
And, for my sake, stay here with Antony.
Do grace to Caesar's corpse, and grace his speech   58
Tending to Caesar's glories, which Mark Antony,   59
By our permission, is allowed to make.
I do entreat you, not a man depart,
Save I alone, till Antony have spoke.   *Exit.*

FIRST PLEBEIAN
Stay, ho, and let us hear Mark Antony.

THIRD PLEBEIAN
Let him go up into the public chair.
We'll hear him. Noble Antony, go up.

ANTONY
For Brutus' sake I am beholding to you.   66
                              [*He goes into the pulpit.*]

FOURTH PLEBEIAN   What does he say of Brutus?

THIRD PLEBEIAN   He says, for Brutus' sake
He finds himself beholding to us all.

FOURTH PLEBEIAN
'Twere best he speak no harm of Brutus here.

FIRST PLEBEIAN
This Caesar was a tyrant.

THIRD PLEBEIAN   Nay, that's certain.
We are blest that Rome is rid of him.

SECOND PLEBEIAN
Peace! Let us hear what Antony can say.

ANTONY
You gentle Romans—

ALL   Peace, ho! Let us hear him.

ANTONY
Friends, Romans, countrymen, lend me your ears.   75
I come to bury Caesar, not to praise him.
The evil that men do lives after them;
The good is oft interrèd with their bones.
So let it be with Caesar. The noble Brutus
Hath told you Caesar was ambitious.
If it were so, it was a grievous fault,
And grievously hath Caesar answered it.   82
Here, under leave of Brutus and the rest—   83
For Brutus is an honorable man,
So are they all, all honorable men—
Come I to speak in Caesar's funeral.
He was my friend, faithful and just to me;
But Brutus says he was ambitious,
And Brutus is an honorable man.
He hath brought many captives home to Rome,
Whose ransoms did the general coffers fill.
Did this in Caesar seem ambitious?
When that the poor have cried, Caesar hath wept;   93
Ambition should be made of sterner stuff.
Yet Brutus says he was ambitious,
And Brutus is an honorable man.
You all did see that on the Lupercal   97
I thrice presented him a kingly crown,
Which he did thrice refuse. Was this ambition?
Yet Brutus says he was ambitious,
And sure he is an honorable man.
I speak not to disprove what Brutus spoke,
But here I am to speak what I do know.
You all did love him once, not without cause.
What cause withholds you then to mourn for him?
O judgment! Thou art fled to brutish beasts,
And men have lost their reason. Bear with me;
My heart is in the coffin there with Caesar,
And I must pause till it come back to me.

FIRST PLEBEIAN
Methinks there is much reason in his sayings.

SECOND PLEBEIAN
If thou consider rightly of the matter,
Caesar has had great wrong.

THIRD PLEBEIAN   Has he, masters?   112
I fear there will a worse come in his place.

FOURTH PLEBEIAN
Marked ye his words? He would not take the crown,
Therefore 'tis certain he was not ambitious.

FIRST PLEBEIAN
If it be found so, some will dear abide it.   116

---

40 enforced exaggerated, insisted upon   **45 lover** friend   **50 SECOND
PLEBEIAN** (Not the same person who exited at line 10; the numbering
here refers to those who stay to hear Brutus.)   **58 Do grace** Show
respect.   **grace his speech** listen courteously to Antony's speech
59 Tending to relating to, dealing with   **66 beholding** beholden

75 Friends (This speech by Antony is thought to illustrate the Asiatic
or "florid" style of speaking. In it Shakespeare gathers various hints
from Plutarch ("Marcus Antonius" and "Dion") and Appian, but the
speech is Shakespeare's invention.)   **82 answered** paid the penalty
for   **83 under leave** by permission   **93 When that** When   **97 Lupercal** (See 1.1.67 and note.)   **112 masters** good sirs.   **116 dear abide it**
pay a heavy penalty for it.

SECOND PLEBEIAN
Poor soul, his eyes are red as fire with weeping.

THIRD PLEBEIAN
There's not a nobler man in Rome than Antony.

FOURTH PLEBEIAN
Now mark him. He begins again to speak.

ANTONY
But yesterday the word of Caesar might
Have stood against the world. Now lies he there,
And none so poor to do him reverence. 122
Oh, masters, if I were disposed to stir
Your hearts and minds to mutiny and rage, 124
I should do Brutus wrong, and Cassius wrong,
Who, you all know, are honorable men.
I will not do them wrong; I rather choose
To wrong the dead, to wrong myself and you,
Than I will wrong such honorable men.
But here's a parchment with the seal of Caesar.
I found it in his closet; 'tis his will. 131
                [He shows the will.]
Let but the commons hear this testament— 132
Which, pardon me, I do not mean to read—
And they would go and kiss dead Caesar's wounds
And dip their napkins in his sacred blood, 135
Yea, beg a hair of him for memory,
And dying, mention it within their wills,
Bequeathing it as a rich legacy
Unto their issue.

FOURTH PLEBEIAN
We'll hear the will! Read it, Mark Antony.

ALL
The will, the will! We will hear Caesar's will.

ANTONY
Have patience, gentle friends: I must not read it.
It is not meet you know how Caesar loved you. 143
You are not wood, you are not stones, but men;
And being men, hearing the will of Caesar,
It will inflame you, it will make you mad.
'Tis good you know not that you are his heirs,
For if you should, oh, what would come of it?

FOURTH PLEBEIAN
Read the will! We'll hear it, Antony.
You shall read us the will, Caesar's will.

ANTONY
Will you be patient? Will you stay awhile?
I have o'ershot myself to tell you of it. 152
I fear I wrong the honorable men
Whose daggers have stabbed Caesar; I do fear it.

FOURTH PLEBEIAN
They were traitors. "Honorable men"!

ALL   The will! The testament!

SECOND PLEBEIAN
They were villains, murderers. The will! Read the will!

ANTONY
You will compel me then to read the will?
Then make a ring about the corpse of Caesar
And let me show you him that made the will.
Shall I descend? And will you give me leave?

ALL   Come down.

SECOND PLEBEIAN   Descend.

THIRD PLEBEIAN   You shall have leave.
        [Antony comes down. They gather around Caesar.]

FOURTH PLEBEIAN   A ring; stand round.

FIRST PLEBEIAN
Stand from the hearse. Stand from the body. 166

SECOND PLEBEIAN
Room for Antony, most noble Antony!

ANTONY
Nay, press not so upon me. Stand farre off. 168

ALL   Stand back! Room! Bear back!

ANTONY
If you have tears, prepare to shed them now.
You all do know this mantle. I remember 171
The first time ever Caesar put it on;
'Twas on a summer's evening in his tent,
That day he overcame the Nervii. 174
Look, in this place ran Cassius' dagger through.
See what a rent the envious Casca made. 176
Through this the well-belovèd Brutus stabbed,
And as he plucked his cursèd steel away,
Mark how the blood of Caesar followed it,
As rushing out of doors to be resolved 180
If Brutus so unkindly knocked or no; 181
For Brutus, as you know, was Caesar's angel. 182
Judge, O you gods, how dearly Caesar loved him!
This was the most unkindest cut of all; 184
For when the noble Caesar saw him stab,
Ingratitude, more strong than traitors' arms,
Quite vanquished him. Then burst his mighty heart,
And in his mantle muffling up his face,
Even at the base of Pompey's statue,
Which all the while ran blood, great Caesar fell.
Oh, what a fall was there, my countrymen!
Then I, and you, and all of us fell down,
Whilst bloody treason flourished over us. 193
Oh, now you weep, and I perceive you feel
The dint of pity. These are gracious drops. 195
Kind souls, what weep you when you but behold 196
Our Caesar's vesture wounded? Look you here, 197
Here is himself, marred as you see with traitors.
               [He lifts Caesar's mantle.]

FIRST PLEBEIAN   Oh, piteous spectacle!

SECOND PLEBEIAN   O noble Caesar!

---

166 **hearse** bier.   168 **farre** farther   171 **mantle** cloak, toga.   174 **the Nervii** the Belgian tribe whose defeat in 57 B.C. is described in Caesar's *Gallic Wars*, 2.15–28   176 **rent** tear, hole   **envious** malicious, spiteful   180 **be resolved** learn for certain   181 **unkindly** cruelly and unnaturally   182 **angel** (1) daimon or genius, guardian angel (2) best beloved.   184 **unkindest** (1) most cruel (2) most unnatural. (The double superlative was grammatically acceptable in Shakespeare's day.)   193 **flourished** (1) triumphed insolently (2) brandished its sword   195 **dint** impression   196 **what** why, or how much   197 **vesture** clothing

---

122 **And none . . . reverence** i.e., and yet no one is below him in fortune now, no one of even the lowest social station to look up to and revere him.   124 **mutiny** riot, tumult   131 **closet** private chamber, study   132 **commons** common people   135 **napkins** handkerchiefs   143 **meet** fitting that   152 **o'ershot myself** gone further than I should

THIRD PLEBEIAN   Oh, woeful day!

FOURTH PLEBEIAN   Oh, traitors, villains!

FIRST PLEBEIAN   Oh, most bloody sight!

SECOND PLEBEIAN   We will be revenged.

ALL   Revenge! About! Seek! Burn! Fire! Kill! Slay! Let 205
not a traitor live!

ANTONY   Stay, countrymen.

FIRST PLEBEIAN   Peace there! Hear the noble Antony.

SECOND PLEBEIAN   We'll hear him, we'll follow him,
we'll die with him!

ANTONY

Good friends, sweet friends, let me not stir you up
To such a sudden flood of mutiny.
They that have done this deed are honorable.
What private griefs they have, alas, I know not,   214
That made them do it. They are wise and honorable,
And will no doubt with reasons answer you.
I come not, friends, to steal away your hearts.
I am no orator, as Brutus is,
But, as you know me all, a plain blunt man
That love my friend, and that they know full well
That gave me public leave to speak of him.   221
For I have neither wit, nor words, nor worth,   222
Action, nor utterance, nor the power of speech   223
To stir men's blood. I only speak right on.
I tell you that which you yourselves do know,
Show you sweet Caesar's wounds, poor poor dumb
      mouths,
And bid them speak for me. But were I Brutus,
And Brutus Antony, there were an Antony
Would ruffle up your spirits and put a tongue   229
In every wound of Caesar that should move
The stones of Rome to rise and mutiny.

ALL

We'll mutiny!

FIRST PLEBEIAN   We'll burn the house of Brutus!

THIRD PLEBEIAN

Away, then! Come, seek the conspirators.

ANTONY

Yet hear me, countrymen. Yet hear me speak.

ALL

Peace, ho! Hear Antony, most noble Antony!

ANTONY

Why, friends, you go to do you know not what.
Wherein hath Caesar thus deserved your loves?
Alas, you know not. I must tell you then:
You have forgot the will I told you of.

ALL

Most true. The will! Let's stay and hear the will.

ANTONY

Here is the will, and under Caesar's seal.
To every Roman citizen he gives,
To every several man, seventy-five drachmas.   243

SECOND PLEBEIAN

Most noble Caesar! We'll revenge his death.

THIRD PLEBEIAN   O royal Caesar!

ANTONY   Hear me with patience.

ALL   Peace, ho!

ANTONY

Moreover, he hath left you all his walks,
His private arbors, and new-planted orchards,
On this side Tiber; he hath left them you,
And to your heirs forever—common pleasures,   251
To walk abroad and recreate yourselves.
Here was a Caesar! When comes such another?

FIRST PLEBEIAN

Never, never! Come, away, away!
We'll burn his body in the holy place
And with the brands fire the traitors' houses.
Take up the body.

SECOND PLEBEIAN   Go fetch fire!

THIRD PLEBEIAN   Pluck down benches!

FOURTH PLEBEIAN   Pluck down forms, windows, any- 259
thing!   Exeunt Plebeians [with the body].

ANTONY

Now let it work. Mischief, thou art afoot.
Take thou what course thou wilt.

          Enter [Octavius'] Servant.

                              How now, fellow?

SERVANT

Sir, Octavius is already come to Rome.

ANTONY   Where is he?

SERVANT

He and Lepidus are at Caesar's house.

ANTONY

And thither will I straight to visit him.   266
He comes upon a wish. Fortune is merry,   267
And in this mood will give us anything.

SERVANT

I heard him say Brutus and Cassius
Are rid like madmen through the gates of Rome.   270

ANTONY

Belike they had some notice of the people,   271
How I had moved them. Bring me to Octavius.
                                        Exeunt.

                    ❖

[3.3]

Enter Cinna the poet, and after him the Plebeians.

CINNA

I dreamt tonight that I did feast with Caesar,   1

---

205 About! To work!   214 griefs grievances   221 public leave permission to speak publicly   222–3 neither . . . speech neither intelligence, vocabulary, moral authority, gesture, rhetorical skill, nor
polished delivery   229 ruffle up stir to anger   243 several individual.   drachmas coins. (This is a substantial bequest.)

251 common pleasures public pleasure gardens (in which)
259 forms, windows benches, window frames and shutters
266 straight straightway, at once   267 upon a wish just when
wanted.   merry favorably disposed   270 Are rid have ridden
271 Belike Likely enough.   of about; or, from
3.3. Location: A street.
1 tonight last night

And things unluckily charge my fantasy. 2
I have no will to wander forth of doors,
Yet something leads me forth.

FIRST PLEBEIAN   What is your name?

SECOND PLEBEIAN   Whither are you going?

THIRD PLEBEIAN   Where do you dwell?

FOURTH PLEBEIAN   Are you a married man or a bachelor?

SECOND PLEBEIAN   Answer every man directly.

FIRST PLEBEIAN   Ay, and briefly.

FOURTH PLEBEIAN   Ay, and wisely.

THIRD PLEBEIAN   Ay, and truly, you were best. 13

CINNA   What is my name? Whither am I going? Where do I dwell? Am I a married man or a bachelor? Then to answer every man directly and briefly, wisely and truly: wisely I say, I am a bachelor.

SECOND PLEBEIAN   That's as much as to say they are fools that marry. You'll bear me a bang for that, I fear. 19 Proceed directly. 20

CINNA   Directly, I am going to Caesar's funeral. 21

FIRST PLEBEIAN   As a friend or an enemy?

CINNA   As a friend.

SECOND PLEBEIAN   That matter is answered directly.

FOURTH PLEBEIAN   For your dwelling—briefly.

CINNA   Briefly, I dwell by the Capitol.

THIRD PLEBEIAN   Your name, sir, truly.

CINNA   Truly, my name is Cinna.

FIRST PLEBEIAN   Tear him to pieces! He's a conspirator!

CINNA   I am Cinna the poet, I am Cinna the poet!

FOURTH PLEBEIAN   Tear him for his bad verses, tear him for his bad verses!

CINNA   I am not Cinna the conspirator.

FOURTH PLEBEIAN   It is no matter, his name's Cinna. Pluck but his name out of his heart, and turn him 35 going. 36

THIRD PLEBEIAN   Tear him, tear him! Come, brands, ho, firebrands! To Brutus', to Cassius'; burn all! Some to Decius' house, and some to Casca's; some to Ligarius'. Away, go!

Exeunt all the Plebeians, [dragging off Cinna].

❖

4.1

Enter Antony [with a list], Octavius, and Lepidus.

ANTONY
These many, then, shall die. Their names are pricked. 1

OCTAVIUS
Your brother too must die. Consent you, Lepidus?

LEPIDUS
I do consent—

OCTAVIUS   Prick him down, Antony.

LEPIDUS
Upon condition Publius shall not live,
Who is your sister's son, Mark Antony.

ANTONY
He shall not live. Look, with a spot I damn him. 6
But Lepidus, go you to Caesar's house.
Fetch the will hither, and we shall determine 8
How to cut off some charge in legacies. 9

LEPIDUS   What, shall I find you here?

OCTAVIUS   Or here or at the Capitol.   *Exit Lepidus.* 11

ANTONY
This is a slight, unmeritable man, 12
Meet to be sent on errands. Is it fit,
The threefold world divided, he should stand 14
One of the three to share it?

OCTAVIUS   So you thought him,
And took his voice who should be pricked to die 16
In our black sentence and proscription. 17

ANTONY
Octavius, I have seen more days than you;
And though we lay these honors on this man
To ease ourselves of divers sland'rous loads, 20
He shall but bear them as the ass bears gold,
To groan and sweat under the business,
Either led or driven as we point the way;
And having brought our treasure where we will,
Then take we down his load, and turn him off,
Like to the empty ass, to shake his ears 26
And graze in commons.

OCTAVIUS   You may do your will; 27
But he's a tried and valiant soldier.

ANTONY
So is my horse, Octavius, and for that
I do appoint him store of provender. 30
It is a creature that I teach to fight,
To wind, to stop, to run directly on, 32
His corporal motion governed by my spirit. 33
And in some taste is Lepidus but so. 34
He must be taught, and trained, and bid go forth—
A barren-spirited fellow, one that feeds
On objects, arts, and imitations, 37
Which, out of use and staled by other men, 38
Begin his fashion. Do not talk of him 39
But as a property. And now, Octavius, 40

---

6 **spot** mark (on the list). **damn** condemn **8–9 determine . . . legacies** find a way to reduce the outlay of Caesar's estate, by altering the will. **11 Or** Either **12 slight, unmeritable** insignificant and undeserving **14 threefold** i.e., consisting of Europe, Africa, and Asia. The Roman world was divided among the triumvirate, with most of Gaul on both sides of the Alps to Antony, Spain and Old Gaul to Lepidus, and Africa, Sardinia, and Sicily to Octavius. **16 took his voice** acceded to his opinion (i.e., about Publius) **17 black sentence** death sentence. **proscription** (Proscription branded a man as an outlaw, confiscated his property, offered a reward for his murder, and prohibited his sons and grandsons from holding public office.) **20 sland'rous** giving cause for slander **26 empty** unloaded **27 commons** public pasture. **30 appoint** assign, provide. **provender** fodder. **32 wind** turn. (Horse trainer's term.) **directly on** straight ahead **33 corporal** bodily **34 taste** degree, sense **37 On . . . imitations** on curiosities, artificial things, and the following of fashion—copied things merely, taken up secondhand **38 staled** made common or cheap **39 Begin his fashion** are for him the ultimate in fashion. **40 property** tool.

---

2 unluckily . . . fantasy oppress my imagination with foreboding. **13 you were best** you'd better. **19 bear . . . bang** get a beating from me **20 directly** without evasion. **21 Directly** (1) Straight there (2) At once **35–6 turn him going** send him packing. **4.1. Location: Rome. A table is perhaps set out. 1 pricked** marked down on a list (with a stylus making an impression on a wax tablet, or piercing a sheet of paper).

Listen great things. Brutus and Cassius   41
Are levying powers. We must straight make head.   42
Therefore let our alliance be combined,   43
Our best friends made, our means stretched;   44
And let us presently go sit in council
How covert matters may be best disclosed   46
And open perils surest answerèd.   47

OCTAVIUS
Let us do so, for we are at the stake   48
And bayed about with many enemies;   49
And some that smile have in their hearts, I fear,
Millions of mischiefs.   *Exeunt.*   51

❦

[4.2]

Drum. Enter Brutus, Lucilius, [Lucius,] and the
army. Titinius and Pindarus meet them.

BRUTUS   Stand, ho!   1
LUCILIUS   Give the word, ho, and stand!   2
BRUTUS
What now, Lucilius, is Cassius near?
LUCILIUS
He is at hand, and Pindarus is come
To do you salutation from his master.
BRUTUS
He greets me well. Your master, Pindarus,   6
In his own change, or by ill officers,   7
Hath given me some worthy cause to wish   8
Things done, undone; but if he be at hand
I shall be satisfied.
PINDARUS   I do not doubt   10
But that my noble master will appear
Such as he is, full of regard and honor.   12
BRUTUS
He is not doubted.—A word, Lucilius.
                    [*Brutus and Lucilius speak apart.*]
How he received you let me be resolved.   14
LUCILIUS
With courtesy and with respect enough,
But not with such familiar instances   16
Nor with such free and friendly conference   17
As he hath used of old.
BRUTUS   Thou hast described

A hot friend cooling. Ever note, Lucilius:
When love begins to sicken and decay
It useth an enforcèd ceremony.   21
There are no tricks in plain and simple faith.
But hollow men, like horses hot at hand,   23
Make gallant show and promise of their mettle;   24
                          Low march within.
But when they should endure the bloody spur,
They fall their crests and like deceitful jades   26
Sink in the trial. Comes his army on?   27
LUCILIUS
They mean this night in Sardis to be quartered.   28
The greater part, the horse in general,   29
Are come with Cassius.

              Enter Cassius and his powers.

BRUTUS   Hark, he is arrived.
March gently on to meet him.   31
CASSIUS   Stand, ho!
BRUTUS   Stand, ho! Speak the word along.
FIRST SOLDIER   Stand!
SECOND SOLDIER   Stand!
THIRD SOLDIER   Stand!
CASSIUS
Most noble brother, you have done me wrong.
BRUTUS
Judge me, you gods! Wrong I mine enemies?
And if not so, how should I wrong a brother?
CASSIUS
Brutus, this sober form of yours hides wrongs;   40
And when you do them—
BRUTUS   Cassius, be content;   41
Speak your griefs softly. I do know you well.   42
Before the eyes of both our armies here,
Which should perceive nothing but love from us,
Let us not wrangle. Bid them move away.
Then in my tent, Cassius, enlarge your griefs,   46
And I will give you audience.
CASSIUS   Pindarus,
Bid our commanders lead their charges off   48
A little from this ground.
BRUTUS
Lucius, do you the like, and let no man
Come to our tent till we have done our conference.
Let Lucilius and Titinius guard our door.   52
              Exeunt. Manent Brutus and Cassius.
              [*Lucilius and Titinius stand guard at the door.*]

41 **Listen** hear   42 **powers** armies.   **straight make head** immediately raise an army.   43 **let . . . combined** let us work as one 44 **made** mustered, made certain.   **stretched** used to fullest advantage, extended to the utmost   46 **How . . . disclosed** (to determine) how hidden dangers may best be discovered   47 **surest answerèd** most safely met.   48 **at the stake** i.e., like a bear in the sport of bearbaiting   49 **bayed about** surrounded as by baying dogs   51 **mischiefs** harms, evils.
4.2. Location: Camp near Sardis, in Asia Minor. Before Brutus's tent. 1–2 **Stand . . . stand!** Halt! Pass the word!   6 **He . . . well** His greetings are welcome.   7 **In . . . officers** whether from an alteration in his feelings toward me or through the acts of unworthy subordinates   8 **worthy** justifiable   10 **be satisfied** have things explained to my satisfaction.   12 **full . . . honor** deserving all respect and honor. 14 **resolved** informed, put out of doubt.   16 **familiar instances** proofs of intimate friendship   17 **conference** conversation

21 **enforcèd** constrained   23 **hollow** insincere.   **hot at hand** restless and full of spirit when held in, at the start   24 **mettle** spirit   26 **fall their crests** lower their necks (literally, the ridge or mane of the neck), hang their heads.   **jades** worthless horses   27 **Sink** give way, fail 28 **Sardis** (The capital city of Lydia in Asia Minor.)   29 **the horse in general** all the cavalry   31 **gently** mildly, not hostilely   40 **sober form** dignified manner, appearance   41 **be content** keep calm 42 **griefs** grievances.   **I . . . well** i.e., We've known one another long and can proceed calmly.   46 **enlarge** speak freely   48 **charges** troops 52 **Lucilius** (The Folio reads *Lucius* here and *Lucillius* in line 50, but, when Shakespeare interpolated a passage in the next scene at lines 124–66, he evidently intended to have Lucilius guarding the door.)

[4.3]

CASSIUS
  That you have wronged me doth appear in this:
  You have condemned and noted Lucius Pella   2
  For taking bribes here of the Sardians,
  Wherein my letters, praying on his side,   4
  Because I knew the man, was slighted off.   5
BRUTUS
  You wronged yourself to write in such a case.
CASSIUS
  In such a time as this it is not meet   7
  That every nice offense should bear his comment.   8
BRUTUS
  Let me tell you, Cassius, you yourself
  Are much condemned to have an itching palm,   10
  To sell and mart your offices for gold   11
  To undeservers.
CASSIUS   I an itching palm?
  You know that you are Brutus that speaks this,
  Or, by the gods, this speech were else your last.   14
BRUTUS
  The name of Cassius honors this corruption,   15
  And chastisement doth therefore hide his head.   16
CASSIUS   Chastisement?
BRUTUS
  Remember March, the ides of March remember.
  Did not great Julius bleed for justice' sake?
  What villain touched his body that did stab   20
  And not for justice? What, shall one of us,   21
  That struck the foremost man of all this world
  But for supporting robbers, shall we now   23
  Contaminate our fingers with base bribes,
  And sell the mighty space of our large honors   25
  For so much trash as may be graspèd thus?   26
  I had rather be a dog and bay the moon   27
  Than such a Roman.
CASSIUS   Brutus, bait not me.   28
  I'll not endure it. You forget yourself
  To hedge me in. I am a soldier, I,   30
  Older in practice, abler than yourself
  To make conditions.   32
BRUTUS   Go to! You are not, Cassius.

CASSIUS I am.
BRUTUS I say you are not.
CASSIUS   36
  Urge me no more; I shall forget myself.   37
  Have mind upon your health. Tempt me no farther.   38
BRUTUS   Away, slight man!
CASSIUS
  Is't possible?
BRUTUS   Hear me, for I will speak.   40
  Must I give way and room to your rash choler?   41
  Shall I be frighted when a madman stares?
CASSIUS
  O ye gods, ye gods! Must I endure all this?
BRUTUS
  All this? Ay, more. Fret till your proud heart break.
  Go show your slaves how choleric you are,   45
  And make your bondmen tremble. Must I budge?   46
  Must I observe you? Must I stand and crouch   47
  Under your testy humor? By the gods,   48
  You shall digest the venom of your spleen
  Though it do split you; for, from this day forth,
  I'll use you for my mirth, yea, for my laughter,
  When you are waspish.   51
CASSIUS   Is it come to this?
BRUTUS
  You say you are a better soldier.   53
  Let it appear so; make your vaunting true,
  And it shall please me well. For mine own part,   55
  I shall be glad to learn of noble men.
CASSIUS
  You wrong me every way! You wrong me, Brutus.
  I said an elder soldier, not a better.
  Did I say "better"?
BRUTUS   If you did, I care not.
CASSIUS   59
  When Caesar lived he durst not thus have moved me.
BRUTUS   60
  Peace, peace! You durst not so have tempted him.
CASSIUS I durst not?
BRUTUS No.
CASSIUS
  What, durst not tempt him?
BRUTUS   For your life you durst not.
CASSIUS
  Do not presume too much upon my love.
  I may do that I shall be sorry for.
BRUTUS
  You have done that you should be sorry for.
  There is no terror, Cassius, in your threats,
  For I am armed so strong in honesty

4.3. Location: The scene is continuous. Brutus and Cassius remain onstage, which now represents the interior of Brutus's tent.
2 noted publicly disgraced.   **Lucius Pella** a Roman praetor in Sardis
4 letters i.e., letter. (See 3.1.281n.)   **praying** entreating   **5 slighted off** slightingly dismissed.   **7 meet** fitting   **8 nice** trivial.   **bear his comment** be taken note of. (*His* means "its.")   **10 condemned to have** accused of having   **11 mart** traffic in   **14 else** otherwise
15 honors lends the appearance of honor to, countenances   **16 And . . . head** and for that reason those who might rebuke such corruption are reluctant to speak out.   **20–1 What . . . justice?** Which of us was villain enough to stab for any cause other than justice?
23 But only.   **robbers** (According to Plutarch, Caesar "was a favorer and suborner of all of them that did rob and spoil by his countenance and authority.")   **25 the mighty . . . honors** the greatness of our honorable reputations and the high offices we have power to confer   **26 trash** i.e., money (despised in Brutus's stoic philosophy)
27 bay howl at   **28 bait** harass   **30 hedge me in** crowd me, limit my authority.   **32 make conditions** i.e., manage affairs, make decisions about Lucius Pella and other officers.

36 Urge Provoke   **37 Tempt** Provoke   **38 slight** insignificant
40 way and room free course and scope.   **choler** wrathful temperament.   **41 stares** looks wildly at me.   **45 bondmen** (Probably not distinguished from "slaves" in line 44.)   **budge** flinch.   **46 observe** defer to.   **crouch** cringe   **47 humor** temperament.   **48 digest** swallow.   **spleen** i.e., irascibility   **51 waspish** hotheaded.   **53 vaunting** boasting   **55 I shall . . . men** (Said sarcastically: "Wouldn't it be a nice surprise to learn that some men can be noble after all?", or, "I am glad to be corrected by such a noble person as yourself.")   **59 moved** angered   **60 tempted** provoked

That they pass by me as the idle wind,   70
Which I respect not. I did send to you
For certain sums of gold, which you denied me;   72
For I can raise no money by vile means.
By heaven, I had rather coin my heart
And drop my blood for drachmas than to wring
From the hard hands of peasants their vile trash   76
By any indirection. I did send
To you for gold to pay my legions,
Which you denied me. Was that done like Cassius?
Should I have answered Caius Cassius so?
When Marcus Brutus grows so covetous   81
To lock such rascal counters from his friends,
Be ready, gods, with all your thunderbolts,
Dash him to pieces!
CASSIUS   I denied you not.
BRUTUS
    You did.
CASSIUS   I did not. He was but a fool
That brought my answer back. Brutus hath rived my   85
    heart.
A friend should bear his friend's infirmities,
But Brutus makes mine greater than they are.
BRUTUS
    I do not, till you practice them on me.
CASSIUS
    You love me not.
BRUTUS   I do not like your faults.
CASSIUS
    A friendly eye could never see such faults.
BRUTUS
    A flatterer's would not, though they do appear
As huge as high Olympus.
CASSIUS
    Come, Antony, and young Octavius, come,
Revenge yourselves alone on Cassius;
For Cassius is aweary of the world,   96
Hated by one he loves, braved by his brother,   97
Checked like a bondman, all his faults observed,   98
Set in a notebook, learned and conned by rote
To cast into my teeth. Oh, I could weep
My spirit from mine eyes! There is my dagger,
                    [offering his unsheathed dagger]
And here my naked breast; within, a heart   102
Dearer than Pluto's mine, richer than gold.
If that thou be'st a Roman, take it forth.   104
I, that denied thee gold, will give my heart.
Strike, as thou didst at Caesar; for I know,
When thou didst hate him worst, thou loved'st him
    better
Than ever thou loved'st Cassius.
BRUTUS   Sheathe your dagger.   108

Be angry when you will, it shall have scope;   109
Do what you will, dishonor shall be humor.   110
Oh, Cassius, you are yokèd with a lamb
That carries anger as the flint bears fire,   112
Who, much enforcèd, shows a hasty spark
And straight is cold again.   113
CASSIUS   Hath Cassius lived
To be but mirth and laughter to his Brutus   115
When grief and blood ill-tempered vexeth him?
BRUTUS
    When I spoke that, I was ill-tempered too.
CASSIUS
    Do you confess so much? Give me your hand.
BRUTUS
    And my heart too.   [They embrace.]
CASSIUS   Oh, Brutus!
BRUTUS   What's the matter?
CASSIUS
    Have not you love enough to bear with me,   120
When that rash humor which my mother gave me
Makes me forgetful?
BRUTUS   Yes, Cassius, and from henceforth,
When you are overearnest with your Brutus,   123
He'll think your mother chides, and leave you so.

        Enter a Poet [followed by Lucilius and Titinius,
        who have been standing guard at the door].

POET
    Let me go in to see the generals!
There is some grudge between 'em; 'tis not meet
They be alone.
LUCILIUS   You shall not come to them.
POET   Nothing but death shall stay me.
CASSIUS   How now? What's the matter?
POET
    For shame, you generals! What do you mean?
Love and be friends, as two such men should be;
For I have seen more years, I'm sure, than ye.
CASSIUS   132
    Ha, ha, how vilely doth this cynic rhyme!
BRUTUS
    Get you hence, sirrah. Saucy fellow, hence!
CASSIUS
    Bear with him, Brutus. 'Tis his fashion.
BRUTUS   135
    I'll know his humor when he knows his time.   136
What should the wars do with these jigging fools?
Companion, hence!   137
CASSIUS   Away, away, begone!   Exit Poet.

---

70 respect not pay no attention to.   **72 can raise no money** i.e., refuse to raise money   **76 indirection** devious or unjust means.   **81 rascal counters** i.e., paltry sums. (*Counters* were uncurrent coins or disks used by shopkeepers as tokens in making reckonings.)   **85 rived** cleft, split   **96 braved** defied   **97 Checked** rebuked   **98 conned by rote** memorized   **102 Dearer** richer.   **Pluto** god of the underworld (fused with Plutus, god of riches)   **104 that denied** i.e., who you insist denied   **108 scope** free rein

109 dishonor . . . humor i.e., I'll regard your dishonorable conduct and self-righteous anger as the effects of temperament, something to be humored.   **110 yokèd with** allied with   **112 enforcèd** provoked, struck upon   **113 straight** at once   **115 blood ill-tempered** disposition imbalanced by the humors of the body   **120 that rash humor** i.e., choler, anger   **123 leave you so** let it go at that.   **132 cynic** i.e., rude fellow; also one claiming to be a Cynic philosopher, hence outspoken   **135 I'll . . . time** I'll indulge his eccentric behavior when he knows the proper time for it.   **136 jigging** rhyming in jerky doggerel   **137 Companion** Fellow

BRUTUS
Lucilius and Titinius, bid the commanders
Prepare to lodge their companies tonight.
CASSIUS
And come yourselves, and bring Messala with you
Immediately to us.   [*Exeunt Lucilius and Titinius.*]
BRUTUS [*to Lucius within*]   Lucius, a bowl of wine.
CASSIUS
I did not think you could have been so angry.
BRUTUS
Oh, Cassius, I am sick of many griefs.
CASSIUS   145
Of your philosophy you make no use
If you give place to accidental evils.
BRUTUS
No man bears sorrow better. Portia is dead.
CASSIUS   Ha? Portia?
BRUTUS   She is dead.   149
CASSIUS
How scaped I killing when I crossed you so?
Oh, insupportable and touching loss!
Upon what sickness?
BRUTUS   Impatient of my absence,   153
And grief that young Octavius with Mark Antony
Have made themselves so strong—for with her death 155
That tidings came—with this she fell distract
And, her attendants absent, swallowed fire.
CASSIUS
And died so?
BRUTUS   Even so.
CASSIUS   O ye immortal gods!

Enter Boy [Lucius] with wine and tapers.

BRUTUS
Speak no more of her.—Give me a bowl of wine.—
In this I bury all unkindness, Cassius.   *Drinks.*
CASSIUS
My heart is thirsty for that noble pledge.   161
Fill, Lucius, till the wine o'erswell the cup;
I cannot drink too much of Brutus' love.
                              [*He drinks. Exit Lucius.*]

Enter Titinius and Messala.

BRUTUS
Come in, Titinius. Welcome, good Messala.   164
Now sit we close about this taper here
And call in question our necessities.   [*They sit.*]
CASSIUS
Portia, art thou gone?   166

BRUTUS   No more, I pray you.
Messala, I have here receivèd letters   168
That young Octavius and Mark Antony   169
Come down upon us with a mighty power,
Bending their expedition toward Philippi.
                              [*He shows a letter.*]
MESSALA
Myself have letters of the selfsame tenor.
BRUTUS   With what addition?   172
MESSALA
That by proscription and bills of outlawry
Octavius, Antony, and Lepidus
Have put to death an hundred senators.
BRUTUS
Therein our letters do not well agree;
Mine speak of seventy senators that died
By their proscriptions, Cicero being one.
CASSIUS
Cicero one?
MESSALA   Cicero is dead,   180
And by that order of proscription.
Had you your letters from your wife, my lord?
BRUTUS   No, Messala.   182
MESSALA
Nor nothing in your letters writ of her?
BRUTUS
Nothing, Messala.
MESSALA   That, methinks, is strange.
BRUTUS
Why ask you? Hear you aught of her in yours?
MESSALA   No, my lord.
BRUTUS
Now, as you are a Roman, tell me true.
MESSALA
Then like a Roman bear the truth I tell,
For certain she is dead, and by strange manner.
BRUTUS   190
Why, farewell, Portia. We must die, Messala.
With meditating that she must die once,
I have the patience to endure it now.   192
MESSALA
Even so great men great losses should endure.   193
CASSIUS   194
I have as much of this in art as you,
But yet my nature could not bear it so.   195
BRUTUS
Well, to our work alive. What do you think

168 power army   **169 Bending** directing.   **expedition** rapid march;
warlike enterprise   **172 proscription** (See the note at 4.1.17.)
180–94 Had . . . so (This passage is sometimes regarded as contradictory to lines 142–65 and redundant. Perhaps it is the original account of
Portia's death, and lines 142–65 are part of a later interpolation, but it is
also possible that both are intended, the first being Brutus's intimate
revelation of the news to his friend and the second being Brutus's
recovery of his stoic reserve now on display for Messala and Titinius.)
182 nothing . . . her nothing written about her in the letter or letters
you've received.   **190 once** at some time   **192 Even so** In just such a
way   **193 art** i.e., the acquired theoretical wisdom of stoical fortitude
(as contrasted with the gifts of *nature* in line 194)   **195 alive** concerning
us who are alive and dealing with present and future realities.

145 place way.   **accidental evils** misfortunes caused by chance
(which should be a matter of indifference to a philosopher like Brutus).   **149 scaped I killing** did I escape being killed   **153 her death**
i.e., news of her death   **155 swallowed fire** (According to Plutarch,
as translated by Thomas North, Portia "took hot burning coals and
cast them in her mouth, and kept her mouth so close that she choked
herself.")   **161.2 Titinius** (Lucilius does not return with Titinius, as he
was ordered to do at lines 140–1, probably because he was not in Shakespeare's original version of this scene.)   **164 call in question** consider,
discuss   **166 letters** (Probably a single letter. See 3.1.281n and 4.3.4n.)

Of marching to Philippi presently?

CASSIUS
I do not think it good.

BRUTUS   Your reason?

CASSIUS   This it is:
'Tis better that the enemy seek us.
So shall he waste his means, weary his soldiers,   200
Doing himself offense, whilst we, lying still,
Are full of rest, defense, and nimbleness.

BRUTUS   202
Good reasons must of force give place to better.
The people twixt Philippi and this ground
Do stand but in a forced affection,
For they have grudged us contribution.
The enemy, marching along by them,
By them shall make a fuller number up,
Come on refreshed, new-added, and encouraged;
From which advantage shall we cut him off
If at Philippi we do face him there,
These people at our back.   211

CASSIUS   Hear me, good brother—

BRUTUS   212
Under your pardon. You must note beside
That we have tried the utmost of our friends;
Our legions are brim full, our cause is ripe.
The enemy increaseth every day;
We, at the height, are ready to decline.
There is a tide in the affairs of men
Which, taken at the flood, leads on to fortune;
Omitted, all the voyage of their life   220
Is bound in shallows and in miseries.
On such a full sea are we now afloat,
And we must take the current when it serves
Or lose our ventures.   223

CASSIUS   Then, with your will, go on.
We'll along ourselves and meet them at Philippi.

BRUTUS
The deep of night is crept upon our talk,
And nature must obey necessity,   227
Which we will niggard with a little rest.
There is no more to say.

CASSIUS   No more. Good night.   229
Early tomorrow will we rise and hence.

BRUTUS
Lucius!

Enter Lucius.

My gown.   [*Exit Lucius.*] 230
                    Farewell, good Messala.
Good night, Titinius. Noble, noble Cassius,
Good night and good repose.

CASSIUS   Oh, my dear brother!
This was an ill beginning of the night.
Never come such division 'tween our souls!
Let it not, Brutus.

Enter Lucius with the gown.

BRUTUS   Everything is well.

CASSIUS   Good night, my lord.

BRUTUS   Good night, good brother.

TITINIUS, MESSALA   Good night, Lord Brutus.

BRUTUS   Farewell, everyone.
                    Exeunt [all but Brutus and Lucius]. 241
Give me the gown. Where is thy instrument?

LUCIUS
Here in the tent.

BRUTUS   What, thou speak'st drowsily!   243
Poor knave, I blame thee not; thou art o'erwatched.
Call Claudius and some other of my men;
I'll have them sleep on cushions in my tent.

LUCIUS [*calling*]   Varro and Claudius!

Enter Varro and Claudius.

VARRO   Calls my lord?

BRUTUS
I pray you, sirs, lie in my tent and sleep.   249
It may be I shall raise you by and by
On business to my brother Cassius.

VARRO   251
So please you, we will stand and watch your pleasure.

BRUTUS
I will not have it so. Lie down, good sirs.   253
It may be I shall otherwise bethink me.
                    [*Varro and Claudius lie down.*]
Look, Lucius, here's the book I sought for so;
I put it in the pocket of my gown.

LUCIUS
I was sure Your Lordship did not give it me.

BRUTUS
Bear with me, good boy, I am much forgetful.
Canst thou hold up thy heavy eyes awhile   259
And touch thy instrument a strain or two?

LUCIUS
Ay, my lord, an't please you.   260

BRUTUS   It does, my boy.
I trouble thee too much, but thou art willing.

LUCIUS   It is my duty, sir.

BRUTUS
I should not urge thy duty past thy might;   264
I know young bloods look for a time of rest.

LUCIUS   I have slept, my lord, already.

BRUTUS
It was well done, and thou shalt sleep again;

---

200 **offense** harm   202 **of force** necessarily   211 **These . . . back** i.e., with the people our enemy would otherwise recruit being instead in territory we control.   212 **Under your pardon** i.e., Excuse me, let me continue.   220 **bound in** confined to   223 **ventures** investments (of enterprise at sea).   **with your will** as you wish   227 **niggard** stint (by sleeping only briefly)   229 **hence** depart.   230 **gown** housecoat.

241 **instrument** i.e., perhaps a lute or cittern.   243 **knave** boy. **o'erwatched** tired from lack of sleep.   249 **raise** rouse   251 **watch your pleasure** wakefully await your commands.   253 **otherwise bethink me** change my mind.   259 **touch** i.e., play on.   **strain** tune, musical phrase   260 **an't** if it   264 **young bloods** youthful constitutions

I will not hold thee long. If I do live,
I will be good to thee.
                Music, and a song. [*Lucius falls asleep.*] 269
This is a sleepy tune. O murd'rous slumber,   270
Layest thou thy leaden mace upon my boy,
That plays thee music? Gentle knave, good night;
I will not do thee so much wrong to wake thee.
If thou dost nod, thou break'st thy instrument;
I'll take it from thee. And, good boy, good night.
            [*He removes Lucius' instrument,*
                 and begins to read.]
Let me see, let me see; is not the leaf turned down
Where I left reading? Here it is, I think.

    Enter the Ghost of Caesar.   277

How ill this taper burns! Ha! Who comes here?
I think it is the weakness of mine eyes
That shapes this monstrous apparition.   280
It comes upon me.—Art thou any thing?
Art thou some god, some angel, or some devil,   282
That mak'st my blood cold and my hair to stare?
Speak to me what thou art.
GHOST
    Thy evil spirit, Brutus.
BRUTUS   Why com'st thou?
GHOST
    To tell thee thou shalt see me at Philippi.
BRUTUS   Well; then I shall see thee again?
GHOST   Ay, at Philippi.
BRUTUS
    Why, I will see thee at Philippi, then.   [*Exit Ghost.*]
Now I have taken heart, thou vanishest.
Ill spirit, I would hold more talk with thee.—
Boy, Lucius! Varro! Claudius! Sirs, awake!
Claudius!   292
LUCIUS   The strings, my lord, are false.
BRUTUS
    He thinks he still is at his instrument.—
Lucius, awake!
LUCIUS   My lord?
BRUTUS
    Didst thou dream, Lucius, that thou so cried'st out?
LUCIUS
    My lord, I do not know that I did cry.
BRUTUS
    Yes, that thou didst. Didst thou see anything?
LUCIUS   Nothing, my lord.
BRUTUS
    Sleep again, Lucius. Sirrah Claudius!
[*To Varro*] Fellow thou, awake!
VARRO   My lord?
CLAUDIUS   My lord?
                        [*They get up.*]

---

269 **murd'rous** producing the likeness of death   **270 leaden mace**
heavy staff of office (used by a sheriff to touch the shoulder of one
being placed under arrest)   **277 How . . . burns!** (Ghostly apparitions
were thought to be accompanied by such effects as lights burning low
and blue.)   **280 upon** toward   **282 stare** stand on end.   **292 false** out
of tune.

BRUTUS
    Why did you so cry out, sirs, in your sleep?
VARRO, CLAUDIUS
    Did we, my lord?
BRUTUS   Ay. Saw you anything?
VARRO
    No, my lord, I saw nothing.
CLAUDIUS   Nor I, my lord.
BRUTUS
    Go and commend me to my brother Cassius.   305
Bid him set on his powers betimes before,   306
And we will follow.
VARRO, CLAUDIUS   It shall be done, my lord.
                       Exeunt.

❖

5.1

    Enter Octavius, Antony, and their army.

OCTAVIUS
    Now, Antony, our hopes are answerèd.
You said the enemy would not come down,
But keep the hills and upper regions.   3
It proves not so. Their battles are at hand;   4
They mean to warn us at Philippi here,   5
Answering before we do demand of them.
ANTONY
    Tut, I am in their bosoms, and I know   7
Wherefore they do it. They could be content
To visit other places, and come down   9
With fearful bravery, thinking by this face   10
To fasten in our thoughts that they have courage;
But 'tis not so.

    Enter a Messenger.

MESSENGER   Prepare you, generals.   12
The enemy comes on in gallant show.
Their bloody sign of battle is hung out,   14
And something to be done immediately.   15
ANTONY
    Octavius, lead your battle softly on   16
Upon the left hand of the even field.
OCTAVIUS
    Upon the right hand, I. Keep thou the left.
ANTONY
    Why do you cross me in this exigent?   19

---

305 commend me deliver my greetings   **306 set . . . before** march
away with his troops early in the morning, before me
5.1 Location: The plains of Philippi, in Macedonia.
3 keep remain in   **4 battles** armies   **5 warn** challenge   **7 bosoms**
secret councils   **9 visit other places** i.e., be elsewhere   **10 fearful
bravery** (1) awesome ostentation (2) a show of bravery to conceal
their fear.   **face** pretense (of courage)   **12 'tis not so** (1) their plan
cannot deceive us (2) they have no courage.   **14 bloody sign** red
flag or crimson coat of arms as battle signal   **15 to be** is to be
16 softly warily, with restraint   **19 cross** contradict.   **exigent** critical
moment.

OCTAVIUS

I do not cross you, but I will do so. *March.* 20

Drum. Enter Brutus, Cassius, and their army;
[*Lucilius, Titinius, Messala, and others*].

BRUTUS They stand and would have parley.

CASSIUS

Stand fast, Titinius. We must out and talk. 22

OCTAVIUS

Mark Antony, shall we give sign of battle?

ANTONY

No, Caesar, we will answer on their charge. 24
Make forth. The generals would have some words. 25

OCTAVIUS [*to his officers*] Stir not until the signal.

[*The two sides advance toward one another.*]

BRUTUS

Words before blows. Is it so, countrymen?

OCTAVIUS

Not that we love words better, as you do.

BRUTUS

Good words are better than bad strokes, Octavius.

ANTONY

In your bad strokes, Brutus, you give good words. 30
Witness the hole you made in Caesar's heart,
Crying "Long live! Hail, Caesar!"

CASSIUS Antony,
The posture of your blows are yet unknown; 33
But for your words, they rob the Hybla bees, 34
And leave them honeyless.

ANTONY Not stingless too?

BRUTUS Oh, yes, and soundless too.
For you have stol'n their buzzing, Antony,
And very wisely threat before you sting. 39

ANTONY

Villains! You did not so when your vile daggers 40
Hacked one another in the sides of Caesar.
You showed your teeth like apes, and fawned like
hounds, 42
And bowed like bondmen, kissing Caesar's feet,
Whilst damnèd Casca, like a cur, behind,
Struck Caesar on the neck. Oh, you flatterers!

CASSIUS

Flatterers? Now, Brutus, thank yourself!
This tongue had not offended so today
If Cassius might have ruled. 48

OCTAVIUS

Come, come, the cause. If arguing make us sweat, 49
The proof of it will turn to redder drops. 50
Look, [*He draws.*]

I draw a sword against conspirators.
When think you that the sword goes up again? 53
Never, till Caesar's three-and-thirty wounds 54
Be well avenged, or till another Caesar 55
Have added slaughter to the sword of traitors. 56

BRUTUS

Caesar, thou canst not die by traitors' hands, 57
Unless thou bring'st them with thee.

OCTAVIUS So I hope. 58
I was not born to die on Brutus' sword. 59

BRUTUS

Oh, if thou wert the noblest of thy strain, 60
Young man, thou couldst not die more honorable.

CASSIUS

A peevish schoolboy, worthless of such honor, 62
Joined with a masker and a reveler! 63

ANTONY

Old Cassius still.

OCTAVIUS Come, Antony, away!— 64
Defiance, traitors, hurl we in your teeth.
If you dare fight today, come to the field;
If not, when you have stomachs. 67

Exeunt Octavius, Antony, and army.

CASSIUS

Why, now, blow wind, swell billow, and swim bark! 68
The storm is up, and all is on the hazard. 69

BRUTUS

Ho, Lucilius! Hark, a word with you.

LUCILIUS (*stands forth*) My lord?

[*Brutus and Lucilius converse apart.*]

CASSIUS Messala!

MESSALA (*stands forth*) What says my general?

CASSIUS Messala,
This is my birthday, as this very day 75
Was Cassius born. Give me thy hand, Messala.
Be thou my witness that against my will,
As Pompey was, am I compelled to set 78
Upon one battle all our liberties.
You know that I held Epicurus strong 80
And his opinion. Now I change my mind
And partly credit things that do presage. 82
Coming from Sardis, on our former ensign 83

---

20 **cross you** contradict you perversely. **do so** do as I said. 22 **out** go out 24 **answer on their charge** respond when they attack. 25 **Make forth** March forward. 30 **In . . . words** i.e., As you deliver cruel blows, Brutus, you use deceiving flattery. 33 **The posture . . . are** how you strike your blows is 34 **for** as for. **Hybla** a mountain and a town in ancient Sicily, famous for honey 39 **very wisely** (Said ironically; Brutus suggests that Antony is all bluster and no action.) **threat** threaten 40 **so** i.e., give warning 42 **showed your teeth** i.e., in smiles 48 **ruled** prevailed (in urging that Antony be killed). 49 **the cause** to our business. 50 **proof** trial

53 **up** in its sheath 54 **three-and-thirty** (Plutarch has it three-and-twenty.) 55 **another Caesar** i.e., myself, Octavius 56 **Have . . . to** has also been slaughtered by 57–8 **thou . . . thee** i.e., the only traitors here are in your own army. 58–9 **So . . . sword** i.e. (sardonically), I'm glad to hear that, since you are the traitor I mean, and since you are not in my army, I cannot, according to your assertion, die at your hands. 60 **if** even if. **strain** lineage 62 **peevish** silly, childish. **schoolboy** (Octavius was eighteen at the time of Caesar's assassination.) **worthless** unworthy 63 **a masker . . . reveler** i.e., Antony, noted for his dissipation. 64 **Old . . . still** i.e., Cassius, as envious and ill-willed as ever. (Said sardonically.) 67 **stomachs** appetites (for fighting), courage. 68 **billow** wave. **swim bark** let the sailing vessel swim for its life. 69 **on the hazard** at stake. 75 **as** inasmuch as 78 **Pompey** (The reference is to the battle of Pharsalus, where Pompey was persuaded to fight Caesar against his own judgment.) **set** stake 80 **Epicurus** Greek philosopher (341–270 B.C.) who, because he held the gods to be indifferent to human affairs, spurned belief in omens or superstitions 82 **presage** foretell events. 83 **former ensign** foremost standard, the legion's *aquila*, a tall standard surmounted by the image of an eagle

Two mighty eagles fell, and there they perched,   84
Gorging and feeding from our soldiers' hands,
Who to Philippi here consorted us.   86
This morning are they fled away and gone,
And in their steads do ravens, crows, and kites   88
Fly o'er our heads and downward look on us
As we were sickly prey. Their shadows seem   90
A canopy most fatal, under which   91
Our army lies, ready to give up the ghost.

MESSALA
Believe not so.

CASSIUS   I but believe it partly,   93
For I am fresh of spirit and resolved
To meet all perils very constantly.   95

BRUTUS
Even so, Lucilius.   [*He rejoins Cassius.*]

CASSIUS   Now, most noble Brutus,   96
The gods today stand friendly, that we may,   97
Lovers in peace, lead on our days to age!   98
But since the affairs of men rest still incertain,   99
Let's reason with the worst that may befall.   100
If we do lose this battle, then is this
The very last time we shall speak together.
What are you then determinèd to do?

BRUTUS
Even by the rule of that philosophy
By which I did blame Cato for the death   105
Which he did give himself—I know not how,
But I do find it cowardly and vile,
For fear of what might fall, so to prevent   108
The time of life—arming myself with patience   109
To stay the providence of some high powers   110
That govern us below.

CASSIUS   Then, if we lose this battle,
You are contented to be led in triumph
Thorough the streets of Rome?   113

BRUTUS
No, Cassius, no. Think not, thou noble Roman,
That ever Brutus will go bound to Rome;
He bears too great a mind. But this same day
Must end that work the ides of March begun.
And whether we shall meet again I know not;
Therefore our everlasting farewell take.
Forever and forever farewell, Cassius!
If we do meet again, why, we shall smile;
If not, why then this parting was well made.

CASSIUS
Forever and forever farewell, Brutus!
If we do meet again, we'll smile indeed;
If not, 'tis true this parting was well made.

BRUTUS
Why, then, lead on. Oh, that a man might know
The end of this day's business ere it come!   127
But it sufficeth that the day will end,
And then the end is known.—Come, ho, away!
                                        Exeunt.

❧

[5.2]

Alarum. Enter Brutus and Messala.

BRUTUS
Ride, ride, Messala, ride, and give these bills   1
Unto the legions on the other side.   2
                    [*He hands him written orders.*]
                                        Loud alarum.
Let them set on at once; for I perceive   3
But cold demeanor in Octavio's wing,   4
And sudden push gives them the overthrow.
Ride, ride, Messala! Let them all come down.   6
                    Exeunt [*separately*].

❧

[5.3]

Alarums. Enter Cassius [*carrying a standard*], *and
Titinius.*

CASSIUS
Oh, look, Titinius, look, the villains fly!   1
Myself have to mine own turned enemy.   2
This ensign here of mine was turning back;   3
I slew the coward and did take it from him.   4

TITINIUS
Oh, Cassius, Brutus gave the word too early,
Who, having some advantage on Octavius,
Took it too eagerly. His soldiers fell to spoil,   7
Whilst we by Antony are all enclosed.   8

Enter Pindarus.

---

84 fell swooped down   **86 consorted** accompanied   **88 kites** scavenger birds (also raptors)   **90 As** as if   **91 fatal** presaging death   **93 but** only   **95 constantly** resolutely.   **96 Even so, Lucilius** (This phrase marks the end of Brutus's private conversation apart with Lucilius.)   **97 The gods** May the gods   **98 Lovers** friends.   **age** old age.   **99 still** always   **100 reason** reckon   **105 Cato** i.e., Marcus Porcius Cato, Brutus's father-in-law, who killed himself to avoid submission to Caesar in 46 B.C. (See 2.1.296 and note.) Brutus's condemnation of Cato's suicide out of fear of failure can perhaps be reconciled with lines 114–17 below and with Brutus's own later suicide (5.5.50), since on that occasion Brutus is responding to certain defeat and disgrace. The seeming contradiction may also be owing to an ambiguity in North's Plutarch.   **108 fall** befall.   **prevent** anticipate the end, cut short   **109 time** term, extent   **110 stay** await   **113 Thorough** through

127 ere before
5.2 Location: The plains of Philippi. The field of battle.
0.1 *Alarum* (This is seemingly an anticipatory stage direction; the battle actually begins with the *Loud alarum* at line 2. An *alarum* is off stage sounds, signifying a battle.)   **1 bills** orders   **2 side** wing (i.e., Cassius's wing).   **3 set on** attack   **4 cold demeanor** faintheartedness
6 come down i.e., from the hills, where the Republican army has been awaiting the signal to attack. (See 5.1.2–3.)
5.3 Location: The field of battle still.
1 the villains i.e., my own troops   **2 mine own** my own men
3 ensign bearer of the standard. (A legion's *aquila*, or "eagle standard," had great significance and needed to be guarded.)   **4 it** i.e., the standard   **7 spoil** looting   **8 enclosed** surrounded.

PINDARUS
　　Fly further off, my lord, fly further off!
　　Mark Antony is in your tents, my lord.
　　Fly therefore, noble Cassius, fly far off.
CASSIUS
　　This hill is far enough. Look, look, Titinius:
　　Are those my tents where I perceive the fire?
TITINIUS
　　They are, my lord.
CASSIUS　　　　　　　Titinius, if thou lovest me,
　　Mount thou my horse, and hide thy spurs in him
　　Till he have brought thee up to yonder troops
　　And here again, that I may rest assured
　　Whether yond troops are friend or enemy.
TITINIUS
　　I will be here again even with a thought.　　*Exit.*　19
CASSIUS
　　Go, Pindarus, get higher on that hill.
　　My sight was ever thick. Regard Titinius,　　　　21
　　And tell me what thou not'st about the field.　　22
　　　　　　　　　　[*Pindarus goes up.*]
　　This day I breathèd first. Time is come round,　23
　　And where I did begin, there shall I end.
　　My life is run his compass.—Sirrah, what news?　25
PINDARUS (*above*)　Oh, my lord!
CASSIUS　What news?
PINDARUS [*above*]
　　Titinius is enclosèd round about
　　With horsemen, that make to him on the spur,　29
　　Yet he spurs on. Now they are almost on him.
　　Now, Titinius! Now some light. Oh, he　　　　31
　　Lights too. He's ta'en. (*Shout.*) And hark! They shout
　　　for joy.
CASSIUS　Come down, behold no more.
　　Oh, coward that I am, to live so long
　　To see my best friend ta'en before my face!　　35

　　　　　Enter Pindarus [*from above*].

　　Come hither, sirrah.
　　In Parthia did I take thee prisoner,　　　　　37
　　And then I swore thee, saving of thy life,　　　38
　　That whatsoever I did bid thee do
　　Thou shouldst attempt it. Come now, keep thine oath;
　　Now be a freeman, and with this good sword,
　　That ran through Caesar's bowels, search this bosom.　42
　　Stand not to answer. Here, take thou the hilts,　　43
　　And when my face is covered, as 'tis now,
　　Guide thou the sword. [*Pindarus does so.*] Caesar, thou
　　　art revenged,
　　Even with the sword that killed thee.　　[*He dies.*]

PINDARUS
　　So, I am free, yet would not so have been,　　47
　　Durst I have done my will. Oh, Cassius!　　48
　　Far from this country Pindarus shall run,
　　Where never Roman shall take note of him.　[*Exit.*]

　　　　　Enter Titinius [*wearing a garland of laurel*] *and
　　　　　Messala.*

MESSALA
　　It is but change, Titinius; for Octavius　　　51
　　Is overthrown by noble Brutus' power,
　　As Cassius' legions are by Antony.
TITINIUS
　　These tidings will well comfort Cassius.
MESSALA
　　Where did you leave him?
TITINIUS　　　　　　　All disconsolate,
　　With Pindarus his bondman, on this hill.
MESSALA
　　Is not that he that lies upon the ground?
TITINIUS
　　He lies not like the living. Oh, my heart!
MESSALA
　　Is not that he?
TITINIUS　　　　No, this was he, Messala,
　　But Cassius is no more. O setting sun,
　　As in thy red rays thou dost sink to night,
　　So in his red blood Cassius' day is set.
　　The sun of Rome is set. Our day is gone;　　63
　　Clouds, dews, and dangers come; our deeds are done.
　　Mistrust of my success hath done this deed.　65
MESSALA
　　Mistrust of good success hath done this deed.
　　O hateful Error, Melancholy's child,　　　　67
　　Why dost thou show to the apt thoughts of men　68
　　The things that are not? O Error, soon conceived,
　　Thou never com'st unto a happy birth,
　　But kill'st the mother that engendered thee.　71
TITINIUS
　　What, Pindarus! Where art thou, Pindarus?
MESSALA
　　Seek him, Titinius, whilst I go to meet
　　The noble Brutus, thrusting this report
　　Into his ears. I may say "thrusting" it,
　　For piercing steel and darts envenomèd
　　Shall be as welcome to the ears of Brutus
　　As tidings of this sight.
TITINIUS　　　　　　　Hie you, Messala,
　　And I will seek for Pindarus the while.
　　　　　　　　　　[*Exit Messala.*]
　　Why didst thou send me forth, brave Cassius?
　　Did I not meet thy friends? And did not they
　　Put on my brows this wreath of victory

---

19 even . . . thought as quick as thought.　**21 thick** imperfect, dim. **Regard** Observe　**22.1 *Pindarus goes up*** (Pindarus may climb to the gallery, or may exit and ascend behind the scenes; see line 35.1 and note.)　**23 I breathèd first** i.e., it is my birthday.　**25 his compass** its circuit, circle (as drawn by a geometer's compass).　**29 make . . . spur** approach him riding rapidly　**31 light** alight, dismount.　**35.1 *Enter*** (Pindarus may descend in full view of the audience; see note at 22.1.)　**37 Parthia** (What is now northern Iran.)　**38 swore . . . of** made you swear, when I spared　**42 search** probe, penetrate　**43 Stand** Delay. **hilts** sword hilt

47 so in this manner　**48 Durst . . . will** if I had dared do what I wished.　**51 change** exchange of advantage, quid pro quo　**63 sun** (With pun on *son.*)　**65 Mistrust** i.e., Cassius's doubt　**67 Melancholy's child** i.e., bred of pessimism　**68 apt** impressionable　**71 the mother** i.e., the melancholy person who too readily believes the worst

And bid me give it thee? Didst thou not hear their
   shouts?
Alas, thou hast misconstrued everything.
But, hold thee, take this garland on thy brow.   85
       [*He places the garland on Cassius's brow.*]
Thy Brutus bid me give it thee, and I
Will do his bidding. Brutus, come apace   87
And see how I regarded Caius Cassius.
By your leave, gods! This is a Roman's part.
Come, Cassius' sword, and find Titinius' heart.
           [*He stabs himself and*] *dies.*

Alarum. Enter Brutus, Messala, young Cato,
Strato, Volumnius, and Lucilius, [Labeo, and
Flavius].

BRUTUS
  Where, where, Messala, doth his body lie?
MESSALA
  Lo, yonder, and Titinius mourning it.
BRUTUS
  Titinius' face is upward.
CATO   He is slain.
BRUTUS
  O Julius Caesar, thou art mighty yet!
  Thy spirit walks abroad and turns our swords
  In our own proper entrails.   *Low alarums.*
CATO   Brave Titinius!   96
  Look whe'er he have not crowned dead Cassius.   97
BRUTUS
  Are yet two Romans living such as these?
  The last of all the Romans, fare thee well!
  It is impossible that ever Rome
  Should breed thy fellow. Friends, I owe more tears
  To this dead man than you shall see me pay.—
  I shall find time, Cassius, I shall find time.—
  Come, therefore, and to Thasos send his body.   104
  His funerals shall not be in our camp,   105
  Lest it discomfort us. Lucilius, come,   106
  And come, young Cato, let us to the field.
  Labeo and Flavius, set our battles on.   108
  'Tis three o'clock, and, Romans, yet ere night   109
  We shall try fortune in a second fight.
               Exeunt [with the bodies].

❖

[5.4]

Alarum. Enter Brutus, Messala, [young] Cato,
Lucilius, and Flavius.

BRUTUS
  Yet, countrymen, oh, yet hold up your heads!
        [*Exit, followed by Messala and Flavius.*]
CATO
  What bastard doth not? Who will go with me?   2
  I will proclaim my name about the field:
  I am the son of Marcus Cato, ho!
  A foe to tyrants, and my country's friend.
  I am the son of Marcus Cato, ho!

     Enter soldiers, and fight.

LUCILIUS
  And I am Brutus, Marcus Brutus I!
  Brutus, my country's friend! Know me for Brutus!
       [*Young Cato is slain by Antony's men.*]
  O young and noble Cato, art thou down?
  Why, now thou diest as bravely as Titinius,
  And mayst be honored, being Cato's son.
FIRST SOLDIER [*capturing Lucilius*]
  Yield, or thou diest.
LUCILIUS [*offering money*]   Only I yield to die.   12
  There is so much that thou wilt kill me straight;   13
  Kill Brutus, and be honored in his death.
FIRST SOLDIER
  We must not. A noble prisoner!
SECOND SOLDIER
  Room, ho! Tell Antony, Brutus is ta'en.

     Enter Antony.

FIRST SOLDIER
  I'll tell the news. Here comes the General.—
  Brutus is ta'en, Brutus is ta'en, my lord.
ANTONY   Where is he?
LUCILIUS
  Safe, Antony, Brutus is safe enough.
  I dare assure thee that no enemy
  Shall ever take alive the noble Brutus.
  The gods defend him from so great a shame!
  When you do find him, or alive or dead,   24
  He will be found like Brutus, like himself.
ANTONY [*to First Soldier*]
  This is not Brutus, friend, but, I assure you,
  A prize no less in worth. Keep this man safe;
  Give him all kindness. I had rather have
  Such men my friends than enemies.—Go on,
  And see whe'er Brutus be alive or dead;   30
  And bring us word unto Octavius' tent
  How everything is chanced.   32
     Exeunt [separately, some bearing Cato's body].

❖

---

85 hold thee wait   **87 apace** quickly   **96 own proper** very own
96 s.d. *Low alarums* Offstage sound effects suggesting the activity
of distant battle.   **97 whe'er** whether   **104 Thasos** an island off
the coast of Thrace, near Philippi   **105 funerals** funeral obsequies
106 discomfort us discourage our troops.   **108 battles** armies
109 yet ere night (The historical battles fought at Philippi were
actually weeks apart.)
5.4. Location: Scene continues at the field of battle.

2 What . . . not? Who is so base that he would not do so?   **12 Only . . .**
die I surrender only on condition that I die at your hands.   **13 There**
. . . straight Here is money if you will kill me at once   **24 or alive**
either alive   **30 whe'er** whether   **32 is chanced** has fallen out.

[5.5]

*Enter Brutus, Dardanius, Clitus, Strato, and
Volumnius.*

BRUTUS
Come, poor remains of friends, rest on this rock.
                                                    [*He sits.*]
CLITUS
Statilius showed the torchlight, but, my lord,   2
He came not back. He is or ta'en or slain.   3
BRUTUS
Sit thee down, Clitus. Slaying is the word.
It is a deed in fashion. Hark thee, Clitus.
                                        [*He whispers.*]
CLITUS
What, I, my lord? No, not for all the world.
BRUTUS
Peace then. No words.
CLITUS   I'll rather kill myself.
BRUTUS
Hark thee, Dardanius.   [*He whispers.*]
DARDANIUS   Shall I do such a deed?
            [*Dardanius and Clitus move away from Brutus.*]
CLITUS   Oh, Dardanius!
DARDANIUS   Oh, Clitus!
CLITUS
What ill request did Brutus make to thee?
DARDANIUS
To kill him, Clitus. Look, he meditates.
CLITUS
Now is that noble vessel full of grief,
That it runs over even at his eyes.
BRUTUS
Come hither, good Volumnius. List a word.   15
VOLUMNIUS
What says my lord?
BRUTUS   Why, this, Volumnius:
The ghost of Caesar hath appeared to me
Two several times by night—at Sardis once,   18
And this last night here in Philippi fields.
I know my hour is come.
VOLUMNIUS   Not so, my lord.
BRUTUS
Nay, I am sure it is, Volumnius.
Thou see'st the world, Volumnius, how it goes;
Our enemies have beat us to the pit.   *Low alarums.*   23
It is more worthy to leap in ourselves
Than tarry till they push us. Good Volumnius,
Thou know'st that we two went to school together.
Even for that our love of old, I prithee,   27

Hold thou my sword hilts whilst I run on it.   28
VOLUMNIUS
That's not an office for a friend, my lord.
                                        Alarum still.
CLITUS
Fly, fly, my lord! There is no tarrying here.
BRUTUS
Farewell to you, and you, and you, Volumnius.
Strato, thou hast been all this while asleep;
Farewell to thee too, Strato. Countrymen,
My heart doth joy that yet in all my life
I found no man but he was true to me.
I shall have glory by this losing day
More than Octavius and Mark Antony
By this vile conquest shall attain unto.
So fare you well at once, for Brutus' tongue   39
Hath almost ended his life's history.
Night hangs upon mine eyes; my bones would rest,
That have but labored to attain this hour.   42
            Alarum. Cry within, "Fly, fly, fly!"
CLITUS
Fly, my lord, fly!
BRUTUS   Hence, I will follow.
            [*Exeunt Clitus, Dardanius, and Volumnius.*]
I prithee, Strato, stay thou by thy lord.
Thou art a fellow of a good respect;   45
Thy life hath had some smatch of honor in it.   46
Hold then my sword, and turn away thy face,
While I do run upon it. Wilt thou, Strato?
STRATO
Give me your hand first. Fare you well, my lord.
BRUTUS
Farewell, good Strato. [*He runs on his sword.*] Caesar,
    now be still.
I killed not thee with half so good a will.   *Dies.*   51

            *Alarum. Retreat. Enter Antony, Octavius;
            Messala, Lucilius [as prisoners]; and the army.*

OCTAVIUS   What man is that?
MESSALA
My master's man. Strato, where is thy master?
STRATO
Free from the bondage you are in, Messala.
The conquerors can but make a fire of him,
For Brutus only overcame himself,   56
And no man else hath honor by his death.
LUCILIUS
So Brutus should be found. I thank thee, Brutus,
That thou hast proved Lucilius' saying true.   59
OCTAVIUS
All that served Brutus, I will entertain them.   60

5.5. Location: The field of battle still.
2–3 Statilius . . . slain (According to Plutarch, a scout named Statilius
has gone through the enemy lines to reconnoitre and to hold up a
torch if all is well at Cassius's camp; he signals back but is then captured and slain.)   3 or ta'en either taken   15 List Listen to   18 several separate   23 beat driven.   pit trap for wild animals; also, a
grave.   27 that our love that friendship of ours

28 hilts hilt   39 at once all together, or without further ado   42 That
. . . hour that have striven all life long only to achieve this moment
of death.   45 respect reputation   46 some smatch some flavor, a
touch   51.1 Retreat signal to retire.   56 Brutus . . . himself only
Brutus conquered Brutus   59 saying (See 5.4.21–5.)   60 entertain
take into service

Fellow, wilt thou bestow thy time with me?

STRATO
Ay, if Messala will prefer me to you.   62

OCTAVIUS   Do so, good Messala.

MESSALA   How died my master, Strato?

STRATO
I held the sword, and he did run on it.

MESSALA
Octavius, then take him to follow thee,   66
That did the latest service to my master.   67

ANTONY
This was the noblest Roman of them all.
All the conspirators save only he
Did that they did in envy of great Caesar;
He only in a general honest thought   71
And common good to all made one of them.

His life was gentle, and the elements   73
So mixed in him that Nature might stand up
And say to all the world, "This was a man!"

OCTAVIUS
According to his virtue let us use him,
With all respect and rites of burial.
Within my tent his bones tonight shall lie,
Most like a soldier, ordered honorably.   79
So call the field to rest, and let's away   80
To part the glories of this happy day.   81

Exeunt omnes [with Brutus's body].

62 prefer recommend   **66 follow** serve   **67 latest** last   **71 general** i.e., selfless. (Cf. 2.1.2 n.)

73 gentle noble.   **elements** (Humankind as a microcosm is made up of earth, air, fire, and water, formed into the four humors of phlegm, blood, yellow bile [or choler], and black bile [or melancholy], whose qualities were mingled in Brutus in due proportions.)   **79 ordered** treated, arranged for; accorded solemn rites. (Cf. 1.2.25 n.)   **80 field** army in the field   **81 part** share.   **happy** fortunate   **81.1** *omnes* all

Hamlet, Prince of Denmark

Arecurring motif in *Hamlet* is of a seemingly healthy exterior concealing an interior sickness. Mere pretense of virtue, as Hamlet warns his mother, "will but skin and film the ulcerous place, / Whiles rank corruption, mining all within, / Infects unseen" (3.4.154–6). Polonius confesses, when he is about to use his daughter as a decoy for Hamlet, that "with devotion's visage / And pious action we do sugar o'er / The devil himself"; and his observation elicits a more anguished mea culpa from Claudius in an aside: "How smart a lash that speech doth give my conscience! / The harlot's cheek, beautied with plast'ring art, / Is not more ugly to the thing that helps it / Than is my deed to my most painted word" (3.1.47–54).

This motif of concealed evil and disease continually reminds us that, in both a specific and a broader sense, "Something is rotten in the state of Denmark" (1.4.90). The specific source of contamination is a poison: the poison with which Claudius has killed Hamlet's father, the poison in the players' enactment of "The Murder of Gonzago," and the two poisons (envenomed sword and poisoned drink) with which Claudius and Laertes plot to rid themselves of young Hamlet. More generally, the poison is an evil nature seeking to destroy humanity's better self, as in the archetypal murder of Abel by Cain. "Oh, my offense is rank! It smells to heaven," laments Claudius, "It hath the primal eldest curse upon't, / A brother's murder" (3.3.36–8). To Hamlet, his father and Claudius typify what is best and worst in humanity; one is the sun-god Hyperion and the other, a satyr. Claudius is a "serpent" and a "mildewed ear, / Blasting his wholesome brother" (1.5.40; 3.4.65–6). Many a person, in Hamlet's view, is tragically destined to behold his or her better qualities corrupted by "some vicious mole of nature" over which the individual seems to have no control. "His virtues else, be they as pure as grace, / As infinite as man may undergo, / Shall in the general censure take corruption / From that particular fault." The "dram of evil" pollutes "all the noble substance" (1.4.24–37). Thus, poison spreads outward to infect the whole individual, just as bad individuals can infect an entire court or nation.

Hamlet, his mind attuned to philosophical matters, is keenly and poetically aware of humanity's fallen condition. He is, moreover, a shrewd observer of the Danish court, familiar with its ways and at the same time newly returned from abroad, looking at Denmark with a stranger's eyes. What particularly darkens his view of humanity, however, is not the general fact of corrupted human nature but rather Hamlet's knowledge of a dreadful secret. Even before he learns of his father's murder, Hamlet senses that there is something more deeply amiss than his mother's overhasty marriage to her deceased husband's brother. This is serious enough, to be sure, for it violates a taboo (parallel to the marriage of a widower to his deceased wife's sister, long regarded as incestuous by the English) and is thus understandably referred to as "incest" by Hamlet and his father's ghost. The appalling spectacle of Gertrude's "wicked speed, to post / With such dexterity to incestuous sheets" (1.2.156–7) overwhelms Hamlet with revulsion at carnal appetite and intensifies the emotional crisis any son would go through when forced to contemplate his father's death and his mother's remarriage. Still, the Ghost's revelation is of something far worse, something Hamlet has subconsciously feared and suspected. "Oh, my prophetic soul! My uncle!" (1.5.42). Now Hamlet believes he has confirming evidence for his intuition that the world itself is "an unweeded garden / That grows to seed. Things rank and gross in nature / Possess it merely" (1.2.135–7).

Something is indeed rotten in the state of Denmark. The monarch on whom the health and safety of the kingdom depend is a murderer. Yet few persons know his secret: Hamlet, Horatio only belatedly, Claudius himself, and ourselves as audience. Many ironies and misunderstandings within the play cannot be understood without a proper awareness of this gap between Hamlet's knowledge and most others' ignorance of the murder. For, according to their own lights, Polonius and the rest behave as courtiers normally behave, obeying and flattering a king who has been chosen by a constitutional process of "election" and therefore can claim to be their legitimate ruler. They do not know that he is a murderer. Hamlet, for his part, is so obsessed with the secret murder that he overreacts to those around him, rejecting overtures of friendship and becoming embittered, callous, brutal, and even violent. His antisocial behavior gives the others good reason to fear him as a menace to the state. Nevertheless, we share with Hamlet a knowledge of the truth and know that he is right, whereas the others are at best unhappily deceived by their own blind complicity in evil.

Rosencrantz and Guildenstern, for instance, are boyhood friends of Hamlet but are now dependent on the favor of King Claudius. Despite their seeming concern for their one-time comrade and Hamlet's initial pleasure in receiving them, they are faceless courtiers whose very names, like their personalities, are virtually interchangeable. "Thanks, Rosencrantz and gentle Guildenstern," says the King, and "Thanks, Guildenstern and gentle Rosencrantz," echoes the Queen (2.2.33–4). They cannot understand why Hamlet increasingly mocks their overtures of friendship, whereas Hamlet cannot stomach their subservience to the King. The secret murder divides Hamlet from them, since only he knows of it. As the confrontation between Hamlet and Claudius grows more deadly, Rosencrantz and Guildenstern, not knowing the true cause, can only interpret Hamlet's behavior as dangerous madness. The wild display he puts on during the performance of "The Murder of Gonzago" and then the killing of Polonius are evidence of a treasonous threat to the crown, eliciting from them staunch assertions of the divine right of kings. "Most holy and religious fear it is / To keep those many many bodies safe / That live and feed upon Your Majesty," professes Guildenstern, and Rosencrantz reiterates the theme: "The cess of majesty / Dies not alone, but like a gulf doth draw / What's near it with it" (3.3.8–17). These sentiments of Elizabethan orthodoxy, similar to ones frequently heard in Shakespeare's history plays, are here undercut by a devastating irony, since they are spoken unwittingly in defense of a murderer. This irony pursues Rosencrantz and Guildenstern to their graves, for they are killed performing what they see as their duty to convey Hamlet safely to England. They are as ignorant of Claudius's secret orders for the murder of Hamlet in England as they are of Claudius's real reason for wishing to be rid of his stepson. That Hamlet should ingeniously remove the secret commission from Rosencrantz and Guildenstern's packet and substitute an order for their execution is ironically fitting, even though they are guiltless of having plotted Hamlet's death. "Why, man, they did make love to this employment," says Hamlet to Horatio. "They are not near my conscience. Their defeat / Does by their own

insinuation grow" (5.2.57–9). They have condemned themselves, in Hamlet's eyes, by interceding officiously in deadly affairs of which they had no comprehension. Hamlet's judgment of them is harsh, and he himself appears hardened and pitiless in his role as agent in their deaths, but he is right that they have courted their own destiny.

Polonius, too, dies for meddling. It seems an unfair fate, since he wishes no physical harm to Hamlet and is only trying to ingratiate himself with Claudius. Yet Polonius's complicity in jaded court politics is deeper than his fatuous parental sententiousness might lead one to suppose. His famous advice to his son, often quoted out of context as though it were wise counsel, is, in fact, a worldly gospel of self-interest and concern for appearances. Like his son, Laertes, he cynically presumes that Hamlet's affection for Ophelia cannot be serious, since princes are not free to marry ladies of the court; accordingly, Polonius obliges his daughter to return the love letters she so cherishes. Polonius's spies are everywhere, seeking to entrap Polonius's own son in fleshly sin or to discover symptoms of Hamlet's presumed lovesickness. Polonius may cut a ridiculous figure as a prattling busybody, but he is wily and even menacing in his intent. He has actually helped Claudius to the throne and is an essential instrument of royal policy. His ineffectuality and ignorance of the murder do not really excuse his guilty involvement.

Ophelia is more innocent than her father and brother, and more truly affectionate toward Hamlet. She earns our sympathy because she is caught between the conflicting wills of the men who are supremely important to her— her wooer, her father, and her brother. Obedient by instinct and training to patriarchal instruction, she is unprepared to cope with divided authority and so takes refuge in passivity. Nevertheless, her pitiable story suggests that weak-willed acquiescence is poisoned by the evil to which it surrenders. However passively, Ophelia becomes an instrument through which Claudius attempts to spy on Hamlet. She is much like Gertrude, for the Queen has yielded to Claudius's importunity without ever knowing fully what awful price Claudius has paid for her and for the throne. The resemblance between Ophelia and Gertrude confirms Hamlet's tendency to generalize about feminine weakness—"frailty, thy name is woman" (1.2.146)—and prompts his misogynistic outburst against Ophelia when he concludes she, too, is spying on him. His rejection of love and friendship (except for Horatio's) seems paranoid in character and yet is at least partially justified by the fact that so many of the court are in fact conspiring to learn what he is up to.

Their oversimplification of his dilemma and their facile analyses vex Hamlet as much as their meddling. When they presume to diagnose his malady, the courtiers actually reveal more about themselves than about Hamlet— something we as readers and viewers might well bear in mind. Rosencrantz and Guildenstern think in political terms, reflecting their own ambitious natures, and Hamlet takes mordant delight in leading them on. "Sir, I lack advancement," he mockingly answers Rosencrantz's questioning as to the cause of his distemper. Rosencrantz is immediately taken in: "How can that be, when you have the voice of the King himself for your succession in Denmark?" (3.2.338–41). Actually, Hamlet does hold a grudge against Claudius for having "Popped in between th'election and my hopes" (5.2.65), using the Danish custom of "election" by the chief lords of the realm to deprive young Hamlet of the succession that would normally have been his. Nevertheless, it is a gross oversimplification to suppose that political frustration is the key to Hamlet's sorrow, and to speculate thus is presumptuous. "Why, look you now, how unworthy a thing you make of me!" Hamlet protests to Rosencrantz and Guildenstern. "You would play upon me, you would seem to know my stops, you would pluck out the heart of my mystery" (3.2.362–5). An even worse offender in the distortion of complex truth is Polonius, whose facile diagnosis of lovesickness appears to have been inspired by recollections of Polonius's own far-off youth. ("Truly in my youth I suffered much extremity for love, very near this," 2.2.189–91). Polonius's fatuous complacency in his own powers of analysis—"If circumstances lead me, I will find / Where truth is hid, though it were hid indeed / Within the center" (2.2.157–9)—reads like a parody of Hamlet's struggle to discover what is true and what is not.

Thus, although Hamlet may seem to react with excessive bitterness toward those who are set to watch over him, the corruption he decries in Denmark is both real and universal. "The time is out of joint," he laments. "Oh, cursèd spite / That ever I was born to set it right!" (1.5.197–8). How is he to proceed in setting things right? Ever since the nineteenth century, it has been fashionable to discover reasons for Hamlet's delaying his revenge. The basic Romantic approach is to find a defect, or tragic flaw, in Hamlet himself. In Coleridge's words, Hamlet suffers from "an overbalance in the contemplative faculty" and is "one who vacillates from sensibility and procrastinates from thought, and loses the power of action in the energy of resolve." More recent psychological critics, such as Freud's disciple Ernest Jones, still seek answers to the Romantics' question by explaining Hamlet's failure of will. In Jones' interpretation, Hamlet is the victim of an Oedipal trauma: he has longed unconsciously to possess his mother and for that very reason cannot bring himself to punish the hated uncle who has supplanted him in his incestuous and forbidden desire. Such interpretations suggest, among other things, that Hamlet continues to serve as a mirror in which analysts who would pluck out the heart of his mystery see an image of their own concerns— just as Rosencrantz and Guildenstern read politics, and Polonius reads lovesickness, into Hamlet's distress.

We can ask, however, not only whether the explanations for Hamlet's supposed delay are valid but also whether the question they seek to answer is itself valid. Is the delay unnecessary or excessive? The question did not even arise until the nineteenth century. Earlier audiences were evidently satisfied that Hamlet must test the Ghost's credibility, since apparitions can tell half-truths to deceive people, and that, once Hamlet has confirmed the Ghost's word, he proceeds as resolutely as his canny adversary allows. More recent criticism, perhaps reflecting a modern absorption in existentialist philosophy, has proposed that Hamlet's dilemma is a matter, not of personal failure, but of the absurdity of action itself in a corrupt world. Does what Hamlet is asked to do make any sense, given the bestial nature of humanity and the impossibility of knowing what is right? In part, it is a matter of style: Claudius's Denmark is crassly vulgar, and to combat this vulgarity on its own terms seems to require the sort of bad histrionics Hamlet derides in actors who mouth their lines or tear a passion to tatters. Hamlet's dilemma of action can best be studied in the play by comparing him with various characters who are obliged to act in situations similar to his own and who respond in meaningfully different ways.

Three young men—Hamlet, Laertes, and Fortinbras— are called upon to avenge their fathers' violent deaths. Ophelia, too, has lost a father by violent means, and her madness and death are another kind of reaction to such a loss. The responses of Laertes and Fortinbras offer rich parallels to Hamlet, in both cases implying the futility of positive and forceful action. Laertes thinks he has received an unambiguous mandate to take revenge, since Hamlet has undoubtedly slain Polonius and helped to deprive Ophelia of her sanity. Accordingly, Laertes comes back to Denmark in a fury, stirring the rabble with his demagoguery and spouting Senecan rant about dismissing conscience "to the profoundest pit" in his quest for vengeance (4.5.135). When Claudius asks what Laertes would do to Hamlet "To show yourself in deed your father's son / More than in words," Laertes fires back: "To cut his throat i'th' church" (4.7.126–7). This resolution is understandable. The pity is, however, that Laertes has only superficially identified the murderer in the case. He is too easily deceived by Claudius, because he has jumped to easy and fallacious conclusions, and so is doomed to become a pawn in Claudius's sly maneuverings. Too late he sees his error and must die for it, begging and receiving Hamlet's forgiveness. Before we accuse Hamlet of thinking too deliberately before acting, we must consider that Laertes does not think enough.

Fortinbras of Norway, as his name implies ("strong in arms"), is one who believes in decisive action. At the beginning of the play, we learn that his father has been slain in battle by old Hamlet and that Fortinbras has collected an army to win back by force the territory fairly won by the Danes in that encounter. Like Hamlet, young Fortinbras does not succeed his father to the throne but must now contend with an uncle-king. When this uncle, at Claudius's instigation, forbids Fortinbras to march against the Danes and rewards him for his restraint with a huge annual income and a commission to fight the Poles instead, Fortinbras sagaciously welcomes the new opportunity. He pockets the money, marches against Poland, and waits for occasion to deliver Denmark as well into his hands. Clearly this is more of a success story than that of Laertes, and Hamlet does, after all, give his blessing to the "election" of Fortinbras to the Danish throne. Fortinbras is the man of the hour, the representative of a restored political stability. Yet Hamlet's admiration for this man on horseback is qualified by a profound reservation. Hamlet's dying prophecy that the election will light on Fortinbras (5.2.357–8) is suffused with ironies, so much so that the incongruity is sometimes made conscious and deliberate in performance. Earlier in the play, the spectacle of Fortinbras marching against Poland "to gain a little patch of ground / That hath in it no profit but the name" prompts Hamlet to berate himself for inaction, but he cannot ignore the absurdity of the effort. "Two thousand souls and twenty thousand ducats / Will not debate the question of this straw." The soldiers will risk their very lives "Even for an eggshell" (4.4.19–54). It is only one step from this view of the vanity of ambitious striving to the speculation that great Caesar or Alexander, dead and turned to dust, may one day produce the loam or clay with which to stop the bunghole of a beer barrel. Fortinbras epitomizes the ongoing political order after Hamlet's death, but is that order of any consequence to us after we have imagined with Hamlet the futility of most human endeavor?

To ask such a question is to seek passive or self-abnegating answers to the riddle of life, and Hamlet is attuned to such inquiries. Even before he learns of his father's murder, he contemplates suicide, wishing "that the Everlasting had not fixed / His canon 'gainst self-slaughter" (1.2.131–2). As with the alternative of action, other characters serve as foils to Hamlet, revealing both the attractions and perils of withdrawal. Ophelia is destroyed by meekly acquiescing in others' desires. Whether she commits suicide is uncertain, but the very possibility reminds us that Hamlet has twice considered and reluctantly rejected this despairing path as forbidden by Christian teaching—the second such occasion being his "To be, or not to be" soliloquy in 3.1. He has also playacted at the madness to which Ophelia succumbs. Gertrude identifies herself with Ophelia and like her has surrendered her will to male aggressiveness. We suspect she knows little of the actual murder (see 3.4.31) but dares not think how deeply she may be implicated. Although her death is evidently not a suicide (see 5.2.291–7), it is passive and expiatory.

A more attractive alternative to decisive action for Hamlet is acting in the theater, and he is full of exuberant advice to the visiting players. The play they perform before Claudius at Hamlet's request and with some lines added by him—a play consciously archaic in style—offers to the Danish court a kind of heightened reflection of itself, a homiletic artifact, rendering in conventional terms the taut anxieties and terrors of murder for the sake of noble passion. Structurally, the play within the play becomes not an escape for Hamlet into inaction but rather the point on which the whole drama pivots and the scene in which contemplation of past events is largely replaced with stirrings toward action. When Lucianus in the Mousetrap play turns out to be nephew rather than brother to the dead king, the audience finds itself face to face, not with history, but with prophecy. We are not surprised when, in his conversations with the players, Hamlet openly professes his admiration for the way in which art holds "the mirror up to nature, to show virtue her feature, scorn her own image, and the very age and body of the time his form and pressure" (3.2.22–4). Hamlet admires the dramatist's ability to transmute raw human feeling into tragic art, depicting and ordering reality as Shakespeare's play of *Hamlet* does for us. Yet playacting can also be, Hamlet recognizes, a self-indulgent escape for him, a way of unpacking his heart with words and of verbalizing his situation without doing something to remedy it. Acting and talking remind him too much of Polonius, who was an actor in his youth and who continues to be, like Hamlet, an inveterate punster.

Of the passive responses in the play, the stoicism of Horatio is by far the most attractive to Hamlet. "More an antique Roman than a Dane" (5.2.343), Horatio is, as Hamlet praises him, immune to flattering or to opportunities for cheap self-advancement. He is "As one, in suffering all, that suffers nothing, / A man that Fortune's buffets and rewards / Hast ta'en with equal thanks" (3.2.65–7). Such a person has a sure defense against the worst that life can offer. Hamlet can trust and love Horatio as he can no one else. Yet even here there are limits, for Horatio's skeptical and Roman philosophy cuts him off from a Christian and metaphysical overview. "There are more things in heaven and earth, Horatio, / Than are dreamt of in your philosophy" (1.5.175–6). After they have beheld together the skulls of Yorick's graveyard, Horatio seemingly does not share with Hamlet the exulting Christian perception that, although human life is indeed vain, Providence will reveal a pattern transcending human sorrow.

Hamlet's path must lie somewhere between the rash suddenness of Laertes or the canny resoluteness of Fortinbras on the one hand, and the passivity of Ophelia or Gertrude and the stoic resignation of Horatio on the other. At first he alternates between action and inaction, finding neither satisfactory. The Ghost has commanded Hamlet to revenge but has not explained how this is to be done; indeed, Gertrude is to be left passively to heaven and her conscience. If this method will suffice for her (and Christian wisdom taught that such a purgation was as thorough as it was sure), why not for Claudius? If Claudius must be killed, should it be while he is at his sin rather than at his prayers? The play is full of questions, stemming chiefly from the enigmatic commands of the Ghost. "Say, why is this? Wherefore? What should we do?" (1.4.57). Hamlet is not incapable of action. He shows unusual strength and cunning on the pirate ship, in his duel with Laertes ("I shall win at the odds"; 5.2.209), and especially in his slaying of Polonius—an action hardly characterized by "thinking too precisely on th'event" (4.4.42). Here is forthright action of the sort Laertes espouses. Yet, when the corpse behind his mother's arras turns out to be Polonius rather than Claudius, Hamlet concludes from the mistake that he has offended heaven. Even if Polonius deserves what he got, Hamlet believes he has made himself into a cruel "scourge" of Providence who must himself suffer retribution as well as deal it out. Swift action has not accomplished what the Ghost commanded.

The Ghost does not appear to speak for Providence in any case. His message is of revenge, a pagan concept deeply embedded in most societies but at odds with Christian teaching. His wish that Claudius be sent to hell and that Gertrude be more gently treated might, in fact, be the judgment of an impartial deity but here comes wrapped in the passionate involvement of a murdered man's restless spirit. This is not to say that Hamlet is being tempted to perform a damnable act, as he fears is possible, but that the Ghost's command cannot readily be reconciled with a complex and balanced view of justice. If Hamlet were to spring on Claudius in the fullness of his vice and cut his throat, we would pronounce Hamlet a murderer. What Hamlet believes he has learned instead is that he must become the instrument of Providence according to *its* plans, not his own. After his return from England, he senses triumphantly that all will be for the best if he allows an unseen power to decide the time and place for his final act. Under these conditions, rash action will be right. "Rashly, / And praised be rashness for it— let us know / Our indiscretion sometime serves us well / When our deep plots do pall, and that should learn us / There's a divinity that shapes our ends, / Rough-hew them how we will" (5.2.6–11). Passivity, too, is now a proper course, for Hamlet puts himself wholly at the disposal of Providence. What had seemed so impossible when Hamlet tried to formulate his own design proves elementary once he trusts to a divine justice in which he now firmly believes. Rashness and passivity are perfectly fused. Hamlet is revenged without having to commit premeditated murder and is relieved of his painful existence without having to commit suicide.

The circumstances of *Hamlet'* s catastrophe do indeed seem to accomplish all that Hamlet desires, by a route so circuitous that no one could ever have foreseen or devised it. Polonius's death, as it turns out, was instrumental after all, for it led to Laertes's angry return to Denmark and the challenge to a duel. Every seemingly unrelated event has its place; "There is special providence in the fall of a sparrow" (5.2.217–18). Repeatedly, the characters stress the role of seeming accident leading to just retribution. Even Horatio, for whom the events of the play suggest a pattern of randomness and violence, of "accidental judgments" and "casual slaughters," can see at last, "in this upshot, purposes mistook / Fall'n on th'inventors' heads" (5.2.384–7). In a similar vein, Laertes confesses himself "a woodcock to mine own springe" (line 309). As Hamlet had said earlier, of Rosencrantz and Guildenstern, " 'tis the sport to have the engineer / Hoist with his own petard" (3.4.213–14). Thus, too, Claudius's poisoned cup, intended for Hamlet, kills the Queen for whom Claudius had done such evil in order to acquire her and the throne. The destiny of evil in this play is to overreach itself.

In its final resolution, *Hamlet* incorporates a broader conception of justice than its revenge formula seemed at first to make possible. Yet, in its origins, *Hamlet* is a revenge story, and these traditions have left some residual savagery in the play. In the *Historia Danica* of Saxo Grammaticus, 1180–1208, and in the rather free translation of Saxo into French by François de Belleforest, *Histoires Tragiques* (1576), Hamlet is cunning and bloodily resolute throughout. He kills an eavesdropper without a qualm during the interview with his mother and exchanges letters on his way to England with characteristic shrewdness. Ultimately, he returns to Denmark, sets fire to his uncle's hall, slays its courtly inhabitants, and claims his rightful throne from a grateful people. The Ghost, absent in this account, may well have been supplied by Thomas Kyd's *The Spanish Tragedy* (c. 1587) and a lost *Hamlet* play in existence by 1589. *The Spanish Tragedy* bears many resemblances to our *Hamlet* and suggests what the lost *Hamlet* may well have contained: a sensational murder, a Senecan Ghost demanding revenge, the avenger hampered by court intrigue, his resort to a feigned madness, and his difficulty in authenticating the ghostly vision. A German version of *Hamlet*, called *Der bestrafte Brudermord* (1710), based seemingly on the older *Hamlet*, includes such details as the play within the play, the sparing of the King at his prayers in order to damn his soul, Ophelia's madness, the fencing match with poisoned swords and poisoned drink, and the final catastrophe of vengeance and death. Similarly, the early unauthorized First Quarto of *Hamlet* (1603) offers some passages seemingly based on the older play by Kyd.

Although this evidence suggests that Shakespeare received most of the material for the plot intact, his transformation of that material was nonetheless immeasurable. To be sure, Kyd's *The Spanish Tragedy* contains many rhetorical passages on the inadequacy of human justice, but the overall effect is still sensational and the outcome is a triumph for the pagan spirit of revenge. So, too, with the many revenge plays of the 1590s and 1600s that Kyd's dramatic genius had inspired, including Shakespeare's own *Titus Andronicus* (c. 1589–1592). *Hamlet,* written in about 1599–1601 (it is not mentioned by Frances Meres in his *Palladis Tamia: Wit's Treasury,* in 1598, and was entered in the Stationers' Register, the official record book of the London Company of Stationers [booksellers and printers], in 1602), is unparalleled in its philosophical richness. Its ending is truly cathartic, for Hamlet dies, not as a bloodied avenger, but as one who has affirmed the tragic dignity of the human race. His courage and faith, maintained in the face of great odds, atone for the dismal corruption in which Denmark has festered. His resolutely honest inquiries have taken him beyond the revulsion and doubt that express so eloquently, among other matters, the fearful response of Shakespeare's own generation to a seeming breakdown of established political, theological, and cosmological beliefs. Hamlet finally perceives that "if it be not now, yet it will come," and that "The readiness is all" (5.2.219–20). This discovery, this revelation of necessity and meaning in Hamlet's great reversal of fortune, enables him to confront the tragic circumstance of his life with understanding and heroism and to demonstrate the triumph of the human spirit even in the moment of his catastrophe.

Such an assertion of the individual will does not lessen the tragic waste with which *Hamlet* ends. Hamlet is dead, and the great promise of his life is forever lost. Few others have survived. Justice has seemingly been fulfilled in the deaths of Claudius, Gertrude, Rosencrantz and Guildenstern, Polonius, Laertes, and perhaps even Ophelia, but in a wild and extravagant way, as though Justice herself, more vengeful than providential, were unceasingly hungry for victims. Hamlet, the minister of that justice, has likewise grown indifferent to the spilling of blood, even if he submits himself at last to the will of a force he recognizes as providential. Denmark faces the kind of political uncertainty with which the play began. However much Hamlet may admire Fortinbras's resolution, the prince of Norway seems an alien choice for Denmark—even an ironic one. Horatio sees so little point in outliving the catastrophe of this play that he would choose death, were it not that he must draw his breath in pain to ensure that Hamlet's story is truly told. Still, that truth has been rescued from oblivion. Amid the ruin of the final scene, we share the artist's vision, through which we struggle to interpret and give order to the tragedy that proves inseparable from human existence.

The performance history of *Hamlet* is extraordinarily rich. It also attests to a variety of interpetations that is equally textured. Eighteenth-century versions by David Garrick and others often took out or severely reduced the Fortinbras plot; indeed, the play is so long that it almost certainly was not acted in its entirety even in Shakespeare's day. Garrick also deleted the Gravediggers' scene and much besides in Act 5. Pictorial scenery in the nineteenth century tended to favor opulent renditions of the play-within-the-play and Ophelia's mad scenes. Hamlet was portrayed in 1864, at the Lyceum Theater, as a Viking in a primitive medieval decor. Henry Irving, undertaking the role of Hamlet from 1864 to 1885, chose a decor of the fifth or sixth century, with castle battlements set among massive rocks glimmering under the soft light of the moon in the first act. John Gielgud became famous as a leading Hamlet of his day, beginning in 1930 at the Old Vic, emphasizing the pale, introspective, sonorous-voiced Hamlet that Coleridge had imagined. More recently, *Hamlet* has been seen from an existential vantage (by Tyrone Guthrie, 1938, at the Old Vic) in the modern-dress context of a Europe precariously trapped between the first World War and a second about to begin. Laurence Olivier, in his film version of 1948, explored the Freudian dimensions of "a man who could not make up his mind"; influenced by Ernest Jones's *Hamlet and Oedipus,* Olivier allowed the camera eye to linger on the Queen's bedchamber and its bed, where Hamlet encountered his mother in a scene (3.4) heavy with incestuous overtones.

Recent productions on stage, in film, and on television amply demonstrate how Shakespeare's best-known play can lend itself to other kinds of relevance to our modern world. Political interpretations sometimes focus on Claudius as a Machiavel in the school of modern spin-doctoring. At the Wisdom Bridge Theater's Chicago production in the 1970s, for example, directed by Robert Falls with Aiden Quinn as Hamlet, Claudius was the Great Communicator in the style of Ronald Reagan. His first scene (1.2) featured the new king on an array of television sets, blandly explaining to the Danish public the reasons for his rapid assumption of power and marriage with the widow of his dead brother. Claudius and Gertrude never appeared onstage in this scene; the audience saw the king on television, while the stage itself was given over to his zealous public relations team, nattily dressed, preparing a reception for the press representatives, making sure the event went smoothly. Fading posters of the dead king offered contrasting reminders of the regime which Claudius had so astutely supplanted.

More recently, in Michael Almereyda's low-budget film of 2000, the setting throughout is the New York world of privilege and high finance. Claudius (Kyle MacLachlan) is a chief executive officer of a superconglomerate financial empire. Gertrude (Diane Venora) is a suburban wife utterly seduced by the expensive privileges she now enjoys, of stretch limosines, private bathing pools in their high-rise empire, and the surroundings of obsequious flattery that immense wealth can command. Hamlet (Ethan Hawke), conversely, is a rebel with a cause, ostentatiously out of step in his moth-eaten ski cap, his scruffy clothes, his mania for the latest film and computer technology, and his disdain for corrupting privilege. The ghost of Hamlet's father (Sam Shepard) eerily appears on the swank penthouse battlements of New York's concrete skyscrapers, berattling the television monitors of up-to-date security systems. The overall effect is indeed strikingly modern and plausible. Another popular film version is that of Franco Zeffirelli (1990), with Mel Gibson as a matinee idol Hamlet, Alan Bates as a believably sexy Claudius, Glenn Close as a Gertrude who is erotically infatuated with her new husband, and some compellingly handsome scenery. Grigori Kozintsev's Russian film version of 1964, based on a script by Boris Pasternak, is visually eloquent in its recurring images of stone, iron, fire, sea, and earth. Kenneth Branagh's four-hour *Hamlet* (1996) is notable for its intrepedity in offering an essentially uncut version and for some superb performances, especially that of Derek Jacobi

as Claudius. Jacobi had starred earlier as Hamlet onstage (Old Vic, 1979) and in the BBC television series of all the plays beginning in 1979. Richard Burton's memorable stage performance (1964, at New York's Lunt-Fontanne Theater) is available on video. This play is especially fortunate in a rich archive of filmed or televised versions that make possible a comparative study in production by some of the greatest Shakespearean actors of the twentieth and twenty-first centuries. These varied interpretations abundantly show how *Hamlet* and its fascinating protagonist can be satirical, rebellious, mordant, funny, disillusioned, melancholic, introspective, and much more. The play that puzzles and fascinates readers is also immensely disturbing in performance.

Hamlet, Prince of Denmark

[*Dramatis Personae*

GHOST *of Hamlet, the former King of Denmark*
CLAUDIUS, *King of Denmark, the former King's brother*
GERTRUDE, *Queen of Denmark, widow of the former King and now wife of Claudius*
HAMLET, *Prince of Denmark, son of the late King and of Gertrude*

POLONIUS, *councillor to the King*
LAERTES, *his son*
OPHELIA, *his daughter*
REYNALDO, *his servant*

HORATIO, *Hamlet's friend and fellow student*

VOLTIMAND,
CORNELIUS,
ROSENCRANTZ,
GUILDENSTERN, } *members of the Danish court*
OSRIC,
A GENTLEMAN,
A LORD,

SCENE: *Denmark*]

BERNARDO,
FRANCISCO, } *officers and soldiers on watch*
MARCELLUS,

FORTINBRAS, *Prince of Norway*
CAPTAIN *in his army*

Three or Four PLAYERS, *taking the roles of* PROLOGUE, PLAYER KING, PLAYER QUEEN, *and* LUCIANUS
Two MESSENGERS
FIRST SAILOR
Two CLOWNS, *a gravedigger and his companion*
PRIEST
FIRST AMBASSADOR *from England*

Lords, Soldiers, Attendants, Guards, other Players, Followers of Laertes, other Sailors, another Ambassador or Ambassadors from England

[1.1]

Enter Bernardo and Francisco, two sentinels,
[meeting].

BERNARDO   Who's there?

FRANCISCO
    Nay, answer me. Stand and unfold yourself.   2

BERNARDO   Long live the King!

FRANCISCO   Bernardo?

BERNARDO   He.

FRANCISCO
    You come most carefully upon your hour.

BERNARDO
    'Tis now struck twelve. Get thee to bed, Francisco.

FRANCISCO
    For this relief much thanks. 'Tis bitter cold,
    And I am sick at heart.

BERNARDO   Have you had quiet guard?

FRANCISCO   Not a mouse stirring.

BERNARDO   Well, good night.
    If you do meet Horatio and Marcellus,
    The rivals of my watch, bid them make haste.   14

Enter Horatio and Marcellus.

FRANCISCO
    I think I hear them.—Stand, ho! Who is there?

HORATIO   Friends to this ground.   16

MARCELLUS   And liegemen to the Dane.   17

FRANCISCO   Give you good night.   18

MARCELLUS
    Oh, farewell, honest soldier. Who hath relieved you?

FRANCISCO
    Bernardo hath my place. Give you good night.

                                            Exit Francisco.

MARCELLUS   Holla! Bernardo!

BERNARDO   Say, what, is Horatio there?

HORATIO   A piece of him.

BERNARDO
    Welcome, Horatio. Welcome, good Marcellus.

HORATIO
    What, has this thing appeared again tonight?

BERNARDO   I have seen nothing.

MARCELLUS
    Horatio says 'tis but our fantasy,   27
    And will not let belief take hold of him
    Touching this dreaded sight twice seen of us.
    Therefore I have entreated him along   30
    With us to watch the minutes of this night,   31
    That if again this apparition come
    He may approve our eyes and speak to it.   33

HORATIO
    Tush, tush, 'twill not appear.

BERNARDO   Sit down awhile

And let us once again assail your ears,
That are so fortified against our story,
What we have two nights seen.

HORATIO   Well, sit we down,
    And let us hear Bernardo speak of this.

BERNARDO   Last night of all,   39
    When yond same star that's westward from the pole   40
    Had made his course t'illume that part of heaven   41
    Where now it burns, Marcellus and myself,
    The bell then beating one—

Enter Ghost.

MARCELLUS
    Peace, break thee off! Look where it comes again!

BERNARDO
    In the same figure like the King that's dead.

MARCELLUS
    Thou art a scholar. Speak to it, Horatio.   46

BERNARDO
    Looks 'a not like the King? Mark it, Horatio.   47

HORATIO
    Most like. It harrows me with fear and wonder.

BERNARDO
    It would be spoke to.

MARCELLUS   Speak to it, Horatio.   49

HORATIO
    What art thou that usurp'st this time of night,   50
    Together with that fair and warlike form
    In which the majesty of buried Denmark   52
    Did sometimes march? By heaven, I charge thee, speak!   53

MARCELLUS
    It is offended.

BERNARDO   See, it stalks away.

HORATIO
    Stay! Speak, speak! I charge thee, speak!   *Exit Ghost.*

MARCELLUS   'Tis gone and will not answer.

BERNARDO
    How now, Horatio? You tremble and look pale.
    Is not this something more than fantasy?
    What think you on't?   59

HORATIO
    Before my God, I might not this believe
    Without the sensible and true avouch   61
    Of mine own eyes.

MARCELLUS   Is it not like the King?

HORATIO   As thou art to thyself.
    Such was the very armor he had on
    When he the ambitious Norway combated.   65
    So frowned he once when, in an angry parle,   66
    He smote the sledded Polacks on the ice.   67
    'Tis strange.

1.1 Location: Elsinore castle. A guard platform.
2 me (Francisco emphasizes that *he* is the sentry currently on watch.)
unfold yourself reveal your identity.   **14 rivals** partners   **16 ground**
country, land.   **17 liegemen to the Dane** men sworn to serve the
Danish king.   **18 Give** May God give   **27 fantasy** imagination
30 along to come along   **31 watch** keep watch during   **33 approve**
corroborate

39 Last . . . all i.e., This *very* last night. (Emphatic.)   **40 pole** polestar,
north star   **41 his** its.   **t'illume** to illuminate   **46 scholar** one
learned enough to know how to question a ghost properly.   **47 'a** he
49 It . . . to (It was commonly believed that a ghost could not speak
until spoken to.)   **50 usurp'st** wrongfully takes over   **52 buried**
Denmark the buried King of Denmark   **53 sometimes** formerly
59 on't of it.   **61 sensible** confirmed by the senses.   **avouch** warrant,
evidence   **65 Norway** King of Norway   **66 parle** parley   **67 sledded**
traveling on sleds.   **Polacks** Poles

MARCELLUS

    Thus twice before, and jump at this dead hour,   69

    With martial stalk hath he gone by our watch.   70

HORATIO

    In what particular thought to work I know not,   71

    But in the gross and scope of mine opinion   72

    This bodes some strange eruption to our state.

MARCELLUS

    Good now, sit down, and tell me, he that knows,   74

    Why this same strict and most observant watch

    So nightly toils the subject of the land,   76

    And why such daily cast of brazen cannon   77

    And foreign mart for implements of war,   78

    Why such impress of shipwrights, whose sore task   79

    Does not divide the Sunday from the week.

    What might be toward, that this sweaty haste   81

    Doth make the night joint-laborer with the day?

    Who is't that can inform me?

HORATIO   That can I;

    At least, the whisper goes so. Our last king,

    Whose image even but now appeared to us,

    Was, as you know, by Fortinbras of Norway,

    Thereto pricked on by a most emulate pride,   87

    Dared to the combat; in which our valiant Hamlet—

    For so this side of our known world esteemed him—   89

    Did slay this Fortinbras; who by a sealed compact   90

    Well ratified by law and heraldry   91

    Did forfeit, with his life, all those his lands

    Which he stood seized of, to the conqueror;   93

    Against the which a moiety competent   94

    Was gagèd by our king, which had returned   95

    To the inheritance of Fortinbras   96

    Had he been vanquisher, as, by the same cov'nant   97

    And carriage of the article designed,   98

    His fell to Hamlet. Now, sir, young Fortinbras,

    Of unimprovèd mettle hot and full,   100

    Hath in the skirts of Norway here and there   101

    Sharked up a list of lawless resolutes   102

    For food and diet to some enterprise   103

    That hath a stomach in't, which is no other—   104

    As it doth well appear unto our state—

    But to recover of us, by strong hand

    And terms compulsatory, those foresaid lands

    So by his father lost. And this, I take it,

    Is the main motive of our preparations,

    The source of this our watch, and the chief head   110

    Of this posthaste and rummage in the land.   111

BERNARDO

    I think it be no other but e'en so.

    Well may it sort that this portentous figure   113

    Comes armèd through our watch so like the King

    That was and is the question of these wars.   115

HORATIO

    A mote it is to trouble the mind's eye.   116

    In the most high and palmy state of Rome,   117

    A little ere the mightiest Julius fell,   118

    The graves stood tenantless, and the sheeted dead   119

    Did squeak and gibber in the Roman streets;

    As stars with trains of fire and dews of blood,   121

    Disasters in the sun; and the moist star   122

    Upon whose influence Neptune's empire stands   123

    Was sick almost to doomsday with eclipse.   124

    And even the like precurse of feared events,   125

    As harbingers preceding still the fates   126

    And prologue to the omen coming on,   127

    Have heaven and earth together demonstrated

    Unto our climatures and countrymen.   129

            Enter Ghost.

    But soft, behold! Lo, where it comes again!   130

    I'll cross it, though it blast me. (*It spreads his arms.*) Stay,

       illusion!   131

    If thou hast any sound or use of voice,

    Speak to me!

    If there be any good thing to be done

    That may to thee do ease and grace to me,

    Speak to me!

    If thou art privy to thy country's fate,   137

    Which, happily, foreknowing may avoid,   138

    Oh, speak!

    Or if thou hast uphoarded in thy life

    Extorted treasure in the womb of earth,

    For which, they say, you spirits oft walk in death,

    Speak of it! (*The cock crows.*) Stay and speak!—Stop it,

       Marcellus.

MARCELLUS

    Shall I strike at it with my partisan?   144

HORATIO   Do, if it will not stand.   [*They strike at it.*]

BERNARDO   'Tis here!   146

HORATIO   'Tis here!   [*Exit Ghost.*]   147

---

69 **jump** exactly   70 **stalk** stride   71 **to work** i.e., to collect my thoughts and try to understand this   72 **gross and scope** general drift   74 **Good now** (An expression denoting entreaty or expostulation.)   76 **toils** causes to toil. **subject** subjects   77 **cast** casting   78 **mart** shopping   79 **impress** impressment, conscription   81 **toward** in preparation   87 **Thereto . . . pride** (Refers to old Fortinbras, not the Danish King.) **pricked on** incited. **emulate** emulous, ambitious   89 **this . . . world** i.e., all Europe, the Western world   90 **sealed** certified, confirmed   91 **heraldry** chivalry   93 **seized** possessed   94 **Against the** in return for. **moiety competent** corresponding portion   95 **gagèd** engaged, pledged. **had returned** would have passed   96 **inheritance** possession   97 **cov'nant** i.e., the *sealed compact* of line 90   98 **carriage . . . designed** purport of the article referred to   100 **unimprovèd mettle** untried, undisciplined spirits   101 **skirts** outlying regions, outskirts   102–4 **Sharked . . . in't** rounded up (as a shark scoops up fish) a troop of lawless desperadoes to feed and supply an enterprise of considerable daring

110 **head** source   111 **posthaste and rummage** frenetic activity and bustle   113 **Well . . . sort** That would explain why   115 **question** focus of contention   116 **mote** speck of dust   117 **palmy** flourishing   118 **Julius** Julius Caesar   119 **sheeted** shrouded   121 **As** (This abrupt transition suggests that matter is possibly omitted between lines 120 and 121.) **trains** trails   122 **Disasters** unfavorable signs or aspects. **moist star** i.e., moon, governing tides   123 **Neptune's . . . stands** the sea depends   124 **Was . . . eclipse** was eclipsed nearly to the cosmic darkness predicted for the second coming of Christ and the ending of the world. (See Matthew 24:29 and Revelation 6:12.)   125 **precurse** heralding, foreshadowing   126 **harbingers** forerunners. **still** always   127 **omen** calamitous event   129 **climatures** climes, regions   130 **soft** i.e., enough, break off   131 **cross** stand in its path, confront. **blast** wither, strike with a curse. 131 s.d. *his* its   137 **privy to** in on the secret of   138 **happily** haply, perchance   144 **partisan** long-handled spear.   146–7 **'Tis Here! / 'Tis here!** (Perhaps they attempt to strike at the Ghost, but are baffled by its seeming ability to be here and there and nowhere.)

MARCELLUS   'Tis gone.
We do it wrong, being so majestical,
To offer it the show of violence,
For it is as the air invulnerable,
And our vain blows malicious mockery.

BERNARDO
It was about to speak when the cock crew.

HORATIO
And then it started like a guilty thing
Upon a fearful summons. I have heard
The cock, that is the trumpet to the morn,   156
Doth with his lofty and shrill-sounding throat
Awake the god of day, and at his warning,
Whether in sea or fire, in earth or air,
Th'extravagant and erring spirit hies   160
To his confine; and of the truth herein
This present object made probation.   162

MARCELLUS
It faded on the crowing of the cock.
Some say that ever 'gainst that season comes   164
Wherein our Savior's birth is celebrated,
This bird of dawning singeth all night long,
And then, they say, no spirit dare stir abroad;
The nights are wholesome, then no planets strike,   168
No fairy takes, nor witch hath power to charm,   169
So hallowed and so gracious is that time.   170

HORATIO
So have I heard and do in part believe it.
But, look, the morn in russet mantle clad   172
Walks o'er the dew of yon high eastward hill.
Break we our watch up, and by my advice
Let us impart what we have seen tonight
Unto young Hamlet; for upon my life,
This spirit, dumb to us, will speak to him.
Do you consent we shall acquaint him with it,
As needful in our loves, fitting our duty?

MARCELLUS
Let's do't, I pray, and I this morning know
Where we shall find him most conveniently.

                                                      Exeunt.

❖

[1.2]

*Flourish. Enter Claudius, King of Denmark,
Gertrude the Queen, [the] Council, as Polonius
and his son Laertes, Hamlet, cum aliis [including
Voltimand and Cornelius].*

KING
Though yet of Hamlet our dear brother's death   1
The memory be green, and that it us befitted
To bear our hearts in grief and our whole kingdom

To be contracted in one brow of woe,
Yet so far hath discretion fought with nature
That we with wisest sorrow think on him
Together with remembrance of ourselves.
Therefore our sometime sister, now our queen,   8
Th'imperial jointress to this warlike state,   9
Have we, as 'twere with a defeated joy—
With an auspicious and a dropping eye,   11
With mirth in funeral and with dirge in marriage,
In equal scale weighing delight and dole—   13
Taken to wife. Nor have we herein barred
Your better wisdoms, which have freely gone
With this affair along. For all, our thanks.
Now follows that you know young Fortinbras,   17
Holding a weak supposal of our worth,   18
Or thinking by our late dear brother's death
Our state to be disjoint and out of frame,   20
Co-leaguèd with this dream of his advantage,   21
He hath not failed to pester us with message
Importing the surrender of those lands   23
Lost by his father, with all bonds of law,   24
To our most valiant brother. So much for him.
Now for ourself and for this time of meeting.
Thus much the business is: we have here writ
To Norway, uncle of young Fortinbras—
Who, impotent and bed-rid, scarcely hears   29
Of this his nephew's purpose—to suppress
His further gait herein, in that the levies,   31
The lists, and full proportions are all made   32
Out of his subject; and we here dispatch   33
You, good Cornelius, and you, Voltimand,
For bearers of this greeting to old Norway,
Giving to you no further personal power
To business with the King more than the scope
Of these dilated articles allow.   [*He gives a paper.*]   38
Farewell, and let your haste commend your duty.   39

CORNELIUS, VOLTIMAND
In that, and all things, will we show our duty.

KING
We doubt it nothing. Heartily farewell.   41
                    [*Exeunt Voltimand and Cornelius.*]
And now, Laertes, what's the news with you?
You told us of some suit; what is't, Laertes?
You cannot speak of reason to the Dane   44
And lose your voice. What wouldst thou beg, Laertes,   45
That shall not be my offer, not thy asking?
The head is not more native to the heart,   47

---

156 **trumpet** trumpeter   160 **extravagant and erring** wandering
beyond bounds. (The words have similar meaning.)   **hies** hastens
162 **probation** proof.   164 **'gainst** just before   168 **strike** destroy by
evil influence   169 **takes** bewitches.   **charm** cast a spell, control by
enchantment   170 **gracious** full of grace   172 **russet** reddish brown
1.2 Location: The castle.
0.2 *as* i.e., such as, including.   0.3 *cum aliis* with others   1 **our** my.
(The royal "we"; also in the following lines.)

8 **sometime** former   9 **jointress** woman possessing property with
her husband   11 **With . . . eye** with one eye smiling and the other
weeping   13 **dole** grief   17 **Now . . . know** Next, you need to be
informed that   18 **weak supposal** low estimate   20 **disjoint . . .
frame** in a state of total disorder   21 **Co-leaguèd . . . advantage**
joined to his illusory sense of having the advantage over us and to
his vision of future success   23 **Importing** having for its substance
24 **with . . . law** (See 1.1.91, "Well ratified by law and heraldry.")
29 **impotent** helpless   31 **His** i.e., Fortinbras'.   **gait** proceeding
31–3 **in that . . . subject** since the levying of troops and supplies is
drawn entirely from the King of Norway's own subjects   38 **dilated**
set out at length   39 **let . . . duty** let your swift obeying of orders,
rather than mere words, express your dutifulness.   41 **nothing** not
at all.   44 **the Dane** the Danish king   45 **lose your voice** waste your
speech.   47 **native** closely connected, related

The hand more instrumental to the mouth,   48
Than is the throne of Denmark to thy father.
What wouldst thou have, Laertes?

LAERTES   My dread lord,
Your leave and favor to return to France,   51
From whence though willingly I came to Denmark
To show my duty in your coronation,
Yet now I must confess, that duty done,
My thoughts and wishes bend again toward France
And bow them to your gracious leave and pardon.   56

KING
Have you your father's leave? What says Polonius?

POLONIUS
H'ath, my lord, wrung from me my slow leave   58
By laborsome petition, and at last
Upon his will I sealed my hard consent.   60
I do beseech you, give him leave to go.

KING
Take thy fair hour, Laertes. Time be thine,   62
And thy best graces spend it at thy will.   63
But now, my cousin Hamlet, and my son—   64

HAMLET
A little more than kin, and less than kind.   65

KING
How is it that the clouds still hang on you?

HAMLET
Not so, my lord. I am too much in the sun.   67

QUEEN
Good Hamlet, cast thy nighted color off,   68
And let thine eye look like a friend on Denmark.   69
Do not forever with thy vailèd lids   70
Seek for thy noble father in the dust.
Thou know'st 'tis common, all that lives must die,   72
Passing through nature to eternity.

HAMLET
Ay, madam, it is common.

QUEEN   If it be,
Why seems it so particular with thee?   75

HAMLET
Seems, madam? Nay, it is. I know not "seems."
'Tis not alone my inky cloak, good mother,
Nor customary suits of solemn black,   78
Nor windy suspiration of forced breath,   79

No, nor the fruitful river in the eye,   80
Nor the dejected havior of the visage,   81
Together with all forms, moods, shapes of grief,   82
That can denote me truly. These indeed seem,
For they are actions that a man might play.
But I have that within which passes show;
These but the trappings and the suits of woe.

KING
'Tis sweet and commendable in your nature, Hamlet,
To give these mourning duties to your father.
But you must know your father lost a father,
That father lost, lost his, and the survivor bound
In filial obligation for some term
To do obsequious sorrow. But to persever   92
In obstinate condolement is a course   93
Of impious stubbornness. 'Tis unmanly grief.
It shows a will most incorrect to heaven,
A heart unfortified, a mind impatient,   96
An understanding simple and unschooled.   97
For what we know must be and is as common
As any the most vulgar thing to sense,   99
Why should we in our peevish opposition
Take it to heart? Fie, 'tis a fault to heaven,
A fault against the dead, a fault to nature,
To reason most absurd, whose common theme
Is death of fathers, and who still hath cried,   104
From the first corpse till he that died today,   105
"This must be so." We pray you, throw to earth
This unprevailing woe and think of us   107
As of a father; for let the world take note,
You are the most immediate to our throne,   109
And with no less nobility of love
Than that which dearest father bears his son
Do I impart toward you. For your intent   112
In going back to school in Wittenberg,   113
It is most retrograde to our desire,   114
And we beseech you bend you to remain   115
Here in the cheer and comfort of our eye,
Our chiefest courtier, cousin, and our son.

QUEEN
Let not thy mother lose her prayers, Hamlet.
I pray thee, stay with us, go not to Wittenberg.

HAMLET
I shall in all my best obey you, madam.   120

KING
Why, 'tis a loving and a fair reply.
Be as ourself in Denmark. Madam, come.
This gentle and unforced accord of Hamlet
Sits smiling to my heart, in grace whereof   124
No jocund health that Denmark drinks today   125

---

48 instrumental serviceable   **51 leave and favor** kind permission **56 bow . . . pardon** entreatingly make a deep bow, asking your permission to depart.   **58 H'ath** He has   **60 sealed** (as if sealing a legal document).   **hard** reluctant   **62 Take thy fair hour** Enjoy your time of youth   **63 And . . . will** and may your time be spent in exercising your best qualities.   **64 cousin** any kin not of the immediate family **65 A little . . . kind** Too close a blood relation, and yet we are less than kinsmen in that our relationship lacks affection and is indeed unnatural. (Hamlet plays on *kind* as [1] kindly [2] belonging to nature, suggesting that Claudius is not the same kind of being as the rest of humanity. The line is often delivered as an aside, though it need not be.)   **67 the sun** i.e., the sunshine of the King's royal favor. (With pun on *son*.)   **68 nighted color** (1) mourning garments of black (2) dark melancholy   **69 Denmark** the King of Denmark.   **70 vailèd lids** lowered eyes   **72 common** of universal occurrence. (But Hamlet plays on the sense of "vulgar" in line 74.)   **75 particular** personal **78 customary** customary to mourning   **79 suspiration** sighing

80 fruitful abundant   **81 havior** expression   **82 moods** outward expression of feeling   **92 obsequious** suited to obsequies or funerals **93 condolement** sorrowing   **96 unfortified** i.e., against adversity **97 simple** ignorant   **99 As . . . sense** as the most ordinary experience **104 still** always   **105 the first corpse** (Abel's)   **107 unprevailing** unavailing, useless   **109 most immediate** next in succession **112 impart toward** liberally bestow on.   **For** As for   **113 to school** i.e., to your studies.   **Wittenberg** famous German university founded in 1502   **114 retrograde** contrary   **115 bend you** incline yourself   **120 in all my best** to the best of my ability   **124 to** i.e., at. **grace** thanksgiving   **125 jocund** merry

But the great cannon to the clouds shall tell,
And the King's rouse the heaven shall bruit again,   127
Respeaking earthly thunder. Come away.   128

Flourish. Exeunt all but Hamlet.

HAMLET
Oh, that this too too sullied flesh would melt,   129
Thaw, and resolve itself into a dew!
Or that the Everlasting had not fixed
His canon 'gainst self-slaughter! Oh, God, God,   132
How weary, stale, flat, and unprofitable
Seem to me all the uses of this world!
Fie on't, ah, fie! 'Tis an unweeded garden
That grows to seed. Things rank and gross in nature
Possess it merely. That it should come to this!   137
But two months dead—nay, not so much, not two.
So excellent a king, that was to this   139
Hyperion to a satyr, so loving to my mother   140
That he might not beteem the winds of heaven   141
Visit her face too roughly. Heaven and earth,
Must I remember? Why, she would hang on him
As if increase of appetite had grown
By what it fed on, and yet within a month—
Let me not think on't; frailty, thy name is woman!—
A little month, or ere those shoes were old   147
With which she followed my poor father's body,
Like Niobe, all tears, why she, even she—   149
Oh, God, a beast, that wants discourse of reason,   150
Would have mourned longer—married with my
    uncle,
My father's brother, but no more like my father
Than I to Hercules. Within a month,
Ere yet the salt of most unrighteous tears
Had left the flushing in her gallèd eyes,   155
She married. Oh, most wicked speed, to post   156
With such dexterity to incestuous sheets!   157
It is not, nor it cannot come to good.
But break, my heart, for I must hold my tongue.

Enter Horatio, Marcellus, and Bernardo.

HORATIO
Hail to Your Lordship!
HAMLET   I am glad to see you well.
Horatio!—or I do forget myself.
HORATIO
The same, my lord, and your poor servant ever.

HAMLET
Sir, my good friend; I'll change that name with you.   163
And what make you from Wittenberg, Horatio?—   164
Marcellus.
MARCELLUS   My good lord.
HAMLET
I am very glad to see you. [*To Bernardo*] Good even,
    sir.—
But what in faith make you from Wittenberg?
HORATIO
A truant disposition, good my lord.
HAMLET
I would not hear your enemy say so,
Nor shall you do my ear that violence
To make it truster of your own report   172
Against yourself. I know you are no truant.
But what is your affair in Elsinore?
We'll teach you to drink deep ere you depart.
HORATIO
My lord, I came to see your father's funeral.
HAMLET
I prithee, do not mock me, fellow student;
I think it was to see my mother's wedding.
HORATIO
Indeed, my lord, it followed hard upon.   179
HAMLET
Thrift, thrift, Horatio! The funeral baked meats   180
Did coldly furnish forth the marriage tables.   181
Would I had met my dearest foe in heaven   182
Or ever I had seen that day, Horatio!   183
My father!—Methinks I see my father.
HORATIO
Where, my lord?
HAMLET   In my mind's eye, Horatio.
HORATIO
I saw him once. 'A was a goodly king.   186
HAMLET
'A was a man. Take him for all in all,
I shall not look upon his like again.
HORATIO
My lord, I think I saw him yesternight.
HAMLET   Saw? Who?
HORATIO   My lord, the King your father.
HAMLET   The King my father?
HORATIO
Season your admiration for a while   193
With an attent ear till I may deliver,   194
Upon the witness of these gentlemen,
This marvel to you.
HAMLET   For God's love, let me hear!
HORATIO
Two nights together had these gentlemen,

127 **rouse** drinking of a draft of liquor.   **bruit again** loudly echo
128 **thunder** i.e., of trumpet and kettledrum, sounded when the King
drinks; see 1.4.8–12.   129 **sullied** defiled. (The early quartos read
"sallied"; the Folio, "solid.")   132 **canon** law   137 **merely** completely.   139 **to** in comparison to   140 **Hyperion** Titan sun-god,
father of Helios.   **satyr** a lecherous creature of classical mythology,
half-human but with a goat's legs, tail, ears, and horns   141 **beteem**
allow   147 **or ere** even before   149 **Niobe** Tantalus's daughter,
Queen of Thebes, who boasted that she had more sons and daughters
than Leto; for this, Apollo and Artemis, children of Leto, slew her
fourteen children. She was turned by Zeus into a stone that continually dropped tears.   150 **wants . . . reason** lacks the faculty of reason
155 **gallèd** irritated, inflamed   156 **post** hasten   157 **incestuous** (In
Shakespeare's day, the marriage of a man like Claudius to his
deceased brother's wife was considered incestuous.)

163 **change that name** i.e., give and receive reciprocally the name of
"friend" rather than talk of "servant." Or Hamlet may be saying,
"No, I am *your* servant."   164 **make you from** are you doing away
from   172 **To . . . of** to make it trust   179 **hard** close   180 **baked
meats** meat pies   181 **coldly** i.e., as cold leftovers   182 **dearest** closest (and therefore deadliest)   183 **Or ever** ere, before   186 **'A** He
193 **Season your admiration** Moderate your astonishment
194 **attent** attentive

Marcellus and Bernardo, on their watch,
In the dead waste and middle of the night,   199
Been thus encountered. A figure like your father,
Armèd at point exactly, cap-à-pie,   201
Appears before them, and with solemn march
Goes slow and stately by them. Thrice he walked
By their oppressed and fear-surprisèd eyes
Within his truncheon's length, whilst they, distilled   205
Almost to jelly with the act of fear,   206
Stand dumb and speak not to him. This to me
In dreadful secrecy impart they did,   208
And I with them the third night kept the watch,
Where, as they had delivered, both in time,
Form of the thing, each word made true and good,
The apparition comes. I knew your father;
These hands are not more like.

HAMLET   But where was this?
MARCELLUS
My lord, upon the platform where we watch.
HAMLET
Did you not speak to it?
HORATIO   My lord, I did,
But answer made it none. Yet once methought
It lifted up it head and did address   217
Itself to motion, like as it would speak;   218
But even then the morning cock crew loud,   219
And at the sound it shrunk in haste away
And vanished from our sight.
HAMLET   'Tis very strange.
HORATIO
As I do live, my honored lord, 'tis true,
And we did think it writ down in our duty
To let you know of it.
HAMLET
Indeed, indeed, sirs. But this troubles me.
Hold you the watch tonight?
ALL   We do, my lord.
HAMLET   Armed, say you?
ALL   Armed, my lord.
HAMLET   From top to toe?
ALL   My lord, from head to foot.
HAMLET   Then saw you not his face?
HORATIO
Oh, yes, my lord, he wore his beaver up.   232
HAMLET   What looked he, frowningly?   233
HORATIO
A countenance more in sorrow than in anger.
HAMLET   Pale or red?
HORATIO   Nay, very pale.
HAMLET   And fixed his eyes upon you?
HORATIO   Most constantly.
HAMLET   I would I had been there.
HORATIO   It would have much amazed you.
HAMLET   Very like, very like. Stayed it long?

HORATIO
While one with moderate haste might tell a hundred. 242
MARCELLUS, BERNARDO   Longer, longer.
HORATIO   Not when I saw't.
HAMLET   His beard was grizzled—no?
HORATIO
It was, as I have seen it in his life,
A sable silvered.
HAMLET   I will watch tonight.
Perchance 'twill walk again.
HORATIO   I warr'nt it will.
HAMLET
If it assume my noble father's person,
I'll speak to it though hell itself should gape
And bid me hold my peace. I pray you all,
If you have hitherto concealed this sight,
Let it be tenable in your silence still,   253
And whatsomever else shall hap tonight,
Give it an understanding but no tongue.
I will requite your loves. So, fare you well.
Upon the platform twixt eleven and twelve
I'll visit you.
ALL   Our duty to Your Honor.
HAMLET
Your loves, as mine to you. Farewell.   259
                         Exeunt [all but Hamlet].
My father's spirit in arms! All is not well.
I doubt some foul play. Would the night were come!   261
Till then sit still, my soul. Foul deeds will rise,
Though all the earth o'erwhelm them, to men's eyes.
                                           Exit.

[1.3]

Enter Laertes and Ophelia, his sister.

LAERTES
My necessaries are embarked. Farewell.
And, sister, as the winds give benefit
And convoy is assistant, do not sleep   3
But let me hear from you.
OPHELIA   Do you doubt that?
LAERTES
For Hamlet, and the trifling of his favor,   5
Hold it a fashion and a toy in blood,   6
A violet in the youth of primy nature,   7
Forward, not permanent, sweet, not lasting,   8
The perfume and suppliance of a minute—   9
No more.
OPHELIA   No more but so?
LAERTES   Think it no more.

---

199 **dead waste** desolate stillness   201 **at point** correctly in every
detail.   **cap-à-pie** from head to foot   205 **truncheon** officer's staff.
distilled dissolved   206 **act** action, operation   208 **dreadful** full
of dread   217 **it** its   217–18 **did . . . speak** prepared to move as
though it was about to speak   219 **even then** at that very instant
232 **beaver** visor on the helmet   233 **What** How

242 **tell** count   253 **tenable** held   259 **Your loves** i.e., Say "Your
loves" to me, not just your "duty."   261 **doubt** suspect
1.3. Location: Polonius's chambers.
3 **convoy is assistant** means of conveyance are available   5 **For** As
for   6 **toy in blood** passing amorous fancy   7 **primy** in its prime,
springtime   8 **Forward** precocious   9 **suppliance** pastime, something to fill the time

For nature crescent does not grow alone	11
In thews and bulk, but as this temple waxes	12
The inward service of the mind and soul	13
Grows wide withal. Perhaps he loves you now,	14
And now no soil nor cautel doth besmirch	15
The virtue of his will; but you must fear,	16
His greatness weighed, his will is not his own.	17
For he himself is subject to his birth.	
He may not, as unvalued persons do,	
Carve for himself, for on his choice depends	20
The safety and health of this whole state,	
And therefore must his choice be circumscribed	
Unto the voice and yielding of that body	23
Whereof he is the head. Then if he says he loves you,	
It fits your wisdom so far to believe it	
As he in his particular act and place	26
May give his saying deed, which is no further	
Than the main voice of Denmark goes withal.	28
Then weigh what loss your honor may sustain	
If with too credent ear you list his songs,	30
Or lose your heart, or your chaste treasure open	
To his unmastered importunity.	32
Fear it, Ophelia, fear it, my dear sister,	
And keep you in the rear of your affection,	34
Out of the shot and danger of desire.	
The chariest maid is prodigal enough	36
If she unmask her beauty to the moon.	37
Virtue itself scapes not calumnious strokes.	
The canker galls the infants of the spring	39
Too oft before their buttons be disclosed,	40
And in the morn and liquid dew of youth	41
Contagious blastments are most imminent.	42
Be wary then; best safety lies in fear.	
Youth to itself rebels, though none else near.	44

OPHELIA
I shall the effect of this good lesson keep
As watchman to my heart. But, good my brother,
Do not, as some ungracious pastors do,   47
Show me the steep and thorny way to heaven,
Whiles like a puffed and reckless libertine   49
Himself the primrose path of dalliance treads,
And recks not his own rede.

Enter Polonius.

LAERTES   Oh, fear me not.   51

11–14 For nature . . . withal For nature, as it ripens, does not grow only in physical strength, but as the body matures the inner qualities of mind and soul grow along with it. (Laertes warns Ophelia that the mature Hamlet may not cling to his youthful interests.)   **15 soil nor cautel** blemish nor deceit   **16 The . . . will** the purity of his desire   **17 His greatness weighed** taking into account his high fortune   **20 Carve** i.e., choose   **23 voice and yielding** assent, approval   **26 in . . . place** in his particular restricted circumstances   **28 main voice** general assent. **withal** along with.   **30 credent** credulous.   **list** listen to   **32 unmastered** uncontrolled   **34 keep . . . affection** don't advance as far as your affection might lead you. (A military metaphor.)   **36 chariest** most scrupulously modest   **37 If she unmask** if she does no more than show her beauty.   **moon** (Symbol of chastity.)   **39 canker galls** cankerworm destroys   **40 buttons be disclosed** buds be opened   **41 liquid dew** i.e., time when dew is fresh and bright   **42 blastments** blights   **44 Youth . . . rebels** Youth yields to the rebellion of the flesh   **47 ungracious** ungodly   **49 puffed** bloated, or swollen with pride   **51 recks** heeds. **rede** counsel.   **fear me not** don't worry on my account.

I stay too long. But here my father comes.	
A double blessing is a double grace;	53
Occasion smiles upon a second leave.	54

POLONIUS

Yet here, Laertes? Aboard, aboard, for shame!	
The wind sits in the shoulder of your sail,	
And you are stayed for. There—my blessing with thee!	
And these few precepts in thy memory	
Look thou character. Give thy thoughts no tongue,	59
Nor any unproportioned thought his act.	60
Be thou familiar, but by no means vulgar.	61
Those friends thou hast, and their adoption tried,	62
Grapple them unto thy soul with hoops of steel,	
But do not dull thy palm with entertainment	64
Of each new-hatched, unfledged courage. Beware	65
Of entrance to a quarrel, but being in,	
Bear't that th'opposèd may beware of thee.	67
Give every man thy ear, but few thy voice;	
Take each man's censure, but reserve thy judgment.	69
Costly thy habit as thy purse can buy,	70
But not expressed in fancy; rich, not gaudy,	71
For the apparel oft proclaims the man,	
And they in France of the best rank and station	
Are of a most select and generous chief in that.	74
Neither a borrower nor a lender be,	
For loan oft loses both itself and friend,	
And borrowing dulleth edge of husbandry.	77
This above all: to thine own self be true,	
And it must follow, as the night the day,	
Thou canst not then be false to any man.	
Farewell. My blessing season this in thee!	81

LAERTES
Most humbly do I take my leave, my lord.
POLONIUS
The time invests you. Go, your servants tend.   83
LAERTES
Farewell, Ophelia, and remember well
What I have said to you.
OPHELIA   'Tis in my memory locked,
And you yourself shall keep the key of it.
LAERTES   Farewell.   *Exit Laertes.*
POLONIUS
What is't, Ophelia, he hath said to you?
OPHELIA
So please you, something touching the Lord Hamlet.
POLONIUS   Marry, well bethought.   91
'Tis told me he hath very oft of late
Given private time to you, and you yourself

53–4 A double . . . leave The goddess Occasion or Opportunity smiles on the happy circumstance of being able to say good-bye twice and thus receive a second blessing.   **59 Look thou character** see to it that you inscribe.   **60 unproportioned** badly calculated, intemperate.   **his** its   **61 familiar** sociable.   **vulgar** common.   **62 and . . . tried** and their suitability to be your friends having been put to the test   **64 dull thy palm** i.e., shake hands so often as to make the gesture meaningless   **65 courage** swashbuckler.   **67 Bear't that** manage it so that   **69 censure** opinion, judgment   **70 habit** clothing   **71 fancy** excessive ornament, decadent fashion   **74 Are . . . that** are of a most refined and well-bred preeminence in choosing what to wear.   **77 husbandry** thrift.   **81 season** mature   **83 invests** besieges, presses upon. **tend** attend, wait.   **91 Marry** i.e., By the Virgin Mary. (A mild oath.)

Have of your audience been most free and bounteous.
If it be so—as so 'tis put on me,   95
And that in way of caution—I must tell you
You do not understand yourself so clearly
As it behooves my daughter and your honor.   98
What is between you? Give me up the truth.

OPHELIA
He hath, my lord, of late made many tenders   100
Of his affection to me.

POLONIUS
Affection? Pooh! You speak like a green girl,
Unsifted in such perilous circumstance.   103
Do you believe his tenders, as you call them?

OPHELIA
I do not know, my lord, what I should think.

POLONIUS
Marry, I will teach you. Think yourself a baby
That you have ta'en these tenders for true pay
Which are not sterling. Tender yourself more dearly,   108
Or—not to crack the wind of the poor phrase,   109
Running it thus—you'll tender me a fool.   110

OPHELIA
My lord, he hath importuned me with love
In honorable fashion.

POLONIUS
Ay, fashion you may call it. Go to, go to.   113

OPHELIA
And hath given countenance to his speech, my lord,   114
With almost all the holy vows of heaven.

POLONIUS
Ay, springes to catch woodcocks. I do know,   116
When the blood burns, how prodigal the soul   117
Lends the tongue vows. These blazes, daughter,
Giving more light than heat, extinct in both
Even in their promise as it is a-making,   120
You must not take for fire. From this time
Be something scanter of your maiden presence.   122
Set your entreatments at a higher rate   123
Than a command to parle. For Lord Hamlet,   124
Believe so much in him that he is young,   125
And with a larger tether may he walk
Than may be given you. In few, Ophelia,   127
Do not believe his vows, for they are brokers,   128
Not of that dye which their investments show,   129
But mere implorators of unholy suits,   130

Breathing like sanctified and pious bawds,   131
The better to beguile. This is for all: 132
I would not, in plain terms, from this time forth
Have you so slander any moment leisure   134
As to give words or talk with the Lord Hamlet.
Look to't, I charge you. Come your ways.   136

OPHELIA   I shall obey, my lord.   *Exeunt.*

❧

[1.4]

Enter Hamlet, Horatio, and Marcellus.

HAMLET
The air bites shrewdly; it is very cold.   1

HORATIO
It is a nipping and an eager air.   2

HAMLET
What hour now?

HORATIO   I think it lacks of twelve.   3

MARCELLUS
No, it is struck.

HORATIO   Indeed? I heard it not.
It then draws near the season   5
Wherein the spirit held his wont to walk.   6
            A flourish of trumpets, and two pieces go off
                                              [*within*].
What does this mean, my lord?

HAMLET
The King doth wake tonight and takes his rouse,   8
Keeps wassail, and the swagg'ring upspring reels;   9
And as he drains his drafts of Rhenish down,   10
The kettledrum and trumpet thus bray out
The triumph of his pledge.

HORATIO   Is it a custom?   12

HAMLET   Ay, marry, is't,
But to my mind, though I am native here
And to the manner born, it is a custom   15
More honored in the breach than the observance.   16
This heavy-headed revel east and west   17
Makes us traduced and taxed of other nations.   18
They clepe us drunkards, and with swinish phrase   19
Soil our addition; and indeed it takes   20
From our achievements, though performed at height,   21
The pith and marrow of our attribute.   22

---

95 **put on** impressed on, told to   98 **behooves** befits   100 **tenders**
offers   103 **Unsifted** i.e., untried   108 **sterling** legal currency.
Tender . . . dearly (1) Bargain for your favors at a higher rate—i.e.,
hold out for marriage (2) Show greater care of yourself   109 **crack
the wind** i.e., run it until it is broken-winded   110 **tender . . . fool** (1)
make a fool of me (2) present me with a *fool* or baby.   113 **fashion**
mere form, pretense.   **Go to** (An expression of impatience.)
114 **countenance** credit, confirmation   116 **springes** snares.
woodcocks birds easily caught; here used to connote gullibility.
117 **prodigal** prodigally   120 **it** i.e., the promise   122 **something**
somewhat   123–4 **Set . . . parle** i.e., As defender of your chastity,
negotiate for something better than a surrender simply because the
besieger requests an interview.   124 **For** As for   125 **so . . . him** this
much concerning him   127 **In few** Briefly   128 **brokers** go-
betweens, procurers   129 **dye** color or sort.   **investments** clothes.
(The vows are not what they seem.)   130 **mere implorators** out-and-
out solicitors

131 **Breathing** speaking   132 **for all** once for all, in sum   134 **slander**
abuse, misuse.   **moment** moment's   136 **Come your ways** Come
along.
1.4 Location: The guard platform.
1 **shrewdly** keenly, sharply   2 **eager** biting   3 **lacks of** is just short of
5 **season** time   6 **held his wont** was accustomed   6.1 *pieces* i.e., of
ordnance, cannon   8 **wake** stay awake and hold revel.   **takes his
rouse** carouses   9 **Keeps . . . reels** carouses, and riotously dances a
German dance called the upspring   10 **Rhenish** Rhine wine   12 **The
triumph . . . pledge** the celebration of his offering a toast.   15 **manner** custom (of drinking)   16 **More . . . observance** better neglected
than followed.   17 **east and west** i.e., everywhere   18 **taxed of** censured by   19 **clepe** call.   **with swinish phrase** i.e., by calling us
swine   20 **addition** reputation   21 **at height** outstandingly   22 **The
pith . . . attribute** the most essential part of the esteem that should be
attributed to us.

So, oft it chances in particular men,

That for some vicious mole of nature in them,   24

As in their birth—wherein they are not guilty,

Since nature cannot choose his origin—   26

By their o'ergrowth of some complexion,   27

Oft breaking down the pales and forts of reason,   28

Or by some habit that too much o'erleavens   29

The form of plausive manners, that these men,   30

Carrying, I say, the stamp of one defect,

Being nature's livery or fortune's star,   32

His virtues else, be they as pure as grace,   33

As infinite as man may undergo,   34

Shall in the general censure take corruption   35

From that particular fault. The dram of evil   36

Doth all the noble substance often dout   37

To his own scandal.

Enter Ghost.

HORATIO   Look, my lord, it comes!   38

HAMLET

Angels and ministers of grace defend us!   39

Be thou a spirit of health or goblin damned,   40

Bring with thee airs from heaven or blasts from hell,   41

Be thy intents wicked or charitable,   42

Thou com'st in such a questionable shape   43

That I will speak to thee. I'll call thee Hamlet,

King, father, royal Dane. Oh, answer me!

Let me not burst in ignorance, but tell

Why thy canonized bones, hearsèd in death,   47

Have burst their cerements; why the sepulcher   48

Wherein we saw thee quietly inurned   49

Hath oped his ponderous and marble jaws

To cast thee up again. What may this mean,

That thou, dead corpse, again in complete steel,   52

Revisits thus the glimpses of the moon,   53

Making night hideous, and we fools of nature   54

So horridly to shake our disposition   55

With thoughts beyond the reaches of our souls?

Say, why is this? Wherefore? What should we do?

[*The Ghost*] *beckons* [*Hamlet*].

HORATIO

It beckons you to go away with it,

As if it some impartment did desire   59

To you alone.

MARCELLUS   Look with what courteous action

It wafts you to a more removèd ground.

But do not go with it.

HORATIO   No, by no means.

HAMLET

It will not speak. Then I will follow it.

HORATIO

Do not, my lord!

HAMLET   Why, what should be the fear?

I do not set my life at a pin's fee,   65

And for my soul, what can it do to that,   66

Being a thing immortal as itself?

It waves me forth again. I'll follow it.

HORATIO

What if it tempt you toward the flood, my lord,   69

Or to the dreadful summit of the cliff

That beetles o'er his base into the sea,   71

And there assume some other horrible form

Which might deprive your sovereignty of reason   73

And draw you into madness? Think of it.

The very place puts toys of desperation,   75

Without more motive, into every brain

That looks so many fathoms to the sea

And hears it roar beneath.

HAMLET

It wafts me still.—Go on, I'll follow thee.

MARCELLUS

You shall not go, my lord.   [*They try to stop him.*]

HAMLET   Hold off your hands!

HORATIO

Be ruled. You shall not go.

HAMLET   My fate cries out,   81

And makes each petty artery in this body   82

As hardy as the Nemean lion's nerve.   83

Still am I called. Unhand me, gentlemen.

By heaven, I'll make a ghost of him that lets me!   85

I say, away!—Go on, I'll follow thee.

Exeunt Ghost and Hamlet.

HORATIO

He waxes desperate with imagination.

MARCELLUS

Let's follow. 'Tis not fit thus to obey him.

HORATIO

Have after. To what issue will this come?   89

MARCELLUS

Something is rotten in the state of Denmark.

---

24 for . . . mole on account of some natural defect in their constitutions   **26 his** its   **27 their o'ergrowth . . . complexion** the excessive growth in individuals of some natural trait   **28 pales** palings, fences (as of a fortification)   **29–30 o'erleavens . . . manners** i.e., infects the way we should behave (much as bad yeast spoils the dough). *Plausive* means "pleasing."   **32 Being . . . star** (that stamp of defect) being a sign identifying one as wearing the livery of, and hence being the servant to, nature (unfortunate inherited qualities) or fortune (mischance)   **33 His virtues else** i.e., the other qualities of *these men* (line 30)   **34 may undergo** can sustain   **35 in . . . censure** in overall appraisal, in people's opinion generally   **36-8 The dram . . . scandal** i.e., The small drop of evil blots out or works against the noble substance of the whole and brings it into disrepute. (To *dout* is to blot out. A famous crux.)   **39 ministers of grace** messengers of God   **40 Be . . . health** Whether you are a good angel   **41 Bring** whether you bring   **42 Be thy intents** whether your intentions are   **43 questionable** inviting question   **47 canonized** buried according to the canons of the church.   **hearsèd** coffined   **48 cerements** grave clothes   **49 inurned** entombed   **52 complete steel** full armor   **53 the glimpses . . . moon** i.e., the sublunary world, all that is beneath the moon   **54 fools of nature** mere mortals, limited to natural knowledge and subject to nature   **55 So . . . disposition** to distress our mental composure so violently

59 impartment communication   **65 fee** value   **66 for** as for   **69 flood** sea   **71 beetles o'er** overhangs threateningly (like bushy eyebrows).   **his** its   **73 deprive . . . reason** take away the rule of reason over your mind   **75 toys of desperation** fancies of desperate acts, i.e., suicide   **81 My fate cries out** My destiny summons me   **82 petty** weak.   **artery** blood vessel system through which the vital spirits were thought to have been conveyed   **83 as the . . . nerve** as a sinew of the huge lion slain by Hercules as the first of his twelve labors.   **85 lets** hinders   **89 Have after** Let's go after him.   **issue** outcome

HORATIO
　　Heaven will direct it.

MARCELLUS　　　　　　　Nay, let's follow him.　　　*Exeunt.* 91

❖

[1.5]

Enter Ghost and Hamlet.

HAMLET
　　Whither wilt thou lead me? Speak. I'll go no further.
GHOST
　　Mark me.
HAMLET　　I will.
GHOST　　　　　My hour is almost come,
　　When I to sulf'rous and tormenting flames
　　Must render up myself.
HAMLET　　　　　　　　Alas, poor ghost!
GHOST
　　Pity me not, but lend thy serious hearing
　　To what I shall unfold.
HAMLET　　Speak. I am bound to hear.　　　　　　　　7
GHOST
　　So art thou to revenge, when thou shalt hear.
HAMLET　　What?
GHOST　　I am thy father's spirit,
　　Doomed for a certain term to walk the night,
　　And for the day confined to fast in fires,　　　　12
　　Till the foul crimes done in my days of nature　　13
　　Are burnt and purged away. But that I am forbid　14
　　To tell the secrets of my prison house,
　　I could a tale unfold whose lightest word
　　Would harrow up thy soul, freeze thy young blood,　17
　　Make thy two eyes like stars start from their spheres,　18
　　Thy knotted and combinèd locks to part,　　　　19
　　And each particular hair to stand on end
　　Like quills upon the fretful porcupine.
　　But this eternal blazon must not be　　　　　22
　　To ears of flesh and blood. List, list, oh, list!
　　If thou didst ever thy dear father love—
HAMLET　　Oh, God!
GHOST
　　Revenge his foul and most unnatural murder.
HAMLET　　Murder?
GHOST
　　Murder most foul, as in the best it is,　　　　28
　　But this most foul, strange, and unnatural.
HAMLET
　　Haste me to know't, that I, with wings as swift
　　As meditation or the thoughts of love,
　　May sweep to my revenge.
GHOST　　　　　　　　　I find thee apt;

And duller shouldst thou be than the fat weed　　33
That roots itself in ease on Lethe wharf,　　　　34
Wouldst thou not stir in this. Now, Hamlet, hear.
'Tis given out that, sleeping in my orchard,　　　36
A serpent stung me. So the whole ear of Denmark
Is by a forgèd process of my death　　　　　38
Rankly abused. But know, thou noble youth,　　39
The serpent that did sting thy father's life
Now wears his crown.
HAMLET　　Oh, my prophetic soul! My uncle!
GHOST
Ay, that incestuous, that adulterate beast,　　　43
With witchcraft of his wit, with traitorous gifts—　44
Oh, wicked wit and gifts, that have the power
So to seduce!—won to his shameful lust
The will of my most seeming-virtuous queen.
Oh, Hamlet, what a falling off was there!
From me, whose love was of that dignity
That it went hand in hand even with the vow　　50
I made to her in marriage, and to decline
Upon a wretch whose natural gifts were poor
To those of mine!　　　　　　　　　　53
But virtue, as it never will be moved,　　　　54
Though lewdness court it in a shape of heaven,　　55
So lust, though to a radiant angel linked,
Will sate itself in a celestial bed　　　　　57
And prey on garbage.
But soft, methinks I scent the morning air.
Brief let me be. Sleeping within my orchard,
My custom always of the afternoon,
Upon my secure hour thy uncle stole,　　　　62
With juice of cursèd hebona in a vial,　　　　63
And in the porches of my ears did pour　　　　64
The leprous distillment, whose effect　　　　65
Holds such an enmity with blood of man
That swift as quicksilver it courses through
The natural gates and alleys of the body,　　　68
And with a sudden vigor it doth posset　　　　69
And curd, like eager droppings into milk,　　　70
The thin and wholesome blood. So did it mine,
And a most instant tetter barked about,　　　72
Most lazar-like, with vile and loathsome crust,　　73
All my smooth body.
Thus was I, sleeping, by a brother's hand
Of life, of crown, of queen at once dispatched,　　76

---

91 it i.e., the outcome.
1.5 Location: The battlements of the castle.
7 bound (1) ready (2) obligated by duty and fate. (The Ghost, in line 8, answers in the second sense.)　**12 fast** do penance by fasting
13 crimes sins.　**of nature** as a mortal　**14 But that** Were it not that
17 harrow up lacerate, tear　**18 spheres** i.e., eye-sockets, here compared to the orbits or transparent revolving spheres in which, according to Ptolemaic astronomy, the heavenly bodies were fixed
19 knotted . . . locks hair neatly arranged and confined　**22 eternal blazon** revelation of the secrets of eternity　**28 in the best** even at best

33 shouldst thou be you would have to be.　**fat** torpid, lethargic
34 Lethe the river of forgetfulness in Hades　**36 orchard** garden
38 forgèd process falsified account　**39 abused** deceived.　**43 adulterate** adulterous　**44 gifts** (1) talents (2) presents　**50 even with the vow** with the very vow　**53 To** compared with　**54 virtue, as it** just as virtue　**55 shape of heaven** heavenly form　**57 sate . . . bed** gratify its lustful appetite to the point of revulsion or ennui, even in a virtuously lawful marriage　**62 secure hour** time of being free from worries　**63 hebona** a poison. (The word seems to be a form of *ebony*, though it is thought perhaps to be related to *henbane*, a poison, or to *ebenus*, "yew.")　**64 porches** gateways　**65 leprous distillment** distillation causing leprosylike disfigurement　**68 gates** entry ways
69–70 posset . . . curd coagulate and curdle　**70 eager** sour, acid
72 tetter eruption of scabs.　**barked** covered with a rough covering, like bark on a tree　**73 lazar-like** leperlike　**76 dispatched** suddenly deprived

Cut off even in the blossoms of my sin,
Unhouseled, disappointed, unaneled,   78
No reck'ning made, but sent to my account   79
With all my imperfections on my head.
Oh, horrible! Oh, horrible, most horrible!
If thou hast nature in thee, bear it not.   82
Let not the royal bed of Denmark be
A couch for luxury and damnèd incest.   84
But, howsomever thou pursues this act,
Taint not thy mind nor let thy soul contrive
Against thy mother aught. Leave her to heaven
And to those thorns that in her bosom lodge,
To prick and sting her. Fare thee well at once.
The glowworm shows the matin to be near,   90
And 'gins to pale his uneffectual fire.   91
Adieu, adieu, adieu! Remember me.   [*Exit.*]

HAMLET
O all you host of heaven! O earth! What else?
And shall I couple hell? Oh, fie! Hold, hold, my heart,   94
And you, my sinews, grow not instant old,   95
But bear me stiffly up. Remember thee?
Ay, thou poor ghost, whiles memory holds a seat
In this distracted globe. Remember thee?   98
Yea, from the table of my memory   99
I'll wipe away all trivial fond records,   100
All saws of books, all forms, all pressures past   101
That youth and observation copied there,
And thy commandment all alone shall live
Within the book and volume of my brain,
Unmixed with baser matter. Yes, by heaven!
Oh, most pernicious woman!
Oh, villain, villain, smiling, damnèd villain!
My tables—meet it is I set it down   108
That one may smile, and smile, and be a villain.
At least I am sure it may be so in Denmark.
So, uncle, there you are. Now to my word: 111
It is "Adieu, adieu! Remember me."
I have sworn't.

Enter Horatio and Marcellus.

HORATIO   My lord, my lord!
MARCELLUS   Lord Hamlet!
HORATIO   Heavens secure him!   116
HAMLET   So be it.
MARCELLUS   Hillo, ho, ho, my lord!
HAMLET   Hillo, ho, ho, boy! Come, bird, come.   119
MARCELLUS   How is't, my noble lord?

HORATIO   What news, my lord?
HAMLET   Oh, wonderful!
HORATIO   Good my lord, tell it.
HAMLET   No, you will reveal it.
HORATIO   Not I, my lord, by heaven.
MARCELLUS   Nor I, my lord.
HAMLET
How say you, then, would heart of man once think it?   127
But you'll be secret?
HORATIO, MARCELLUS   Ay, by heaven, my lord.
HAMLET
There's never a villain dwelling in all Denmark
But he's an arrant knave.   130
HORATIO
There needs no ghost, my lord, come from the grave
To tell us this.
HAMLET   Why, right, you are in the right.
And so, without more circumstance at all,   133
I hold it fit that we shake hands and part,
You as your business and desire shall point you—
For every man hath business and desire,
Such as it is—and for my own poor part,
Look you, I'll go pray.
HORATIO
These are but wild and whirling words, my lord.
HAMLET
I am sorry they offend you, heartily;
Yes, faith, heartily.
HORATIO   There's no offense, my lord.
HAMLET
Yes, by Saint Patrick, but there is, Horatio,   142
And much offense too. Touching this vision here,   143
It is an honest ghost, that let me tell you.   144
For your desire to know what is between us,
O'ermaster't as you may. And now, good friends,
As you are friends, scholars, and soldiers,
Give me one poor request.
HORATIO   What is't, my lord? We will.
HAMLET
Never make known what you have seen tonight.
HORATIO, MARCELLUS   My lord, we will not.
HAMLET   Nay, but swear't.
HORATIO   In faith, my lord, not I.   153
MARCELLUS   Nor I, my lord, in faith.
HAMLET   Upon my sword.   [*He holds out his sword.*]   155
MARCELLUS   We have sworn, my lord, already.   156
HAMLET   Indeed, upon my sword, indeed.
GHOST (*cries under the stage*)   Swear.
HAMLET
Ha, ha, boy, say'st thou so? Art thou there, truepenny?   159

---

78 Unhouseled . . . unaneled without having received the Sacrament or other last rites including confession, absolution, and the holy oil of extreme unction   **79 reck'ning** settling of accounts   **82 nature** i.e., the promptings of a son   **84 luxury** lechery   **90 matin** morning   **91 his** its   **94 couple** add.   **Hold** Hold together   **95 instant** instantly   **98 globe** (1) head (2) world (3) Globe Theater.   **99 table** tablet, slate   **100 fond** foolish   **101 All . . . past** all wise sayings, all shapes or images imprinted on the tablets of my memory, all past impressions   **108 My tables . . . down** (Editors often specify that Hamlet makes a note in his writing tablet, but he may simply mean that he is making a mental observation of lasting impression.)   **111 there you are** i.e., there, I've noted that against you.   **116 secure him** keep him safe.   **119 Hillo . . . come** (A falconer's call to a hawk in air. Hamlet mocks the hallooing as though it were a part of hawking.)

127 once ever   **130 But . . . knave** (Hamlet jokingly gives a self-evident answer: every villain is a thoroughgoing knave.)   **133 circumstance** ceremony, elaboration   **142 Saint Patrick** the keeper of Purgatory   **143 offense** (Hamlet deliberately changes Horatio's "no offense taken" to "an offense against all decency.")   **144 honest** genuine   **153 In faith . . . I** i.e., I swear not to tell what I have seen. (Horatio is not refusing to swear.)   **155 sword** i.e., the hilt in the form of a cross.   **156 We . . . already** i.e., We swore *in faith*.   **159 truepenny** honest old fellow.

Come on, you hear this fellow in the cellarage.
Consent to swear.

HORATIO   Propose the oath, my lord.

HAMLET

Never to speak of this that you have seen,
Swear by my sword.

GHOST [*beneath*]   Swear.   [*They swear.*] 164

HAMLET

Hic et ubique? Then we'll shift our ground.   165

                      [*He moves to another spot.*]

Come hither, gentlemen,
And lay your hands again upon my sword.
Swear by my sword
Never to speak of this that you have heard.

GHOST [*beneath*]   Swear by his sword.   [*They swear.*]

HAMLET

Well said, old mole. Canst work i'th'earth so fast?
A worthy pioneer!—Once more remove, good friends. 172

                       [*He moves again.*]

HORATIO

Oh, day and night, but this is wondrous strange!

HAMLET

And therefore as a stranger give it welcome.   174
There are more things in heaven and earth, Horatio,
Than are dreamt of in your philosophy.   176
But come;
Here, as before, never, so help you mercy,   178
How strange or odd some'er I bear myself—
As I perchance hereafter shall think meet
To put an antic disposition on—   181
That you, at such times seeing me, never shall,
With arms encumbered thus, or this headshake,   183
Or by pronouncing of some doubtful phrase
As "Well, we know," or "We could, an if we would," 185
Or "If we list to speak," or "There be, an if they
   might,"   186
Or such ambiguous giving out, to note   187
That you know aught of me—this do swear,   188
So grace and mercy at your most need help you.

GHOST [*beneath*]   Swear.   [*They swear.*]

HAMLET

Rest, rest, perturbèd spirit!—So, gentlemen,
With all my love I do commend me to you;   192
And what so poor a man as Hamlet is
May do t'express his love and friending to you,   194
God willing, shall not lack. Let us go in together,   195
And still your fingers on your lips, I pray.   196

The time is out of joint. Oh, cursèd spite   197
That ever I was born to set it right!

             [*They wait for him to leave first.*]

Nay, come, let's go together.   *Exeunt.* 199

[2.1]

Enter old Polonius with his man [Reynaldo].

POLONIUS

Give him this money and these notes, Reynaldo.

             [*He gives money and papers.*]

REYNALDO   I will, my lord.

POLONIUS

You shall do marvelous wisely, good Reynaldo,   3
Before you visit him, to make inquire   4
Of his behavior.

REYNALDO   My lord, I did intend it.

POLONIUS

Marry, well said, very well said. Look you, sir,
Inquire me first what Danskers are in Paris,   7
And how, and who, what means, and where they
   keep,   8
What company, at what expense; and finding
By this encompassment and drift of question   10
That they do know my son, come you more nearer   11
Than your particular demands will touch it.   12
Take you, as 'twere, some distant knowledge of him,   13
As thus, "I know his father and his friends,
And in part him." Do you mark this, Reynaldo?

REYNALDO   Ay, very well, my lord.

POLONIUS

"And in part him, but," you may say, "not well.
But if't be he I mean, he's very wild,
Addicted so and so," and there put on him   19
What forgeries you please—marry, none so rank   20
As may dishonor him, take heed of that,
But, sir, such wanton, wild, and usual slips   22
As are companions noted and most known
To youth and liberty.

REYNALDO   As gaming, my lord.

POLONIUS   Ay, or drinking, fencing, swearing,
Quarreling, drabbing—you may go so far.   27

REYNALDO   My lord, that would dishonor him.

POLONIUS

Faith, no, as you may season it in the charge.   29
You must not put another scandal on him
That he is open to incontinency;   31

---

164 s.d. *They swear* (Seemingly they swear here, and at lines 170 and 190, as they lay their hands on Hamlet's sword. Triple oaths would have particular force; these three oaths deal with what they have seen, what they have heard, and what they promise about Hamlet's *antic disposition*.) **165** *Hic et ubique?* Here and everywhere? (Latin.) **172 pioneer** foot soldier assigned to dig tunnels and excavations. **174 as a stranger** i.e., needing your hospitality **176 your philosophy** this subject that is called "natural philosophy" or "science." (*Your* is not personal.) **178 so help you mercy** as you hope for God's mercy when you are judged **181 antic** grotesque, strange **183 encumbered** folded **185 an if** if **186 list** wished. **There . . . might** There are those who could talk if they were at liberty to do so **187 note** indicate **188 aught** anything **192 commend . . . you** give you my best wishes **194 friending** friendliness **195 lack** be lacking. **196 still** always

197 out of joint in utter disorder.   **199 let's go together** (Probably they wait for him to leave first, but he refuses this ceremoniousness.) **2.1 Location:** Polonius's chambers.
3 marvelous marvelously **4 inquire** inquiry **7 Danskers** Danes **8 what means** what wealth (they have). **keep** dwell **10 encompassment . . . question** roundabout way of questioning **11-12 come . . . it** you will find out more this way than by asking pointed questions (*particular demands*). **13 Take you** Assume, pretend **19 put on** impute to **20 forgeries** invented tales. **rank** gross **22 wanton** sportive, unrestrained **27 drabbing** whoring **29 season** temper, soften **31 incontinency** habitual sexual excess

That's not my meaning. But breathe his faults so
    quaintly   32
That they may seem the taints of liberty,   33
The flash and outbreak of a fiery mind,
A savageness in unreclaimèd blood,   35
Of general assault.   36
REYNALDO   But, my good lord—
POLONIUS   Wherefore should you do this?
REYNALDO   Ay, my lord, I would know that.
POLONIUS   Marry, sir, here's my drift,
And I believe it is a fetch of warrant.   41
You laying these slight sullies on my son,
As 'twere a thing a little soiled wi'th' working,   43
Mark you,
Your party in converse, him you would sound,   45
Having ever seen in the prenominate crimes   46
The youth you breathe of guilty, be assured   47
He closes with you in this consequence: 48
"Good sir," or so, or "friend," or "gentleman,"
According to the phrase or the addition   50
Of man and country.
REYNALDO   Very good, my lord.
POLONIUS   And then, sir, does 'a this—'a does—what
was I about to say? By the Mass, I was about to say
something. Where did I leave?
REYNALDO   At "closes in the consequence."
POLONIUS
At "closes in the consequence," ay, marry.
He closes thus: "I know the gentleman,
I saw him yesterday," or "th'other day,"
Or then, or then, with such or such, "and as you say,
There was 'a gaming," "there o'ertook in 's rouse,"   60
"There falling out at tennis," or perchance   61
"I saw him enter such a house of sale,"
Videlicet a brothel, or so forth. See you now,   63
Your bait of falsehood takes this carp of truth;   64
And thus do we of wisdom and of reach,   65
With windlasses and with assays of bias,   66
By indirections find directions out.   67
So by my former lecture and advice   68
Shall you my son. You have me, have you not?   69
REYNALDO
My lord, I have.
POLONIUS   God b'wi'ye; fare ye well.
REYNALDO   Good my lord.

POLONIUS
Observe his inclination in yourself.   72
REYNALDO   I shall, my lord.
POLONIUS   And let him ply his music.
REYNALDO   Well, my lord.
POLONIUS
Farewell.   *Exit Reynaldo.*

    Enter Ophelia.

          How now, Ophelia, what's the matter?
OPHELIA
Oh, my lord, my lord, I have been so affrighted!
POLONIUS   With what, i'th' name of God?
OPHELIA
My lord, as I was sewing in my closet,   79
Lord Hamlet, with his doublet all unbraced,   80
No hat upon his head, his stockings fouled,
Ungartered, and down-gyvèd to his ankle,   82
Pale as his shirt, his knees knocking each other,
And with a look so piteous in purport   84
As if he had been loosèd out of hell
To speak of horrors—he comes before me.
POLONIUS
Mad for thy love?
OPHELIA   My lord, I do not know,
But truly I do fear it.
POLONIUS   What said he?
OPHELIA
He took me by the wrist and held me hard.
Then goes he to the length of all his arm,
And, with his other hand thus o'er his brow
He falls to such perusal of my face
As 'a would draw it. Long stayed he so.   93
At last, a little shaking of mine arm
And thrice his head thus waving up and down,
He raised a sigh so piteous and profound
As it did seem to shatter all his bulk   97
And end his being. That done, he lets me go,
And with his head over his shoulder turned
He seemed to find his way without his eyes,
For out o' doors he went without their helps,
And to the last bended their light on me.
POLONIUS
Come, go with me. I will go seek the King.
This is the very ecstasy of love,   104
Whose violent property fordoes itself   105
And leads the will to desperate undertakings
As oft as any passion under heaven
That does afflict our natures. I am sorry.
What, have you given him any hard words of late?
OPHELIA
No, my good lord, but as you did command
I did repel his letters and denied

32 **quaintly** artfully, subtly   33 **taints of liberty** faults resulting from
free living   35-6 **A savageness . . . assault** a wildness in untamed
youth that assails all indiscriminately.   41 **fetch of warrant** legitimate
trick.   43 **wi'th' working** in the process of being made, i.e., in everyday experience   45 **Your . . . converse** the person you are conversing
with.   **sound** sound out   46 **Having ever** if he has ever.   **prenominate
crimes** aforenamed offenses   47 **breathe** speak   48 **closes . . . consequence** takes you into his confidence as follows   50 **addition** title
60 **o'ertook in 's rouse** overcome by drink   61 **falling out** quarreling
63 **Videlicet** namely   64 **carp** a fish   65 **reach** capacity, ability
66 **windlasses** i.e., circuitous paths. (Literally, circuits made to head
off the game in hunting.)   **assays of bias** attempts through indirection (like the curving path of the bowling ball, which is biased or
weighted to one side)   67 **directions** i.e., the way things really are
68 **former lecture** just-ended set of instructions   69 **have** understand

72 **in yourself** in your own person (as well as by asking questions of
others).   79 **closet** private chamber   80 **doublet** close-fitting jacket.
unbraced unfastened   82 **down-gyvèd** fallen to the ankles (like gyves
or fetters)   84 **in purport** in what it expressed   93 **As 'a** as if he
97 **As** that.   **bulk** body   104 **ecstasy** madness   105 **property fordoes** nature destroys

His access to me.
POLONIUS   That hath made him mad.
I am sorry that with better heed and judgment
I had not quoted him. I feared he did but trifle   114
And meant to wrack thee. But beshrew my jealousy!   115
By heaven, it is as proper to our age   116
To cast beyond ourselves in our opinions   117
As it is common for the younger sort
To lack discretion. Come, go we to the King.
This must be known, which, being kept close, might
    move   120
More grief to hide than hate to utter love.   121
Come.   *Exeunt.*

❖

[2.2]

*Flourish. Enter King and Queen, Rosencrantz,
and Guildenstern [with others].*

KING
Welcome, dear Rosencrantz and Guildenstern.
Moreover that we much did long to see you,   2
The need we have to use you did provoke
Our hasty sending. Something have you heard
Of Hamlet's transformation—so call it,
Sith nor th'exterior nor the inward man   6
Resembles that it was. What it should be,   7
More than his father's death, that thus hath put him
So much from th'understanding of himself,
I cannot dream of. I entreat you both
That, being of so young days brought up with him,   11
And sith so neighbored to his youth and havior,   12
That you vouchsafe your rest here in our court   13
Some little time, so by your companies
To draw him on to pleasures, and to gather
So much as from occasion you may glean,   16
Whether aught to us unknown afflicts him thus
That, opened, lies within our remedy.   18
QUEEN
Good gentlemen, he hath much talked of you,
And sure I am two men there is not living
To whom he more adheres. If it will please you
To show us so much gentry and good will
As to expend your time with us awhile   22
For the supply and profit of our hope,   24

Your visitation shall receive such thanks
As fits a kings's remembrance.
ROSENCRANTZ   Both Your Majesties   26
Might, by the sovereign power you have of us,   27
Put your dread pleasures more into command   28
Than to entreaty.
GUILDENSTERN   But we both obey,
And here give up ourselves in the full bent   30
To lay our service freely at your feet,
To be commanded.
KING
Thanks, Rosencrantz and gentle Guildenstern.
QUEEN
Thanks, Guildenstern and gentle Rosencrantz.
And I beseech you instantly to visit
My too much changèd son.—Go, some of you,
And bring these gentlemen where Hamlet is.
GUILDENSTERN
Heavens make our presence and our practices   38
Pleasant and helpful to him!
QUEEN   Ay, amen!
              *Exeunt Rosencrantz and Guildenstern [with some
                                              attendants].*

Enter Polonius.

POLONIUS
Th'ambassadors from Norway, my good lord,
Are joyfully returned.
KING
Thou still hast been the father of good news.   42
POLONIUS
Have I, my lord? I assure my good liege
I hold my duty, as I hold my soul,
Both to my God and to my gracious king;
And I do think, or else this brain of mine
Hunts not the trail of policy so sure   47
As it hath used to do, that I have found
The very cause of Hamlet's lunacy.
KING
Oh, speak of that! That do I long to hear.
POLONIUS
Give first admittance to th'ambassadors.
My news shall be the fruit to that great feast.   52
KING
Thyself do grace to them and bring them in.   53
                              [Exit Polonius.]
He tells me, my dear Gertrude, he hath found
The head and source of all your son's distemper.
QUEEN
I doubt it is no other but the main,   56
His father's death and our o'erhasty marriage.

*Enter Ambassadors [Voltimand and Cornelius,
with Polonius].*

---

114 quoted observed   **115 wrack** ruin, seduce.   **beshrew my jealousy!** a plague upon my suspicious nature!   **116 proper . . . age** characteristic of us (old) men   **117 cast beyond** overshoot, miscalculate.
(A metaphor from hunting.)   **120 known** made known (to the King).
close secret   **120-1 might . . . love** might cause more grief
(because of what Hamlet might do) by hiding the knowledge of Hamlet's strange behavior to Ophelia than unpleasantness by telling it.
2.2 Location: The castle.
2 Moreover that Besides the fact that   **6 Sith nor** since neither   **7 that**
what   **11–12 That . . . havior** that, seeing as you were brought up
with him from early youth (see 3.4.209, where Hamlet refers to
Rosencrantz and Guildenstern as "my two schoolfellows"), and since
you have been intimately acquainted with his youthful ways
13 vouchsafe your rest consent to stay   **16 occasion** opportunity
18 opened being revealed   **22 gentry** courtesy   **24 supply . . . hope**
aid and furtherance of what we hope for

26 As fits . . . remembrance as would be a fitting gift of a king who
rewards true service.   **27 of** over   **28 dread** inspiring awe   **30 in . . .
bent** to the utmost degree of our capacity. (An archery metaphor.)
38 practices doings   **42 still** always   **47 policy** statecraft   **52 fruit**
dessert   **53 grace** honor. (Punning on *grace* said before a *feast*, line
52.)   **56 doubt** fear, suspect

KING
    Well, we shall sift him.—Welcome, my good friends!   58
    Say, Voltimand, what from our brother Norway?   59
VOLTIMAND
    Most fair return of greetings and desires.   60
    Upon our first, he sent out to suppress   61
    His nephew's levies, which to him appeared
    To be a preparation 'gainst the Polack,
    But, better looked into, he truly found
    It was against Your Highness. Whereat grieved
    That so his sickness, age, and impotence   66
    Was falsely borne in hand, sends out arrests   67
    On Fortinbras, which he, in brief, obeys,
    Receives rebuke from Norway, and in fine   69
    Makes vow before his uncle never more
    To give th'assay of arms against Your Majesty.   71
    Whereon old Norway, overcome with joy,
    Gives him three thousand crowns in annual fee
    And his commission to employ those soldiers,
    So levied as before, against the Polack,
    With an entreaty, herein further shown,
                                        [giving a paper]
    That it might please you to give quiet pass
    Through your dominions for this enterprise
    On such regards of safety and allowance   79
    As therein are set down.
KING   It likes us well,   80
    And at our more considered time we'll read,   81
    Answer, and think upon this business.
    Meantime we thank you for your well-took labor.
    Go to your rest; at night we'll feast together.
    Most welcome home!   Exeunt Ambassadors.
POLONIUS   This business is well ended.
    My liege, and madam, to expostulate   86
    What majesty should be, what duty is,
    Why day is day, night night, and time is time,
    Were nothing but to waste night, day, and time.
    Therefore, since brevity is the soul of wit,   90
    And tediousness the limbs and outward flourishes,
    I will be brief. Your noble son is mad.
    Mad call I it, for, to define true madness,
    What is't but to be nothing else but mad?
    But let that go.
QUEEN   More matter, with less art.
POLONIUS
    Madam, I swear I use no art at all.
    That he's mad, 'tis true; 'tis true 'tis pity,
    And pity 'tis 'tis true—a foolish figure,   98
    But farewell it, for I will use no art.
    Mad let us grant him, then, and now remains
    That we find out the cause of this effect,

Or rather say, the cause of this defect,
For this effect defective comes by cause.   103
Thus it remains, and the remainder thus.
Perpend.   105
I have a daughter—have while she is mine—
Who, in her duty and obedience, mark,
Hath given me this. Now gather and surmise.   108
[He reads the letter.] "To the celestial and my soul's
idol, the most beautified Ophelia"—
That's an ill phrase, a vile phrase; "beautified" is a
vile phrase. But you shall hear. Thus: [He reads.]
"In her excellent white bosom, these, etc."   113
QUEEN   Came this from Hamlet to her?
POLONIUS
    Good madam, stay awhile, I will be faithful.   115
                                        [He reads.]
        "Doubt thou the stars are fire,
            Doubt that the sun doth move,
        Doubt truth to be a liar,   118
            But never doubt I love.
O dear Ophelia, I am ill at these numbers. I have not   120
art to reckon my groans. But that I love thee best, O   121
most best, believe it. Adieu.
            Thine evermore, most dear lady, whilst this
                        machine is to him, Hamlet."   124
This in obedience hath my daughter shown me,
And, more above, hath his solicitings,   126
As they fell out by time, by means, and place,   127
All given to mine ear.
KING   But how hath she   128
Received his love?
POLONIUS   What do you think of me?
KING
    As of a man faithful and honorable.
POLONIUS
    I would fain prove so. But what might you think,   131
    When I had seen this hot love on the wing—
    As I perceived it, I must tell you that,
    Before my daughter told me—what might you,
    Or my dear Majesty your queen here, think,
    If I had played the desk or table book,   136
    Or given my heart a winking, mute and dumb,   137
    Or looked upon this love with idle sight?   138
    What might you think? No, I went round to work,   139
    And my young mistress thus I did bespeak: 140
    "Lord Hamlet is a prince out of thy star;   141
    This must not be." And then I prescripts gave her,   142

---

58 **sift him** question Polonius (or Hamlet) closely.   59 **brother** fellow
king   60 **desires** good wishes.   61 **Upon our first** At our first words
on the business   66 **impotence** weakness   67 **borne in hand**
deluded, taken advantage of.   **arrests** orders to desist   69 **in fine** in
conclusion   71 **give th'assay** make trial of strength, challenge
79 **On . . . allowance** i.e., with such considerations for the safety of
Denmark and permission for Fortinbras   80 **likes** pleases   81 **considered** suitable for deliberation   86 **expostulate** expound, inquire
into   90 **wit** sense or judgment   98 **figure** figure of speech

103 **For . . . cause** i.e., for this defective behavior, this madness, must
have a cause.   105 **Perpend** Consider.   108 **gather and surmise**
draw your own conclusions.   113 **"In . . . etc."** (The letter is poetically addressed to her heart, where a letter would be kept by a young
lady.)   115 **stay . . . faithful** i.e., hold on, I will do as you wish.
118 **Doubt** suspect   120 **ill . . . numbers** unskilled at writing verses.
121 **reckon** (1) count (2) number metrically, scan   124 **machine** i.e.,
body   126–8 **And . . . ear** and moreover she has told me when, how,
and where his solicitings of her occurred.   131 **fain** gladly   136–7 **If . . .
dumb** if I had acted as go-between, passing love notes, or if I had
refused to let my heart acknowledge what my eyes could see
138 **with idle sight** complacently or incomprehendingly.   139 **round**
roundly, plainly   140 **bespeak** address   141 **out of thy star** above
your sphere, position   142 **prescripts** orders

That she should lock herself from his resort,
Admit no messengers, receive no tokens.
Which done, she took the fruits of my advice;
And he, repellèd—a short tale to make—
Fell into a sadness, then into a fast,
Thence to a watch, thence into a weakness, 148
Thence to a lightness, and by this declension 149
Into the madness wherein now he raves,
And all we mourn for.

KING [to the Queen]   Do you think 'tis this?

QUEEN   It may be, very like.

POLONIUS
Hath there been such a time—I would fain know
    that—
That I have positively said "'Tis so,"
When it proved otherwise?

KING   Not that I know.

POLONIUS
Take this from this, if this be otherwise. 156
If circumstances lead me, I will find
Where truth is hid, though it were hid indeed
Within the center.

KING   How may we try it further? 159

POLONIUS
You know sometimes he walks four hours together
Here in the lobby.

QUEEN   So he does indeed.

POLONIUS
At such a time I'll loose my daughter to him. 162
Be you and I behind an arras then. 163
Mark the encounter. If he love her not
And be not from his reason fall'n thereon, 165
Let me be no assistant for a state,
But keep a farm and carters.

KING   We will try it. 167

Enter Hamlet [reading on a book].

QUEEN
But look where sadly the poor wretch comes reading.

POLONIUS
Away, I do beseech you both, away.
I'll board him presently. Oh, give me leave. 170
        Exeunt King and Queen [with attendants].
How does my good Lord Hamlet?

HAMLET   Well, God-a-mercy. 172

POLONIUS   Do you know me, my lord?

HAMLET   Excellent well. You are a fishmonger. 174

POLONIUS   Not I, my lord.

HAMLET   Then I would you were so honest a man.

POLONIUS   Honest, my lord?

HAMLET   Ay, sir. To be honest, as this world goes, is to
be one man picked out of ten thousand.

POLONIUS   That's very true, my lord.

HAMLET   For if the sun breed maggots in a dead dog,
being a good kissing carrion—Have you a daughter? 182

POLONIUS   I have, my lord.

HAMLET   Let her not walk i'th' sun. Conception is a 184
blessing, but as your daughter may conceive, friend,
look to't.

POLONIUS [aside]   How say you by that? Still harping
on my daughter. Yet he knew me not at first; 'a said
I was a fishmonger. 'A is far gone. And truly in my
youth I suffered much extremity for love, very near
this. I'll speak to him again.—What do you read,
my lord?

HAMLET   Words, words, words.

POLONIUS   What is the matter, my lord? 194

HAMLET   Between who?

POLONIUS   I mean, the matter that you read, my lord.

HAMLET   Slanders, sir; for the satirical rogue says here
that old men have gray beards, that their faces are wrinkled, their eyes purging thick amber and plum-tree 199
gum, and that they have a plentiful lack of wit, to- 200
gether with most weak hams. All which, sir, though I
most powerfully and potently believe, yet I hold it not
honesty to have it thus set down, for yourself, sir, shall 203
grow old as I am, if like a crab you could go backward. 204

POLONIUS [aside]   Though this be madness, yet there is
method in't.—Will you walk out of the air, my lord? 206

HAMLET   Into my grave.

POLONIUS   Indeed, that's out of the air. [Aside] How
pregnant sometimes his replies are! A happiness that 209
often madness hits on, which reason and sanity could
not so prosperously be delivered of. I will leave him 211
and suddenly contrive the means of meeting between 212
him and my daughter.—My honorable lord, I will
most humbly take my leave of you.

HAMLET   You cannot, sir, take from me anything that I
will more willingly part withal—except my life, except 216
my life, except my life.

Enter Guildenstern and Rosencrantz.

POLONIUS   Fare you well, my lord.

HAMLET   These tedious old fools!

POLONIUS   You go to seek the Lord Hamlet. There he is.

ROSENCRANTZ [to Polonius]   God save you, sir!
                                [Exit Polonius.]

GUILDENSTERN   My honored lord!

---

148 **watch** state of sleeplessness   149 **lightness** lightheadedness.
declension decline, deterioration. (With a pun on the grammatical
sense.)   156 **Take this from this** (The actor probably gestures, indicating that he means his head from his shoulders, or his staff of office
or chain from his hands or neck, or something similar.)   159 **center**
center of the earth, traditionally an extraordinarily inaccessible place.
try test   162 **loose** (As one might release an animal that is being
mated.)   163 **arras** hanging, tapestry   165 **thereon** on that account
167 **carters** wagon drivers.   170 **I'll . . . leave** I'll accost him at once.
Please leave us alone; leave him to me.   172 **God-a-mercy** God have
mercy, i.e., thank you.   174 **fishmonger** fish merchant.

182 **a good kissing carrion** i.e., a good piece of flesh for kissing, or for
the sun to kiss   184 **i'th' sun** in public. (With additional implication
of the sunshine of princely favors.)   **Conception** (1) Understanding
(2) Pregnancy   194 **matter** substance. (But Hamlet plays on the sense
of "basis for a dispute.")   199 **purging** discharging.   **amber** i.e.,
resin, like the resinous *plum-tree gum*   200 **wit** understanding
203 **honesty** decency, decorum   204 **old** as old   206 **out of the air**
(The open air was considered dangerous for sick people.)   209 **pregnant** quick-witted, full of meaning.   **happiness** felicity of expression
211 **prosperously** successfully   212 **suddenly** immediately
216 **withal** with

ROSENCRANTZ　My most dear lord!

HAMLET　My excellent good friends! How dost thou, Guildenstern? Ah, Rosencrantz! Good lads, how do you both?

ROSENCRANTZ
As the indifferent children of the earth. 227

GUILDENSTERN
Happy in that we are not overhappy.
On Fortune's cap we are not the very button.

HAMLET　Nor the soles of her shoe?

ROSENCRANTZ　Neither, my lord.

HAMLET　Then you live about her waist, or in the mid- 232
dle of her favors? 233

GUILDENSTERN　Faith, her privates we. 234

HAMLET　In the secret parts of Fortune? Oh, most true, she is a strumpet. What news? 236

ROSENCRANTZ　None, my lord, but the world's grown honest.

HAMLET　Then is doomsday near. But your news is not true. Let me question more in particular. What have you, my good friends, deserved at the hands of Fortune that she sends you to prison hither?

GUILDENSTERN　Prison, my lord?

HAMLET　Denmark's a prison.

ROSENCRANTZ　Then is the world one.

HAMLET　A goodly one, in which there are many confines, wards, and dungeons, Denmark being one 247
o'th' worst.

ROSENCRANTZ　We think not so, my lord.

HAMLET　Why then 'tis none to you, for there is nothing either good or bad but thinking makes it so. To me it is a prison.

ROSENCRANTZ　Why then, your ambition makes it one. 'Tis too narrow for your mind.

HAMLET　Oh, God, I could be bounded in a nutshell and count myself a king of infinite space, were it not that I have bad dreams.

GUILDENSTERN　Which dreams indeed are ambition, for the very substance of the ambitious is merely the 259
shadow of a dream.

HAMLET　A dream itself is but a shadow.

ROSENCRANTZ　Truly, and I hold ambition of so airy and light a quality that it is but a shadow's shadow.

HAMLET　Then are our beggars bodies, and our mon- 264
archs and outstretched heroes the beggars' shadows. 265
Shall we to th' court? For, by my fay, I cannot reason. 266

ROSENCRANTZ, GUILDENSTERN　We'll wait upon you. 267

HAMLET　No such matter. I will not sort you with the 268
rest of my servants, for, to speak to you like an honest man, I am most dreadfully attended. But, in the 270
beaten way of friendship, what make you at Elsinore? 271

ROSENCRANTZ　To visit you, my lord, no other occasion.

HAMLET　Beggar that I am, I am even poor in thanks; but I thank you, and sure, dear friends, my thanks are too dear a halfpenny. Were you not sent for? Is it your 275
own inclining? Is it a free visitation? Come, come, deal 276
justly with me. Come, come. Nay, speak.

GUILDENSTERN　What should we say, my lord?

HAMLET　Anything but to th' purpose. You were sent 279
for, and there is a kind of confession in your looks which your modesties have not craft enough to color. 281
I know the good King and Queen have sent for you.

ROSENCRANTZ　To what end, my lord?

HAMLET　That you must teach me. But let me conjure 284
you, by the rights of our fellowship, by the consonancy 285
of our youth, by the obligation of our ever-preserved 286
love, and by what more dear a better proposer 287
could charge you withal, be even and direct with me 288
whether you were sent for or no.

ROSENCRANTZ [aside to Guildenstern]　What say you?

HAMLET [aside]　Nay, then, I have an eye of you.—If 291
you love me, hold not off. 292

GUILDENSTERN　My lord, we were sent for.

HAMLET　I will tell you why; so shall my anticipation 294
prevent your discovery, and your secrecy to the King 295
and Queen molt no feather. I have of late—but 296
wherefore I know not—lost all my mirth, forgone all custom of exercises; and indeed it goes so heavily with my disposition that this goodly frame, the earth, seems to me a sterile promontory; this most excellent canopy, the air, look you, this brave o'erhanging 301
firmament, this majestical roof fretted with golden 302
fire, why, it appeareth nothing to me but a foul and pestilent congregation of vapors. What a piece of work 304
is a man! How noble in reason, how infinite in faculties, in form and moving how express and admirable, in 306
action how like an angel, in apprehension how like a 307
god! The beauty of the world, the paragon of animals! And yet, to me, what is this quintessence of dust? 309
Man delights not me—no, nor woman neither, though by your smiling you seem to say so.

227 indifferent ordinary, at neither extreme of fortune or misfortune
232–3 the middle . . . favors i.e., her genitals.　**234 her privates we**
(1) we dwell in her privates, her genitals, in the middle of her favors
(2) we are her ordinary footsoldiers.　**236 strumpet** (Fortune was
proverbially thought of as fickle.)　**247 confines** places of confinement　**259 the very . . . ambitious** that seemingly very substantial
thing that the ambitious pursue　**264–5 Then . . . shadows** (Hamlet
pursues their argument about ambition to its absurd extreme: if ambition is only a shadow of a shadow, then beggars (who are presumably
without ambition) must be real, whereas monarchs and heroes are
only their shadows—*outstretched* like elongated shadows, made to
look bigger than they are.)　**266 fay** faith　**267 wait upon** accompany, attend. (But Hamlet uses the phrase in the sense of providing
menial service.)

268 sort class, categorize　**270 dreadfully attended** waited upon in
slovenly fashion.　**271 beaten way** familiar path, tried-and-true
course.　**make** do　**275 too dear a halfpenny** (1) too expensive at
even a halfpenny, i.e., of little worth (2) too expensive by a halfpenny
in return for worthless kindness.　**276 free** voluntary　**279 Anything
but to th' purpose** Anything except a straightforward answer. (Said
ironically.)　**281 color** disguise.　**284 conjure** adjure, entreat
285–6 the consonancy of our youth our closeness in our younger
days　**287 better** more skillful　**288 charge** urge.　**even** straight,
honest　**291 of** on　**292 hold not off** don't hold back.　**294–5 so . . .
discovery** in that way my saying it first will spare you from having to
reveal the truth　**296 molt no feather** i.e., not diminish in the least.
301 brave splendid　**302 fretted** adorned (with fretwork, as in a
vaulted ceiling)　**304 congregation** mass.　**piece of work** masterpiece　**306 express** well-framed, exact, expressive　**307 apprehension** power of comprehending　**309 quintessence** very essence.
(Literally, the fifth essence beyond earth, water, air, and fire, supposed to be extractable from them.)

ROSENCRANTZ   My lord, there was no such stuff in my thoughts.

HAMLET   Why did you laugh, then, when I said man delights not me?

ROSENCRANTZ   To think, my lord, if you delight not in man, what Lenten entertainment the players shall 317 receive from you. We coted them on the way, and 318 hither are they coming to offer you service.

HAMLET   He that plays the king shall be welcome; His Majesty shall have tribute of me. The adventurous 321 knight shall use his foil and target, the lover shall not 322 sigh gratis, the humorous man shall end his part in 323 peace, the clown shall make those laugh whose lungs 324 are tickle o'th' sear, and the lady shall say her mind 325 freely, or the blank verse shall halt for't. What players 326 are they?

ROSENCRANTZ   Even those you were wont to take such delight in, the tragedians of the city. 329

HAMLET   How chances it they travel? Their residence, 330 both in reputation and profit, was better both ways.

ROSENCRANTZ   I think their inhibition comes by the 332 means of the late innovation. 333

HAMLET   Do they hold the same estimation they did when I was in the city? Are they so followed?

ROSENCRANTZ   No, indeed are they not.

HAMLET   How comes it? Do they grow rusty? 337

ROSENCRANTZ   Nay, their endeavor keeps in the wonted 338 pace. But there is, sir, an aerie of children, little eyases, 339 that cry out on the top of question and are most tyran- 340 nically clapped for't. These are now the fashion, and 341 so berattle the common stages—so they call them— 342 that many wearing rapiers are afraid of goose quills 343 and dare scarce come thither.

HAMLET   What, are they children? Who maintains 'em? How are they escotted? Will they pursue the quality no 346 longer than they can sing? Will they not say after- 347

wards, if they should grow themselves to common 348 players—as it is most like, if their means are no 349 better—their writers do them wrong to make them 350 exclaim against their own succession? 351

ROSENCRANTZ   Faith, there has been much to-do on 352 both sides, and the nation holds it no sin to tar them to 353 controversy. There was for a while no money bid for 354 argument unless the poet and the player went to cuffs 355 in the question. 356

HAMLET   Is't possible?

GUILDENSTERN   Oh, there has been much throwing about of brains.

HAMLET   Do the boys carry it away? 360

ROSENCRANTZ   Ay, that they do, my lord—Hercules 361 and his load too. 362

HAMLET   It is not very strange; for my uncle is King of Denmark, and those that would make mouths at him 364 while my father lived give twenty, forty, fifty, a hundred ducats apiece for his picture in little. 'Sblood, 366 there is something in this more than natural, if philos- ophy could find it out.

A flourish [of trumpets within].

GUILDENSTERN   There are the players.

HAMLET   Gentlemen, you are welcome to Elsinore. Your hands, come then. Th'appurtenance of welcome is 371 fashion and ceremony. Let me comply with you in this 372 garb, lest my extent to the players, which, I tell you, 373 must show fairly outwards, should more appear like 374 entertainment than yours. You are welcome. But my 375 uncle-father and aunt-mother are deceived.

GUILDENSTERN   In what, my dear lord?

HAMLET   I am but mad north-north-west. When the 378 wind is southerly I know a hawk from a handsaw. 379

Enter Polonius.

POLONIUS   Well be with you, gentlemen!

HAMLET   Hark you, Guildenstern, and you too; at each ear a hearer. That great baby you see there is not yet out of his swaddling clouts. 383

ROSENCRANTZ   Haply he is the second time come to 384 them, for they say an old man is twice a child.

---

317 **Lenten entertainment** meager reception (appropriate to Lent) 318 **coted** overtook and passed by   321 **tribute** (1) applause (2) homage paid in money.   **of** from   322 **foil and target** sword and shield   323 **gratis** for nothing.   **humorous man** eccentric character, dominated by one trait or "humor"   323–4 **in peace** i.e., with full license   325 **tickle o'th' sear** hair trigger, ready to laugh easily. (A *sear* is part of a gun-lock.)   326 **halt** limp   329 **tragedians** actors 330 **residence** remaining in their usual place, i.e., in the city 332 **inhibition** formal prohibition (from acting plays in the city) 333 **late innovation** i.e., recent new fashion in satirical plays per- formed by boy actors in the "private" theaters; or the Earl of Essex's abortive rebellion in 1601 against Elizabeth's government. (A much debated passage of seemingly topical reference.)   337 **How . . . rusty?** Have they lost their polish, gone out of fashion? (This passage, through line 362, alludes to the rivalry between the children's compa- nies and the adult actors, given strong impetus by the reopening of the Children of the Chapel at the Blackfriars Theater in late 1600.) 338 **keeps . . . wonted** continues in the usual   339 **aerie** nest.   **eyases** young hawks   340 **cry . . . question** speak shrilly, dominating the controversy (in decrying the public theaters)   340–1 **tyrannically** vehemently   342 **berattle . . . stages** clamor against the public the- aters   343 **many wearing rapiers** i.e., many men of fashion, afraid to patronize the common players for fear of being satirized by the poets writing for the boy actors.   **goose quills** i.e., pens of satirists 346 **escotted** maintained.   **quality** (acting) profession   346–7 **no longer . . . sing** i.e., only until their voices change.

348 **common** regular, adult   349 **like** likely   349–50 **if . . . better** if they find no better way to support themselves   351 **succession** i.e., future careers.   352 **to-do** ado   353 **tar** incite (as in inciting dogs to attack a chained bear)   354–6 **There . . . question** i.e., For a while, no money was offered by the acting companies to playwrights for the plot to a play unless the satirical poets who wrote for the boys and the adult actors came to blows in the play itself.   360 **carry it away** i.e., win the day.   361–2 **Hercules . . . load** (Thought to be an allusion to the sign of the Globe Theatre, which allegedly was Hercules bear- ing the world on his shoulders.)   364 **mouths** faces   366 **ducats** gold coins.   **in little** in miniature.   **'Sblood** By God's (Christ's) blood 371 **Th'appurtenance** The proper accompaniment   372 **comply** observe the formalities of courtesy   373 **garb** i.e., manner.   **my extent** that which I extend, i.e., my polite behavior   374 **show fairly outwards** show every evidence of cordiality   375 **entertainment** a (warm) reception   378 **north-north-west** just off true north, only partly.   379 **I . . . handsaw** (Speaking in his mad guise, Hamlet per- haps suggests that he can tell true from false. A *handsaw* may be a *hernshaw* or heron. Still, a supposedly mad disposition might com- pare hawks and handsaws.)   383 **swaddling clouts** cloths in which to wrap a newborn baby.   384 **Haply** Perhaps

HAMLET   I will prophesy he comes to tell me of the
players. Mark it.—You say right, sir, o' Monday 387
morning, 'twas then indeed.   388

POLONIUS   My lord, I have news to tell you.

HAMLET   My lord, I have news to tell you. When Roscius 390
was an actor in Rome—

POLONIUS   The actors are come hither, my lord.

HAMLET   Buzz, buzz!   393

POLONIUS   Upon my honor—

HAMLET   Then came each actor on his ass.

POLONIUS   The best actors in the world, either for
tragedy, comedy, history, pastoral, pastoral-comical,
historical-pastoral, tragical-historical, tragical-comical-
historical-pastoral, scene individable, or poem unlim- 399
ited. Seneca cannot be too heavy, nor Plautus too 400
light. For the law of writ and the liberty, these are the 401
only men.

HAMLET   O Jephthah, judge of Israel, what a treasure 403
hadst thou!

POLONIUS   What a treasure had he, my lord?

HAMLET   Why,
    "One fair daughter, and no more,
    The which he lovèd passing well."   408

POLONIUS [aside]   Still on my daughter.

HAMLET   Am I not i'th' right, old Jephthah?

POLONIUS   If you call me Jephthah, my lord, I have a
daughter that I love passing well.

HAMLET   Nay, that follows not.   413

POLONIUS   What follows then, my lord?   414

HAMLET   Why,
    "As by lot, God wot,"   416
and then, you know,
    "It came to pass, as most like it was"—   418
the first row of the pious chanson will show you more, 419
for look where my abridgment comes.   420

        Enter the Players.

You are welcome, masters; welcome, all. I am glad to 421
see thee well. Welcome, good friends. Oh, old friend!
Why, thy face is valanced since I saw thee last. Com'st 423
thou to beard me in Denmark? What, my young lady 424

and mistress! By'r Lady, Your Ladyship is nearer to 425
heaven than when I saw you last, by the altitude of a 426
chopine. Pray God your voice, like a piece of uncur- 427
rent gold, be not cracked within the ring. Masters, you 428
are all welcome. We'll e'en to't like French falconers, 429
fly at anything we see. We'll have a speech straight. 430
Come, give us a taste of your quality. Come, a 431
passionate speech.

FIRST PLAYER   What speech, my good lord?

HAMLET   I heard thee speak me a speech once, but it
was never acted, or if it was, not above once, for the
play, I remember, pleased not the million; 'twas cav- 436
iar to the general. But it was—as I received it, and 437
others, whose judgments in such matters cried in the 438
top of mine—an excellent play, well digested in the 439
scenes, set down with as much modesty as cunning. I 440
remember one said there were no sallets in the lines to 441
make the matter savory, nor no matter in the phrase
that might indict the author of affectation, but called it 443
an honest method, as wholesome as sweet, and by very
much more handsome than fine. One speech in't I 445
chiefly loved: 'twas Aeneas' tale to Dido, and there-
about of it especially when he speaks of Priam's 447
slaughter. If it live in your memory, begin at this line: 448
let me see, let me see—
    "The rugged Pyrrhus, like th' Hyrcanian beast"— 450
'Tis not so. It begins with Pyrrhus:
    "The rugged Pyrrhus, he whose sable arms,   452
    Black as his purpose, did the night resemble
    When he lay couchèd in th' ominous horse,   454
    Hath now this dread and black complexion
        smeared
    With heraldry more dismal. Head to foot   456
    Now is he total gules, horridly tricked   457
    With blood of fathers, mothers, daughters, sons,
    Baked and impasted with the parching streets, 459
    That lend a tyrannous and a damnèd light   460

387–8 You say . . . then indeed (Said to impress upon Polonius the idea
that Hamlet is in serious conversation with his friends.) 390 Roscius a
famous Roman actor who died in 62 B.C. 393 Buzz (An interjection
used to denote stale news.) 399–400 scene . . . unlimited plays that
are unclassifiable and all-inclusive. (An absurdly catchall conclusion to
Polonius's pompous list of categories.) 400 Seneca writer of Latin
tragedies. Plautus writer of Latin comedies 401 law . . . liberty dramatic composition both according to the rules and disregarding the
rules. these i.e., the actors 403 Jephthah . . . Israel (Jephthah had to
sacrifice his daughter; see Judges 11. Hamlet goes on to quote from a
ballad on the theme.) 408 passing surpassingly 413 that follows not
i.e., just because you resemble Jephthah in having a daughter does not
logically prove that you love her. 414 What . . . lord? What does follow logically? (But Hamlet, pretending madness, answers with a fragment of a ballad, as if Polonius had asked, "What comes next?" See
419n.) 416 lot chance. wot knows 418 like likely, probable
419 the first . . . more the first stanza of this biblically based ballad will
satisfy your stated desire to know what follows (line 414) 420 my
abridgment something that cuts short my conversation; also, a diversion 421 masters good sirs 423 valanced fringed (with a beard)
424 beard confront, challenge. (With obvious pun.) young lady i.e.,
boy playing women's parts

425 By'r Lady By Our Lady 425–6 nearer to heaven i.e., taller
427 chopine thick-soled shoe of Italian fashion. 427–8 uncurrent not
passable as lawful coinage 428 cracked . . . ring i.e., changed from
adolescent to male voice, no longer suitable for women's roles. (Coins
featured rings enclosing the sovereign's head; if the coin was sufficiently clipped to invade within this ring, it was unfit for currency.)
429 e'en to't go at it 430 straight at once. 431 quality professional
skill. 436–7 caviar to the general i.e., an expensive delicacy not generally palatable to uneducated tastes. 438–9 cried in the top of i.e.,
spoke with greater authority than 439 digested arranged, ordered
440 modesty moderation, restraint. cunning skill. 441 sallets i.e.,
something savory, spicy improprieties 443 indict convict
445 handsome well-proportioned. fine elaborately ornamented,
showy. 447–8 Priam's slaughter the slaying of the ruler of Troy,
when the Greeks finally took the city. 450 Pyrrhus a Greek hero in
the Trojan War, also known as Neoptolemus, son of Achilles—another
avenging son. th' Hyrcanian beast i.e., the tiger. (On the death of
Priam, see Virgil, Aeneid, 2.506 ff.; compare the whole speech with
Marlowe's Dido Queen of Carthage, 2.1.214 ff. On the Hyrcanian tiger,
see Aeneid, 4.366–7. Hyrcania is on the Caspian Sea.) 452 rugged
shaggy, savage. sable black (for reasons of camouflage during the
episode of the Trojan horse) 454 couchèd concealed. ominous
horse fateful Trojan horse, by which the Greeks gained access to Troy
456 dismal calamitous. 457 total gules entirely red. (A heraldic
term.) tricked spotted and smeared. (Heraldic.) 459 Baked . . .
streets roasted and encrusted, like a thick paste, by the parching heat
of the streets (because of the fires everywhere) 460 tyrannous cruel

To their lord's murder. Roasted in wrath and fire, 461
And thus o'ersizèd with coagulate gore, 462
With eyes like carbuncles, the hellish Pyrrhus 463
Old grandsire Priam seeks."
So proceed you.

POLONIUS   'Fore God, my lord, well spoken, with good accent and good discretion.

FIRST PLAYER   "Anon he finds him
Striking too short at Greeks. His antique sword, 469
Rebellious to his arm, lies where it falls,
Repugnant to command. Unequal matched, 471
Pyrrhus at Priam drives, in rage strikes wide,
But with the whiff and wind of his fell sword 473
Th'unnervèd father falls. Then senseless Ilium, 474
Seeming to feel this blow, with flaming top
Stoops to his base, and with a hideous crash 476
Takes prisoner Pyrrhus' ear. For, lo! His sword,
Which was declining on the milky head 478
Of reverend Priam, seemed i'th'air to stick.
So as a painted tyrant Pyrrhus stood, 480
And, like a neutral to his will and matter, 481
Did nothing.
But as we often see against some storm 483
A silence in the heavens, the rack stand still, 484
The bold winds speechless, and the orb below 485
As hush as death, anon the dreadful thunder
Doth rend the region, so, after Pyrrhus' pause, 487
A rousèd vengeance sets him new a-work,
And never did the Cyclops' hammers fall 489
On Mars's armor forged for proof eterne 490
With less remorse than Pyrrhus' bleeding sword 491
Now falls on Priam.
Out, out, thou strumpet Fortune! All you gods
In general synod take away her power! 494
Break all the spokes and fellies from her wheel, 495
And bowl the round nave down the hill of heaven 496
As low as to the fiends!"

POLONIUS   This is too long.

HAMLET   It shall to the barber's with your beard.—Prithee, say on. He's for a jig or a tale of bawdry, or he 500
sleeps. Say on; come to Hecuba. 501

FIRST PLAYER
"But who, ah woe! had seen the moblèd queen"— 502

HAMLET   "The moblèd queen"?

POLONIUS   That's good. "Moblèd queen" is good.

FIRST PLAYER
"Run barefoot up and down, threat'ning the flames 505
With bisson rheum, a clout upon that head 506
Where late the diadem stood, and, for a robe, 507
About her lank and all o'erteemèd loins 508
A blanket, in the alarm of fear caught up—
Who this had seen, with tongue in venom steeped,
'Gainst Fortune's state would treason have
     pronounced. 511
But if the gods themselves did see her then
When she saw Pyrrhus make malicious sport
In mincing with his sword her husband's limbs,
The instant burst of clamor that she made,
Unless things mortal move them not at all,
Would have made milch the burning eyes of heaven, 517
And passion in the gods." 518

POLONIUS   Look whe'er he has not turned his color and 519
has tears in 's eyes. Prithee, no more.

HAMLET   'Tis well; I'll have thee speak out the rest of this soon.—Good my lord, will you see the players well bestowed? Do you hear, let them be well used, for they 523
are the abstract and brief chronicles of the time. After 524
your death you were better have a bad epitaph than their ill report while you live.

POLONIUS   My lord, I will use them according to their desert.

HAMLET   God's bodikin, man, much better. Use every 529
man after his desert, and who shall scape whipping? Use them after your own honor and dignity. The less 531
they deserve, the more merit is in your bounty. Take them in.

POLONIUS   Come, sirs.   [*Exit.*]

HAMLET   Follow him, friends. We'll hear a play tomorrow. [*As they start to leave, Hamlet detains the First Player.*] Dost thou hear me, old friend? Can you play *The Murder of Gonzago?*

FIRST PLAYER   Ay, my lord.

HAMLET   We'll ha 't tomorrow night. You could, for a 540
need, study a speech of some dozen or sixteen lines 541
which I would set down and insert in 't, could you not?

FIRST PLAYER   Ay, my lord.

HAMLET   Very well. Follow that lord, and look you mock him not.   *Exeunt players.*
My good friends, I'll leave you till night. You are welcome to Elsinore.

ROSENCRANTZ   Good my lord!
     Exeunt [*Rosencrantz and Guildenstern*].

HAMLET
Ay, so, goodbye to you.—Now I am alone.
Oh, what a rogue and peasant slave am I!

---

461 their lord's i.e., Priam's   **462 o'ersizèd** covered as with size or glue   **463 carbuncles** large fiery-red precious stones thought to emit their own light   **469 antique** ancient, long-used   **471 Repugnant** disobedient, resistant   **473 fell** cruel   **474 Th'unnervèd** the strengthless.   **senseless Ilium** inanimate citadel of Troy   **476 his** its **478 declining** descending.   **milky** white-haired   **480 painted** motionless, as in a painting   **481 like . . . matter** i.e., as though suspended between his intention and its fulfillment   **483 against** just before   **484 rack** mass of clouds   **485 orb** globe, earth   **487 region** sky   **489 Cyclops** giant armor makers in the smithy of Vulcan **490 proof** proven or tested resistance to assault   **491 remorse** pity **494 synod** assembly   **495 fellies** pieces of wood forming the rim of a wheel   **496 nave** hub.   **hill of heaven** Mount Olympus   **500 jig** comic song and dance often given at the end of a play   **501 Hecuba** wife of Priam.   **502 who . . . had** anyone who had. (Also in line 510.) **moblèd** muffled

505 threat'ning the flames i.e., weeping hard enough to dampen the flames   **506 bisson rheum** blinding tears.   **clout** cloth   **507 late** lately   **508 all o'erteemèd** utterly worn out with bearing children **511 state** rule, managing.   **pronounced** proclaimed.   **517 milch** milky, moist with tears.   **burning eyes of heaven** i.e., stars, heavenly bodies   **518 passion** overpowering emotion   **519 whe'er** whether **523 bestowed** lodged.   **524 abstract** summary account   **529 God's bodikin** By God's (Christ's) little body, *bodykin*. (Not to be confused with *bodkin,* "dagger.")   **531 after** according to   **540 ha 't** have it **541 study** memorize

Is it not monstrous that this player here,
But in a fiction, in a dream of passion,   552
Could force his soul so to his own conceit   553
That from her working all his visage wanned,   554
Tears in his eyes, distraction in his aspect,   555
A broken voice, and his whole function suiting   556
With forms to his conceit? And all for nothing!   557
For Hecuba!
What's Hecuba to him, or he to Hecuba,
That he should weep for her? What would he do
Had he the motive and the cue for passion
That I have? He would drown the stage with tears
And cleave the general ear with horrid speech,   563
Make mad the guilty and appall the free,   564
Confound the ignorant, and amaze indeed   565
The very faculties of eyes and ears. Yet I,
A dull and muddy-mettled rascal, peak   567
Like John-a-dreams, unpregnant of my cause,   568
And can say nothing—no, not for a king
Upon whose property and most dear life   570
A damned defeat was made. Am I a coward?   571
Who calls me villain? Breaks my pate across?   572
Plucks off my beard and blows it in my face?
Tweaks me by the nose? Gives me the lie i'th' throat   574
As deep as to the lungs? Who does me this?
Ha, 'swounds, I should take it; for it cannot be   576
But I am pigeon-livered and lack gall   577
To make oppression bitter, or ere this   578
I should ha' fatted all the region kites   579
With this slave's offal. Bloody, bawdy villain!   580
Remorseless, treacherous, lecherous, kindless villain!   581
Oh, vengeance!
Why, what an ass am I! This is most brave,   583
That I, the son of a dear father murdered,
Prompted to my revenge by heaven and hell,
Must like a whore unpack my heart with words
And fall a-cursing, like a very drab,   587
A scullion! Fie upon't, foh! About, my brains!   588
Hum, I have heard
That guilty creatures sitting at a play
Have by the very cunning of the scene   591
Been struck so to the soul that presently   592

They have proclaimed their malefactions;
For murder, though it have no tongue, will speak
With most miraculous organ. I'll have these players
Play something like the murder of my father
Before mine uncle. I'll observe his looks;
I'll tent him to the quick. If 'a do blench,   598
I know my course. The spirit that I have seen
May be the devil, and the devil hath power
T'assume a pleasing shape; yea, and perhaps,
Out of my weakness and my melancholy,
As he is very potent with such spirits,   603
Abuses me to damn me. I'll have grounds   604
More relative than this. The play's the thing   605
Wherein I'll catch the conscience of the King.   *Exit.*

[3.1]

Enter King, Queen, Polonius, Ophelia,
Rosencrantz, Guildenstern, lords.

KING
And can you by no drift of conference   1
Get from him why he puts on this confusion,
Grating so harshly all his days of quiet
With turbulent and dangerous lunacy?

ROSENCRANTZ
He does confess he feels himself distracted,
But from what cause 'a will by no means speak.

GUILDENSTERN
Nor do we find him forward to be sounded,   7
But with a crafty madness keeps aloof
When we would bring him on to some confession
Of his true state.

QUEEN   Did he receive you well?
ROSENCRANTZ   Most like a gentleman.
GUILDENSTERN
But with much forcing of his disposition.   12

ROSENCRANTZ
Niggard of question, but of our demands   13
Most free in his reply.

QUEEN   Did you assay him   14
To any pastime?

ROSENCRANTZ
Madam, it so fell out that certain players
We o'erraught on the way. Of these we told him,   17
And there did seem in him a kind of joy
To hear of it. They are here about the court,
And, as I think, they have already order
This night to play before him.

POLONIUS   'Tis most true,
And he beseeched me to entreat Your Majesties
To hear and see the matter.

---

552 But merely   **553 force . . . conceit** bring his innermost being so
entirely into accord with his conception (of the role)   **554 from her
working** as a result of, or in response to, his soul's activity.   **wanned**
grew pale   **555 aspect** look, glance   **556–7 his whole . . . conceit** all
his bodily powers responding with actions to suit his thought.
563 the general ear everyone's ear.   **horrid** horrible   **564 appall** (Literally, make pale.)   **free** innocent   **565 Confound the ignorant** i.e.,
dumbfound those who know nothing of the crime that has been
committed.   **amaze** stun   **567 muddy-mettled** dull-spirited
567–8 peak . . . cause mope, like a dreaming idler, not quickened by
my cause   **570 property** person and function   **571 damned defeat**
damnable act of destruction   **572 pate** head   **574 Gives . . . throat**
Calls me an out-and-out liar   **576 'swounds** by his (Christ's) wounds
577 pigeon-livered (The pigeon or dove was popularly supposed to
be mild because it secreted no gall.)   **578 To . . . bitter** to make things
bitter for oppressors   **579 region kites** kites (birds of prey) of the air
580 offal entrails.   **581 Remorseless** Pitiless.   **kindless** unnatural
583 brave fine, admirable. (Said ironically.)   **587 drab** whore
588 scullion menial kitchen servant. (Apt to be foul-mouthed.)
About About it, to work   **591 cunning** art, skill.   **scene** dramatic
presentation   **592 presently** at once

598 tent probe.   **the quick** the tender part of a wound, the core.
blench quail, flinch   **603 spirits** humors (of melancholy)
604 Abuses deludes   **605 relative** cogent, pertinent
3.1 Location: The castle.
1 drift of conference course of talk   **7 forward** willing.   **sounded**
questioned   **12 disposition** inclination.   **13 Niggard of question**
Laconic.   **demands** questions   **14 assay** try to win   **17 o'erraught**
overtook

KING
   With all my heart, and it doth much content me
   To hear him so inclined.
   Good gentlemen, give him a further edge   26
   And drive his purpose into these delights.

ROSENCRANTZ
   We shall, my lord.
                    Exeunt Rosencrantz and Guildenstern.

KING   Sweet Gertrude, leave us too,
   For we have closely sent for Hamlet hither,   29
   That he, as 'twere by accident, may here
   Affront Ophelia.   31
   Her father and myself, lawful espials,   32
   Will so bestow ourselves that seeing, unseen,
   We may of their encounter frankly judge,
   And gather by him, as he is behaved,
   If't be th'affliction of his love or no
   That thus he suffers for.

QUEEN   I shall obey you.
   And for your part, Ophelia, I do wish
   That your good beauties be the happy cause
   Of Hamlet's wildness. So shall I hope your virtues
   Will bring him to his wonted way again,
   To both your honors.

OPHELIA   Madam, I wish it may.
                                    [*Exit Queen.*]

POLONIUS
   Ophelia, walk you here.—Gracious, so please you, 43
   We will bestow ourselves. [*To Ophelia*] Read on this
      book,   [*giving her a book*]   44
   That show of such an exercise may color   45
   Your loneliness. We are oft to blame in this—   46
   'Tis too much proved—that with devotion's visage 47
   And pious action we do sugar o'er
   The devil himself.

KING [*aside*]   Oh, 'tis too true!
   How smart a lash that speech doth give my
      conscience!
   The harlot's cheek, beautied with plast'ring art,
   Is not more ugly to the thing that helps it   53
   Than is my deed to my most painted word.   54
   Oh, heavy burden!

POLONIUS
   I hear him coming. Let's withdraw, my lord.   56
                    [*The King and Polonius withdraw.*]

      Enter Hamlet. [*Ophelia pretends to read a book.*]

HAMLET
   To be, or not to be, that is the question:
   Whether 'tis nobler in the mind to suffer
   The slings and arrows of outrageous fortune,

   Or to take arms against a sea of troubles
   And by opposing end them. To die, to sleep—
   No more—and by a sleep to say we end
   The heartache and the thousand natural shocks
   That flesh is heir to. 'Tis a consummation
   Devoutly to be wished. To die, to sleep;
   To sleep, perchance to dream. Ay, there's the rub, 66
   For in that sleep of death what dreams may come,
   When we have shuffled off this mortal coil,   68
   Must give us pause. There's the respect   69
   That makes calamity of so long life.   70
   For who would bear the whips and scorns of time,
   Th'oppressor's wrong, the proud man's contumely, 72
   The pangs of disprized love, the law's delay,   73
   The insolence of office, and the spurns   74
   That patient merit of th'unworthy takes,   75
   When he himself might his quietus make   76
   With a bare bodkin? Who would fardels bear,   77
   To grunt and sweat under a weary life,
   But that the dread of something after death,
   The undiscovered country from whose bourn   80
   No traveler returns, puzzles the will,
   And makes us rather bear those ills we have
   Than fly to others that we know not of?
   Thus conscience does make cowards of us all;
   And thus the native hue of resolution   85
   Is sicklied o'er with the pale cast of thought, 86
   And enterprises of great pitch and moment   87
   With this regard their currents turn awry   88
   And lose the name of action.—Soft you now,   89
   The fair Ophelia.—Nymph, in thy orisons   90
   Be all my sins remembered.

OPHELIA   Good my lord,   91
   How does Your Honor for this many a day?

HAMLET
   I humbly thank you; well, well, well.

OPHELIA
   My lord, I have remembrances of yours,
   That I have longèd long to redeliver.
   I pray you, now receive them.   [*She offers tokens.*]

HAMLET
   No, not I, I never gave you aught.

OPHELIA
   My honored lord, you know right well you did,
   And with them words of so sweet breath composed
   As made the things more rich. Their perfume lost,
   Take these again, for to the noble mind

---

26 edge incitement   **29 closely** privately   **31 Affront** confront, meet   **32 espials** spies   **43 Gracious** Your Grace (i.e., the King)   **44 bestow** conceal   **45 exercise** religious exercise. (The book she reads is one of devotion.)   **color** give a plausible appearance to   **46 loneliness** being alone.   **47 too much proved** too often shown to be true, too often practiced   **53 to . . . helps it** in comparison with the cosmetic that fashions the cheek's false beauty   **54 painted word** deceptive utterances.   **56.1 *withdraw*** (The King and Polonius may retire behind an arras. The stage directions specify that they "enter" again near the end of the scene.)

66 rub (Literally, an obstacle in the game of bowls.)   **68 shuffled** sloughed, cast.   **coil** turmoil   **69 respect** consideration   **70 of . . . life** so long-lived, something we willingly endure for so long. (Also suggesting that long life is itself a calamity.)   **72 contumely** insolent abuse   **73 disprized** unvalued   **74 office** officialdom.   **spurns** insults   **75 of . . . takes** receives from unworthy persons   **76 quietus** acquittance; here, death   **77 a bare bodkin** a mere dagger, unsheathed.   **fardels** burdens   **80 bourn** frontier, boundary   **85 native hue** natural color, complexion   **86 cast** tinge, shade of color   **87 pitch** height (as of a falcon's flight).   **moment** importance   **88 regard** respect, consideration.   **currents** courses   **89 Soft you** i.e., Wait a minute, gently   **90–1 in . . . remembered** i.e., pray for me, sinner that I am.

Rich gifts wax poor when givers prove unkind.
There, my lord.   [*She gives tokens.*]

HAMLET   Ha, ha! Are you honest?   104

OPHELIA   My lord?

HAMLET   Are you fair?   106

OPHELIA   What means Your Lordship?

HAMLET   That if you be honest and fair, your honesty   108
should admit no discourse to your beauty.   109

OPHELIA   Could beauty, my lord, have better commerce   110
than with honesty?

HAMLET   Ay, truly, for the power of beauty will sooner
transform honesty from what it is to a bawd than the
force of honesty can translate beauty into his likeness.   114
This was sometime a paradox, but now the time gives   115
it proof. I did love you once.   116

OPHELIA   Indeed, my lord, you made me believe so.

HAMLET   You should not have believed me, for virtue   118
cannot so inoculate our old stock but we shall relish of   119
it. I loved you not.   120

OPHELIA   I was the more deceived.

HAMLET   Get thee to a nunnery. Why wouldst thou be a   122
breeder of sinners? I am myself indifferent honest, but   123
yet I could accuse me of such things that it were better
my mother had not borne me: I am very proud,
revengeful, ambitious, with more offenses at my beck   126
than I have thoughts to put them in, imagination to
give them shape, or time to act them in. What should
such fellows as I do crawling between earth and
heaven? We are arrant knaves all; believe none of us.
Go thy ways to a nunnery. Where's your father?

OPHELIA   At home, my lord.

HAMLET   Let the doors be shut upon him, that he may
play the fool nowhere but in 's own house. Farewell.

OPHELIA   Oh, help him, you sweet heavens!

HAMLET   If thou dost marry, I'll give thee this plague for
thy dowry: be thou as chaste as ice, as pure as snow,
thou shalt not escape calumny. Get thee to a nunnery,
farewell. Or, if thou wilt needs marry, marry a fool, for
wise men know well enough what monsters you   140
make of them. To a nunnery, go, and quickly too.
Farewell.

OPHELIA   Heavenly powers, restore him!

HAMLET   I have heard of your paintings too, well   144
enough. God hath given you one face, and you make
yourselves another. You jig, you amble, and you   146
lisp, you nickname God's creatures, and make your   147
wantonness your ignorance. Go to, I'll no more on't;   148

it hath made me mad. I say we will have no more
marriage. Those that are married already—all but
one—shall live. The rest shall keep as they are. To a
nunnery, go.   *Exit.*

OPHELIA
Oh, what a noble mind is here o'erthrown!
The courtier's, soldier's, scholar's, eye, tongue, sword,
Th'expectancy and rose of the fair state,   155
The glass of fashion and the mold of form,   156
Th'observed of all observers, quite, quite down!   157
And I, of ladies most deject and wretched,
That sucked the honey of his music vows,   159
Now see that noble and most sovereign reason
Like sweet bells jangled out of tune and harsh,
That unmatched form and feature of blown youth   162
Blasted with ecstasy. Oh, woe is me,   163
T'have seen what I have seen, see what I see!

Enter King and Polonius.

KING
Love? His affections do not that way tend;   165
Nor what he spake, though it lacked form a little,
Was not like madness. There's something in his soul
O'er which his melancholy sits on brood,   168
And I do doubt the hatch and the disclose   169
Will be some danger; which for to prevent,
I have in quick determination
Thus set it down: he shall with speed to England   172
For the demand of our neglected tribute.
Haply the seas and countries different
With variable objects shall expel   175
This something-settled matter in his heart,   176
Whereon his brains still beating puts him thus   177
From fashion of himself. What think you on't?   178

POLONIUS
It shall do well. But yet do I believe
The origin and commencement of his grief
Sprung from neglected love.—How now, Ophelia?
You need not tell us what Lord Hamlet said;
We heard it all.—My lord, do as you please,
But, if you hold it fit, after the play
Let his queen-mother all alone entreat him
To show his grief. Let her be round with him;   186
And I'll be placed, so please you, in the ear
Of all their conference. If she find him not,   188
To England send him, or confine him where

---

104 **honest** (1) truthful (2) chaste.   106 **fair** (1) beautiful (2) just, honorable.   108 **your honesty** your chastity   109 **discourse to** familiar dealings with   110 **commerce** dealings, intercourse   114 **his** its   115–16 **This . . . proof** This was formerly an unfashionable view, but now the present age confirms how true it is.   118–20 **virtue . . . of it** virtue cannot be grafted onto our sinful condition without our retaining some taste of the old stock.   122 **nunnery** convent. (With an awareness that the word was also used derisively to denote a brothel.)   123 **indifferent honest** reasonably virtuous   126 **beck** command   140 **monsters** (An illusion to the horns of a cuckold.) **you** i.e., you women   144 **paintings** use of cosmetics   146–8 **You jig . . . ignorance** i.e., You prance about frivolously and speak with affected coyness, you put new labels on God's creatures (by your use of cosmetics), and you excuse your affectations on the grounds of pretended ignorance.   148 **on't** of it

155 **Th'expectancy and rose** the hope and ornament   156 **The glass . . . form** the mirror of true self-fashioning and the pattern of courtly behavior   157 **Th'observed . . . observers** i.e., the center of attention and honor in the court   159 **music** musical, sweetly uttered   162 **blown** blossoming   163 **Blasted with ecstasy** blighted with madness.   165 **affections** emotions, feelings   168 **sits on brood** sits like a bird on a nest, about to *hatch* mischief (line 169)   169 **doubt** suspect, fear.   **disclose** disclosure, hatching   172 **set it down** resolved   175 **variable objects** various sights and surroundings to divert him   176 **This something . . . heart** the strange matter settled in his heart   177 **still** continually   178 **From . . . himself** out of his natural manner.   186 **round** blunt   188 **find him not** fails to discover what is troubling him

Your wisdom best shall think.

KING   It shall be so.

Madness in great ones must not unwatched go.

Exeunt.

❧

[3.2]

Enter Hamlet and three of the Players.

HAMLET   Speak the speech, I pray you, as I pronounced it to you, trippingly on the tongue. But if you mouth it, as many of our players do, I had as lief the town crier 3 spoke my lines. Nor do not saw the air too much with your hand, thus, but use all gently; for in the very torrent, tempest, and, as I may say, whirlwind of your passion, you must acquire and beget a temperance that may give it smoothness. Oh, it offends me to the soul to hear a robustious periwig-pated fellow tear a 9 passion to tatters, to very rags, to split the ears of the groundlings, who for the most part are capable of 11 nothing but inexplicable dumb shows and noise. I 12 would have such a fellow whipped for o'erdoing Ter- 13 magant. It out-Herods Herod. Pray you, avoid it. 14

FIRST PLAYER   I warrant Your Honor.

HAMLET   Be not too tame neither, but let your own discretion be your tutor. Suit the action to the word, the word to the action, with this special observance, that you o'erstep not the modesty of nature. For 19 anything so o'erdone is from the purpose of playing, 20 whose end, both at the first and now, was and is to hold as 'twere the mirror up to nature, to show virtue her feature, scorn her own image, and the very age 23 and body of the time his form and pressure. Now this 24 overdone or come tardy off, though it makes the 25 unskillful laugh, cannot but make the judicious grieve, 26 the censure of the which one must in your allowance 27 o'erweigh a whole theater of others. Oh, there be players that I have seen play, and heard others praise, and that highly, not to speak it profanely, that, neither 30 having th'accent of Christians nor the gait of Chris- 31 tian, pagan, nor man, have so strutted and bellowed 32 that I have thought some of nature's journeymen had 33

made men and not made them well, they imitated humanity so abominably. 35

FIRST PLAYER   I hope we have reformed that indifferently 36 with us, sir.

HAMLET   Oh, reform it altogether. And let those that play your clowns speak no more than is set down for them; for there be of them that will themselves laugh, to set 40 on some quantity of barren spectators to laugh too, 41 though in the meantime some necessary question of the play be then to be considered. That's villainous, and shows a most pitiful ambition in the fool that uses it. Go make you ready.   [*Exeunt Players.*]

Enter Polonius, Guildenstern, and Rosencrantz.

How now, my lord, will the King hear this piece of work?

POLONIUS   And the Queen too, and that presently. 48

HAMLET   Bid the players make haste.   [*Exit Polonius.*]
Will you two help to hasten them?

ROSENCRANTZ
Ay, my lord.   *Exeunt they two.*

HAMLET   What ho, Horatio!

Enter Horatio.

HORATIO   Here, sweet lord, at your service.

HAMLET
Horatio, thou art e'en as just a man
As e'er my conversation coped withal. 54

HORATIO
Oh, my dear lord—

HAMLET   Nay, do not think I flatter,
For what advancement may I hope from thee
That no revenue hast but thy good spirits
To feed and clothe thee? Why should the poor be
    flattered?
No, let the candied tongue lick absurd pomp, 59
And crook the pregnant hinges of the knee 60
Where thrift may follow fawning. Dost thou hear? 61
Since my dear soul was mistress of her choice
And could of men distinguish her election, 63
Sh' hath sealed thee for herself, for thou hast been 64
As one, in suffering all, that suffers nothing,
A man that Fortune's buffets and rewards
Hast ta'en with equal thanks; and blest are those
Whose blood and judgment are so well commeddled 68
That they are not a pipe for Fortune's finger
To sound what stop she please. Give me that man 70
That is not passion's slave, and I will wear him
In my heart's core, ay, in my heart of heart,
As I do thee.—Something too much of this.—
There is a play tonight before the King.
One scene of it comes near the circumstance
Which I have told thee of my father's death.

3.2 Location: The castle.
3 our players players nowadays.   **I had as lief** I would just as soon   **9 robustious** violent, boisterous.   **periwig-pated** wearing a wig   **11 groundlings** spectators who paid least and stood in the yard of the theater.   **capable of** able to understand   **12 dumb shows and noise** noisy spectacle (rather than thoughtful drama).   **13–14 Termagant** a supposed deity of the Mohammedans, not found in any English medieval play but elsewhere portrayed as violent and blustering. **14 Herod** Herod of Jewry. (A character in *The Slaughter of the Innocents* and other cycle plays. The part was played with great noise and fury.) **19 modesty** restraint, moderation   **20 from** contrary to   **23 scorn** i.e., something foolish and deserving of scorn   **23–4 and the . . . pressure** and the present state of affairs its likeness as seen in an impression, such as wax.   **25 come tardy off** falling short   **25–6 the unskillful** those lacking in judgment   **27 the censure . . . one** the judgment of even one of whom.   **your allowance** your scale of values   **30 not . . . profanely** (Hamlet anticipates his idea in lines 33–4 that some men were not made by God at all.)   **31-2 Christians** i.e., ordinary decent folk   **32 nor man** i.e., nor any human being at all   **33 journeymen** common workmen

35 abominably (Shakespeare's usual spelling, "abhominably," suggests a literal though etymologically incorrect meaning, "removed from human nature.")   **36 indifferently** tolerably   **40 of them** some among them   **41 barren** i.e., of wit   **48 presently** at once.   **54 my . . . withal** my dealings encountered.   **59 candied** sugared, flattering **60 pregnant** compliant   **61 thrift** profit   **63 could . . . election** could make distinguishing choices among persons   **64 sealed thee** (Literally, as one would seal a legal document to mark possession.) **68 blood** passion.   **commeddled** commingled   **70 stop** hole in a wind instrument for controlling the sound

I prithee, when thou see'st that act afoot,
Even with the very comment of thy soul 78
Observe my uncle. If his occulted guilt 79
Do not itself unkennel in one speech, 80
It is a damnèd ghost that we have seen,
And my imaginations are as foul
As Vulcan's stithy. Give him heedful note, 83
For I mine eyes will rivet to his face,
And after we will both our judgments join
In censure of his seeming.
HORATIO   Well, my lord. 86
If 'a steal aught the whilst this play is playing 87
And scape detecting, I will pay the theft.

> [*Flourish.*] *Enter trumpets and kettledrums, King,
> Queen, Polonius, Ophelia, [Rosencrantz,
> Guildenstern, and other lords, with guards
> carrying torches*].

HAMLET   They are coming to the play. I must be idle. 89
Get you a place.   [*The King, Queen, and courtiers sit.*]
KING   How fares our cousin Hamlet? 91
HAMLET   Excellent, i'faith, of the chameleon's dish: I eat 92
the air, promise-crammed. You cannot feed capons so. 93
KING   I have nothing with this answer, Hamlet. These 94
words are not mine. 95
HAMLET   No, nor mine now. [*To Polonius*] My lord, you 96
played once i'th'university, you say?
POLONIUS   That did I, my lord, and was accounted a
good actor.
HAMLET   What did you enact?
POLONIUS   I did enact Julius Caesar. I was killed i'th' 101
Capitol; Brutus killed me. 102
HAMLET   It was a brute part of him to kill so capital a 103
calf there.—Be the players ready? 104
ROSENCRANTZ   Ay, my lord. They stay upon your 105
patience.
QUEEN   Come hither, my dear Hamlet, sit by me.
HAMLET   No, good mother, here's metal more attractive. 108
POLONIUS [*to the King*]   Oho, do you mark that?
HAMLET   Lady, shall I lie in your lap? 110
                    [*Lying down at Ophelia's feet.*]

OPHELIA   No, my lord.
HAMLET   I mean, my head upon your lap?
OPHELIA   Ay, my lord.
HAMLET   Do you think I meant country matters? 114
OPHELIA   I think nothing, my lord.
HAMLET   That's a fair thought to lie between maids'
legs.
OPHELIA   What is, my lord?
HAMLET   Nothing. 119
OPHELIA   You are merry, my lord.
HAMLET   Who, I?
OPHELIA   Ay, my lord.
HAMLET   Oh, God, your only jig maker. What should a 123
man do but be merry? For look you how cheerfully my
mother looks, and my father died within 's two hours. 125
OPHELIA   Nay, 'tis twice two months, my lord.
HAMLET   So long? Nay then, let the devil wear black, for
I'll have a suit of sables. O heavens! Die two months 128
ago, and not forgotten yet? Then there's hope a great
man's memory may outlive his life half a year. But, by'r
Lady, 'a must build churches, then, or else shall 'a
suffer not thinking on, with the hobbyhorse, whose 132
epitaph is "For oh, for oh, the hobbyhorse is forgot." 133

> *The trumpets sound. Dumb show follows.*

> *Enter a King and a Queen [very lovingly]; the
> Queen embracing him, and he her. [She kneels,
> and makes show of protestation unto him.] He
> takes her up, and declines his head upon her neck.
> He lies him down upon a bank of flowers. She,
> seeing him asleep, leaves him. Anon comes in
> another man, takes off his crown, kisses it, pours
> poison in the sleeper's ears, and leaves him. The
> Queen returns, finds the King dead, makes
> passionate action. The Poisoner with some three or
> four come in again, seem to condole with her. The
> dead body is carried away. The Poisoner woos the
> Queen with gifts; she seems harsh awhile, but in
> the end accepts love.*

>   [*Exeunt players.*]

OPHELIA   What means this, my lord?
HAMLET   Marry, this' miching mallico; it means mis- 135
chief.

---

78 very . . . soul your most penetrating observation and consideration
79 occulted hidden   **80 unkennel** (As one would say of a fox driven
from its lair.)   **83 Vulcan's stithy** the smithy, the place of stiths (anvils)
of the Roman god of fire and metalworking.   **86 censure of his seeming** judgment of his appearance or behavior.   **87 If 'a steal aught** If he
gets away with anything   **89 idle** (1) unoccupied (2) mad.   **91 cousin**
i.e., close relative   **92 chameleon's dish** (Chameleons were supposed
to feed on air. Hamlet deliberately misinterprets the King's *fares* as
"feeds." By his phrase *eat the air* he also plays on the idea of feeding
himself with the promise of succession, of being the *heir*.)   **93 capons**
roosters castrated and *crammed* with feed to make them succulent
94 have . . . with make nothing of, or gain nothing from   **95 are not
mine** do not respond to what I asked.   **96 nor mine now** (Once spoken, words are proverbially no longer the speaker's own—and hence
should be uttered warily.)   **101–2 i'th' Capitol** (Where Caesar was
assassinated, according to *Julius Caesar*, 3.1, but see 1.3.126n in that
play)   **103 brute** (The Latin meaning of *brutus*, "stupid," was often
used punningly with the name Brutus.)   **part** (1) deed (2) role
104 calf fool   **105 stay upon** await   **108 metal** substance that is
attractive, i.e., magnetic, but with suggestion also of *mettle*, "disposition"   **110 Lady . . . lap?** Onstage, Hamlet often lies at Ophelia's feet,
but he could instead offer to do this and continue to stand.

114 country matters sexual intercourse. (With a bawdy pun on the
first syllable of *country*.)   **119 Nothing** The figure zero or naught,
suggesting the female sexual anatomy. (*Thing* not infrequently has a
bawdy connotation of male or female anatomy, and the reference here
could be male.)   **123 only jig maker** very best composer of jigs, i.e.,
pointless merriment. (Hamlet replies sardonically to Ophelia's observation that he is merry by saying, "If you're looking for someone who
is really merry, you've come to the right person.")   **125 within 's**
within this (i.e., these)   **128 suit of sables** garments trimmed with
the dark fur of the sable and hence suited for a person in mourning.
132 suffer . . . on undergo oblivion   **133 "For . . . forgot"** (Verse of a
song occurring also in *Love's Labor's Lost*, 3.1.27–8. The hobbyhorse
was a character made up to resemble a horse and rider, appearing in
the morris dance and such May-game sports. This song laments the
disappearance of such customs under pressure from the Puritans.)
133.12 condole with offer sympathy to   **135 this' miching mallico**
this is sneaking mischief

OPHELIA   Belike this show imports the argument of the 137
play.

      Enter Prologue.

HAMLET   We shall know by this fellow. The players cannot keep counsel; they'll tell all.   140

OPHELIA   Will 'a tell us what this show meant?

HAMLET   Ay, or any show that you will show him. Be 142
not you ashamed to show, he'll not shame to tell you 143
what it means.

OPHELIA   You are naught, you are naught. I'll mark the 145
play.

PROLOGUE

      For us, and for our tragedy,
      Here stooping to your clemency,   148
      We beg your hearing patiently.   [*Exit.*]

HAMLET   Is this a prologue, or the posy of a ring?   150

OPHELIA   'Tis brief, my lord.

HAMLET   As woman's love.

      Enter [two Players as] King and Queen.

PLAYER KING

      Full thirty times hath Phoebus' cart gone round   153
      Neptune's salt wash and Tellus' orbèd ground,   154
      And thirty dozen moons with borrowed sheen   155
      About the world have times twelve thirties been,
      Since love our hearts and Hymen did our hands   157
      Unite commutual in most sacred bands.   158

PLAYER QUEEN

      So many journeys may the sun and moon
      Make us again count o'er ere love be done!
      But, woe is me, you are so sick of late,
      So far from cheer and from your former state,
      That I distrust you. Yet, though I distrust,   163
      Discomfort you, my lord, it nothing must.   164
      For women's fear and love hold quantity;   165
      In neither aught, or in extremity.   166
      Now, what my love is, proof hath made you know,   167
      And as my love is sized, my fear is so.
      Where love is great, the littlest doubts are fear;   169
      Where little fears grow great, great love grows there.

PLAYER KING

      Faith, I must leave thee, love, and shortly too;
      My operant powers their functions leave to do.   172
      And thou shalt live in this fair world behind,   173
      Honored, beloved; and haply one as kind
      For husband shalt thou—

PLAYER QUEEN   Oh, confound the rest!

Such love must needs be treason in my breast.
In second husband let me be accurst!
None wed the second but who killed the first.   178

HAMLET   Wormwood, wormwood.   179

PLAYER QUEEN

      The instances that second marriage move   180
      Are base respects of thrift, but none of love.   181
      A second time I kill my husband dead
      When second husband kisses me in bed.

PLAYER KING

      I do believe you think what now you speak,
      But what we do determine oft we break.
      Purpose is but the slave to memory,   186
      Of violent birth, but poor validity,   187
      Which now, like fruit unripe, sticks on the tree,   188
      But fall unshaken when they mellow be.
      Most necessary 'tis that we forget   190
      To pay ourselves what to ourselves is debt.   191
      What to ourselves in passion we propose,
      The passion ending, doth the purpose lose.
      The violence of either grief or joy
      Their own enactures with themselves destroy.   195
      Where joy most revels, grief doth most lament;   196
      Grief joys, joy grieves, on slender accident.   197
      This world is not for aye, nor 'tis not strange   198
      That even our loves should with our fortunes change;
      For 'tis a question left us yet to prove,
      Whether love lead fortune, or else fortune love.
      The great man down, you mark his favorite flies;   202
      The poor advanced makes friends of enemies.   203
      And hitherto doth love on fortune tend;   204
      For who not needs shall never lack a friend,   205
      And who in want a hollow friend doth try   206
      Directly seasons him his enemy.   207
      But, orderly to end where I begun,
      Our wills and fates do so contrary run   209
      That our devices still are overthrown;   210
      Our thoughts are ours, their ends none of our own.   211
      So think thou wilt no second husband wed,
      But die thy thoughts when thy first lord is dead.

PLAYER QUEEN

      Nor earth to me give food, nor heaven light,   214
      Sport and repose lock from me day and night,   215

---

178 None (1) Let no woman; or (2) No woman does.   **but who** except the one who   **179 Wormwood** i.e., How bitter. (Literally, a bitter-tasting plant.)   **180 instances** motives.   **move** motivate   **181 base . . . thrift** ignoble considerations of material prosperity   **186 Purpose . . . memory** Our good intentions are subject to forgetfulness   **187 validity** strength, durability   **188 Which** i.e., purpose   **190–1 Most . . . debt** It's inevitable that in time we forget the obligations we have imposed on ourselves.   **195 enactures** fulfillments   **196–7 Where . . . accident** The capacity for extreme joy and grief go together, and often one extreme is instantly changed into its opposite on the slightest provocation.   **198 aye** ever   **202 down** fallen in fortune   **203 The poor . . . enemies** when one of humble station is promoted, you see his enemies suddenly becoming his friends.   **204 hitherto** up to this point in the argument, or, to this extent.   **tend** attend   **205 who not needs** he who is not in need (of wealth)   **206 who in want** he who, being in need.   **try** test (his generosity)   **207 seasons him** ripens him into   **209 Our . . . run** what we want and what we get go so contrarily   **210 devices** intentions.   **still** continually   **211 ends** results   **214 Nor** Let neither   **215 Sport . . . night** may day deny me its pastimes and night its repose

---

137 Belike Probably.   **argument** plot   **140 counsel** secret   **142–3 Be not you** Provided you are not   **145 naught** indecent. (Ophelia is reacting to Hamlet's pointed remarks about not being ashamed to show all.)   **148 stooping** bowing   **150 posy . . . ring** brief motto in verse inscribed in a ring.   **153 Phoebus' cart** the sun-god's chariot, making its yearly cycle   **154 salt wash** the sea.   **Tellus** goddess of the earth, of the *orbèd ground*   **155 borrowed** i.e., reflected   **157 Hymen** god of matrimony   **158 commutual** mutually.   **bands** bonds.   **163 distrust** am anxious about   **164 Discomfort . . . must** it must not distress you at all.   **165 hold quantity** keep proportion with one another   **166 In . . . extremity** (women feel) either no anxiety if they do not love or extreme anxiety if they do love.   **167 proof** experience   **169 the littlest** even the littlest   **172 My . . . to do** my vital functions are shutting down.   **173 behind** after I have gone

To desperation turn my trust and hope,
An anchor's cheer in prison be my scope!   217
Each opposite that blanks the face of joy   218
Meet what I would have well and it destroy!   219
Both here and hence pursue me lasting strife   220
If, once a widow, ever I be wife!

HAMLET   If she should break it now!

PLAYER KING
'Tis deeply sworn. Sweet, leave me here awhile;
My spirits grow dull, and fain I would beguile   224
The tedious day with sleep.

PLAYER QUEEN   Sleep rock thy brain,
And never come mischance between us twain!
                          [*He sleeps.*] *Exit* [*Player Queen*].

HAMLET   Madam, how like you this play?

QUEEN   The lady doth protest too much, methinks.   228

HAMLET   Oh, but she'll keep her word.

KING   Have you heard the argument? Is there no   230
offense in't?

HAMLET   No, no, they do but jest, poison in jest. No of- 232
fense i'th' world.   233

KING   What do you call the play?

HAMLET   *The Mousetrap*. Marry, how? Tropically.   235
This play is the image of a murder done in Vienna.
Gonzago is the Duke's name, his wife, Baptista. You   237
shall see anon. 'Tis a knavish piece of work, but what
of that? Your Majesty, and we that have free souls, it   239
touches us not. Let the galled jade wince, our withers   240
are unwrung.   241

        Enter Lucianus.

This is one Lucianus, nephew to the King.

OPHELIA   You are as good as a chorus, my lord.   243

HAMLET   I could interpret between you and your love,   244
if I could see the puppets dallying.   245

OPHELIA   You are keen, my lord, you are keen.   246

HAMLET   It would cost you a groaning to take off mine
edge.

OPHELIA   Still better, and worse.   249

HAMLET   So you mis-take your husbands.—Begin, mur-   250
derer; leave thy damnable faces and begin. Come, the
croaking raven doth bellow for revenge.

LUCIANUS
Thoughts black, hands apt, drugs fit, and time
        agreeing,
Confederate season, else no creature seeing,   254
Thou mixture rank, of midnight weeds collected,
With Hecate's ban thrice blasted, thrice infected,   256
Thy natural magic and dire property   257
On wholesome life usurp immediately.
        [*He pours the poison into the sleeper's ear.*]

HAMLET   'A poisons him i'th' garden for his estate. His 259
name's Gonzago. The story is extant, and written in
very choice Italian. You shall see anon how the
murderer gets the love of Gonzago's wife.
                          [*Claudius rises.*]

OPHELIA   The King rises.

HAMLET   What, frighted with false fire?   264

QUEEN   How fares my lord?

POLONIUS   Give o'er the play.

KING   Give me some light. Away!

POLONIUS   Lights, lights, lights!
                Exeunt all but Hamlet and Horatio.

HAMLET
        "Why, let the strucken deer go weep,   269
                The hart ungallèd play.   270
        For some must watch, while some must sleep;   271
                Thus runs the world away."   272
Would not this, sir, and a forest of feathers—if the   273
rest of my fortunes turn Turk with me—with two   274
Provincial roses on my razed shoes, get me a fellow-   275
ship in a cry of players?   276

HORATIO   Half a share.

HAMLET   A whole one, I.
        "For thou dost know, O Damon dear,   279
                This realm dismantled was   280
        Of Jove himself, and now reigns here   281
                A very, very—pajock."   282

---

217 **anchor's cheer** anchorite's or hermit's fare.   **my scope** the extent of my happiness.   **218–19** Each . . . destroy! May every adverse thing that causes the face of joy to turn pale meet and destroy everything that I desire to see prosper!   **220 hence** in the life hereafter   **224 spirits** vital spirits   **228 doth . . . much** makes too many promises and protestations   **230 argument** plot.   **232 jest** make believe. **232–3 offense** crime, injury. (Hamlet playfully alters the King's use of the word in line 231 to mean "cause for objection.")   **235 Tropically** Figuratively. (The First Quarto reading, "trapically," suggests a pun on *trap* in *Mousetrap*.)   **237 Duke's** i.e., King's. (An inconsistency that may be due to Shakespeare's possible acquaintance with a historical incident, the alleged murder of the Duke of Urbino by Luigi Gonzaga in 1538.)   **239 free** guiltless   **240 galled jade** horse whose hide is rubbed by saddle or harness.   **withers** the part between the horse's shoulder blades   **241 unwrung** not rubbed sore.   **243 chorus** (In many Elizabethan plays, the forthcoming action was explained by an actor known as the "chorus"; at a puppet show, the actor who spoke the dialogue was known as an "interpreter," as indicated by the lines following.)   **244 interpret** (1) ventriloquize the dialogue, as in a puppet show (2) act as pander   **245 puppets dallying** (With suggestion of sexual play, continued in *keen*, "sexually aroused," *groaning*, "moaning in pregnancy," and *edge*, "sexual desire" or "impetuosity.") **246 keen** sharp, bitter   **249 Still . . . worse** More keen, always *bettering* what other people say with witty wordplay, but at the same time more offensive.

250 **So** Even thus (in marriage).   **mis-take** take falseheartedly and cheat on. (The marriage vows say "for better, for worse.")   **254 Confederate . . . seeing** the time and occasion conspiring (to assist me), and also no one seeing me   **256 Hecate's ban** the curse of Hecate, the goddess of witchcraft   **257 dire property** baleful quality   **259 estate** i.e., the kingship.   **His** i.e., the King's   **264 false fire** the blank discharge of a gun loaded with powder but no shot.   **269–72 Why . . . away** (Perhaps from an old ballad, with allusion to the popular belief that a wounded deer retires to weep and die; compare with *As You Like It*, 2.1.33–66.)   **270 ungallèd** unafflicted   **271 watch** remain awake   **272 Thus . . . away** Thus the world goes.   **273 this** i.e., this success with the play I have just presented.   **feathers** (Allusion to the plumes that Elizabethan actors were fond of wearing.)   **274 turn Turk with** turn renegade against, go back on   **275 Provincial roses** rosettes of ribbon, named for roses grown in a part of France.   **razed** with ornamental slashing   **275–6 fellowship . . . players** partnership in a theatrical company.   **276 cry** pack (of hounds, etc.)   **279 Damon** the friend of Pythias, as Horatio is friend of Hamlet; or, a traditional pastoral name   **280–2 This realm . . . pajock** i.e., Jove, representing divine authority and justice, has abandoned this realm to its own devices, leaving in his stead only a peacock or vain pretender to virtue (though the rhyme-word expected in place of *pajock* or "peacock" suggests that the realm is now ruled over by an "ass"). **280 dismantled** stripped, divested

HORATIO   You might have rhymed.

HAMLET   Oh, good Horatio, I'll take the ghost's word for a thousand pound. Didst perceive?

HORATIO   Very well, my lord.

HAMLET   Upon the talk of the poisoning?

HORATIO   I did very well note him.

Enter Rosencrantz and Guildenstern.

HAMLET   Aha! Come, some music! Come, the recorders.

"For if the King like not the comedy,
Why then, belike, he likes it not, perdy."   292
Come, some music.

GUILDENSTERN   Good my lord, vouchsafe me a word with you.

HAMLET   Sir, a whole history.

GUILDENSTERN   The King, sir—

HAMLET   Ay, sir, what of him?

GUILDENSTERN   Is in his retirement marvelous dis- 299
tempered.   300

HAMLET   With drink, sir?

GUILDENSTERN   No, my lord, with choler.   302

HAMLET   Your wisdom should show itself more richer to signify this to the doctor, for for me to put him to his purgation would perhaps plunge him into more 305 choler.

GUILDENSTERN   Good my lord, put your discourse into some frame and start not so wildly from my affair.   308

HAMLET   I am tame, sir. Pronounce.

GUILDENSTERN   The Queen, your mother, in most great affliction of spirit, hath sent me to you.

HAMLET   You are welcome.

GUILDENSTERN   Nay, good my lord, this courtesy is not of the right breed. If it shall please you to make me a 314 wholesome answer, I will do your mother's command-ment; if not, your pardon and my return shall be the 316 end of my business.

HAMLET   Sir, I cannot.

ROSENCRANTZ   What, my lord?

HAMLET   Make you a wholesome answer; my wit's dis-eased. But, sir, such answer as I can make, you shall command, or rather, as you say, my mother. Therefore no more, but to the matter. My mother, you say—

ROSENCRANTZ   Then thus she says: your behavior hath struck her into amazement and admiration.   325

HAMLET   Oh, wonderful son, that can so 'stonish a mother! But is there no sequel at the heels of this mother's ad-miration? Impart.

ROSENCRANTZ   She desires to speak with you in her closet ere you go to bed.   330

HAMLET   We shall obey, were she ten times our mother. Have you any further trade with us?

ROSENCRANTZ   My lord, you once did love me.

HAMLET   And do still, by these pickers and stealers.   334

ROSENCRANTZ   Good my lord, what is your cause of distemper? You do surely bar the door upon your own liberty if you deny your griefs to your friend.   337

HAMLET   Sir, I lack advancement.

ROSENCRANTZ   How can that be, when you have the voice of the King himself for your succession in Denmark?

HAMLET   Ay, sir, but "While the grass grows"—the 342 proverb is something musty.   343

Enter the Players with recorders.

Oh, the recorders. Let me see one. [*He takes a recorder.*] To withdraw with you: why do you go about to recover 345 the wind of me, as if you would drive me into a toil?   346

GUILDENSTERN   Oh, my lord, if my duty be too bold, my 347 love is too unmannerly.   348

HAMLET   I do not well understand that. Will you play 349 upon this pipe?

GUILDENSTERN   My lord, I cannot.

HAMLET   I pray you.

GUILDENSTERN   Believe me, I cannot.

HAMLET   I do beseech you.

GUILDENSTERN   I know no touch of it, my lord.

HAMLET   It is as easy as lying. Govern these ventages 356 with your fingers and thumb, give it breath with your mouth, and it will discourse most eloquent music. Look you, these are the stops.

GUILDENSTERN   But these cannot I command to any utterance of harmony. I have not the skill.

HAMLET   Why, look you now, how unworthy a thing you make of me! You would play upon me, you would seem to know my stops, you would pluck out the heart of my mystery, you would sound me from my lowest 365 note to the top of my compass, and there is much 366 music, excellent voice, in this little organ, yet cannot 367 you make it speak. 'Sblood, do you think I am easier to be played on than a pipe? Call me what instrument you will, though you can fret me, you cannot play 370 upon me.

Enter Polonius.

God bless you, sir!

---

292 perdy (A corruption of the French *par dieu*, "by God.")
299 retirement withdrawal to his chambers   **299–300 distempered** out of humor. (But Hamlet deliberately plays on the wider applica-tion to any illness of mind or body, as in lines 335–6, especially to drunkenness.)   **302 choler** anger. (But Hamlet takes the word in its more basic humoral sense of "bilious disorder.")   **305 purgation** (Hamlet hints at something going beyond medical treatment to bloodletting and the extraction of confession.)   **308 frame** order. **start** shy or jump away (like a horse; the opposite of *tame* in line 309) **314 breed** (1) kind (2) breeding, manners.   **316 pardon** permission to depart   **325 admiration** bewilderment.   **330 closet** private chamber

334 pickers and stealers i.e., hands. (So called from the catechism, "to keep my hands from picking and stealing.")   **337 liberty** i.e., being freed from *distemper*, line 336; but perhaps with a veiled threat as well. **deny** refuse to share   **342 "While . . . grows"** (The rest of the proverb is "the silly horse starves"; Hamlet implies that his hopes of succession are distant in time at best.)   **343 something** somewhat   **343.1** *Players* actors   **345 withdraw** speak privately   **345–6 recover the wind** get to the windward side (thus allowing the game to scent the hunter and thereby be driven in the opposite direction into the *toil* or net)   **346 toil** snare.   **347–8 if . . . unmannerly** if I am using an unmannerly boldness, it is my love that occasions it.   **349 I . . . that** i.e., I don't understand how genuine love can be unmannerly.   **356 ventages** finger-holes or *stops* (line 359) of the recorder   **365 sound** (1) fathom (2) produce sound in   **366 compass** range (of voice)   **367 organ** musical instrument **370 fret** irritate. (With a quibble on the *frets* or ridges on the fingerboard of some stringed instruments to regulate the fingering.)

POLONIUS My lord, the Queen would speak with you,
and presently.   374

HAMLET Do you see yonder cloud that's almost in
shape of a camel?

POLONIUS By th' Mass, and 'tis, like a camel indeed.

HAMLET Methinks it is like a weasel.

POLONIUS It is backed like a weasel.

HAMLET Or like a whale.

POLONIUS Very like a whale.

HAMLET Then I will come to my mother by and by.
[*Aside*] They fool me to the top of my bent.—I will 383
come by and by.

POLONIUS I will say so.   [*Exit.*]

HAMLET "By and by" is easily said. Leave me, friends.
                                   [*Exeunt all but Hamlet.*]
'Tis now the very witching time of night,   387
When churchyards yawn and hell itself breathes out
Contagion to this world. Now could I drink hot
    blood
And do such bitter business as the day
Would quake to look on. Soft, now to my mother.
O heart, lose not thy nature! Let not ever   392
The soul of Nero enter this firm bosom.   393
Let me be cruel, not unnatural;
I will speak daggers to her, but use none.
My tongue and soul in this be hypocrites:
How in my words somever she be shent,   397
To give them seals never my soul consent!   *Exit.* 398

❧

[3.3]

Enter King, Rosencrantz, and Guildenstern.

KING
I like him not, nor stands it safe with us   1
To let his madness range. Therefore prepare you.
I your commission will forthwith dispatch,   3
And he to England shall along with you.
The terms of our estate may not endure   5
Hazard so near 's as doth hourly grow
Out of his brows.

GUILDENSTERN   We will ourselves provide.   7
Most holy and religious fear it is   8
To keep those many many bodies safe
That live and feed upon Your Majesty.

ROSENCRANTZ
The single and peculiar life is bound   11

With all the strength and armor of the mind
To keep itself from noyance, but much more   13
That spirit upon whose weal depends and rests   14
The lives of many. The cess of majesty   15
Dies not alone, but like a gulf doth draw   16
What's near it with it; or it is a massy wheel   17
Fixed on the summit of the highest mount,
To whose huge spokes ten thousand lesser things
Are mortised and adjoined, which, when it falls,   20
Each small annexment, petty consequence,   21
Attends the boist'rous ruin. Never alone   22
Did the King sigh, but with a general groan.

KING
Arm you, I pray you, to this speedy voyage,   24
For we will fetters put about this fear,
Which now goes too free-footed.

ROSENCRANTZ   We will haste us.
Exeunt gentlemen [Rosencrantz and Guildenstern].

Enter Polonius.

POLONIUS
My lord, he's going to his mother's closet.
Behind the arras I'll convey myself   28
To hear the process. I'll warrant she'll tax him home, 29
And, as you said—and wisely was it said—
'Tis meet that some more audience than a mother,   31
Since nature makes them partial, should o'erhear
The speech of vantage. Fare you well, my liege.   33
I'll call upon you ere you go to bed
And tell you what I know.

KING   Thanks, dear my lord.
                                   Exit [Polonius].
Oh, my offense is rank! It smells to heaven.
It hath the primal eldest curse upon't,   37
A brother's murder. Pray can I not,
Though inclination be as sharp as will;   39
My stronger guilt defeats my strong intent,
And like a man to double business bound   41
I stand in pause where I shall first begin,
And both neglect. What if this cursèd hand
Were thicker than itself with brother's blood,
Is there not rain enough in the sweet heavens
To wash it white as snow? Whereto serves mercy   46
But to confront the visage of offense?   47
And what's in prayer but this twofold force,

---

374 **presently** at once.   383 **They fool . . . bent** They humor my odd
behavior to the limit of my ability or endurance. (Literally, the extent
to which a bow may be bent.)   387 **witching time** time when spells
are cast and evil is abroad   392 **nature** natural feeling.   393 **Nero**
(This infamous Roman emperor put to death his mother, Agrippina,
who had murdered her husband, Claudius.)   397–8 **How . . . consent!** however much she is to be rebuked by my words, may my soul
never consent to ratify those words with deeds of violence!
3.3. Location: The castle.
1 **him** i.e., his behavior   3 **dispatch** prepare, cause to be drawn up
5 **terms of our estate** circumstances of my royal position   7 **Out . . .
brows** i.e., from his brain, in the form of plots and threats.   **We . . .
provide** We'll put ourselves in readiness.   8 **religious fear** sacred
concern   11 **single and peculiar** individual and private

13 **noyance** harm   14 **weal** well-being   15 **cess** decease, cessation
16 **gulf** whirlpool   17 **massy** massive   20 **mortised** fastened (as with
a fitted joint).   **when it falls** i.e., when it descends, like the wheel of
Fortune, bringing a king down with it   21 **Each . . . consequence** i.e.,
every hanger-on and unimportant person or thing connected with the
King   22 **Attends** participates in   24 **Arm** Provide, prepare
28 **arras** screen of tapestry placed around the walls of household
apartments. (On the Elizabethan stage, the arras was presumably
over a door or aperture in the tiring-house facade.)   29 **process** proceedings.   **tax him home** reprove him severely   31 **meet** fitting
33 **of vantage** from an advantageous place, or, in addition.   37 **the
primal eldest curse** the curse of Cain, the first murderer; he killed his
brother Abel   39 **Though . . . will** though my desire is as strong as
my determination   41 **bound** (1) destined (2) obliged. (The King
wants to repent and still enjoy what he has gained.)   46–7 **Whereto . . .
offense?** What function does mercy serve other than to meet sin face
to face?

To be forestallèd ere we come to fall,   49
Or pardoned being down? Then I'll look up.
My fault is past. But oh, what form of prayer
Can serve my turn? "Forgive me my foul murder"?
That cannot be, since I am still possessed
Of those effects for which I did the murder:
My crown, mine own ambition, and my queen.
May one be pardoned and retain th'offense?   56
In the corrupted currents of this world   57
Offense's gilded hand may shove by justice,   58
And oft 'tis seen the wicked prize itself   59
Buys out the law. But 'tis not so above.
There is no shuffling, there the action lies   61
In his true nature, and we ourselves compelled,   62
Even to the teeth and forehead of our faults,   63
To give in evidence. What then? What rests?   64
Try what repentance can. What can it not?
Yet what can it, when one cannot repent?
O wretched state, O bosom black as death,
O limèd soul that, struggling to be free,   68
Art more engaged! Help, angels! Make assay.   69
Bow, stubborn knees, and heart with strings of steel,
Be soft as sinews of the newborn babe!
All may be well.   [*He kneels.*]

Enter Hamlet.

HAMLET
Now might I do it pat, now 'a is a-praying;   73
And now I'll do't. [*He draws his sword.*] And so 'a goes
    to heaven,
And so am I revenged. That would be scanned: 75
A villain kills my father, and for that,
I, his sole son, do this same villain send
To heaven.
Why, this is hire and salary, not revenge.
'A took my father grossly, full of bread,   80
With all his crimes broad blown, as flush as May;   81
And how his audit stands who knows save heaven?   82
But in our circumstance and course of thought   83
'Tis heavy with him. And am I then revenged,
To take him in the purging of his soul,
When he is fit and seasoned for his passage?   86
No!
Up, sword, and know thou a more horrid hent.   88
                                    [*He puts up his sword.*]

When he is drunk asleep, or in his rage,   89
Or in th'incestuous pleasure of his bed,
At game, a-swearing, or about some act   91
That has no relish of salvation in't—   92
Then trip him, that his heels may kick at heaven,
And that his soul may be as damned and black
As hell, whereto it goes. My mother stays.   95
This physic but prolongs thy sickly days.   *Exit.*   96
KING
My words fly up, my thoughts remain below.
Words without thoughts never to heaven go.   *Exit.*

❖

[3.4]

Enter [Queen] Gertrude and Polonius.

POLONIUS
'A will come straight. Look you lay home to him.   1
Tell him his pranks have been too broad to bear with,   2
And that Your Grace hath screened and stood
    between
Much heat and him. I'll silence me even here.   4
Pray you, be round with him.   5
HAMLET (*within*)   Mother, mother, mother!
QUEEN   I'll warrant you, fear me not.
Withdraw, I hear him coming.
                        [*Polonius hides behind the arras.*]

Enter Hamlet.

HAMLET   Now, mother, what's the matter?
QUEEN
Hamlet, thou hast thy father much offended.   10
HAMLET
Mother, you have my father much offended.
QUEEN
Come, come, you answer with an idle tongue.   12
HAMLET
Go, go, you question with a wicked tongue.
QUEEN
Why, how now, Hamlet?
HAMLET   What's the matter now?
QUEEN
Have you forgot me?
HAMLET   No, by the rood, not so: 15
You are the Queen, your husband's brother's wife,
And—would it were not so!—you are my mother.
QUEEN
Nay, then, I'll set those to you that can speak.   18

49 forestallèd prevented (from sinning)   **56 th'offense** the thing for which one offended.   **57 currents** courses of events   **58 gilded hand** hand offering gold as a bribe.   **shove by** thrust aside   **59 wicked prize** prize won by wickedness   **61 There . . . lies** There in heaven can be no evasion, there the deed lies exposed to view   **62 his** its   **63 to the teeth and forehead** face to face, concealing nothing   **64 give in** provide.   **rests** remains.   **68 limèd** caught as with birdlime, a sticky substance used to ensnare birds   **69 engaged** entangled.   **assay** trial. (Said to himself, or to the angels to try him.)   **73 pat** opportunely   **75 would be scanned** needs to be looked into, or, would be interpreted as follows   **80 grossly, full of bread** i.e., enjoying his worldly pleasures rather than fasting. (See Ezekiel 16:49.)   **81 crimes broad blown** sins in full bloom.   **flush** vigorous   **82 audit** account.   **save** except for   **83 in . . . thought** as we see it from our mortal perspective   **86 seasoned** matured, readied   **88 know . . . hent** await to be grasped by me on a more horrid occasion. (*Hent* means "act of seizing.")

89 drunk . . . rage dead drunk, or in a fit of sexual passion   **91 game** gambling   **92 relish** trace, savor   **95 stays** awaits (me).   **96 physic** purging (by prayer), or, Hamlet's postponement of the killing   **3.4. Location: The Queen's private chamber.**
1 lay . . . him reprove him soundly   **2 broad** unrestrained   **4 Much heat** i.e., the King's anger.   **I'll silence me** I'll quietly conceal myself. (Ironic, since it is his crying out at line 24 that leads to his death. Some editors emend *silence* to "sconce." The First Quarto's reading, "shroud," is attractive.)   **5 round** blunt   **10 thy father** i.e., your step-father, Claudius   **12 idle** foolish   **15 forgot me** i.e., forgotten that I am your mother.   **rood** cross of Christ   **18 speak** i.e., speak to someone so rude.

HAMLET
    Come, come, and sit you down; you shall not budge.
    You go not till I set you up a glass
    Where you may see the inmost part of you.
QUEEN
    What wilt thou do? Thou wilt not murder me?
    Help, ho!
POLONIUS [*behind the arras*]   What ho! Help!
HAMLET [*drawing*]
    How now? A rat? Dead for a ducat, dead!   25
                    [*He thrusts his rapier through the arras.*]
POLONIUS [*behind the arras*]
    Oh, I am slain!   [*He falls and dies.*]
QUEEN   Oh, me, what hast thou done?
HAMLET   Nay, I know not. Is it the King?
QUEEN
    Oh, what a rash and bloody deed is this!
HAMLET
    A bloody deed—almost as bad, good mother,
    As kill a king, and marry with his brother.
QUEEN
    As kill a king!
HAMLET   Ay, lady, it was my word.
            [*He parts the arras and discovers Polonius.*]
    Thou wretched, rash, intruding fool, farewell!
    I took thee for thy better. Take thy fortune.
    Thou find'st to be too busy is some danger.—   34
    Leave wringing of your hands. Peace, sit you down,
    And let me wring your heart, for so I shall,
    If it be made of penetrable stuff,
    If damnèd custom have not brazed it so   38
    That it be proof and bulwark against sense.   39
QUEEN
    What have I done, that thou dar'st wag thy tongue
    In noise so rude against me?
HAMLET   Such an act
    That blurs the grace and blush of modesty,
    Calls virtue hypocrite, takes off the rose
    From the fair forehead of an innocent love
    And sets a blister there, makes marriage vows   45
    As false as dicers' oaths. Oh, such a deed
    As from the body of contraction plucks   47
    The very soul, and sweet religion makes   48
    A rhapsody of words. Heaven's face does glow   49
    O'er this solidity and compound mass   50
    With tristful visage, as against the doom,   51
    Is thought-sick at the act.
QUEEN   Ay me, what act,   52
    That roars so loud and thunders in the index?   53
HAMLET [*showing her two likenesses*]
    Look here upon this picture, and on this,

The counterfeit presentment of two brothers.   55
See what a grace was seated on this brow:
Hyperion's curls, the front of Jove himself,   57
An eye like Mars to threaten and command,   58
A station like the herald Mercury   59
New-lighted on a heaven-kissing hill—   60
A combination and a form indeed
Where every god did seem to set his seal   62
To give the world assurance of a man.
This was your husband. Look you now what follows:
Here is your husband, like a mildewed ear,   65
Blasting his wholesome brother. Have you eyes?   66
Could you on this fair mountain leave to feed   67
And batten on this moor? Ha, have you eyes?   68
You cannot call it love, for at your age
The heyday in the blood is tame, it's humble,   70
And waits upon the judgment, and what judgment
Would step from this to this? Sense, sure, you have,   72
Else could you not have motion, but sure that sense
Is apoplexed, for madness would not err,   74
Nor sense to ecstasy was ne'er so thralled,   75
But it reserved some quantity of choice   76
To serve in such a difference. What devil was't   77
That thus hath cozened you at hoodman-blind?   78
Eyes without feeling, feeling without sight,
Ears without hands or eyes, smelling sans all,   80
Or but a sickly part of one true sense
Could not so mope. O shame, where is thy blush?   82
Rebellious hell,
If thou canst mutine in a matron's bones,   84
To flaming youth let virtue be as wax   85
And melt in her own fire. Proclaim no shame   86
When the compulsive ardor gives the charge,   87
Since frost itself as actively doth burn,   88
And reason panders will.   89
QUEEN   Oh, Hamlet, speak no more!
    Thou turn'st mine eyes into my very soul,
    And there I see such black and grainèd spots   92

---

25 **Dead for a ducat** i.e., I bet a ducat he's dead; or, a ducat is his life's fee.   34 **busy** nosey   38 **damnèd custom** habitual wickedness. **brazed** brazened, hardened   39 **proof** impenetrable, like *proof* or tested armor.   **sense** feeling.   45 **sets a blister** i.e., brands as a harlot   47 **contraction** the marriage contract   48 **sweet religion makes** i.e., makes marriage vows   49 **rhapsody** senseless string   49–52 **Heaven's . . . act** Heaven's face blushes at this solid world compounded of the various elements, with sorrowful face as though the day of doom were near, and is sick with horror at the deed (i.e., Gertrude's marriage).   53 **index** table of contents, prelude or preface.

---

55 **counterfeit presentment** representation in portraiture   57 **Hyperion's** the sun-god's.   **front** brow   58 **Mars** god of war   59 **station** manner of standing.   **Mercury** winged messenger of the gods   60 **New-lighted** newly alighted.   **heaven-kissing** reaching to the sky   62 **set his seal** i.e., affix his approval   65 **ear** i.e., of grain   66 **Blasting** blighting   67 **leave** cease   68 **batten** gorge.   **moor** barren or marshy ground. (Suggesting also "dark-skinned.")   70 **The heyday . . . blood** (The blood was thought to be the source of sexual desire.)   72 **Sense** Perception through the five senses (the functions of the middle or sensible soul)   74 **apoplexed** paralyzed.   **err** so err   75–7 **Nor . . . difference** nor could your physical senses ever have been so enthralled to *ecstasy* or lunacy that they could not distinguish to some degree between Hamlet Senior and Claudius.   78 **cozened** cheated. **hoodman-blind** blindman's buff. (In this game, says Hamlet, the devil must have pushed Claudius toward Gertrude while she was blindfolded.)   80 **sans** without   82 **mope** be dazed, act aimlessly.   84 **mutine** mutiny   85–6 **To . . . fire** when it comes to sexually passionate youth, let virtue melt like a candle or stick of sealing wax held over a candle flame. (There's no point in hoping for self-restraint among young people when matronly women set such a bad example.)   86–9 **Proclaim . . . will** Call it no shameful business when the compelling ardor of youth delivers the attack, i.e., commits lechery, since the *frost* of advanced age burns with as active a fire of lust and reason perverts itself by fomenting lust rather than restraining it.   92 **grainèd** ingrained, indelible

As will not leave their tinct.

HAMLET   Nay, but to live   93
In the rank sweat of an enseamèd bed,   94
Stewed in corruption, honeying and making love   95
Over the nasty sty!   96

QUEEN   Oh, speak to me no more!
These words like daggers enter in my ears.
No more, sweet Hamlet!

HAMLET   A murderer and a villain,
A slave that is not twentieth part the tithe   100
Of your precedent lord, a vice of kings,   101
A cutpurse of the empire and the rule,
That from a shelf the precious diadem stole
And put it in his pocket!

QUEEN   No more!   105

Enter Ghost [*in his nightgown*].

HAMLET   A king of shreds and patches—   106
Save me, and hover o'er me with your wings,
You heavenly guards! What would your gracious
     figure?

QUEEN   Alas, he's mad!

HAMLET
Do you not come your tardy son to chide,
That, lapsed in time and passion, lets go by   111
Th'important acting of your dread command?   112
Oh, say!

GHOST
Do not forget. This visitation
Is but to whet thy almost blunted purpose.   115
But look, amazement on thy mother sits.   116
Oh, step between her and her fighting soul!
Conceit in weakest bodies strongest works.   118
Speak to her, Hamlet.

HAMLET   How is it with you, lady?

QUEEN   Alas, how is't with you,
That you do bend your eye on vacancy,
And with th'incorporal air do hold discourse?   122
Forth at your eyes your spirits wildly peep,
And, as the sleeping soldiers in th'alarm,   124
Your bedded hair, like life in excrements,   125
Start up and stand on end. O gentle son,
Upon the heat and flame of thy distemper   127
Sprinkle cool patience. Whereon do you look?

HAMLET
On him, on him! Look you how pale he glares!
His form and cause conjoined, preaching to stones,   130
Would make them capable.—Do not look upon me,   131
Lest with this piteous action you convert   132
My stern effects. Then what I have to do   133
Will want true color—tears perchance for blood.   134

QUEEN   To whom do you speak this?

HAMLET   Do you see nothing there?

QUEEN
Nothing at all, yet all that is I see.

HAMLET   Nor did you nothing hear?

QUEEN   No, nothing but ourselves.

HAMLET
Why, look you there, look how it steals away!
My father, in his habit as he lived!   141
Look where he goes even now out at the portal!
                                        Exit Ghost.

QUEEN
This is the very coinage of your brain.   143
This bodiless creation ecstasy   144
Is very cunning in.   145

HAMLET   Ecstasy?
My pulse as yours doth temperately keep time,
And makes as healthful music. It is not madness
That I have uttered. Bring me to the test,
And I the matter will reword, which madness   150
Would gambol from. Mother, for love of grace,   151
Lay not that flattering unction to your soul   152
That not your trespass but my madness speaks.
It will but skin and film the ulcerous place,   154
Whiles rank corruption, mining all within,   155
Infects unseen. Confess yourself to heaven,
Repent what's past, avoid what is to come,
And do not spread the compost on the weeds   158
To make them ranker. Forgive me this my virtue;   159
For in the fatness of these pursy times   160
Virtue itself of vice must pardon beg,
Yea, curb and woo for leave to do him good.   162

QUEEN
Oh, Hamlet, thou hast cleft my heart in twain.

HAMLET
Oh, throw away the worser part of it,
And live the purer with the other half.
Good night. But go not to my uncle's bed;
Assume a virtue, if you have it not.
That monster, custom, who all sense doth eat,   168
Of habits devil, is angel yet in this,   169

---

93 leave their tinct surrender their dark stain.   **94 enseamèd** saturated in the grease and filth of passionate lovemaking   **95 Stewed** soaked, bathed. (With a suggestion of "stew," brothel.)   **96 Over . . . sty** (Like barnyard animals.)   **100 tithe** tenth part   **101 precedent lord** former husband.   **vice** (From the morality plays, a model of iniquity and a buffoon.)   **105.1 *nightgown*** a robe for indoor wear.   **106 A king . . . patches** i.e., a king whose splendor is all sham; a clown or fool dressed in motley   **111 lapsed . . . passion** having let time and passion slip away   **112 Th'important** the importunate, urgent   **115 whet** sharpen   **116 amazement** distraction   **118 Conceit** Imagination   **122 th'incorporal** the immaterial   **124 as . . . th'alarm** like soldiers called out of sleep by an alarum   **125 bedded** laid flat. **like life in excrements** i.e., as though hair, an outgrowth of the body, had a life of its own. (Hair was thought to be lifeless because it lacks sensation, and so its standing on end would be unnatural and ominous.)   **127 distemper** disorder

130 His . . . conjoined His appearance joined to his cause for speaking   **131 capable** capable of feeling, receptive.   **132–3 convert . . . effects** divert me from my stern duty.   **134 want . . . blood** lack plausibility so that (with a play on the normal sense of *color*) I shall shed colorless tears instead of blood.   **141 habit** clothes.   **as . . . when**   **143 very mere**   **144–5 This . . . in** Madness is skillful in creating this kind of hallucination.   **150 reword** repeat word for word   **151 gambol** skip away   **152 unction** ointment   **154 skin** grow a skin over   **155 mining** working under the surface   **158 compost** manure   **159 this my virtue** my virtuous talk in reproving you   **160 fatness** grossness. **pursy** flabby, out of shape   **162 curb** bow, bend the knee.   **leave** permission   **168 who . . . eat** which consumes and overwhelms the physical senses   **169 Of habits devil** devil-like in prompting evil habits

That to the use of actions fair and good
He likewise gives a frock or livery   171
That aptly is put on. Refrain tonight,   172
And that shall lend a kind of easiness
To the next abstinence; the next more easy;
For use almost can change the stamp of nature,   175
And either . . . the devil, or throw him out   176
With wondrous potency. Once more, good night;
And when you are desirous to be blest,   178
I'll blessing beg of you. For this same lord,   179
[pointing to Polonius]
I do repent; but heaven hath pleased it so
To punish me with this, and this with me,   181
That I must be their scourge and minister.   182
I will bestow him, and will answer well   183
The death I gave him. So, again, good night.
I must be cruel only to be kind.
This bad begins, and worse remains behind.   186
One word more, good lady.

QUEEN   What shall I do?

HAMLET
Not this by no means that I bid you do:
Let the bloat king tempt you again to bed,   189
Pinch wanton on your cheek, call you his mouse,   190
And let him, for a pair of reechy kisses,   191
Or paddling in your neck with his damned fingers,   192
Make you to ravel all this matter out   193
That I essentially am not in madness,
But mad in craft. 'Twere good you let him know,   195
For who that's but a queen, fair, sober, wise,
Would from a paddock, from a bat, a gib,   197
Such dear concernings hide? Who would do so?   198
No, in despite of sense and secrecy,   199
Unpeg the basket on the house's top,   200
Let the birds fly, and like the famous ape,   201
To try conclusions, in the basket creep   202
And break your own neck down.   203

QUEEN
Be thou assured, if words be made of breath,
And breath of life, I have no life to breathe
What thou hast said to me.

HAMLET
I must to England. You know that?

QUEEN   Alack,
I had forgot. 'Tis so concluded on.

HAMLET
There's letters sealed, and my two schoolfellows,
Whom I will trust as I will adders fanged,
They bear the mandate; they must sweep my way   211
And marshal me to knavery. Let it work.   212
For 'tis the sport to have the engineer   213
Hoist with his own petard, and 't shall go hard   214
But I will delve one yard below their mines   215
And blow them at the moon. Oh, 'tis most sweet
When in one line two crafts directly meet.   217
This man shall set me packing.   218
I'll lug the guts into the neighbor room.
Mother, good night indeed. This counselor
Is now most still, most secret, and most grave,
Who was in life a foolish prating knave.—
Come, sir, to draw toward an end with you.—   223
Good night, mother.
Exeunt [separately, Hamlet dragging in Polonius].

[4.1]

*Enter King and Queen, with Rosencrantz and
Guildenstern.*

KING
There's matter in these sighs, these profound heaves.   1
You must translate; 'tis fit we understand them.
Where is your son?

QUEEN
Bestow this place on us a little while.
[Exeunt Rosencrantz and Guildenstern.]
Ah, mine own lord, what have I seen tonight!

---

171 **livery** an outer appearance, a customary garb (and hence a predisposition easily assumed in time of stress)   172 **aptly** readily   175 **use** habit.   **the stamp of nature** our inborn traits   176 **And either** (A defective line, often emended by inserting the word "master" after *either*, following the Third Quarto and early editors, or some other word such as "shame," "lodge," "curb," or "house.")   178–9 **when . . . you** i.e., when you are ready to be penitent and seek God's blessing, I will ask your blessing as a dutiful son should.   181 **To punish . . . with me** to seek retribution from me for killing Polonius, and from him through my means   182 **their scourge and minister** i.e., agent of heavenly retribution.   183 **bestow** stow, dispose of.   **answer** account or pay for   186 **This** i.e., The killing of Polonius.   **behind** to come.   189 **bloat** bloated   190 **Pinch wanton** i.e., leave his love pinches on your cheeks, branding you as wanton   191 **reechy** dirty, filthy   192 **paddling** fingering amorously   193 **ravel . . . out** unravel, disclose   195 **in craft** by cunning.   **good** (Said sarcastically; also the following eight lines.)   197 **paddock** toad.   **gib** tomcat   198 **dear concernings** important affairs   199 **sense and secrecy** secrecy that common sense requires   200 **Unpeg the basket** open the cage, i.e., let out the secret   201 **famous ape** (In a story now lost.)   202 **try conclusions** test the outcome (in which the ape apparently enters a cage from which birds have been released and then tries to fly out of the cage as they have done, falling to its death)   203 **down** in the fall.

211–12 **sweep . . . knavery** sweep a path before me and conduct me to some *knavery* or treachery prepared for me.   212 **work** proceed.   213 **engineer** maker of *engines* of war   214 **Hoist with** blown up by.   **petard** an explosive used to blow in a door or make a breach   214–15 **'t shall . . . will** unless luck is against me, I will   215 **mines** tunnels used in warfare to undermine the enemy's emplacements; Hamlet will countermine by going under their mines   217 **in one line** i.e., mines and countermines on a collision course, or the countermines directly below the mines.   **crafts** acts of guile, plots   218 **set me packing** set me to making schemes, and set me to lugging (him), and, also, send me off in a hurry.   223 **draw . . . end** finish up. (With a pun on *draw*, "pull.")
4.1 Location: The castle.
0.1 Enter . . . Queen (Some editors argue that Gertrude does not in fact exit at the end of 3.4 and that the scene is continuous here. It is true that the Folio ends 3.4 with *"Exit Hamlet tugging in Polonius,"* not naming Gertrude, and opens 4.1 with *"Enter King."* Yet the Second Quarto concludes 3.4 with a simple *"Exit,"* which often stands ambiguously for a single exit or an exeunt in early modern texts, and then starts 4.1 with *"Enter King, and Queene, with Rosencraus and Guyldensterne."* The King's opening lines in 4.1 suggest that he has had time, during a brief intervening pause, to become aware of Gertrude's highly wrought emotional state. In line 35, the King refers to Gertrude's *closet* as though it were elsewhere. The differences between the Second Quarto and the Folio offer an alternative staging. In either case, 4.1 follows swiftly upon 3.4.)   1 **matter** significance.   **heaves** heavy sighs.

KING
  What, Gertrude? How does Hamlet?
QUEEN
  Mad as the sea and wind when both contend
  Which is the mightier. In his lawless fit,
  Behind the arras hearing something stir,
  Whips out his rapier, cries, "A rat, a rat!"
  And in this brainish apprehension kills   11
  The unseen good old man.
KING   Oh, heavy deed!   12
  It had been so with us, had we been there.   13
  His liberty is full of threats to all—
  To you yourself, to us, to everyone.
  Alas, how shall this bloody deed be answered?   16
  It will be laid to us, whose providence   17
  Should have kept short, restrained, and out of haunt   18
  This mad young man. But so much was our love,
  We would not understand what was most fit,
  But, like the owner of a foul disease,
  To keep it from divulging, let it feed   22
  Even on the pith of life. Where is he gone?
QUEEN
  To draw apart the body he hath killed,
  O'er whom his very madness, like some ore   25
  Among a mineral of metals base,   26
  Shows itself pure: 'a weeps for what is done.
KING   Oh, Gertrude, come away!
  The sun no sooner shall the mountains touch
  But we will ship him hence, and this vile deed
  We must with all our majesty and skill
  Both countenance and excuse.—Ho, Guildenstern!   32

          Enter Rosencrantz and Guildenstern.

  Friends both, go join you with some further aid.
  Hamlet in madness hath Polonius slain,
  And from his mother's closet hath he dragged him.
  Go seek him out, speak fair, and bring the body   36
  Into the chapel. I pray you, haste in this.
              [*Exeunt Rosencrantz and Guildenstern.*]
  Come, Gertrude, we'll call up our wisest friends
  And let them know both what we mean to do
  And what's untimely done   40
  Whose whisper o'er the world's diameter,   41
  As level as the cannon to his blank,   42
  Transports his poisoned shot, may miss our name
  And hit the woundless air. Oh, come away!   44
  My soul is full of discord and dismay.   *Exeunt.*

---

11 **brainish apprehension** frenzied misapprehension   12 **heavy** grievous   13 **us** i.e., me. (The royal "we"; also in line 15.)   16 **answered** explained.   17 **providence** foresight   18 **short** i.e., on a short tether. **out of haunt** secluded   22 **from divulging** from becoming publicly known   25 **ore** vein of gold   26 **mineral** mine   32 **countenance** put the best face on   36 **fair** gently, courteously   40 **And . . . done** (A defective line; conjectures as to the missing words include "So, haply, slander" [Capell and others]; "For, haply, slander" [Theobald and others]; and "So envious slander" [Jenkins].)   41 **diameter** extent from side to side   42 **As level** with as direct aim. **his blank** its target at point-blank range   44 **woundless** invulnerable

---

[4.2]

          Enter Hamlet.

HAMLET   Safely stowed.
ROSENCRANTZ, GUILDENSTERN (*within*)   Hamlet! Lord
  Hamlet!
HAMLET   But soft, what noise? Who calls on Hamlet? Oh,
  here they come.

          Enter Rosencrantz and Guildenstern.

ROSENCRANTZ
  What have you done, my lord, with the dead body?
HAMLET
  Compounded it with dust, whereto 'tis kin.
ROSENCRANTZ
  Tell us where 'tis, that we may take it thence
  And bear it to the chapel.
HAMLET   Do not believe it.
ROSENCRANTZ   Believe what?
HAMLET   That I can keep your counsel and not mine   12
  own. Besides, to be demanded of a sponge, what rep-   13
  lication should be made by the son of a king?   14
ROSENCRANTZ   Take you me for a sponge, my lord?
HAMLET   Ay, sir, that soaks up the King's countenance, 16
  his rewards, his authorities. But such officers do the 17
  King best service in the end. He keeps them, like an
  ape, an apple, in the corner of his jaw, first mouthed
  to be last swallowed. When he needs what you have
  gleaned, it is but squeezing you, and, sponge, you
  shall be dry again.
ROSENCRANTZ   I understand you not, my lord.
HAMLET   I am glad of it. A knavish speech sleeps in a   24
  foolish ear.
ROSENCRANTZ   My lord, you must tell us where the
  body is and go with us to the King.
HAMLET   The body is with the King, but the King is not 28
  with the body. The King is a thing—   29
GUILDENSTERN   A thing, my lord?
HAMLET   Of nothing. Bring me to him. Hide fox, and all 31
  after!   *Exeunt* [*running*]. 32

                    ♣

[4.3]

          Enter King, and two or three.

4.2 Location: The castle.
12–13 That . . . own i.e., Don't expect me to do as you bid me and not follow my own counsel.   **13 demanded of** questioned by   **13–14 replication** reply   **16 countenance** favor   **17 authorities** delegated power, influence.   **24 sleeps in** has no meaning to   **28–9 The . . . body** (Perhaps alludes to the legal commonplace of "the king's two bodies," which drew a distinction between the sacred office of kingship and the particular mortal who possessed it at any given time. Hence, although Claudius's body is necessarily a part of him, true kingship is not contained in it. Similarly, Claudius will have Polonius's body when it is found, but there is no kingship in this business either.)   **31 Of nothing** (1) Of no account (2) Lacking the essence of kingship, as in lines 28–9 and note.   **31–2 Hide . . . after** (An old signal cry in the game of hide-and-seek, suggesting that Hamlet now runs away from them.)
4.3. Location: The castle.

KING
I have sent to seek him, and to find the body.
How dangerous is it that this man goes loose!
Yet must not we put the strong law on him.
He's loved of the distracted multitude,   4
Who like not in their judgment, but their eyes,   5
And where 'tis so, th'offender's scourge is weighed,   6
But never the offense. To bear all smooth and even,   7
This sudden sending him away must seem
Deliberate pause. Diseases desperate grown   9
By desperate appliance are relieved,   10
Or not at all.

Enter Rosencrantz, [Guildenstern,]
and all the rest.

How now, what hath befall'n?

ROSENCRANTZ
Where the dead body is bestowed, my lord,
We cannot get from him.
KING   But where is he?
ROSENCRANTZ
Without, my lord; guarded, to know your pleasure.   14
KING
Bring him before us.
ROSENCRANTZ [*calling*]   Ho! Bring in the lord.

They enter [with Hamlet].

KING   Now, Hamlet, where's Polonius?
HAMLET   At supper.
KING   At supper? Where?
HAMLET   Not where he eats, but where 'a is eaten. A
certain convocation of politic worms are e'en at him.   20
Your worm is your only emperor for diet. We fat all   21
creatures else to fat us, and we fat ourselves for mag-
gots. Your fat king and your lean beggar is but
variable service—two dishes, but to one table. That's   24
the end.
KING   Alas, alas!
HAMLET   A man may fish with the worm that hath eat   27
of a king, and eat of the fish that hath fed of that
worm.
KING   What dost thou mean by this?
HAMLET   Nothing but to show you how a king may go
a progress through the guts of a beggar.   32
KING   Where is Polonius?
HAMLET   In heaven. Send thither to see. If your messenger find him not there, seek him i'th'other place yourself. But if indeed you find him not within this month,

you shall nose him as you go up the stairs into the   37
lobby.
KING [*to some attendants*]   Go seek him there.
HAMLET   'A will stay till you come. [*Exeunt attendants.*]
KING
Hamlet, this deed, for thine especial safety—
Which we do tender, as we dearly grieve   42
For that which thou hast done—must send thee hence
With fiery quickness. Therefore prepare thyself.
The bark is ready, and the wind at help,   45
Th'associates tend, and everything is bent   46
For England.
HAMLET   For England!
KING   Ay, Hamlet.
HAMLET   Good.
KING
So is it, if thou knew'st our purposes.
HAMLET   I see a cherub that sees them. But come, for   52
England! Farewell, dear mother.
KING   Thy loving father, Hamlet.
HAMLET   My mother. Father and mother is man and
wife, man and wife is one flesh, and so, my mother.
Come, for England!   *Exit.*
KING
Follow him at foot; tempt him with speed aboard.   58
Delay it not. I'll have him hence tonight.
Away! For everything is sealed and done
That else leans on th'affair. Pray you, make haste.   61
                                    [*Exeunt all but the King.*]
And, England, if my love thou hold'st at aught—   62
As my great power thereof may give thee sense,   63
Since yet thy cicatrice looks raw and red   64
After the Danish sword, and thy free awe   65
Pays homage to us—thou mayst not coldly set   66
Our sovereign process, which imports at full,   67
By letters congruing to that effect,   68
The present death of Hamlet. Do it, England,   69
For like the hectic in my blood he rages,   70
And thou must cure me. Till I know 'tis done,
Howe'er my haps, my joys were ne'er begun.   *Exit.* 72

❖

[4.4]

Enter Fortinbras with his army over the stage.

FORTINBRAS
Go, Captain, from me greet the Danish king.

4 **of** by.   **distracted** fickle, unstable   5 **Who . . . eyes** who choose not
by judgment but by appearance   6–7 **th'offender's . . . offense** i.e.,
the populace often takes umbrage at the severity of a punishment
without taking into account the gravity of the crime.   7 **To . . . even**
To manage the business in an unprovocative way   9 **Deliberate**
pause carefully considered action.   10 **appliance** remedies   14 **With-**
out Outside   20 **politic worms** crafty worms (suited to a master spy
like Polonius).   **e'en** even now   21 **Your worm** Your average worm.
(Compare *your fat king and your lean beggar* in line 23.)   **diet** food, eating. (With a punning reference to the Diet of Worms, a famous
convocation held in 1521.)   24 **service** food served at table. (Worms
feed on kings and beggars alike.)   27 **eat** eaten. (Pronounced *et*.)
32 **progress** royal journey of state

37 **nose** smell   42 **tender** regard, hold dear.   **dearly** intensely
45 **bark** sailing vessel   46 **tend** wait.   **bent** in readiness   52 **cherub**
(Cherubim are angels of knowledge. Hamlet hints that both he and
heaven are onto Claudius's tricks.)   58 **at foot** close behind, at heel
61 **leans on** bears upon, is related to   62 **England** i.e., King of England.   **at aught** at any value   63 **As . . . sense** for so my great power
may give you a just appreciation of the importance of valuing my
love   64 **cicatrice** scar   65 **free awe** unconstrained show of respect
66 **coldly set** regard with indifference   67 **process** command.
imports at full conveys specific directions for   68 **congruing** agreeing   69 **present** immediate   70 **hectic** persistent fever   72 **Howe'er**
. . . begun whatever else happens, I cannot begin to be happy.
4.4 **Location: The coast of Denmark.**

Tell him that by his license Fortinbras 2
Craves the conveyance of a promised march 3
Over his kingdom. You know the rendezvous.
If that His Majesty would aught with us,
We shall express our duty in his eye; 6
And let him know so.
CAPTAIN   I will do't, my lord.
FORTINBRAS   Go softly on.   [*Exeunt all but the Captain.*] 9

    Enter Hamlet, Rosencrantz, [Guildenstern,] etc.

HAMLET   Good sir, whose powers are these? 10
CAPTAIN   They are of Norway, sir.
HAMLET   How purposed, sir, I pray you?
CAPTAIN   Against some part of Poland.
HAMLET   Who commands them, sir?
CAPTAIN
The nephew to old Norway, Fortinbras.
HAMLET
Goes it against the main of Poland, sir, 16
Or for some frontier?
CAPTAIN
Truly to speak, and with no addition, 18
We go to gain a little patch of ground
That hath in it no profit but the name.
To pay five ducats, five, I would not farm it; 21
Nor will it yield to Norway or the Pole
A ranker rate, should it be sold in fee. 23
HAMLET
Why, then the Polack never will defend it.
CAPTAIN
Yes, it is already garrisoned.
HAMLET
Two thousand souls and twenty thousand ducats
Will not debate the question of this straw 27
This is th'impostume of much wealth and peace, 28
That inward breaks, and shows no cause without 29
Why the man dies. I humbly thank you, sir.
CAPTAIN
God b'wi'you, sir.   [*Exit.*]
ROSENCRANTZ   Will't please you go, my lord?
HAMLET
I'll be with you straight. Go a little before.
    [*Exeunt all except Hamlet.*]
How all occasions do inform against me 33
And spur my dull revenge! What is a man,
If his chief good and market of his time 35
Be but to sleep and feed? A beast, no more.
Sure he that made us with such large discourse, 37
Looking before and after, gave us not 38
That capability and godlike reason

To fust in us unused. Now, whether it be 40
Bestial oblivion, or some craven scruple 41
Of thinking too precisely on th'event— 42
A thought which, quartered, hath but one part
    wisdom
And ever three parts coward—I do not know
Why yet I live to say "This thing's to do,"
Sith I have cause, and will, and strength, and means 46
To do't. Examples gross as earth exhort me: 47
Witness this army of such mass and charge, 48
Led by a delicate and tender prince, 49
Whose spirit with divine ambition puffed
Makes mouths at the invisible event, 51
Exposing what is mortal and unsure
To all that fortune, death, and danger dare, 53
Even for an eggshell. Rightly to be great 54
Is not to stir without great argument, 55
But greatly to find quarrel in a straw 56
When honor's at the stake. How stand I, then, 57
That have a father killed, a mother stained,
Excitements of my reason and my blood, 59
And let all sleep, while to my shame I see
The imminent death of twenty thousand men
That for a fantasy and trick of fame 62
Go to their graves like beds, fight for a plot 63
Whereon the numbers cannot try the cause, 64
Which is not tomb enough and continent 65
To hide the slain? Oh, from this time forth
My thoughts be bloody or be nothing worth!   *Exit.*

❧

[4.5]

    Enter Horatio, [Queen] Gertrude, and a Gentleman.

QUEEN
I will not speak with her.
GENTLEMAN   She is importunate,
Indeed distract. Her mood will needs be pitied. 2
QUEEN   What would she have?
GENTLEMAN
She speaks much of her father, says she hears
There's tricks i'th' world, and hems, and beats her
    heart, 5
Spurns enviously at straws, speaks things in doubt 6

40 **fust** grow moldy   41 **oblivion** forgetfulness.   **craven** cowardly
42 **precisely** scrupulously.   **th'event** the outcome   46 **Sith** since
47 **gross** obvious   48 **charge** expense   49 **delicate and tender** of fine
and youthful qualities   51 **Makes mouths** makes scornful faces.
invisible event unforeseeable outcome   53 **dare** could do (to him)
54–7 **Rightly . . . stake** True greatness is not a matter of being moved
to action solely by a great cause; rather, it is to respond greatly to an
apparently trivial cause when honor is at the stake.   59 **blood** (The
supposed seat of the passions.)   62 **fantasy** fanciful caprice, illusion.
trick trifle, deceit   63 **plot** plot of ground   64 **Whereon . . . cause** on
which there is insufficient room for the soldiers needed to fight for it
65 **continent** receptacle, container
4.5 Location: The castle.
2 **distract** out of her mind.   5 **tricks** deceptions.   **hems** clears her
throat, makes "hmm" sounds.   **heart** i.e., breast   6 **Spurns . . .
straws** kicks spitefully, takes offense at trifles.   **in doubt** of obscure
meaning

2 **license** permission   3 **conveyance** unhindered passage   6 **We . . .
eye** I will come about pay my respects in person   9 **softly** slowly, circum-
spectly   10 **powers** forces   16 **main** main part   18 **addition** exaggeration   21 **To pay** i.e., For a yearly rental of.   **farm it** take a lease
of it   23 **ranker** higher.   **in fee** fee simple, outright.   27 **debate . . .
straw** argue about this trifling matter.   28 **th'impostume** the abscess
29 **inward breaks** festers within.   **without** externally   33 **inform
against** denounce; take shape against   35 **market of** profit of
37 **discourse** power of reasoning   38 **Looking before and after** able
to review past events and anticipate the future

That carry but half sense. Her speech is nothing,
Yet the unshapèd use of it doth move   8
The hearers to collection; they yawn at it,   9
And botch the words up fit to their own thoughts,   10
Which, as her winks and nods and gestures yield
   them,   11
Indeed would make one think there might be thought,   12
Though nothing sure, yet much unhappily.   13
HORATIO
'Twere good she were spoken with, for she may strew
Dangerous conjectures in ill-breeding minds.   15
QUEEN   Let her come in.   [Exit Gentleman.]
   [Aside] To my sick soul, as sin's true nature is,
Each toy seems prologue to some great amiss.   18
So full of artless jealousy is guilt,   19
It spills itself in fearing to be spilt.   20

             Enter Ophelia [distracted].

OPHELIA
Where is the beauteous majesty of Denmark?
QUEEN   How now, Ophelia?
OPHELIA (she sings)
       "How should I your true love know
           From another one?
       By his cockle hat and staff,   25
           And his sandal shoon."   26
QUEEN   Alas, sweet lady, what imports this song?
OPHELIA   Say you? Nay, pray you, mark.
       "He is dead and gone, lady,   (Song.)
           He is dead and gone;
       At his head a grass-green turf,
           At his heels a stone."
   Oho!   33
QUEEN   Nay, but Ophelia—
OPHELIA   Pray you, mark.
   [Sings] "White his shroud as the mountain snow"—

             Enter King.

QUEEN   Alas, look here, my lord.
OPHELIA
       "Larded with sweet flowers;   (Song.) 38
       Which bewept to the ground did not go
           With true-love showers."   40
KING   How do you, pretty lady?
OPHELIA   Well, God 'ild you! They say the owl was a   42

baker's daughter. Lord, we know what we are, but
know not what we may be. God be at your table!
KING   Conceit upon her father.   45
OPHELIA   Pray let's have no words of this; but when
   they ask you what it means, say you this:
       "Tomorrow is Saint Valentine's day,   (Song.)
           All in the morning betime,   49
       And I a maid at your window,
           To be your Valentine.
       Then up he rose, and donned his clothes,
           And dupped the chamber door,   53
       Let in the maid, that out a maid
           Never departed more."
KING   Pretty Ophelia—
OPHELIA   Indeed, la, without an oath, I'll make an end
   on't:
   [Sings]   "By Gis and by Saint Charity,   59
           Alack, and fie for shame!
       Young men will do't, if they come to't;
           By Cock, they are to blame.   62
       Quoth she, 'Before you tumbled me,
           You promised me to wed.'"
   He answers:
       "'So would I ha' done, by yonder sun,
           An thou hadst not come to my bed.'"   67
KING   How long hath she been thus?
OPHELIA   I hope all will be well. We must be patient,
   but I cannot choose but weep to think they would lay
   him i'th' cold ground. My brother shall know of it.
   And so I thank you for your good counsel. Come, my
   coach! Good night, ladies, good night, sweet ladies,
   good night, good night.   [Exit.]
KING   [to Horatio]
Follow her close. Give her good watch, I pray you.
                                            [Exit Horatio.]
Oh, this is the poison of deep grief; it springs
All from her father's death—and now behold!
Oh, Gertrude, Gertrude,
When sorrows come, they come not single spies,   79
But in battalions. First, her father slain;
Next, your son gone, and he most violent author
Of his own just remove; the people muddied,   82
Thick and unwholesome in their thoughts and
   whispers
For good Polonius' death—and we have done but
   greenly,   84
In hugger-mugger to inter him; poor Ophelia   85
Divided from herself and her fair judgment,
Without the which we are pictures or mere beasts;
Last, and as much containing as all these,   88
Her brother is in secret come from France,

8 **unshapèd use** incoherent manner 9 **collection** inference, a guess
at some sort of meaning. **yawn** gape, wonder; grasp. (The Folio
reading, "aim," is possible.) 10 **botch** patch 11 **Which** which
words. **yield** deliver, represent 12–13 **there might . . . unhappily**
that a great deal could be guessed at of a most unfortunate nature,
even if one couldn't be at all sure. 15 **ill-breeding** prone to suspect
the worst and to make mischief 18 **toy** trifle. **amiss** calamity.
19–20 **So . . . spilt** Guilt is so burdened with conscience and guileless
fear of detection that it reveals itself through apprehension of disaster. 20.1 **Enter Ophelia** (In the First Quarto, Ophelia enters "*playing
on a lute, and her hair down, singing.*") 25 **cockle hat** hat with cock-
leshell stuck in it as a sign that the wearer had been a pilgrim to the
shrine of Saint James of Compostella in Spain 26 **shoon** shoes.
33 **Oho!** (Perhaps a sigh.) 38 **Larded** strewn, bedecked 40 **showers**
i.e., tears. 42 **God 'ild** God yield or reward. **owl** (Refers to a legend about a baker's daughter who was turned into an owl for being
ungenerous when Jesus begged a loaf of bread.)

45 **Conceit** Fancy, brooding 49 **betime** early 53 **dupped** did up,
opened 59 **Gis** Jesus 62 **Cock** (A perversion of "God" in oaths;
here also with a quibble on the slang word for penis.) 67 **An** if
79 **spies** scouts sent in advance of the main force 82 **remove**
removal. **muddied** stirred up, confused 84 **greenly** foolishly
85 **hugger-mugger** secret haste 88 **as much containing** as full of
serious matter

Feeds on this wonder, keeps himself in clouds,   90
And wants not buzzers to infect his ear   91
With pestilent speeches of his father's death,
Wherein necessity, of matter beggared,   93
Will nothing stick our person to arraign   94
In ear and ear. Oh, my dear Gertrude, this,   95
Like to a murd'ring piece, in many places   96
Gives me superfluous death.   *A noise within.*   97

QUEEN   Alack, what noise is this?

KING   Attend!   99
Where is my Switzers? Let them guard the door.   100

Enter a Messenger.

What is the matter?

MESSENGER   Save yourself, my lord!
The ocean, overpeering of his list,   102
Eats not the flats with more impetuous haste   103
Than young Laertes, in a riotous head,   104
O'erbears your officers. The rabble call him lord,
And, as the world were now but to begin,   106
Antiquity forgot, custom not known,   107
The ratifiers and props of every word,   108
They cry, "Choose we! Laertes shall be king!"
Caps, hands, and tongues applaud it to the clouds,   110
"Laertes shall be king, Laertes king!"

QUEEN
How cheerfully on the false trail they cry!
                                    A noise within.
Oh, this is counter, you false Danish dogs!   113

Enter Laertes with others.

KING   The doors are broke.

LAERTES
Where is this King?—Sirs, stand you all without.

ALL   No, let's come in.

LAERTES   I pray you, give me leave.

ALL   We will, we will.

LAERTES   I thank you. Keep the door. [*Exeunt followers.*]
                          Oh, thou vile king,
Give me my father!

QUEEN [*restraining him*]   Calmly, good Laertes.

LAERTES
That drop of blood that's calm proclaims me bastard,

Cries cuckold to my father, brands the harlot
Even here between the chaste unsmirchèd brow   123
Of my true mother.

KING   What is the cause, Laertes,
That thy rebellion looks so giantlike?   125
Let him go, Gertrude. Do not fear our person.   126
There's such divinity doth hedge a king   127
That treason can but peep to what it would,   128
Acts little of his will. Tell me, Laertes,   129
Why thou art thus incensed. Let him go, Gertrude.
Speak, man.

LAERTES   Where is my father?

KING   Dead.

QUEEN
But not by him.

KING   Let him demand his fill.

LAERTES
How came he dead? I'll not be juggled with.   133
To hell, allegiance! Vows, to the blackest devil!
Conscience and grace, to the profoundest pit!
I dare damnation. To this point I stand,   136
That both the worlds I give to negligence,   137
Let come what comes, only I'll be revenged
Most throughly for my father.   139

KING   Who shall stay you?

LAERTES   My will, not all the world's.   141
And for my means, I'll husband them so well   142
They shall go far with little.

KING   Good Laertes,
If you desire to know the certainty
Of your dear father, is't writ in your revenge
That, swoopstake, you will draw both friend and foe,   146
Winner and loser?

LAERTES   None but his enemies.

KING   Will you know them, then?

LAERTES
To his good friends thus wide I'll ope my arms,
And like the kind life-rendering pelican   151
Repast them with my blood.

KING   Why, now you speak   152
Like a good child and a true gentleman.
That I am guiltless of your father's death,
And am most sensibly in grief for it,   155
It shall as level to your judgment 'pear   156
As day does to your eye.   *A noise within.*

---

90 Feeds . . . clouds feeds his resentment on this whole shocking turn of events, keeps himself aloof and mysterious **91 wants** lacks. **buzzers** gossipers, informers **93 necessity** i.e., the need to invent some plausible explanation. **of matter beggared** unprovided with facts **94–5 Will . . . ear** will not hesitate to accuse my (royal) person in everybody's ears. **96 murd'ring piece** cannon loaded so as to scatter its shot **97 Gives . . . death** kills me over and over. **99 Attend!** Guard me! **100 Switzers** Swiss guards, mercenaries. **102 overpeering of his list** overflowing its shore, boundary **103 flats** i.e., flatlands near shore. **impetuous** violent (perhaps also with the meaning of *impiteous* ["impitious," Q2], "pitiless") **104 riotous head** insurrectionary advance **106–8 And . . . word** and, as if the world were to be started all over afresh, utterly setting aside all ancient traditional customs that should confirm and underprop our every word and promise **110 Caps** (The caps are thrown in the air.) **113 counter** (A hunting term, meaning to follow the trail in a direction opposite to that which the game has taken.)

123 between amidst **125 giantlike** (Recalling the rising of the giants of Greek mythology against Olympus.) **126 fear our** fear for my **127 hedge** protect, as with a surrounding barrier **128 can . . . would** can only peep furtively, as through a barrier, at what it would intend **129 Acts . . . will** (but) performs little of what it intends. **133 juggled with** cheated, deceived. **136 To . . . stand** I am resolved in this **137 both . . . negligence** i.e., both this world and the next are of no consequence to me **139 throughly** thoroughly **141 My will . . . world's** I'll stop (*stay*) when my will is accomplished, not for anyone else's. **142 for** as for **146 swoopstake** i.e., indiscriminately. (Literally, taking all stakes on the gambling table at once. *Draw* is also a gambling term, meaning "take from.") **151 pelican** (Refers to the belief that the female pelican fed its young with its own blood.) **152 Repast** feed **155 sensibly** feelingly **156 level** plain

LAERTES
How now, what noise is that?

Enter Ophelia.

KING   Let her come in.
LAERTES
O heat, dry up my brains! Tears seven times salt
Burn out the sense and virtue of mine eye!   160
By heaven, thy madness shall be paid with weight   161
Till our scale turn the beam. O rose of May!   162
Dear maid, kind sister, sweet Ophelia!
O heavens, is't possible a young maid's wits
Should be as mortal as an old man's life?
Nature is fine in love, and where 'tis fine   166
It sends some precious instance of itself   167
After the thing it loves.   168
OPHELIA
        "They bore him barefaced on the bier,   (*Song.*)
               Hey non nonny, nonny, hey nonny,
               And in his grave rained many a tear—"
Fare you well, my dove!
LAERTES
Hadst thou thy wits and didst persuade revenge,
It could not move thus.
OPHELIA   You must sing "A-down a-down," and you 175
"call him a-down-a." Oh, how the wheel becomes it! It 176
is the false steward that stole his master's daughter. 177
LAERTES   This nothing's more than matter.   178
OPHELIA   There's rosemary, that's for remembrance; 179
pray you, love, remember. And there is pansies; that's 180
for thoughts.
LAERTES   A document in madness, thoughts and re- 182
membrance fitted.
OPHELIA   There's fennel for you, and columbines. 184
There's rue for you, and here's some for me; we may 185
call it herb of grace o' Sundays. You must wear your
rue with a difference. There's a daisy. I would give 187
you some violets, but they withered all when my 188
father died. They say 'a made a good end—

[*Sings*] "For bonny sweet Robin is all my joy."
LAERTES
Thought and affliction, passion, hell itself,   191
She turns to favor and to prettiness.   192
OPHELIA
        "And will 'a not come again?   (*Song.*)
               And will 'a not come again?
               No, no, he is dead.
               Go to thy deathbed,
               He never will come again.

               "His beard was as white as snow,
               All flaxen was his poll.   199
               He is gone, he is gone,
               And we cast away moan.
               God ha' mercy on his soul!"
And of all Christian souls, I pray God. God b'wi'you.
               [*Exit, followed by Gertrude.*]
LAERTES   Do you see this, O God?
KING
Laertes, I must commune with your grief,
Or you deny me right. Go but apart,
Make choice of whom your wisest friends you will,   207
And they shall hear and judge twixt you and me.
If by direct or by collateral hand   209
They find us touched, we will our kingdom give,   210
Our crown, our life, and all that we call ours
To you in satisfaction; but if not,
Be you content to lend your patience to us,
And we shall jointly labor with your soul
To give it due content.   Let this be so.
LAERTES
His means of death, his obscure funeral—
No trophy, sword, nor hatchment o'er his bones,   217
No noble rite, nor formal ostentation—   218
Cry to be heard, as 'twere from heaven to earth,
That I must call't in question.
KING   So you shall,   220
And where th'offense is, let the great ax fall.
I pray you, go with me.   *Exeunt.*

[4.6]

Enter Horatio and others.

HORATIO
What are they that would speak with me?
GENTLEMAN   Seafaring men, sir. They say they have
letters for you.   3
HORATIO   Let them come in.   [*Exit Gentleman.*]
I do not know from what part of the world

---

160 virtue faculty, power   **161 paid with weight** repaid, avenged
equally or more   **162 beam** crossbar of a balance.   **166–8 Nature . . .
loves** Human nature is exquisitely sensitive in matters of love, and in
cases of sudden loss it sends some precious part of itself after the lost
object of that love. (In this case, Ophelia's sanity deserts her out of
sorrow for her lost father and perhaps too out of her love for Hamlet.)
175–6 You . . . a-down-a (Ophelia assigns the singing of refrains, like
her own "Hey non nonny," to others present.)   **176 wheel** spinning
wheel as accompaniment to the song, or refrain   **177 false steward**
(The story is unknown.)   **178 This . . . matter** This seeming nonsense
is more eloquent than sane utterance.   **179 rosemary** (Used as a symbol of remembrance both at weddings and at funerals.)   **180 pansies**
(Emblems of love and courtship; perhaps from French *pensées*,
"thoughts.")   **182 document** instruction, lesson   **184 There's fennel
. . . columbines** (*Fennel* betokens flattery; *columbines*, unchastity or
ingratitude. Throughout, Ophelia addresses her various listeners,
giving one flower to one and another to another, perhaps with particular symbolic significance in each case.)   **185 rue** (Emblem of repentance—a signification that is evident in its popular name, *herb of
grace*.)   **187 with a difference** (A device used in heraldry to distinguish one family from another on the coat of arms, here suggesting
that Ophelia and the others have different causes of sorrow and
repentance; perhaps with a play on *rue* in the sense of "ruth," "pity.")
daisy (Emblem of love's victims and of faithlessness.)   **188 violets**
(Emblems of faithfulness.)

191 Thought Melancholy.   **passion** suffering   **192 favor** grace,
beauty   **199 poll** head.   **207 whom** whichever of   **209 collateral
hand** indirect agency   **210 us touched** me implicated   **217 trophy**
memorial.   **hatchment** tablet displaying the armorial bearings of a
deceased person   **218 ostentation** ceremony   **220 That** so that.
call't in question demand an explanation.
4.6. Location: The castle.
3 letters a letter

I should be greeted, if not from Lord Hamlet.

Enter Sailors.

FIRST SAILOR   God bless you, sir.

HORATIO   Let him bless thee too.

FIRST SAILOR   'A shall, sir, an't please him. There's a   9
letter for you, sir—it came from th'ambassador that   10
was bound for England—if your name be Horatio, as
I am let to know it is.   [*He gives a letter.*]

HORATIO [*reads*]   "Horatio, when thou shalt have over-   13
looked this, give these fellows some means to the King;   14
they have letters for him. Ere we were two days old at
sea, a pirate of very warlike appointment gave us   16
chase. Finding ourselves too slow of sail, we put on a
compelled valor, and in the grapple I boarded them.
On the instant they got clear of our ship, so I alone
became their prisoner. They have dealt with me like
thieves of mercy, but they knew what they did: I am to   21
do a good turn for them. Let the King have the letters
I have sent, and repair thou to me with as much speed   23
as thou wouldest fly death. I have words to speak in
thine ear will make thee dumb, yet are they much too
light for the bore of the matter. These good fellows will   26
bring thee where I am. Rosencrantz and Guildenstern
hold their course for England. Of them I have much to
tell thee. Farewell.
            He that thou knowest thine, Hamlet."
Come, I will give you way for these your letters,   31
And do't the speedier that you may direct me
To him from whom you brought them.   *Exeunt.*

[4.7]

Enter King and Laertes.

KING
Now must your conscience my acquittance seal,   1
And you must put me in your heart for friend,
Sith you have heard, and with a knowing ear,   3
That he which hath your noble father slain
Pursued my life.

LAERTES   It well appears. But tell me
Why you proceeded not against these feats   6
So crimeful and so capital in nature,   7
As by your safety, greatness, wisdom, all things else,
You mainly were stirred up.   9

KING   Oh, for two special reasons,
Which may to you perhaps seem much unsinewed,   11
But yet to me they're strong. The Queen his mother
Lives almost by his looks, and for myself—
My virtue or my plague, be it either which—

She is so conjunctive to my life and soul   15
That, as the star moves not but in his sphere,   16
I could not but by her. The other motive
Why to a public count I might not go   18
Is the great love the general gender bear him,   19
Who, dipping all his faults in their affection,
Work like the spring that turneth wood to stone,   21
Convert his gyves to graces, so that my arrows,   22
Too slightly timbered for so loud a wind,   23
Would have reverted to my bow again
But not where I had aimed them.

LAERTES
And so have I a noble father lost,
A sister driven into desp'rate terms,   27
Whose worth, if praises may go back again,   28
Stood challenger on mount of all the age   29
For her perfections. But my revenge will come.

KING
Break not your sleeps for that. You must not think
That we are made of stuff so flat and dull
That we can let our beard be shook with danger
And think it pastime. You shortly shall hear more.
I loved your father, and we love ourself;
And that, I hope, will teach you to imagine—

Enter a Messenger with letters.

How now? What news?

MESSENGER   Letters, my lord, from Hamlet:
This to Your Majesty, this to the Queen.
            [*He gives letters.*]

KING   From Hamlet? Who brought them?

MESSENGER
Sailors, my lord, they say. I saw them not.
They were given me by Claudio. He received them
Of him that brought them.

KING   Laertes, you shall hear them.—
Leave us.   [*Exit Messenger.*]
[*He reads.*] "High and mighty, you shall know I am set
naked on your kingdom. Tomorrow shall I beg leave   45
to see your kingly eyes, when I shall, first asking your
pardon, thereunto recount the occasion of my sudden   47
and more strange return.   Hamlet."
What should this mean? Are all the rest come back?
Or is it some abuse, and no such thing?   50

LAERTES
Know you the hand?

KING   'Tis Hamlet's character. "Naked!"   51
And in a postscript here he says "alone."

---

9 **an't** if it   10 **th'ambassador** (Hamlet's ostensible role; see 3.1.172–3.)
13–14 **overlooked** looked over   14 **means** means of access
16 **appointment** equipage   21 **thieves of mercy** merciful thieves
23 **repair** come   26 **bore** caliber, i.e., importance   31 **way** means of
access
4.7. Location: The castle.
1 **my acquittance seal** confirm or acknowledge my innocence   3 **Sith**
since   6 **feats** acts   7 **capital** punishable by death   9 **mainly** greatly
11 **unsinewed** weak

15 **conjunctive** closely united. (An astronomical metaphor.)   16 **his**
its.   **sphere** one of the hollow spheres in which, according to Ptolemaic astronomy, the planets were supposed to move   18 **count**
account, reckoning, indictment   19 **general gender** common people
21 **Work** operate, act.   **spring** i.e., a spring with such a concentration
of lime that it coats a piece of wood with limestone, in effect gilding
and petrifying it   22 **gyves** fetters (which, gilded by the people's
praise, would look like badges of honor)   23 **Too . . . wind** with too
light a shaft for so powerful a gust (of popular sentiment)   27 **terms**
state, condition   28 **go back** recall what she was   29 **on mount** set
up on high   45 **naked** destitute, unarmed, without following
47 **pardon** (for returning without authorization)   50 **abuse** deceit.
no such thing not what the letter says.   51 **character** handwriting.

Can you devise me?   53

LAERTES
I am lost in it, my lord. But let him come.
It warms the very sickness in my heart
That I shall live and tell him to his teeth,
"Thus didst thou."

KING   If it be so, Laertes—   57
As how should it be so? How otherwise?—   58
Will you be ruled by me?

LAERTES   Ay, my lord,
So you will not o'errule me to a peace.   60

KING
To thine own peace. If he be now returned,
As checking at his voyage, and that he means   62
No more to undertake it, I will work him
To an exploit, now ripe in my device,   64
Under the which he shall not choose but fall;
And for his death no wind of blame shall breathe,
But even his mother shall uncharge the practice   67
And call it accident.

LAERTES   My lord, I will be ruled,
The rather if you could devise it so
That I might be the organ.

KING   It falls right.   70
You have been talked of since your travel much,
And that in Hamlet's hearing, for a quality
Wherein they say you shine. Your sum of parts   73
Did not together pluck such envy from him
As did that one, and that, in my regard,
Of the unworthiest siege.   76

LAERTES   What part is that, my lord?

KING
A very ribbon in the cap of youth,
Yet needful too, for youth no less becomes   79
The light and careless livery that it wears
Than settled age his sables and his weeds   81
Importing health and graveness. Two months since   82
Here was a gentleman of Normandy.
I have seen myself, and served against, the French,
And they can well on horseback, but this gallant   85
Had witchcraft in't; he grew unto his seat,
And to such wondrous doing brought his horse
As had he been incorpsed and demi-natured   88
With the brave beast. So far he topped my thought   89
That I in forgery of shapes and tricks   90
Come short of what he did.

LAERTES   A Norman was't?

KING   A Norman.   53

LAERTES
Upon my life, Lamord.

KING   The very same.

LAERTES
I know him well. He is the brooch indeed   94
And gem of all the nation.

KING   He made confession of you,   96
And gave you such a masterly report
For art and exercise in your defense,   98
And for your rapier most especial,
That he cried out 'twould be a sight indeed
If one could match you. Th'escrimers of their nation, 101
He swore, had neither motion, guard, nor eye
If you opposed them. Sir, this report of his
Did Hamlet so envenom with his envy
That he could nothing do but wish and beg
Your sudden coming o'er, to play with you.   106
Now, out of this—

LAERTES   What out of this, my lord?

KING
Laertes, was your father dear to you?
Or are you like the painting of a sorrow,
A face without a heart?

LAERTES   Why ask you this?

KING
Not that I think you did not love your father,
But that I know love is begun by time,   112
And that I see, in passages of proof,   113
Time qualifies the spark and fire of it.   114
There lives within the very flame of love
A kind of wick or snuff that will abate it,   116
And nothing is at a like goodness still,   117
For goodness, growing to a pleurisy,   118
Dies in his own too much. That we would do,   119
We should do when we would; for this "would"
    changes
And hath abatements and delays as many   121
As there are tongues, are hands, are accidents,   122
And then this "should" is like a spendthrift sigh,   123
That hurts by easing. But, to the quick o'th'ulcer: 124
Hamlet comes back. What would you undertake
To show yourself in deed your father's son
More than in words?

LAERTES   To cut his throat i'th' church.

53 devise explain to   **57 Thus didst thou** i.e., Here's for what you did to my father.   **58 As . . . otherwise?** how can this (Hamlet's return) be true? Yet how otherwise than true (since we have the evidence of his letter)?   **60 So** provided that   **62 checking at** i.e., turning aside from (like a falcon leaving the quarry to fly at a chance bird).   **that if**   **64 device** devising, invention   **67 uncharge the practice** acquit the stratagem of being a plot   **70 organ** agent, instrument.   **73 Your . . . parts** All your other virtues   **76 unworthiest siege** least important rank.   **79 no less becomes** is no less adorned by   **81–2 his sables . . . graveness** its rich robes furred with sable and its garments denoting dignified well-being and seriousness.   **85 can well** are skilled   **88–9 As . . . beast** as if, centaurlike, he had been made into one body with the horse, possessing half its nature.   **89 topped** surpassed   **90 forgery** fabrication

94 brooch ornament   **96 confession** testimonial, admission of superiority   **98 For . . . defense** with respect to your skill and practice with your weapon   **101 Th'escrimers** The fencers   **106 sudden** immediate.   **play** fence   **112 begun by time** i.e., created by the right circumstance and hence subject to change   **113 passages of proof** actual well-attested instances   **114 qualifies** weakens, moderates   **116 snuff** the charred part of a candlewick   **117 nothing . . . still** nothing remains at a constant level of perfection   **118 pleurisy** excess, plethora. (Literally, a chest inflammation.)   **119 in . . . much** of its own excess.   **That** That which   **121 abatements** diminutions   **122 As . . . accidents** as there are tongues to dissuade, hands to prevent, and chance events to intervene   **123 spendthrift sigh** (An allusion to the belief that sighs draw blood from the heart.)   **124 hurts by easing** i.e., costs the heart blood and wastes precious opportunity even while it affords emotional relief.   **quick o'th'ulcer** i.e., heart of the matter

KING
No place, indeed, should murder sanctuarize;   128
Revenge should have no bounds. But good Laertes,
Will you do this, keep close within your chamber.   130
Hamlet returned shall know you are come home.
We'll put on those shall praise your excellence   132
And set a double varnish on the fame
The Frenchman gave you, bring you in fine together,   134
And wager on your heads. He, being remiss,   135
Most generous, and free from all contriving,   136
Will not peruse the foils, so that with ease,
Or with a little shuffling, you may choose
A sword unbated, and in a pass of practice   139
Requite him for your father.

LAERTES   I will do't,
And for that purpose I'll anoint my sword.
I bought an unction of a mountebank   142
So mortal that, but dip a knife in it,
Where it draws blood no cataplasm so rare,   144
Collected from all simples that have virtue   145
Under the moon, can save the thing from death   146
That is but scratched withal. I'll touch my point
With this contagion, that if I gall him slightly,   148
It may be death.

KING   Let's further think of this,
Weigh what convenience both of time and means
May fit us to our shape. If this should fail,   151
And that our drift look through our bad performance,   152
'Twere better not assayed. Therefore this project
Should have a back or second, that might hold
If this did blast in proof. Soft, let me see.   155
We'll make a solemn wager on your cunnings—   156
I ha 't!
When in your motion you are hot and dry—
As make your bouts more violent to that end—   159
And that he calls for drink, I'll have prepared him
A chalice for the nonce, whereon but sipping,   161
If he by chance escape your venomed stuck,   162
Our purpose may hold there. [*A cry within.*] But stay,
what noise?

Enter Queen.

QUEEN
One woe doth tread upon another's heel,
So fast they follow. Your sister's drowned, Laertes.

LAERTES   Drowned! Oh, where?

QUEEN
There is a willow grows askant the brook,   167
That shows his hoar leaves in the glassy stream;   168
Therewith fantastic garlands did she make
Of crowflowers, nettles, daisies, and long purples,   170
That liberal shepherds give a grosser name,   171
But our cold maids do dead men's fingers call them.   172
There on the pendent boughs her crownet weeds   173
Clamb'ring to hang, an envious sliver broke,   174
When down her weedy trophies and herself   175
Fell in the weeping brook. Her clothes spread wide,
And mermaidlike awhile they bore her up,
Which time she chanted snatches of old lauds,   178
As one incapable of her own distress,   179
Or like a creature native and endued   180
Unto that element. But long it could not be
Till that her garments, heavy with their drink,
Pulled the poor wretch from her melodious lay   183
To muddy death.

LAERTES   Alas, then she is drowned?

QUEEN   Drowned, drowned.

LAERTES
Too much of water hast thou, poor Ophelia,
And therefore I forbid my tears. But yet
It is our trick; nature her custom holds,   188
Let shame say what it will. [*He weeps.*] When these
are gone,   189
The woman will be out. Adieu, my lord.   190
I have a speech of fire that fain would blaze,
But that this folly douts it.   *Exit.*

KING   Let's follow, Gertrude.   192
How much I had to do to calm his rage!
Now fear I this will give it start again;
Therefore let's follow.   *Exeunt.*

[5.1]

Enter two Clowns [with spades and mattocks].

FIRST CLOWN   Is she to be buried in Christian burial,
when she willfully seeks her own salvation?   2

128 **sanctuarize** protect from punishment. (Alludes to the right of sanctuary with which certain religious places were invested.)
130 **Will you do this** if you wish to do this   132 **put on those shall** arrange for some to   134 **in fine** finally   135 **remiss** negligently unsuspicious   136 **generous** noble-minded   139 **unbated** not blunted, having no button.   **pass of practice** treacherous thrust in an arranged bout   142 **unction** ointment.   **mountebank** quack doctor
144 **cataplasm** plaster or poultice   145 **simples** herbs.   **virtue** potency   146 **Under the moon** i.e., anywhere (with reference perhaps to the belief that herbs gathered at night had a special power)
148 **gall** graze, wound   151 **shape** part we propose to act.   152 **drift ... performance** intention should be made visible by our bungling
155 **blast in proof** come to grief when put to the test.   156 **cunnings** respective skills   159 **As** i.e., and you should   161 **nonce** occasion
162 **stuck** thrust. (From *stoccado*, a fencing term.)

167 **askant** aslant   168 **hoar leaves** white or gray undersides of the leaves   170 **long purples** early purple orchids   171 **liberal** free-spoken.   **a grosser name** (The testicle-resembling tubers of the orchid, which also in some cases resemble *dead men's fingers*, have earned various slang names like "dogstones" and "cullions.")   172 **cold** chaste
173 **pendent** overhanging.   **crownet** made into a chaplet or coronet
174 **envious sliver** malicious branch   175 **weedy** i.e., of plants
178 **lauds** hymns   179 **incapable of** lacking capacity to apprehend
180 **endued** adapted by nature   183 **lay** ballad, song   188 **It is our trick** i.e., weeping is our natural way (when sad)   189–90 **When ... out** When my tears are all shed, the woman in me will be expended, satisfied.   192 **douts** extinguishes. (The Second Quarto reads "drownes.")
5.1 Location: A churchyard.
0.1 *Clowns* rustics   2 **salvation** (A blunder for "damnation," or perhaps a suggestion that Ophelia was taking her own shortcut to heaven.)

SECOND CLOWN   I tell thee she is; therefore make her grave straight. The crowner hath sat on her, and finds it Christian burial.   4 5

FIRST CLOWN   How can that be, unless she drowned herself in her own defense?

SECOND CLOWN   Why, 'tis found so.   8

FIRST CLOWN   It must be *se offendendo*, it cannot be else. For here lies the point: if I drown myself wittingly, it argues an act, and an act hath three branches—it is to act, to do, and to perform. Argal, she drowned herself wittingly.   9   12

SECOND CLOWN   Nay, but hear you, goodman delver—   14

FIRST CLOWN   Give me leave. Here lies the water; good. Here stands the man; good. If the man go to this water and drown himself, it is, will he, nill he, he goes, mark you that. But if the water come to him and drown him, he drowns not himself. Argal, he that is not guilty of his own death shortens not his own life.   17

SECOND CLOWN   But is this law?

FIRST CLOWN   Ay, marry, is't—crowner's quest law.   22

SECOND CLOWN   Will you ha' the truth on't? If this had not been a gentlewoman, she should have been buried out o' Christian burial.

FIRST CLOWN   Why, there thou say'st. And the more pity that great folk should have countenance in this world to drown or hang themselves, more than their even-Christian. Come, my spade. There is no ancient gentlemen but gardeners, ditchers, and grave makers. They hold up Adam's profession.   26   27   29   31

SECOND CLOWN   Was he a gentleman?

FIRST CLOWN   'A was the first that ever bore arms.   33

SECOND CLOWN   Why, he had none.

FIRST CLOWN   What, art a heathen? How dost thou understand the Scripture? The Scripture says Adam digged. Could he dig without arms? I'll put another question to thee. If thou answerest me not to the purpose, confess thyself—   37   39

SECOND CLOWN   Go to.

FIRST CLOWN   What is he that builds stronger than either the mason, the shipwright, or the carpenter?

SECOND CLOWN   The gallows maker, for that frame outlives a thousand tenants.   43

FIRST CLOWN   I like thy wit well, in good faith. The gallows does well. But how does it well? It does well to those that do ill. Now thou dost ill to say the gallows   46

is built stronger than the church. Argal, the gallows may do well to thee. To't again, come.

SECOND CLOWN   "Who builds stronger than a mason, a shipwright, or a carpenter?"

FIRST CLOWN   Ay, tell me that, and unyoke.   52

SECOND CLOWN   Marry, now I can tell.

FIRST CLOWN   To't.

SECOND CLOWN   Mass, I cannot tell.   55

Enter Hamlet and Horatio [at a distance].

FIRST CLOWN   Cudgel thy brains no more about it, for your dull ass will not mend his pace with beating; and when you are asked this question next, say "a grave maker." The houses he makes lasts till doomsday. Go get thee in and fetch me a stoup of liquor.   60

[*Exit Second Clown. First Clown digs.*]
Song.

"In youth, when I did love, did love,
    Methought it was very sweet,
To contract—oh—the time for—a—my behove,
    Oh, methought there—a—was nothing—a—
        meet."   61   63   64

HAMLET   Has this fellow no feeling of his business, 'a sings in grave-making?   65

HORATIO   Custom hath made it in him a property of easiness.   67   68

HAMLET   'Tis e'en so. The hand of little employment hath the daintier sense.   70

FIRST CLOWN   *Song.*
"But age with his stealing steps
    Hath clawed me in his clutch,
And hath shipped me into the land,
    As if I had never been such."   73

[*He throws up a skull.*]

HAMLET   That skull had a tongue in it and could sing once. How the knave jowls it to the ground, as if 'twere Cain's jawbone, that did the first murder! This might be the pate of a politician, which this ass now o'erreaches, one that would circumvent God, might it not?   76   78   79

HORATIO   It might, my lord.

HAMLET   Or of a courtier, which could say, "Good morrow, sweet lord! How dost thou, sweet lord?" This might be my Lord Such-a-one, that praised my Lord Such-a-one's horse when 'a meant to beg it, might it not?

HORATIO   Ay, my lord.

4 straight straightway, immediately. (But with a pun on *strait*, "narrow.") **crowner** coroner. **sat on her** conducted an inquest on her case **4–5 finds it** gives his official verdict that her means of death was consistent with **8 found so** determined so in the coroner's verdict. **9 se offendendo** (A comic mistake for *se defendendo,* a term used in verdicts of self-defense.) **12 Argal** (Corruption of *ergo,* "therefore.") **14 goodman** (An honorific title often used with the name of a profession or craft.) **17 will he, nill he** whether he will or no, willy-nilly **22 quest** inquest **26 there thou say'st** i.e., that's right. **27 countenance** privilege **29 even-Christian** fellow Christians. **ancient** going back to ancient times **31 hold up** maintain **33 bore arms** (To be entitled to bear a coat of arms would make Adam a gentleman, but as one who bore a spade, our common ancestor was an ordinary delver in the earth.) **37 arms** i.e., the arms of the body. **39 confess thyself** (The saying continues, "and be hanged.") **43 frame** (1) gallows (2) structure **46 does well** (1) is an apt answer (2) does a good turn.

52 **unyoke** i.e., after this great effort, you may unharness the team of your wits. **55 Mass** By the Mass **60 stoup** two-quart measure **61 In . . . love** (This and the two following stanzas, with nonsensical variations, are from a poem attributed to Lord Vaux and printed in *Tottel's Miscellany,* 1557. The *oh* and *a* [for "ah"] seemingly are the grunts of the digger.) **63 To contract . . . behove** i.e., to shorten the time for my own advantage. (Perhaps he means to *prolong* it.) **64 meet** suitable, i.e., more suitable. **65 'a** that he **67–8 property of easiness** something he can do easily and indifferently. **70 daintier sense** more delicate sense of feeling. **73 into the land** i.e., toward my grave (?) (But note the lack of rhyme in *steps, land.*) **76 jowls** dashes. (With a pun on *jowl,* "jawbone.") **78 politician** schemer, plotter **79 o'erreaches** circumvents, gets the better of

HAMLET   Why, e'en so, and now my Lady Worm's,
chapless, and knocked about the mazard with a sex-   89
ton's spade. Here's fine revolution, an we had the trick   90
to see't. Did these bones cost no more the breeding   91
but to play at loggets with them? Mine ache to think   92
on't.

FIRST CLOWN   *Song.*
     "A pickax and a spade, a spade,
           For and a shrouding sheet;   95
     Oh, a pit of clay for to be made
           For such a guest is meet."
                          [*He throws up another skull.*]

HAMLET   There's another. Why may not that be the skull
of a lawyer? Where be his quiddities now, his quilli-   99
ties, his cases, his tenures, and his tricks? Why does   100
he suffer this mad knave now to knock him about the
sconce with a dirty shovel, and will not tell him of his   102
action of battery? Hum, this fellow might be in 's time   103
a great buyer of land, with his statutes, his recogni-   104
zances, his fines, his double vouchers, his recoveries.   105
Is this the fine of his fines and the recovery of his   106
recoveries, to have his fine pate full of fine dirt? Will   107
his vouchers vouch him no more of his purchases, and   108
double ones too, than the length and breadth of a   109
pair of indentures? The very conveyances of his lands   110
will scarcely lie in this box, and must th'inheritor   111
himself have no more, ha?

HORATIO   Not a jot more, my lord.

HAMLET   Is not parchment made of sheepskins?

HORATIO   Ay, my lord, and of calves' skins too.

HAMLET   They are sheep and calves which seek out as-   116
surance in that. I will speak to this fellow.—Whose   117
grave's this, sirrah?   118

FIRST CLOWN   Mine, sir.
     [*Sings*] "Oh, pit of clay for to be made
           For such a guest is meet."

HAMLET   I think it be thine, indeed, for thou liest in't.

FIRST CLOWN   You lie out on't, sir, and therefore 'tis
not yours. For my part, I do not lie in't, yet it is mine.

HAMLET   Thou dost lie in't, to be in't and say it is
thine. 'Tis for the dead, not for the quick; therefore   126
thou liest.

FIRST CLOWN   'Tis a quick lie, sir; 'twill away again
from me to you.

HAMLET   What man dost thou dig it for?

FIRST CLOWN   For no man, sir.

HAMLET   What woman, then?

FIRST CLOWN   For none, neither.

HAMLET   Who is to be buried in't?

FIRST CLOWN   One that was a woman, sir, but, rest her
soul, she's dead.

HAMLET   How absolute the knave is! We must speak by   137
the card, or equivocation will undo us. By the Lord,   138
Horatio, this three years I have took note of it: the age   139
is grown so picked that the toe of the peasant comes so   140
near the heel of the courtier he galls his kibe.—How   141
long hast thou been grave maker?

FIRST CLOWN   Of all the days i'th' year, I came to't that
day that our last king Hamlet overcame Fortinbras.

HAMLET   How long is that since?

FIRST CLOWN   Cannot you tell that? Every fool can tell
that. It was that very day that young Hamlet was
born—he that is mad and sent into England.

HAMLET   Ay, marry, why was he sent into England?

FIRST CLOWN   Why, because 'a was mad. 'A shall
recover his wits there, or if 'a do not, 'tis no great
matter there.

HAMLET   Why?

FIRST CLOWN   'Twill not be seen in him there. There the
men are as mad as he.

HAMLET   How came he mad?

FIRST CLOWN   Very strangely, they say.

HAMLET   How strangely?

FIRST CLOWN   Faith, e'en with losing his wits.

HAMLET   Upon what ground?   160

FIRST CLOWN   Why, here in Denmark. I have been
sexton here, man and boy, thirty years.

HAMLET   How long will a man lie i'th'earth ere he rot?

FIRST CLOWN   Faith, if 'a be not rotten before 'a die—as
we have many pocky corpses nowadays, that will   165
scarce hold the laying in—'a will last you some eight   166
year or nine year. A tanner will last you nine year.

HAMLET   Why he more than another?

FIRST CLOWN   Why, sir, his hide is so tanned with his
trade that 'a will keep out water a great while, and

---

89 **chapless** having no lower jaw. **mazard** i.e., head. (Literally, a
drinking vessel.) 90 **revolution** turn of Fortune's wheel, change.
trick knack 91–2 **cost ... but** involve so little expense and care in
upbringing that we may 92 **loggets** a game in which pieces of hard
wood shaped like Indian clubs or bowling pins are thrown to lie as
near as possible to a stake 95 **For and** and moreover 99–100 **his
quiddities . . . quillities** his subtleties, his legal niceties 100 **tenures**
the holding of a piece of property or office, or the conditions or
period of such holding 102 **sconce** head 103 **action of battery** lawsuit about physical assault. 104 **his statutes** his legal documents
acknowledging obligation of a debt 104–5 **recognizances** bonds
undertaking to repay debts 105 **fines** procedures for converting
entailed estates into "fee simple" or freehold. **double vouchers**
vouchers signed by two signatories guaranteeing the legality of real
estate titles. **recoveries** suits to obtain the authority of a court judgment for the holding of land. 106–7 **Is this ... dirt?** Is this the end of
his legal maneuvers and profitable land deals, to have the skull of his
elegant head filled full of minutely sifted dirt? (With multiple wordplay on *fine* and *fines*.) 107–10 **Will . . . indentures?** Will his vouchers, even double ones, guarantee him no more land than is needed to
bury him in, being no bigger than the deed of conveyance? (An
indenture is literally a legal document drawn up in duplicate on a single sheet and then cut apart on a zigzag line so that each pair was
uniquely matched.) 111 **box** (1) deed box (2) coffin. **th'inheritor**
the acquirer, owner 116–17 **assurance in that** safety in legal parch-
ments. 118 **sirrah** (A term of address to inferiors.)

126 **quick** living 137 **absolute** strict, precise 137–8 **by the card** i.e.,
with precision. (Literally, by the mariner's compass-card, on which
the points of the compass were marked.) 138 **equivocation** ambiguity in the use of terms 139 **took** taken 139–41 **the age . . . kibe** i.e.,
the age has grown so finical and mannered that the lower classes ape
their social betters, chafing at their heels. (*Kibes* are chilblains on the
heels.) 160 **ground** cause. (But, in the next line, the gravedigger
takes the word in the sense of "land," "country.") 165 **pocky** rotten,
diseased. (Literally, with the pox, or syphilis.) 166 **hold the laying
in** hold together long enough to be interred. **last you** last. (*You* is
used colloquially here and in the following lines.)

your water is a sore decayer of your whoreson dead 171
body. [*He picks up a skull.*] Here's a skull now hath
lien you i'th'earth three-and-twenty years. 173

HAMLET   Whose was it?

FIRST CLOWN   A whoreson mad fellow's it was. Whose
do you think it was?

HAMLET   Nay, I know not.

FIRST CLOWN   A pestilence on him for a mad rogue! 'A
poured a flagon of Rhenish on my head once. This 179
same skull, sir, was, sir, Yorick's skull, the King's jester.

HAMLET   This?

FIRST CLOWN   E'en that.

HAMLET   Let me see. [*He takes the skull.*] Alas, poor
Yorick! I knew him, Horatio, a fellow of infinite jest, of
most excellent fancy. He hath bore me on his back a 185
thousand times, and now how abhorred in my
imagination it is! My gorge rises at it. Here hung those 187
lips that I have kissed I know not how oft. Where be
your gibes now? Your gambols, your songs, your 189
flashes of merriment that were wont to set the table on
a roar? Not one now, to mock your own grinning?
Quite chopfallen? Now get you to my lady's chamber 192
and tell her, let her paint an inch thick, to this favor 193
she must come. Make her laugh at that. Prithee,
Horatio, tell me one thing.

HORATIO   What's that, my lord?

HAMLET   Dost thou think Alexander looked o' this
fashion i'th'earth?

HORATIO   E'en so.

HAMLET   And smelt so? Pah! [*He throws down the skull.*]

HORATIO   E'en so, my lord.

HAMLET   To what base uses we may return, Horatio!
Why may not imagination trace the noble dust of
Alexander till 'a find it stopping a bunghole? 204

HORATIO   'Twere to consider too curiously to consider 205
so.

HAMLET   No, faith, not a jot, but to follow him thither
with modesty enough, and likelihood to lead it. As 208
thus: Alexander died, Alexander was buried, Alexander returneth to dust, the dust is earth, of earth we
make loam, and why of that loam whereto he was 211
converted might they not stop a beer barrel?
Imperious Caesar, dead and turned to clay, 213
Might stop a hole to keep the wind away.
Oh, that that earth which kept the world in awe
Should patch a wall t'expel the winter's flaw! 216

Enter King, Queen, Laertes, and the corpse [of
Ophelia, in procession, with Priest, lords, etc.].

But soft, but soft awhile! Here comes the King, 217

The Queen, the courtiers. Who is this they follow?
And with such maimèd rites? This doth betoken 219
The corpse they follow did with desperate hand
Fordo it own life. 'Twas of some estate. 221
Couch we awhile and mark. 222

[*He and Horatio conceal themselves.*
Ophelia's body is taken to the grave.]

LAERTES   What ceremony else?

HAMLET [*to Horatio*]
That is Laertes, a very noble youth. Mark.

LAERTES   What ceremony else?

PRIEST
Her obsequies have been as far enlarged
As we have warranty. Her death was doubtful, 227
And but that great command o'ersways the order 228
She should in ground unsanctified been lodged 229
Till the last trumpet. For charitable prayers, 230
Shards, flints, and pebbles should be thrown on her. 231
Yet here she is allowed her virgin crants, 232
Her maiden strewments, and the bringing home 233
Of bell and burial. 234

LAERTES
Must there no more be done?

PRIEST   No more be done.
We should profane the service of the dead
To sing a requiem and such rest to her 237
As to peace-parted souls.

LAERTES   Lay her i'th'earth, 238
And from her fair and unpolluted flesh
May violets spring! I tell thee, churlish priest, 240
A ministering angel shall my sister be
When thou liest howling.

HAMLET [*to Horatio*]   What, the fair Ophelia! 242

QUEEN [*scattering flowers*]   Sweets to the sweet! Farewell.
I hoped thou shouldst have been my Hamlet's wife.
I thought thy bride-bed to have decked, sweet maid,
And not t' have strewed thy grave.

LAERTES   Oh, treble woe
Fall ten times treble on that cursèd head
Whose wicked deed thy most ingenious sense 248
Deprived thee of! Hold off the earth awhile,
Till I have caught her once more in mine arms.

[*He leaps into the grave and embraces Ophelia.*]
Now pile your dust upon the quick and dead,
Till of this flat a mountain you have made
T' o'ertop old Pelion or the skyish head 253
Of blue Olympus.

---

219 maimèd mutilated, incomplete   **221 Fordo it** destroy its.   **estate** rank.   **222 Couch we** Let's hide, lie low   **227 warranty** i.e., ecclesiastical authority.   **228 order** (1) prescribed practice (2) religious order of clerics   **229 She should . . . lodged** she should have been buried in unsanctified ground   **230 For** In place of   **231 Shards** broken bits of pottery   **232 crants** garlands betokening maidenhood   **233 strewments** flowers strewn on a coffin   **233–4 bringing . . . burial** laying the body to rest, to the sound of the bell.   **237 such rest** i.e., to pray for such rest   **238 peace-parted souls** those who have died at peace with God.   **240 violets** (See 4.5.188 and note.)   **242 howling** i.e., in hell.   **248 ingenious sense** a mind that is quick, alert, of fine qualities   **253 Pelion** a mountain in northern Thessaly; compare *Olympus* and *Ossa* in lines 254 and 286. (In their rebellion against the Olympian gods, the giants attempted to heap Ossa on Pelion in order to scale Olympus.)

---

171 sore keen, veritable.   **whoreson** (An expression of contemptuous familiarity.)   **173 lien you** lain. (See the note at line 166.)   **179 Rhenish** Rhine wine   **185 bore** borne   **187 My gorge rises** i.e., I feel nauseated   **189 gibes** taunts   **192 chopfallen** (1) lacking the lower jaw (2) dejected.   **193 favor** aspect, appearance   **204 bunghole** hole for filling or emptying a cask.   **205 curiously** minutely   **208 with . . . lead it** with moderation and plausibility.   **211 loam** a mixture of clay, straw, sand, etc. used to mold bricks, or, in this case, bungs for a beer barrel   **213 Imperious** Imperial   **216 flaw** gust of wind.   **217 soft** i.e., wait, be careful

HAMLET [*coming forward*]   What is he whose grief
   Bears such an emphasis, whose phrase of sorrow   255
   Conjures the wandering stars and makes them stand   256
   Like wonder-wounded hearers? This is I,   257
   Hamlet the Dane.   258
LAERTES [*grappling with him*]   The devil take thy soul!   259
HAMLET   Thou pray'st not well.
   I prithee, take thy fingers from my throat,
   For though I am not splenitive and rash,   262
   Yet have I in me something dangerous,
   Which let thy wisdom fear. Hold off thy hand.
KING   Pluck them asunder.
QUEEN   Hamlet, Hamlet!
ALL   Gentlemen!
HORATIO   Good my lord, be quiet.
           [*Hamlet and Laertes are parted.*]
HAMLET
   Why, I will fight with him upon this theme
   Until my eyelids will no longer wag.   270
QUEEN   Oh, my son, what theme?
HAMLET
   I loved Ophelia. Forty thousand brothers
   Could not with all their quantity of love
   Make up my sum. What wilt thou do for her?
KING   Oh, he is mad, Laertes.
QUEEN   For love of God, forbear him.   276
HAMLET
   'Swounds, show me what thou'lt do.   277
   Woo't weep? Woo't fight? Woo't fast? Woo't tear
     thyself?   278
   Woo't drink up eisel? Eat a crocodile?   279
   I'll do't. Dost come here to whine?
   To outface me with leaping in her grave?
   Be buried quick with her, and so will I.   282
   And if thou prate of mountains, let them throw
   Millions of acres on us, till our ground,
   Singeing his pate against the burning zone,   285
   Make Ossa like a wart! Nay, an thou'lt mouth,   286
   I'll rant as well as thou.
QUEEN   This is mere madness,   287
   And thus awhile the fit will work on him;
   Anon, as patient as the female dove

When that her golden couplets are disclosed,   290
   His silence will sit drooping.
HAMLET   Hear you, sir.
   What is the reason that you use me thus?
   I loved you ever. But it is no matter.
   Let Hercules himself do what he may,   294
   The cat will mew, and dog will have his day.   295
                Exit Hamlet.
KING
   I pray thee, good Horatio, wait upon him.
               [*Exit*] *Horatio.*
   [*To Laertes*] Strengthen your patience in our last
     night's speech;   297
   We'll put the matter to the present push.—   298
   Good Gertrude, set some watch over your son.—
   This grave shall have a living monument.   300
   An hour of quiet shortly shall we see;   301
   Till then, in patience our proceeding be.   *Exeunt.*

                    ❧

[5.2]

Enter Hamlet and Horatio.

HAMLET
   So much for this, sir; now shall you see the other.   1
   You do remember all the circumstance?
HORATIO   Remember it, my lord!
HAMLET
   Sir, in my heart there was a kind of fighting
   That would not let me sleep. Methought I lay
   Worse than the mutines in the bilboes. Rashly,   6
   And praised be rashness for it—let us know   7
   Our indiscretion sometime serves us well   8
   When our deep plots do pall, and that should learn us 9
   There's a divinity that shapes our ends,
   Rough-hew them how we will—
HORATIO   That is most certain.   11
HAMLET   Up from my cabin,
   My sea-gown scarfed about me, in the dark   13
   Groped I to find out them, had my desire,   14
   Fingered their packet, and in fine withdrew   15
   To mine own room again, making so bold,
   My fears forgetting manners, to unseal
   Their grand commission; where I found, Horatio—
   Ah, royal knavery!—an exact command,

---

255 emphasis i.e., rhetorical and florid emphasis. (*Phrase* has a similar rhetorical connotation.)   **256 wandering stars** planets   **257 wonder-wounded** struck with amazement   **258 the Dane** (This title normally signifies the King; see 1.1.17 and note.)   **259 s.d. *grappling with him*** The testimony of the First Quarto that "*Hamlet leaps in after Laertes*" and of the ballad "Elegy on Burbage," published in *Gentleman's Magazine* in 1825 ("Oft have I seen him leap into a grave") seem to indicate one way in which this fight was staged; however, the difficulty of fitting two contenders with Ophelia's body into a confined space (probably the trapdoor) suggests to many editors the alternative, that Laertes jumps out of the grave to attack Hamlet.)   **262 splenitive** quick-tempered   **270 wag** move. (A fluttering eyelid is a conventional sign that life has not yet gone.)   **276 forbear him** leave him alone.   **277 'Swounds** By His (Christ's) wounds   **278 Woo't** Wilt thou   **279 Woo't . . . eisel?** Will you drink up a whole draft of vinegar? (An extremely self-punishing task as a way of expressing grief.) **crocodile** (Crocodiles were tough and dangerous, and were supposed to shed crocodile tears.)   **282 quick** alive   **285 his pate** its head, i.e., top.   **burning zone** zone in the celestial sphere containing the sun's orbit, between the tropics of Cancer and Capricorn   **286 Ossa** (See 253n.)   **an thou'lt mouth** if you want to rant   **287 mere** utter

290 golden couplets two baby pigeons, covered with yellow down. **disclosed** hatched   **294–5 Let . . . day** i.e., (1) Even Hercules couldn't stop Laertes's theatrical rant (2) I, too, will have my turn; i.e., despite any blustering attempts at interference, every person will sooner or later do what he or she must do.   **297 in** i.e., by recalling   **298 present push** immediate test.   **300 living** lasting. (For Laertes' private understanding, Claudius also hints that Hamlet's death will serve as such a monument.)   **301 hour of quiet** time free of conflict
5.2 Location: The castle.
1 see the other hear the other news. (See 4.6.24–6.)   **6 mutines** mutineers.   **bilboes** shackles.   **Rashly** On impulse. (This adverb goes with lines 12 ff.)   **7 know** acknowledge   **8 indiscretion** lack of foresight and judgment (not an indiscreet act)   **9 pall** fail, falter, go stale. **learn** teach   **11 Rough-hew** shape roughly   **13 sea-gown** seaman's coat.   **scarfed** loosely wrapped   **14 them** i.e., Rosencrantz and Guildenstern   **15 Fingered** pilfered, pinched.   **in fine** finally, in conclusion

Larded with many several sorts of reasons   20
Importing Denmark's health and England's too,   21
With, ho! such bugs and goblins in my life,   22
That on the supervise, no leisure bated,   23
No, not to stay the grinding of the ax,   24
My head should be struck off.
HORATIO   Is't possible?
HAMLET [*giving a document*]
  Here's the commission. Read it at more leisure.
  But wilt thou hear now how I did proceed?
HORATIO   I beseech you.
HAMLET
  Being thus benetted round with villainies—
  Ere I could make a prologue to my brains,   30
  They had begun the play—I sat me down,   31
  Devised a new commission, wrote it fair.   32
  I once did hold it, as our statists do,   33
  A baseness to write fair, and labored much   34
  How to forget that learning, but, sir, now
  It did me yeoman's service. Wilt thou know
  Th'effect of what I wrote?
HORATIO   Ay, good my lord.
HAMLET
  An earnest conjuration from the King,   38
  As England was his faithful tributary,
  As love between them like the palm might flourish,   40
  As peace should still her wheaten garland wear   41
  And stand a comma 'tween their amities,   42
  And many suchlike "as"es of great charge,   43
  That on the view and knowing of these contents,
  Without debatement further more or less,
  He should those bearers put to sudden death,
  Not shriving time allowed.
HORATIO   How was this sealed?   47
HAMLET
  Why, even in that was heaven ordinant.   48
  I had my father's signet in my purse,   49
  Which was the model of that Danish seal;   50
  Folded the writ up in the form of th'other,   51
  Subscribed it, gave't th'impression, placed it safely,   52
  The changeling never known. Now, the next day   53
  Was our sea fight, and what to this was sequent   54
  Thou knowest already.

HORATIO
  So Guildenstern and Rosencrantz go to't.
HAMLET
  Why, man, they did make love to this employment.
  They are not near my conscience. Their defeat   58
  Does by their own insinuation grow.   59
  'Tis dangerous when the baser nature comes   60
  Between the pass and fell incensèd points   61
  Of mighty opposites.
HORATIO   Why, what a king is this!   62
HAMLET
  Does it not, think thee, stand me now upon—   63
  He that hath killed my king and whored my mother,
  Popped in between th'election and my hopes,   65
  Thrown out his angle for my proper life,   66
  And with such coz'nage—is't not perfect conscience   67
  To quit him with this arm? And is't not to be damned   68
  To let this canker of our nature come   69
  In further evil?   70
HORATIO
  It must be shortly known to him from England
  What is the issue of the business there.
HAMLET
  It will be short. The interim is mine,
  And a man's life's no more than to say "one."   74
  But I am very sorry, good Horatio,
  That to Laertes I forgot myself,
  For by the image of my cause I see
  The portraiture of his. I'll court his favors.
  But, sure, the bravery of his grief did put me   79
  Into a tow'ring passion.
HORATIO   Peace, who comes here?

Enter a Courtier [*Osric*].

OSRIC   Your Lordship is right welcome back to Denmark.
HAMLET   I humbly thank you, sir. [*To Horatio*] Dost
  know this water fly?
HORATIO   No, my good lord.
HAMLET   Thy state is the more gracious, for 'tis a vice to
  know him. He hath much land, and fertile. Let a beast   86
  be lord of beasts, and his crib shall stand at the King's 87
  mess. 'Tis a chuff, but, as I say, spacious in the   88
  possession of dirt.
OSRIC   Sweet lord, if Your Lordship were at leisure, I
  should impart a thing to you from His Majesty.
HAMLET   I will receive it, sir, with all diligence of spirit.
  Put your bonnet to his right use; 'tis for the head.   93

---

20 Larded garnished.   **several** different   **21 Importing** relating to
22 With . . . life i.e., with all sorts of warnings of imaginary dangers if
I were allowed to continue living. (*Bugs* are bugbears, hobgoblins.)
23 That . . . bated that on the reading of this commission, no delay
being allowed   **24 stay** await   **30–1 Ere . . . play** before I could consciously turn my brain to the matter, it had started working on a plan
32 fair in a clear hand.   **33 statists** politicians, men of public affairs
34 A baseness beneath my dignity   **38 conjuration** entreaty
40 palm (An image of health; see Psalm 92:12.)   **41 still** always.
wheaten garland (Symbolic of fruitful agriculture, of peace and
plenty.)   **42 comma** (Indicating continuity, link.)   **43 "as"es** (1) the
"whereases" of a formal document (2) asses.   **charge** (1) import (2)
burden (appropriate to asses)   **47 shriving time** time for confession
and absolution   **48 ordinant** directing.   **49 signet** small seal
50 model replica   **51 writ** writing   **52 Subscribed** signed (with
forged signature).   **impression** i.e., with a wax seal   **53 changeling**
i.e., substituted letter. (Literally, a fairy child substituted for a human
one.)   **54 was sequent** followed

58 defeat destruction   **59 insinuation** intrusive intervention, sticking
their noses in my business   **60 baser** of lower social station   **61 pass**
thrust.   **fell** fierce   **62 opposites** antagonists.   **63 stand me now
upon** become incumbent on me now   **65 th'election** (The Danish
monarch was "elected" by a small number of high-ranking electors.)
66 angle fishhook.   **proper** very   **67 coz'nage** trickery   **68 quit**
requite, pay back   **69 canker** ulcer   **69–70 come In** grow into
74 a man's . . . "one" one's whole life occupies such a short time, only
as long as it takes to count to 1.   **79 bravery** bravado   **86–8 Let . . .
mess** i.e., If a man, no matter how beastlike, is as rich in livestock and
possessions as Osric, he may eat at the King's table.   **87 crib** manger
88 chuff boor, churl. (The Second Quarto spelling, "chough," is a
variant spelling that also suggests the meaning here of "chattering
jackdaw.")   **93 bonnet** any kind of cap or hat.   **his** its

OSRIC   I thank Your Lordship, it is very hot.

HAMLET   No, believe me, 'tis very cold. The wind is northerly.

OSRIC   It is indifferent cold, my lord, indeed.   97

HAMLET   But yet methinks it is very sultry and hot for my complexion.   99

OSRIC   Exceedingly, my lord. It is very sultry, as 'twere—I cannot tell how. My lord, His Majesty bade me signify to you that 'a has laid a great wager on your head. Sir, this is the matter—

HAMLET   I beseech you, remember.

[Hamlet moves him to put on his hat.]

OSRIC   Nay, good my lord; for my ease, in good faith.   105 Sir, here is newly come to court Laertes—believe me, an absolute gentleman, full of most excellent differ-   107 ences, of very soft society and great showing. Indeed,   108 to speak feelingly of him, he is the card or calendar of   109 gentry, for you shall find in him the continent of what   110 part a gentleman would see.   111

HAMLET   Sir, his definement suffers no perdition in   112 you, though I know to divide him inventorially would   113 dozy th'arithmetic of memory, and yet but yaw   114 neither in respect of his quick sail. But, in the verity of   115 extolment, I take him to be a soul of great article, and   116 his infusion of such dearth and rareness as, to make   117 true diction of him, his semblable is his mirror and   118 who else would trace him his umbrage, nothing   119 more.   120

OSRIC   Your Lordship speaks most infallibly of him.

HAMLET   The concernancy, sir? Why do we wrap the   122 gentleman in our more rawer breath?   123

OSRIC   Sir?

HORATIO   Is't not possible to understand in another   125 tongue? You will do't, sir, really.   126

HAMLET   What imports the nomination of this gentle-   127 man?

OSRIC   Of Laertes?

HORATIO *[to Hamlet]* His purse is empty already; all 's golden words are spent.

HAMLET   Of him, sir.

OSRIC   I know you are not ignorant—

HAMLET   I would you did, sir. Yet in faith if you did,   134 it would not much approve me. Well, sir?   135

OSRIC   You are not ignorant of what excellence Laertes is—

HAMLET   I dare not confess that, lest I should compare   138 with him in excellence. But to know a man well were   139 to know himself.   140

OSRIC   I mean, sir, for his weapon; but in the imputation   141 laid on him by them, in his meed he's unfellowed.   142

HAMLET   What's his weapon?

OSRIC   Rapier and dagger.

HAMLET   That's two of his weapons—but well.   145

OSRIC   The King, sir, hath wagered with him six Barbary horses, against the which he has impawned, as I take   147 it, six French rapiers and poniards, with their assigns,   148 as girdle, hangers, and so. Three of the carriages, in   149 faith, are very dear to fancy, very responsive to the   150 hilts, most delicate carriages, and of very liberal con-   151 ceit.   152

HAMLET   What call you the carriages?   153

HORATIO *[to Hamlet]* I knew you must be edified by the margent ere you had done.   155

OSRIC   The carriages, sir, are the hangers.

HAMLET   The phrase would be more germane to the matter if we could carry a cannon by our sides; I would it might be hangers till then. But, on: six Barbary horses against six French swords, their assigns, and three lib- eral-conceited carriages; that's the French bet against the Danish. Why is this impawned, as you call it?

OSRIC   The King, sir, hath laid, sir, that in a dozen   163 passes between yourself and him, he shall not exceed   164 you three hits. He hath laid on twelve for nine, and it would come to immediate trial, if Your Lordship would vouchsafe the answer.   167

HAMLET   How if I answer no?

---

97 indifferent somewhat **99 complexion** constitution. **105 for my ease** (A conventional reply declining the invitation to put the hat back on.) **107 absolute** perfect **107–8 differences** special qualities **108 soft society** agreeable manners. **great showing** distinguished appearance. **109 feelingly** with just perception **109–10 the card . . . gentry** the model or paradigm (literally, a chart or directory) of good breeding **110–11 the continent . . . see** one who contains in himself all the qualities a gentleman would like to see. (A *continent* is that which contains.) **112–15 his definement . . . sail** the task of defining Laertes's excellences suffers no diminution in your description of him, though I know that to enumerate all his graces would stupify one's powers of memory, and even so could do no more than veer unsteadily off course in a vain attempt to keep up with his rapid forward motion. (Hamlet mocks Osric by parodying his jargon-filled speeches.) **115–20 But . . . more** But, in true praise of him, I take him to be a person of remarkable value, and his essence of such rarity and excellence as, to speak truly of him, none can compare with him other than his own mirror; anyone following in his footsteps can only hope to be the shadow to his substance, nothing more. **122 concernancy** import, relevance **123 rawer breath** unrefined speech that can only come short in praising him. **125–6 Is't . . . tongue?** i.e., Is it not possible for you, Osric, to understand and communicate in any other tongue than the overblown rhetoric you have used? (Alternatively, Horatio could be asking Hamlet to speak more plainly.) **126 You will do't** i.e., You can if you try, or, you may well have to try (to speak plainly). **127 nomination** naming

134–5 I would . . . approve me (Responding to Osric's incompleted sentence as though it were a complete statement, Hamlet says, with mock politeness, "I wish you did know me to be not ignorant [i.e., to be knowledgeable] about matters," and then turns this into an insult: "But if you did, your recommendation of me would be of little value in any case.") **138–40 I dare . . . himself** I dare not boast of knowing Laertes's excellence lest I seem to imply a comparable excellence in myself. Certainly, to know another person well, one must know oneself. **141–2 I mean . . . unfellowed** I mean his excellence with his rapier, not his general excellence; in the reputation he enjoys for use of his weapons, his merit is unequaled. **145 but well** but never mind. **147 he** i.e., Laertes. **impawned** staked, wagered **148 poniards** daggers. **assigns** appurtenances **149 hangers** straps on the sword belt (*girdle*), from which the sword hung. **and so** and so on. **149–52 Three . . . conceit** Three of the hangers, truly, are very pleasing to the fancy, decoratively matched with the hilts, delicate in workmanship, and made with elaborate ingenuity. **153 What call you** What do you refer to when you say **155 margent** margin of a book, place for explanatory notes **163 laid** wagered **164 passes** bouts. (The odds of the betting are hard to explain. Possibly the King bets that Hamlet will win at least five out of twelve, at which point Laertes raises the odds against himself by betting he will win nine.) **167 vouchsafe the answer** be so good as to accept the challenge. (Hamlet deliberately takes the phrase in its literal sense of replying.)

OSRIC   I mean, my lord, the opposition of your person
in trial.
HAMLET   Sir, I will walk here in the hall. If it please His
Majesty, it is the breathing time of day with me. Let   172
the foils be brought, the gentleman willing, and the
King hold his purpose, I will win for him an I can; if
not, I will gain nothing but my shame and the odd
hits.
OSRIC   Shall I deliver you so?   177
HAMLET   To this effect, sir—after what flourish your
nature will.
OSRIC   I commend my duty to Your Lordship.   180
HAMLET   Yours, yours.   [*Exit Osric.*]
'A does well to commend it himself; there are no tongues
else for 's turn.   183
HORATIO   This lapwing runs away with the shell on his   184
head.
HAMLET   'A did comply with his dug before 'a sucked   186
it. Thus has he—and many more of the same breed   187
that I know the drossy age dotes on—only got the   188
tune of the time, and, out of an habit of encounter, a   189
kind of yeasty collection, which carries them through   190
and through the most fanned and winnowed opin-   191
ions; and do but blow them to their trial, the bubbles   192
are out.   193

Enter a Lord.

LORD   My lord, His Majesty commended him to you by
young Osric, who brings back to him that you attend
him in the hall. He sends to know if your pleasure
hold to play with Laertes, or that you will take longer   197
time.
HAMLET   I am constant to my purposes; they follow the
King's pleasure. If his fitness speaks, mine is ready;   200
now or whensoever, provided I be so able as now.
LORD   The King and Queen and all are coming down.
HAMLET   In happy time.   203
LORD   The Queen desires you to use some gentle enter-   204
tainment to Laertes before you fall to play.   205
HAMLET   She well instructs me.   [*Exit Lord.*]
HORATIO   You will lose, my lord.
HAMLET   I do not think so. Since he went into France, I
have been in continual practice; I shall win at the odds.

---

172 breathing time exercise period.   **Let** i.e., If   **177 deliver you**
report what you say   **180 commend** commit to your favor. (A conventional salutation, but Hamlet wryly uses a more literal meaning,
"recommend," "praise," in line 182.)   **183 for 's turn** for his purposes, i.e., to do it for him.   **184 lapwing** (A proverbial type of
youthful forwardness. Also, a bird that draws intruders away from
its nest and was thought to run about with its head in the shell when
newly hatched; a seeming reference to Osric's hat.)   **186 comply . . .
dug** observe ceremonious formality toward his nurse's or mother's
teat   **187–93 Thus . . . are out** Thus has he—and many like him of the
sort our frivolous age dotes on—acquired the trendy manner of
speech of the time, and, out of habitual conversation with courtiers of
their own kind, have collected together a kind of frothy medley of
current phrases, which enables such gallants to hold their own
among persons of the most select and well-sifted views; and yet do
but test them by merely blowing on them, and their bubbles burst.
197 play fence.   **that** if   **200 If . . . ready** If he declares his readiness,
my convenience waits on his   **203 In happy time** (A phrase of courtesy indicating that the time is convenient.)   **204–5 entertainment**
greeting

But thou wouldst not think how ill all's here about my
heart; but it is no matter.
HORATIO   Nay, good my lord—
HAMLET   It is but foolery, but it is such a kind of gain-   213
giving as would perhaps trouble a woman.   214
HORATIO   If your mind dislike anything, obey it. I will
forestall their repair hither and say you are not fit.   216
HAMLET   Not a whit, we defy augury. There is special   217
providence in the fall of a sparrow. If it be now, 'tis
not to come; if it be not to come, it will be now; if it
be not now; yet it will come. The readiness is all. Since   220
no man of aught he leaves knows, what is't to leave   221
betimes? Let be.   222

*A table prepared. [Enter] trumpets, drums, and
officers with cushions; King, Queen, [Osric,] and
all the state; foils, daggers, [and wine borne in;]
and Laertes.*

KING
Come, Hamlet, come and take this hand from me.
[*The King puts Laertes's hand into Hamlet's.*]
HAMLET [*to Laertes*]
Give me your pardon, sir. I have done you wrong,
But pardon't as you are a gentleman.
This presence knows,   226
And you must needs have heard, how I am punished   227
With a sore distraction. What I have done
That might your nature, honor, and exception   229
Roughly awake, I here proclaim was madness.
Was't Hamlet wronged Laertes? Never Hamlet.
If Hamlet from himself be ta'en away,
And when he's not himself does wrong Laertes,
Then Hamlet does it not, Hamlet denies it.
Who does it, then? His madness. If't be so,
Hamlet is of the faction that is wronged;   236
His madness is poor Hamlet's enemy.
Sir, in this audience
Let my disclaiming from a purposed evil
Free me so far in your most generous thoughts
That I have shot my arrow o'er the house
And hurt my brother.
LAERTES   I am satisfied in nature,   242
Whose motive in this case should stir me most   243
To my revenge. But in my terms of honor
I stand aloof, and will no reconcilement
Till by some elder masters of known honor
I have a voice and precedent of peace   247
To keep my name ungored. But till that time   248
I do receive your offered love like love,

213–14 gaingiving misgiving   **216 repair** coming   **217 augury** the
attempt to read signs of future events in order to avoid predicted
trouble.   **220–2 Since . . . Let be** Since no one has knowledge of what
he is leaving behind, what does an early death matter after all?
Enough; forbear.   **222.1 trumpets, drums** trumpeters, drummers
222.3 all the state the entire court   **226 presence** royal assembly
227 punished afflicted   **229 exception** disapproval   **236 faction**
party   **242 in nature** i.e., as to my personal feelings   **243 motive**
prompting   **247 voice** authoritative pronouncement.   **of peace** for
reconciliation   **248 name ungored** reputation unwounded.

And will not wrong it.

HAMLET   I embrace it freely,
And will this brothers' wager frankly play.—   251
Give us the foils. Come on.

LAERTES   Come, one for me.

HAMLET
I'll be your foil, Laertes. In mine ignorance   253
Your skill shall, like a star i'th' darkest night,
Stick fiery off indeed.

LAERTES   You mock me, sir.   255

HAMLET   No, by this hand.

KING
Give them the foils, young Osric. Cousin Hamlet,
You know the wager?

HAMLET   Very well, my lord.
Your Grace has laid the odds o'th' weaker side.   259

KING
I do not fear it; I have seen you both.
But since he is bettered, we have therefore odds.   261

LAERTES
This is too heavy. Let me see another.
                    [He exchanges his foil for another.]

HAMLET
This likes me well. These foils have all a length?   263
                    [They prepare to fence.]

OSRIC   Ay, my good lord.

KING
Set me the stoups of wine upon that table.
If Hamlet give the first or second hit,
Or quit in answer of the third exchange,   267
Let all the battlements their ordnance fire.
The King shall drink to Hamlet's better breath,   269
And in the cup an union shall he throw   270
Richer than that which four successive kings
In Denmark's crown have worn. Give me the cups,
And let the kettle to the trumpet speak,   273
The trumpet to the cannoneer without,
The cannons to the heavens, the heaven to earth,
"Now the King drinks to Hamlet." Come, begin.
                    Trumpets the while.
And you, the judges, bear a wary eye.

HAMLET   Come on, sir.

LAERTES   Come, my lord. [They fence. Hamlet scores a hit.]

HAMLET   One.

LAERTES   No.

HAMLET   Judgment.

OSRIC   A hit, a very palpable hit.   282
                    Drum, trumpets, and shot. Flourish.
                    A piece goes off.

LAERTES   Well, again.

KING
Stay, give me drink. Hamlet, this pearl is thine.
                    [He drinks, and throws a pearl in Hamlet's cup.]
Here's to thy health. Give him the cup.

HAMLET
I'll play this bout first. Set it by awhile.
Come. [They fence.] Another hit; what say you?

LAERTES   A touch, a touch, I do confess't.

KING
Our son shall win.

QUEEN   He's fat and scant of breath.   289
Here, Hamlet, take my napkin, rub thy brows.   290
The Queen carouses to thy fortune, Hamlet.   291

HAMLET   Good madam!

KING   Gertrude, do not drink.

QUEEN
I will, my lord, I pray you pardon me.   [She drinks.]

KING [aside]
It is the poisoned cup. It is too late.

HAMLET
I dare not drink yet, madam; by and by.

QUEEN   Come, let me wipe thy face.

LAERTES [aside to the King]
My lord, I'll hit him now.

KING   I do not think't.

LAERTES [aside]
And yet it is almost against my conscience.

HAMLET
Come, for the third, Laertes. You do but dally.
I pray you, pass with your best violence;   301
I am afeard you make a wanton of me.   302

LAERTES   Say you so? Come on.   [They fence.]

OSRIC   Nothing neither way.

LAERTES
Have at you now!   305
                    [Laertes wounds Hamlet; then, in scuffling,
                    they change rapiers, and Hamlet wounds Laertes.]

KING   Part them! They are incensed.

HAMLET
Nay, come, again.   [The Queen falls.]

OSRIC   Look to the Queen there, ho!

HORATIO
They bleed on both sides. How is it, my lord?

OSRIC   How is't, Laertes?

LAERTES
Why, as a woodcock to mine own springe, Osric;   309
I am justly killed with mine own treachery.

HAMLET
How does the Queen?

KING   She swoons to see them bleed.

---

251 **frankly** without ill feeling or the burden of rancor   253 **foil** thin
metal background which sets a jewel off. (With pun on the blunted
rapier for fencing.)   255 **Stick fiery off** stand out brilliantly
259 **laid . . . side** backed the weaker side.   261 **is bettered** is the
odds-on favorite. (Laertes's handicap is the "three hits" specified in
line 165.)   263 **likes** pleases   267 **Or . . . exchange** or draws even
with Laertes by winning the third exchange   269 **better breath**
improved vigor   270 **union** pearl. (So called, according to Pliny's
Natural History, 9, because pearls are *unique,* never identical.)
273 **kettle** kettledrum   282.2 *A piece* A cannon

289 **fat** not physically fit, out of training   290 **napkin** handkerchief
291 **carouses** drinks a toast   301 **pass** thrust   302 **make . . . me** i.e.,
treat me like a spoiled child, trifle with me.   305.1–2 *in scuffling, they
change rapiers* (This stage direction occurs in the Folio. According to
a widespread stage tradition, Hamlet receives a scratch, realizes that
Laertes's sword is unbated, and accordingly forces an exchange.)
309 **woodcock** a bird, a type of stupidity or as a decoy.   **springe**
trap, snare

QUEEN
    No, no, the drink, the drink—Oh, my dear Hamlet—
    The drink, the drink! I am poisoned.   [*She dies.*]
HAMLET
    Oh, villainy! Ho, let the door be locked!
    Treachery! Seek it out.   [*Laertes falls. Exit Osric.*]
LAERTES
    It is here, Hamlet. Hamlet, thou art slain.
    No med'cine in the world can do thee good;
    In thee there is not half an hour's life.
    The treacherous instrument is in thy hand,
    Unbated and envenomed. The foul practice   320
    Hath turned itself on me. Lo, here I lie,
    Never to rise again. Thy mother's poisoned.
    I can no more. The King, the King's to blame.
HAMLET
    The point envenomed too? Then, venom, to thy work.
                                    [*He stabs the King.*]
ALL   Treason! Treason!
KING
    Oh, yet defend me, friends! I am but hurt.
HAMLET [*forcing the King to drink*]
    Here, thou incestuous, murderous, damnèd Dane,
    Drink off this potion. Is thy union here?   328
    Follow my mother.   [*The King dies.*]
LAERTES   He is justly served.
    It is a poison tempered by himself.   330
    Exchange forgiveness with me, noble Hamlet.
    Mine and my father's death come not upon thee,
    Nor thine on me!   [*He dies.*]
HAMLET
    Heaven make thee free of it! I follow thee.
    I am dead, Horatio. Wretched Queen, adieu!
    You that look pale and tremble at this chance,   336
    That are but mutes or audience to this act,   337
    Had I but time—as this fell sergeant, Death,   338
    Is strict in his arrest—oh, I could tell you—   339
    But let it be. Horatio, I am dead;
    Thou livest. Report me and my cause aright
    To the unsatisfied.
HORATIO   Never believe it.
    I am more an antique Roman than a Dane.   343
    Here's yet some liquor left.
            [*He attempts to drink from the poisoned cup.
                            Hamlet prevents him.*]
HAMLET   As thou'rt a man,
    Give me the cup! Let go! By heaven, I'll ha 't.
    Oh, God, Horatio, what a wounded name,
    Things standing thus unknown, shall I leave behind
        me!
    If thou didst ever hold me in thy heart,
    Absent thee from felicity awhile,

And in this harsh world draw thy breath in pain
To tell my story. *A march afar off* [*and a volley within*].
    What warlike noise is this?

            Enter Osric.

OSRIC
    Young Fortinbras, with conquest come from Poland,
    To th'ambassadors of England gives
    This warlike volley.
HAMLET   Oh, I die, Horatio!
    The potent poison quite o'ercrows my spirit.   355
    I cannot live to hear the news from England,
    But I do prophesy th'election lights
    On Fortinbras. He has my dying voice.   358
    So tell him, with th'occurrents more and less   359
    Which have solicited. The rest is silence.   [*He dies.*] 360
HORATIO
    Now cracks a noble heart. Good night, sweet prince,
    And flights of angels sing thee to thy rest!
                                    [*March within.*]
    Why does the drum come hither?

            Enter Fortinbras, with the [*English*] *Ambassadors*
            [*with drum, colors, and attendants*].

FORTINBRAS
    Where is this sight?
HORATIO   What is it you would see?
    If aught of woe or wonder, cease your search.
FORTINBRAS
    This quarry cries on havoc. O proud Death,   366
    What feast is toward in thine eternal cell,   367
    That thou so many princes at a shot
    So bloodily hast struck?
FIRST AMBASSADOR   The sight is dismal,
    And our affairs from England come too late.
    The ears are senseless that should give us hearing,
    To tell him his commandment is fulfilled,
    That Rosencrantz and Guildenstern are dead.
    Where should we have our thanks?
HORATIO   Not from his mouth, 374
    Had it th'ability of life to thank you.
    He never gave commandment for their death.
    But since, so jump upon this bloody question,   377
    You from the Polack wars and you from England
    Are here arrived, give order that these bodies
    High on a stage be placèd to the view,   380
    And let me speak to th' yet unknowing world
    How these things came about. So shall you hear
    Of carnal, bloody, and unnatural acts,
    Of accidental judgments, casual slaughters,   384

---

320 **Unbated** not blunted with a button.   **practice** plot   **328 union**
pearl. (See line 270; with grim puns on the word's other meanings:
marriage, shared death.)   **330 tempered** mixed   **336 chance** mischance   **337 mutes** silent observers. (Literally, actors with nonspeak-
ing parts.)   **338 fell sergeant** remorseless arresting officer   **339 strict**
(1) severely just (2) unavoidable.   **arrest** (1) taking into custody (2)
stopping my speech   **343 Roman** (Suicide was an honorable choice
for many Romans as an alternative to a dishonorable life.)

355 o'ercrows triumphs over (like the winner in a cockfight)
358 voice vote.   **359 th'occurrents** the events, incidents
360 solicited moved, urged. (Hamlet doesn't finish saying what the
events have prompted—presumably, his acts of vengeance, or his
reporting of those events to Fortinbras.)   **366 This . . . havoc** This
heap of dead bodies loudly proclaims a general slaughter.   **367 feast**
i.e., Death feasting on those who have fallen.   **toward** in preparation
374 his Claudius's   **377 so jump . . . question** so hard on the heels of
this bloody business   **380 stage** platform   **384 judgments** retribu-
tions.   **casual** occurring by chance

Of deaths put on by cunning and forced cause,   385
And, in this upshot, purposes mistook
Fall'n on th'inventors' heads. All this can I
Truly deliver.
FORTINBRAS   Let us haste to hear it,
And call the noblest to the audience.
For me, with sorrow I embrace my fortune.
I have some rights of memory in this kingdom,   391
Which now to claim my vantage doth invite me.   392
HORATIO
Of that I shall have also cause to speak,
And from his mouth whose voice will draw on more. 394
But let this same be presently performed,   395

Even while men's minds are wild, lest more
    mischance
On plots and errors happen.
FORTINBRAS   Let four captains   397
Bear Hamlet, like a soldier, to the stage,
For he was likely, had he been put on,   399
To have proved most royal; and for his passage,   400
The soldiers' music and the rite of war
Speak loudly for him.   402
Take up the bodies. Such a sight as this
Becomes the field, but here shows much amiss.   404
Go bid the soldiers shoot.
        Exeunt [*marching, bearing off the dead bodies;*
                    a peal of ordnance is shot off].

---

385 put on instigated.   **forced cause** contrivance   **391 of memory**
traditional, remembered, unforgotten   **392 vantage** favorable opportunity   **394 voice . . . more** vote will influence still others.
395 presently immediately

397 On on top of   **399 put on** i.e., invested in royal office and so put
to the test   **400 for his passage** to mark his passing   **402 Speak** (let
them) speak   **404 Becomes the field** suits the field of battle

Othello, the Moor of Venice

thello differs in several respects from the other three major Shakespearean tragedies with which it is usually ranked. Written seemingly about the time of its performance at court by the King's Men (Shakespeare's acting company) on November 1, 1604, after *Hamlet* (c. 1599–1601) and before *King Lear* (1605–1606) and *Macbeth* (c. 1606–1607), *Othello* shares with these other plays a fascination with evil in its most virulent and universal aspect. These plays study the devastating effects of ambitious pride, ingratitude, wrath, jealousy, and vengeful hate—the deadly sins of the spirit—with only a passing interest in the political strife to which Shakespeare's Roman or classical tragedies are generally devoted. Of the four, *Othello* is the most concentrated upon one particular evil. The action concerns sexual jealousy, and, although human sinfulness is such that jealousy ceaselessly touches on other forms of depravity, the center of interest always returns in *Othello* to the destruction of a love through jealousy. *Othello* is a tragic portrait of a marriage. The protagonist is not a king or a prince, as in the tragedies already mentioned, but a general recently married. There are no supernatural visitations, as in *Hamlet* and *Macbeth*. Ideas of divine justice, while essential to *Othello*'s portrayal of a battle between good and evil for the allegiance of the protagonist, do not encompass the wide sweep of *King Lear*, nor do we find here the same broad indictment of humanity. Social order is not seriously shaken by Othello's tragedy. The fair-minded Duke of Venice remains firmly in control, and his deputy Lodovico oversees a just conclusion on Cyprus.

By the same token, *Othello* does not offer the remorseless questioning about humanity's relationship to the cosmos that we find in *King Lear, Hamlet,* and *Macbeth.* The battle of good and evil is, of course, cosmic, but in *Othello* that battle is realized through a taut narrative of jealousy and murder. Its poetic images are accordingly focused to a large extent on the natural world. One cluster of images is domestic and animal, having to do with goats, mon-

keys, wolves, baboons, guinea hens, wildcats, spiders, flies, asses, dogs, copulating horses and sheep, serpents, and toads; other images, more wide-ranging in scope, include green-eyed monsters, devils, poisons, money purses, tarnished jewels, music untuned, and light extinguished. The story is immediate and direct, retaining the sensational atmosphere of its Italian prose source by Giovanni Baptista Giraldi Cinthio, in his *Hecatommithi* of 1565 (translated into French in 1584). Events move even more swiftly than in Cinthio's work, for Shakespeare has compressed the story into two or three nights and days (albeit with an intervening sea journey and with an elastic use of stage time to allow for the maturing of long-term plans, as when we learn that Iago has begged Emilia "a hundred times" to steal Desdemona's handkerchief, 3.3.308, or that Iago has accused Cassio of making love to Desdemona "A thousand times," 5.2.219). *Othello* does not have a fully developed double plot, as in *King Lear,* or a comparatively large group of characters serving as foils to the protagonist, as in *Hamlet.* *Othello*'s cast is small, and the plot is concentrated to an unusual degree on Othello, Desdemona, and Iago. What *Othello* may lose in breadth it gains in dramatic intensity.

Daringly, Shakespeare opens this tragedy of love, not with a direct and sympathetic portrayal of the lovers themselves, but with a scene of vicious insinuation about their marriage. The images employed by Iago to describe the coupling of Othello and Desdemona are revoltingly animalistic, sodomistic. "Even now, now, very now, an old black ram / Is tupping your white ewe," he taunts Desdemona's father, Brabantio. (Tupping is a word used specifically for the copulating of sheep.) "You'll have your daughter covered with a Barbary horse; you'll have your nephews neigh to you"; "your daughter and the Moor are now making the beast with two backs"; "the devil will make a grandsire of you" (1.1.90–3, 113–20). This degraded view reduces the marriage to one of utter carnality, with repeated emphasis on the word "gross": Desdemona has yielded "to the gross clasps of a lascivious Moor" and has made "a gross revolt" against her family and society (lines 129, 137). Iago's second theme, one that is habitual with him, is money. "What ho, Brabantio! Thieves, thieves, thieves! / Look to your house, your daughter, and your bags" (lines 81–2). The implication is of a sinister bond between thievery in sex and thievery in gold. Sex and money are both commodities to be protected by watchful fathers against libidinous and opportunistic children.

We as audience make plentiful allowance for Iago's bias in all this, since he has admitted to Roderigo his knavery and resentment of Othello. Even so, the carnal vision of love we confront is calculatedly disturbing, because it seems so equated with a pejorative image of blackness. Othello is unquestionably a black man, referred to disparagingly by his detractors as the "thick-lips," with a "sooty bosom" (1.1.68; 1.2.71); Elizabethan usage applied the term "Moor" without attempting to distinguish between Arabian and African peoples. From the ugly start of the play, Othello and Desdemona have to prove the worth of their love in the face of preset attitudes against miscegenation. Brabantio takes refuge in the thought that Othello must have bewitched Desdemona. His basic assumption—one to be echoed later by Iago and when Othello's confidence is undermined by Othello himself—is that miscegenation is unnatural by definition. In confronting and accusing Othello, he repeatedly appeals "to all things of sense" (that is, to common sense) and asks if it is not "gross in sense" (self-evident) that Othello has practiced magic on her, since nothing else could prompt human nature so to leave its natural path. "For nature so preposterously to err, / Being not deficient, blind, or lame of sense, / Sans witchcraft could not" (1.2.65, 73; 1.3.64–6). We as audience can perceive the racial bias in Brabantio's view and can recognize also in him the type of imperious father who conventionally opposes romantic love. It is sadly ironic that he should now prefer Roderigo as a son-in-law, evidently concluding that any white Venetian would be preferable to the prince of blacks. Still, Brabantio has been hospitable to the Moor and trusting of his daughter. He is a sorrowful rather than ridiculous figure, and the charge he levels at the married pair, however much it is based on a priori assumptions of what is "natural" in human behavior, remains to be answered.

After all, we find ourselves wondering, what did attract Othello and Desdemona to one another? Even though he certainly did not use witchcraft, may Othello not have employed a subtler kind of enchantment in the exotic character of his travels among "the Cannibals that each other eat, / The Anthropophagi, and men whose heads / Do grow beneath their shoulders" (1.3.145–7)? These "passing strange" events fascinate Desdemona as they do everyone, including the Duke of Venice ("I think

this tale would win my daughter too"). Othello has not practiced unfairly on her—"This only is the witchcraft I have used" (lines 162, 171–3). Yet may he not represent for Desdemona a radical novelty, being a man at once less devious and more interesting than the dissolute Venetian swaggerers, such as Roderigo and the "wealthy curlèd darlings of our nation" (1.2.69), who follow her about? Was her deceiving of her father by means of the elopement a protest, an escape from conventionality? Why has she been attracted to a man older than herself? For his part, Othello gives the impression of being inexperienced with women, at least of Desdemona's rank and complexion, and is both intrigued and flattered by her attentions. "She loved me for the dangers I had passed, / And I loved her that she did pity them" (1.3.169–70). Desdemona fulfills a place in Othello's view of himself. Does she also represent status for him in Venetian society, where he has been employed as a military commander but treated nonetheless as something of an alien?

These subtle but impertinent ways of doubting the motivations of Othello and Desdemona, adding to the difficulties that are inherent in an attempt to understand the mysteries of attraction in any relationship, are thrust upon us by the play's opening and are later crucial to Iago's strategy of breeding mistrust. Just as importantly, however, these insinuations are refuted by Othello and especially by Desdemona. Whatever others may think, she never gives the slightest indication of regarding her husband as different because he is black and old. In fact, the images of blackness and age are significantly reversed during the play's early scenes. Othello has already embraced the Christian faith, whereas Iago, a white Italian in a Christian culture, emerges as innately evil from the very start of the play. Othello's first appearance onstage, when he confronts a party of torch-bearing men coming to arrest him and bids his followers sheathe their swords (1.2.60), is perhaps reminiscent of Christ's arrest in the Garden of Gethsemane; if so, it suggests a fleeting comparison between Othello and the Christian God whose charity and forbearance he seeks to emulate. Othello's blackness may be used in part as an emblem of fallen humanity, but so are we all fallen. His age similarly strengthens our impression of his wisdom, restraint, and leadership. Any suggestions of comic sexual infidelity in the marriage of an older man and an attractive young bride are confuted by what we see in Desdemona's chaste yet sensual regard for the good man she has chosen.

Desdemona is devoted to Othello, admiring, and faithful. We believe her when she says that she does not even know what it means to be unfaithful; the word *whore* is not in her vocabulary. She is defenseless against the charges brought against her because she does not even comprehend them and cannot believe that anyone would imagine such things. Her love, both erotic and chaste, is of that transcendent wholesomeness common to several late Shakespearean heroines, such as Cordelia in *King Lear* and Hermione in *The Winter's Tale.* Her "preferring" Othello to her father, like Cordelia's placing her duty to a husband before that to a father, is not ungrateful but natural and proper. And Othello, however much he may regard Desdemona in terms of his own identity (he calls her "my fair warrior"), does cherish Desdemona as she deserves. "I cannot speak enough of this content," he exclaims when he rejoins her on Cyprus. "It stops me here; it is too much of joy" (2.1.182, 196–7). The passionate intensity of his love prepares the way for his tragedy; he speaks more truly than he knows in saying, "when I love thee not, / Chaos is come again" (3.3.99–100). Iago speaks truly also when he observes that Othello "Is of a constant, loving, noble nature" (2.1.290). Othello's tragedy is not that he is easily duped, but that his strong faith can be destroyed at such terrible cost. Othello never forgets how much he is losing. The threat to his love is not an initial lack of his being happily married, but rather the insidious assumption that Desdemona cannot love him because such a love might be unnatural. The fear of being unlovable exists in Othello's mind, but the human instrument of this vicious gospel is Iago.

Iago belongs to a select group of villains in Shakespeare who, while plausibly motivated in human terms, also take delight in evil for its own sake: Aaron the Moor in *Titus Andronicus,* Richard III, Don John in *Much Ado about Nothing,* Edmund in *King Lear.* They are not, like Macbeth or like Claudius in *Hamlet,* men driven by ambition to commit crimes they clearly recognize to be wrong. Although Edmund does belatedly try to make amends, these villains are essentially conscienceless, sinister, and amused by their own cunning. They are related to one another by a stage metaphor of personified evil derived from the Vice of the morality play, whose typical role is to win the Mankind figure away from virtue and to corrupt him with worldly enticements. Like that engaging tempter, Shakespeare's villains in these plays take the audience into their confidence, boast in soliloquy of their cleverness, exult in the triumph of evil, and improvise plans with daring and resourcefulness. They are all superb actors, deceiving virtually every character onstage until late in the action with their protean and hypocritical display. They take pleasure in this "sport" and amaze us by their virtuosity. The role is paradoxically comic in its use of ingenious and resourceful deception—the grim and ironic comedy of vice. We know that we are to condemn morally even while we applaud the skill.

This theatrical tradition of the Vice may best explain a puzzling feature of Iago, noted long ago and memorably phrased by Samuel Taylor Coleridge as "the motive hunting of a motiveless malignity." To be sure, Iago does offer plausible motives for what he does. Despite his resemblance to the morality Vice, he is no allegorized abstraction but an ensign in the army, a junior field officer who hates being out-ranked by a theoretician or staff officer. As an old-school professional, he also resents that he has not been promoted on the basis of seniority, the "old gradation" (1.1.38). Even his efforts at using influence with Othello have come to naught, and Iago can scarcely be blamed for supposing that Cassio's friendship with Othello has won him special favor. Thus, Iago has reason to plot against Cassio as well as Othello. Nevertheless a further dimension is needed to explain Iago's gloating, his utter lack of moral reflection, his concentration on destroying Desdemona (who has not wronged Iago), his absorption in ingenious methods of plotting, his finesse and style. Hatred precedes any plausible motive in Iago and ultimately does not depend on psychological causality. Probably the tradition of the stage Machiavel (another type of gloating villain based on stereotyped attitudes toward the heretical political ideas of Niccolò Machiavelli), as in Marlowe's *The Jew of Malta,* contributes to the portraiture; this tradition was readily assimilated with that of the Vice.

Iago's machinations yield him both "sport" and "profit" (1.3.387); that is, he enjoys his evildoing, although he is also driven by a motive. This Vice-like behavior in human garb creates a restless sense of a destructive metaphysical reality lying behind his visible exterior. Even his stated motives do not always make sense. When in an outburst of hatred he soliloquizes that "I hate the Moor; / And it is thought abroad that twixt my sheets / He's done my office," Iago goes on to concede the unlikelihood of this charge. "I know not if't be true; / But I, for mere suspicion in that kind, / Will do as if for surety" (lines 387–91). The charge is so absurd, in fact, that we have to look into Iago himself for the origin of this jealous paranoia. The answer may be partly emblematic: as the embodiment and genius of sexual jealousy, Iago suffers with ironic appropriateness from the evil he preaches, and without external cause. Emilia understands that jealousy is not a rational affliction but a self-induced disease of the mind. Jealous persons, she tells Desdemona, "are not ever jealous for the cause, / But jealous for they're jealous. It is a monster / Begot upon itself, born on itself" (3.4.161–3). Iago's own testimonial bears this out, for his jealousy is at once wholly irrational and agonizingly self-destructive. "I do suspect the lusty Moor / Hath leaped into my seat, the thought whereof / Doth, like a poisonous mineral, gnaw my innards" (2.1.296–8). In light of this nightmare, we can see that even his seemingly plausible resentment of Cassio's promotion is jealous envy. The "daily beauty" in Cassio's life makes Iago feel "ugly" by comparison (5.1.19–20), engendering in Iago a profound sense of lack of worth from which he can temporarily find relief only by reducing Othello and others to his own miserable condition. He is adept at provoking self-hatred in others because he suffers from it himself. His declaration to Othello that "I am your own forever"

(3.3.495) is, of course, cynical, but it also signals the extent to which Iago has succeeded in wooing Othello away from Desdemona and Cassio into a murderous union between two women-hating men. The Iago who thus dedicates himself as partner in the fulfillment of Othello's homicidal fantasies is, we learn, capable of fantasizing a bizarre amorous encounter between himself and Cassio (lines 429–41).

Othello comes at last to regard Iago as a "demi-devil" who has tempted Othello to damn himself "beneath all depth in hell"; Lodovico speaks of Iago in the closing lines of the play as a "hellish villain" (5.2.142, 309, 379); and Iago himself boasts that "When devils will the blackest sins put on, / They do suggest at first with heavenly shows, / As I do now" (2.3.345–7). Iago thus bears some affinity to both Vice and the devil, suggesting his relationship both to Othello's inner temptation and to a pre-existent evil force in the universe itself. Conversely, Desdemona is in Emilia's words an "angel," purely chaste; "So come my soul to bliss as I speak true" (5.2.134, 259). When Desdemona lands on Cyprus, she is greeted in words that echo the *Ave Maria:* "Hail to thee, lady! And the grace of heaven . . . Enwheel thee round" (2.1.87–9). These images introduce metaphorically a conflict of good and evil in which Othello, typical of fallen humanity, has chosen evil and destroyed the good at the prompting of a diabolical counselor. Again we see the heritage of the morality play, especially of the later morality play in which the Mankind figure was sometimes damned rather than saved. Even so, to allegorize *Othello* is to obscure and misread its clash of human passion. In fact, we see that the impulse to reduce human complexity to simplistic moral absolutes is a fatal weakness in Othello; by insisting on viewing Desdemona as a type or abstraction, he loses sight of her wonderful humanity. The theological issue of salvation or damnation is not relevant in dramatic terms; the play is not a homily on the dangers of jealousy. The metaphysical dimensions of a homiletic tradition are transmuted into human drama. Acknowledging these limitations, we can notwithstanding see a spiritual analogy in Iago's devil-like method of undoing his victims.

His trick resembles that of the similarly mischief-making Don John in *Much Ado About Nothing:* an optical illusion by which the blameless heroine is impugned as an adulteress. The concealed Othello must watch Cassio boasting of sexual triumphs and believe he is talking about Desdemona. Like the devil, Iago is given power over people's frail senses, especially the eyes. He can create illusions to induce Othello to see what Iago wants him to see, as Don John does with Claudio, but Othello's acceptance of the lie must be his own responsibility, a failure of his corrupted will. Iago practices on Othello with an a priori logic used before on Brabantio and Roderigo, urging the proneness of all mortals to sin and the alleged

unnaturalness of a black-white marriage. All women have appetites; Desdemona is a woman; hence, Desdemona has appetites. "The wine she drinks is made of grapes," he scoffs to Roderigo. "If she had been blessed, she would never have loved the Moor" (2.1.253–5). She is a Venetian, and "In Venice they do let God see the pranks / They dare not show their husbands" (3.3.216–17). Therefore, she, too, is a hypocrite; "She did deceive her father" (line 220). Most of all, it stands to reason that she must long for a man of her own race. Iago succeeds in getting Othello to concur: "And yet, how nature erring from itself—" (line 243). This proposition that Nature teaches all persons, including Desdemona, to seek a harmonious matching of "clime, complexion, and degree" strikes a responsive chord in Othello, since he knows that even though he has authority as a general serving his adopted city he is also black and in some senses a foreigner, an alien. "Haply, for I am black / And have not those soft parts of conversation / That chamberers have." Then, too, he is sensitive that he is older than she, "declined / Into the vale of years" (lines 246, 279–82), "the young affects / In me defunct" (1.3.266–7). And so, if one must conclude from the preceding that Desdemona will seek a lover, the only question is who. "This granted—as it is a most pregnant and unforced position—who stands so eminent in the degree of this fortune as Cassio does?" (2.1.236–9). Once Othello has accepted this syllogistic sequence of proofs, specious not through any lapse in logic but because the axiomatic assumptions about human nature are degraded and do not apply to Desdemona, Othello has arrived at an unshakable conclusion to which all subsequent evidence must be applied. "Villain, be sure thou prove my love a whore," he commissions Iago (3.3.375). Desdemona's innocent pleading for Cassio only makes things look worse. Cassio's reputed muttering while asleep, like the handkerchief seen in his possession or his giddy talk about his mistress Bianca, "speaks against her [Desdemona] with the other proofs" (line 456).

How has Othello fallen so far? His bliss with Desdemona as they are rejoined on Cyprus knows no limit. These two persons represent married love at its very best, erotic and spiritual, she enhancing his manliness, he cherishing her beauty and virtue. His blackness and age are positive images in him, despite earlier insinuations to the contrary. Indeed, we have no reason to suppose that Othello is what we would call "old," despite his worries about being "declined / Into the vale of years" and having lost the "young effects" of sexual desire; he appears to be middle-aged and vigorous, so much so that Desdemona is attracted to him sexually as well as in other ways. He is a man of public worthiness, of command, of self-assurance. Desdemona is the most domestic of Shakespeare's tragic heroines, even while she is also representative of so much that is transcendent. Husband and wife are bound happily in one of Shakespeare's few detailed portraits of serious commitment in marriage. Othello initially has the wisdom to know that Desdemona's feminine attractiveness ought not to be threatening to him: he need not be jealous because she is beautiful, "free of speech," and loves dancing and music, since "Where virtue is, these are more virtuous." Nor does he see any reason at first to fear her "revolt" simply because he is black and older than his wife; "she had eyes, and chose me" (3.3.197–203). Othello's self-assurance through the love he perceives in Desdemona is the strongest sign of his happiness in marriage.

What then gives way? We look at Iago for one important insight, but ultimately the cause must be in Othello himself. Arthur Kirsch has argued persuasively (in *Shakespeare and the Experience of Love*, 1981) that Othello's most grave failing is an insufficient regard for himself. It is in part an inability to counter the effects on him of a culture that regards him as an outsider; he is at last persuaded to see himself with the eyes of Venice, not just of Iago, but of Brabantio (who gladly entertains Othello until he has the presumption to elope with Brabantio's white daughter) and others. The resulting destruction of self-regard is devastating. Othello's jealousy stems from a profound suspicion that others cannot love him because he does not deem himself lovable.

Othello has loved Desdemona as an extention of himself, and, in his moments of greatest contentedness, his marriage is sustained by an idealized vision of himself serving as the object of his exalted romantic passion. When he destroys Desdemona, as he realizes with a terrible clarity, Othello destroys himself; the act is a prelude to his actual suicide. Iago's means of temptation, then, is to persuade Othello to regard himself with the eyes of Venice, to accept the view that Othello is himself alien and that any woman who loves him does so perversely. In Othello's tainted state of mind, Desdemona's very sexuality becomes an unbearable threat to him, her warmth and devotion a "proof" of disloyalty. Othello's most tortured speeches (3.4.57–77, 4.2.49–66) reveal the extent to which he equates the seemingly betraying woman, whom he has so depended on for happiness, with his own mother, who gave Othello's father a handkerchief and threatened him with loss of her love if he should lose it. Othello has briefly learned and then forgotten the precious art of harmonizing erotic passion and spiritual love, and, as these two great aims of love are driven apart in him, he comes to loathe and fear the sexuality that puts him so much in mind of his physical frailty and dependence on woman. The horror and pity of *Othello* rests, above all, in the spectacle of a love that was once so whole and noble made filthy by self-hatred. The tragic flaw thus lies in Othello's maleness, in his fear of betrayal by the innocent woman he loves, and his apparent need to degrade her for the very thing he finds desirable in her— a tendency so common among men that Freud, in the early twentieth century, could declare it to be "the most prevalent form of degradation in erotic life" (in Freud's *Sammlung*, volume 4).

The increasing surrender of Othello's judgment to passion can be measured in three successive trial scenes in the play: the entirely fair trial of Othello himself by the Venetian Senate concerning the elopement, Othello's trial of Cassio for drinking and rioting (when, ominously, Othello's "blood begins my safer guides to rule," 2.3.199), and finally the prejudged sentencing of Desdemona without providing her any opportunity to defend herself. In a corollary decline, Othello falls from the Christian compassion of the opening scenes (he customarily confesses to heaven "the vices of my blood," 1.3.125) to the pagan savagery of his vengeful and ritualistic execution of his wife. "My heart is turned to stone" (4.1.184–5), he vows, and at the play's end he grievingly characterizes himself as a "base Indian" who "threw a pearl away / Richer than all his tribe" (5.2.357–8). Iago knows that he must persuade Othello to sentence and to execute Desdemona himself, for only by active commitment to evil will Othello damn himself. In nothing does Iago so resemble the devil as in his wish to see Othello destroy the innocence and goodness on which his happiness depends.

The fate of some of the lesser characters echoes that of Othello, for Iago's evil intent is to "enmesh them all" (2.3.356). Cassio, in particular, is, like Othello, an attractive man with a single, vulnerable weakness—in his case, a fleshly appetite for wine and women. For him, alternately idolizing and depreciating women as he does, the gap between spiritual and sensual love remains vast, but he is essentially good-natured and trustworthy. His seemingly genial flaws lead to disaster, because they put him at the mercy of a remorseless enemy. Iago is, with fitting irony, the apostle of absolute self-control: "Our bodies are our gardens, to the which our wills are gardeners" (1.3.323–4). Thus, Cassio's tragedy is anything but a straightforward homily on the virtues of temperance. Similarly, Bianca is undone, not through any simple cause-and-effect punishment of her sexual conduct—she is, after all, fond of Cassio and loyal to him, even if he will not marry her—but because Iago is able to turn appearances against her. With his usual appeal to a priori logic, he builds a case that she and Cassio are in cahoots: "I do suspect this trash / To be a party in this injury . . . This is the fruits of whoring" (5.1.86–7, 118). Roderigo is another of Iago's victims, a contemptible one, led by the nose because he, too, has surrendered reason to passion. Emilia cannot escape Iago's evil influence and steals the handkerchief for him, despite knowing its value for Desdemona. Flaws are magnified into disasters by a remorseless evil intelligence. Men and women both must be ceaselessly circumspect; a good reputation is sooner lost than recovered. Emilia is a conventionally decent enough woman—she jests to Desdemona that she would be faithless in marriage only for a very high price—and yet her one small compromise with her conscience contributes to the murder of her mistress. Like Othello, she offers atonement too late, by denouncing her husband in a gesture of defiance toward male authority that says much about the tragic consequences of male mistrust of women. Desdemona is the only person in the play too good to be struck down through some inner flaw, which may explain why Iago is so intent on destroying her along with Othello and Cassio.

As a tragic hero, Othello obtains self-knowledge at a terrible price. He knows finally that what he has destroyed was ineffably good. The discovery is too late for him to make amends, and he dies by his own hand as atonement. The deaths of Othello and Desdemona are, in their separate ways, equally devastating: he is in part the victim of racism, though he nobly refuses to deny his own culpability, and she is the victim of sexism, lapsing sadly into the stereotypical role of passive and silent sufferer that the Venetian world expects of women. Despite the loss, however, Othello's reaffirmation of faith in Desdemona's goodness undoes what the devil-like Iago had most hoped to achieve: the separation of Othello from his loving trust in one who is good. In this important sense, Othello's self-knowledge is cathartic and a compensation for the terrible price he has paid. The very existence of a person as good as Desdemona gives the lie to Iago's creed that everyone has his or her price. She is the sacrificial victim who must die for Othello's loss of faith and, by dying, rekindle that faith. ("My life upon her faith!" Othello prophetically affirms, in response to her father's warning that she may deceive [1.3.297].) She cannot restore him to himself, for self-hatred has done its ugly work, but she is the means by which he understands at last the chimerical and wantonly destructive nature of his jealousy. His greatness appears in his acknowledgment of this truth and in the heroic struggle with which he has confronted an inner darkness we all share.

Onstage and in film and television, *Othello* proves itself to be jarringly relevant to modern concerns about racial conflict and about men's mistreatment of women. Janet Suzman chose to produce the play onstage and subsequently for educational television in Johannesburg, South Africa, at a time when apartheid was soon to be dismantled, even though that surprising if inevitable event was not yet discernible. A racially mixed audience came to see a racially mixed cast, with John Kani, a well-known South African Black actor, as Othello, and a very fair-haired South African actress as Desdemona. Iago unmistakably represented the mindset of a state police officer obsessed with preserving the purity of the White race and therefore venemous in his racial hatred of Othello for his miscegenated marriage with a White woman. The explosively powerful emotions of that production carry over into a memorable film version. Orson Welles's 1951 film version, recently remastered, featured Othello in blackface as the protagonist; so did Laurence Olivier's film of 1965, based on a National Theatre stage production of 1964 with Frank Finlay as Iago and Maggie Smith as Desdemona. Indeed, most Othellos onstage over the centuries have been White actors (including Edmund Kean, John Philip Kemble, Edwin Booth, Charles Macready, Edwin Forrest, Henry Irving, Tommaso Salvini, and Paul Scofield, many of whom also played Iago), with notable exceptions that include Ira Aldridge, Earle Hyman, and Paul Robeson. Robeson's galvanizing performances at the Savoy Theatre in 1930 with Peggy Ashcroft as Desdemona, and then in Margaret Webster's New York production of 1943–1945 with Uta Hagen as Desdemona and José Ferrer as Iago, helped establish the role of Othello as one that great Black actors could perform. Today racially mixed casting allows for all sorts of permutations, though Kenneth Branagh's recent film chooses the more recognizable pattern with Branagh himself as Iago and Laurence Fishburne as Othello. In another recent development, Emilia has stood out in several productions as the raisonneur and heroic figure in the play, speaking as she does on behalf of maltreated women, urging Desdemona to stand up for her rights. One recent Chicago production went so far as to rewrite the ending: Othello and Iago both survive unpunished for what they have done, while Desdemona and Emilia lie dead as their innocent victims. This deliberate and provocative overstatement might seem extreme to some viewers, but unquestionably did signal the direction of recent performance history of this profoundly disturbing play.

Othello, the Moor of Venice

The Names of the Actors

OTHELLO, *the Moor*
BRABANTIO, *[a senator,] father to Desdemona*
CASSIO, *an honorable lieutenant [to Othello]*
IAGO, *[Othello's ancient,] a villain*
RODERIGO, *a gulled gentleman*
DUKE OF VENICE
SENATORS *[of Venice]*
MONTANO, *Governor of Cyprus*
GENTLEMEN *of Cyprus*
LODOVICO *and* GRATIANO, *[kinsmen to Brabantio,] two noble Venetians*
SAILORS
CLOWN

DESDEMONA, *[daughter to Brabantio and] wife to Othello*
EMILIA, *wife to Iago*
BIANCA, *a courtesan [and mistress to Cassio]*

[A MESSENGER
A HERALD
A MUSICIAN

Servants, Attendants, Officers, Senators, Musicians, Gentlemen

SCENE: *Venice; a seaport in Cyprus]*

1.1

Enter Roderigo and Iago.

RODERIGO
 Tush, never tell me! I take it much unkindly   1
 That thou, Iago, who hast had my purse
 As if the strings were thine, shouldst know of this. 3
IAGO 'Sblood, but you'll not hear me.   4
 If ever I did dream of such a matter,
 Abhor me.
RODERIGO
 Thou told'st me thou didst hold him in thy hate.   7
IAGO   Despise me
 If I do not. Three great ones of the city,
 In personal suit to make me his lieutenant,
 Off-capped to him; and by the faith of man,
 I know my price, I am worth no worse a place.
 But he, as loving his own pride and purposes,
 Evades them with a bombast circumstance   14

 Horribly stuffed with epithets of war,   15
 And, in conclusion,
 Nonsuits my mediators. For, "Certes," says he,   17
 "I have already chose my officer."
 And what was he?
 Forsooth, a great arithmetician,   20
 One Michael Cassio, a Florentine,
 A fellow almost damned in a fair wife,   22
 That never set a squadron in the field
 Nor the division of a battle knows   24
 More than a spinster—unless the bookish theoric,   25
 Wherein the togaed consuls can propose   26
 As masterly as he. Mere prattle without practice
 Is all his soldiership. But he, sir, had th'election;
 And I, of whom his eyes had seen the proof   29
 At Rhodes, at Cyprus, and on other grounds

1.1 Location: Venice. A street.
1 never tell me (An expression of incredulity, like "tell me another one.") **3 this** i.e., Desdemona's elopement. **4 'Sblood** By His (Christ's) blood **7 him** Othello **14 bombast circumstance** wordy evasion. (*Bombast* is cotton padding.)

15 epithets of war military expressions **17 Nonsuits** rejects the petition of. **Certes** Certainly **20 arithmetician** i.e., a man whose military knowledge is merely theoretical, based on books of tactics **22 A . . . wife** (Cassio does not seem to be married, but his counterpart in Shakespeare's source does have a woman in his house. See also 4.1.131.) **24 division of a battle** disposition of a military unit **25 a spinster** i.e., a housewife, one whose regular occupation is spinning. **theoric** theory **26 togaed consuls** toga-wearing counselors or senators. **propose** discuss **29 his** Othello's

1156

Christened and heathen, must be beleed and calmed 31
By debitor and creditor. This countercaster, 32
He, in good time, must his lieutenant be, 33
And I—God bless the mark!—His Moorship's ancient. 34

RODERIGO
By heaven, I rather would have been his hangman. 35

IAGO
Why, there's no remedy. 'Tis the curse of service;
Preferment goes by letter and affection, 37
And not by old gradation, where each second 38
Stood heir to th' first. Now, sir, be judge yourself
Whether I in any just term am affined 40
To love the Moor.

RODERIGO   I would not follow him then.

IAGO   Oh, sir, content you. 43
I follow him to serve my turn upon him.
We cannot all be masters, nor all masters
Cannot be truly followed. You shall mark 46
Many a duteous and knee-crooking knave
That, doting on his own obsequious bondage,
Wears out his time, much like his master's ass,
For naught but provender, and when he's old,
    cashiered. 50
Whip me such honest knaves. Others there are 51
Who, trimmed in forms and visages of duty, 52
Keep yet their hearts attending on themselves,
And, throwing but shows of service on their lords,
Do well thrive by them, and when they have lined
    their coats, 55
Do themselves homage. These fellows have some
    soul, 56
And such a one do I profess myself. For, sir,
It is as sure as you are Roderigo,
Were I the Moor I would not be Iago. 59
In following him, I follow but myself—
Heaven is my judge, not I for love and duty,
But seeming so for my peculiar end. 62
For when my outward action doth demonstrate
The native act and figure of my heart 64
In compliment extern, 'tis not long after 65

But I will wear my heart upon my sleeve
For daws to peck at. I am not what I am. 67

RODERIGO
What a full fortune does the thick-lips owe 68
If he can carry't thus!

IAGO   Call up her father. 69
Rouse him, make after him, poison his delight,
Proclaim him in the streets; incense her kinsmen,
And, though he in a fertile climate dwell, 72
Plague him with flies. Though that his joy be joy, 73
Yet throw such changes of vexation on't 74
As it may lose some color. 75

RODERIGO
Here is her father's house. I'll call aloud.

IAGO
Do, with like timorous accent and dire yell 77
As when, by night and negligence, the fire 78
Is spied in populous cities.

RODERIGO
What ho, Brabantio! Signor Brabantio, ho!

IAGO
Awake! What ho, Brabantio! Thieves, thieves, thieves!
Look to your house, your daughter, and your bags!
Thieves, thieves! 83

Brabantio [enters] above [at a window].

BRABANTIO
What is the reason of this terrible summons?
What is the matter there?

RODERIGO
Signor, is all your family within?

IAGO
Are your doors locked?

BRABANTIO   Why, wherefore ask you this?

IAGO
Zounds, sir, you're robbed. For shame, put on your
    gown! 88
Your heart is burst; you have lost half your soul.
Even now, now, very now, an old black ram
Is tupping your white ewe. Arise, arise! 91
Awake the snorting citizens with the bell, 92
Or else the devil will make a grandsire of you. 93
Arise, I say!

BRABANTIO   What, have you lost your wits?

RODERIGO
Most reverend signor, do you know my voice?

---

31 beleed and calmed left to leeward without wind, becalmed. (A sailing metaphor.)   **32 debitor and creditor** (A name for a system of bookkeeping, here used as a contemptuous nickname for Cassio.) **countercaster** i.e., bookkeeper, one who tallies with *counters*, or "metal disks." (Said contemptuously.)   **33 in good time** opportunely, i.e., forsooth   **34 God bless the mark** (Perhaps originally a formula to ward off evil; here an expression of impatience.)   **ancient** standard-bearer, ensign.   **35 his hangman** the executioner of him. **37 Preferment** promotion.   **letter and affection** personal influence and favoritism   **38 old gradation** step-by-step seniority, the traditional way   **40 term** respect.   **affined** bound   **43 content you** don't you worry about that.   **46 truly** faithfully   **50 cashiered** dismissed from service.   **51 Whip me** Whip, as far as I'm concerned **52 trimmed . . . duty** dressed up in the mere form and show of dutifulness   **55 lined their coats** i.e., stuffed their purses   **56 Do themselves homage** i.e., attend to self-interest solely.   **59 Were . . . Iago** i.e., if I were able to assume command, I certainly would not choose to remain a subordinate, or, I would keep a suspicious eye on a flattering subordinate.   **62 peculiar** particular, personal   **64 native** innate.   **figure** shape, intent   **65 compliment extern** outward show (conforming in this case to the inner workings and intention of the heart)

67 daws small crowlike birds, proverbially stupid and avaricious. **I am not what I am** i.e., I am not one who wears his heart on his sleeve.   **68 full** swelling.   **thick-lips** (Elizabethans often applied the term "Moor" to Negroes.)   **owe** own   **69 carry't thus** carry this off. **72–3 though . . . flies** though he seems prosperous and happy now, vex him with misery.   **73 Though . . . be joy** Although he seems fortunate and happy. (Repeats the idea of line 72.)   **74 changes of vexation** vexing changes   **75 As . . . color** that may cause it to lose some of its first gloss.   **77 timorous** frightening   **78 As . . . fire** as when a fire, having gained hold by negligence at night   **83.1 at a window** (This stage direction, from the Quarto, probably calls for an appearance on the gallery above and rearstage.)   **88 Zounds** By His (Christ's) wounds   **91 tupping** covering, copulating with. (Said of sheep.)   **92 snorting** snoring   **93 the devil** (The devil was conventionally pictured as black.)

BRABANTIO   Not I. What are you?

RODERIGO   My name is Roderigo.

BRABANTIO   The worser welcome.
I have charged thee not to haunt about my doors.
In honest plainness thou hast heard me say
My daughter is not for thee; and now, in madness,
Being full of supper and distemp'ring drafts,   102
Upon malicious bravery dost thou come   103
To start my quiet.   104

RODERIGO
Sir, sir, sir—

BRABANTIO   But thou must needs be sure
My spirits and my place have in their power   106
To make this bitter to thee.

RODERIGO   Patience, good sir.

BRABANTIO
What tell'st thou me of robbing? This is Venice;
My house is not a grange.

RODERIGO   Most grave Brabantio,   109
In simple and pure soul I come to you.   110

IAGO   Zounds, sir, you are one of those that will not
serve God if the devil bid you. Because we come to do
you service and you think we are ruffians, you'll have
your daughter covered with a Barbary horse; you'll   114
have your nephews neigh to you; you'll have coursers   115
for cousins and jennets for germans.   116

BRABANTIO   What profane wretch art thou?

IAGO   I am one, sir, that comes to tell you your daughter
and the Moor are now making the beast with two
backs.

BRABANTIO
Thou art a villain.

IAGO   You are—a senator.   121

BRABANTIO
This thou shalt answer. I know thee, Roderigo.   122

RODERIGO
Sir, I will answer anything. But I beseech you,
If't be your pleasure and most wise consent—   124
As partly I find it is—that your fair daughter,
At this odd-even and dull watch o'th' night,   126
Transported with no worse nor better guard   127
But with a knave of common hire, a gondolier,   128
To the gross clasps of a lascivious Moor—
If this be known to you and your allowance   130
We then have done you bold and saucy wrongs.   131
But if you know not this, my manners tell me
We have your wrong rebuke. Do not believe

That, from the sense of all civility,   134
I thus would play and trifle with your reverence.   135
Your daughter, if you have not given her leave,
I say again, hath made a gross revolt,
Tying her duty, beauty, wit, and fortunes   138
In an extravagant and wheeling stranger   139
Of here and everywhere. Straight satisfy yourself.   140
If she be in her chamber or your house,
Let loose on me the justice of the state
For thus deluding you.

BRABANTIO [calling]   Strike on the tinder, ho!   144
Give me a taper! Call up all my people!
This accident is not unlike my dream.   146
Belief of it oppresses me already.
Light, I say, light!   Exit [above].

IAGO   Farewell, for I must leave you.
It seems not meet nor wholesome to my place   149
To be produced—as, if I stay, I shall—   150
Against the Moor. For I do know the state,
However this may gall him with some check,   152
Cannot with safety cast him, for he's embarked   153
With such loud reason to the Cyprus wars,   154
Which even now stands in act, that, for their souls,   155
Another of his fathom they have none   156
To lead their business; in which regard,   157
Though I do hate him as I do hell pains,
Yet for necessity of present life   159
I must show out a flag and sign of love,
Which is indeed but sign. That you shall surely find
    him,
Lead to the Sagittary the raisèd search,   162
And there will I be with him. So farewell.   Exit.   163

    Enter [below] Brabantio [in his nightgown] with
    servants and torches.

BRABANTIO
It is too true an evil. Gone she is;
And what's to come of my despisèd time   165
Is naught but bitterness. Now, Roderigo,
Where didst thou see her?—Oh, unhappy girl!—
With the Moor, say'st thou?—Who would be a father!—
How didst thou know 'twas she?—Oh, she deceives
    me
Past thought!—What said she to you?—Get more
    tapers.
Raise all my kindred.—Are they married, think you?

---

102 distemp'ring intoxicating   **103 Upon malicious bravery** with hostile intent to defy me   **104 start** startle, disrupt   **106 My . . . power** my temperament and my authority of office have it in their power   **109 grange** isolated country house.   **110 simple** sincere   **114 Barbary** from northern Africa (and hence associated with Othello)   **115 nephews** i.e., grandsons   **115–16 you'll . . . germans** you'll consent to have powerful horses for kinfolks and small Spanish horses for near relatives.   **121 a senator** (Said with mock politeness, as though the word itself were an insult.)   **122 answer** be held accountable for.   **124 wise** well-informed   **126 At . . . night** at this hour that is between day and night, neither the one nor the other   **127 with** by   **128 But with a knave** than by a low fellow, a servant   **130 and your allowance** and has your permission   **131 saucy** insolent

134 from contrary to.   **civility** good manners, decency   **135 your reverence** (1) the respect due to you (2) Your Reverence.   **138 wit** intelligence   **139–40 In . . . everywhere** to a wandering and vagabond foreigner of uncertain origins.   **140 Straight** Straightaway   **144 tinder** charred linen ignited by a spark from flint and steel, used to light torches or *tapers* (lines 145, 170)   **146 accident** occurrence, event   **149 meet** fitting.   **place** position (as ensign)   **150 produced** produced (as a witness)   **152 gall** rub; oppress.   **check** rebuke   **153 cast** dismiss.   **embarked** engaged   **154 loud** urgent   **155 stands in act** have started.   **for their souls** to save their souls   **156 fathom** i.e., ability, depth of experience   **157 in which regard** out of regard for which   **159 life** livelihood   **162 Sagittary** (An inn or house where Othello and Desdemona are staying, named for its sign of Sagittarius, or Centaur.)   **raisèd search** search party roused out of sleep   **163.1 nightgown** dressing gown. (This costuming is specified in the Quarto text.)   **165 time** i.e., remainder of life

RODERIGO Truly, I think they are.

BRABANTIO

Oh, heaven! How got she out? Oh, treason of the
    blood!
Fathers, from hence trust not your daughters' minds
By what you see them act. Is there not charms   175
By which the property of youth and maidhood   176
May be abused? Have you not read, Roderigo,   177
Of some such thing?

RODERIGO   Yes, sir, I have indeed.

BRABANTIO

Call up my brother.—Oh, would you had had her!—
Some one way, some another.—Do you know
Where we may apprehend her and the Moor?

RODERIGO

I think I can discover him, if you please   182
To get good guard and go along with me.

BRABANTIO

Pray you, lead on. At every house I'll call;
I may command at most.—Get weapons, ho!   185
And raise some special officers of night.—
On, good Roderigo. I will deserve your pains.   187

                                 Exeunt.

❖

1.2

Enter Othello, Iago, attendants with torches.

IAGO

Though in the trade of war I have slain men,
Yet do I hold it very stuff o'th' conscience   2
To do no contrived murder. I lack iniquity   3
Sometimes to do me service. Nine or ten times
I had thought t'have yerked him here under the ribs. 5

OTHELLO

'Tis better as it is.

IAGO   Nay, but he prated,
And spoke such scurvy and provoking terms
Against your honor
That, with the little godliness I have,
I did full hard forbear him. But, I pray you, sir,   10
Are you fast married? Be assured of this,
That the magnifico is much beloved,   12
And hath in his effect a voice potential   13
As double as the Duke's. He will divorce you,
Or put upon you what restraint or grievance
The law, with all his might to enforce it on,
Will give him cable.

OTHELLO   Let him do his spite.   17
My services which I have done the seigniory   18

Shall out-tongue his complaints. 'Tis yet to know—   19
Which, when I know that boasting is an honor,
I shall promulgate—I fetch my life and being
From men of royal siege, and my demerits   22
May speak unbonneted to as proud a fortune   23
As this that I have reached. For know, Iago,
But that I love the gentle Desdemona,
I would not my unhousèd free condition   26
Put into circumscription and confine   27
For the seas' worth. But look, what lights come yond? 28

    Enter Cassio [and officers] with torches.

IAGO

Those are the raisèd father and his friends.
You were best go in.

OTHELLO   Not I. I must be found.
My parts, my title, and my perfect soul   31
Shall manifest me rightly. Is it they?

IAGO By Janus, I think no.   33

OTHELLO

The servants of the Duke? And my lieutenant?
The goodness of the night upon you, friends!
What is the news?

CASSIO   The Duke does greet you, General,
And he requires your haste-post-haste appearance
Even on the instant.

OTHELLO   What is the matter, think you?

CASSIO

Something from Cyprus, as I may divine.   39
It is a business of some heat. The galleys   40
Have sent a dozen sequent messengers   41
This very night at one another's heels,
And many of the consuls, raised and met,   43
Are at the Duke's already. You have been hotly called
    for;
When, being not at your lodging to be found,
The Senate hath sent about three several quests   46
To search you out.

OTHELLO   'Tis well I am found by you.
I will but spend a word here in the house
And go with you.   [*Exit.*]

CASSIO   Ancient, what makes he here?   49

IAGO

Faith, he tonight hath boarded a land carrack.   50
If it prove lawful prize, he's made forever.   51

19 yet to know not yet widely known   **22 siege** i.e., rank. (Literally, a seat used by a person of distinction.)   **demerits** deserts   **23 unbonneted** without removing the hat, i.e., on equal terms. (Or "with hat off," "in all due modesty.")   **26 unhousèd** unconfined, undomesticated   **27 circumscription and confine** restriction and confinement   **28 the seas' worth** all the riches at the bottom of the sea.   **28.1** *officers* (The Quarto text specifies, "*Enter Cassio with lights, Officers, and torches.*")   **31 My . . . soul** My natural gifts, my position or reputation, and my unflawed conscience   **33 Janus** Roman two-faced god of beginnings   **39 divine** guess.   **40 heat** urgency.   **41 sequent** successive   **43 consuls** senators   **46 about** all over the city.   **several** separate   **49 makes** does   **50 boarded** gone aboard and seized as an act of piracy. (With sexual suggestion.)   **carrack** large merchant ship.   **51 prize** booty

175 charms spells   **176 property** special quality, nature   **177 abused** deceived.   **182 discover** reveal, uncover   **185 command** demand assistance   **187 deserve** show gratitude for
1.2. Location: Venice. Another street, before Othello's lodgings.
2 very stuff essence, basic material. (Continuing the metaphor of *trade* from line 1.)   **3 contrived** premeditated   **5 yerked** stabbed. **him** i.e., Roderigo   **10 I . . . him** I restrained myself with great difficulty from assaulting him.   **12 magnifico** Venetian grandee, i.e., Brabantio   **13 in his effect** at his command.   **potential** powerful
17 cable i.e., scope.   **18 seigniory** Venetian government

CASSIO
I do not understand.
IAGO   He's married.
CASSIO   To who?

[*Enter Othello.*]

IAGO
Marry, to—Come, Captain, will you go?   53
OTHELLO   Have with you.   54
CASSIO
Here comes another troop to seek for you.   55

Enter Brabantio, Roderigo, with officers and
torches.

IAGO
It is Brabantio. General, be advised.   56
He comes to bad intent.
OTHELLO   Holla! Stand there!
RODERIGO
Signor, it is the Moor.
BRABANTIO   Down with him, thief!
                                  [*They draw on both sides.*]
IAGO
You, Roderigo! Come, sir, I am for you.
OTHELLO
Keep up your bright swords, for the dew will rust
      them.   60
Good signor, you shall more command with years
Than with your weapons.
BRABANTIO
O thou foul thief, where hast thou stowed my
      daughter?
Damned as thou art, thou hast enchanted her!
For I'll refer me to all things of sense,   65
If she in chains of magic were not bound
Whether a maid so tender, fair, and happy,
So opposite to marriage that she shunned
The wealthy curlèd darlings of our nation,
Would ever have, t'incur a general mock,
Run from her guardage to the sooty bosom   71
Of such a thing as thou—to fear, not to delight.
Judge me the world if 'tis not gross in sense   73
That thou hast practiced on her with foul charms,
Abused her delicate youth with drugs or minerals   75
That weakens motion. I'll have't disputed on;   76
'Tis probable and palpable to thinking.
I therefore apprehend and do attach thee   78
For an abuser of the world, a practicer   79
Of arts inhibited and out of warrant.—   80
Lay hold upon him! If he do resist,

Subdue him at his peril.
OTHELLO   Hold your hands,
Both you of my inclining and the rest.   83
Were it my cue to fight, I should have known it
Without a prompter.—Whither will you that I go
To answer this your charge?
BRABANTIO   To prison, till fit time
Of law and course of direct session   88
Call thee to answer.
OTHELLO   What if I do obey?
How may the Duke be therewith satisfied,
Whose messengers are here about my side
Upon some present business of the state
To bring me to him?
OFFICER   'Tis true, most worthy signor.
The Duke's in council, and your noble self,
I am sure, is sent for.
BRABANTIO   How? The Duke in council?
In this time of the night? Bring him away.   96
Mine's not an idle cause. The Duke himself,   97
Or any of my brothers of the state,
Cannot but feel this wrong as 'twere their own;
For if such actions may have passage free,   100
Bondslaves and pagans shall our statesmen be.
                                        Exeunt.

1.3

*Enter Duke [and] Senators [and sit at a table, with
lights], and Officers. [The Duke and Senators
are reading dispatches.]*

DUKE
There is no composition in these news   1
That gives them credit.
FIRST SENATOR   Indeed, they are disproportioned.   3
My letters say a hundred and seven galleys.
DUKE
And mine, a hundred forty.
SECOND SENATOR   And mine, two hundred.
But though they jump not on a just account—   6
As in these cases, where the aim reports   7
'Tis oft with difference—yet do they all confirm
A Turkish fleet, and bearing up to Cyprus.
DUKE
Nay, it is possible enough to judgment.
I do not so secure me in the error   11
But the main article I do approve   12
In fearful sense.

---

53 Marry (An oath, originally "by the Virgin Mary"; here used
with wordplay on *married*.)   **54 Have with you** i.e., Let's go.
55.1–2 *officers and torches* (The Quarto text calls for *"others with lights
and weapons."*)   **56 be advised** be on your guard.   **60 Keep up** Keep
in the sheath   **65 I'll . . . sense** I'll submit my case to one and all
71 guardage guardianship   **73 gross in sense** obvious
75 minerals i.e., poisons   **76 weakens motion** impair the vital faculties.   **disputed on** argued in court by professional counsel, debated
by experts   **78 attach** arrest   **79 abuser** deceiver   **80 arts inhibited**
prohibited arts, black magic.   **out of warrant** illegal.

83 inclining following, party   **88 course of direct session** regular or
specially convened legal proceedings   **96 away** right along.   **97 idle**
trifling   **100 may . . . free** are allowed to go unchecked
1.3. Location: Venice. A council chamber.
0.1–2 *Enter . . . Officers* (The Quarto text calls for the Duke and senators to *"set at a Table with lights and Attendants."*)   **1 composition** consistency   **3 disproportioned** inconsistent.   **6 jump** agree.   **just** exact
7 the aim conjecture   **11–12 I do not . . . approve** I do not take such
(false) comfort in the discrepancies that I fail to perceive the main
point, i.e., that the Turkish fleet is threatening

SAILOR (*within*) What ho, what ho, what ho!

Enter Sailor.

OFFICER   A messenger from the galleys.

DUKE   Now, what's the business?

SAILOR

The Turkish preparation makes for Rhodes.   16
So was I bid report here to the state
By Signor Angelo.

DUKE

How say you by this change?

FIRST SENATOR   This cannot be   19
By no assay of reason. 'Tis a pageant   20
To keep us in false gaze. When we consider   21
Th'importancy of Cyprus to the Turk,
And let ourselves again but understand
That, as it more concerns the Turk than Rhodes,
So may he with more facile question bear it,   25
For that it stands not in such warlike brace,   26
But altogether lacks th'abilities   27
That Rhodes is dressed in—if we make thought of this,   28
We must not think the Turk is so unskillful   29
To leave that latest which concerns him first,   30
Neglecting an attempt of ease and gain
To wake and wage a danger profitless.   32

DUKE

Nay, in all confidence, he's not for Rhodes.

OFFICER   Here is more news.

Enter a Messenger.

MESSENGER

The Ottomites, reverend and gracious,
Steering with due course toward the isle of Rhodes,
Have there injointed them with an after fleet.   37

FIRST SENATOR

Ay, so I thought. How many, as you guess?

MESSENGER

Of thirty sail; and now they do restem   39
Their backward course, bearing with frank
    appearance   40
Their purposes toward Cyprus. Signor Montano,
Your trusty and most valiant servitor,   42
With his free duty recommends you thus,   43
And prays you to believe him.

DUKE   'Tis certain then for Cyprus.
Marcus Luccicos, is not he in town?

FIRST SENATOR   He's now in Florence.

DUKE

Write from us to him, post-post-haste. Dispatch.

FIRST SENATOR

Here comes Brabantio and the valiant Moor.

Enter Brabantio, Othello, Cassio, Iago,
Roderigo, and officers.

DUKE

Valiant Othello, we must straight employ you   50
Against the general enemy Ottoman.   51
[*To Brabantio*] I did not see you; welcome, gentle
    signor.   52
We lacked your counsel and your help tonight.

BRABANTIO

So did I yours. Good Your Grace, pardon me;
Neither my place nor aught I heard of business   55
Hath raised me from my bed, nor doth the general
    care
Take hold on me, for my particular grief   57
Is of so floodgate and o'erbearing nature   58
That it engluts and swallows other sorrows   59
And it is still itself.

DUKE   Why, what's the matter?   60

BRABANTIO

My daughter! Oh, my daughter!

DUKE AND SENATORS   Dead?

BRABANTIO   Ay, to me.
She is abused, stol'n from me, and corrupted   62
By spells and medicines bought of mountebanks;
For nature so preposterously to err,
Being not deficient, blind, or lame of sense,   65
Sans witchcraft could not.   66

DUKE

Whoe'er he be that in this foul proceeding
Hath thus beguiled your daughter of herself,
And you of her, the bloody book of law
You shall yourself read in the bitter letter
After your own sense—yea, though our proper son   71
Stood in your action.

BRABANTIO   Humbly I thank Your Grace.   72
Here is the man, this Moor, whom now it seems
Your special mandate for the state affairs
Hath hither brought.

ALL   We are very sorry for't.

DUKE [*to Othello*]

What, in your own part, can you say to this?

BRABANTIO   Nothing, but this is so.

OTHELLO

Most potent, grave, and reverend signors,
My very noble and approved good masters: 79
That I have ta'en away this old man's daughter,
It is most true; true, I have married her.
The very head and front of my offending   82

---

16 **preparation** fleet prepared for battle   19 **by** about   20 **assay** test.
pageant mere show   21 **in false gaze** looking the wrong way.   25 **So
may . . . it** so also he (the Turk) can more easily capture it (Cyprus)
26 **For that** since.   **brace** state of defense   27 **th'abilities** the means
of self-defense   28 **dressed in** equipped with   29 **unskillful** deficient in judgment   30 **latest** last   32 **wake and wage** stir up and risk
37 **injointed them** joined themselves.   **after** second, following
39–40 **restem . . . course** retrace their original course   40 **frank
appearance** undisguised intent   42 **servitor** officer under your command   43 **free duty** freely given and loyal service.   **recommends**
commends himself and reports to

50 **straight** straightaway   51 **general enemy** universal enemy to all
Christendom   52 **gentle** noble   55 **place** official position   57 **particular** personal   58 **floodgate** i.e., overwhelming (as when floodgates
are opened)   59 **engluts** engulfs   60 **is still itself** remains undiminished.   62 **abused** deceived   65 **deficient** defective.   **lame of sense**
deficient in sensory perception   66 **Sans** without   71 **After . . .
sense** according to your own interpretation.   **our proper** my own
72 **Stood . . . action** were under your accusation.   79 **approved**
proved, esteemed   82 **head and front** height and breadth, entire
extent

Hath this extent, no more. Rude am I in my speech,   83
And little blessed with the soft phrase of peace;
For since these arms of mine had seven years' pith,   85
Till now some nine moons wasted, they have used   86
Their dearest action in the tented field;   87
And little of this great world can I speak
More than pertains to feats of broils and battle,
And therefore little shall I grace my cause
In speaking for myself. Yet, by your gracious patience,
I will a round unvarnished tale deliver   92
Of my whole course of love—what drugs, what
    charms,
What conjuration, and what mighty magic,
For such proceeding I am charged withal,   95
I won his daughter.

BRABANTIO   A maiden never bold;
Of spirit so still and quiet that her motion   97
Blushed at herself; and she, in spite of nature,   98
Of years, of country, credit, everything,   99
To fall in love with what she feared to look on!
It is a judgment maimed and most imperfect
That will confess perfection so could err   102
Against all rules of nature, and must be driven
To find out practices of cunning hell   104
Why this should be. I therefore vouch again   105
That with some mixtures powerful o'er the blood,   106
Or with some dram conjured to this effect,   107
He wrought upon her.

DUKE   To vouch this is no proof,
Without more wider and more overt test   109
Than these thin habits and poor likelihoods   110
Of modern seeming do prefer against him.   111

FIRST SENATOR   But Othello, speak.
Did you by indirect and forcèd courses   113
Subdue and poison this young maid's affections?
Or came it by request and such fair question   115
As soul to soul affordeth?

OTHELLO   I do beseech you,
Send for the lady to the Sagittary
And let her speak of me before her father.
If you do find me foul in her report,
The trust, the office I do hold of you
Not only take away, but let your sentence
Even fall upon my life.

DUKE   Fetch Desdemona hither.

OTHELLO [to Iago]
Ancient, conduct them. You best know the place.

[Exeunt Iago and attendants.]

And, till she come, as truly as to heaven
I do confess the vices of my blood,   125
So justly to your grave ears I'll present   126
How I did thrive in this fair lady's love,
And she in mine.

DUKE   Say it, Othello.

OTHELLO
Her father loved me, oft invited me,
Still questioned me the story of my life   131
From year to year—the battles, sieges, fortunes
That I have passed.
I ran it through, even from my boyish days
To th' very moment that he bade me tell it,
Wherein I spoke of most disastrous chances,
Of moving accidents by flood and field,   137
Of hairbreadth scapes i'th'imminent deadly breach,   138
Of being taken by the insolent foe
And sold to slavery, of my redemption thence,
And portance in my travels' history,   141
Wherein of antres vast and deserts idle,   142
Rough quarries, rocks, and hills whose heads touch
    heaven,   143
It was my hint to speak—such was my process—   144
And of the Cannibals that each other eat,
The Anthropophagi, and men whose heads   146
Do grow beneath their shoulders. These things to hear
Would Desdemona seriously incline;
But still the house affairs would draw her thence,
Which ever as she could with haste dispatch
She'd come again, and with a greedy ear
Devour up my discourse. Which I, observing,
Took once a pliant hour, and found good means   153
To draw from her a prayer of earnest heart
That I would all my pilgrimage dilate,   155
Whereof by parcels she had something heard,   156
But not intentively. I did consent,   157
And often did beguile her of her tears,
When I did speak of some distressful stroke
That my youth suffered. My story being done,
She gave me for my pains a world of sighs.
She swore, in faith, 'twas strange, 'twas passing
    strange,   162
'Twas pitiful, 'twas wondrous pitiful.
She wished she had not heard it, yet she wished
That heaven had made her such a man. She thanked
    me,   165
And bade me, if I had a friend that loved her,
I should but teach him how to tell my story,
And that would woo her. Upon this hint I spake.   168
She loved me for the dangers I had passed,

---

83 **Rude** Unpolished   85 **since . . . pith** i.e., since I was seven. (*Pith* means "strength, vigor.")   86 **Till . . . wasted** until some nine months ago (since when Othello has evidently not been on active duty, but in Venice)   87 **dearest** most valuable   92 **round** plain   95 **withal** with   97–8 **her . . . herself** i.e., she blushed easily at herself. (*Motion* can suggest the impulse of the soul or of the emotions, or physical movement.)   99 **years** i.e., difference in age.   **credit** virtuous reputation   102 **confess** concede (that)   104 **practices** plots   105 **vouch** assert   106 **blood** passions   107 **dram . . . effect** dose made by magical spells to have this effect   109 **more wider** fuller.   **test** testimony   110 **habits** garments, i.e., appearances.   **poor likelihoods** weak inferences   111 **modern seeming** commonplace assumption.   **prefer** bring forth   113 **forcèd courses** means used against her will   115 **question** conversation

125 **blood** passions, human nature   126 **justly** truthfully, accurately   131 **Still** continually   137 **moving accidents** stirring happenings   138 **i'th'imminent . . . breach** in death-threatening gaps made in a fortification   141 **portance** conduct   142 **antres** caverns.   **idle** barren, desolate   143 **Rough quarries** rugged rock formations   144 **hint** occasion, opportunity   146 **Anthropophagi** man-eaters. (A term from Pliny's *Natural History*.)   153 **pliant** well-suiting   155 **dilate** relate in detail   156 **by parcels** piecemeal   157 **intentively** with full attention, continuously   162 **passing** exceedingly   165 **made her** (1) created her to be (2) made for her   168 **hint** (1) opportunity (2) hint (in the modern sense)

And I loved her that she did pity them.
This only is the witchcraft I have used.
Here comes the lady. Let her witness it.

Enter Desdemona, Iago, [and] attendants.

DUKE
I think this tale would win my daughter too.
Good Brabantio,
Take up this mangled matter at the best.   175
Men do their broken weapons rather use
Than their bare hands.

BRABANTIO   I pray you, hear her speak.
If she confess that she was half the wooer,
Destruction on my head if my bad blame
Light on the man!—Come hither, gentle mistress.
Do you perceive in all this noble company
Where most you owe obedience?

DESDEMONA   My noble father,
I do perceive here a divided duty.
To you I am bound for life and education;   184
My life and education both do learn me   185
How to respect you. You are the lord of duty;   186
I am hitherto your daughter. But here's my husband,
And so much duty as my mother showed
To you, preferring you before her father,
So much I challenge that I may profess   190
Due to the Moor my lord.

BRABANTIO   God be with you! I have done.
Please it Your Grace, on to the state affairs.
I had rather to adopt a child than get it.   194
Come hither, Moor.   *[He joins the hands of Othello*
                                      and Desdemona.]
I here do give thee that with all my heart   196
Which, but thou hast already, with all my heart   197
I would keep from thee.—For your sake, jewel,   198
I am glad at soul I have no other child,
For thy escape would teach me tyranny,   200
To hang clogs on them.—I have done, my lord.   201

DUKE
Let me speak like yourself, and lay a sentence   202
Which, as a grece or step, may help these lovers   203
Into your favor.
When remedies are past, the griefs are ended   205
By seeing the worst, which late on hopes depended.   206
To mourn a mischief that is past and gone   207
Is the next way to draw new mischief on.   208
What cannot be preserved when fortune takes,   209
Patience her injury a mock'ry makes.   210

The robbed that smiles steals something from the thief;
He robs himself that spends a bootless grief.   212

BRABANTIO
So let the Turk of Cyprus us beguile,
We lose it not, so long as we can smile.
He bears the sentence well that nothing bears   215
But the free comfort which from thence he hears,   216
But he bears both the sentence and the sorrow   217
That, to pay grief, must of poor patience borrow.   218
These sentences, to sugar or to gall,   219
Being strong on both sides, are equivocal.   220
But words are words. I never yet did hear
That the bruisèd heart was piercèd through the ear.   222
I humbly beseech you, proceed to th'affairs of state.

DUKE   The Turk with a most mighty preparation makes
for Cyprus. Othello, the fortitude of the place is best   225
known to you; and though we have there a substitute   226
of most allowed sufficiency, yet opinion, a sovereign   227
mistress of effects, throws a more safer voice on you.   228
You must therefore be content to slubber the gloss of   229
your new fortunes with this more stubborn and   230
boisterous expedition.   231

OTHELLO
The tyrant custom, most grave senators,
Hath made the flinty and steel couch of war
My thrice-driven bed of down. I do agnize   234
A natural and prompt alacrity
I find in hardness, and do undertake   236
These present wars against the Ottomites.
Most humbly therefore bending to your state,   238
I crave fit disposition for my wife,
Due reference of place and exhibition,   240
With such accommodation and besort   241
As levels with her breeding.   242

DUKE
Why, at her father's.

BRABANTIO   I will not have it so.

OTHELLO
Nor I.

DESDEMONA   Nor I. I would not there reside,
To put my father in impatient thoughts
By being in his eye. Most gracious Duke,
To my unfolding lend your prosperous ear,   247

---

175 Take . . . best make the best of a bad bargain.   **184 education**
upbringing   **185 learn** teach   **186 of duty** to whom duty is due
190 challenge claim   **194 get** beget   **196 with all my heart** wherein
my whole affection has been engaged   **197 with all my heart** willingly, gladly   **198 For your sake** Because of you   **200 escape** elopement   **201 clogs** (Literally, blocks of wood fastened to the legs of
criminals or animals to inhibit escape.)   **202 like yourself** i.e., as you
would, in your proper temper.   **lay a sentence** apply a maxim
203 grece step   **205–6 When . . . depended** When all hope of remedy
is past, our sorrows are ended by realizing that the worst has already
happened which lately we hoped would not happen.   **207 mischief**
misfortune, injury   **208 next** nearest   **209–10 What . . . makes** When
fortune takes away what cannot be saved, patience makes a mockery
of fortune's wrongdoing.

212 spends a bootless grief indulges in unavailing grief.   **215–18 He
bears . . . borrow** A person can easily be comforted by your maxim
that enjoys its platitudinous comfort without having to experience
the misfortune that occasions sorrow, but anyone whose grief bankrupts his poor patience is left with your saying and his sorrow, too.
(*Bears the sentence* also plays on the judicial meaning, "receives judicial sentence.")   **219–20 These . . . equivocal** These fine maxims are equivocal, being equally appropriate to happiness or bitterness.
222 piercèd . . . ear relieved by mere words reaching it through the
ear.   **225 fortitude** strength   **226 substitute** deputy   **227 allowed**
acknowledged   **227–8 opinion . . . on you** general opinion, an important determiner of affairs, chooses you as the best man.   **229 slubber**
soil, sully   **230–1 stubborn . . . expedition** rough and violent expedition, for which haste is needed.   **234 thrice-driven** thrice sifted, winnowed.   **agnize** know in myself, acknowledge   **236 hardness**
hardship   **238 bending . . . state** bowing or kneeling to your authority   **240–2 Due . . . breeding** proper respect for her place (as my
wife) and maintenance, with such suitable provision and attendance
as befits her upbringing.   **247 my unfolding** what I shall unfold or
say.   **prosperous** favorable

And let me find a charter in your voice,   248
T'assist my simpleness.
DUKE   What would you, Desdemona?
DESDEMONA
That I did love the Moor to live with him,
My downright violence and storm of fortunes   252
May trumpet to the world. My heart's subdued
Even to the very quality of my lord.   254
I saw Othello's visage in his mind,
And to his honors and his valiant parts   256
Did I my soul and fortunes consecrate.
So that, dear lords, if I be left behind
A moth of peace, and he go to the war,   259
The rites for why I love him are bereft me,   260
And I a heavy interim shall support   261
By his dear absence. Let me go with him.   262
OTHELLO   Let her have your voice.   263
Vouch with me, heaven, I therefor beg it not
To please the palate of my appetite,
Nor to comply with heat—the young affects   266
In me defunct—and proper satisfaction,   267
But to be free and bounteous to her mind.   268
And heaven defend your good souls that you think   269
I will your serious and great business scant
When she is with me. No, when light-winged toys
Of feathered Cupid seel with wanton dullness   272
My speculative and officed instruments,   273
That my disports corrupt and taint my business,   274
Let huswives make a skillet of my helm,
And all indign and base adversities   276
Make head against my estimation!   277
DUKE
Be it as you shall privately determine,
Either for her stay or going. Th'affair cries haste,
And speed must answer it.
A SENATOR   You must away tonight.
DESDEMONA
Tonight, my lord?
DUKE   This night.
OTHELLO   With all my heart.
DUKE
At nine i'th' morning here we'll meet again.
Othello, leave some officer behind,
And he shall our commission bring to you,
With such things else of quality and respect   285
As doth import you.
OTHELLO   So please Your Grace, my ancient; 286

A man he is of honesty and trust.
To his conveyance I assign my wife,
With what else needful Your Good Grace shall think
To be sent after me.
DUKE   Let it be so.
Good night to everyone. [*To Brabantio*] And, noble
   signor,
If virtue no delighted beauty lack,   292
Your son-in-law is far more fair than black.
FIRST SENATOR
Adieu, brave Moor. Use Desdemona well.
BRABANTIO
Look to her, Moor, if thou hast eyes to see.
She has deceived her father, and may thee.
                   Exeunt [Duke, Brabantio, Cassio, Senators, and
                                                officers].
OTHELLO
My life upon her faith!—Honest Iago,
My Desdemona must I leave to thee.
I prithee, let thy wife attend on her,
And bring them after in the best advantage.   300
Come, Desdemona. I have but an hour
Of love, of worldly matters and direction,   302
To spend with thee. We must obey the time.   303
                                Exit [with Desdemona].
RODERIGO   Iago—
IAGO   What say'st thou, noble heart?
RODERIGO   What will I do, think'st thou?
IAGO   Why, go to bed and sleep.
RODERIGO   I will incontinently drown myself.   308
IAGO   If thou dost, I shall never love thee after. Why,
   thou silly gentleman?
RODERIGO   It is silliness to live when to live is torment;
   and then have we a prescription to die when death is   312
   our physician.
IAGO   Oh, villainous! I have looked upon the world for   314
   four times seven years, and, since I could distinguish
   betwixt a benefit and an injury, I never found man
   that knew how to love himself. Ere I would say I
   would drown myself for the love of a guinea hen, I   318
   would change my humanity with a baboon.   319
RODERIGO   What should I do? I confess it is my shame
   to be so fond, but it is not in my virtue to amend it. 321
IAGO   Virtue? A fig! 'Tis in ourselves that we are thus or 322
   thus. Our bodies are our gardens, to the which our
   wills are gardeners; so that if we will plant nettles or
   sow lettuce, set hyssop and weed up thyme, supply it   325
   with one gender of herbs or distract it with many,   326
   either to have it sterile with idleness or manured with 327

---

248 **charter** privilege, authorization   252 **My . . . fortunes** my plain and total breach of social custom   254 **quality** moral and spiritual identity   256 **parts** qualities   259 **moth** i.e., one who consumes merely   260 **rites** rites of love. (With a suggestion, too, of "rights," sharing.)   261 **heavy** burdensome   262 **dear** grievous   263 **voice** consent.   266 **heat** sexual passion.   **young affects** passions of youth, adolescent desires   267 **defunct** done with, at an end.   **proper** personal   268 **free** generous   269 **defend** forbid.   **think** should think   272 **seel** i.e., make blind (as in falconry, by sewing up the eyes of the hawk during training)   273 **My . . . instruments** my eyes, whose function is to see   274 **That . . . business** in such a way that my sexual pastimes interfere with my official duties   276 **indign** unworthy, shameful   277 **Make head** raise an army.   **estimation** reputation.   285 **of quality and respect** of importance and relevance   286 **import** concern

292 **delighted** capable of delighting   300 **in . . . advantage** at the most favorable opportunity.   302 **direction** instructions   303 **the time** the urgency of the present crisis.   308 **incontinently** immediately, without self-restraint   312 **prescription** (1) right based on long-established custom (2) doctor's prescription   314 **villainous** i.e., what perfect nonsense.   318 **guinea hen** (A slang term for a prostitute.)   319 **change** exchange   321 **fond** infatuated.   **virtue** strength, nature   322 **fig** (To give a fig is to thrust the thumb between the first and second fingers in a vulgar and insulting gesture.)   325 **hyssop** a herb of the mint family   326 **gender** kind.   **distract it with** divide it among   327 **idleness** want of cultivation

industry—why, the power and corrigible authority of 328
this lies in our wills. If the beam of our lives had not 329
one scale of reason to poise another of sensuality, the 330
blood and baseness of our natures would conduct us 331
to most preposterous conclusions. But we have reason
to cool our raging motions, our carnal stings, our 333
unbitted lusts, whereof I take this that you call love to 334
be a sect or scion.   335

RODERIGO   It cannot be.

IAGO   It is merely a lust of the blood and a permission
of the will. Come, be a man. Drown thyself? Drown
cats and blind puppies. I have professed me thy friend, 339
and I confess me knit to thy deserving with cables of
perdurable toughness. I could never better stead thee 341
than now. Put money in thy purse. Follow thou the
wars; defeat thy favor with an usurped beard. I say, 343
put money in thy purse. It cannot be long that Desdemona should continue her love to the Moor—put
money in thy purse—nor he his to her. It was a violent commencement in her, and thou shalt see an an- 347
swerable sequestration—put but money in thy purse. 348
These Moors are changeable in their wills—fill thy 349
purse with money. The food that to him now is as
luscious as locusts shall be to him shortly as bitter as 351
coloquintida. She must change for youth; when she is 352
sated with his body, she will find the error of her
choice. She must have change, she must. Therefore
put money in thy purse. If thou wilt needs damn thyself, do it a more delicate way than drowning. Make 356
all the money thou canst. If sanctimony and a frail vow 357
betwixt an erring barbarian and a supersubtle Vene- 358
tian be not too hard for my wits and all the tribe of
hell, thou shalt enjoy her. Therefore make money. A
pox of drowning thyself! It is clean out of the way. 361
Seek thou rather to be hanged in compassing thy joy 362
than to be drowned and go without her.

RODERIGO   Wilt thou be fast to my hopes if I depend on 364
the issue?   365

IAGO   Thou art sure of me. Go, make money. I have
told thee often, and I retell thee again and again, I hate
the Moor. My cause is hearted; thine hath no less rea- 368
son. Let us be conjunctive in our revenge against him. 369
If thou canst cuckold him, thou dost thyself a pleasure,
me a sport. There are many events in the womb of
time which will be delivered. Traverse, go, provide thy 372
money. We will have more of this tomorrow. Adieu.

RODERIGO   Where shall we meet i'th' morning?

IAGO   At my lodging.

RODERIGO   I'll be with thee betimes. [*He starts to leave.*] 376

IAGO   Go to, farewell.—Do you hear, Roderigo?   377

RODERIGO   What say you?

IAGO   No more of drowning, do you hear?

RODERIGO   I am changed.

IAGO   Go to, farewell. Put money enough in your
purse.

RODERIGO   I'll sell all my land.   *Exit.*

IAGO
Thus do I ever make my fool my purse;
For I mine own gained knowledge should profane
If I would time expend with such a snipe   386
But for my sport and profit. I hate the Moor;
And it is thought abroad that twixt my sheets   388
He's done my office. I know not if't be true;   389
But I, for mere suspicion in that kind,
Will do as if for surety. He holds me well;   391
The better shall my purpose work on him.
Cassio's a proper man. Let me see now: 393
To get his place and to plume up my will   394
In double knavery—How, how?—Let's see:
After some time, to abuse Othello's ear   396
That he is too familiar with his wife.   397
He hath a person and a smooth dispose   398
To be suspected, framed to make women false.   399
The Moor is of a free and open nature,   400
That thinks men honest that but seem to be so,
And will as tenderly be led by the nose   402
As asses are.
I have't. It is engendered. Hell and night
Must bring this monstrous birth to the world's light.
                                                    [*Exit.*]

❖

2.1

Enter Montano and two Gentlemen.

MONTANO
What from the cape can you discern at sea?

FIRST GENTLEMAN
Nothing at all. It is a high-wrought flood.   2
I cannot, twixt the heaven and the main,   3
Descry a sail.

MONTANO
Methinks the wind hath spoke aloud at land;
A fuller blast ne'er shook our battlements.
If it hath ruffianed so upon the sea,   7

---

328 **corrigible authority** power to correct   329 **beam** balance
330 **poise** counterbalance   331 **blood** natural passions   333 **motions**
appetites   334 **unbitted** unbridled, uncontrolled   335 **sect or scion**
cutting or offshoot.   339 **blind** i.e., newborn and helpless   341 **perdurable** very durable.   **stead** assist   343 **defeat thy favor** disguise
your face.   **usurped** (The suggestion is that Roderigo is not man
enough to have a beard of his own.)   347–8 **an answerable sequestration** a corresponding cutting off or estrangement   349 **wills** carnal
appetites   351 **locusts** fruit of the carob tree (see Matthew 3:4), or
perhaps honeysuckle   352 **coloquintida** colocynth or bitter apple, a
purgative.   356 **Make** Raise, collect   357 **sanctimony** (1) an aura of
goodness (2) love-worship   358 **erring** wandering, vagabond,
unsteady   361 **clean . . . way** entirely unsuitable as a course of action.
362 **compassing** encompassing, embracing   364 **fast** true   365 **issue**
(successful) outcome.   368 **hearted** fixed in the heart, heartfelt
369 **conjunctive** united   372 **Traverse** (A military marching term.)

376 **betimes** early.   377 **Go to** (An expression of impatience or jolly-
ing along others.)   386 **snipe** woodcock, i.e., fool   388 **it is thought
abroad** it is rumored   389 **my office** i.e., my sexual function as husband.   391 **do . . . surety** act as if on certain knowledge.   **holds me
well** regards me favorably   393 **proper** handsome   394 **plume up**
put a feather in the cap of, i.e., glorify, gratify   396 **abuse** deceive
397 **he** Cassio.   **his** Othello's   398 **dispose** disposition   399 **framed**
formed, made   400 **free and open** frank and unsuspecting   402 **tenderly** readily
2.1. Location: A seaport in Cyprus. An open place near the quay.
2 **high-wrought flood** very agitated sea.   3 **main** ocean. (Also at line
41.)   7 **ruffianed** raged

What ribs of oak, when mountains melt on them,   8
Can hold the mortise? What shall we hear of this?   9

SECOND GENTLEMAN
A segregation of the Turkish fleet.   10
For do but stand upon the foaming shore,
The chidden billow seems to pelt the clouds;   12
The wind-shaked surge, with high and monstrous
    mane,   13
Seems to cast water on the burning Bear   14
And quench the guards of th'ever-fixèd pole.
I never did like molestation view   16
On the enchafèd flood.   17

MONTANO   If that the Turkish fleet   18
Be not ensheltered and embayed, they are drowned;   19
It is impossible to bear it out.   20

Enter a [Third] Gentleman.

THIRD GENTLEMAN   News, lads! Our wars are done.
The desperate tempest hath so banged the Turks
That their designment halts. A noble ship of Venice   23
Hath seen a grievous wreck and sufferance   24
On most part of their fleet.

MONTANO   How? Is this true?

THIRD GENTLEMAN   The ship is here put in,
A Veronesa; Michael Cassio,   28
Lieutenant to the warlike Moor Othello,
Is come on shore; the Moor himself at sea,
And is in full commission here for Cyprus.

MONTANO
I am glad on't. 'Tis a worthy governor.

THIRD GENTLEMAN
But this same Cassio, though he speak of comfort
Touching the Turkish loss, yet he looks sadly   34
And prays the Moor be safe, for they were parted
With foul and violent tempest.

MONTANO   Pray heaven he be,
For I have served him, and the man commands
Like a full soldier. Let's to the seaside, ho!   38
As well to see the vessel that's come in
As to throw out our eyes for brave Othello,
Even till we make the main and th'aerial blue   41
An indistinct regard.

THIRD GENTLEMAN   Come, let's do so,   42
For every minute is expectancy   43

Of more arrivance.   44

Enter Cassio.

CASSIO
Thanks, you the valiant of this warlike isle,
That so approve the Moor! Oh, let the heavens   46
Give him defense against the elements,
For I have lost him on a dangerous sea.

MONTANO   Is he well shipped?

CASSIO
His bark is stoutly timbered, and his pilot
Of very expert and approved allowance;   51
Therefore my hopes, not surfeited to death,   52
Stand in bold cure.
                    [*A cry*] *within:* "A sail, a sail, a sail!"   53

CASSIO   What noise?

A GENTLEMAN
The town is empty. On the brow o'th' sea   55
Stand ranks of people, and they cry "A sail!"

CASSIO
My hopes do shape him for the governor.   57
                            [*A shot within.*]

SECOND GENTLEMAN
They do discharge their shot of courtesy;   58
Our friends at least.

CASSIO   I pray you, sir, go forth,
And give us truth who 'tis that is arrived.

SECOND GENTLEMAN   I shall.   *Exit.*

MONTANO
But, good Lieutenant, is your general wived?

CASSIO
Most fortunately. He hath achieved a maid
That paragons description and wild fame,   64
One that excels the quirks of blazoning pens,   65
And in th'essential vesture of creation   66
Does tire the engineer.

Enter [Second] Gentleman.

                            How now? Who has put in?   67

SECOND GENTLEMAN
'Tis one Iago, ancient to the General.

CASSIO
He's had most favorable and happy speed.
Tempests themselves, high seas, and howling winds,
The guttered rocks and congregated sands—   71
Traitors ensteeped to clog the guiltless keel—   72
As having sense of beauty, do omit   73
Their mortal natures, letting go safely by   74

---

8 **mountains** i.e., of water   9 **hold the mortise** hold their joints
together. (A *mortise* is the socket hollowed out in fitting timbers.)
10 **segregation** dispersal   12 **chidden** i.e., rebuked, repelled (by the
shore), and thus shot into the air   13 **monstrous mane** (The surf is
like the mane of a wild beast.)   14 **the burning Bear** i.e., the constellation Ursa Minor or the Little Bear, which includes the polestar (and
hence regarded as the *guards of th'ever-fixèd pole* in the next line; sometimes the term *guards* is applied to the two "pointers" of the Big Bear
or Dipper, which may be intended here.)   16 **like molestation** comparable disturbance   17 **enchafèd** angry   18 **If that** If   19 **embayed**
sheltered by a bay   20 **bear it out** survive, weather the storm.
23 **designment halts** enterprise is crippled. (Literally, "is lame.")
24 **wreck** shipwreck.   **sufferance** damage, disaster   28 **Veronesa**
from Verona (and perhaps in service with Venice)   34 **sadly** gravely
38 **full** perfect   41 **the main . . . blue** the sea and the sky   42 **An
indistinct regard** indistinguishable in our view.   43 **is expectancy**
gives expectation

44 **arrivance** arrival.   46 **approve** admire, honor   51 **approved
allowance** tested reputation   52–3 **not . . . cure** not worn thin
through repeated application or delayed fulfillment, strongly persist.
55 **brow o'th' sea** cliff-edge   57 **My . . . governor** I hope and imagine
this ship to be Othello's.   58 **discharge . . . courtesy** fire a salute in
token of respect and courtesy   64 **paragons** surpasses.   **wild fame**
extravagant report   65 **quirks** witty conceits.   **blazoning** setting
forth as though in heraldic language   66–7 **And in . . . engineer** and
in her real, God-given, beauty, (she) defeats any attempt to praise her.
(An *engineer* is one who devises, here a poet.)   67 **put in** i.e., to harbor.   71 **guttered** jagged, trenched   72 **ensteeped** lying under water
73 **As** as if.   **omit** forbear to exercise   74 **mortal** deadly

The divine Desdemona.
MONTANO   What is she?
CASSIO
She that I spake of, our great captain's captain,
Left in the conduct of the bold Iago,
Whose footing here anticipates our thoughts   78
A sennight's speed. Great Jove, Othello guard,   79
And swell his sail with thine own powerful breath,
That he may bless this bay with his tall ship,   81
Make love's quick pants in Desdemona's arms,
Give renewed fire to our extincted spirits,
And bring all Cyprus comfort!

        Enter Desdemona, Iago, Roderigo, and Emilia.

                              Oh, behold,
The riches of the ship is come on shore!
You men of Cyprus, let her have your knees.
        [*The gentlemen make curtsy to Desdemona.*]
Hail to thee, lady! And the grace of heaven
Before, behind thee, and on every hand
Enwheel thee round!
DESDEMONA   I thank you, valiant Cassio.
What tidings can you tell me of my lord?
CASSIO
He is not yet arrived, nor know I aught
But that he's well and will be shortly here.
DESDEMONA
Oh, but I fear—How lost you company?
CASSIO
The great contention of the sea and skies
Parted our fellowship.
                    (*Within*) "A sail, a sail!" [*A shot.*]
                    But hark. A sail!
SECOND GENTLEMAN
They give their greeting to the citadel.
This likewise is a friend.
CASSIO   See for the news.
                    [*Exit Second Gentleman.*]
Good Ancient, you are welcome. [*Kissing Emilia.*]
    Welcome, mistress.
Let it not gall your patience, good Iago,
That I extend my manners; 'tis my breeding   100
That gives me this bold show of courtesy.
IAGO
Sir, would she give you so much of her lips
As of her tongue she oft bestows on me,
You would have enough.
DESDEMONA   Alas, she has no speech!   105
IAGO   In faith, too much.
I find it still, when I have list to sleep.   107
Marry, before Your Ladyship, I grant,
She puts her tongue a little in her heart
And chides with thinking.
EMILIA   You have little cause to say so. 110

IAGO
Come on, come on. You are pictures out of doors,   111
Bells in your parlors, wildcats in your kitchens,   112
Saints in your injuries, devils being offended,   113
Players in your huswifery, and huswives in your beds. 114
DESDEMONA   Oh, fie upon thee, slanderer!
IAGO
Nay, it is true, or else I am a Turk.   116
You rise to play, and go to bed to work.
EMILIA
You shall not write my praise.
IAGO   No, let me not.
DESDEMONA
What wouldst write of me, if thou shouldst praise me?
IAGO
Oh, gentle lady, do not put me to't,
For I am nothing if not critical.   121
DESDEMONA
Come on, essay.—There's one gone to the harbor?   122
IAGO   Ay, madam.
DESDEMONA
I am not merry, but I do beguile
The thing I am by seeming otherwise.   125
Come, how wouldst thou praise me?
IAGO
I am about it, but indeed my invention
Comes from my pate as birdlime does from frieze—   128
It plucks out brains and all. But my Muse labors,   129
And thus she is delivered:
If she be fair and wise, fairness and wit,
The one's for use, the other useth it.   132
DESDEMONA
Well praised! How if she be black and witty?   133
IAGO
If she be black, and thereto have a wit,
She'll find a white that shall her blackness fit.   135
DESDEMONA
Worse and worse.
EMILIA   How if fair and foolish?
IAGO
She never yet was foolish that was fair,
For even her folly helped her to an heir.   138
DESDEMONA   These are old fond paradoxes to make fools 139

78–9 **Whose . . . speed** whose arrival here has happened a week
sooner than we expected.   81 **tall** tall-masted   100 **extend** give scope
to.   **breeding** training in the niceties of etiquette   105 **she has no
speech** i.e., she's not a chatterbox, as you allege.   107 **still** always.
list desire   110 **with thinking** i.e., in her thoughts only.

111 **pictures out of doors** i.e., as pretty as pictures, and silently well-
behaved in public   112 **Bells** i.e., jangling, noisy, and brazen.   **in
your kitchens** i.e., in domestic affairs. (Ladies would not do the cooking.)   113 **Saints . . . injuries** i.e., putting on airs of sanctity and innocence when wronged by others   114 **Players . . . beds** play-actors at
domesticity and truly energetic only as lovers in bed.   116 **a Turk** an
infidel, not to be believed.   121 **critical** censorious.   122 **essay** try.
125 **The thing I am** i.e., my anxious self   128 **birdlime** sticky substance used to catch small birds.   **frieze** coarse woolen cloth
129 **labors** (1) exerts herself (2) prepares to deliver a child. (With a following pun on *delivered* in line 130.)   132 **The one's . . . it** i.e., her
cleverness will make use of her beauty.   133 **black** dark-complex-
ioned, brunette   135 **She'll . . . fit** she will find a fair-complexioned
mate suited to her dark complexion. (Punning on *wight*, person, and
contrasting *white* and *black*, with suggestion of sexual coupling.)
138 **folly** (With added meaning of "lechery, wantonness.")   **to an
heir** i.e., to bear a child.   139 **fond** foolish

laugh i'th'alehouse. What miserable praise hast thou
for her that's foul and foolish?   141

IAGO
There's none so foul and foolish thereunto,   142
But does foul pranks which fair and wise ones do.   143

DESDEMONA   Oh, heavy ignorance! Thou praisest the worst
best. But what praise couldst thou bestow on a deserving woman indeed, one that, in the authority of her mer-
it, did justly put on the vouch of very malice itself?   147

IAGO
She that was ever fair, and never proud,
Had tongue at will, and yet was never loud,   149
Never lacked gold and yet went never gay,   150
Fled from her wish, and yet said, "Now I may,"   151
She that being angered, her revenge being nigh,
Bade her wrong stay and her displeasure fly,   153
She that in wisdom never was so frail
To change the cod's head for the salmon's tail,   155
She that could think and ne'er disclose her mind,
See suitors following and not look behind,
She was a wight, if ever such wight were—

DESDEMONA   To do what?

IAGO
To suckle fools and chronicle small beer.   160

DESDEMONA   Oh, most lame and impotent conclusion! Do
not learn of him, Emilia, though he be thy husband.
How say you, Cassio? Is he not a most profane and   163
liberal counselor?   164

CASSIO   He speaks home, madam. You may relish him   165
more in the soldier than in the scholar.   166

[Cassio and Desdemona stand together,
conversing intimately.]

IAGO [*aside*]   He takes her by the palm. Ay, well said,   167
whisper. With as little a web as this will I ensnare as
great a fly as Cassio. Ay, smile upon her, do; I will
gyve thee in thine own courtship. You say true; 'tis so,   170
indeed. If such tricks as these strip you out of your
lieutenantry, it had been better you had not kissed
your three fingers so oft, which now again you are
most apt to play the sir in. Very good; well kissed! An   174
excellent courtesy! 'Tis so, indeed. Yet again your fingers to your lips? Would they were clyster pipes for   176
your sake! [*Trumpet within.*] The Moor! I know his
trumpet.

CASSIO   'Tis truly so.

DESDEMONA   Let's meet him and receive him.

---

141 foul ugly   142 thereunto in addition   143 foul sluttish   147 put
. . . vouch compel the approval   149 Had . . . will was never at a loss
for words   150 gay extravagantly clothed   151 Fled . . . may avoided
temptation where the choice was hers   153 Bade . . . stay i.e.,
resolved to put up with her injury and bade her anger to cease
155 To . . . tail i.e., to be selfishly demanding and ambitious. (The
fish's lower body, below the rib cage, has fewest bones and is generally the succulent portion. With sexual implication as well: cod's head
can be slang for "penis," and tail for "pudendum.")   160 To . . . beer
i.e., To breastfeed babies and keep petty household accounts.
163–4 profane and liberal irreverent and licentious   165 home right
to the target. (A term from fencing.)   relish appreciate   166 in in the
character of   167 well said well done   170 gyve fetter, shackle.
courtship courtesy, show of courtly manners.   You say true i.e.,
That's right, go ahead   174 the sir i.e., the fine gentleman
176 clyster pipes tubes used for enemas and douches

CASSIO   Lo, where he comes!

Enter Othello and attendants.

OTHELLO
Oh, my fair warrior!

DESDEMONA   My dear Othello!

OTHELLO
It gives me wonder great as my content
To see you here before me. O my soul's joy,
If after every tempest come such calms,
May the winds blow till they have wakened death,
And let the laboring bark climb hills of seas
Olympus-high, and duck again as low
As hell's from heaven! If it were now to die,
'Twere now to be most happy, for I fear
My soul hath her content so absolute
That not another comfort like to this
Succeeds in unknown fate.

DESDEMONA   The heavens forbid   193
But that our loves and comforts should increase
Even as our days do grow!

OTHELLO   Amen to that, sweet powers!
I cannot speak enough of this content.
It stops me here; it is too much of joy.
And this, and this, the greatest discords be   199
                                    [*They kiss.*]
That e'er our hearts shall make!

IAGO [*aside*]   Oh, you are well tuned now!
But I'll set down the pegs that make this music,   202
As honest as I am.   203

OTHELLO   Come, let us to the castle.
News, friends! Our wars are done, the Turks are
drowned.
How does my old acquaintance of this isle?—
Honey, you shall be well desired in Cyprus;   207
I have found great love amongst them. Oh, my sweet,
I prattle out of fashion, and I dote   209
In mine own comforts.—I prithee, good Iago,
Go to the bay and disembark my coffers.   211
Bring thou the master to the citadel;   212
He is a good one, and his worthiness
Does challenge much respect.—Come, Desdemona.—   214
Once more, well met at Cyprus!

Exeunt Othello and Desdemona [and all
but Iago and Roderigo].

IAGO [*to a departing attendant*]   Do thou meet me presently at
the harbor. [*To Roderigo*] Come hither. If thou be'st
valiant—as, they say, base men being in love have   218
then a nobility in their natures more than is native to
them—list me. The Lieutenant tonight watches on   220
the court of guard. First, I must tell thee this: 221
Desdemona is directly in love with him.

---

193 Succeeds . . . fate i.e., can follow in the unknown future.
199.1 They kiss (The direction is from the Quarto.)   202 set down
loosen (and hence untune the instrument)   203 As . . . I am for all my
supposed honesty.   207 desired sought after   209 out of fashion
indecorously, incoherently   211 coffers chests, baggage.   212 master
ship's captain   214 challenge lay claim to, deserve   218 base men
even ignoble men   220 list listen to   221 court of guard guardhouse.
(Cassio is in charge of the watch.)

RODERIGO   With him? Why, 'tis not possible.

IAGO   Lay thy finger thus, and let thy soul be instructed. 224
Mark me with what violence she first loved the Moor,
but for bragging and telling her fantastical lies. To love 226
him still for prating? Let not thy discreet heart think it.
Her eye must be fed; and what delight shall she have
to look on the devil? When the blood is made dull with
the act of sport, there should be, again to inflame it 230
and to give satiety a fresh appetite, loveliness in favor, 231
sympathy in years, manners, and beauties—all which 232
the Moor is defective in. Now, for want of these
required conveniences, her delicate tenderness will 234
find itself abused, begin to heave the gorge, disrelish 235
and abhor the Moor. Very nature will instruct her in it 236
and compel her to some second choice. Now, sir, this
granted—as it is a most pregnant and unforced 238
position—who stands so eminent in the degree of this 239
fortune as Cassio does? A knave very voluble, no 240
further conscionable than in putting on the mere form 241
of civil and humane seeming for the better compass- 242
ing of his salt and most hidden loose affection. Why, 243
none, why, none. A slipper and subtle knave, a finder 244
out of occasions, that has an eye can stamp and 245
counterfeit advantages, though true advantage never 246
present itself; a devilish knave. Besides, the knave is
handsome, young, and hath all those requisites in him
that folly and green minds look after. A pestilent 249
complete knave, and the woman hath found him 250
already.

RODERIGO   I cannot believe that in her. She's full of
most blessed condition.   253

IAGO   Blessed fig's end! The wine she drinks is made of 254
grapes. If she had been blessed, she would never have
loved the Moor. Blessed pudding! Didst thou not see 256
her paddle with the palm of his hand? Didst not mark
that?

RODERIGO   Yes, that I did; but that was but courtesy.

IAGO   Lechery, by this hand. An index and obscure pro- 260
logue to the history of lust and foul thoughts. They
met so near with their lips that their breaths embraced
together. Villainous thoughts, Roderigo! When these
mutualities so marshal the way, hard at hand comes 264
the master and main exercise, th'incorporate conclu- 265
sion. Pish! But, sir, be you ruled by me. I have brought

you from Venice. Watch you tonight; for the com- 267
mand, I'll lay't upon you. Cassio knows you not. I'll 268
not be far from you. Do you find some occasion to
anger Cassio, either by speaking too loud, or tainting 270
his discipline, or from what other course you please,
which the time shall more favorably minister.   272

RODERIGO   Well.

IAGO   Sir, he's rash and very sudden in choler, and haply 274
may strike at you. Provoke him that he may, for
even out of that will I cause these of Cyprus to mutiny, 276
whose qualification shall come into no true taste again 277
but by the displanting of Cassio. So shall you have a
shorter journey to your desires by the means I shall
then have to prefer them, and the impediment most 280
profitably removed, without the which there were no
expectation of our prosperity.

RODERIGO   I will do this, if you can bring it to any
opportunity.

IAGO   I warrant thee. Meet me by and by at the citadel. 285
I must fetch his necessaries ashore. Farewell.

RODERIGO   Adieu.   *Exit.*

IAGO
That Cassio loves her, I do well believe't;
That she loves him, 'tis apt and of great credit.   289
The Moor, howbeit that I endure him not,
Is of a constant, loving, noble nature,
And I dare think he'll prove to Desdemona
A most dear husband. Now, I do love her too,
Not out of absolute lust—though peradventure
I stand accountant for as great a sin—   295
But partly led to diet my revenge   296
For that I do suspect the lusty Moor
Hath leaped into my seat, the thought whereof
Doth, like a poisonous mineral, gnaw my innards;
And nothing can or shall content my soul
Till I am evened with him, wife for wife,
Or failing so, yet that I put the Moor
At least into a jealousy so strong
That judgment cannot cure. Which thing to do,
If this poor trash of Venice, whom I trace   305
For his quick hunting, stand the putting on,   306
I'll have our Michael Cassio on the hip,   307
Abuse him to the Moor in the rank garb—   308
For I fear Cassio with my nightcap too—   309
Make the Moor thank me, love me, and reward me
For making him egregiously an ass
And practicing upon his peace and quiet   312

---

224 thus i.e., on your lips   **226 but** only   **230 the act of sport** sex
231 favor appearance   **232 sympathy** correspondence, similarity
234 required conveniences things conducive to sexual compatibility
235 abused cheated, revolted.   **heave the gorge** experience nausea
236 Very nature Her very instincts   **238 pregnant** evident, cogent
239 in . . . of as next in line for   **240 voluble** facile, glib   **241 conscionable** conscientious, conscience-bound   **242 humane** polite,
courteous   **243 salt** licentious.   **affection** passion.   **244 slipper** slippery   **245 an eye can stamp** an eye that can coin, create   **246 advantages** favorable opportunities   **249 folly** wantonness.   **green**
immature   **250 found him** sized him up, perceived his intent
253 condition disposition.   **254 fig's end** (See 1.3.322 for the vulgar
gesture of the fig.)   **256 pudding** sausage.   **260 index** table of contents.   **obscure** veiled, hidden   **264 mutualities** exchanges, intima-
cies.   **hard at hand** closely following   **265 th'incorporate** the carnal

267 Watch you Stand watch   **267–8 for . . . you** I'll arrange for you to
be appointed, given orders; or, I'll put you in charge.   **270 tainting**
disparaging   **272 minister** provide.   **274 choler** wrath.   **haply** perhaps   **276 mutiny** riot   **277 qualification** pacification.   **true taste**
i.e., acceptable state   **280 prefer** advance   **285 warrant** assure.
by and by immediately   **289 apt** probable.   **credit** credibility.
295 accountant accountable   **296 diet** feed   **305 trace** i.e., pursue,
dog; or, keep hungry (?) or perhaps *trash,* a hunting term, meaning to
put weights on a hunting dog in order to slow him down   **306 For** to
make more eager for.   **stand . . . on** responds properly when I incite
him to quarrel   **307 on the hip** at my mercy, where I can throw him.
(A wrestling term.)   **308 Abuse** slander.   **rank garb** coarse manner,
gross fashion   **309 with my nightcap** i.e., as a rival in my bed, as one
who gives me cuckold's horns   **312 practicing upon** plotting against

Even to madness. 'Tis here, but yet confused.
Knavery's plain face is never seen till used.   *Exit.*

❖

2.2

Enter Othello's Herald with a proclamation.

HERALD   It is Othello's pleasure, our noble and valiant
general, that, upon certain tidings now arrived, importing the mere perdition of the Turkish fleet, every   3
man put himself into triumph: some to dance, some to   4
make bonfires, each man to what sport and revels his
addiction leads him. For, besides these beneficial   6
news, it is the celebration of his nuptial. So much was
his pleasure should be proclaimed. All offices are open,   8
and there is full liberty of feasting from this present
hour of five till the bell have told eleven. Heaven bless
the isle of Cyprus and our noble general Othello!
                                                    Exit.

❖

[2.3]

*Enter Othello, Desdemona, Cassio, and
attendants.*

OTHELLO
Good Michael, look you to the guard tonight.
Let's teach ourselves that honorable stop   2
Not to outsport discretion.   3
CASSIO
Iago hath direction what to do,
But notwithstanding, with my personal eye
Will I look to't.
OTHELLO   Iago is most honest.
Michael, good night. Tomorrow with your earliest   7
Let me have speech with you. [*To Desdemona*] Come,
my dear love,
The purchase made, the fruits are to ensue;   9
That profit's yet to come 'tween me and you.—   10
Good night.
          Exit [*Othello, with Desdemona and attendants*].

          Enter Iago.

CASSIO   Welcome, Iago. We must to the watch.
IAGO   Not this hour, Lieutenant; 'tis not yet ten o'th'   13
clock. Our general cast us thus early for the love of his   14
Desdemona; who let us not therefore blame. He hath   15
not yet made wanton the night with her, and she is
sport for Jove.
CASSIO   She's a most exquisite lady.
IAGO   And, I'll warrant her, full of game.

CASSIO   Indeed, she's a most fresh and delicate creature.
IAGO   What an eye she has! Methinks it sounds a parley   21
to provocation.
CASSIO   An inviting eye, and yet methinks right modest.
IAGO   And when she speaks, is it not an alarum to love?   24
CASSIO   She is indeed perfection.
IAGO   Well, happiness to their sheets! Come, Lieutenant,
I have a stoup of wine, and here without are a brace of   27
Cyprus gallants that would fain have a measure to the   28
health of black Othello.
CASSIO   Not tonight, good Iago. I have very poor and
unhappy brains for drinking. I could well wish cour-
tesy would invent some other custom of entertain-
ment.
IAGO   Oh, they are our friends. But one cup! I'll drink for   34
you.   35
CASSIO   I have drunk but one cup tonight, and that was
craftily qualified too, and behold what innovation it   37
makes here. I am unfortunate in the infirmity and   38
dare not task my weakness with any more.
IAGO   What, man? 'Tis a night of revels. The gallants
desire it.
CASSIO   Where are they?
IAGO   Here at the door. I pray you, call them in.
CASSIO   I'll do't, but it dislikes me.   *Exit.*   44
IAGO
If I can fasten but one cup upon him,
With that which he hath drunk tonight already,
He'll be as full of quarrel and offense   47
As my young mistress' dog. Now, my sick fool
Roderigo,
Whom love hath turned almost the wrong side out,
To Desdemona hath tonight caroused   50
Potations pottle-deep; and he's to watch.   51
Three lads of Cyprus—noble swelling spirits,   52
That hold their honors in a wary distance,   53
The very elements of this warlike isle—   54
Have I tonight flustered with flowing cups,
And they watch too. Now, 'mongst this flock of
drunkards   56
Am I to put our Cassio in some action
That may offend the isle.—But here they come.

          Enter Cassio, Montano, and gentlemen; [*servants
following with wine*].

If consequence do but approve my dream,   59
My boat sails freely both with wind and stream.   60
CASSIO   'Fore God, they have given me a rouse already.   61

2.2. Location: Cyprus.
3 mere perdition complete destruction   **4 triumph** public celebration
6 addiction inclination   **8 offices** rooms where food and drink are kept
2.3. Location: Cyprus. The citadel.
2 stop restraint   **3 outsport** celebrate beyond the bounds of   **7 with
your earliest** at your earliest convenience   **9–10 The purchase . . .
you** i.e., though married, we haven't yet consummated our love.
(Possibly, too, Othello is referring to pregnancy. At all events, his
desire for sexual union is manifest.)   **13 Not this hour** Not for an
hour yet   **14 cast** dismissed   **15 who** i.e., Othello

21 sounds a parley calls for a conference, issues an invitation
24 alarum signal calling men to arms. (Continuing the military
metaphor of *parley*, line 21.)   **27 stoup** measure of liquor, two quarts.
without outside.   **brace** pair   **28 fain have a measure** gladly drink a
toast   **34–5 for you** in your place. (Iago will do the steady drinking
to keep the gallants company while Cassio has only one cup.)
37 qualified diluted.   **innovation** disturbance, insurrection   **38 here**
i.e., in my head.   **44 it dislikes me** i.e., I'm reluctant.   **47 offense**
readiness to give or take offense   **50 caroused** drunk off   **51 pottle-
deep** to the bottom of the tankard.   **watch** stand watch.
52 swelling proud   **53 hold . . . distance** i.e., are extremely sensitive
of their honor   **54 elements** lifeblood   **56 watch** are members of the
guard   **59 If . . . dream** If subsequent events will only confirm my
dreams and hopes   **60 stream** current.   **61 rouse** full draft of liquor

MONTANO   Good faith, a little one; not past a pint, as I
am a soldier.
IAGO   Some wine, ho!
[*He sings.*]   "And let me the cannikin clink, clink,   65
          And let me the cannikin clink.
             A soldier's a man,
             Oh, man's life's but a span;   68
          Why, then, let a soldier drink."
Some wine, boys!
CASSIO   'Fore God, an excellent song.
IAGO   I learned it in England, where indeed they are
most potent in potting. Your Dane, your German, and   73
your swag-bellied Hollander—drink, ho!—are noth-
ing to your English.
CASSIO   Is your Englishman so exquisite in his drinking?
IAGO   Why, he drinks you, with facility, your Dane   77
dead drunk; he sweats not to overthrow your Almain;   78
he gives your Hollander a vomit ere the next pottle can
be filled.
CASSIO   To the health of our general!
MONTANO   I am for it, Lieutenant, and I'll do you justice.   82
IAGO   O sweet England! [*He sings.*]

"King Stephen was and-a worthy peer,
   His breeches cost him but a crown;
He held them sixpence all too dear,
   With that he called the tailor lown.   87

He was a wight of high renown,
   And thou art but of low degree.
'Tis pride that pulls the country down;   90
   Then take thy auld cloak about thee."   91

Some wine, ho!
CASSIO   'Fore God, this is a more exquisite song than
the other.
IAGO   Will you hear't again?
CASSIO   No, for I hold him to be unworthy of his place
that does those things. Well, God's above all; and
there be souls must be saved, and there be souls must
not be saved.
IAGO   It's true, good Lieutenant.
CASSIO   For mine own part—no offense to the General,
nor any man of quality—I hope to be saved.   102
IAGO   And so do I too, Lieutenant.
CASSIO   Ay, but, by your leave, not before me; the lieutenant is to be saved before the ancient. Let's have no
more of this; let's to our affairs.—God forgive us our
sins!—Gentlemen, let's look to our business. Do not
think, gentlemen, I am drunk. This is my ancient; this
is my right hand, and this is my left. I am not drunk
now. I can stand well enough, and speak well enough.

GENTLEMEN   Excellent well.
CASSIO   Why, very well then; you must not think then
that I am drunk.   *Exit.*
MONTANO
To th' platform, masters. Come, let's set the watch.   114
                                  [*Exeunt Gentlemen.*]
IAGO
You see this fellow that is gone before.
He's a soldier fit to stand by Caesar
And give direction; and do but see his vice.
'Tis to his virtue a just equinox,   118
The one as long as th'other. 'Tis pity of him.
I fear the trust Othello puts him in,
On some odd time of his infirmity,
Will shake this island.
MONTANO   But is he often thus?
IAGO
'Tis evermore the prologue to his sleep.
He'll watch the horologe a double set,   124
If drink rock not his cradle.
MONTANO   It were well
The General were put in mind of it.
Perhaps he sees it not, or his good nature
Prizes the virtue that appears in Cassio
And looks not on his evils. Is not this true?

Enter Roderigo.

IAGO [*aside to him*]   How now, Roderigo?
I pray you, after the Lieutenant; go.   [*Exit Roderigo.*]
MONTANO
And 'tis great pity that the noble Moor
Should hazard such a place as his own second   133
With one of an engraffed infirmity.   134
It were an honest action to say so
To the Moor.
IAGO   Not I, for this fair island.
I do love Cassio well and would do much
To cure him of this evil.   [*Cry within:* "Help! Help!"]
                        But, hark! What noise?   138

Enter Cassio, pursuing Roderigo.

CASSIO   Zounds, you rogue! You rascal!
MONTANO   What's the matter, Lieutenant?
CASSIO   A knave teach me my duty? I'll beat the knave
into a twiggen bottle.   142
RODERIGO   Beat me?
CASSIO   Dost thou prate, rogue?   [*He strikes Roderigo.*]
MONTANO   Nay, good Lieutenant. [*Restraining him.*] I
pray you, sir, hold your hand.
CASSIO   Let me go, sir, or I'll knock you o'er the
mazard.   148

---

65 cannikin small drinking vessel   **68 span** brief span of time. (Compare Psalm 39:5 as rendered in the Book of Common Prayer: "Thou
hast made my days as it were a span long.")   **73 potting** drinking.
77 drinks you drinks.   **your Dane** your typical Dane   **78 sweats not**
i.e., need not exert himself.   **Almain** German   **82 I'll . . . justice** i.e.,
I'll drink as much as you.   **87 lown** lout, rascal.   **90 pride** i.e.,
extravagance in dress   **91 auld** old   **102 quality** rank

114 set the watch mount the guard.   **118 just equinox** exact counterpart. (*Equinox* is an equal length of days and nights.)   **124 watch . . .
set** stay awake twice around the clock or *horologe*   **133–4 hazard . . .
With** risk giving such an important position as his second in command to   **134 engraffed** engrafted, inveterate   **138.1 pursuing** (The
Quarto text reads, "*driuing in.*")   **142 twiggen** wicker-covered. (Cassio vows to assail Roderigo until his skin resembles wickerwork or
until he has driven Roderigo through the holes in a wickerwork.)
148 mazard i.e., head. (Literally, a drinking vessel.)

MONTANO Come, come, you're drunk.

CASSIO Drunk? [They fight.]

IAGO [aside to Roderigo]

Away, I say. Go out and cry a mutiny. 151

[Exit Roderigo.]

Nay, good Lieutenant—God's will, gentlemen—
Help, ho!—Lieutenant—sir—Montano—sir—
Help, masters!—Here's a goodly watch indeed! 154

[A bell rings.]

Who's that which rings the bell?—Diablo, ho! 155
The town will rise. God's will, Lieutenant, hold! 156
You'll be ashamed forever.

Enter Othello and attendants [with weapons].

OTHELLO

What is the matter here?

MONTANO Zounds, I bleed still.

I am hurt to th' death. He dies! [He thrusts at Cassio.]

OTHELLO Hold, for your lives!

IAGO

Hold, ho! Lieutenant—sir—Montano—gentlemen—
Have you forgot all sense of place and duty?
Hold! The General speaks to you. Hold, for shame!

OTHELLO

Why, how now, ho! From whence ariseth this?
Are we turned Turks, and to ourselves do that 164
Which heaven hath forbid the Ottomites? 165
For Christian shame, put by this barbarous brawl!
He that stirs next to carve for his own rage 167
Holds his soul light; he dies upon his motion. 168
Silence that dreadful bell. It frights the isle
From her propriety. What is the matter, masters? 170
Honest Iago, that looks dead with grieving,
Speak. Who began this? On thy love, I charge thee.

IAGO

I do not know. Friends all but now, even now,
In quarter and in terms like bride and groom 174
Devesting them for bed; and then, but now— 175
As if some planet had unwitted men—
Swords out, and tilting one at others' breasts
In opposition bloody. I cannot speak 178
Any beginning to this peevish odds; 179
And would in action glorious I had lost
Those legs that brought me to a part of it!

OTHELLO

How comes it, Michael, you are thus forgot? 182

CASSIO

I pray you, pardon me. I cannot speak.

OTHELLO

Worthy Montano, you were wont be civil; 184
The gravity and stillness of your youth 185
The world hath noted, and your name is great
In mouths of wisest censure. What's the matter 187
That you unlace your reputation thus 188
And spend your rich opinion for the name 189
Of a night-brawler? Give me answer to it.

MONTANO

Worthy Othello, I am hurt to danger.
Your officer, Iago, can inform you—
While I spare speech, which something now offends
me— 193
Of all that I do know; nor know I aught
By me that's said or done amiss this night,
Unless self-charity be sometimes a vice,
And to defend ourselves it be a sin
When violence assails us.

OTHELLO Now, by heaven,

My blood begins my safer guides to rule, 199
And passion, having my best judgment collied, 200
Essays to lead the way. Zounds, if I stir, 201
Or do but lift this arm, the best of you
Shall sink in my rebuke. Give me to know
How this foul rout began, who set it on; 204
And he that is approved in this offense, 205
Though he had twinned with me, both at a birth,
Shall lose me. What? In a town of war 207
Yet wild, the people's hearts brim full of fear,
To manage private and domestic quarrel? 209
In night, and on the court and guard of safety? 210
'Tis monstrous. Iago, who began't?

MONTANO [to Iago]

If partially affined, or leagued in office, 212
Thou dost deliver more or less than truth,
Thou art no soldier.

IAGO Touch me not so near.

I had rather have this tongue cut from my mouth
Than it should do offense to Michael Cassio;
Yet, I persuade myself, to speak the truth
Shall nothing wrong him. Thus it is, General:
Montano and myself being in speech,
There comes a fellow crying out for help,
And Cassio following him with determined sword
To execute upon him. Sir, this gentleman 222

[indicating Montano]

Steps in to Cassio and entreats his pause. 223
Myself the crying fellow did pursue,
Lest by his clamor—as it so fell out—
The town might fall in fright. He, swift of foot,

151 mutiny riot. 154 masters sirs. 154.1 A bell rings (This direction is from the Quarto, as are Exit Roderigo at line 131, They fight at line 150, and with weapons at line 157.1.) 155 Diablo The devil 156 rise grow riotous. 164–5 to ourselves . . . Ottomites inflict on ourselves the harm that heaven has prevented the Turks from doing (by destroying their fleet). 167 carve for i.e., indulge, satisfy with his sword 168 Holds . . . light i.e., places little value on his life. upon his motion if he moves. 170 propriety proper state or condition. 174 In quarter . . . terms in conduct and speech 175 Devesting them undressing themselves 178 speak explain 179 peevish odds childish quarrel 182 are thus forgot have forgotten yourself thus.

184 wont be accustomed to be 185 stillness sobriety 187 censure judgment. 188 unlace undo, lay open (as one might loose the strings of a purse containing reputation) 189 opinion reputation 193 something somewhat. offends pains 199 blood passion (of anger). guides i.e., reason 200 collied darkened 201 Essays undertakes 204 rout riot 205 approved in found guilty of 207 town of town garrisoned for 209 manage undertake 210 on . . . safety at the main guardhouse or headquarters and on watch. 212 If . . . office If made partial by personal relationship or by your being fellow officers 222 execute upon him (1) proceed violently against him (2) execute him. 223 his pause him to stop.

Outran my purpose, and I returned, the rather   227
For that I heard the clink and fall of swords
And Cassio high in oath, which till tonight
I ne'er might say before. When I came back—
For this was brief—I found them close together
At blow and thrust, even as again they were
When you yourself did part them.
More of this matter cannot I report.
But men are men; the best sometimes forget.   235
Though Cassio did some little wrong to him,
As men in rage strike those that wish them best,   237
Yet surely Cassio, I believe, received
From him that fled some strange indignity,
Which patience could not pass.
OTHELLO   I know, Iago,   240
Thy honesty and love doth mince this matter,
Making it light to Cassio. Cassio, I love thee,
But nevermore be officer of mine.

Enter Desdemona, attended.

Look if my gentle love be not raised up.
I'll make thee an example.
DESDEMONA
What is the matter, dear?
OTHELLO   All's well now, sweeting;
Come away to bed. [*To Montano*] Sir, for your hurts,
Myself will be your surgeon.—Lead him off.   248
                              [*Montano is led off.*]
Iago, look with care about the town
And silence those whom this vile brawl distracted.
Come, Desdemona. 'Tis the soldiers' life
To have their balmy slumbers waked with strife.
                              Exit [*with all but Iago and Cassio*].
IAGO   What, are you hurt, Lieutenant?
CASSIO   Ay, past all surgery.
IAGO   Marry, God forbid!
CASSIO   Reputation, reputation, reputation! Oh, I have
lost my reputation! I have lost the immortal part of
myself, and what remains is bestial. My reputation,
Iago, my reputation!
IAGO   As I am an honest man, I thought you had
received some bodily wound; there is more sense in
that than in reputation. Reputation is an idle and most
false imposition, oft got without merit and lost with-   263
out deserving. You have lost no reputation at all,
unless you repute yourself such a loser. What, man,
there are more ways to recover the General again. You   266
are but now cast in his mood—a punishment more in   267
policy than in malice, even so as one would beat his   268
offenseless dog to affright an imperious lion. Sue to   269
him again and he's yours.

CASSIO   I will rather sue to be despised than to deceive
so good a commander with so slight, so drunken, and   272
so indiscreet an officer. Drunk? And speak parrot?   273
And squabble? Swagger? Swear? And discourse fus-
tian with one's own shadow? O thou invisible spirit
of wine, if thou hast no name to be known by, let us
call thee devil!
IAGO   What was he that you followed with your sword?
What had he done to you?
CASSIO   I know not.
IAGO   Is't possible?
CASSIO   I remember a mass of things, but nothing
distinctly; a quarrel, but nothing wherefore. Oh, God,   283
that men should put an enemy in their mouths to steal
away their brains! That we should, with joy, pleas-
ance, revel, and applause transform ourselves into   286
beasts!
IAGO   Why, but you are now well enough. How came
you thus recovered?
CASSIO   It hath pleased the devil drunkenness to give
place to the devil wrath. One unperfectness shows me
another, to make me frankly despise myself.
IAGO   Come, you are too severe a moraler. As the time,   293
the place, and the condition of this country stands, I
could heartily wish this had not befallen; but since it is
as it is, mend it for your own good.
CASSIO   I will ask him for my place again; he shall tell
me I am a drunkard. Had I as many mouths as Hydra,   298
such an answer would stop them all. To be now a
sensible man, by and by a fool, and presently a beast!
Oh, strange! Every inordinate cup is unblessed, and the   301
ingredient is a devil.
IAGO   Come, come, good wine is a good familiar
creature, if it be well used. Exclaim no more against it.
And, good Lieutenant, I think you think I love you.
CASSIO   I have well approved it, sir. I drunk!   306
IAGO   You or any man living may be drunk at a time,   307
man. I'll tell you what you shall do. Our general's wife
is now the general—I may say so in this respect, for   309
that he hath devoted and given up himself to the   310
contemplation, mark, and denotement of her parts   311
and graces. Confess yourself freely to her; importune
her help to put you in your place again. She is of so
free, so kind, so apt, so blessed a disposition, she   314
holds it a vice in her goodness not to do more than she
is requested. This broken joint between you and her
husband entreat her to splinter; and, my fortunes   317
against any lay worth naming, this crack of your love   318
shall grow stronger than it was before.
CASSIO   You advise me well.

---

227 **rather** sooner   235 **forget** forget themselves.   237 **those . . . best**
i.e., even those who are well disposed toward them   240 **pass** pass
over, overlook.   248 **be your surgeon** i.e., make sure you receive
medical attention.   263 **false imposition** thing artificially imposed
and of no real value   266 **recover** regain favor with   267 **cast in his**
mood dismissed in a moment of anger   267–8 **in policy** done for
expediency's sake and as a public gesture   268–9 **would . . . lion** i.e.,
would make an example of a minor offender in order to deter more
important and dangerous offenders.   269 **Sue** Petition

272 **slight** worthless   273 **speak parrot** talk nonsense, rant. (*Discourse*
fustian, lines 274–5, has much the same meaning.)   283 **wherefore**
why.   286 **applause** desire for applause   293 **moraler** moralizer.
298 **Hydra** the Lernaean Hydra, a monster with many heads and the
ability to grow two heads when one was cut off, slain by Hercules
as the second of his twelve labors   301 **inordinate** immoderate
306 **approved** proved by experience   307 **at a time** at one time or
another   309–10 **for that** that   311 **mark, and denotement** (Both
words mean "observation.")   **parts** qualities   314 **free** generous
317 **splinter** bind with splints   318 **lay** stake, wager

IAGO   I protest, in the sincerity of love and honest 321
kindness.
CASSIO   I think it freely; and betimes in the morning I 323
will beseech the virtuous Desdemona to undertake for
me. I am desperate of my fortunes if they check me 325
here.
IAGO   You are in the right. Good night, Lieutenant. I
must to the watch.
CASSIO   Good night, honest Iago.   *Exit Cassio.*
IAGO
And what's he then that says I play the villain,
When this advice is free I give, and honest,   331
Probal to thinking, and indeed the course   332
To win the Moor again? For 'tis most easy
Th'inclining Desdemona to subdue   334
In any honest suit; she's framed as fruitful   335
As the free elements. And then for her   336
To win the Moor—were't to renounce his baptism,
All seals and symbols of redeemèd sin—   338
His soul is so enfettered to her love
That she may make, unmake, do what she list,
Even as her appetite shall play the god   341
With his weak function. How am I then a villain,   342
To counsel Cassio to this parallel course   343
Directly to his good? Divinity of hell!   344
When devils will the blackest sins put on,   345
They do suggest at first with heavenly shows,   346
As I do now. For whiles this honest fool
Plies Desdemona to repair his fortune,
And she for him pleads strongly to the Moor,
I'll pour this pestilence into his ear,
That she repeals him for her body's lust;   351
And by how much she strives to do him good,
She shall undo her credit with the Moor.
So will I turn her virtue into pitch,   354
And out of her own goodness make the net
That shall enmesh them all.

          Enter Roderigo.

                    How now, Roderigo?
RODERIGO   I do follow here in the chase, not like a
hound that hunts, but one that fills up the cry. My 358
money is almost spent; I have been tonight exceedingly well cudgeled; and I think the issue will be I shall 360
have so much experience for my pains, and so, 361
with no money at all and a little more wit, return again
to Venice.

IAGO
How poor are they that have not patience!
What wound did ever heal but by degrees?
Thou know'st we work by wit, and not by witchcraft,
And wit depends on dilatory time.
Does't not go well? Cassio hath beaten thee,
And thou, by that small hurt, hast cashiered Cassio.   369
Though other things grow fair against the sun,   370
Yet fruits that blossom first will first be ripe.   371
Content thyself awhile. By the Mass, 'tis morning!
Pleasure and action make the hours seem short.
Retire thee; go where thou art billeted.
Away, I say! Thou shalt know more hereafter.
Nay, get thee gone.   *Exit Roderigo.*
          Two things are to be done.
My wife must move for Cassio to her mistress;   377
I'll set her on;
Myself the while to draw the Moor apart
And bring him jump when he may Cassio find   380
Soliciting his wife. Ay, that's the way.
Dull not device by coldness and delay.   *Exit.* 382

                    ❖

3.1

          Enter Cassio [and] Musicians.

CASSIO
Masters, play here—I will content your pains—   1
Something that's brief, and bid "Good morrow,
     General."   [*They play.*]

          [*Enter*] *Clown.*

CLOWN   Why, masters, have your instruments been in
Naples, that they speak i'th' nose thus?   4
A MUSICIAN   How, sir, how?
CLOWN   Are these, I pray you, wind instruments?
A MUSICIAN   Ay, marry, are they, sir.
CLOWN   Oh, thereby hangs a tail.
A MUSICIAN   Whereby hangs a tale, sir?
CLOWN   Marry, sir, by many a wind instrument that I 10
know. But, masters, here's money for you. [*He gives
money.*] And the General so likes your music that he
desires you, for love's sake, to make no more noise
with it.
A MUSICIAN   Well, sir, we will not.
CLOWN   If you have any music that may not be heard, 16
to't again; but, as they say, to hear music the General
does not greatly care.
A MUSICIAN   We have none such, sir.

---

321 protest insist, declare   **323 freely** unreservedly   **325 check**
repulse   **331 free** (1) free from guile (2) freely given   **332 Probal**
probable, reasonable   **334 Th'inclining** the favorably disposed.
subdue persuade   **335 framed as fruitful** created as generous
336 free elements i.e., earth, air, fire, and water, unrestrained and
spontaneous.   **338 seals** tokens   **341 her appetite** her desire, or, perhaps, his desire for her   **342 function** exercise of faculties (weakened
by his fondness for her).   **343 parallel** i.e., seemingly in his best interests but at the same time threatening   **344 Divinity of hell!** Inverted
theology of hell (which seduces the soul to its damnation)!   **345 put
on** further, instigate   **346 suggest** tempt   **351 repeals him** attempts
to get him restored   **354 pitch** i.e., (1) foul blackness (2) a snaring
substance   **358 fills up the cry** merely takes part as one of the pack.
360 issue outcome   **361 so much** just so much and no more

369 cashiered dismissed from service   **370–1 Though . . . ripe** i.e.,
Plans that are well prepared and set expeditiously in motion will
soonest ripen into success.   **377 move** plead   **380 jump** precisely
382 device plot.   **coldness** lack of zeal
3.1. Location: Before the chamber of Othello and Desdemona.
1 Masters Good sirs.   **content your pains** reward your efforts
4 speak i'th' nose (1) sound nasal (2) sound like one whose nose has
been attacked by syphilis. (Naples was popularly supposed to have a
high incidence of venereal disease.)   **10 wind instrument** (With a
joke on flatulence. The *tail*, line 8, that hangs nearby the *wind instrument* suggests the penis.)   **16 may not** cannot

CLOWN Then put up your pipes in your bag, for I'll
away. Go, vanish into air, away!   *Exeunt Musicians.*
CASSIO Dost thou hear, mine honest friend?
CLOWN No, I hear not your honest friend; I hear you.
CASSIO Prithee, keep up thy quillets. There's a poor   24
piece of gold for thee. [*He gives money.*] If the gentlewoman that attends the General's wife be stirring, tell
her there's one Cassio entreats her a little favor of   27
speech. Wilt thou do this?   28
CLOWN She is stirring, sir. If she will stir hither, I shall   29
seem to notify unto her.   30
CASSIO
Do, good my friend.   *Exit Clown.*

Enter Iago.

In happy time, Iago.   31
IAGO You have not been abed, then?
CASSIO Why, no. The day had broke
Before we parted. I have made bold, Iago,
To send in to your wife. My suit to her
Is that she will to virtuous Desdemona
Procure me some access.
IAGO I'll send her to you presently;
And I'll devise a mean to draw the Moor
Out of the way, that your converse and business
May be more free.
CASSIO
I humbly thank you for't.   *Exit [Iago].*
I never knew
A Florentine more kind and honest.   43

Enter Emilia.

EMILIA
Good morrow, good Lieutenant. I am sorry
For your displeasure; but all will sure be well.   45
The General and his wife are talking of it,
And she speaks for you stoutly. The Moor replies   47
That he you hurt is of great fame in Cyprus   48
And great affinity, and that in wholesome wisdom   49
He might not but refuse you; but he protests he loves
you   50
And needs no other suitor but his likings
To take the safest occasion by the front   52
To bring you in again.
CASSIO   Yet I beseech you,
If you think fit, or that it may be done,
Give me advantage of some brief discourse
With Desdemon alone.
EMILIA   Pray you, come in.
I will bestow you where you shall have time
To speak your bosom freely.   58

CASSIO I am much bound to you.   [*Exeunt.*]

❖

3.2

Enter Othello, Iago, and Gentlemen.

OTHELLO [*giving letters*]
These letters give, Iago, to the pilot,
And by him do my duties to the Senate.   2
That done, I will be walking on the works;   3
Repair there to me.
IAGO   Well, my good lord, I'll do't.   4
OTHELLO
This fortification, gentlemen, shall we see't?
GENTLEMEN We'll wait upon Your Lordship.   *Exeunt.*   6

❖

3.3

Enter Desdemona, Cassio, and Emilia.

DESDEMONA
Be thou assured, good Cassio, I will do
All my abilities in thy behalf.
EMILIA
Good madam, do. I warrant it grieves my husband
As if the cause were his.
DESDEMONA
Oh, that's an honest fellow. Do not doubt, Cassio,
But I will have my lord and you again
As friendly as you were.
CASSIO   Bounteous madam,
Whatever shall become of Michael Cassio,
He's never anything but your true servant.
DESDEMONA
I know't. I thank you. You do love my lord;
You have known him long, and be you well assured
He shall in strangeness stand no farther off   12
Than in a politic distance.
CASSIO   Ay, but, lady,   13
That policy may either last so long,
Or feed upon such nice and waterish diet,   15
Or breed itself so out of circumstance,   16
That, I being absent and my place supplied,   17
My general will forget my love and service.
DESDEMONA
Do not doubt that. Before Emilia here   19
I give thee warrant of thy place. Assure thee,   20
If I do vow a friendship I'll perform it
To the last article. My lord shall never rest.
I'll watch him tame and talk him out of patience;   23

---

24 **keep . . . quillets** refrain from quibbling.   **27–8 a little . . . speech**
the favor of a brief talk.   **29 stir** bestir herself. (With a play on
stirring, "rousing herself from rest.")   **30 seem** deem it good, think fit
31 In happy time i.e., Well met   **43 Florentine** i.e., even a fellow Florentine. (Iago is a Venetian; Cassio is a Florentine.)   **45 displeasure**
fall from favor   **47 stoutly** spiritedly.   **48 fame** reputation, importance   **49 affinity** kindred, family connection   **50 protests** insists
52 occasion . . . front opportunity by the forelock   **58 bosom** inmost
thoughts

3.2. Location: The citadel.
2 do my duties convey my respects   **3 works** breastworks, fortifications   **4 Repair** return, come   **6 wait upon** attend
3.3. Location: The garden of the citadel.
12 strangeness aloofness   **13 politic** required by wise policy
15 Or . . . diet or sustain itself at length upon such trivial and meager
technicalities   **16 breed . . . circumstance** continually renew itself so
out of chance events, or yield so few chances for my being pardoned
17 supplied filled by another person   **19 doubt** fear   **20 warrant**
guarantee   **23 watch him tame** tame him by keeping him from sleeping. (A term from falconry.)   **out of patience** past his endurance

His bed shall seem a school, his board a shrift;   24
I'll intermingle everything he does
With Cassio's suit. Therefore be merry, Cassio,
For thy solicitor shall rather die   27
Than give thy cause away.   28

Enter Othello and Iago [at a distance].

EMILIA   Madam, here comes my lord.
CASSIO   Madam, I'll take my leave.
DESDEMONA   Why, stay, and hear me speak.
CASSIO
Madam, not now. I am very ill at ease,
Unfit for mine own purposes.
DESDEMONA   Well, do your discretion.   *Exit Cassio.*   34
IAGO   Ha? I like not that.
OTHELLO   What dost thou say?
IAGO
Nothing, my lord; or if—I know not what.
OTHELLO
Was not that Cassio parted from my wife?
IAGO
Cassio, my lord? No, sure, I cannot think it,
That he would steal away so guiltylike,
Seeing you coming.
OTHELLO   I do believe 'twas he.
DESDEMONA *[joining them]*   How now, my lord?
I have been talking with a suitor here,
A man that languishes in your displeasure.
OTHELLO   Who is't you mean?
DESDEMONA
Why, your lieutenant, Cassio. Good my lord,
If I have any grace or power to move you,
His present reconciliation take;   49
For if he be not one that truly loves you,
That errs in ignorance and not in cunning,   51
I have no judgment in an honest face.
I prithee, call him back.
OTHELLO   Went he hence now?
DESDEMONA   Yes, faith, so humbled
That he hath left part of his grief with me
To suffer with him. Good love, call him back.
OTHELLO
Not now, sweet Desdemon. Some other time.
DESDEMONA   But shall't be shortly?
OTHELLO   The sooner, sweet, for you.
DESDEMONA   Shall't be tonight at supper?
OTHELLO   No, not tonight.
DESDEMONA   Tomorrow dinner, then?   63
OTHELLO   I shall not dine at home.
I meet the captains at the citadel.
DESDEMONA
Why, then, tomorrow night, or Tuesday morn,
On Tuesday noon, or night, on Wednesday morn.
I prithee, name the time, but let it not
Exceed three days. In faith, he's penitent;

And yet his trespass, in our common reason—   70
Save that, they say, the wars must make example   71
Out of her best—is not almost a fault   72
T'incur a private check. When shall he come?   73
Tell me, Othello. I wonder in my soul
What you would ask me that I should deny,
Or stand so mamm'ring on. What? Michael Cassio,   76
That came a-wooing with you, and so many a time,
When I have spoke of you dispraisingly,
Hath ta'en your part—to have so much to do
To bring him in! By'r Lady, I could do much—   80
OTHELLO
Prithee, no more. Let him come when he will;
I will deny thee nothing.
DESDEMONA   Why, this is not a boon.
'Tis as I should entreat you wear your gloves,
Or feed on nourishing dishes, or keep you warm,
Or sue to you to do a peculiar profit   86
To your own person. Nay, when I have a suit
Wherein I mean to touch your love indeed,   88
It shall be full of poise and difficult weight,   89
And fearful to be granted.
OTHELLO   I will deny thee nothing.
Whereon, I do beseech thee, grant me this,   92
To leave me but a little to myself.
DESDEMONA
Shall I deny you? No. Farewell, my lord.
OTHELLO
Farewell, my Desdemona. I'll come to thee straight.   95
DESDEMONA
Emilia, come.—Be as your fancies teach you;   96
Whate'er you be, I am obedient.   *Exit [with Emilia].*
OTHELLO
Excellent wretch! Perdition catch my soul   98
But I do love thee! And when I love thee not,   99
Chaos is come again.   100
IAGO   My noble lord—
OTHELLO   What dost thou say, Iago?
IAGO
Did Michael Cassio, when you wooed my lady,
Know of your love?
OTHELLO
He did, from first to last. Why dost thou ask?
IAGO
But for a satisfaction of my thought;
No further harm.
OTHELLO   Why of thy thought, Iago?

---

70 **common reason** everyday judgments   71–2 **Save . . . best** were it
not that, as the saying goes, military discipline requires making an
example of the very best men. (*Her* refers to wars as a singular concept.)   72 **not almost** scarcely   73 **a private check** even a private
reprimand.   76 **mamm'ring on** wavering or muttering about.
80 **bring him in** restore him to favor.   86 **peculiar** particular, personal   88 **touch** test   89 **poise . . . weight** delicacy and weightiness
92 **Whereon** In return for which   95 **straight** straightaway.   96 **fancies** inclinations   98 **wretch** (A term of affectionate endearment.)
99–100 **And . . . again** i.e., My love for you will last forever, until the
end of time when chaos will return. (But with an unconscious, ironic
suggestion that, if anything should induce Othello to cease loving
Desdemona, the result would be chaos.)

---

24 **board** dining table.   **shrift** confessional   27 **solicitor** advocate
28 **away** up.   34 **do your discretion** do as you think fit.   49 **His . . .
take** let him be reconciled to you right away   51 **in cunning** wittingly   63 **dinner** (The noontime meal.)

IAGO

I did not think he had been acquainted with her.

OTHELLO

Oh, yes, and went between us very oft.

IAGO   Indeed?

OTHELLO

Indeed? Ay, indeed. Discern'st thou aught in that?
Is he not honest?

IAGO   Honest, my lord?

OTHELLO   Honest. Ay, honest.

IAGO   My lord, for aught I know.

OTHELLO   What dost thou think?

IAGO   Think, my lord?

OTHELLO

"Think, my lord?" By heaven, thou echo'st me,
As if there were some monster in thy thought
Too hideous to be shown. Thou dost mean something.
I heard thee say even now, thou lik'st not that,
When Cassio left my wife. What didst not like?
And when I told thee he was of my counsel   123
In my whole course of wooing, thou cried'st "Indeed?"
And didst contract and purse thy brow together   125
As if thou then hadst shut up in thy brain
Some horrible conceit. If thou dost love me,   127
Show me thy thought.

IAGO   My lord, you know I love you.

OTHELLO   I think thou dost;
And, for I know thou'rt full of love and honesty,   131
And weigh'st thy words before thou giv'st them
    breath,
Therefore these stops of thine fright me the more; 133
For such things in a false disloyal knave
Are tricks of custom, but in a man that's just   135
They're close dilations, working from the heart   136
That passion cannot rule.

IAGO   For Michael Cassio,   137
I dare be sworn I think that he is honest.

OTHELLO

I think so too.

IAGO   Men should be what they seem;
Or those that be not, would they might seem none!   140

OTHELLO

Certain, men should be what they seem.

IAGO

Why, then, I think Cassio's an honest man.

OTHELLO   Nay, yet there's more in this.
I prithee, speak to me as to thy thinkings,
As thou dost ruminate, and give thy worst of thoughts
The worst of words.

IAGO   Good my lord, pardon me.
Though I am bound to every act of duty,
I am not bound to that all slaves are free to.   148
Utter my thoughts? Why, say they are vile and false,
As where's that palace whereinto foul things

Sometimes intrude not? Who has that breast so pure
But some uncleanly apprehensions
Keep leets and law days, and in sessions sit   153
With meditations lawful?   154

OTHELLO

Thou dost conspire against thy friend, Iago,   155
If thou but think'st him wronged and mak'st his ear
A stranger to thy thoughts.

IAGO   I do beseech you,
Though I perchance am vicious in my guess—   158
As I confess it is my nature's plague
To spy into abuses, and oft my jealousy   160
Shapes faults that are not—that your wisdom then,
From one that so imperfectly conceits,   162
Would take no notice, nor build yourself a trouble
Out of his scattering and unsure observance.   164
It were not for your quiet nor your good,
Nor for my manhood, honesty, and wisdom,
To let you know my thoughts.

OTHELLO   What dost thou mean?

IAGO

Good name in man and woman, dear my lord,
Is the immediate jewel of their souls.   169
Who steals my purse steals trash; 'tis something,
    nothing;
'Twas mine, 'tis his, and has been slave to thousands;
But he that filches from me my good name
Robs me of that which not enriches him
And makes me poor indeed.

OTHELLO   By heaven, I'll know thy thoughts.

IAGO

You cannot, if my heart were in your hand,   176
Nor shall not, whilst 'tis in my custody.

OTHELLO   Ha?

IAGO   Oh, beware, my lord, of jealousy.
It is the green-eyed monster, which doth mock   179
The meat it feeds on. That cuckold lives in bliss   180
Who, certain of his fate, loves not his wronger;   181
But oh, what damnèd minutes tells he o'er   182
Who dotes, yet doubts, suspects, yet fondly loves!

OTHELLO   Oh, misery!

IAGO

Poor and content is rich, and rich enough,   185
But riches fineless is as poor as winter   186
To him that ever fears he shall be poor.

---

153 **Keep leets and law days** i.e., hold court, set up their authority in one's heart. (*Leets* are a kind of manor court; *law days* are the days courts sit in session, or those sessions.)   153–4 **and . . . lawful** i.e., and coexist in a kind of spiritual conflict with virtuous thoughts. 155 **thy friend** i.e., Othello   158 **vicious** wrong   160 **jealousy** suspicious nature   162 **one** i.e., myself, Iago.   **conceits** judges, conjectures 164 **scattering** random   169 **immediate** essential, most precious 176 **if** even if   179–80 **which . . . feeds on** (Jealousy mocks both itself and the sufferer of jealousy; it is self-devouring and is its own punishment.)   180–1 **That . . . wronger** A cuckolded husband who knows his wife to be unfaithful can at least take comfort in knowing the truth, so that he will not continue to love her or to befriend her lover. (Othello echoes this sentiment in lines 204–6, when he vows that he would end uncertainty and cease to love an unfaithful wife.) 182 **tells** counts   185 **Poor . . . enough** To be content with what little one has is the greatest wealth of all. (Proverbial.)   186 **fineless** boundless

---

123 **of my counsel** in my confidence   125 **purse** knit   127 **conceit** fancy.   131 **for** because   133 **stops** pauses   135 **of custom** customary   136–7 **They're . . . rule** they are secret or involuntary expressions of feeling that are too strong to be kept back.   137 **For** As for 140 **seem none** not seem at all, not seem to be honest.   148 **that** that which.   **free to** free with respect to.

Good God, the souls of all my tribe defend
From jealousy!
OTHELLO   Why, why is this?
Think'st thou I'd make a life of jealousy,
To follow still the changes of the moon   192
With fresh suspicions? No! To be once in doubt   193
Is once to be resolved. Exchange me for a goat   194
When I shall turn the business of my soul
To such exsufflicate and blown surmises   196
Matching thy inference. 'Tis not to make me jealous   197
To say my wife is fair, feeds well, loves company,
Is free of speech, sings, plays, and dances well;
Where virtue is, these are more virtuous.
Nor from mine own weak merits will I draw
The smallest fear or doubt of her revolt,   202
For she had eyes, and chose me. No, Iago,
I'll see before I doubt; when I doubt, prove;
And on the proof, there is no more but this—
Away at once with love or jealousy.

IAGO
I am glad of this, for now I shall have reason
To show the love and duty that I bear you
With franker spirit. Therefore, as I am bound,
Receive it from me. I speak not yet of proof.
Look to your wife; observe her well with Cassio.
Wear your eyes thus, not jealous nor secure.   212
I would not have your free and noble nature,
Out of self-bounty, be abused. Look to't.   214
I know our country disposition well;
In Venice they do let God see the pranks
They dare not show their husbands; their best
    conscience
Is not to leave't undone, but keep't unknown.
OTHELLO   Dost thou say so?
IAGO
She did deceive her father, marrying you;
And when she seemed to shake and fear your looks,
She loved them most.
OTHELLO   And so she did.
IAGO   Why, go to, then!   222
She that, so young, could give out such a seeming,   223
To seel her father's eyes up close as oak,   224
He thought 'twas witchcraft! But I am much to blame.
I humbly do beseech you of your pardon
For too much loving you.
OTHELLO   I am bound to thee forever.   228
IAGO
I see this hath a little dashed your spirits.

OTHELLO
Not a jot, not a jot.
IAGO   I'faith, I fear it has.
I hope you will consider what is spoke
Comes from my love. But I do see you're moved.
I am to pray you not to strain my speech
To grosser issues nor to larger reach   234
Than to suspicion.
OTHELLO   I will not.
IAGO   Should you do so, my lord,
My speech should fall into such vile success   238
Which my thoughts aimed not. Cassio's my worthy
    friend.
My lord, I see you're moved.
OTHELLO   No, not much moved.
I do not think but Desdemona's honest.   241
IAGO
Long live she so! And long live you to think so!
OTHELLO
And yet, how nature erring from itself—
IAGO
Ay, there's the point! As—to be bold with you—
Not to affect many proposèd matches   245
Of her own clime, complexion, and degree,   246
Whereto we see in all things nature tends—
Foh! One may smell in such a will most rank,   248
Foul disproportion, thoughts unnatural.   249
But pardon me. I do not in position   250
Distinctly speak of her, though I may fear
Her will, recoiling to her better judgment,   252
May fall to match you with her country forms   253
And happily repent.
OTHELLO   Farewell, farewell!   254
If more thou dost perceive, let me know more.
Set on thy wife to observe. Leave me, Iago.
IAGO [going]   My lord, I take my leave.
OTHELLO
Why did I marry? This honest creature doubtless
Sees and knows more, much more, than he unfolds.
IAGO [returning]
My lord, I would I might entreat Your Honor
To scan this thing no farther. Leave it to time.   261
Although 'tis fit that Cassio have his place—
For, sure, he fills it up with great ability—
Yet, if you please to hold him off awhile,
You shall by that perceive him and his means.   265
Note if your lady strain his entertainment   266
With any strong or vehement importunity;
Much will be seen in that. In the meantime,
Let me be thought too busy in my fears—   269

192–3 To follow . . . suspicions? to be constantly imagining new causes for suspicion, changing incessantly like the moon? 194 once once and for all.   resolved free of doubt, having settled the matter. 196 exsufflicate and blown inflated and blown up or flyblown, hence, loathsome, disgusting   197 inference description or allegation.   202 doubt . . . revolt fear of her unfaithfulness   212 not neither.   secure free from uncertainty.   214 self-bounty inherent or natural goodness and generosity.   abused deceived.   222 go to (An expression of impatience.)   223 seeming false appearance   224 seel blind. (A term from falconry.)   oak (A close-grained wood.) 228 bound indebted. (But perhaps with ironic sense of "tied.")

234 issues significances.   reach meaning, scope   238 success effect, result   241 honest chaste.   245 affect prefer, desire   246 clime . . . degree country, temperament or skin color, and social position 248 will sensuality, appetite   249 disproportion abnormality   250 in position in making this argument or proposition   252 recoiling reverting.   better i.e., more natural and reconsidered   253 fall . . . forms undertake to compare you with Venetian norms of handsomeness   254 happily repent haply repent her marriage   261 scan scrutinize   265 his means the method he uses (to regain his post). 266 strain his entertainment urge his reinstatement   269 busy officious

As worthy cause I have to fear I am—
And hold her free, I do beseech Your Honor.   271
OTHELLO   Fear not my government.   272
IAGO   I once more take my leave.   *Exit.*
OTHELLO
This fellow's of exceeding honesty,
And knows all qualities, with a learnèd spirit,   275
Of human dealings. If I do prove her haggard,   276
Though that her jesses were my dear heartstrings,   277
I'd whistle her off and let her down the wind   278
To prey at fortune. Haply, for I am black   279
And have not those soft parts of conversation   280
That chamberers have, or for I am declined   281
Into the vale of years—yet that's not much—
She's gone. I am abused, and my relief   283
Must be to loathe her. Oh, curse of marriage,
That we can call these delicate creatures ours
And not their appetites! I had rather be a toad
And live upon the vapor of a dungeon
Than keep a corner in the thing I love
For others' uses. Yet, 'tis the plague of great ones;
Prerogatived are they less than the base.   290
'Tis destiny unshunnable, like death.
Even then this forkèd plague is fated to us   292
When we do quicken. Look where she comes.   293

Enter Desdemona and Emilia.

If she be false, oh, then heaven mocks itself!
I'll not believe't.
DESDEMONA   How now, my dear Othello?
Your dinner, and the generous islanders   296
By you invited do attend your presence.   297
OTHELLO
I am to blame.
DESDEMONA   Why do you speak so faintly?
Are you not well?
OTHELLO
I have a pain upon my forehead here.
DESDEMONA
Faith, that's with watching. 'Twill away again.   301
               [She offers her handkerchief.]
Let me but bind it hard, within this hour
It will be well.
OTHELLO   Your napkin is too little.   303
Let it alone. Come, I'll go in with you.   304
    [He puts the handkerchief from him, and it drops.]

DESDEMONA
I am very sorry that you are not well.
                     Exit [with Othello].
EMILIA *[picking up the handkerchief]*
I am glad I have found this napkin.
This was her first remembrance from the Moor.
My wayward husband hath a hundred times   308
Wooed me to steal it, but she so loves the token—
For he conjured her she should ever keep it—
That she reserves it evermore about her
To kiss and talk to. I'll have the work ta'en out,   312
And give't Iago. What he will do with it
Heaven knows, not I;
I nothing but to please his fantasy.   315

Enter Iago.

IAGO
How now? What do you here alone?
EMILIA
Do not you chide. I have a thing for you.
IAGO
You have a thing for me? It is a common thing—   318
EMILIA   Ha?
IAGO   To have a foolish wife.
EMILIA
Oh, is that all? What will you give me now
For that same handkerchief?
IAGO   What handkerchief?
EMILIA   What handkerchief?
Why, that the Moor first gave to Desdemona;
That which so often you did bid me steal.
IAGO   Hast stolen it from her?
EMILIA
No, faith. She let it drop by negligence,
And to th'advantage I, being here, took't up.   329
Look, here 'tis.
IAGO   A good wench! Give it me.
EMILIA
What will you do with't, that you have been so earnest
To have me filch it?
IAGO *[snatching it]*   Why, what is that to you?
EMILIA
If it be not for some purpose of import,
Give't me again. Poor lady, she'll run mad
When she shall lack it.
IAGO   Be not acknown on't.   335
I have use for it. Go, leave me.   *Exit Emilia.*
I will in Cassio's lodging lose this napkin   337
And let him find it. Trifles light as air
Are to the jealous confirmations strong
As proofs of Holy Writ. This may do something.
The Moor already changes with my poison.

---

271 hold her free regard her as innocent   **272 government** self-control, conduct.   **275 qualities** natures, types   **276 haggard** wild (like a wild female hawk)   **277 jesses** straps fastened around the legs of a trained hawk   **278 I'd . . . wind** i.e., I'd let her go forever. (To release a hawk downwind was to turn it loose.)   **279 prey at fortune** fend for herself in the wild.   **Haply, for** Perhaps because   **280 soft . . . conversation** pleasing social graces   **281 chamberers** drawing-room gallants   **283 abused** deceived   **290 Prerogatived** privileged (to have honest wives).   **the base** ordinary citizens. (Socially prominent men are especially prone to the common destiny of being cuckolded and to the public shame that goes with it.)   **292 forkèd** (An allusion to the horns of the cuckold.)   **293 quicken** receive life. (*Quicken* may also mean to swarm with maggots as the body festers, as in 4.2.69, in which case lines 292–3 suggest that *even then*, in death, we are cuckolded by *forkèd* worms.)   **296 generous** noble   **297 attend** await   **301 watching** too little sleep.   **303 napkin** handkerchief   **304 Let it alone** i.e., Never mind.

308 wayward capricious   **312 work ta'en out** design of the embroidery copied   **315 fantasy** whim.   **318 common thing** (With bawdy suggestion; *common* suggests coarseness and availability to all comers, and *thing* is a slang term for the pudendum.)   **329 to th'advantage** taking the opportunity   **335 lack** miss.   **Be . . . on't** Do not confess knowledge of it; keep out of this.   **337 lose** (The Folio spelling, "loose," is a normal spelling for "lose," but it may also contain the idea of "let go," "release.")

Dangerous conceits are in their natures poisons,   342
Which at the first are scarce found to distaste,   343
But with a little act upon the blood   344
Burn like the mines of sulfur.

    Enter Othello.

                       I did say so.
Look where he comes! Not poppy nor mandragora   346
Nor all the drowsy syrups of the world
Shall ever medicine thee to that sweet sleep
Which thou owed'st yesterday.

OTHELLO   Ha, ha, false to me?   349

IAGO
    Why, how now, General? No more of that.

OTHELLO
    Avaunt! Begone! Thou hast set me on the rack.
    I swear 'tis better to be much abused
    Than but to know't a little.

IAGO   How now, my lord?

OTHELLO
    What sense had I of her stolen hours of lust?
    I saw't not, thought it not, it harmed not me.
    I slept the next night well, fed well, was free and
        merry;   356
    I found not Cassio's kisses on her lips.
    He that is robbed, not wanting what is stolen,   358
    Let him not know't and he's not robbed at all.

IAGO   I am sorry to hear this.

OTHELLO
    I had been happy if the general camp,
    Pioneers and all, had tasted her sweet body,   362
    So I had nothing known. Oh, now, forever   363
    Farewell the tranquil mind! Farewell content!
    Farewell the plumèd troops and the big wars   365
    That makes ambition virtue! Oh, farewell!
    Farewell the neighing steed and the shrill trump,
    The spirit-stirring drum, th'ear-piercing fife,
    The royal banner, and all quality,   369
    Pride, pomp, and circumstance of glorious war!   370
    And O you mortal engines, whose rude throats   371
    Th'immortal Jove's dread clamors counterfeit,   372
    Farewell! Othello's occupation's gone.

IAGO   Is't possible, my lord?

OTHELLO
    Villain, be sure thou prove my love a whore!
    Be sure of it. Give me the ocular proof,
    Or, by the worth of mine eternal soul,
    Thou hadst been better have been born a dog
    Than answer my waked wrath!

IAGO   Is't come to this?

OTHELLO
    Make me to see't, or at the least so prove it

That the probation bear no hinge nor loop   381
To hang a doubt on, or woe upon thy life!

IAGO   My noble lord—

OTHELLO
    If thou dost slander her and torture me,
    Never pray more; abandon all remorse;   385
    On horror's head horrors accumulate;   386
    Do deeds to make heaven weep, all earth amazed;   387
    For nothing canst thou to damnation add
    Greater than that.

IAGO   O grace! O heaven forgive me!
    Are you a man? Have you a soul or sense?
    God b'wi'you; take mine office. O wretched fool,   391
    That lov'st to make thine honesty a vice!   392
    O monstrous world! Take note, take note, O world,
    To be direct and honest is not safe.
    I thank you for this profit, and from hence   395
    I'll love no friend, sith love breeds such offense.   396

OTHELLO   Nay, stay. Thou shouldst be honest.   397

IAGO
    I should be wise, for honesty's a fool
    And loses that it works for.

OTHELLO   By the world,   399
    I think my wife be honest and think she is not;
    I think that thou art just and think thou art not.
    I'll have some proof. My name, that was as fresh
    As Dian's visage, is now begrimed and black   403
    As mine own face. If there be cords, or knives,
    Poison, or fire, or suffocating streams,
    I'll not endure it. Would I were satisfied!

IAGO
    I see, sir, you are eaten up with passion.
    I do repent me that I put it to you.
    You would be satisfied?

OTHELLO   Would? Nay, and I will.

IAGO
    And may; but how? How satisfied, my lord?
    Would you, the supervisor, grossly gape on?   411
    Behold her topped?

OTHELLO   Death and damnation! Oh!

IAGO
    It were a tedious difficulty, I think,
    To bring them to that prospect. Damn them then,   414
    If ever mortal eyes do see them bolster   415
    More than their own. What then? How then?   416
    What shall I say? Where's satisfaction?
    It is impossible you should see this,
    Were they as prime as goats, as hot as monkeys,   419

---

342 **conceits** fancies, ideas   343 **distaste** be distasteful   344 **act** action, working   346 **mandragora** an opiate made of the mandrake root   349 **thou owed'st** you did own   356 **free** carefree   358 **wanting** missing   362 **Pioneers** diggers of mines, the lowest grade of soldiers   363 **So** provided   365 **big** mighty   369 **quality** character, essential nature   370 **Pride** rich display.   **circumstance** pageantry   371 **mortal engines** i.e., cannon. (*Mortal* means "deadly.")   372 **Jove's dread clamors** i.e., thunder

381 **probation** proof   385 **remorse** pity, penitent hope for salvation   386 **horrors accumulate** add still more horrors   387 **amazed** confounded with horror   391 **O wretched fool** (Iago addresses himself as a fool for having carried honesty too far.)   392 **vice** failing, something overdone.   395 **profit** profitable instruction.   **hence** henceforth   396 **sith** since.   **offense** i.e., harm to the one who offers help and friendship.   397 **Thou shouldst be** It appears that you are. (But Iago replies in the sense of "ought to be.")   399 **that** what   403 **Dian** Diana, goddess of the moon and of chastity   411 **supervisor** onlooker   414 **Damn them then** i.e., They would have to be really incorrigible   415 **bolster** go to bed together, share a bolster   416 **More** other.   **own** own eyes.   419 **prime** lustful

As salt as wolves in pride, and fools as gross 420
As ignorance made drunk. But yet I say,
If imputation and strong circumstances 422
Which lead directly to the door of truth
Will give you satisfaction, you might have't.

OTHELLO
Give me a living reason she's disloyal.

IAGO   I do not like the office.
But sith I am entered in this cause so far, 427
Pricked to't by foolish honesty and love, 428
I will go on. I lay with Cassio lately,
And being troubled with a raging tooth
I could not sleep. There are a kind of men
So loose of soul that in their sleeps will mutter
Their affairs. One of this kind is Cassio.
In sleep I heard him say, "Sweet Desdemona,
Let us be wary, let us hide our loves!"
And then, sir, would he grip and wring my hand,
Cry "O sweet creature!", then kiss me hard,
As if he plucked up kisses by the roots
That grew upon my lips; then laid his leg
Over my thigh, and sighed, and kissed, and then
Cried, "Cursèd fate that gave thee to the Moor!"

OTHELLO
Oh, monstrous! Monstrous!

IAGO   Nay, this was but his dream.

OTHELLO
But this denoted a foregone conclusion. 443
'Tis a shrewd doubt, though it be but a dream. 444

IAGO
And this may help to thicken other proofs
That do demonstrate thinly.

OTHELLO   I'll tear her all to pieces.

IAGO
Nay, but be wise. Yet we see nothing done;
She may be honest yet. Tell me but this:
Have you not sometimes seen a handkerchief
Spotted with strawberries in your wife's hand? 450

OTHELLO
I gave her such a one. 'Twas my first gift.

IAGO
I know not that; but such a handkerchief—
I am sure it was your wife's—did I today
See Cassio wipe his beard with.

OTHELLO   If it be that—

IAGO
If it be that, or any that was hers,
It speaks against her with the other proofs.

OTHELLO
Oh, that the slave had forty thousand lives! 457
One is too poor, too weak for my revenge.
Now do I see 'tis true. Look here, Iago,
All my fond love thus do I blow to heaven. 460

'Tis gone.
Arise, black vengeance, from the hollow hell!
Yield up, O love, thy crown and hearted throne 463
To tyrannous hate! Swell, bosom, with thy freight, 464
For 'tis of aspics' tongues! 465

IAGO   Yet be content. 466

OTHELLO   Oh, blood, blood, blood!

IAGO
Patience, I say. Your mind perhaps may change.

OTHELLO
Never, Iago. Like to the Pontic Sea, 469
Whose icy current and compulsive course
Ne'er feels retiring ebb, but keeps due on
To the Propontic and the Hellespont, 472
Even so my bloody thoughts with violent pace
Shall ne'er look back, ne'er ebb to humble love,
Till that a capable and wide revenge 475
Swallow them up. Now, by yond marble heaven, 476
[*Kneeling*] In the due reverence of a sacred vow
I here engage my words.

IAGO   Do not rise yet.
[*He kneels.*] Witness, you ever-burning lights above, 479
You elements that clip us round about, 480
Witness that here Iago doth give up
The execution of his wit, hands, heart, 482
To wronged Othello's service. Let him command,
And to obey shall be in me remorse, 484
What bloody business ever.   [*They rise.*]

OTHELLO   I greet thy love, 485
Not with vain thanks, but with acceptance bounteous,
And will upon the instant put thee to't. 487
Within these three days let me hear thee say
That Cassio's not alive.

IAGO   My friend is dead;
'Tis done at your request. But let her live.

OTHELLO
Damn her, lewd minx! Oh, damn her, damn her! 491
Come, go with me apart. I will withdraw
To furnish me with some swift means of death
For the fair devil. Now art thou my lieutenant.

IAGO   I am your own forever.   *Exeunt.*

❧

3.4

Enter Desdemona, Emilia, and Clown.

DESDEMONA   Do you know, sirrah, where Lieutenant 1
Cassio lies? 2

---

420 **salt** wanton, sensual.   **pride** heat   422 **imputation . . . circumstances** strong circumstantial evidence   427 **sith** since   428 **Pricked**
spurred   443 **foregone conclusion** previous experience or action.
444 **shrewd doubt** suspicious circumstance   450 **Spotted with strawberries** embroidered with a strawberry pattern   457 **the slave** i.e.,
Cassio   460 **fond** foolish. (But also suggesting "affectionate.")

463 **hearted** fixed in the heart   464 **freight** burden   465 **aspics'**
venomous serpents'   466 **content** calm.   469 **Pontic Sea** Black Sea
472 **Propontic** Sea of Marmora, between the Black Sea and the
Aegean.   **Hellespont** Dardanelles, straits where the Sea of Marmora
joins with the Aegean   475 **capable** ample, comprehensive
476 **marble** i.e., gleaming, polished, and indifferent to human suffering   479 **s.d.** *He kneels* (In the Quarto text, Iago kneels here after
Othello has knelt at line 477.)   480 **clip** encompass   482 **execution**
exercise, action.   **wit** mind   484 **remorse** pity (for Othello's wrongs)
485 **ever** soever.   487 **to't** to the proof.   491 **minx** wanton.
3.4. Location: Before the citadel.
1 **sirrah** (A form of address to an inferior.)   2 **lies** lodges. (But the
Clown makes the obvious pun.)

CLOWN   I dare not say he lies anywhere.

DESDEMONA   Why, man?

CLOWN   He's a soldier, and for me to say a soldier lies, 'tis stabbing.

DESDEMONA   Go to. Where lodges he?

CLOWN   To tell you where he lodges is to tell you where I lie.

DESDEMONA   Can anything be made of this?

CLOWN   I know not where he lodges, and for me to de-
vise a lodging and say he lies here, or he lies there,
were to lie in mine own throat.   13

DESDEMONA   Can you inquire him out, and be edified by report?

CLOWN   I will catechize the world for him; that is, make questions, and by them answer.

DESDEMONA   Seek him, bid him come hither. Tell him I
have moved my lord on his behalf and hope all will be   19
well.

CLOWN   To do this is within the compass of man's wit,
and therefore I will attempt the doing it.   *Exit Clown.*

DESDEMONA
Where should I lose that handkerchief, Emilia?

EMILIA   I know not, madam.

DESDEMONA
Believe me, I had rather have lost my purse
Full of crusadoes; and but my noble Moor   26
Is true of mind and made of no such baseness
As jealous creatures are, it were enough
To put him to ill thinking.

EMILIA   Is he not jealous?

DESDEMONA
Who, he? I think the sun where he was born
Drew all such humors from him.

EMILIA   Look where he comes.   31

      Enter Othello.

DESDEMONA
I will not leave him now till Cassio
Be called to him.—How is't with you, my lord?

OTHELLO
Well, my good lady. [*Aside*] Oh, hardness to
    dissemble!—
How do you, Desdemona?

DESDEMONA   Well, my good lord.

OTHELLO
Give me your hand. [*She gives her hand.*] This hand is
    moist, my lady.

DESDEMONA
It yet hath felt no age nor known no sorrow.

OTHELLO
This argues fruitfulness and liberal heart.   38
Hot, hot, and moist. This hand of yours requires
A sequester from liberty, fasting and prayer,   40

Much castigation, exercise devout;   41
For here's a young and sweating devil here
That commonly rebels. 'Tis a good hand,
A frank one.

DESDEMONA   You may indeed say so,   44
For 'twas that hand that gave away my heart.

OTHELLO
A liberal hand. The hearts of old gave hands,   46
But our new heraldry is hands, not hearts.   47

DESDEMONA
I cannot speak of this. Come now, your promise.

OTHELLO   What promise, chuck?   49

DESDEMONA
I have sent to bid Cassio come speak with you.

OTHELLO
I have a salt and sorry rheum offends me;   51
Lend me thy handkerchief.

DESDEMONA   Here, my lord.   [*She offers a handkerchief.*]

OTHELLO
That which I gave you.

DESDEMONA   I have it not about me.

OTHELLO   Not?

DESDEMONA   No, faith, my lord.

OTHELLO
That's a fault. That handkerchief
Did an Egyptian to my mother give.
She was a charmer, and could almost read   59
The thoughts of people. She told her, while she kept it
'Twould make her amiable and subdue my father   61
Entirely to her love, but if she lost it
Or made a gift of it, my father's eye
Should hold her loathèd and his spirits should hunt
After new fancies. She, dying, gave it me,   65
And bid me, when my fate would have me wived,
To give it her. I did so; and take heed on't;   67
Make it a darling like your precious eye.
To lose't or give't away were such perdition   69
As nothing else could match.

DESDEMONA   Is't possible?

OTHELLO
'Tis true. There's magic in the web of it.   71
A sibyl, that had numbered in the world
The sun to course two hundred compasses,   73
In her prophetic fury sewed the work;   74
The worms were hallowed that did breed the silk,
And it was dyed in mummy which the skillful   76
Conserved of maidens' hearts.

DESDEMONA   I'faith! Is't true?   77

---

13 lie . . . throat lie egregiously and deliberately.   **19 moved my lord** petitioned Othello   **26 crusadoes** Portuguese gold coins   **31 humors** (Refers to the four bodily fluids thought to determine temperament.) **38 argues** gives evidence of.   **fruitfulness** generosity, amorousness, and fecundity.   **liberal** generous and sexually free   **40 sequester** sequestration

41 castigation corrective discipline.   **exercise devout** i.e., prayer, religious meditation, etc.   **44 frank** generous, open. (With sexual suggestion.)   **46–7 The hearts . . . hearts** i.e., In former times, people would give their hearts when they gave their hands to something, but in our decadent present age the joining of hands no longer has that spiritual sense.   **49 chuck** (A term of endearment.)   **51 salt . . . rheum** distressful head cold or watering of the eyes   **59 charmer** sorceress   **61 amiable** desirable   **65 fancies** loves.   **67 her** i.e., to my wife.   **69 perdition** loss   **71 web** fabric, weaving   **73 compasses** annual circlings. (The *sibyl*, or prophetess, was two hundred years old.)   **74 prophetic fury** frenzy of prophetic inspiration.   **work** embroidered pattern **76 mummy** medicinal or magical preparation drained from mummified bodies   **77 Conserved of** prepared or preserved out of

OTHELLO
Most veritable. Therefore look to't well.

DESDEMONA
Then would to God that I had never seen't!

OTHELLO   Ha? Wherefore?

DESDEMONA
Why do you speak so startingly and rash?   81

OTHELLO
Is't lost? Is't gone? Speak, is't out o'th' way?   82

DESDEMONA   Heaven bless us!

OTHELLO   Say you?

DESDEMONA
It is not lost; but what an if it were?   85

OTHELLO   How?

DESDEMONA
I say it is not lost.

OTHELLO   Fetch't, let me see't.

DESDEMONA
Why, so I can, sir, but I will not now.
This is a trick to put me from my suit.
Pray you, let Cassio be received again.

OTHELLO
Fetch me the handkerchief! My mind misgives.

DESDEMONA   Come, come,
You'll never meet a more sufficient man.   93

OTHELLO
The handkerchief!

DESDEMONA   I pray, talk me of Cassio.   94

OTHELLO
The handkerchief!

DESDEMONA   A man that all his time   95
Hath founded his good fortunes on your love,   96
Shared dangers with you—

OTHELLO   The handkerchief!

DESDEMONA   I'faith, you are to blame.

OTHELLO   Zounds!   Exit Othello.

EMILIA   Is not this man jealous?

DESDEMONA   I ne'er saw this before.
Sure, there's some wonder in this handkerchief.
I am most unhappy in the loss of it.   104

EMILIA
'Tis not a year or two shows us a man.   105
They are all but stomachs, and we all but food;   106
They eat us hungerly, and when they are full   107
They belch us.

        Enter Iago and Cassio.

                Look you, Cassio and my husband.

IAGO [to Cassio]
There is no other way; 'tis she must do't.
And, lo, the happiness! Go and importune her.   110

DESDEMONA
How now, good Cassio? What's the news with you?

CASSIO
Madam, my former suit. I do beseech you
That by your virtuous means I may again   113
Exist and be a member of his love
Whom I, with all the office of my heart,   115
Entirely honor. I would not be delayed.
If my offense be of such mortal kind   117
That nor my service past, nor present sorrows,   118
Nor purposed merit in futurity
Can ransom me into his love again,
But to know so must be my benefit;   121
So shall I clothe me in a forced content,
And shut myself up in some other course,   123
To fortune's alms.

DESDEMONA   Alas, thrice-gentle Cassio,   124
My advocation is not now in tune.   125
My lord is not my lord; nor should I know him,
Were he in favor as in humor altered.   127
So help me every spirit sanctified   128
As I have spoken for you all my best
And stood within the blank of his displeasure   130
For my free speech! You must awhile be patient.   131
What I can do I will, and more I will
Than for myself I dare. Let that suffice you.

IAGO
Is my lord angry?

EMILIA   He went hence but now,
And certainly in strange unquietness.

IAGO
Can he be angry? I have seen the cannon
When it hath blown his ranks into the air,
And like the devil from his very arm
Puffed his own brother—and is he angry?
Something of moment then. I will go meet him.   140
There's matter in't indeed, if he be angry.

DESDEMONA
I prithee, do so.   Exit [Iago].
                Something, sure, of state,   142
Either from Venice, or some unhatched practice   143
Made demonstrable here in Cyprus to him,
Hath puddled his clear spirit; and in such cases   145
Men's natures wrangle with inferior things,
Though great ones are their object. 'Tis even so;
For let our finger ache, and it indues   148
Our other, healthful members even to a sense
Of pain. Nay, we must think men are not gods,

---

81 **startingly and rash** disjointedly and impetuously, excitedly.
82 **out o'th' way** lost, misplaced.   85 **an if** if   93 **sufficient** able,
complete   94 **talk** talk to   95–6 **A man . . . love** A man who throughout his career has relied on your favor for his advancement
104 **unhappy** (1) unfortunate (2) sad   105 **'Tis . . . man** A year or two
is not enough time for us to know what men really are.
106 **but** nothing but   107 **hungerly** hungrily   110 **the happiness** in
happy time, fortunately met.

113 **virtuous** (1) efficacious (2) morally good   115 **office** loyal service
117 **mortal** fatal   118 **nor . . . nor** neither . . . nor   121 **But . . . benefit**
merely to know that my case is hopeless will have to content me (and
will be better than uncertainty)   123 **shut . . . in** commit myself to
124 **To fortune's alms** throwing myself on the mercy of fortune.   125
advocation advocacy   127 **favor** appearance.   **humor** mood   128
So . . . sanctified So help me all the heavenly host   130 **within the
blank** within point-blank range. (The *blank* is the center of the target.)
131 **free** frank   140 **of moment** of immediate importance, momentous   142 **of state** concerning state affairs   143 **unhatched practice**
as yet unexecuted or undiscovered plot   145 **puddled** muddied
148 **indues** endows, brings to the same condition

Nor of them look for such observancy 151
As fits the bridal. Beshrew me much, Emilia, 152
I was, unhandsome warrior as I am, 153
Arraigning his unkindness with my soul; 154
But now I find I had suborned the witness, 155
And he's indicted falsely.

EMILIA   Pray heaven it be
State matters, as you think, and no conception
Nor no jealous toy concerning you. 158

DESDEMONA
Alas the day! I never gave him cause.

EMILIA
But jealous souls will not be answered so;
They are not ever jealous for the cause,
But jealous for they're jealous. It is a monster 162
Begot upon itself, born on itself. 163

DESDEMONA
Heaven keep that monster from Othello's mind!

EMILIA   Lady, amen.

DESDEMONA
I will go seek him. Cassio, walk hereabout.
If I do find him fit, I'll move your suit
And seek to effect it to my uttermost.

CASSIO
I humbly thank Your Ladyship.

Exit [Desdemona with Emilia].

Enter Bianca.

BIANCA
Save you, friend Cassio!

CASSIO   What make you from home? 170
How is't with you, my most fair Bianca?
I' faith, sweet love, I was coming to your house.

BIANCA
And I was going to your lodging, Cassio.
What, keep a week away? Seven days and nights?
Eightscore-eight hours? And lovers' absent hours 175
More tedious than the dial eightscore times? 176
Oh, weary reck'ning!

CASSIO   Pardon me, Bianca.
I have this while with leaden thoughts been pressed;
But I shall, in a more continuate time, 179
Strike off this score of absence. Sweet Bianca, 180
          [*giving her Desdemona's handkerchief*]
Take me this work out.

BIANCA   Oh, Cassio, whence came this? 181
This is some token from a newer friend. 182
To the felt absence now I feel a cause.
Is't come to this? Well, well.

CASSIO   Go to, woman!
Throw your vile guesses in the devil's teeth,

From whence you have them. You are jealous now
That this is from some mistress, some remembrance.
No, by my faith, Bianca.

BIANCA   Why, whose is it?

CASSIO
I know not, neither. I found it in my chamber.
I like the work well. Ere it be demanded— 190
As like enough it will—I would have it copied. 191
Take it and do't, and leave me for this time.

BIANCA   Leave you? Wherefore?

CASSIO
I do attend here on the General,
And think it no addition, nor my wish, 195
To have him see me womaned.

BIANCA   Why, I pray you?

CASSIO   Not that I love you not.

BIANCA   But that you do not love me.
I pray you, bring me on the way a little, 200
And say if I shall see you soon at night.

CASSIO
'Tis but a little way that I can bring you,
For I attend here; but I'll see you soon.

BIANCA
'Tis very good. I must be circumstanced. 204

                    Exeunt omnes.

❧

4.1

Enter Othello and Iago.

IAGO
Will you think so?

OTHELLO   Think so, Iago?

IAGO   What,
To kiss in private?

OTHELLO   An unauthorized kiss!

IAGO
Or to be naked with her friend in bed
An hour or more, not meaning any harm?

OTHELLO
Naked in bed, Iago, and not mean harm?
It is hypocrisy against the devil.
They that mean virtuously and yet do so,
The devil their virtue tempts, and they tempt heaven.

IAGO
If they do nothing, 'tis a venial slip. 9
But if I give my wife a handkerchief—

OTHELLO   What then?

IAGO
Why then, 'tis hers, my lord, and being hers,
She may, I think, bestow't on any man.

OTHELLO
She is protectress of her honor too.
May she give that?

---

151 **observancy** attentiveness   152 **bridal** wedding (when a bridegroom is newly attentive to his bride).   **Beshrew me** (A mild oath.)
153 **unhandsome** insufficient, unskillful   154 **with** before the bar of
155 **suborned the witness** induced the witness to give false testimony
158 **toy** fancy   162 **for** because   163 **Begot upon itself** generated solely from itself   170 **Save** God save.   **make** do   175 **Eightscore-eight** one hundred sixty-eight, the number of hours in a week
176 **the dial** a complete revolution of the clock   179 **continuate** uninterrupted   180 **Strike . . . score** settle this account   181 **Take . . . out** copy this embroidery for me.   182 **friend** mistress.

190 **demanded** inquired for   191 **like** likely   195 **addition** i.e., addition to my reputation   200 **bring** accompany   204 **be circumstanced** be governed by circumstance, yield to your conditions.
4.1. Location: Before the citadel.
9 **venial** pardonable

IAGO
　　Her honor is an essence that's not seen;
　　They have it very oft that have it not.　　　　　　　　17
　　But, for the handkerchief—
OTHELLO
　　By heaven, I would most gladly have forgot it.
　　Thou said'st—Oh, it comes o'er my memory
　　As doth the raven o'er the infectious house,　　　　21
　　Boding to all—he had my handkerchief.
IAGO
　　Ay, what of that?
OTHELLO　　　　　　That's not so good now.
IAGO　　　　　　　　　　　　　　　What
　　If I had said I had seen him do you wrong?
　　Or heard him say—as knaves be such abroad,　　　25
　　Who having, by their own importunate suit,　　　　26
　　Or voluntary dotage of some mistress,　　　　　　27
　　Convincèd or supplied them, cannot choose　　　　28
　　But they must blab—
OTHELLO　　　　　　　　Hath he said anything?　　29
IAGO
　　He hath, my lord; but, be you well assured,
　　No more than he'll unswear.
OTHELLO　　　　　　　　　　What hath he said?
IAGO
　　Faith, that he did—I know not what he did.
OTHELLO　　What? What?
IAGO
　　Lie—
OTHELLO　　With her?
IAGO　　　　　　　　With her, on her; what you will.
OTHELLO　　Lie with her? Lie on her? We say "lie on her"
　　when they belie her. Lie with her? Zounds, that's ful-　36
　　some.—Handkerchief—confessions—handkerchief!　37
　　—To confess and be hanged for his labor—first to be　38
　　hanged and then to confess.—I tremble at it. Nature　39
　　would not invest herself in such shadowing passion　40
　　without some instruction. It is not words that shakes　41
　　me thus. Pish! Noses, ears, and lips.—Is't possible?
　　—Confess—handkerchief!—O devil!

　　　　　　　　　　　　　　　　　　Falls in a trance.

IAGO　　Work on,
　　My medicine, work! Thus credulous fools are caught,
　　And many worthy and chaste dames even thus,
　　All guiltless, meet reproach.—What, ho! My lord!
　　My lord, I say! Othello!

　　　　　　Enter Cassio.

　　　　　　How now, Cassio?

CASSIO　　What's the matter?
IAGO
　　My lord is fall'n into an epilepsy.
　　This is his second fit. He had one yesterday.
CASSIO
　　Rub him about the temples.
IAGO　　　　　　　　　　　　　No, forbear.
　　The lethargy must have his quiet course.　　　　　　53
　　If not, he foams at mouth, and by and by
　　Breaks out to savage madness. Look, he stirs.
　　Do you withdraw yourself a little while.
　　He will recover straight. When he is gone,
　　I would on great occasion speak with you.　　　　　58

　　　　　　　　　　　　　　　　　　[Exit Cassio.]

　　How is it, General? Have you not hurt your head?
OTHELLO
　　Dost thou mock me?
IAGO　　　　　　　　　　I mock you not, by heaven.　　60
　　Would you would bear your fortune like a man!
OTHELLO
　　A hornèd man's a monster and a beast.
IAGO
　　There's many a beast then in a populous city,
　　And many a civil monster.　　　　　　　　　　　64
OTHELLO　　Did he confess it?
IAGO　　Good sir, be a man.
　　Think every bearded fellow that's but yoked　　　67
　　May draw with you. There's millions now alive　68
　　That nightly lie in those unproper beds　　　　　69
　　Which they dare swear peculiar. Your case is better.　70
　　Oh, 'tis the spite of hell, the fiend's arch-mock,
　　To lip a wanton in a secure couch　　　　　　　72
　　And to suppose her chaste! No, let me know,
　　And knowing what I am, I know what she shall be.　74
OTHELLO　　Oh, thou art wise. 'Tis certain.
IAGO　　Stand you awhile apart;
　　Confine yourself but in a patient list.　　　　　77
　　Whilst you were here o'erwhelmèd with your grief—
　　A passion most unsuiting such a man—
　　Cassio came hither. I shifted him away,　　　　80
　　And laid good 'scuse upon your ecstasy,　　　　81
　　Bade him anon return and here speak with me,
　　The which he promised. Do but encave yourself　83
　　And mark the fleers, the gibes, and notable scorns　84
　　That dwell in every region of his face;
　　For I will make him tell the tale anew,
　　Where, how, how oft, how long ago, and when
　　He hath and is again to cope your wife.　　　　　88

17 They have it i.e., They enjoy a reputation for it　21 raven . . . house (Allusion to the belief that the raven hovered over a house of sickness or infection, such as one visited by the plague.)　25–9 as . . . blab— since there are rascals enough who, having seduced a woman either through their own importunity or through the woman's willing infatuation, cannot keep quiet about it—　36 belie slander 36–7 fulsome foul.　38–9 first . . . to confess (Othello reverses the proverbial confess and be hanged; Cassio is to be given no time to confess before he dies.)　39–41 Nature . . . instruction i.e., Without some foundation in fact, nature would not have dressed herself in such an overwhelming passion that comes over me now and fills my mind with images, or in such a lifelike fantasy as Cassio had in his dream of lying with Desdemona.　41 words mere words

53 lethargy coma.　his its　58 on great occasion on a matter of great importance　60 mock me (Othello takes Iago's question about hurting his head to be a mocking reference to the cuckold's horns.)　64 civil i.e., dwelling in a city　67 yoked (1) married (2) put into the yoke of infamy and cuckoldry　68 draw with you pull as you do, like oxen who are yoked, i.e., share your fate as cuckold.　69 unproper not exclusively their own　70 peculiar private, their own.　better i.e., because you know the truth.　72 lip kiss.　secure free from suspicion　74 And . . . shall be and, knowing myself to be a cuckold, I'll know for certain that she's a whore.　77 in . . . list within the bounds of patience.　80–1 I shifted . . . ecstasy I got him out of the way, using your fit as my excuse for doing so　83 encave conceal 84 fleers sneers　88 cope encounter with, have sex with

I say, but mark his gesture. Marry, patience!
Or I shall say you're all-in-all in spleen,   90
And nothing of a man.
OTHELLO   Dost thou hear, Iago?
I will be found most cunning in my patience;
But—dost thou hear?—most bloody.
IAGO   That's not amiss;
But yet keep time in all. Will you withdraw?   94
                              [*Othello stands apart.*]
Now will I question Cassio of Bianca,
A huswife that by selling her desires   96
Buys herself bread and clothes. It is a creature
That dotes on Cassio—as 'tis the strumpet's plague
To beguile many and be beguiled by one.
He, when he hears of her, cannot restrain   100
From the excess of laughter. Here he comes.

          Enter Cassio.

As he shall smile, Othello shall go mad;
And his unbookish jealousy must conster   103
Poor Cassio's smiles, gestures, and light behaviors
Quite in the wrong.—How do you now, Lieutenant?
CASSIO
The worser that you give me the addition   106
Whose want even kills me.   107
IAGO
Ply Desdemona well and you are sure on't.
[*Speaking lower*] Now, if this suit lay in Bianca's power,
How quickly should you speed!
CASSIO [*laughing*]   Alas, poor caitiff!   111
OTHELLO [*aside*]   Look how he laughs already!
IAGO
I never knew a woman love man so.
CASSIO
Alas, poor rogue! I think, i'faith, she loves me.
OTHELLO [*aside*]
Now he denies it faintly, and laughs it out.
IAGO
Do you hear, Cassio?
OTHELLO [*aside*]   Now he importunes him
To tell it o'er. Go to! Well said, well said.   117
IAGO
She gives it out that you shall marry her.
Do you intend it?
CASSIO   Ha, ha, ha!
OTHELLO [*aside*]
Do you triumph, Roman? Do you triumph?   121
CASSIO   I marry her? What? A customer? Prithee, bear   122
some charity to my wit; do not think it so unwhole-   123
some. Ha, ha, ha!

OTHELLO [*aside*]   So, so, so, so! They laugh that win.   125
IAGO   Faith, the cry goes that you shall marry her.   126
CASSIO   Prithee, say true.
IAGO   I am a very villain else.   128
OTHELLO [*aside*]   Have you scored me? Well.   129
CASSIO   This is the monkey's own giving out. She is
persuaded I will marry her out of her own love and
flattery, not out of my promise.   132
OTHELLO [*aside*]   Iago beckons me. Now he begins the   133
story.
CASSIO   She was here even now; she haunts me in every
place. I was the other day talking on the seabank with   136
certain Venetians, and thither comes the bauble, and,   137
by this hand, she falls me thus about my neck—   138
                              [*He embraces Iago.*]
OTHELLO [*aside*]   Crying, "Oh, dear Cassio!" as it were; his
gesture imports it.
CASSIO   So hangs and lolls and weeps upon me, so
shakes and pulls me. Ha, ha, ha!
OTHELLO [*aside*]   Now he tells how she plucked him to my
chamber. Oh, I see that nose of yours, but not that dog   144
I shall throw it to.   145
CASSIO   Well, I must leave her company.
IAGO   Before me, look where she comes.   147

          Enter Bianca [with Desdemona's handkerchief].

CASSIO   'Tis such another fitchew! Marry, a perfumed   148
one.—What do you mean by this haunting of me?
BIANCA   Let the devil and his dam haunt you! What did   150
you mean by that same handkerchief you gave me
even now? I was a fine fool to take it. I must take out
the work? A likely piece of work, that you should find   153
it in your chamber and know not who left it there!
This is some minx's token, and I must take out the
work? There; give it your hobbyhorse. [*She gives him   156
the handkerchief.*] Wheresoever you had it, I'll take out
no work on't.
CASSIO   How now, my sweet Bianca? How now? How
now?
OTHELLO [*aside*]   By heaven, that should be my hand-   161
kerchief!
BIANCA   If you'll come to supper tonight, you may; if
you will not, come when you are next prepared for.   164
                                        Exit.
IAGO   After her, after her.
CASSIO   Faith, I must. She'll rail in the streets else.
IAGO   Will you sup there?
CASSIO   Faith, I intend so.
IAGO   Well, I may chance to see you, for I would very
fain speak with you.

---

90 all-in-all in spleen utterly governed by passionate impulses
94 keep time keep yourself steady (as in music)   **96 huswife** hussy
100 restrain refrain   **103 his unbookish** Othello's uninstructed.
conster construe   **106 addition** title   **107 Whose want** the lack of
which   **111 caitiff** wretch.   **117 Go to** (An expression of remonstrance.)   **Well said** Well done. (Sarcastic.)   **121 Roman** (The
Romans were noted for their *triumphs* or triumphal processions.)
122 A customer? Who, I, the whore's customer? (Or, *customer* could
mean "prostitute.")   **122–3 bear . . . wit** be more charitable to my
judgment

125 They . . . win i.e., They that laugh last laugh best.   **126 cry** rumor
128 I . . . else Call me a complete rogue if I'm not telling the truth.
129 scored me scored off me, beaten me, made up my reckoning,
branded me.   **132 flattery** self-flattery, self-deception   **133 beckons**
signals to   **136 seabank** seashore   **137 bauble** plaything   **138 by
this hand** I make my vow   **144–5 not . . . to** (Othello imagines himself cutting off Cassio's nose and throwing it to a dog.)   **147 Before
me** i.e., On my soul   **148 'Tis . . . fitchew!** What a whore she is! Just
like all the others. (*Fitchew* or "polecat" was a common term of contempt for a courtesan or prostitute.)   **150 dam** mother   **153 A likely
. . . work** A fine story   **156 hobbyhorse** harlot.   **161 should be** must
be   **164 when . . . for** when I'm ready for you (i.e., never).

CASSIO   Prithee, come. Will you?

IAGO   Go to. Say no more.   [*Exit Cassio.*] 172

OTHELLO [*advancing*]   How shall I murder him, Iago?

IAGO   Did you perceive how he laughed at his vice?

OTHELLO   Oh, Iago!

IAGO   And did you see the handkerchief?

OTHELLO   Was that mine?

IAGO   Yours, by this hand. And to see how he prizes the foolish woman your wife! She gave it him, and he hath given it his whore.

OTHELLO   I would have him nine years a-killing. A fine woman! A fair woman! A sweet woman!

IAGO   Nay, you must forget that.

OTHELLO   Ay, let her rot and perish, and be damned tonight, for she shall not live. No, my heart is turned to stone; I strike it, and it hurts my hand. Oh, the world hath not a sweeter creature! She might lie by an emperor's side and command him tasks.

IAGO   Nay, that's not your way.   189

OTHELLO   Hang her! I do but say what she is. So delicate with her needle! An admirable musician! Oh, she will sing the savageness out of a bear. Of so high and plenteous wit and invention!   193

IAGO   She's the worse for all this.

OTHELLO   Oh, a thousand, a thousand times! And then, of so gentle a condition!   196

IAGO   Ay, too gentle.   197

OTHELLO   Nay, that's certain. But yet the pity of it, Iago! Oh, Iago, the pity of it, Iago!

IAGO   If you are so fond over her iniquity, give her patent 200 to offend, for if it touch not you it comes near nobody.

OTHELLO   I will chop her into messes. Cuckold me?   202

IAGO   Oh, 'tis foul in her.

OTHELLO   With mine officer?

IAGO   That's fouler.

OTHELLO   Get me some poison, Iago, this night. I'll not expostulate with her, lest her body and beauty unpro- 207 vide my mind again. This night, Iago.   208

IAGO   Do it not with poison. Strangle her in her bed, even the bed she hath contaminated.

OTHELLO   Good, good! The justice of it pleases. Very good.

IAGO   And for Cassio, let me be his undertaker. You 212 shall hear more by midnight.

OTHELLO   Excellent good. [*A trumpet within.*] What trumpet is that same?

IAGO   I warrant, something from Venice.

Enter Lodovico, Desdemona, and attendants.

'Tis Lodovico. This comes from the Duke. See, your wife's with him.

LODOVICO   God save you, worthy General!

OTHELLO   With all my heart, sir. 218

LODOVICO [*giving him a letter*]   The Duke and the senators of Venice greet you.

OTHELLO   I kiss the instrument of their pleasures.
                    [*He opens the letter, and reads.*]

DESDEMONA   And what's the news, good cousin Lodovico?

IAGO   I am very glad to see you, signor. Welcome to Cyprus.

LODOVICO   I thank you. How does Lieutenant Cassio?

IAGO   Lives, sir.

DESDEMONA   Cousin, there's fall'n between him and my lord An unkind breach; but you shall make all well.   227

OTHELLO   Are you sure of that?

DESDEMONA   My lord?

OTHELLO [*reads*]   "This fail you not to do, as you will—"

LODOVICO   He did not call; he's busy in the paper. Is there division twixt my lord and Cassio?

DESDEMONA   A most unhappy one. I would do much T'atone them, for the love I bear to Cassio.   234

OTHELLO   Fire and brimstone!

DESDEMONA   My lord?

OTHELLO   Are you wise?

DESDEMONA   What, is he angry?

LODOVICO   Maybe the letter moved him; For, as I think, they do command him home, Deputing Cassio in his government.   240

DESDEMONA   By my troth, I am glad on't.   241

OTHELLO   Indeed?

DESDEMONA   My lord?

OTHELLO   I am glad to see you mad.   244

DESDEMONA   Why, sweet Othello—

OTHELLO [*striking her*]   Devil!

DESDEMONA   I have not deserved this.

LODOVICO   My lord, this would not be believed in Venice, Though I should swear I saw't. 'Tis very much. 249 Make her amends; she weeps.

OTHELLO   Oh, devil, devil! If that the earth could teem with woman's tears, 251 Each drop she falls would prove a crocodile.   252 Out of my sight!

DESDEMONA   I will not stay to offend you. [*Going.*]

172 **Go to** (An expression of remonstrance.)   189 **your way** i.e., the way you should think of her.   193 **invention** imagination.   196 **gentle a condition** wellborn and well-bred.   197 **gentle** generous, yielding (to other men).   200 **fond** foolish.   **patent** license   202 **messes** portions of meat, i.e., bits.   207–8 **unprovide** weaken, disarm   212 **be his undertaker** undertake to dispatch him.

218 **With all my heart** i.e., I thank you most heartily   227 **unkind** unnatural, contrary to their natures; hurtful   234 **T'atone** to reconcile   240 **government** office.   241 **on't** of it.   244 **I am . . . mad** i.e., I am glad to see that you are insane enough to rejoice in Cassio's promotion. (? Othello bitterly plays on Desdemona's *I am glad*.)   249 **very much** too much, outrageous.   251 **teem** breed, be impregnated   252 **falls** lets fall.   **crocodile** (Crocodiles were supposed to weep hypocritical tears for their victims.)

LODOVICO   Truly, an obedient lady.
　I do beseech Your Lordship, call her back.
OTHELLO [*calling*]   Mistress!
DESDEMONA [*returning*]   My lord?
OTHELLO   What would you with her, sir?   258
LODOVICO   Who, I, my lord?
OTHELLO
　Ay, you did wish that I would make her turn.
　Sir, she can turn, and turn, and yet go on
　And turn again; and she can weep, sir, weep;
　And she's obedient, as you say, obedient,   263
　Very obedient.—Proceed you in your tears.—
　Concerning this, sir—Oh, well-painted passion!—   265
　I am commanded home.—Get you away;
　I'll send for you anon.—Sir, I obey the mandate
　And will return to Venice.—Hence, avaunt!
　　　　　　　　　　　　　　　[*Exit Desdemona.*]
　Cassio shall have my place. And, sir, tonight
　I do entreat that we may sup together.
　You are welcome, sir, to Cyprus.—Goats and
　　monkeys!   *Exit.* 271
LODOVICO
　Is this the noble Moor whom our full Senate
　Call all in all sufficient? Is this the nature
　Whom passion could not shake? Whose solid virtue
　The shot of accident nor dart of chance
　Could neither graze nor pierce?
IAGO   He is much changed.
LODOVICO
　Are his wits safe? Is he not light of brain?
IAGO
　He's that he is. I may not breathe my censure   278
　What he might be. If what he might he is not,   279
　I would to heaven he were!
LODOVICO   What, strike his wife?   280
IAGO
　Faith, that was not so well; yet would I knew
　That stroke would prove the worst!
LODOVICO   Is it his use?   282
　Or did the letters work upon his blood   283
　And new-create his fault?
IAGO   Alas, alas!
　It is not honesty in me to speak
　What I have seen and known. You shall observe him,
　And his own courses will denote him so   287
　That I may save my speech. Do but go after,
　And mark how he continues.
LODOVICO
　I am sorry that I am deceived in him.   *Exeunt.*

❧

4.2

Enter Othello and Emilia.

OTHELLO   You have seen nothing, then?
EMILIA
　Nor ever heard, nor ever did suspect.
OTHELLO
　Yes, you have seen Cassio and she together.
EMILIA
　But then I saw no harm, and then I heard
　Each syllable that breath made up between them.
OTHELLO   What, did they never whisper?
EMILIA   Never, my lord.
OTHELLO   Nor send you out o'th' way?
EMILIA   Never.
OTHELLO
　To fetch her fan, her gloves, her mask, nor nothing?
EMILIA   Never, my lord.
OTHELLO   That's strange.
EMILIA
　I durst, my lord, to wager she is honest,
　Lay down my soul at stake. If you think other,   14
　Remove your thought; it doth abuse your bosom.   15
　If any wretch have put this in your head,
　Let heaven requite it with the serpent's curse!   17
　For if she be not honest, chaste, and true,
　There's no man happy; the purest of their wives
　Is foul as slander.
OTHELLO   Bid her come hither. Go.
　　　　　　　　　　　　　　　Exit Emilia.
　She says enough; yet she's a simple bawd   21
　That cannot say as much. This is a subtle whore,   22
　A closet lock and key of villainous secrets.   23
　And yet she'll kneel and pray; I have seen her do't.

Enter Desdemona and Emilia.

DESDEMONA   My lord, what is your will?
OTHELLO   Pray you, chuck, come hither.
DESDEMONA
　What is your pleasure?
OTHELLO   Let me see your eyes.
　Look in my face.
DESDEMONA   What horrible fancy's this?
OTHELLO [*to Emilia*]   Some of your function, mistress.   29
　Leave procreants alone and shut the door;   30
　Cough or cry "hem" if anybody come.
　Your mystery, your mystery! Nay, dispatch.   32
　　　　　　　　　　　　　　　Exit Emilia.
DESDEMONA [*kneeling*]
　Upon my knees, what doth your speech import?

I understand a fury in your words,
But not the words.

OTHELLO
Why, what art thou?

DESDEMONA   Your wife, my lord, your true
And loyal wife.

OTHELLO   Come, swear it, damn thyself,
Lest, being like one of heaven, the devils themselves   38
Should fear to seize thee. Therefore be double
    damned:
Swear thou art honest.

DESDEMONA   Heaven doth truly know it.

OTHELLO
Heaven truly knows that thou art false as hell.

DESDEMONA
To whom, my lord? With whom? How am I false?

OTHELLO [weeping]
Ah, Desdemon! Away, away, away!

DESDEMONA
Alas the heavy day! Why do you weep?
Am I the motive of these tears, my lord?   45
If haply you my father do suspect
An instrument of this your calling back,
Lay not your blame on me. If you have lost him,
I have lost him too.

OTHELLO   Had it pleased heaven
To try me with affliction, had they rained   50
All kinds of sores and shames on my bare head,
Steeped me in poverty to the very lips,
Given to captivity me and my utmost hopes,
I should have found in some place of my soul
A drop of patience. But, alas, to make me
A fixèd figure for the time of scorn   56
To point his slow and moving finger at!   57
Yet could I bear that too, well, very well.
But there where I have garnered up my heart,   59
Where either I must live or bear no life,
The fountain from the which my current runs   61
Or else dries up—to be discarded thence!
Or keep it as a cistern for foul toads   63
To knot and gender in! Turn thy complexion there,   64
Patience, thou young and rose-lipped cherubin—   65
Ay, there look grim as hell!   66

DESDEMONA
I hope my noble lord esteems me honest.   67

OTHELLO
Oh, ay, as summer flies are in the shambles,   68
That quicken even with blowing. O thou weed,   69
Who art so lovely fair and smell'st so sweet
That the sense aches at thee, would thou hadst ne'er
    been born!

DESDEMONA
Alas, what ignorant sin have I committed?   72

OTHELLO
Was this fair paper, this most goodly book,
Made to write "whore" upon? What committed?
Committed? Oh, thou public commoner!   75
I should make very forges of my cheeks,
That would to cinders burn up modesty,
Did I but speak thy deeds. What committed?
Heaven stops the nose at it and the moon winks;   79
The bawdy wind, that kisses all it meets,   80
Is hushed within the hollow mine of earth   81
And will not hear't. What committed?
Impudent strumpet!

DESDEMONA   By heaven, you do me wrong.

OTHELLO
Are not you a strumpet?

DESDEMONA   No, as I am a Christian.
If to preserve this vessel for my lord   86
From any other foul unlawful touch
Be not to be a strumpet, I am none.

OTHELLO   What, not a whore?

DESDEMONA   No, as I shall be saved.

OTHELLO   Is't possible?

DESDEMONA
Oh, heaven forgive us!

OTHELLO   I cry you mercy, then.   92
I took you for that cunning whore of Venice
That married with Othello. [Calling out] You, mistress,
That have the office opposite to Saint Peter
And keep the gate of hell!

        Enter Emilia.

                        You, you, ay, you!
We have done our course. There's money for your
    pains.   [He gives money.]   97
I pray you, turn the key and keep our counsel.   Exit.

EMILIA
Alas, what does this gentleman conceive?   99
How do you, madam? How do you, my good lady?

DESDEMONA   Faith, half asleep.   101

EMILIA
Good madam, what's the matter with my lord?

DESDEMONA   With who?

EMILIA   Why, with my lord, madam.

DESDEMONA
Who is thy lord?

EMILIA   He that is yours, sweet lady.

DESDEMONA
I have none. Do not talk to me, Emilia.
I cannot weep, nor answers have I none
But what should go by water. Prithee, tonight   108

---

38 being . . . heaven looking like an angel   45 motive cause   50 they
the heavenly powers   56–7 A fixèd . . . finger at a figure of ridicule
to be pointed at scornfully for all of eternity by the slowly moving
finger of Time.   59 garnered stored   61 fountain spring   63 cistern
cesspool   64 To . . . gender in to couple sexually and conceive in.
64–6 Turn . . . hell! Direct your gaze there, Patience, and your youthful and rosy cherubic countenance will turn grim and pale at this
hellish spectacle!   67 honest chaste.   68 shambles slaughterhouse
69 That . . . blowing that come to life with the puffing up of the rotten
meat on which the flies and their maggots are breeding.

72 ignorant sin sin in ignorance   75 commoner prostitute.
79 winks closes her eyes. (The moon symbolizes chastity.)
80 bawdy kissing one and all   81 mine cave (where the winds were
thought to dwell)   86 vessel body   92 cry you mercy beg your pardon. (Sarcastic.)   97 course business. (With an indecent suggestion of
"trick," turn at sex.)   99 conceive suppose, think.   101 half asleep
i.e., dazed.   108 go by water be conveyed by tears.

Lay on my bed my wedding sheets, remember;
And call thy husband hither.

EMILIA   Here's a change indeed!   *Exit.*

DESDEMONA
'Tis meet I should be used so, very meet.   112
How have I been behaved, that he might stick   113
The small'st opinion on my least misuse?   114

Enter Iago and Emilia.

IAGO
What is your pleasure, madam? How is't with you?

DESDEMONA
I cannot tell. Those that do teach young babes
Do it with gentle means and easy tasks.
He might have chid me so, for, in good faith,
I am a child to chiding.

IAGO   What is the matter, lady?

EMILIA
Alas, Iago, my lord hath so bewhored her,
Thrown such despite and heavy terms upon her,
That true hearts cannot bear it.

DESDEMONA   Am I that name, Iago?

IAGO   What name, fair lady?

DESDEMONA
Such as she said my lord did say I was.

EMILIA
He called her whore. A beggar in his drink
Could not have laid such terms upon his callet.   128

IAGO   Why did he so?

DESDEMONA [*weeping*]
I do not know. I am sure I am none such.

IAGO   Do not weep, do not weep. Alas the day!

EMILIA
Hath she forsook so many noble matches,
Her father and her country and her friends,
To be called whore? Would it not make one weep?

DESDEMONA
It is my wretched fortune.

IAGO   Beshrew him for't!   135
How comes this trick upon him?

DESDEMONA   Nay, heaven doth know.   136

EMILIA
I will be hanged if some eternal villain,   137
Some busy and insinuating rogue,   138
Some cogging, cozening slave, to get some office,   139
Have not devised this slander. I will be hanged else.

IAGO
Fie, there is no such man. It is impossible.

DESDEMONA
If any such there be, heaven pardon him!

EMILIA
A halter pardon him! And hell gnaw his bones!   143

Why should he call her whore? Who keeps her
  company?
What place? What time? What form? What
  likelihood?   145
The Moor's abused by some most villainous knave,
Some base notorious knave, some scurvy fellow.
Oh, heavens, that such companions thou'dst unfold,   148
And put in every honest hand a whip
To lash the rascals naked through the world
Even from the east to th' west!

IAGO   Speak within door.   151

EMILIA
Oh, fie upon them! Some such squire he was   152
That turned your wit the seamy side without   153
And made you to suspect me with the Moor.

IAGO
You are a fool. Go to.

DESDEMONA   Oh, God, Iago,   155
What shall I do to win my lord again?
Good friend, go to him; for, by this light of heaven,
I know not how I lost him. Here I kneel.   [*She kneels.*]
If e'er my will did trespass 'gainst his love,
Either in discourse of thought or actual deed,   160
Or that mine eyes, mine ears, or any sense   161
Delighted them in any other form;   162
Or that I do not yet, and ever did,   163
And ever will—though he do shake me off
To beggarly divorcement—love him dearly,
Comfort forswear me! Unkindness may do much,   166
And his unkindness may defeat my life,   167
But never taint my love. I cannot say "whore."
It does abhor me now I speak the word;   169
To do the act that might the addition earn   170
Not the world's mass of vanity could make me.   171
                    [*She rises.*]

IAGO
I pray you, be content. 'Tis but his humor.   172
The business of the state does him offense,
And he does chide with you.

DESDEMONA   If 'twere no other—

IAGO   It is but so, I warrant.   [*Trumpets within.*]
Hark, how these instruments summon you to supper!
The messengers of Venice stays the meat.   178
Go in, and weep not. All things shall be well.
                    Exeunt Desdemona and Emilia.

Enter Roderigo.

How now, Roderigo?

RODERIGO   I do not find that thou deal'st justly with me.

IAGO   What in the contrary?

---

112 'Tis . . . very meet i.e., It must be I somehow have deserved this.
113–14 How . . . misuse? What have I done that prompts Othello to
attach even the slightest censure to whatever little fault I may have
committed?   128 callet whore.   135 Beshrew May evil befall. (An
oath.)   136 trick strange behavior, delusion   137 eternal inveterate
138 insinuating ingratiating, fawning, wheedling   139 cogging, cozening cheating, defrauding   143 halter hangman's noose

145 form manner, circumstance.   148 that . . . unfold would that you
would expose such fellows   151 within door i.e., not so loud.
152 squire fellow   153 seamy side without wrong side out   155 Go
to i.e., That's enough.   160 discourse of thought process of thinking
161 that if. (Also in line 163.)   162 Delighted them took delight
163 yet still   166 Comfort forswear may heavenly comfort forsake
167 defeat destroy   169 abhor (1) fill me with abhorrence (2) make
me whorelike   170 addition title   171 vanity showy splendor
172 humor mood.   178 stays the meat are waiting to dine.

RODERIGO   Every day thou daff'st me with some device, 183
Iago, and rather, as it seems to me now, keep'st
from me all conveniency than suppliest me with the 185
least advantage of hope. I will indeed no longer 186
endure it, nor am I yet persuaded to put up in peace 187
what already I have foolishly suffered.

IAGO   Will you hear me, Roderigo?

RODERIGO   Faith, I have heard too much, for your words
and performances are no kin together.

IAGO   You charge me most unjustly.

RODERIGO   With naught but truth. I have wasted myself
out of my means. The jewels you have had from me to
deliver Desdemona would half have corrupted a vo- 195
tarist. You have told me she hath received them and 196
returned me expectations and comforts of sudden re- 197
spect and acquaintance, but I find none. 198

IAGO   Well, go to, very well.

RODERIGO   "Very well"! "Go to"! I cannot go to, man, 200
nor 'tis not very well. By this hand, I think it is scurvy,
and begin to find myself fopped in it. 202

IAGO   Very well.

RODERIGO   I tell you 'tis not very well. I will make myself 204
known to Desdemona. If she will return me my jewels,
I will give over my suit and repent my unlawful solicitation; if not, assure yourself I will seek satisfaction 207
of you.

IAGO   You have said now? 209

RODERIGO   Ay, and said nothing but what I protest 210
intendment of doing. 211

IAGO   Why, now I see there's mettle in thee, and even
from this instant do build on thee a better opinion
than ever before. Give me thy hand, Roderigo. Thou
hast taken against me a most just exception; but yet I
protest I have dealt most directly in thy affair.

RODERIGO   It hath not appeared.

IAGO   I grant indeed it hath not appeared, and your
suspicion is not without wit and judgment. But,
Roderigo, if thou hast that in thee indeed which I have
greater reason to believe now than ever—I mean
purpose, courage, and valor—this night show it. If
thou the next night following enjoy not Desdemona,
take me from this world with treachery and devise
engines for my life. 225

RODERIGO   Well, what is it? Is it within reason and
compass?

IAGO   Sir, there is especial commission come from
Venice to depute Cassio in Othello's place.

RODERIGO   Is that true? Why, then Othello and Desdemona return again to Venice.

IAGO   Oh, no; he goes into Mauritania and takes away
with him the fair Desdemona, unless his abode be
lingered here by some accident; wherein none can be
so determinate as the removing of Cassio. 235

RODERIGO   How do you mean, removing of him?

IAGO   Why, by making him uncapable of Othello's
place—knocking out his brains.

RODERIGO   And that you would have me to do?

IAGO   Ay, if you dare do yourself a profit and a right.
He sups tonight with a harlotry, and thither will I go to 241
him. He knows not yet of his honorable fortune. If
you will watch his going thence, which I will fashion
to fall out between twelve and one, you may take him 244
at your pleasure. I will be near to second your attempt,
and he shall fall between us. Come, stand not amazed
at it, but go along with me. I will show you such a
necessity in his death that you shall think yourself
bound to put it on him. It is now high suppertime, 249
and the night grows to waste. About it. 250

RODERIGO   I will hear further reason for this.

IAGO   And you shall be satisfied.   *Exeunt.*

4.3

*Enter Othello, Lodovico, Desdemona, Emilia, and
attendants.*

LODOVICO
I do beseech you, sir, trouble yourself no further.

OTHELLO
Oh, pardon me; 'twill do me good to walk.

LODOVICO
Madam, good night. I humbly thank Your Ladyship.

DESDEMONA
Your Honor is most welcome.

OTHELLO   Will you walk, sir?
Oh, Desdemona!

DESDEMONA   My lord?

OTHELLO   Get you to bed on th'instant. I will be returned forthwith. Dismiss your attendant there. Look't
be done.

DESDEMONA   I will, my lord.
        Exit [Othello, with Lodovico and attendants].

EMILIA   How goes it now? He looks gentler than he did.

DESDEMONA
He says he will return incontinent, 12
And hath commanded me to go to bed,
And bid me to dismiss you.

EMILIA   Dismiss me?

DESDEMONA
It was his bidding. Therefore, good Emilia,
Give me my nightly wearing, and adieu.
We must not now displease him.

EMILIA   I would you had never seen him!

183 **thou daff'st me** you put me off.   **device** excuse, trick
185 **conveniency** advantage, opportunity   **186 advantage** increase
187 **put up** submit to, tolerate   **195 deliver** deliver to   **195–6 votarist**
nun.   **197-8 sudden respect** immediate consideration   **200 I cannot
go to** (Roderigo changes Iago's *go to*, an expression urging patience,
to *I cannot go to*, "I have no opportunity for success in wooing.")
202 fopped fooled, duped   **204 not very well** (Roderigo changes
Iago's *Very well*, "All right, then," to *not very well*, "not at all good.")
207 satisfaction repayment. (The term normally means settling of
accounts in a duel.)   **209 You . . . now?** Have you finished?
210–11 protest intendment avow my intention   **225 engines** plots,
snares

235 **determinate** conclusive, instrumental   **241 harlotry** slut
244 **fall out** occur   **249 high** fully   **250 grows to waste** wastes away.
4.3 Location: The citadel.
12 incontinent immediately

DESDEMONA
So would not I. My love doth so approve him
That even his stubbornness, his checks, his frowns—   21
Prithee, unpin me—have grace and favor in them.
                [*Emilia prepares Desdemona for bed.*]
EMILIA   I have laid those sheets you bade me on the
bed.
DESDEMONA
All's one. Good faith, how foolish are our minds!   25
If I do die before thee, prithee shroud me
In one of these same sheets.
EMILIA   Come, come, you talk.   27
DESDEMONA
My mother had a maid called Barbary.
She was in love, and he she loved proved mad   29
And did forsake her. She had a song of "Willow."
An old thing 'twas, but it expressed her fortune,
And she died singing it. That song tonight
Will not go from my mind; I have much to do   33
But to go hang my head all at one side   34
And sing it like poor Barbary. Prithee, dispatch.
EMILIA   Shall I go fetch your nightgown?   36
DESDEMONA   No, unpin me here.
This Lodovico is a proper man.   38
EMILIA   A very handsome man.
DESDEMONA   He speaks well.
EMILIA   I know a lady in Venice would have walked
barefoot to Palestine for a touch of his nether lip.
DESDEMONA [*singing*]
    "The poor soul sat sighing by a sycamore tree,
        Sing all a green willow;   44
    Her hand on her bosom, her head on her knee,
        Sing willow, willow, willow.
    The fresh streams ran by her and murmured her
        moans;
        Sing willow, willow, willow;
    Her salt tears fell from her, and softened the
        stones—"
Lay by these.
[*Singing*] "Sing willow, willow, willow—"
Prithee, hie thee. He'll come anon.   52
[*Singing*] "Sing all a green willow must be my garland.
    Let nobody blame him; his scorn I approve—"
Nay, that's not next.—Hark! Who is't that knocks?
EMILIA   It's the wind.
DESDEMONA [*singing*]
    "I called my love false love; but what said he
        then?
        Sing willow, willow, willow;
    If I court more women, you'll couch with more
        men."
So, get thee gone. Good night. Mine eyes do itch;
Doth that bode weeping?
EMILIA   'Tis neither here nor there.

DESDEMONA
I have heard it said so. Oh, these men, these men!
Dost thou in conscience think—tell me, Emilia—
That there be women do abuse their husbands   64
In such gross kind?
EMILIA   There be some such, no question.
DESDEMONA
Wouldst thou do such a deed for all the world?
EMILIA
Why, would not you?
DESDEMONA   No, by this heavenly light!
EMILIA
Nor I neither by this heavenly light;
I might do't as well i'th' dark.
DESDEMONA
Wouldst thou do such a deed for all the world?
EMILIA
The world's a huge thing. It is a great price
For a small vice.
DESDEMONA
Good troth, I think thou wouldst not.
EMILIA   By my troth, I think I should, and undo't when
I had done. Marry, I would not do such a thing for a
joint ring, nor for measures of lawn, nor for gowns,   76
petticoats, nor caps, nor any petty exhibition. But for   77
all the whole world! Uds pity, who would not make   78
her husband a cuckold to make him a monarch? I
should venture purgatory for't.
DESDEMONA
Beshrew me if I would do such a wrong
For the whole world.
EMILIA   Why, the wrong is but a wrong i'th' world, and
having the world for your labor, 'tis a wrong in your
own world, and you might quickly make it right.
DESDEMONA
I do not think there is any such woman.
EMILIA   Yes, a dozen, and as many   87
To th' vantage as would store the world they played
for.   88
But I do think it is their husbands' faults
If wives do fall. Say that they slack their duties   90
And pour our treasures into foreign laps,   91
Or else break out in peevish jealousies,
Throwing restraint upon us? Or say they strike us,   93
Or scant our former having in despite?   94
Why, we have galls, and though we have some grace,   95
Yet have we some revenge. Let husbands know
Their wives have sense like them. They see, and smell,   97
And have their palates both for sweet and sour,
As husbands have. What is it that they do   99

---

21 **stubbornness** roughness. **checks** rebukes   25 **All's one** All right. It doesn't really matter. **27 talk** i.e., prattle. **29 mad** wild, lunatic 33-4 **I . . . hang** I can scarcely keep myself from hanging **36 nightgown** dressing gown. **38 proper** handsome **44 willow** (A conventional emblem of disappointed love.) **52 hie thee** hurry. **anon** right away.

64 **abuse** deceive **76 joint ring** a ring made in separate halves. **lawn** fine linen **77 exhibition** gift. **78 Uds** God's **87-8 and . . . played for** and enough additionally to stock the world men have gambled and sported sexually for. **90 they** our husbands. **duties** marital duties **91 pour . . . laps** i.e., are unfaithful, give what is rightfully ours (semen) to other women **93 Throwing . . . us** jealously restricting our freedom. **94 Or . . . despite** or spitefully take away from us whatever we enjoyed before. **95 have galls** i.e., are capable of resenting injury and insult. **grace** inclination to be merciful **97 sense** sensory perception and appetite **99 they** husbands

When they change us for others? Is it sport? 100
I think it is. And doth affection breed it? 101
I think it doth. Is't frailty that thus errs?
It is so, too. And have not we affections,
Desires for sport, and frailty, as men have?
Then let them use us well; else let them know,
The ills we do, their ills instruct us so.

DESDEMONA
Good night, good night. God me such uses send 107
Not to pick bad from bad, but by bad mend! 108

Exeunt.

♣

5.1

Enter Iago and Roderigo.

IAGO
Here stand behind this bulk. Straight will he come. 1
Wear thy good rapier bare, and put it home. 2
Quick, quick! Fear nothing. I'll be at thy elbow.
It makes us or it mars us. Think on that,
And fix most firm thy resolution.

RODERIGO
Be near at hand. I may miscarry in't.

IAGO
Here, at thy hand. Be bold, and take thy stand.
[*Iago stands aside, Roderigo conceals himself.*]

RODERIGO
I have no great devotion to the deed;
And yet he hath given me satisfying reasons.
'Tis but a man gone. Forth, my sword! He dies.
[*He draws.*]

IAGO
I have rubbed this young quat almost to the sense, 11
And he grows angry. Now, whether he kill Cassio
Or Cassio him, or each do kill the other,
Every way makes my gain. Live Roderigo, 14
He calls me to a restitution large
Of gold and jewels that I bobbed from him 16
As gifts to Desdemona.
It must not be. If Cassio do remain,
He hath a daily beauty in his life
That makes me ugly; and besides, the Moor
May unfold me to him; there stand I in much peril. 21
No, he must die. Be't so. I hear him coming.

Enter Cassio.

RODERIGO [*coming forth*]
I know his gait, 'tis he.—Villain, thou diest!
[*He attacks Cassio.*]

CASSIO
That thrust had been mine enemy indeed,
But that my coat is better than thou know'st. 25
I will make proof of thine.
[*He draws, and wounds Roderigo.*]

RODERIGO   Oh, I am slain! [*He falls.* 26
*Iago, from behind, wounds Cassio
in the leg, and exit.*]

CASSIO
I am maimed forever. Help, ho! Murder! Murder!

Enter Othello.

OTHELLO   The voice of Cassio! Iago keeps his word.
RODERIGO   Oh, villain that I am!
OTHELLO   It is even so.
CASSIO   Oh, help, ho! Light! A surgeon!
OTHELLO
'Tis he. O brave Iago, honest and just,
That hast such noble sense of thy friend's wrong!
Thou teachest me.—Minion, your dear lies dead, 34
And your unblest fate hies. Strumpet, I come. 35
Forth of my heart those charms, thine eyes, are blotted; 36
Thy bed, lust-stained, shall with lust's blood be
spotted.   *Exit Othello.*

Enter Lodovico and Gratiano.

CASSIO
What ho! No watch? No passage? Murder! Murder! 38
GRATIANO
'Tis some mischance. The voice is very direful.
CASSIO   Oh, help!
LODOVICO   Hark!
RODERIGO   Oh, wretched villain!
LODOVICO
Two or three groan. 'Tis heavy night; 43
These may be counterfeits. Let's think't unsafe
To come in to the cry without more help. 45
[*They remain near the entrance.*]

RODERIGO
Nobody come? Then shall I bleed to death.

Enter Iago [in his shirtsleeves, with a light].

LODOVICO   Hark!
GRATIANO
Here's one comes in his shirt, with light and weapons.
IAGO
Who's there? Whose noise is this that cries on murder? 49
LODOVICO
We do not know.
IAGO   Did not you hear a cry?
CASSIO
Here, here! For heaven's sake, help me!
IAGO   What's the matter?
[*He moves toward Cassio.*]

---

100 **change** exchange.   **sport** sexual pastime.   101 **affection** passion
107 **uses** habit, practice   108 **Not . . . mend** i.e., not to learn bad conduct from others' badness (as Emilia has suggested women learn
from men), but to mend my ways by perceiving what badness is,
making spiritual benefit out of evil and adversity.
5.1 Location: A street in Cyprus.
1 **bulk** framework projecting from the front of a shop.   **2 bare**
unsheathed.   **home** all the way into the target.   **11 quat** pimple,
pustule.   **to the sense** to the quick   **14 Live Roderigo** If Roderigo
lives   **16 bobbed** swindled   **21 unfold** expose

25 **coat** (Possibly a garment of mail under the outer clothing, or simply a tougher coat than Roderigo expected.)   **26 proof** a test
34 Minion Hussy (i.e., Desdemona)   **35 hies** hastens on.   **36 Forth**
of From out   **38 passage** people passing by.   **43 heavy** thick, dark
45 come in to approach   **49 cries** cries out

GRATIANO [*to Lodovico*]
  This is Othello's ancient, as I take it.
LODOVICO [*to Gratiano*]
  The same indeed, a very valiant fellow.
IAGO [*to Cassio*]
  What are you here that cry so grievously?   54
CASSIO
  Iago? Oh, I am spoiled, undone by villains!   55
  Give me some help.
IAGO
  Oh, me, Lieutenant! What villains have done this?
CASSIO
  I think that one of them is hereabout,
  And cannot make away.
IAGO   Oh, treacherous villains!   59
  [*To Lodovico and Gratiano*] What are you there? Come
    in, and give some help.   [*They advance.*]
RODERIGO   Oh, help me there!
CASSIO
  That's one of them.
IAGO   Oh, murderous slave! Oh, villain!
                        [*He stabs Roderigo.*]
RODERIGO
  Oh, damned Iago! Oh, inhuman dog!
IAGO
  Kill men i'th' dark?—Where be these bloody thieves?—
  How silent is this town!—Ho! Murder, murder!—
  [*To Lodovico and Gratiano*] What may you be? Are you
    of good or evil?
LODOVICO   As you shall prove us, praise us.   67
IAGO   Signor Lodovico?
LODOVICO   He, sir.
IAGO
  I cry you mercy. Here's Cassio hurt by villains.   70
GRATIANO   Cassio?
IAGO   How is't, brother?
CASSIO   My leg is cut in two.
IAGO   Marry, heaven forbid!
  Light, gentlemen! I'll bind it with my shirt.
            [*He hands them the light, and tends to Cassio's
                                              wound.*]

            Enter Bianca.

BIANCA
  What is the matter, ho? Who is't that cried?
IAGO   Who is't that cried?
BIANCA   Oh, my dear Cassio!
  My sweet Cassio! Oh, Cassio, Cassio, Cassio!
IAGO
  Oh, notable strumpet! Cassio, may you suspect
  Who they should be that have thus mangled you?
CASSIO   No.
GRATIANO
  I am sorry to find you thus. I have been to seek you.

IAGO
  Lend me a garter. [*He applies a tourniquet.*] So.—Oh, for
    a chair,   83
  To bear him easily hence!
BIANCA
  Alas, he faints! Oh, Cassio, Cassio, Cassio!
IAGO
  Gentlemen all, I do suspect this trash
  To be a party in this injury.—
  Patience awhile, good Cassio.—Come, come;
  Lend me a light. [*He shines the light on Roderigo.*] Know
    we this face or no?
  Alas, my friend and my dear countryman
  Roderigo! No.—Yes, sure.—Oh, heaven! Roderigo!
GRATIANO   What, of Venice?
IAGO   Even he, sir. Did you know him?
GRATIANO   Know him? Ay.
IAGO
  Signor Gratiano? I cry your gentle pardon.   95
  These bloody accidents must excuse my manners   96
  That so neglected you.
GRATIANO   I am glad to see you.
IAGO
  How do you, Cassio?—Oh, a chair, a chair!
GRATIANO   Roderigo!
IAGO
  He, he, 'tis he. [*A litter is brought in.*] Oh, that's well
    said; the chair.   100
  Some good man bear him carefully from hence;
  I'll fetch the General's surgeon. [*To Bianca*] For you,
    mistress,   102
  Save you your labor.—He that lies slain here, Cassio,   103
  Was my dear friend. What malice was between you?   104
CASSIO
  None in the world, nor do I know the man.
IAGO [*to Bianca*]
  What, look you pale?—Oh, bear him out o'th'air.   106
                  [*Cassio and Roderigo are borne off.*]
  Stay you, good gentlemen.—Look you pale,
    mistress?—   107
  Do you perceive the gastness of her eye?—   108
  Nay, if you stare, we shall hear more anon.—   109
  Behold her well; I pray you, look upon her.
  Do you see, gentlemen? Nay, guiltiness
  Will speak, though tongues were out of use.

            [*Enter Emilia.*]

EMILIA
  'Las, what's the matter? What's the matter, husand?
IAGO
  Cassio hath here been set on in the dark
  By Roderigo and fellows that are scaped.
  He's almost slain, and Roderigo dead.

---

83 chair litter   **95 gentle** noble   **96 accidents** sudden events
100 well said well done   **102 For** As for   **103 Save . . . labor** i.e.,
never you mind tending Cassio.   **104 malice** enmity   **106 bear . . .
air** (Fresh air was thought to be dangerous for a wound.)   **107 Stay
you** (Lodovico and Gratiano are evidently about to leave.)   **108 gastness** terror   **109 stare** (Iago pretends to interpret Bianca's wild looks
as an involuntary confession of guilt.)

---

54 What Who. (Also at lines 60 and 66.)   **55 spoiled** ruined, done for
59 make get   **67 prove us** prove us to be.   **praise** appraise   **70 I cry
you mercy** I beg your pardon.

EMILIA
Alas, good gentleman! Alas, good Cassio!

IAGO
This is the fruits of whoring. Prithee, Emilia,
Go know of Cassio where he supped tonight.   119
[To Bianca] What, do you shake at that?

BIANCA
He supped at my house, but I therefore shake not.

IAGO
Oh, did he so? I charge you go with me.

EMILIA   Oh, fie upon thee, strumpet!

BIANCA
I am no strumpet, but of life as honest   124
As you that thus abuse me.

EMILIA   As I? Faugh! Fie upon thee!

IAGO
Kind gentlemen, let's go see poor Cassio dressed.—   127
Come, mistress, you must tell 's another tale.—
Emilia, run you to the citadel
And tell my lord and lady what hath happed.—
Will you go on afore? [Aside] This is the night
That either makes me or fordoes me quite.   *Exeunt.* 132

❖

5.2

*Enter Othello [with a light], and Desdemona in
her bed.*

OTHELLO
It is the cause, it is the cause, my soul.   1
Let me not name it to you, you chaste stars!
It is the cause. Yet I'll not shed her blood,
Nor scar that whiter skin of hers than snow,
And smooth as monumental alabaster.   5
Yet she must die, else she'll betray more men.
Put out the light, and then put out the light.   7
If I quench thee, thou flaming minister,   8
I can again thy former light restore,
Should I repent me; but once put out thy light,   10
Thou cunning'st pattern of excelling nature,   11
I know not where is that Promethean heat   12
That can thy light relume. When I have plucked thy
     rose,   13
I cannot give it vital growth again;
It needs must wither. I'll smell thee on the tree.
     [He kisses her.]
Oh, balmy breath, that dost almost persuade
Justice to break her sword! One more, one more.

119 **know** learn   124 **honest** chaste   127 **Cassio dressed** Cassio's
wounds dressed.   132 **fordoes** undoes, ruins
5.2. Location: A bedchamber in the citadel.
0.1–2 *in her bed* (Either the curtains are drawn back to reveal the bed
in a recessed area backstage, or the bed is "thrust out" onstage as the
scene begins.)   1 **cause** i.e., cause of justice, the offense itself, which
must be corrected in the name of justice   5 **monumental** i.e., used in
making tombs and funeral monuments   7 **the light . . . light** the
torch or lamp . . . Desdemona's life.   8 **minister** servant   10 **repent
me** change my mind   11 **Thou . . . pattern** you skillfully wrought
perfect example   12 **Promethean heat** (Alludes to two myths: that of
Prometheus stealing fire from heaven for humanity, and that of his
creating humankind.)   13 **relume** rekindle.

Be thus when thou art dead, and I will kill thee,
And love thee after. One more, and that's the last.
     [He kisses her.]
So sweet was ne'er so fatal. I must weep,
But they are cruel tears. This sorrow's heavenly;   21
It strikes where it doth love. She wakes.   22

DESDEMONA   Who's there? Othello?

OTHELLO   Ay, Desdemona.

DESDEMONA   Will you come to bed, my lord?

OTHELLO   Have you prayed tonight, Desdemon?

DESDEMONA   Ay, my lord.

OTHELLO
If you bethink yourself of any crime   28
Unreconciled as yet to heaven and grace,
Solicit for it straight.   30

DESDEMONA
Alack, my lord, what may you mean by that?

OTHELLO
Well, do it, and be brief. I will walk by.
I would not kill thy unprepared spirit.
No, heaven forfend! I would not kill thy soul.   34

DESDEMONA
Talk you of killing?

OTHELLO   Ay, I do.

DESDEMONA   Then heaven
Have mercy on me!

OTHELLO   Amen, with all my heart!

DESDEMONA
If you say so, I hope you will not kill me.

OTHELLO   Humh!

DESDEMONA
And yet I fear you; for you're fatal then
When your eyes roll so. Why I should fear I know not,
Since guiltiness I know not; but yet I feel I fear.

OTHELLO
Think on thy sins.

DESDEMONA   They are loves I bear to you.   42

OTHELLO   Ay, and for that thou diest.

DESDEMONA
That death's unnatural that kills for loving.
Alas, why gnaw you so your nether lip?
Some bloody passion shakes your very frame.
These are portents; but yet I hope, I hope,
They do not point on me.

OTHELLO   Peace, and be still!

DESDEMONA   I will so. What's the matter?

OTHELLO
That handkerchief which I so loved and gave thee
Thou gav'st to Cassio.

DESDEMONA   No, by my life and soul!
Send for the man and ask him.

OTHELLO
Sweet soul, take heed, take heed of perjury.
Thou art on thy deathbed.

21 **they are cruel tears** these tears betoken a sorrowful cruelty, regrettable but just.   22 **It . . . love** (Compare Hebrews 12:6: "For whom the
Lord loveth he chasteneth.")   28 **crime** sin   30 **Solicit** petition, pray.
straight immediately.   34 **forfend** forbid.   42 **They . . . you** i.e., My
only sins are my idolatry of loving you too much.

DESDEMONA
  Ay, but not yet to die.
OTHELLO   Yes, presently.   56
  Therefore confess thee freely of thy sin;
  For to deny each article with oath
  Cannot remove nor choke the strong conception   59
  That I do groan withal. Thou art to die.   60
DESDEMONA
  Then Lord have mercy on me!
OTHELLO   I say, amen.
DESDEMONA
  And have you mercy too! I never did
  Offend you in my life; never loved Cassio
  But with such general warranty of heaven   64
  As I might love. I never gave him token.
OTHELLO
  By heaven, I saw my handkerchief in 's hand.
  Oh, perjured woman! Thou dost stone my heart,   67
  And makes me call what I intend to do
  A murder, which I thought a sacrifice.
  I saw the handkerchief.
DESDEMONA   He found it, then.
  I never gave it him. Send for him hither;
  Let him confess a truth.
OTHELLO   He hath confessed.
DESDEMONA   What, my lord?
OTHELLO
  That he hath used thee.
DESDEMONA   How? Unlawfully?
OTHELLO   Ay.
DESDEMONA
  He will not say so.
OTHELLO   No, his mouth is stopped;
  Honest Iago hath ta'en order for't.   76
DESDEMONA
  Oh, my fear interprets. What, is he dead?
OTHELLO
  Had all his hairs been lives, my great revenge
  Had stomach for them all.
DESDEMONA
  Alas, he is betrayed and I undone!   [She weeps.]
OTHELLO
  Out, strumpet! Weep'st thou for him to my face?
DESDEMONA
  Oh, banish me, my lord, but kill me not!
OTHELLO   Down, strumpet!
DESDEMONA
  Kill me tomorrow; let me live tonight!
OTHELLO   Nay, if you strive—
DESDEMONA
  But half an hour!
OTHELLO   Being done, there is no pause.   86

DESDEMONA
  But while I say one prayer!
OTHELLO   It is too late.
                                   Smothers her.
EMILIA (at the door)
  My lord, my lord! What, ho! My lord, my lord!
OTHELLO
  What noise is this? Not dead? Not yet quite dead?
  I that am cruel am yet merciful;
  I would not have thee linger in thy pain.
                              [He dispatches her.]
  So, so.
EMILIA (within)   What, ho! My lord, my lord!
OTHELLO   Who's there?
EMILIA [within]
  Oh, good my lord, I would speak a word with you!
OTHELLO
  Yes, 'tis Emilia.—By and by.—She's dead.
  'Tis like she comes to speak of Cassio's death.—   95
  The noise was here. Ha! No more moving?   96
  Still as the grave. Shall she come in? Were't good?—
  I think she stirs again. No. What's best to do?
  If she come in, she'll sure speak to my wife.
  My wife! My wife! What wife? I have no wife.
  Oh, insupportable! Oh, heavy hour!
  Methinks it should be now a huge eclipse
  Of sun and moon, and that th'affrighted globe
  Should yawn at alteration.
EMILIA [within]   I do beseech you   104
  That I may speak with you, O good my lord!
OTHELLO
  I had forgot thee. Oh, come in, Emilia.—
  Soft, by and by. Let me the curtains draw.—   107
          [He closes the bedcurtains and opens the door.]
  Where art thou?

          Enter Emilia.

                      What's the matter with thee now?
EMILIA
  Oh, my good lord, yonder's foul murders done!
OTHELLO   What, now?
EMILIA   But now, my lord.
OTHELLO
  It is the very error of the moon;   112
  She comes more nearer earth than she was wont,   113
  And makes men mad.   114
EMILIA
  Cassio, my lord, hath killed a young Venetian
  Called Roderigo.
OTHELLO   Roderigo killed?

---

56 presently immediately.   59 conception (1) belief in your guilt
(2) plan in my mind   60 groan withal (1) groan at in sorrow
(2) groan as in giving birth.   64 warranty sanction   67 stone turn to
stone, harden   76 ta'en order taken measures   86 Being done i.e.,
Since justice has begun its relentless course

95 like likely that   96 here (The Folio's "high" is possible, suggesting
that the commotion of the attack on Cassio was loud.)   104 Should . . .
alteration should gape wide in an earthquake, as if expressing
amazement at an eclipse. (According to Pliny, earthquakes often happen during eclipses. The cataclismic event here is especially terrifying
in that it imagines the impossible concurrence of a solar and lunar
eclipse—an apocalyptic scenario befitting the horror of Desdemona's
death.)   107 Soft Wait a minute   112 error aberration, irregularity
113 She Luna, the moon goddess   114 mad i.e., "lunatic."

And Cassio killed?

EMILIA   No, Cassio is not killed.

OTHELLO
Not Cassio killed? Then murder's out of tune,
And sweet revenge grows harsh.

DESDEMONA   Oh, falsely, falsely murdered!

EMILIA   Oh, Lord, what cry is that?

OTHELLO   That? What?

EMILIA
Out and alas, that was my lady's voice.   123
                    [*She opens the bedcurtains.*]
Help, help, ho, help! O lady, speak again!
Sweet Desdemona! O sweet mistress, speak!

DESDEMONA   A guiltless death I die.

EMILIA   Oh, who hath done this deed?

DESDEMONA   Nobody; I myself. Farewell.
Commend me to my kind lord. Oh, farewell! [*She dies.*]

OTHELLO
Why, how should she be murdered?

EMILIA   Alas, who knows?

OTHELLO
You heard her say herself it was not I.

EMILIA
She said so. I must needs report the truth.

OTHELLO
She's like a liar gone to burning hell!
'Twas I that killed her.

EMILIA   Oh, the more angel she,
And you the blacker devil!

OTHELLO
She turned to folly, and she was a whore.   136

EMILIA
Thou dost belie her, and thou art a devil.   137

OTHELLO   She was false as water.

EMILIA   Thou art rash as fire to say
That she was false. Oh, she was heavenly true!

OTHELLO
Cassio did top her. Ask thy husband else.   141
Oh, I were damned beneath all depth in hell
But that I did proceed upon just grounds
To this extremity. Thy husband knew it all.

EMILIA   My husband?

OTHELLO   Thy husband.

EMILIA   That she was false to wedlock?

OTHELLO
Ay, with Cassio. Nay, had she been true,
If heaven would make me such another world
Of one entire and perfect chrysolite,   150
I'd not have sold her for it.

EMILIA   My husband?

OTHELLO
Ay, 'twas he that told me on her first.
An honest man he is, and hates the slime
That sticks on filthy deeds.

EMILIA   My husband?

OTHELLO
What needs this iterance, woman? I say thy husband.   157

EMILIA
Oh, mistress, villainy hath made mocks with love!   158
My husband say she was false?

OTHELLO   He, woman;
I say thy husband. Dost understand the word?
My friend, thy husband, honest, honest Iago.

EMILIA
If he say so, may his pernicious soul
Rot half a grain a day! He lies to th' heart.
She was too fond of her most filthy bargain.

OTHELLO   Ha?   [*He draws.*]

EMILIA   Do thy worst!
This deed of thine is no more worthy heaven
Than thou wast worthy her.

OTHELLO   Peace, you were best.   168

EMILIA
Thou hast not half that power to do me harm
As I have to be hurt. O gull! O dolt!   170
As ignorant as dirt! Thou hast done a deed—
I care not for thy sword; I'll make thee known,
Though I lost twenty lives.—Help! Help, ho, help!
The Moor hath killed my mistress! Murder, murder!

Enter Montano, Gratiano, and Iago.

MONTANO
What is the matter? How now, General?

EMILIA
Oh, are you come, Iago? You have done well,
That men must lay their murders on your neck.   177

GRATIANO   What is the matter?

EMILIA [*to Iago*]
Disprove this villain, if thou be'st a man.
He says thou told'st him that his wife was false.
I know thou didst not; thou'rt not such a villain.   181
Speak, for my heart is full.

IAGO
I told him what I thought, and told no more
Than what he found himself was apt and true.   184

EMILIA
But did you ever tell him she was false?

IAGO   I did.

EMILIA
You told a lie, an odious, damnèd lie!
Upon my soul, a lie, a wicked lie.
She false with Cassio? Did you say with Cassio?

IAGO
With Cassio, mistress. Go to, charm your tongue.   190

EMILIA
I will not charm my tongue; I am bound to speak.
My mistress here lies murdered in her bed—

ALL   Oh, heavens forfend!

EMILIA
And your reports have set the murder on.

---

123 **Out** (A cry of dismay, intensifying *alas*.)   136 **folly** i.e., wantonness, fleshly sin   137 **belie** slander   141 **else** i.e., if you don't believe me.   150 **chrysolite** precious topaz

157 **iterance** iteration, repetition   158 **made mocks with** made a mockery of   168 **Peace . . . best** You'd better be quiet.   170 **to be hurt** i.e., to endure hurt.   **gull** dupe.   177 **on your neck** to your charge.   181 **such a villain** such a villain as all that.   184 **apt** plausible   190 **charm** control

OTHELLO
Nay, stare not, masters. It is true indeed.
GRATIANO   'Tis a strange truth.
MONTANO
Oh, monstrous act!
EMILIA   Villainy, villainy, villainy!
I think upon't—I think I smell't! Oh, villainy!
I thought so then—I'll kill myself for grief—   199
Oh, villainy, villainy!
IAGO
What, are you mad? I charge you, get you home.
EMILIA
Good gentlemen, let me have leave to speak.
'Tis proper I obey him, but not now.
Perchance, Iago, I will ne'er go home.
OTHELLO
Oh! Oh! Oh!   [Othello falls on the bed.]
EMILIA   Nay, lay thee down and roar,   205
For thou hast killed the sweetest innocent
That e'er did lift up eye.
OTHELLO [rising]   Oh, she was foul!   207
I scarce did know you, uncle. There lies your niece,
Whose breath indeed these hands have newly
    stopped.
I know this act shows horrible and grim.   210
GRATIANO
Poor Desdemon! I am glad thy father's dead.
Thy match was mortal to him, and pure grief
Shore his old thread in twain. Did he live now,   213
This sight would make him do a desperate turn,   214
Yea, curse his better angel from his side,
And fall to reprobance.   216
OTHELLO
'Tis pitiful. But yet Iago knows
That she with Cassio hath the act of shame
A thousand times committed. Cassio confessed it;
And she did gratify his amorous works   220
With that recognizance and pledge of love   221
Which I first gave her. I saw it in his hand;
It was a handkerchief, an antique token
My father gave my mother.
EMILIA   Oh, God! Oh, heavenly God!
IAGO
Zounds, hold your peace.
EMILIA   'Twill out, 'twill out! I peace?
No, I will speak as liberal as the north.   227
Let heaven and men and devils, let them all,
All, all, cry shame against me, yet I'll speak.
IAGO
Be wise, and get you home.
EMILIA   I will not.
                          [Iago threatens Emilia.]
GRATIANO   Fie,

Your sword upon a woman?
EMILIA
Oh, thou dull Moor! That handkerchief thou speak'st of
I found by fortune and did give my husband;
For often, with a solemn earnestness,
More than indeed belonged to such a trifle,   235
He begged of me to steal't.
IAGO   Villainous whore!
EMILIA
She give it Cassio? No, alas! I found it,
And I did give't my husband.
IAGO   Filth, thou liest!
EMILIA
By heaven, I do not, I do not, gentlemen.
Oh, murderous coxcomb! What should such a fool   240
Do with so good a wife?
OTHELLO   Are there no stones in heaven   242
But what serves for the thunder?—Precious villain!   243
        [He runs at Iago; Montano disarms Othello. Iago,
                          from behind, stabs Emilia.]
GRATIANO
The woman falls! Sure he hath killed his wife.
EMILIA
Ay, ay. Oh, lay me by my mistress' side.
                          [Exit Iago.]
GRATIANO   He's gone, but his wife's killed.
MONTANO
'Tis a notorious villain. Take you this weapon,
Which I have here recovered from the Moor.
Come, guard the door without. Let him not pass,
But kill him rather. I'll after that same villain,
For 'tis a damnèd slave.
                Exit [with all but Othello and Emilia,
                who has been laid by Desdemona's side].
OTHELLO   I am not valiant neither,
But every puny whipster gets my sword.   253
But why should honor outlive honesty?   254
Let it go all.
EMILIA   What did thy song bode, lady?
Hark, canst thou hear me? I will play the swan,   256
And die in music. [She sings] "Willow, willow, willow."
Moor, she was chaste. She loved thee, cruel Moor.
So come my soul to bliss as I speak true.
So speaking as I think, alas, I die.   [She dies.]
OTHELLO
I have another weapon in this chamber;
It was a sword of Spain, the ice-brook's temper—   262
Oh, here it is. [He finds a sword.] Uncle, I must come
    forth.
GRATIANO [within]
If thou attempt it, it will cost thee dear.

199 then (Perhaps at 3.3.331–2 and 4.2.137–54.)   **205 s.d. Othello . . . bed**
(This direction is from the Quarto, as also *He kisses her* at line 19 and *She dies* at line 129.)   **207 lift up eye** i.e., lift her eyes to heaven.   **210 shows** looks   **213 Shore . . . thread** sheared the thread of his old age (as Atropos, one of the three Fates, was thought to do)   **214 turn** deed   **216 reprobance** damnation, i.e., suicide.   **220 gratify** reward   **221 recognizance** token   **227 liberal as the north** freely as the north wind (blows).

235 belonged was appropriate   **240 coxcomb** fool. (Addressed to Othello.)   **242 stones** bolts, such as those used for thunderbolts   **243 Precious** i.e., Arrant, utter   **243.1–2 He . . . Emilia** (The Quarto text reads, "*The Moore runnes at* Iago. Iago *kils his wife.*" The Quarto also specifies the exit of Iago at line 245 and the death of Emilia at line 260.)   **253 every . . . sword** every whipper-snapper can get the better of me and my sword.   **254 why . . . honesty?** why should a soldier's reputation for bravery outlive true integrity?   **256 play the swan** (The swan was fabled to sing only at its death.)   **262 the icebrook's temper** tempered in ice-cold water

Thou hast no weapon, and perforce must suffer.

OTHELLO
Look in upon me then and speak with me,
Or, naked as I am, I will assault thee.   267

    [Enter Gratiano.]

GRATIANO
What is the matter?

OTHELLO   Behold, I have a weapon;
A better never did itself sustain
Upon a soldier's thigh. I have seen the day
That, with this little arm and this good sword,
I have made my way through more impediments
Than twenty times your stop. But oh, vain boast!   273
Who can control his fate? 'Tis not so now.
Be not afraid, though you do see me weaponed;
Here is my journey's end, here is my butt   276
And very seamark of my utmost sail.   277
                                          [Gratiano steps back.]
Do you go back dismayed? 'Tis a lost fear;   278
Man but a rush against Othello's breast   279
And he retires. Where should Othello go?
                              [He turns to Desdemona.]
Now, how dost thou look now? Oh, ill-starred wench!
Pale as thy smock! When we shall meet at compt,   282
This look of thine will hurl my soul from heaven,
And fiends will snatch at it. Cold, cold, my girl?
Even like thy chastity. Oh, cursèd, cursèd slave!   285
Whip me, ye devils,
From the possession of this heavenly sight!
Blow me about in winds! Roast me in sulfur!
Wash me in steep-down gulfs of liquid fire!
Oh, Desdemon! Dead, Desdemon! Dead! Oh! Oh!   290

    Enter Lodovico, Cassio [carried in a litter],
    Montano, and Iago [prisoner], with officers.

LODOVICO
Where is this rash and most unfortunate man?

OTHELLO
That's he that was Othello. Here I am.

LODOVICO
Where is that viper? Bring the villain forth.
                              [Iago is led forward.]

OTHELLO
I look down towards his feet; but that's a fable.   294
If that thou be'st a devil, I cannot kill thee.
                              [He wounds Iago.]

LODOVICO
Wrench his sword from him.   [Othello is disarmed.]

IAGO   I bleed, sir, but not killed.

OTHELLO
I am not sorry neither. I'd have thee live,

For in my sense 'tis happiness to die.   298

LODOVICO
O thou Othello, that was once so good,
Fall'n in the practice of a cursèd slave,   300
What shall be said to thee?

OTHELLO   Why, anything.
An honorable murderer, if you will,
For naught I did in hate, but all in honor.

LODOVICO
This wretch hath part confessed his villainy.
Did you and he consent in Cassio's death?   305

OTHELLO   Ay.

CASSIO
Dear General, I never gave you cause.

OTHELLO
I do believe it, and I ask your pardon.
Will you, I pray, demand that demi-devil
Why he hath thus ensnared my soul and body?

IAGO
Demand me nothing. What you know, you know.
From this time forth I never will speak word.

LODOVICO   What, not to pray?

GRATIANO   Torments will ope your lips.   314

OTHELLO   Well, thou dost best.   315

LODOVICO
Sir, you shall understand what hath befall'n,
Which, as I think, you know not. Here is a letter
Found in the pocket of the slain Roderigo;
And here another. [He produces letters.] The one of them
    imports
The death of Cassio, to be undertook
By Roderigo.

OTHELLO
Oh, villain!

CASSIO   Most heathenish and most gross!   322

LODOVICO [showing another paper]
Now here's another discontented paper   323
Found in his pocket too. And this, it seems,
Roderigo meant t'have sent this damnèd villain;
But that belike Iago in the interim   326
Came in and satisfied him.   327

OTHELLO [to Iago]   Oh, thou pernicious caitiff!—
How came you, Cassio, by that handkerchief
That was my wife's?

CASSIO   I found it in my chamber;
And he himself confessed but even now
That there he dropped it for a special purpose
Which wrought to his desire.

OTHELLO   Oh, fool, fool, fool!   333

CASSIO
There is besides in Roderigo's letter
How he upbraids Iago, that he made him

267 **naked** unarmed   273 **your stop** the obstruction you present.
276 **butt** goal, limit. (An archery term.)   277 **seamark** beacon (mark-
ing his destination or limit)   278 **lost** groundless   279 **Man . . . rush**
wield no more than a reed   282 **compt** account, judgment day
285 **slave** i.e., Othello himself.   290.1 **in a litter** (The Quarto specifies
that Cassio is "in a Chaire.")   294 **towards his feet** i.e., to see if they
are cloven, as the devil's are fabled to be

298 **in my sense** to one who feels as I do   300 **in the practice** through
the plotting, into the snare.   **slave** villain   305 **consent** agree
314 **Torments** Torture   315 **thou dost best** you (Iago) do best not to
talk.   322 **gross** monstrous.   323 **discontented** full of discontent
326 **belike** most likely   327 **Came . . . him** interposed and gave him
satisfactory explanation.   333 **wrought . . . desire** worked out as he
wished, fitted in with his plan.

Brave me upon the watch, whereon it came   336
That I was cast; and even but now he spake,   337
After long seeming dead, Iago hurt him,
Iago set him on.

LODOVICO [*to Othello*]
You must forsake this room and go with us.
Your power and your command is taken off,   341
And Cassio rules in Cyprus. For this slave,
If there be any cunning cruelty
That can torment him much and hold him long,   344
It shall be his. You shall close prisoner rest   345
Till that the nature of your fault be known
To the Venetian state.—Come, bring away.

OTHELLO
Soft you; a word or two before you go.   348
I have done the state some service, and they know't.
No more of that. I pray you, in your letters,
When you shall these unlucky deeds relate,   351
Speak of me as I am; nothing extenuate,
Nor set down aught in malice. Then must you speak
Of one that loved not wisely but too well;
Of one not easily jealous but, being wrought,   355
Perplexed in the extreme; of one whose hand,   356
Like the base Indian, threw a pearl away   357
Richer than all his tribe; of one whose subdued eyes,   358
Albeit unusèd to the melting mood,
Drops tears as fast as the Arabian trees

Their medicinable gum. Set you down this;   361
And say besides that in Aleppo once,
Where a malignant and a turbaned Turk
Beat a Venetian and traduced the state,
I took by th' throat the circumcisèd dog
And smote him, thus.   [*He stabs himself.*] 366

LODOVICO   Oh, bloody period!   367
GRATIANO   All that is spoke is marred.

OTHELLO
I kissed thee ere I killed thee. No way but this,
Killing myself, to die upon a kiss.
                    [*He kisses Desdemona and*] *dies.*

CASSIO
This did I fear, but thought he had no weapon;
For he was great of heart.

LODOVICO [*to Iago*]   O Spartan dog,   372
More fell than anguish, hunger, or the sea!   373
Look on the tragic loading of this bed.
This is thy work. The object poisons sight;
Let it be hid. Gratiano, keep the house,   376
                    [*The bedcurtains are drawn.*]
And seize upon the fortunes of the Moor,   377
For they succeed on you. [*To Cassio*] To you, Lord
    Governor,   378
Remains the censure of this hellish villain,   379
The time, the place, the torture. Oh, enforce it!
Myself will straight aboard, and to the state
This heavy act with heavy heart relate.   *Exeunt.*

---

336 Brave defy.   **whereon it came** whereof it came about   **337 cast** dismissed   **341 taken off** taken away   **344 hold him long** keep him alive a long time (during his torture)   **345 rest** remain   **348 Soft you** One moment   **351 unlucky** unfortunate   **355 wrought** worked upon, worked into a frenzy   **356 Perplexed** distraught   **357 Indian** (This reading from the Quarto pictures an ignorant savage who cannot recognize the value of a precious jewel. The Folio reading, "Iudean," i.e., infidel or disbeliever, may refer to Herod, who slew Miriamne in a fit of jealousy, or to Judas Iscariot, the betrayer of Christ.)   **358 subdued** i.e., overcome by grief

361 gum i.e., myrrh.   **366 s.d.** *He stabs himself* (This direction is in the Quarto text.)   **367 period** termination, conclusion.   **372 Spartan dog** (Spartan dogs were noted for their savagery and silence.)   **373 fell** cruel   **376 Let it be hid** i.e., draw the bedcurtains. (No stage direction specifies that the dead are to be carried offstage at the end of the play.)   **keep** guard   **377 seize upon** take legal possession of   **378 succeed on** pass as though by inheritance to   **379 censure** sentencing

King Lear

In *King Lear*, Shakespeare pushes to its limit the hypothesis of a malign or at least indifferent universe in which human life is meaningless and brutal. Few plays other than *Hamlet* and *Macbeth* approach *King Lear* in evoking the wretchedness of human existence, and even they cannot match the devastating spectacle of the Earl of Gloucester blinded or Cordelia dead in Lear's arms. The responses of the chief characters are correspondingly searing. "Is man no more than this?" rages Lear. "Unaccommodated man is no more but such a poor, bare, forked animal as thou art" (3.4.101–7). Life he calls a "great stage of fools," an endless torment: "the first time that we smell the air / We wawl and cry" (4.6.179–83). Gloucester's despair takes the form of accusing the gods of gleeful malice toward humanity: "As flies to wanton boys are we to th' gods; / They kill us for their sport" (4.1.36–7). Gloucester's ministering son Edgar can offer him no greater consolation than stoic resolve: "Men must endure / Their going hence, even as their coming hither; / Ripeness is all" (5.2.9–11). These statements need not be read as choric expressions of meaning for the play as a whole, but they do attest to the depth of suffering. In no other Shakespearean play does injustice appear to triumph so ferociously, for so long, and with such impunity. Will the heavens countenance this reign of injustice on earth? Retribution is late in coming and is not certainly the work of the heavens themselves. For, at the last, we must confront the wanton death of the innocent Cordelia—a death no longer willed even by the villain who arranged her execution. "Is this the promised end?" (5.3.268) asks the Earl of Kent, stressing the unparalleled horror of the catastrophe.

Throughout its earlier history, the ancient story of King Lear had always ended happily. In the popular folktale of Cinderella, to which the legend of Lear's daughters bears a significant resemblance, the youngest and virtuous daughter triumphs over her two older wicked sisters and is married to her princely wooer. Geoffrey of Monmouth's *Historia Regum Britanniae* (c. 1136), the earliest known version of the Lear story, records that, after Lear is overthrown by his sons-in-law (more than by his daughters), he is restored to his throne by the intervention of the French King and is allowed to enjoy his kingdom and Cordelia's love until his natural death. (Cordelia, as his successor, is later dethroned and murdered by her wicked nephews, but that is another story.) Sixteenth-century Tudor versions of the Lear story with which Shakespeare was familiar—John Higgins's account in *The First Part of the Mirror for Magistrates* (1574), Raphael Holinshed's *Chronicles* (1587), Edmund Spenser's *The Faerie Queene*, 2.10.27–32, and a play called *The True Chronicle History of King Leir* (by 1594, published 1605)—all retain the happy ending. The tragic pattern may have been suggested instead by Shakespeare's probable source for the Gloucester-Edgar-Edmund plot, Sir Philip Sidney's *Arcadia*, 2.10, in which the Paphlagonian King is the victim of filial ingratitude and deceit.

Yet even Shakespeare's authority was not sufficient to put down the craving for a happy resolution. Nahum Tate's adaptation (1681), which banished the Fool as indecorous for a tragedy and united Edgar and Cordelia in marriage, placing Lear once again on his throne, held the English stage for about 150 years. David Garrick restored some of Shakespeare's lines, and Edmund Kean restored the tragic ending, but it was not until 1838 that *King Lear* was again performed more or less as the dramatist wrote it. One of Shakespeare's editors, Dr. Samuel Johnson, evidently spoke for most eighteenth-century audiences when he confessed that he could hardly bring himself to read Shakespeare's text. Cordelia's slaughter violated that age's longing for "poetic justice." Her death implied a wanton universe and so counseled philosophic despair. Today, Shakespeare's relentless honesty and refusal to accept easy answers convince us that he was right to defy the conventions of his source, though no doubt we, too, distort the play to conform with our supposed toughness of vision.

Shakespeare evidently wrote *King Lear* some time before it was performed at court in December of 1606, probably in 1605 and certainly no earlier than 1603–1604; Edgar's speeches as Tom o' Bedlam contain references to Samuel Harsnett's *Declaration of Egregious Popish Impostures,* which was registered for publication in March of 1603. Thus, *King Lear* was probably written between *Othello* (c. 1603–1604) and *Macbeth* (c. 1606–1607), when Shakespeare was at the height of his literary power in the writing of tragedies.

When we look at the play in formal terms, we are apt to be struck first by its complex double plot. Nowhere else in Shakespearean tragedy do we find anything approaching the rich orchestration of the double plotting in *King Lear.* The links and parallels between the two plots are established on a narrative level early in the play and continue to the end. King Lear misjudges his children and disinherits his loving daughter Cordelia in favor of her duplicitous sisters, whereas Gloucester falls prey to Edmund's deceptions and disinherits his loyal son Edgar; Lear is turned out into the storm by his false daughters, while Gloucester is branded as a traitor by Edmund and deprived of his eyesight; Lear in his madness realizes his fault against Cordelia, while the blind Gloucester "sees" at last the truth about Edgar; and both fathers are cared for by their loving children and are belatedly reconciled to them, but then die brokenhearted. As recent criticism has noted, these narrative parallels are not especially significant in themselves; we are moved, not by the mere repetition of events, but by the enlargement of tragic vision that results from the counterpointing of two such actions. When we see juxtaposed to each other two scenes of trial, Lear's mad arraignment of the absent Goneril and Regan and then the cruel imposition of the mere "form of justice" on the pinioned Gloucester (3.6 and 3.7), we begin to measure the extent to which justice and injustice are inverted by cruelty. When at last the two old men come together, during the storm scenes and especially at Dover, the sad comfort they derive from sharing the wreckage of their lives calls forth piercing eloquence against the stench of mortality. The sight is "most pitiful in the meanest wretch, / Past speaking of in a king" (4.6.204–5).

The play's double structure suggests another duality central to *King Lear:* an opposition of parable and realism, in which "divided and distinguished worlds" are bound together for instructive contrast. (These terms are Maynard Mack's, in his *King Lear in Our Time,* 1965.) To a remarkable degree, this play derives its story from folklore and legend, with many of the wondrous and implausible circumstances of popular romance. A prose rendition might almost begin, "Once upon a time there was a king who had three daughters . . . ." Yet Shakespeare arouses romantic expectation only to crush it by aborting the conventional happy ending, setting up a dramatic tension between an idealized world of make-believe and the actual world of disappointed hopes. We are aware of artifice and convention, and yet are deeply moved by the "truth" of suffering, love, and hatred. The characters pull us two ways at once; we regard them as types with universalized characteristics—a king and father, his cruel daughters, his loving daughter, and the like—and yet we scrutinize them for psychological motivation because they seem so real and individual.

This duality appears in both the central and the secondary characters. The King of France is in part a hero out of romance, who makes selfless choices and rescues the heroine Cordelia from her distress; yet his motive must also be appraised in the context of a bitter struggle for power. Why does he leave the English court "in choler," and why does he return to England with an army? Is it only to aid his wife and her beleaguered father, or is he negotiating for military advantage? Certainly, a French invasion of England on behalf of Lear complicates the issues of loyalty for the well-meaning Duke of Albany (and perhaps as well for an English Renaissance audience, with its habitual mistrust of the French). The dual focus of the play invites conflicting interpretation. Similarly, Edgar is presented to us on the one hand as the traduced victim in a starkly pessimistic story, dominated by his rationalistic brother, Edmund, who scoffs at religion and undertakes to manipulate those around him for personal gain; on the other hand, Edgar's story grows increasingly improbable as he undertakes a series of disguises and emerges finally as an anonymous champion of chivalry, challenging his brother in the lists like a knight-errant out of Arthurian romance. Edgar's motives are hard to follow. Is he the hero of a fabulous story whose disguises and contriving of illusions for his father are simply part of that storytelling tradition, or is he, in more realistic terms, a man whose disguises are a defensive mask and whose elaborate contrivances defeat themselves? Edmund, his brother, is no less complex. Onstage today he is usually interpreted as smooth and plausible, well-motivated by his father's condescending attitude and by the arbitrariness of the law that has excluded him from legitimacy and inheritance. Yet parable elevates Edmund into something monstrous. He becomes an embodiment of gleeful villainy, like Iago in *Othello,* malignantly evil simply because the evil that is in the universe must find a human form through which to express itself. Edmund's belated attempt to do some good adds to our difficulties in appraising his character, but the restless power of the dual conception supplies a vitality not to be found in pure fable or in realistic literature.

What we see then in Edmund and in others is the union of the universal and the particular, making *King Lear* at once parable and compellingly real. The parable or folktale element is prominent at the beginning of the play and focuses attention on the archetypal situations with which the story is concerned: rivalry between siblings, fear of parental rejection, and, at the same time, parental fear of children's callousness. The "unrealistic" contrast between Cordelia and her wicked sisters, or between Edgar and Edmund, is something we accept as a convention of storytelling, because it expresses vividly the psychic truth of rivalry between brothers and sisters. We identify with Cordelia and Edgar as virtuous children whose worth is misjudged, and who are losing to wicked siblings the contest for parental approval. (In folklore, the rejecting parent is usually a stepparent, which signifies our conviction that he or she is not a true parent at all.) Similarly, we accept as a meaningful convention of storytelling the equally "unrealistic" device by which Lear tests the love of his daughters. Like any parent, he wishes to be loved and appreciated in response to the kindnesses he has performed. The tension between fathers and their marriageable daughters is a recurrent pattern in Shakespeare's late plays, as in *Othello* (in which Brabantio accuses Desdemona of deceiving and deserting him), in *Pericles, Cymbeline,* and *The Winter's Tale,* and in *The Tempest,* in which the pattern is best resolved. In *King Lear,* Shakespeare explores the inherently explosive situation of an imperious father who, having provided for his children and having grown old, assumes he has a right to expect that those children will express their love and gratitude by looking after him.

The difficulty is that the parable of Lear and his children presents two contrasting viewpoints—that of the unappreciated child and that of the unwanted aging parent. Tragic misunderstanding is inevitable, and it outweighs the question of assessing blame. From Lear's point of view, Cordelia's silence is a truculent scanting of obedience. What he has devised is, after all, only a prearranged formality, with Cordelia to receive the richest third of England. Cannot such a ceremony be answered with the conventional hyperbole of courtly language, to which the King's ear is attuned? Don't parents have a right to be verbally reassured of their children's love? How can children be so laconic about such a precious matter? For her part, however, Cordelia senses that Lear is demanding love as payment for his parental kindliness, quid pro quo. Genuine love ought rather to be selfless, as the King of France tells the Duke of Burgundy: "Love's not love / When it is mingled with regards that stands / Aloof from th'entire point" (1.1.242–4). Is Cordelia being asked to prefer Lear before her own husband-to-be? Is this the price she must pay for her upbringing? Lear's ego seems fully capable of demanding this sacrifice from his daughters, especially from his favorite, Cordelia; he has given them his whole kingdom, now let them care for him as befits his royal rank and patriarchal role. The "second childishness" of his old age brings with it a self-centered longing to monopolize the lives of his children and to be a child again. Besides, as king, Lear has long grown accustomed to flattery and absolute obedience. Goneril

and Regan are content to flatter and promise obedience, knowing they will turn him out once he has relinquished his authority. Cordelia refuses to lie in this fashion, but she also will not yield to Lear's implicit request for her undivided affection. Part of her must be loyal to her own husband and her children, in the natural cycle of the generations. "When I shall wed, / That lord whose hand must take my plight shall carry / Half my love with him, half my care and duty" (1.1.100–2). Marriage will not prevent her from obeying, loving, and honoring her father as is fit but will establish for her a new priority. To Lear, as to other fathers contemplating a daughter's marriage in late Shakespearean plays, this savors of desertion.

Lear is sadly deficient in self-knowledge. As Regan dryly observes, "he hath ever but slenderly known himself" (1.1.296–7) and has grown ever more changeable and imperious with age. By dividing his kingdom in three, ostensibly so that "future strife / May be prevented now" (lines 44–5), he instead sets in motion a civil war and French invasion. His intention of putting aside his regal authority while still retaining "The name and all th'addition to a king" (line 136) perhaps betrays a lack of comprehension of the realities of power, although Lear may also have plausible political reasons for what he does, in view of the restive ambitions of the Dukes of Cornwall, Albany, and Burgundy. In any case, he welcomes poisoned flattery but interprets well-intended criticism, whether from Cordelia or Kent, as treason. These failures in no sense justify what Lear's ungrateful children do to him; as he later says, just before going mad, "I am a man / More sinned against than sinning" (3.2.59–60). His failures are, however, tokens of his worldly insolence, for which he must fall. The process is a painful one, but, since it brings self-discovery, it is not without its compensations. Indeed, a central paradox of the play is that by no other way could Lear have learned what human suffering and need are all about.

Lear's Fool is instrumental in elucidating this paradox. The Fool offers Lear advice in palatable form as mere foolery or entertainment and thus obtains a hearing when Kent and Cordelia have been angrily dismissed. Beneath his seemingly innocent jibes, however, are plain warnings of the looming disaster Lear blindly refuses to acknowledge. The Fool knows, as indeed any fool could tell, that Goneril and Regan are remorseless and unnatural. The real fool, therefore, is Lear himself, for having placed himself in their power. In a paradox familiar to Renaissance audiences—as in Erasmus's *In Praise of Folly,* Cervantes's *Don Quixote,* and Shakespeare's own earlier *As You Like It* and *Twelfth Night*—folly and wisdom exchange places. By a similar inversion of logic, the Fool offers his coxcomb to the Earl of Kent for siding with Lear in his exile, "for taking one's part that's out of favor" (1.4.97). Worldly wisdom suggests that we serve those whose fortunes are on the rise, as the obsequious and servile Oswald does.

Indeed, the sinister progress of the first half of the play seems to confirm the Fool's contention that kindness and love are a sure way to exile and poverty. "Let go thy hold when a great wheel runs down a hill lest it break thy neck with following; but the great one that goes upward, let him draw thee after" (2.4.70–3). Yet the Fool resolves to ignore his own sardonic advice; "I would have none but knaves follow it, since a fool gives it" (lines 74–5). Beneath his mocking, the Fool expresses the deeper truth that it is better to be a "fool" and suffer than to win on the cynical world's terms. The greatest fools truly are those who prosper through cruelty and become hardened in sin. As the Fool puts it, deriving a seemingly contrary lesson from Lear's rejection of Cordelia: "Why, this fellow has banished two on 's daughters and did the third a blessing against his will" (1.4.99–101).

These inversions find a parallel in Christian teaching, although the play is nominally pagan in setting. (The lack of explicit Christian reference may be in part the result of a parliamentary order in 1606 banning references to "God" onstage as blasphemous.) Christianity does not hold a monopoly on the idea that one must lose the world in order to win a better world, but its expressions of that idea were plentifully available to Shakespeare: "Blessed are the meek, for they shall inherit the earth" (the Sermon on the Mount); "Go and sell that thou hast, and give to the poor, and thou shalt have treasure in heaven" (Matthew 19:21); "He hath put down the mighty from their seats, and exalted them of low degree" (Luke 1:52). Cordelia's vision of genuine love is of this exalted spiritual order. She is, as the King of France extols her, "most rich being poor, / Most choice, forsaken, and most loved, despised" (1.1.254–5). This is the sense in which Lear has bestowed on her an unintended blessing, by exiling her from a worldly prosperity that is inherently pernicious. Now, with poetic fitness, Lear must learn the same lesson himself. He does so, paradoxically, at the very moment he goes mad, parting ways with the conventional truths of the corrupted world. "My wits begin to turn," he says (3.2.67), and then speaks his first kind words to the Fool, who is his companion in the storm. Lear senses companionship with a fellow mortal who is cold and outcast as he is. In his madness, he perceives both the worth of this insight and the need for suffering to attain it: "The art of our necessities is strange, / And can make vile things precious" (lines 70–1). Misery teaches Lear things he never could know as king about other "Poor naked wretches" who "bide the pelting of this pitiless storm." How are such poor persons to be fed and clothed? "Oh, I have ta'en / Too little care of this! Take physic, pomp; / Expose thyself to feel what wretches feel, / That thou mayst shake the superflux to them / And show the heavens more just" (3.4.28–36). This vision of perfect justice is visionary and utopian, utterly mad, in fact, but it is also spiritual wisdom dearly bought.

Gloucester learns a similar truth and expresses it in much the same way. Like Lear, he has driven into exile a virtuous child and has placed himself in the power of the wicked. Enlightenment comes only through suffering. Just as Lear achieves spiritual wisdom when he goes mad, Gloucester achieves spiritual vision when he is physically blinded. His eyes having been ground out by the heel of Cornwall's boot, Gloucester asks for Edmund only to learn that Edmund has betrayed him in return for siding with Lear in the approaching civil war. Gloucester's response, however, is not to accuse Edmund of treachery but to beg forgiveness of the wronged Edgar. No longer does Gloucester need eyes to see this truth: "I stumbled when I saw." Although the discovery is shattering, Gloucester perceives, as does Lear, that adversity is paradoxically of some benefit, since prosperity had previously caused him to be so spiritually blind. "Full oft 'tis seen / Our means secure us, and our mere defects / Prove our commodities" (4.1.19–21). And this realization leads him, as it does Lear, to express a longing for utopian social justice in which arrogant men will be humbled and the poor raised up by redistributed wealth. "Heavens, deal so still! / Let the superfluous and lust-dieted man, / That slaves your ordinance, that will not see / Because he does not feel, feel your pow'r quickly! / So distribution should undo excess / And each man have enough" (lines 65–70).

To say that Lear and Gloucester learn something precious is not, however, to deny that they are also devastated and broken by their savage humiliation. Indeed, Gloucester is driven to a despairing attempt at suicide, and Lear remains obsessed with the rotten stench of his own mortality, "bound / Upon a wheel of fire" (4.7.47–8). Every decent value that we like to associate with civilization is grotesquely inverted during the storm scenes. Justice, for example, is portrayed in two sharply contrasting scenes: the mere "form of justice" by which Cornwall condemns Gloucester for treason (3.7.26) and the earnestly playacted trial by which the mad Lear arraigns Goneril and Regan of filial ingratitude (3.6). The appearance and the reality of justice have exchanged places, as have folly and wisdom or blindness and seeing. The trial of Gloucester is outwardly correct, for Cornwall possesses the legal authority to try his subjects and at least goes through the motions of interrogating his prisoner. The outcome is, however, cruelly predetermined. In the playacting trial concurrently taking place in a wretched hovel, the outward appearance of justice is pathetically absurd. Here, justice on earth is personified by a madman (Lear), Edgar disguised as another madman (Tom o' Bedlam), and a Fool, of whom the latter two are addressed by Lear as "Thou robèd man of justice" and "thou, his yokefellow of equity" (lines 36–7). They are caught up in a pastime of illusion, using a footstool to represent Lear's ungrateful daughters. Yet true justice is here and not inside the manor house.

Similar contrasts invert the values of loyalty, obedience, and family bonds. Edmund becomes, in the language of the villains, the "loyal" son whose loyalty is demonstrated by turning on his own "traitorous" father. Cornwall becomes a new father to Edmund ("thou shalt find a dearer father in my love," 3.5.25–6). Conversely, a servant who tries to restrain Cornwall from blinding Gloucester is, in Regan's eyes, monstrously insubordinate. "A peasant stand up thus?" (3.7.83). Personal and sexual relationships betray signs of the universal malaise. The explicitly sexual ties in the play, notably those of Goneril, Regan, and Edmund, are grossly carnal and lead to jealousy and murder, while in Cordelia's wifely role the sensual is underplayed. The relationships we are invited to cherish—those of Cordelia, Kent, the Fool, and Gloucester to King Lear, and Edgar to Gloucester—are filial or are characterized by loyal service, both of which are pointedly nonsexual. Nowhere do we find an embodiment of love that is both sensual and spiritual, as in Desdemona in *Othello* or Hermione in *The Winter's Tale*. The Fool's and Tom o' Bedlam's (i.e., Edgar's) gibes about codpieces and plackets (3.2.27–40, 3.4.96) anticipate Lear's towering indictment of carnality, in which his fear of woman's insatiable appetite and his revulsion at her body "Down from the waist" ("there is the sulfurous pit, burning, scalding, stench, consumption. Fie, fie, fie! Pah, pah!") combine with a destructive self-hatred (4.6.124–30).

All these inversions and polarizations are subsumed in the inversion of the word "natural." Edmund is the "natural" son of Gloucester, meaning literally that he is illegitimate. Figuratively, he therefore represents a violation of traditional moral order. In appearance he is smooth and plausible, but in reality he is an archdeceiver like the Vice in a morality play, a superb actor who boasts to the audience in soliloquy of his protean villainy. "Nature" is Edmund's goddess, and by this he means something like a naturalistic universe in which the race goes to the swiftest and in which conscience, morality, and religion are empty myths. Whereas Lear invokes Nature as a goddess who will punish ungrateful daughters and defend rejected fathers (1.4.274–88) and whereas Gloucester believes in a cosmic correspondence between eclipses of the moon or sun and mutinous discords among people (1.2.106–17), Edmund scoffs at all such metaphysical speculations. He spurns, in other words, the Boethian conception of a divine harmony uniting the cosmos and humankind, with humankind at the center of the universe. As a rationalist, Edmund echoes Jacobean disruptions of the older world order in politics and religion as well as in science. He is Machiavellian, an atheist, and Epicurean—everything inimical to traditional Elizabethan ideals of order. To him, "natural" means precisely what Lear and Gloucester call "unnatural."

His creed provides the play with its supreme test. Which definition of "natural" is true? Does heaven exist, and will it let Edmund and the other villainous persons get away with their evil? The question is frequently asked, but the answers are ambiguous. "If you do love old men," Lear implores the gods, "if your sweet sway / Allow obedience, if you yourselves are old, / Make it your cause" (2.4.191–3). His exhortations mount into frenzied rant, until finally the heavens do send down a terrible storm—on Lear himself. Witnesses agree that the absence of divine order in the universe would have the gravest consequences. "If that the heavens do not their visible spirits / Send quickly down to tame these vile offenses," says Albany of Lear's ordeal, "It will come, / Humanity must perforce prey on itself, / Like monsters of the deep" (4.2.47–51). And Cornwall's servants (in a passage missing from the Folio text) have perceived earlier the dire implications of their masters' evil deeds. "I'll never care what wickedness I do, / If this man come to good," says one, and his fellow agrees: "If she [Regan] live long, / And in the end meet the old course of death, / Women will all turn monsters" (3.7.102–5). Yet these servants do, in fact, obey their own best instincts, turning on Cornwall and ministering to Gloucester despite danger to themselves. Similarly, Albany abandons his mild attempts to conciliate his domineering wife and instead uses his power for good. Cordelia's ability to forgive and cherish her father, and Edgar's comparable ministering to Gloucester, give the lie to Edmund's "natural" or amoral view of humanity; a few people, at least, are capable of charity, even when it does not serve their own material self-interest. Conversely, the play suggests that villainy will at last destroy itself, and not simply because the gods are just; Albany's hopeful insistence that "This shows you are above, / You justicers" (4.2.79–80) may be a little more than wishful thinking, to be undercut by some fresh disaster, but at least the insatiable ambitions of Edmund, Goneril, Regan, Cornwall, and Oswald do lead to their violent deaths. Edmund's belated attempt to save the life of Cordelia, though unsuccessful, suggests that this intelligent villain has at last begun to understand the great flaw in his naturalistic creed and to see that, like Goneril and Regan, he has been consumed by his own lust.

Even with such reassurances that villainy will eventually undo itself, the devastation at the end of *King Lear* is so appalling that our questions about justice remain finally unanswered. To ask the question "Who must pay for Lear's self-knowledge?" is to remind ourselves that women must often die in Shakespeare's tragedies so that men may learn, and to perceive even further that, in the absurdist world of *Lear*, the Cartesian logic of cause and effect and poetic justice simply will not account for all that we long to understand. As Roland Barthes well expresses the matter in an essay on Racine, "tragedy is only a means of reclaiming human unhappiness, of subsuming it, thus justifying it under the form of necessity, or wisdom, or purification." Tragedy cannot explain away the death of

Cordelia and the heartbreak of her father. The last tableau is a vision of doomsday, with Cordelia strangled, Lear broken and dying, and the "gored state" in such disarray that we cannot be sure what restoration can occur. The very question of political order is dwarfed by the enormity of the personal disaster of Lear and Cordelia. No one wishes longer life for the King: "He hates him / That would upon the rack of this tough world / Stretch him out longer." He is dead; "The wonder is he hath endured so long" (5.3.319–26). Lear's view of life's terrible corruption, pronounced in his madness, seems confirmed in his end. Perhaps the only way in which this tragedy can reclaim so much unhappiness is to suggest that, given the incurable badness of the world, we can at least choose whether to attempt to be like Cordelia and Edgar (knowing what the price may be for such courage) or to settle for being our worst selves, like Edmund, Goneril, and Regan. Overwhelmed as we are by the testimonial before us of humankind's vicious capacity for self-destruction, we are stirred nonetheless by the ability of some men and women to confront their fearful destiny with probity and stoic renunciation, adhering to what they believe to be good and expecting Fortune to give them absolutely nothing. The power of love, though learned too late to avert catastrophe, is at last discovered in its very defeat.

King Lear has become a fable for our times, onstage, in film and television, and in fictional adaptations in novel form. The role of Lear has been a compelling one for so many great Shakespearean actors, including Philip Kemble, Henry Irving, Edwin Forrest, John Gielgud, Donald Wolfit, Donald Sinden, Brian Cox, Michael Gambon, Robert Stephens, and John Wood. Peter Brook's film version of 1970, based on a stage production of 1962, with Paul Scofield as Lear, did much to equate the play's bleak vision with that of our modern existential world. Stimulated by Jan Kott's *Shakespeare Our Contemporary* (translated 1964), a post–World War II apocalyptic interpretation of Shakespeare from the perspective of an ideologically embattled eastern Europe, Brook unfolds a narrative of unrelieved disillusionment. The medium of film enables him to show what it would be like, for example, to have a hundred knights and all their followers descend on Albany's castle at the same time, demanding to be fed and quarreling with the servants of Goneril and Albany; the din and confusion are overwhelming, to such an extent that one can see Goneril's point in wanting to cut back on the King's retinue. A barren, wintry landscape adds visual reinforcement to the savage energies of family and dynastic conflict. Grigori Kozintsev's film of 1971, the work of a great Soviet director, sees the larger movements of the play in Marxist terms as the dialectical imperatives of political and social history; again, the medium of film makes it possible for Kozintsev to do what the stage can-

not do, deploy huge casts of anonymous soldiers and workers as both victims and movers of social change. Laurence Olivier's performance of Lear for Grenada Television (directed by Michael Elliott, 1983, Granada Video, 1984) came at the very end of Olivier's life, as his climactic and final role; his interpretation is deeply enhanced by one's perception that the actor is literally dying of cancer. Olivier, weakened but determined, had to be helped through the rigors of the screening, with the result that his Lear is tender, vulnerable, frail, though capable of the outbursts of rage that often come with advanced age. His *King Lear* is about the approach of death. Akira Kurosawa, in his epic *Ran* (1985), chose a more radical adaptation, that of telling a story of a Japanese warlord and his three sons, one of them (like Cordelia) dear but misunderstood, the others treacherous. One of their wives (the Lady Kaede) turns out to be another Edmund, Goneril, Regan, and Lady Macbeth all combined in one, fiercely and murderously determined that her husband succeed by whatever means possible. Kurosawa's vision of evil in the human heart is meant to be terrifying, and it is. The Royal National Theatre production of *King Lear* won several awards for Best Actor (Ian Holm as Lear) and Best Director (Richard Eyre), and is available on video from the BBC and Mobil Masterpiece Theatre (1998). In fiction, Jane Smiley's *A Thousand Acres* (1991) features a similar transposition, in this case to a midwestern American farm run by an aging farmer who transfers his land to his daughters and then sinks into alcoholism and insanity as two daughters squabble over their inheritance and end up losing everything, including their husbands, while their sister Caroline (Cordelia), unwilling to take part in the dividing of the farm, tries unsuccessfully as a lawyer to have the property restored to her father. Edward Bond's stage play called *Lear* (1971) accentuated *King Lear*'s already formidable bleakness by adding to its cruelty and violence; in it, war became a never-ending cycle of repression and escalating oppression. In these varied reworkings, we see the remarkable malleability of *King Lear* as an endlessly fascinating subject for new historicist, cultural materialist, deconstructive, and feminist readings that open up topics of misogyny and patriarchy, political ideologies, and philosophical pessimism.

King Lear exists in two early texts, the Quarto of 1608 and the considerably changed Folio version of 1623. Similar disparities appear in *Hamlet, Othello, Troilus and Cressida, Henry IV Part II*, and a number of other plays, but the problem is especially acute in *King Lear*. Shakespeare must have had a hand in the revisions that led to the Folio text. It contains new material. At the same time, the Quarto text contains passages not found in the Folio. The revisions may have resulted from a number of circumstances: cutting for performance (the play as it stands in either version is too long to have been produced in its entirety on the Jacobean stage), censorship, errors in transcription, and still more. The Folio version does alter some matters especially having to do with the French invasion; characters like Albany appear in a different light. The very ending is changed as to which characters speak the concluding lines.

Given these factors, many editions today present two or even three texts for the reader, or mark the text with brackets and other indicators of textual variation. This edition does not do so, though the textual notes do indicate the differences that occur. The reasons for choosing to present here the more traditional composite or eclectic text are these: *King Lear*'s textual variations between Quarto and Folio are more extensive than in some other plays, but are not always different in kind, so that it is a distortion to treat this play alone as a multiple-text play.

To choose either Quarto or Folio is to lose important material that is unquestionably Shakespeare's. To print two or even three versions is to add pages to an already weighty collection. And the presentation of multiple texts, or of a single text that is flagged with bracketed markers, also imposes on the reader a task of sorting out a complex and uncertain textual history that, however important ultimately in studying Shakespeare as a writer and as a reviser, is perhaps best left to subsequent investigation in a full-scale critical edition after one has absorbed the greatness of this play as a piece of writing for the theater. The present composite *King Lear*, based on the Folio text but including the 300 or so lines found only in the First Quarto along with some Quarto readings where the Folio version seems less textually reliable, is in a sense a compromise, but it is one that seems well suited to the purposes of this present edition.

King Lear

[*Dramatis Personae*

KING LEAR
GONERIL,
REGAN,   } *Lear's daughters*
CORDELIA,
DUKE OF ALBANY, *Goneril's husband*
DUKE OF CORNWALL, *Regan's husband*
KING OF FRANCE, *Cordelia's suitor and husband*
DUKE OF BURGUNDY, *suitor to Cordelia*

EARL OF KENT, *later disguised as Caius*
EARL OF GLOUCESTER
EDGAR, *Gloucester's son and heir, later disguised as poor Tom*
EDMUND, *Gloucester's bastard son*

SCENE: *Britain*]

OSWALD, *Goneril's steward*
A KNIGHT *serving King Lear*
Lear's FOOL
CURAN, *in Gloucester's household*
GENTLEMEN
Three SERVANTS
OLD MAN, *a tenant of Gloucester*
Three MESSENGERS
A GENTLEMAN *attending Cordelia as a Doctor*
Two CAPTAINS
HERALD

Knights, Gentlemen, Attendants, Servants, Officers, Soldiers, Trumpeters

1.1

Enter Kent, Gloucester, and Edmund.

KENT   I thought the King had more affected the Duke of   1
Albany than Cornwall.   2

GLOUCESTER   It did always seem so to us; but now in
the division of the kingdom it appears not which of
the dukes he values most, for equalities are so weighed   5
that curiosity in neither can make choice of either's   6
moiety.   7

KENT   Is not this your son, my lord?

GLOUCESTER   His breeding, sir, hath been at my charge.   9
I have so often blushed to acknowledge him that now
I am brazed to't.   11

KENT   I cannot conceive you.   12

GLOUCESTER   Sir, this young fellow's mother could;
whereupon she grew round-wombed and had indeed,
sir, a son for her cradle ere she had a husband
for her bed. Do you smell a fault?   16

KENT   I cannot wish the fault undone, the issue of it   17
being so proper.   18

GLOUCESTER   But I have a son, sir, by order of law, some   19
year elder than this, who yet is no dearer in my ac-   20
count. Though this knave came something saucily to   21
the world before he was sent for, yet was his mother
fair, there was good sport at his making, and the
whoreson must be acknowledged.—Do you know this   24
noble gentleman, Edmund?

EDMUND   No, my lord.

GLOUCESTER   My lord of Kent. Remember him hereafter
as my honorable friend.

EDMUND   My services to Your Lordship.   29

KENT   I must love you, and sue to know you better.   30

EDMUND   Sir, I shall study deserving.   31

GLOUCESTER   He hath been out nine years, and away   32
he shall again. The King is coming.   33

*Sennet. Enter [one bearing a coronet, then] King
Lear, Cornwall, Albany, Goneril, Regan, Cordelia,
and attendants.*

LEAR
Attend the lords of France and Burgundy, Gloucester.   34

GLOUCESTER   I shall, my liege.   *Exit.*

LEAR
Meantime we shall express our darker purpose.   36
Give me the map there. [*He takes a map.*] Know that we
have divided
In three our kingdom; and 'tis our fast intent   38
To shake all cares and business from our age,
Conferring them on younger strengths while we
Unburdened crawl toward death. Our son of
Cornwall,
And you, our no less loving son of Albany,
We have this hour a constant will to publish   43
Our daughters' several dowers, that future strife   44
May be prevented now. The princes, France and
Burgundy,
Great rivals in our youngest daughter's love,
Long in our court have made their amorous sojourn
And here are to be answered. Tell me, my
daughters—
Since now we will divest us both of rule,
Interest of territory, cares of state—   50
Which of you shall we say doth love us most,
That we our largest bounty may extend
Where nature doth with merit challenge? Goneril,   53
Our eldest born, speak first.

GONERIL
Sir, I love you more than words can wield the matter,
Dearer than eyesight, space, and liberty,   56
Beyond what can be valued, rich or rare,
No less than life, with grace, health, beauty, honor;
As much as child e'er loved, or father found;   59
A love that makes breath poor and speech unable.   60
Beyond all manner of so much I love you.

CORDELIA [*aside*]
What shall Cordelia speak? Love and be silent.

LEAR [*indicating on map*]
Of all these bounds, even from this line to this,
With shadowy forests and with champains riched,   64
With plenteous rivers and wide-skirted meads,   65
We make thee lady. To thine and Albany's issue
Be this perpetual.—What says our second daughter,
Our dearest Regan, wife of Cornwall? Speak.

REGAN
I am made of that self mettle as my sister,   69
And prize me at her worth. In my true heart   70
I find she names my very deed of love;   71
Only she comes too short, that I profess   72
Myself an enemy to all other joys
Which the most precious square of sense possesses,   74

1.1. Location: King Lear's palace.
1 affected favored   **2 Albany** i.e., Scotland   **5–7 equalities . . .
moiety** the shares balance so equally that close scrutiny cannot find
advantage in either's portion.   **9 breeding** raising, care.   **charge**
expense.   **11 brazed** hardened   **12 conceive** understand. (But
Gloucester puns in the sense of "become pregnant.")   **16 fault** (1) sin
(2) loss of scent by the hounds.   **17 issue** (1) result (2) offspring
18 proper (1) excellent (2) handsome.   **19 by order of law** legitimate
19–20 some year about a year   **20–1 account** estimation.   **21 knave**
young fellow. (Not said disapprovingly, though the word is ironic.)
something somewhat   **24 whoreson** low fellow; suggesting bastardy, but (like *knave* above) used with affectionate condescension
29 services duty   **30 sue** petition, beg   **31 study deserving** strive to
be worthy (of your esteem).   **32 out** i.e., abroad, absent.   **33.1** *Sennet*
trumpet signal heralding a procession.   *one . . . then* (This direction
is from the Quarto. The *coronet* is perhaps intended for Cordelia or
her betrothed. A coronet signifies nobility below the rank of king.)
34 Attend Wait upon, usher ceremoniously

36 we, our (The royal plural; also in lines 37–44, etc.)   **darker purpose** undeclared intention.   **38 fast** firm   **43 constant . . . publish**
firm resolve to proclaim   **44 several** individual   **50 Interest of** right
or title to, possession of   **53 Where . . . challenge** where both natural
affection and merit claim our bounty as its due.   **56 space, and liberty** possession of land, and freedom of action   **59 found** i.e., found
himself to be loved   **60 breath . . . unable** utterance impoverished
and speech inadequate.   **64 shadowy** shady.   **champains riched** fertile plains   **65 plenteous . . . meads** abundant rivers bordered with
wide meadows   **69 that self mettle** that same spirited temperament
70 prize . . . worth value myself as her equal (in love for you). (*Prize*
suggests "price.")   **71 names . . . love** describes my love in action
72 that in that   **74 Which . . . possesses** which the most delicately
sensitive part of my nature can enjoy

And find I am alone felicitate 75
In your dear Highness' love.
CORDELIA [aside]   Then poor Cordelia!
And yet not so, since I am sure my love's
More ponderous than my tongue. 78
LEAR
To thee and thine hereditary ever
Remain this ample third of our fair kingdom,
No less in space, validity, and pleasure 81
Than that conferred on Goneril.—Now, our joy,
Although our last and least, to whose young love 83
The vines of France and milk of Burgundy 84
Strive to be interested, what can you say to draw 85
A third more opulent than your sisters'? Speak.
CORDELIA   Nothing, my lord.
LEAR   Nothing?
CORDELIA   Nothing.
LEAR
Nothing will come of nothing. Speak again.
CORDELIA
Unhappy that I am, I cannot heave
My heart into my mouth. I love Your Majesty
According to my bond, no more nor less. 93
LEAR
How, how, Cordelia? Mend your speech a little,
Lest you may mar your fortunes.
CORDELIA   Good my lord,
You have begot me, bred me, loved me. I
Return those duties back as are right fit, 97
Obey you, love you, and most honor you.
Why have my sisters husbands if they say
They love you all? Haply, when I shall wed, 100
That lord whose hand must take my plight shall carry 101
Half my love with him, half my care and duty.
Sure I shall never marry like my sisters,
To love my father all.
LEAR
But goes thy heart with this?
CORDELIA   Ay, my good lord.
LEAR   So young, and so untender?
CORDELIA   So young, my lord, and true.
LEAR
Let it be so! Thy truth then be thy dower!
For, by the sacred radiance of the sun,
The mysteries of Hecate and the night, 110
By all the operation of the orbs 111
From whom we do exist and cease to be, 112
Here I disclaim all my paternal care,
Propinquity, and property of blood, 114
And as a stranger to my heart and me

Hold thee from this forever. The barbarous Scythian, 116
Or he that makes his generation messes 117
To gorge his appetite, shall to my bosom
Be as well neighbored, pitied, and relieved 119
As thou my sometime daughter.
KENT   Good my liege— 120
LEAR   Peace, Kent!
Come not between the dragon and his wrath.
I loved her most, and thought to set my rest 123
On her kind nursery. [To Cordelia] Hence, and avoid
my sight!— 124
So be my grave my peace, as here I give 125
Her father's heart from her. Call France. Who stirs? 126
Call Burgundy.   [Exit one.]
Cornwall and Albany,
With my two daughters' dowers digest the third. 128
Let pride, which she calls plainness, marry her. 129
I do invest you jointly with my power,
Preeminence, and all the large effects 131
That troop with majesty. Ourself by monthly course, 132
With reservation of an hundred knights 133
By you to be sustained, shall our abode
Make with you by due turns. Only we shall retain
The name and all th'addition to a king. 136
The sway, revenue, execution of the rest, 137
Belovèd sons, be yours, which to confirm,
This coronet part between you.
KENT   Royal Lear, 139
Whom I have ever honored as my king,
Loved as my father, as my master followed,
As my great patron thought on in my prayers—
LEAR
The bow is bent and drawn. Make from the shaft. 143
KENT
Let it fall rather, though the fork invade 144
The region of my heart. Be Kent unmannerly
When Lear is mad. What wouldst thou do, old man?
Think'st thou that duty shall have dread to speak
When power to flattery bows?
To plainness honor's bound 149
When majesty falls to folly. Reserve thy state, 150
And in thy best consideration check 151
This hideous rashness. Answer my life my judgment, 152

75 **felicitate** made happy   78 **ponderous** weighty   81 **validity** value.
pleasure pleasing features   83 **least** youngest   84 **vines** vineyards.
milk pastures (?)   85 **be interested** be affiliated, establish a claim, be
admitted as to a privilege.   **draw** win   93 **bond** filial obligation
97 **right fit** proper and fitting   100 **all** exclusively, and with all of
themselves.   **Haply** Perhaps, with luck   101 **plight** pledge in marriage   110 **mysteries** secret rites.   **Hecate** goddess of witchcraft and
the moon   111 **operation** influence.   **orbs** planets and stars
112 **From whom** under whose influence   114 **Propinquity . . . blood**
close kinship, and rights and duties entailed in blood ties

116 **this** this time forth.   **Scythian** (Scythians were famous in antiquity for savagery.)   117 **makes . . . messes** makes meals of his children or parents   119 **neighbored** helped in a neighborly way
120 **sometime** former   123 **set my rest** rely wholly. (A phrase from a
game of cards, meaning "to stake all.")   124 **nursery** nursing, care.
avoid get out of   125 **So . . . peace, as** As I hope to rest peacefully in
my grave   126 **Who stirs?** i.e., Jump to it; don't just stand there.
128 **digest** assimilate, incorporate   129 **Let . . . her** Let pride, which
she calls plain speaking, be her dowry and get her a husband.
131 **effects** outward shows   132 **troop with** accompany, serve.
Ourself (The royal "we.")   133 **With reservation of** reserving to
myself the right to be attended by   136 **th'addition** the honors and
prerogatives   137 **sway** sovereign authority   139 **coronet** (Perhaps
Lear gestures toward this coronet that was to have symbolized
Cordelia's dowry and marriage, hands it to his sons-in-law, or actually attempts to divide it.)   143 **Make from** Get out of the way of
144 **fall** strike.   **fork** barbed head of an arrow   149 **To . . . bound**
Loyalty demands frankness   150 **Reserve thy state** Retain your royal
authority   151 **And . . . check** and with wise deliberation restrain
152 **Answer . . . judgment** I wager my life on my judgment that

Thy youngest daughter does not love thee least,
Nor are those emptyhearted whose low sounds
Reverb no hollowness.

LEAR   Kent, on thy life, no more.   155

KENT

My life I never held but as a pawn   156
To wage against thine enemies, nor fear to lose it,   157
Thy safety being motive.

LEAR   Out of my sight!   158

KENT

See better, Lear, and let me still remain
The true blank of thine eye.   160

LEAR   Now, by Apollo—

KENT   Now, by Apollo, King,
Thou swear'st thy gods in vain.

LEAR   Oh, vassal! Miscreant!   164

[*Laying his hand on his sword.*]

ALBANY, CORNWALL   Dear sir, forbear.

KENT

Kill thy physician, and the fee bestow
Upon the foul disease. Revoke thy gift,
Or whilst I can vent clamor from my throat
I'll tell thee thou dost evil.

LEAR

Hear me, recreant, on thine allegiance hear me!   170
That thou hast sought to make us break our vows,   171
Which we durst never yet, and with strained pride   172
To come betwixt our sentence and our power,   173
Which nor our nature nor our place can bear,   174
Our potency made good, take thy reward.   175
Five days we do allot thee for provision
To shield thee from disasters of the world,
And on the sixth to turn thy hated back
Upon our kingdom. If on the tenth day following
Thy banished trunk be found in our dominions,   180
The moment is thy death. Away! By Jupiter,
This shall not be revoked.

KENT

Fare thee well, King. Sith thus thou wilt appear,   183
Freedom lives hence and banishment is here.

[*To Cordelia*] The gods to their dear shelter take thee,
    maid,
That justly think'st and hast most rightly said!

[*To Regan and Goneril*] And your large speeches may
    your deeds approve,   187
That good effects may spring from words of love.
Thus Kent, O princes, bids you all adieu.

He'll shape his old course in a country new.   *Exit.* 190

Flourish. Enter Gloucester, with France and
Burgundy; attendants.

GLOUCESTER

Here's France and Burgundy, my noble lord.

LEAR   My lord of Burgundy,
We first address toward you, who with this king   193
Hath rivaled for our daughter. What in the least   194
Will you require in present dower with her
Or cease your quest of love?

BURGUNDY   Most royal Majesty,
I crave no more than hath Your Highness offered,
Nor will you tender less.

LEAR   Right noble Burgundy,   198
When she was dear to us we did hold her so,   199
But now her price is fallen. Sir, there she stands.
If aught within that little-seeming substance,   201
Or all of it, with our displeasure pieced,   202
And nothing more, may fitly like Your Grace,   203
She's there, and she is yours.

BURGUNDY   I know no answer.

LEAR

Will you, with those infirmities she owes,   205
Unfriended, new-adopted to our hate,
Dowered with our curse and strangered with our
    oath,   207
Take her, or leave her?

BURGUNDY   Pardon me, royal sir.
Election makes not up in such conditions.   209

LEAR

Then leave her, sir, for by the power that made me,
I tell you all her wealth. [*To France*] For you, great King,   211
I would not from your love make such a stray   212
To match you where I hate; therefore beseech you   213
T'avert your liking a more worthier way   214
Than on a wretch whom Nature is ashamed
Almost t'acknowledge hers.

FRANCE   This is most strange,
That she whom even but now was your best object,
The argument of your praise, balm of your age,   218
The best, the dearest, should in this trice of time   219
Commit a thing so monstrous to dismantle   220
So many folds of favor. Sure her offense
Must be of such unnatural degree
That monsters it, or your forevouched affection   223
Fall into taint, which to believe of her   224

155 **Reverb no hollowness** do not reverberate like a hollow drum, insincerely.   **156–7 My . . . wage** I never regarded my life other than as a pledge to hazard in warfare   **158 motive** that which prompts me to act.   **160 The true . . . eye** i.e., the means to enable you to see better. (*Blank* means "the white center of the target," or, "the true direct aim," as in "point-blank," traveling in a straight line.)   **164 vassal** i.e., wretch.   **Miscreant** (Literally, infidel, heretic; hence, villain, rascal.)   **170 recreant** traitor   **171 That** In that, since   **172 strained** excessive   **173 To . . . power** i.e., to block my power to command and judge   **174 Which . . . place** which neither my temperament nor my office as king   **175 Our . . . good** my power enacted, demonstrated   **180 trunk** body   **183 Sith** Since   **187 your . . . approve** may your deeds confirm your speeches with their vast claims

190 **shape . . . course** follow his traditional plainspoken ways   **190.1 *Flourish*** trumpet fanfare used for the entrance or exit of important persons   **193 address** address myself   **194 rivaled** competed.   **in the least** at the lowest   **198 tender** offer   **199 so** i.e., *dear*, beloved and valued at a high price   **201 little-seeming substance** one who seems substantial but whose substance is, in fact, little, or, one who refuses to flatter   **202 pieced** added, joined   **203 like** please   **205 owes** owns   **207 strangered** disowned   **209 Election . . . conditions** No choice is possible under such conditions.   **211 tell you** (1) inform you of (2) enumerate for you.   **For** As for   **212 make such a stray** stray so far   **213 To** as to.   **beseech** I beseech   **214 T'avert your liking** to turn your affections   **218 argument** theme   **219 trice** moment   **220 to** as to   **223 monsters it** makes it monstrous   **223–4 or . . . taint** or else the affection for her you have hitherto affirmed must fall into suspicion

Must be a faith that reason without miracle
Should never plant in me.

CORDELIA   I yet beseech Your Majesty—
If for I want that glib and oily art   228
To speak and purpose not, since what I well intend   229
I'll do't before I speak—that you make known
It is no vicious blot, murder, or foulness,   231
No unchaste action or dishonored step
That hath deprived me of your grace and favor,
But even for want of that for which I am richer: 234
A still-soliciting eye and such a tongue   235
That I am glad I have not, though not to have it
Hath lost me in your liking.

LEAR   Better thou
Hadst not been born than not t'have pleased me better.

FRANCE
Is it but this? A tardiness in nature
Which often leaves the history unspoke   240
That it intends to do?—My lord of Burgundy,
What say you to the lady? Love's not love
When it is mingled with regards that stands   243
Aloof from th'entire point. Will you have her?   244
She is herself a dowry.

BURGUNDY [to Lear]   Royal King,
Give but that portion which yourself proposed,
And here I take Cordelia by the hand,
Duchess of Burgundy.

LEAR
Nothing. I have sworn. I am firm.

BURGUNDY [to Cordelia]
I am sorry, then, you have so lost a father
That you must lose a husband.

CORDELIA   Peace be with Burgundy!
Since that respects of fortune are his love,   252
I shall not be his wife.

FRANCE
Fairest Cordelia, that art most rich being poor,
Most choice, forsaken, and most loved, despised,
Thee and thy virtues here I seize upon,
Be it lawful I take up what's cast away.   257
                                        [He takes her hand.]
Gods, gods! 'Tis strange that from their cold'st neglect   258
My love should kindle to inflamed respect.—   259
Thy dowerless daughter, King, thrown to my chance,   260
Is queen of us, of ours, and our fair France.
Not all the dukes of wat'rish Burgundy   262
Can buy this unprized precious maid of me.—   263
Bid them farewell, Cordelia, though unkind.   264
Thou losest here, a better where to find.   265

LEAR
Thou hast her, France. Let her be thine, for we
Have no such daughter, nor shall ever see
That face of hers again. Therefore begone
Without our grace, our love, our benison.   269
Come, noble Burgundy.
               Flourish. Exeunt [all but France, Goneril, Regan,
                                                           and Cordelia].

FRANCE   Bid farewell to your sisters.

CORDELIA
Ye jewels of our father, with washed eyes   272
Cordelia leaves you. I know you what you are,
And like a sister am most loath to call   274
Your faults as they are named. Love well our father.   275
To your professèd bosoms I commit him.   276
But yet, alas, stood I within his grace,
I would prefer him to a better place.   278
So, farewell to you both.

REGAN
Prescribe not us our duty.

GONERIL   Let your study
Be to content your lord, who hath received you
At Fortune's alms. You have obedience scanted,   282
And well are worth the want that you have wanted.   283

CORDELIA
Time shall unfold what plighted cunning hides;   284
Who covers faults, at last shame them derides.   285
Well may you prosper!

FRANCE   Come, my fair Cordelia.
                              Exeunt France and Cordelia.

GONERIL   Sister, it is not little I have to say of what most
nearly appertains to us both. I think our father will
hence tonight.

REGAN   That's most certain, and with you; next month
with us.

GONERIL   You see how full of changes his age is; the
observation we have made of it hath not been little.
He always loved our sister most, and with what
poor judgment he hath now cast her off appears too grossly.   295

REGAN   'Tis the infirmity of his age. Yet he hath ever
but slenderly known himself.

GONERIL   The best and soundest of his time hath been   298
but rash. Then must we look from his age to receive   299
not alone the imperfections of long-ingraffed condi-   300
tion, but therewithal the unruly waywardness that in-   301
firm and choleric years bring with them.

REGAN   Such unconstant starts are we like to have from   303
him as this of Kent's banishment.

---

228 **for I want** because I lack   229 **purpose not** not intend to do what
I say   231 **foulness** immorality   234 **for which** for lack of which
235 **still-soliciting** ever begging   240 **history** tale, narrative
243–4 **regards . . . point** irrelevant considerations.   252 **Since . . . fortune** Since concern for wealth and position   257 **Be it lawful** if it be
lawful that   258 **from . . . neglect** out of the cold neglect of the gods
259 **inflamed respect** ardent regard.   260 **chance** lot   262 **wat'rish**
(1) well-watered with rivers (2) feeble, watery   263 **unprized** not
appreciated. (With perhaps a sense also of "priceless.")   264 **though
unkind** though they have behaved unnaturally.   265 **here** this place.
where place elsewhere

269 **benison** blessing.   272 **washed** tear-washed   274 **like a sister** i.e.,
because I am your sister   275 **as . . . named** by their true names.
276 **professèd bosoms** publicly avowed love   278 **prefer** advance,
recommend   282 **At . . . alms** as a pittance or dole from Fortune.
283 **And well . . . wanted** i.e., and well deserve to be without the
dowry and the parental affection that you have both lacked and
flouted.   284–5 **Time . . . derides** Time will bring to light what cunning attempts to conceal as if in the folds of a cloak; those who hide
their faults may do so for a while, but in time they will be shamed and
derided.   295 **grossly** obviously.   298–9 **The best . . . rash** Even in the
prime of his life, he was stormy and unpredictable.   300–1 **long-
ingraffed condition** long-implanted habit   301 **therewithal** added
thereto   303 **unconstant starts** impulsive outbursts.   **like** likely

GONERIL   There is further compliment of leave-taking 305
between France and him. Pray you, let us hit together. 306
If our father carry authority with such disposition as 307
he bears, this last surrender of his will but offend us. 308
REGAN   We shall further think of it.
GONERIL   We must do something, and i'th' heat. 310

Exeunt.

❖

1.2

Enter Bastard [Edmund, with a letter].

EDMUND
Thou, Nature, art my goddess; to thy law   1
My services are bound. Wherefore should I
Stand in the plague of custom and permit   3
The curiosity of nations to deprive me,   4
For that I am some twelve or fourteen moonshines   5
Lag of a brother? Why bastard? Wherefore base?   6
When my dimensions are as well compact,   7
My mind as generous, and my shape as true,   8
As honest madam's issue? Why brand they us   9
With base? With baseness? Bastardy? Base, base?
Who in the lusty stealth of nature take   11
More composition and fierce quality   12
Than doth within a dull, stale, tirèd bed
Go to th' creating a whole tribe of fops   14
Got 'tween asleep and wake? Well, then,   15
Legitimate Edgar, I must have your land.
Our father's love is to the bastard Edmund
As to th' legitimate. Fine word, "legitimate"!
Well, my legitimate, if this letter speed   19
And my invention thrive, Edmund the base   20
Shall top th' legitimate. I grow, I prosper.
Now, gods, stand up for bastards!

Enter Gloucester.

GLOUCESTER
Kent banished thus? And France in choler parted?
And the King gone tonight? Prescribed his power,   24
Confined to exhibition? All this done   25
Upon the gad? Edmund, how now? What news?   26
EDMUND   So please Your Lordship, none.

[Putting up the letter.]

GLOUCESTER   Why so earnestly seek you to put up that
letter?
EDMUND   I know no news, my lord.
GLOUCESTER   What paper were you reading?
EDMUND   Nothing, my lord.
GLOUCESTER   No? What needed then that terrible dis- 33
patch of it into your pocket? The quality of nothing 34
hath not such need to hide itself. Let's see. Come, if it
be nothing I shall not need spectacles.
EDMUND   I beseech you, sir, pardon me. It is a letter
from my brother, that I have not all o'erread; and for 38
so much as I have perused, I find it not fit for your
o'erlooking.   40
GLOUCESTER   Give me the letter, sir.
EDMUND   I shall offend either to detain or give it. The
contents, as in part I understand them, are to blame. 43
GLOUCESTER   Let's see, let's see.

[Edmund gives the letter.]

EDMUND   I hope for my brother's justification he wrote
this but as an essay or taste of my virtue.   46
GLOUCESTER *(reads)* "This policy and reverence of age 47
makes the world bitter to the best of our times, keeps 48
our fortunes from us till our oldness cannot relish
them. I begin to find an idle and fond bondage in the 50
oppression of aged tyranny, who sways not as it hath 51
power but as it is suffered. Come to me, that of this I 52
may speak more. If our father would sleep till I waked
him, you should enjoy half his revenue forever and live
the beloved of your brother,   Edgar."
Hum! Conspiracy! "Sleep till I waked him, you should
enjoy half his revenue." My son Edgar! Had he
a hand to write this? A heart and brain to breed it
in? When came you to this? Who brought it?   59
EDMUND   It was not brought me, my lord; there's the
cunning of it. I found it thrown in at the casement of 61
my closet.   62
GLOUCESTER   You know the character to be your 63
brother's?
EDMUND   If the matter were good, my lord, I durst 65
swear it were his; but in respect of that I would fain 66
think it were not.
GLOUCESTER   It is his.
EDMUND   It is his hand, my lord, but I hope his heart is
not in the contents.
GLOUCESTER   Has he never before sounded you in this
business?
EDMUND   Never, my lord. But I have heard him oft
maintain it to be fit that, sons at perfect age and fathers 74
declined, the father should be as ward to the son, and 75
the son manage his revenue.

---

305 compliment ceremony   **306 hit** agree   **307–8 If ... offend us** If
our father continues to boss us around with his accustomed imperi-
ousness, this most recent display of willfulness will do us nothing but
harm.   **310 i'th' heat** i.e., while the iron is hot.
1.2. Location: The Earl of Gloucester's house.
1 Nature i.e., the sanction that governs the material world through
mechanistic amoral forces   **3 Stand ... custom** submit to the vexa-
tious injustice of convention   **4 The curiosity of nations** arbitrary
social gradations   **5 For that** because.   **moonshines** months
6 Lag of lagging behind   **7 dimensions** proportions.   **compact** knit
together, fitted   **8 generous** noble, refined   **9 honest** chaste
11–12 Who ... quality Whose begetting in the sexual act both
requires and engenders a fuller mixture and more energetic force
14 fops fools   **15 Got** begotten   **19 speed** succeed, prosper
20 invention thrive scheme prosper   **24 tonight** last night.
Prescribed Limited   **25 exhibition** an allowance, pension.
26 Upon the gad suddenly, as if pricked by a gad or spur.

33–4 terrible dispatch fearful quick disposal   **38 for** as for   **40 o'erlooking** perusal.   **43 to blame** (The Folio reading, "too blame," "too
blameworthy to be shown," may be correct.)   **46 essay or taste** assay,
test   **47 policy and reverence of** policy of reverencing   **48 the best ...
times** the best years of our lives, i.e., our youth   **50 idle and fond**
useless and foolish   **51 who sways** which rules   **52 suffered** permitted.   **59 to this** upon this (letter).   **61 casement** window   **62 closet**
private room.   **63 character** handwriting   **65 matter** contents   **66 in
... that** considering what the contents are.   **fain** gladly   **74 fit** fitting, appropriate.   **perfect age** full maturity   **75 declined** having
become feeble

GLOUCESTER   Oh, villain, villain! His very opinion in the 77
letter! Abhorred villain! Unnatural, detested, brutish 78
villain! Worse than brutish! Go, sirrah, seek him. I'll 79
apprehend him. Abominable villain! Where is he?

EDMUND   I do not well know, my lord. If it shall please
you to suspend your indignation against my brother
till you can derive from him better testimony of his
intent, you should run a certain course; where, if you 84
violently proceed against him, mistaking his purpose,
it would make a great gap in your own honor and
shake in pieces the heart of his obedience. I dare pawn 87
down my life for him that he hath writ this to feel my 88
affection to Your Honor, and to no other pretense of 89
danger. 90

GLOUCESTER   Think you so?

EDMUND   If Your Honor judge it meet, I will place you 92
where you shall hear us confer of this, and by an 93
auricular assurance have your satisfaction, and that 94
without any further delay than this very evening.

GLOUCESTER   He cannot be such a monster—

EDMUND   Nor is not, sure.

GLOUCESTER   To his father, that so tenderly and entirely loves him. Heaven and earth! Edmund, seek
him out; wind me into him, I pray you. Frame the 100
business after your own wisdom. I would unstate 101
myself to be in a due resolution. 102

EDMUND   I will seek him, sir, presently, convey the 103
business as I shall find means, and acquaint you
withal. 105

GLOUCESTER   These late eclipses in the sun and moon 106
portend no good to us. Though the wisdom of nature 107
can reason it thus and thus, yet nature finds itself
scourged by the sequent effects. Love cools, friend- 109
ship falls off, brothers divide; in cities, mutinies; in
countries, discord; in palaces, treason; and the bond
cracked twixt son and father. This villain of mine
comes under the prediction; there's son against father.
The King falls from bias of nature; there's father 114
against child. We have seen the best of our time.
Machinations, hollowness, treachery, and all ruinous
disorders follow us disquietly to our graves. Find out
this villain, Edmund; it shall lose thee nothing. Do it 118
carefully. And the noble and truehearted Kent banished! His offense, honesty! 'Tis strange.   *Exit.*

EDMUND   This is the excellent foppery of the world, that 121

when we are sick in fortune—often the surfeits of our 122
own behavior—we make guilty of our disasters the 123
sun, the moon, and stars, as if we were villains on 124
necessity, fools by heavenly compulsion, knaves,
thieves, and treachers by spherical predominance, 126
drunkards, liars, and adulterers by an enforced obedience of planetary influence, and all that we are evil
in, by a divine thrusting on. An admirable evasion of 129
whoremaster man, to lay his goatish disposition on 130
the charge of a star! My father compounded with my 131
mother under the Dragon's tail and my nativity was 132
under Ursa Major, so that it follows I am rough and 133
lecherous. Fut, I should have been that I am, had the 134
maidenliest star in the firmament twinkled on my
bastardizing. Edgar—

Enter Edgar.

and pat he comes like the catastrophe of the old 137
comedy. My cue is villainous melancholy, with a sigh
like Tom o' Bedlam.—Oh, these eclipses do portend 139
these divisions! Fa, sol, la, mi. 140

EDGAR   How now, brother Edmund, what serious
contemplation are you in?

EDMUND   I am thinking, brother, of a prediction I read
this other day, what should follow these eclipses. 144

EDGAR   Do you busy yourself with that?

EDMUND   I promise you, the effects he writes of succeed 146
unhappily, as of unnaturalness between the child and 147
the parent, death, dearth, dissolutions of ancient amities, divisions in state, menaces and maledictions
against king and nobles, needless diffidences, banish- 150
ment of friends, dissipation of cohorts, nuptial 151
breaches, and I know not what.

EDGAR   How long have you been a sectary astronom- 153
ical? 154

EDMUND   Come, come, when saw you my father last?

EDGAR   The night gone by.

EDMUND   Spake you with him?

EDGAR   Ay, two hours together.

EDMUND   Parted you in good terms? Found you no
displeasure in him by word nor countenance? 160

EDGAR   None at all.

---

77 **villain** vile wretch, diabolical schemer   78 **Abhorred** Abhorrent.
detested hated and hateful   79 **sirrah** (Form of address used to inferiors or children.)   84 **run a certain course** proceed with safety and
certainty.   **where** whereas   87–8 **pawn down** stake   88 **feel** feel out
89–90 **pretense of danger** dangerous purpose.   92 **meet** fitting,
proper   93–4 **by an . . . satisfaction** satisfy yourself as to the truth by
what you hear   100 **wind me into him** insinuate yourself into his
confidence. (*Me* is used colloquially.)   **Frame** Arrange   101 **after
your own wisdom** as you think best.   101–2 **I would . . . resolution** I
would give up my wealth and rank to know the truth, have my
doubts resolved.   103 **presently** immediately.   **convey** manage
105 **withal** therewith.   106 **late** recent   107 **the wisdom of nature**
natural science   109 **sequent effects** i.e., devastating consequences.
114 **bias of nature** natural inclination   118 **lose thee nothing** i.e.,
earn you a reward.   121 **foppery** foolishness

122–3 **surfeits . . . behavior** consequences of our own overindulgence
124 **on** by   126 **treachers** traitors.   **spherical predominance** astrological determinism, because a certain planet was ascendant at the
hour of our birth   129 **divine** supernatural   130 **goatish** lecherous
130–1 **on the charge** to the responsibility   131–2 **compounded . . .
Dragon's tail** had sex with my mother under the constellation Draco
(not one of the regular signs of the zodiac), or under the descending
point at which the moon's orbit intersects with the ecliptic or apparent orbit of the sun (when an eclipse might occur)   133 **Ursa Major**
the big bear or dipper—not one of the regular signs of the zodiac
134 **Fut** i.e., 'Sfoot, by Christ's foot.   **that** what   137 **pat** on cue.
catastrophe conclusion, resolution (of a play)   139 **Tom o' Bedlam** a
lunatic patient of Bethlehem Hospital in London turned out to beg for
his bread.   140 **divisions** social and family conflicts. (But with a
musical sense also of florid variations on a theme, thus prompting
Edmund's singing.)   144 **this other day** the other day   146 **promise**
assure   146–7 **succeed unhappily** follow unluckily   150 **needless
diffidences** groundless distrust of others   151 **dissipation of cohorts**
breaking up of military companies, large-scale desertions   153–4 **sectary astronomical** believer in astrology.   160 **countenance** demeanor.

EDMUND   Bethink yourself wherein you may have offended him, and at my entreaty forbear his presence 163
until some little time hath qualified the heat of his 164
displeasure, which at this instant so rageth in him that
with the mischief of your person it would scarcely 166
allay. 167

EDGAR   Some villain hath done me wrong.

EDMUND   That's my fear. I pray you, have a continent 169
forbearance till the speed of his rage goes slower; and, 170
as I say, retire with me to my lodging, from whence I
will fitly bring you to hear my lord speak. Pray ye, go! 172
There's my key. [*He gives a key.*] If you do stir abroad,
go armed.

EDGAR   Armed, brother?

EDMUND   Brother, I advise you to the best. I am no honest man if there be any good meaning toward you. I 177
have told you what I have seen and heard, but faintly, 178
nothing like the image and horror of it. Pray you, 179
away.

EDGAR   Shall I hear from you anon?

EDMUND
I do serve you in this business.   *Exit* [*Edgar*].
A credulous father and a brother noble,
Whose nature is so far from doing harms
That he suspects none; on whose foolish honesty
My practices ride easy. I see the business.   186
Let me, if not by birth, have lands by wit.   187
All with me's meet that I can fashion fit.   *Exit.* 188

❧

1.3

Enter Goneril, and [Oswald, her] steward.

GONERIL   Did my father strike my gentleman for chiding of his fool?

OSWALD   Ay, madam.

GONERIL   By day and night he wrongs me! Every hour
He flashes into one gross crime or other   5
That sets us all at odds. I'll not endure it.
His knights grow riotous, and himself upbraids us
On every trifle. When he returns from hunting
I will not speak with him. Say I am sick.
If you come slack of former services   10
You shall do well; the fault of it I'll answer.   11
          [*Horns within.*]

OSWALD   He's coming, madam. I hear him.

GONERIL
Put on what weary negligence you please,
You and your fellows. I'd have it come to question.   14
If he distaste it, let him to my sister,   15

Whose mind and mine, I know, in that are one,
Not to be overruled. Idle old man,   17
That still would manage those authorities   18
That he hath given away! Now, by my life,
Old fools are babes again, and must be used
With checks as flatteries, when they are seen abused.   21
Remember what I have said.

OSWALD   Well, madam.

GONERIL
And let his knights have colder looks among you.
What grows of it, no matter. Advise your fellows so.
I would breed from hence occasions, and I shall,   26
That I may speak. I'll write straight to my sister   27
To hold my very course. Prepare for dinner.   *Exeunt.*

1.4

Enter Kent [disguised].

KENT
If but as well I other accents borrow   1
That can my speech diffuse, my good intent   2
May carry through itself to that full issue   3
For which I razed my likeness. Now, banished Kent,   4
If thou canst serve where thou dost stand condemned,
So may it come thy master, whom thou lov'st,   6
Shall find thee full of labors.

*Horns within. Enter Lear, [Knights,] and
attendants.*

LEAR   Let me not stay a jot for dinner. Go get it ready.   8
          [*Exit an Attendant.*]
[*To Kent*] How now, what art thou?

KENT   A man, sir.

LEAR   What dost thou profess? What wouldst thou with 11
us?

KENT   I do profess to be no less than I seem: to serve
him truly that will put me in trust, to love him that is
honest, to converse with him that is wise and says 15
little, to fear judgment, to fight when I cannot choose, 16
and to eat no fish. 17

LEAR   What art thou?

KENT   A very honest-hearted fellow, and as poor as the
King.

---

163 **forbear his presence** avoid meeting him   164 **qualified** moder-
ated   166 **with . . . person** with the harmful effect of your presence;
or, even if there were injury done to you   167 **allay** be allayed.
169–70 **have . . . forbearance** keep a wary distance   172 **fitly** at a fit
time.   **my lord** our father   177 **meaning** intention   178 **but faintly**
only with a faint impression   179 **image and horror** horrid reality
186 **practices** plots.   **the business** i.e., how my plots should proceed.
187 **wit** cleverness.   188 **meet** justifiable.   **fit** to my purpose.
1.3. **Location:** The Duke of Albany's palace.
5 **crime** offense   10 **come slack** fall short   11 **answer** be answerable
for.   14 **come to question** be made an issue.   15 **distaste** dislike

17 **Idle** Foolish   18 **manage those authorities** exercise those prerogatives   21 **With . . . abused** with rebukes in place of flattering attentiveness, when such flattery is seen to be taken advantage of.
26 **occasions** opportunities for taking offense   27 **speak** speak
bluntly.   **straight** immediately
1.4. **Location:** The Duke of Albany's palace still. The sense of time
is virtually continuous.
1 **as well** i.e., as well as I have disguised myself by means of costume
2 **diffuse** render confused or indistinct   3–4 **May . . . likeness** may
achieve the desired result for which I scraped off my beard and
erased my outward appearance.   6 **come** come to pass that   8 **stay**
wait   8.1 *Attendant* (This attendant may be a knight; certainly the
one who speaks at line 50 is a knight.)   11 **What . . . profess?** What is
your special calling? (But Kent puns in his answer on *profess* meaning
to "claim.")   15 **honest** honorable.   **converse** associate   16 **judgment** i.e., God's judgment.   **choose** i.e., choose but to fight   17 **eat
no fish** i.e., eat a manly diet (?), be a good Protestant (?).

LEAR   If thou be'st as poor for a subject as he's for a
king, thou'rt poor enough. What wouldst thou?

KENT   Service.

LEAR   Who wouldst thou serve?

KENT   You.

LEAR   Dost thou know me, fellow?

KENT   No, sir, but you have that in your countenance 27
which I would fain call master.

LEAR   What's that?

KENT   Authority.

LEAR   What services canst do?

KENT   I can keep honest counsel, ride, run, mar a curi- 32
ous tale in telling it, and deliver a plain message 33
bluntly. That which ordinary men are fit for I am
qualified in, and the best of me is diligence.

LEAR   How old art thou?

KENT   Not so young, sir, to love a woman for singing, 37
nor so old to dote on her for anything. I have years on
my back forty-eight.

LEAR   Follow me; thou shalt serve me. If I like thee no
worse after dinner, I will not part from thee yet.—
Dinner, ho, dinner! Where's my knave, my fool? Go
you and call my fool hither.   [Exit one.]

Enter steward [Oswald].

You! You, sirrah, where's my daughter?

OSWALD   So please you—   Exit.

LEAR   What says the fellow there? Call the clodpoll back. 46
[Exit a knight.]

Where's my fool, ho? I think the world's asleep.

[Enter Knight.]

How now? Where's that mongrel?

KNIGHT   He says, my lord, your daughter is not well.

LEAR   Why came not the slave back to me when I called
him?

KNIGHT   Sir, he answered me in the roundest manner, 53
he would not.

LEAR   He would not?

KNIGHT   My lord, I know not what the matter is, but to
my judgment Your Highness is not entertained with 57
that ceremonious affection as you were wont. There's
a great abatement of kindness appears as well in the
general dependents as in the Duke himself also and 60
your daughter.

LEAR   Ha? Say'st thou so?

KNIGHT   I beseech you, pardon me, my lord, if I be
mistaken, for my duty cannot be silent when I think
Your Highness wronged.

LEAR   Thou but rememberest me of mine own concep- 66
tion. I have perceived a most faint neglect of late, 67
which I have rather blamed as mine own jealous 68

curiosity than as a very pretense and purpose of 69
unkindness. I will look further into't. But where's my
fool? I have not seen him this two days.   71

KNIGHT   Since my young lady's going into France, sir,
the Fool hath much pined away.

LEAR   No more of that. I have noted it well. Go you and
tell my daughter I would speak with her. [Exit one.]
Go you call hither my fool.   [Exit one.]

Enter steward [Oswald].

Oh, you, sir, you, come you hither, sir. Who am I, sir?

OSWALD   My lady's father.

LEAR   "My lady's father"? My lord's knave! You whoreson dog, you slave, you cur!

OSWALD   I am none of these, my lord, I beseech your
pardon.

LEAR   Do you bandy looks with me, you rascal?   83
[He strikes Oswald.]

OSWALD   I'll not be strucken, my lord.   84

KENT   Nor tripped neither, you base football player.   85
[He trips up Oswald's heels.]

LEAR   I thank thee, fellow. Thou serv'st me, and I'll love
thee.

KENT   Come, sir, arise, away! I'll teach you differences. 88
Away, away! If you will measure your lubber's length 89
again, tarry; but away! Go to. Have you wisdom? So. 90
[He pushes Oswald out.]

LEAR   Now, my friendly knave, I thank thee. There's
earnest of thy service.   [He gives Kent money.] 92

Enter Fool.

FOOL   Let me hire him too. Here's my coxcomb.   93
[Offering Kent his cap.]

LEAR   How now, my pretty knave, how dost thou?

FOOL [to Kent]   Sirrah, you were best take my coxcomb. 95

KENT   Why, Fool?

FOOL   Why? For taking one's part that's out of favor.
Nay, an thou canst not smile as the wind sits, thou'lt 98
catch cold shortly. There, take my coxcomb. Why, this 99
fellow has banished two on 's daughters and did the 100
third a blessing against his will. If thou follow him, thou 101
must needs wear my coxcomb.—How now, nuncle? 102
Would I had two coxcombs and two daughters.

LEAR   Why, my boy?

69 **very pretense** true intention   71 **this** these   83 **bandy looks**
exchange glances (in such a way as to imply that Oswald and Lear
are social equals)   84 **strucken** struck   85 **football** (A raucous street
game played by the lower classes.)   88 **differences** distinctions in
rank.   89–90 **If . . . again** i.e., If you want to be laid out flat again, you
clumsy ox   90 **Go to** (An expression of impatience or anger.)   **Have
you wisdom?** i.e., Wise up.   92 **earnest of** a first payment for
93 **coxcomb** fool's cap, crested with a red comb.   95 **you were best**
you had better   98–9 **an . . . shortly** i.e., if you can't play along with
those in power, you'll find yourself out in the cold.   100 **banished**
(Paradoxically, by giving Goneril and Regan his kingdom, Lear has
lost them, given them power over him.)   **on 's** of his   101 **blessing**
i.e., bestowing Cordelia on France and saving her from the curse of
insolent prosperity   102 **nuncle** (Contraction of "mine uncle," the
Fool's way of addressing Lear.)

27 **countenance** face and bearing   32 **keep honest counsel** respect
confidences   32–3 **curious** ornate, elaborate   37 **to love** as to love
46 **clodpoll** blockhead   53 **roundest** bluntest   57 **entertained** treated
60 **general dependents** servants generally   66 **rememberest** remind
66–7 **conception** idea, thought.   67 **faint** halfhearted   68–9 **jealous
curiosity** overscrupulous regard for matters of etiquette

FOOL If I gave them all my living, I'd keep my 105
coxcombs myself. There's mine; beg another of thy 106
daughters. 107

LEAR Take heed, sirrah—the whip.

FOOL Truth's a dog must to kennel. He must be
whipped out, when the Lady Brach may stand by th' 110
fire and stink.

LEAR A pestilent gall to me! 112

FOOL Sirrah, I'll teach thee a speech.

LEAR Do.

FOOL Mark it, nuncle:
Have more than thou showest, 116
Speak less than thou knowest,
Lend less than thou owest, 118
Ride more than thou goest, 119
Learn more than thou trowest, 120
Set less than thou throwest; 121
Leave thy drink and thy whore,
And keep in-a-door, 123
And thou shalt have more 124
Than two tens to a score. 125

KENT This is nothing, Fool.

FOOL Then 'tis like the breath of an unfee'd lawyer; you 127
gave me nothing for't. Can you make no use of nothing, nuncle?

LEAR Why, no, boy. Nothing can be made out of
nothing.

FOOL [to Kent] Prithee, tell him; so much the rent of his 132
land comes to. He will not believe a fool. 133

LEAR A bitter fool! 134

FOOL Dost know the difference, my boy, between a
bitter fool and a sweet one?

LEAR No, lad. Teach me.

FOOL
That lord that counseled thee
To give away thy land,
Come place him here by me;
Do thou for him stand. 141
The sweet and bitter fool
Will presently appear: 143
The one in motley here, 144
The other found out there. 145

LEAR Dost thou call me fool, boy?

FOOL All thy other titles thou hast given away; that
thou wast born with.

KENT This is not altogether fool, my lord.

FOOL No, faith, lords and great men will not let me; if 150
I had a monopoly out, they would have part on't. And 151
ladies too, they will not let me have all the fool to myself; they'll be snatching. Nuncle, give me an egg and 153
I'll give thee two crowns.

LEAR What two crowns shall they be?

FOOL Why, after I have cut the egg i'th' middle and eat 156
up the meat, the two crowns of the egg. When thou 157
clovest thy crown i'th' middle and gav'st away both
parts, thou bor'st thine ass on thy back o'er the dirt. 159
Thou hadst little wit in thy bald crown when thou
gav'st thy golden one away. If I speak like myself in 161
this, let him be whipped that first finds it so. 162
[Sings.] "Fools had ne'er less grace in a year, 163
For wise men are grown foppish 164
And know not how their wits to wear, 165
Their manners are so apish." 166

LEAR When were you wont to be so full of songs,
sirrah?

FOOL I have used it, nuncle, e'er since thou mad'st thy 169
daughters thy mothers; for when thou gav'st them the
rod and putt'st down thine own breeches,
[Sings] "Then they for sudden joy did weep,
And I for sorrow sung,
That such a king should play bo-peep 174
And go the fools among."
Prithee, nuncle, keep a schoolmaster that can teach
thy fool to lie. I would fain learn to lie.

LEAR An you lie, sirrah, we'll have you whipped. 178

FOOL I marvel what kin thou and thy daughters are.
They'll have me whipped for speaking true, thou'lt
have me whipped for lying, and sometimes I am
whipped for holding my peace. I had rather be any
kind o' thing than a fool. And yet I would not be thee,
nuncle. Thou hast pared thy wit o' both sides and left
nothing i'th' middle. Here comes one o' th' parings.

Enter Goneril.

LEAR
How now, daughter? What makes that frontlet on? 186
You are too much of late i'th' frown.

---

105 living property **105–6 keep my coxcombs** (as proof of my folly)
106–7 beg . . . daughters i.e., beg for the coxcomb that you deserve for
dealing with your daughters as you did. **110 Brach** bitch hound
(here likened to Goneril and Regan, who have been given favored
places despite their reeking of dishonest flattery) **112 gall** irritation,
bitterness—literally, a painful swelling, or bile. (Lear is stung by the
Fool's gibe because it is so true.) **116 Have . . . showest** don't display your wealth ostentatiously **118 owest** own **119 goest** i.e., on
foot. (Travel unostentatiously on horseback, not afoot.) **120 Learn**
i.e., listen to. **trowest** believe **121 Set . . . throwest** don't stake
everything on a single throw **123 in-a-door** indoors, at home
124–5 And . . . score and you will do better than break even (since a
score equals two tens, or twenty). **127 'tis . . . lawyer** i.e., it is free—
and useless—advice. (Lawyers, being proverbially mercenary, would
not give good advice unless paid well.) **132–3 so . . . to** (Because
Lear has given away his land, he can collect no rent.) **134 bitter**
satirical **141 Do . . . stand** take his place. **143 presently** immediately **144 motley** the parti-colored dress of the professional fool.
(The Fool identifies himself as the sweet fool, Lear as the bitter fool
who counseled himself to give away his kingdom.) **145 found out
there** discovered there. (The Fool points at Lear.)

150 No . . . let me i.e., Great persons at court will not let me monopolize folly; I am not *altogether fool* in the sense of being "all the fool
there is" **151 a monopoly out** a corner on the market. (The granting
of monopolies was a common abuse under King James and Queen
Elizabeth.) **on't** of it. **153 snatching** seizing their share (including
sexual pleasure). **156–7 and eat . . . meat** and have eaten the edible
part **159 bor'st . . . dirt** i.e., bore the ass instead of letting the ass
bear you. **161–2 If . . . so** If I speak like a fool in saying this, let the
first person to discover the truth of this be whipped (since in this corrupt world those who speak truth are punished for doing so).
163–6 "Fools . . . apish" "Fools have never been so out of favor, for
wise men foppishly trade places with the fools and no longer know
how to show off their wit to advantage, they have grown so foolish
in their manners." **169 used** practiced **174 bo-peep** (A child's
game.) **178 An** If **186 What . . . on?** What is that frown doing on
your forehead?

FOOL   Thou wast a pretty fellow when thou hadst no
need to care for her frowning; now thou art an O with- 189
out a figure. I am better than thou art now; I am a fool, 190
thou art nothing. [*To Goneril*] Yes, forsooth, I will
hold my tongue; so your face bids me, though you say
nothing.

      Mum, mum,
      He that keeps nor crust nor crumb,   195
      Weary of all, shall want some.   196
[*Pointing to Lear*] That's a shelled peascod.   197

GONERIL
Not only, sir, this your all-licensed fool,   198
But other of your insolent retinue
Do hourly carp and quarrel, breaking forth   200
In rank and not-to-be-endurèd riots. Sir,   201
I had thought by making this well known unto you
To have found a safe redress, but now grow fearful,   203
By what yourself too late have spoke and done,   204
That you protect this course and put it on   205
By your allowance; which if you should, the fault   206
Would not scape censure, nor the redresses sleep   207
Which in the tender of a wholesome weal   208
Might in their working do you that offense,   209
Which else were shame, that then necessity   210
Will call discreet proceeding.   211

FOOL   For you know, nuncle,
      "The hedge sparrow fed the cuckoo so long   213
      That it had it head bit off by it young."   214
So, out went the candle, and we were left darkling.   215

LEAR [*to Goneril*]   Are you our daughter?

GONERIL
I would you would make use of your good wisdom,
Whereof I know you are fraught, and put away   218
These dispositions which of late transport you   219
From what you rightly are.

FOOL   May not an ass know when the cart draws the 221
horse? Whoop, Jug! I love thee.   222

LEAR
Does any here know me? This is not Lear.
Does Lear walk thus, speak thus? Where are his eyes?
Either his notion weakens, or his discernings   225
Are lethargied—Ha! Waking? 'Tis not so.   226
Who is it that can tell me who I am?

FOOL   Lear's shadow.

LEAR
I would learn that; for, by the marks of sovereignty,   229
Knowledge, and reason, I should be false persuaded   230
I had daughters.   231

FOOL   Which they will make an obedient father.   232

LEAR   Your name, fair gentlewoman?

GONERIL
This admiration, sir, is much o'th' savor   234
Of other your new pranks. I do beseech you   235
To understand my purposes aright.
As you are old and reverend, should be wise.   237
Here do you keep a hundred knights and squires,
Men so disordered, so debauched and bold   239
That this our court, infected with their manners,
Shows like a riotous inn. Epicurism and lust   241
Makes it more like a tavern or a brothel
Than a graced palace. The shame itself doth speak   243
For instant remedy. Be then desired,   244
By her that else will take the thing she begs,
A little to disquantity your train,   246
And the remainders that shall still depend   247
To be such men as may besort your age,   248
Which know themselves and you.

LEAR   Darkness and devils! 249
Saddle my horses! Call my train together! [*Exit one.*] 250
Degenerate bastard, I'll not trouble thee.
Yet have I left a daughter.

GONERIL
You strike my people, and your disordered rabble
Make servants of their betters.

      Enter Albany.

LEAR
Woe, that too late repents!—Oh, sir, are you come?   255
Is it your will? Speak, sir.—Prepare my horses.
                  [*Exit one.*]
Ingratitude, thou marble-hearted fiend,
More hideous when thou show'st thee in a child
Than the sea monster!

ALBANY   Pray, sir, be patient.

LEAR [*to Goneril*]   Detested kite, thou liest!   261
My train are men of choice and rarest parts,   262
That all particulars of duty know
And in the most exact regard support   264
The worships of their name. Oh, most small fault,   265

189–90 **O without a figure** zero, cipher of no value unless preceded by
a digit.   195–6 **He . . . some** i.e., That person who, having grown weary
of his possessions, gives all away, will find himself in need of part of
what is gone.   196 **want** lack   197 **shelled peascod** shelled pea pod,
empty of its contents.   198 **all-licensed** allowed to speak or act as he
pleases   200 **carp** find fault   201 **rank** gross, excessive   203 **safe** certain   204 **too late** all too recently   205 **put it on** encourage it
206 **allowance** approval   207–11 **nor . . . proceeding** nor would the
punishments lie dormant which, out of care for the common welfare,
might prove unpleasant to you—proceedings that the stern necessity of
the times will regard as prudent even if under normal circumstances
they might seem shameful.   213 **cuckoo** a bird that lays its eggs in
other birds' nests   214 **it** its.   **it young** i.e., the young cuckoo. (A cautionary fable about ungrateful children.)   215 **darkling** in the dark.
218 **fraught** freighted, provided   219 **dispositions** inclinations, moods
221–2 **May . . . horse?** i.e., May not even a fool see that matters are
backwards when a daughter lectures her father?   222 **Jug** i.e., Joan.
(The origin of this phrase is uncertain.)   225 **notion** intellectual power
225–6 **or his . . . lethargied** or his faculties are asleep   226 **Waking?** i.e.,
Am I really awake?

229 **that** i.e., who I am.   **marks of sovereignty** outward and visible
evidence of being king   230–1 **I should . . . daughters** i.e., all these
outward signs of sanity and status would seem to suggest (falsely)
that I am the king who had obedient daughters.   232 **Which** Whom
234 **admiration** (guise of) wonderment   235 **other** other of
237 **should** i.e., you should   239 **Men . . . bold** men so disorderly, so
depraved and impudent   241 **Shows** appears.   **Epicurism** Excess,
hedonism   243 **graced** dignified   244 **desired** requested   246 **disquantity your train** diminish the number of your attendants   247 **the
remainders . . . depend** those who remain to attend you   248 **besort**
befit   249 **Which . . . you** servants who have proper self-knowledge
and an awareness of how they should serve you.   250 **train** retinue
255 **Woe, that** Woe to the person who   261 **kite** bird of prey
262 **parts** qualities   264–5 **And . . . name** and with utter scrupulous-
ness may uphold the honor of their reputation.

How ugly didst thou in Cordelia show!
Which, like an engine, wrenched my frame of nature 267
From the fixed place, drew from my heart all love, 268
And added to the gall. Oh, Lear, Lear, Lear! 269
Beat at this gate [*striking his head*] that let thy folly in
And thy dear judgment out!—Go, go, my people. 271

                  [*Exeunt some.*]

ALBANY
My lord, I am guiltless as I am ignorant
Of what hath moved you.
LEAR   It may be so, my lord.—
Hear, Nature, hear! Dear goddess, hear!
Suspend thy purpose if thou didst intend
To make this creature fruitful!
Into her womb convey sterility;
Dry up in her the organs of increase,
And from her derogate body never spring 279
A babe to honor her! If she must teem, 280
Create her child of spleen, that it may live 281
And be a thwart disnatured torment to her! 282
Let it stamp wrinkles in her brow of youth,
With cadent tears fret channels in her cheeks, 284
Turn all her mother's pains and benefits 285
To laughter and contempt, that she may feel
How sharper than a serpent's tooth it is
To have a thankless child! Away, away!

    Exit [*with Kent and the rest of Lear's followers*].

ALBANY
Now, gods that we adore, whereof comes this?
GONERIL
Never afflict yourself to know more of it, 290
But let his disposition have that scope 291
As dotage gives it. 292

     Enter Lear.

LEAR
What, fifty of my followers at a clap?
Within a fortnight?
ALBANY   What's the matter, sir?
LEAR
I'll tell thee. [*To Goneril*] Life and death! I am ashamed
That thou hast power to shake my manhood thus,
That these hot tears, which break from me perforce,
Should make thee worth them. Blasts and fogs upon
    thee! 298
Th'untented woundings of a father's curse 299
Pierce every sense about thee! Old fond eyes, 300
Beweep this cause again, I'll pluck ye out 301
And cast you, with the waters that you loose, 302

To temper clay. Yea, is't come to this? 303
Ha! Let it be so. I have another daughter,
Who, I am sure, is kind and comfortable. 305
When she shall hear this of thee, with her nails
She'll flay thy wolvish visage. Thou shalt find
That I'll resume the shape which thou dost think 308
I have cast off forever.   *Exit.*
GONERIL [*to Albany*]   Do you mark that? 309
ALBANY
I cannot be so partial, Goneril,
To the great love I bear you— 311
GONERIL
Pray you, content.—What, Oswald, ho!
[*To the Fool*] You, sir, more knave than fool, after your
    master.
FOOL   Nuncle Lear, nuncle Lear! Tarry, take the Fool 314
    with thee. 315
      A fox, when one has caught her,
      And such a daughter
      Should sure to the slaughter, 318
      If my cap would buy a halter. 319
      So the Fool follows after.   *Exit.*
GONERIL
This man hath had good counsel. A hundred knights? 321
'Tis politic and safe to let him keep 322
At point a hundred knights—yes, that on every
    dream, 323
Each buzz, each fancy, each complaint, dislike, 324
He may enguard his dotage with their powers 325
And hold our lives in mercy.—Oswald, I say! 326
ALBANY   Well, you may fear too far. 327
GONERIL   Safer than trust too far.
Let me still take away the harms I fear, 329
Not fear still to be taken. I know his heart. 330
What he hath uttered I have writ my sister.
If she sustain him and his hundred knights
When I have showed th'unfitness—

     Enter steward [*Oswald*].

                      How now, Oswald?
What, have you writ that letter to my sister?
OSWALD   Ay, madam.
GONERIL
Take you some company and away to horse.
Inform her full of my particular fear,
And thereto add such reasons of your own
As may compact it more. Get you gone, 339

267–8 **Which . . . place** which, like a powerful mechanical contrivance, wrenched my natural affection away from where it belonged   **269 gall** bitterness.   **271 dear** precious   **279 derogate** debased   **280 teem** produce offspring   **281 spleen** violent ill nature   **282 thwart disnatured** obstinate, perverse, and unnatural, unfilial   **284 cadent** cascading.   **fret** wear away   **285 benefits** pleasures of motherhood   **290 Never . . . know** Don't distress yourself by seeking to know   **291 disposition** humor, mood   **292 As** that   **298 Should . . . them** should seem to suggest that you are worth a king's tears. **Blasts and fogs** Infectious blights and disease-bearing fogs   **299 untented** too deep to be probed and cleansed   **300 fond** foolish   **301 Beweep** if you weep for   **302 loose** let loose (in tears)

303 **To temper clay** to mix with earth. (Lear threatens to cast both his eyes and their tears to the ground.)   **305 comfortable** comforting.   **308 the shape** i.e., the kingship   **309 Do . . . that?** i.e., Did you hear his threat to resume royal power?   **311 To** because of   **314–15 take . . . thee** (1) take me with you (2) take the name "fool" with you. (A stock phrase of taunting farewell.)   **318 Should sure** should certainly be sent   **319 halter** (1) rope for leading an animal (2) hangman's noose.   **321 This . . . counsel** (Said sarcastically.)   **322 politic** prudent. (Said ironically.)   **323 At point** armed and ready.   **dream** i.e., imagined wrong   **324 buzz** idle rumor   **325 enguard** protect   **326 in mercy** at his mercy.   **327 fear too far** overestimate the danger.   **329 still take away** always remove   **330 Not . . . taken** rather than dwell continually in the fear of being taken prisoner by such harms.   **339 compact** confirm

And hasten your return.   [*Exit Oswald.*]

No, no, my lord,

This milky gentleness and course of yours   341

Though I condemn not, yet, under pardon,   342

You're much more attasked for want of wisdom   343

Than praised for harmful mildness.   344

ALBANY

How far your eyes may pierce I cannot tell.   345

Striving to better, oft we mar what's well.

GONERIL   Nay, then—

ALBANY   Well, well, th'event.   *Exeunt.* 348

❦

1.5

Enter Lear, Kent [disguised as Caius], and Fool.

LEAR [*giving a letter to Kent*]   Go you before to Gloucester   1
with these letters. Acquaint my daughter no further   2
with anything you know than comes from her demand   3
out of the letter. If your diligence be not speedy, I shall   4
be there afore you.

KENT   I will not sleep, my lord, till I have delivered your
letter.   *Exit.*

FOOL   If a man's brains were in 's heels, were't not in   8
danger of kibes?   9

LEAR   Ay, boy.

FOOL   Then, I prithee, be merry. Thy wit shall not go   11
slipshod.   12

LEAR   Ha, ha, ha!

FOOL   Shalt see thy other daughter will use thee kindly,   14
for though she's as like this as a crab's like an apple,   15
yet I can tell what I can tell.

LEAR   What canst tell, boy?

FOOL   She will taste as like this as a crab does to a crab.
Thou canst tell why one's nose stands i'th' middle
on 's face?   20

LEAR   No.

FOOL   Why, to keep one's eyes of either side 's nose,   22
that what a man cannot smell out he may spy into.

LEAR   I did her wrong.   24

FOOL   Canst tell how an oyster makes his shell?

LEAR   No.

FOOL   Nor I neither. But I can tell why a snail has a
house.

LEAR   Why?

FOOL   Why, to put 's head in, not to give it away to his   30
daughters and leave his horns without a case.   31

LEAR   I will forget my nature. So kind a father!—Be my   32
horses ready?

FOOL   Thy asses are gone about 'em. The reason why   34
the seven stars are no more than seven is a pretty   35
reason.

LEAR   Because they are not eight.

FOOL   Yes, indeed. Thou wouldst make a good fool.

LEAR   To take't again perforce! Monster ingratitude!   39

FOOL   If thou wert my fool, nuncle, I'd have thee beaten
for being old before thy time.

LEAR   How's that?

FOOL   Thou shouldst not have been old till thou hadst
been wise.

LEAR

Oh, let me not be mad, not mad, sweet heaven!

Keep me in temper; I would not be mad!   46

[*Enter Gentleman.*]

How now, are the horses ready?

GENTLEMAN   Ready, my lord.

LEAR   Come, boy.   [*Exeunt Lear and Gentleman.*]

FOOL

She that's a maid now, and laughs at my departure,

Shall not be a maid long, unless things be cut

shorter.   *Exit.* 51

❦

2.1

Enter Bastard [Edmund] and Curan, severally.

EDMUND   Save thee, Curan.   1

CURAN   And you, sir. I have been with your father and
given him notice that the Duke of Cornwall and Regan
his duchess will be here with him this night.

EDMUND   How comes that?

CURAN   Nay, I know not. You have heard of the news
abroad—I mean the whispered ones, for they are yet   7
but ear-kissing arguments?   8

EDMUND   Not I. Pray you, what are they?

CURAN   Have you heard of no likely wars toward twixt   10
the Dukes of Cornwall and Albany?

EDMUND   Not a word.

CURAN   You may do, then, in time. Fare you well, sir.

       Exit.

---

341 milky . . . course effeminate and gentle way   **342 under pardon**
if you'll excuse my saying so   **343 attasked** taken to task for, blamed
344 harmful mildness mildness that causes harm.   **345 pierce** i.e.,
see into matters   **348 th'event** i.e., time will tell.
1.5. Location: Before Albany's palace.
1 Gloucester i.e., the place in Gloucestershire   **2 these letters** this letter.   **3 demand** inquiry   **4 out of** prompted by   **8–9 were't . . .
kibes?** wouldn't his brains be in danger of that common affliction of
the heel called chilblains?   **11–12 Thy wit . . . slipshod** i.e., Your
brains would have no need for slippers to avoid chafing the
chilblains, since you have no brains. (Anyone who journeys to Regan
in hopes of kind treatment is utterly brainless.)   **14 Shalt** Thou shalt.
kindly (1) with filial kindness (2) according to her own nature
15 crab crab apple   **20 on 's** of his   **22 of either side 's** on either side
of his   **24 her** i.e., Cordelia

30–1 Why, to . . . case i.e., The snail's head and horns are unendan-
gered with its *case* or shell; Lear, conversely, has given away his
crown to his daughters, leaving his brows unadorned and vulnerable.
(With a suggestion too of the cuckold's horned head, as though
Lear's victimization had a sexual dimension.)   **32 nature** natural
affection. (Compare line 14 and note.)   **34 Thy . . . 'em** i.e., Your servants (who labor like asses in your service) have gone about readying
the horses.   **35 seven stars** Pleiades   **39 To take't . . . perforce!** i.e.,
To think that Goneril would forcibly take back again the privileges
guaranteed to me! (Or perhaps Lear is meditating an armed restoration of his monarchy.)   **46 temper** mental equilibrium
51 things i.e., penises.   **cut shorter** (A bawdy joke addressed to the
audience.)
2.1 Location: The Earl of Gloucester's house.
0.1 *severally* separately.   **1 Save** God save   **7 abroad** going the
rounds.   **ones** i.e., the news, regarded as plural   **8 ear-kissing arguments** lightly whispered topics.   **10 toward** impending

EDMUND
The Duke be here tonight? The better! Best!   14
This weaves itself perforce into my business.
My father hath set guard to take my brother,
And I have one thing, of a queasy question,   17
Which I must act. Briefness and fortune, work!—   18
Brother, a word. Descend. Brother, I say!

     Enter Edgar.

My father watches. Oh, sir, fly this place!
Intelligence is given where you are hid.
You have now the good advantage of the night.
Have you not spoken 'gainst the Duke of Cornwall?
He's coming hither, now, i'th' night, i'th' haste,   24
And Regan with him. Have you nothing said
Upon his party 'gainst the Duke of Albany?   26
Advise yourself.
EDGAR   I am sure on't, not a word.   27
EDMUND
I hear my father coming. Pardon me;
In cunning I must draw my sword upon you.
Draw. Seem to defend yourself. Now, quit you well.—
                   [They draw.]   30
Yield! Come before my father!—Light, ho, here!—   31
Fly, brother.—Torches, torches!—So, farewell.   32
                Exit Edgar.
Some blood drawn on me would beget opinion   33
Of my more fierce endeavor. I have seen drunkards   34
Do more than this in sport. *[He wounds himself in the
    arm.]* Father, father!
Stop, stop! No help?

     Enter Gloucester, and servants with torches.

GLOUCESTER   Now, Edmund, where's the villain?
EDMUND
Here stood he in the dark, his sharp sword out,
Mumbling of wicked charms, conjuring the moon
To stand 's auspicious mistress.
GLOUCESTER   But where is he?   39
EDMUND
Look, sir, I bleed.
GLOUCESTER   Where is the villain, Edmund?
EDMUND
Fled this way, sir. When by no means he could—
GLOUCESTER   Pursue him, ho! Go after.
              [Exeunt some servants.]
             By no means what?
EDMUND
Persuade me to the murder of Your Lordship,
But that I told him the revenging gods   44

'Gainst parricides did all the thunder bend,   45
Spoke with how manifold and strong a bond
The child was bound to th' father; sir, in fine,   47
Seeing how loathly opposite I stood   48
To his unnatural purpose, in fell motion   49
With his preparèd sword he charges home   50
My unprovided body, latched mine arm;   51
And when he saw my best alarumed spirits,   52
Bold in the quarrel's right, roused to th'encounter, 53
Or whether ghasted by the noise I made,   54
Full suddenly he fled.
GLOUCESTER   Let him fly far.   55
Not in this land shall he remain uncaught;
And found—dispatch. The noble Duke my master,   57
My worthy arch and patron, comes tonight.   58
By his authority I will proclaim it
That he which finds him shall deserve our thanks,
Bringing the murderous coward to the stake;   61
He that conceals him, death.
EDMUND
When I dissuaded him from his intent
And found him pight to do it, with curst speech   64
I threatened to discover him. He replied,   65
"Thou unpossessing bastard, dost thou think,   66
If I would stand against thee, would the reposal   67
Of any trust, virtue, or worth in thee
Make thy words faithed? No. What I should deny—   69
As this I would, ay, though thou didst produce
My very character—I'd turn it all   71
To thy suggestion, plot, and damnèd practice;   72
And thou must make a dullard of the world   73
If they not thought the profits of my death   74
Were very pregnant and potential spirits   75
To make thee seek it."
GLOUCESTER   Oh, strange and fastened villain! 76
Would he deny his letter, said he?
I never got him.   *Tucket within.* 78
Hark, the Duke's trumpets! I know not why he comes.
All ports I'll bar; the villain shall not scape.   80
The Duke must grant me that. Besides, his picture   81
I will send far and near, that all the kingdom
May have due note of him; and of my land,

---

14 The better! Best! So much the better; in fact, the best that could happen!   **17 queasy question** matter not for queasy stomachs   **18 Briefness and fortune** Expeditious dispatch and good luck   **24 i'th' haste** in great haste   **26 Upon his party** i.e., recklessly on Cornwall's behalf (? It would be dangerous to speak on either side.)   **27 Advise yourself** Consider your situation.   **on't** of it   **30 quit you** defend, acquit yourself   **31–2 Yield . . . farewell** (Edmund speaks loudly as though trying to arrest Edgar, calls for others to help, and privately bids Edgar to flee.)   **33–4 beget . . . endeavor** create an impression of my having fought fiercely.   **39 stand 's** stand his, act as his   **44 that** when

45 bend aim   **47 in fine** in conclusion   **48 loathly opposite** loathingly opposed   **49 fell motion** deadly thrust   **50 preparèd** unsheathed and ready.   **home** to the very heart   **51 unprovided** unprotected.   **latched** nicked, lanced   **52 best alarumed** thoroughly aroused to action, as by a trumpet   **53 quarrel's right** justice of the cause   **54 ghasted** frightened   **55 Let him fly far** i.e., Any fleeing, no matter how far, will be in vain.   **57 dispatch** i.e., that will be the end for him.   **58 arch and patron** chief patron   **61 to the stake** i.e., to reckoning   **64 pight** determined.   **curst** angry   **65 discover** expose   **66 unpossessing** unable to inherit, beggarly   **67 reposal** placing   **69 faithed** believed.   **What** That which, whatever   **71 character** written testimony, handwriting.   **turn** attribute   **72 suggestion** instigation.   **practice** scheming   **73–6 And . . . seek it** and you must think everyone slow-witted indeed not to suppose that they would see how the profits to be gained by my death would be fertile and potent tempters to make you seek my death.   **76 strange and fastened** unnatural and hardened   **78 got** begot.   **s.d. *Tucket*** series of notes on the trumpet, here indicating Cornwall's arrival   **80 ports** seaports, or gateways   **81 picture** description

Loyal and natural boy, I'll work the means   84
To make thee capable.   85

Enter Cornwall, Regan, and attendants.

CORNWALL
How now, my noble friend? Since I came hither,
Which I can call but now, I have heard strange news.
REGAN
If it be true, all vengeance comes too short
Which can pursue th'offender. How dost, my lord?
GLOUCESTER
Oh madam, my old heart is cracked, it's cracked!
REGAN
What, did my father's godson seek your life?
He whom my father named? Your Edgar?
GLOUCESTER
Oh, lady, lady, shame would have it hid!
REGAN
Was he not companion with the riotous knights
That tended upon my father?
GLOUCESTER
I know not, madam. 'Tis too bad, too bad.
EDMUND
Yes, madam, he was of that consort.   97
REGAN
No marvel, then, though he were ill affected.   98
'Tis they have put him on the old man's death,   99
To have th'expense and spoil of his revenues.   100
I have this present evening from my sister
Been well informed of them, and with such cautions
That if they come to sojourn at my house
I'll not be there.
CORNWALL   Nor I, assure thee, Regan.
Edmund, I hear that you have shown your father
A childlike office.
EDMUND   It was my duty, sir.   106
GLOUCESTER [*to Cornwall*]
He did bewray his practice, and received   107
This hurt you see striving to apprehend him.   108
CORNWALL   Is he pursued?
GLOUCESTER   Ay, my good lord.
CORNWALL
If he be taken, he shall never more
Be feared of doing harm. Make your own purpose,   112
How in my strength you please. For you, Edmund,   113
Whose virtue and obedience doth this instant
So much commend itself, you shall be ours.
Natures of such deep trust we shall much need;
You we first seize on.
EDMUND   I shall serve you, sir,
Truly, however else.   118
GLOUCESTER   For him I thank Your Grace.

CORNWALL
You know not why we came to visit you—
REGAN
—Thus out of season, threading dark-eyed night:
Occasions, noble Gloucester, of some poise,   122
Wherein we must have use of your advice.
Our father he hath writ, so hath our sister,
Of differences, which I least thought it fit   125
To answer from our home. The several messengers   126
From hence attend dispatch. Our good old friend,   127
Lay comforts to your bosom, and bestow
Your needful counsel to our businesses,
Which craves the instant use.   130
GLOUCESTER   I serve you, madam.
Your Graces are right welcome.   *Flourish. Exeunt.*

❖

2.2

*Enter Kent [disguised as Caius] and steward
[Oswald], severally.*

OSWALD   Good dawning to thee, friend. Art of this   1
house?
KENT   Ay.
OSWALD   Where may we set our horses?
KENT   I'th' mire.
OSWALD   Prithee, if thou lov'st me, tell me.   6
KENT   I love thee not.
OSWALD   Why then, I care not for thee.
KENT   If I had thee in Lipsbury pinfold, I would make 9
thee care for me.   10
OSWALD   Why dost thou use me thus? I know thee not.
KENT   Fellow, I know thee.   12
OSWALD   What dost thou know me for?
KENT   A knave, a rascal, an eater of broken meats;   14
a base, proud, shallow, beggarly, three-suited,   15
hundred-pound, filthy worsted-stocking knave; a   16
lily-livered, action-taking, whoreson, glass-gazing,   17
superserviceable, finical rogue; one-trunk-inheriting   18
slave; one that wouldst be a bawd in way of good ser-   19
vice, and art nothing but the composition of a knave,   20
beggar, coward, pander, and the son and heir of a

---

84 natural (1) prompted by natural feelings of loyalty and affection (2) bastard **85 capable** legally able to become the inheritor. **97 consort** crew. **98 though** if. **ill affected** ill-disposed, disloyal. **99 put him on** incited him to **100 th'expense and spoil** the squandering **106 childlike** filial **107 bewray his practice** expose his (Edgar's) plot **108 apprehend** arrest **112–13 Make . . . please** Go about achieving your purpose, making free use of my authority and resources. **113 For** As for **118 however else** above all else.

122 poise weight **125 differences** quarrels. **which** which letters **126 from our home** while still at our palace in Cornwall. **127 attend dispatch** wait to be dispatched. **130 the instant use** immediate attention.
2.2 Location: Before Gloucester's house.
0.1 *severally* at separate doors. **1 dawning** (It is not yet day.) **6 if thou lov'st me** i.e., if you bear good will toward me. (But Kent deliberately takes the phrase in its literal, not courtly, sense.) **9 in Lipsbury pinfold** i.e., within the pinfold of the lips, between my teeth. (A *pinfold* is a pound for stray animals.) **10 care for** i.e., be wary of. (Playing on *care not for*, "do not like," in line 8.) **12 I know thee** i.e., I know you for what you are. (Playing on *know thee not*, "am unacquainted with you," in line 11.) **14 broken meats** scraps of food (such as were passed out to the most lowly) **15–16 three-suited . . . knave** i.e., a steward of a household, with an allowance of three suits a year and a comfortable income of one hundred pounds, dressed in dirty wool stockings appropriate to the servant class **16–19 a lily-livered . . . slave** a cowardly, litigious, insufferable, self-infatuated, officious, foppish rogue, whose personal property all fits into one trunk **19–20 bawd . . . service** i.e., pimp or pander as a way of providing whatever is wanted **20 composition** compound

mongrel bitch; one whom I will beat into clamorous
whining if thou deny'st the least syllable of thy addi-   23
tion.   24

OSWALD   Why, what a monstrous fellow art thou thus
to rail on one that is neither known of thee nor knows
thee!

KENT   What a brazen-faced varlet art thou to deny thou
knowest me! Is it two days since I tripped up thy heels
and beat thee before the King? Draw, you rogue, for
though it be night, yet the moon shines. I'll make a
sop o'th' moonshine of you, you whoreson, cullionly   32
barbermonger. Draw!   [*He brandishes his sword.*]   33

OSWALD   Away! I have nothing to do with thee.

KENT   Draw, you rascal! You come with letters against
the King, and take Vanity the puppet's part against   36
the royalty of her father. Draw, you rogue, or I'll so
carbonado your shanks—draw, you rascal! Come   38
your ways.   39

OSWALD   Help, ho! Murder! Help!

KENT   Strike, you slave! Stand, rogue, stand, you neat   41
slave, strike!   [*He beats him.*]

OSWALD   Help, ho! Murder! Murder!

Enter Bastard [*Edmund, with his rapier
drawn*], *Cornwall, Regan, Gloucester, servants.*

EDMUND   How now, what's the matter? Part!   44

KENT   With you, goodman boy, an you please! Come,   45
I'll flesh ye. Come on, young master.   46

GLOUCESTER   Weapons? Arms? What's the matter here?

CORNWALL   Keep peace, upon your lives! [*Kent and
Oswald are parted.*] He dies that strikes again. What is
the matter?

REGAN   The messengers from our sister and the King.

CORNWALL   What's your difference? Speak.   52

OSWALD   I am scarce in breath, my lord.

KENT   No marvel, you have so bestirred your valor.
You cowardly rascal, nature disclaims in thee. A tailor   55
made thee.

CORNWALL   Thou art a strange fellow. A tailor make a
man?

KENT   A tailor, sir. A stonecutter or a painter could not
have made him so ill, though they had been but two
years o'th' trade.

CORNWALL   Speak yet, how grew your quarrel?

OSWALD   This ancient ruffian, sir, whose life I have
spared at suit of his gray beard—

KENT   Thou whoreson zed! Thou unnecessary letter!—   65
My lord, if you'll give me leave, I will tread this un-   66
bolted villain into mortar and daub the wall of a jakes   67
with him.—Spare my gray beard, you wagtail?   68

CORNWALL   Peace, sirrah!
You beastly knave, know you no reverence?

KENT
Yes, sir, but anger hath a privilege.

CORNWALL   Why art thou angry?

KENT
That such a slave as this should wear a sword,
Who wears no honesty. Such smiling rogues as these,
Like rats, oft bite the holy cords atwain   75
Which are too intrinse t'unloose; smooth every
passion   76
That in the natures of their lords rebel,   77
Bring oil to fire, snow to their colder moods,   78
Renege, affirm, and turn their halcyon beaks   79
With every gale and vary of their masters,   80
Knowing naught, like dogs, but following.—   81
A plague upon your epileptic visage!   82
Smile you my speeches, as I were a fool?   83
Goose, an I had you upon Sarum plain,   84
I'd drive ye cackling home to Camelot.   85

CORNWALL   What, art thou mad, old fellow?

GLOUCESTER   How fell you out? Say that.

KENT
No contraries hold more antipathy
Than I and such a knave.

CORNWALL
Why dost thou call him knave? What is his fault?

KENT   His countenance likes me not.   91

CORNWALL
No more, perchance, does mine, nor his, nor hers.

KENT
Sir, 'tis my occupation to be plain:
I have seen better faces in my time
Than stands on any shoulder that I see
Before me at this instant.

CORNWALL   This is some fellow
Who, having been praised for bluntness, doth affect   97

23–4 thy addition the titles I've given you.   **32 sop o'th' moonshine**
something so perforated that it will soak up moonshine as a sop
(floating piece of toast) soaks up liquor   **32–3 cullionly barbermonger** base frequenter of barber shops, fop. (*Cullion* originally meant
"testicle.")   **36 Vanity . . . part** i.e., the part of Goneril (here personified as a character in a morality play)   **38 carbonado** cut crosswise,
like meat for broiling   **38–9 Come your ways** Come on.   **41 neat**
(1) foppish (2) calflike. (*Neat* means "horned cattle.")   **44 matter** i.e.,
trouble. (But Kent takes the meaning "cause for quarrel.")   **45 With
you** I'll fight with you; my quarrel is with you.   **goodman boy** (A
contemptuous epithet, a title of mock respect, addressed seemingly to
Edmund.)   **an** if   **46 flesh** initiate into combat   **52 difference** quarrel.   **55 disclaims in** disowns

65 zed the letter z (regarded as unnecessary and often not included in
dictionaries of the time).   **66–7 unbolted** unsifted; hence, coarse
67 daub plaster.   **jakes** privy   **68 wagtail** i.e., bird wagging its tail
feathers in pert obsequiousness.   **75 holy cords** sacred bonds of loyalty and order   **76 intrinse** intricate, tightly knotted.   **smooth** flatter,
humor   **77 rebel** rebel against reason   **78 Bring . . . moods** flatteringly fuel the flame of their masters' angry passions, while similarly
exacerbating their downward mood swings   **79 Renege, affirm** nay-
say one moment (when their lords are in a denying mood) and serve
as yes-men the next.   **halcyon beaks** (The halcyon or kingfisher, if
hung up, would supposedly turn its beak into the wind.)   **80 gale
and vary** shifting wind   **81 following** fawning and flattery.   **82
epileptic** i.e., trembling and pale with fright and distorted with a grin
83 Smile you Do you smile at.   **as** as if   **84–5 Goose . . . Camelot**
(The reference is obscure, but the general sense is that Kent, if given
space and opportunity, would send Oswald packing like a cackling
goose. Camelot, the legendary seat of King Arthur and his Knights of
the Round Table, was thought to have been in the general vicinity of
Salisbury, Sarum, and Gloucester.)   **91 likes** pleases
97 affect adopt the style of

A saucy roughness, and constrains the garb   98
Quite from his nature. He cannot flatter, he;   99
An honest mind and plain, he must speak truth!
An they will take't, so; if not, he's plain.   101
These kind of knaves I know, which in this plainness
Harbor more craft and more corrupter ends
Than twenty silly-ducking observants   104
That stretch their duties nicely.   105

KENT
Sir, in good faith, in sincere verity,   106
Under th'allowance of your great aspect,   107
Whose influence, like the wreath of radiant fire   108
On flickering Phoebus' front—

CORNWALL   What mean'st by this?   109

KENT   To go out of my dialect, which you discommend
so much. I know, sir, I am no flatterer. He that be-   111
guiled you in a plain accent was a plain knave, which   112
for my part I will not be, though I should win your   113
displeasure to entreat me to't.   114

CORNWALL [to Oswald] What was th'offense you gave him?

OSWALD   I never gave him any.
It pleased the King his master very late   117
To strike at me, upon his misconstruction;   118
When he, compact, and flattering his displeasure,   119
Tripped me behind; being down, insulted, railed,   120
And put upon him such a deal of man   121
That worthied him, got praises of the King   122
For him attempting who was self-subdued;   123
And, in the fleshment of this dread exploit,   124
Drew on me here again.

KENT   None of these rogues and cowards   126
But Ajax is their fool.

CORNWALL   Fetch forth the stocks!   127

You stubborn, ancient knave, you reverend braggart,   128
We'll teach you.

KENT   Sir, I am too old to learn.
Call not your stocks for me. I serve the King,
On whose employment I was sent to you.
You shall do small respect, show too bold malice
Against the grace and person of my master,   133
Stocking his messenger.

CORNWALL
Fetch forth the stocks! As I have life and honor,
There shall he sit till noon.

REGAN
Till noon? Till night, my lord, and all night too.

KENT
Why, madam, if I were your father's dog
You should not use me so.   139

REGAN   Sir, being his knave, I will.   140

CORNWALL
This is a fellow of the selfsame color   141
Our sister speaks of.—Come, bring away the stocks!   142
                              Stocks brought out.

GLOUCESTER
Let me beseech Your Grace not to do so.
His fault is much, and the good King his master
Will check him for't. Your purposed low correction   145
Is such as basest and contemned'st wretches   146
For pilferings and most common trespasses
Are punished with. The King must take it ill
That he, so slightly valued in his messenger,
Should have him thus restrained.

CORNWALL   I'll answer that.   150

REGAN
My sister may receive it much more worse
To have her gentleman abused, assaulted,
For following her affairs. Put in his legs.
                              [Kent is put in the stocks.]
Come, my good lord, away.
                    Exeunt [all but Gloucester and Kent].

GLOUCESTER
I am sorry for thee, friend. 'Tis the Duke's pleasure,
Whose disposition, all the world well knows,
Will not be rubbed nor stopped. I'll entreat for thee.   157

KENT
Pray, do not, sir. I have watched and traveled hard.   158
Some time I shall sleep out; the rest I'll whistle.
A good man's fortune may grow out at heels.   160
Give you good morrow!   161

GLOUCESTER
The Duke's to blame in this. 'Twill be ill taken.   *Exit.*

98–9 constrains . . . nature i.e., distorts plainness quite from its true purpose so that it becomes instead a way of deceiving the listener. 99 He . . . he He professes to be one who abhors the use of flattering speech. (Said sardonically.)   101 An . . . plain If people will take his rudeness, fine; if not, his excuse is that he speaks plain truth. 104–5 Than . . . nicely than twenty foolishly bowing, obsequious courtiers who outdo themselves in the punctilious performance of their courtly duties.   106 Sir, in good faith (Kent assumes the wordy mannerisms of courtly flattery.)   107 th'allowance the approval. aspect (1) countenance (2) astrological position   108 influence astrological power   109 Phoebus' front i.e., the sun's forehead   111–14 He . . . to't The man who used plain speech to you craftily (see lines 102–5) and thereby taught you to suspect plain speakers of being deceitful was in fact a plain rascal, which part I will not play, much as it would please me to incur your displeasure if speaking thus would have that effect. (Kent would prefer to displease Cornwall, since Cornwell is pleased only by flatterers, and Kent has assumed until now that plain speech was the best way to offend, but he now argues mockingly that he can no longer speak plainly, since his honest utterance would be interpreted as duplicity.)   117 late recently   118 upon his misconstruction as a result of the King's misunderstanding (me)   119 When . . . displeasure whereupon Kent, in cahoots with the King and his party, and wishing to gratify the King's anger at me   120 being down, insulted when I was down, he exulted over me   121–2 And put . . . him and acted with a bravado that earned him an accolade   123 For . . . self-subdued for assailing me (i.e., myself) who chose not to resist   124 And . . . exploit and, in the excitement of his first success in this fearless deed. (Said ironically.)   126–7 None . . . fool i.e., You never find any rogues and cowards of this sort who do not outdo the blustering Ajax in their boasting.

128 reverend (because old)   133 grace sovereignty, royal grace 139 should would   140 being since you are   141 color complexion, character   142 away along   145 check rebuke, correct   146 contemned'st most despised   150 answer be answerable for 157 rubbed hindered, obstructed. (A term from bowls.) 158 watched gone sleepless   160 A . . . heels i.e., Even good men suffer decline in fortune at times. (To be out at heels is literally to be threadbare, coming through one's stockings.)   161 Give you i.e., God give you

KENT

    Good King, that must approve the common saw,   163
    Thou out of heaven's benediction com'st
    To the warm sun!   [*He takes out a letter.*]
    Approach, thou beacon to this under globe,   166
    That by thy comfortable beams I may   167
    Peruse this letter. Nothing almost sees miracles   168
    But misery. I know 'tis from Cordelia,   169
    Who hath most fortunately been informed
    Of my obscurèd course, "and shall find time   171
    From this enormous state, seeking to give   172
    Losses their remedies." All weary and o'erwatched,   173
    Take vantage, heavy eyes, not to behold   174
    This shameful lodging.   175
    Fortune, good night. Smile once more; turn thy wheel!   176
                 [*He sleeps.*]

[2.3]

Enter Edgar.

EDGAR   I heard myself proclaimed,
    And by the happy hollow of a tree   2
    Escaped the hunt. No port is free, no place   3
    That guard and most unusual vigilance   4
    Does not attend my taking. Whiles I may scape   5
    I will preserve myself, and am bethought   6
    To take the basest and most poorest shape
    That ever penury, in contempt of man,   8
    Brought near to beast. My face I'll grime with filth,
    Blanket my loins, elf all my hairs in knots,   10
    And with presented nakedness outface   11
    The winds and persecutions of the sky.
    The country gives me proof and precedent   13
    Of Bedlam beggars who with roaring voices   14
    Strike in their numbed and mortifièd arms   15
    Pins, wooden pricks, nails, sprigs of rosemary;   16
    And with this horrible object, from low farms,   17

    Poor pelting villages, sheepcotes, and mills,   18
    Sometimes with lunatic bans, sometimes with prayers,   19
    Enforce their charity. Poor Turlygod! Poor Tom!   20
    That's something yet. Edgar I nothing am.   *Exit.*   21

[2.4]

Enter Lear, Fool, and Gentleman.

LEAR

    'Tis strange that they should so depart from home   1
    And not send back my messenger.
GENTLEMAN   As I learned,
    The night before there was no purpose in them
    Of this remove.
KENT   Hail to thee, noble master!   4
LEAR   Ha?
    Mak'st thou this shame thy pastime?
KENT   No, my lord.
FOOL   Ha, ha, he wears cruel garters. Horses are tied by   7
    the heads, dogs and bears by th' neck, monkeys by
    th' loins, and men by th' legs. When a man's over-   9
    lusty at legs, then he wears wooden netherstocks.   10
LEAR

    What's he that hath so much thy place mistook
    To set thee here?
KENT   It is both he and she: 12
    Your son and daughter.
LEAR   No.
KENT   Yes.
LEAR   No, I say.
KENT   I say yea.
LEAR   No, no, they would not.
KENT   Yes, they have.
LEAR   By Jupiter, I swear no.
KENT

    By Juno, I swear ay.
LEAR   They durst not do't!
    They could not, would not do't. 'Tis worse than
       murder
    To do upon respect such violent outrage.   23
    Resolve me with all modest haste which way   24
    Thou mightst deserve, or they impose, this usage,
    Coming from us.

---

163 approve prove true.   **saw** proverb (i.e., "To run out of God's blessing into the warm sun," meaning "to go from better to worse," from a state of bliss into the pitiless world. Kent sees Lear as heading for trouble.)   **166 beacon . . . globe** i.e., the sun. (Daylight is coming soon.)   **167 comfortable** comforting   **168–9 Nothing . . . misery** Scarcely anything can make one appreciate miracles like being in a state of misery; to the miserable, any relief seems miraculous.
171 obscurèd disguised   **171–3 "and shall . . . remedies"** i.e., "and who, in the fullness of time, will bring relief from the monstrous state of affairs under which we suffer, seeking to remedy what has been destroyed." (The passage may be corrupt. Kent may be reading from his letter.)   **173 o'erwatched** exhausted with staying awake
174 vantage advantage (of sleep)   **175 lodging** i.e., the stocks.
176 wheel (Since Kent is at the bottom of Fortune's wheel, any turning should improve his situation.)
2.3 Location: Scene continues. Kent is dozing in the stocks.
2 happy luckily found   **3 port** (See 2.1.80 and note.)   **4 That** in which   **5 attend my taking** lie in wait to capture me.   **6 bethought** resolved   **8 in . . . man** in order to show how contemptible humankind is   **10 elf** tangle into elflocks   **11 presented** exposed to view, displayed   **13 proof** example   **14 Bedlam** (See the note to 1.2.139.)   **15 Strike** stick.   **mortifièd** deadened   **16 wooden pricks** skewers   **17 object** spectacle.   **low** lowly

18 pelting paltry   **19 bans** curses   **20 Enforce their charity** manage to beg something.   **Poor . . . Tom** (Edgar practices the begging role he is about to adopt. Beggars were known as "poor Toms.")
Turlygod (Meaning unknown.)   **21 That's . . . am** There's some kind of existence for me as poor Tom. I am Edgar no longer.
2.4 Location: Scene continues before Gloucester's house. Kent still dozing in the stocks.
1 they Cornwall and Regan   **4 remove** change of residence.   **7 cruel** (1) unkind (2) crewel (compare the Quarto spelling, "crewell"), a thin yarn of which hose were made   **9–10 overlusty at legs** given to running away, or overly active sexually   **10 netherstocks** stockings.
12 To as to   **23 upon respect** i.e., against my officers (who deserve respect)   **24 Resolve** Enlighten.   **modest** moderate

KENT   My lord, when at their home   26
I did commend Your Highness' letters to them,   27
Ere I was risen from the place that showed   28
My duty kneeling, came there a reeking post,   29
Stewed in his haste, half breathless, panting forth   30
From Goneril his mistress salutations;
Delivered letters, spite of intermission,   32
Which presently they read; on whose contents   33
They summoned up their meiny, straight took horse,   34
Commanded me to follow and attend
The leisure of their answer, gave me cold looks;
And meeting here the other messenger,
Whose welcome, I perceived, had poisoned mine—
Being the very fellow which of late
Displayed so saucily against Your Highness—   40
Having more man than wit about me, drew.   41
He raised the house with loud and coward cries.
Your son and daughter found this trespass worth
The shame which here it suffers.

FOOL   Winter's not gone yet if the wild geese fly that   45
way.   46
        Fathers that wear rags
            Do make their children blind,   48
        But fathers that bear bags   49
            Shall see their children kind.
        Fortune, that arrant whore,
        Ne'er turns the key to th' poor.   52
But, for all this, thou shalt have as many dolors for thy   53
daughters as thou canst tell in a year.   54

LEAR
Oh, how this mother swells up toward my heart!   55
Hysterica passio, down, thou climbing sorrow!   56
Thy element's below.—Where is this daughter?   57

KENT   With the Earl, sir, here within.

LEAR   Follow me not. Stay here.   *Exit.*

GENTLEMAN
Made you no more offense but what you speak of?

KENT   None.
How chance the King comes with so small a number?   62

FOOL   An thou hadst been set i'th' stocks for that ques-   63
tion, thou'dst well deserved it.

KENT   Why, Fool?

FOOL   We'll set thee to school to an ant to teach thee   66
there's no laboring i'th' winter. All that follow their   67
noses are led by their eyes but blind men, and there's   68
not a nose among twenty but can smell him that's   69
stinking. Let go thy hold when a great wheel runs   70
down a hill lest it break thy neck with following; but
the great one that goes upward, let him draw thee after. When a wise man gives thee better counsel, give
me mine again. I would have none but knaves follow
it, since a fool gives it.
        That sir which serves and seeks for gain,
            And follows but for form,
        Will pack when it begins to rain   78
            And leave thee in the storm.
        But I will tarry; the fool will stay,
            And let the wise man fly.
        The knave turns fool that runs away;   82
            The fool no knave, pardie.   83

Enter Lear and Gloucester.

KENT   Where learned you this, Fool?
FOOL   Not i'th' stocks, fool.
LEAR
Deny to speak with me? They are sick? They are
    weary?
They have traveled all the night? Mere fetches,   87
The images of revolt and flying off.   88
Fetch me a better answer.
GLOUCESTER   My dear lord,
You know the fiery quality of the Duke,
How unremovable and fixed he is
In his own course.
LEAR
Vengeance! Plague! Death! Confusion!   93
Fiery? What quality? Why, Gloucester, Gloucester,
I'd speak with the Duke of Cornwall and his wife.
GLOUCESTER
Well, my good lord, I have informed them so.
LEAR
Informed them? Dost thou understand me, man?
GLOUCESTER   Ay, my good lord.
LEAR
The King would speak with Cornwall. The dear father
Would with his daughter speak, commands, tends
    service.   100
Are they informed of this? My breath and blood!   101
Fiery? The fiery Duke? Tell the hot Duke that—
No, but not yet. Maybe he is not well.
Infirmity doth still neglect all office   104
Whereto our health is bound; we are not ourselves   105

26 their home (Kent and Oswald went first to Cornwall's palace after leaving Albany's palace.)   **27 commend** deliver   **28–9 from . . . kneeling** from the kneeling posture that showed my duty   **29 reeking** steaming (with heat of travel)   **30 Stewed** i.e., thoroughly heated, soaked   **32 spite of intermission** in disregard of interrupting me, or, in spite of the interruptions caused by his being out of breath   **33 presently** instantly.   **on** on the basis of   **34 meiny** retinue of servants, household   **40 Displayed so saucily** behaved so insolently   **41 more man than wit** more courage than good sense   **45–6 Winter's . . . way** i.e., The signs still point to continued and worsening fortune; the wild geese are still flying south.   **48 blind** i.e., indifferent to their father's needs   **49 bags** i.e., of gold   **52 turns the key** opens the door   **53 dolors** griefs. (With pun on "dollars," English word for an Austrian or Spanish coin.)   **for** (1) on account of (2) in exchange for   **54 tell** (1) relate (2) count   **55, 56 mother,** *Hysterica passio* i.e., hysteria, giving the sensation of choking or suffocating   **57 element's** proper place is. (Hysteria, from the Greek *hystera*, womb, was thought to be produced by vapors ascending from the uterus or abdomen.)   **62 chance** chances it   **63 An** If

66–7 We'll . . . winter i.e., Just as the ant knows not to labor in the winter, the wise man knows not to labor for one whose fortunes are fallen.   **67–70 All . . . stinking** i.e., One who is out of favor can be easily detected (he smells of misfortune) and so is easily avoided by timeservers.   **78 pack** be off   **82 The knave . . . away** i.e., Deserting one's master is the greatest folly   **83 pardie** *par Dieu* (French), "by God."   **87 fetches** pretexts, dodges   **88 images** signs.   **flying off** desertion.   **93 Confusion!** Destruction!   **100 tends** attends, waits for   **101 My . . . blood!** i.e., By my very life. (An oath.)   **104–5 Infirmity . . . bound** Sickness always prompts us to neglect all duties which in good health we are bound to perform

When nature, being oppressed, commands the mind
To suffer with the body. I'll forbear,
And am fallen out with my more headier will,   108
To take the indisposed and sickly fit   109
For the sound man. [*Looking at Kent*] Death on my
    state! Wherefore   110
Should he sit here? This act persuades me
That this remotion of the Duke and her   112
Is practice only. Give me my servant forth.   113
Go tell the Duke and 's wife I'd speak with them,
Now, presently. Bid them come forth and hear me,   115
Or at their chamber door I'll beat the drum
Till it cry sleep to death.   117
GLOUCESTER   I would have all well betwixt you.   *Exit.*
LEAR
    Oh, me, my heart, my rising heart! But down!
FOOL   Cry to it, nuncle, as the cockney did to the eels   120
    when she put 'em i'th' paste alive. She knapped 'em   121
    o'th' coxcombs with a stick and cried, "Down, wan-   122
    tons, down!" 'Twas her brother that, in pure kindness   123
    to his horse, buttered his hay.   124

        Enter Cornwall, Regan, Gloucester, [and]
        servants.

LEAR   Good morrow to you both.
CORNWALL   Hail to Your Grace!
                            Kent here set at liberty.
REGAN   I am glad to see Your Highness.
LEAR
    Regan, I think you are. I know what reason
    I have to think so. If thou shouldst not be glad,
    I would divorce me from thy mother's tomb,   130
    Sepulch'ring an adultress. [*To Kent*] Oh, are you free?   131
    Some other time for that.—Belovèd Regan,
    Thy sister's naught. Oh, Regan, she hath tied   133
    Sharp-toothed unkindness, like a vulture, here.
                        [*He lays his hand on his heart.*]
    I can scarce speak to thee. Thou'lt not believe
    With how depraved a quality—Oh, Regan!   136

REGAN
    I pray you, sir, take patience. I have hope   137
    You less know how to value her desert   138
    Than she to scant her duty.
LEAR   Say? How is that?   139
REGAN
    I cannot think my sister in the least
    Would fail her obligation. If, sir, perchance
    She have restrained the riots of your followers,
    'Tis on such ground and to such wholesome end
    As clears her from all blame.
LEAR   My curses on her!
REGAN   Oh, sir, you are old;
    Nature in you stands on the very verge   147
    Of his confine. You should be ruled and led   148
    By some discretion that discerns your state   149
    Better than you yourself. Therefore, I pray you,
    That to our sister you do make return.
    Say you have wronged her.
LEAR   Ask her forgiveness?
    Do you but mark how this becomes the house: 153
    [*Kneeling*] "Dear daughter, I confess that I am old;
    Age is unnecessary. On my knees I beg
    That you'll vouchsafe me raiment, bed, and food."
REGAN
    Good sir, no more. These are unsightly tricks.
    Return you to my sister.
LEAR [*rising*]   Never, Regan.
    She hath abated me of half my train,   159
    Looked black upon me, struck me with her tongue
    Most serpentlike upon the very heart.
    All the stored vengeances of heaven fall
    On her ingrateful top! Strike her young bones,   163
    You taking airs, with lameness!
CORNWALL   Fie, sir, fie!   164
LEAR
    You nimble lightnings, dart your blinding flames
    Into her scornful eyes! Infect her beauty,
    You fen-sucked fogs drawn by the powerful sun   167
    To fall and blister!   168
REGAN
    O the blest gods! So will you wish on me
    When the rash mood is on.
LEAR
    No, Regan, thou shalt never have my curse.
    Thy tender-hafted nature shall not give   172
    Thee o'er to harshness. Her eyes are fierce, but thine
    Do comfort and not burn. 'Tis not in thee
    To grudge my pleasures, to cut off my train,

108–10 And . . . man and now disapprove of my more impetuous will
in having rashly supposed that those who are indisposed and sickly
were in sound health.   **110 Death . . . state!** (A common oath, here
ironically appropriate to a king whose royal authority is dying.)
112 remotion removal, inaccessibility   **113 practice** deception.
forth out of the stocks.   **115 presently** at once.   **117 cry sleep to
death** i.e., puts an end to sleep by the noise.   **120 cockney** i.e., a
Londoner, ignorant of ways of cooking eels   **121 paste** pastry pie.
knapped rapped   **122 coxcombs** heads   **122–3 wantons** playful
creatures, sexy rogues. (A term of affectionate abuse. The cockney
wife is trying to coax and wheedle the eels into laying down their lives
for the making of the pastry pie—a plea that is about as ineffectual as
Lear's imploring his rising heart to subside.)   **123–4 'Twas
. . . hay** (Another city ignorance; the act is well intended, but
horses do not like greasy hay. As with Lear, good intentions are
not enough. The *brother* is related to the cockney wife in that
they are both misguidedly tenderhearted.)   **130–1 I would . . . adultress** i.e., I would cease to honor your dead mother's tomb, since it
would surely contain the dead body of an adultress. (Only such
a fantasy of illegitimacy could explain to Lear filial ingratitude of
the monstrous sort that now confronts him.)   **133 naught** wicked.
136 quality disposition

137–9 I have . . . duty I trust this is more a matter of your undervalu-
ing her merit than of her falling slack in her duty to you.   **139 Say?**
Come again?   **147–8 Nature . . . confine** i.e., Your life has almost
completed its allotted scope.   **149 By . . . state** by some discreet person who understands your situation and condition   **153 becomes the
house** suits domestic decorum and the royal family line. (Said with
bitter irony.)   **159 abated** deprived   **163 ingrateful top** ungrateful
head.   **164 taking** infectious   **167 fen-sucked** (It was supposed that
the sun sucked up poisons from fens or marshes.)   **168 To fall and
blister** to fall upon her and blister her beauty.   **172 tender-hafted**
gentle. (Literally, set in a tender *haft*, i.e., handle or frame.)

To bandy hasty words, to scant my sizes,   176
And, in conclusion, to oppose the bolt   177
Against my coming in. Thou better know'st
The offices of nature, bond of childhood,   179
Effects of courtesy, dues of gratitude.   180
Thy half o'th' kingdom hast thou not forgot,
Wherein I thee endowed.

REGAN   Good sir, to th' purpose.   182

LEAR
Who put my man i'th' stocks?   *Tucket within.*

CORNWALL   What trumpet's that?

REGAN
I know't—my sister's. This approves her letter,   184
That she would soon be here.

        Enter steward [Oswald].

                              Is your lady come?

LEAR
This is a slave, whose easy-borrowed pride   186
Dwells in the fickle grace of her he follows.—   187
Out, varlet, from my sight!

CORNWALL   What means Your Grace?   188

LEAR
Who stocked my servant? Regan, I have good hope
Thou didst not know on't.

        Enter Goneril.

                              Who comes here? O heavens,
If you do love old men, if your sweet sway
Allow obedience, if you yourselves are old,   192
Make it your cause; send down, and take my part!
[*To Goneril*] Art not ashamed to look upon this beard?
                      [*Goneril and Regan join hands.*] 194
Oh, Regan, will you take her by the hand?

GONERIL
Why not by th' hand, sir? How have I offended?
All's not offense that indiscretion finds   197
And dotage terms so.

LEAR   O sides, you are too tough!   198
Will you yet hold?—How came my man i'th' stocks?

CORNWALL
I set him there, sir; but his own disorders
Deserved much less advancement.

LEAR   You? Did you?   201

REGAN
I pray you, father, being weak, seem so.   202
If till the expiration of your month
You will return and sojourn with my sister,
Dismissing half your train, come then to me.

I am now from home, and out of that provision   206
Which shall be needful for your entertainment.   207

LEAR
Return to her? And fifty men dismissed?
No! Rather I abjure all roofs, and choose
To wage against the enmity o'th'air,   210
To be a comrade with the wolf and owl—
Necessity's sharp pinch. Return with her?
Why, the hot-blooded France, that dowerless took   213
Our youngest born—I could as well be brought
To knee his throne and, squirelike, pension beg   215
To keep base life afoot. Return with her?
Persuade me rather to be slave and sumpter   217
To this detested groom.   [*He points to Oswald.*]

GONERIL   At your choice, sir.

LEAR
I prithee, daughter, do not make me mad.
I will not trouble thee, my child. Farewell.
We'll no more meet, no more see one another.
But yet thou art my flesh, my blood, my daughter—
Or rather a disease that's in my flesh,
Which I must needs call mine. Thou art a boil,
A plague-sore, or embossèd carbuncle   225
In my corrupted blood. But I'll not chide thee;
Let shame come when it will, I do not call it.   227
I do not bid the thunder-bearer shoot,   228
Nor tell tales of thee to high-judging Jove.   229
Mend when thou canst; be better at thy leisure.
I can be patient. I can stay with Regan,
I and my hundred knights.

REGAN   Not altogether so.
I looked not for you yet, nor am provided   234
For your fit welcome. Give ear, sir, to my sister;
For those that mingle reason with your passion   236
Must be content to think you old, and so—   237
But she knows what she does.

LEAR   Is this well spoken?

REGAN
I dare avouch it, sir. What, fifty followers?   239
Is it not well? What should you need of more?
Yea, or so many, sith that both charge and danger   241
Speak 'gainst so great a number? How in one house
Should many people under two commands
Hold amity? 'Tis hard, almost impossible.

GONERIL
Why might not you, my lord, receive attendance
From those that she calls servants, or from mine?

REGAN
Why not, my lord? If then they chanced to slack ye,   247
We could control them. If you will come to me—   248
For now I spy a danger—I entreat you

---

176 **bandy** volley, exchange.   **scant my sizes** diminish my
allowances   177 **oppose the bolt** lock the door   179 **The offices . . .
childhood** the natural duties and filial obligations due to parents
180 **Effects** outward manifestations   182 **to th' purpose** get to the
point.   184 **approves** confirms   186 **easy-borrowed** easily put on
187 **grace** favor   188 **varlet** worthless fellow   192 **Allow** approve,
sanction   194 **beard** (A sign of age and presumed entitlement to
respect.)   197–8 **All's . . . so** Not everything that the poor judgment
and dotage of old age deem offensive is actually so.   198 **sides** i.e.,
sides of the chest (stretched by the swelling heart)   201 **much less
advancement** far less honor, i.e., far worse treatment.   202 **seem so**
i.e., don't act as if you were strong.

206 **from** away from   207 **entertainment** proper reception.
210 **wage** wage war   213 **hot-blooded** spirited, youthful; choleric
215 **knee** fall on my knees before   217 **sumpter** packhorse; hence,
drudge   225 **embossèd** swollen, tumid   227 **call** summon   228 **the
thunder-bearer** i.e., Jove   229 **high-judging** judging from on high
234 **looked not for** did not expect   236–7 **For . . . old** for those who
dispassionately consider your intemperate outbursts must conclude
that you are old   239 **avouch** vouch for   241 **sith that** since.   **charge**
expense   247 **slack** neglect   248 **control** correct

To bring but five-and-twenty. To no more
Will I give place or notice.   251

LEAR
I gave you all—

REGAN   And in good time you gave it.

LEAR
Made you my guardians, my depositaries,   253
But kept a reservation to be followed   254
With such a number. What, must I come to you
With five-and-twenty? Regan, said you so?

REGAN
And speak't again, my lord. No more with me.

LEAR
Those wicked creatures yet do look well-favored   258
When others are more wicked; not being the worst
Stands in some rank of praise. [*To Goneril*] I'll go with
    thee.   260
Thy fifty yet doth double five-and-twenty,
And thou art twice her love.

GONERIL   Hear me, my lord:
What need you five-and-twenty, ten, or five,
To follow in a house where twice so many   264
Have a command to tend you?

REGAN   What need one?

LEAR
Oh, reason not the need! Our basest beggars   266
Are in the poorest thing superfluous.   267
Allow not nature more than nature needs,   268
Man's life is cheap as beast's. Thou art a lady;
If only to go warm were gorgeous,   270
Why, nature needs not what thou gorgeous wear'st,   271
Which scarcely keeps thee warm. But, for true need—   272
You heavens, give me that patience, patience I need!
You see me here, you gods, a poor old man,
As full of grief as age, wretched in both.
If it be you that stirs these daughters' hearts
Against their father, fool me not so much   277
To bear it tamely; touch me with noble anger,   278
And let not women's weapons, water drops,
Stain my man's cheeks. No, you unnatural hags,
I will have such revenges on you both
That all the world shall—I will do such things—
What they are yet I know not, but they shall be
The terrors of the earth. You think I'll weep;
No, I'll not weep.   *Storm and tempest.*
I have full cause of weeping; but this heart
Shall break into a hundred thousand flaws   287

Or ere I'll weep. Oh, Fool, I shall go mad!   288
           Exeunt [*Lear, Gloucester, Kent, Gentleman,*
                                 and Fool].

CORNWALL
Let us withdraw. 'Twill be a storm.

REGAN
This house is little. The old man and 's people
Cannot be well bestowed.   291

GONERIL
'Tis his own blame hath put himself from rest,   292
And must needs taste his folly.   293

REGAN
For his particular, I'll receive him gladly,   294
But not one follower.

GONERIL
So am I purposed. Where is my lord of Gloucester?

CORNWALL
Followed the old man forth.

               Enter Gloucester.

                         He is returned.

GLOUCESTER
The King is in high rage.

CORNWALL   Whither is he going?

GLOUCESTER
He calls to horse, but will I know not whither.

CORNWALL
'Tis best to give him way. He leads himself.   300

GONERIL [*to Gloucester*]
My lord, entreat him by no means to stay.   301

GLOUCESTER
Alack, the night comes on, and the bleak winds
Do sorely ruffle. For many miles about   303
There's scarce a bush.

REGAN   Oh, sir, to willful men
The injuries that they themselves procure
Must be their schoolmasters. Shut up your doors.
He is attended with a desperate train,
And what they may incense him to, being apt   308
To have his ear abused, wisdom bids fear.   309

CORNWALL
Shut up your doors, my lord; 'tis a wild night.
My Regan counsels well. Come out o'th' storm.
                                  Exeunt.

                      ❖

3.1

       Storm still. Enter Kent [*disguised as Caius*]
       and a Gentleman, severally.

KENT   Who's there, besides foul weather?

251 **place or notice** houseroom or recognition.   253 **depositaries** trustees   254 **kept a reservation** reserved a right   258 **well-favored** attractive, fair of feature   260 **Stands . . . praise** achieves, by necessity, some relative deserving of praise.   264 **follow** be your attendants   266 **reason not** do not dispassionately analyze   266–7 **Our . . . superfluous** Even our most destitute beggars have some wretched possessions beyond what they absolutely need.   268 **Allow not** If you do not allow.   **needs** i.e., to survive   270–2 **If . . . warm** If fashions in clothes were determined only by the need for warmth, this natural standard wouldn't justify the rich robes you wear to be gorgeous—which don't serve well for warmth in any case.   277–8 **fool . . . To** do not make me so foolish as to   287 **flaws** fragments

288 **Or ere** before   291 **bestowed** lodged.   292 **blame** fault.   **hath** that he has, or, that has.   **from rest** i.e., out of the house; also, lacking peace of mind   293 **taste** experience   294 **For his particular** As for him individually   300 **give . . . himself** give him his own way. He is guided only by his own willfulness.   301 **entreat . . . means** by no means entreat him   303 **ruffle** bluster.   308–9 **being . . . abused** (he) being inclined to hearken to wild counsel
3.1. Location: An open place in Gloucestershire.
0.2 *severally* at separate doors.

GENTLEMAN
One minded like the weather, most unquietly.
KENT   I know you. Where's the King?
GENTLEMAN
Contending with the fretful elements;
Bids the wind blow the earth into the sea
Or swell the curlèd waters 'bove the main,   6
That things might change or cease; tears his white hair,   7
Which the impetuous blasts with eyeless rage
Catch in their fury and make nothing of;   9
Strives in his little world of man to outstorm   10
The to-and-fro-conflicting wind and rain.
This night, wherein the cub-drawn bear would couch,   12
The lion and the belly-pinchèd wolf
Keep their fur dry, unbonneted he runs
And bids what will take all.
KENT   But who is with him?   15
GENTLEMAN
None but the Fool, who labors to outjest   16
His heart-struck injuries.
KENT   Sir, I do know you,   17
And dare upon the warrant of my note   18
Commend a dear thing to you. There is division,   19
Although as yet the face of it is covered
With mutual cunning, twixt Albany and Cornwall;
Who have—as who have not, that their great stars   22
Throned and set high?—servants, who seem no less,   23
Which are to France the spies and speculations   24
Intelligent of our state. What hath been seen,   25
Either in snuffs and packings of the dukes,   26
Or the hard rein which both of them hath borne   27
Against the old kind King, or something deeper,   28
Whereof perchance these are but furnishings—   29
But true it is, from France there comes a power   30
Into this scattered kingdom, who already,   31
Wise in our negligence, have secret feet   32
In some of our best ports and are at point   33
To show their open banner. Now to you:
If on my credit you dare build so far   35
To make your speed to Dover, you shall find
Some that will thank you, making just report   37
Of how unnatural and bemadding sorrow
The King hath cause to plain.   39
I am a gentleman of blood and breeding,   40

And from some knowledge and assurance offer   41
This office to you.   42
GENTLEMAN
I will talk further with you.
KENT   No, do not.
For confirmation that I am much more
Than my outwall, open this purse and take   45
What it contains. [*He gives a purse and a ring.*] If you
   shall see Cordelia—
As fear not but you shall—show her this ring,   47
And she will tell you who that fellow is   48
That yet you do not know. Fie on this storm!
I will go seek the King.
GENTLEMAN
Give me your hand. Have you no more to say?
KENT
Few words, but, to effect, more than all yet: 52
That when we have found the King—in which your
   pain   53
That way, I'll this—he that first lights on him   54
Holla the other.   *Exeunt [separately].*

❧

3.2

Storm still. Enter Lear and Fool.

LEAR
Blow, winds, and crack your cheeks! Rage, blow!
You cataracts and hurricanoes, spout   2
Till you have drenched our steeples, drowned the
   cocks!   3
You sulfurous and thought-executing fires,   4
Vaunt-couriers of oak-cleaving thunderbolts,   5
Singe my white head! And thou, all-shaking thunder,
Strike flat the thick rotundity o'th' world!
Crack nature's molds, all germens spill at once   8
That makes ingrateful man!
FOOL   Oh, nuncle, court holy water in a dry house is bet-   10
ter than this rainwater out o'door. Good nuncle, in,
ask thy daughters blessing. Here's a night pities   12
neither wise men nor fools.
LEAR
Rumble thy bellyful! Spit, fire! Spout, rain!
Nor rain, wind, thunder, fire are my daughters.   15
I tax not you, you elements, with unkindness;   16
I never gave you kingdom, called you children.
You owe me no subscription. Then let fall   18

---

6 **main** mainland   7 **things** all things   9 **make nothing of** blow about contemptuously   10 **little world of man** i.e., microcosm, which is an epitome of the macrocosm or universe   12 **cub-drawn** famished, with udders sucked dry (and hence ravenous). **couch** lie close in its den   15 **bids . . . all** (A cry of desperate defiance; "take all" is the cry of a gambler in staking his last.)   16 **outjest** exorcise or relieve by jesting   17 **heart-struck injuries** injuries that strike to the very heart.   18–19 **And . . . to you** and dare, on the strength of what I know about you, entrust a precious undertaking to you.   22–3 **as . . . high** as who does not, among those whom a mighty destiny has enthroned on high   23 **no less** i.e., no other than servants   24 **speculations** scouts, spies   25 **Intelligent of** supplying intelligence pertinent to   26 **snuffs and packings** resentments and intrigues   27–8 **Or . . . King** or the harsh reining in they both have inflicted on King Lear   29 **furnishings** outward shows   30 **power** army   31 **scattered** divided   32 **Wise in** taking advantage of   **feet** footholds   33 **at point** ready   35 **credit** trustworthiness.   **so far** so far as   37 **making just report** for making an accurate report   39 **plain** complain.   40 **blood and breeding** good family and education

41 **assurance** confidence, certainty   42 **office** assignment   45 **outwall** exterior appearance   47 **fear not but** be assured that   48 **fellow** i.e., Kent   52 **to effect** in their consequences   53–4 **in which . . . this** in which task, you search in that direction while I go this way
3.2. Location: An open place, as before.
2 **hurricanoes** waterspouts   3 **drenched** drowned.   **cocks** weathercocks.   4 **thought-executing fires** lightning that acts with the quickness of thought   5 **Vaunt-couriers** forerunners   8 **Crack . . . at once** Crack the molds in which nature makes all life; destroy all seeds at once   10 **court holy water** flattery   12 **ask . . . blessing** (For Lear to do so would be to acknowledge their authority.)   15 **Nor** Neither   16 **tax** accuse.   **with** of   18 **subscription** allegiance.

Your horrible pleasure. Here I stand your slave,
A poor, infirm, weak, and despised old man.
But yet I call you servile ministers,   21
That will with two pernicious daughters join
Your high-engendered battles 'gainst a head   23
So old and white as this. Oho! 'Tis foul.

FOOL   He that has a house to put 's head in has a good
headpiece.   26
     The codpiece that will house   27
       Before the head has any,   28
     The head and he shall louse;   29
       So beggars marry many.   30
     The man that makes his toe   31
       What he his heart should make   32
     Shall of a corn cry woe,   33
       And turn his sleep to wake.   34
For there was never yet fair woman but she made 35
mouths in a glass.   36

LEAR
No, I will be the pattern of all patience;
I will say nothing.

     Enter Kent, [disguised as Caius].

KENT   Who's there?
FOOL   Marry, here's grace and a codpiece; that's a wise   40
man and a fool.
KENT
Alas, sir, are you here? Things that love night
Love not such nights as these. The wrathful skies
Gallow the very wanderers of the dark   44
And make them keep their caves. Since I was man, 45
Such sheets of fire, such bursts of horrid thunder,
Such groans of roaring wind and rain I never
Remember to have heard. Man's nature cannot carry 48
Th'affliction nor the fear.
LEAR   Let the great gods,   49
That keep this dreadful pother o'er our heads,   50
Find out their enemies now. Tremble, thou wretch,
That hast within thee undivulgèd crimes
Unwhipped of justice! Hide thee, thou bloody hand,
Thou perjured, and thou simular of virtue   54
That art incestuous! Caitiff, to pieces shake,   55
That under covert and convenient seeming   56

Has practiced on man's life! Close pent-up guilts,   57
Rive your concealing continents and cry   58
These dreadful summoners grace! I am a man   59
More sinned against than sinning.
KENT   Alack, bareheaded?
Gracious my lord, hard by here is a hovel;
Some friendship will it lend you 'gainst the tempest.
Repose you there while I to this hard house—
More harder than the stones whereof 'tis raised,
Which even but now, demanding after you,   65
Denied me to come in—return and force
Their scanted courtesy.
LEAR   My wits begin to turn.   67
Come on, my boy. How dost, my boy? Art cold?
I am cold myself.—Where is this straw, my fellow?
The art of our necessities is strange,
And can make vile things precious. Come, your
    hovel.—
Poor fool and knave, I have one part in my heart
That's sorry yet for thee.
FOOL   [*sings*]
    "He that has and a little tiny wit,   74
      With heigh-ho, the wind and the rain,
    Must make content with his fortunes fit,
      Though the rain it raineth every day."   77
LEAR
True, boy.—Come, bring us to this hovel.
     Exit [with Kent].
FOOL   This is a brave night to cool a courtesan. I'll speak 79
a prophecy ere I go:

    When priests are more in word than matter;   81
    When brewers mar their malt with water;   82
    When nobles are their tailors' tutors,   83
    No heretics burned but wenches' suitors,   84
    Then shall the realm of Albion   85
    Come to great confusion.

    When every case in law is right,   87
    No squire in debt, nor no poor knight;
    When slanders do not live in tongues,   89
    Nor cutpurses come not to throngs;

---

21 ministers agents   **23 high-engendered battles** battalions engendered in the heavens   **26 headpiece** (1) helmetlike covering for the head (2) head for common sense.   **27–30 The codpiece . . . many** i.e., A man who houses his genitals in a sexual embrace before he has a roof over his head can expect the lice-infested penury of a penniless marriage. (The *codpiece* is a covering for the genitals worn by men with their close-fitting hose; here representing the genitals themselves.)   **31–4 The man . . . wake** i.e., Anyone who unwisely places his affection on base things will be afflicted with sorrow and sleeplessness. (The *corn* is a bunion on the toe.)   **35–6 made . . . glass** practiced making attractive faces in a mirror.   **40 Marry** (An oath, originally "by the Virgin Mary.")   **grace** royal grace.   **codpiece** (Often prominent in the Fool's costume.)   **44 Gallow . . . dark** frighten the very wild beasts of the night   **45 keep** occupy, remain inside   **48 carry** endure   **49 Th'affliction** the physical affliction   **50 pother** hubbub, turmoil   **54 simular** pretender   **55 Caitiff** Wretch   **56 convenient seeming** deception fitted to the purpose

57 practiced on plotted against   **57–9 Close . . . grace!** O you secret and buried consciousnesses of guilt, burst open the hiding places that conceal you, and pray for mercy! (*Summoners* are the officers who cited offenders to appear before ecclesiastical courts.)   **65 Which** i.e., the occupants of which.   **demanding** I inquiring   **67 scanted** stinted   **74–7 "He . . . day"** (Derived from the popular song that Feste sings in *Twelfth Night*, 5.1.389 ff.)   **79 This . . . courtesan** i.e., This night is stormy enough to cool even the lust of a courtesan. (*Brave* means "fine, excellent.")   **81 When priests . . . matter** i.e., When priests do not practice what they preach. (This and the next three lines satirize the present state of affairs.)   **82 mar** adulterate   **83 are . . . tutors** can instruct their own tailors about fashion   **84 No heretics . . . suitors** i.e., when the prevailing heresy is lechery (a heresy, in other words, against love rather than against true religion), punished by burning not at the stake but by means of venereal infection   **85 realm of Albion** kingdom of England. (The Fool is parodying a pseudo-Chaucerian prophetic verse.)   **87 right** just. (This and the next five lines offer a utopian vision of justice and charity that will never be realized in this corrupted world.)   **89 When slanders . . . tongues** when no tongues speak slanders

When usurers tell their gold i'th' field,   91
And bawds and whores do churches build,
Then comes the time, who lives to see't,   93
That going shall be used with feet.   94

This prophecy Merlin shall make, for I live before his   95
time.   *Exit.*

❖

3.3

Enter Gloucester and Edmund [with lights].

GLOUCESTER   Alack, alack, Edmund, I like not this unnatural dealing. When I desired their leave that I might
pity him, they took from me the use of mine own   3
house, charged me on pain of perpetual displeasure
neither to speak of him, entreat for him, or any way
sustain him.

EDMUND   Most savage and unnatural!

GLOUCESTER   Go to; say you nothing. There is division   8
between the dukes, and a worse matter than that. I
have received a letter this night; 'tis dangerous to be
spoken; I have locked the letter in my closet. These in- 11
juries the King now bears will be revenged home;   12
there is part of a power already footed. We must in-   13
cline to the King. I will look him and privily relieve   14
him. Go you and maintain talk with the Duke, that
my charity be not of him perceived. If he ask for me,   16
I am ill and gone to bed. If I die for't, as no less is
threatened me, the King my old master must be relieved. There is strange things toward, Edmund. Pray   19
you, be careful.   *Exit.*

EDMUND
This courtesy forbid thee shall the Duke   21
Instantly know, and of that letter too.
This seems a fair deserving, and must draw me   23
That which my father loses—no less than all.   24
The younger rises when the old doth fall.   *Exit.*

❖

3.4

Enter Lear, Kent [disguised as Caius], and Fool.

KENT
Here is the place, my lord. Good my lord, enter.

The tyranny of the open night's too rough
For nature to endure.   *Storm still.*
LEAR   Let me alone.   3
KENT
Good my lord, enter here.
LEAR   Wilt break my heart?   4
KENT
I had rather break mine own. Good my lord, enter.
LEAR
Thou think'st 'tis much that this contentious storm
Invades us to the skin. So 'tis to thee,
But where the greater malady is fixed   8
The lesser is scarce felt. Thou'dst shun a bear,
But if thy flight lay toward the roaring sea
Thou'dst meet the bear i'th' mouth. When the mind's
    free,   11
The body's delicate. This tempest in my mind   12
Doth from my senses take all feeling else
Save what beats there. Filial ingratitude!
Is it not as this mouth should tear this hand   15
For lifting food to't? But I will punish home.   16
No, I will weep no more. In such a night
To shut me out? Pour on; I will endure.
In such a night as this? Oh, Regan, Goneril,
Your old kind father, whose frank heart gave all—   20
Oh, that way madness lies; let me shun that!
No more of that.
KENT   Good my lord, enter here.
LEAR
Prithee, go in thyself; seek thine own ease.
This tempest will not give me leave to ponder   24
On things would hurt me more. But I'll go in.   25
[*To the Fool*] In, boy; go first. You houseless poverty—
Nay, get thee in. I'll pray, and then I'll sleep.
                            Exit [Fool into the hovel].
Poor naked wretches, wheresoe'er you are,
That bide the pelting of this pitiless storm,   29
How shall your houseless heads and unfed sides,   30
Your looped and windowed raggedness, defend you   31
From seasons such as these? Oh, I have ta'en
Too little care of this! Take physic, pomp;   33
Expose thyself to feel what wretches feel,
That thou mayst shake the superflux to them   35
And show the heavens more just.
EDGAR [*within*]   Fathom and half, fathom and half!   37
Poor Tom!

Enter Fool [from the hovel].

FOOL   Come not in here, nuncle; here's a spirit. Help
me, help me!

KENT   Give me thy hand. Who's there?

FOOL   A spirit, a spirit! He says his name's poor Tom.

KENT
What art thou that dost grumble there i'th' straw?   43
Come forth.

Enter Edgar [disguised as a madman].

EDGAR   Away! The foul fiend follows me! Through the   45
sharp hawthorn blows the cold wind. Hum! Go to thy   46
bed and warm thee.

LEAR   Didst thou give all to thy daughters? And art
thou come to this?

EDGAR   Who gives anything to poor Tom? Whom the
foul fiend hath led through fire and through flame,
through ford and whirlpool, o'er bog and quagmire;
that hath laid knives under his pillow and halters in   53
his pew, set ratsbane by his porridge, made him   54
proud of heart to ride on a bay trotting horse over   55
four-inched bridges to course his own shadow for a   56
traitor. Bless thy five wits! Tom's a-cold. Oh, do de,   57
do de, do de. Bless thee from whirlwinds, star-blast-   58
ing, and taking! Do poor Tom some charity, whom the   59
foul fiend vexes. There could I have him now—and   60
there—and there again—and there.   *Storm still.*

LEAR
Has his daughters brought him to this pass?—   62
Couldst thou save nothing? Wouldst thou give 'em
all?

FOOL   Nay, he reserved a blanket, else we had been all   64
shamed.

LEAR
Now, all the plagues that in the pendulous air   66
Hang fated o'er men's faults light on thy daughters!   67

KENT   He hath no daughters, sir.

LEAR
Death, traitor! Nothing could have subdued nature
To such a lowness but his unkind daughters.
Is it the fashion that discarded fathers
Should have thus little mercy on their flesh?   72
Judicious punishment! 'Twas this flesh begot   73
Those pelican daughters.   74

EDGAR   Pillicock sat on Pillicock Hill. Alow, alow, loo,   75
loo!

FOOL   This cold night will turn us all to fools and madmen.

EDGAR   Take heed o'th' foul fiend. Obey thy parents;
keep thy word's justice; swear not; commit not with   80
man's sworn spouse; set not thy sweet heart on proud
array. Tom's a-cold.

LEAR   What hast thou been?

EDGAR   A servingman, proud in heart and mind, that   84
curled my hair, wore gloves in my cap, served the lust   85
of my mistress' heart, and did the act of darkness with
her; swore as many oaths as I spake words, and broke
them in the sweet face of heaven. One that slept in the
contriving of lust and waked to do it. Wine loved I
deeply, dice dearly, and in woman out-paramoured   90
the Turk. False of heart, light of ear, bloody of hand;   91
hog in sloth, fox in stealth, wolf in greediness, dog in
madness, lion in prey. Let not the creaking of shoes   93
nor the rustling of silks betray thy poor heart to   94
woman. Keep thy foot out of brothels, thy hand out of
plackets, thy pen from lenders' books, and defy the   96
foul fiend. Still through the hawthorn blows the cold
wind; says suum, mun, nonny. Dolphin my boy, boy,   98
sessa! Let him trot by.   *Storm still.*   99

LEAR   Thou wert better in a grave than to answer with
thy uncovered body this extremity of the skies. Is man
no more than this? Consider him well. Thou ow'st the   102
worm no silk, the beast no hide, the sheep no wool,   103
the cat no perfume. Ha! Here's three on 's are sophis-   104
ticated; thou art the thing itself. Unaccommodated   105
man is no more but such a poor, bare, forked animal
as thou art. Off, off, you lendings! Come, unbutton
here.   *[Tearing off his clothes.]*

FOOL   Prithee, nuncle, be contented; 'tis a naughty night   109
to swim in. Now a little fire in a wild field were like   110
an old lecher's heart—a small spark, all the rest on 's   111
body cold.

Enter Gloucester, with a torch.

Look, here comes a walking fire.

---

43 grumble mutter, mumble   **45 Away!** Keep away!   **45–6 Through . . . wind** (Possibly a line from a ballad.)   **53–4 that hath . . . porridge** (The fiend has laid in poor Tom's way tempting means to despairing suicide, the most damnable of sins: knives under his pillow when he is asleep, nooses in his church pew when he should be at prayer, and rat poison set beside his soup when he should eat.)   **54–7 made him . . . traitor** (The next temptation is a prideful act of great bravado that would be impossible without the devil's aid: riding a horse over bridges only four inches wide in pursuit of one's own shadow.)   **57 five wits** (Either the five physical senses—sight, hearing, etc.—or the five faculties of the mind: common wit, imagination, fantasy, estimation, and memory.)   **58–9 star-blasting** being blighted by influence of the stars   **59 taking** infection, evil influence, enchantment.   **60 There** (Perhaps he slaps at lice and other vermin as if they were devils.)   **62 pass** miserable plight.   **64 reserved a blanket** kept a wrap (for his nakedness)   **66 pendulous** suspended, overhanging   **67 fated** having the power of fate   **72 have . . . flesh** i.e., punish themselves, as Edgar has done (probably with pins and thorns stuck in his flesh).   **73 Judicious** Appropriate to the crime   **74 pelican** greedy. (Young pelicans supposedly smote their parents and fed on the blood of their mothers' breasts.)

75 Pillicock (From an old rhyme, suggested by the sound of *pelican*. *Pillicock* in nursery rhyme seems to have been a euphemism for penis; *Pillicock Hill*, for the Mount of Venus.)   **80 justice** integrity.   **commit not** i.e., do not commit adultery. (Edgar's mad homily contains fragments of the Ten Commandments.)   **84 servingman** either a "servant" in the language of courtly love or an ambitious servant in a household   **85 gloves** i.e., my mistress's favors   **90–1 out-paramoured the Turk** outdid the Sultan in keeping mistresses.   **91 light of ear** i.e., listening intently for information that can be used criminally   **93 prey** preying.   **93–4 creaking . . . silks** (Telltale noises of lovers in a secret assignation.)   **96 plackets** slits in skirts or petticoats.   **thy pen . . . books** i.e., do not sign a contract for a loan   **98 suum . . . nonny** (Imitative of the wind?)   **Dolphin my boy** (A slang phrase or bit of song?)   **99 sessa** i.e., away, cease (?).   **102–4 Thou . . . perfume** Stripped of your finery, you are not indebted to the silkworm for silk, cattle for hide, the sheep for wool, or the civet cat for the perfume derived from its anal pouch.   **104–5 Here . . . itself** The three of us here (Kent, the Fool, and Lear) are decked out in the sophistication of supposedly civilized society; you (Edgar) are the unadorned, natural essence, the natural man.   **105 Unaccommodated** Unfurnished with the trappings of civilization, such as clothing   **109 naughty** bad, nasty   **110 wild** barren, uncultivated   **111 on 's** of his

EDGAR This is the foul fiend Flibbertigibbet! He begins 114
at curfew and walks till the first cock; he gives the web 115
and the pin, squinnies the eye and makes the harelip, 116
mildews the white wheat, and hurts the poor creature 117
of earth.
　　　Swithold footed thrice the 'old; 119
　　　He met the nightmare and her ninefold; 120
　　　　Bid her alight,
　　　　And her troth plight,
　　　And aroint thee, witch, aroint thee! 123
KENT How fares Your Grace?
LEAR What's he?
KENT Who's there? What is't you seek?
GLOUCESTER What are you there? Your names?
EDGAR Poor Tom, that eats the swimming frog, the
toad, the tadpole, the wall newt and the water; that in 129
the fury of his heart, when the foul fiend rages, eats
cow dung for salads, swallows the old rat and the
ditch-dog, drinks the green mantle of the standing 132
pool; who is whipped from tithing to tithing and 133
stock-punished and imprisoned; who hath had three 134
suits to his back, six shirts to his body, 135
　　　Horse to ride, and weapon to wear;
　　　But mice and rats and such small deer 137
　　　Have been Tom's food for seven long year.
Beware my follower. Peace, Smulkin! Peace, thou fiend! 139
GLOUCESTER
What, hath Your Grace no better company?
EDGAR The Prince of Darkness is a gentleman. Modo 141
he's called, and Mahu.
GLOUCESTER [to Lear]
Our flesh and blood, my lord, is grown so vile 143
That it doth hate what gets it. 144
EDGAR Poor Tom's a-cold.
GLOUCESTER
Go in with me. My duty cannot suffer 146
T'obey in all your daughters' hard commands. 147
Though their injunction be to bar my doors
And let this tyrannous night take hold upon you,

Yet have I ventured to come seek you out
And bring you where both fire and food is ready.
LEAR
First let me talk with this philosopher.
[To Edgar] What is the cause of thunder?
KENT　　　　　　　　　　　　　　　　Good my lord,
Take his offer. Go into th' house.
LEAR
I'll talk a word with this same learnèd Theban. 155
[To Edgar] What is your study? 156
EDGAR How to prevent the fiend, and to kill vermin. 157
LEAR Let me ask you one word in private.
　　　　　　　　　　　　[Lear and Edgar talk apart.]
KENT [to Gloucester]
Importune him once more to go, my lord.
His wits begin t'unsettle.
GLOUCESTER　　　　　　　　Canst thou blame him?
　　　　　　　　　　　　　　　　　Storm still.
His daughters seek his death. Ah, that good Kent!
He said it would be thus, poor banished man.
Thou sayest the King grows mad; I'll tell thee, friend,
I am almost mad myself. I had a son,
Now outlawed from my blood; he sought my life 165
But lately, very late. I loved him, friend,
No father his son dearer. True to tell thee,
The grief hath crazed my wits. What a night's this!—
I do beseech Your Grace—
LEAR Oh, cry you mercy, sir. 170
[To Edgar] Noble philosopher, your company.
EDGAR Tom's a-cold.
GLOUCESTER [to Edgar]
In, fellow, there, in th' hovel. Keep thee warm.
LEAR [starting toward the hovel]
Come, let's in all.
KENT　　　　　　　This way, my lord.
LEAR　　　　　　　　　　　　　　With him!
I will keep still with my philosopher.
KENT [to Gloucester]
Good my lord, soothe him. Let him take the fellow. 176
GLOUCESTER [to Kent] Take you him on. 177
KENT [to Edgar]
Sirrah, come on. Go along with us.
LEAR Come, good Athenian. 179
GLOUCESTER No words, no words! Hush.
EDGAR
Child Rowland to the dark tower came; 181
His word was still, "Fie, foh, and fum, 182
I smell the blood of a British man."　　Exeunt. 183

❧

114 Flibbertigibbet (A devil from Elizabethan folklore whose name appears in Samuel Harsnett's *Declaration of Egregious Popish Impostures*, 1603, and elsewhere.) 114–15 He . . . cock He walks from nightfall till dawn 115–16 web and the pin cataract of the eye 116 squinnies squints 117 white ripening, ready for harvest 119 Swithold Saint Withold, an Anglo-Saxon exorcist, who here provides defense against the *nightmare*, or demon thought to afflict sleepers, by commanding the nightmare to *alight*, i.e., stop riding over the sleeper, and *plight* her *troth*, i.e., vow true faith, promise to do no harm. (Or, an error for *Swithin*.) footed . . . 'old thrice traversed the wold (tract of hilly upland) 120 ninefold nine offspring. (With possible pun on *fold, foal*.) 123 aroint thee begone 129 water water newt 132 ditch-dog dead dog in a ditch. mantle scum. standing stagnant 133 from . . . to tithing from one ward or parish to another 134 stock-punished placed in the stocks 134–5 three suits (Like the menial servant at 2.2.15.) 137 deer animals 139 follower familiar, attendant devil. Smulkin a devil's name (in Samuel Harsnet's *Declaration*, as are *Modo* and *Mahu* in lines 141–2). 141 The Prince of Darkness The devil 143–4 Our . . . gets it (1) Children have become so hardened in sin that they hate their parents (2) Life is so intolerable that humans cry out at having been born. 146 suffer permit me 147 in all in all matters

155 Theban i.e., one deeply versed in "philosophy" or natural science. 156 study special competence. 157 prevent thwart 165 outlawed . . . blood disowned, disinherited, and legally outlawed 170 cry you mercy I beg your pardon 176 soothe humor 177 Take . . . on i.e., Go on ahead with Edgar. 179 Athenian i.e., philosopher. 181 Child Rowland, etc. (Probably a fragment of a ballad about the hero of the Charlemagne legends. A *child* is a candidate for knighthood.) 182 word watchword 182–3 "Fie . . . man" (This is essentially what the Giant says in "Jack, the Giant Killer.")

3.5

Enter Cornwall and Edmund [with a letter].

CORNWALL   I will have my revenge ere I depart his
house.

EDMUND   How, my lord, I may be censured, that nature   3
thus gives way to loyalty, something fears me to   4
think of.

CORNWALL   I now perceive it was not altogether your
brother's evil disposition made him seek his death,   7
but a provoking merit set awork by a reprovable   8
badness in himself.   9

EDMUND   How malicious is my fortune, that I must   10
repent to be just! This is the letter he spoke of, which   11
approves him an intelligent party to the advantages   12
of France. Oh, heavens! That this treason were not, or   13
not I the detector!

CORNWALL   Go with me to the Duchess.

EDMUND   If the matter of this paper be certain, you have
mighty business in hand.

CORNWALL   True or false, it hath made thee Earl of
Gloucester. Seek out where thy father is, that he may
be ready for our apprehension.   20

EDMUND   [aside]   If I find him comforting the King, it   21
will stuff his suspicion more fully.—I will persevere   22
in my course of loyalty, though the conflict be sore
between that and my blood.   24

CORNWALL   I will lay trust upon thee, and thou shalt
find a dearer father in my love.   *Exeunt.*

3.6

*Enter Kent [disguised as Caius] and
Gloucester.*

GLOUCESTER   Here is better than the open air; take it
thankfully. I will piece out the comfort with what   2
addition I can. I will not be long from you.

KENT   All the power of his wits have given way to his
impatience. The gods reward your kindness!   5
Exit [Gloucester].

Enter Lear, Edgar [as poor Tom], and Fool.

EDGAR   Fraretetto calls me, and tells me Nero is an   6
angler in the lake of darkness. Pray, innocent, and   7
beware the foul fiend.

FOOL   Prithee, nuncle, tell me whether a madman be a
gentleman or a yeoman?   10

LEAR   A king, a king!

FOOL   No, he's a yeoman that has a gentleman to his
son; for he's a mad yeoman that sees his son a
gentleman before him.

LEAR
To have a thousand with red burning spits
Come hizzing in upon 'em—   16

EDGAR   The foul fiend bites my back.   17

FOOL   He's mad that trusts in the tameness of a wolf, a   18
horse's health, a boy's love, or a whore's oath.   19

LEAR
It shall be done; I will arraign them straight.   20
[To Edgar] Come, sit thou here, most learnèd justicer.   21
[To the Fool] Thou, sapient sir, sit here. Now, you she-
foxes!   22

EDGAR   Look where he stands and glares! Want'st thou   23
eyes at trial, madam?   24
[Sings.] "Come o'er the burn, Bessy, to me—"   25

FOOL [sings]
Her boat hath a leak,
And she must not speak
Why she dares not come over to thee.

EDGAR   The foul fiend haunts poor Tom in the voice of a
nightingale. Hoppedance cries in Tom's belly for two   30
white herring. Croak not, black angel; I have no food   31
for thee.

KENT [to Lear]
How do you, sir? Stand you not so amazed.   33
Will you lie down and rest upon the cushions?

LEAR
I'll see their trial first. Bring in their evidence.   35
[To Edgar] Thou robèd man of justice, take thy place;   36
[To the Fool] And thou, his yokefellow of equity,   37

3.5 Location: Gloucester's house.
3 censured judged.   **nature** attachment to family   **4 something
fears** somewhat frightens   **7 his** his father's   **8–9 but ... himself**
but the promptings of self-worth stimulated by the reprehensible
badness of the Earl of Gloucester.   **10–11 How ... just!** i.e., How
cruel of fate to oblige me to be upright and loyal by betraying my
own father!   **11–13 which ... France** which proves him to be a spy
on behalf of the French.   **20 for our apprehension** for our arresting
of him.   **21 If ... comforting** If I find Gloucester giving aid and comfort to   **22 his suspicion** suspicion of him   **24 blood** family loyalty,
filial instincts.
3.6. Location: Within a building on Gloucester's estate, near or
adjoining his house, or part of the house itself. See 3.4.146–54.
Cushions are provided, and stools.
2 piece eke   **5 impatience** rage, inability to endure more.

6 Fraretetto (Another of the fiends from Harsnett.)   **6–7 Nero is an
angler** (Chaucer's "Monk's Tale," lines 2474–5, tells how Nero fished
in the Tiber with nets of gold thread; in Rabelais, 2.30, Nero is
described as a hurdy-gurdy player and Trajan an angler for frogs in
the underworld.)   **7 innocent** simpleton, fool (i.e., the Fool)   **10 yeoman** property owner below the rank of gentleman. (The Fool's bitter
jest in lines 12–14 is that such a man might go mad to see his son
advanced over him.)   **16 hizzing** hissing. (Lear imagines his wicked
daughters suffering torments in hell or being attacked by enemies.)
17 bites (i.e., in the shape of a louse)   **18–19 tameness ... health**
(Wolves are untamable, and horses are prone to disease.)   **20 arraign
them** (Lear now imagines the trial of his cruel daughters.)   **21 justicer** judge, justice.   **22 sapient** wise   **23 he** (Probably one of Edgar's
devils, or, Lear.)   **23–4 Want'st ... trial** Do you lack spectators at
your trial? or, Can't you see who's looking at you?   **25 Come ... me**
(First line of a ballad by William Birche, 1558. A *burn* is a brook. The
Fool makes a ribald reply, in which the *leaky boat* suggests the
woman's easy virtue or perhaps her menstrual period.)   **30 nightingale** (Edgar pretends to take the Fool's singing for that of a fiend disguised as a nightingale.)   **Hoppedance** (Harsnett mentions
"Hoberdidance.")   **31 white** unsmoked (contrasted with *black angel*,
a demon).   **Croak** (Refers to the rumbling in Edgar's stomach,
denoting hunger.)   **33 amazed** bewildered.   **35 their evidence** the
witnesses against them.   **36 robèd man** i.e., Edgar, with his blanket
37 yokefellow of equity partner in the law

Bench by his side. [*To Kent*] You are o'th' commission; 38
Sit you, too.   [*They sit.*]
EDGAR   Let us deal justly.   [*He sings.*]
    Sleepest or wakest thou, jolly shepherd?
      Thy sheep be in the corn;   42
    And for one blast of thy minikin mouth,   43
      Thy sheep shall take no harm.   44
Purr the cat is gray.   45
LEAR   Arraign her first; 'tis Goneril, I here take my oath
before this honorable assembly, kicked the poor King 47
her father.
FOOL   Come hither, mistress. Is your name Goneril?
LEAR   She cannot deny it.
FOOL   Cry you mercy, I took you for a joint stool.   51
LEAR
And here's another, whose warped looks proclaim   52
What store her heart is made on. Stop her there!   53
Arms, arms, sword, fire! Corruption in the place!   54
False justicer, why hast thou let her scape?
EDGAR   Bless thy five wits!
KENT
Oh, pity! Sir, where is the patience now
That you so oft have boasted to retain?
EDGAR [*aside*]
My tears begin to take his part so much
They mar my counterfeiting.
LEAR   The little dogs and all,
Tray, Blanch, and Sweetheart, see, they bark at me.
EDGAR   Tom will throw his head at them.—Avaunt, you 63
curs!
    Be thy mouth or black or white,   65
    Tooth that poisons if it bite,
    Mastiff, greyhound, mongrel grim,
    Hound or spaniel, brach or lym,   68
    Bobtail tike or trundle-tail,   69
    Tom will make him weep and wail;
    For, with throwing thus my head,
    Dogs leap the hatch, and all are fled.   72
Do de, de, de. Sessa! Come, march to wakes and fairs 73
and market towns. Poor Tom, thy horn is dry.   74
LEAR   Then let them anatomize Regan; see what breeds 75
about her heart. Is there any cause in nature that makes
these hard hearts? [*To Edgar*] You, sir, I entertain 77

for one of my hundred; only I do not like the fashion of
your garments. You will say they are Persian; but let 79
them be changed.
KENT
Now, good my lord, lie here and rest awhile.
LEAR [*lying on cushions*]   Make no noise, make no
noise. Draw the curtains. So, so. We'll go to supper 83
i'th' morning.   [*He sleeps.*]
FOOL   And I'll go to bed at noon.

    Enter Gloucester.

GLOUCESTER [*to Kent*]
Come hither, friend. Where is the King my master?
KENT
Here, sir, but trouble him not; his wits are gone.
GLOUCESTER
Good friend, I prithee, take him in thy arms.
I have o'erheard a plot of death upon him.   89
There is a litter ready; lay him in't
And drive toward Dover, friend, where thou shalt
    meet
Both welcome and protection. Take up thy master.
If thou shouldst dally half an hour, his life,
With thine and all that offer to defend him,
Stand in assurèd loss. Take up, take up,   95
And follow me, that will to some provision   96
Give thee quick conduct.
KENT   Oppressèd nature sleeps.   97
This rest might yet have balmed thy broken sinews,   98
Which, if convenience will not allow,   99
Stand in hard cure. [*To the Fool*] Come, help to bear thy
    master.   100
Thou must not stay behind.   [*They pick up Lear.*]
GLOUCESTER   Come, come, away!
                 Exeunt [*all but Edgar*].
EDGAR
When we our betters see bearing our woes,   102
We scarcely think our miseries our foes.   103
Who alone suffers suffers most i'th' mind,   104
Leaving free things and happy shows behind;   105
But then the mind much sufferance doth o'erskip   106
When grief hath mates, and bearing fellowship.   107
How light and portable my pain seems now,   108
When that which makes me bend makes the King
    bow—
He childed as I fathered. Tom, away!   110

---

38 Bench take your place on the bench. **o'th' commission** one commissioned to be a justice **42 corn** grainfield **43–4 And . . . harm** i.e., one shout from your dainty (*minikin*) mouth can recall the sheep from the grainfield and thus save them from dangerous overeating. **45 Purr the cat** (A devil or familiar from Harsnett; see the note for 3.4.114. *Purr* may be the sound the familiar makes.) **47 kicked** who kicked **51 joint stool** low stool made by a joiner, or maker of furniture with joined parts. (Proverbially, the phrase "I took . . . stool" meant "I beg your pardon for failing to notice you." The reference is also presumably to a real stool onstage.) **52 another** i.e., Regan **53 store** abundance, material. **on** of. **54 Corruption in the place!** i.e., There is iniquity or bribery in this court! **63 throw his head at** i.e., threaten **65 or black** either black **68 brach or lym** bitch-hound or bloodhound **69 Bobtail . . . trundle-tail** mongrel dog with a docked or bobbed tail, or one that is curly-tailed **72 hatch** lower half of a divided door **73 Sessa** i.e., Away, cease. **wakes** parish festivals **74 horn** horn-bottle, used by beggars to drink from and to beg for alms **75 anatomize** dissect **77 entertain** take into my service

79 Persian (Lear madly asks if Edgar's wretched blanket is a rich Persian fabric.) **83 curtains** bedcurtains. (They presumably exist only in Lear's mad imagination.) **89 upon** against **95 Stand . . . loss** will assuredly be lost. **96 provision** supplies, or, means of providing for safety **97 conduct** guidance. **98 balmed** soothed, healed. **sinews** nerves **99 convenience** circumstances **100 Stand . . . cure** will be hard to cure. **102 our woes** woes like ours **103 We . . . foes** we almost forget our own miseries (since we see how human suffering afflicts even the great). **104–7 Who . . . fellowship** Anyone who has no companionship in suffering undergoes the mental anguish of forgetting entirely the carefree ways and happy scenes that were once enjoyed, whereas fellowship in grief enables the mind to rise above such suffering. (I.e., Misery loves company.) **108 portable** bearable, endurable **110 He . . . fathered** he suffering cruelty from his children as I from my father.

Mark the high noises, and thyself bewray 111
When false opinion, whose wrong thoughts defile
   thee, 112
In thy just proof repeals and reconciles thee. 113
What will hap more tonight, safe scape the King! 114
Lurk, lurk. [*Exit.*] 115

❧

3.7

Enter Cornwall, Regan, Goneril, Bastard
[Edmund], and Servants.

CORNWALL [*to Goneril*]   Post speedily to my lord your hus- 1
band; show him this letter. [*He gives a letter.*] The army
of France is landed.—Seek out the traitor Gloucester.
            [*Exeunt some Servants.*]
REGAN   Hang him instantly.
GONERIL   Pluck out his eyes.
CORNWALL   Leave him to my displeasure. Edmund,
keep you our sister company. The revenges we are 7
bound to take upon your traitorous father are not fit 8
for your beholding. Advise the Duke, where you are 9
going, to a most festinate preparation; we are bound 10
to the like. Our posts shall be swift and intelligent 11
betwixt us. Farewell, dear sister; farewell, my lord of 12
Gloucester. 13

Enter steward [Oswald].

How now? Where's the King?
OSWALD
My lord of Gloucester hath conveyed him hence.
Some five- or six-and-thirty of his knights, 16
Hot questrists after him, met him at gate, 17
Who, with some other of the lord's dependents, 18
Are gone with him toward Dover, where they boast
To have well-armèd friends.
CORNWALL   Get horses for your mistress. [*Exit Oswald.*]
GONERIL   Farewell, sweet lord, and sister.
CORNWALL
Edmund, farewell.   *Exeunt* [*Goneril and Edmund*].
       Go seek the traitor Gloucester.
Pinion him like a thief; bring him before us.
             [*Exeunt Servants.*]
Though well we may not pass upon his life 25
Without the form of justice, yet our power

Shall do a court'sy to our wrath, which men 27
May blame but not control.

Enter Gloucester, and Servants [leading him].

                  Who's there? The traitor?
REGAN   Ingrateful fox! 'Tis he.
CORNWALL   Bind fast his corky arms. 30
GLOUCESTER
What means Your Graces? Good my friends, consider
You are my guests. Do me no foul play, friends.
CORNWALL
Bind him, I say. [*Servants bind him.*]
REGAN   Hard, hard. Oh, filthy traitor!
GLOUCESTER
Unmerciful lady as you are, I'm none.
CORNWALL
To this chair bind him.—Villain, thou shalt find—
          [*Regan plucks Gloucester's beard.*]
GLOUCESTER
By the kind gods, 'tis most ignobly done
To pluck me by the beard.
REGAN
So white, and such a traitor?
GLOUCESTER   Naughty lady, 38
These hairs which thou dost ravish from my chin
Will quicken and accuse thee. I am your host. 40
With robbers' hands my hospitable favors 41
You should not ruffle thus. What will you do? 42
CORNWALL
Come, sir, what letters had you late from France? 43
REGAN
Be simple-answered, for we know the truth. 44
CORNWALL
And what confederacy have you with the traitors
Late footed in the kingdom?
REGAN   To whose hands 46
You have sent the lunatic King. Speak.
GLOUCESTER
I have a letter guessingly set down, 48
Which came from one that's of a neutral heart,
And not from one opposed.
CORNWALL   Cunning.
REGAN   And false.
CORNWALL   Where hast thou sent the King?
GLOUCESTER   To Dover.
REGAN
Wherefore to Dover? Wast thou not charged at peril— 55
CORNWALL
Wherefore to Dover? Let him answer that.
GLOUCESTER
I am tied to th' stake, and I must stand the course. 57

111–13 Mark . . . thee Observe what is being said about those in high places or about great events, and reveal your identity only when the general opinion that now slanders you, at length establishing your innocence, recalls you from banishment and restores you to favor. **114 What . . . King!** Whatever else happens tonight, may the King escape safely!   **115 Lurk** Keep out of sight
3.7. Location: Gloucester's house.
1 Post speedily Hurry   **7 sister** sister-in-law, Goneril   **8 bound** intending; obliged   **9 the Duke** Albany   **10 festinate** hasty.   **are bound** intend, are committed   **11 posts** messengers.   **intelligent** serviceable in bearing information, knowledgeable   **12–13 my . . . Gloucester.** i.e., Edmund, the recipient now of his father's forfeited estate and title. (Two lines later, Oswald uses the same title to refer to Edmund's father.)   **16 his** Lear's   **17 questrists after him** searchers for Lear   **18 the lord's** i.e., Gloucester's   **25 pass upon his life** pass the death sentence upon him

27 do a court'sy i.e., bow before, yield precedence   **30 corky** withered with age   **38 white** white-haired, venerable.   **Naughty** Wicked   **40 quicken** come to life   **41–2 With . . . thus** You should not roughly handle my welcoming face with your hands as though you were robbers.   **43 late** lately   **44 simple-answered** straightforward in your answers   **46 Late footed** recently landed   **48 guessingly set down** conjecturally written   **55 charged at peril** commanded on peril of your life   **57 tied to th' stake** i.e., like a bear to be baited with dogs. **the course** the dogs' attack.

REGAN   Wherefore to Dover?

GLOUCESTER
Because I would not see thy cruel nails
Pluck out his poor old eyes, nor thy fierce sister
In his anointed flesh rash boarish fangs.   61
The sea, with such a storm as his bare head
In hell-black night endured, would have buoyed up   63
And quenched the stellèd fires;   64
Yet, poor old heart, he holp the heavens to rain.   65
If wolves had at thy gate howled that dern time,   66
Thou shouldst have said, "Good porter, turn the key."   67
All cruels else subscribe. But I shall see   68
The wingèd Vengeance overtake such children.   69

CORNWALL
See't shalt thou never.—Fellows, hold the chair.
Upon these eyes of thine I'll set my foot.

GLOUCESTER
He that will think to live till he be old,   72
Give me some help!

[Servants hold the chair as Cornwall grinds
out one of Gloucester's eyes with his boot.]
Oh, cruel! O you gods!

REGAN
One side will mock another. Th'other too.

CORNWALL [to Gloucester]
If you see Vengeance—

FIRST SERVANT   Hold your hand, my lord!
I have served you ever since I was a child;
But better service have I never done you
Than now to bid you hold.

REGAN   How now, you dog?

FIRST SERVANT [to Regan]
If you did wear a beard upon your chin,
I'd shake it on this quarrel.—What do you mean?   80

CORNWALL   My villain?   [He draws his sword.]   81

FIRST SERVANT [drawing]
Nay, then, come on, and take the chance of anger.   82
[They fight. Cornwall is wounded.]

REGAN [to another Servant]
Give me thy sword. A peasant stand up thus?   83
[She takes a sword and runs at him behind.]

FIRST SERVANT
Oh, I am slain! My lord, you have one eye left
To see some mischief on him. Oh!   [He dies.]   85

CORNWALL
Lest it see more, prevent it. Out, vile jelly!
[He puts out Gloucester's other eye.]

Where is thy luster now?

GLOUCESTER
All dark and comfortless. Where's my son Edmund?
Edmund, enkindle all the sparks of nature   89
To quit this horrid act.

REGAN   Out, treacherous villain!   90
Thou call'st on him that hates thee. It was he
That made the overture of thy treasons to us,   92
Who is too good to pity thee.

GLOUCESTER
Oh, my follies! Then Edgar was abused.   94
Kind gods, forgive me that, and prosper him!

REGAN [to a Servant]
Go thrust him out at gates and let him smell
His way to Dover.   Exit [a Servant] with Gloucester.
How is't, my lord? How look you?   97

CORNWALL
I have received a hurt. Follow me, lady.—
Turn out that eyeless villain. Throw this slave
Upon the dunghill.—Regan, I bleed apace.
Untimely comes this hurt. Give me your arm.
Exeunt [Cornwall, supported by Regan].

SECOND SERVANT
I'll never care what wickedness I do,
If this man come to good.

THIRD SERVANT   If she live long,
And in the end meet the old course of death,   104
Women will all turn monsters.

SECOND SERVANT
Let's follow the old Earl, and get the Bedlam   106
To lead him where he would. His roguish madness   107
Allows itself to anything.   108

THIRD SERVANT
Go thou. I'll fetch some flax and whites of eggs
To apply to his bleeding face. Now, heaven help him! 110
Exeunt [with the body].

❧

4.1

Enter Edgar [as poor Tom].

EDGAR
Yet better thus, and known to be contemned,   1
Than still contemned and flattered. To be worst,   2
The lowest and most dejected thing of fortune,   3
Stands still in esperance, lives not in fear.   4

---

61 anointed consecrated with holy oil.   **rash** slash, stick
63–4 would . . . fires would have swelled high enough, like a wave-lifted buoy, to quench the stars. (*Stellèd* means "starry" or "fixed.")
65 holp helped   **66 dern** dire, dread   **67 turn the key** i.e., let them in.   **68 All . . . subscribe** All other cruel creatures would show forgiveness except you; this cruelty is unparalleled.   **69 The wingèd Vengeance** the swift vengeance of the avenging angel of divine wrath
72 will think hopes   **80 I'd . . . quarrel** i.e., I'd pull your beard in vehement defiance in this cause.   **What do you mean?** i.e., What are you thinking of, what do you think you're doing? (Said perhaps to Cornwall.)   **81 villain** servant, bondman. (Cornwall's question implies, "How dare you do such a thing?")   **82 the chance of anger** the risks of an angry encounter.   **83.1 She . . . behind** (This stage direction appears in the Quarto.)   **85 mischief** injury

89 nature i.e., filial love   **90 quit** requite.   **Out** (An exclamation of anger or impatience.)   **92 overture** disclosure   **94 abused** wronged.
97 How look you? How is it with you?   **104 old** customary, natural
106 Bedlam i.e., lunatic discharged from the insane asylum and licensed to beg   **107–8 His . . . anything** His being a madman and derelict allows him to do anything we ask.   **110.1 Exeunt** (At some point after lines 99–100, the body of the slain First Servant must be removed.)
4.1. Location: An open place.
1–2 Yet . . . flattered It is better to be openly despised as a beggar than continually despised behind one's back and flattered to one's face.
3 dejected cast down   **4 Stands . . . fear** gives one some cause for hope, having nothing to fear (since everything is already lost).

The lamentable change is from the best;   5
The worst returns to laughter. Welcome, then,   6
Thou unsubstantial air that I embrace!
The wretch that thou hast blown unto the worst
Owes nothing to thy blasts.

Enter Gloucester, and an Old Man [leading him].

           But who comes here?   9
My father, poorly led? World, world, O world!
But that thy strange mutations make us hate thee,   11
Life would not yield to age.   12

OLD MAN
Oh, my good lord, I have been your tenant
And your father's tenant these fourscore years.

GLOUCESTER
Away, get thee away! Good friend, begone.
Thy comforts can do me no good at all;
Thee they may hurt.

OLD MAN   You cannot see your way.

GLOUCESTER
I have no way and therefore want no eyes;
I stumbled when I saw. Full oft 'tis seen
Our means secure us, and our mere defects   20
Prove our commodities. O dear son Edgar,   21
The food of thy abusèd father's wrath!   22
Might I but live to see thee in my touch,   23
I'd say I had eyes again!

OLD MAN   How now? Who's there?

EDGAR [aside]
O gods! Who is't can say, "I am at the worst"?
I am worse than e'er I was.

OLD MAN   'Tis poor mad Tom.

EDGAR [aside]
And worse I may be yet. The worst is not   27
So long as we can say, "This is the worst."   28

OLD MAN [to Edgar]
Fellow, where goest?

GLOUCESTER   Is it a beggar-man?

OLD MAN   Madman and beggar too.

GLOUCESTER
He has some reason, else he could not beg.   31
I'th' last night's storm I such a fellow saw,
Which made me think a man a worm. My son
Came then into my mind, and yet my mind
Was then scarce friends with him. I have heard more
     since.
As flies to wanton boys are we to th' gods;   36

They kill us for their sport.

EDGAR [aside]   How should this be?   37
Bad is the trade that must play fool to sorrow,   38
Ang'ring itself and others.—Bless thee, master!   39

GLOUCESTER
Is that the naked fellow?

OLD MAN   Ay, my lord.

GLOUCESTER
Then, prithee, get thee gone. If for my sake
Thou wilt o'ertake us hence a mile or twain   42
I'th' way toward Dover, do it for ancient love,   43
And bring some covering for this naked soul,
Which I'll entreat to lead me.

OLD MAN   Alack, sir, he is mad.

GLOUCESTER
'Tis the time's plague, when madmen lead the blind.   46
Do as I bid thee, or rather do thy pleasure;
Above the rest, begone.   48

OLD MAN
I'll bring him the best 'parel that I have,
Come on't what will.   *Exit.*

GLOUCESTER   Sirrah, naked fellow—   50

EDGAR
Poor Tom's a-cold. [Aside] I cannot daub it further.   51

GLOUCESTER   Come hither, fellow.

EDGAR [aside]
And yet I must.—Bless thy sweet eyes, they bleed.

GLOUCESTER   Know'st thou the way to Dover?

EDGAR   Both stile and gate, horseway and footpath.
Poor Tom hath been scared out of his good wits. Bless
thee, good man's son, from the foul fiend! Five fiends
have been in poor Tom at once: of lust, as Obidicut;   58
Hobbididance, prince of dumbness; Mahu, of stealing;   59
Modo, of murder; Flibbertigibbet, of mopping   60
and mowing, who since possesses chambermaids and   61
waiting women. So, bless thee, master!

GLOUCESTER [giving a purse]
Here, take this purse, thou whom the heavens'
     plagues
Have humbled to all strokes. That I am wretched   64
Makes thee the happier. Heavens, deal so still!
Let the superfluous and lust-dieted man,   66

5–6 **The lamentable . . . laughter** Any change from the best is grievous, just as any change from the worst is bound to be for the better. 9 **Owes nothing** can pay no more, is free of obligation   11–12 **But . . . age** If it were not for your hateful inconstancy, we would never be reconciled to old age and death.   20–1 **Our . . . commodities** Our prosperity makes us proudly overconfident, whereas the sheer afflictions we suffer prove beneficial (by teaching us humility).   22 **The . . . wrath** on whom thy deceived father's wrath fed, the object of his anger.   23 **in** by means of   27–8 **The worst . . . worst** So long as we can speak and act and delude ourselves with false hopes, our fortunes can, in fact, grow worse.   31 **reason** sanity   36 **wanton** childishly cruel

37 **How . . . be?** i.e., How can he have suffered so much, changed so much?   38–9 **Bad . . . others** It's a bad business to have to play the fool to my sorrowing father, vexing myself and others (with this delay in revealing my true identity).   42 **o'ertake us** catch up to us (after you have found clothing for Tom o' Bedlam)   43 **ancient love** i.e., the mutually trusting relationship of master and tenant that you and I have long enjoyed   46 **'Tis the time's plague** It well expresses the spreading sickness of our present state   48 **the rest** all   50 **Come . . . will** whatever comes of this as regards myself.   51 **I . . . further** i.e., I cannot keep up this pretense any longer. (Literally, "I cannot plaster up the wall.")   58–60 **Obidicut . . . Flibbertigibbet** (Fiends borrowed, as before in 3.4.114 and 139–42, from Harsnett.) 60–1 **mopping and mowing** making grimaces and mouths   61 **since** ever since then   64 **Have . . . strokes** have brought so low as to bear every blow of Fortune.   66 **superfluous and lust-dieted** immoderately gluttonous and luxuriously fed

That slaves your ordinance, that will not see   67
Because he does not feel, feel your pow'r quickly!   68
So distribution should undo excess
And each man have enough. Dost thou know Dover?

EDGAR   Ay, master.

GLOUCESTER
There is a cliff, whose high and bending head   72
Looks fearfully in the confinèd deep.   73
Bring me but to the very brim of it
And I'll repair the misery thou dost bear
With something rich about me. From that place   76
I shall no leading need.

EDGAR   Give me thy arm.
Poor Tom shall lead thee.   *Exeunt.*

❖

4.2

Enter Goneril [and] Bastard [Edmund].

GONERIL
Welcome, my lord. I marvel our mild husband   1
Not met us on the way.

       [Enter] steward [Oswald].

              Now, where's your master?   2

OSWALD
Madam, within, but never man so changed.
I told him of the army that was landed;
He smiled at it. I told him you were coming;
His answer was "The worse." Of Gloucester's
   treachery
And of the loyal service of his son
When I informed him, then he called me sot   8
And told me I had turned the wrong side out.
What most he should dislike seems pleasant to him;
What like, offensive.

GONERIL *[to Edmund]*   Then shall you go no further.
It is the cowish terror of his spirit,   12
That dares not undertake. He'll not feel wrongs   13
Which tie him to an answer. Our wishes on the way   14
May prove effects. Back, Edmund, to my brother;   15
Hasten his musters and conduct his powers.   16
I must change names at home and give the distaff   17

Into my husband's hands. This trusty servant
Shall pass between us. Ere long you are like to hear,   19
If you dare venture in your own behalf,
A mistress's command. Wear this; spare speech.   21
            [She gives him a favor.]
Decline your head. *[She kisses him.]* This kiss, if it durst
   speak,
Would stretch thy spirits up into the air.
Conceive, and fare thee well.   24

EDMUND
Yours in the ranks of death.   *Exit.*

GONERIL   My most dear Gloucester!
Oh, the difference of man and man!
To thee a woman's services are due;
My fool usurps my body.   28

OSWALD   Madam, here comes my lord.   *[Exit.]*   29

       Enter Albany.

GONERIL
I have been worth the whistling.

ALBANY   Oh, Goneril,   30
You are not worth the dust which the rude wind
Blows in your face. I fear your disposition;   32
That nature which contemns its origin   33
Cannot be bordered certain in itself.   34
She that herself will sliver and disbranch   35
From her material sap perforce must wither   36
And come to deadly use.   37

GONERIL   No more. The text is foolish.   38

ALBANY
Wisdom and goodness to the vile seem vile;
Filths savor but themselves. What have you done?   40
Tigers, not daughters, what have you performed?
A father, and a gracious agèd man,
Whose reverence even the head-lugged bear would
   lick,   43
Most barbarous, most degenerate, have you madded.   44
Could my good brother suffer you to do it?   45
A man, a prince, by him so benefited?
If that the heavens do not their visible spirits   47
Send quickly down to tame these vile offenses,
It will come,
Humanity must perforce prey on itself,
Like monsters of the deep.

GONERIL   Milk-livered man,   51

---

67 That . . . ordinance who enslaves your divine ordinances to his own corrupt will   **67–8 that . . . feel** who is resistant to spiritual insight because, not having suffered himself, he lacks the sympathy of fellow feeling   **72 bending** overhanging   **73 in . . . deep** i.e., into the sea below, which is confined by its shores.   **76 about me** on my person.
4.2. Location: Before the Duke of Albany's palace.
1 Welcome (Goneril, who has just arrived home from Gloucestershire escorted by Edmund, bids him brief welcome before he must return.) **2 Not met** has not met   **8 sot** fool   **12 cowish** cowardly   **13 undertake** venture.   **13–14 He'll . . . answer** He will ignore insults that, if he took notice, would oblige him to respond, to fight.   **14–15 Our . . . effects** The hopes we discussed on our journey here (presumably concerning the supplanting of Albany by Edmund) may come to pass.   **15 brother** brother-in-law, Cornwall   **16 musters** assembling of troops.   **powers** armed forces.   **17 change names** i.e., exchange the roles of master and mistress of the household, and exchange the insignia of man and woman: the sword and the *distaff*.   **distaff** spinning staff, symbolizing the wife's role

19 like likely   **21 mistress's** (With sexual double meaning.)   **24 Conceive** Understand, take my meaning. (With sexual double entendre, continuing from *stretch thy spirits* in the previous line and continued in *death*, line 25, and *a woman's services*, line 27.)   **28 My fool . . . body** i.e., my husband claims possession of me but is unfitted to do so.   **29 s.d. Exit** (Oswald could exit later with Goneril, at line 88.)   **30 worth the whistling** i.e., worth the attentions of men. (Alludes to the proverb, "it is a poor dog that is not worth the whistling.")   **32 fear your disposition** mistrust your nature   **33 contemns** spurns   **34 bordered certain** safely restrained, kept within bounds   **35 sliver** tear off   **36 material sap** nourishing substance, the stock from which she grew   **37 to deadly use** to a bad end, to a destructive purpose.   **38 The text** i.e., on which you have been preaching   **40 savor but themselves** hunger only for that which is filthy.   **43 head-lugged** dragged by the head (or by the ring in its nose) and infuriated   **44 madded** driven mad.   **45 brother** brother-in-law (Cornwall)   **47 If that** If.   **visible** manifested   **51 Milk-livered** White-livered, cowardly

That bear'st a cheek for blows, a head for wrongs,
Who hast not in thy brows an eye discerning   53
Thine honor from thy suffering, that not know'st   54
Fools do those villains pity who are punished   55
Ere they have done their mischief. Where's thy drum?   56
France spreads his banners in our noiseless land,   57
With plumèd helm thy state begins to threat,   58
Whilst thou, a moral fool, sits still and cries,   59
"Alack, why does he so?"
ALBANY   See thyself, devil!   60
Proper deformity shows not in the fiend   61
So horrid as in woman.
GONERIL   Oh, vain fool!   62
ALBANY
Thou changèd and self-covered thing, for shame,   63
Bemonster not thy feature. Were't my fitness   64
To let these hands obey my blood,   65
They are apt enough to dislocate and tear   66
Thy flesh and bones. Howe'er thou art a fiend,   67
A woman's shape doth shield thee.   68
GONERIL   Marry, your manhood! Mew!   69

        Enter a Messenger.

ALBANY   What news?
MESSENGER
Oh, my good lord, the Duke of Cornwall's dead,
Slain by his servant, going to put out
The other eye of Gloucester.
ALBANY   Gloucester's eyes!
MESSENGER
A servant that he bred, thrilled with remorse,   74
Opposed against the act, bending his sword   75
To his great master, who, thereat enraged,   76
Flew on him and amongst them felled him dead,   77
But not without that harmful stroke which since
Hath plucked him after.
ALBANY   This shows you are above,   79

You justicers, that these our nether crimes   80
So speedily can venge! But, oh, poor Gloucester!
Lost he his other eye?
MESSENGER   Both, both, my lord.—
This letter, madam, craves a speedy answer;
'Tis from your sister.   [*He gives her a letter.*]
GONERIL [*aside*]   One way I like this well;   84
But being widow, and my Gloucester with her,   85
May all the building in my fancy pluck   86
Upon my hateful life. Another way   87
The news is not so tart.—I'll read, and answer.   88
                                    [*Exit.*]
ALBANY
Where was his son when they did take his eyes?   89
MESSENGER
Come with my lady hither.
ALBANY   He is not here.
MESSENGER
No, my good lord. I met him back again.   91
ALBANY   Knows he the wickedness?
MESSENGER
Ay, my good lord. 'Twas he informed against him,
And quit the house on purpose that their punishment
Might have the freer course.
ALBANY   Gloucester, I live   95
To thank thee for the love thou show'dst the King
And to revenge thine eyes.—Come hither, friend.
Tell me what more thou know'st.   *Exeunt.*

                          ♣

4.[3]

        Enter Kent [disguised] and a Gentleman.

KENT   Why the King of France is so suddenly gone back
    know you no reason?
GENTLEMAN   Something he left imperfect in the state,   3
    which since his coming forth is thought of, which im-   4
    ports to the kingdom so much fear and danger that his   5
    personal return was most required and necessary.
KENT
Who hath he left behind him general?
GENTLEMAN
The Marshal of France, Monsieur la Far.
KENT   Did your letters pierce the Queen to any demon-
    stration of grief?
GENTLEMAN
Ay, sir. She took them, read them in my presence,
And now and then an ample tear trilled down   12
Her delicate cheek. It seemed she was a queen

53–4 **discerning . . . suffering** able to tell the difference between an insult to your honor and something you should tolerate   54–6 **that not . . . mischief** you who fail to understand that only fools like yourself are so tenderhearted as to pity villains (like Gloucester, Lear, and Cordelia) who are apprehended and punished before they have committed a crime.   56 **Where's thy drum?** Where is your military preparedness?   57 **noiseless** peaceful, unprepared for war   58 **thy state . . . threat** (France) begins to threaten your kingdom   59 **moral** moralizing   60 **"Alack . . . so?"** (An utterly ineffectual response to invasion.)   61–2 **Proper . . . woman** The deformity that is appropriate in a fiend's features is even uglier in a woman's (since it is so at variance with her nominally feminine appearance).   63–4 **Thou . . . feature** i.e., You creature whose transformation into a fiend now overwhelms your womanliness, do not, however evil you are, take on the outward form of a monster or fiend.   64 **Were't my fitness** If it were suitable for me   65 **blood** passion   66 **apt** ready   67 **Howe'er . . . fiend** However much you may be a fiend in reality   68 **shield** (Since I, as a gentleman, cannot lay violent hands on a lady.)   69 **Mew** (An exclamation of disgust, a derisive catcall: You speak of manhood in shielding me as a woman. Some manhood!)   74 **bred** kept in his household.   **thrilled with remorse** deeply moved with pity   75 **Opposed** opposed himself   75–6 **bending . . . To** directing his sword against   77 **amongst them** together with the others (?) in their midst (?) out of their number (?)   79 **after** along (to death).

80 **justicers** (heavenly) judges.   **nether** i.e., committed here below, on earth   84 **One way** (i.e., because Edmund is now Duke of Gloucester, and Cornwall, a dangerous rival for the throne, is dead)   85–7 **But . . . life** but she being now a widow, and Edmund in her company, may pull down my imagined happiness (of having the entire kingdom with Edmund), leaving my hopes in ruins.   88 **tart** bitter, sour. (See line 84 and note.)   89 **his son** Edmund.   **his** Gloucester's.   91 **back again** on the way back (from Albany's palace).   95 **Gloucester** The old Earl of Gloucester
4.3. Location: The French camp near Dover.
3 **imperfect in the state** unsettled in state affairs   4–5 **imports** portends   12 **trilled** trickled

Over her passion, who, most rebel-like,
Sought to be king o'er her. 14

KENT   Oh, then it moved her?

GENTLEMAN
Not to a rage. Patience and sorrow strove
Who should express her goodliest. You have seen 17
Sunshine and rain at once. Her smiles and tears
Were like a better way; those happy smilets 19
That played on her ripe lip seemed not to know 20
What guests were in her eyes, which parted thence 21
As pearls from diamonds dropped. In brief,
Sorrow would be a rarity most beloved 23
If all could so become it. 24

KENT   Made she no verbal question? 25

GENTLEMAN
Faith, once or twice she heaved the name of "father" 26
Pantingly forth, as if it pressed her heart;
Cried, "Sisters, sisters! Shame of ladies, sisters!
Kent! Father! Sisters! What, i'th' storm, i'th' night?
Let pity not be believed!" There she shook 30
The holy water from her heavenly eyes,
And, clamor-moistened, then away she started 32
To deal with grief alone.

KENT   It is the stars,
The stars above us, govern our conditions, 34
Else one self mate and make could not beget 35
Such different issues. You spoke not with her since? 36

GENTLEMAN   No.

KENT
Was this before the King returned?

GENTLEMAN   No, since. 38

KENT
Well, sir, the poor distressèd Lear's i'th' town,
Who sometime in his better tune remembers 40
What we are come about, and by no means
Will yield to see his daughter.

GENTLEMAN   Why, good sir? 42

KENT
A sovereign shame so elbows him—his own
unkindness 43
That stripped her from his benediction, turned her 44
To foreign casualties, gave her dear rights 45
To his dog-hearted daughters—these things sting
His mind so venomously that burning shame
Detains him from Cordelia. 48

GENTLEMAN   Alack, poor gentleman!

KENT
Of Albany's and Cornwall's powers you heard not? 50

GENTLEMAN   'Tis so. They are afoot. 51

KENT
Well, sir, I'll bring you to our master Lear
And leave you to attend him. Some dear cause 53
Will in concealment wrap me up awhile.
When I am known aright, you shall not grieve 55
Lending me this acquaintance. I pray you, go 56
Along with me.   Exeunt.

❖

4.[4]

Enter, with drum and colors, Cordelia,
Gentleman, and soldiers.

CORDELIA
Alack, 'tis he! Why, he was met even now
As mad as the vexed sea, singing aloud,
Crowned with rank fumiter and furrow weeds, 3
With hardocks, hemlock, nettles, cuckooflowers, 4
Darnel, and all the idle weeds that grow 5
In our sustaining corn. A century send forth! 6
Search every acre in the high-grown field
And bring him to our eye.   [*Exit a soldier or soldiers.*]
                    What can man's wisdom 8
In the restoring his bereavèd sense,
He that helps him take all my outward worth. 10

GENTLEMAN   There is means, madam.
Our foster nurse of nature is repose,
The which he lacks. That to provoke in him 13
Are many simples operative, whose power 14
Will close the eye of anguish.

CORDELIA   All blest secrets,
All you unpublished virtues of the earth, 16
Spring with my tears! Be aidant and remediate 17
In the good man's distress! Seek, seek for him,
Lest his ungoverned rage dissolve the life 19
That wants the means to lead it.

Enter Messenger.

MESSENGER   News, madam. 20
The British powers are marching hitherward. 21

50 **powers** troops, armies   51 **afoot** on the march.   53 **dear cause** important purpose   55–6 **grieve . . . acquaintance** regret having made my acquaintance.
4.4. Location: The French camp.
0.2 Gentleman (The Quarto specifies "Doctor" here and at line 11.)
3 **fumiter** fumitory, a weed or herb.   **furrow weeds** weeds growing in plowed furrows   4 **hardocks** probably burdock, a coarse weedy plant.   **cuckooflowers** flowers of late spring, when the cuckoo is heard   5 **Darnel** weed of the grass kind.   **idle** worthless   6 **sustaining corn** sustenance-giving grain.   **A century** (Literally, a troop of one hundred men.)   8 **What . . . wisdom** i.e., What medical knowledge can accomplish   10 **outward** material   13 **That to provoke** To induce that   14 **Are . . . operative** many herbal remedies are efficacious; or, there are many effective remedies. (*Simples* are prepared from a single herb.)   16 **unpublished virtues** little-known benign herbs   17 **Spring** grow.   **aidant and remediate** helpful and remedial   19 **rage** frenzy   20 **That . . . lead it** that lacks the means to live sanely.
21 **powers** armies

14 **who** which   17 **Who . . . goodliest** which of the two could portray her best.   19 **like a better way** better than that, though similar   20–1 **seemed . . . eyes** seemed oblivious of her tears   23 **a rarity** i.e., a precious thing, like a jewel   24 **If . . . it** i.e., if all persons were as attractive in sorrow as she.   25 **verbal** i.e., as distinguished from her tears and looks   26 **heaved** breathed out with difficulty   30 **Let . . . believed!** i.e., Let no show of pity be trusted (since they are proved to be so false)!   32 **clamor-moistened** i.e., her outcry of grief assuaged by tears.   **started** i.e., went   34 **conditions** characters   35 **Else . . . make** otherwise, one couple (husband and wife)   36 **issues** offspring.   38 **before . . . returned** before the King of France returned to his kingdom.   40 **better tune** more composed state of mind   42 **yield** consent   43 **sovereign** overruling.   **elbows him** i.e., prods his memory, jostles him, thrusts him back   44 **turned her** turned her out   45 **foreign casualties** chances of fortune abroad   48 **Detains him from** holds him back from seeing

CORDELIA
'Tis known before. Our preparation stands
In expectation of them. O dear father,
It is thy business that I go about;
Therefore great France
My mourning and importuned tears hath pitied.   26
No blown ambition doth our arms incite,   27
But love, dear love, and our aged father's right.
Soon may I hear and see him!   *Exeunt.*

❦

4.[5]

Enter Regan and steward [Oswald].

REGAN   But are my brother's powers set forth?   1
OSWALD   Ay, madam.
REGAN   Himself in person there?
OSWALD   Madam, with much ado.   4
Your sister is the better soldier.
REGAN
Lord Edmund spake not with your lord at home?
OSWALD   No, madam.
REGAN
What might import my sister's letters to him?   8
OSWALD   I know not, lady.
REGAN
Faith, he is posted hence on serious matter.   10
It was great ignorance, Gloucester's eyes being out,   11
To let him live. Where he arrives he moves
All hearts against us. Edmund, I think, is gone,
In pity of his misery, to dispatch   14
His nighted life; moreover to descry   15
The strength o'th'enemy.
OSWALD
I must needs after him, madam, with my letter.
REGAN
Our troops set forth tomorrow. Stay with us;
The ways are dangerous.
OSWALD   I may not, madam.
My lady charged my duty in this business.   20
REGAN
Why should she write to Edmund? Might not you
Transport her purposes by word? Belike   22
Something—I know not what. I'll love thee much;
Let me unseal the letter.
OSWALD   Madam, I had rather—
REGAN
I know your lady does not love her husband,
I am sure of that; and at her late being here   26
She gave strange oeillades and most speaking looks   27
To noble Edmund. I know you are of her bosom.   28
OSWALD   I, madam?

REGAN
I speak in understanding; y'are, I know't.   30
Therefore I do advise you, take this note: 31
My lord is dead; Edmund and I have talked,   32
And more convenient is he for my hand   33
Than for your lady's. You may gather more.   34
If you do find him, pray you, give him this;   35
And when your mistress hears thus much from you,   36
I pray, desire her call her wisdom to her.   37
So, fare you well.
If you do chance to hear of that blind traitor,
Preferment falls on him that cuts him off.   40
OSWALD
Would I could meet him, madam! I should show
What party I do follow.
REGAN   Fare thee well.
                    Exeunt [separately].

❦

4.[6]

Enter Gloucester, and Edgar [in peasant's clothes, leading his father].

GLOUCESTER
When shall I come to th' top of that same hill?   1
EDGAR
You do climb up it now. Look how we labor.
GLOUCESTER
Methinks the ground is even.
EDGAR   Horrible steep.
Hark, do you hear the sea?
GLOUCESTER   No, truly.
EDGAR
Why, then, your other senses grow imperfect
By your eyes' anguish.
GLOUCESTER   So may it be, indeed.
Methinks thy voice is altered, and thou speak'st
In better phrase and matter than thou didst.
EDGAR
You're much deceived. In nothing am I changed
But in my garments.
GLOUCESTER   Methinks you're better spoken.
EDGAR
Come on, sir, here's the place. Stand still. How fearful
And dizzy 'tis to cast one's eyes so low!
The crows and choughs that wing the midway air   13
Show scarce so gross as beetles. Halfway down   14
Hangs one that gathers samphire—dreadful trade!   15
Methinks he seems no bigger than his head.
The fishermen that walk upon the beach

---

26 importuned importunate   **27 blown** swollen
4.5. Location; Gloucester's house.
1 my brother's powers Albany's forces   **4 with much ado** after much fuss and persuasion.   **8 import** bear as their purport, express   **10 is posted** has hurried   **11 ignorance** error, folly   **14 his** Gloucester's **15 nighted** benighted, blinded.   **descry** spy out   **20 charged my duty** laid great stress on my obedience   **22 Belike** It may be   **26 late** recently   **27 oeillades** amorous glances   **28 of her bosom** in her confidence.

30 y'are you are   **31 take this note** take note of this   **32 have talked** have come to an understanding   **33 convenient** fitting   **34 gather more** infer what I am trying to suggest.   **35 this** i.e., this information, or a love token, or possibly a letter (though only one letter, Goneril's, is found on his dead body at 4.6.262)   **36 thus much** what I have told you   **37 call . . . to her** recall herself to her senses.   **40 Preferment** advancement
4.6. Location: Open place near Dover.
1 that same hill i.e., the cliff we talked about (4.1.72–4).   **13 choughs** jackdaws.   **midway** halfway down   **14 gross** large   **15 samphire** (A herb used in pickling.)

Appear like mice, and yond tall anchoring bark 18
Diminished to her cock; her cock, a buoy 19
Almost too small for sight. The murmuring surge,
That on th'unnumbered idle pebble chafes, 21
Cannot be heard so high. I'll look no more,
Lest my brain turn, and the deficient sight 23
Topple down headlong.

GLOUCESTER   Set me where you stand. 24

EDGAR
Give me your hand. You are now within a foot
Of th'extreme verge. For all beneath the moon 26
Would I not leap upright.

GLOUCESTER   Let go my hand. 27
Here, friend, 's another purse; in it a jewel
Well worth a poor man's taking.   [He gives a purse.]
Fairies and gods 29
Prosper it with thee! Go thou further off. 30
Bid me farewell, and let me hear thee going.

EDGAR [moving away]
Now fare ye well, good sir.

GLOUCESTER   With all my heart.

EDGAR [aside]
Why I do trifle thus with his despair
Is done to cure it.

GLOUCESTER [kneeling]   O you mighty gods!
This world I do renounce, and in your sights
Shake patiently my great affliction off.
If I could bear it longer and not fall
To quarrel with your great opposeless wills, 38
My snuff and loathèd part of nature should 39
Burn itself out. If Edgar live, oh, bless him!
Now, fellow, fare thee well.   [He falls forward.]

EDGAR   Gone, sir. Farewell.—
And yet I know not how conceit may rob 42
The treasury of life, when life itself
Yields to the theft. Had he been where he thought, 44
By this had thought been past. Alive or dead?— 45
Ho, you, sir! Friend! Hear you, sir! Speak!—
Thus might he pass indeed; yet he revives.— 47
What are you, sir?

GLOUCESTER   Away, and let me die. 48

EDGAR
Hadst thou been aught but gossamer, feathers, air,
So many fathom down precipitating,
Thou'dst shivered like an egg; but thou dost breathe,
Hast heavy substance, bleed'st not, speak'st, art
  sound. 52

Ten masts at each make not the altitude 53
Which thou hast perpendicularly fell.
Thy life's a miracle. Speak yet again.

GLOUCESTER   But have I fall'n or no?

EDGAR
From the dread summit of this chalky bourn. 57
Look up aheight; the shrill-gorged lark so far 58
Cannot be seen or heard. Do but look up.

GLOUCESTER   Alack, I have no eyes.
Is wretchedness deprived that benefit
To end itself by death? 'Twas yet some comfort
When misery could beguile the tyrant's rage 63
And frustrate his proud will.

EDGAR   Give me your arm.
                          [He lifts him up.]
Up—so. How is't? Feel you your legs? You stand.

GLOUCESTER
Too well, too well.

EDGAR   This is above all strangeness.
Upon the crown o'th' cliff what thing was that
Which parted from you?

GLOUCESTER   A poor unfortunate beggar.

EDGAR
As I stood here below, methought his eyes
Were two full moons; he had a thousand noses,
Horns whelked and waved like the enridgèd sea. 71
It was some fiend. Therefore, thou happy father, 72
Think that the clearest gods, who make them honors 73
Of men's impossibilities, have preserved thee. 74

GLOUCESTER
I do remember now. Henceforth I'll bear
Affliction till it do cry out itself 76
"Enough, enough," and die. That thing you speak of, 77
I took it for a man; often 'twould say
"The fiend, the fiend." He led me to that place.

EDGAR
Bear free and patient thoughts.

Enter Lear [mad, fantastically dressed with wild
  flowers].

                          But who comes here? 80
The safer sense will ne'er accommodate 81
His master thus. 82

LEAR   No, they cannot touch me for coining. I am the 83
King himself. 84

EDGAR   Oh, thou side-piercing sight! 85

---

18 bark small sailing vessel   19 Diminished . . . cock reduced to the size of her cockboat, small ship's boat   21 th'unnumbered idle pebble innumerable, randomly shifting, pebbles   23–4 Lest . . . headlong lest I become dizzy, and my failing sight topple me headlong. 26 For . . . moon i.e., For the whole world   27 upright i.e., up and down, much less forward.   29–30 Fairies . . . thee! May the fairies and gods cause this to multiply in your possession!   38 To quarrel with into rebellion against.   opposeless irresistible   39 snuff i.e., useless residue. (Literally, the smoking wick of a candle.)   of nature i.e., of my life   42 conceit imagination   44 Yields consents   45 By this by this time   47 pass die   48 What Who. (Edgar now speaks in a new voice, differing from that of "poor Tom" and also from the "altered" voice he used at the start of this scene; see lines 7–10.) 52 heavy substance the substance of the flesh

53 at each end to end   57 bourn limit, boundary (i.e., the edge of the sea).   58 aheight on high.   shrill-gorged shrill-throated   63 beguile outwit   71 whelked twisted, convoluted.   enridgèd furrowed (by the wind)   72 happy father lucky old man   73 clearest purest, most righteous   73–4 who . . . impossibilities who win our awe and reverence by doing things impossible to men   76–7 till . . . die i.e., until affliction itself has had enough, or until I die.   80 free i.e., free from despair   81–2 The safer . . . thus i.e., A person in his right senses would never dress himself in such a fashion. (His master is the owner of the safer sense or sane mind. His means "its.")   83–4 they . . . himself they cannot prosecute me for minting coins. As king, I enjoy the exclusive royal prerogative for doing so. (Lear goes on to discuss his need for money to pay his imaginary soldiers.)   85 side-piercing heartrending. (With a suggestion of Christ's suffering on the cross.)

LEAR Nature's above art in that respect. There's your 86
press money. That fellow handles his bow like a crow- 87
keeper. Draw me a clothier's yard. Look, look, a 88
mouse! Peace, peace; this piece of toasted cheese will
do't. There's my gauntlet; I'll prove it on a giant. Bring 90
up the brown bills. Oh, well flown, bird! I'th' clout, 91
i'th' clout—hewgh! Give the word. 92

EDGAR Sweet marjoram. 93

LEAR Pass.

GLOUCESTER I know that voice.

LEAR Ha! Goneril with a white beard? They flattered
me like a dog and told me I had white hairs in my 97
beard ere the black ones were there. To say ay and 98
no to everything that I said ay and no to was 99
no good divinity. When the rain came to wet me 100
once and the wind to make me chatter, when the 101
thunder would not peace at my bidding, there I found 102
'em, there I smelt 'em out. Go to, they are not men o' 103
their words. They told me I was everything. 'Tis a
lie. I am not ague-proof. 105

GLOUCESTER

The trick of that voice I do well remember. 106
Is't not the King?

LEAR   Ay, every inch a king.
When I do stare, see how the subject quakes.
I pardon that man's life. What was thy cause? 109
Adultery?
Thou shalt not die. Die for adultery? No.
The wren goes to't, and the small gilded fly
Does lecher in my sight.
Let copulation thrive; for Gloucester's bastard son
Was kinder to his father than my daughters
Got 'tween the lawful sheets.
To't, luxury, pell-mell, for I lack soldiers. 117
Behold yond simpering dame,
Whose face between her forks presages snow, 119
That minces virtue and does shake the head 120
To hear of pleasure's name; 121
The fitchew nor the soilèd horse goes to't 122

With a more riotous appetite.
Down from the waist they're centaurs, 124
Though women all above.
But to the girdle do the gods inherit; 126
Beneath is all the fiend's.
There's hell, there's darkness, there is the sulfurous pit,
burning, scalding, stench, consumption. Fie, fie, fie!
Pah, pah! Give me an ounce of civet, good apothecary, 130
sweeten my imagination. There's money for thee.

GLOUCESTER Oh, let me kiss that hand!

LEAR Let me wipe it first; it smells of mortality.

GLOUCESTER

Oh, ruined piece of nature! This great world 134
Shall so wear out to naught. Dost thou know me? 135

LEAR I remember thine eyes well enough. Dost thou
squinny at me? No, do thy worst, blind Cupid; I'll not 137
love. Read thou this challenge. Mark but the penning
of it.

GLOUCESTER

Were all thy letters suns, I could not see.

EDGAR [aside]

I would not take this from report. It is, 141
And my heart breaks at it.

LEAR Read.

GLOUCESTER What, with the case of eyes? 144

LEAR Oho, are you there with me? No eyes in your 145
head, nor no money in your purse? Your eyes are in a
heavy case, your purse in a light, yet you see how this 147
world goes.

GLOUCESTER I see it feelingly. 149

LEAR What, art mad? A man may see how this world
goes with no eyes. Look with thine ears. See how
yond justice rails upon yond simple thief. Hark in 152
thine ear: change places and, handy-dandy, which is 153
the justice, which is the thief? Thou hast seen a
farmer's dog bark at a beggar?

GLOUCESTER Ay, sir.

LEAR And the creature run from the cur? There thou 157
mightst behold the great image of authority: a dog's 158
obeyed in office. 159
Thou rascal beadle, hold thy bloody hand! 160
Why dost thou lash that whore? Strip thine own back;
Thou hotly lusts to use her in that kind 162
For which thou whipp'st her. The usurer hangs the
cozener. 163

---

86 Nature's . . . respect Real life can offer more heart-piercing examples than art. **87 press money** enlistment bonus. **87–8 crowkeeper** laborer hired to scare away the crows. **88 Draw . . . yard** i.e., Draw your bow to the full length of the arrow, a cloth-yard long. **90 do't** i.e., capture the mouse, an imagined enemy. **gauntlet** armored glove thrown down as a challenge. **prove it on** maintain it against **91 brown bills** soldiers carrying pikes (painted brown), or the pikes themselves. **well flown, bird** (Lear uses the language of hawking to describe the flight of an arrow.) **clout** target, bull's-eye **92 hewgh** (The arrow's noise.) **word** password. **93 Sweet marjoram** (A herb used to cure madness.) **97 like a dog** as a dog fawns **97–8 told . . . there** i.e., told me I had the white-haired wisdom of old age before I had even attained the manliness of a beard. **98–100 To . . . divinity** i.e., To agree flatteringly with everything I said was not good theology, since the Bible teaches us to "let your yea be yea and your nay, nay" (James 5:12; see also Matthew 5:37 and 2 Cor. 1:18). **100–3 When . . . out** i.e., Suffering wet, cold, and storm have taught me about the frailty of the human condition. **103 Go to** (An expression of impatience.) **105 ague-proof** immune against illness (literally, fever). **106 trick** peculiar characteristic **109 cause** offense. **117 luxury** lechery **119 Whose . . . snow** whose frosty countenance seems to suggest frigidity between her legs **120 minces** affects, mimics **121 of pleasure's name** the very name of pleasure **122 The fitchew . . . to't** neither the polecat nor the well-pastured horse indulges in sexual pleasure

124 centaurs fabulous creatures with the head, trunk, and arms of a man joined to the body and legs of a horse **126 But** Only. **girdle** waist. **inherit** have possession **130 civet** musk perfume **134 piece** (1) fragment (2) masterpiece **134–5 This . . . naught** Even so will the whole universe come to an apocalyptic end. **137 squinny** squint **141 take** believe, credit. **It is** It is taking place, incredibly enough **144 case** sockets **145 are . . . me?** is that your meaning, the point you are making? **147 heavy case** sad plight. (With pun on *case* in line 144.) **149 feelingly** (1) by touch (2) keenly, painfully. **152 simple** of humble station **153 handy-dandy** take your choice of hands (as in a well-known child's game) **157 creature** poor fellow **158–9 a dog's . . . office** i.e., even currish power commands submission. **160 beadle** parish officer, responsible for giving whippings **162 kind** way **163 The usurer . . . cozener** The moneylender (who can buy out justice) hangs the con man.

Through tattered clothes small vices do appear;   164
Robes and furred gowns hide all. Plate sin with gold,   165
And the strong lance of justice hurtless breaks;   166
Arm it in rags, a pygmy's straw does pierce it.
None does offend, none, I say, none. I'll able 'em.   168
Take that of me, my friend, who have the power   169
To seal th'accuser's lips. Get thee glass eyes,   170
And like a scurvy politician seem   171
To see the things thou dost not. Now, now, now, now!   172
Pull off my boots. Harder, harder! So.

EDGAR [aside]
Oh, matter and impertinency mixed,   174
Reason in madness!

LEAR
If thou wilt weep my fortunes, take my eyes.
I know thee well enough; thy name is Gloucester.
Thou must be patient. We came crying hither.
Thou know'st the first time that we smell the air
We wawl and cry. I will preach to thee. Mark.

GLOUCESTER   Alack, alack the day!

LEAR
When we are born, we cry that we are come
To this great stage of fools.—This' a good block.   183
It were a delicate stratagem to shoe   184
A troop of horse with felt. I'll put 't in proof,   185
And when I have stol'n upon these son-in-laws,
Then, kill, kill, kill, kill, kill, kill!

Enter a Gentleman [with attendants].

GENTLEMAN
Oh, here he is. Lay hand upon him.—Sir,
Your most dear daughter—

LEAR
No rescue? What, a prisoner? I am even
The natural fool of fortune. Use me well;   191
You shall have ransom. Let me have surgeons;
I am cut to th' brains.

GENTLEMAN   You shall have anything.   193

LEAR   No seconds? All myself?   194
Why, this would make a man a man of salt   195
To use his eyes for garden waterpots,
Ay, and laying autumn's dust.
I will die bravely, like a smug bridegroom. What?   198

I will be jovial. Come, come, I am a king,   199
Masters, know you that?   200

GENTLEMAN
You are a royal one, and we obey you.

LEAR   Then there's life in't. Come, an you get it, you   202
shall get it by running. Sa, sa, sa, sa.   203
                    Exit [running, followed by attendants].

GENTLEMAN
A sight most pitiful in the meanest wretch,
Past speaking of in a king! Thou hast one daughter
Who redeems nature from the general curse   206
Which twain have brought her to.   207

EDGAR   Hail, gentle sir.   208

GENTLEMAN   Sir, speed you. What's your will?   209

EDGAR
Do you hear aught, sir, of a battle toward?   210

GENTLEMAN
Most sure and vulgar. Everyone hears that   211
Which can distinguish sound.

EDGAR   But, by your favor,   212
How near's the other army?

GENTLEMAN
Near and on speedy foot. The main descry   214
Stands on the hourly thought.   215

EDGAR   I thank you, sir; that's all.

GENTLEMAN
Though that the Queen on special cause is here,   217
Her army is moved on.

EDGAR   I thank you, sir.
                    Exit [Gentleman].

GLOUCESTER
You ever-gentle gods, take my breath from me;
Let not my worser spirit tempt me again   220
To die before you please!

EDGAR   Well pray you, father.   222

GLOUCESTER   Now, good sir, what are you?   223

EDGAR
A most poor man, made tame to fortune's blows,   224
Who, by the art of known and feeling sorrows,   225
Am pregnant to good pity. Give me your hand.   226
I'll lead you to some biding.   *[He offers his arm.]*

GLOUCESTER   Hearty thanks.   227

164–5 Through . . . all i.e., Beggars' small vices are apparent for all to
see; rich folk, in expensive clothes, succeed in hiding a great deal.
165 Plate Arm in plate armor   166 hurtless breaks splinters harm-
lessly   168 able empower, give warrant to   169 Take . . . me
(1) Learn that from me (2) Take that protection from me   170–2 Get
. . . dost not If Gloucester were to fit himself out with spectacles (or
perhaps with glass eyeballs, though they are not mentioned elsewhere until later in the seventeenth century), he would look wise like
a hypocritical politician.   174 matter and impertinency sense and
nonsense   183 This' This is.   block mold for a felt hat. (Lear may
refer to the weeds strewn in his hair, which he removes as though
doffing a hat before preaching a sermon.)   184 delicate subtle
185 felt i.e., padding to deaden the sound of the footfall.   in proof to
the test   191 natural fool born plaything   193 cut wounded
194 seconds supporters.   195 of salt of salt tears   198 bravely (1)
courageously (2) splendidly attired.   smug trimly dressed.
(*Bridegroom* continues the punning sexual suggestion of *die bravely*,
"have sex successfully.")

199 jovial (1) Jovelike, majestic (2) jolly.   200 Masters good sirs
202 life i.e., hope still.   an if   203 Sa . . . sa (A hunting cry.)
206 general curse fallen condition of the human race   207 twain
(1) Goneril and Regan (2) Adam and Eve   208 gentle noble   209 speed
you Godspeed, may God prosper you.   210 toward imminent.
211 vulgar in everyone's mouth, generally known.   212 Which who
214–15 The main . . . thought The full view of the main body is
expected any hour now.   217 Though that Although.   on special
cause for a special reason, i.e., to minister to Lear   220 worser spirit
bad angel, or ill thoughts   222 father (A term of respect to older
men, as also in lines 72, 259, and 290, though with ironic double
meaning throughout the scene.)   223 what who. (Again, Edgar alters
his voice to personate a new stranger assisting Gloucester. See line 48,
above, and note.)   224 tame submissive   225 known and feeling
personally experienced and heartfelt   226 pregnant prone   227 biding abode.

The bounty and the benison of heaven   228
To boot, and boot!

Enter steward [Oswald].

OSWALD   A proclaimed prize! Most happy!   229
                              [He draws his sword.]
That eyeless head of thine was first framed flesh   230
To raise my fortunes. Thou old unhappy traitor,
Briefly thyself remember. The sword is out   232
That must destroy thee.

GLOUCESTER   Now let thy friendly hand   233
Put strength enough to't.   *[Edgar intervenes.]*

OSWALD   Wherefore, bold peasant,
Durst thou support a published traitor? Hence,   235
Lest that th'infection of his fortune take   236
Like hold on thee. Let go his arm.   237

EDGAR 'Chill not let go, zir, without vurther 'cagion.   238

OSWALD Let go, slave, or thou diest!

EDGAR Good gentleman, go your gait, and let poor volk   240
pass. An 'chud ha' bin zwaggered out of my life,   241
'twould not ha' bin zo long as 'tis by a vortnight. Nay,   242
come not near th' old man; keep out, 'che vor ye, or   243
Ise try whether your costard or my ballow be the   244
harder. 'Chill be plain with you.

OSWALD Out, dunghill!

EDGAR 'Chill pick your teeth, zir. Come, no matter vor
your foins. *[They fight. Edgar fells him with his cudgel.]*   248

OSWALD
Slave, thou hast slain me. Villain, take my purse.   249
If ever thou wilt thrive, bury my body
And give the letters which thou find'st about me   251
To Edmund, Earl of Gloucester. Seek him out
Upon the English party. Oh, untimely death!   253
Death!   *[He dies.]*

EDGAR
I know thee well: a serviceable villain,   255
As duteous to the vices of thy mistress
As badness would desire.

GLOUCESTER What, is he dead?

EDGAR Sit you down, father. Rest you. *[Gloucester sits.]*
Let's see these pockets; the letters that he speaks of
May be my friends. He's dead; I am only sorry
He had no other deathsman. Let us see.   262
                    [He finds a letter and opens it.]
Leave, gentle wax, and, manners, blame us not.   263

To know our enemies' minds we rip their hearts;
Their papers is more lawful.   *(Reads the letter.)*
          "Let our reciprocal vows be remembered. You have
many opportunities to cut him off; if your will want   267
not, time and place will be fruitfully offered. There is   268
nothing done if he return the conqueror. Then am I   269
the prisoner, and his bed my jail, from the loathed
warmth whereof deliver me and supply the place for   271
your labor.   272
          Your—wife, so I would say—affectionate servant,
          and for you her own for venture, Goneril."   274
Oh, indistinguished space of woman's will!   275
A plot upon her virtuous husband's life,
And the exchange my brother! Here in the sands
Thee I'll rake up, the post unsanctified   278
Of murderous lechers; and in the mature time   279
With this ungracious paper strike the sight   280
Of the death-practiced Duke. For him 'tis well   281
That of thy death and business I can tell.
                              [Exit with the body.]

GLOUCESTER
The King is mad. How stiff is my vile sense,   283
That I stand up and have ingenious feeling   284
Of my huge sorrows! Better I were distract;   285
So should my thoughts be severed from my griefs,
And woes by wrong imaginations lose   287
The knowledge of themselves.   *Drum afar off.*

          [Enter Edgar.]

EDGAR   Give me your hand.
Far off, methinks, I hear the beaten drum.
Come, father, I'll bestow you with a friend.   290
                    Exeunt, [Edgar leading his father].

❧

4.7

*Enter Cordelia, Kent [dressed still in his disguise
costume], and Gentleman.*

CORDELIA
O thou good Kent, how shall I live and work
To match thy goodness? My life will be too short,
And every measure fail me.   3

228–9 **The bounty . . . and boot!** In addition to my thanks, I wish you the bounty and blessings of heaven. **229 proclaimed prize** one with a price on his head. **happy** fortunate. **230 framed flesh** born **232 thyself remember** i.e., say your prayers. **233 friendly** i.e., welcome, since I desire death **235 published** proclaimed **236 Lest that** lest **237 Like** similar **238 'Chill** I will. (Literally, a contraction of *Ich will*. Edgar adopts Somerset dialect, a stage convention regularly used for peasants.) **vurther 'cagion** further occasion. **240 go your gait** go your own way **241 An 'chud** If I could. **zwaggered** swaggered, bullied **242 'twould . . . vortnight** it (my life) wouldn't have lasted a fortnight. **243 'che vor ye** I warrant you **244 Ise** I shall. **costard** head. (Literally, an apple.) **ballow** cudgel **248 foins** thrusts. **249 Villain** Serf **251 letters** letter. (See 4.5.35 and note.) **about me** upon my person **253 Upon** on. **party** side. **255 serviceable** officious **262 deathsman** executioner. **263 Leave** By your leave. **wax** wax seal on the letter

267 **him** Albany **267–8 want not** is not lacking **268 fruitfully** plentifully and with results **268–9 There is nothing done** i.e., We will have accomplished nothing **271 supply** fill **271–2 for your labor** (1) as recompense for your efforts (2) as a place for your amorous labors. **274 and for . . . venture** and one ready to venture her own fortunes for your sake **275 indistinguished . . . will** limitless and incalculable expanse of woman's appetite. **278 rake up** cover up. **post unsanctified** unholy messenger **279 in . . . time** when the time is ripe **280 ungracious** wicked. **strike** blast **281 Of . . . well** of Albany, whose death is plotted. It's a good thing for him **283 How . . . sense** How obstinate is my deplorable sanity and power of sensation **284 ingenious** conscious. (Gloucester laments that he remains sane and hence fully conscious of his troubles, unlike Lear.) **285 distract** distracted, crazy **287 wrong imaginations** delusions **290 bestow** lodge. (At the scene's end, Edgar leads off Gloucester; presumably, at line 282 or else here, he must also dispose of Oswald's body in the trapdoor or by lugging it offstage.)
4.7. Location: The French camp.
0.2 *Gentleman* ("Doctor" in Q.) **3 every . . . me** every attempt (to match your goodness) will fall short.

KENT
  To be acknowledged, madam, is o'erpaid.
  All my reports go with the modest truth,   5
  Nor more nor clipped, but so.
CORDELIA   Be better suited.   6
  These weeds are memories of those worser hours;   7
  I prithee, put them off.
KENT   Pardon, dear madam;
  Yet to be known shortens my made intent.   9
  My boon I make it that you know me not   10
  Till time and I think meet.   11
CORDELIA
  Then be't so, my good lord. [*To the Gentleman*] How
      does the King?
GENTLEMAN   Madam, sleeps still.
CORDELIA   O you kind gods,
  Cure this great breach in his abusèd nature!
  Th'untuned and jarring senses, oh, wind up   16
  Of this child-changèd father!   17
GENTLEMAN   So please Your Majesty
  That we may wake the King? He hath slept long.
CORDELIA
  Be governed by your knowledge, and proceed
  I'th' sway of your own will.—Is he arrayed?   21

        Enter Lear in a chair carried by servants.

GENTLEMAN
  Ay, madam. In the heaviness of sleep
  We put fresh garments on him.
  Be by, good madam, when we do awake him.
  I doubt not of his temperance.
CORDELIA   Very well.   [*Music.*] 25
GENTLEMAN
  Please you, draw near.—Louder the music there!
CORDELIA [*kissing him*]
  O my dear father! Restoration hang
  Thy medicine on my lips, and let this kiss
  Repair those violent harms that my two sisters
  Have in thy reverence made!
KENT   Kind and dear princess!   30
CORDELIA
  Had you not been their father, these white flakes   31
  Did challenge pity of them. Was this a face   32
  To be opposed against the warring winds?
  To stand against the deep dread-bolted thunder   34
  In the most terrible and nimble stroke

Of quick cross lightning? To watch—poor perdu!—   36
  With this thin helm? Mine enemy's dog,   37
  Though he had bit me, should have stood that night
  Against my fire; and wast thou fain, poor father,   39
  To hovel thee with swine and rogues forlorn   40
  In short and musty straw? Alack, alack!   41
  'Tis wonder that thy life and wits at once
  Had not concluded all.—He wakes! Speak to him.   43
GENTLEMAN   Madam, do you; 'tis fittest.
CORDELIA
  How does my royal lord? How fares Your Majesty?
LEAR
  You do me wrong to take me out o'th' grave.
  Thou art a soul in bliss; but I am bound
  Upon a wheel of fire, that mine own tears   48
  Do scald like molten lead.
CORDELIA   Sir, do you know me?
LEAR
  You are a spirit, I know. Where did you die?
CORDELIA   Still, still, far wide!   51
GENTLEMAN
  He's scarce awake. Let him alone awhile.
LEAR
  Where have I been? Where am I? Fair daylight?
  I am mightily abused. I should ev'n die with pity   54
  To see another thus. I know not what to say.   55
  I will not swear these are my hands. Let's see;
  I feel this pinprick. Would I were assured
  Of my condition!
CORDELIA [*kneeling*]   Oh, look upon me, sir,
  And hold your hands in benediction o'er me.
                        [*He attempts to kneel.*]
  No, sir, you must not kneel.
LEAR   Pray, do not mock me.
  I am a very foolish fond old man,   61
  Fourscore and upward, not an hour more nor less;
  And, to deal plainly,
  I fear I am not in my perfect mind.
  Methinks I should know you, and know this man,
  Yet I am doubtful; for I am mainly ignorant   66
  What place this is, and all the skill I have
  Remembers not these garments, nor I know not
  Where I did lodge last night. Do not laugh at me,
  For, as I am a man, I think this lady
  To be my child Cordelia.
CORDELIA [*weeping*]   And so I am, I am.
LEAR
  Be your tears wet? Yes, faith. I pray, weep not.
  If you have poison for me I will drink it.
  I know you do not love me, for your sisters
  Have, as I do remember, done me wrong.
  You have some cause, they have not.

5 All my reports go All my reports (of my service as Caius to Lear) conform   **6 Nor . . . clipped** i.e., neither more nor less.   **suited** dressed.   **7 weeds** garments.   **memories** remembrances   **9 Yet . . . intent** to reveal my true identity now would alter my carefully made plan.   **10 My . . . it** The favor I seek is.   **know** acknowledge   **11 meet** appropriate.   **16 wind up** tune (as by tightening the slackened string of an instrument)   **17 child-changèd** changed by children's cruelty   **21 I'th' sway** under the direction   **25 temperance** self-control, calm behavior.   **30 reverence** venerable condition   **31 Had you** Even if you had.   **flakes** locks of hair   **32 Did challenge** would have demanded   **34 deep** bass-voiced.   **dread-bolted** furnished with the dreadful thunderbolt

36 cross zigzag.   **watch** stay awake (like a sentry on duty).   **perdu** lost one; a sentinel placed in a position of peculiar danger.   **37 helm** helmet, i.e., scanty hair.   **39 Against** before, in front of.   **fain** constrained   **40 rogues forlorn** abandoned vagabonds   **41 short** broken up and hence uncomfortable   **43 concluded all** come to an end altogether.   **48 wheel of fire** (A hellish torment for the eternally damned.)   **that** so that   **51 wide** wide of the mark, wandering.   **54 abused** confused, deluded.   **55 thus** i.e., thus confused, bewildered.   **61 fond** in my dotage   **66 mainly** entirely

CORDELIA   No cause, no cause.

LEAR   Am I in France?

KENT   In your own kingdom, sir.

LEAR   Do not abuse me.   81

GENTLEMAN
Be comforted, good madam. The great rage,   82
You see, is killed in him, and yet it is danger
To make him even o'er the time he has lost.   84
Desire him to go in. Trouble him no more
Till further settling.   86

CORDELIA   Will't please Your Highness walk?   87

LEAR   You must bear with me.
Pray you now, forget and forgive.
I am old and foolish.
                          Exeunt [all but Kent and Gentleman].

GENTLEMAN   Holds it true, sir, that the Duke of Corn-   91
wall was so slain?

KENT   Most certain, sir.

GENTLEMAN   Who is conductor of his people?   94

KENT   As 'tis said, the bastard son of Gloucester.

GENTLEMAN   They say Edgar, his banished son, is with
the Earl of Kent in Germany.

KENT   Report is changeable. 'Tis time to look about; the   98
powers of the kingdom approach apace.   99

GENTLEMAN   The arbitrament is like to be bloody. Fare   100
you well, sir.   [*Exit.*]

KENT
My point and period will be throughly wrought,   102
Or well or ill, as this day's battle's fought.   *Exit.*   103

❧

5.1

*Enter, with drum and colors, Edmund, Regan,
Gentlemen, and soldiers.*

EDMUND   [*to a Gentleman*]
Know of the Duke if his last purpose hold,   1
Or whether since he is advised by aught   2
To change the course. He's full of alteration   3
And self-reproving. Bring his constant pleasure.   4
                                       [*Exit Gentleman.*]

REGAN
Our sister's man is certainly miscarried.   5

EDMUND
'Tis to be doubted, madam.

REGAN   Now, sweet lord,   6
You know the goodness I intend upon you.   7
Tell me, but truly—but then speak the truth—
Do you not love my sister?

EDMUND   In honored love.   9

REGAN
But have you never found my brother's way
To the forfended place?   11

EDMUND   That thought abuses you.   12

REGAN
I am doubtful that you have been conjunct   13
And bosomed with her, as far as we call hers.   14

EDMUND   No, by mine honor, madam.

REGAN
I never shall endure her. Dear my lord,
Be not familiar with her.   17

EDMUND
Fear me not.—She and the Duke her husband!   18

*Enter, with drum and colors, Albany, Goneril,
[and] soldiers.*

GONERIL   [*aside*]
I had rather lose the battle than that sister
Should loosen him and me.

ALBANY   [*to Regan*]
Our very loving sister, well bemet.   21
[*To Edmund*] Sir, this I heard: the King is come to his
     daughter,
With others whom the rigor of our state   23
Forced to cry out. Where I could not be honest,   24
I never yet was valiant. For this business,   25
It touches us as France invades our land,   26
Not bolds the King, with others whom, I fear,   27
Most just and heavy causes make oppose.   28

EDMUND   Sir, you speak nobly.

REGAN   Why is this reasoned?   30

GONERIL
Combine together 'gainst the enemy;
For these domestic and particular broils   32
Are not the question here.

ALBANY   Let's then determine
With th'ancient of war on our proceeding.   34

EDMUND
I shall attend you presently at your tent.

REGAN   Sister, you'll go with us?

GONERIL   No.

---

81 abuse deceive. (Or perhaps Lear feels hurt by the reminder of his having divided the kingdom.)   **82 rage** frenzy   **84 even o'er** fill in, go over in his mind   **86 settling** composing of his mind.   **87 walk** withdraw.   **91 Holds it true** Is it still held to be true   **94 conductor** leader, general   **98 look about** be wary, take stock of the situation   **99 powers of the kingdom** British armies (marching against the French invaders)   **100 arbitrament** decision by arms, decisive encounter   **102 My . . . wrought** i.e., The conclusion of my destiny (literally, the full stop at the end of my life's sentence) will be thoroughly shaped   **103 Or** either.   **as** according as
5.1. Location: The British camp near Dover.
1 Know Inquire.   **last purpose hold** most recent intention (to fight) remains firm   **2 since** since then.   **advised by aught** persuaded by any consideration   **3 alteration** vacillation   **4 constant pleasure** settled decision.   **5 man** i.e., Oswald.   **miscarried** lost, perished.

6 doubted feared   **7 intend** intend to confer   **9 honored** honorable
11 forfended forbidden (by the commandment against adultery)
12 abuses degrades, wrongs   **13–14 I . . . hers** I fear that you have been sexually intimate with her to the fullest extent possible.
17 familiar intimate   **18 Fear me not** Don't worry about me on that score.   **21 bemet** met.   **23 rigor of our state** harshness of our rule   **24 cry out** rebel.   **Where** In a case where.   **honest** honorable
25 For As for   **26 touches us as** concerns us insofar as   **27–8 Not . . . oppose** not because the matter emboldens the King and others who, I fear, are driven into opposition by just and weighty grievances.
30 Why . . . reasoned? i.e., Why are we arguing about reasons for fighting, instead of fighting?   **32 particular broils** private quarrels
34 th'ancient of war the veteran officers

REGAN
'Tis most convenient. Pray, go with us.   38
GONERIL [aside]
Oho, I know the riddle.—I will go.   39

[As they are going out,] enter Edgar [disguised].

EDGAR [to Albany]
If e'er Your Grace had speech with man so poor,
Hear me one word.
ALBANY [to the others]   I'll overtake you.
                                        Exeunt both the armies.
                                        Speak.
EDGAR [giving a letter]
Before you fight the battle, ope this letter.   42
If you have victory, let the trumpet sound   43
For him that brought it. Wretched though I seem,
I can produce a champion that will prove   45
What is avouchèd there. If you miscarry,   46
Your business of the world hath so an end,
And machination ceases. Fortune love you!   48
ALBANY   Stay till I have read the letter.
EDGAR   I was forbid it.
When time shall serve, let but the herald cry
And I'll appear again.   Exit [Edgar].
ALBANY
Why, fare thee well. I will o'erlook thy paper.   53

Enter Edmund.

EDMUND
The enemy's in view. Draw up your powers.
                          [He offers Albany a paper.]
Here is the guess of their true strength and forces   55
By diligent discovery; but your haste   56
Is now urged on you.
ALBANY   We will greet the time.   Exit.   57
EDMUND
To both these sisters have I sworn my love,
Each jealous of the other as the stung   59
Are of the adder. Which of them shall I take?
Both? One? Or neither? Neither can be enjoyed
If both remain alive. To take the widow
Exasperates, makes mad her sister Goneril,
And hardly shall I carry out my side,   64
Her husband being alive. Now then, we'll use
His countenance for the battle, which being done,   66
Let her who would be rid of him devise
His speedy taking off. As for the mercy   68
Which he intends to Lear and to Cordelia,
The battle done and they within our power,

Shall never see his pardon, for my state   71
Stands on me to defend, not to debate.   72
                                        Exit.

❖

5.2

Alarum within. Enter, with drum and colors, Lear,
Cordelia, and soldiers, over the stage; and exeunt.

Enter Edgar and Gloucester.

EDGAR
Here, father, take the shadow of this tree   1
For your good host. Pray that the right may thrive.   2
If ever I return to you again,
I'll bring you comfort.
GLOUCESTER   Grace go with you, sir!   4
                                        Exit [Edgar].

Alarum and retreat within. Enter Edgar.

EDGAR
Away, old man! Give me thy hand. Away!
King Lear hath lost, he and his daughter ta'en.
Give me thy hand. Come on.
GLOUCESTER
No further, sir. A man may rot even here.
EDGAR
What, in ill thoughts again? Men must endure
Their going hence, even as their coming hither;
Ripeness is all. Come on.
GLOUCESTER   And that's true too.   11
                                        Exeunt.

❖

5.3

Enter, in conquest, with drum and colors, Edmund;
Lear and Cordelia, as prisoners; soldiers, Captain.

EDMUND
Some officers take them away. Good guard   1
Until their greater pleasures first be known   2
That are to censure them.
CORDELIA [to Lear]   We are not the first   3
Who with best meaning have incurred the worst.   4
For thee, oppressèd King, I am cast down;
Myself could else outfrown false Fortune's frown.
Shall we not see these daughters and these sisters?   7

---

38 **convenient** proper, fitting.   39 **I know the riddle** i.e., I understand the reason for Regan's enigmatic demand that I accompany her,
which is that she wants to keep me away from Edmund.   42 **this let-**
ter i.e., Goneril's letter to Edmund found on Oswald's body.
43 **sound** sound a summons   45 **prove** i.e., in trial by combat
46 **avouchèd** affirmed.   **miscarry** lose the battle and die   48 **machi-**
nation plotting (against your life)   53 **o'erlook** peruse   55 **guess**
estimate   56 **discovery** reconnoitering   57 **We . . . time** We will be
ready for whatever happens.   59 **jealous** suspicious   64 **carry . . .**
side carry out my end of the bargain in our *reciprocal vows* (4.6.266)
66 **countenance** backing, authority of his name   68 **taking off** killing.

71 **Shall** they shall   71–2 **my state . . . debate** my position depends
upon maintenance by forceful action, not by talk.
5.2. Location: The battlefield.
0.1 *Alarum* trumpet call to arms   1 **father** i.e., reverend old man
2 **host** shelterer.   4.2 *retreat* trumpet signal for withdrawal
11 **Ripeness** (Humans shouldn't die before their time, just as fruit
doesn't fall until it's ripe.)
5.3. Location: The British camp.
1 **Good guard** Guard them well   2 **their greater pleasures** the wishes
of those in command   3 **censure** judge   4 **meaning** intentions
7 **Shall . . . sisters?** i.e., Aren't we even allowed to speak to Goneril
and Regan before they order to prison their own father and sister?

LEAR
No, no, no, no! Come, let's away to prison.
We two alone will sing like birds i'th' cage.
When thou dost ask me blessing, I'll kneel down
And ask of thee forgiveness. So we'll live,
And pray, and sing, and tell old tales, and laugh
At gilded butterflies, and hear poor rogues   13
Talk of court news; and we'll talk with them too—
Who loses and who wins; who's in, who's out—
And take upon 's the mystery of things,   16
As if we were God's spies; and we'll wear out,   17
In a walled prison, packs and sects of great ones,   18
That ebb and flow by th' moon.
EDMUND   Take them away.   19
LEAR
Upon such sacrifices, my Cordelia,
The gods themselves throw incense. Have I caught
    thee?   21
He that parts us shall bring a brand from heaven   22
And fire us hence like foxes. Wipe thine eyes;   23
The good years shall devour them, flesh and fell,   24
Ere they shall make us weep. We'll see 'em starved
    first.   25
Come.   *Exit [with Cordelia, guarded].*
EDMUND   Come hither, Captain. Hark.
Take thou this note. [*He gives a paper.*] Go follow them
    to prison.
One step I have advanced thee; if thou dost
As this instructs thee, thou dost make thy way
To noble fortunes. Know thou this: that men
Are as the time is. To be tender-minded   32
Does not become a sword. Thy great employment   33
Will not bear question; either say thou'lt do 't   34
Or thrive by other means.
CAPTAIN   I'll do 't, my lord.
EDMUND   About it, and write "happy" when th' hast done. 36
Mark, I say, instantly, and carry it so   37
As I have set it down.
CAPTAIN
I cannot draw a cart, nor eat dried oats;
If it be man's work, I'll do 't.   *Exit Captain.*

*Flourish. Enter Albany, Goneril, Regan, [another
Captain, and] soldiers.*

ALBANY
Sir, you have showed today your valiant strain,
And fortune led you well. You have the captives
Who were the opposites of this day's strife;   43
I do require them of you, so to use them
As we shall find their merits and our safety
May equally determine.
EDMUND   Sir, I thought it fit
To send the old and miserable King
To some retention and appointed guard,   49
Whose age had charms in it, whose title more,   50
To pluck the common bosom on his side   51
And turn our impressed lances in our eyes   52
Which do command them. With him I sent the Queen, 53
My reason all the same; and they are ready
Tomorrow, or at further space, t'appear   55
Where you shall hold your session. At this time
We sweat and bleed; the friend hath lost his friend,
And the best quarrels in the heat are cursed   58
By those that feel their sharpness.   59
The question of Cordelia and her father
Requires a fitter place.
ALBANY   Sir, by your patience,   61
I hold you but a subject of this war,   62
Not as a brother.
REGAN   That's as we list to grace him.   63
Methinks our pleasure might have been demanded   64
Ere you had spoke so far. He led our powers,
Bore the commission of my place and person,
The which immediacy may well stand up   67
And call itself your brother.
GONERIL   Not so hot!
In his own grace he doth exalt himself
More than in your addition.
REGAN   In my rights,   70
By me invested, he compeers the best.   71
GONERIL
That were the most if he should husband you.   72
REGAN
Jesters do oft prove prophets.
GONERIL   Holla, holla!   73
That eye that told you so looked but asquint.   74
REGAN
Lady, I am not well, else I should answer
From a full-flowing stomach. [*To Edmund*] General,   76

---

13 gilded butterflies i.e., gaily dressed courtiers and other ephemeral types, or perhaps actual butterflies   **16 take upon 's** assume the burden of, or profess to understand   **17 God's spies** i.e., detached observers surveying the deeds of humanity from an eternal vantage point.   **wear out** outlast   **18–19 packs . . . moon** i.e., followers and cliques attached to persons of high station, whose fortunes change erratically and constantly.   **21 The gods . . . incense** (The gods make offerings to Cordelia instead of receiving them.)   **22–3 He . . . foxes** i.e., Nothing short of a firebrand from heaven will ever part us again. (Firebrands were used to smoke foxes from their lairs; compare also Samson's use of firebrands tied to the tails of foxes in order to punish the Philistines for denying him his wife, in Judges 15:4–5.)   **24–5 The good . . . weep** i.e., the years will be good to us and will utterly foil our enemies' attempts to make us sorrowful as long as we are together (?).   **32 Are . . . is** i.e., must adapt themselves to stern exigencies.   **33 become a sword** i.e., suit a warrior.   **34 bear question** admit of discussion   **36 write "happy"** call yourself fortunate.   **th'** thou   **37 carry it** carry it out

43 opposites enemies   **49 retention** confinement   **50–3 Whose . . . them** whose advanced age had magic in it, and whose title as king had even more, to win the sympathy of the commoners and turn against us the weapons of those very troops whom we impressed into service. (*In our eyes* may suggest retaliation for the blinding of Gloucester.)   **55 space** interval of time   **58–9 And . . . sharpness** and even the best of causes, at this moment when the passions of battle have not cooled, are viewed with hatred by those who have suffered the painful consequences. (Edmund pretends to worry that Lear and Cordelia would not receive a fair trial.)   **61 by your patience** if you please   **62 subject of** subordinate in   **63 list** please   **64 pleasure** wish.   **demanded** asked about   **67 immediacy** nearness of connection   **70 your addition** the titles you confer.   **71 compeers** is equal with   **72 That . . . most** That investiture would be most complete   **73 prove** turn out to be   **74 asquint** (Jealousy proverbially makes the eye look *asquint*, "furtively, suspiciously.")   **76 full-flowing stomach** full tide of angry rejoinder.

Take thou my soldiers, prisoners, patrimony;   77
Dispose of them, of me; the walls is thine.   78
Witness the world that I create thee here
My lord and master.

GONERIL   Mean you to enjoy him?

ALBANY
The let-alone lies not in your good will.   81

EDMUND
Nor in thine, lord.

ALBANY   Half-blooded fellow, yes.   82

REGAN [to Edmund]
Let the drum strike and prove my title thine.

ALBANY
Stay yet; hear reason. Edmund, I arrest thee
On capital treason; and, in thy attaint   85
This gilded serpent. [Pointing to Goneril] For your
    claim, fair sister,
I bar it in the interest of my wife;
'Tis she is subcontracted to this lord,
And I, her husband, contradict your banns.   89
If you will marry, make your loves to me;   90
My lady is bespoke.

GONERIL   An interlude!   91

ALBANY
Thou art armed, Gloucester. Let the trumpet sound.
If none appear to prove upon thy person
Thy heinous, manifest, and many treasons,
There is my pledge. [He throws down a glove.] I'll make
    it on thy heart,   95
Ere I taste bread, thou art in nothing less   96
Than I have here proclaimed thee.

REGAN   Sick, oh, sick!

GONERIL [aside]   If not, I'll ne'er trust medicine.   99

EDMUND [throwing down a glove]
There's my exchange. What in the world he is   100
That names me traitor, villain-like he lies.
Call by the trumpet. He that dares approach,
On him, on you—who not?—I will maintain
My truth and honor firmly.

ALBANY
A herald, ho!

EDMUND   A herald, ho, a herald!

        Enter a Herald.

ALBANY [to Edmund]
Trust to thy single virtue; for thy soldiers,   106
All levied in my name, have in my name
Took their discharge.

REGAN   My sickness grows upon me.

ALBANY [to Soldiers]
She is not well. Convey her to my tent.
                        [Exit Regan, supported.]
Come hither, herald. Let the trumpet sound,
And read out this.   [He gives a paper.]

CAPTAIN   Sound, trumpet!   A trumpet sounds.

HERALD (reads)   "If any man of quality or degree within   113
the lists of the army will maintain upon Edmund, sup-   114
posed Earl of Gloucester, that he is a manifold traitor,
let him appear by the third sound of the trumpet. He
is bold in his defense."

EDMUND   Sound!   First trumpet.
HERALD   Again!   Second trumpet.
HERALD   Again!   Third trumpet.
                        Trumpet answers within.

        Enter Edgar, armed, [with a trumpeter before
        him].

ALBANY
Ask him his purposes, why he appears
Upon this call o'th' trumpet.

HERALD   What are you?   122
Your name, your quality, and why you answer
This present summons?

EDGAR   Know my name is lost,
By treason's tooth bare-gnawn and canker-bit.   125
Yet am I noble as the adversary
I come to cope.

ALBANY   Which is that adversary?   127

EDGAR
What's he that speaks for Edmund, Earl of
    Gloucester?

EDMUND
Himself. What say'st thou to him?

EDGAR   Draw thy sword,
That, if my speech offend a noble heart,
Thy arm may do thee justice. Here is mine.
                        [He draws his sword.]
Behold, it is the privilege of mine honors,   132
My oath, and my profession. I protest,   133
Maugre thy strength, place, youth, and eminence,   134
Despite thy victor sword and fire-new fortune,   135
Thy valor, and thy heart, thou art a traitor—   136
False to thy gods, thy brother, and thy father,
Conspirant 'gainst this high-illustrious prince,
And from th'extremest upward of thy head   139
To the descent and dust below thy foot   140
A most toad-spotted traitor. Say thou no,   141
This sword, this arm, and my best spirits are bent   142
To prove upon thy heart, whereto I speak,
Thou liest.

---

77 **patrimony** inheritance   78 **the walls is thine** i.e., the citadel of my heart and body surrenders completely to you.   81 **let-alone** preventing, denying   82 **Half-blooded** Only partly of noble blood, bastard   85 **in thy attaint** i.e., as partner in your corruption and as one who has (unwittingly) provided the *attaint* or impeachment against you   89 **banns** public announcement of a proposed marriage.   90 **make . . . me**, sue to me for permission   91 **An interlude!** A play; i.e., you are being melodramatic, or, what a farce this is!   95 **make** prove   96 **in nothing less** in no respect less guilty   99 **medicine** i.e., poison.   100 **What** Whoever   106 **single virtue** unaided prowess

113 **quality or degree** noble birth or rank. (Also in line 123.)   114 **lists** roster   122 **What** Who   125 **canker-bit** eaten as by the caterpillar.   127 **cope** encounter.   132 **of mine honors** i.e., of my knighthood   133 **profession** i.e., knighthood.   134 **Maugre** in spite of   135 **victor** victorious.   **fire-new** newly minted   136 **heart** courage   139 **upward** top   140 **descent** lowest extreme   141 **toad-spotted** venomous, or having spots of infamy.   **Say thou** If you say   142 **bent** prepared

EDMUND   In wisdom I should ask thy name.   144
  But since thy outside looks so fair and warlike,
  And that thy tongue some say of breeding breathes,   146
  What safe and nicely I might well delay   147
  By rule of knighthood, I disdain and spurn.   148
  Back do I toss those treasons to thy head,   149
  With the hell-hated lie o'erwhelm thy heart,   150
  Which—for they yet glance by and scarcely bruise—   151
  This sword of mine shall give them instant way,   152
  Where they shall rest forever.—Trumpets, speak!   153
        [He draws.] Alarums. Fight. [Edmund falls.]
ALBANY *[to Edgar]*
  Save him, save him!
GONERIL   This is practice, Gloucester.   154
  By th' law of arms thou wast not bound to answer
  An unknown opposite. Thou art not vanquished,
  But cozened and beguiled.
ALBANY   Shut your mouth, dame,   157
  Or with this paper shall I stopple it.—Hold, sir.   158
  Thou worse than any name, read thine own evil.
             [He shows the letter.]
  [To Goneril] No tearing, lady; I perceive you know it.
GONERIL
  Say if I do, the laws are mine, not thine.
  Who can arraign me for't?
ALBANY   Most monstrous! Oh!
  Know'st thou this paper?
GONERIL   Ask me not what I know.
                    Exit.
ALBANY
  Go after her. She's desperate; govern her.   164
              [Exit a soldier.]
EDMUND
  What you have charged me with, that have I done,
  And more, much more. The time will bring it out.
  'Tis past, and so am I. But what art thou
  That hast this fortune on me? If thou'rt noble,   168
  I do forgive thee.
EDGAR   Let's exchange charity.   169
  I am no less in blood than thou art, Edmund;
  If more, the more th' hast wronged me.   171
  My name is Edgar, and thy father's son.
  The gods are just, and of our pleasant vices   173
  Make instruments to plague us.
  The dark and vicious place where thee he got   175

  Cost him his eyes.
EDMUND   Th' hast spoken right. 'Tis true.
  The wheel is come full circle; I am here.   177
ALBANY *[to Edgar]*
  Methought thy very gait did prophesy
  A royal nobleness. I must embrace thee.
                [They embrace.]
  Let sorrow split my heart if ever I
  Did hate thee or thy father!
EDGAR   Worthy prince, I know't.
ALBANY   Where have you hid yourself?
  How have you known the miseries of your father?
EDGAR
  By nursing them, my lord. List a brief tale,   185
  And when 'tis told, oh, that my heart would burst!
  The bloody proclamation to escape   187
  That followed me so near—oh, our lives' sweetness,   188
  That we the pain of death would hourly die   189
  Rather than die at once!—taught me to shift   190
  Into a madman's rags, t'assume a semblance
  That very dogs disdained; and in this habit   192
  Met I my father with his bleeding rings,   193
  Their precious stones new lost; became his guide,   194
  Led him, begged for him, saved him from despair;
  Never—oh, fault!—revealed myself unto him
  Until some half hour past, when I was armed.
  Not sure, though hoping, of this good success,   198
  I asked his blessing, and from first to last
  Told him our pilgrimage. But his flawed heart—   200
  Alack, too weak the conflict to support—
  Twixt two extremes of passion, joy and grief,
  Burst smilingly.
EDMUND   This speech of yours hath moved me,
  And shall perchance do good. But speak you on;
  You look as you had something more to say.
ALBANY
  If there be more, more woeful, hold it in,
  For I am almost ready to dissolve,   207
  Hearing of this.
EDGAR   This would have seemed a period   208
  To such as love not sorrow; but another,   209
  To amplify too much, would make much more   210
  And top extremity. Whilst I   211
  Was big in clamor, came there in a man   212
  Who, having seen me in my worst estate,
  Shunned my abhorred society; but then, finding
  Who 'twas that so endured, with his strong arms
  He fastened on my neck and bellowed out

144 wisdom prudence   **146 say** smack, taste, indication   **147 safe and nicely** prudently and punctiliously   **148 I . . . spurn** i.e., I disdain to insist on my right to refuse combat with one of lower rank. **149 treasons . . . head** i.e., accusations of treason in your teeth **150 hell-hated** hated as hell is hated   **151 Which . . . bruise** i.e., which charges of treason—since as yet they merely glance off my armor and do no harm   **152 give . . . way** provide them an immediate pathway (to your heart)   **153 Where . . . forever** i.e., my victory in trial by combat will prove forever that the charges of treason apply to you.   **154 Save** Spare. (Albany wishes to spare Edmund's life so that he may confess and be found guilty.)   **practice** trickery, or (said sardonically) astute management   **157 cozened** tricked   **158 stopple** stop up.   **Hold, sir** (Addressed to Edgar or, more probably, Edmund.) **164 govern** restrain   **168 fortune on** victory over   **169 charity** forgiveness (for Edmund's wickedness toward Edgar and Edgar's having slain Edmund).   **171 th' hast** thou hast   **173 pleasant** pleasurable   **175 got** begot

177 The wheel . . . here (Alludes both to the wheel of fortune and to the idea of a completed circle whereby crime meets its appropriate punishment. Edmund sees that everything has at last come around to where it began.)   **185 List** Listen to   **187 The . . . escape** In order to escape the death-threatening proclamation   **188–90 oh . . . at once!** oh, the perversity of our attachment to our lives' sweetness, that we prefer to suffer continually the fear of death rather than die at once and be done with it!   **192 habit** garb   **193 rings** sockets   **194 stones** i.e., eyeballs   **198 success** outcome   **200 flawed** cracked   **207 dissolve** i.e., in tears   **208 a period** the limit   **209–11 but . . . extremity** i.e., but another sorrowful circumstance, adding to what is already too much, would increase it and exceed the limit.   **212 big in clamor** loud in my lamenting

As he'd burst heaven, threw him on my father,   217
Told the most piteous tale of Lear and him
That ever ear received, which in recounting
His grief grew puissant, and the strings of life   220
Began to crack. Twice then the trumpets sounded,
And there I left him tranced.

ALBANY   But who was this?   222

EDGAR
Kent, sir, the banished Kent, who in disguise
Followed his enemy king and did him service   224
Improper for a slave.

        Enter a Gentleman [with a bloody knife].

GENTLEMAN
Help, help, oh, help!

EDGAR   What kind of help?

ALBANY   Speak, man.

EDGAR
What means this bloody knife?

GENTLEMAN   'Tis hot, it smokes.   227
It came even from the heart of—Oh, she's dead!

ALBANY   Who dead? Speak, man.

GENTLEMAN
Your lady, sir, your lady! And her sister
By her is poisoned; she confesses it.

EDMUND
I was contracted to them both. All three
Now marry in an instant.

EDGAR   Here comes Kent.

            Enter Kent.

ALBANY
Produce the bodies, be they alive or dead.
                    [Exit Gentleman.]
This judgment of the heavens, that makes us tremble,
Touches us not with pity.—Oh, is this he?
[To Kent] The time will not allow the compliment   237
Which very manners urges.

KENT   I am come   238
To bid my king and master aye good night.   239
Is he not here?

ALBANY   Great thing of us forgot!
Speak, Edmund, where's the King? And where's
    Cordelia?
            Goneril and Regan's bodies [are] brought out.
See'st thou this object, Kent?   242

KENT   Alack, why thus?

EDMUND   Yet Edmund was beloved.
The one the other poisoned for my sake
And after slew herself.

ALBANY   Even so. Cover their faces.

EDMUND
I pant for life. Some good I mean to do,
Despite of mine own nature. Quickly send—
Be brief in it—to th' castle, for my writ
Is on the life of Lear and on Cordelia.
Nay, send in time.

ALBANY   Run, run, oh, run!

EDGAR
To who, my lord? Who has the office? *[To Edmund]*
    Send   253
Thy token of reprieve.

EDMUND   Well thought on. Take my sword. The captain!
Give it the Captain.

EDGAR   Haste thee, for thy life.
                [Exit one with Edmund's sword.]

EDMUND
He hath commission from thy wife and me
To hang Cordelia in the prison and
To lay the blame upon her own despair,
That she fordid herself.   260

ALBANY
The gods defend her! Bear him hence awhile.
                    [Edmund is borne off.]

    Enter Lear, with Cordelia in his arms; [Captain].

LEAR
Howl, howl, howl! Oh, you are men of stones!
Had I your tongues and eyes, I'd use them so
That heaven's vault should crack. She's gone forever.
I know when one is dead and when one lives;
She's dead as earth. Lend me a looking glass;
If that her breath will mist or stain the stone,   267
Why, then she lives.

KENT   Is this the promised end?   268

EDGAR
Or image of that horror?

ALBANY   Fall and cease!   269

LEAR
This feather stirs; she lives! If it be so,
It is a chance which does redeem all sorrows
That ever I have felt.

KENT *[kneeling]*   O my good master!

LEAR
Prithee, away.

EDGAR   'Tis noble Kent, your friend.

LEAR
A plague upon you, murderers, traitors all!
I might have saved her; now she's gone forever!
Cordelia, Cordelia! Stay a little. Ha?
What is't thou say'st? Her voice was ever soft,
Gentle, and low, an excellent thing in woman.
I killed the slave that was a-hanging thee.

CAPTAIN
'Tis true, my lords, he did.

LEAR   Did I not, fellow?

---

217 As as if.   **threw . . . father** threw himself on my father's body
220 His i.e., Kent's.   **puissant** powerful.   **strings of life** heartstrings
222 tranced entranced, senseless.   **224 his enemy king** i.e., the king
who had rejected and banished him   **227 smokes** steams.   **237 compliment** ceremony   **238 Which . . . urges** which common courtesy
requires.   **239 aye good night** farewell forever. (Kent believes he
himself is near death, his heartstrings having begun to crack.)
242 object sight

253 office commission.   **260 fordid** destroyed   **267 stone** crystal or
polished stone of which the mirror is made   **268 Is . . . end?** (Kent
may mean "Is this what all our hopes have come to?" Edgar replies
by invoking the Last Judgment.)   **269 image** representation.   **Fall
and cease!** i.e., Let all things cease to be!

I have seen the day, with my good biting falchion 281
I would have made them skip. I am old now,
And these same crosses spoil me.—Who are you? 283
Mine eyes are not o'th' best; I'll tell you straight. 284

KENT
If Fortune brag of two she loved and hated, 285
One of them we behold. 286

LEAR
This is a dull sight. Are you not Kent?

KENT   The same, 287
Your servant Kent. Where is your servant Caius? 288

LEAR
He's a good fellow, I can tell you that;
He'll strike, and quickly too. He's dead and rotten.

KENT
No, my good lord, I am the very man—

LEAR   I'll see that straight. 292

KENT
That from your first of difference and decay 293
Have followed your sad steps—

LEAR   You are welcome hither.

KENT
Nor no man else. All's cheerless, dark, and deadly. 295
Your eldest daughters have fordone themselves, 296
And desperately are dead.

LEAR   Ay, so I think. 297

ALBANY
He knows not what he says, and vain is it
That we present us to him.

EDGAR   Very bootless. 299

Enter a Messenger.

MESSENGER   Edmund is dead, my lord.
ALBANY   That's but a trifle here.
You lords and noble friends, know our intent:
What comfort to this great decay may come 303

Shall be applied. For us, we will resign, 304
During the life of this old majesty,
To him our absolute power; [*to Edgar and Kent*] you, to
    your rights,
With boot and such addition as your honors 307
Have more than merited. All friends shall taste
The wages of their virtue, and all foes
The cup of their deservings.—Oh, see, see!

LEAR
And my poor fool is hanged! No, no, no life? 311
Why should a dog, a horse, a rat have life,
And thou no breath at all? Thou'lt come no more,
Never, never, never, never, never!
Pray you, undo this button. Thank you, sir.
Do you see this? Look on her, look, her lips,
Look there, look there!   *He dies.*

EDGAR   He faints.—My lord, my lord!

KENT
Break, heart, I prithee, break!

EDGAR   Look up, my lord.

KENT
Vex not his ghost. Oh, let him pass! He hates him 319
That would upon the rack of this tough world 320
Stretch him out longer.

EDGAR   He is gone indeed.

KENT
The wonder is he hath endured so long.
He but usurped his life.

ALBANY
Bear them from hence. Our present business
Is general woe. [*To Kent and Edgar*] Friends of my soul,
    you twain
Rule in this realm, and the gored state sustain.

KENT
I have a journey, sir, shortly to go. 327
My master calls me; I must not say no.

EDGAR
The weight of this sad time we must obey;
Speak what we feel, not what we ought to say.
The oldest hath borne most; we that are young
Shall never see so much nor live so long. 332

Exeunt, with a dead march.

---

281 **falchion** light sword   283 **crosses spoil me** adversities take away my strength.   284 **I'll . . . straight** I'll recognize you in a moment. 285–6 **If . . . behold** If Fortune were to brag of two persons whom she has subjected to the greatest fall from her favor into her hatred, Lear would have to be one of them.   287 **This . . . sight** i.e., My vision is clouding, or, this is a dismal spectacle.   288 **Caius** (Kent's disguise name.)   292 **see that straight** attend to that in a moment.   293 **from . . . decay** from the beginning of your quarrel (with Cordelia) to your decline of fortune   295 **Nor . . . else** No, not I nor anyone else, or, I am the *very man* (line 291), him and no one else.   296 **fordone** destroyed   297 **desperately** in despair   299 **bootless** in vain. 303 **What . . . come** i.e., whatever means of comforting this ruined king and state of affairs may present themselves

304 **For** As for   307 **With . . . honors** with advantage and such further distinctions or titles as your honorable conduct in this war 311 **poor fool** i.e., Cordelia. (*Fool* is here a term of endearment.) 319 **ghost** departing spirit.   320 **rack** torture rack. (With suggestion, in the Folio and Quarto spelling, "wracke," of shipwreck, disaster.) 327 **journey** i.e., to another world, to death   332.1 *Exeunt* (Presumably the dead bodies are borne out in procession.)

Macbeth

Macbeth is seemingly the last of four great Shakespearean tragedies—*Hamlet* (c. 1599–1601), *Othello* (c. 1603–1604), *King Lear* (1605–1606), and *Macbeth* (c. 1606–1607)—that examine the dimensions of spiritual evil, as distinguished from the political strife of Roman tragedies such as *Julius Caesar, Antony* and *Cleopatra,* and *Coriolanus.* Whether or not Shakespeare intended *Macbeth* as a culmination of a series of tragedies on evil, the play does offer a particularly terse and gloomy view of humanity's encounter with the powers of darkness. Macbeth, more consciously than any other of Shakespeare's major tragic protagonists, has to face the temptation of committing what he knows to be a monstrous crime. Like Doctor Faustus in Christopher Marlowe's play, *The Tragedy of Doctor Faustus* (c. 1588), and to a lesser extent like Adam in John Milton's *Paradise Lost* (1667), Macbeth understands the reasons for resisting evil and yet goes ahead with his disastrous plan. His awareness and sensitivity to moral issues, together with his conscious choice of evil, produce an unnerving account of human failure, all the more distressing because Macbeth is so representatively human. He seems to possess freedom of will and accepts personal responsibility for his fate, and yet his tragic doom seems unavoidable. Nor is there eventual salvation to be hoped for, as there is in *Paradise Lost*, since Macbeth's crime is too heinous and his heart too hardened. He is more like Doctor Faustus—damned and in despair.

To an extent not found in the other tragedies, the issue is stated in terms of salvation versus damnation. Macbeth knows before he acts that King Duncan's virtues "Will plead like angels, trumpet-tongued, against / The deep damnation of his taking-off" (1.7.19–20). After the murder, he is equally aware that he has "Put rancors in the vessel of my peace . . . and mine eternal jewel / Given to the common enemy of man" (3.1.68–70). His enemies later describe him as a devil and a "hellhound" (5.8.3). He, like Marlowe's Doctor Faustus before him, has knowingly sold his soul for gain. And, although as a mortal he still has time to repent his crimes, horrible as they are,

Macbeth cannot find the words to be penitent. "Wherefore could not I pronounce 'Amen'?" he implores his wife after they have committed the murder. "I had most need of blessing, and 'Amen' / Stuck in my throat" (2.2.35–7). Macbeth's own answer seems to be that he has committed himself so inexorably to evil that he cannot turn back. Sentence has been pronounced: "Glamis hath murdered sleep, and therefore Cawdor / Shall sleep no more; Macbeth shall sleep no more" (lines 46–7).

Macbeth is not a conventional morality play (even less so than *Doctor Faustus*) and is not concerned primarily with preaching against sinfulness or demonstrating that Macbeth is finally damned for what he does. A tradition of moral and religious drama has been transformed into an intensely human study of the psychological effects of evil on a particular man and, to a lesser extent, on his wife. That moral tradition nevertheless provides as its legacy a perspective on the operation of evil in human affairs. A perverse ambition seemingly inborn in Macbeth himself is abetted by dark forces dwelling in the universe, waiting to catch him off guard. Among Shakespeare's tragedies, indeed, *Macbeth* is remarkable for its focus on evil in the protagonist and on his relationship to the sinister forces tempting him. In no other Shakespearean play is the audience asked to identify to such an extent with the evildoer himself. *Richard III* also focuses on an evil protagonist, but in that play the spectators are distanced by the character's gloating and are not partakers in the introspective soliloquies of a man confronting his own ambition. Macbeth is more representatively human. If he betrays an inclination toward brutality, he also humanely attempts to resist that urge. We witness and struggle to understand his downfall through two phases: the spiritual struggle before he actually commits the crime and the despairing aftermath, with its vain quest for security through continued violence. Evil is thus presented in two aspects: first as an insidious suggestion leading Macbeth on toward an illusory promise of gain and then as a frenzied addiction to the hated thing by which he is possessed.

In the first phase, before the commission of the crime, we wonder to what extent the powers of darkness are a determining factor in what Macbeth does. Can he avoid the fate the witches proclaim? Evidently, he and Lady Macbeth have previously considered murdering Duncan; the witches appear after the thought, not before. Lady Macbeth reminds her wavering husband that he was the first to "break this enterprise" to her, on some previous occasion when "Nor time nor place / Did then adhere, and yet you would make both" (1.7.49–53). Elizabethans would probably understand that evil spirits such as witches appear when summoned, whether by our conscious or unconscious minds. Macbeth is ripe for their insinuations: a mind free of taint would see no sinister invitation in their prophecy of greatness to come. And, in a saner moment, Macbeth knows that his restless desire to interfere with destiny is arrogant and useless. "If chance will have me king, why, chance may crown me / Without my stir" (1.3.145–6). Banquo, his companion, serves as his dramatic opposite by consistently displaying a more stoical attitude toward the witches. "Speak then to me," he addresses them, "who neither beg nor fear / Your favors nor your hate" (lines 60–1). Like Horatio in *Hamlet*, Banquo strongly resists the blandishments of fortune as well as its buffets, though not without an agonizing night of moral struggle. Indeed, promises of success are often more ruinous than setbacks—as in the seemingly paradoxical instance of the farmer, cited by Macbeth's porter, who "hanged himself on th'expectation of plenty" (2.3.4–5). It is by showing Macbeth that he is two-thirds of his way to the throne that the witches tempt him to seize the last third at whatever cost. "Glamis, and Thane of Cawdor! / The greatest is behind" (1.3.116–17).

Banquo comprehends the nature of temptation. "To win us to our harm," he observes, "The instruments of darkness tell us truths, / Win us with honest trifles, to betray 's / In deepest consequence" (1.3.123–6). The devil can speak true, and his strategy is to invite us into a trap we help prepare. Without our active consent in evil (as Othello also learns), we cannot fall. Yet in what sense are the witches trifling with Macbeth or prevaricating? When they address him as one "that shalt be king hereafter" (line 50), they are stating a certainty, for they can "look into the seeds of time / And say which grain will grow and which will not," as Banquo says (lines 58–9). They know that Banquo will be "Lesser than Macbeth, and greater. / Not so happy, yet much happier" (lines 65–6), since Banquo will beget a race of kings and Macbeth will not. How then do they know that Macbeth will be king? If we consider the hypothetical question, what if Macbeth does *not* murder Duncan, we can gain some understanding of the relationship between character and fate; for the only valid answer is that the question remains hypothetical—Macbeth *does* kill Duncan, the witches are right in their prediction. It is idle to speculate that Providence would have found another way to make Macbeth king, for the witches' prophecy is self-fulfilling in the very way they foresee. Character is fate; they know Macbeth's fatal weakness and know they can "enkindle" him to seize the crown by laying irresistible temptations before him. This does not mean that they determine his choice but, rather, that Macbeth's choice is predictable and therefore unvoidable, even though not preordained. He has free choice, but that choice will, in fact, go only one way—as with Adam and Eve in Milton's *Paradise Lost* and in the medieval tradition from which this poem was derived.

Although the powers of evil cannot determine Macbeth's choice, they can influence the external conditions affecting that choice. By a series of apparently circumstantial events, well timed in their effect, they can repeatedly assail him just when he is about to rally to the call of conscience. The witches, armed with supernatural knowledge, inform Macbeth of his new title shortly before the King's ambassadors confirm that he is to be the Thane of Cawdor. Duncan chooses this night to lodge under Macbeth's roof. And, just when Macbeth resolves to abandon even this unparalleled opportunity, his wife intervenes on the side of the witches. Macbeth commits the murder in part to keep his word to her and to prove he is no coward (like Donwald, the slayer of King Duff in one of Shakespeare's chief sources, Raphael Holinshed's *Chronicles*). Not only the opportunities presented to Macbeth, but also the obstacles put in his way are cannily timed to overwhelm his conscience. When King Duncan announces that his son Malcolm is now Prince of Cumberland and official heir to the throne (1.4.36–42), the unintended threat deflects Macbeth's mood from one of gratitude and acceptance to one of hostility. These are mitigating circumstances that affect our judgment of Macbeth, and, even though they cannot excuse him, they certainly increase our sympathetic identification.

We are moved, too, by the poetic intensity of Macbeth's moral vision. His soliloquies are memorable as poetry, not merely because Shakespeare wrote them, but because Macbeth is sensitive and aware. The horror, indeed, of his crime is that his cultivated self is revolted by what he cannot prevent himself from doing. He understands with a terrible clarity, not only the moral wrong of what he is about to do, but also the inescapably destructive consequences for himself. He is as reluctant as we to see the crime committed, and yet he goes to it with a sad and rational deliberateness rather than in a self-blinding fury. For Macbeth, there is no seeming loss of perspective, and yet there is total alienation of the act from his moral consciousness. The arguments for and against murdering Duncan, as Macbeth pictures them in his acutely visual imagination, when weighed, are overwhelmingly opposed to the deed. Duncan is his king and his guest, deserving Macbeth's duty and hospitality. The King is virtuous and able. He has shown every favor to

Macbeth, thereby removing any sane motive for striving after further promotion. All human history shows that murders of this sort "return / To plague th'inventor" (1.7.9–10), that is, provide only guilt and punishment rather than satisfaction. Finally, judgment in "the life to come" includes the prospect of eternal torment. On the other side of the argument is nothing but Macbeth's "Vaulting ambition, which o'erleaps itself" (line 27)—a perverse refusal to be content with his present good fortune because there is more that beckons. Who could weigh the issues so dispassionately and still choose the wrong? Yet the failure is, in fact, predictable; Macbeth is presented to us as typically human, both in his understanding and in his perverse ambition.

Macbeth's clarity of moral imagination is contrasted with his wife's imperceptiveness. He is always seeing visions or hearing voices—a dagger in the air, the ghost of Banquo, a voice crying "Sleep no more!"—and she is always denying them. "The sleeping and the dead / Are but as pictures," she insists. He knows that "all great Neptune's ocean" cannot wash the blood from his hands; "No, this my hand will rather / The multitudinous seas incarnadine, / Making the green one red." To Lady Macbeth, contrastingly, "A little water clears us of this deed. / How easy is it, then!" (2.2.57–72). Macbeth knows that the murder of Duncan is but the beginning: "We have scorched the snake, not killed it." Lady Macbeth would prefer to believe that "What's done is done" (3.2.14–15). Ironically, it is she, finally, who must endure visions of the most agonizing sort, sleepwalking in her distress and trying to rub away the "damned spot" that before seemed so easy to remove. "All the perfumes of Arabia will not sweeten this little hand," she laments (5.1.33–52). This relationship between Macbeth and Lady Macbeth owes much to traditional contrasts between male and female principles. As in the pairing of Adam and Eve, the man is putatively the more rational of the two but knowingly shares his wife's sin through fondness for her. She has failed to foresee the long-range consequences of sinful ambition and so becomes a temptress to her husband. The fall of man and woman into the bondage of sin takes place in an incongruous atmosphere of domestic intimacy and mutual concern; Lady Macbeth is motivated by ambition for her husband in much the same way that he sins to win her approbation.

The fatal disharmony flawing this domestic accord is conveyed through images of sexual inversion. Lady Macbeth prepares for her ordeal with the incantation, "Come, you spirits / That tend on mortal thoughts, unsex me here . . . Come to my woman's breasts / And take my milk for gall" (1.5.40–8). When she accuses her husband of unmanly cowardice and vows she would dash out the brains of her own infant for such effeminacy as he has displayed, he extols her with "Bring forth men-children only! / For thy undaunted mettle should compose / Nothing but males" (1.7.73–5). She takes the initiative,

devising and then carrying out the plan to drug Duncan's chamber-guards with wine. This assumption of the dominant male role by the woman might well remind Elizabethan spectators of numerous biblical, medieval, and classical parallels deploring the ascendancy of passion over reason: Eve choosing for Adam, Noah's wife taking command of the ark, the Wife of Bath dominating her husbands, Venus emasculating Mars, and others.

In *Macbeth*, sexual inversion also allies Lady Macbeth with the witches or weird sisters, the bearded women. Their unnaturalness betokens disorder in nature, for they can sail in a sieve and "look not like th'inhabitants o'th'earth / And yet are on't" (1.3.41–2). Characteristically, they speak in paradoxes: "When the battle's lost and won," "Fair is foul, and foul is fair" (1.1.4,11). Shakespeare probably drew on numerous sources to depict the witches: Holinshed's *Chronicles* (from which he conflated two accounts, one of Duncan and Macbeth, and the other of King Duff slain by Donwald with the help of his wife), King James's writings on witchcraft, Samuel Harsnett's *Declaration of Egregious Popish Impostures* (used also for *King Lear*), and the accounts of the Scottish witch trials published around 1590. In the last, particularly, Shakespeare could have found mention of witches raising storms and sailing in sieves to endanger vessels at sea, performing threefold rituals blaspheming the Trinity, and brewing witches' broth. Holinshed's *Chronicles* refer to the Weird Sisters as "goddesses of destiny," associating them with the three fates, Clotho, Lachesis, and Atropos, who hold the spinning distaff, draw off the thread of life, and cut it. In *Macbeth*, the Weird Sisters' power to control fortune is curtailed, and they are portrayed as witches according to popular contemporary understanding, rather than as goddesses of destiny; nonetheless, witches were thought to be servants of the devil (Banquo wonders if the devil can speak true in their utterances, 1.3.107), and through them Macbeth has made an ominous pact with evil itself. His visit to their seething cauldron in 4.1 brings him to the witches' masters, those unknown powers that know his very thought and who tempt him with those equivocations of which Banquo has warned Macbeth. The popularity of witchlore tempted Shakespeare's acting company to expand the witches' scenes with spectacles of song and dance; even the Folio text we have evidently contains interpolations derived in part from Thomas Middleton's *The Witch* (see especially 3.5 and part of 4.1, containing mention of Middleton's songs "Come away" and "Black spirits"). Nevertheless, Shakespeare's original theme of a disharmony in nature remains clearly visible.

The disharmonies of gender relations in *Macbeth* suggest another disturbing dimension of this tragedy. The play is filled with what Janet Adelman (in *Cannibals, Witches, and Divorce*, edited by Marjorie Garber, 1985) aptly calls fantasies of maternal power. Macbeth, like many males, attempts to cope with his imaginings of a destructive maternal power and his fantasies of escape into a world fashioned and controlled solely by himself. Initially, he submits to his wife's idea of manliness and commits murder in order to win her approval, destroying in the process a fatherly figure whose manhood is nonetheless ambivalently presented to us: Duncan is to be sure a nurturing father-king, but he is also too soft and trusting for his own good. Macbeth chooses to side with his masculinized wife against the gentler side of human nature, lauding her as a woman who should "Bring forth men-children only," since her "undaunted mettle should compose / Nothing but males" (1.7.73–5), but, in the longer term, Macbeth finds himself desiccated by his own vulnerability to this masculinized mother. He turns unsuccessfully to the witches for the power he needs to make him author of himself; in the process of attempting to make himself wholly "masculine," he manages instead to strip away from himself "honor, love, obedience, troops of friends," and all the graces that should "accompany old age" (5.3.24–5). His nemesis is appropriately one who was not, in the normal sense, "of woman born," since Macduff "was from his mother's womb / Untimely ripped" (5.8.13–16). Macduff represents, in other words, the self-creating and invulnerable masculinity that Macbeth cannot fashion for himself. The ending of the play is distressingly absolute in its consolidation of male power—a reestablishment of control that seems necessary in view of the virulence of the maternal power the play has dared to unleash.

Patterns of imagery throughout the play point similarly to disorders in nature and in human relationships. The murder of Duncan, like that of Caesar in *Julius Caesar*, is accompanied by signs of the heavens' anger. Various observers report that chimneys blow down during the unruly night, that owls clamor and attack falcons, that the earth shakes, and that Duncan's horses devour each other. (Some of these portents are from Holinshed.) Banquo's ghost returns from the dead to haunt his murderer, prompting Macbeth to speak in metaphors of charnel houses and graves that send back their dead and of birds of prey that devour the corpses. The drunken porter who opens the gate to Macduff and Lennox after the murder (2.3) invokes images of judgment and everlasting bonfire, through which the scene takes on the semblance of hell gate and the Harrowing of Hell. Owls appear repeatedly in the imagery, along with other creatures associated with nighttime and horror: wolves, serpents, scorpions, bats, toads, beetles, crows, rooks. Darkness itself assumes tangible and menacing shapes of hidden stars or extinguished candles, a thick blanket shrouded "in the dunnest smoke of hell" (1.5.51), an entombment of the earth in place of "living light" (2.4.10), a scarf to hoodwink the eye of "pitiful day" (3.2.50), and a "bloody and invisible hand" to tear to pieces the lives of the virtuous (3.2.51–2). Sleep is transformed from "great nature's second course" and a "nourisher" of life that "knits up the raveled sleeve

of care" (2.2.41–4) into "death's counterfeit" (2.3.77) and a living hell for Lady Macbeth. Life becomes sterile for Macbeth, a denial of harvest, the lees or dregs of the wine and "the sere, the yellow leaf" (5.3.23). In a theatrical metaphor, life becomes for him unreal, "a walking shadow, a poor player / That struts and frets his hour upon the stage / And then is heard no more" (5.5.24–6). This theme of empty illusion carries over into the recurring image of borrowed or ill-fitting garments that belie the wearer. Macbeth is an actor, a hypocrite, whose "False face must hide what the false heart doth know" (1.7.83) and who must "Look like th'innocent flower, / But be the serpent under't" (1.5.65–6). Even the show of grief is an assumed mask whereby evildoers deceive the virtuous, so much so that Malcolm, Donalbain, and Macduff learn to conceal their true feelings rather than be thought to "show an unfelt sorrow" (2.3.138).

Blood is not only a literal sign of disorder but an emblem of Macbeth's remorseless butchery, a "damned spot" on the conscience, and a promise of divine vengeance: "It will have blood, they say; blood will have blood" (3.4.123). The emphasis on corrupted blood also suggests disease, in which Macbeth's tyranny is a sickness to his country as well as to himself. Scotland bleeds (4.3.32), needing a physician; Macduff and his allies call themselves "the med'cine of the sickly weal" (5.2.27). Lady Macbeth's disease is incurable, something spiritually corrupt wherein "the patient / Must minister to himself" (5.3.47–8). Conversely, the English King Edward is renowned for his divine gift of curing what was called the king's evil, or scrofula (4.3.147–8). These images are generally paternalistic in their invocation of kings and fathers who heal and unite.

Throughout, the defenders of righteousness are associated with positive images of natural order and with patriarchal control. Duncan rewards his subjects by saying, "I have begun to plant thee, and will labor / To make thee full of growing" (1.4.28–9). His arrival at Inverness Castle is heralded by signs of summer, sweet air, and "the temple-haunting martlet" (1.6.4). He is a fatherly figure, so much so that even Lady Macbeth balks at an act so like patricide. Macduff, too, is a father and husband whose family is butchered. The forest of Birnam marching to confront Macbeth, although rationally explainable as a device of camouflage for Macduff's army, is emblematic of the natural order itself rising up against the monstrosity of Macbeth's crimes. Banquo is, above all, a patriarchal figure, ancestor of the royal line governing Scotland and England at the time the play was written. These harmonies are to an extent restorative. Even the witches' riddling prophecies, "th'equivocation of the fiend" (5.5.43), luring Macbeth into further atrocities with the vain promise of security, anticipate a just retribution.

Nonetheless, the play's vision of evil shakes us deeply. Scotland's peace has been violated, so much so that "to do harm / Is often laudable, to do good sometime /

Accounted dangerous folly" (4.2.76–8). Macduff has been forced to deny his proper manly role of protecting his wife and family; Lady Macduff and her son, along with young Siward, have had to pay with their innocent lives the terrible price of Scotland's tyranny. In his frenzied attempt to prevent the fulfillment of the prophecy about Banquo's lineage inheriting the kingdom, Macbeth has, like King Herod, slaughtered much of the younger generation on whom the future depends. We can only hope that the stability to which Scotland returns after his death will be lasting. Banquo's line is to rule eventually and to produce a line of kings reaching down to the royal occupant to whom Shakespeare will present his play, but, when *Macbeth* ends, it is Malcolm who is king. The killing of a traitor (Macbeth) and the placing of his head on a pole replicate the play's beginning in the treason and beheading of the Thane of Cawdor—a gentleman on whom Duncan built "An absolute trust" (1.4.14). Most troublingly, the humanly representative nature of Macbeth's crime leaves us with little assurance that we could resist his temptation. The most that can be said is that wise and good persons such as Banquo and Macduff have learned to know the evil in themselves and to resist it as nobly as they can.

Along with its timeless interest in murder and the human conscience, *Macbeth* is an intensely political play. It surely was viewed as such when it was first produced in 1606–1607. The drunken porter in 2.3 seemingly refers to the infamous attempt to blow up the houses of Parliament known as the Gunpowder Plot of 1605, and to the subsequent trial of the Jesuit Henry Garnet, the notorious "equivocator," for his part in the conspiracy (2.3.8). Banquo fulfills a historical role as progenitor of the dynastic line that would lead eventually to James VI of Scotland, who had become James I of England in 1603. The pageant of *"eight Kings and Banquo last"* that Macbeth must witness on the occasion of his final visit to the Weird Sisters (4.1.111.1) ends with a *glass* or magic mirror showing many more kings bearing the appurtenances of royal office, including the "twofold balls and treble scepters" (4.1.121) that seemingly refer to James's double coronation in 1603 as King of England and Scotland. James was keenly interested in witchcraft. Scotland was a constant worry on England's northern border, aligning itself with France, marauding across the English border, tearing itself apart through clan violence, and, from an English point of view, manifesting the kind of tyranny that the English especially feared. The Scotland of this play thus helps to define, largely by contrast, what is thought to be truly English. The English King who is described as doing "A most miraculous work" in curing "the evil," or scrofula, by his touch (4.3.147–8) suggests a flattering reference to James, who claimed this power of curing. This unnamed English king lends his support to the military attack against Macbeth through which the tyrant is finally overthrown. The play simultaneously incorporates an uneasy attitude of hostility toward Scotland along with a vision of union between the two countries that is brought about by the subjugation of Scotland to her southern neighbor. A rough kind of harmony is achieved out of disharmony. Macbeth's act of murderous regicide is answered by another regicide in the name of English law. The quandaries of such a resolution may point to the ambivalence that many English people felt about their odd ruler from the north, the man who came to be known as "the wisest fool in Christendom."

Macbeth is a difficult play to present on stage, at least according to stage tradition: ever since the early twentieth century, actors have referred to it superstitiously as "the Scottish play" as a way of avoiding bad luck that otherwise can hover menacingly over the acting company. Presumably this is a theatrical response to the play's dark probing of irrational magic, fatal determinism, and human frailty. Not coincidentally, perhaps, some of the greatest successes in performance have been on film. Akira Kurosawa's *Throne of Blood* (1957) retells the story of Macbeth, in black and white, as a devastating exploration of ambitious strife among Japanese warlords. Although the dialogue and characters' names of Shakespeare's play are altered throughout, this version captures magnificently the mysterious and malign intent of the prophetic figure Macbeth encounters in a forest, tempting him to evil by the ambiguous promises of future greatness. The forest itself is a striking presence in this film, invested as it is with supernatural terror in the midst of a thunderstorm. The Lady Asaji, wife to Washizu (the Macbeth figure), is horrifyingly obsessed with ambition for her husband; her seeming role as an obedient and decorously aristocratic Japanese wife accentuates the contrast between the surfaces of civilized behavior and the dark inner promptings of competitive self-assertion. A film version with Ian McKellen and Judi Dench as Macbeth and his wife, based on a stage version directed by Trevor Nunn (1976–1978) at Stratford-upon-Avon, London, and Newcastle-upon-Tyne, emphasizes the demonic in such a way as to give the Weird Sisters a real power that is both psychologically plausible and frighteningly irrational. Roman Polanski's film version (1971), though faulted for its sponsorship by Playboy Productions and its consequent flaunting of some grotesque nakedness, does successfully portray Macbeth and Lady Macbeth as a vitally young couple for whom sexuality is integral to their ambition. And of course there have been great stage productions, despite the shibboleth of the bad-luck legend, notably Glen Byam Shaw's production at Stratford-upon-Avon in 1955 starring Laurence Olivier and Vivien Leigh that invited admiration for husband and wife as magnificent, courageous, loyal, and of genuinely tragic stature even if fatally flawed by their hearkening to the voice of evil.

Macbeth

[*Dramatis Personae*

DUNCAN, *King of Scotland*
MALCOLM, } *his sons*
DONALBAIN, }

MACBETH, *Thane of Glamis, later of Cawdor, later King of Scotland*
LADY MACBETH

BANQUO, *a thane of Scotland*
FLEANCE, *his son*
MACDUFF, *Thane of Fife*
LADY MACDUFF
SON *of Macduff and Lady Macduff*

LENNOX, }
ROSS, }
MENTEITH, } *thanes and noblemen of Scotland*
ANGUS, }
CAITHNESS, }

SIWARD, *Earl of Northumberland*
YOUNG SIWARD, *his son*

SEYTON, *an officer attending Macbeth*
Another LORD
ENGLISH DOCTOR
SCOTTISH DOCTOR
GENTLEWOMAN *attending Lady Macbeth*
CAPTAIN *serving Duncan*
PORTER
OLD MAN
Three MURDERERS *of Banquo*
FIRST MURDERER *at Macduff's castle*
MESSENGER *to Lady Macbeth*
MESSENGER *to Lady Macduff*
SERVANT *to Macbeth*
SERVANT *to Lady Macbeth*
Three WITCHES *or* WEIRD SISTERS
HECATE
Three APPARITIONS

Lords, Gentlemen, Officers, Soldiers, Murderers, and Attendants

SCENE: *Scotland; England*]

1.1

Thunder and lightning. Enter three Witches.

FIRST WITCH
When shall we three meet again?
In thunder, lightning, or in rain?
SECOND WITCH
When the hurlyburly's done,
When the battle's lost and won.
THIRD WITCH
That will be ere the set of sun.   3

FIRST WITCH
Where the place?
SECOND WITCH   Upon the heath.
THIRD WITCH
There to meet with Macbeth.
FIRST WITCH   I come, Grimalkin!   8
SECOND WITCH   Paddock calls.   9
THIRD WITCH   Anon.   10

1.1 Location: An open place.
3 hurlyburly tumult

8 Grimalkin i.e., gray cat, name of the witch's familiar—a demon or evil spirit supposed to answer a witch's call and to allow him or her to perform black magic.   **9 Paddock** toad; also a familiar   **10 Anon** At once, right away.

ALL
Fair is foul, and foul is fair.
Hover through the fog and filthy air.   *Exeunt.*

❖

1.2

Alarum within. Enter King [Duncan], Malcolm,
Donalbain, Lennox, with attendants, meeting a
bleeding Captain.

DUNCAN
What bloody man is that? He can report,
As seemeth by his plight, of the revolt
The newest state.

MALCOLM   This is the sergeant   3
Who like a good and hardy soldier fought
'Gainst my captivity.—Hail, brave friend!
Say to the King the knowledge of the broil   6
As thou didst leave it.

CAPTAIN   Doubtful it stood,
As two spent swimmers that do cling together   8
And choke their art. The merciless Macdonwald—   9
Worthy to be a rebel, for to that   10
The multiplying villainies of nature   11
Do swarm upon him—from the Western Isles   12
Of kerns and gallowglasses is supplied;   13
And Fortune, on his damnèd quarrel smiling,   14
Showed like a rebel's whore. But all's too weak;   15
For brave Macbeth—well he deserves that name—   16
Disdaining Fortune, with his brandished steel,
Which smoked with bloody execution,
Like valor's minion carved out his passage   19
Till he faced the slave,   20
Which ne'er shook hands nor bade farewell to him   21
Till he unseamed him from the nave to th' chops,   22
And fixed his head upon our battlements.

DUNCAN
Oh, valiant cousin, worthy gentleman!   24

CAPTAIN
As whence the sun 'gins his reflection   25
Shipwrecking storms and direful thunders break,   26
So from that spring whence comfort seemed to come   27
Discomfort swells. Mark, King of Scotland, mark.   28
No sooner justice had, with valor armed,
Compelled these skipping kerns to trust their heels   30
But the Norweyan lord, surveying vantage,   31
With furbished arms and new supplies of men,
Began a fresh assault.

DUNCAN
Dismayed not this our captains, Macbeth and
Banquo?

CAPTAIN
Yes, as sparrows eagles, or the hare the lion.   35
If I say sooth, I must report they were   36
As cannons overcharged with double cracks,   37
So they doubly redoubled strokes upon the foe.
Except they meant to bathe in reeking wounds   39
Or memorize another Golgotha,   40
I cannot tell.
But I am faint. My gashes cry for help.

DUNCAN
So well thy words become thee as thy wounds;
They smack of honor both.—Go get him surgeons.
                              [*Exit Captain, attended.*]

Enter Ross and Angus.

Who comes here?

MALCOLM   The worthy Thane of Ross.   45

LENNOX   What a haste looks through his eyes!
So should he look that seems to speak things strange.   47

ROSS   God save the King!

DUNCAN   Whence cam'st thou, worthy thane?

ROSS   From Fife, great King,
Where the Norweyan banners flout the sky   51
And fan our people cold.   52
Norway himself, with terrible numbers,   53
Assisted by that most disloyal traitor,
The Thane of Cawdor, began a dismal conflict,   55
Till that Bellona's bridegroom, lapped in proof,   56
Confronted him with self-comparisons,   57

1.2. Location: A camp near Forres.
0.1 *Alarum* trumpet call to arms   **3 newest state** latest news.
sergeant i.e., staff officer. (There may be no inconsistency with his rank of "captain" in the stage direction and speech prefixes in the Folio.)   **6 broil** battle   **8 spent** tired out   **9 choke their art** render their skill in swimming useless.   **9–13 The merciless . . . supplied** The merciless Macdonwald—worthy of the hated name of rebel, for in the cause of rebellion an ever-increasing number of villainous persons and unnatural qualities swarm about him like vermin—is joined by light-armed Irish footsoldiers and ax-armed horsemen from the western islands of Scotland (the Hebrides and perhaps Ireland)
14–15 And Fortune . . . whore i.e., Fortune, proverbially a false strumpet, smiles at first on Macdonwald's damned rebellion but deserts him in his hour of need.   **16 well . . . name** well he deserves a name that is synonymous with "brave"   **19 minion** darling. (Macbeth is Valor's darling, not Fortune's.)   **20 the slave** i.e., Macdonwald   **21 Which . . . to him** i.e., Macbeth paused for no ceremonious greeting or farewell to Macdonwald   **22 nave** navel.   **chops** jaws
24 cousin kinsman

25–8 As . . . swells Just as terrible storms at sea arise out of the east, from the place where the sun first shows itself in the seeming comfort of the dawn, even thus did a new military threat come on the heels of the seeming good news of Macdonwald's execution.   **30 skipping** (1) lightly armed, quick at maneuvering (2) skittish   **31 surveying vantage** seeing an opportunity   **35 Yes . . . eagles** Yes, about as much as sparrows terrify eagles. (Said ironically.)   **36 say sooth** tell the truth   **37 cracks** charges of explosive   **39 Except** Unless   **40 memorize** make memorable or famous.   **Golgotha** "place of a skull," where Christ was crucified. (Mark 15:22.)   **45 Thane** Scottish title of honor, roughly equivalent to "Earl"   **47 seems to** seems about to   **51 flout** mock, insult   **52 fan . . . cold** fan cold fear into our troops.   **53 Norway** The King of Norway.   **terrible numbers** terrifying numbers of troops   **55 dismal** ominous   **56 Till . . . proof** i.e., until Macbeth, clad in well-tested armor. (Bellona was the Roman goddess of war.)   **57 him** i.e., the King of Norway.   **self-comparisons** i.e., matching counterthrusts

Point against point, rebellious arm 'gainst arm,
Curbing his lavish spirit; and to conclude,
The victory fell on us.
DUNCAN   Great happiness!
ROSS   That now
Sweno, the Norways' king, craves composition;   62
Nor would we deign him burial of his men
Till he disbursèd at Saint Colme's Inch   64
Ten thousand dollars to our general use.   65
DUNCAN
No more that Thane of Cawdor shall deceive
Our bosom interest. Go pronounce his present death,   67
And with his former title greet Macbeth.
ROSS   I'll see it done.
DUNCAN
What he hath lost noble Macbeth hath won.
                    Exeunt.

❖

1.3

Thunder. Enter the three Witches.

FIRST WITCH   Where hast thou been, sister?
SECOND WITCH   Killing swine.
THIRD WITCH   Sister, where thou?
FIRST WITCH
A sailor's wife had chestnuts in her lap,
And munched, and munched, and munched. "Give
    me," quoth I.
"Aroint thee, witch!" the rump-fed runnion cries.   6
Her husband's to Aleppo gone, master o'th' *Tiger*;   7
But in a sieve I'll thither sail,
And like a rat without a tail   9
I'll do, I'll do, and I'll do.   10
SECOND WITCH
I'll give thee a wind.
FIRST WITCH
Thou'rt kind.
THIRD WITCH
And I another.
FIRST WITCH
I myself have all the other,   14
And the very ports they blow,   15
All the quarters that they know   16
I'th' shipman's card.   17
I'll drain him dry as hay.   18

---

62 Norways' Norwegians'.   **composition** agreement, treaty of peace
64 Saint Colme's Inch Inchcolm, the Isle of St. Columba in the Firth
of Forth   **65 dollars** Spanish or Dutch coins   **67 Our** (The royal
"we.")   **bosom** close and intimate.   **present** immediate
1.3. Location: A heath near Forres.
6 Aroint thee Begone.   **rump-fed runnion** fat-rumped baggage
7 *Tiger* (A ship's name.)   **9–10 like . . . do** (Suggestive of the witches'
deformity and sexual insatiability. Witches were thought to seduce
men sexually. *Do* means [1] act [2] perform sexually.)   **14–17 I . . .
card** I can summon all other winds, wherever they blow and from
whatever *quarter* in the shipman's compass card.   **18 I'll . . . hay**
(With a suggestion of sexually draining the seaman's semen.)

Sleep shall neither night nor day
Hang upon his penthouse lid.   20
He shall live a man forbid.   21
Weary sev'nnights nine times nine   22
Shall he dwindle, peak, and pine.   23
Though his bark cannot be lost,
Yet it shall be tempest-tossed.
Look what I have.
SECOND WITCH   Show me, show me.
FIRST WITCH
Here I have a pilot's thumb,
Wrecked as homeward he did come.   *Drum within.*
THIRD WITCH
A drum, a drum!
Macbeth doth come.
ALL [*dancing in a circle*]
The Weird Sisters, hand in hand,   32
Posters of the sea and land,   33
Thus do go about, about,
Thrice to thine, and thrice to mine,
And thrice again, to make up nine.
Peace! The charm's wound up.

Enter Macbeth and Banquo.

MACBETH
So foul and fair a day I have not seen.
BANQUO
How far is't called to Forres?—What are these,   39
So withered and so wild in their attire,
That look not like th'inhabitants o'th'earth
And yet are on't?—Live you? Or are you aught
That man may question? You seem to understand me
By each at once her choppy finger laying   44
Upon her skinny lips. You should be women,
And yet your beards forbid me to interpret
That you are so.
MACBETH   Speak, if you can. What are you?
FIRST WITCH
All hail, Macbeth! Hail to thee, Thane of Glamis!
SECOND WITCH
All hail, Macbeth! Hail to thee, Thane of Cawdor!
THIRD WITCH
All hail, Macbeth, that shalt be king hereafter!
BANQUO
Good sir, why do you start and seem to fear
Things that do sound so fair?—I'th' name of truth,
Are ye fantastical or that indeed   53
Which outwardly ye show? My noble partner   54
You greet with present grace and great prediction   55
Of noble having and of royal hope,
That he seems rapt withal. To me you speak not.   57
If you can look into the seeds of time

---

20 penthouse lid i.e., eyelid (which projects out over the eye like a
penthouse or slope-roofed structure).   **21 forbid** accursed.   **22 sev'n-
nights** weeks   **23 peak** grow peaked or thin   **32 Weird Sisters**
women connected with fate or destiny; also women having a mysterious or unearthly, uncanny appearance   **33 Posters of** swift travelers
over   **39 is't called** is it said to be   **44 choppy** chapped   **53 fantastical** creatures of fantasy or imagination   **54 show** appear.   **55 grace**
honor   **57 rapt withal** entranced.

And say which grain will grow and which will not,
Speak then to me, who neither beg nor fear   60
Your favors nor your hate.   61

FIRST WITCH   Hail!

SECOND WITCH   Hail!

THIRD WITCH   Hail!

FIRST WITCH
Lesser than Macbeth, and greater.

SECOND WITCH
Not so happy, yet much happier.   66

THIRD WITCH
Thou shalt get kings, though thou be none.   67
So all hail, Macbeth and Banquo!

FIRST WITCH
Banquo and Macbeth, all hail!

MACBETH
Stay, you imperfect speakers, tell me more!   70
By Sinel's death I know I am Thane of Glamis,   71
But how of Cawdor? The Thane of Cawdor lives
A prosperous gentleman; and to be king
Stands not within the prospect of belief,
No more than to be Cawdor. Say from whence   75
You owe this strange intelligence, or why   76
Upon this blasted heath you stop our way   77
With such prophetic greeting? Speak, I charge you.
                                          Witches vanish.

BANQUO
The earth hath bubbles, as the water has,
And these are of them. Whither are they vanished?

MACBETH
Into the air; and what seemed corporal melted,   81
As breath into the wind. Would they had stayed!

BANQUO
Were such things here as we do speak about?
Or have we eaten on the insane root   84
That takes the reason prisoner?

MACBETH
Your children shall be kings.

BANQUO   You shall be king.

MACBETH
And Thane of Cawdor too. Went it not so?

BANQUO
To th' selfsame tune and words.—Who's here?

                    Enter Ross and Angus.

ROSS
The King hath happily received, Macbeth,
The news of thy success; and when he reads   90
Thy personal venture in the rebels' fight,   91
His wonders and his praises do contend   92
Which should be thine or his. Silenced with that,   93
In viewing o'er the rest o'th' selfsame day

He finds thee in the stout Norweyan ranks,   95
Nothing afeard of what thyself didst make,   96
Strange images of death. As thick as tale   97
Came post with post, and every one did bear   98
Thy praises in his kingdom's great defense,
And poured them down before him.

ANGUS   We are sent
To give thee from our royal master thanks,
Only to herald thee into his sight,
Not pay thee.

ROSS
And, for an earnest of a greater honor,   104
He bade me, from him, call thee Thane of Cawdor;
In which addition, hail, most worthy thane,   106
For it is thine.

BANQUO   What, can the devil speak true?

MACBETH
The Thane of Cawdor lives. Why do you dress me
In borrowed robes?

ANGUS   Who was the thane lives yet,   109
But under heavy judgment bears that life
Which he deserves to lose. Whether he was combined 111
With those of Norway, or did line the rebel   112
With hidden help and vantage, or that with both
He labored in his country's wrack, I know not;   114
But treasons capital, confessed and proved,   115
Have overthrown him.

MACBETH [*aside*]   Glamis, and Thane of Cawdor!
The greatest is behind. [*To Ross and Angus*] Thanks for
    your pains.   117
[*Aside to Banquo*] Do you not hope your children shall
    be kings
When those that gave the Thane of Cawdor to me
Promised no less to them?

BANQUO [*to Macbeth*]   That, trusted home,   120
Might yet enkindle you unto the crown,
Besides the Thane of Cawdor. But 'tis strange;
And oftentimes to win us to our harm
The instruments of darkness tell us truths,
Win us with honest trifles, to betray 's
In deepest consequence.—   126
Cousins, a word, I pray you.   127
            [*He converses apart with Ross and Angus.*]

MACBETH [*aside*]   Two truths are told,
As happy prologues to the swelling act   129
Of the imperial theme.—I thank you, gentlemen.
[*Aside*] This supernatural soliciting   131
Cannot be ill, cannot be good. If ill,
Why hath it given me earnest of success

60–1 beg . . . hate beg your favors nor fear your hate.   66 happy fortunate   67 get beget   70 imperfect cryptic   71 Sinel's (Sinel was
Macbeth's father.)   75–6 Say . . . intelligence Say from what source
you have this disturbing information   77 blasted blighted   81 corporal corporeal   84 on of.   insane root root causing insanity; variously identified   90–3 and when . . . his and when he reads of your
extraordinary valor in fighting the rebels, he concludes that your
wondrous deeds outdo any praise he could offer.

95 stout haughty, determined, valiant   96 Nothing not at all
97–8 As . . . with post As fast as could be told, i.e., counted, came
messenger after messenger. (Unless the text should be amended to
"As thick as hail.")   104 earnest token payment   106 addition title
109 Who He who   111 combined confederate   112 line the rebel
reinforce Macdonwald   114 in . . . wrack to bring about his country's
ruin   115 capital deserving death   117 The greatest is behind either
(1) Two of the three prophecies (and thus the greatest number of
them) have already been fulfilled, or (2) The greatest one, the kingship, is still to come.   120 home all the way   126 In deepest consequence in the profoundly important sequel.   127 Cousins i.e., Fellow
lords   129 swelling act stately drama   131 soliciting tempting

Commencing in a truth? I am Thane of Cawdor.
If good, why do I yield to that suggestion
Whose horrid image doth unfix my hair   136
And make my seated heart knock at my ribs,
Against the use of nature? Present fears   138
Are less than horrible imaginings.
My thought, whose murder yet is but fantastical,   140
Shakes so my single state of man   141
That function is smothered in surmise,   142
And nothing is but what is not.   143

BANQUO   Look how our partner's rapt.

MACBETH [*aside*]
If chance will have me king, why, chance may crown
    me
Without my stir.

BANQUO   New honors come upon him,   146
Like our strange garments, cleave not to their mold   147
But with the aid of use.

MACBETH [*aside*]   Come what come may,   148
Time and the hour runs through the roughest day.   149

BANQUO
Worthy Macbeth, we stay upon your leisure.   150

MACBETH
Give me your favor. My dull brain was wrought   151
With things forgotten. Kind gentlemen, your pains
Are registered where every day I turn   153
The leaf to read them. Let us toward the King.
[*Aside to Banquo*]   Think upon what hath chanced,
    and at more time,   155
The interim having weighed it, let us speak   156
Our free hearts each to other.   157

BANQUO [*to Macbeth*]   Very gladly.

MACBETH [*to Banquo*]   Till then, enough.—Come, friends.
                                        Exeunt.

❖

1.4

*Flourish. Enter King [Duncan], Lennox, Malcolm,
Donalbain, and attendants.*

DUNCAN
Is execution done on Cawdor? Are not
Those in commission yet returned?

MALCOLM   My liege,   2
They are not yet come back. But I have spoke

With one that saw him die, who did report
That very frankly he confessed his treasons,
Implored Your Highness' pardon, and set forth
A deep repentance. Nothing in his life
Became him like the leaving it. He died   8
As one that had been studied in his death   9
To throw away the dearest thing he owed   10
As 'twere a careless trifle.

DUNCAN   There's no art   11
To find the mind's construction in the face.
He was a gentleman on whom I built
An absolute trust.

Enter Macbeth, Banquo, Ross, and Angus.

                    O worthiest cousin!
The sin of my ingratitude even now
Was heavy on me. Thou art so far before   16
That swiftest wing of recompense is slow
To overtake thee. Would thou hadst less deserved,
That the proportion both of thanks and payment   19
Might have been mine! Only I have left to say,   20
More is thy due than more than all can pay.

MACBETH
The service and the loyalty I owe,
In doing it, pays itself. Your Highness' part
Is to receive our duties; and our duties
Are to your throne and state children and servants,   25
Which do but what they should by doing everything
Safe toward your love and honor.

DUNCAN   Welcome hither!   27
I have begun to plant thee, and will labor
To make thee full of growing. Noble Banquo,
That hast no less deserved, nor must be known
No less to have done so, let me infold thee
And hold thee to my heart.

BANQUO   There if I grow,
The harvest is your own.

DUNCAN   My plenteous joys,
Wanton in fullness, seek to hide themselves   34
In drops of sorrow.—Sons, kinsmen, thanes,
And you whose places are the nearest, know
We will establish our estate upon   37
Our eldest, Malcolm, whom we name hereafter
The Prince of Cumberland; which honor must   39
Not unaccompanied invest him only,   40
But signs of nobleness, like stars, shall shine
On all deservers.—From hence to Inverness,   42
And bind us further to you.   43

---

136 unfix my hair make my hair stand on end   **138 use** custom.
fears things feared   **140 whose . . . fantastical** in which the conception of murder is merely imaginary at this point   **141 single . . . man**
weak human condition   **142 function** normal power of action.
surmise speculation, imaginings   **143 And . . . not** and everything
seems unreal.   **146 stir** bestirring (myself).   **come** i.e., which have
come   **147–8 cleave . . . use** do not take the shape of the wearer until
often worn. (Macbeth is often connected in the text with clothes that
don't really fit him.)   **149 Time . . . day** time moves relentlessly on,
no matter what else happens.   **150 stay** wait
151 favor pardon.   **wrought** shaped, preoccupied   **153 registered**
recorded (in my memory)   **155 at more time** at a time of greater
leisure   **156 weighed it** given oportunity for reflection on its meaning   **157 Our free hearts** our hearts freely
1.4. Location: Forres. The palace.
2 in commission having warrant (to see to the execution of Cawdor)

8 Became graced, befitted   **9 been studied** made it his study
10 owed owned   **11 careless** uncared for   **16 before** ahead (in
deserving)   **19–20 That . . . mine** that I might have thanked and
rewarded you in ample proportion to your worth.   **25 Are . . . servants** are like children and servants in relation to your throne and
dignity, existing only to serve you   **27 Safe . . . honor** to safeguard
you whom we love and honor.   **34 Wanton** unrestrained   **37 We**
(The royal "we.")   **establish our estate** fix the succession of our state
39 Prince of Cumberland title of the heir apparent to the Scottish
throne   **40 Not . . . only** not be bestowed on Malcolm alone; other
deserving nobles are to share honors   **42 Inverness** the seat or location of Macbeth's castle, Dunsinane   **43 bind . . . you** put me further
in your (Macbeth's) obligation by your hospitality.

MACBETH
The rest is labor which is not used for you.   44
I'll be myself the harbinger and make joyful   45
The hearing of my wife with your approach;
So humbly take my leave.
DUNCAN   My worthy Cawdor!
MACBETH [aside]
The Prince of Cumberland! That is a step
On which I must fall down or else o'erleap,
For in my way it lies. Stars, hide your fires;   50
Let not light see my black and deep desires.
The eye wink at the hand; yet let that be   52
Which the eye fears, when it is done, to see.   Exit.   53
DUNCAN
True, worthy Banquo. He is full so valiant,   54
And in his commendations I am fed;   55
It is a banquet to me. Let's after him,
Whose care is gone before to bid us welcome.
It is a peerless kinsman.   Flourish. Exeunt.

❖

1.5

Enter Macbeth's Wife, alone, with a letter.

LADY MACBETH [reads] "They met me in the day of success; and I have learned by the perfect'st report they   2
have more in them than mortal knowledge. When I
burnt in desire to question them further, they made
themselves air, into which they vanished. Whiles I
stood rapt in the wonder of it came missives from the   6
King, who all-hailed me 'Thane of Cawdor,' by which
title, before, these Weird Sisters saluted me, and referred me to the coming on of time with 'Hail, king
that shalt be!' This have I thought good to deliver thee,   10
my dearest partner of greatness, that thou mightst not
lose the dues of rejoicing by being ignorant of what
greatness is promised thee. Lay it to thy heart, and
farewell."
Glamis thou art, and Cawdor, and shalt be
What thou art promised. Yet do I fear thy nature;   16
It is too full o'th' milk of human kindness
To catch the nearest way. Thou wouldst be great,
Art not without ambition, but without
The illness should attend it. What thou wouldst
highly,   20
That wouldst thou holily; wouldst not play false,

And yet wouldst wrongly win. Thou'dst have, great
Glamis,
That which cries "Thus thou must do," if thou have it,   23
And that which rather thou dost fear to do   24
Than wishest should be undone. Hie thee hither,   25
That I may pour my spirits in thine ear
And chastise with the valor of my tongue
All that impedes thee from the golden round   28
Which fate and metaphysical aid doth seem   29
To have thee crowned withal.

Enter [a servant as] Messenger.

What is your tidings?   30
MESSENGER
The King comes here tonight.
LADY MACBETH   Thou'rt mad to say it!
Is not thy master with him, who, were't so,
Would have informed for preparation?   33
MESSENGER
So please you, it is true. Our thane is coming.
One of my fellows had the speed of him,   35
Who, almost dead for breath, had scarcely more
Than would make up his message.
LADY MACBETH   Give him tending;   37
He brings great news.   Exit Messenger.
                    The raven himself is hoarse
That croaks the fatal entrance of Duncan
Under my battlements. Come, you spirits
That tend on mortal thoughts, unsex me here   41
And fill me from the crown to the toe top-full
Of direst cruelty! Make thick my blood;
Stop up th'access and passage to remorse,   44
That no compunctious visitings of nature   45
Shake my fell purpose, nor keep peace between   46
Th'effect and it! Come to my woman's breasts   47
And take my milk for gall, you murd'ring ministers,   48
Wherever in your sightless substances   49
You wait on nature's mischief! Come, thick night,   50
And pall thee in the dunnest smoke of hell,   51
That my keen knife see not the wound it makes,
Nor heaven peep through the blanket of the dark
To cry "Hold, hold!"

Enter Macbeth.

                    Great Glamis! Worthy Cawdor!   54
Greater than both by the all-hail hereafter!
Thy letters have transported me beyond   56

44 **The rest . . . you** All activity not devoted to serving you is mere
tediousness and hard work.   45 **harbinger** forerunner, messenger
50 **in my way it lies** (The monarchy was not hereditary, and Macbeth
had a right to believe that he himself might be chosen as Duncan's
successor; he here questions whether he will interfere with the
course of events.)   52–3 **The eye . . . see** Let the eye shut itself and
not see the hand's deed; yet when the deed is done, let it be fearful to
behold.   54 **full so valiant** fully as valiant as you say. (Apparently,
Duncan and Banquo have been conversing privately on this subject
during Macbeth's soliloquy.)   55 **in . . . fed** it nourishes me to hear
him praised
1.5. Location: Inverness. Macbeth's castle.
2 **perfect'st** most accurate   6 **missives** messengers   10 **deliver thee**
inform you of   16 **do I fear** I mistrust   20 **illness** evil (that).
highly greatly

23 **have** are to have, want to have   24–5 **And that . . . undone** i.e.,
and the thing you ambitiously crave frightens you more in terms of
the means needed to achieve it than in the idea of having it; if you
could have it without those means, you certainly wouldn't wish it
undone.   25 **Hie** Hasten   28 **round** crown   29 **metaphysical** supernatural   30 **withal** with.   33 **informed for preparation** i.e., sent me
word so that I might get things ready.   35 **had . . . of** outstripped
37 **Give him tending** Tend to his needs   41 **tend . . . thoughts** attend
on, act as the instruments of, deadly or murderous thoughts
44 **remorse** pity   45 **nature** natural feelings   46 **fell** fierce, cruel
46–7 **nor . . . and it** nor intervene between my *fell purpose* and its
accomplishment.   48 **for gall** in exchange for gall, or perhaps *as* gall.
ministers agents   49 **sightless** invisible   50 **You . . . mischief** you
aid and abet the wickedness of human nature.   51 **pall** envelop.
dunnest darkest   54 **Hold** Stop   56 **letters have** i.e., letter has

<table>
<tr><td>

This ignorant present, and I feel now
The future in the instant.

MACBETH   My dearest love,
Duncan comes here tonight.

LADY MACBETH   And when goes hence?

MACBETH
Tomorrow, as he purposes.

LADY MACBETH   Oh, never
Shall sun that morrow see!
Your face, my thane, is as a book where men
May read strange matters. To beguile the time,   63
Look like the time; bear welcome in your eye,   64
Your hand, your tongue. Look like th'innocent flower,
But be the serpent under't. He that's coming
Must be provided for; and you shall put
This night's great business into my dispatch,   68
Which shall to all our nights and days to come
Give solely sovereign sway and masterdom.

MACBETH
We will speak further.

LADY MACBETH   Only look up clear.   71
To alter favor ever is to fear.   72
Leave all the rest to me.   *Exeunt.*

</td><td>

How you shall bid God 'ild us for your pains,   13
And thank us for your trouble.

LADY MACBETH   All our service
In every point twice done, and then done double,
Were poor and single business to contend   16
Against those honors deep and broad wherewith   17
Your Majesty loads our house. For those of old,   18
And the late dignities heaped up to them,   19
We rest your hermits.

DUNCAN   Where's the Thane of Cawdor? 20
We coursed him at the heels, and had a purpose   21
To be his purveyor; but he rides well,   22
And his great love, sharp as his spur, hath holp him 23
To his home before us. Fair and noble hostess,
We are your guest tonight.

LADY MACBETH   Your servants ever   25
Have theirs, themselves, and what is theirs in compt 26
To make their audit at Your Highness' pleasure,   27
Still to return your own.

DUNCAN   Give me your hand.   28
Conduct me to mine host. We love him highly,
And shall continue our graces towards him.
By your leave, hostess.   *Exeunt.*

</td></tr>
</table>

❖

1.6

Hautboys and torches. Enter King [Duncan],
Malcolm, Donalbain, Banquo, Lennox, Macduff,
Ross, Angus, and attendants.

DUNCAN
This castle hath a pleasant seat. The air   1
Nimbly and sweetly recommends itself
Unto our gentle senses.

BANQUO   This guest of summer,   3
The temple-haunting martlet, does approve   4
By his loved mansionry that the heaven's breath   5
Smells wooingly here. No jutty, frieze,   6
Buttress, nor coign of vantage but this bird   7
Hath made his pendent bed and procreant cradle.   8
Where they most breed and haunt, I have observed
The air is delicate.

Enter Lady [Macbeth].

DUNCAN   See, see, our honored hostess!
The love that follows us sometime is our trouble,   11
Which still we thank as love. Herein I teach you   12

❖

1.7

Hautboys. Torches. Enter a sewer, and divers
servants with dishes and service, [and pass] over
the stage. Then enter Macbeth.

MACBETH
If it were done when 'tis done, then 'twere well
It were done quickly. If th'assassination   2
Could trammel up the consequence, and catch   3
With his surcease success—that but this blow   4
Might be the be-all and the end-all!—here,   5
But here, upon this bank and shoal of time,
We'd jump the life to come. But in these cases   7

63–4 To beguile . . . time To deceive everyone, look the way people expect you to look   **68 dispatch** management   **71–2 Only . . . fear** Whatever else you do, keep a cheerful countenance. To alter one's countenance is to betray a guilty conscience.
1.6. Location: Before Macbeth's castle.
0.1 *Hautboys* oboelike instruments   **1 seat** site.   **3 gentle** (1) noble (2) refined (by the delicate air)   **4–5 The . . . mansionry** The house martin, that loves to nest in churches, proves by his devoted nest building   **6 jutty** projection of wall or building   **7 coign of vantage** convenient corner, i.e., for nesting   **8 pendent** hanging, suspended. **procreant** for breeding   **11–12 The love . . . love** The love that sometimes forces itself inconveniently upon us we still appreciate, since it is meant as love. (Duncan is graciously suggesting that his visit is a bother, but, he hopes, a welcome one.)

13 bid . . . pains ask God to reward me for the trouble I'm giving you. (This is said in the same gently jocose spirit as lines 11–12.)   **'ild** yield, repay   **16–17 Were . . . Against** would be poor and small when compared with   **18–20 For . . . hermits** In gratitude for the dignities heaped upon us in former days and still others more recently added to them, we are your thankful worshipers who pray for you like hermits or beadsmen.   **21 coursed** followed (as in a hunt)   **22 purveyor** an officer sent ahead to provide for entertainment; here, forerunner   **23 holp** helped   **25 We** (the royal "we," also in lines 13–14 and 29)   **25–8 Your . . . own** Those who serve you hold their own servants, themselves, and all their possessions in trust from you, and can render an account whenever you wish, ready always to render back to you what is yours. (A feudal concept of obligation.)
1.7. Location: Macbeth's castle; an inner courtyard.
0.1 *sewer* chief waiter, butler   **2–4 If . . . success** i.e., If only the assassination of Duncan could proceed without further consequences and end the matter with the completion of the deed itself. (To *trammel* is to bind up or entangle in a net; *surcease* means "cessation"; *success* means "what succeeds or follows.")   **4 that but** so that only   **5 here** in this world   **7 jump** risk. (But imaging the physical act is characteristic of Macbeth; compare this with line 27.)

We still have judgment here, that we but teach   8
Bloody instructions, which, being taught, return   9
To plague th'inventor. This evenhanded justice   10
Commends th'ingredience of our poisoned chalice   11
To our own lips. He's here in double trust:
First, as I am his kinsman and his subject,
Strong both against the deed; then, as his host,
Who should against his murderer shut the door,
Not bear the knife myself. Besides, this Duncan
Hath borne his faculties so meek, hath been   17
So clear in his great office, that his virtues   18
Will plead like angels, trumpet-tongued, against
The deep damnation of his taking-off;   20
And Pity, like a naked newborn babe
Striding the blast, or heaven's cherubin, horsed   22
Upon the sightless couriers of the air,   23
Shall blow the horrid deed in every eye,
That tears shall drown the wind. I have no spur   25
To prick the sides of my intent, but only
Vaulting ambition, which o'erleaps itself
And falls on th'other—   28

Enter Lady [Macbeth].

How now, what news?

LADY MACBETH
He has almost supped. Why have you left the
   chamber?

MACBETH
Hath he asked for me?

LADY MACBETH   Know you not he has?

MACBETH
We will proceed no further in this business.
He hath honored me of late, and I have bought   33
Golden opinions from all sorts of people,
Which would be worn now in their newest gloss,   35
Not cast aside so soon.

LADY MACBETH   Was the hope drunk
Wherein you dressed yourself? Hath it slept since?
And wakes it now, to look so green and pale   38
At what it did so freely? From this time
Such I account thy love. Art thou afeard
To be the same in thine own act and valor
As thou art in desire? Wouldst thou have that
Which thou esteem'st the ornament of life,   43
And live a coward in thine own esteem,
Letting "I dare not" wait upon "I would,"   45

Like the poor cat i'th' adage?

MACBETH   Prithee, peace!   46
I dare do all that may become a man;
Who dares do more is none.

LADY MACBETH   What beast was't, then,
That made you break this enterprise to me?   49
When you durst do it, then you were a man;
And, to be more than what you were, you would
Be so much more the man. Nor time nor place   52
Did then adhere, and yet you would make both.   53
They have made themselves, and that their fitness
   now   54
Does unmake you. I have given suck, and know
How tender 'tis to love the babe that milks me;
I would, while it was smiling in my face,
Have plucked my nipple from his boneless gums
And dashed the brains out, had I so sworn as you
Have done to this.

MACBETH   If we should fail?

LADY MACBETH   We fail?
But screw your courage to the sticking place   61
And we'll not fail. When Duncan is asleep—
Whereto the rather shall his day's hard journey
Soundly invite him—his two chamberlains   64
Will I with wine and wassail so convince   65
That memory, the warder of the brain,   66
Shall be a fume, and the receipt of reason   67
A limbeck only. When in swinish sleep   68
Their drenchèd natures lies as in a death,   69
What cannot you and I perform upon
Th'unguarded Duncan? What not put upon
His spongy officers, who shall bear the guilt   72
Of our great quell?

MACBETH   Bring forth men-children only!   73
For thy undaunted mettle should compose   74
Nothing but males. Will it not be received,   75
When we have marked with blood those sleepy two
Of his own chamber and used their very daggers,
That they have done't?

LADY MACBETH   Who dares receive it other, 78
As we shall make our griefs and clamor roar   79
Upon his death?

MACBETH   I am settled, and bend up   80
Each corporal agent to this terrible feat.   81

8–10 **We . . . th'inventor** i.e., we still have punishment for crime in this world, whereby our bloody acts establish guilty precedents and thereby invite the just reciprocity of punishing blood with blood. 11 **Commends** presents.   **th'ingredience** the contents of a mixture 17 **faculties** powers of office   18 **clear** free of taint   20 **taking-off** murder   22 **Striding the blast** bestriding the tempest. (Putti and cherubs are often portrayed this way in Renaissance graphic arts.) 23 **sightless couriers** invisible steeds or runners, i.e., the winds 25 **tears . . . wind** (Showers of rain were popularly supposed to still the wind.)   28 **th'other** the other side. (The image is of a horseman vaulting into his saddle and ignominiously falling on the opposite side.)   33 **bought** acquired (by bravery in battle)   35 **would** ought to, should   38 **green** sickly   43 **the ornament of life** i.e., the crown 45 **wait upon** accompany, always follow

46 **adage** (i.e., "The cat would eat fish but she will not wet her feet.") 49 **break** broach   52 **Nor** Neither   53 **adhere** agree, suit.   **would** wanted to   54 **that their fitness** that very suitability of time and place   61 **But** Only.   **the sticking place** the notch into which is fitted the string of a crossbow cranked taut for shooting   64 **chamberlains** attendants on the bedchamber   65 **wassail** carousal, drink. **convince** overpower   66–8 **warder . . . only** (The brain was thought to be divided into three ventricles: imagination in front, memory at the back, and between them the seat of reason. The fumes of wine, arising from the stomach, would deaden memory and judgment.) 67 **receipt** receptacle, ventricle   68 **limbeck** device for distilling liquids   69 **drenchèd** drowned (in wine)   72 **spongy** soaked, drunken 73 **quell** murder.   74 **mettle** (the same word as *metal*): substance, temperament   75 **received** i.e., as truth   78 **other** otherwise 79 **As** inasmuch as   80–1 **bend up . . . agent** harness and direct every part of me

Away, and mock the time with fairest show.   82
False face must hide what the false heart doth know.
Exeunt.

❧

2.1

Enter Banquo, and Fleance, with a torch before him.

BANQUO   How goes the night, boy?

FLEANCE
The moon is down. I have not heard the clock.

BANQUO
And she goes down at twelve.

FLEANCE   I take't, 'tis later, sir.

BANQUO
Hold, take my sword. [*He gives him his sword.*] There's
    husbandry in heaven;   4
Their candles are all out. Take thee that too.
                    [*He gives him his belt and dagger.*]
A heavy summons lies like lead upon me,   6
And yet I would not sleep. Merciful powers,   7
Restrain in me the cursèd thoughts that nature
Gives way to in repose!

Enter Macbeth, and a Servant with a torch.

Give me my sword. Who's there? [*He takes his sword.*]

MACBETH   A friend.

BANQUO
What, sir, not yet at rest? The King's abed.
He hath been in unusual pleasure,
And sent forth great largess to your offices.   14
This diamond he greets your wife withal,
By the name of most kind hostess, and shut up   16
In measureless content.   [*He gives a diamond.*]

MACBETH   Being unprepared,   17
Our will became the servant to defect,   18
Which else should free have wrought.   19

BANQUO   All's well.
I dreamt last night of the three Weird Sisters.
To you they have showed some truth.

MACBETH   I think not of them.
Yet, when we can entreat an hour to serve,
We would spend it in some words upon that business,
If you would grant the time.

BANQUO   At your kind'st leisure.

MACBETH
If you shall cleave to my consent when 'tis,   26
It shall make honor for you.

BANQUO   So I lose none   27
In seeking to augment it, but still keep
My bosom franchised and allegiance clear,   29
I shall be counseled.

MACBETH   Good repose the while!   30

BANQUO   Thanks, sir. The like to you.
                    Exit Banquo [*with Fleance*].

MACBETH [*to Servant*]
Go bid thy mistress, when my drink is ready,   32
She strike upon the bell. Get thee to bed.
                    Exit [*Servant*].
Is this a dagger which I see before me,
The handle toward my hand? Come, let me clutch
    thee.
I have thee not, and yet I see thee still.
Art thou not, fatal vision, sensible   37
To feeling as to sight? Or art thou but
A dagger of the mind, a false creation,
Proceeding from the heat-oppressèd brain?   40
I see thee yet, in form as palpable
As this which now I draw.   [*He draws a dagger.*]
Thou marshall'st me the way that I was going,   43
And such an instrument I was to use.
Mine eyes are made the fools o'th'other senses,
Or else worth all the rest. I see thee still,
And on thy blade and dudgeon gouts of blood,   47
Which was not so before. There's no such thing.
It is the bloody business which informs
Thus to mine eyes. Now o'er the one half world
Nature seems dead, and wicked dreams abuse   51
The curtained sleep. Witchcraft celebrates   52
Pale Hecate's offerings, and withered Murder,   53
Alarumed by his sentinel, the wolf,   54
Whose howl's his watch, thus with his stealthy pace,   55
With Tarquin's ravishing strides, towards his design   56
Moves like a ghost. Thou sure and firm-set earth,
Hear not my steps which way they walk, for fear
Thy very stones prate of my whereabout
And take the present horror from the time   60
Which now suits with it. Whiles I threat, he lives;   61

---

82 mock deceive
**2.1 Location: Inner courtyard of Macbeth's castle. Time is virtually
continuous from the previous scene.**
0.1 torch (This may mean "torchbearer," although it does not at line
9.1.)   **4 husbandry** thrift (careful management of resources in the
domestic economy)   **6 summons** i.e., to sleep   **7 would not** am
reluctant to (owing to my uneasy fears).   **powers** order of angels
deputed by God to resist demons   **14 largess** gifts, gratuities.
offices quarters used for the household work.   **16–17 and shut . . .
content** and went to bed professing himself endlessly pleased.
18–19 Our . . . wrought our good will (to entertain the King) was limited by our meager resources (on such short notice), which otherwise
would have poured forth hospitality without restraint.

26 cleave . . . 'tis give me your support, adhere to my view, when the
time comes   **27 So** Provided that   **29 franchised** free (from guilt).
clear unstained   **30 counseled** receptive to suggestion.   **32 drink**
i.e., posset or bedtime drink of hot spiced milk curdled with ale or
wine, as also in 2.2.6   **37 fatal** ominous.   **sensible** perceivable by the
senses   **40 heat-oppressèd** fevered   **43 Thou . . . going** You seem to
guide me toward the destiny I intended, toward Duncan's chambers
47 dudgeon hilt of a dagger.   **gouts** drops   **51 abuse** deceive
52 curtained curtained by night (and by bedcurtains)   **53 Pale
Hecate's offerings** sacrificial offerings to Hecate, the goddess of night
and witchcraft. (She is *pale* because she is identified with the pale
moon.)   **withered** (Murder is pictured as in images of Death,
shrunken and wasted.)   **54 Alarumed** given the signal to action
55 watch watchword or cry   **56 Tarquin's** (Tarquin was a Roman
tyrant who ravished Lucrece.)   **60–1 And take . . . with it** and thus
echo and augment the horror which is so suited to this evil hour, or,
usurp the present horror by breaking the silence.   **61 threat** i.e.,
merely threaten to kill Duncan

Words to the heat of deeds too cold breath gives.   62
                                           A bell rings.

I go, and it is done. The bell invites me.
Hear it not, Duncan, for it is a knell
That summons thee to heaven or to hell.   *Exit.*

❧

2.2

Enter Lady [Macbeth].

LADY MACBETH
That which hath made them drunk hath made me
   bold;
What hath quenched them hath given me fire. Hark!
   Peace!
It was the owl that shrieked, the fatal bellman,   3
Which gives the stern'st good-night. He is about it. 4
The doors are open; and the surfeited grooms   5
Do mock their charge with snores. I have drugged
   their possets,   6
That death and nature do contend about them
Whether they live or die.

MACBETH [*within*]   Who's there? What, ho!

LADY MACBETH
Alack, I am afraid they have awaked,
And 'tis not done. Th'attempt and not the deed
Confounds us. Hark! I laid their daggers ready;   11
He could not miss 'em. Had he not resembled
My father as he slept, I had done't.

Enter Macbeth, [bearing bloody daggers].

My husband!

MACBETH
I have done the deed. Didst thou not hear a noise?

LADY MACBETH
I heard the owl scream and the crickets cry.   16
Did not you speak?

MACBETH   When?

LADY MACBETH   Now.

MACBETH   As I descended?

LADY MACBETH   Ay.

MACBETH   Hark! Who lies i'th' second chamber?

LADY MACBETH   Donalbain.

MACBETH [*looking at his hands*]   This is a sorry sight.

LADY MACBETH
A foolish thought, to say a sorry sight.

MACBETH
There's one did laugh in 's sleep, and one cried
   "Murder!"
That they did wake each other. I stood and heard
   them.

But they did say their prayers, and addressed them   28
Again to sleep.

LADY MACBETH   There are two lodged together.

MACBETH
One cried "God bless us!" and "Amen!" the other,
As they had seen me with these hangman's hands.   31
List'ning their fear, I could not say "Amen"
When they did say "God bless us!"

LADY MACBETH   Consider it not so deeply.

MACBETH
But wherefore could not I pronounce "Amen"?
I had most need of blessing, and "Amen"
Stuck in my throat.

LADY MACBETH   These deeds must not be thought 37
After these ways; so, it will make us mad.   38

MACBETH
Methought I heard a voice cry "Sleep no more!
Macbeth does murder sleep," the innocent sleep,
Sleep that knits up the raveled sleave of care,   41
The death of each day's life, sore labor's bath,   42
Balm of hurt minds, great nature's second course,   43
Chief nourisher in life's feast—

LADY MACBETH   What do you mean?

MACBETH
Still it cried "Sleep no more!" to all the house;
"Glamis hath murdered sleep, and therefore Cawdor
Shall sleep no more; Macbeth shall sleep no more."

LADY MACBETH
Who was it that thus cried? Why, worthy thane,
You do unbend your noble strength to think   49
So brainsickly of things. Go get some water
And wash this filthy witness from your hand.   51
Why did you bring these daggers from the place?
They must lie there. Go, carry them and smear
The sleepy grooms with blood.

MACBETH   I'll go no more.
I am afraid to think what I have done;
Look on't again I dare not.

LADY MACBETH   Infirm of purpose!
Give me the daggers. The sleeping and the dead
Are but as pictures. 'Tis the eye of childhood
That fears a painted devil. If he do bleed,
I'll gild the faces of the grooms withal,   60
For it must seem their guilt.
          [*She takes the daggers, and*] *exit. Knock within.*

MACBETH   Whence is that knocking?
How is't with me, when every noise appalls me?
What hands are here? Ha! They pluck out mine eyes.
Will all great Neptune's ocean wash this blood
Clean from my hand? No, this my hand will rather
The multitudinous seas incarnadine,   66

---

62 Words . . . gives Words give only lifeless expression to live deeds,
are no substitute for deeds.
2.2. Location: Scene continues.
3 bellman one who rings a bell to announce a death or to mark the
hours of the night   **4 Which . . . good-night** i.e., that announces the
last good-night, death.   **5 grooms** servants   **6 mock their charge**
make a mockery of their guard duty.   **possets** hot bedtime drinks (as
in 2.1.32)   **11 Confounds** ruins   **16 owl, crickets** (The sounds of
both could be ominous and prophetic of death.)

28 addressed them settled themselves   **31 As** as if.   **hangman's
hands** bloody hands of the executioner.   **37 thought** thought about
38 so if we do so   **41 raveled sleave** tangled skein   **42 bath** i.e., to
relieve the soreness   **43 second course** (Ordinary feasts had two
courses, of which the second was the *chief nourisher;* here, sleep is
seen as following eating in a restorative process.)   **49 unbend**
slacken (as one would a bow; contrast with "bend up" in 1.7.80)
51 witness evidence   **60 gild** smear, coat, as if with a thin layer of
gold. (Gold was ordinarily spoken of as red.)   **66 multitudinous**
numerous and teeming.   **incarnadine** stain red

Making the green one red.   67

Enter Lady [Macbeth].

LADY MACBETH
My hands are of your color, but I shame
To wear a heart so white. (*Knock.*) I hear a knocking
At the south entry. Retire we to our chamber.
A little water clears us of this deed.
How easy is it, then! Your constancy   72
Hath left you unattended. (*Knock.*) Hark! More
    knocking.   73
Get on your nightgown, lest occasion call us   74
And show us to be watchers. Be not lost   75
So poorly in your thoughts.

MACBETH
To know my deed, 'twere best not know myself.   77
                                                          Knock.

Wake Duncan with thy knocking! I would thou
    couldst!   *Exeunt.*

❖

2.3

Knocking within. Enter a Porter.

PORTER   Here's a knocking indeed! If a man were porter
of hell gate, he should have old turning the key.   2
(*Knock.*) Knock, knock, knock! Who's there, i'th'
name of Beelzebub? Here's a farmer that hanged   4
himself on th'expectation of plenty. Come in time!   5
Have napkins enough about you; here you'll sweat for't.   6
(*Knock.*) Knock, knock! Who's there, in th'other
devil's name? Faith, here's an equivocator, that could   8
swear in both the scales against either scale, who
committed treason enough for God's sake, yet could
not equivocate to heaven. Oh, come in, equivocator.
(*Knock.*) Knock, knock, knock! Who's there? Faith,
here's an English tailor come hither for stealing out of   13
a French hose. Come in, tailor. Here you may roast   14
your goose. (*Knock.*) Knock, knock! Never at quiet!   15

What are you? But this place is too cold for hell. I'll
devil-porter it no further. I had thought to have let in
some of all professions that go the primrose way to
th'everlasting bonfire. (*Knock.*) Anon, anon! [*He opens the
gate.*] I pray you, remember the porter.

Enter Macduff and Lennox.

MACDUFF
Was it so late, friend, ere you went to bed,
That you do lie so late?
PORTER   Faith, sir, we were carousing till the second   23
cock; and drink, sir, is a great provoker of three things.   24
MACDUFF   What three things does drink especially
provoke?
PORTER   Marry, sir, nose-painting, sleep, and urine.   27
Lechery, sir, it provokes and unprovokes: it provokes
the desire but it takes away the performance. Therefore much drink may be said to be an equivocator
with lechery: it makes him and it mars him; it sets him
on and it takes him off; it persuades him and disheartens him, makes him stand to and not stand to;   33
in conclusion, equivocates him in a sleep and, giving   34
him the lie, leaves him.   35
MACDUFF   I believe drink gave thee the lie last night.   36
PORTER   That it did, sir, i'the very throat on me. But I   37
requited him for his lie, and, I think, being too strong
for him, though he took up my legs sometimes, yet I   39
made a shift to cast him.   40
MACDUFF   Is thy master stirring?

Enter Macbeth.

Our knocking has awaked him. Here he comes.
                                                  [*Exit Porter.*]
LENNOX
Good morrow, noble sir.
MACDUFF   Good morrow, both.
MACDUFF
Is the King stirring, worthy thane?
MACBETH   Not yet.
MACDUFF
He did command me to call timely on him.   45
I have almost slipped the hour.
MACBETH   I'll bring you to him.   46
MACDUFF
I know this is a joyful trouble to you,
But yet 'tis one.

---

67 one red one all-pervading red.   **72–3 Your . . . unattended** Your
preoccupation with yourself has left you inattentive to other matters.
74 nightgown dressing gown   **75 to be watchers** to have been awake
and not abed.   **77 To know . . . myself** To come to terms with what I
have done, I would do best to shut out the horror entirely and deny
who I am.
**2.3. Location: Scene continues. The knocking at the door has
already been heard in 2.2. It is not necessary to assume literally,
however, that Macbeth and Lady Macbeth have been talking near
the** *south entry* **(2.2.70) where the knocking is heard.**
2 old plenty of   **4 Beelzebub** a devil.   **4–5 Here's . . . plenty** i.e., Here's
a farmer who has hoarded in anticipation of a scarcity and will be justly
punished by a crop surplus and low prices.   **5 Come in time!** i.e., You
have come in good time!   **6 napkins** handkerchiefs or towels (to mop
up the sweat)   **8 equivocator** (This is regarded by many editors as an
allusion to the trial of the Jesuit Henry Garnet for treason in the spring of
1606 and to the doctrine of equivocation said to have been presented in
his defense; according to this doctrine, a lie was not a lie if the utterer
had in his mind a different meaning in which the utterance was true.)
13–14 for stealing . . . hose (French fashions, much in demand by style-
conscious courtiers, no doubt provided opportunities for tailors to skimp
in the making of garments while charging customers the full amount.)
14–15 roast your goose heat your tailor's smoothing iron—something
easily done in the flames of hell. (With a pun on the sense, "cook your
goose." A *goose* could also be a long-handled iron, or a prostitute.)

23–4 second cock second crowing of the cock before dawn   **27 Marry**
(Originally, an oath, "by the Virgin Mary.")   **nose-painting** i.e., red-
dening of the nose through drink   **33 makes . . . not stand to** arouses
him sexually but then takes away the ability to perform sexually.
(Repeating the idea of the previous phrases about how it *makes him
and mars him*, etc.)   **34 equivocates . . . sleep** (1) lulls him asleep
(2) gives him an erotic experience in dream only   **34–5 giving him
the lie** (1) deceiving him (2) laying him out flat   **35 leaves him**
(1) dissipates as intoxication (2) is passed off as urine.   **36 gave thee
the lie** (1) called you a liar (2) made you unable to stand and put you
to sleep   **37 i'the . . . me** (1) giving me the deepest insult imaginable
(2) literally, going down my throat. (*On* means "of.")   **39 took . . .
legs** tripped me up and threw me to the ground as a
wrestler might do   **40 made a shift** managed.   **cast** (1) throw, as in
wrestling (2) vomit   **45 timely** betimes, early   **46 slipped** let slip

MACBETH

  The labor we delight in physics pain.   49
  This is the door.

MACDUFF   I'll make so bold to call,
  For 'tis my limited service.   *Exit Macduff.*   51

LENNOX   Goes the King hence today?

MACBETH   He does; he did appoint so.

LENNOX

  The night has been unruly. Where we lay,
  Our chimneys were blown down, and, as they say,
  Lamentings heard i'th'air, strange screams of death,
  And prophesying with accents terrible   57
  Of dire combustion and confused events   58
  New hatched to the woeful time. The obscure bird   59
  Clamored the livelong night. Some say the earth
  Was feverous and did shake.

MACBETH   'Twas a rough night.

LENNOX

  My young remembrance cannot parallel
  A fellow to it.

        Enter Macduff.

MACDUFF   Oh, horror, horror, horror!
  Tongue nor heart cannot conceive nor name thee!

MACBETH AND LENNOX   What's the matter?

MACDUFF

  Confusion now hath made his masterpiece!   66
  Most sacrilegious murder hath broke ope
  The Lord's anointed temple and stole thence
  The life o'th' building!

MACBETH   What is't you say? The life?

LENNOX   Mean you His Majesty?

MACDUFF

  Approach the chamber and destroy your sight
  With a new Gorgon. Do not bid me speak;   73
  See, and then speak yourselves.
                        Exeunt Macbeth and Lennox.
                        Awake, awake!
  Ring the alarum bell. Murder and treason!
  Banquo and Donalbain, Malcolm, awake!
  Shake off this downy sleep, death's counterfeit,   77
  And look on death itself! Up, up, and see
  The great doom's image! Malcolm, Banquo,   79
  As from your graves rise up and walk like sprites   80
  To countenance this horror! Ring the bell.   *Bell rings.*   81

        Enter Lady [Macbeth].

LADY MACBETH   What's the business,
  That such a hideous trumpet calls to parley   83

The sleepers of the house? Speak, speak!

MACDUFF   Oh, gentle lady,
  'Tis not for you to hear what I can speak.
  The repetition in a woman's ear   87
  Would murder as it fell.

        Enter Banquo.

                        Oh, Banquo, Banquo,
  Our royal master's murdered!

LADY MACBETH   Woe, alas!
  What, in our house?

BANQUO   Too cruel anywhere.
  Dear Duff, I prithee, contradict thyself
  And say it is not so.

        Enter Macbeth, Lennox, and Ross.

MACBETH

  Had I but died an hour before this chance   93
  I had lived a blessèd time; for from this instant
  There's nothing serious in mortality.   95
  All is but toys. Renown and grace is dead;   96
  The wine of life is drawn, and the mere lees   97
  Is left this vault to brag of.   98

        Enter Malcolm and Donalbain.

DONALBAIN

  What is amiss?

MACBETH   You are, and do not know't.
  The spring, the head, the fountain of your blood
  Is stopped, the very source of it is stopped.

MACDUFF

  Your royal father's murdered.

MALCOLM   Oh, by whom?

LENNOX

  Those of his chamber, as it seemed, had done't.
  Their hands and faces were all badged with blood;   104
  So were their daggers, which unwiped we found
  Upon their pillows. They stared and were distracted;
  No man's life was to be trusted with them.

MACBETH

  Oh, yet I do repent me of my fury,
  That I did kill them.

MACDUFF   Wherefore did you so?

MACBETH

  Who can be wise, amazed, temp'rate and furious,   110
  Loyal and neutral, in a moment? No man.
  Th'expedition of my violent love   112
  Outran the pauser, reason. Here lay Duncan,
  His silver skin laced with his golden blood,   114
  And his gashed stabs looked like a breach in nature   115
  For ruin's wasteful entrance; there the murderers,   116
  Steeped in the colors of their trade, their daggers

---

49 physics pain i.e., cures that labor of its troublesome aspect.
51 limited appointed   **57 accents terrible** terrifying utterances
58 combustion tumult   **59 New . . . time** newly born to accompany
the woeful nature of the time.   **obscure bird** owl, the bird of darkness
66 Confusion Destruction   **73 Gorgon** one of three monsters with
hideous faces (Medusa was a Gorgon), whose look turned the behold-
ers to stone.   **77 downy** feathery, unsubstantial   **79 great doom's
image** simulacrum of the Last Judgment, of Doomsday.   **80 As . . .
rise up** (At the Last Judgment, the dead will rise from their graves to
be judged.)   **sprites** souls, ghosts   **81 countenance** (1) be in keeping
with (2) witness   **83 trumpet** (Another metaphorical suggestion of
the Last Judgment; the *trumpet* here is the shouting and the bell.)

87 repetition recital, report   **93 chance** occurrence   **95 serious in
mortality** worthwhile in mortal life.   **96 toys** trifles.   **97 lees** dregs
98 vault (1) wine-vault (2) earth, with its vaulted sky   **104 badged**
marked, as with a badge or emblem   **110 amazed** bewildered
112 Th'expedition The haste   **114 golden** (See the note for 2.2.60.)
115 breach in nature gap in the defenses of life. (A metaphor of military siege.)   **116 wasteful** destructive

Unmannerly breeched with gore. Who could refrain   118
That had a heart to love, and in that heart
Courage to make 's love known?
LADY MACBETH [*fainting*]   Help me hence, ho!   120
MACDUFF
   Look to the lady.
MALCOLM [*aside to Donalbain*]
                     Why do we hold our tongues,
   That most may claim this argument for ours?   122
DONALBAIN [*aside to Malcolm*]
   What should be spoken here, where our fate,
   Hid in an auger hole, may rush and seize us?   124
   Let's away. Our tears are not yet brewed.   125
MALCOLM [*aside to Donalbain*]
   Nor our strong sorrow upon the foot of motion.   126
BANQUO   Look to the lady.
                     [*Lady Macbeth is helped out.*]
   And when we have our naked frailties hid,   128
   That suffer in exposure, let us meet
   And question this most bloody piece of work   130
   To know it further. Fears and scruples shake us.   131
   In the great hand of God I stand, and thence   132
   Against the undivulged pretense I fight   133
   Of treasonous malice.
MACDUFF   And so do I.
ALL   So all.   134
MACBETH
   Let's briefly put on manly readiness   135
   And meet i'th' hall together.
ALL   Well contented.
             Exeunt [all but Malcolm and Donalbain].
MALCOLM
   What will you do? Let's not consort with them.   137
   To show an unfelt sorrow is an office
   Which the false man does easy. I'll to England.   139
DONALBAIN
   To Ireland, I. Our separated fortune
   Shall keep us both the safer. Where we are,
   There's daggers in men's smiles; the nea'er in blood,   142
   The nearer bloody.
MALCOLM   This murderous shaft that's shot   143
   Hath not yet lighted, and our safest way   144
   Is to avoid the aim. Therefore to horse,
   And let us not be dainty of leave-taking,   146
   But shift away. There's warrant in that theft   147

---

118 **breeched with gore** covered (as with breeches) to the hilts with
gore.   120 **make 's love known** make manifest his love.   122 **That . . .
ours** we to whom this business matters most.   124 **in an auger hole**
i.e., in some hiding place, in ambush. (An *auger* is a hole-drilling
tool.)   125 **Our . . . brewed** i.e., Our real sorrow has not yet ripened.
126 **upon . . . motion** yet prepared to express itself fully.   128 **our
naked frailties hid** clothed our poor, shivering bodies (which remind
us of our human frailty)   130 **question** discuss   131 **scruples**
doubts, suspicions   132–4 **thence . . . malice** with God's help, I will
fight against the as-yet-unknown purpose that prompted this treason.
133 **pretense** design   134 **malice** enmity.   135 **briefly** quickly.
manly readiness men's clothing and resolute purpose   137 **consort**
keep company, associate   139 **easy** easily.   142–3 **the nea'er . . .
bloody** the closer the relationship, the greater the danger to be feared
of bloody intent.   144 **lighted** alighted, descended   146 **dainty of**
tediously ceremonious in   147 **shift away** disappear by stealth.
warrant justification

Which steals itself when there's no mercy left.
                          Exeunt.

                     ❧

2.4

             Enter Ross with an Old Man.

OLD MAN
   Threescore and ten I can remember well,
   Within the volume of which time I have seen
   Hours dreadful and things strange, but this sore night   3
   Hath trifled former knowings.
ROSS   Ha, good father,   4
   Thou see'st the heavens, as troubled with man's act,   5
   Threatens his bloody stage. By th' clock 'tis day,   6
   And yet dark night strangles the traveling lamp.   7
   Is't night's predominance or the day's shame
   That darkness does the face of earth entomb
   When living light should kiss it?
OLD MAN   'Tis unnatural,
   Even like the deed that's done. On Tuesday last
   A falcon, tow'ring in her pride of place,   12
   Was by a mousing owl hawked at and killed.   13
ROSS
   And Duncan's horses—a thing most strange and
        certain—
   Beauteous and swift, the minions of their race,   15
   Turned wild in nature, broke their stalls, flung out,
   Contending 'gainst obedience, as they would   17
   Make war with mankind.
OLD MAN   'Tis said they eat each other.   18
ROSS
   They did so, to th'amazement of mine eyes
   That looked upon't.

             Enter Macduff.

                     Here comes the good Macduff.—
   How goes the world, sir, now?
MACDUFF   Why, see you not?
ROSS
   Is't known who did this more than bloody deed?
MACDUFF
   Those that Macbeth hath slain.
ROSS   Alas the day,
   What good could they pretend?
MACDUFF   They were suborned.   24
   Malcolm and Donalbain, the King's two sons,
   Are stol'n away and fled, which puts upon them
   Suspicion of the deed.
ROSS   'Gainst nature still!

2.4. Location: Outside Macbeth's castle of Inverness.
3 **sore** dreadful, grievous   4 **trifled former knowings** made trivial all
former experiences.   **father** old man   5–6 **the heavens . . . stage** a
solar eclipse threatens disapprovingly our human scene of murder.
(With a theatrical metaphor in *heavens* [the decorated roof over the
stage], *act*, and *stage*.)   7 **traveling lamp** i.e., sun.   12 **tow'ring** circling higher and higher. (A term in falconry.)   **place** pitch, highest
point in the falcon's flight   13 **mousing** i.e., ordinarily preying on
mice   15 **minions** darlings   17 **as** as if   18 **eat** ate. (Pronounced
"et.")   24 **What . . . pretend?** i.e., what could they hope to gain by it?
suborned bribed, hired.

Thriftless ambition, that will ravin up   28
Thine own life's means! Then 'tis most like   29
The sovereignty will fall upon Macbeth.

MACDUFF
He is already named and gone to Scone   31
To be invested.

ROSS   Where is Duncan's body?

MACDUFF   Carried to Colmekill,   33
The sacred storehouse of his predecessors
And guardian of their bones.

ROSS   Will you to Scone?

MACDUFF
No, cousin, I'll to Fife.

ROSS   Well, I will thither.   36

MACDUFF
Well, may you see things well done there. Adieu,
Lest our old robes sit easier than our new!

ROSS   Farewell, father.

OLD MAN
God's benison go with you, and with those   40
That would make good of bad, and friends of foes!
                                        Exeunt omnes.

                         ❖

3.1

         Enter Banquo.

BANQUO
Thou hast it now—King, Cawdor, Glamis, all
As the weird women promised, and I fear
Thou played'st most foully for't. Yet it was said
It should not stand in thy posterity,   4
But that myself should be the root and father
Of many kings. If there come truth from them—
As upon thee, Macbeth, their speeches shine—   7
Why, by the verities on thee made good,
May they not be my oracles as well
And set me up in hope? But hush, no more.   10

         Sennet sounded. Enter Macbeth as King, Lady
         [Macbeth], Lennox, Ross, lords, and attendants.

MACBETH
Here's our chief guest.

LADY MACBETH   If he had been forgotten,
It had been as a gap in our great feast
And all-thing unbecoming.   13

MACBETH
Tonight we hold a solemn supper, sir,   14
And I'll request your presence.

BANQUO   Let Your Highness
Command upon me, to the which my duties   16

Are with a most indissoluble tie
Forever knit.

MACBETH   Ride you this afternoon?

BANQUO   Ay, my good lord.

MACBETH
We should have else desired your good advice,
Which still hath been both grave and prosperous,   22
In this day's council; but we'll take tomorrow.
Is't far you ride?

BANQUO
As far, my lord, as will fill up the time
Twixt this and supper. Go not my horse the better,   26
I must become a borrower of the night
For a dark hour or twain.

MACBETH   Fail not our feast.

BANQUO   My lord, I will not.

MACBETH
We hear our bloody cousins are bestowed   31
In England and in Ireland, not confessing
Their cruel parricide, filling their hearers
With strange invention. But of that tomorrow,   34
When therewithal we shall have cause of state   35
Craving us jointly. Hie you to horse. Adieu,   36
Till you return at night. Goes Fleance with you?

BANQUO
Ay, my good lord. Our time does call upon 's.

MACBETH
I wish your horses swift and sure of foot,
And so I do commend you to their backs.   40
Farewell.   *Exit Banquo.*
Let every man be master of his time
Till seven at night. To make society
The sweeter welcome, we will keep ourself   44
Till suppertime alone. While then, God be with you!   45
         Exeunt Lords [and all but Macbeth and a Servant].
Sirrah, a word with you. Attend those men   46
Our pleasure?

SERVANT
They are, my lord, without the palace gate.

MACBETH
Bring them before us.   *Exit Servant.*
                        To be thus is nothing,   49
But to be safely thus.—Our fears in Banquo   50
Stick deep, and in his royalty of nature   51
Reigns that which would be feared. 'Tis much he
    dares;   52
And to that dauntless temper of his mind   53
He hath a wisdom that doth guide his valor
To act in safety. There is none but he
Whose being I do fear; and under him
My genius is rebuked, as it is said   57

---

28 Thriftless Spendthrift. **ravin up** devour ravenously **29 like**
likely **31 named** chosen. (See the note for 1.4.50.) **Scone** ancient
royal city of Scotland near Perth **33 Colmekill** Icolmkill, i.e., Cell of
St. Columba, the barren islet of Iona in the Western Islands, a sacred
spot where the kings were buried; here, called a *storehouse* **36 Fife**
(Of which Macduff is Thane.) **40 bension** blessing
3.1. Location: Forres. The palace.
4 stand stay, remain **7 shine** beam favorably **10.1** *Sennet* trumpet
call **13 all-thing** in every way **14 solemn** ceremonious **16 Command** lay your command

22 still always. **grave and prosperous** weighty and profitable
26 this this present moment. **Go . . . better** Unless my horse makes
better time than I expect **31 bestowed** lodged **34 invention** falsehood. **35 therewithal** besides that **35–6 cause . . . jointly** questions
of state occupying our joint attention. **40 commend** commit, entrust
44 we . . . ourself I will keep to myself **45 While** Till **46 Sirrah** (A
form of address to a social inferior.) **49 thus** i.e., king **50 But**
unless. **in** concerning **51 royalty of nature** natural kingly bearing
52 would be deserves to be **53 to** added to **57 My genius is
rebuked** my guardian spirit is daunted or abashed

Mark Antony's was by Caesar. He chid the sisters 58
When first they put the name of king upon me,
And bade them speak to him. Then, prophetlike,
They hailed him father to a line of kings.
Upon my head they placed a fruitless crown
And put a barren scepter in my grip,
Thence to be wrenched with an unlineal hand, 64
No son of mine succeeding. If't be so,
For Banquo's issue have I filed my mind; 66
For them the gracious Duncan have I murdered,
Put rancors in the vessel of my peace 68
Only for them, and mine eternal jewel 69
Given to the common enemy of man 70
To make them kings, the seeds of Banquo kings.
Rather than so, come fate into the list, 72
And champion me to th'utterance!—Who's there? 73

Enter Servant and two Murderers.

Now go to the door, and stay there till we call.
                                   Exit Servant.
Was it not yesterday we spoke together?
MURDERERS
It was, so please Your Highness.
MACBETH   Well then, now
Have you considered of my speeches? Know
That it was he in the times past which held you
So under fortune, which you thought had been 79
Our innocent self. This I made good to you
In our last conference, passed in probation with you 81
How you were borne in hand, how crossed, the
    instruments, 82
Who wrought with them, and all things else that
    might 83
To half a soul and to a notion crazed 84
Say, "Thus did Banquo."
FIRST MURDERER   You made it known to us.
MACBETH
I did so, and went further, which is now
Our point of second meeting. Do you find
Your patience so predominant in your nature
That you can let this go? Are you so gospeled 89
To pray for this good man and for his issue,
Whose heavy hand hath bowed you to the grave
And beggared yours forever?
FIRST MURDERER   We are men, my liege. 92
MACBETH
Ay, in the catalogue ye go for men, 93
As hounds and greyhounds, mongrels, spaniels, curs,

Shoughs, water-rugs, and demi-wolves are clept 95
All by the name of dogs. The valued file 96
Distinguishes the swift, the slow, the subtle,
The housekeeper, the hunter, every one 98
According to the gift which bounteous nature
Hath in him closed, whereby he does receive 100
Particular addition from the bill 101
That writes them all alike; and so of men. 102
Now, if you have a station in the file, 103
Not i'th' worst rank of manhood, say't, 104
And I will put that business in your bosoms
Whose execution takes your enemy off, 106
Grapples you to the heart and love of us,
Who wear our health but sickly in his life, 108
Which in his death were perfect.
SECOND MURDERER   I am one, my liege,
Whom the vile blows and buffets of the world
Hath so incensed that I am reckless what
I do to spite the world.
FIRST MURDERER   And I another,
So weary with disasters, tugged with fortune, 113
That I would set my life on any chance 114
To mend it or be rid on't.
MACBETH   Both of you
Know Banquo was your enemy.
BOTH MURDERERS   True, my lord.
MACBETH
So is he mine, and in such bloody distance 117
That every minute of his being thrusts 118
Against my near'st of life. And though I could 119
With barefaced power sweep him from my sight 120
And bid my will avouch it, yet I must not, 121
For certain friends that are both his and mine, 122
Whose loves I may not drop, but wail his fall 123
Who I myself struck down. And thence it is 124
That I to your assistance do make love, 125
Masking the business from the common eye
For sundry weighty reasons.
SECOND MURDERER   We shall, my lord,
Perform what you command us.
FIRST MURDERER   Though our lives—
MACBETH
Your spirits shine through you. Within this hour at
    most 129
I will advise you where to plant yourselves,

---

58 **Caesar** Octavius Caesar.   64 **with** by.   **unlineal** not of lineal descent from me   66 **filed** defiled   68 **rancors** malignant enemies (here visualized as a poison added to a vessel full of wholesome drink)   69 **eternal jewel** i.e., soul   70 **common . . . man** i.e., devil   72 **list** lists, place of combat   73 **champion me** fight with me in single combat.   **to th'utterance** to the last extremity (French, *à l'outrance*).   79 **under fortune** down in your fortunes   81–3 **passed . . . with them** went over the proof with you how you were deceived by false promises, how you were thwarted, who the agents were, who directed their activities   84 **To . . . crazed** even to a half-wit of unsound mind   89 **gospeled** imbued with the gospel spirit   92 **yours** your family   93 **go for** pass for, are entered for

95 **Shoughs . . . clept** shaggy lap-dogs, long-haired water dogs, and dogs that have been crossbred with wolves are called   96 **valued file** list classified according to value   98 **housekeeper** watchdog   100 **in him closed** enclosed in him   101–2 **Particular . . . alike** particular qualification apart from the catalog that lists them all indiscriminately   103–4 **if . . . manhood** if you occupy not the worst of places in the *rank and file* of men   106 **Whose execution** the doing of which   108 **in his life** while he lives   113 **tugged with** pulled about by (as in wrestling)   114 **set** risk, stake   117 **distance** (1) hostility, enmity (2) interval of distance between fencers   118–19 **thrusts . . . life** stabs me to the heart.   120 **With barefaced power** by open use of my supreme royal authority   121 **And . . . avouch it** and use my mere wish as my justification   122 **For** because of, for the sake of   123–4 **wail . . . Who** I must bewail the death of him whom   125 **That . . . love** that I woo your aid   129 **Your . . . you** i.e., Enough; I can see your determination in your faces.

Acquaint you with the perfect spy o'th' time,   131
The moment on't, for't must be done tonight,   132
And something from the palace; always thought   133
That I require a clearness. And with him—   134
To leave no rubs nor botches in the work—   135
Fleance his son, that keeps him company,
Whose absence is no less material to me
Than is his father's, must embrace the fate
Of that dark hour. Resolve yourselves apart;   139
I'll come to you anon.
BOTH MURDERERS   We are resolved, my lord.
MACBETH
I'll call upon you straight. Abide within.
                              Exeunt [*Murderers*].
It is concluded. Banquo, thy soul's flight,
If it find heaven, must find it out tonight.   [*Exit.*]

❧

3.2

Enter Macbeth's Lady and a Servant.

LADY MACBETH   Is Banquo gone from court?
SERVANT
Ay, madam, but returns again tonight.
LADY MACBETH
Say to the King I would attend his leisure
For a few words.
SERVANT   Madam, I will.   *Exit.*
LADY MACBETH   Naught's had, all's spent,
Where our desire is got without content.   7
'Tis safer to be that which we destroy
Than by destruction dwell in doubtful joy.   9

Enter Macbeth.

How now, my lord? Why do you keep alone,
Of sorriest fancies your companions making,   11
Using those thoughts which should indeed have died   12
With them they think on? Things without all remedy
Should be without regard. What's done is done.   14
MACBETH
We have scorched the snake, not killed it.   15
She'll close and be herself, whilst our poor malice   16
Remains in danger of her former tooth.   17
But let the frame of things disjoint, both the worlds
    suffer,
Ere we will eat our meal in fear and sleep   18
In the affliction of these terrible dreams

That shake us nightly. Better be with the dead,
Whom we, to gain our peace, have sent to peace,   22
Than on the torture of the mind to lie   23
In restless ecstasy. Duncan is in his grave;   24
After life's fitful fever he sleeps well.
Treason has done his worst; nor steel, nor poison,   26
Malice domestic, foreign levy, nothing   27
Can touch him further.
LADY MACBETH   Come on,
Gentle my lord, sleek o'er your rugged looks.   30
Be bright and jovial among your guests tonight.
MACBETH
So shall I, love, and so, I pray, be you.
Let your remembrance apply to Banquo;   33
Present him eminence, both with eye and tongue—   34
Unsafe the while, that we   35
Must lave our honors in these flattering streams   36
And make our faces vizards to our hearts,   37
Disguising what they are.
LADY MACBETH   You must leave this.
MACBETH
Oh, full of scorpions is my mind, dear wife!
Thou know'st that Banquo and his Fleance lives.
LADY MACBETH
But in them nature's copy's not eterne.   41
MACBETH
There's comfort yet; they are assailable.
Then be thou jocund. Ere the bat hath flown
His cloistered flight, ere to black Hecate's summons   44
The shard-borne beetle with his drowsy hums   45
Hath rung night's yawning peal, there shall be done   46
A deed of dreadful note.
LADY MACBETH   What's to be done?
MACBETH
Be innocent of the knowledge, dearest chuck,   48
Till thou applaud the deed. Come, seeling night,   49
Scarf up the tender eye of pitiful day,   50
And with thy bloody and invisible hand
Cancel and tear to pieces that great bond   52
Which keeps me pale! Light thickens,   53
And the crow makes wing to th' rooky wood;   54
Good things of day begin to droop and drowse,

131–2 **with ... on't** with full and precise instructions as to when it is to be done. (*Spy* means "espial, observation.")   133 **something from** some distance removed from.   **thought** being borne in mind   134 **clearness** freedom from suspicion.   135 **rubs** defects, rough spots   139 **Resolve yourselves apart** Make up your minds in private conference
3.2. Location: The palace.
7 **content** contentedness.   9 **Than ... joy** than by destroying achieve only an apprehensive joy.   11 **sorriest** most despicable or wretched   12 **Using** keeping company with, entertaining   14 **without regard** not pondered upon.   15 **scorched** slashed, cut   16 **close** heal, close up again.   **poor malice** feeble hostility   17 **her former tooth** her fang, just as before.   18 **let ... suffer** let the universe itself fall apart, both heaven and earth perish

22 **to gain ... to peace** to gain contentedness through satisfied ambition, have sent to eternal rest   23 **torture** rack   24 **ecstasy** frenzy.   26 **nor steel** neither steel   27 **Malice domestic** civil war.   **foreign levy** the levying of troops abroad (against Scotland)   30 **Gentle ... looks** my noble lord, smooth over your rough looks.   33 **Let ... apply** Remember to pay special attention   34 **eminence** favor   35–6 **Unsafe ... streams** we being unsafe at present, we must put on a show of flattering cordiality to make clean our honor. (To *lave* is to wash.)   37 **vizards** masks   41 **nature's ... eterne** nature's pattern will not continue forever.   44 **cloistered** secluded.   **Hecate** goddess of night and witchcraft, as in 2.1.53   45 **shard-borne** borne on shards, or horny wing cases, or, *shard-born*, bred in cow-droppings (shards)   46 **yawning** drowsy   48 **chuck** (A term of endearment.)   49 **seeling** eye-closing. (Night is pictured here as a falconer sewing up the eyes of day lest it should struggle against the deed that is to be done.)   50 **Scarf up** blindfold.   **pitiful** compassionate   52 **that ... bond** i.e., the bond of natural and moral law (here associated with the full light of day)   53 **pale** sickly, pallid (like moonlight, contrasted with the full light of day); also, pallid from fear.   **Light thickens** Darkness is coming on   54 **crow** rook.   **rooky** full of rooks

Whiles night's black agents to their preys do rouse.   56
Thou marvel'st at my words, but hold thee still.
Things bad begun make strong themselves by ill.
So, prithee, go with me.   *Exeunt.*

❖

3.3

Enter three Murderers.

FIRST MURDERER [*to the Third Murderer*]
But who did bid thee join with us?
THIRD MURDERER   Macbeth.
SECOND MURDERER [*to the First Murderer*]
He needs not our mistrust, since he delivers   2
Our offices and what we have to do   3
To the direction just.
FIRST MURDERER   Then stand with us.   4
The west yet glimmers with some streaks of day.
Now spurs the lated traveler apace   6
To gain the timely inn, and near approaches   7
The subject of our watch.
THIRD MURDERER   Hark, I hear horses.
BANQUO (*within*)   Give us a light there, ho!
SECOND MURDERER   Then 'tis he. The rest
That are within the note of expectation   12
Already are i'th' court.
FIRST MURDERER   His horses go about.   14
THIRD MURDERER
Almost a mile; but he does usually—
So all men do—from hence to th' palace gate
Make it their walk.

Enter Banquo and Fleance, with a torch.

SECOND MURDERER   A light, a light!
THIRD MURDERER   'Tis he.
FIRST MURDERER   Stand to't.
BANQUO   It will be rain tonight.
FIRST MURDERER   Let it come down!
                        [*They attack Banquo.*]
BANQUO
Oh, treachery! Fly, good Fleance, fly, fly, fly!
Thou mayst revenge.—Oh, slave!
                        [*He dies. Fleance escapes.*]
THIRD MURDERER
Who did strike out the light?
FIRST MURDERER   Was't not the way?   25
THIRD MURDERER
There's but one down; the son is fled.
SECOND MURDERER
We have lost best half of our affair.

FIRST MURDERER
Well, let's away and say how much is done.   28
                        Exeunt.

❖

3.4

*Banquet prepared. Enter Macbeth, Lady
[Macbeth], Ross, Lennox, Lords, and attendants.*

MACBETH
You know your own degrees; sit down. At first   1
And last, the hearty welcome.   [*They sit.*]
LORDS   Thanks to Your Majesty.   2
MACBETH
Ourself will mingle with society   3
And play the humble host.
Our hostess keeps her state, but in best time   5
We will require her welcome.   6
LADY MACBETH
Pronounce it for me, sir, to all our friends,
For my heart speaks they are welcome.

Enter First Murderer [to the door].

MACBETH
See, they encounter thee with their hearts' thanks.   9
Both sides are even. Here I'll sit i'th' midst.   10
Be large in mirth; anon we'll drink a measure   11
The table round. [*He goes to the Murderer.*] There's
    blood upon thy face.
MURDERER   'Tis Banquo's, then.
MACBETH
'Tis better thee without than he within.   14
Is he dispatched?
MURDERER
My lord, his throat is cut. That I did for him.
MACBETH   Thou art the best o'th' cutthroats.
Yet he's good that did the like for Fleance;
If thou didst it, thou art the nonpareil.   19
MURDERER   Most royal sir, Fleance is scaped.
MACBETH
Then comes my fit again. I had else been perfect,
Whole as the marble, founded as the rock,   22
As broad and general as the casing air.   23
But now I am cabined, cribbed, confined, bound in   24
To saucy doubts and fears. But Banquo's safe?   25

---

56 **to . . . rouse** bestir themselves to hunt their prey.
3.3. Location: A park near the palace.
2–4 He . . . just We need not mistrust this man, since the instructions he brings from Macbeth are so precise.   **6 lated** belated   **7 timely** arrived at in good time   **12 within . . . expectation** in the list of those expected   **14 go about** i.e., can be heard as servants take the horses to the stables (while Banquo and Fleance, provided with a torch, walk from the palace gate to the castle).   **25 way** i.e., thing to do.

28.1 *Exeunt* (Presumably, the murderers drag the body of Banquo offstage as they go.)
3.4. Location: A room of state in the palace.
1 degrees ranks (as a determinant of seating)   **1–2 At . . . last** Once for all   **3 mingle with society** i.e., leave the chair of state and circulate among the guests   **5 keeps her state** remains in her canopied chair of state.   **in best time** when it is most appropriate   **6 require her welcome** call upon her to give the welcome.   **9 encounter** respond to   **10 even** full, with equal numbers on both sides.
11 large liberal, free.   **measure** i.e., cup filled to the brim for a toast
14 'Tis . . . within It is better to have his blood on you than he to have it within him.   **19 the nonpareil** without equal.   **22 founded** firmly established   **23 broad and general** unconfined.   **casing** encasing, enveloping   **24 cribbed** shut in   **25 saucy** sharp, impudent, importunate

MURDERER

Ay, my good lord. Safe in a ditch he bides,
With twenty trenchèd gashes on his head,
The least a death to nature.

MACBETH   Thanks for that.

There the grown serpent lies; the worm that's fled   29
Hath nature that in time will venom breed,
No teeth for th' present. Get thee gone. Tomorrow
We'll hear ourselves again.   *Exit Murderer.*

LADY MACBETH   My royal lord,   32

You do not give the cheer. The feast is sold   33
That is not often vouched, while 'tis a-making,   34
'Tis given with welcome. To feed were best at home;   35
From thence, the sauce to meat is ceremony;   36
Meeting were bare without it.

*Enter the Ghost of Banquo, and sits in Macbeth's
place.*

MACBETH   Sweet remembrancer!   37

Now, good digestion wait on appetite,   38
And health on both!

LENNOX   May't please Your Highness sit?

MACBETH

Here had we now our country's honor roofed   40
Were the graced person of our Banquo present,
Who may I rather challenge for unkindness   42
Than pity for mischance.

ROSS   His absence, sir,

Lays blame upon his promise. Please't Your Highness
To grace us with your royal company?

MACBETH [*seeing his place occupied*]

The table's full.

LENNOX   Here is a place reserved, sir.

MACBETH   Where?

LENNOX

Here, my good lord. What is't that moves Your
    Highness?

MACBETH

Which of you have done this?

LORDS   What, my good lord?

MACBETH

Thou canst not say I did it. Never shake
Thy gory locks at me.

ROSS

Gentlemen, rise. His Highness is not well.
                           [*They start to rise.*]

LADY MACBETH

Sit, worthy friends. My lord is often thus,
And hath been from his youth. Pray you, keep seat.
The fit is momentary; upon a thought   55
He will again be well. If much you note him

You shall offend him and extend his passion.   57
Feed, and regard him not.—[*She confers apart with
    Macbeth.*] Are you a man?

MACBETH

Ay, and a bold one, that dare look on that
Which might appall the devil.

LADY MACBETH   Oh, proper stuff!   60

This is the very painting of your fear.
This is the air-drawn dagger which, you said,   62
Led you to Duncan. Oh, these flaws and starts,   63
Impostors to true fear, would well become   64
A woman's story at a winter's fire,
Authorized by her grandam. Shame itself!   66
Why do you make such faces? When all's done,
You look but on a stool.

MACBETH   Prithee, see there!

Behold, look! Lo, how say you?—
Why, what care I? If thou canst nod, speak too.   70
If charnel houses and our graves must send   71
Those that we bury back, our monuments   72
Shall be the maws of kites.   [*Exit Ghost.*]   73

LADY MACBETH   What, quite unmanned in folly?

MACBETH

If I stand here, I saw him.

LADY MACBETH   Fie, for shame!

MACBETH

Blood hath been shed ere now, i'th'olden time,
Ere humane statute purged the gentle weal;   77
Ay, and since too, murders have been performed
Too terrible for the ear. The time has been
That, when the brains were out, the man would die,
And there an end; but now they rise again
With twenty mortal murders on their crowns,   82
And push us from our stools. This is more strange
Than such a murder is.

LADY MACBETH   My worthy lord,

Your noble friends do lack you.

MACBETH   I do forget.

Do not muse at me, my most worthy friends;
I have a strange infirmity, which is nothing
To those that know me. Come, love and health to all!
Then I'll sit down. Give me some wine. Fill full.
                           [*He is given wine.*]

Enter Ghost.

I drink to th' general joy o'th' whole table,
And to our dear friend Banquo, whom we miss.
Would he were here! To all, and him, we thirst,   92

---

29 **worm** small serpent   32 **hear ourselves** personally confer
33 **give the cheer** welcome your guests.   33–5 **The feast . . . welcome**
A feast seems grudgingly and mercenarily given unless it is repeatedly graced with assurances of welcome.   35–7 **To feed . . . without
it** Plain eating is best done in one's own domestic setting; on more
social occasions, the spice to a feast is ceremony; gatherings are too
unadorned without it.   38 **wait on** attend   40 **roofed** under one roof
42 **Who . . . unkindness** whom I hope I may sooner reprove for negligence   55 **upon a thought** in a moment

57 **offend him** make him worse   60 **Oh, proper stuff!** Oh, nonsense!
62 **air-drawn** made of thin air, or floating disembodied in space
63 **flaws** gusts, outbursts   64 **to** compared with.   **become** befit
66 **Authorized by** told on the authority of   70 **thou** Banquo
71 **charnel houses** depositories for bones or bodies   72–3 **our . . .
kites** i.e., we will have to leave the unburied bodies to scavenging
birds of prey.   77 **Ere . . . weal** before the institution of law cleansed
the commonwealth of violence and made it civilized. (*Humane*, interchangeable with *human*, means both "appertaining to humankind"
and "benevolent, civilizing.")   82 **mortal murders** deadly wounds.
crowns heads   92 **thirst** desire to drink

And all to all.

LORDS   Our duties and the pledge.   93

                                 [*They drink.*]

MACBETH [*seeing the Ghost*]

Avaunt, and quit my sight! Let the earth hide thee!

Thy bones are marrowless, thy blood is cold;

Thou hast no speculation in those eyes   96

Which thou dost glare with!

LADY MACBETH   Think of this, good peers,

But as a thing of custom. 'Tis no other;

Only it spoils the pleasure of the time.

MACBETH   What man dare, I dare.

Approach thou like the rugged Russian bear,

The armed rhinoceros, or th' Hyrcan tiger;   102

Take any shape but that, and my firm nerves   103

Shall never tremble. Or be alive again

And dare me to the desert with thy sword.   105

If trembling I inhabit then, protest me   106

The baby of a girl. Hence, horrible shadow!   107

Unreal mockery, hence!   [*Exit Ghost.*]

                    Why, so; being gone,

I am a man again. Pray you, sit still.

LADY MACBETH

You have displaced the mirth, broke the good meeting

With most admired disorder.

MACBETH   Can such things be,   111

And overcome us like a summer's cloud,   112

Without our special wonder? You make me strange   113

Even to the disposition that I owe,   114

When now I think you can behold such sights

And keep the natural ruby of your cheeks

When mine is blanched with fear.

ROSS   What sights, my lord?

LADY MACBETH

I pray you, speak not. He grows worse and worse;

Question enrages him. At once, good night.   119

Stand not upon the order of your going,   120

But go at once.

LENNOX   Good night, and better health

Attend His Majesty!

LADY MACBETH   A kind good night to all!

                    Exeunt Lords [*and attendants*].

MACBETH

It will have blood, they say; blood will have blood.

Stones have been known to move, and trees to speak;   124

Augurs and understood relations have   125

By maggotpies and choughs and rooks brought forth   126

The secret'st man of blood. What is the night?   127

LADY MACBETH

Almost at odds with morning, which is which.

MACBETH

How say'st thou, that Macduff denies his person   129

At our great bidding?

LADY MACBETH   Did you send to him, sir?

MACBETH

I hear it by the way; but I will send.   131

There's not a one of them but in his house   132

I keep a servant fee'd. I will tomorrow—   133

And betimes I will—to the Weird Sisters.   134

More shall they speak, for now I am bent to know   135

By the worst means the worst. For mine own good

All causes shall give way. I am in blood   137

Stepped in so far that, should I wade no more,   138

Returning were as tedious as go o'er.   139

Strange things I have in head, that will to hand,

Which must be acted ere they may be scanned.   141

LADY MACBETH

You lack the season of all natures, sleep.   142

MACBETH

Come, we'll to sleep. My strange and self-abuse   143

Is the initiate fear that wants hard use.   144

We are yet but young in deed.   *Exeunt.*

❧

3.5

*Thunder. Enter the three Witches, meeting
Hecate.*

FIRST WITCH

Why, how now, Hecate? You look angerly.   1

HECATE

Have I not reason, beldams as you are?   2

Saucy and overbold, how did you dare

To trade and traffic with Macbeth

In riddles and affairs of death,

And I, the mistress of your charms,

The close contriver of all harms,   7

Was never called to bear my part

Or show the glory of our art?

And, which is worse, all you have done

Hath been but for a wayward son,

Spiteful and wrathful, who, as others do,

Loves for his own ends, not for you.

But make amends now. Get you gone,

And at the pit of Acheron   15

93 **all to all** all good wishes to all, or, let all drink to everyone else.
96 **speculation** power of sight   102 **armed** armor-plated.   **Hyrcan** of
Hyrcania, in ancient times a region near the Caspian Sea   103 **nerves**
sinews   105 **the desert** some solitary place   106–7 **If . . . girl** If then I
tremble, proclaim me a baby girl, or a girl's doll.   111 **admired disorder**
wondered-at lack of self-control.   112 **overcome** come over   113–14 **You
make . . . owe** You cause me to feel I do not know my own nature (which
I had presumed to be that of a brave man)   119 **At once** To you all; now
120 **Stand . . . going** Do not take the time to leave in ceremonious order
of rank, as you entered   124 **Stones . . . speak** i.e., Even inanimate
nature speaks in such a way as to reveal the unnatural act of murder
125–7 **Augurs . . . blood** Prophets versed in the interpretation of occult
mysteries have, by reading the signs of magpies and jackdaws, revealed
secret murderers.   127 **the night** i.e., the time of night.

129 **How say'st thou** What do you say to the fact   131 **by the way**
indirectly   132 **them** my Scottish nobles   133 **fee'd** i.e., paid to spy.
134 **betimes** (1) early (2) while there is still time   135 **bent** determined   137 **All causes** all other considerations   138 **should . . . more**
even if I were to wade no farther   139 **were** would be.   **go o'er** to
proceed.   141 **acted . . . scanned** put into performance even before
there is time to scrutinize them.   142 **season** preservative   143–4 **My
. . . use** My strange self-punishing fear is that felt by a novice who
lacks toughening experience.
3.5. Location: A heath. (This scene is probably by another author.)
1 **angerly** angrily, angry.   2 **beldams** hags   7 **close** secret
15 **Acheron** the river of sorrows in Hades; here, hell itself

Meet me i'th' morning. Thither he
Will come to know his destiny.
Your vessels and your spells provide,
Your charms and everything beside.
I am for th'air. This night I'll spend
Unto a dismal and a fatal end.   21
Great business must be wrought ere noon.
Upon the corner of the moon
There hangs a vap'rous drop profound;   24
I'll catch it ere it come to ground,
And that, distilled by magic sleights,
Shall raise such artificial sprites   27
As by the strength of their illusion
Shall draw him on to his confusion.   29
He shall spurn fate, scorn death, and bear
His hopes 'bove wisdom, grace, and fear.
And you all know, security   32
Is mortals' chiefest enemy.   *Music and a song.*
Hark! I am called. My little spirit, see,
Sits in a foggy cloud and stays for me.   [*Exit.*]   35
            Sing within, "Come away, come away," *etc.*

FIRST WITCH
Come, let's make haste. She'll soon be back again.
                                                   Exeunt.

❧

3.6

Enter Lennox and another Lord.

LENNOX
My former speeches have but hit your thoughts,   1
Which can interpret farther. Only I say   2
Things have been strangely borne. The gracious
    Duncan   3
Was pitied of Macbeth; marry, he was dead.   4
And the right valiant Banquo walked too late,
Whom you may say, if't please you, Fleance killed,
For Fleance fled. Men must not walk too late.
Who cannot want the thought how monstrous   8
It was for Malcolm and for Donalbain
To kill their gracious father? Damnèd fact!   10
How it did grieve Macbeth! Did he not straight   11
In pious rage the two delinquents tear
That were the slaves of drink and thralls of sleep?   13
Was not that nobly done? Ay, and wisely too;
For 'twould have angered any heart alive
To hear the men deny't. So that I say

He has borne all things well; and I do think   17
That had he Duncan's sons under his key—
As, an't please heaven, he shall not—they should find   19
What 'twere to kill a father. So should Fleance.
But peace! For from broad words, and 'cause he failed   21
His presence at the tyrant's feast, I hear   22
Macduff lives in disgrace. Sir, can you tell
Where he bestows himself?
LORD   The son of Duncan,   24
From whom this tyrant holds the due of birth,   25
Lives in the English court, and is received
Of the most pious Edward with such grace   27
That the malevolence of fortune nothing
Takes from his high respect. Thither Macduff   29
Is gone to pray the holy king, upon his aid,   30
To wake Northumberland and warlike Siward,   31
That by the help of these—with Him above
To ratify the work—we may again
Give to our tables meat, sleep to our nights,   34
Free from our feasts and banquets bloody knives,   35
Do faithful homage, and receive free honors—   36
All which we pine for now. And this report
Hath so exasperate the King that he   38
Prepares for some attempt of war.
LENNOX   Sent he to Macduff?
LORD
He did; and with an absolute "Sir, not I,"   41
The cloudy messenger turns me his back   42
And hums, as who should say, "You'll rue the time   43
That clogs me with this answer."
LENNOX   And that well might   44
Advise him to a caution, t' hold what distance   45
His wisdom can provide. Some holy angel   46
Fly to the court of England and unfold
His message ere he come, that a swift blessing   48
May soon return to this our suffering country   49
Under a hand accursed!   50
LORD   I'll send my prayers with him.   *Exeunt.*

❧

---

21 **dismal** disastrous, ill-omened   24 **profound** i.e., heavily pendent, ready to drop off   27 **artificial sprites** spirits produced by magical arts   29 **confusion** ruin.   32 **security** overconfidence   35.1 **"Come away," etc.** (The song occurs in Thomas Middleton's *The Witch.*)
3.6. Location: Somewhere in Scotland.
1–2 **My . . . farther** What I've just said has coincided with your own thought. I needn't say more; you can surmise the rest.   3 **borne** carried on.   3–4 **The gracious . . . dead** (Lennox ironically implies that Macbeth's show of sorrow was hypocritical and came only after the murder.)   8 **cannot . . . thought** can help thinking   10 **fact** deed, crime.   11 **straight** straightaway, at once   13 **thralls** slaves

17 **borne all things well** managed everything cleverly   19 **an't** if it. **should** would be sure to   21 **from broad words** on account of plain speech   22 **His presence** i.e., to be present   24 **bestows himself** is quartered, has taken refuge.   25 **holds . . . birth** withholds the birthright (i.e., the Scottish crown)   27 **Of** by.   **Edward** Edward the Confessor, King of England   29 **his high respect** the high respect paid to him. (Being out of fortune has not lessened the dignity with which Malcolm is received in England.)   30 **upon his aid** in aid of Malcolm   31 **wake Northumberland** rouse the people of Northumberland   34 **meat** food   35 **Free . . . banquets** free our feasts and banquets from   36 **free** freely bestowed, or, pertaining to freemen   38 **exasperate the King** exasperated Macbeth   41 **with . . . I** i.e., when Macduff answered the messenger curtly with a refusal   42 **cloudy** louring, scowling.   **turns me** i.e., turns. (*Me* is used colloquially for emphasis.)   43 **hums . . . say** says "umph!" as if to say   44 **clogs** encumbers, loads   45–6 **Advise . . . provide** warn him (Macduff) to keep what safe distance he can (from Macbeth).   48 **His message** i.e., the request for aid against Scotland that Macduff is going to present to King Edward (see lines 29 ff.)   49–50 **suffering country Under** country suffering under

4.1

[*A cauldron.*] *Thunder. Enter the three Witches.*

FIRST WITCH
Thrice the brinded cat hath mewed.   1
SECOND WITCH
Thrice, and once the hedgepig whined.   2
THIRD WITCH
Harpier cries. "'Tis time, 'tis time!"   3
FIRST WITCH
Round about the cauldron go;
In the poisoned entrails throw.
Toad, that under cold stone
Days and nights has thirty-one   7
Sweltered venom sleeping got,   8
Boil thou first i'th' charmèd pot.
ALL [*as they dance round the cauldron*]
Double, double, toil and trouble;
Fire burn, and cauldron bubble.
SECOND WITCH
Fillet of a fenny snake,   12
In the cauldron boil and bake;
Eye of newt and toe of frog,
Wool of bat and tongue of dog,
Adder's fork and blindworm's sting,   16
Lizard's leg and owlet's wing,
For a charm of powerful trouble,
Like a hell-broth boil and bubble.
ALL
Double, double, toil and trouble;
Fire burn, and cauldron bubble.
THIRD WITCH
Scale of dragon, tooth of wolf,
Witches' mummy, maw and gulf   23
Of the ravined salt-sea shark,   24
Root of hemlock digged i'th' dark,
Liver of blaspheming Jew,
Gall of goat, and slips of yew   27
Slivered in the moon's eclipse,   28
Nose of Turk and Tartar's lips,
Finger of birth-strangled babe
Ditch-delivered by a drab,   31
Make the gruel thick and slab.   32
Add thereto a tiger's chaudron   33
For th'ingredience of our cauldron.   34

ALL
Double, double, toil and trouble;
Fire burn, and cauldron bubble.
SECOND WITCH
Cool it with a baboon's blood,
Then the charm is firm and good.   38

Enter Hecate to the other three Witches.

HECATE
Oh, well done! I commend your pains,   39
And everyone shall share i'th' gains.
And now about the cauldron sing
Like elves and fairies in a ring,
Enchanting all that you put in.   43
Music and a song: "Black spirits," etc.
[*Exit Hecate.*]
SECOND WITCH
By the pricking of my thumbs,
Something wicked this way comes.
Open, locks,
Whoever knocks!

Enter Macbeth.

MACBETH
How now, you secret, black, and midnight hags?   48
What is't you do?
ALL   A deed without a name.
MACBETH
I conjure you, by that which you profess,
Howe'er you come to know it, answer me.
Though you untie the winds and let them fight
Against the churches, though the yeasty waves   53
Confound and swallow navigation up,   54
Though bladed corn be lodged and trees blown down,   55
Though castles topple on their warders' heads,   56
Though palaces and pyramids do slope   57
Their heads to their foundations, though the treasure
Of nature's germens tumble all together   59
Even till destruction sicken, answer me   60
To what I ask you.
FIRST WITCH   Speak.
SECOND WITCH   Demand.
THIRD WITCH   We'll answer.
FIRST WITCH
Say if thou'dst rather hear it from our mouths
Or from our masters?
MACBETH   Call 'em. Let me see 'em.
FIRST WITCH
Pour in sow's blood, that hath eaten
Her nine farrow; grease that's sweaten   65

4.1. Location: A cavern (see 3.5.15). In the middle, a boiling cauldron (provided presumably by means of the trapdoor; see 4.1.106. The trapdoor must also be used in this scene for the apparitions.) **1 brinded** marked by streaks (as by fire), brindled   **2 hedgepig** hedgehog   **3 Harpier** (The name of a familiar spirit; probably derived from *harpy*.)   **cries** i.e., gives the signal to begin   **7–8 Days . . . got** for thirty-one days and nights has exuded venom formed during sleep   **12 Fillet** Slice.   **fenny** inhabiting fens or swamps   **16 fork** forked tongue.   **blindworm** slowworm, a harmless burrowing lizard   **23 mummy** mummified flesh made into a magical potion.   **maw and gulf** gullet and stomach   **24 ravined** ravenous, or glutted with prey (?)   **27 Gall** gall bladder.   **slips** cuttings for grafting or planting.   **yew** (A tree often planted in churchyards and associated with mourning.)   **28 Slivered** broken off (as a branch)   **31 Ditch . . . drab** born in a ditch of a harlot   **32 slab** viscous.   **33 chaudron** entrails   **34 th'ingredience** the ingredients

38.1 *other* (Said because Hecate is a witch, too, not because more witches enter.)   **39–43 Oh . . . in** (These lines are universally regarded as non-Shakespearean.)   **43.1 "Black spirits," etc.** (This song is found in Middleton's *The Witch*.)   **48 black** i.e., dealing in black magic   **53 yeasty** foamy   **54 Confound** destroy   **55 Though . . . lodged** though unripe grain be laid flat   **56 warders'** guardsmen's   **57 slope** bend   **59 nature's germens** seed or elements from which all nature operates   **60 sicken** be surfeited with its own excess   **65 nine farrow** litter of nine.   **sweaten** sweated

From the murderer's gibbet throw 66
Into the flame.
ALL   Come high or low, 67
Thyself and office deftly show! 68

Thunder. First Apparition, an armed Head.

MACBETH
Tell me, thou unknown power—
FIRST WITCH   He knows thy thought.
Hear his speech, but say thou naught.
FIRST APPARITION
Macbeth! Macbeth! Macbeth! Beware Macduff,
Beware the Thane of Fife. Dismiss me. Enough. 72
                              He descends.

MACBETH
Whate'er thou art, for thy good caution, thanks;
Thou hast harped my fear aright. But one word
     more— 74
FIRST WITCH
He will not be commanded. Here's another,
More potent than the first. 76

Thunder. Second Apparition, a bloody Child.

SECOND APPARITION   Macbeth! Macbeth! Macbeth!
MACBETH   Had I three ears, I'd hear thee.
SECOND APPARITION
Be bloody, bold, and resolute; laugh to scorn
The power of man, for none of woman born
Shall harm Macbeth.   *Descends.*
MACBETH
Then live, Macduff; what need I fear of thee?
But yet I'll make assurance double sure,
And take a bond of fate. Thou shalt not live, 84
That I may tell pale-hearted fear it lies,
And sleep in spite of thunder. 86

*Thunder. Third Apparition, a Child crowned, with
a tree in his hand.*

                         What is this
That rises like the issue of a king 87
And wears upon his baby brow the round 88
And top of sovereignty?
ALL   Listen, but speak not to't. 89
THIRD APPARITION
Be lion-mettled, proud, and take no care
Who chafes, who frets, or where conspirers are.
Macbeth shall never vanquished be until

Great Birnam Wood to high Dunsinane Hill
Shall come against him.   *Descends.*
MACBETH   That will never be.
Who can impress the forest, bid the tree 95
Unfix his earthbound root? Sweet bodements, good! 96
Rebellious dead, rise never till the wood 97
Of Birnam rise, and our high-placed Macbeth 98
Shall live the lease of nature, pay his breath 99
To time and mortal custom. Yet my heart 100
Throbs to know one thing. Tell me, if your art
Can tell so much: shall Banquo's issue ever
Reign in this kingdom?
ALL   Seek to know no more.
MACBETH
I will be satisfied. Deny me this,
And an eternal curse fall on you! Let me know. 105
          [The cauldron descends.] Hautboys.
Why sinks that cauldron? And what noise is this? 106
FIRST WITCH   Show!
SECOND WITCH   Show!
THIRD WITCH   Show!
ALL
Show his eyes, and grieve his heart;
Come like shadows, so depart! 111

*A show of eight kings and Banquo last; [the eighth
King] with a glass in his hand.*

MACBETH
Thou art too like the spirit of Banquo. Down!
Thy crown does sear mine eyeballs. And thy hair,
Thou other gold-bound brow, is like the first. 114
A third is like the former. Filthy hags,
Why do you show me this? A fourth? Start, eyes! 116
What, will the line stretch out to th' crack of doom? 117
Another yet? A seventh? I'll see no more.
And yet the eighth appears, who bears a glass
Which shows me many more; and some I see
That twofold balls and treble scepters carry. 121
Horrible sight! Now I see 'tis true,
For the blood-boltered Banquo smiles upon me 123
And points at them for his. *[The apparitions vanish.]*
     What, is this so? 124

66 **gibbet** gallows   67 **high or low** of the upper or lower air, from under the earth or in hell; or, one and all   68 **office** function   68.1 *armed Head* (Perhaps symbolizes the head of Macbeth cut off by Macduff and presented by him to Malcolm, or else the head of Macduff, armed in rebellion against Macbeth.)   72.1 *He descends* (i.e., by means of the trapdoor).   74 **harped** hit, touched (as in touching a harp to make it sound)   76.1 *bloody Child* (Symbolizes Macduff untimely ripped from his mother's womb; see 5.8.15–16.)   84 **take a bond of** get a guarantee from (i.e., by killing Macduff, to make doubly sure he can do no harm)   86.1-2 *Child . . . hand* (Symbolizes Malcolm, the royal child; the tree anticipates the cutting of boughs in Birnam Wood, 5.4.)   87 **like** in the likeness of   88–9 **round And top** crown

95 **impress** press into service, like soldiers   96 **bodements** prophecies   97–8 **Rebellious . . . rise** i.e., May the souls of those I have murdered (Banquo, Duncan) never rise again, since trees themself cannot rise. (An image of the Day of Judgment, when bodies are prophesied to rise again; see *Henry V*, 4.1.135–8.)   99–100 **Shall . . . custom** will live out his full life span until it is time for him to expire (*pay his breath*) in the way of all mortals.   105.1 **Hautboys** oboelike instruments.   106 **noise** music   111.1 *eight kings* (Banquo was the supposed ancestor of the Stuart dynasty, leading forward to King James VI of Scotland and James I of England, the *eighth King* here.)   111.2 *glass* (magic) mirror (also in line 119)   114 **other** i.e., second   116 **Start** Bulge from their sockets   117 **th' crack of doom** the thunder-peal of Doomsday at the end of time.   121 **twofold balls** (A probable reference to the double coronation of James at Scone and Westminster, as King of England and Scotland.)   **treble scepters** (Probably refers to James' assumed title as King of Great Britain, France, and Ireland.)   123 **blood-boltered** having his hair matted with blood   124 **for his** as his descendants.

FIRST WITCH

Ay, sir, all this is so. But why   125
Stands Macbeth thus amazedly?   126
Come, sisters, cheer we up his sprites   127
And show the best of our delights.
I'll charm the air to give a sound,
While you perform your antic round,   130
That this great king may kindly say
Our duties did his welcome pay.   132

                   Music. The Witches dance, and vanish.

MACBETH

Where are they? Gone? Let this pernicious hour
Stand aye accursèd in the calendar!
Come in, without there!

        Enter Lennox.

LENNOX   What's Your Grace's will?

MACBETH

Saw you the Weird Sisters?

LENNOX   No, my lord.

MACBETH

Came they not by you?

LENNOX   No, indeed, my lord.

MACBETH

Infected be the air whereon they ride,
And damned all those that trust them! I did hear
The galloping of horse. Who was't came by?   140

LENNOX

'Tis two or three, my lord, that bring you word
Macduff is fled to England.

MACBETH   Fled to England!

LENNOX

Ay, my good lord.

MACBETH [*aside*]

Time, thou anticipat'st my dread exploits.   144
The flighty purpose never is o'ertook   145
Unless the deed go with it. From this moment   146
The very firstlings of my heart shall be   147
The firstlings of my hand. And even now,   148
To crown my thoughts with acts, be it thought and
    done:
The castle of Macduff I will surprise,   150
Seize upon Fife, give to th'edge o'th' sword
His wife, his babes, and all unfortunate souls
That trace him in his line. No boasting like a fool; 153
This deed I'll do before this purpose cool.
But no more sights!—Where are these gentlemen?
Come, bring me where they are.   *Exeunt.*

               ❖

4.2

      Enter Macduff's Wife, her Son, and Ross.

LADY MACDUFF

What had he done to make him fly the land?

ROSS

You must have patience, madam.

LADY MACDUFF   He had none.
His flight was madness. When our actions do not,   3
Our fears do make us traitors.

ROSS   You know not   4
Whether it was his wisdom or his fear.

LADY MACDUFF

Wisdom? To leave his wife, to leave his babes,
His mansion, and his titles in a place   7
From whence himself does fly? He loves us not,
He wants the natural touch; for the poor wren,   9
The most diminutive of birds, will fight,
Her young ones in her nest, against the owl.   11
All is the fear and nothing is the love,
As little is the wisdom, where the flight
So runs against all reason.

ROSS   My dearest coz,   14
I pray you, school yourself. But, for your husband, 15
He is noble, wise, judicious, and best knows
The fits o'th' season. I dare not speak much further, 17
But cruel are the times when we are traitors   18
And do not know ourselves, when we hold rumor   19
From what we fear, yet know not what we fear,   20
But float upon a wild and violent sea
Each way and none. I take my leave of you;   22
Shall not be long but I'll be here again.   23
Things at the worst will cease, or else climb upward
To what they were before.—My pretty cousin,
Blessing upon you!

LADY MACDUFF

Fathered he is, and yet he's fatherless.

ROSS

I am so much a fool, should I stay longer
It would be my disgrace and your discomfort.   29
I take my leave at once.   *Exit Ross.*

LADY MACDUFF   Sirrah, your father's dead;   31
And what will you do now? How will you live?

SON

As birds do, mother.

LADY MACDUFF   What, with worms and flies?

SON

With what I get, I mean; and so do they.

4.2. Location: Fife. Macduff's castle.
3–4 When . . . traitors Even when we have committed no treasonous
act, our fearful responses make us look guilty.   **7 titles** possessions to
which he has title   **9 wants . . . touch** lacks the natural instinct to protect his family   **11 Her . . . nest** when her young ones are in the nest
14 coz kinswoman   **15 school** control.   **for** as for   **17 fits o'th' season** violent convulsions of the time.   **18–19 are traitors . . . ourselves**
are alienated from one another by a climate of fear and suspected
treason   **19–20 hold . . . From what we fear** believe every fearful
rumor on the basis of what we fear might be   **22 Each . . . none** this
way and that.   **23 Shall** it shall.   **but** before   **29 It . . . discomfort** I
should disgrace my manhood by weeping and cause you distress.
31 Sirrah (Here, an affectionate form of address to a child.)

125–32 Ay . . . pay (These lines are assumed to have been written by
someone other than Shakespeare.)   **126 amazedly** stunned.
127 sprites spirits   **130 antic round** grotesque dance in a circle
132 pay repay.   **140 horse** horses.   **144 thou anticipat'st** you forestall
145 flighty fleeting   **146 Unless . . . it** unless the execution of the
deed accompanies the conception of it immediately.   **147–8 The
very . . . hand** the firstborn promptings of my heart will become my
first of deeds.   **150 surprise** attack without warning   **153 trace . . .
line** follow him in the line of inheritance.

LADY MACDUFF   Poor bird! Thou'dst never fear   35
The net nor lime, the pitfall nor the gin.   36

SON
Why should I, mother? Poor birds they are not set for.   37
My father is not dead, for all your saying.

LADY MACDUFF
Yes, he is dead. How wilt thou do for a father?

SON   Nay, how will you do for a husband?

LADY MACDUFF   Why, I can buy me twenty at any
market.

SON   Then you'll buy 'em to sell again.

LADY MACDUFF
Thou speak'st with all thy wit,
And yet, i'faith, with wit enough for thee.

SON   Was my father a traitor, mother?

LADY MACDUFF   Ay, that he was.

SON   What is a traitor?

LADY MACDUFF   Why, one that swears and lies.

SON   And be all traitors that do so?

LADY MACDUFF
Every one that does so is a traitor,
And must be hanged.

SON
And must they all be hanged that swear and lie?

LADY MACDUFF   Every one.

SON   Who must hang them?

LADY MACDUFF   Why, the honest men.

SON   Then the liars and swearers are fools, for there are
liars and swearers enough to beat the honest men and
hang up them.

LADY MACDUFF   Now, God help thee, poor monkey!
But how wilt thou do for a father?

SON   If he were dead, you'd weep for him; if you would
not, it were a good sign that I should quickly have a
new father.

LADY MACDUFF   Poor prattler, how thou talk'st!

Enter a Messenger.

MESSENGER
Bless you, fair dame! I am not to you known,
Though in your state of honor I am perfect.   67
I doubt some danger does approach you nearly.   68
If you will take a homely man's advice,   69
Be not found here. Hence with your little ones!
To fright you thus, methinks, I am too savage;
To do worse to you were fell cruelty,   72
Which is too nigh your person. Heaven preserve you!   73
I dare abide no longer.   *Exit Messenger.*

LADY MACDUFF   Whither should I fly?
I have done no harm. But I remember now
I am in this earthly world, where to do harm
Is often laudable, to do good sometime
Accounted dangerous folly. Why then, alas,

Do I put up that womanly defense
To say I have done no harm?

Enter Murderers.

What are these faces?

FIRST MURDERER   Where is your husband?

LADY MACDUFF
I hope in no place so unsanctified
Where such as thou mayst find him.

FIRST MURDERER   He's a traitor.

SON
Thou liest, thou shag-haired villain!

FIRST MURDERER   What, you egg?
[*He stabs him.*]
Young fry of treachery!

SON   He has killed me, mother.   85
Run away, I pray you!   [*He dies.*]
Exit [*Lady Macduff*] *crying "Murder!"*
[*followed by the Murderers with the Son's body*].

❖

4.3

Enter Malcolm and Macduff.

MALCOLM
Let us seek out some desolate shade, and there
Weep our sad bosoms empty.

MACDUFF   Let us rather
Hold fast the mortal sword, and like good men   3
Bestride our downfall'n birthdom. Each new morn   4
New widows howl, new orphans cry, new sorrows
Strike heaven on the face, that it resounds   6
As if it felt with Scotland and yelled out   7
Like syllable of dolor.

MALCOLM   What I believe, I'll wail;   8
What know, believe; and what I can redress,   9
As I shall find the time to friend, I will.   10
What you have spoke it may be so, perchance.
This tyrant, whose sole name blisters our tongues,   12
Was once thought honest. You have loved him well;
He hath not touched you yet. I am young; but
something   14
You may deserve of him through me, and wisdom   15
To offer up a weak, poor, innocent lamb
T'appease an angry god.

MACDUFF   I am not treacherous.

MALCOLM   But Macbeth is.

---

35 **Thou'dst never fear** You are too innocent to be prudently wary of
36 **lime** birdlime (a sticky substance put on branches to snare birds).
gin snare.   37 **Poor . . . for** i.e., Traps are not set for *poor* birds, as you
call me.   67 **Though . . . perfect** though I am perfectly acquainted
with your honorable state.   68 **doubt** fear   69 **homely** plain
72–3 **To . . . person** to frighten you still further would be savage cruelty, which cruelty is all too near at hand.

85 **fry** spawn, progeny
4.3. Location: England. Before King Edward the Confessor's palace.
3 **mortal** deadly   4 **Bestride** stand over in defense.   **birthdom** native
land.   6 **that it resounds** so that it echoes   7–8 **As . . . dolor** as if
heaven, feeling itself the blow delivered to Scotland, cried out with a
similar cry of pain.   8–9 **What . . . believe** i.e., What I believe to be
amiss in Scotland I will grieve for, and anything I am certain to be
true I will believe. (But one must be cautious in these duplicitous
times.)   10 **to friend** opportune, congenial   12 **sole** mere   14 **He . . .
yet** i.e., the fact that Macbeth hasn't hurt you yet makes me suspicious of your loyalties.   **young** i.e., inexperienced   14–15 **something
. . . me** i.e., you may win favor with Macbeth by delivering me to him
15 **wisdom** i.e., it would be worldly-wise

A good and virtuous nature may recoil 20
In an imperial charge. But I shall crave your pardon. 21
That which you are my thoughts cannot transpose; 22
Angels are bright still, though the brightest fell. 23
Though all things foul would wear the brows of grace, 24
Yet grace must still look so.
MACDUFF   I have lost my hopes. 25
MALCOLM
Perchance even there where I did find my doubts. 26
Why in that rawness left you wife and child, 27
Those precious motives, those strong knots of love,
Without leave-taking? I pray you,
Let not my jealousies be your dishonors, 30
But mine own safeties. You may be rightly just, 31
Whatever I shall think.
MACDUFF   Bleed, bleed, poor country!
Great tyranny, lay thou thy basis sure, 33
For goodness dare not check thee; wear thou thy
     wrongs, 34
The title is affeered! Fare thee well, lord. 35
I would not be the villain that thou think'st
For the whole space that's in the tyrant's grasp,
And the rich East to boot.
MALCOLM   Be not offended. 38
I speak not as in absolute fear of you. 39
I think our country sinks beneath the yoke;
It weeps, it bleeds, and each new day a gash
Is added to her wounds. I think withal 42
There would be hands uplifted in my right; 43
And here from gracious England have I offer 44
Of goodly thousands. But, for all this,
When I shall tread upon the tyrant's head,
Or wear it on my sword, yet my poor country
Shall have more vices than it had before,
More suffer, and more sundry ways than ever, 49
By him that shall succeed.
MACDUFF   What should he be? 50
MALCOLM
It is myself I mean, in whom I know

All the particulars of vice so grafted 52
That, when they shall be opened, black Macbeth 53
Will seem as pure as snow, and the poor state
Esteem him as a lamb, being compared
With my confineless harms.
MACDUFF   Not in the legions 56
Of horrid hell can come a devil more damned
In evils to top Macbeth.
MALCOLM   I grant him bloody, 58
Luxurious, avaricious, false, deceitful, 59
Sudden, malicious, smacking of every sin 60
That has a name. But there's no bottom, none,
In my voluptuousness. Your wives, your daughters,
Your matrons, and your maids could not fill up
The cistern of my lust, and my desire
All continent impediments would o'erbear 65
That did oppose my will. Better Macbeth 66
Than such an one to reign.
MACDUFF   Boundless intemperance
In nature is a tyranny; it hath been 68
Th'untimely emptying of the happy throne
And fall of many kings. But fear not yet 70
To take upon you what is yours. You may
Convey your pleasures in a spacious plenty, 72
And yet seem cold; the time you may so hoodwink. 73
We have willing dames enough. There cannot be
That vulture in you to devour so many
As will to greatness dedicate themselves,
Finding it so inclined.
MALCOLM   With this there grows
In my most ill-composed affection such 78
A stanchless avarice that, were I king, 79
I should cut off the nobles for their lands,
Desire his jewels and this other's house, 81
And my more-having would be as a sauce
To make me hunger more, that I should forge 83
Quarrels unjust against the good and loyal,
Destroying them for wealth.
MACDUFF   This avarice
Sticks deeper, grows with more pernicious root
Than summer-seeming lust, and it hath been 87
The sword of our slain kings. Yet do not fear; 88
Scotland hath foisons to fill up your will 89
Of your mere own. All these are portable, 90
With other graces weighed. 91
MALCOLM
But I have none. The king-becoming graces,
As justice, verity, temperance, stableness,

20–1 A good . . . charge i.e., Even as good a virtuous nature as you have, Macduff, may give way to the insinuations of a royal command from Macbeth. (With wordplay on the *recoil* of a firearm that is *charged* with power and shot.)   **22 That . . . transpose** My suspicious thoughts cannot change you from what you are, cannot make you evil   **23 the brightest** i.e., Lucifer   **24–5 Though . . . so** Even though evil puts on the appearance of good so often as to cast that appearance into deep suspicion, yet goodness must go on looking and acting like itself.   **25 hopes** i.e., hopes of persuading Malcolm to lead the cause against Macbeth.   **26 Perchance even there** i.e., Perhaps in that same mistrustful frame of mind.   **doubts** i.e., fears such as that Macduff may covertly be on Macbeth's side.   **27 rawness** unprotected condition. (Malcolm suggests that Macduff's leaving his family unprotected could be construed as more evidence of his not having anything to fear from Macbeth.)   **30–1 Let . . . safeties** may it be true that my suspicions of your lack of honor are founded only in my own wariness.   **33 basis** foundation   **34 check** rebuke, call to account.   **wear . . . wrongs** continue to enjoy your wrongfully gained powers   **35 affeered** confirmed, certified.   **38 to boot** in addition.   **39 absolute fear** complete mistrust   **42 withal** in addition   **43 right cause**   **44 England** the King of England   **49 More . . . ways** suffer more grievously and in more varied ways   **50 What . . . be?** Whom could you possibly mean?

52 grafted (1) engrafted, indissolubly mixed (2) grafted like a plant that will then *open* or unfold   **53 opened** unfolded (like a bud)   **56 confineless** limitless   **58 top** surpass   **59 Luxurious** lecherous   **60 Sudden** violent, impetuous   **65 continent** (1) chaste (2) restraining, containing   **66 will** lust. (Also in line 89.)   **68 nature** human nature   **70 yet** nevertheless   **72 Convey** manage with secrecy   **73 cold** chaste.   **the time . . . hoodwink** you may thus deceive the age.   **78 ill-composed affection** evil disposition   **79 stanchless** insatiable   **81 his** one man's.   **this other's** another's   **83 that** so that   **87 summer-seeming** appropriate to youth (and lessening in later years)   **88 sword** i.e., cause of overthrow   **89 foisons** resources, plenty   **90 Of . . . own** out of your own royal estates alone.   **portable** bearable   **91 weighed** counterbalanced.

Bounty, perseverance, mercy, lowliness,   94
Devotion, patience, courage, fortitude,
I have no relish of them, but abound   96
In the division of each several crime,   97
Acting it many ways. Nay, had I power, I should
Pour the sweet milk of concord into hell,
Uproar the universal peace, confound   100
All unity on earth.
MACDUFF   O Scotland, Scotland!
MALCOLM
If such a one be fit to govern, speak.
I am as I have spoken.
MACDUFF   Fit to govern?
No, not to live. O nation miserable,
With an untitled tyrant bloody-sceptered,   105
When shalt thou see thy wholesome days again,
Since that the truest issue of thy throne
By his own interdiction stands accurst   108
And does blaspheme his breed? Thy royal father   109
Was a most sainted king; the queen that bore thee,
Oft'ner upon her knees than on her feet,
Died every day she lived. Fare thee well.   112
These evils thou repeat'st upon thyself
Hath banished me from Scotland. O my breast,   114
Thy hope ends here!
MALCOLM   Macduff, this noble passion,
Child of integrity, hath from my soul   116
Wiped the black scruples, reconciled my thoughts
To thy good truth and honor. Devilish Macbeth
By many of these trains hath sought to win me   119
Into his power, and modest wisdom plucks me   120
From overcredulous haste. But God above
Deal between thee and me! For even now
I put myself to thy direction and
Unspeak mine own detraction, here abjure   124
The taints and blames I laid upon myself
For strangers to my nature. I am yet   126
Unknown to woman, never was forsworn,   127
Scarcely have coveted what was mine own,
At no time broke my faith, would not betray
The devil to his fellow, and delight
No less in truth than life. My first false speaking
Was this upon myself. What I am truly   132
Is thine and my poor country's to command—
Whither indeed, before thy here-approach,
Old Siward with ten thousand warlike men,
Already at a point, was setting forth.   136

Now we'll together; and the chance of goodness   137
Be like our warranted quarrel!—Why are you silent?   138
MACDUFF
Such welcome and unwelcome things at once
'Tis hard to reconcile.

        Enter a Doctor.

MALCOLM
Well, more anon.—Comes the King forth, I pray you?
DOCTOR
Ay, sir. There are a crew of wretched souls
That stay his cure. Their malady convinces   143
The great essay of art; but at his touch—   144
Such sanctity hath heaven given his hand—
They presently amend.
MALCOLM   I thank you, Doctor.   146
                                    Exit [Doctor].
MACDUFF
What's the disease he means?
MALCOLM   'Tis called the evil.   147
A most miraculous work in this good king,
Which often, since my here-remain in England,   149
I have seen him do. How he solicits heaven   150
Himself best knows; but strangely-visited people,   151
All swoll'n and ulcerous, pitiful to the eye,
The mere despair of surgery, he cures,   153
Hanging a golden stamp about their necks   154
Put on with holy prayers; and 'tis spoken,   155
To the succeeding royalty he leaves   156
The healing benediction. With this strange virtue   157
He hath a heavenly gift of prophecy,
And sundry blessings hang about his throne
That speak him full of grace.

        Enter Ross.

MACDUFF   See who comes here.
MALCOLM
My countryman, but yet I know him not.   161
MACDUFF
My ever-gentle cousin, welcome hither.   162
MALCOLM
I know him now. Good God betimes remove   163
The means that makes us strangers!
ROSS   Sir, amen.
MACDUFF
Stands Scotland where it did?
ROSS   Alas, poor country,
Almost afraid to know itself. It cannot

---

94 **lowliness** humility   96 **relish** flavor or trace   97 **division** subdivisions, various possible forms.   **several** separate   100 **Uproar** throw into an uproar   105 **untitled** lacking rightful title, usurping   108 **interdiction** debarring of self   109 **does blaspheme his breed** defames his breeding, i.e., is a disgrace to his royal lineage.
112 **Died . . . lived** lived a life of daily mortification.   114 **breast** heart   116 **Child of integrity** a product of your integrity of spirit; or, you person of perfect integrity   119 **trains** plots, artifices
120 **modest . . . me** wise prudence holds me back   124 **Unspeak . . . detraction** take back all I said in detraction of myself   126 **For** as
127 **Unknown to woman** a virgin   132 **upon** against   136 **at a point** prepared

137–8 **the chance . . . quarrel** may our chance of success be proportionate to the justice of our cause.   143 **stay** wait for.   **convinces** conquers   144 **essay of art** efforts of medical skill   146 **presently** immediately   147 **evil** i.e., scrofula, supposedly cured by the royal touch; James I claimed this power.   149 **here-remain** stay   150 **solicits** prevails by prayer with   151 **strangely-visited** afflicted by strange diseases   153 **mere** utter   154 **stamp** minted coin   155–7 **'tis . . . benediction** it is said that he bequeaths this healing blessedness to his royal progeny.   157 **virtue** healing power   161 **My countryman** (So identified by his dress.)   **know** recognize   162 **gentle** noble   163 **betimes** speedily

Be called our mother, but our grave; where nothing   167
But who knows nothing is once seen to smile;   168
Where sighs and groans and shrieks that rend the air
Are made, not marked; where violent sorrow seems   170
A modern ecstasy. The dead man's knell   171
Is there scarce asked for who, and good men's lives
Expire before the flowers in their caps,   173
Dying or ere they sicken.
MACDUFF   Oh, relation   174
Too nice, and yet too true!
MALCOLM   What's the newest grief?   175
ROSS
That of an hour's age doth hiss the speaker;   176
Each minute teems a new one.
MACDUFF   How does my wife?   177
ROSS
Why, well.
MACDUFF   And all my children?
ROSS   Well too.   178
MACDUFF
The tyrant has not battered at their peace?
ROSS
No, they were well at peace when I did leave 'em.
MACDUFF
Be not a niggard of your speech. How goes't?
ROSS
When I came hither to transport the tidings
Which I have heavily borne, there ran a rumor   183
Of many worthy fellows that were out,   184
Which was to my belief witnessed the rather   185
For that I saw the tyrant's power afoot.   186
Now is the time of help. [*To Malcolm*] Your eye in
    Scotland
Would create soldiers, make our women fight,   188
To doff their dire distresses.
MALCOLM   Be't their comfort   189
We are coming thither. Gracious England hath   190
Lent us good Siward and ten thousand men;
An older and a better soldier none   192
That Christendom gives out.
ROSS   Would I could answer   193
This comfort with the like! But I have words
That would be howled out in the desert air,   195
Where hearing should not latch them.
MACDUFF   What concern they?   196

The general cause? Or is it a fee-grief   197
Due to some single breast?
ROSS   No mind that's honest   198
But in it shares some woe, though the main part
Pertains to you alone.
MACDUFF   If it be mine,
Keep it not from me; quickly let me have it.
ROSS
Let not your ears despise my tongue forever,
Which shall possess them with the heaviest sound   203
That ever yet they heard.
MACDUFF   Hum! I guess at it.
ROSS
Your castle is surprised, your wife and babes
Savagely slaughtered. To relate the manner
Were, on the quarry of these murdered deer,   207
To add the death of you.
MALCOLM   Merciful heaven!
What, man, ne'er pull your hat upon your brows;   209
Give sorrow words. The grief that does not speak
Whispers the o'erfraught heart and bids it break.   211
MACDUFF
My children too?
ROSS   Wife, children, servants, all
That could be found.
MACDUFF   And I must be from thence!   213
My wife killed too?
ROSS   I have said.
MALCOLM   Be comforted.
Let's make us med'cines of our great revenge
To cure this deadly grief.
MACDUFF
He has no children. All my pretty ones?   217
Did you say all? O hell-kite! All?   218
What, all my pretty chickens and their dam
At one fell swoop?   220
MALCOLM   Dispute it like a man.   221
MACDUFF   I shall do so;
But I must also feel it as a man.
I cannot but remember such things were,
That were most precious to me. Did heaven look on
And would not take their part? Sinful Macduff,
They were all struck for thee! Naught that I am,   227
Not for their own demerits, but for mine,
Fell slaughter on their souls. Heaven rest them now!
MALCOLM
Be this the whetstone of your sword. Let grief
Convert to anger; blunt not the heart, enrage it.

167–8 nothing But who nobody except a person who   **168 once** ever
170 marked noticed (because they are so common)   **171 modern
ecstasy** commonplace emotion.   **173 flowers** (Often worn in Elizabethan caps.)   **174 or ere they sicken** before they have had time to
fall ill.   **relation** report   **175 nice** minutely accurate, elaborately
phrased   **176 That . . . speaker** The speaker of news that is scarcely
an hour old is hissed at for reporting stale news   **177 teems** teems
with, yields   **178 well** (Ross quibbles, in his reluctance to tell the bad
news. "The dead are well" means they are at rest.)   **183 heavily**
sadly   **184–6 Of . . . afoot** about many worthy Scots who have been
driven into exile and armed rebellion, which rumor was strengthened
all the more when I saw Macbeth's army on the move (in anticipation
of being attacked).   **188 our women** even our women   **189 doff** put
off, get rid of   **190 Gracious England** i.e., Edward the Confessor
192 none there is none   **193 gives out** tells of, proclaims.   **195 would**
should   **196 latch** catch (the sound of)

197 fee-grief a grief with an individual owner, having absolute ownership   **198 Due to** i.e., owned by   **203 possess them with** put them
in possession of   **207 quarry** heap of slaughtered deer at a hunt.
(With a pun on *dear, deer*.)   **209 pull your hat** (A conventional gesture
of grief.)   **211 Whispers** whispers to.   **o'erfraught** overburdened
213 must had to   **217 He has no children** (Referring either to Macbeth, who must not be a father if he can do such a thing, or, to Malcolm, who speaks comfortingly without knowing what such a loss
feels like to a father.)   **218 hell-kite** (The *kite* is a rapacious bird of
prey; a term of disdain and dislike.)   **220 fell** cruel   **221 Dispute**
Strive against, debate   **227 for thee** i.e., as divine punishment for
your sins.   **Naught** Wicked

MACDUFF
Oh, I could play the woman with mine eyes
And braggart with my tongue! But, gentle heavens,
Cut short all intermission. Front to front   234
Bring thou this fiend of Scotland and myself;
Within my sword's length set him. If he scape,   236
Heaven forgive him too!
MALCOLM   This tune goes manly.   237
Come, go we to the King. Our power is ready;   238
Our lack is nothing but our leave. Macbeth   239
Is ripe for shaking, and the powers above
Put on their instruments. Receive what cheer you may.   241
The night is long that never finds the day.   *Exeunt.*

❖

5.1

Enter a Doctor of Physic and a Waiting-
Gentlewoman.

DOCTOR   I have two nights watched with you, but can
perceive no truth in your report. When was it she last
walked?
GENTLEWOMAN   Since His Majesty went into the field, I
have seen her rise from her bed, throw her nightgown
upon her, unlock her closet, take forth paper, fold it,   6
write upon't, read it, afterwards seal it, and again
return to bed; yet all this while in a most fast sleep.
DOCTOR   A great perturbation in nature, to receive at
once the benefit of sleep and do the effects of   10
watching! In this slumbery agitation, besides her   11
walking and other actual performances, what, at any
time, have you heard her say?
GENTLEWOMAN   That, sir, which I will not report after her.
DOCTOR   You may to me, and 'tis most meet you should.   16
GENTLEWOMAN   Neither to you nor anyone, having no
witness to confirm my speech.

Enter Lady [*Macbeth*], *with a taper.*

Lo you, here she comes! This is her very guise, and,
upon my life, fast asleep. Observe her. Stand close.   20
                    [*They stand aside.*]
DOCTOR   How came she by that light?
GENTLEWOMAN   Why, it stood by her. She has light by
her continually. 'Tis her command.
DOCTOR   You see her eyes are open.
GENTLEWOMAN   Ay, but their sense are shut.
DOCTOR   What is it she does now? Look how she rubs
her hands.
GENTLEWOMAN   It is an accustomed action with her to
seem thus washing her hands. I have known her
continue in this a quarter of an hour.

LADY MACBETH   Yet here's a spot.
DOCTOR   Hark, she speaks. I will set down what comes
from her, to satisfy my remembrance the more   33
strongly.
LADY MACBETH   Out, damned spot! Out, I say! One—
two—why then, 'tis time to do't. Hell is murky.—
Fie, my lord, fie, a soldier, and afeard? What need we
fear who knows it, when none can call our power to
account? Yet who would have thought the old man to
have had so much blood in him?
DOCTOR   Do you mark that?
LADY MACBETH   The Thane of Fife had a wife. Where is
she now?—What, will these hands ne'er be
clean?—No more o'that, my lord, no more o' that;
you mar all with this starting.   45
DOCTOR   Go to, go to. You have known what you   46
should not.
GENTLEWOMAN   She has spoke what she should not, I
am sure of that. Heaven knows what she has known!
LADY MACBETH   Here's the smell of the blood still. All
the perfumes of Arabia will not sweeten this little
hand. Oh, oh, oh!
DOCTOR   What a sigh is there! The heart is sorely   53
charged.   54
GENTLEWOMAN   I would not have such a heart in my
bosom for the dignity of the whole body.   56
DOCTOR   Well, well, well.
GENTLEWOMAN   Pray God it be, sir.   58
DOCTOR   This disease is beyond my practice. Yet I have
known those which have walked in their sleep who
have died holily in their beds.
LADY MACBETH   Wash your hands, put on your night-
gown; look not so pale! I tell you yet again, Banquo's
buried. He cannot come out on 's grave.   64
DOCTOR   Even so?
LADY MACBETH   To bed, to bed! There's knocking at the
gate. Come, come, come, come, give me your hand.
What's done cannot be undone. To bed, to bed,
to bed!   *Exit Lady.*
DOCTOR   Will she go now to bed?
GENTLEWOMAN   Directly.
DOCTOR
Foul whisperings are abroad. Unnatural deeds
Do breed unnatural troubles. Infected minds
To their deaf pillows will discharge their secrets.
More needs she the divine than the physician.
God, God forgive us all! Look after her;
Remove from her the means of all annoyance,   77
And still keep eyes upon her. So, good night.   78
My mind she has mated, and amazed my sight.   79
I think, but dare not speak.
GENTLEWOMAN   Good night, good Doctor.
                                    Exeunt.

---

234 intermission delay, interval.   **Front to front** Face to face
236–7 If . . . too! If I let him escape, may he find forgiveness not only
from me but from heaven itself! (This is a condition that Macduff will
not allow to happen.)   **238 power** army   **239 Our . . . leave** we need
only to take our leave (of the English King).   **241 Put . . . instruments**
set us on as their agents, or, arm themselves.
5.1. Location: Dunsinane. Macbeth's castle.
0.1 *Physic* medicine   **6 closet** chest or cabinet   **10–11 do . . . watching** act as though awake.   **16 meet** suitable   **20 close** concealed.

33 satisfy confirm, support   **45 this starting** these startled movements.
46 Go to (An exclamation of reproof, directed at Lady Macbeth.)
53–4 sorely charged heavily burdened.   **56 dignity** worth, value   **58 Pray
. . . sir** Pray God it will turn out well, as you say, sir. (Playing on the
Doctor's *"Well, well,"* i.e., "Dear, dear.")   **64 on 's** of his   **77 annoyance**
i.e., harming herself   **78 still** constantly   **79 mated** bewildered, stupefied

5.2

Drum and colors. Enter Menteith, Caithness,
Angus, Lennox, [and] soldiers.

MENTEITH
The English power is near, led on by Malcolm,
His uncle Siward, and the good Macduff.
Revenges burn in them, for their dear causes   3
Would to the bleeding and the grim alarm   4
Excite the mortified man.

ANGUS   Near Birnam Wood   5
Shall we well meet them; that way are they coming.   6

CAITHNESS
Who knows if Donalbain be with his brother?

LENNOX
For certain, sir, he is not. I have a file   8
Of all the gentry. There is Siward's son,
And many unrough youths that even now   10
Protest their first of manhood.

MENTEITH   What does the tyrant? 11

CAITHNESS
Great Dunsinane he strongly fortifies.
Some say he's mad, others that lesser hate him
Do call it valiant fury; but for certain
He cannot buckle his distempered cause   15
Within the belt of rule.

ANGUS   Now does he feel
His secret murders sticking on his hands;
Now minutely revolts upbraid his faith-breach.   18
Those he commands move only in command,   19
Nothing in love. Now does he feel his title
Hang loose about him, like a giant's robe
Upon a dwarfish thief.

MENTEITH   Who then shall blame
His pestered senses to recoil and start,   23
When all that is within him does condemn
Itself for being there?

CAITHNESS   Well, march we on
To give obedience where 'tis truly owed.
Meet we the med'cine of the sickly weal,   27
And with him pour we in our country's purge   28
Each drop of us.

LENNOX   Or so much as it needs   29
To dew the sovereign flower and drown the weeds.   30
Make we our march towards Birnam.

Exeunt, marching.

❖

5.3

Enter Macbeth, Doctor, and attendants.

MACBETH
Bring me no more reports. Let them fly all!   1
Till Birnam Wood remove to Dunsinane,
I cannot taint with fear. What's the boy Malcolm?   3
Was he not born of woman? The spirits that know
All mortal consequences have pronounced me thus: 5
"Fear not, Macbeth. No man that's born of woman
Shall e'er have power upon thee." Then fly, false
    thanes,
And mingle with the English epicures!   8
The mind I sway by and the heart I bear   9
Shall never sag with doubt nor shake with fear.

Enter Servant.

The devil damn thee black, thou cream-faced loon!   11
Where got'st thou that goose look?

SERVANT
There is ten thousand—

MACBETH   Geese, villain?

SERVANT   Soldiers, sir.

MACBETH
Go prick thy face and over-red thy fear,   14
Thou lily-livered boy. What soldiers, patch?   15
Death of thy soul! Those linen cheeks of thine   16
Are counselors to fear. What soldiers, whey-face?   17

SERVANT   The English force, so please you.

MACBETH   Take thy face hence.   [*Exit Servant.*]
                [*Calling*] Seyton!—I am sick at heart
When I behold—Seyton, I say!—This push   20
Will cheer me ever, or disseat me now.   21
I have lived long enough. My way of life   22
Is fall'n into the sere, the yellow leaf,   23
And that which should accompany old age,
As honor, love, obedience, troops of friends,   25
I must not look to have, but in their stead
Curses, not loud but deep, mouth-honor, breath
Which the poor heart would fain deny and dare not.
Seyton!

Enter Seyton.

SEYTON
What's your gracious pleasure?

MACBETH   What news more?

5.2. Location: The country near Dunsinane.
3–5 their . . . man their grievous wrongs would awaken even the dead to answer the bloody and grim call to battle. **6 well** conveniently **8 file** list, roster **10 unrough** beardless **11 Protest** assert publicly **15 distempered** disease-swollen, dropsical **18 Now . . . faith-breach** every minute now, revolts upbraid him for his violation of all trust and sacred vows. **19 in command** under orders **23 pestered** troubled, tormented **27 Meet we . . . weal** i.e., Let us join forces with Malcolm, the physician of our sick land **28–9 pour . . . of us** i.e., let us shed all our blood as a bloodletting or *purge* of our country. **30 dew** bedew, water. **sovereign** (1) royal (2) medically efficacious

5.3. Location: Dunsinane. Macbeth's castle.
1 Let . . . all! Let all the thanes desert! **3 taint with** become imbued or infected with, weakened by **5 All . . . consequences** all that happens in this mortal life **8 English epicures** luxury-loving Englishmen. **9 sway** rule myself **11 loon** stupid fellow. **14 Go . . . fear** i.e., Go prick or pinch your pale cheeks to bring some color into them. (Current medical theory held that fear caused a retreat of the blood to the abdominal organs, leaving the countenance pale or *lily-livered*, line 15.) **15 patch** domestic fool. **16 Death . . . soul!** May your soul die an eternal death! (An oath.) **linen** i.e., pale, white **17 Are . . . fear** (The fear is contagious to the rest of the body and to other observers.) **20 behold** (Macbeth does not finish this thought.) **push** effort, crisis **21 cheer** (With a suggestion of "chair.") **disseat** dethrone **22 way** course **23 sere** dry and withered **25 As** such as

SEYTON
    All is confirmed, my lord, which was reported.
MACBETH
    I'll fight till from my bones my flesh be hacked.
    Give me my armor.
SEYTON   'Tis not needed yet.
MACBETH   I'll put it on.
    Send out more horses. Skirr the country round.   36
    Hang those that talk of fear. Give me mine armor.
    How does your patient, Doctor?
DOCTOR   Not so sick, my lord,
    As she is troubled with thick-coming fancies
    That keep her from her rest.
MACBETH   Cure her of that.
    Canst thou not minister to a mind diseased,
    Pluck from the memory a rooted sorrow,
    Raze out the written troubles of the brain,   44
    And with some sweet oblivious antidote   45
    Cleanse the stuffed bosom of that perilous stuff
    Which weighs upon the heart?
DOCTOR   Therein the patient
    Must minister to himself.
MACBETH
    Throw physic to the dogs! I'll none of it.   49
    Come, put mine armor on. Give me my staff.   50
                    [*Attendants arm him.*]
    Seyton, send out. Doctor, the thanes fly from me.—
    Come, sir, dispatch.—If thou couldst, Doctor, cast   52
    The water of my land, find her disease,   53
    And purge it to a sound and pristine health,
    I would applaud thee to the very echo,
    That should applaud again.—Pull't off, I say.—   56
    What rhubarb, senna, or what purgative drug   57
    Would scour these English hence? Hear'st thou of
      them?   58
DOCTOR
    Ay, my good lord. Your royal preparation
    Makes us hear something.
MACBETH   Bring it after me.—   60
    I will not be afraid of death and bane   61
    Till Birnam Forest come to Dunsinane.
                    Exeunt [all but the Doctor].
DOCTOR
    Were I from Dunsinane away and clear,
    Profit again should hardly draw me here.   [*Exit.*]

❧

5.4

*Drum and colors. Enter Malcolm, Siward,
Macduff, Siward's Son, Menteith, Caithness,
Angus, [Lennox, Ross,] and soldiers, marching.*

MALCOLM
    Cousins, I hope the days are near at hand   1
    That chambers will be safe.
MENTEITH   We doubt it nothing.   2
SIWARD
    What wood is this before us?
MENTEITH   The wood of Birnam.
MALCOLM
    Let every soldier hew him down a bough
    And bear't before him. Thereby shall we shadow
    The numbers of our host and make discovery   6
    Err in report of us.
SOLDIERS   It shall be done.
SIWARD
    We learn no other but the confident tyrant   8
    Keeps still in Dunsinane and will endure   9
    Our setting down before't.
MALCOLM   'Tis his main hope;   10
    For where there is advantage to be given,   11
    Both more and less have given him the revolt,   12
    And none serve with him but constrainèd things
    Whose hearts are absent too.
MACDUFF   Let our just censures   14
    Attend the true event, and put we on   15
    Industrious soldiership.
SIWARD   The time approaches
    That will with due decision make us know
    What we shall say we have and what we owe.   18
    Thoughts speculative their unsure hopes relate,   19
    But certain issue strokes must arbitrate—   20
    Towards which advance the war.   *Exeunt, marching.*   21

❧

5.5

*Enter Macbeth, Seyton, and soldiers, with drum
and colors.*

MACBETH
    Hang out our banners on the outward walls.
    The cry is still, "They come!" Our castle's strength
    Will laugh a siege to scorn. Here let them lie
    Till famine and the ague eat them up.   4
    Were they not forced with those that should be ours,   5
    We might have met them dareful, beard to beard,   6

---

36 Skirr Scour   **44 Raze** scrape; erase.   **written troubles of** troubles recorded in   **45 oblivious** causing forgetfulness   **49 physic** medicine   **50 staff** lance or baton of office.   **52 dispatch** hurry.   **52–3 cast The water** diagnose disease by the inspection of urine   **56 Pull't off** (Refers to some part of the armor not properly put on.)   **57 senna** a purgative drug   **58 scour** purge, cleanse, rid   **60 it** i.e., the armor not yet put on   **61 bane** ruin
5.4. Location: Country near Birnam Wood.

1 Cousins Kinsmen, peers   **2 chambers . . . safe** i.e., we may sleep safely in our bedchambers.   **nothing** not at all.   **6 discovery** scouting reports   **8 no other but** no other news but that   **9 Keeps** remains.   **endure** allow, not attempt to prevent   **10 setting down before't** laying siege to it.   **11 advantage** opportunity (i.e., in military operations outside Macbeth's castle in which it is possible for would-be deserters to slip away; in a siege, his forces will be more confined to the castle and under his watchful eye)   **12 more and less** high and low   **14–15 Let . . . event** Let us postpone judgment about these uncertain matters until we've achieved our goal   **18 What . . . owe** what we only claim to have, as distinguished from what we actually have. (*Owe* can mean "own.")   **19–20 Thoughts . . . arbitrate** Speculating can only convey our sense of hope; blows must decide the actual outcome   **21 war** army.
5.5. Location: Dunsinane. Macbeth's castle.
4 the ague fever, disease   **5 forced** reinforced   **6 dareful** boldly, in open battle

And beat them backward home.

A cry within of women.
What is that noise?

SEYTON

It is the cry of women, my good lord.

[He goes to the door.]

MACBETH

I have almost forgot the taste of fears.
The time has been my senses would have cooled   10
To hear a night-shriek, and my fell of hair   11
Would at a dismal treatise rouse and stir   12
As life were in't. I have supped full with horrors;   13
Direness, familiar to my slaughterous thoughts,
Cannot once start me.

[Seyton returns.]

Wherefore was that cry?   15

SEYTON   The Queen, my lord, is dead.

MACBETH   She should have died hereafter;   17
There would have been a time for such a word.
Tomorrow, and tomorrow, and tomorrow   19
Creeps in this petty pace from day to day   20
To the last syllable of recorded time,
And all our yesterdays have lighted fools   22
The way to dusty death. Out, out, brief candle!   23
Life's but a walking shadow, a poor player
That struts and frets his hour upon the stage
And then is heard no more. It is a tale
Told by an idiot, full of sound and fury,
Signifying nothing.   28

Enter a Messenger.

Thou com'st to use thy tongue; thy story quickly.

MESSENGER   Gracious my lord,
I should report that which I say I saw,
But know not how to do't.

MACBETH   Well, say, sir.

MESSENGER

As I did stand my watch upon the hill,
I looked toward Birnam, and anon, methought,
The wood began to move.

MACBETH   Liar and slave!

MESSENGER

Let me endure your wrath if't be not so.
Within this three mile may you see it coming;
I say, a moving grove.

MACBETH   If thou speak'st false,
Upon the next tree shalt thou hang alive
Till famine cling thee. If thy speech be sooth,   40
I care not if thou dost for me as much.

I pull in resolution, and begin   42
To doubt th'equivocation of the fiend
That lies like truth. "Fear not, till Birnam Wood
Do come to Dunsinane," and now a wood
Comes toward Dunsinane. Arm, arm, and out!
If this which he avouches does appear,
There is nor flying hence nor tarrying here.
I 'gin to be aweary of the sun,
And wish th'estate o'th' world were now undone.   50
Ring the alarum bell! Blow wind, come wrack,   51
At least we'll die with harness on our back.   *Exeunt.*   52

❧

5.6

*Drum and colors. Enter Malcolm, Siward,
Macduff, and their army, with boughs.*

MALCOLM

Now near enough. Your leafy screens throw down,
And show like those you are. You, worthy uncle,   2
Shall with my cousin, your right noble son,
Lead our first battle. Worthy Macduff and we   4
Shall take upon 's what else remains to do,
According to our order.

SIWARD   Fare you well.   6
Do we but find the tyrant's power tonight,   7
Let us be beaten, if we cannot fight.

MACDUFF

Make all our trumpets speak! Give them all breath,
Those clamorous harbingers of blood and death!   10

Exeunt. Alarums continued.

❧

5.7

Enter Macbeth.

MACBETH

They have tied me to a stake. I cannot fly,
But bearlike I must fight the course. What's he   2
That was not born of woman? Such a one
Am I to fear, or none.

Enter young Siward.

YOUNG SIWARD   What is thy name?

MACBETH   Thou'lt be afraid to hear it.

YOUNG SIWARD

No, though thou call'st thyself a hotter name
Than any is in hell.

MACBETH   My name's Macbeth.

---

10 **cooled** felt the chill of terror   11 **my fell of hair** the hair of my
scalp   12 **dismal treatise** sad story   13 **As** as if   15 **start me** make
me start.   17 **She . . . hereafter** She would have died someday, or, she
should have died at some more appropriate time, freed from the
relentless pressures of the moment   19–28 **Tomorrow . . . nothing**
(For biblical echoes in this speech, see Psalms 18:28, 22:15, 90:9; Job
8:9, 14:1–2, 18:6.)   20 **in this** in at this   22 **lighted** (The metaphor is
of a candle used to light one to bed, just as life is a brief transit for
wretched mortals to their deathbeds.)   23 **dusty** (Since life, made out
of dust, returns to dust.)   40 **cling** cause to shrivel.   **sooth** truth

42 **pull in resolution** can no longer give free rein to my self-confident
determination   50 **th'estate** the settled order   51 **wrack** ruin
52 **harness** armor
5.6. Location: Dunsinane. Before Macbeth's castle.
2 **show** appear.   **uncle** i.e., Siward   4 **battle** battalion.   6 **order**
plan of battle.   7 **Do we** If we do.   **power** army   10 **harbingers**
forerunners
**5.7. Location: Before Macbeth's castle; the battle action is continu-
ous here.**
2 **course** bout or round of bearbaiting, in which the bear was tied to a
stake and dogs were set upon him.

YOUNG SIWARD
    The devil himself could not pronounce a title
    More hateful to mine ear.
MACBETH   No, nor more fearful.
YOUNG SIWARD
    Thou liest, abhorrèd tyrant! With my sword
    I'll prove the lie thou speak'st.
                            Fight, and young Siward slain.
MACBETH   Thou wast born of woman.   12
    But swords I smile at, weapons laugh to scorn,
    Brandished by man that's of a woman born.   *Exit.*

            Alarums. Enter Macduff.

MACDUFF
    That way the noise is. Tyrant, show thy face!
    If thou be'st slain, and with no stroke of mine,
    My wife and children's ghosts will haunt me still.
    I cannot strike at wretched kerns, whose arms   18
    Are hired to bear their staves. Either thou, Macbeth,   19
    Or else my sword with an unbattered edge
    I sheathe again undeeded. There thou shouldst be;   21
    By this great clatter one of greatest note
    Seems bruited. Let me find him, Fortune,   23
    And more I beg not.   *Exit. Alarums.*

            Enter Malcolm and Siward.

SIWARD
    This way, my lord. The castle's gently rendered: 25
    The tyrant's people on both sides do fight,
    The noble thanes do bravely in the war,
    The day almost itself professes yours,   28
    And little is to do.
MALCOLM   We have met with foes
    That strike beside us.
SIWARD   Enter, sir, the castle.   30
                            Exeunt. Alarum.

[5.8]

            Enter Macbeth.

MACBETH
    Why should I play the Roman fool and die   1
    On mine own sword? Whiles I see lives, the gashes   2

Do better upon them.

            Enter Macduff.

MACDUFF   Turn, hellhound, turn!
MACBETH
    Of all men else I have avoided thee.
    But get thee back! My soul is too much charged
    With blood of thine already.
MACDUFF   I have no words;
    My voice is in my sword, thou bloodier villain
    Than terms can give thee out!   *Fight. Alarum.*
MACBETH   Thou losest labor.   8
    As easy mayst thou the intrenchant air   9
    With thy keen sword impress as make me bleed.   10
    Let fall thy blade on vulnerable crests;
    I bear a charmèd life, which must not yield
    To one of woman born.
MACDUFF   Despair thy charm,   13
    And let the angel whom thou still hast served   14
    Tell thee, Macduff was from his mother's womb
    Untimely ripped.   16
MACBETH
    Accursèd be that tongue that tells me so,
    For it hath cowed my better part of man!   18
    And be these juggling fiends no more believed   19
    That palter with us in a double sense,   20
    That keep the word of promise to our ear   21
    And break it to our hope. I'll not fight with thee.   22
MACDUFF   Then yield thee, coward,
    And live to be the show and gaze o'th' time!   24
    We'll have thee, as our rarer monsters are,
    Painted upon a pole, and underwrit,   26
    "Here may you see the tyrant."
MACBETH   I will not yield
    To kiss the ground before young Malcolm's feet
    And to be baited with the rabble's curse.
    Though Birnam Wood be come to Dunsinane,
    And thou opposed, being of no woman born,
    Yet I will try the last. Before my body   32
    I throw my warlike shield. Lay on, Macduff,
    And damned be him that first cries, "Hold, enough!"   34
                    Exeunt, fighting. Alarums.

            *Enter fighting, and Macbeth slain. [Exit Macduff
            with Macbeth's body.] Retreat, and flourish. Enter,
            with drum and colors, Malcolm, Siward, Ross,
            thanes, and soldiers.*

---

12 s.d. *young Siward slain* (In some unspecified way, young Siward's body must be removed from the stage; his own father enters at line 24.1 and perceives nothing amiss, and in 5.8.38 young Siward is reported *missing* in action. Perhaps Macbeth drags off the body, or perhaps it is removed by soldiers during the alarums.)   18 kerns (Properly, Irish foot soldiers; here, applied contemptuously to the rank and file.)   19 staves spears.   Either thou i.e., Either I find you and sheathe my sword in you   21 undeeded having seen no action. shouldst be ought to be (judging by the noise)   23 bruited announced.   25 gently rendered surrendered without fighting 28 professes declares itself   30 strike beside us fight on our side, or miss us deliberately.
5.8. Location: Before Macbeth's castle, as the battle continues; after line 34, within the castle.
1 Roman fool i.e., suicide, like Brutus, Mark Antony, and others
2 Whiles . . . lives i.e., As long as I see any enemy living

8 give thee out name you, describe you.   9 intrenchant that cannot be cut, indivisible   10 impress make an impression on   13 Despair Despair of   14 angel evil angel, Macbeth's genius.   still always 16 Untimely prematurely, i.e., by Caesarian delivery   18 better . . . man i.e., courage.   19 juggling deceiving   20 palter . . . sense equivocate with us   21–2 That . . . hope that make promises we hear (and think we understand) but then break promise with what we hoped and expected.   24 gaze o'th' time spectacle or sideshow of the age. 26 Painted . . . pole i.e., painted on a board or cloth and suspended on a pole   32 the last i.e., my last resort: my own strength and resolution.   34.3 *Retreat* a trumpet call ordering an end to the fighting. 34.3–4 *Enter, with drum and colors, etc.* (The remainder of the play is perhaps imagined as taking place in Macbeth's castle and could be marked as a separate scene. In Shakespeare's theater, however, the shift is so nonrepresentational and without scenic alteration that the action is virtually continuous.)

MALCOLM
    I would the friends we miss were safe arrived.
SIWARD
    Some must go off; and yet, by these I see   36
    So great a day as this is cheaply bought.
MALCOLM
    Macduff is missing, and your noble son.
ROSS   [to Siward]
    Your son, my lord, has paid a soldier's debt.
    He only lived but till he was a man,
    The which no sooner had his prowess confirmed
    In the unshrinking station where he fought,   42
    But like a man he died.
SIWARD   Then he is dead?
ROSS
    Ay, and brought off the field. Your cause of sorrow
    Must not be measured by his worth, for then
    It hath no end.
SIWARD   Had he his hurts before?
ROSS
    Ay, on the front.
SIWARD   Why then, God's soldier be he!
    Had I as many sons as I have hairs
    I would not wish them to a fairer death.
    And so, his knell is knolled.
MALCOLM   He's worth more sorrow,
    And that I'll spend for him.
SIWARD   He's worth no more.
    They say he parted well and paid his score,   52
    And so, God be with him! Here comes newer comfort.

    Enter Macduff, with Macbeth's head.

36 go off die.   **by these** to judge by these (assembled)   **42 unshrink-
ing station** post from which he did not shrink   **52 parted** departed,
died.   **score** reckoning

MACDUFF
    Hail, King! For so thou art. Behold where stands   54
    Th'usurper's cursèd head. The time is free.   55
    I see thee compassed with thy kingdom's pearl,   56
    That speak my salutation in their minds,
    Whose voices I desire aloud with mine:
    Hail, King of Scotland!
ALL   Hail, King of Scotland!   *Flourish.*
MALCOLM
    We shall not spend a large expense of time
    Before we reckon with your several loves   62
    And make us even with you. My thanes and kinsmen,   63
    Henceforth be earls, the first that ever Scotland
    In such an honor named. What's more to do
    Which would be planted newly with the time,   66
    As calling home our exiled friends abroad
    That fled the snares of watchful tyranny,
    Producing forth the cruel ministers   69
    Of this dead butcher and his fiendlike queen—
    Who, as 'tis thought, by self and violent hands   71
    Took off her life—this, and what needful else
    That calls upon us, by the grace of Grace
    We will perform in measure, time, and place.
    So, thanks to all at once and to each one,
    Whom we invite to see us crowned at Scone.   76
                        Flourish. Exeunt omnes.

54 stands i.e., on a pole   **55 free** released from tyranny.   **56 com-
passed . . . pearl** surrounded by the nobles of your kingdom
(literally, the pearls encircling a crown)   **62 reckon** come to a
reckoning.   **several** individual   **63 make . . . you** repay your worthiness.   **66 would . . . time** should be established at the commencement of this new era   **69 Producing forth** bringing forward to
trial.   **ministers** agents   **71 self and violent** her own violent
76.1 *omnes* all.

Timon of Athens

*T*imon of Athens is Shakespeare's most relentless study in misanthropy. It expresses, with *King Lear*, a moral outrage at human depravity but refuses to soften anger with compassionate tears. The protagonist learns little other than bitterness from his encounters with avarice and ingratitude. In its mordant vision of human folly, *Timon of Athens* resembles a number of other Roman or classical plays. As in *Julius Caesar, Coriolanus*, and *Troilus and Cressida*, and to a lesser extent *Titus Andronicus*, the dominant mood is one of futility. Political conflicts end in stalemate or a victory for opportunists; the populace and their leaders are fickle and craven; private virtues of noble men must yield to crass considerations of statecraft. Banishment or self-exile is too often the reward of those who have given their lives to public service. Shakespeare's misanthropic vision in *Timon of Athens* is, then, integral to his portrayal of humanity's political and social nature in the ancient classical world. This is a world to which Shakespeare turned often during his writing career, especially during the period from about 1599 to 1608. As a group, the Roman and classical plays tend to differ from the great tragedies written during this same period (*Hamlet, Othello, King Lear, Macbeth*) in that the classical plays focus on a sardonic and dispiriting view of life's tragic absurdity. Even in *Antony and Cleopatra*, in which Shakespeare offers us an ennobling dream of greatness to offset the worldly failure of his protagonists, the arena of human conflict remains pitiless and disillusioning. *Timon of Athens* offers little compensatory vision; despite the attempts of Flavius and Alcibiades to ameliorate matters, the play remains bleak and dispiriting right to the very end.

Timon of Athens appears to have been written between 1605 and 1608. Evidently Shakespeare collaborated with Thomas Middleton in writing this play. Although the evidence is chiefly internal, and although specific attributions of various parts of the play to one writer or the other remain in dispute, Middleton's style reveals itself in char-

acteristic sexual wordplay and Calvinist moralizing. Shakespeare appears to have been the senior partner at all events, the initiator and deviser of the overall scheme, so that, with qualifications, we can study the play as an integral part of the Shakespeare canon. It is often grouped with *King Lear* (c. 1605) on grounds of stylistic and thematic similarity. For its chief source, it uses Thomas North's translation of Plutarch's *Lives of the Noble Grecians and Romans*, a source also for *Julius Caesar, Antony and Cleopatra, Coriolanus*, and parts of other plays. *Timon of Athens* also makes use, through intermediary versions, of the dialogue called *Timon*, or *The Misanthrope*, by the Greek satirist Lucian. The play may not have been produced; the text, not printed until the 1623 Folio, appears to have been taken from the author's unfinished manuscript, with contradictory uncanceled lines (see Timon's will, 5.4.70–3), unresolved discrepancies as to the amount of money Timon gives or requests, and passages of half-versified prose. Whatever the exact date and circumstance of composition, the play certainly belongs to a period in Shakespeare's artistic career devoted to an unsparing portrayal of human villainy and corruption. The collaboration with Middleton may have given particular impetus to this. Like *Troilus and Cressida, Timon of Athens* defies the conventional categories of tragedy, comedy, and history. Generically, the play stands chiefly between tragedy and satire in its preoccupation with dying and sterility. The play portrays a tragic fall from greatness, and presents us with a tragic hero who learns through suffering, but the learning is less about the hero himself than about the failings of humanity. Moreover, Timon's shift from fulsome generosity to embittered misogyny deprives him of the sympathy that is essential to a fully tragic protagonist; as Apemantus says to Timon, "The middle of humanity thou never knewest, but the extremity of both ends" (4.3.305–6). The vision is thus primarily satiric rather than cathartic in its exposure of an unfeeling society. Satire prompts a comic response; we are invited to laugh sardonically at the hypocrisies of Timon's fair-weather friends, and even Timon is himself a problematic figure. The resemblance of his eventual dwelling place *"in the woods"* outside Athens (4.3.0.1) to the forest outside Athens in *A Midsummer Night's Dream* accentuates the difference in genre between romantic comedy and a dark, brooding satire. The play is also a history, drawn from historical sources, as its Folio title, *The Life of Timon of Athens*, suggests. We ought to see or read it with the expectations not simply of tragedy but also of satire and ironic history.

As a genre, in fact, the play most resembles those works that the Painter and the Poet wish to offer Timon himself: a "moral painting" and a "satire against the softness of prosperity" (1.1.95 and 5.1.32–3). Such a deliberately old-fashioned genre recalls the medieval morality plays and the "hybrid" morality plays of the 1570s and 1580s, like Thomas Lupton's *All for Money* (c. 1577) or Thomas Lodge and Robert Greene's *A Looking Glass for London and England* (1587–1591), which inveigh against usury and the neglect of military heroes. John Marston's later quasi-morality, *Histriomastix* (c. 1599), proclaims the decline of civilization through worldly insolence. Ben Jonson's *Volpone* (1605–1606), though "comical" rather than "tragical" in its satire, similarly castigates human greed. The *Parnassus* trilogy (1598–1603), a series of three mordantly satirical plays written to be acted by students at Cambridge, indulges in a massive venting of spleen against a philistine culture. Satire against governmental policies and politicians led to reprisals in the form of prohibitions, imprisonments, and book burning. *Timon of Athens*, though not topically controversial in this sense, follows a tradition of social satire derived from both English and classical models. Like most satire of the 1600s, both dramatic and nondramatic, it is crabbed in style, features a railing protagonist, and denounces through exaggerated caricature an ugly array of types representing a broad social spectrum. The genre of satiric morality play accords well with the play's acerbic view of decadence and "softness."

Human greed, with which *Timon of Athens* is so occupied, lends itself readily to satiric treatment. Avarice does not ordinarily seem terrifying at first, like the spiritual sins of jealousy or prideful ambition as portrayed in *Othello* and *Macbeth*; instead, it is disgusting, ludicrous, and incredibly tenacious. Avarice is, after all, one of the Deadly Sins. Chaucer, in his "Pardoner's Tale," follows a long tradition of medieval commentary in referring to Avarice as the pivotal Sin, the *radix malorum*, or root of all evils. Along with Pride and Envy, it is one of the sins of the spirit. It is insidious and all-embracing. We see its corrupting effects in Timon's friends. Those who sponge off him and then desert him are quick to return when he is rumored to have found gold in his exile. Greed is also self-deceiving and hypocritical. Many are the excuses offered for failing to come to Timon's aid: one friend rates Timon as a bad credit risk, another happens to be short of ready cash at the moment, a third insists that Timon's generosity to him wasn't as great as people suppose, and so on. No wonder Timon feels he must devise for such hypocrites a suitable comeuppance, consisting of a farewell banquet in which their crass expectations are rewarded with a mocking litany of curses and a dinner of water and stones.

Appropriately for this satirical depiction of human greed, the characters are virtually all types or social abstractions. Several represent the crafts and professions and are abstractly labeled as such: the Poet, the Painter, the Jeweler, the Merchant. Others are "flattering lords" or "false friends" or "thieves." Seldom in Shakespeare do we find so many characters without proper names. They are depersonalized, and we are distanced from them. Apemantus is another type, a "churlish philosopher," recognizable in all his appearances by this one feature; we learn little about him other than that he professes to scoff at worldliness with a scabrous wit, derived in part from legends about Diogenes the Cynic philosopher and other devotees of an extravagantly simple mode of life. Abstraction of this sort is close to allegory, especially an allegory of social malaise. Timon himself becomes a type in his conversion to misanthropy, "infected," as Apemantus says, by "A poor unmanly melancholy sprung / From change of fortune" (4.3.204–6). Apemantus's remark appeals to a view of personality as governed by "humors" or dominant traits, such as melancholy or irascibility, which are generated by imbalance in the body of the four "humors": blood, phlegm, bile, and black bile. Images of disease and cannibalism, prominent throughout the play, are often derived from such "humorous" imbalances. The imagery also associates character types, as in Jonson's *Volpone*, with various beasts: the lion, the fox, the ass, the wolf, the bear, and, most of all, the dog.

The nearly total absence of women in the play adds greatly to its bleakness; the tone of the play is distinctly misogynistic as well as misanthropic. Timon addresses the two women named Phrynia and Timandra who appear before him with Alcibiades as "whores" (4.3.84, 142, 170), linking them imagistically with that "common whore of mankind" called gold (line 43). The women are indeed Alcibiades's mistresses, and are content to put up with Timon's sermonizing as long as he pays them: "More counsel with more money, bounteous Timon" (line 169). Timon's invective against them, as against women generally and all of mankind as well, is rife with images of venereal infection, painful attempts at cures, and the devastating physical consequences of the advanced stages of the disease: a collapsed nose, baldness, boneache, and sterility (see lines 145–66). The ladies who enter as Amazons in the masque at Timon's house in Act 1, scene 2 remain silent other than in a brief expression of thanks for their handsome entertainment; they function as tokens of idle evening pleasure, evoking from Apemantus an outburst against a "sweep of vanity" (1.2.131). The misogyny remains unalleviated by any positive example.

By means of such techniques, Shakespeare portrays those whom Timon comes to despise with a seemingly intentional one-sidedness; the caricatures of avarice are vivid and amusing, with little allowance for subtlety or change. The plot, too, is, by Shakespeare's standard, unusually lacking in complication: Timon discovers the ingratitude and greed of his fellow humans and retires from a world he can no longer tolerate, breathing upon it his dying curse. The dramatic tension of this uneventful story lies instead in Timon's own tortured spiritual saga, in the painful process of realization, in the revulsion, the refusal to compromise, the spurning even of honest friendship, the bitter renunciation and longing for oblivion. Alcibiades, too, is a character who interests us, offering as he does the alternatives of vengeful action against an ungrateful world or of successful conciliation. Then, too, the debate between Apemantus and Timon in which Timon rejects even the companionship of one who wishes, like him, to be the castigator of a corrupt world (4.3.200–402), is an essential part of Timon's working toward total rejection of hope. The true drama of such philosophical debate is increasingly contrasted with a static and superficial society toward which we are asked to feel revulsion.

There are no villains in *Timon of Athens*, though there are plenty of weak and foolish people. What is depressing about greed, in fact, is its insidious normality. Those who desert Timon have many prudent arguments on their side. After all, his original generosity is excessive and reckless. If his friends take advantage of him, they can at least say they have tried to warn him. Even a fool can see what lies in store. Much of Timon's wealth goes into drunken and gluttonous debauchery, into "feasts, pomps, and vainglories" (1.2.247–8). Timon does not know how to use prosperity wisely, and even his loyal servants deplore the "riot" (2.2.3). He is deaf to the friendly counsel of his steward, Flavius. For one who is so open-handed, Timon is surprisingly churlish with his creditors. And is he not presumptuous to assume that his friends will come to his aid when such vast sums are needed? Are they to be blamed for not emulating his prodigal decline into poverty? Clearly, Timon expects too much. We readily though sadly perceive, as do all Timon's friends, that commerce is a god worshiped by all; need he be so shocked at this? As bystanders, we share with Timon's choric servants the certainty that his large requests for help will be refused. And yet, no matter how stupid or blind Timon may be, the desertion of him is still monstrous. Timon suffers, partly at least, from being an idealist, in expecting that people will repay kindness with

gratitude. Even Timon's well-intentioned servants know all too well that most people are not like that.

Timon thus tears himself apart in a rage at what we consider the way of the world. We find his misanthropy intemperate, and yet we cannot help being moved by his sweeping indictment of human pettiness and inhumanity. Timon's furor carries him beyond satire. He is, like Lear, all the more clear-sighted for being near to madness. Wisdom and folly exchange places, as Apemantus's friend the Fool has already pointed out (2.2.99–120). In Timon's nearly mad vision, beggars and lords are interchangeable, distinguished only by wealth and position. Love of gold, he sees, inverts everything decent in human life, making "Black white, foul fair, wrong right, / Base noble, old young, coward valiant" (4.3.29–30). Thieves and whores are at least more honest than their counterparts in everyday life, the respectable citizens of Athens and their wives, and so Timon mockingly rewards the thieves and insults the hypocrites. Yet Timon also inveighs furiously against women and all sexuality in a way that suggests feelings of betrayal. Though women occupy virtually no place in Timon's life, he himself has sought to displace women by serving as the generous source of comfort for all his friends—a self-created and narcissistic role that is destined to collapse into self-hatred and dread of all human feeling. His curse embraces the cosmos as well as humanity, inverting all semblance of hierarchical order: obedience must turn to rebellion, fidelity to incontinence, virginity to lasciviousness. "Degrees, observances, customs, and laws" must "Decline to your confounding contraries" (4.1.19–20). Clothing and cosmetics must be stripped away, as in *King Lear*, so that human monstrosity may be revealed for what it truly is.

Three persons, Apemantus, Alcibiades, and Flavius, serve as chief foils to Timon in his estrangement from humanity. Apemantus the Cynic, who first taught Timon to rail at greed, now counsels him to find stoic contentment in renunciation of desire or, conversely, to thrive as a flatterer by preying on those who have undone him (4.3.200–34). Alcibiades, the military commander banished by an ungrateful Athenian Senate for presuming to beg the life of one who had rashly shed blood in a quarrel, offers Timon the example of revenge against his enemies; subsequently, he offers Athens the olive branch with the sword, making "war breed peace" (5.4.83), in an accommodating move that is important for the conclusion of the play and its final mitigating tone. Timon, although resembling both men as railer and as victim of ingratitude, rejects their counsels as too politic, too worldly. His stand is unflinching, absolute, so lacking in compromise that his sole choice can be to curse, die, and hope for oblivion. Only Flavius, his steward, offers brief consolation. Flavius comes to him, like Kent to King Lear, offering love and service in exile. Flavius even speaks in paradoxes reminiscent of *King Lear*, calling Timon "My dearest lord, blest to be most accurst, / Rich only to be wretched" (4.2.43–4). These are precious words, showing that humanity is not utterly irredeemable. Still, this consolation is evidently too late to offset the nightmarish truth that Timon has learned. Timon experiences little of the compassionate love that comes to Lear in his madness, but he at least faces the bleakness of human existence with unbending honesty.

Stage productions in recent years have sought out instructive visual contrasts between the complacent prosperity of the play's first half and the apocalyptic barrenness of Timon's isolated hermitage at the end. The first half works easily in modern dress. Timon in his prosperity has appeared in black-tie evening dress among his money-conscious acquaintances, as in Trevor Nunn's 1971 Young Vic production with David Suchet as Timon. At other times Timon has been represented as a Texas oil tycoon (Jerry Turner's production at Ashland, Oregon, in 1978). Gregory Doran, at Stratford-upon-Avon in 1999, provided a nightclub atmosphere complete with a nightclub pianist, music by Duke Ellington, Apemantus as a master of ceremonies in dark glasses and with a wireless microphone, and a show of Cupid with Amazons in male drag. Conversely, the play's second half has invited desolation: Timon in a loincloth (Michael Pennington in Doran's 1999 production), Timon taking up his abode in a burned-out truck chassis from an automobile graveyard (Larry Yando, directed by Barbara Gaines at the Chicago Shakespeare Theatre in 2000), Timon in the ruins of a dilapidated theater building (Peter Brook's production at Les-Bouffes-du-Nord, Paris, in 1973). Through such contrastive settings, this sometimes neglected play has been shown to have a devastating relevance for a postmodern world of disillusionment.

Timon of Athens

The Actors' Names

TIMON OF ATHENS
LUCIUS *and* ⎱ *two flattering lords*
LUCULLUS, ⎰
SEMPRONIUS, *another flattering lord*
VENTIDIUS, *one of Timon's false friends*
APEMANTUS, *a churlish philosopher*
ALCIBIADES, *an Athenian captain*
[PHRYNIA, ⎱ *mistresses of Alcibiades*
TIMANDRA, ⎰
AN OLD ATHENIAN]
Certain SENATORS [*and* LORDS]
[FLAVIUS, *steward to Timon*]
POET, PAINTER, JEWELER, [*and*] MERCHANT
FLAMINIUS, *one of Timon's servants*
[LUCILIUS, *another*]
SERVILIUS, *another*

CAPHIS,
PHILOTUS'S [SERVANT],
TITUS'S [SERVANT], ⎱ *several servants*
HORTENSIUS'S [SERVANT], ⎰ *to usurers*
[ISIDORE'S SERVANT, [*Timon's creditors*]
Two of] VARRO'S [SERVANTS],
[A PAGE
A FOOL
Three STRANGERS
Two MESSENGERS]
Certain THIEVES [*or* BANDITTI]
CUPID [*and*] *certain* MASKERS [*as Amazons*]

With divers other Servants and Attendants, [*other Lords, Officers, Soldiers*]

[SCENE: *Athens, and the neighboring woods*]

1.1

Enter Poet, Painter, Jeweler, and Merchant, at several doors. [The Poet and Painter form one group, the Jeweler and Merchant another.]

POET　Good day, sir.

PAINTER　I am glad you're well.

POET

I have not seen you long. How goes the world?　3

PAINTER

It wears, sir, as it grows.

POET　　　　　　　　　　　　　Ay, that's well known.　4
But what particular rarity? What strange,　5
Which manifold record not matches? See,　6
Magic of bounty, all these spirits thy power　7
Hath conjured to attend! I know the merchant.

PAINTER

I know them both. Th'other's a jeweler.

MERCHANT [*to the Jeweler*]
Oh, 'tis a worthy lord!

JEWELER　　　　　　　　　　Nay, that's most fixed.　10

MERCHANT

A most incomparable man, breathed, as it were,　11
To an untirable and continuate goodness.　12
He passes.　13

JEWELER　I have a jewel here—

MERCHANT

Oh, pray, let's see't. For the Lord Timon, sir?

JEWELER

If he will touch the estimate. But for that—　16

POET [*reciting to himself*]
"When we for recompense have praised the vile,
It stains the glory in that happy verse　18
Which aptly sings the good."

MERCHANT [*looking at the jewel*]　'Tis a good form.　19

JEWELER　And rich. Here is a water, look ye.　20

PAINTER [*to the Poet*]
You are rapt, sir, in some work, some dedication　21
To the great lord.

POET　　　　　　　　　　A thing slipped idly from me.　22
Our poesy is as a gum which oozes　23
From whence 'tis nourished. The fire i'th' flint　24

Shows not till it be struck; our gentle flame
Provokes itself and like the current flies　26
Each bound it chafes. What have you there?　27

PAINTER

A picture, sir. When comes your book forth?

POET

Upon the heels of my presentment, sir.　29
Let's see your piece.　　　[*He examines the painting.*]

PAINTER　'Tis a good piece.

POET

So 'tis. This comes off well and excellent.

PAINTER

Indifferent.

POET　　　　　　　Admirable! How this grace　33
Speaks his own standing! What a mental power　34
This eye shoots forth! How big imagination　35
Moves in this lip! To th' dumbness of the gesture　36
One might interpret.　37

PAINTER

It is a pretty mocking of the life.　38
Here is a touch; is't good?

POET　　　　　　　　　　I will say of it,
It tutors nature. Artificial strife　40
Lives in these touches, livelier than life.

Enter certain Senators.

PAINTER　How this lord is followed!

POET

The senators of Athens. Happy man!

PAINTER　Look, more!
　　　　　[*The Senators pass over the stage, and exeunt.*]

POET

You see this confluence, this great flood of visitors.
　　　　　　　　　　　　　[*He shows his poem.*]
I have in this rough work shaped out a man
Whom this beneath world doth embrace and hug　47
With amplest entertainment. My free drift　48
Halts not particularly, but moves itself　49
In a wide sea of tax. No leveled malice　50
Infects one comma in the course I hold,　51
But flies an eagle flight, bold and forth on,　52
Leaving no tract behind.　53

PAINTER　How shall I understand you?　54

POET　I will unbolt to you.　55

1.1. Location: Athens. Timon's house.
0.2 *several* separate　**3 long** for a long time.　**How . . . world?** i.e., How are things? (But the Painter quibbles on the literal sense.)　**4 wears** decays.　**grows** ages.　**5 rarity** unusual occurrence.　**strange** strange event　**6 Which . . . matches** which all recorded history cannot equal.　**7 Magic of bounty** the remarkable attractive power of generosity.　**spirits** i.e., beings, persons (spoken of as if they were spirits conjured by magic)　**10 worthy lord** i.e., Timon.　**fixed** certain.　**11 breathed** conditioned or trained so as not to be wearied (as one "breathes" horses by exercising them)　**12 untirable and continuate** inexhaustible and habitual　**13 passes** surpasses.　**16 touch the estimate** offer or meet the price.　**18 happy** felicitous, matching truthful praise to a worthy object　**19 form** shape, appearance. (Refers to the jewel.)　**20 water** luster　**21 dedication** (Such works were regularly dedicated to great nobles.)　**22 idly** casually　**23–4 Our . . . nourished** The poetry we write oozes like gummy sap from the tree that nourishes it.　**24 The fire i'th' flint** (Flint, struck against a stone, yields a spark, and so may seem to have fire latent in it.)

26 Provokes itself is self-generating　**26–7 flies . . . chafes** seeks escape from the riverbanks that confine it.　**29 Upon . . . presentment** As soon as I have presented it (to Lord Timon, in hopes of obtaining his patronage)　**33 Indifferent** Not bad, so-so.　**this grace** i.e., of the person in the picture　**34 Speaks . . . standing** conveys the dignity of its subject.　**35 big** largely　**36–7 To . . . interpret** One might easily supply words to express this silent gesture.　**38 mocking** mirroring　**40 Artificial strife** The striving of art to surpass nature　**47 beneath** sublunar, beneath the moon　**48 entertainment** welcome.　**drift** design　**49 Halts not particularly** doesn't concern itself with criticizing anyone individually　**50 tax** censure. (The Poet's defense of satire is a familiar one from classical poets like Horace and neoclassicists like Ben Jonson, that the satirist is a moral guardian of society who is entitled to free speech so long as he satirizes types of abuses rather than libeling individuals.)　**leveled** aimed, as a gun is aimed at a particular object　**51 comma** i.e., detail　**52 forth on** straight on　**53 tract** track, trace　**54 How . . . you?** What do you mean?　**55 unbolt** unlock, interpret

You see how all conditions, how all minds,   56
As well of glib and slippery creatures as
Of grave and austere quality, tender down   58
Their services to Lord Timon. His large fortune,
Upon his good and gracious nature hanging,   60
Subdues and properties to his love and tendance   61
All sorts of hearts; yea, from the glass-faced flatterer   62
To Apemantus, that few things loves better
Than to abhor himself—even he drops down
The knee before him and returns in peace   65
Most rich in Timon's nod.   66
PAINTER   I saw them speak together.
POET
    Sir, I have upon a high and pleasant hill
    Feigned Fortune to be throned. The base o'th' mount   69
    Is ranked with all deserts, all kind of natures,   70
    That labor on the bosom of this sphere   71
    To propagate their states. Amongst them all   72
    Whose eyes are on this sovereign lady fixed,
    One do I personate of Lord Timon's frame,   74
    Whom Fortune with her ivory hand wafts to her,   75
    Whose present grace to present slaves and servants   76
    Translates his rivals.
PAINTER   'Tis conceived to scope.   77
    This throne, this Fortune, and this hill, methinks,
    With one man beckoned from the rest below,
    Bowing his head against the steepy mount   80
    To climb his happiness, would be well expressed   81
    In our condition.
POET   Nay, sir, but hear me on.   82
    All those which were his fellows but of late—
    Some better than his value—on the moment   84
    Follow his strides, his lobbies fill with tendance,   85
    Rain sacrificial whisperings in his ear,   86
    Make sacred even his stirrup, and through him   87
    Drink the free air.
PAINTER   Ay, marry, what of these?   88
POET
    When Fortune in her shift and change of mood

Spurns down her late beloved, all his dependents,   90
Which labored after him to the mountain's top
Even on their knees and hands, let him slip down,
Not one accompanying his declining foot.
PAINTER   'Tis common.
    A thousand moral paintings I can show   95
    That shall demonstrate these quick blows of Fortune's
    More pregnantly than words. Yet you do well
    To show Lord Timon that mean eyes have seen   98
    The foot above the head.   99

    Trumpets sound. Enter Lord Timon, addressing
    himself courteously to every suitor; [a Messenger
    from Ventidius talking with him; Lucilius and
    other servants following].

TIMON   Imprisoned is he, say you?
MESSENGER
    Ay, my good lord. Five talents is his debt,   101
    His means most short, his creditors most strait.   102
    Your honorable letter he desires   103
    To those have shut him up, which failing   104
    Periods his comfort.
TIMON   Noble Ventidius! Well,   105
    I am not of that feather to shake off   106
    My friend when he must need me. I do know him   107
    A gentleman that well deserves a help,
    Which he shall have. I'll pay the debt and free him.
MESSENGER   Your Lordship ever binds him.   110
TIMON
    Commend me to him. I will send his ransom;
    And being enfranchised, bid him come to me.   112
    'Tis not enough to help the feeble up,
    But to support him after. Fare you well.   114
MESSENGER   All happiness to Your Honor!   *Exit.*

    Enter an Old Athenian.

OLD ATHENIAN
    Lord Timon, hear me speak.
TIMON   Freely, good father.   116
OLD ATHENIAN
    Thou hast a servant named Lucilius.
TIMON   I have so. What of him?
OLD ATHENIAN
    Most noble Timon, call the man before thee.
TIMON
    Attends he here or no? Lucilius!

56 **conditions** ranks, temperaments   58 **quality** nature.   **tender down** tender, offer   60 **hanging** depending. (The Poet suggests that good nature counts for little without a large fortune to attend it.) 61 **properties** appropriates.   **love and tendance** loving and being in attendance on him   62 **glass-faced** reflecting superficially the tastes and whims of his patron   65 **returns** departs   66 **in Timon's nod** for having been acknowledged by Timon.   69 **Feigned** imagined, supposed   70 **ranked . . . deserts** filled with persons of all degrees of merit standing in ranks   71 **this sphere** i.e., the earth   72 **propagate their states** enlarge their fortunes.   74 **personate** represent.   **frame** mold, shape   75 **ivory** white.   **wafts** beckons, waves   76–7 **Whose . . . rivals** whose (Fortune's) present gracious favor transforms his (Timon's) rivals immediately into followers and servants.   77 **to scope** to the purpose, in correct proportion.   80 **Bowing his head** i.e., bending forward with the effort.   **steepy** steep   81 **his happiness** to his good fortune   81–2 **would . . . condition** would find a striking parallel in the human condition.   82 **hear me on** hear me speak further.   84 **better . . . value** of more worth, and worth more, than he. **on the moment** immediately   85 **his lobbies . . . tendance** fill the anterooms of his house with their attentive presence   86 **Rain . . . ear** whisper reverentially to him as if he were a god to be sacrificed to   87 **stirrup** i.e., as they help him to his horse   87–8 **through . . . air** seem to breathe the free air only through his bounty.   88 **marry** (A mild oath, originally "By the Virgin Mary.")

90 **Spurns down** kicks or thrusts down   95 **moral paintings** paintings pointing out a moral   98 **mean eyes** even the eyes of persons of low degree   99 **The foot . . . head** i.e., highest fortune tumbling headlong downward by the turn of Fortune's wheel, or, the foot of Fortune poised over the head of the once-prosperous man.   101 **talents** units of money today worth $2,000 or more. (But Shakespeare was evidently uncertain about the *talent's* value as he wrote this play. *Talents* is also a biblical term; see, for example, Matthew 2:14–29.) 102 **short** limited.   **strait** severe, exacting.   103 **Your . . . letter** A letter from your honor   104 **those** those who   104–5 **which failing Periods** the lack of which puts an end to   106 **feather** i.e., disposition (as in "birds of a feather")   107 **know him** know him to be   110 **binds him** i.e., to grateful obligation.   112 **enfranchised** set free 114 **But** i.e., but one must continue   116 **Freely** Readily, gladly. **father** (Respectful term of address to an old man.)

LUCILIUS   Here, at Your Lordship's service.

OLD ATHENIAN
This fellow here, Lord Timon, this thy creature,   122
By night frequents my house. I am a man
That from my first have been inclined to thrift,
And my estate deserves an heir more raised   125
Than one which holds a trencher.

TIMON   Well, what further?   126

OLD ATHENIAN
One only daughter have I, no kin else
On whom I may confer what I have got.   128
The maid is fair, o'th' youngest for a bride,   129
And I have bred her at my dearest cost   130
In qualities of the best. This man of thine
Attempts her love. I prithee, noble lord,   132
Join with me to forbid him her resort;   133
Myself have spoke in vain.

TIMON   The man is honest.

OLD ATHENIAN   Therefore he will be, Timon.   136
His honesty rewards him in itself;
It must not bear my daughter.   138

TIMON   Does she love him?

OLD ATHENIAN   She is young and apt.   140
Our own precedent passions do instruct us   141
What levity's in youth.

TIMON [to Lucilius]   Love you the maid?

LUCILIUS
Ay, my good lord, and she accepts of it.   143

OLD ATHENIAN
If in her marriage my consent is missing,
I call the gods to witness, I will choose
Mine heir from forth the beggars of the world
And dispossess her all.   147

TIMON   How shall she be endowed   148
If she be mated with an equal husband?   149

OLD ATHENIAN
Three talents on the present; in future, all.   150

TIMON
This gentleman of mine hath served me long;
To build his fortune I will strain a little,
For 'tis a bond in men. Give him thy daughter.   153
What you bestow, in him I'll counterpoise,   154
And make him weigh with her.

OLD ATHENIAN   Most noble lord,   155
Pawn me to this your honor, she is his.   156

TIMON
My hand to thee; mine honor on my promise.

LUCILIUS
Humbly I thank Your Lordship. Never may
That state or fortune fall into my keeping   159
Which is not owed to you!   160

                Exeunt [Lucilius and Old Athenian].

POET [presenting his poem]
Vouchsafe my labor, and long live Your Lordship!   161

TIMON
I thank you; you shall hear from me anon.   162
Go not away.—What have you there, my friend?

PAINTER
A piece of painting, which I do beseech   164
Your Lordship to accept.   [He presents his painting.]

TIMON   Painting is welcome.
The painting is almost the natural man;   166
For since dishonor traffics with man's nature,   167
He is but outside; these penciled figures are   168
Even such as they give out. I like your work,   169
And you shall find I like it. Wait attendance   170
Till you hear further from me.

PAINTER   The gods preserve ye!

TIMON
Well fare you, gentleman. Give me your hand;
We must needs dine together.—Sir, your jewel   173
Hath suffered under praise.

JEWELER   What, my lord, dispraise?   174

TIMON
A mere satiety of commendations.   175
If I should pay you for't as 'tis extolled,
It would unclew me quite.

JEWELER   My lord, 'tis rated   177
As those which sell would give; but you well know   178
Things of like value differing in the owners
Are prizèd by their masters. Believe't, dear lord,   180
You mend the jewel by the wearing it.
                [He presents a jewel.]

TIMON   Well mocked.   182

MERCHANT
No, my good lord, he speaks the common tongue   183
Which all men speak with him.

                Enter Apemantus.

TIMON   Look who comes here. Will you be chid?   185

JEWELER   We'll bear, with Your Lordship.   186

MERCHANT   He'll spare none.

---

122 **creature** dependent, hanger-on   125 **more raised** of higher social position   126 **holds a trencher** i.e., serves at table, handling wooden dishes.   128 **got** acquired.   129 **o'th'... bride** just of marriageable age   130 **bred ... cost** brought her up at great expense   132 **Attempts** tries to win   133 **her resort** access to her   136 **Therefore ... be** If he really is honest he will continue to be so for honesty's sake   138 **bear my daughter** carry off my daughter into the bargain.   140 **apt** easily wooed, impressionable.   141 **precedent** former (when we were young)   143 **accepts of** accepts   147 **all** wholly.   148 **How ... endowed** What dowry will she be given   149 **an equal husband** one of equal estate.   150 **on the present** immediately   153 **bond in** obligation among   154 **counterpoise** match, counterbalance   155 **weigh with her** be equal to her in estate.   156 **Pawn ... honor** If you'll pledge your word of honor to do as you have said

159 **That** i.e., any   160 **owed to you** acknowledged to be from you.   161 **Vouchsafe** Deign to accept   162 **anon** shortly.   164 **piece** example, specimen   166–9 **The painting ... out** Painting reveals the truth about human nature; for, since deception is inherent in human nature, our outward appearances necessarily conceal much within, whereas paintings are exactly what they show themselves to be.   170 **Wait** Remain in   173 **must needs** must   174 **Hath ... praise** has been overvalued, to the would-be purchaser's disadvantage. (But the Jeweler misunderstands as "suffered underpraise.")   175 **mere** utter   177 **unclew** unwind, i.e., ruin   178 **As ... give** at a price which merchants would pay, i.e., at cost   180 **prizèd ... masters** valued differently by different owners. (Accordingly, the gem will increase in value because Timon will wear it.)   182 **Well mocked** A well-turned bit of flattery, well counterfeited.   183 **common tongue** general opinion   185 **Will you be chid?** Are you prepared to be scolded?   186 **We'll .. Lordship** i.e., We'll put up with it if Your Lordship can.

TIMON
 Good morrow to thee, gentle Apemantus!
APEMANTUS
 Till I be gentle, stay thou for thy good morrow— 189
 When thou art Timon's dog, and these knaves honest. 190
TIMON
 Why dost thou call them knaves? Thou know'st them
 not.
APEMANTUS Are they not Athenians?
TIMON Yes.
APEMANTUS Then I repent not. 194
JEWELER You know me, Apemantus?
APEMANTUS Thou know'st I do. I called thee by thy 196
 name. 197
TIMON Thou art proud, Apemantus.
APEMANTUS Of nothing so much as that I am not like
 Timon.
TIMON Whither art going?
APEMANTUS To knock out an honest Athenian's brains.
TIMON That's a deed thou'lt die for.
APEMANTUS Right, if doing nothing be death by th' law. 204
TIMON How lik'st thou this picture, Apemantus?
APEMANTUS The best, for the innocence. 206
TIMON Wrought he not well that painted it?
APEMANTUS He wrought better that made the painter,
 and yet he's but a filthy piece of work.
PAINTER You're a dog. 210
APEMANTUS Thy mother's of my generation. What's 211
 she, if I be a dog? 212
TIMON Wilt dine with me, Apemantus?
APEMANTUS No. I eat not lords. 214
TIMON An thou shouldst, thou'dst anger ladies. 215
APEMANTUS Oh, they eat lords. So they come by great 216
 bellies. 217
TIMON That's a lascivious apprehension. 218
APEMANTUS So thou apprehend'st it. Take it for thy labor. 219
TIMON How dost thou like this jewel, Apemantus?
APEMANTUS Not so well as plain dealing, which will
 not cost a man a doit. 222
TIMON What dost thou think 'tis worth?
APEMANTUS Not worth my thinking.—How now,
 poet?
POET How now, philosopher?
APEMANTUS Thou liest.

POET Art not one?
APEMANTUS Yes.
POET Then I lie not.
APEMANTUS Art not a poet?
POET Yes.
APEMANTUS Then thou liest. Look in thy last work, 233
 where thou hast feigned him a worthy fellow. 234
POET That's not feigned. He is so.
APEMANTUS Yes, he is worthy of thee, and to pay thee
 for thy labor. He that loves to be flattered is worthy
 o'th' flatterer. Heavens, that I were a lord!
TIMON What wouldst do then, Apemantus?
APEMANTUS E'en as Apemantus does now: hate a lord
 with my heart.
TIMON What, thyself?
APEMANTUS Ay.
TIMON Wherefore?
APEMANTUS That I had no angry wit to be a lord.—Art 245
 not thou a merchant?
MERCHANT Ay, Apemantus.
APEMANTUS Traffic confound thee, if the gods will not! 248
MERCHANT If traffic do it, the gods do it. 249
APEMANTUS Traffic's thy god, and thy god confound
 thee!

   Trumpet sounds. Enter a Messenger.

TIMON What trumpet's that?
MESSENGER
 'Tis Alcibiades and some twenty horse, 253
 All of companionship. 254
TIMON
 Pray, entertain them; give them guide to us. 255
      [Exeunt some attendants.]
 [*To his guests*] You must needs dine with me. Go not
  you hence
 Till I have thanked you.—When dinner's done,
 Show me this piece.—I am joyful of your sights. 258

   Enter Alcibiades, with the rest.

 Most welcome, sir!
APEMANTUS   So, so, there! Aches contract 259
 And starve your supple joints! That there should be 260
 Small love amongst these sweet knaves, and all
 This courtesy! The strain of man's bred out 262
 Into baboon and monkey.
ALCIBIADES [*to Timon*]
 Sir, you have saved my longing, and I feed 264

189–90 Till . . . honest i.e., You must wait for my "good morrow" until I have become free of satirical sharpness and until men are free of the faults I criticize, something as likely to happen as Timon changing places with his dog. **194 repent not** don't regret what I said. **196–7 thy name** i.e., "knave." (See line 190.) **204 Right . . . law** i.e., Since Athenians have no brains or honesty, I will be doing nothing that is a capital offense. **206 innocence** innocuous character, inability to do harm. **210 dog** (*Cynic* is derived from the Greek for "dog.") **211 generation** species. **211–12 What's she** i.e., Isn't she a bitch **214 I . . . lords** i.e., I refuse to dine (in sycophantic fashion) at the tables of influential men and consume their wealth. **215 An** If **216 eat** (1) take into their bellies (sexually) (2) consume the substance of. **come by** acquire **216–17 great bellies** (1) pregnant wombs (2) bellies plump from eating. **218 apprehension** interpretation. **219 So . . . labor** That's your interpretation, not mine. You can keep it for your pains. (With a pun on *apprehending* as seizing, and on *labor*, "giving birth.") **222 doit** half a farthing, coin of slight value.

233 Then thou liest (Because poets are supposed to feign.) **234 him** i.e., Timon **245 That . . . lord** (Apemantus quips that since he professes to hate lords, if he were himself a lord he could hate himself with all his angry wit.) **248 Traffic confound** May business or trade ruin **249 If . . . do it** i.e., If I were to suffer financial ruin in merchant shipping (by shipwreck or other disaster), it would be at the behest of the gods. **253 horse** horsemen **254 of companionship** of a company, coming in a body. **255 Pray . . . us** Please receive them hospitably and show them in. **258 of your sights** to see you. **259 So, so, there** Well, well, look at that (i.e., at all the bowing and scraping). **260 starve** destroy **262 strain** race, stock. **bred out** degenerated **264 saved** anticipated and thus prevented

Most hungerly on your sight.

TIMON   Right welcome, sir!   265
Ere we depart, we'll share a bounteous time   266
In different pleasures. Pray you, let us in.   267

Exeunt [all except Apemantus].

Enter two Lords.

FIRST LORD   What time o'day is't, Apemantus?
APEMANTUS   Time to be honest.
FIRST LORD   That time serves still.   270
APEMANTUS   The most accursèd thou, that still omitt'st it. 271
SECOND LORD   Thou art going to Lord Timon's feast?
APEMANTUS   Ay, to see meat fill knaves and wine heat
fools.
SECOND LORD   Fare thee well, fare thee well.
APEMANTUS   Thou art a fool to bid me farewell twice.
SECOND LORD   Why, Apemantus?
APEMANTUS   Shouldst have kept one to thyself, for I
mean to give thee none.
FIRST LORD   Hang thyself!
APEMANTUS   No, I will do nothing at thy bidding. Make
thy requests to thy friend.
SECOND LORD   Away, unpeaceable dog, or I'll spurn 283
thee hence!
APEMANTUS   I will fly, like a dog, the heels o'th' ass. 285

[Exit.]

FIRST LORD
He's opposite to humanity. Come, shall we in   286
And taste Lord Timon's bounty? He outgoes   287
The very heart of kindness.   288
SECOND LORD
He pours it out. Plutus, the god of gold,
Is but his steward. No meed but he repays   290
Sevenfold above itself; no gift to him
But breeds the giver a return exceeding
All use of quittance.
FIRST LORD   The noblest mind he carries 293
That ever governed man.
SECOND LORD
Long may he live in fortunes! Shall we in?
FIRST LORD   I'll keep you company.   *Exeunt.*

❦

[1.2]

*Hautboys playing loud music. A great banquet
served in, [Flavius and others attending]; and
then enter Lord Timon, the states, the Athenian
Lords, [Alcibiades, and] Ventidius (which Timon
redeemed from prison). Then comes, dropping after
all, Apemantus, discontentedly, like himself.*

265 **hungerly . . . on your sight** hungrily on the sight of you.
266 **depart** part company   267 **different** various.   **in** enter.
270 **still** always.   271 **The . . . it** The more accursed are you, for continually failing to make good use of time.   283 **unpeaceable** quarrel-
some, incessantly barking.   **spurn** kick   285 **fly** flee   286 **opposite
to** antagonistic to and out of step with   287 **outgoes** surpasses
288 **heart** essence   290 **meed** merit, or, gift   293 **use of quittance**
usual rates of repayment with interest.
1.2. Location: A banqueting room in Timon's house.
0.1 *Hautboys* oboelike instruments.   0.3 *states* i.e., rulers of the state,
senators.   0.5 *dropping* entering casually   0.6 *like himself* not in finery.

VENTIDIUS   Most honored Timon,
It hath pleased the gods to remember my father's age
And call him to long peace.   3
He is gone happy and has left me rich.
Then, as in grateful virtue I am bound
To your free heart, I do return those talents,   6
Doubled with thanks and service, from whose help
I derived liberty.   *[He offers money.]*
TIMON   Oh, by no means,
Honest Ventidius. You mistake my love.
I gave it freely ever, and there's none
Can truly say he gives if he receives.   12
If our betters play at that game, we must not dare 13
To imitate them. Faults that are rich are fair.   14
VENTIDIUS   A noble spirit!
[They all stand ceremoniously looking on Timon.]
TIMON
Nay, my lords, ceremony was but devised at first
To set a gloss on faint deeds, hollow welcomes,   17
Recanting goodness, sorry ere 'tis shown;   18
But where there is true friendship, there needs none. 19
Pray, sit. More welcome are ye to my fortunes
Than my fortunes to me.   *[They sit.]*
FIRST LORD
My lord, we always have confessed it.   22
APEMANTUS
Ho, ho, confessed it? Hanged it, have you not?   23
TIMON
Oh, Apemantus, you are welcome.
APEMANTUS   No,
You shall not make me welcome.
I come to have thee thrust me out of doors.   26
TIMON
Fie, thou'rt a churl. You've got a humor there   27
Does not become a man; 'tis much to blame.   28
They say, my lords, *Ira furor brevis est*, but yond 29
man is ever angry. Go, let him have a table by himself,
for he does neither affect company nor is he fit for't, 31
indeed.
APEMANTUS   Let me stay at thine apperil, Timon. I come 33
to observe; I give thee warning on't.
TIMON   I take no heed of thee. Thou'rt an Athenian,
therefore welcome. I myself would have no power;   36
prithee, let my meat make thee silent.   37
APEMANTUS   I scorn thy meat; 'twould choke me, for I 38
should ne'er flatter thee. O you gods, what a number 39

3 **long peace** eternal rest.   6 **free** generous   12 **gives . . . receives**
(Compare with Acts 20:35: "It is more blessed to give than to receive.")
13 **at that game** i.e., at taking in wealth while seeming to be generous
14 **Faults . . . fair** Faults in rich persons are overlooked because they
are wealthy.   17 **set a gloss on** give a speciously fair appearance to
18 **Recanting goodness** generosity that takes back what it has offered
19 **there needs none** there is no need for ceremony.   22 **confessed it**
acknowledged the truth of what you say.   23 **Hanged it** i.e., Killed it
instead. (Apemantus replies with a jesting allusion to the saying,
"Confess and be hanged.")   26 **have thee thrust** provoke you into
thrusting   27 **churl** surly person.   **humor** disposition   28 **Does** that
does   29 *Ira furor brevis est* Wrath is a brief madness (Horace's *Epistles*, 1.2.62)   31 **affect** desire, seek   33 **thine apperil** your peril, risk
36 **would . . . power** do not wish the power (to silence you)   37 **meat**
food   38–9 **'twould . . . thee** (Apemantus implies that Timon's food is
to reward flatterers; Apemantus, being none, would choke on it.)

of men eats Timon, and he sees 'em not! It grieves me
to see so many dip their meat in one man's blood; and 41
all the madness is, he cheers them up, too. 42
I wonder men dare trust themselves with men.
Methinks they should invite them without knives; 44
Good for their meat, and safer for their lives. 45
There's much example for't. The fellow that sits next
him, now parts bread with him, pledges the breath of 47
him in a divided draft, is the readiest man to kill 48
him. 'T has been proved. If I were a huge man, I 49
should fear to drink at meals,
Lest they should spy my windpipe's dangerous notes. 51
Great men should drink with harness on their throats. 52

TIMON [*toasting a Lord who drinks to him*]
My lord, in heart! And let the health go round. 53

SECOND LORD
Let it flow this way, my good lord. 54

APEMANTUS   Flow this way? A brave fellow! He keeps 55
his tides well. Those healths will make thee and thy 56
state look ill, Timon. 57
Here's that which is too weak to be a sinner: 58
Honest water, which ne'er left man i'th' mire. 59
This and my food are equals; there's no odds. 60
Feasts are too proud to give thanks to the gods. 61

Apemantus' grace.

Immortal gods, I crave no pelf. 62
I pray for no man but myself.
Grant I may never prove so fond 64
To trust man on his oath or bond, 65
Or a harlot for her weeping,
Or a dog that seems a-sleeping,
Or a keeper with my freedom, 68
Or my friends, if I should need 'em.
Amen. So fall to't. 70
Rich men sin, and I eat root. [*He eats and drinks.*] 71
Much good dich thy good heart, Apemantus! 72

TIMON   Captain Alcibiades, your heart's in the field 73
now.

ALCIBIADES   My heart is ever at your service, my lord.

TIMON   You had rather be at a breakfast of enemies 76
than a dinner of friends. 77

ALCIBIADES   So they were bleeding new, my lord, 78
there's no meat like 'em. I could wish my best friend
at such a feast.

APEMANTUS   Would all those flatterers were thine enemies then, that then thou mightst kill 'em—and bid
me to 'em! 83

FIRST LORD   Might we but have that happiness, my lord,
that you would once use our hearts, whereby we 85
might express some part of our zeals, we should think 86
ourselves forever perfect. 87

TIMON   Oh, no doubt, my good friends, but the gods
themselves have provided that I shall have much help
from you. How had you been my friends else? Why
have you that charitable title from thousands, did not 91
you chiefly belong to my heart? I have told more of 92
you to myself than you can with modesty speak in 93
your own behalf; and thus far I confirm you. O you 94
gods, think I, what need we have any friends if we 95
should ne'er have need of 'em? They were the most
needless creatures living should we ne'er have use for 97
'em, and would most resemble sweet instruments 98
hung up in cases, that keeps their sounds to themselves. Why, I have often wished myself poorer, that I
might come nearer to you. We are born to do benefits; 101
and what better or properer can we call our own than 102
the riches of our friends? Oh, what a precious comfort
'tis to have so many, like brothers, commanding one 104
another's fortunes! Oh, joy's e'en made away ere't can 105
be born! Mine eyes cannot hold out water, methinks.
To forget their faults, I drink to you. 107
          [*He weeps, and drinks a toast.*]

APEMANTUS   Thou weep'st to make them drink, Timon. 108

SECOND LORD [*to Timon*]
Joy had the like conception in our eyes,
And at that instant like a babe sprung up. 110

APEMANTUS
Ho, ho! I laugh to think that babe a bastard. 111

THIRD LORD [*to Timon*]
I promise you, my lord, you moved me much. 112

APEMANTUS   Much!   *Sound tucket* [*within*]. 113

---

41 one man's blood (Possible allusion to the Last Supper; the *fellow* in lines 46–9, who shares food and drink only to betray his host, is like Judas.)   **42 all . . . too** the craziest aspect of his behavior is that he encourages them.   **44 without knives** (Refers to the Renaissance custom of guests bringing their own knives.)   **45 Good . . . lives** Without knives, the guests will consume less food and be less likely to use the knives to commit mayhem.   **47 parts** shares.   **pledges the breath** i.e., drinks to the health   **48 a divided draft** a cup that they share   **49 'T has been proved** There are precedents for it. (Compare with line 143.)   **huge** great in rank and wealth   **51 Lest . . . notes** i.e., lest they should be able to discern where best to slit my throat at the windpipe. (It is the spying that is dangerous, not the *notes* or sounds made by the windpipe.)   **52 harness** armor   **53 in heart** heartily.   **health** toast, and the cup   **54 flow** circulate   **55 brave** fine, foppish. (Said ironically.)   **56 tides** times, seasons. (With quibbling reference to *flow* of tides; Apemantus comments sardonically that the Second Lord is making sure that he will get plenty to drink.)   **57 state** (1) physical condition (2) fortune, estate   **58 a sinner** an incentive to sin   **59 i'th' mire** i.e., in trouble.   **60–1 This . . . gods** There's nothing to choose between this simple water and the honest plain food I eat; feasts, as the products of insolent worldliness, are not a fit offering to the gods.   **62 pelf** property, possessions.   **64 fond** foolish   **65 To** as to   **68 keeper** jailer   **70 fall to't** i.e., begin to eat.   **71 Rich . . root** i.e., The rich sin in gluttony, while I eat sparingly.   **72 dich** may it do. (Originally a contraction of "d' it ye" in the phrase "much good do it you.")

73 field battlefield   **76 a breakfast of enemies** a feast of slaughter on the battlefield   **77 of** among   **78 So** Provided that   **83 to 'em** i.e., to eat them.   **85 use our hearts** make trial of our love   **86 zeals** love   **87 forever perfect** completely happy.   **91 charitable . . . from** beloved name from among   **92 told** (1) recited (2) counted   **92–3 of you** i.e., concerning your deservings   **94 confirm you** endorse your claim (to be my worthy friends).   **95 what** why   **97 needless** useless   **98 instruments** musical instruments   **101 come . . . you** come to you in need.   **102 properer** more fittingly   **104 commanding** having at their disposal   **105 made away** undone, i.e., turned to tears   **107 To . . . faults** i.e., To mask my weakness in giving way to tears   **108 Thou . . . drink** i.e., You ought to weep at the way your absurd sentimentalizing is just giving them an excuse to drink up your substance   **110 sprung up** (1) leaped from the womb (2) welled up like a spring of tears.   **111 bastard** i.e., illegitimate, without genuine source. (Refers to the guests' tears.)   **112 promise** assure   **113 Much** (An expression of contemptuous disbelief; playing on *much* in the previous line.)   **s.d. tucket** trumpet call

TIMON
What means that trump?

Enter Servant.

How now?   114

SERVANT   Please you, my lord, there are certain ladies
most desirous of admittance.

TIMON   Ladies? What are their wills?

SERVANT   There comes with them a forerunner, my
lord, which bears that office to signify their pleasures. 119

TIMON   I pray, let them be admitted.   [*Exit Servant.*]

Enter Cupid.

CUPID
Hail to thee, worthy Timon, and to all
That of his bounties taste! The five best senses
Acknowledge thee their patron, and come freely
To gratulate thy plenteous bosom. Th'ear,   124
Taste, touch, and smell, pleased from thy table rise;
They only now come but to feast thine eyes.   126

TIMON
They're welcome all. Let 'em have kind admittance.
Music, make their welcome!

[*Cupid summons the maskers.*]

FIRST LORD
You see, my lord, how ample you're beloved.   129

[*Music.*] *Enter a masque of Ladies* [*as*] *Amazons,
with lutes in their hands, dancing and playing.*

APEMANTUS   Hoyday!   130
What a sweep of vanity comes this way!
They dance? They are madwomen.
Like madness is the glory of this life   133
As this pomp shows to a little oil and root.   134
We make ourselves fools to disport ourselves   135
And spend our flatteries to drink those men   136
Upon whose age we void it up again   137
With poisonous spite and envy.   138
Who lives that's not depravèd or depraves?   139
Who dies that bears not one spurn to their graves 140
Of their friends' gift?   141
I should fear those that dance before me now
Would one day stamp upon me. 'T has been done;
Men shut their doors against a setting sun.   144

*The Lords rise from table, with much adoring of
Timon; and to show their loves each singles out an
Amazon, and all dance, men with women, a lofty
strain or two to the hautboys, and cease.*

TIMON
You have done our pleasures much grace, fair ladies,
Set a fair fashion on our entertainment,   146
Which was not half so beautiful and kind.   147
You have added worth unto't and luster,
And entertained me with mine own device.   149
I am to thank you for't.   150

FIRST LADY
My lord, you take us even at the best.   151

APEMANTUS   Faith, for the worst is filthy and would not 152
hold taking, I doubt me.   153

TIMON
Ladies, there is an idle banquet attends you;   154
Please you to dispose yourselves.   155

ALL LADIES   Most thankfully, my lord.

Exeunt [*Cupid and Ladies*].

TIMON   Flavius!

FLAVIUS   My lord?

TIMON   The little casket bring me hither.

FLAVIUS   Yes, my lord. [*Aside*] More jewels yet?
There is no crossing him in 's humor;   160
Else I should tell him well, i'faith I should,   161
When all's spent, he'd be crossed then, an he could. 162
'Tis pity bounty had not eyes behind,   163
That man might ne'er be wretched for his mind.   164

Exit.

FIRST LORD   Where be our men?

SERVANT   Here, my lord, in readiness.

SECOND LORD
Our horses!

Enter Flavius [*with the casket*].

TIMON   Oh, my friends, I have one word
To say to you. Look you, my good lord,
I must entreat you honor me so much   169
As to advance this jewel; accept it and wear it,   170
Kind my lord.   [*He offers a jewel.*] 171

FIRST LORD
I am so far already in your gifts—   172

ALL   So are we all.

Enter a Servant.

SERVANT
My lord, there are certain nobles of the Senate

---

114 trump trumpet blast.   **119 which** who.   **office** function.   **pleasures**
wishes.   **124 To . . . bosom** to greet your generosity of heart.   **126 They**
. . . but the maskers come now only   **129 ample** amply   **130 Hoyday**
(Exclamation denoting surprise; a variety of "heyday.")   **133–4 Like . . .**
root i.e., The insane vaingloriousness of this life is made plain when we
compare the pomp of this lavish entertainment with the bare necessities
needed to maintain life.   **135–8 We . . . envy** We foolishly devise entertainments and lavish our flattering attentions in drinking toasts to men
upon whom, when they are old, we will vomit up what we have drunk
in poisonous spite and malice.   **139 Who . . . depraves?** Who is there
alive that is not either vilified himself or vilifies others?   **140–1 Who . . .**
gift? Who is there that does not go to his grave bearing the injuries of
his dearest friends?   **144.1 adoring of** paying homage to

146 Set . . . on given grace and elegance to   **147 was not** i.e., before
your arrival was not.   **kind** gracious.   **149 And . . . device** (This
could mean that Timon designed the masque himself to surprise his
guests, but more probably he is expressing pleasure at a masque
especially designed for him.)   **150 am to** am under obligation to
151 take . . . best i.e., praise us most generously.   **152–3 Faith . . .**
doubt me i.e., Truly, if you were to take your guests at their worst,
take them sexually, you'd find them filthy and rotten with venereal
disease, I fear.   **154 idle** trifling, slight   **155 dispose yourselves** take
your places.   **160 humor** frame of mind   **161 well** plainly
162 When . . . could when all the money is gone, he'd be glad enough
to have me try to stop him, if it weren't too late. (Or, he'd be happy to
have someone cross his palm with silver, give him money.)
163–4 'Tis . . . mind It's a pity his bounty was not wary, so that he
might not have to suffer privation on account of his bounteous inclination.   **169 you honor** you to honor   **170 advance** raise in value by
accepting   **171 Kind my lord** my kind lord.   **172 in your gifts**
indebted to you for your gifts

Newly alighted and come to visit you.

TIMON

They are fairly welcome.   [*Exit Servant.*]

FLAVIUS   I beseech Your Honor,   176
Vouchsafe me a word; it does concern you near.   177

TIMON

Near? Why then, another time I'll hear thee.
I prithee, let's be provided to show them
entertainment.

FLAVIUS [*aside*]   I scarce know how.

Enter another Servant.

SECOND SERVANT

May it please Your Honor, Lord Lucius,
Out of his free love, hath presented to you
Four milk-white horses trapped in silver.   183

TIMON

I shall accept them fairly. Let the presents   184
Be worthily entertained.   [*Exit Servant.*]

Enter a third Servant.

                        How now? What news?   185

THIRD SERVANT   Please you, my lord, that honorable
gentleman, Lord Lucullus, entreats your company tomorrow to hunt with him and has sent Your Honor
two brace of greyhounds.   189

TIMON

I'll hunt with him; and let them be received,
Not without fair reward.   [*Exit Servant.*]

FLAVIUS [*aside*]   What will this come to?
He commands us to provide, and give great gifts,
And all out of an empty coffer;
Nor will he know his purse, or yield me this,   194
To show him what a beggar his heart is,
Being of no power to make his wishes good.
His promises fly so beyond his state   197
That what he speaks is all in debt; he owes
For every word. He is so kind that he now
Pays interest for't; his land's put to their books. 200
Well, would I were gently put out of office
Before I were forced out!
Happier is he that has no friend to feed
Than such that do e'en enemies exceed.   204
I bleed inwardly for my lord.   *Exit.*

TIMON [*to the Lords*]   You do yourselves
Much wrong, you bate too much of your own
    merits.—   206
Here, my lord, a trifle of our love.   [*He offers a gift.*]

SECOND LORD

With more than common thanks I will receive it.

THIRD LORD   Oh, he's the very soul of bounty!

TIMON   And now I remember, my lord, you gave good 210
words the other day of a bay courser I rode on. 'Tis 211
yours because you liked it.

THIRD LORD

Oh, I beseech you, pardon me, my lord, in that.   213

TIMON

You may take my word, my lord: I know no man
Can justly praise but what he does affect.   215
I weigh my friends' affection with mine own.   216
I'll tell you true, I'll call to you.   217

ALL LORDS   Oh, none so welcome.

TIMON

I take all and your several visitations   219
So kind to heart, 'tis not enough to give.   220
Methinks I could deal kingdoms to my friends
And ne'er be weary. Alcibiades,
Thou art a soldier, therefore seldom rich.
It comes in charity to thee; for all thy living   224
Is 'mongst the dead, and all the lands thou hast
Lie in a pitched field.   226

ALCIBIADES   Ay, defiled land, my lord.   227

FIRST LORD   We are so virtuously bound—

TIMON   And so am I to you.

SECOND LORD   So infinitely endeared—   230

TIMON   All to you. [*To servants*] Lights, more lights! 231

FIRST LORD

The best of happiness, honor, and fortunes
Keep with you, Lord Timon!   233

TIMON   Ready for his friends.   234

          Exeunt lords [and all but Apemantus and Timon].

APEMANTUS   What a coil's here!   235
Serving of becks and jutting-out of bums!   236
I doubt whether their legs be worth the sums   237
That are given for 'em. Friendship's full of dregs.
Methinks false hearts should never have sound legs. 239
Thus honest fools lay out their wealth on curtsies. 240

TIMON

Now, Apemantus, if thou wert not sullen,
I would be good to thee.

APEMANTUS   No, I'll nothing; for if I should be bribed
too, there would be none left to rail upon thee, and
then thou wouldst sin the faster. Thou giv'st so long,
Timon, I fear me thou wilt give away thyself in paper 246
shortly. What needs these feasts, pomps, and vain- 247
glories?

---

176 **fairly** sincerely   177 **near** closely.   183 **trapped in silver** in
silver-mounted trappings.   184 **fairly** graciously.   185 **entertained**
received.   189 **brace** pair   194 **purse** financial situation.   **yield me
this** grant me opportunity   197 **state** financial state   200 **put . . .
books** mortgaged to those whom he has befriended with gifts.
204 **Than . . . exceed** i.e., than he that feeds so-called "friends" who,
by consuming his wealth, outdo his enemies in ruining him.
206 **bate . . . of** belittle too much

210–11 **gave good words** spoke praisingly   211 **bay courser** reddish-
brown horse   213 **pardon . . . that** i.e., forgive my mentioning the
horse; it was not meant as a hint.   215 **Can . . . affect** who can justly
praise a thing unless he likes and desires it.   216 **I . . . own** I judge
my friends' desires by my own and give them equal weight.   217 **I'll
call to you** I'll call on you when I have need.   219 **all . . . several** your
joint and individual   220 **kind** kindly.   **'tis . . . give** there isn't
enough wealth in my possession to match my wish to be generous.
224 **It . . . thee** i.e., You have need of charity.   **living** (1) existence
(2) property, wealth   226 **pitched field** battlefield.   227 **defiled**
(1) defiled by dead bodies (2) arrayed with files or rows of soldiers
230 **endeared** obligated   231 **All to you** i.e., The obligation is entirely
mine, or, all mine is yours.   233 **Keep** dwell, remain   234 **Ready for**
Ready to assist   235 **coil** fuss   236 **Serving of becks** Bowing
237 **legs** (1) limbs (2) bows, curtsies   239 **sound legs** i.e., healthy legs
able to make deceptively flattering bows.   240 **curtsies** (1) bows
(2) courtesies.   246 **I fear me** I fear.   **paper** bonds, promises to pay
247 **What needs** What necessity is there for

TIMON Nay, an you begin to rail on society once, I am 249
sworn not to give regard to you. Farewell, and come 250
with better music.   *Exit.*
APEMANTUS So.
Thou wilt not hear me now; thou shalt not then. 253
I'll lock thy heaven from thee. 254
Oh, that men's ears should be
To counsel deaf, but not to flattery!   *Exit.*

❖

[2.1]

Enter a Senator [with papers in his hand].

SENATOR
And late, five thousand. To Varro and to Isidore 1
He owes nine thousand, besides my former sum,
Which makes it five-and-twenty. Still in motion 3
Of raging waste? It cannot hold; it will not. 4
If I want gold, steal but a beggar's dog 5
And give it Timon, why, the dog coins gold.
If I would sell my horse and buy twenty more
Better than he, why, give my horse to Timon—
Ask nothing, give it him—it foals me straight, 9
And able horses. No porter at his gate, 10
But rather one that smiles and still invites 11
All that pass by. It cannot hold. No reason 12
Can sound his state in safety.—Caphis, ho! 13
Caphis, I say!

Enter Caphis.

CAPHIS   Here, sir. What is your pleasure?
SENATOR
Get on your cloak and haste you to Lord Timon.
Importune him for my moneys. Be not ceased 16
With slight denial, nor then silenced when 17
"Commend me to your master" and the cap 18
Plays in the right hand, thus, but tell him 19
My uses cry to me; I must serve my turn 20
Out of mine own. His days and times are past, 21
And my reliances on his fracted dates 22
Have smit my credit. I love and honor him, 23
But must not break my back to heal his finger.
Immediate are my needs, and my relief
Must not be tossed and turned to me in words, 26

But find supply immediate. Get you gone.
Put on a most importunate aspect,
A visage of demand, for I do fear
When every feather sticks in his own wing 30
Lord Timon will be left a naked gull, 31
Which flashes now a phoenix. Get you gone. 32
CAPHIS I go, sir.
SENATOR *[giving him bonds]*
Ay, go, sir. Take the bonds along with you
And have the dates in compt.
CAPHIS   I will, sir.
SENATOR   Go.   *Exeunt.* 35

❖

[2.2]

*Enter steward [Flavius] with many bills in his
hand.*

FLAVIUS
No care, no stop! So senseless of expense
That he will neither know how to maintain it 2
Nor cease his flow of riot, takes no account 3
How things go from him nor resumes no care 4
Of what is to continue. Never mind 5
Was to be so unwise to be so kind. 6
What shall be done? He will not hear till feel. 7
I must be round with him, now he comes from
hunting. 8
Fie, fie, fie, fie!

*Enter Caphis [and the Servants of] Isidore and
Varro.*

CAPHIS
Good even, Varro. What, you come for money? 10
VARRO'S SERVANT Is't not your business too?
CAPHIS It is. And yours too, Isidore?
ISIDORE'S SERVANT It is so.
CAPHIS Would we were all discharged! 14
VARRO'S SERVANT I fear it. 15
CAPHIS Here comes the lord.

Enter Timon and his train [with Alcibiades].

TIMON
So soon as dinner's done we'll forth again, 17
My Alcibiades.—With me? What is your will?
CAPHIS *[presenting a bill]*
My lord, here is a note of certain dues. 19
TIMON Dues? Whence are you?

---

249 an . . . once if once you begin to criticize **250 give regard to** take notice of **253 thou shalt not then** you won't have the opportunity later. **254 thy heaven** i.e., my saving advice
2.1. Location: Athens. A Senator's house.
1 late lately **3–4 Still . . . waste?** Perpetually and ceaselessly squandering? **4 hold** hold out, last. (Also in line 12.) **5 steal but** I need only steal **9 foals me straight** at once yields me foals, i.e., more horses (as gifts) **10 And able horses** i.e., and what's more, they are full-grown horses, not literally foals. **porter** i.e., one who sternly denies entrance **11 still** constantly **12–13 No . . . safety** No reasonable fathoming of his estate can get to the bottom of Timon's financial position. **16 ceased** silenced, put off **17 slight** negligent, offhand **17–19 when . . . thus** i.e., when he offers fair greetings and flattering gestures in lieu of real payment **20 uses** needs **20–1 I must . . . own** I must address my own necessities with my own money.
21 His . . . times The deadlines for repayments of his loans **22 fracted** broken (by failure to meet payments on notes due) **23 smit** smitten, hurt **26 tossed and turned** bandied back

30 When . . . wing i.e., when everything is in the hands of its rightful possessor **31 gull** (1) unfledged bird (2) dupe **32 Which . . . phoenix** who now showily looks like a phoenix, a one-of-a-kind mythical bird, a rare and precious creature that is eventually consumed in flames (according to myth). **35 in compt** reckoned.
2.2. Location: Athens. Before Timon's house.
2 know learn **3 riot** uncontrolled reveling **4–5 resumes . . . continue** makes no provision for how it is to continue. **5–6 Never . . . kind** Never was there a mind so unwise in being so kind. **7 till feel** until he suffers feelingly. **8 round** plainspoken. **now** now that **10 Good even** (A greeting used any time after noon.) **14 discharged** paid. **15 fear it** i.e., am apprehensive about our being paid.
17 forth go forth **19 dues** debts.

CAPHIS   Of Athens here, my lord.

TIMON   Go to my steward.

CAPHIS
Please it Your Lordship, he hath put me off
To the succession of new days this month.   24
My master is awaked by great occasion   25
To call upon his own, and humbly prays you   26
That with your other noble parts you'll suit   27
In giving him his right.

TIMON   Mine honest friend,
I prithee but repair to me next morning.   29

CAPHIS
Nay, good my lord—

TIMON   Contain thyself, good friend.

VARRO'S SERVANT
One Varro's servant, my good lord—

ISIDORE'S SERVANT
From Isidore; he humbly prays your speedy payment.

CAPHIS
If you did know, my lord, my master's wants—

VARRO'S SERVANT
'Twas due on forfeiture, my lord, six weeks and past.   34

ISIDORE'S SERVANT
Your steward puts me off, my lord, and I
Am sent expressly to Your Lordship.

TIMON   Give me breath.—   37
I do beseech you, good my lords, keep on;   38
I'll wait upon you instantly.
                        [*Exeunt Alcibiades and Lords.*]
                [*To Flavius*]   Come hither. Pray you,   39
How goes the world, that I am thus encountered
With clamorous demands of broken bonds
And the detention of long-since-due debts   42
Against my honor?

FLAVIUS [*to the Servants*]   Please you, gentlemen,   43
The time is unagreeable to this business.
Your importunacy cease till after dinner,   45
That I may make His Lordship understand   46
Wherefore you are not paid.

TIMON   Do so, my friends.—   47
See them well entertained.   [*Exit.*]

FLAVIUS   Pray, draw near.   *Exit.*   48

Enter Apemantus and Fool.

CAPHIS   Stay, stay, here comes the Fool with Apemantus.
Let's ha' some sport with 'em.

VARRO'S SERVANT   Hang him! He'll abuse us.   51

ISIDORE'S SERVANT   A plague upon him, dog!

VARRO'S SERVANT   How dost, Fool?

APEMANTUS   Dost dialogue with thy shadow?   54

VARRO'S SERVANT   I speak not to thee.

APEMANTUS   No, 'tis to thyself. [*To the Fool*] Come away.   56

ISIDORE'S SERVANT [*to Varro's Servant*]   There's the fool   57
hangs on your back already.   58

APEMANTUS   No, thou stand'st single; thou'rt not on   59
him yet.   60

CAPHIS [*to Isidore's Servant*]   Where's the fool now?   61

APEMANTUS   He last asked the question. Poor rogues   62
and usurers' men, bawds between gold and want!   63

ALL THE SERVANTS   What are we, Apemantus?

APEMANTUS   Asses.

ALL THE SERVANTS   Why?

APEMANTUS   That you ask me what you are, and do not
know yourselves. Speak to 'em, Fool.

FOOL   How do you, gentlemen?

ALL THE SERVANTS   Gramercies, good Fool. How does   70
your mistress?

FOOL   She's e'en setting on water to scald such chickens   72
as you are. Would we could see you at Corinth!   73

APEMANTUS   Good! Gramercy.

Enter Page.

FOOL   Look you, here comes my mistress' page.

PAGE [*to the Fool*]   Why, how now, captain? What do
you in this wise company?—How dost thou,
Apemantus?

APEMANTUS   Would I had a rod in my mouth, that I   79
might answer thee profitably.   80

PAGE   Prithee, Apemantus, read me the superscription   81
of these letters. I know not which is which.
                        [*He shows two letters.*]

APEMANTUS   Canst not read?

PAGE   No.

APEMANTUS   There will little learning die then that day
thou art hanged. This is to Lord Timon, this to
Alcibiades. Go, thou wast born a bastard and thou'lt
die a bawd.

PAGE   Thou wast whelped a dog, and thou shalt famish   89
a dog's death. Answer not; I am gone.   *Exit.*

---

24 To . . . month from one day to another all month.   25 awaked
roused, driven   26 his own i.e., that which he has lent you   27 with
. . . parts in conformity to your other noble qualities   29 but repair
only come   34 on forfeiture on penalty of forfeiting the security for
it if not paid on the date prescribed   37 breath breathing space, time
to breathe.   38 keep on go ahead without me   39 wait . . . instantly
be with you in a moment.   42 the detention the charge of withholding payment   43 Against my honor contrary to my honorable reputation.   45 Your . . . cease Cease your importunate demands
46 That so that   47 Wherefore why   48 entertained received,
treated.   51 abuse vilify

54 Dost . . . shadow? i.e., Are you talking with an image of yourself
when you say "Fool"?   56 No . . . thyself No, you are speaking to
yourself when you say "fool." (Said to Varro's Servant.)
57–8 There's . . . already i.e., You've just been labeled fool; Apemantus has pinned the label on you.   59–60 No . . . yet i.e., No, I didn't
put you, fool that you are, on the back of Varro's Servant; you're still
standing on your own two feet. (Said to Isidore's Servant.)
61 Where's . . . now? i.e., Who is the fool now after what Apemantus
just said to you?   62 He He who (i.e., Caphis, who has now been
called a fool like the others)   63 bawds . . . want middlemen who,
like panders, bring together usurers and needy men.   70 Gramercies
Many thanks   72 e'en . . . water just putting water on the fire.   scald
such chickens (Allusion to the sweating-tub treatment for venereal
disease, which causes loss of hair, just as a chicken loses its feathers
through scalding. The Fool also implies that they are fools deserving
to be plucked.)   73 Corinth a city noted for its brothels; hence, a
brothel or the district for such houses   79–80 Would . . . profitably
i.e., I wish that the verbal tongue-lashing I habitually give were an
actual stick to beat you with, that I might teach you a useful lesson.
81 superscription address   89 whelped born.   famish die

APEMANTUS   E'en so thou outrun'st grace. Fool, I will 91
go with you to Lord Timon's.

FOOL   Will you leave me there?

APEMANTUS   If Timon stay at home.—You three serve 94
three usurers?

ALL THE SERVANTS   Ay. Would they served us! 96

APEMANTUS   So would I—as good a trick as ever
hangman served thief.

FOOL   Are you three usurers' men?

ALL THE SERVANTS   Ay, Fool.

FOOL   I think no usurer but has a fool to his servant; my 101
mistress is one, and I am her fool. When men come to 102
borrow of your masters, they approach sadly and go
away merry, but they enter my mistress' house
merrily and go away sadly. The reason of this?

VARRO'S SERVANT   I could render one. 106

APEMANTUS   Do it then, that we may account thee a
whoremaster and a knave; which notwithstanding,
thou shalt be no less esteemed. 109

VARRO'S SERVANT   What is a whoremaster, Fool?

FOOL   A fool in good clothes, and something like thee.
'Tis a spirit; sometime 't appears like a lord, some- 112
time like a lawyer, sometime like a philosopher,
with two stones more than 's artificial one. He is very 114
often like a knight; and generally, in all shapes that
man goes up and down in from fourscore to thirteen, 116
this spirit walks in.

VARRO'S SERVANT   Thou art not altogether a fool.

FOOL   Nor thou altogether a wise man. As much
foolery as I have, so much wit thou lack'st.

APEMANTUS   That answer might have become Ape- 121
mantus.

ALL THE SERVANTS   Aside, aside! Here comes Lord Timon.
                        [*They stand aside.*]

        Enter Timon and steward [*Flavius*].

APEMANTUS   Come with me, Fool, come.

FOOL   I do not always follow lover, elder brother, and 125
woman; sometime the philosopher. 126
                [*Exeunt Apemantus and Fool.*]

FLAVIUS [*to Servants*]
        Pray you, walk near. I'll speak with you anon. 127
                        Exeunt [*Servants*].

TIMON
        You make me marvel wherefore ere this time
        Had you not fully laid my state before me, 129
        That I might so have rated my expense 130
        As I had leave of means.

FLAVIUS   You would not hear me. 131
        At many leisures I proposed—

TIMON   Go to! 132
        Perchance some single vantages you took, 133
        When my indisposition put you back,
        And that unaptness made your minister 135
        Thus to excuse yourself.

FLAVIUS   O my good lord, 136
        At many times I brought in my accounts,
        Laid them before you. You would throw them off
        And say you found them in mine honesty. 139
        When for some trifling present you have bid me
        Return so much, I have shook my head and wept; 141
        Yea, 'gainst th'authority of manners prayed you 142
        To hold your hand more close. I did endure 143
        Not seldom nor no slight checks when I have 144
        Prompted you in the ebb of your estate 145
        And your great flow of debts. My lovèd lord,
        Though you hear now too late, yet now's a time; 147
        The greatest of your having lacks a half 148
        To pay your present debts.

TIMON   Let all my land be sold.

FLAVIUS
        'Tis all engaged, some forfeited and gone, 151
        And what remains will hardly stop the mouth 152
        Of present dues. The future comes apace; 153
        What shall defend the interim? And at length 154
        How goes our reck'ning? 155

TIMON
        To Lacedaemon did my land extend. 156

FLAVIUS
        Oh, my good lord, the world is but a word.
        Were it all yours to give it in a breath,
        How quickly were it gone!

TIMON   You tell me true.

91 E'en . . . grace That's just the way you run away from instruction that might save you. (Said to the departing Page.)   94 If . . . home i.e., While Timon remains at home, a fool is there.   You three Do you three   96 Would . . . us! Would that they looked after us adequately! (But Apemantus deliberately misunderstands *serve*, answering, "It would serve you right to be hanged.")   101–2 my mistress is one (A bawd is a kind of usurer from whom customers "borrow" pleasure at great personal expense.)   106 one (Implies that the Fool's mistress's house is a bawdy house, where men come merrily but leave diseased and poorer.)   109 no less esteemed i.e., no less esteemed than at present, since these professions are highly regarded in Athens and since a usurer's servant is universally despised.   112 spirit i.e., one that can assume various shapes   114 with . . . one i.e., with two testicles besides the philosopher's *stone*, the quintessence, supposed to change other metals into gold.   116 from . . . thirteen (The Fool playfully inverts the normal "from thirteen to eighty," the life span of an adult male.)   121 become been worthy of, done credit to   125–6 lover . . . woman (Various sorts of persons proverbially associated with folly; an *elder brother* is the counterpart of the proverbially wiser younger brother.)

127 walk near remain nearby.   129 fully . . . state completely detailed my financial position   130 rated estimated and regulated   131 As . . . means as my means permitted.   132 leisures times when you were free.   Go to (An exclamation of impatience.)   133 single vantages occasional opportunities   135–6 that . . . yourself i.e., my disinclination to listen on those occasions served as your excuse thereafter for remaining silent. (*Made your minister* means "became your agent or means.")   139 found . . . honesty i.e., found warrant for believing the books properly kept in knowing me to be honest. 141 Return so much give as in repayment a large gift   142 'gainst . . . manners contrary to what decorum dictated   143–4 I did . . . checks I have had to endure rebukes not seldom or slight in nature   145 in in regard to   147 yet . . . time i.e., late as it is, it is necessary that you be made acquainted with it   148 The greatest . . . having your total wealth at a most optimistic reckoning   151 engaged mortgaged 152–3 stop . . . Of satisfy   153 dues debts.   apace quickly 154–5 And . . . reckoning? And how are we to provide for the long term?   156 Lacedaemon Sparta

FLAVIUS
If you suspect my husbandry of falsehood,   160
Call me before th'exactest auditors
And set me on the proof. So the gods bless me,   162
When all our offices have been oppressed   163
With riotous feeders, when our vaults have wept   164
With drunken spilth of wine, when every room   165
Hath blazed with lights and brayed with minstrelsy,
I have retired me to a wasteful cock   167
And set mine eyes at flow.
TIMON   Prithee, no more.
FLAVIUS
Heavens, have I said, the bounty of this lord!
How many prodigal bits have slaves and peasants   170
This night englutted! Who is not Timon's?   171
What heart, head, sword, force, means, but is Lord
     Timon's?   172
Great Timon, noble, worthy, royal Timon!
Ah, when the means are gone that buy this praise,
The breath is gone whereof this praise is made.
Feast-won, fast-lost; one cloud of winter showers,   176
These flies are couched.   [He weeps.]
TIMON   Come, sermon me no further. 177
No villainous bounty yet hath passed my heart;   178
Unwisely, not ignobly, have I given.
Why dost thou weep? Canst thou the conscience lack   180
To think I shall lack friends? Secure thy heart.   181
If I would broach the vessels of my love   182
And try the argument of hearts by borrowing,   183
Men and men's fortunes could I frankly use   184
As I can bid thee speak.
FLAVIUS   Assurance bless your thoughts!   186
TIMON
And in some sort these wants of mine are crowned,   187
That I account them blessings; for by these   188
Shall I try friends. You shall perceive how you   189
Mistake my fortunes; I am wealthy in my friends.—
Within there! Flaminius! Servilius!

          Enter three servants [Flaminius, Servilius, and
          another].

SERVANTS
My lord? My lord?
TIMON   I will dispatch you severally: [to Servilius] you 193
to Lord Lucius; [to Flaminius] to Lord Lucullus you—
I hunted with His Honor today; [to the other] you to

Sempronius. Commend me to their loves, and, I am
proud, say, that my occasions have found time to use   197
'em toward a supply of money. Let the request be fifty 198
talents.
FLAMINIUS   As you have said, my lord.   200
                              [Exeunt Servants.]
FLAVIUS [aside]   Lord Lucius and Lucullus? Humh!
TIMON   Go you, sir, to the senators,
Of whom, even to the state's best health, I have   203
Deserved this hearing. Bid 'em send o'th'instant   204
A thousand talents to me.
FLAVIUS   I have been bold—
For that I knew it the most general way—   206
To them to use your signet and your name,   207
But they do shake their heads, and I am here
No richer in return.
TIMON   Is't true? Can 't be?
FLAVIUS
They answer, in a joint and corporate voice,   210
That now they are at fall, want treasure, cannot   211
Do what they would, are sorry; you are honorable,
But yet they could have wished—they know not—
Something hath been amiss—a noble nature
May catch a wrench—would all were well—'tis pity.   215
And so, intending other serious matters,   216
After distasteful looks and these hard fractions,   217
With certain half-caps and cold-moving nods   218
They froze me into silence.
TIMON   You gods, reward them!
Prithee, man, look cheerly. These old fellows   220
Have their ingratitude in them hereditary.
Their blood is caked, 'tis cold, it seldom flows;   222
'Tis lack of kindly warmth they are not kind;   223
And nature, as it grows again toward earth,   224
Is fashioned for the journey, dull and heavy.
Go to Ventidius. Prithee, be not sad.
Thou art true and honest—ingeniously I speak—   227
No blame belongs to thee. Ventidius lately
Buried his father, by whose death he's stepped
Into a great estate. When he was poor,   230
Imprisoned, and in scarcity of friends,
I cleared him with five talents. Greet him from me.   232
Bid him suppose some good necessity   233
Touches his friend, which craves to be remembered   234
With those five talents. That had, give't these fellows   235

---

160 **husbandry** management, stewardship 162 **set . . . proof** put me
to the test. 163 **offices** rooms, especially the kitchen and pantries
164 **vaults** wine cellars 165 **spilth** spilling 167 **retired . . . cock**
withdrawn to sit beside the wastefully flowing faucet of a barrel
170 **prodigal bits** wasteful morsels 171 **is not** i.e., does not profess
himself to be 172 **means** financial resources 176 **fast-lost** (1) lost in
time of fast (2) lost quickly and for good 177 **are couched** hide
themselves (to avoid Timon's requests for help). **sermon** lecture
178 **villainous bounty** generosity that I am ashamed of 180 **conscience** faith, or judgment 181 **Secure** Set at ease 182 **broach** tap,
open. **my love** the love others have for me 183 **try . . . hearts** test
protestations of love 184 **frankly** as freely 186 **Assurance . . .
thoughts!** May your hopes prove well founded! 187 **sort** manner,
sense. **crowned** given a special dignity 188 **That** so that 189 **try**
test 193 **severally** separately

197 **occasions** needs. **time** opportunity 198 **toward** for 200 **As** We
will do as 203 **to . . . health** i.e., for my services in behalf of the state's
welfare. (Compare with 4.3.93–6, where Alcibiades refers to Timon's
sword and fortune offered in the defense of Athens.) 204 **o'th'instant**
at once 206 **For . . . way** because I knew it to be the best overall plan,
trying many at a time 207 **signet** signet ring and seal, token of authority 210 **corporate** united 211 **at fall** at low ebb. **want** lack
215 **catch a wrench** be twisted from its natural course, run into misfortune 216 **intending** turning their attention to, or pretending 217 **hard
fractions** harsh broken sentences 218 **half-caps** i.e., salutations half-
heartedly given. **cold-moving** chilling 220 **cheerly** cheerful.
222 **caked** congealed 223 **'Tis . . . kind** it is lack of natural warmth that
makes them not generous. (With pun on *kind*, "natural," "of humankind.") 224 **earth** i.e., the grave 227 **ingeniously** frankly 230–2 **When
. . . talents** (These lines echo Matthew 25:34–7 where Jesus discusses the
Last Judgment.) 233 **good** genuine 234–5 **which . . . talents** which
necessity of mine calls out for the return of those five talents. 235 **That
had** When you have that

To whom 'tis instant due. Ne'er speak or think
That Timon's fortunes 'mong his friends can sink.
FLAVIUS   I would I could not think it.
That thought is bounty's foe;   239
Being free itself, it thinks all others so.   *Exeunt.* 240

❖

[3.1]

*[Enter] Flaminius, waiting to speak with a lord,
[Lucullus,] from his master. Enter a Servant to
him.*

LUCULLUS'S SERVANT   I have told my lord of you. He is
coming down to you.
FLAMINIUS   I thank you, sir.

Enter Lucullus.

LUCULLUS'S SERVANT   Here's my lord.
LUCULLUS *[aside]*   One of Lord Timon's men? A gift, I
warrant. Why, this hits right; I dreamt of a silver basin   6
and ewer tonight.—Flaminius, honest Flaminius, you   7
are very respectively welcome, sir. *[To Servant]* Fill me   8
some wine.   *[Exit Servant.]*
And how does that honorable, complete, free-hearted   10
gentleman of Athens, thy very bountiful good lord
and master?
FLAMINIUS   His health is well, sir.
LUCULLUS   I am right glad that his health is well, sir.
And what hast thou there under thy cloak, pretty
Flaminius?
FLAMINIUS   Faith, nothing but an empty box, sir,
which, in my lord's behalf, I come to entreat Your
Honor to supply; who, having great and instant   18
occasion to use fifty talents, hath sent to Your Lordship   19
to furnish him, nothing doubting your present assis-   20
tance therein.
LUCULLUS   La, la, la la! "Nothing doubting," says he?
Alas, good lord! A noble gentleman 'tis, if he would   23
not keep so good a house. Many a time and often I ha'   24
dined with him and told him on't, and come again to   25
supper to him of purpose to have him spend less, and   26
yet he would embrace no counsel, take no warning by   27
my coming. Every man has his fault, and honesty is   28
his. I ha' told him on't, but I could ne'er get him
from't.   30

Enter Servant, with wine.

SERVANT   Please Your Lordship, here is the wine.
LUCULLUS   Flaminius, I have noted thee always wise.
Here's to thee.   *[He offers a toast.]*
FLAMINIUS   Your Lordship speaks your pleasure.   34

LUCULLUS   I have observed thee always for a towardly   35
prompt spirit—give thee thy due—and one that   36
knows what belongs to reason; and canst use the time   37
well, if the time use thee well. Good parts in thee! *[To*   38
Servant] Get you gone, sirrah.   *[Exit Servant.]*
Draw nearer, honest Flaminius. Thy lord's a bountiful
gentleman; but thou art wise, and thou know'st well
enough, although thou com'st to me, that this is no
time to lend money, especially upon bare friendship,   43
without security. Here's three solidares for thee. *[He*   44
gives a tip.] Good boy, wink at me, and say thou   45
saw'st me not. Fare thee well.
FLAMINIUS
Is't possible the world should so much differ,   47
And we alive that lived? Fly, damnèd baseness,   48
To him that worships thee! *[He throws the money back.]*
LUCULLUS   Ha? Now I see thou art a fool, and fit for thy
master.   *Exit Lucullus.*
FLAMINIUS
May these add to the number that may scald thee!   52
Let molten coin be thy damnation,
Thou disease of a friend and not himself!   54
Has friendship such a faint and milky heart
It turns in less than two nights? O you gods!   56
I feel my master's passion. This slave   57
Unto his honor has my lord's meat in him.   58
Why should it thrive and turn to nutriment
When he is turned to poison?   60
Oh, may diseases only work upon't!   61
And, when he's sick to death, let not that part of
nature   62
Which my lord paid for be of any power
To expel sickness, but prolong his hour!   *Exit.*

❖

3.2

Enter Lucius, with three Strangers.

LUCIUS   Who, the Lord Timon? He is my very good
friend and an honorable gentleman.
FIRST STRANGER   We know him for no less, though we   3
are but strangers to him. But I can tell you one thing,
my lord, and which I hear from common rumors: now

239 **That . . . foe** i.e., Such naive trusting is the fatal weakness of the
generous mind   **240 free** generous
3.1. Location: Athens. Lucullus's house.
6 hits right accords perfectly   **7 ewer** pitcher.   **tonight** last night.
8 respectively respectfully   **10 complete** accomplished   **18 supply**
fill   **18–19 instant occasion** urgent need   **20 nothing** not at all.
present immediate   **23 'tis** he is   **24 keep . . . house** be so lavish in
his entertaining.   **25 on't** of it   **26 of** on.   **have him** persuade him to
27 by from   **28 honesty** liberality   **30 from't** away from it.   **34 Your**
. . . pleasure It pleases Your Lordship to say so.

35–6 towardly prompt alacritous   **36–8 one . . . thee!** one that knows
how to be sensible; and can make the most of an opportunity if it presents itself. These are fine qualities in you!   **43 bare** mere   **44 soli-**
dares small coins. (A term invented by Shakespeare, evidently.)
45 wink at me pretend not to see me   **47–8 Is't . . . lived?** Is it possible that so much has changed in a short lifetime?   **52 May . . . thee!**
i.e., May these gold coins be added to the molten gold that will be
poured down your throat in hell!   **54 Thou . . . himself** you who are
no true friend at all but only a diseased resemblance.   **56 It turns**
that it sours like milk. (With quibble on the idea of *turn* as in "turn-
coat.")   **57 feel . . . passion** i.e., feel angry on my master's behalf,
share his anger and his suffering.   **57–8 slave Unto his honor** person
slavishly devoted to his own dignity. (Said ironically.)   **58 meat** i.e.,
food of a feast   **60 When . . . poison** when his behavior is so poisonous.   **61 may . . . upon't!** i.e., may diseases only thrive on the food
he has eaten at Timon's table!   **62 that . . . nature** i.e., that sustenance
3.2. Location: Athens. A public place.
3 for no less to be no less than you say

Lord Timon's happy hours are done and past, and his estate shrinks from him.

LUCIUS   Fie, no, do not believe it! He cannot want for money. 8

SECOND STRANGER   But believe you this, my lord, that not long ago one of his men was with the Lord Lucullus to borrow so many talents, nay, urged extremely 12 for't, and showed what necessity belonged to't, and 13 yet was denied.

LUCIUS   How? 15

SECOND STRANGER   I tell you, denied, my lord.

LUCIUS   What a strange case was that! Now, before the gods, I am ashamed on't. Denied that honorable man? There was very little honor showed in't. For my own part, I must needs confess, I have received some small kindnesses from him, as money, plate, jewels, and suchlike trifles, nothing comparing to his; yet had 22 he mistook him and sent to me, I should ne'er have 23 denied his occasion so many talents. 24

Enter Servilius.

SERVILIUS   See, by good hap, yonder's my lord. I have 25 sweat to see his honor. [*To Lucius*] My honored lord— 26

LUCIUS   Servilius? You are kindly met, sir. Fare thee well. Commend me to thy honorable virtuous lord, my very exquisite friend.   [*He starts to go.*] 29

SERVILIUS   May it please Your Honor, my lord hath sent—

LUCIUS   Ha? What has he sent? I am so much endeared 32 to that lord; he's ever sending. How shall I thank him, think'st thou? And what has he sent now?

SERVILIUS   He's only sent his present occasion now, my lord, requesting Your Lordship to supply his instant 36 use with so many talents. 37

LUCIUS
I know His Lordship is but merry with me;
He cannot want fifty—five hundred—talents. 39

SERVILIUS
But in the meantime he wants less, my lord.
If his occasion were not virtuous, 41
I should not urge it half so faithfully.

LUCIUS
Dost thou speak seriously, Servilius?

SERVILIUS   Upon my soul, 'tis true, sir.

LUCIUS   What a wicked beast was I to disfurnish myself 45 against such a good time, when I might ha' shown 46

myself honorable! How unluckily it happened that I 47 should purchase the day before for a little part, and 48 undo a great deal of honor! Servilius, now before the 49 gods, I am not able to do—the more beast, I say—I was sending to use Lord Timon myself, these gentle- 51 men can witness; but I would not for the wealth of 52 Athens I had done't now. Commend me bountifully to His good Lordship, and I hope His Honor will con- 54 ceive the fairest of me, because I have no power to be 55 kind. And tell him this from me: I count it one of my greatest afflictions, say, that I cannot pleasure such an 57 honorable gentleman. Good Servilius, will you be- friend me so far as to use mine own words to him?

SERVILIUS   Yes, sir, I shall.

LUCIUS   I'll look you out a good turn, Servilius. 61
Exit Servilius.
True, as you said, Timon is shrunk indeed; 62
And he that's once denied will hardly speed. 63
Exit.

FIRST STRANGER   Do you observe this, Hostilius?

SECOND STRANGER   Ay, too well.

FIRST STRANGER   Why, this is the world's soul, 66
And just of the same piece 67
Is every flatterer's sport. Who can call him his friend 68
That dips in the same dish? For, in my knowing, 69
Timon has been this lord's father 70
And kept his credit with his purse, 71
Supported his estate; nay, Timon's money
Has paid his men their wages. He ne'er drinks
But Timon's silver treads upon his lip. 74
And yet—Oh, see the monstrousness of man
When he looks out in an ungrateful shape!— 76
He does deny him, in respect of his, 77
What charitable men afford to beggars.

THIRD STRANGER
Religion groans at it.

FIRST STRANGER   For mine own part,
I never tasted Timon in my life, 80
Nor came any of his bounties over me 81
To mark me for his friend; yet I protest,
For his right noble mind, illustrious virtue, 83
And honorable carriage, 84
Had his necessity made use of me,

---

8 **want for** lack   12 **urged extremely** begged insistently   13 **what . . . to't** how necessary it was   15 **How?** What's that you say?   22 **his** i.e., Lucullus's receiving of generosity   23 **mistook . . . me** i.e., mistakenly sent to me, who owe him less   24 **occasion** need. (As also in line 35.)   25 **hap** fortune   25–6 **I have sweat** i.e., I have been hurrying   29 **exquisite** sought after, extraordinary   32 **endeared** obliged   36–7 **supply . . . use** provide for his immediate need   39 **He cannot . . . talents** (Probably an indication of Shakespeare's uncertainty over the value of this currency; see also *so many* above in lines 12, 24, and 37.)   41 **were not virtuous** were due to a fault instead of a virtue, i.e., generosity   45–6 **disfurnish . . . time** leave myself unprepared for such an excellent opportunity

47–9 **that I . . . honor** i.e., that I just yesterday laid out a sum of money in a small investment and thus made it impossible now to acquire a great honor by helping Timon.   51 **use** borrow from   52 **would not** could not bring myself to wish   54–5 **conceive the fairest** think the best   55 **because** i.e., even though   57 **pleasure** satisfy   61 **look you out** seek occasion to do you   62 **shrunk** brought low   63 **speed** prosper.   66 **soul** real essence, vital principle   67 **just . . . piece** exactly the same, cut from the same piece of cloth   68 **sport** plaything, diversion.   69 **dips . . . dish** (Alludes to Judas's betrayal of Christ; see Matthew 26:23.)   **in my knowing** to my knowledge   70 **father** i.e., patron   71 **And . . . purse** and maintained Lucius's credit with Timon's wealth   74 **But . . . lip** without drinking from a silver cup paid for by Timon.   76 **When . . . shape** when he appears in his ungrateful aspect.   77 **He . . . his** Lucius denies Timon an amount that equals, in relation to Lucius's total wealth   80 **tasted Timon** i.e., sampled Timon's liberality   81 **Nor . . . me** nor did any of his generosities light on me   83 **For** because of   84 **carriage** conduct

I would have put my wealth into donation   86
And the best half should have returned to him,
So much I love his heart. But I perceive
Men must learn now with pity to dispense,
For policy sits above conscience.   *Exeunt.*   90

❧

[3.3]

*Enter a third Servant [of Timon's] with
Sempronius, another of Timon's friends.*

SEMPRONIUS
Must he needs trouble me in't? Hum! 'Bove all others?
He might have tried Lord Lucius or Lucullus;
And now Ventidius is wealthy too,
Whom he redeemed from prison. All these
Owe their estates unto him.
SERVANT   My lord,
They have all been touched and found base metal,   7
For they have all denied him.
SEMPRONIUS   How? Have they denied him?
Has Ventidius and Lucullus denied him?
And does he send to me? Three? Humh!
It shows but little love or judgment in him.
Must I be his last refuge? His friends, like physicians,
Thrive, give him over. Must I take th' cure upon me?   14
He's much disgraced me in't. I'm angry at him,
That might have known my place. I see no sense for't   16
But his occasions might have wooed me first;   17
For, in my conscience, I was the first man   18
That e'er received gift from him.
And does he think so backwardly of me now   20
That I'll requite it last? No!   21
So it may prove an argument of laughter   22
To th' rest, and I 'mongst lords be thought a fool.
I'd rather than the worth of thrice the sum
He'd sent to me first, but for my mind's sake;   25
I'd such a courage to do him good. But now return,   26
And with their faint reply this answer join:
Who bates mine honor shall not know my coin.   28
Exit.

SERVANT   Excellent! Your Lordship's a goodly villain.   29
The devil knew not what he did when he made man
politic; he crossed himself by't, and I cannot think but   31
in the end the villainies of man will set him clear.   32

How fairly this lord strives to appear foul! Takes vir-   33
tuous copies to be wicked, like those that under hot   34
ardent zeal would set whole realms on fire!   35
Of such a nature is his politic love.
This was my lord's best hope; now all are fled,
Save only the gods. Now his friends are dead,   38
Doors that were ne'er acquainted with their wards   39
Many a bounteous year must be employed   40
Now to guard sure their master.   41
And this is all a liberal course allows: 42
Who cannot keep his wealth must keep his house.   43
Exit.

❧

[3.4]

*Enter [two of] Varro's Men, meeting [Titus's
Servant and] others, all [being servants of] Timon's
creditors, to wait for his coming out. Then enter
Lucius's [Servant] and Hortensius's [Servant].*

VARRO'S FIRST SERVANT
Well met. Good morrow, Titus and Hortensius.
TITUS'S SERVANT
The like to you, kind Varro.
HORTENSIUS'S SERVANT   Lucius!
What, do we meet together?
LUCIUS'S SERVANT   Ay, and I think
One business does command us all;
For mine is money.
TITUS'S SERVANT   So is theirs and ours.

Enter Philotus's [Servant].

LUCIUS'S SERVANT
And Sir Philotus too!
PHILOTUS'S SERVANT   Good day at once.   6
LUCIUS'S SERVANT   Welcome, good brother.
What do you think the hour?
PHILOTUS'S SERVANT   Laboring for nine.   8
LUCIUS'S SERVANT
So much?
PHILOTUS'S SERVANT   Is not my lord seen yet?
LUCIUS'S SERVANT   Not yet.   9
PHILOTUS'S SERVANT
I wonder on't. He was wont to shine at seven.   10
LUCIUS'S SERVANT
Ay, but the days are waxed shorter with him.   11
You must consider that a prodigal course

---

86 I . . . donation i.e., I would have supposed all my wealth to have
come from him (and thus to be considered his when he needs it back)
90 policy self-interest
3.3. Location: Athens. Sempronius's house.
7 touched (Metaphor derived from testing metals with a touchstone
to see if they are gold.)   14 Thrive . . . over i.e., thrive on his wealth,
but now give him up as beyond help.   16 That . . . place who should
have acknowledged my position (among his friends).   sense reason
17 But his occasions but that he, in his need   18 in my conscience to
my knowledge   20 think . . . me (1) think I am so backward (2) think
of me last   21 That . . . last? that I will repay him when he has
applied last to me among his friends?   22 argument of subject for
25 but . . . sake if only to satisfy my mind   26 courage desire
28 Who bates whoever abates, detracts from   29 goodly proper.
(Said ironically.)   31 politic cunning.   crossed foiled (by making
man his rival in treachery)   32 set him clear make even the devil
look innocent.

33 How fairly With what a plausible appearance of virtue
33–5 Takes . . . fire! How this lord appears to model himself on the
virtuous only for wicked purposes, like religious bigots who for zealous purposes would burn down whole kingdoms!   38 Now Now
that.   dead dead to him, alienated   39–41 Doors . . . master doors
that for those many years of Timon's bounty never knew a single bolt
or lock must now be shut tight to shield Timon against arrest for debt
(and also to shield his erstwhile friends from Timon's importunities).
42 liberal generous   43 keep . . . keep preserve . . . stay inside
3.4. Location: Athens. Timon's house.
6 at once to one and all.   8 Laboring for Moving toward   9 much
i.e., late.   10 was . . . shine used to be up   11 are waxed have grown

Is like the sun's,
But not, like his, recoverable. I fear   14
'Tis deepest winter in Lord Timon's purse;
That is, one may reach deep enough and yet
Find little.

PHILOTUS'S SERVANT   I am of your fear for that.   17

TITUS'S SERVANT
I'll show you how t'observe a strange event.
Your lord sends now for money?

HORTENSIUS'S SERVANT   Most true, he does.

TITUS'S SERVANT
And he wears jewels now of Timon's gift,
For which I wait for money.   21

HORTENSIUS'S SERVANT   It is against my heart.   22

LUCIUS'S SERVANT   Mark how strange it shows:
Timon in this should pay more than he owes,
And e'en as if your lord should wear rich jewels   25
And send for money for 'em.   26

HORTENSIUS'S SERVANT
I'm weary of this charge, the gods can witness.   27
I know my lord hath spent of Timon's wealth,
And now ingratitude makes it worse than stealth.   29

VARRO'S FIRST SERVANT
Yes, mine's three thousand crowns. What's yours?

LUCIUS'S SERVANT   Five thousand, mine.

VARRO'S FIRST SERVANT
'Tis much deep, and it should seem by th' sum   32
Your master's confidence was above mine,   33
Else surely his had equaled.   34

Enter Flaminius.

TITUS'S SERVANT   One of Lord Timon's men.

LUCIUS'S SERVANT   Flaminius? Sir, a word. Pray, is my
lord ready to come forth?

FLAMINIUS   No, indeed, he is not.

TITUS'S SERVANT   We attend His Lordship. Pray signify   39
so much.

FLAMINIUS   I need not tell him that. He knows you are
too diligent.   [*Exit.*]   41

Enter steward [*Flavius*] *in a cloak, muffled.*

LUCIUS'S SERVANT
Ha! Is not that his steward muffled so?
He goes away in a cloud. Call him, call him.   43

TITUS'S SERVANT [*to Flavius*]   Do you hear, sir?

VARRO'S SECOND SERVANT [*to Flavius*]   By your leave, sir.

FLAVIUS
What do ye ask of me, my friend?

TITUS'S SERVANT
We wait for certain money here, sir.

FLAVIUS   Ay,   47
If money were as certain as your waiting,
'Twere sure enough.
Why then preferred you not your sums and bills   50
When your false masters eat of my lord's meat?   51
Then they could smile and fawn upon his debts,
And take down th'interest into their glutt'nous maws.   53
You do yourselves but wrong to stir me up.   54
Let me pass quietly.
Believe't, my lord and I have made an end;   56
I have no more to reckon, he to spend.   57

LUCIUS'S SERVANT   Ay, but this answer will not serve.   58

FLAVIUS
If 'twill not serve, 'tis not so base as you,
For you serve knaves.   [*Exit.*]

VARRO'S FIRST SERVANT   How? What does His cashiered   61
Worship mutter?

VARRO'S SECOND SERVANT   No matter what; he's poor,   64
and that's revenge enough. Who can speak broader   64
than he that has no house to put his head in? Such   65
may rail against great buildings.   66

Enter Servilius.

TITUS'S SERVANT   Oh, here's Servilius. Now we shall
know some answer.

SERVILIUS   If I might beseech you, gentlemen, to repair   69
some other hour, I should derive much from't. For   70
take't of my soul, my lord leans wondrously to discon-   71
tent. His comfortable temper has forsook him; he's   72
much out of health and keeps his chamber.   73

LUCIUS'S SERVANT
Many do keep their chambers are not sick,   74
And if it be so far beyond his health,   75
Methinks he should the sooner pay his debts
And make a clear way to the gods.

SERVILIUS   Good gods!   77

TITUS'S SERVANT
We cannot take this for an answer, sir.

FLAMINIUS (*within*)   Servilius, help! My lord, my lord!

Enter Timon, in a rage.

---

14 **But . . . recoverable** i.e., the sun will return from its wintry path,
but Timon cannot recover (since his funds are not *recoverable*).   17 **am
of** share   21 **For . . . money** i.e., while I wait for the money used to
buy those jewels.   22 **It is . . . heart** It goes against my conscience.
25–6 **e'en . . . for 'em** i.e., it's just as though your master should both
wear the jewels Timon gave him and simultaneously demand the
money that paid for those jewels.   27 **charge** commission   29 **stealth**
theft.   32 **much deep** very great   33 **mine** my master's   34 **his had
equaled** i.e., my master's loan would have equaled in amount your
master's.   39 **attend** are waiting for   41 **diligent** i.e., officious.
43 **in a cloud** (1) muffled (2) in a state of gloom and ignominy.

47 **certain** certain sums of. (But Flavius puns bitterly in the next line
on the sense of "reliable," "predictable.")   50 **preferred** presented
51 **eat** ate. (Pronounced *et*.)   53 **th'interest** i.e., the food and drink
they consumed as though it were interest on a loan.   **maws** stomachs. (A term used of animals.)   54 **do yourselves but** only do yourselves   56 **made an end** severed our relationship   57 **reckon** keep
account of   58 **serve** do. (But Flavius punningly replies in the sense
of "act as servant.")   61 **How?** What's this?   **cashiered** dismissed.
(*His cashiered Worship* is offered sardonically as if it were a title of dignity.)   64 **broader** (1) more freely (2) more in the open, abroad
65–6 **Such . . . buildings** i.e., A man who is houseless and out of service, like Flavius, has nothing to lose and can inveigh against injustice
and inequality.   69 **repair** return   70 **derive** benefit   71 **take't . . . soul**
i.e., believe I speak sincerely   72 **comfortable temper** cheerful disposition   73 **keeps** stays in   74 **are** who are   75 **if . . . health** if his difficulty is something other than poor physical health   77 **make . . .
gods** i.e., pay all his debts to smooth his way to heaven.   **Good gods!**
(1) The gods are good! (2) Good God!

TIMON
What, are my doors opposed against my passage?
Have I been ever free, and must my house
Be my retentive enemy, my jail?   82
The place which I have feasted, does it now,
Like all mankind, show me an iron heart?

LUCIUS'S SERVANT   Put in now, Titus.   85

TITUS'S SERVANT   My lord, here is my bill.

LUCIUS'S SERVANT   Here's mine.

HORTENSIUS'S SERVANT   And mine, my lord.

BOTH VARRO'S SERVANTS   And ours, my lord.

PHILOTUS'S SERVANT   All our bills.

TIMON
Knock me down with 'em! Cleave me to the girdle!   91

LUCIUS'S SERVANT   Alas, my lord—

TIMON   Cut my heart in sums!   93

TITUS'S SERVANT   Mine, fifty talents.

TIMON   Tell out my blood!   95

LUCIUS'S SERVANT   Five thousand crowns, my lord.

TIMON
Five thousand drops pays that. What yours? And
    yours?

VARRO'S FIRST SERVANT   My lord—

VARRO'S SECOND SERVANT   My lord—

TIMON
Tear me, take me, and the gods fall upon you!   100
                                    Exit Timon.

HORTENSIUS'S SERVANT   Faith, I perceive our masters
may throw their caps at their money. These debts   102
may well be called desperate ones, for a madman owes   103
'em.   Exeunt.

        Enter Timon [and Flavius].

TIMON
They have e'en put my breath from me, the slaves.   105
Creditors? Devils!

FLAVIUS   My dear lord—

TIMON   What if it should be so?   108

FLAVIUS   My lord—

TIMON
I'll have it so. My steward!

FLAVIUS   Here, my lord.

TIMON
So fitly? Go, bid all my friends again,   111
Lucius, Lucullus, and Sempronius—all.
I'll once more feast the rascals.

FLAVIUS   Oh, my lord,
You only speak from your distracted soul;
There's not so much left to furnish out   115
A moderate table.

TIMON   Be it not in thy care. Go,   117
I charge thee, invite them all. Let in the tide
Of knaves once more. My cook and I'll provide.
                                    Exeunt.

                        ❧

[3.5]

*Enter three Senators at one door, Alcibiades
meeting them, with attendants.*

FIRST SENATOR   [*to another Senator*]
My lord, you have my voice to't.   1
The fault's bloody;   2
'Tis necessary he should die.
Nothing emboldens sin so much as mercy.

SECOND SENATOR   Most true. The law shall bruise 'em.   5

ALCIBIADES
Honor, health, and compassion to the Senate!   6

FIRST SENATOR   Now, Captain?

ALCIBIADES
I am an humble suitor to your virtues;
For pity is the virtue of the law,   9
And none but tyrants use it cruelly.
It pleases time and fortune to lie heavy   11
Upon a friend of mine, who in hot blood   12
Hath stepped into the law, which is past depth   13
To those that without heed do plunge into't.   14
He is a man, setting his fate aside,   15
Of comely virtues;
Nor did he soil the fact with cowardice—   17
An honor in him which buys out his fault—   18
But with a noble fury and fair spirit,
Seeing his reputation touched to death,   20
He did oppose his foe;
And with such sober and unnoted passion   22
He did behave his anger, ere 'twas spent,   23
As if he had but proved an argument.   24

FIRST SENATOR
You undergo too strict a paradox,   25
Striving to make an ugly deed look fair.
Your words have took such pains as if they labored
To bring manslaughter into form and set quarreling   28
Upon the head of valor—which indeed   29
Is valor misbegot, and came into the world
When sects and factions were newly born.

---

82 **retentive** confining   85 **Put in** i.e., Make payment; let me put in
my bill   91 **Knock, Cleave** (Timon puns on *bills* as weapons.)
girdle belt.   93 **in sums** into sums of money.   95 **Tell out** Count out
by the drop   100 **the gods fall upon you** i.e., may the gods attack
you as with an army.   102 **throw . . . at** i.e., give up hope of recovering   103 **desperate** (1) unlikely to be recovered (2) resulting from
desperate madness   105 **e'en . . . me** left me breathless   108 **What
. . . so?** i.e., What is there to do in that case? (Timon has evidently
thought of the mock banquet he will serve in 3.6.)   111 **fitly** conveniently.   115 **furnish out** supply

117 **Be . . . care** Don't you worry about it.
3.5. Location: Athens. The Senate House.
1 voice to't vote in favor of it (the death sentence under consideration).   **2 fault's bloody** crime involved bloodshed   **5 'em** i.e., all
such offenders.   **6 compassion to the Senate** i.e., may the Senate
have compassion.   **9 virtue** chief merit, essence   **11–12 lie . . . Upon**
oppress   **13 stepped into** incurred the penalties of   **13–14 past
depth To** over the heads of   **15 setting . . . aside** setting aside his ill-
fated action   **17 fact** deed   **18 buys out** redeems   **20 touched to
death** fatally threatened   **22 unnoted** imperceptible   **23 behave** control   **24 but . . . argument** only been arguing a point.   **25 You . . .
paradox** You split hairs   **28–9 To . . . valor** to make manslaughter
appear legally defensible and dueling the very height of honor

He's truly valiant that can wisely suffer   32
The worst that man can breathe,   33
And make his wrongs his outsides,   34
To wear them like his raiment, carelessly,   35
And ne'er prefer his injuries to his heart,   36
To bring it into danger.   37
If wrongs be evils and enforce us kill,   38
What folly 'tis to hazard life for ill!   39

ALCIBIADES
My lord—

FIRST SENATOR   You cannot make gross sins look clear.   40
To revenge is no valor, but to bear.   41

ALCIBIADES
My lords, then, under favor, pardon me   42
If I speak like a captain.
Why do fond men expose themselves to battle,   44
And not endure all threats? Sleep upon't,   45
And let the foes quietly cut their throats
Without repugnancy? If there be   47
Such valor in the bearing, what make we   48
Abroad? Why then, women are more valiant   49
That stay at home, if bearing carry it,   50
And the ass more captain than the lion, the felon
Loaden with irons wiser than the judge,   52
If wisdom be in suffering. O my lords,
As you are great, be pitifully good.   54
Who cannot condemn rashness in cold blood?
To kill, I grant, is sin's extremest gust,   56
But in defense, by mercy, 'tis most just.   57
To be in anger is impiety,
But who is man that is not angry?   59
Weigh but the crime with this.

SECOND SENATOR   You breathe in vain.   61

ALCIBIADES   In vain? His service done
At Lacedaemon and Byzantium
Were a sufficient briber for his life.

FIRST SENATOR   What's that?

ALCIBIADES
Why, I say, my lords, he's done fair service
And slain in fight many of your enemies.
How full of valor did he bear himself
In the last conflict, and made plenteous wounds!

SECOND SENATOR
He has made too much plenty with 'em.   70

He's a sworn rioter; he has a sin that often   71
Drowns him and takes his valor prisoner.
If there were no foes, that were enough   73
To overcome him. In that beastly fury
He has been known to commit outrages
And cherish factions. 'Tis inferred to us   76
His days are foul and his drink dangerous.

FIRST SENATOR
He dies.

ALCIBIADES   Hard fate! He might have died in war.
My lords, if not for any parts in him—   79
Though his right arm might purchase his own time   80
And be in debt to none—yet, more to move you,
Take my deserts to his and join 'em both;   82
And, for I know your reverend ages love   83
Security, I'll pawn my victories, all   84
My honors, to you, upon his good returns.   85
If by this crime he owes the law his life,
Why, let the war receive't in valiant gore,   87
For law is strict, and war is nothing more.

FIRST SENATOR
We are for law. He dies; urge it no more,
On height of our displeasure. Friend or brother,   90
He forfeits his own blood that spills another.   91

ALCIBIADES
Must it be so? It must not be. My lords,
I do beseech you, know me.

SECOND SENATOR   How?

ALCIBIADES   Call me to your remembrances.

THIRD SENATOR   What?

ALCIBIADES
I cannot think but your age has forgot me.   97
It could not else be I should prove so base   98
To sue and be denied such common grace.   99
My wounds ache at you.

FIRST SENATOR   Do you dare our anger?
'Tis in few words, but spacious in effect: 101
We banish thee forever.

ALCIBIADES   Banish me?
Banish your dotage, banish usury,
That makes the Senate ugly.

FIRST SENATOR
If after two days' shine Athens contain thee,
Attend our weightier judgment.   106
And, not to swell our spirit,   107
He shall be executed presently.   *Exeunt [Senators].*   108

32–7 He's . . . danger That person is truly valiant who can endure grave insults with equanimity and treat such injuries as merely external, bearing them lightly and casually as though they were garments, and never take such injuries to heart in such a way as to lead to a dangerous confrontation.   38 kill to kill   39 What . . . ill! what a folly it is to let this code of honor put life itself at risk in a bad cause!   40 clear innocent.   41 to bear bearing insults calmly is true valor.   42 under favor by your leave   44 fond foolish   45 Sleep upon't i.e., Why do they not disregard danger   47 repugnancy resistance.   47–9 If . . . Abroad? If it's valorous to put up with insults, what are we men doing abroad in the world?   50 bearing (1) putting up with insults (2) child-bearing (3) bearing the weight of a man in sex.   carry it wins the day   52 Loaden with irons weighed down with shackles   54 pitifully good good by showing mercy.   56 gust outburst   57 defense self-defense.   by mercy by a merciful interpretation of law   59 not not sometimes   61 breathe speak   70 He . . . 'em He has been too free in making wounds, and has rioted too freely after victory.

71 sworn rioter inveterate debauchee.   a sin i.e., drunkenness   73 If . . . enough Even without enemies, his drinking is enough   76 cherish factions encourage dissension and conspiracy.   inferred alleged   79 parts admirable traits   80 his . . . time his ability as a soldier should redeem him   82 to in addition to   83 for because   84 Security (1) safety (2) collateral for a loan (using a financial metaphor found also in *purchase, pawn, good returns,* etc.)   85 upon . . . returns as a pledge that he will make a good return on your investment in him, i.e., fight bravely in war.   87 let . . . gore i.e., let him pay his debt by bleeding as a soldier   90 On . . . our on pain of our highest   91 another i.e., another's.   97 your age has you, in your advanced age, have   98 else be otherwise be (that).   prove i.e., be considered   99 To sue as to plead for   101 spacious in effect of great import. (With quibble on the spacious world to which Alcibiades is banished.)   106 Attend . . . judgment expect our more severe sentence.   107 spirit anger   108 presently immediately.

ALCIBIADES

 Now the gods keep you old enough   109
 That you may live
 Only in bone, that none may look on you!—   111
 I'm worse than mad. I have kept back their foes,
 While they have told their money and let out   113
 Their coin upon large interest, I myself
 Rich only in large hurts. All those for this?   115
 Is this the balsam that the usuring Senate   116
 Pours into captains' wounds? Banishment!
 It comes not ill; I hate not to be banished.   118
 It is a cause worthy my spleen and fury,   119
 That I may strike at Athens. I'll cheer up
 My discontented troops and lay for hearts.   121
 'Tis honor with most lands to be at odds.   122
 Soldiers should brook as little wrongs as gods.   *Exit.*   123

❧

[3.6]

[Music. Tables and seats set out; servants attending.] Enter divers friends [of Timon] at several doors.

FIRST LORD The good time of day to you, sir.

SECOND LORD I also wish it to you. I think this honorable lord did but try us this other day.   3

FIRST LORD Upon that were my thoughts tiring when   4
we encountered. I hope it is not so low with him as he   5
made it seem in the trial of his several friends.

SECOND LORD It should not be, by the persuasion of   7
his new feasting.

FIRST LORD I should think so. He hath sent me an earnest inviting, which many my near occasions did urge   10
me to put off; but he hath conjured me beyond them,   11
and I must needs appear.   12

SECOND LORD In like manner was I in debt to my importunate business, but he would not hear my excuse.   13
I am sorry, when he sent to borrow of me, that my
provision was out.   16

FIRST LORD I am sick of that grief too, as I understand   17
how all things go.   18

SECOND LORD Every man here's so. What would he
have borrowed of you?

FIRST LORD A thousand pieces.   21

---

109 **keep . . . enough** preserve you to such an old age 111 **Only . . . you** i.e., mere skeletons, forgotten or avoided by everyone. 113 **told** reckoned. **let** lent 115 **hurts** injuries. 116 **balsam** balm, medicine 118 **It . . . ill** It is not such a bad thing after all 119 **worthy** worthy of 121 **lay for hearts** endeavor to win their affection. 122 **'Tis . . . odds** It's honorable to be at variance with a country (and its political leaders) in most instances. 123 **brook . . . gods** endure insults as little as the gods do.
3.6. Location: Athens. A banqueting room in Timon's house.
0.3 *several* separate **3 did . . . us** was only testing us **4 tiring** preying, feeding, i.e., busily engaged **5 I . . . him** I hope his financial situation is not as desperate **7 persuasion** evidence **10 inviting** invitation. **many . . . occasions** my many urgent necessities or business **11 conjured . . . them** summoned me so urgently as to overcome my previous commitments **12 needs** necessarily **13 in debt to** obligated to **16 provision was out** resources were exhausted.
17–18 as . . . go particularly as I now understand the state of affairs. (Perhaps hinting at Timon's seeming ability to entertain lavishly again.) **21 pieces** i.e., gold coins.

SECOND LORD A thousand pieces?

FIRST LORD What of you?

SECOND LORD He sent to me, sir—Here he comes.

Enter Timon and attendants. [Music plays.]

TIMON With all my heart, gentlemen both! And how fare you?

FIRST LORD Ever at the best, hearing well of Your Lordship.

SECOND LORD The swallow follows not summer more willing than we Your Lordship.

TIMON *[aside]* Nor more willingly leaves winter, such summer birds are men.—Gentlemen, our dinner will not recompense this long stay. Feast your ears   33
with the music awhile, if they will fare so harshly o'th'   34
trumpet's sound. We shall to't presently.   35

FIRST LORD I hope it remains not unkindly with Your Lordship that I returned you an empty messenger.

TIMON Oh, sir, let it not trouble you.

SECOND LORD My noble lord—

TIMON Ah, my good friend, what cheer?

         The banquet brought in.

SECOND LORD My most honorable lord, I am e'en sick of shame that when Your Lordship this other day sent to me I was so unfortunate a beggar.   43

TIMON Think not on't, sir.

SECOND LORD If you had sent but two hours before—

TIMON Let it not cumber your better remembrance.—   46
Come, bring in all together.

SECOND LORD All covered dishes!   48

FIRST LORD Royal cheer, I warrant you.

THIRD LORD Doubt not that, if money and the season can yield it.

FIRST LORD How do you? What's the news?

THIRD LORD Alcibiades is banished. Hear you of it?

FIRST AND SECOND LORDS Alcibiades banished?

THIRD LORD 'Tis so, be sure of it.

FIRST LORD How? How?

SECOND LORD I pray you, upon what?   57

TIMON My worthy friends, will you draw near?

THIRD LORD I'll tell you more anon. Here's a noble feast toward.   60

SECOND LORD This is the old man still.   61

THIRD LORD Will't hold? Will't hold?   62

SECOND LORD It does; but time will—and so—   63

THIRD LORD I do conceive.   64

TIMON Each man to his stool, with that spur as he   65
would to the lip of his mistress. Your diet shall be in   66
all places alike. Make not a city feast of it, to let the   67
meat cool ere we can agree upon the first place; sit, sit.   68
[They sit.] The gods require our thanks.

---

33 stay delay. **34–5 if . . . sound** if your ears will deign to feast on so harsh a sound as that of the trumpet. **43 so . . . beggar** so unfortunate as to be out of ready reserves. **46 cumber . . . remembrance** trouble your happier thoughts, memories. **48 covered** lidded. (Implies particularly elegant fare.) **57 what** what ground.
60 toward imminent. **61 old man still** man we once knew. **62 hold** last. **63 will** i.e., will tell **64 conceive** understand. **65 that spur** the same eagerness **66 diet** food **66–7 in . . . alike** the same wherever you sit to eat. **67 city feast** formal occasion, with seating by rank **68 first place** place of honor

You great benefactors, sprinkle our society with
thankfulness. For your own gifts, make yourselves
praised; but reserve still to give, lest your deities be   72
despised. Lend to each man enough, that one need not
lend to another; for, were your godheads to borrow of
men, men would forsake the gods. Make the meat be
beloved more than the man that gives it. Let no assembly of twenty be without a score of villains. If there sit   77
twelve women at the table, let a dozen of them be—as
they are. The rest of your fees, O gods—the senators   79
of Athens, together with the common tag of people—   80
what is amiss in them, you gods, make suitable for
destruction. For these my present friends, as they are   82
to me nothing, so in nothing bless them, and to nothing are they welcome.

Uncover, dogs, and lap!
> [*The dishes are uncovered and seen to contain
> warm water and stones.*]

SOME SPEAK   What does His Lordship mean?
SOME OTHERS   I know not.
TIMON
May you a better feast never behold,
You knot of mouth-friends! Smoke and lukewarm
     water   89
Is your perfection. This is Timon's last,   90
Who, stuck and spangled with your flatteries,   91
Washes it off and sprinkles in your faces
Your reeking villainy.
> [*He throws the water in their faces.*]
               Live loathed and long,
Most smiling, smooth, detested parasites,
Courteous destroyers, affable wolves, meek bears,
You fools of fortune, trencher-friends, time's flies,   96
Cap-and-knee slaves, vapors, and minute-jacks!   97
Of man and beast the infinite malady   98
Crust you quite o'er! What, dost thou go?
Soft! Take thy physic first! Thou too, and thou!   100
Stay, I will lend thee money, borrow none.
> [*He assaults them and drives them out.*]
What, all in motion? Henceforth be no feast
Whereat a villain's not a welcome guest.
Burn, house! Sink, Athens! Henceforth hated be
Of Timon, man, and all humanity!   *Exit.* 105

Enter the Senators, with other Lords, [*returning*].

FIRST LORD   How now, my lords?

SECOND LORD   Know you the quality of Lord Timon's   107
     fury?
THIRD LORD   Push! Did you see my cap?   109
FOURTH LORD   I have lost my gown.
FIRST LORD   He's but a mad lord, and naught but hu-   111
mors sways him. He gave me a jewel th'other day,   112
and now he has beat it out of my hat. Did you see my
jewel?   [*They search for their belongings.*]
THIRD LORD   Did you see my cap?
SECOND LORD   Here 'tis.
FOURTH LORD   Here lies my gown.
FIRST LORD   Let's make no stay.
SECOND LORD
Lord Timon's mad.
THIRD LORD   I feel't upon my bones.
FOURTH LORD
One day he gives us diamonds, next day stones.
                         Exeunt the Senators [*etc.*].

4.1

Enter Timon.

TIMON
Let me look back upon thee. O thou wall
That girdles in those wolves, dive in the earth
And fence not Athens! Matrons, turn incontinent!   3
Obedience fail in children! Slaves and fools,   4
Pluck the grave wrinkled Senate from the bench
And minister in their steads! To general filths   6
Convert o'th'instant, green virginity!   7
Do't in your parents' eyes. Bankrupts, hold fast;
Rather than render back, out with your knives
And cut your trusters' throats! Bound servants, steal!   10
Large-handed robbers your grave masters are,   11
And pill by law. Maid, to thy master's bed!   12
Thy mistress is o'th' brothel. Son of sixteen,
Pluck the lined crutch from thy old limping sire;   14
With it beat out his brains! Piety and fear,   15
Religion to the gods, peace, justice, truth,   16
Domestic awe, night rest, and neighborhood,   17
Instruction, manners, mysteries, and trades,   18
Degrees, observances, customs, and laws,   19
Decline to your confounding contraries,   20
And yet confusion live! Plagues, incident to men,   21
Your potent and infectious fevers heap
On Athens, ripe for stroke! Thou cold sciatica,   23

---

72 reserve . . . give always hold back something   **77 a score** twenty
79 fees i.e., what is held in fee from you, your gifts or benefactions,
or, those who hold their lives in fee from you   **80 tag** rabble   **82 For**
As for   **89 knot of mouth-friends** group of friends in words only.
Smoke Steam, i.e., "hot air"   **90 Is your perfection** suits you perfectly.   **91 stuck and spangled** bespattered and decorated   **96–7 You
. . . minute-jacks!** you toadies and dupes of Dame Fortune, you
friends only so long as you're being fed, you fair-weather insects, you
obsequious flatterers doffing your caps and bowing your knees, you
vapid creatures, you timeservers like the mannikins that strike the
bell on the outside of a clock!   **98 Of . . . malady** May every loathsome disease known to humanity and beasts   **100 Soft!** Wait a
minute!   **physic** medicine   **105 Of** by

107 quality original nature, occasion   **109 Push!** Pshaw!
111–12 humors caprice, an imbalance in his physiological humors
4.1. Location: Outside the walls of Athens.
3 fence (1) enclose (2) defend.   **incontinent** lascivious.   **4 Obedience fail** Let obedience fail   **6 general filths** common prostitutes
7 green young   **10 trusters'** creditors'.   **Bound** Indentured
11 Large-handed Rapacious   **12 pill by law** plunder by legal means.
to go to   **14 lined** stuffed, padded   **15 fear** religious awe   **16 Religion to** veneration of   **17 Domestic awe** respect for the seniors of a
household.   **neighborhood** neighborliness   **18 mysteries** crafts
19 Degrees established ranks of society   **20 confounding contraries**
opposites that reduce all to chaos   **21 yet** i.e., henceforth still let
23 cold chilling, or caused by chill.   **sciatica** nerve pain in hip and leg

Cripple our senators, that their limbs may halt   24
As lamely as their manners! Lust and liberty   25
Creep in the minds and marrows of our youth,   26
That 'gainst the stream of virtue they may strive   27
And drown themselves in riot! Itches, blains,   28
Sow all th'Athenian bosoms, and their crop   29
Be general leprosy! Breath infect breath,
That their society, as their friendship, may   31
Be merely poison! Nothing I'll bear from thee   32
But nakedness, thou detestable town!
                                    [*He strips off his garments.*]
Take thou that too, with multiplying bans!   34
Timon will to the woods, where he shall find
Th'unkindest beast more kinder than mankind.   36
The gods confound—hear me, you good gods all—
Th'Athenians both within and out that wall!
And grant, as Timon grows, his hate may grow
To the whole race of mankind, high and low!
Amen.   *Exit.*

❧

[4.2]

*Enter steward [Flavius], with two or three
Servants.*

FIRST SERVANT
Hear you, Master Steward, where's our master?
Are we undone, cast off, nothing remaining?

FLAVIUS
Alack, my fellows, what should I say to you?
Let me be recorded by the righteous gods,   4
I am as poor as you.

FIRST SERVANT   Such a house broke?   5
So noble a master fall'n? All gone, and not
One friend to take his fortune by the arm   7
And go along with him?

SECOND SERVANT   As we do turn our backs
From our companion thrown into his grave,
So his familiars to his buried fortunes   11
Slink all away, leave their false vows with him
Like empty purses picked; and his poor self,
A dedicated beggar to the air,   14
With his disease of all-shunned poverty,
Walks, like contempt, alone. More of our fellows.   16

Enter other Servants.

FLAVIUS
All broken implements of a ruined house.

THIRD SERVANT
Yet do our hearts wear Timon's livery;   18
That see I by our faces. We are fellows still,
Serving alike in sorrow. Leaked is our bark,   20
And we, poor mates, stand on the dying deck,   21
Hearing the surges threat. We must all part   22
Into this sea of air.

FLAVIUS   Good fellows all,
The latest of my wealth I'll share amongst you.   24
Wherever we shall meet, for Timon's sake,
Let's yet be fellows. Let's shake our heads and say,   26
As 'twere a knell unto our master's fortunes,   27
"We have seen better days." Let each take some.
                                    [*He gives them money.*]
Nay, put out all your hands. Not one word more.   29
Thus part we rich in sorrow, parting poor.   30
                        [*Servants*] embrace, and part several ways.
Oh, the fierce wretchedness that glory brings us!
Who would not wish to be from wealth exempt,
Since riches point to misery and contempt?   33
Who would be so mocked with glory, or to live
But in a dream of friendship,
To have his pomp and all what state compounds   36
But only painted, like his varnished friends?   37
Poor honest lord, brought low by his own heart,
Undone by goodness! Strange, unusual blood,   39
When man's worst sin is he does too much good!
Who then dares to be half so kind again?
For bounty, that makes gods, do still mar men.   42
My dearest lord, blest to be most accurst,   43
Rich only to be wretched, thy great fortunes
Are made thy chief afflictions. Alas, kind lord!
He's flung in rage from this ingrateful seat   46
Of monstrous friends,
Nor has he with him to supply his life,   48
Or that which can command it.   49
I'll follow and inquire him out.
I'll ever serve his mind with my best will;   51
Whilst I have gold, I'll be his steward still.   *Exit.*

❧

[4.3]

Enter Timon, in the woods [with a spade].

TIMON
O blessèd breeding sun, draw from the earth

24 **halt** limp   25 **liberty** licentiousness   26 **marrows** soft tissues filling the cavities of bone (thought of as the source of vitality and
strength)   27 **stream** current   28 **riot** dissoluteness.   **blains** blisters
29 **Sow** fall like seed in   31 **society** associating with one another
32 **merely** entirely   34 **bans** curses.   36 **Th'unkindest** (1) the cru-
ellest (2) the most unnatural, turning against kin and kind. (*Kinder*
continues the wordplay.)
4.2. Location: Athens. Timon's house.
4 **Let . . . gods** May the gods note down and confirm what I say
5 **house broke** household disbanded.   7 **his fortune** i.e., Timon in his
misfortune. (The dialogue here fulfills the allegorical scene of fallen
fortune imagined by the Poet in 1.1.68–93.)   11 **his familiars . . . fortunes** those close to him when he was fortunate, now perceiving his
ruin   14 **dedicated . . . air** beggar having nothing and nowhere to go
16 **like contempt** as if he were contemptibility itself

18 **livery** uniform worn by male household servants (here used
metaphorically)   20 **bark** sailing vessel   21 **mates** (1) fellows
(2) mates of a vessel.   **dying** i.e., sinking   22 **surges** waves
24 **latest** last remnant   26 **yet** still.   **shake our heads** (in sorrow)
27 **knell** tolling of a bell, announcing a death or other misfortune
29 **put out all** all put out   30.1 *several* separate   33 **point to** tend to
36 **what state compounds** that which constitutes dignity and splendor   37 **But only** nothing more than   39 **blood** nature   42 **bounty
. . . men** i.e., generosity, a godlike attribute, brings mere mortals to
ruin.   43 **to be** only to be   46 **flung** rushed off   48 **Nor . . . life** nor
has he anything to maintain himself with   49 **that . . . it** i.e., money.
51 **serve his mind** execute his wishes
**4.3. Location: Woods and cave, near the seashore; in front of
Timon's cave.**

Rotten humidity; below thy sister's orb 2
Infect the air! Twinned brothers of one womb, 3
Whose procreation, residence, and birth 4
Scarce is dividant, touch them with several fortunes, 5
The greater scorns the lesser. Not nature, 6
To whom all sores lay siege, can bear great fortune 7
But by contempt of nature. 8
Raise me this beggar, and deny't that lord; 9
The senator shall bear contempt hereditary, 10
The beggar native honor. 11
It is the pasture lards the brother's sides, 12
The want that makes him lean. Who dares, who dares 13
In purity of manhood stand upright
And say "This man's a flatterer"? If one be,
So are they all, for every grece of fortune 16
Is smoothed by that below. The learnèd pate 17
Ducks to the golden fool. All's obliquy; 18
There's nothing level in our cursèd natures 19
But direct villainy. Therefore, be abhorred
All feasts, societies, and throngs of men!
His semblable, yea, himself, Timon disdains. 22
Destruction fang mankind! Earth, yield me roots! 23
                                    [*He digs.*]
Who seeks for better of thee, sauce his palate 24
With thy most operant poison! [*He finds gold.*] What
    is here? 25
Gold? Yellow, glittering, precious gold?
No, gods, I am no idle votarist. 27
Roots, you clear heavens! Thus much of this will make 28
Black white, foul fair, wrong right,
Base noble, old young, coward valiant.
Ha, you gods! Why this? What this, you gods? Why,
    this
Will lug your priests and servants from your sides,
Pluck stout men's pillows from below their heads. 33

This yellow slave 34
Will knit and break religions, bless th'accurst, 35
Make the hoar leprosy adored, place thieves 36
And give them title, knee, and approbation 37
With senators on the bench. This is it 38
That makes the wappened widow wed again; 39
She whom the spital house and ulcerous sores 40
Would cast the gorge at, this embalms and spices 41
To th'April day again. Come, damnèd earth, 42
Thou common whore of mankind, that puts odds 43
Among the rout of nations, I will make thee 44
Do thy right nature. (*March afar off.*) Ha? A drum?
    Thou'rt quick, 45
But yet I'll bury thee. Thou'lt go, strong thief, 46
When gouty keepers of thee cannot stand. 47
                        [*He buries the gold.*]
Nay, stay thou out for earnest.   [*He keeps some gold.*] 48

*Enter Alcibiades, with drum and fife, in warlike
manner, and Phrynia and Timandra.*

ALCIBIADES   What art thou there? Speak.
TIMON
A beast, as thou art. The canker gnaw thy heart 50
For showing me again the eyes of man!
ALCIBIADES
What is thy name? Is man so hateful to thee
That art thyself a man?
TIMON
I am Misanthropos and hate mankind. 54
For thy part, I do wish thou wert a dog, 55
That I might love thee something.
ALCIBIADES   I know thee well, 56
But in thy fortunes am unlearned and strange. 57
TIMON
I know thee too; and more than that I know thee
I not desire to know. Follow thy drum;
With man's blood paint the ground gules, gules. 60
Religious canons, civil laws, are cruel; 61
Then what should war be? This fell whore of thine 62
Hath in her more destruction than thy sword,

---

2 Rotten humidity rot-causing damp.   **thy sister's** i.e., the moon's
3–6 Twinned . . . lesser If, as a test, one were to give unequal fortunes
to identical twins whose lives are otherwise indivisible, the wealthier
twin would end up scorning his poorer twin. (The lust for power and
wealth is greater than the closest of blood ties.)   **6–8 Not . . . nature**
Human nature, subject as it is to such antagonisms and competitive
instincts, cannot experience good fortune without scorning fellow
creatures who are less fortunate.   **9–11 Raise . . . honor** i.e., If Fortune were to raise a beggar to great fortune while simultaneously
impoverishing a lord, the senator would find himself treated with
contempt and the beggar with honor as though this were their
birthright. (*Raise me* means "raise"; the *me* is colloquial.)   **12–13 It is
. . . lean** i.e., It is the inheritance and possessing of pasture that makes
one brother fat, the lack (want) that makes the younger brother lean.
(The Folio reads "leaue" for "lean," which could mean that the
younger brother has to leave in search of riches elsewhere.)   **16 grece**
step   **17 smoothed** assiduously prepared   **17–18 The learnèd . . .
obliquy** The head of the scholar bows obsequiously to the rich fool.
All things deviate from the right path. (*Obliquy* may mean "obliq-
uity," i.e., deviation, or "oblique," or perhaps is a variant of "oblo-
quy," evil-speaking or being spoken against.)   **19 level** direct. (The
contrary to *obliquy*.)   **22 His semblable** i.e., His own kind, his own
image   **23 fang** seize   **24 Who** Whoever.   **sauce** stimulate, tickle
25 operant active, potent   **27 no idle votarist** no trifler in my vows
(of wishing to lead a spare existence).   **28 clear** pure.   **this** i.e., the
gold   **33 Pluck . . . heads** i.e., expedite the death of healthy men by
pulling the pillows from beneath their heads as they sleep (supposedly a way of suffocating them).

34–8 This . . . bench Gold will build up some religious movements
and destroy others, smile with favor on the wicked, cause even lepers
with their white scaly skins to be venerated (if they are rich), and give
to wealthy thieves high office and obsequious attention worthy of a
senator.   **39 makes** enables.   **wappened** worn out   **40–2 She . . .
again** A diseased old woman, whom even hospital inmates with horrible ulcers would vomit to behold, can be so embalmed and spiced
by gold that her greedy wooers will think her as fresh and marriageable as a day in April. (A *spital-house* was usually an unwholesome
institution for foul diseases.)   **42 damnèd earth** i.e., gold   **43–4 puts
. . . nations** causes strife among various peoples   **44–5 I will . . .
nature** i.e., (1) I will make you do according to your true nature as a
whore (2) I will return you to the earth, whence you came and where
you belong.   **45 quick** (1) swift to act (2) alive   **46–7 Thou'lt . . .
stand** i.e., I will put you in the earth where you will dwell unchanged
while those who long to possess you grow gouty and infirm.   **48 for
earnest** for token payments, or as a deposit to secure goods or services.   **48.1 *drum and fife*** i.e., soldiers playing drum and fife
50 The canker May a spreading ulcer   **54 Misanthropos** hater of
mankind   **55 For thy part** As for you   **56 something** somewhat,
a little.   **57 unlearned and strange** uninformed and ignorant.
60 gules (Heraldic name for "red.")   **61 canons** rules, laws
62 fell deadly

For all her cherubin look.
PHRYNIA   Thy lips rot off!   64
TIMON
I will not kiss thee; then the rot returns   65
To thine own lips again.   66
ALCIBIADES
How came the noble Timon to this change?
TIMON
As the moon does, by wanting light to give.   68
But then renew I could not, like the moon;   69
There were no suns to borrow of.   70
ALCIBIADES   Noble Timon, what friendship may I do thee?
TIMON   None, but to maintain my opinion.
ALCIBIADES   What is it, Timon?
TIMON   Promise me friendship, but perform none. If   74
thou wilt not promise, the gods plague thee, for thou 75
art a man! If thou dost perform, confound thee, for   76
thou art a man!   77
ALCIBIADES
I have heard in some sort of thy miseries.
TIMON
Thou saw'st them when I had prosperity.   79
ALCIBIADES
I see them now. Then was a blessèd time.
TIMON
As thine is now, held with a brace of harlots.   81
TIMANDRA
Is this th'Athenian minion whom the world   82
Voiced so regardfully?
TIMON   Art thou Timandra?
TIMANDRA   Yes.   83
TIMON
Be a whore still. They love thee not that use thee;
Give them diseases, leaving with thee their lust.   85
Make use of thy salt hours. Season the slaves   86
For tubs and baths; bring down rose-cheeked youth   87
To the tub-fast and the diet.
TIMANDRA   Hang thee, monster!
ALCIBIADES
Pardon him, sweet Timandra, for his wits
Are drowned and lost in his calamities.—
I have but little gold of late, brave Timon,
The want whereof doth daily make revolt   92
In my penurious band. I have heard and grieved   93
How cursèd Athens, mindless of thy worth,
Forgetting thy great deeds, when neighbor states,

But for thy sword and fortune, trod upon them—   96
TIMON
I prithee, beat thy drum and get thee gone.
ALCIBIADES
I am thy friend and pity thee, dear Timon.
TIMON
How dost thou pity him whom thou dost trouble?
I had rather be alone.
ALCIBIADES
Why, fare thee well. Here is some gold for thee.
                                        [He offers gold.]
TIMON   Keep it. I cannot eat it.
ALCIBIADES
When I have laid proud Athens on a heap—
TIMON
Warr'st thou 'gainst Athens?
ALCIBIADES   Ay, Timon, and have cause.
TIMON
The gods confound them all in thy conquest,   105
And thee after, when thou hast conquered!
ALCIBIADES   Why me, Timon?
TIMON   That by killing of villains   108
Thou wast born to conquer my country.   109
Put up thy gold. Go on—here's gold—go on.
                                        [He offers gold.]
Be as a planetary plague, when Jove   111
Will o'er some high-viced city hang his poison   112
In the sick air. Let not thy sword skip one.
Pity not honored age for his white beard;
He is an usurer. Strike me the counterfeit matron;   115
It is her habit only that is honest,   116
Herself's a bawd. Let not the virgin's cheek
Make soft thy trenchant sword; for those milk paps, 118
That through the window bars bore at men's eyes,   119
Are not within the leaf of pity writ,   120
But set them down horrible traitors. Spare not the
   babe,   121
Whose dimpled smiles from fools exhaust their mercy; 122
Think it a bastard, whom the oracle
Hath doubtfully pronounced thy throat shall cut,   124
And mince it sans remorse. Swear against objects;   125
Put armor on thine ears and on thine eyes,
Whose proof nor yells of mothers, maids, nor babes, 127
Nor sight of priests in holy vestments bleeding,

---

64 **cherubin** angelic. **Thy lips** May thy lips **65–6 I . . . again** Since I will not kiss you (and thereby contract venereal disease), your curse rebounds back on to yourself. **68 wanting** lacking **69 renew** become new again. (With a quibble on the idea of renewing a loan.) **70 suns** (Punning on *sons*, i.e., "men.") **74–7 If . . . a man!** i.e., May the gods plague you for being a man whether you perform your promises or don't even make promises! **79 Thou . . . prosperity** i.e., Prosperity itself was my true misery. **81 brace** pair. (With a quibble on the meaning "clamp," one that holds Alcibiades in its grip.) **82 th'Athenian minion** the darling of Athens **83 Voiced so regardfully** spoke of so respectfully. **85 leaving** since they are leaving **86 salt** lecherous. **Season the slaves** i.e., Pickle and spice the villains as if preparing them for the pickling tub; make them ready **87 tubs and baths** (Allusion to the treatments for venereal diseases, as also in *tub-fast* and *diet* in the next line.) **92 want** lack. **make revolt** provoke mutiny **93 penurious** poverty-stricken

96 **But . . . fortune** (A suggestion of Timon's history as a great military leader, for which Athens ought to be grateful.) **105 confound** destroy **108–9 That . . . country** (Timon sees Alcibiades as a scourge, one who is destined to destroy the corrupt city of Athens and then himself be destroyed by the angry gods.) **111 planetary plague** (Allusion to the belief in the malignant influence of planets.) **112 high-viced** extremely vicious **115 Strike me** Strike. **counterfeit** pretending respectability **116 habit** costume, outward appearance. **honest** chaste **118 trenchant** sharp. **milk paps** nipples **119 window bars** i.e., latticework of her bodice, or of her window **120 Are . . . writ** are not written down on the list of those to whom pity is to be shown **121 traitors** i.e., betrayers of men. **122 exhaust** draw forth **124 doubtfully** ambiguously. **thy . . . cut** will cut your throat. (However, the phrase can also be ambiguously reversed.) **125 And . . . remorse** and slash it in small bits without pity. **Swear . . . objects** Bind yourself by oath to resist any objections or appeals; curse objects of compassion **127 Whose proof** the tested strength of which armor. **nor yells** neither the yells

Shall pierce a jot. There's gold to pay thy soldiers.
Make large confusion; and, thy fury spent, 130
Confounded be thyself! Speak not, begone. 131

ALCIBIADES
Hast thou gold yet? I'll take the gold thou givest me,
Not all thy counsel. 　　　　　　　　　[*He takes gold.*]

TIMON
Dost thou or dost thou not, heaven's curse upon thee! 134

PHRYNIA AND TIMANDRA
Give us some gold, good Timon. Hast thou more?

TIMON
Enough to make a whore forswear her trade, 136
And to make whores, a bawd. Hold up, you sluts, 137
Your aprons mountant. [*He throws gold into their
　　aprons.*] You are not oathable, 138
Although I know you'll swear—terribly swear—
Into strong shudders and to heavenly agues 140
Th'immortal gods that hear you. Spare your oaths;
I'll trust to your conditions. Be whores still; 142
And he whose pious breath seeks to convert you,
Be strong in whore, allure him, burn him up. 144
Let your close fire predominate his smoke, 145
And be no turncoats. Yet may your pains six months 146
Be quite contrary. And thatch your poor thin roofs 147
With burdens of the dead—some that were hanged, 148
No matter; wear them, betray with them. Whore still; 149
Paint till a horse may mire upon your face. 150
A pox of wrinkles!

PHRYNIA AND TIMANDRA 　　Well, more gold. What then? 151
Believe't that we'll do anything for gold.

TIMON 　　Consumptions sow 153
In hollow bones of man; strike their sharp shins,
And mar men's spurring. Crack the lawyer's voice, 155
That he may never more false title plead,
Nor sound his quillets shrilly. Hoar the flamen, 157

That scolds against the quality of flesh 158
And not believes himself. Down with the nose, 159
Down with it flat; take the bridge quite away
Of him that, his particular to foresee, 161
Smells from the general weal. Make curled-pate
　　ruffians bald, 162
And let the unscarred braggarts of the war
Derive some pain from you. Plague all,
That your activity may defeat and quell
The source of all erection. There's more gold. 166
　　　　　　　　　　　　　[*He gives gold.*]
Do you damn others, and let this damn you,
And ditches grave you all! 168

PHRYNIA AND TIMANDRA
More counsel with more money, bounteous Timon. 169

TIMON
More whore, more mischief first. I have given you
　　earnest. 170

ALCIBIADES
Strike up the drum towards Athens. Farewell, Timon.
If I thrive well, I'll visit thee again.

TIMON
If I hope well, I'll never see thee more. 173

ALCIBIADES 　　I never did thee harm.

TIMON
Yes, thou spok'st well of me.

ALCIBIADES 　　　　　　　　　Call'st thou that harm?

TIMON
Men daily find it. Get thee away, and take 176
Thy beagles with thee.

ALCIBIADES 　　　　　　We but offend him. Strike! 177
　　　　[*Drum beats.*] *Exeunt* [*Alcibiades,
　　　　　　　Phrynia, and Timandra*].

TIMON
That nature, being sick of man's unkindness, 178
Should yet be hungry! [*He digs.*] Common mother,
　　thou 179
Whose womb unmeasurable and infinite breast
Teems and feeds all, whose selfsame mettle 181
Whereof thy proud child, arrogant man, is puffed 182
Engenders the black toad and adder blue,
The gilded newt and eyeless venomed worm, 184
With all th'abhorrèd births below crisp heaven 185

---

130 large confusion wholesale destruction　**131 Confounded** destroyed　**134 Dost . . . not** Whether you do or not　**136–7 Enough . . . bawd** Enough to let a whore retire from her whoring and turn madam instead (or, retire from her profession of turning women into whores).　**138 mountant** (A heraldic coinage, with sexual suggestion of raising up for erotic purposes; see also *erection* in line 166.) **oathable** to be believed on your oath　**140 strong** violent.　**agues** feverish shivers　**142 your conditions** what you are, your characters. **144 Be . . . whore** be resolute in whoring.　**burn him up** (1) inflame him with desire (2) infect him with venereal disease.　**145 Let . . . smoke** (1) Combat the smoke of the enemy with your close-range musketry (2) Use your transmitting of venereal infection to overcome his hypocritical rhetoric, his smokescreen of pious utterances　**146 be no turncoats** i.e. (continuing the military metaphor), don't betray your profession of whoring; whore still.　**146–7 Yet . . . contrary** (Unclear. The *six months* may refer to the time required for syphilitic infection to take hold, or the time needed to cure a painful venereal infection, or a prolonged period of menstrual cramping, or the length of a sentence in a correctional institution.)　**147–8 thatch . . . dead** cover your balding heads (caused by venereal disease) with wigs made of the hair of corpses　**149 betray with them** use these wigs to create false beauty to betray more men.　**150 mire upon** bog down in. (Timon sardonically urges so thick a cosmetic covering that even a horse would become mired.)　**151 A pox of wrinkles!** i.e., May you be plagued with wrinkles!　**153 Consumptions sow** Plant wasting diseases such as syphilis. (Addressed to Phrynia and Timandra.) **155 spurring** i.e., riding (here used as a sexual metaphor).　**157 quillets** quibbles.　**Hoar the flamen** Whiten (with venereal disease or leprosy) the priest. (With a pun on *hoar*, "whore.")

158 quality of flesh fleshly desire　**159 And . . . himself** i.e., and doesn't practice what he preaches.　**Down . . . nose** (An effect of syphilis.)　**161–2 Of . . . weal** of him that, in furthering his narrow self-interest, loses the scent of the general welfare, goes down the wrong path.　**162 curled-pate** curly-headed　**166 erection** (1) advancement (2) sexual erection.　**168 grave** enclose in the grave. (With a pun on "ditches" and "damming" continued from line 167.) **169 More . . . money** i.e., We're glad to listen to your sermon as long as the money keeps coming　**170 More . . . first** i.e., That's a bargain, but I insist on more whoring and spreading of disease before I give more money.　**earnest** earnest money.　**173 If I hope well** If my hopes are realized　**176 find it** i.e., find it harmful to be spoken well of.　**177 beagles** i.e., beagle hounds, fawning followers—the prostitutes　**178–9 That . . . hungry!** To think that my human constitution, sick though it is man's ingratitude and unnaturalness, should still require food!　**179 Common mother** i.e., The earth　**181 Teems** abundantly bears offspring.　**mettle** spirit, essence　**182 Whereof** with which　**184 gilded** iridescent.　**eyeless venomed worm** the blindworm (wrongly supposed poisonous, as were the toad and the newt)　**185 crisp** rippled, curled

Whereon Hyperion's quick'ning fire doth shine: 186
Yield him who all thy human sons do hate, 187
From forth thy plenteous bosom, one poor root!
Ensear thy fertile and conceptious womb; 189
Let it no more bring out ingrateful man!
Go great with tigers, dragons, wolves, and bears; 191
Teem with new monsters, whom thy upward face 192
Hath to the marbled mansion all above 193
Never presented! [*He finds a root.*] Oh, a root! Dear
thanks!—
Dry up thy marrows, vines, and plow-torn leas, 195
Whereof ingrateful man with liquorish drafts 196
And morsels unctuous greases his pure mind, 197
That from it all consideration slips— 198

Enter Apemantus.

More man? Plague, plague!
APEMANTUS
I was directed hither. Men report
Thou dost affect my manners and dost use them. 201
TIMON
'Tis, then, because thou dost not keep a dog, 202
Whom I would imitate. Consumption catch thee! 203
APEMANTUS
This is in thee a nature but infected, 204
A poor unmanly melancholy sprung
From change of fortune. Why this spade? This place?
This slavelike habit and these looks of care? 207
Thy flatterers yet wear silk, drink wine, lie soft,
Hug their diseased perfumes, and have forgot 209
That ever Timon was. Shame not these woods
By putting on the cunning of a carper. 211
Be thou a flatterer now and seek to thrive
By that which has undone thee. Hinge thy knee, 213
And let his very breath whom thou'lt observe 214
Blow off thy cap. Praise his most vicious strain 215
And call it excellent. Thou wast told thus. 216
Thou gav'st thine ears, like tapsters that bade
welcome,
To knaves and all approachers. 'Tis most just 218
That thou turn rascal; hadst thou wealth again,
Rascals should have't. Do not assume my likeness. 220

TIMON
Were I like thee, I'd throw away myself.
APEMANTUS
Thou hast cast away thyself, being like thyself—
A madman so long, now a fool. What, think'st 223
That the bleak air, thy boisterous chamberlain, 224
Will put thy shirt on warm? Will these mossed trees, 225
That have outlived the eagle, page thy heels 226
And skip when thou point'st out? Will the cold brook, 227
Candied with ice, caudle thy morning taste 228
To cure thy o'ernight's surfeit? Call the creatures
Whose naked natures live in all the spite 230
Of wreakful heaven, whose bare unhousèd trunks, 231
To the conflicting elements exposed,
Answer mere nature; bid them flatter thee. 233
Oh, thou shalt find—
TIMON   A fool of thee. Depart. 234
APEMANTUS
I love thee better now than e'er I did.
TIMON
I hate thee worse.
APEMANTUS   Why?
TIMON   Thou flatter'st misery.
APEMANTUS
I flatter not, but say thou art a caitiff. 237
TIMON
Why dost thou seek me out?
APEMANTUS   To vex thee.
TIMON
Always a villain's office or a fool's.
Dost please thyself in't?
APEMANTUS   Ay.
TIMON   What, a knave too? 241
APEMANTUS
If thou didst put this sour cold habit on 242
To castigate thy pride, 'twere well, but thou 243
Dost it enforcedly. Thou'dst courtier be again
Wert thou not beggar. Willing misery 245
Outlives incertain pomp, is crowned before: 246
The one is filling still, never complete, 247
The other at high wish. Best state, contentless, 248
Hath a distracted and most wretched being, 249
Worse than the worst, content. 250
Thou shouldst desire to die, being miserable.

186 Hyperion's i.e., the sun's. **quick'ning** life-giving **187 who . . . hate** who hates all your human offspring **189 Ensear** Dry up. **conceptious** fertile **191 Go great** Be pregnant **192 upward** upturned **193 the marbled . . . above** i.e., the heavens **195 marrows** gourds, squash. (Also, figuratively, the vital strength of the earth.) **plow-torn leas** plowed-up pastureland **196–8 Whereof . . . slips** from which ingrateful man, with his delight in alcoholic drink and tasty morsels of meat, greasily indulges his appetites to the point of losing all rationality **201 affect** put on **202 dog** (*Cynic* is derived from the Greek for "dog"; see 1.1.210.) **203 would** would prefer to. **Consumption catch thee!** May a wasting illness lay hold on you! **204 but infected** i.e., not inborn and philosophical but induced by misery and hence shallow **207 habit** garment **209 perfumes** perfumed mistresses **211 putting . . . carper** assuming the manner and profession of a fault-finding cynic. **213–5 Hinge . . . cap** Bow deeply, so low that the breath of the great lord to whom you are so obsequious will virtually blow off your cap. **215 strain** quality **216 Thou . . . thus** This is what you used to be told; you were warned of this. **217–18 Thou . . . approachers** You imprudently gave ear to any rascals that approached you, like a barkeep who welcomes any comer to a tavern. **220 Do . . . likeness** Don't be poor, churlish, and misanthropic, like me.

223–5 think'st . . . warm (Alludes to the practice of having a servant warm one's garment by the fire.) **226 page thy heels** follow at your heels like a page **227 skip . . . out** jump to fulfill your command. **228 Candied** encrusted, as if with sugar. **caudle . . . taste** i.e., provide you with a caudle, a hot spiced drink **230 in** exposed to **231 wreakful** vengeful. **trunks** i.e., bodies **233 Answer . . . nature** contend with nature in its natural state **234 of** in **237 caitiff** wretch. **241 a knave too?** (It is knavish to take pleasure in vexing others rather than doing so with moral intent.) **242 habit** disposition **243 'twere well** it would be a commendable thing **245–6 Willing . . . before** Willingly embraced poverty outlasts the life of insecure ceremony and wealth, and is sooner crowned with spiritual reward **247 The one . . . still** Uncertain pomp is never satisfied **248 at high wish** at the height of contentment. **248–50 Best . . . content** Being at the height of prosperity without contentment means a wretched existence, worse than being at the bottom of prosperity with contentment.

TIMON
　　Not by his breath that is more miserable.　　　　　　　252
　　Thou art a slave whom Fortune's tender arm　　　　　　253
　　With favor never clasped but bred a dog.　　　　　　　254
　　Hadst thou, like us from our first swathe, proceeded　255
　　The sweet degrees that this brief world affords
　　To such as may the passive drudges of it　　　　　　　257
　　Freely command, thou wouldst have plunged thyself　258
　　In general riot, melted down thy youth　　　　　　　　259
　　In different beds of lust, and never learned　　　　　　260
　　The icy precepts of respect, but followed
　　The sugared game before thee. But myself—　　　　　　262
　　Who had the world as my confectionary,　　　　　　　263
　　The mouths, the tongues, the eyes, and hearts of men
　　At duty, more than I could frame employment,　　　　　265
　　That numberless upon me stuck, as leaves
　　Do on the oak, have with one winter's brush　　　　　267
　　Fell from their boughs and left me open, bare　　　　　268
　　For every storm that blows—I to bear this,　　　　　　269
　　That never knew but better, is some burden.　　　　　　270
　　Thy nature did commence in sufferance; time　　　　　271
　　Hath made thee hard in't. Why shouldst thou hate
　　　　men?　　　　　　　　　　　　　　　　　　　　　272
　　They never flattered thee. What hast thou given?
　　If thou wilt curse, thy father, that poor rag,　　　　　274
　　Must be thy subject, who in spite put stuff　　　　　　275
　　To some she-beggar and compounded thee　　　　　　276
　　Poor rogue hereditary. Hence, begone!　　　　　　　　277
　　If thou hadst not been born the worst of men,　　　　　278
　　Thou hadst been a knave and flatterer.
APEMANTUS
　　Art thou proud yet?
TIMON　　　　　　　　　　Ay, that I am not thee.
APEMANTUS　　I, that I was no prodigal.
TIMON　　I, that I am one now.　　　　　　　　　　　　282
　　Were all the wealth I have shut up in thee,　　　　　　283
　　I'd give thee leave to hang it. Get thee gone.　　　　　284
　　That the whole life of Athens were in this!　　　　　　285
　　Thus would I eat it.　　　　　　　[He eats a root.]
APEMANTUS [offering food]　　Here, I will mend thy feast.
TIMON
　　First mend my company: take away thyself.

252 Not . . . miserable Not when he who speaks (Apemantus) is more wretched than I.　253–4 Thou . . . dog i.e., You are a wretch whom Fortune has never treated any better than a dog. (See note 202 above.) 255 like . . . swathe like us who were born aristocrats. (Swathe means "swaddling clothes.")　proceeded passed through (like a student taking an academic degree)　257–8 To such . . . command i.e., to the status of those who have the world and its sycophants at command 259 riot debauchery　260 different various　262 sugared game sweet-tasting quarry　263 confectionary sweetmeat shop　265 At duty subservient to my wishes.　frame provide with　267 winter's brush gust of wintry wind　268 Fell fallen.　open exposed 269 I . . . this that I should bear this　270 That . . . better who have known only better fortune　271 sufferance suffering, poverty 272 hard in't hardened to it.　274 rag i.e., wretch　275–7 who . . . hereditary who spitefully fornicated with some beggarly woman and begot you as a rogue by right of inheritance.　278 worst lowest in station　282–4 I, that . . . hang it (Timon declares himself now a prodigal in the sense of wishing to give away all his worldly posses-sions. If that wealth were all contained in Apemantus, Timon would be glad to see Apemantus hanged and thereby have done with the whole lot.)　285 That I wish that

APEMANTUS
　　So I shall mend mine own by th' lack of thine.
TIMON
　　'Tis not well mended so; it is but botched.　　　　　　289
　　If not, I would it were.　　　　　　　　　　　　　　290
APEMANTUS　　What wouldst thou have to Athens?　291
TIMON
　　Thee thither in a whirlwind. If thou wilt,
　　Tell them there I have gold. Look, so I have.
　　　　　　　　　　　　　　　　[He shows his gold.]
APEMANTUS
　　Here is no use for gold.
TIMON　　　　　　　　　　The best and truest,
　　For here it sleeps and does no hirèd harm.
APEMANTUS　　Where liest anights, Timon?　　　　　　296
TIMON　　Under that's above me. Where feed'st thou 297
　　adays, Apemantus?　　　　　　　　　　　　　　　　298
APEMANTUS　　Where my stomach finds meat; or, rather,
　　where I eat it.
TIMON　　Would poison were obedient and knew my
　　mind!
APEMANTUS　　Where wouldst thou send it?
TIMON　　To sauce thy dishes.　　　　　　　　　　　304
APEMANTUS　　The middle of humanity thou never knew-
　　est, but the extremity of both ends. When thou wast
　　in thy gilt and thy perfume, they mocked thee for too 307
　　much curiosity; in thy rags thou know'st none, but art 308
　　despised for the contrary. There's a medlar for thee. 309
　　Eat it.　　　　　　　　　　　　[He gives a fruit.]
TIMON　　On what I hate I feed not.
APEMANTUS　　Dost hate a medlar?
TIMON　　Ay, though it look like thee.　　　　　　　　313
APEMANTUS　　An thou'dst hated meddlers sooner, thou 314
　　shouldst have loved thyself better now. What man
　　didst thou ever know unthrift that was beloved after 316
　　his means?　　　　　　　　　　　　　　　　　　　317
TIMON　　Who, without those means thou talk'st of, didst
　　thou ever know beloved?
APEMANTUS　　Myself.
TIMON　　I understand thee: thou hadst some means to 321
　　keep a dog.　　　　　　　　　　　　　　　　　　322
APEMANTUS　　What things in the world canst thou
　　nearest compare to thy flatterers?
TIMON　　Women nearest. But men—men are the things

289 botched badly mended (since you remain in your own company). 290 If not If it isn't botched　291 What . . . have What would you have me convey. (But Timon caustically jests in a more literal sense of the phrase.)　296 anights at night　297 that's that which is 298 adays by day　304 sauce flavor　307 gilt fine trappings 308 curiosity fastidiousness, refinement　309 medlar fruit like a small brown-skinned apple, eaten when nearly decayed. (Used here, as often, for the sake of a quibble on meddler, one given to sexual promiscuity.)　313 like thee i.e., in a state of decay, or, as one who meddles.　314 An thou'dst If thou hadst.　meddlers busybodies. (With sexual meaning also.)　316 unthrift to be unthrifty 316–17 after his means (1) after his wealth was gone (2) according to his means.　321–2 thou . . . dog i.e., even in your poverty you were able to keep a dog, and it loved you.

themselves. What wouldst thou do with the world, Apemantus, if it lay in thy power?

APEMANTUS   Give it the beasts, to be rid of the men.

TIMON   Wouldst thou have thyself fall in the confusion 329 of men and remain a beast with the beasts? 330

APEMANTUS   Ay, Timon.

TIMON   A beastly ambition, which the gods grant thee t'attain to! If thou wert the lion, the fox would beguile thee. If thou wert the lamb, the fox would eat thee. If thou wert the fox, the lion would suspect thee when peradventure thou wert accused by the ass. If thou 336 wert the ass, thy dullness would torment thee, and still 337 thou lived'st but as a breakfast to the wolf. If thou wert 338 the wolf, thy greediness would afflict thee, and oft thou shouldst hazard thy life for thy dinner. Wert thou the unicorn, pride and wrath would confound thee 341 and make thine own self the conquest of thy fury. Wert thou a bear, thou wouldst be killed by the horse. Wert thou a horse, thou wouldst be seized by the leopard. Wert thou a leopard, thou wert germane to the lion, 345 and the spots of thy kindred were jurors on thy life; all 346 thy safety were remotion and thy defense absence. 347 What beast couldst thou be, that were not subject to a beast? And what a beast art thou already, that see'st not thy loss in transformation! 350

APEMANTUS   If thou couldst please me with speaking to 351 me, thou mightst have hit upon it here. The common- 352 wealth of Athens is become a forest of beasts.

TIMON   How, has the ass broke the wall, that thou art 354 out of the city?

APEMANTUS   Yonder comes a poet and a painter. The 356 plague of company light upon thee! I will fear to catch it, and give way. When I know not what else to do, I'll 358 see thee again.

TIMON   When there is nothing living but thee, thou shalt be welcome. I had rather be a beggar's dog than Apemantus.

APEMANTUS   Thou art the cap of all the fools alive. 363

TIMON   Would thou wert clean enough to spit upon!

APEMANTUS   A plague on thee! Thou art too bad to curse.

TIMON   All villains that do stand by thee are pure. 366

APEMANTUS   There is no leprosy but what thou speak'st.

TIMON   If I name thee. I'd beat thee, but I should infect my hands.

APEMANTUS   I would my tongue could rot them off!

TIMON   Away, thou issue of a mangy dog! 371 Choler does kill me that thou art alive; I swoon to see thee.

APEMANTUS   Would thou wouldst burst!

TIMON   Away, thou tedious rogue! I am sorry I shall lose a stone by thee.
            [He throws a stone at Apemantus.]

APEMANTUS   Beast!

TIMON   Slave!

APEMANTUS   Toad!

TIMON   Rogue, rogue, rogue! I am sick of this false world, and will love naught But even the mere necessities upon't. 381 Then, Timon, presently prepare thy grave. 382 Lie where the light foam of the sea may beat Thy gravestone daily. Make thine epitaph, That death in me at others' lives may laugh. 385
[To the gold] O thou sweet king-killer and dear divorce Twixt natural son and sire! Thou bright defiler 387 Of Hymen's purest bed! Thou valiant Mars! 388 Thou ever young, fresh, loved, and delicate wooer, Whose blush doth thaw the consecrated snow 390 That lies on Dian's lap! Thou visible god, 391 That sold'rest close impossibilities 392 And mak'st them kiss; that speak'st with every tongue To every purpose! O thou touch of hearts! 394 Think thy slave, man, rebels, and by thy virtue 395 Set them into confounding odds, that beasts 396 May have the world in empire!

APEMANTUS   Would 'twere so! But not till I am dead. I'll say thou'st gold; 398 Thou wilt be thronged to shortly.

TIMON   Thronged to?

APEMANTUS   Ay.

TIMON   Thy back, I prithee.

APEMANTUS   Live, and love thy misery. 400

TIMON   Long live so, and so die! I am quit. 401

            Enter the Banditti.

329–30 in . . . men i.e., in the destruction of mankind you've just wished for   336 peradventure by chance   337 still continually 338 lived'st wouldst live   341 unicorn a legendary creature, suppos- edly caught by being goaded into charging a tree and embedding its horn in the tree trunk   345 germane akin, related   346 the spots . . . life i.e., the crimes of those closely related to you would bring down a sentence of death upon you. (With a pun on *spots*, meaning "leop- ard's spots" and "stains, crimes.")   346–7 all . . . remotion your only safety would consist in your constantly going from place to place 350 in transformation in being changed into a beast.   351–2 If . . . here If it were possible for anything you say to please me, what you've just said (comparing men with beasts) would be pleasing. 354 How What is this   356 Yonder . . . painter (In fact, they do not appear until 5.1; this line may give evidence of an incompletely revised manuscript.)   358 give way (I will) retire.   363 cap acme, summit. (With wordplay on "fool's cap.")   366 that . . . thee com- pared to you

371 issue offspring   381 But even except   382 presently immedi- ately   385 That in order that.   in through   387 natural truly begot- ten (not illegitimate)   388 Hymen god of marriage.   Mars i.e., as the adulterous lover of Venus   390 blush i.e., reddish glow of gold 391 Dian Diana, goddess of the hunt and patroness of chastity 392 That . . . impossibilities you who solder tightly together things incapable apparently of being united   394 touch touchstone 395 Think Consider the fact that.   virtue power   396 Set . . . odds set men in self-destroying conflict with one another   398 thou'st thou hast   400 Thy back i.e., Show me your back   401 quit rid (of Apemantus).

APEMANTUS
More things like men! Eat, Timon, and abhor them.   402

Exit Apemantus.

FIRST BANDIT   Where should he have this gold? It is   403
some poor fragment, some slender ort of his remain-   404
der. The mere want of gold and the falling-from of his   405
friends drove him into this melancholy.

SECOND BANDIT   It is noised he hath a mass of treasure.   407

THIRD BANDIT   Let us make the assay upon him. If he   408
care not for't, he will supply us easily. If he covetously   409
reserve it, how shall 's get it?   410

SECOND BANDIT   True, for he bears it not about him.
'Tis hid.

FIRST BANDIT   Is not this he?

BANDITTI   Where?

SECOND BANDIT   'Tis his description.

THIRD BANDIT   He. I know him.

BANDITTI [*coming forward*]   Save thee, Timon.   417

TIMON   Now, thieves?

BANDITTI
Soldiers, not thieves.

TIMON   Both, too, and women's sons.   419

BANDITTI
We are not thieves, but men that much do want.   420

TIMON
Your greatest want is, you want much of meat.   421
Why should you want? Behold, the earth hath roots;
Within this mile break forth a hundred springs;
The oaks bear mast, the briers scarlet hips.   424
The bounteous huswife Nature on each bush
Lays her full mess before you. What? Why want?   426

FIRST BANDIT
We cannot live on grass, on berries, water,
As beasts and birds and fishes.

TIMON
Nor on the beasts themselves, the birds and fishes;
You must eat men. Yet thanks I must you con   430
That you are thieves professed, that you work not
In holier shapes; for there is boundless theft
In limited professions. [*He gives gold.*] Rascal thieves,   433
Here's gold. Go, suck the subtle blood o'th' grape   434
Till the high fever seethe your blood to froth,   435
And so scape hanging. Trust not the physician;   436
His antidotes are poison, and he slays
More than you rob. Take wealth and lives together.   438
Do villainy, do, since you protest to do't,   439

Like workmen. I'll example you with thievery.   440
The sun's a thief, and with his great attraction   441
Robs the vast sea. The moon's an arrant thief,   442
And her pale fire she snatches from the sun.
The sea's a thief, whose liquid surge resolves   444
The moon into salt tears. The earth's a thief,
That feeds and breeds by a composture stol'n   446
From gen'ral excrement. Each thing's a thief.
The laws, your curb and whip, in their rough power   448
Has unchecked theft. Love not yourselves. Away!   449
Rob one another. There's more gold. Cut throats.
All that you meet are thieves. To Athens go,
Break open shops; nothing can you steal
But thieves do lose it. Steal less for this I give you,   453
And gold confound you howsoe'er! Amen.   454

THIRD BANDIT   He's almost charmed me from my pro-   455
fession by persuading me to it.

FIRST BANDIT   'Tis in the malice of mankind that he   457
thus advises us, not to have us thrive in our mystery.   458

SECOND BANDIT   I'll believe him as an enemy, and give   459
over my trade.

FIRST BANDIT   Let us first see peace in Athens. There is   461
no time so miserable but a man may be true.   462

Exeunt Thieves.

Enter the steward [Flavius] to Timon.

FLAVIUS   O you gods!
Is yond despised and ruinous man my lord?   464
Full of decay and failing? O monument   465
And wonder of good deeds evilly bestowed!   466
What an alteration of honor has desp'rate want made!
What viler thing upon the earth than friends,
Who can bring noblest minds to basest ends!   469
How rarely does it meet with this time's guise,   470
When man was wished to love his enemies!   471
Grant I may ever love, and rather woo   472
Those that would mischief me than those that do!—   473
He's caught me in his eye. I will present
My honest grief unto him, and as my lord
Still serve him with my life.—My dearest master!

---

402 **them** i.e., the bandits.   403 **should he have** can he have obtained
404 **ort** fragment   405 **mere** utter   407 **noised** rumored   408 **assay**
trial, test (as one would test gold ore for its content)   409 **for't** for the
gold   410 **shall 's** shall we   417 **Save** God save   419 **Both, too** You
are both   420 **much do want** are greatly in need. (But Timon answers
as if they meant "want too much.")   421 **Your . . . meat** Your main
need arises from the fact that you crave such rich food (as Timon goes
on to explain).   424 **mast** acorns.   **hips** fruit of the rosebush.
426 **mess** food, meal   430 **thanks . . . con** I must offer you thanks
433 **limited** regulated, legalized. (With a play on *boundless*, line 432,
as the opposite of *limited*.)   434 **subtle** (1) delicate (2) treacherous in
its influence   435 **high fever** (Induced by intoxication.)   **seethe** boil
436 **scape hanging** i.e., avoid execution by dying of excess drinking.
438 **Take . . . together** i.e., Murder your robbery victims.   439 **protest**
openly profess

440 **example you with** give you instances of   441 **attraction** power to
draw up   442 **arrant** notorious   444 **resolves** melts, dissolves.
(Alludes to the belief that the moon draws moisture from the air and
deposits it in the sea, thus creating the effect of tides.)   446 **composture** compost, manure   448–9 **The laws . . . theft** The laws, which
restrain and punish men, provide opportunity for unlimited abuse to
those who administer them.   453 **But . . . it** i.e., without robbing from
persons who are themselves thieves.   453–4 **Steal . . . howsoe'er!** If
you steal less because of my giving you this gold, may gold destroy
you no matter what happens!   455 **charmed** dissuaded (as if by
means of enchantment)   457 **the malice of** i.e., his hating of
458 **mystery** trade.   459 **as** as I would. (One can learn even from an
enemy.)   461–2 **Let . . . true** i.e., Let's not rush into reformation, at
least not until there is peace in Athens; besides, there will always be
time to repent.   464 **ruinous** brought to ruin   465 **failing** downfall.
465–6 **O . . . bestowed!** O admonishing memorial of charitable deeds
sorely misdirected!   469 **bring . . . ends** reduce even the noblest-
minded (like Timon) to wretchedness.   470–1 **How . . . enemies!**
How strangely does the commandment to love one's enemies suit
this degenerate age!   472–3 **Grant . . . do!** May the gods grant that I
continue to love my enemies, but preferring to deal with those who
only intend me harm rather than those who actually do harm!

TIMON
Away! What art thou?

FLAVIUS   Have you forgot me, sir?

TIMON
Why dost ask that? I have forgot all men.
Then, if thou grant'st thou'rt a man, I have forgot thee.

FLAVIUS   An honest poor servant of yours.

TIMON   Then I know thee not.
I never had honest man about me, I; all
I kept were knaves, to serve in meat to villains.

FLAVIUS   The gods are witness,
Ne'er did poor steward wear a truer grief
For his undone lord than mine eyes for you.
                                        [*He weeps.*]

TIMON
What, dost thou weep? Come nearer, then, I love thee
Because thou art a woman and disclaim'st
Flinty mankind, whose eyes do never give   489
But thorough lust and laughter. Pity's sleeping.   490
Strange times, that weep with laughing, not with
    weeping!

FLAVIUS
I beg of you to know me, good my lord,
T'accept my grief, and whilst this poor wealth lasts
To entertain me as your steward still.   494
                                    [*He offers money.*]

TIMON   Had I a steward
So true, so just, and now so comfortable?   496
It almost turns my dangerous nature mild.   497
Let me behold thy face. Surely, this man
Was born of woman.
Forgive my general and exceptless rashness,   500
You perpetual-sober gods! I do proclaim   501
One honest man—mistake me not, but one;   502
No more, I pray—and he's a steward.
How fain would I have hated all mankind,   504
And thou redeem'st thyself! But all, save thee,
I fell with curses.   506
Methinks thou art more honest now than wise,
For by oppressing and betraying me
Thou mightst have sooner got another service;   509
For many so arrive at second masters
Upon their first lord's neck. But tell me true—   511
For I must ever doubt, though ne'er so sure—   512
Is not thy kindness subtle, covetous,
A usuring kindness, and, as rich men deal gifts,
Expecting in return twenty for one?

FLAVIUS
No, my most worthy master, in whose breast
Doubt and suspect, alas, are placed too late.   517
You should have feared false times when you did
    feast.   518

Suspect still comes where an estate is least.   519
That which I show, heaven knows, is merely love,   520
Duty, and zeal to your unmatchèd mind,
Care of your food and living; and believe it,   522
My most honored lord,
For any benefit that points to me,   524
Either in hope or present, I'd exchange   525
For this one wish: that you had power and wealth
To requite me by making rich yourself.   527

TIMON
Look thee, 'tis so. Thou singly honest man,   528
Here, take. [*He offers gold.*] The gods out of my misery
Has sent thee treasure. Go, live rich and happy,
But thus conditioned: thou shalt build from men,   531
Hate all, curse all, show charity to none,
But let the famished flesh slide from the bone
Ere thou relieve the beggar. Give to dogs
What thou deniest to men. Let prisons swallow 'em,
Debts wither 'em to nothing. Be men like blasted
    woods,   536
And may diseases lick up their false bloods!
And so farewell and thrive.

FLAVIUS   Oh, let me stay
And comfort you, my master.

TIMON   If thou hat'st curses,
Stay not; fly, whilst thou art blest and free.
Ne'er see thou man, and let me ne'er see thee.
                    Exit [*Flavius; Timon retires to his cave*].

[5.1]

Enter Poet and Painter. [*Timon enters at some
point to watch them from his cave.*]

PAINTER   As I took note of the place, it cannot be far
where he abides.

POET   What's to be thought of him? Does the rumor
hold for true that he's so full of gold?

PAINTER   Certain. Alcibiades reports it. Phrynia and
Timandra had gold of him. He likewise enriched poor
straggling soldiers with great quantity. 'Tis said he
gave unto his steward a mighty sum.

POET   Then this breaking of his has been but a try for   9
his friends?

PAINTER   Nothing else. You shall see him a palm in Ath- 11
ens again, and flourish with the highest. Therefore 'tis
not amiss we tender our loves to him in this supposed   13
distress of his. It will show honestly in us and is very

489 **Flinty** hardhearted.   **give** give forth tears   490 **But thorough**
except through   494 **entertain** receive, employ   496 **comfortable**
comforting.   497 **dangerous** savage   500 **exceptless** making no
exception   501 **perpetual-sober** eternally grave and sedate   502 **but**
only   504 **fain** gladly   506 **fell** cut down   509 **service** position
511 **Upon . . . neck** by stepping on the bowed neck of their former
master.   512 **though . . . sure** however persuasive the evidence
517 **suspect** suspicion   518 **feast** entertain lavishly.

519 **Suspect . . . least** Wariness inevitably arrives (too late) when
one's fortunes are ruined.   520 **merely** purely   522 **Care . . . living**
concern for your having food and maintenance   524 **For** as for.
points to me appears in prospect for me   525 **in hope** in the future
527 **requite** repay   528 **singly** (1) uniquely (2) earnestly   531 **thus**
conditioned upon this condition.   **from** away from   536 **Be men** Let
men be.   **blasted** withered
5.1. Location: The woods. Before Timon's cave. The scene is virtually continuous; Timon may well remain visible to the audience.
9 **breaking** bankruptcy.   **try** test   11 **a palm** a dignitary. (Probably
referring to Psalm 92:12: "The righteous man shall flourish like a
palm.")   13 **we tender** that we should offer

likely to load our purposes with what they travail for,   15
if it be a just and true report that goes of his having.   16

POET   What have you now to present unto him?

PAINTER   Nothing at this time but my visitation. Only I
will promise him an excellent piece.

POET   I must serve him so too, tell him of an intent   20
that's coming toward him.   21

PAINTER   Good as the best. Promising is the very air o'th'   22
time; it opens the eyes of expectation. Performance
is ever the duller for his act, and but in the plainer   24
and simpler kind of people the deed of saying is quite   25
out of use. To promise is most courtly and fashionable.   26
Performance is a kind of will or testament which   27
argues a great sickness in his judgment that makes it.

Enter Timon from his cave.

TIMON [*aside*]   Excellent workman! Thou canst not
paint a man so bad as is thyself.

POET   I am thinking what I shall say I have provided for   31
him. It must be a personating of himself, a satire   32
against the softness of prosperity, with a discovery of   33
the infinite flatteries that follow youth and opulency.

TIMON [*aside*]   Must thou needs stand for a villain in   35
thine own work? Wilt thou whip thine own faults in   36
other men? Do so, I have gold for thee.

POET   Nay, let's seek him.
Then do we sin against our own estate   39
When we may profit meet and come too late.   40

PAINTER True.
When the day serves, before black-cornered night,   42
Find what thou want'st by free and offered light.   43
Come.

TIMON [*aside*]
I'll meet you at the turn. What a god's gold,   45
That he is worshiped in a baser temple   46
Than where swine feed!
'Tis thou that rigg'st the bark and plow'st the foam,   48
Settlest admirèd reverence in a slave.   49
To thee be worship, and thy saints for aye   50
Be crowned with plagues, that thee alone obey!   51
Fit I meet them.   [*He comes forward.*]   52

POET   Hail, worthy Timon!

PAINTER   Our late noble master!

TIMON
Have I once lived to see two honest men?   55

POET   Sir,
Having often of your open bounty tasted,
Hearing you were retired, your friends fall'n off,   58
Whose thankless natures—oh, abhorrèd spirits!
Not all the whips of heaven are large enough—
What, to you,
Whose starlike nobleness gave life and influence   62
To their whole being? I am rapt, and cannot cover   63
The monstrous bulk of this ingratitude
With any size of words.   65

TIMON
Let it go naked; men may see't the better.
You that are honest, by being what you are
Make them best seen and known.

PAINTER   He and myself   68
Have traveled in the great show'r of your gifts   69
And sweetly felt it.

TIMON   Ay, you are honest men.

PAINTER
We are hither come to offer you our service.

TIMON
Most honest men! Why, how shall I requite you?
Can you eat roots and drink cold water? No.

BOTH
What we can do we'll do to do you service.

TIMON
You're honest men. You've heard that I have gold;
I am sure you have. Speak truth; you're honest men.

PAINTER
So it is said, my noble lord, but therefor   77
Came not my friend nor I.

TIMON
Good honest men! [*To the Painter*] Thou draw'st a
counterfeit   79
Best in all Athens. Thou'rt indeed the best;
Thou counterfeit'st most lively.

PAINTER   So-so, my lord.   81

TIMON
E'en so, sir, as I say. [*To the Poet*] And for thy fiction,   82
Why, thy verse swells with stuff so fine and smooth   83
That thou art even natural in thine art.   84
But for all this, my honest-natured friends,
I must needs say you have a little fault.
Marry, 'tis not monstrous in you, neither wish I
You take much pains to mend.

BOTH   Beseech Your Honor   88

15 **load our purposes** i.e., crown our efforts. **travail** labor   16 **goes of his having** is current about his wealth.   20 **intent** project   21 **coming toward** intended for   22 **Good as the best** i.e., That's perfect. **air** style   24 **for his act** for its being completed. **but in** except among   25 **deed of saying** actions fulfilling words or promises   26 **use** fashion.   27 **a kind . . . testament** i.e., a desperate attempt to settle accounts, as if one were about to die   31 **provided** planned   32 **personating of himself** representation of his case   33 **discovery** disclosure   35 **needs** necessarily. **stand for** serve as a model for   36 **in** your portrayal of   39 **estate** worldly well-being   40 **may profit meet** have a chance to make a profit   42 **black-cornered night** night which darkens as in corners   43 **free and offered light** the light of day, freely offered to all.   45 **at the turn** i.e., trick for trick in a cheating game.   46 **a baser temple** i.e., the human body, or, the marketplace   48 **rigg'st the bark** sets the ship's sail   49 **Settlest . . . slave** engenders in the servile worshiper a wondering awe of money.   50–1 **thy saints . . . obey!** may your saints (i.e., members of your sect) who obey you only, be eternally crowned with plagues!   52 **Fit** It is fit that

55 **once** actually   58 **fall'n off** estranged   62–3 **Whose . . . being?** whose nobility of character was of such power as to ennoble men. (An astrological metaphor.)   65 **size** (1) quantity (2) covering glue applied by painters   68 **them** i.e., the ungrateful men you condemn, or, ungrateful acts   69 **traveled** walked. (With a suggestion also of "worked, travailed," as one would labor for a patron.)   77 **therefor** for that reason   79 **counterfeit** picture, likeness. (With quibble on the idea of "fraudulent imitation.")   81 **So-so** Passably   82 **fiction** any creative writing; here, poetry. (With connotation of "lying.")   83 **swells . . . smooth** (1) is elegantly styled and adorned (2) is a vainglorious concoction of specious fabrication   84 **thou . . . thine art** (1) your art is a triumph of natural verisimilitude and has become second nature to you (2) you're a born fool and a liar in your art.   88 **mend** mend your ways.

To make it known to us.

TIMON   You'll take it ill.

BOTH   Most thankfully, my lord.

TIMON   Will you, indeed?

BOTH   Doubt it not, worthy lord.

TIMON

There's never a one of you but trusts a knave   93
That mightily deceives you.

BOTH   Do we, my lord?

TIMON

Ay, and you hear him cog, see him dissemble,   95
Know his gross patchery, love him, feed him,   96
Keep in your bosom; yet remain assured   97
That he's a made-up villain.   98

PAINTER   I know none such, my lord.

POET   Nor I.

TIMON

Look you, I love you well. I'll give you gold;
Rid me these villains from your companies,   100
Hang them or stab them, drown them in a draft,   101
Confound them by some course, and come to me,   102
I'll give you gold enough.

BOTH   Name them, my lord, let's know them.

TIMON

You that way and you this, but two in company;   105
Each man apart, all single and alone,   106
Yet an archvillain keeps him company.   107
[To one] If where thou art two villains shall not be, 108
Come not near him. [To the other] If thou wouldst not
   reside   109
But where one villain is, then him abandon.—
Hence, pack! There's gold. You came for gold, ye
   slaves.   111
[To one] You have work for me; there's payment.
   Hence!   112
[To the other] You are an alchemist; make gold of that. 113
Out, rascal dogs!

            Exeunt [Poet and Painter, beaten out by Timon,
                        who retires to his cave].

      Enter steward [Flavius] and two Senators.

FLAVIUS

It is in vain that you would speak with Timon;
For he is set so only to himself   116
That nothing but himself which looks like man
Is friendly with him.

FIRST SENATOR   Bring us to his cave.   118
It is our part and promise to th'Athenians   119

---

93 There's . . . but i.e., Each of you   95 cog cheat   96 patchery knavery   97 Keep keep him   98 made-up utter, complete   100 Rid me If
you'll rid   101 draft privy, cesspool   102 Confound destroy.
course means   105–7 You . . . him company (Timon riddlingly suggests that, if the two of them stand apart from each other with no one
else around, each has an archvillain—himself—to keep him company.)
108 shall not be are not to be   109 him i.e., the other one.   111 pack
be off.   112 there's payment i.e., here's a beating or a thrown stone.
113 alchemist i.e., one who transmutes nature into poetry and art, as
the alchemist is supposed to transmute base metals into gold.   that
i.e., a beating or a thrown stone.   116 set . . . himself so self-absorbed
118 friendly with congenial to   119 our . . . promise the part we have
promised to undertake

To speak with Timon.

SECOND SENATOR   At all times alike
Men are not still the same. 'Twas time and griefs   121
That framed him thus. Time with his fairer hand   122
Offering the fortunes of his former days,
The former man may make him. Bring us to him,   124
And chance it as it may.

FLAVIUS   Here is his cave.—   125
Peace and content be here! Lord Timon! Timon!
Look out, and speak to friends. Th'Athenians,
By two of their most reverend Senate, greet thee.
Speak to them, noble Timon.

            Enter Timon out of his cave.

TIMON

Thou sun that comforts, burn! Speak and be hanged!
For each true word a blister, and each false   131
Be as a cauterizing to the root o'th' tongue,
Consuming it with speaking!

FIRST SENATOR   Worthy Timon—   133

TIMON

Of none but such as you, and you of Timon.   134

FIRST SENATOR

The senators of Athens greet thee, Timon.

TIMON

I thank them, and would send them back the plague,
Could I but catch it for them.

FIRST SENATOR   Oh, forget   137
What we are sorry for ourselves in thee.   138
The senators with one consent of love   139
Entreat thee back to Athens, who have thought
On special dignities which vacant lie
For thy best use and wearing.

SECOND SENATOR   They confess
Toward thee forgetfulness too general gross;   143
Which now the public body, which doth seldom   144
Play the recanter, feeling in itself   145
A lack of Timon's aid, hath sense withal   146
Of its own fail, restraining aid to Timon,   147
And send forth us to make their sorrowed render,   148
Together with a recompense more fruitful
Than their offense can weigh down by the dram—   150
Ay, even such heaps and sums of love and wealth
As shall to thee blot out what wrongs were theirs   152
And write in thee the figures of their love,   153

---

121 still always   122 framed made, fashioned   124 The former . . .
him may turn him into his former self.   125 chance it let it happen
131 each false may each false word   133 Worthy Noble. (But Timon
deliberately mistakes the meaning as "deserving.")   134 Of . . .
Timon We are worthy of nothing better than each other (each of us
being worthless, since we are human).   137 catch (1) snare in such a
way that I could send it back (2) contract, as a disease   138 What . . .
thee those wrongs that we regret having done you.   139 consent
unanimous voice   143 too general gross too all-encompassing and
evident   144 public body state   145 Play the recanter i.e., change its
mind and apologize   146 Timon's aid aid to Timon. (But suggesting
also "aid to be given by Timon to Athens.")   withal in addition
147 fail failing.   restraining in withholding   148 sorrowed render
sorrowful rendering of apologies   150 can . . . dram can outweigh
under the most scrupulous measurement   152 theirs of their making
153 figures (1) representations (2) numbers written in a ledger

Ever to read them thine.

TIMON   You witch me in it,   154
Surprise me to the very brink of tears.
Lend me a fool's heart and a woman's eyes,
And I'll beweep these comforts, worthy senators.   157

FIRST SENATOR
Therefore, so please thee to return with us,   158
And of our Athens, thine and ours, to take
The captainship, thou shalt be met with thanks,
Allowed with absolute power, and thy good name   161
Live with authority. So soon we shall drive back   162
Of Alcibiades th'approaches wild,   163
Who, like a boar too savage, doth root up
His country's peace.

SECOND SENATOR   And shakes his threat'ning sword
Against the walls of Athens.

FIRST SENATOR   Therefore, Timon—

TIMON
Well, sir, I will; therefore, I will, sir; thus:
If Alcibiades kill my countrymen,
Let Alcibiades know this of Timon,
That Timon cares not. But if he sack fair Athens
And take our goodly agèd men by th' beards,
Giving our holy virgins to the stain   172
Of contumelious, beastly, mad-brained war,   173
Then let him know, and tell him Timon speaks it
In pity of our agèd and our youth,
I cannot choose but tell him that I care not,
And let him take't at worst—for their knives care not,   177
While you have throats to answer. For myself,   178
There's not a whittle in th'unruly camp   179
But I do prize it at my love before   180
The reverend'st throat in Athens. So I leave you
To the protection of the prosperous gods,   182
As thieves to keepers.

FLAVIUS [to Senators]   Stay not; all's in vain.   183

TIMON
Why, I was writing of my epitaph;
It will be seen tomorrow. My long sickness
Of health and living now begins to mend,
And nothing brings me all things. Go, live still;   187
Be Alcibiades your plague, you his,
And last so long enough!

FIRST SENATOR   We speak in vain.   189

TIMON
But yet I love my country and am not
One that rejoices in the common wrack,   191
As common bruit doth put it.

FIRST SENATOR   That's well spoke.   192

TIMON
Commend me to my loving countrymen—

FIRST SENATOR
These words become your lips as they pass through
them.   194

SECOND SENATOR
And enter in our ears like great triumphers   195
In their applauding gates.

TIMON   Commend me to them,   196
And tell them that, to ease them of their griefs,
Their fears of hostile strokes, their aches, losses,
Their pangs of love, with other incident throes   199
That nature's fragile vessel doth sustain   200
In life's uncertain voyage, I will some kindness do
them:
I'll teach them to prevent wild Alcibiades' wrath.   202

FIRST SENATOR [to the Second Senator]
I like this well. He will return again.

TIMON
I have a tree which grows here in my close,   204
That mine own use invites me to cut down,   205
And shortly must I fell it. Tell my friends,
Tell Athens, in the sequence of degree   207
From high to low throughout, that whoso please
To stop affliction, let him take his haste,
Come hither ere my tree hath felt the ax,
And hang himself. I pray you, do my greeting.

FLAVIUS [to Senators]
Trouble him no further. Thus you still shall find him.

TIMON
Come not to me again. But say to Athens,
Timon hath made his everlasting mansion   214
Upon the beachèd verge of the salt flood,   215
Who once a day with his embossèd froth   216
The turbulent surge shall cover. Thither come,
And let my gravestone be your oracle.   218
Lips, let four words go by and language end!   219
What is amiss, plague and infection mend!
Graves only be men's works and death their gain!
Sun, hide thy beams! Timon hath done his reign.

                              Exit Timon [into his cave].

FIRST SENATOR
His discontents are unremovably
Coupled to nature.   224

SECOND SENATOR
Our hope in him is dead. Let us return
And strain what other means is left unto us

---

154 Ever . . . thine i.e., to provide a perpetual record of the Athenians' love for you.   **witch** bewitch   **157 beweep these comforts** weep gratefully at these comforting tidings   **158 so** if it   **161 Allowed** vested   **162 Live with authority** enjoy full authority.   **163 Of . . . wild** the savage attacks of Alcibiades   **172 stain** pollution   **173 contumelious** despiteful   **177 take't at worst** put the worst possible construction on what I say, or, do the worst destruction possible.   **their** of Alcibiades' troops   **178 answer** suffer the consequences.
179 whittle small clasp-knife   **180 at** in.   **before** above   **182 prosperous** auspicious, favorable   **183 As . . . keepers** as I would leave thieves to the mercy of their hardhearted jailers.   **187 nothing** oblivion, death   **189 last . . . enough** remain in that state as long as possible.   **191 wrack** destruction   **192 bruit** rumor

194 become grace, do credit to   **195 triumphers** those coming in triumph   **196 applauding gates** i.e., (1) gates crowded with applauding citizens (2) porches of the ears.   **199 incident throes** naturally occurring agonies   **200 nature's . . . vessel** i.e., the body   **202 prevent** frustrate, forestall. (With a quibble on "anticipate.")   **204 close** enclosure   **205 use** need   **207 in . . . degree** in order of social rank   **214 everlasting mansion** i.e., grave   **215 verge . . . flood** boundary or margin of the sea. (See 5.4.66.)   **216 Who** whom or which, i.e., Timon or his grave, his *everlasting mansion* (line 214), both of which the foaming tide will cover daily.   **his** its.   **embossèd** foaming (like a hunted animal, foaming at the mouth)   **218 oracle** source of wisdom.   **219 four words** i.e., few words   **224 Coupled to nature** integrally part of him.

In our dear peril.

FIRST SENATOR   It requires swift foot.   *Exeunt.* 227

❧

[5.2]

Enter two other Senators, with a Messenger.

THIRD SENATOR
Thou hast painfully discovered. Are his files   1
As full as thy report?

MESSENGER   I have spoke the least.   2
Besides, his expedition promises   3
Present approach.   4

FOURTH SENATOR
We stand much hazard if they bring not Timon.   5

MESSENGER
I met a courier, one mine ancient friend,   6
Whom, though in general part we were opposed,   7
Yet our old love made a particular force   8
And made us speak like friends. This man was riding
From Alcibiades to Timon's cave
With letters of entreaty which imported   11
His fellowship i'th' cause against your city,   12
In part for his sake moved.

Enter the other Senators [from Timon].

THIRD SENATOR   Here come our brothers.   13

FIRST SENATOR
No talk of Timon; nothing of him expect.
The enemies' drum is heard, and fearful scouring   15
Doth choke the air with dust. In, and prepare.   16
Ours is the fall, I fear, our foe's the snare.   *Exeunt.* 17

❧

[5.3]

Enter a Soldier in the woods, seeking Timon.

SOLDIER
By all description this should be the place.
Who's here? Speak, ho! No answer? What is this?
                    [*He finds a rude tomb.*]
"Timon is dead, who hath outstretched his span.   3
Some beast read this; there does not live a man."   4

Dead, sure, and this his grave. What's on this tomb
I cannot read. The character I'll take with wax.   6
                    [*He makes a wax impression.*]
Our captain hath in every figure skill,   7
An aged interpreter, though young in days.   8
Before proud Athens he's set down by this,   9
Whose fall the mark of his ambition is.   *Exit.* 10

❧

[5.4]

*Trumpets sound. Enter Alcibiades with his powers
before Athens.*

ALCIBIADES
Sound to this coward and lascivious town   1
Our terrible approach.   *Sounds a parley.* 2

The Senators appear on the walls.

Till now you have gone on and filled the time
With all licentious measure, making your wills   4
The scope of justice. Till now myself and such   5
As slept within the shadow of your power   6
Have wandered with our traversed arms and
          breathed   7
Our sufferance vainly. Now the time is flush,   8
When crouching marrow in the bearer strong   9
Cries of itself, "No more!" Now breathless wrong   10
Shall sit and pant in your great chairs of ease,
And pursy insolence shall break his wind   12
With fear and horrid flight.

FIRST SENATOR   Noble and young,   13
When thy first griefs were but a mere conceit,   14
Ere thou hadst power or we had cause of fear,
We sent to thee, to give thy rages balm,
To wipe out our ingratitude with loves   17
Above their quantity.

SECOND SENATOR   So did we woo   18
Transformèd Timon to our city's love
By humble message and by promised means.   20

---

227 **dear** costly, dire.   **foot** i.e., action.
5.2. Location: Before the walls of Athens.
1 **painfully discovered** revealed unsettling news, or, reconnoitered
with painstaking effort.   **files** military ranks   2 **spoke the least**
given the lowest estimate.   3 **expedition** speed   4 **Present** immediate   5 **stand much hazard** are at great risk.   **they** i.e., the senators
who were sent to Timon   6 **one mine ancient friend** a friend of mine
of long standing   7 **Whom** with whom.   **in general part** on many
public issues   8 **made . . . force** exerted a strong personal influence
11–13 **which . . . moved** which importuned Timon to join Alcibiades
in an attack on Athens, undertaken in part on Timon's behalf.
13 **brothers** fellow senators.   15 **scouring** hurrying along, aggressive
movement   16 **In** Let us go in   17 **Ours . . . snare** Our part, I fear, is
to fall; our foe's part is to set the trap.
**5.3. Location: The woods. Seemingly near Timon's cave but also at
the edge of the sea; see 5.1.214–17 and 5.4.66. A rude tomb is seen.**
3 **outstretched his span** stretched out his span of life to its limit.
4 **Some . . . man** i.e., Whoever reads this will be a beast, since all men
are beasts.

6 **I cannot read** (Suggests there is another inscription in another language, perhaps Latin, or that this scene shows signs of incomplete
revision and hence apparent inconsistency.)   **The . . . wax** I'll take an
impression of the inscription in wax.   7 **every figure** all kinds of writing   8 **aged** experienced   9 **Before . . . this** By this time he has laid
siege to proud Athens   10 **Whose fall** the fall of which.   **mark** goal
**5.4. Location: Before the walls of Athens. Appearances *on the walls*
are presumably located in the gallery, above, to the rear of the stage.**
0.1 *powers* armed forces   1 **Sound** Proclaim.   **coward** cowardly
2 **terrible** terrifying.   **s.d.** *parley* trumpet call to a negotiation.   4 **all
licentious measure** every kind of licentious behavior   4–5 **making
. . . justice** equating justice with your wills.   6 **slept** i.e., dwelled
7 **traversed arms** weapons not in firing position. (A term in military
drill.)   7–8 **breathed Our sufferance** voiced our sufferings   8 **flush**
at flood, ripe   9–10 **When . . . more!** i.e., when the vital spirit of even
the brave man, crouching in terror, cries out of its own accord, "No
more!" (*Marrow* is literally the fatty substance in the bones.)
10 **breathless wrong** wrongdoers (i.e., you senators) who are frightened into breathlessness   12 **pursy** short-winded.   **break his wind**
pant for breath. (Perhaps suggesting also to void air from the bowels
in fright.)   13 **horrid** terrified   14 **When . . . conceit** when your
grievances were as yet new and scarcely imagined by us
17–18 **loves . . . quantity** offers of friendship exceeding the quantity
of your grievances.   20 **means** rewards.

We were not all unkind, nor all deserve
The common stroke of war.
FIRST SENATOR   These walls of ours   22
Were not erected by their hands from whom
You have received your grief; nor are they such
That these great tow'rs, trophies, and schools should
    fall   25
For private faults in them.
SECOND SENATOR   Nor are they living   26
Who were the motives that you first went out.   27
Shame, that they wanted cunning, in excess   28
Hath broke their hearts. March, noble lord,
Into our city with thy banners spread.
By decimation and a tithèd death—   31
If thy revenges hunger for that food
Which nature loathes—take thou the destined tenth,
And by the hazard of the spotted die   34
Let die the spotted.
FIRST SENATOR   All have not offended.   35
For those that were, it is not square to take   36
On those that are, revenge. Crimes, like lands,   37
Are not inherited. Then, dear countryman,   38
Bring in thy ranks, but leave without thy rage.   39
Spare thy Athenian cradle and those kin   40
Which in the bluster of thy wrath must fall
With those that have offended. Like a shepherd
Approach the fold and cull th'infected forth,   43
But kill not all together.
SECOND SENATOR   What thou wilt,
Thou rather shalt enforce it with thy smile
Than hew to't with thy sword.
FIRST SENATOR   Set but thy foot
Against our rampired gates and they shall ope,   47
So thou wilt send thy gentle heart before   48
To say thou'lt enter friendly.
SECOND SENATOR   Throw thy glove,   49
Or any token of thine honor else,   50
That thou wilt use the wars as thy redress
And not as our confusion, all thy powers   52
Shall make their harbor in our town till we   53
Have sealed thy full desire.
ALCIBIADES [throwing a glove]   Then there's my glove. 54
Descend, and open your unchargèd ports.   55

Those enemies of Timon's and mine own
Whom you yourselves shall set out for reproof   57
Fall, and no more; and, to atone your fears   58
With my more noble meaning, not a man   59
Shall pass his quarter or offend the stream   60
Of regular justice in your city's bounds   61
But shall be remedied to your public laws   62
At heaviest answer.
BOTH   'Tis most nobly spoken.   63
ALCIBIADES   Descend, and keep your words.   64
          [The Senators descend, and open the gates.]

     Enter [Soldier as] a messenger [with a wax tablet].

SOLDIER
My noble general, Timon is dead,
Entombed upon the very hem o'th' sea;   66
And on his gravestone this insculpture, which   67
With wax I brought away, whose soft impression
Interprets for my poor ignorance.
ALCIBIADES (reads the epitaph)
"Here lies a wretched corpse, of wretched soul bereft. 70
Seek not my name. A plague consume you wicked
    caitiffs left!   71
Here lie I, Timon, who, alive, all living men did hate.
Pass by and curse thy fill, but pass and stay not here
    thy gait."   73
These well express in thee thy latter spirits.   74
Though thou abhorredst in us our human griefs,
Scorned'st our brains' flow and those our droplets
    which   76
From niggard nature fall, yet rich conceit   77
Taught thee to make vast Neptune weep for aye   78
On thy low grave, on faults forgiven. Dead
Is noble Timon, of whose memory
Hereafter more. Bring me into your city,
And I will use the olive with my sword,   82
Make war breed peace, make peace stint war, make
    each   83
Prescribe to other as each other's leech.   84
Let our drums strike.   [Drums.] Exeunt.

22 common indiscriminate   25 trophies monuments   26 them i.e.,
those from whom you have received your injuries.   27 motives . . .
out instigators that prompted your banishment.   28 Shame . . .
excess i.e., An excess of shame for their lack of astuteness in statecraft
31 decimation . . . tithèd death selection of every tenth to die. (The
two phrases mean the same thing.)   34 die singular of dice. (With a
play on the verb die.)   35 the spotted the corrupt, wicked. (With a
play on the spots on the dice in line 34.)   36 were were living then
(and were your enemies).   square just   37 are are now alive   37–8
like . . . inherited are not inherited, as lands are.   39 without outside
40 thy Athenian cradle Athens, your birthplace   43 cull . . . forth
pick out the tainted   47 rampired barricaded.   ope open   48 So if
only   49 Throw If you will throw   50 token pledge   52 confusion
overthrow.   powers armed forces   53 make their harbor find safe
lodging   54 sealed satisfied, ratified   55 unchargèd ports unat-
tacked gates.

57 set out for reproof pick out for punishment   58 atone appease,
make "at one"   59–63 not . . . answer no soldier of mine will be
allowed to leave his assigned duty area or violate the norms set by
established law without being remanded to Athenian justice to
receive severest punishment.   64.1 open the gates (Presumably, the
gates are a door in the tiring-house facade representing here the walls
of Athens; the gallery above is on the walls.)   66 hem i.e., edge, shore
67 insculpture inscription   70–3 "Here . . . gait" (Of these two
inscriptions, both found in Plutarch, Shakespeare would presumably
have deleted one, since they contradict one another.)   71 caitiffs
wretches   73 gait journey.   74 thy latter spirits your bitter views at
the end of your life.   76–7 Scorned'st . . . fall scorned our sentiments
and our tears, both of which you considered craven and worldly,
stemming from our impoverished human spirit   77 conceit imagination, fancy   78 Neptune the god of the sea in Roman mythology.
aye ever   82 olive . . . sword (Symbols of peace and war.)   83 Make
. . . peace use war to bring about the security needed for peace (and
also, perhaps, to cure the decadent softness of a prolonged peace-
time).   stint stop   84 leech physician.

Antony and Cleopatra

Shakespeare probably wrote *Antony and Cleopatra* in 1606 or 1607; it was registered for publication on May 20, 1608, and apparently influenced a revision of Samuel Daniel's *Cleopatra* that was published "newly altered" in 1607. *Antony and Cleopatra* was thus roughly contemporary with *King Lear* and *Macbeth*. Yet the contrast between those two tragedies and *Antony and Cleopatra* is immense. Unlike *Macbeth*, with its taut focus on a murderer and his wife, *Antony and Cleopatra* moves back and forth across the Mediterranean in its epic survey of characters and events, bringing together the fates of Pompey, Octavius Caesar, Octavia, and Lepidus with those of the protagonists. *King Lear* gives proper names to fourteen characters, *Macbeth* to eighteen, *Antony and Cleopatra* to thirty-one. The Roman play requires no less than forty-two separate scenes, of which most occur in what modern editors label Acts 3 and 4, although no play is less suited to the classical rigors of five-act structure, and these divisions are not found in the reliable Folio text of 1623. Indeed, it is as though Shakespeare resolved at the height of his career to show that he could dispense entirely with the classical "rules," which had never taken serious hold of the English popular stage in any case. The flouting of the unities is so extreme that John Dryden, in his *All for Love or The World Well Lost* (1678), undertook not so much to revise Shakespeare as to start afresh on the same subject. Dryden's play is restricted to the last few hours of the protagonists' lives, at Cleopatra's tomb in Alexandria, with a severely limited cast of characters and much of the narrative revealed through recollection. Although a substantial achievement in its own right, *All for Love* surely demonstrates that Shakespeare knew what he was doing, for Dryden has excised a good deal of the panorama, the excitement, and the "infinite variety" (2.2.246).

Shakespeare departs also from the somber tone of his tragedies of evil. He creates, instead, a world that bears affinities to the ambiguous conflicts of the other Roman plays, to the varying humorous perspectives of the come-

dies, and to the imaginative reconstructions of the late romances. As protagonists, Antony and Cleopatra lack tragic stature, or so it first appears: she is a tawny gypsy temptress and he a "strumpet's fool," a once-great general now bound in "strong Egyptian fetters" and lost in "dotage" (1.1.13; 1.2.122–3). Several scenes, especially those set in Egypt, are comic and delightfully bawdy: Charmian learning her fortune from the soothsayer, Cleopatra practicing her charms in vain to keep Antony from leaving Egypt or raunchily daydreaming of being Antony's horse "to bear the weight of Antony" (1.5.22), Cleopatra flying into a magnificent rage at the news of Antony's marriage to Octavia and then consoling herself with catty reflections on Octavia's reported low voice and shortness of stature ("I think so, Charmian. Dull of tongue, and dwarfish," 3.3.17). In its comic texture, the play somewhat resembles *Romeo and Juliet*, an earlier play about a younger pair of lovers, although there the bawdry is used chiefly to characterize the lovers' companions and confidants, whereas in *Antony and Cleopatra* it is central to our vision of Cleopatra especially. In any case, the later play is a tragedy about lovers who, despite their quarrels and uncertainties and betrayals of self, are reconciled in a vision of the greatness of their love. In its depiction of two contrasting worlds, also, *Antony and Cleopatra* recalls the movement of several earlier comedies from the realistic world of political conniving to a dreamworld of the romantic and the unexpected. We can endorse neither world fully in *Antony and Cleopatra,* and, accordingly, the vision of life presented is often ambivalent and ironic as much as it is tragic. The contrast of values separating Egypt and Rome underscores the paradox of humanity's quest for seemingly irreconcilable goals. The ending is neither a triumph nor a defeat for the lovers but something of both. If Antony and Cleopatra seem in one way too small to be tragic protagonists, in another way they seem too large, creating imaginative visions of themselves and their union that escape the realm of tragedy altogether. Our attention is focused less on the way in which the protagonists come to understand some meaningful relationship between their character and the fate required of them by a tragic universe than on the almost comic way in which the absurdities of Roman worldly striving and Egyptian dissipation are transfigured in the world of the imagination.

The Roman point of view opens the play and never entirely loses its force. At first, it may seem superior to that of Egypt. Demetrius and Philo, who invite us to view the play's first encounter between Antony and Cleopatra (1.1) from the perspective of the professional Roman soldier, lament the decline of Antony into Circean enslavement. Their tragic concept is of the Fall of Princes, all the more soberly edifying because of the height from which Antony has toppled. "You shall see in him / The triple pillar of the world transformed / Into a strumpet's fool" (1.1.11–13). Egypt is enchanting but clearly enervating— a bizarre assemblage of soothsayers, eunuchs, and waiting-gentlewomen who wish to be "married to three kings in a forenoon and widow them all" (1.2.28–9). Their mirth is all bawdry, tinged with practices, such as transvestitism, that Roman custom views as licentious. The prevailing images are of procreation in various shapes, sleep (mandragora, Lethe), the oriental opulence of Cleopatra's barge (a golden poop, purple sails, silver oars, divers-colored fans), Epicurean feasting, and drinking. As Enobarbus says, "Mine, and most of our fortunes tonight, shall be—drunk to bed" (1.2.47–8).

Antony, for all his reckless defiance of Rome, agrees in his more reflective moments with what Demetrius and Philo have said. "A Roman thought hath struck him," Cleopatra observantly remarks, and Antony has indeed determined that "I must from this enchanting queen break off" (1.2.88, 135). His later return to Cleopatra is at least in part a surrender, a betrayal of his marriage vows to Octavia and his political assurances to Caesar. In the ensuing battles, Antony submits himself dangerously to Cleopatra's governance, and this inversion of dominance in sexual roles, as conventionally understood by the Roman patriarchal world, is emblematic of a deeper disorder within Antony. As Enobarbus concludes bitterly, Antony "would make his will / Lord of his reason" and so has subverted his "judgment" (3.13.3–4, 37) to passion.

From the beginning, Cleopatra has sought dominance over Antony in the war of the sexes. When Antony first came to her on the River Cydnus, we learn, he was so overcome in all his senses that he was "barbered ten times o'er" (2.2.234). Cleopatra boasts that she "angled" for Antony on many occasions, catching him the way fishermen "betray" fish, and that, when she had "drunk him to his bed," she "put my tires and mantles on him, whilst / I wore his sword Philippan" (2.5.10–23). Caesar, affronted by such transvestite debauchery, charges that Antony "is not more manlike / Than Cleopatra, nor the queen of Ptolemy / More womanly than he" (1.4.5–7). During the battle scenes, Antony's followers complain that "Photinus, an eunuch" (probably Mardian), and Cleopatra's maids manage the war: "So our leader's led, / And we are women's men" (3.7.14–15, 70–1). Antony confesses too late that they were right. He becomes a "doting mallard," one whose heart is "tied by th' strings" to Cleopatra's rudder when her ships retreat in the first naval engagement (3.10.20, 3.11.56). In the mythic images used to raise their relationship to heroic proportions, Antony is like Mars to Cleopatra's Venus (1.5.19), both in a positive and a negative sense. The image has positive connotations of the way in which, as Milton puts it, the "two great sexes animate the world," the masterful soldier and his attractive consort complementing one another in a right relationship of martial prowess and beauty, bravery and love, reason and will; however, to the Renaissance, the myth of Mars and Venus could also be read in a destructive sense, as an adulterous relationship in which reason is subverted to appetite. In another mythic comparison, Antony is like Hercules, not in his prime, but with the shirt of Nessus on his back—a poisoned shirt given to Hercules by his wife in a mistaken hope of thereby assuring his love for her (4.12.43). Antony's soldiers understandably believe that the god Hercules has deserted his reputed descendant and onetime champion (4.3.21–2).

Despite Antony's shameful violation of manhood, honor, attention to duty, self-knowledge, and all that Rome stands for, however, the end of his story is anything but a one-sided endorsement for the Roman point of view. The actual Rome, disfigured by political conniving, falls far short of the ideal. Antony has a point when he protests that "Kingdoms are clay" (1.1.37). Alliances are unstable and are governed by mere political expediency. At first, Antony's wife Fulvia and his brother Lucius have fought one another until forced to unite against the greater threat of Octavius Caesar. Similarly, Antony and Caesar come together only because Pompey has become dangerously powerful at sea and has won the favor of the fickle mob, "Our slippery people" (1.2.192). This detente is not meant to last. As Enobarbus bluntly puts it, "if you borrow one another's love for the instant, you may, when you hear no more words of Pompey, return it again" (2.2.109–11). Enobarbus is rebuked for his unstatesmanlike tone, but no one denies the validity of what he says. In this cynical negotiation, Octavia is a pawn between husband and brother, shabbily treated by both. Caesar coldly bargains away the happiness of the one person of whom he protests that "no brother / Did ever love so dearly" (2.2.159–60). Antony, although hating false promises and resolving to be loyal to Octavia, knows within himself that it won't work. To make matters worse for the fair-minded Antony, he has received great favors from Pompey that he must now uncharitably repudiate in the interests of politics. Pompey does not miss the opportunity to remind Antony of his ingratitude, but the prevailing mood is not so much of bitterness as of ironic futility. Old friendships must be sacrificed; no one seems wholly to blame, and no one can stop the game. Pompey is as much in the wrong as anyone and as powerless. Despite his idealistic hope of restoring republican government to Rome, he has had to ally himself with pirates who offer him sinister temptations. He could be "lord of all the world" (2.7.62) if he would only murder on occasion, but Pompey is destined to be trapped between lofty ends and ignoble means. Lepidus is still another dismaying victim of political callousness, used condescendingly by Caesar and permitted to drink himself into oblivion, until he is cashiered on a trumped-up charge and imprisoned for life.

Octavius Caesar embodies most of all the ironic limits of political ambition. He has avoided enslavement to passion at the very real cost of enslaving himself to his public career as general, triumvir, and future emperor. His ideal warrior is one who, driven by military necessity, would "drink / The stale [urine] of horses and the gilded puddle / Which beasts would cough at" (1.4.62–4). As a general, he is Antony's opposite in every way. He attacks only when he has the advantage and places those who have deserted Antony in his own front lines so "That Antony may seem to spend his fury / Upon himself" (4.6.10–11). He controls his supplies cannily, believing it a "waste" to feast his army (4.1.17). He, of course, declines Antony's offers of single combat. Antony meantime recklessly accepts Caesar's challenge to fight at sea, feasts debauchingly in one "gaudy night" after another (3.13.186), and generously refuses to blame or penalize those who leave him. His sending Enobarbus's belongings after him into Caesar's camp convinces that honest soldier he has made a fatal error, for, however imprudent Antony's chivalry may be, it is unquestionably noble and great-hearted. Caesar is a superb general and political genius, but he is also a military automaton, a logistical reckoner, a Machiavellian pragmatist. In his personal life, he is no less austere and puritanical. He deplores loosening his tongue with alcohol. About women, he is deeply cynical, believing that "want will perjure / The ne'er-touched vestal" (3.12.30–1). Between him and Cleopatra, there is a profound antipathy, based in part on his revulsion at her earlier affair with his namesake and adoptive father, Julius Caesar (3.6.6). Cleopatra may entertain briefly the notion of trying to seduce this new Caesar (3.13.46 ff.), for like Charmian she loves long life "better than figs"(1.2.34), but, if so, she soon discovers that she and Caesar are not compatible. All that he represents she must instead grandly repudiate, choosing death and the fantasy of an eternity with Antony as her way to "call great Caesar ass / Unpolicied" (5.2.307–8).

Cleopatra is a "lass unparalleled" (5.2.316), whose greatness is elusive and all the more enthralling because it is so mysterious. She rises above her counterpart in Shakespeare's source, Plutarch's *Lives of the Noble Grecians and Romans,* in which she is an impressive queenly woman but still essentially a temptress causing the lamentable fall of the hero. Shakespeare's Cleopatra is that but is also something indefinable that can be gotten at only through paradox. Her very character is the essence of contradiction: she knows how "to chide, to laugh, / To weep" (1.1.51–2), to be sullen or violent, like a skillful actor keeping Antony continually off guard. Dispassionately examined, she is a woman no longer young who abuses messengers like an oriental despot, who sends Antony a false report of her death out of fear for her own safety, who will not risk leaving her monument even when Antony lies outside mortally wounded, and who lies about her wealth when captured by Caesar (what is she planning to do with that wealth, anyway?). We cannot be sure that she would not have "packed cards with Caesar" (4.14.19) if she had found him susceptible to her charms. Yet we are not invited to see her dispassionately. Her charm is eternal, and so are the myths surrounding that charm. Observers evoking her splendor do not describe her person directly but, rather, her effects and surroundings: Enobarbus says simply that "For her own person, / It beggared all description" and goes on to catalogue her cloth-of-gold pavilion and her mermaidlike attendants. Most of all, she is a paradox: she makes defect perfection, age cannot wither her, and "vilest things / Become themselves in her, that the holy priests / Bless her when she is riggish" (2.2.207–50). She is both a whore and the Lucretian Venus; both sluttish and holy.

Inspired by Cleopatra, Antony shows himself ready to break down conventional barriers between the sexes and to explore new emotional territory by giving up part of his self-protective masculinity. Antony's embracing of an attractive but sexually dangerous woman is all the more remarkable in a play that follows the harrowing depictions of sexual conflict in *Hamlet, Othello,* and *Lear* and the degrading portrait of erotic enslavement in the "Dark Lady" sonnets, for here the relationship of the lovers, though doomed, is also triumphant. Shakespeare takes a look at something like midlife crisis, conceding freely how ridiculous the male appears to himself and to others in his compulsive tendency to polarize women into saints and whores. Yet Shakespeare also explores ways in which the man and the woman attempt to become increasingly like each other, enabling the man to participate in a vision of union with the feminine principle of generative, erotic, fertile, life-giving vitality, and enabling the woman to join her "husband" in the noble resolve of a Roman suicide.

In Cleopatra, "fancy" exceeds "nature"; the fertility of her Egypt overflows the measure, exceeding the sterility of Rome as her own imaginative fertility exceeds reality itself. When she protests that she will not go to Rome to behold herself in a wretched play and thus see "Some squeaking Cleopatra boy my greatness / I'th' posture of a whore" (5.2.220–1), we realize that Shakespeare is calling attention to his own art as well, pointing out how Elizabethan boy actors on a bare stage can transform reality into a dream that we believe. Cleopatra's mystery is like that of poetry itself. The "real" world pales into insignificance of a "little O, the earth," something "No better than a sty," full of illusory shadows that "mock our eyes with air" (5.2.80, 4.15.64, 4.14.7); and Caesar's triumph vanishes with it. In its place, Antony and Cleopatra raise up a vision of themselves as lovers who, through art, have indeed become eternal. Together they will over-picture Venus and Mars, and will be so renowned that "Dido and her Aeneas shall want troops, / And all the haunt be ours" (4.14.53–4). They are virtually husband and wife—"Husband, I come!" exclaims Cleopatra just before she dies (5.2.287)—united at last in a re-creative vision almost appropriate to comedy; and in their marriage they find a kind of redemption for the defeat that history can inflict. Antony is no longer dying Hercules but the god of Cleopatra's dream whose "legs bestrid the ocean; his reared arm / Crested the world; his voice was propertied / As all the tunèd spheres" (lines 81–3). Through Cleopatra's vision, we realize how all the characteristics that made Antony at once so noble and so sure to fall before Caesar—his generosity amounting to imprudence, his spontaneity, his impatience with the ordinary, his staking his all on love when he hears of Cleopatra's supposed death—have not deserted him. His death serves to reaffirm the magnificence of the very qualities that have brought him down. His essential nobility is confirmed, even if it must be defined in non-Roman ways. He and Cleopatra share the "immortal longings" for which she goes willingly to her death, dressed in her "best attires" like a queen (lines 281, 228), for neither lover will accept anything less than greatness.

Antony and Cleopatra is a daunting play to stage, because the main characters take on a mythic character that seems larger than life, larger than art itself. Michael Goldman imagines what it would be like for an actor to try out for the part of Antony only to be instructed by the casting director, "Now, stand there and be a triple pillar of the world." How can an actor convey the charisma of a man whose very name is legendary? The problem in acting Cleopatra is even more acute. The great actresses who have taken on the assignment have all been praised for many things but also faulted for lacking other dimensions of this amazing character. Vivien Leigh, playing opposite Laurence Olivier's Antony at the St. James Theatre, London, in 1951, was applauded by the critics for her coquettish sexiness and magnetism but perhaps deficient in animal heat and duskiness. Peggy Ashcroft, in Glen Byam Shaw's production at Stratford-upon-Avon in 1953, was lauded as impressively intelligent and capable of huge emotional variation, but was seen as physically small and not as sexually glamorous as Leigh. Margaret Whiting, at the Old Vic in 1957, was regarded by most viewers as simply too young for the part. Vanessa Redgrave, at the Bankside Globe Playhouse in 1973, threw cola bottles at her servants in her fits of temper, and somehow lacked dignity for the final scenes. Glenda Jackson, playing Cleopatra in Peter Brook's de-romanticized version at Stratford-upon-Avon in 1978, was brilliant for her iciness of tone and angularity in wit combat, but at the expense of tenderness and erotic feeling. The role has attracted the greatest of talent, from Janet Suzman to Helen Mirren to Judi Dench, with similar praise and qualifications. These limits are a tribute to the play itself but a thorny problem for those who are producing the play. Film versions have tended to succumb to the temptations of visual splendor, in the style of Cecil B. DeMille, thus missing the point of the play's verbal and theatrical invocation of the ineffable. One singularly successful production is that on audiotape with Michael Redgrave as Antony and Peggy Ashcroft as Cleopatra; here the listener can imagine the lovers to be as toweringly great as the play's language suggests, magnificently assisted by the voices of two great actors. This is not to say that *Antony and Cleopatra* is unplayable; to the contrary, it shows Shakespeare at the very height of his powers as a professional writer for the theater. At the same time, few plays have ever posed a greater challenge for an acting ensemble.

Antony and Cleopatra

[*Dramatis Personae*

MARK ANTONY,
OCTAVIUS CAESAR, } *triumvirs*
LEPIDUS,

CLEOPATRA,
CHARMIAN,
IRAS,
ALEXAS,
MARDIAN, *a eunuch,* } *Cleopatra's attendants*
DIOMEDES,
SELEUCUS, *Cleopatra's treasurer,*

OCTAVIA, *sister of Octavius Caesar and wife of
Antony*

DEMETRIUS,
PHILO,
DOMITIUS ENOBARBUS,
VENTIDIUS,
SILIUS, } *Antony's friends and followers*
EROS,
CANIDIUS,
SCARUS,
DERCETUS,
A SCHOOLMASTER, *Antony's* AMBASSADOR *to Caesar*

MAECENAS,
AGRIPPA,
TAURUS,
THIDIAS, } *Octavius Caesar's friends and followers*
DOLABELLA,
GALLUS,
PROCULEIUS,

SEXTUS POMPEIUS *or* POMPEY
MENAS,
MENECRATES, } *Pompey's friends*
VARRIUS,

MESSENGERS *to Antony, Octavius, Caesar, and Cleopatra*
A SOOTHSAYER
Two SERVANTS *of Pompey*
SERVANTS *of Antony and Cleopatra*
A BOY
SOLDIERS, SENTRIES, GUARDSMEN *of Antony
and Octavius Caesar*
A CAPTAIN *in Antony's army*
An EGYPTIAN
A CLOWN *with figs*

*Ladies attending Cleopatra, Eunuchs, Servants, Sol-
diers, Captains, Officers, silent named characters
(Rannius, Lucillius, Lamprius)*

SCENE: *In several parts of the Roman Empire*]

1.1

Enter Demetrius and Philo.

PHILO
Nay, but this dotage of our general's   1
O'erflows the measure. Those his goodly eyes,   2

That o'er the files and musters of the war   3
Have glowed like plated Mars, now bend, now turn   4
The office and devotion of their view   5
Upon a tawny front. His captain's heart,   6
Which in the scuffles of great fights hath burst
The buckles on his breast, reneges all temper   8

1.1. Location: Alexandria. Cleopatra's palace.
1 dotage foolish affection, sometimes associated with old age
2 O'erflows the measure exceeds moderation, exceeds the means of measuring it.

3 files and musters orderly formations   **4 plated** clothed in armor
5 office function   **6 tawny front** dark face. (Literally, forehead.)
8 reneges all temper renounces all moderation

And is become the bellows and the fan
To cool a gypsy's lust.

    Flourish. Enter Antony, Cleopatra, her ladies, the
    train, with eunuchs fanning her.

                 Look, where they come.   10
Take but good note, and you shall see in him
The triple pillar of the world transformed   12
Into a strumpet's fool. Behold and see.   13

CLEOPATRA
If it be love indeed, tell me how much.

ANTONY
There's beggary in the love that can be reckoned.   15

CLEOPATRA
I'll set a bourn how far to be beloved.   16

ANTONY
Then must thou needs find out new heaven, new
   earth.   17

    Enter a Messenger.

MESSENGER   News, my good lord, from Rome.
ANTONY   Grates me! The sum.   19
CLEOPATRA   Nay, hear them, Antony.   20
Fulvia perchance is angry, or who knows   21
If the scarce-bearded Caesar have not sent   22
His powerful mandate to you, "Do this, or this;
Take in that kingdom, and enfranchise that;   24
Perform't, or else we damn thee."   25
ANTONY   How, my love?   26
CLEOPATRA   Perchance? Nay, and most like.   27
You must not stay here longer; your dismission   28
Is come from Caesar. Therefore hear it, Antony.
Where's Fulvia's process? Caesar's, I would say. Both?   30
Call in the messengers. As I am Egypt's queen,
Thou blushest, Antony, and that blood of thine
Is Caesar's homager; else so thy cheek pays shame   33
When shrill-tongued Fulvia scolds. The messengers!
ANTONY
Let Rome in Tiber melt and the wide arch
Of the ranged empire fall! Here is my space.   36
Kingdoms are clay; our dungy earth alike
Feeds beast as man. The nobleness of life

Is to do thus; when such a mutual pair   39
And such a twain can do't, in which I bind,   40
On pain of punishment, the world to weet   41
We stand up peerless.
CLEOPATRA   Excellent falsehood!   42
Why did he marry Fulvia, and not love her?   43
I'll seem the fool I am not. Antony   44
Will be himself.
ANTONY   But stirred by Cleopatra.   45
Now, for the love of Love and her soft hours,
Let's not confound the time with conference harsh.   47
There's not a minute of our lives should stretch   48
Without some pleasure now. What sport tonight?
CLEOPATRA
Hear the ambassadors.
ANTONY   Fie, wrangling queen!
Whom everything becomes—to chide, to laugh,
To weep; whose every passion fully strives
To make itself, in thee, fair and admired!
No messenger but thine; and all alone
Tonight we'll wander through the streets and note
The qualities of people. Come, my queen,
Last night you did desire it.—Speak not to us.
    Exeunt [Antony and Cleopatra] with the train.
DEMETRIUS
Is Caesar with Antonius prized so slight?   58
PHILO
Sir, sometimes when he is not Antony
He comes too short of that great property   60
Which still should go with Antony.
DEMETRIUS   I am full sorry   61
That he approves the common liar, who   62
Thus speaks of him at Rome; but I will hope
Of better deeds tomorrow. Rest you happy!   *Exeunt.*   64

[1.2]

    Enter Enobarbus, Lamprius, a Soothsayer, Ran-
    nius, Lucillius, Charmian, Iras, Mardian the
    eunuch, and Alexas.

CHARMIAN   Lord Alexas, sweet Alexas, most anything
Alexas, almost most absolute Alexas, where's the   2
soothsayer that you praised so to th' Queen? Oh, that

---

10 gypsy's (Gypsies were widely believed to have come from Egypt,
to enjoy magical powers, and to be lustful and cunning.)   **s.d.**
Flourish trumpet fanfare announcing the arrival or departure of
important person.   *train* retinue   **12 triple** one of three. (Alludes to
the triumvirate of Antony, Lepidus, and Octavius Caesar; also to tri-
partite division of the world into Asia, Africa, and Europe.)   **13 fool**
plaything.   **15 There's . . . reckoned** i.e., Love that can be quantified
is paltry; ours is infinite.   **16 bourn** boundary, limit   **17 Then . . .
earth** i.e., Only in some new universe could you find a limit to my
love. (The language echoes Revelation 21:1 and other biblical passages.)   **19 Grates . . . sum** It annoys me! Be brief.   **20 them** i.e., the
news   **21 Fulvia** Antony's wife   **22 scarce-bearded Caesar** (Octavius
Caesar was twenty-three in 40 B.C., at the time of the play's opening.
Antony was forty-three.)   **24 Take in** conquer.   **enfranchise** set free
25 damn condemn to death   **26 How** i.e., What's that you say?
27 Perchance (Cleopatra reconsiders what she has said in line 21.)
like likely.   **28 dismission** order to depart   **30 process** writ to
appear in court.   **33 Is . . . shame** is Caesar's vassal, doing homage to
him; or else your blushing pays the tribute of shame   **36 ranged** well
ordered and far-extending

39 thus (May indicate an embrace, or Antony may refer more generally to their way of life.)   **40–2 in which . . . peerless** with respect to
which I insist that the world, under penalty of punishment if it fails
to do so, acknowledge us to be peerless.   **43 and not** if he did not
44 I'll . . . not i.e., I'll pretend to be gullible and believe him, though I
know better.   **45 be himself** i.e., be the Roman Antony, the fool
and deceiver he always is, etc.   **stirred** (1) prompted to noble deeds
(2) moved to folly (3) sexually stirred   **47 confound** ruin, waste.
conference conversation   **48 should stretch** that should be prolonged   **58 prized** valued   **60 property** quality, distinction   **61 still**
always   **62 approves** corroborates   **64 Of** for
1.2. Location: Alexandria. Cleopatra's palace.
0.1–2 Lamprius . . . Lucillius (Lamprius may possibly be the soothsayer, but Rannius and Lucillius have no speaking parts here and do
not appear again in the play. Mardian is mute here but does speak in
later scenes.)   **2 absolute** perfect

I knew this husband, which, you say, must charge his   4
horns with garlands!   5

ALEXAS   Soothsayer!

SOOTHSAYER   Your will?

CHARMIAN
Is this the man?—Is't you, sir, that know things?

SOOTHSAYER
In nature's infinite book of secrecy
A little I can read.

ALEXAS [to Charmian]   Show him your hand.

ENOBARBUS [to servants within]
Bring in the banquet quickly; wine enough   12
Cleopatra's health to drink.

CHARMIAN [giving her hand to the Soothsayer]   Good sir,
give me good fortune.

SOOTHSAYER   I make not, but foresee.

CHARMIAN   Pray, then, foresee me one.

SOOTHSAYER
You shall be yet far fairer than you are.

CHARMIAN   He means in flesh.   19

IRAS   No, you shall paint when you are old.   20

CHARMIAN   Wrinkles forbid!

ALEXAS   Vex not his prescience. Be attentive.

CHARMIAN   Hush!

SOOTHSAYER
You shall be more beloving than beloved.

CHARMIAN   I had rather heat my liver with drinking.   25

ALEXAS   Nay, hear him.

CHARMIAN   Good now, some excellent fortune! Let me   27
be married to three kings in a forenoon and widow
them all. Let me have a child at fifty, to whom Herod   29
of Jewry may do homage. Find me to marry me with   30
Octavius Caesar, and companion me with my mis-   31
tress.   32

SOOTHSAYER
You shall outlive the lady whom you serve.

CHARMIAN   Oh, excellent! I love long life better than figs.   34

SOOTHSAYER
You have seen and proved a fairer former fortune   35
Than that which is to approach.

CHARMIAN   Then belike my children shall have no   37
names. Prithee, how many boys and wenches must I   38
have?   39

SOOTHSAYER
If every of your wishes had a womb,
And fertile every wish, a million.

CHARMIAN   Out, fool! I forgive thee for a witch.   42

ALEXAS   You think none but your sheets are privy to   43
your wishes.

CHARMIAN   Nay, come, tell Iras hers.

ALEXAS   We'll know all our fortunes.

ENOBARBUS   Mine, and most of our fortunes tonight,
shall be—drunk to bed.

IRAS [giving her hand to the Soothsayer]   There's a palm
presages chastity, if nothing else.

CHARMIAN   E'en as the o'erflowing Nilus presageth   51
famine.   52

IRAS   Go, you wild bedfellow, you cannot soothsay.   53

CHARMIAN   Nay, if an oily palm be not a fruitful prog-   54
nostication, I cannot scratch mine ear. Prithee, tell her   55
but a workaday fortune.   56

SOOTHSAYER   Your fortunes are alike.

IRAS   But how, but how? Give me particulars.

SOOTHSAYER   I have said.   59

IRAS   Am I not an inch of fortune better than she?

CHARMIAN   Well, if you were but an inch of fortune better than I, where would you choose it?

IRAS   Not in my husband's nose.   63

CHARMIAN   Our worser thoughts heavens mend! Al-   64
exas—come, his fortune, his fortune! Oh, let him marry
a woman that cannot go, sweet Isis, I beseech thee,   66
and let her die too, and give him a worse, and let
worse follow worse till the worst of all follow him
laughing to his grave, fiftyfold a cuckold! Good Isis,
hear me this prayer, though thou deny me a matter of   70
more weight; good Isis, I beseech thee!

IRAS   Amen, dear goddess, hear that prayer of the people! For, as it is a heart-breaking to see a handsome
man loose-wived, so it is a deadly sorrow to behold a   74
foul knave uncuckolded. Therefore, dear Isis, keep de-   75
corum, and fortune him accordingly!   76

CHARMIAN   Amen.

ALEXAS   Lo now, if it lay in their hands to make me a
cuckold, they would make themselves whores but   79
they'd do't.   80

Enter Cleopatra.

ENOBARBUS
Hush! Here comes Antony.

CHARMIAN   Not he. The Queen.

CLEOPATRA   Saw you my lord?

---

4 this husband (Evidently Alexas has told Charmian that the Sooth-sayer will prophesy a husband for her.)   **4–5 must . . . garlands** i.e., must decorate his cuckold's horns with a garland of flowers, like a sacrificial beast. (Cuckolded men were derisively thought of as grow-ing horns, as a badge of their infamy.)   **12 banquet** light repast, dessert   **19 in flesh** i.e., by putting on weight.   **20 paint** i.e., use makeup   **25 heat . . . drinking** i.e., heat my liver with wine rather than with unrequited love. (The liver was believed to be the seat of sexual desire.)   **27 Good now** Come on, now   **29–30 Herod of Jewry** i.e., even the blustering tyrant who massacred the children of Judea   **30 Find me** i.e., Find in my palm   **31–2 companion . . . mistress** give me equal fortune with Cleopatra; or, perhaps, let Cleopatra become my "companion" or attendant.   **34 better than figs** (Probably a proverbial expression; with genital suggestion.)   **35 proved** experi-enced   **37 belike** probably   **37–8 have no names** be illegitimate.   **38 wenches** girls   **38–9 must I have** am I to have.

42 Out . . . witch (Charmian jokingly says that, since soothsayers, like fools, are allowed to speak freely without penalty, she will forgive him for slander.)   **43 privy to** in on the secret of   **51–2 E'en . . . famine** (Charmian speaks ironically; the overflowing Nile presages abundance. See 2.7.17–23.)   **53 wild** wanton   **54 oily palm** sweaty or moist palm (indicating a sensual disposition)   **54–5 fruitful prognos-tication** omen of fertility   **56 workaday** ordinary   **59 I have said** I have no more to say.   **63 Not . . . nose** (Iras bawdily hints at some place other than in the nose where she would prefer to see her hus-band well endowed.)   **64 Our . . . mend!** (Charmian pretends to be shocked: May heaven improve our dirty minds!)   **66 cannot go** (1) is lame (2) cannot make love satisfactorily or cannot bear children.   **Isis** Egyptian goddess usually identified with fertility and the moon   **70 hear me** hear (on my behalf)   **74 loose-wived** with an unfaithful wife   **75 foul** ugly   **75–6 keep decorum** deal suitably with the case   **76 fortune him** grant him fortune   **79–80 they . . . do't** i.e., they would stop at nothing, even becoming whores, to cuckold me.

ENOBARBUS   No, lady.
CLEOPATRA   Was he not here?
CHARMIAN   No, madam.
CLEOPATRA
He was disposed to mirth, but on the sudden
A Roman thought hath struck him. Enobarbus!
ENOBARBUS   Madam?
CLEOPATRA
Seek him and bring him hither. Where's Alexas?
ALEXAS
Here at your service.—My lord approaches.

Enter Antony with a Messenger.

CLEOPATRA
We will not look upon him. Go with us.
            Exeunt [all but Antony and the Messenger].
FIRST MESSENGER
Fulvia thy wife first came into the field.   93
ANTONY   Against my brother Lucius?
FIRST MESSENGER   Ay.
But soon that war had end, and the time's state   96
Made friends of them, jointing their force 'gainst
   Caesar,   97
Whose better issue in the war from Italy   98
Upon the first encounter drave them.   99
ANTONY   Well, what worst?
FIRST MESSENGER
The nature of bad news infects the teller.   101
ANTONY
When it concerns the fool or coward. On.
Things that are past are done with me. 'Tis thus:
Who tells me true, though in his tale lie death,
I hear him as he flattered.
FIRST MESSENGER   Labienus—   105
This is stiff news—hath with his Parthian force
Extended Asia; from Euphrates   107
His conquering banner shook, from Syria
To Lydia and to Ionia,
Whilst—
ANTONY   Antony, thou wouldst say.
FIRST MESSENGER   Oh, my lord!
ANTONY
Speak to me home; mince not the general tongue.   111
Name Cleopatra as she is called in Rome;
Rail thou in Fulvia's phrase, and taunt my faults   113
With such full license as both truth and malice
Have power to utter. Oh, then we bring forth weeds
When our quick minds lie still, and our ills told us   116
Is as our earing. Fare thee well awhile.   117

FIRST MESSENGER   At your noble pleasure.
                        Exit [First] Messenger.

        Enter another Messenger.

ANTONY
From Sicyon, ho, the news! Speak there.
SECOND MESSENGER
The man from Sicyon—is there such an one?   120
THIRD MESSENGER [*at the door*]
He stays upon your will.
ANTONY   Let him appear.—   121
        [*Exeunt Second and Third Messengers.*]
These strong Egyptian fetters I must break,
Or lose myself in dotage.

        Enter another Messenger, with a letter.

                        What are you?
FOURTH MESSENGER   Fulvia thy wife is dead.
ANTONY   Where died she?
FOURTH MESSENGER   In Sicyon.
Her length of sickness, with what else more serious
Importeth thee to know, this bears.   [*He gives a letter.*]
ANTONY   Forbear me.   128
            [*Exit Fourth Messenger.*]
There's a great spirit gone! Thus did I desire it.
What our contempts doth often hurl from us
We wish it ours again. The present pleasure,
By revolution lowering, does become   132
The opposite of itself. She's good, being gone;
The hand could pluck her back that shoved her on.   134
I must from this enchanting queen break off.
Ten thousand harms more than the ills I know
My idleness doth hatch.—How now, Enobarbus!

        Enter Enobarbus.

ENOBARBUS   What's your pleasure, sir?
ANTONY   I must with haste from hence.
ENOBARBUS   Why, then, we kill all our women. We see
how mortal an unkindness is to them; if they suffer
our departure, death's the word.
ANTONY   I must be gone.
ENOBARBUS   Under a compelling occasion, let women
die. It were pity to cast them away for nothing, though
between them and a great cause they should be esteemed nothing. Cleopatra, catching but the least noise 147
of this, dies instantly; I have seen her die twenty times 148
upon far poorer moment. I do think there is mettle in   149

---

93 field battlefield.   **96 time's state** circumstances prevailing at the
moment   **97 jointing** uniting   **98–9 Whose . . . them** whose better
military success drove them from Italy upon the very first encounter.
101 infects the teller i.e., makes the teller seem unwelcome.   **105 as** as
if.   **Labienus** (Brutus and Cassius [see *Julius Caesar*] had sent Quintus
Labienus to Orodes, King of Parthia, to seek aid against Antony and
Octavius Caesar; with a force thus obtained, he is now overrunning the
Roman provinces in the Middle East.)   **107 Extended** seized upon. (A
legal phrase.)   **111 Speak . . . tongue** Speak bluntly; don't minimize the
common report.   **113 Rail . . . phrase** Scold me as Fulvia would   **116 quick**
alive, inventive   **116–17 our ills . . . earing** hearing our faults told to us
improves us, as plowing (*earing*) improves land by rooting out the weeds.

120 The man from Sicyon (The messenger who has just entered, not
being from Sicyon, realizes in some confusion that Antony wants to
hear the news from Sicyon. This second messenger therefore calls out
to ask if the messenger from Sicyon is to be found. Another messenger at the door replies that such a man is indeed waiting, and in a
moment that messenger from Sicyon enters with his report. Some editors change the second and third messengers into attendants.) *Sicyon*
is an ancient city in Greece, where Antony left Fulvia.   **121 stays
upon** awaits   **128 Importeth** concerns.   **Forbear** Leave   **132 By revolution lowering** sinking in our estimation in the course of time and
Fortune's turning wheel   **134 could** would be willing to   **147 noise**
hint, rumor   **148 die** (Playing on a common second meaning of
"achieve sexual orgasm.")   **149 poorer moment** lesser cause.
mettle i.e., sexual vigor

death, which commits some loving act upon her, she
hath such a celerity in dying.

ANTONY   She is cunning past man's thought.

ENOBARBUS   Alack, sir, no, her passions are made of
nothing but the finest part of pure love. We cannot call
her winds and waters sighs and tears; they are greater 155
storms and tempests than almanacs can report. This
cannot be cunning in her; if it be, she makes a shower
of rain as well as Jove.

ANTONY   Would I had never seen her!

ENOBARBUS   Oh, sir, you had then left unseen a wonderful piece of work, which not to have been blessed
withal would have discredited your travel.

ANTONY   Fulvia is dead.

ENOBARBUS   Sir?

ANTONY   Fulvia is dead.

ENOBARBUS   Fulvia?

ANTONY   Dead.

ENOBARBUS   Why, sir, give the gods a thankful sacrifice.
When it pleaseth their deities to take the wife of a man
from him, it shows to man the tailors of the earth; 170
comforting therein, that when old robes are worn out,
there are members to make new. If there were no more 172
women but Fulvia, then had you indeed a cut, and the
case to be lamented. This grief is crowned with consolation; your old smock brings forth a new petticoat, 175
and indeed the tears live in an onion that should water 176
this sorrow. 177

ANTONY
The business she hath broachèd in the state 178
Cannot endure my absence.

ENOBARBUS   And the business you have broached here
cannot be without you, especially that of Cleopatra's,
which wholly depends on your abode. 182

ANTONY
No more light answers. Let our officers 183
Have notice what we purpose. I shall break 184
The cause of our expedience to the Queen 185
And get her leave to part. For not alone 186
The death of Fulvia, with more urgent touches, 187
Do strongly speak to us, but the letters too
Of many our contriving friends in Rome 189
Petition us at home. Sextus Pompeius 190
Hath given the dare to Caesar and commands
The empire of the sea. Our slippery people, 192

Whose love is never linked to the deserver
Till his deserts are past, begin to throw 194
Pompey the Great and all his dignities 195
Upon his son, who—high in name and power,
Higher than both in blood and life—stands up 197
For the main soldier; whose quality, going on, 198
The sides o'th' world may danger. Much is breeding, 199
Which, like the courser's hair, hath yet but life, 200
And not a serpent's poison. Say our pleasure, 201
To such whose place is under us, requires 202
Our quick remove from hence. 203

ENOBARBUS   I shall do't.   [*Exeunt separately.*]

[1.3]

Enter Cleopatra, Charmian, Alexas, and Iras.

CLEOPATRA
Where is he?

CHARMIAN   I did not see him since. 1

CLEOPATRA [*to Alexas*]
See where he is, who's with him, what he does.
I did not send you. If you find him sad, 3
Say I am dancing; if in mirth, report
That I am sudden sick. Quick, and return. 5
                    [*Exit Alexas.*]

CHARMIAN
Madam, methinks, if you did love him dearly,
You do not hold the method to enforce 7
The like from him.

CLEOPATRA   What should I do I do not? 8

CHARMIAN
In each thing give him way. Cross him in nothing.

CLEOPATRA
Thou teachest like a fool: the way to lose him.

CHARMIAN
Tempt him not so too far. I wish, forbear; 11
In time we hate that which we often fear.

        Enter Antony.

But here comes Antony.

CLEOPATRA   I am sick and sullen. 13

ANTONY
I am sorry to give breathing to my purpose— 14

155 **sighs** i.e., mere sighs   170 **tailors** (The gods can fashion a new
wife for a man, much as a tailor can mend or replace a worn-out garment.)   172 **members** (The word has a bawdy suggestion, pursued
in lines 173–4 and 180 in *cut, case, business,* and *broached; cut* and *case*
suggest the female sexual organs; *broached* suggests something that is
stabbed, pricked, opened.)   175 **smock** undergarment. (Also used
defamatorily of women.)   176–7 **the tears . . . sorrow** i.e., only an
onion could produce tears on this occasion of Fulvia's death.
178 **broachèd** opened up. (But see the note for line 172.)   182 **abode**
staying.   183 **light** frivolous, indelicate   184 **break** i.e., break the
news of   185 **expedience** haste   186 **leave** consent   187 **urgent
touches** pressing matters   189 **Of . . . friends** from many friends
working in our interest   190 **at home** to come home.   **Sextus Pompeius** son of Pompey the Great, who, though outlawed, has been able
to exploit the division between Antony and Octavius and thereby
gain command of Sicily and the sea; he appears in Act 2
192 **slippery** fickle

194 **throw** bestow   195 **Pompey the Great** i.e., the title and honored
status of "Pompey the Great"   197 **blood and life** mettle and vitality
197–8 **stands . . . soldier** lays claim to being the greatest soldier
198–9 **whose . . . danger** whose aspiring character and situation, if
allowed to continue unchecked, may endanger the frame of the
Roman world.   200 **like . . . hair** (Allusion to the popular belief that a
horsehair put into water would turn to a snake.)   200–1 **hath . . .
poison** is alive at this point but not yet a poisonous full-grown serpent.   201–3 **Say . . . hence** Tell those who serve me that my wish is
to depart quickly.
1.3 Location: Alexandria. Cleopatra's palace.
1 **since** lately.   3 **I did . . . you** i.e., Do not let him know I sent you.
sad serious   5 **sudden** suddenly taken   7 **hold the method** follow
the right course   8 **I do not** that I am not doing.   11 **Tempt** Try.
I wish I wish you would   13 **sullen** depressed, melancholy.
14 **breathing** utterance

CLEOPATRA
Help me away, dear Charmian! I shall fall.
It cannot be thus long; the sides of nature 16
Will not sustain it.
ANTONY   Now, my dearest queen—
CLEOPATRA
Pray you, stand farther from me.
ANTONY   What's the matter? 18
CLEOPATRA
I know by that same eye there's some good news.
What, says the married woman you may go? 20
Would she had never given you leave to come!
Let her not say 'tis I that keep you here.
I have no power upon you; hers you are.
ANTONY
The gods best know—
CLEOPATRA   Oh, never was there queen
So mightily betrayed! Yet at the first
I saw the treasons planted.
ANTONY   Cleopatra—
CLEOPATRA
Why should I think you can be mine, and true—
Though you in swearing shake the thronèd gods—
Who have been false to Fulvia? Riotous madness, 29
To be entangled with those mouth-made vows 30
Which break themselves in swearing!
ANTONY   Most sweet queen— 31
CLEOPATRA
Nay, pray you, seek no color for your going, 32
But bid farewell and go. When you sued staying, 33
Then was the time for words. No going then.
Eternity was in our lips and eyes, 35
Bliss in our brows' bent; none our parts so poor 36
But was a race of heaven. They are so still, 37
Or thou, the greatest soldier of the world,
Art turned the greatest liar.
ANTONY   How now, lady?
CLEOPATRA
I would I had thy inches. Thou shouldst know 40
There were a heart in Egypt.
ANTONY   Hear me, Queen: 41
The strong necessity of time commands
Our services awhile, but my full heart
Remains in use with you. Our Italy 44
Shines o'er with civil swords; Sextus Pompeius 45
Makes his approaches to the port of Rome;

Equality of two domestic powers 47
Breed scrupulous faction; the hated, grown to
strength, 48
Are newly grown to love; the condemned Pompey, 49
Rich in his father's honor, creeps apace 50
Into the hearts of such as have not thrived
Upon the present state, whose numbers threaten; 52
And quietness, grown sick of rest, would purge 53
By any desperate change. My more particular, 54
And that which most with you should safe my going, 55
Is Fulvia's death.
CLEOPATRA
Though age from folly could not give me freedom,
It does from childishness. Can Fulvia die?
ANTONY   She's dead, my queen.   [He offers letters.]
Look here, and at thy sovereign leisure read
The garboils she awaked, at the last, best, 61
See when and where she died.
CLEOPATRA   Oh, most false love!
Where be the sacred vials thou shouldst fill 63
With sorrowful water? Now I see, I see,
In Fulvia's death how mine received shall be.
ANTONY
Quarrel no more, but be prepared to know
The purposes I bear, which are or cease 67
As you shall give th'advice. By the fire 68
That quickens Nilus' slime, I go from hence 69
Thy soldier, servant, making peace or war
As thou affects.
CLEOPATRA   Cut my lace, Charmian, come! 71
But let it be; I am quickly ill, and well,
So Antony loves.
ANTONY   My precious queen, forbear, 73
And give true evidence to his love which stands 74
An honorable trial.
CLEOPATRA   So Fulvia told me. 75
I prithee, turn aside and weep for her;
Then bid adieu to me, and say the tears
Belong to Egypt. Good now, play one scene 78

---

16 It . . . long I can't last long at this rate. sides of nature human body, frame 18 stand farther from me give me air. 20 the married woman Fulvia 29 Who you who. Riotous madness What folly on my part 30 mouth-made insincerely spoken 31 in swearing even while they are being sworn. 32 color pretext 33 sued staying begged to stay 35 our i.e., my. (The royal plural.) 36 bent arch, curve. none . . . poor none of my features, however poor 37 race of heaven of heavenly origin, or, possibly, of the flavor of heaven. 40 inches (1) height (2) manly strength. (With perhaps a bawdy suggestion.) 41 a heart in Egypt a mighty courage in the Queen of Egypt. 44 in use with you for your use. 45 Shines . . . swords glitters everywhere with weapons of civil war

47–8 Equality . . . faction the equal splitting of domestic power between two (Antony and Caesar) breeds petty bickering 48–9 the hated . . . love those (like Pompey) who were out of favor, being now strong, have recently come back into popular favor 49–50 Pompey . . . apace i.e., Sextus Pompeius, richly inheriting the honor once accorded Pompey the Great, quickly insinuates himself 52 state government (of the triumvirate). whose i.e., those supporting Pompey 53–4 And quietness . . . change and peace, bored with its own long continuance, longs to purge itself by the violence of war (medically speaking, by vomiting, bowel evacuation, or bloodletting). 54 particular personal concern 55 safe make safe 61 garboils disturbances, commotions. best i.e., best of all 63 sacred vials (Alludes to the supposed Roman custom of putting bottles filled with tears in the tombs of the departed.) 67 which are which will proceed 68 fire i.e., sun 69 quickens . . . slime brings to life the mud left by the overflow of the Nile 71 thou affects you desire. lace cord or laces fastening the bodice. (Cleopatra pretends she is fainting.) 73 So provided that, or, possibly, "in the same way, with changes as sudden as my own" 74–5 And . . . trial and bear true witness to the love of one who withstands any honorable test. 75 So . . . me i.e., So Fulvia would have said, no doubt. (Said as a taunt.) 78 Belong to Egypt are shed for the Queen of Egypt. Good now (An expression of entreaty.)

Of excellent dissembling, and let it look
Like perfect honor.

ANTONY   You'll heat my blood. No more.   80

CLEOPATRA
You can do better yet; but this is meetly.   81

ANTONY
Now, by my sword—

CLEOPATRA   And target. Still he mends.   82
But this is not the best. Look, prithee, Charmian,
How this Herculean Roman does become   84
The carriage of his chafe.   85

ANTONY   I'll leave you, lady.

CLEOPATRA   Courteous lord, one word.
Sir, you and I must part, but that's not it;
Sir, you and I have loved, but there's not it;
That you know well. Something it is I would—   90
Oh, my oblivion is a very Antony,   91
And I am all forgotten.

ANTONY   But that your royalty   92
Holds idleness your subject, I should take you   93
For idleness itself.

CLEOPATRA   'Tis sweating labor   94
To bear such idleness so near the heart   95
As Cleopatra this. But sir, forgive me,   96
Since my becomings kill me when they do not   97
Eye well to you. Your honor calls you hence;   98
Therefore be deaf to my unpitied folly,
And all the gods go with you! Upon your sword
Sit laurel victory, and smooth success   101
Be strewed before your feet!

ANTONY   Let us go. Come;
Our separation so abides and flies   103
That thou, residing here, goes yet with me,
And I, hence fleeting, here remain with thee.
Away!   *Exeunt.*

❦

[1.4]

*Enter Octavius [Caesar], reading a letter, Lepidus,
and their train.*

CAESAR
You may see, Lepidus, and henceforth know,
It is not Caesar's natural vice to hate

Our great competitor. From Alexandria   3
This is the news: he fishes, drinks, and wastes
The lamps of night in revel; is not more manlike
Than Cleopatra, nor the queen of Ptolemy   6
More womanly than he; hardly gave audience, or   7
Vouchsafed to think he had partners. You shall find
    there
A man who is the abstract of all faults   9
That all men follow.

LEPIDUS   I must not think there are
Evils enough to darken all his goodness.
His faults in him seem as the spots of heaven,   12
More fiery by night's blackness, hereditary   13
Rather than purchased, what he cannot change   14
Than what he chooses.

CAESAR
You are too indulgent. Let's grant it is not   16
Amiss to tumble on the bed of Ptolemy,
To give a kingdom for a mirth, to sit   18
And keep the turn of tippling with a slave,   19
To reel the streets at noon, and stand the buffet   20
With knaves that smells of sweat. Say this becomes
    him—
As his composure must be rare indeed   22
Whom these things cannot blemish—yet must Antony
No way excuse his foils when we do bear   24
So great weight in his lightness. If he filled   25
His vacancy with his voluptuousness,   26
Full surfeits and the dryness of his bones   27
Call on him for't. But to confound such time   28
That drums him from his sport and speaks as loud   29
As his own state and ours, 'tis to be chid   30
As we rate boys who, being mature in knowledge,   31
Pawn their experience to their present pleasure   32
And so rebel to judgment.

Enter a Messenger.

LEPIDUS   Here's more news.   33

FIRST MESSENGER
Thy biddings have been done, and every hour,
Most noble Caesar, shalt thou have report
How 'tis abroad. Pompey is strong at sea,

---

80 heat my blood i.e., anger me.   **81 meetly** i.e., fairly well acted.
(Said mockingly.)   **82 target** shield.   **mends** improves (in his "scene
/ Of excellent dissembling").   **84–5 How . . . chafe** i.e., how Antony,
who claims descent from Hercules, plays the role of his enraged
ancestor well. (Hercules had become a stock figure of the enraged
hero or tyrant.)   **chafe** rage.   **90 would** wished to say   **91 my . . .
Antony** my forgetful memory is like Antony (who is now leaving and
thus forgetting me)   **92 I . . . forgotten** (1) I have forgotten what I
was going to say (2) I am entirely forgotten (by Antony).   **92–4 But . . .
itself** Since you are a queen, your frivolousness must be your subject
(i.e., ruled by you); otherwise, I'd think you were frivolousness itself.
94–6 'Tis . . . this i.e., I am not being frivolous; this is hard for me to
bear. (*Sweating, labor,* and *bear* are all associated with pregnancy.)
97 my becomings (1) those qualities that become me (2) the various
roles that I adopt   **98 Eye** appear   **101 laurel** wreathed with laurel
103 so abides and flies mingles remaining and going in such a paradoxical fashion
1.4 Location: Rome.

3 competitor partner. (With a suggestion also of "rival.")   **6 Ptolemy**
(Cleopatra's royal brother, to whom she had been married according
to Egyptian custom.)   **7 gave audience** i.e., received messengers
9 abstract epitome   **12–13 His . . . blackness** His faults are enhanced
by contrast with his virtues, just as the stars in the sky stand out from
the darkness   **14 purchased** acquired   **16 Let's grant** Even if we
were to grant   **18 mirth** jest, diversion   **19 keep . . . of** take turns
20 stand the buffet exchange blows   **22 As his composure** and a
man's composition or temperament   **24 foils** blemishes   **24–5 when
. . . lightness** when we have to carry the heavy burden imposed by
his levity.   **26 His vacancy** his leisure time   **27–8 Full . . . for't** the
physical disabilities resulting from such voluptuousness (such as
venereal disease) would call him to account and would be adequate
punishment.   **28 confound** waste   **sport** amorous pastime   **29–30 speaks . . . ours** summons him urgently in view of his political position and ours as well
30 chid chided, reprimanded   **31 rate** berate.   **mature in knowledge**
old enough to know better   **32 Pawn . . . pleasure** risk for the sake of
immediate gratification what experience tells them will be ultimately
painful   **33 to judgment** against better judgment.

And it appears he is beloved of those 37
That only have feared Caesar. To the ports 38
The discontents repair, and men's reports 39
Give him much wronged.   [*Exit.*]
CAESAR   I should have known no less. 40
It hath been taught us from the primal state 41
That he which is was wished until he were; 42
And the ebbed man, ne'er loved till ne'er worth love, 43
Comes deared by being lacked. This common body, 44
Like to a vagabond flag upon the stream, 45
Goes to and back, lackeying the varying tide 46
To rot itself with motion.

[*Enter a Second Messenger.*]

SECOND MESSENGER   Caesar, I bring thee word
Menecrates and Menas, famous pirates, 49
Makes the sea serve them, which they ear and wound 50
With keels of every kind. Many hot inroads
They make in Italy. The borders maritime 52
Lack blood to think on't, and flush youth revolt. 53
No vessel can peep forth but 'tis as soon
Taken as seen; for Pompey's name strikes more 55
Than could his war resisted.   [*Exit.*]
CAESAR   Antony, 56
Leave thy lascivious wassails. When thou once 57
Was beaten from Modena, where thou slew'st
Hirtius and Pansa, consuls, at thy heel
Did famine follow, whom thou fought'st against, 60
Though daintily brought up, with patience more
Than savages could suffer. Thou didst drink 62
The stale of horses and the gilded puddle 63
Which beasts would cough at. Thy palate then did
    deign 64
The roughest berry on the rudest hedge.
Yea, like the stag, when snow the pasture sheets, 66
The barks of trees thou browsèd. On the Alps 67
It is reported thou didst eat strange flesh,
Which some did die to look on. And all this—
It wounds thine honor that I speak it now—
Was borne so like a soldier that thy cheek
So much as lanked not. 72
LEPIDUS   'Tis pity of him. 73
CAESAR   Let his shames quickly
Drive him to Rome. 'Tis time we twain
Did show ourselves i'th' field, and to that end

---

37 **of** by   38 **That . . . Caesar** that have obeyed Caesar only through fear.   39 **discontents** discontented. (See 1.3.48–52.)   40 **Give him** represent him as   41–4 **It . . . lacked** It is an ironic lesson of history from the earliest times that the man currently in the public eye is avidly sought after only until he becomes ruler, whereas the public figure whose fortunes have decayed, sought after only when he is no longer worthy of love, becomes loved once he is gone.   44 **common body** populace   45 **vagabond flag** shifting and undependable weeds   46 **lackeying** following in servile fashion, like a lackey   49 **famous** notorious   50 **ear** plow   52 **borders maritime** coastal territories   53 **Lack blood** turn pale.   **flush** vigorous; flushed, ruddy (contrasted with those who *Lack blood*)   55–6 **strikes . . . resisted** inflicts more damage than his forces could against our resistance.   57 **wassails** carousals.   60 **whom** i.e., famine   62 **suffer** show in suffering.   63 **stale** urine.   **gilded** covered with iridescent slime   64 **deign** not disdain   66 **sheets** covers   67 **browsèd** fed upon.   72 **lanked not** did not become thin.   73 **of** about

---

Assemble we immediate council. Pompey
Thrives in our idleness.
LEPIDUS   Tomorrow, Caesar,
I shall be furnished to inform you rightly
Both what by sea and land I can be able 80
To front this present time.
CAESAR   Till which encounter 81
It is my business too. Farewell.
LEPIDUS
Farewell, my lord. What you shall know meantime
Of stirs abroad, I shall beseech you, sir, 84
To let me be partaker.
CAESAR
Doubt not, sir, I knew it for my bond. 86
                        Exeunt [*separately*].

❧

[1.5]

Enter Cleopatra, Charmian, Iras, and Mardian.

CLEOPATRA   Charmian!
CHARMIAN   Madam?
CLEOPATRA
Ha, ha! Give me to drink mandragora. 3
CHARMIAN   Why, madam?
CLEOPATRA
That I might sleep out this great gap of time
My Antony is away.
CHARMIAN   You think of him too much.
CLEOPATRA
Oh, 'tis treason!
CHARMIAN   Madam, I trust not so.
CLEOPATRA
Thou, eunuch Mardian!
MARDIAN   What's Your Highness' pleasure?
CLEOPATRA
Not now to hear thee sing. I take no pleasure
In aught an eunuch has. 'Tis well for thee 11
That, being unseminared, thy freer thoughts 12
May not fly forth of Egypt. Hast thou affections? 13
MARDIAN   Yes, gracious madam.
CLEOPATRA   Indeed?
MARDIAN
Not in deed, madam, for I can do nothing 16
But what indeed is honest to be done. 17
Yet have I fierce affections, and think
What Venus did with Mars.
CLEOPATRA   Oh, Charmian,
Where think'st thou he is now? Stands he or sits he?
Or does he walk? Or is he on his horse?
Oh, happy horse, to bear the weight of Antony!

---

80 **be able** be capable of mustering   81 **front** confront, deal with   84 **stirs** commotions   86 **knew** already knew.   **bond** duty, obligation.   **1.5 Location:** Egypt. Cleopatra's palace.   3 **mandragora** juice of the mandrake (a narcotic).   11 **aught** (With bawdy suggestion.)   12 **unseminared** castrated   13 **of** from.   **affections** passions.   16 **Not in deed** (Mardian punningly takes the *deed* of *Indeed* in line 15 to mean "physical act.")   **do** (With suggestion of sexual intercourse.)   17 **honest** chaste

Do bravely, horse, for wot'st thou whom thou mov'st?   23
The demi-Atlas of this earth, the arm   24
And burgonet of men. He's speaking now,   25
Or murmuring, "Where's my serpent of old Nile?"
For so he calls me. Now I feed myself
With most delicious poison. Think on me,   28
That am with Phoebus' amorous pinches black   29
And wrinkled deep in time. Broad-fronted Caesar,   30
When thou wast here above the ground, I was
A morsel for a monarch. And great Pompey   32
Would stand and make his eyes grow in my brow;   33
There would he anchor his aspect, and die   34
With looking on his life.   35

    Enter Alexas.

ALEXAS   Sovereign of Egypt, hail!
CLEOPATRA
How much unlike art thou Mark Antony!
Yet, coming from him, that great med'cine hath   38
With his tinct gilded thee.   39
How goes it with my brave Mark Antony?   40
ALEXAS   Last thing he did, dear Queen,
He kissed—the last of many doubled kisses—
This orient pearl. [*He gives a pearl.*] His speech sticks in
 my heart.   43
CLEOPATRA
Mine ear must pluck it thence.
ALEXAS   "Good friend," quoth he,
"Say the firm Roman to great Egypt sends   45
This treasure of an oyster; at whose foot,
To mend the petty present, I will piece   47
Her opulent throne with kingdoms. All the East,
Say thou, shall call her mistress." So he nodded,
And soberly did mount an arm-gaunt steed,   50
Who neighed so high that what I would have spoke
Was beastly dumbed by him.   52
CLEOPATRA   What, was he sad, or merry?
ALEXAS
Like to the time o'th' year between the extremes
Of hot and cold, he was nor sad nor merry.   55

CLEOPATRA
Oh, well-divided disposition! Note him,   56
Note him, good Charmian, 'tis the man; but note him.   57
He was not sad, for he would shine on those   58
That make their looks by his; he was not merry,   59
Which seemed to tell them his remembrance lay
In Egypt with his joy; but between both.
Oh, heavenly mingle! Be'st thou sad or merry,
The violence of either thee becomes,   63
So does it no man else.—Met'st thou my posts?   64
ALEXAS
Ay, madam, twenty several messengers.   65
Why do you send so thick?
CLEOPATRA   Who's born that day   66
When I forget to send to Antony
Shall die a beggar. Ink and paper, Charmian.   68
Welcome, my good Alexas. Did I, Charmian,
Ever love Caesar so?
CHARMIAN   Oh, that brave Caesar!
CLEOPATRA
Be choked with such another emphasis!   71
Say, "the brave Antony."
CHARMIAN   The valiant Caesar!
CLEOPATRA
By Isis, I will give thee bloody teeth
If thou with Caesar paragon again   74
My man of men.
CHARMIAN   By your most gracious pardon,
I sing but after you.
CLEOPATRA   My salad days,
When I was green in judgment, cold in blood,   77
To say as I said then. But, come, away,
Get me ink and paper.
He shall have every day a several greeting,
Or I'll unpeople Egypt.   *Exeunt.*   81

          ❖

[2.1]

*Enter Pompey, Menecrates, and Menas, in war-
like manner.*

POMPEY
If the great gods be just, they shall assist
The deeds of justest men.
MENAS   Know, worthy Pompey,   2
That what they do delay they not deny.   3

---

23 Do (With sexual suggestion, as in line 16.)   **wot'st thou** do you
know   **24 demi-Atlas** one who (together with Caesar) supports the
weight of the whole world, as Atlas did. (Cleopatra disregards Lepidus as a triumvir.)   **arm** strong right arm or weapon   **25 burgonet**
light helmet or steel cap, i.e., protector   **28–30 Think . . . time**
(Cleopatra reflects on her ability to attract Antony, given the fact that
she is dark-skinned [as from the amorous pinches of her lover, the
sun] and increasingly wrinkled with age.)   **29 Phoebus'** the sun's
30 Broad-fronted Caesar Broad-foreheaded Julius Caesar   **32 great
Pompey** Gnaeus Pompey, oldest son of Pompey the Great. (Shakespeare may conflate the two.)   **33 make . . . brow** i.e., rivet his eyes
on my face   **34 aspect** look, gaze.   **die** i.e., suffer the extremity of
love. (And with suggestion of orgasm, as at 1.2.148.)   **35 his life** that
which he lived for.   **38 great med'cine** the philosopher's stone, the
supposed substance by which alchemists hoped to turn all baser metals into gold   **39 his tinct** its alchemical potency; also, its color
40 brave splendid   **43 orient** shining, bright. (The best pearls were
from the East or Orient.)   **45 firm** constant, true.   **Egypt** the Queen
of Egypt   **47 piece** augment   **50 arm-gaunt** made trim and hard by
warlike service, or hungry for battle   **52 dumbed** drowned out,
made inaudible   **55 nor sad** neither sad

56 well-divided disposition well-balanced temperament.   **57 the
man** i.e., perfectly characteristic of him.   **but** do but, only   **58 would**
wished to   **59 make . . . his** model their demeanor on his look
63 thee becomes is becoming to you   **64 posts** messengers.   **65 several** separate, distinct. (Also in line 80.)   **66 Who's** Anyone who is
68 Shall . . . beggar (since that day, sure never to come, would be ill-
omened)   **71 emphasis** emphatic expression.   **74 paragon** match or
compare   **77 green** immature   **81 Or . . . Egypt** Or I will send so
many messengers that Egypt will be unpeopled. (Perhaps too with a
darker threat of violence.)
2.1 Location: Pompey's camp, probably at Messina, Sicily.
2 MENAS (The Folio assigns the speeches in this scene to "*Mene.*";
some could be for Menecrates, but Pompey ignores him entirely at
lines 43–52, and Menecrates never reappears in the play.)   **3 not
deny** i.e., do not necessarily deny.

POMPEY
    Whiles we are suitors to their throne, decays   4
    The thing we sue for.
MENAS   We, ignorant of ourselves,   5
    Beg often our own harms, which the wise powers
    Deny us for our good; so find we profit
    By losing of our prayers.
POMPEY   I shall do well.
    The people love me, and the sea is mine;
    My powers are crescent, and my auguring hope   10
    Says it will come to th' full. Mark Antony   11
    In Egypt sits at dinner, and will make
    No wars without doors. Caesar gets money where   13
    He loses hearts. Lepidus flatters both,
    Of both is flattered; but he neither loves,   15
    Nor either cares for him.
MENAS   Caesar and Lepidus
    Are in the field. A mighty strength they carry.   17
POMPEY
    Where have you this? 'Tis false.
MENAS   From Silvius, sir.
POMPEY
    He dreams. I know they are in Rome together
    Looking for Antony. But all the charms of love,   20
    Salt Cleopatra, soften thy waned lip!   21
    Let witchcraft joined with beauty, lust with both,
    Tie up the libertine in a field of feasts,   23
    Keep his brain fuming. Epicurean cooks,   24
    Sharpen with cloyless sauce his appetite,   25
    That sleep and feeding may prorogue his honor   26
    Even till a Lethe'd dullness—

    Enter Varrius.

              How now, Varrius?   27
VARRIUS
    This is most certain that I shall deliver: 28
    Mark Antony is every hour in Rome
    Expected. Since he went from Egypt 'tis
    A space for further travel.   31
POMPEY   I could have given less matter   32
    A better ear. Menas, I did not think
    This amorous surfeiter would have donned his helm   34
    For such a petty war. His soldiership
    Is twice the other twain. But let us rear   36
    The higher our opinion, that our stirring   37
    Can from the lap of Egypt's widow pluck   38

    The ne'er-lust-wearied Antony.
MENAS   I cannot hope   39
    Caesar and Antony shall well greet together.   40
    His wife that's dead did trespasses to Caesar;   41
    His brother warred upon him, although, I think,   42
    Not moved by Antony.
POMPEY   I know not, Menas,   43
    How lesser enmities may give way to greater.
    Were't not that we stand up against them all,
    'Twere pregnant they should square between
        themselves,   46
    For they have entertainèd cause enough   47
    To draw their swords. But how the fear of us
    May cement their divisions and bind up
    The petty difference, we yet not know.
    Be't as our gods will have't! It only stands   51
    Our lives upon to use our strongest hands.   52
    Come, Menas.   *Exeunt.*

❖

[2.2]

    Enter Enobarbus and Lepidus.

LEPIDUS
    Good Enobarbus, 'tis a worthy deed,
    And shall become you well, to entreat your captain
    To soft and gentle speech.
ENOBARBUS   I shall entreat him
    To answer like himself. If Caesar move him,   4
    Let Antony look over Caesar's head   5
    And speak as loud as Mars. By Jupiter,
    Were I the wearer of Antonio's beard,
    I would not shave't today.   8
LEPIDUS
    'Tis not a time for private stomaching.
ENOBARBUS   Every time   9
    Serves for the matter that is then born in't.
LEPIDUS
    But small to greater matters must give way.
ENOBARBUS
    Not if the small come first.
LEPIDUS   Your speech is passion;
    But pray you stir no embers up. Here comes
    The noble Antony.

    Enter Antony and Ventidius [in conversation].

ENOBARBUS   And yonder, Caesar.

    *Enter Caesar, Maecenas, and Agrippa, [also in
    conversation, by another door].*

4–5 Whiles . . . for While we are praying, that for which we pray is being destroyed.   **10 My . . . crescent** My armed forces are on the increase. **auguring** prophesying **11 it** i.e., my powers or fortune (seen as a crescent moon, becoming full) **13 without doors** outdoors, i.e., in the battlefield, rather than in the bedroom. **15 Of** by. **neither loves** loves neither **17 A . . . carry** They command a mighty army. **20 Looking for** Awaiting. **charms** spells **21 Salt** lustful. **waned** faded, withered **23 Tie . . . feasts** i.e., tether him like an animal in a rich pasture **24 Epicurean** Let epicurean **25 cloyless** i.e., which will not satiate **26 prorogue** defer the operation of **27 Lethe'd** oblivious. (From the river of the underworld whose waters cause forgetfulness in those who drink.) **28 deliver** report **31 space . . . travel** time enough for an even longer journey and labor (travail). **32 less** less important **34 helm** helmet **36 rear** raise **37 opinion** i.e., of ourselves **38 Egypt's widow** i.e., Cleopatra, widow of the young King Ptolemy

39 hope expect **40 well greet** greet one another kindly **41 did trespasses to** wronged **42 brother** i.e., Lucius Antonius. (See 1.2.94 ff.) **43 moved** provoked, incited **46 pregnant** clear, obvious. **square** quarrel **47 entertainèd** maintained **51–2 It . . . hands** Our very lives depend upon our using our greatest strength.
2.2 Location: Rome. Furniture is put out on which Antony and Caesar are to sit.
4 like himself i.e., in a way befitting his greatness. **move him** i.e., to anger **5 look . . . head** i.e., condescend to Caesar as a smaller man **8 I . . . shave't** i.e., I would continue to wear it and thereby dare Caesar to pluck it (in a symbolic gesture for starting a fight) **9 private stomaching** personal resentment.

ANTONY
  If we compose well here, to Parthia.   15
  Hark, Ventidius.   *[They confer apart.]*

CAESAR
  I do not know, Maecenas, ask Agrippa.

LEPIDUS Noble friends,
  That which combined us was most great, and let not
  A leaner action rend us. What's amiss,   20
  May it be gently heard. When we debate
  Our trivial difference loud, we do commit
  Murder in healing wounds. Then, noble partners,   23
  The rather for I earnestly beseech,   24
  Touch you the sourest points with sweetest terms,
  Nor curstness grow to th' matter.

ANTONY   'Tis spoken well.   26
  Were we before our armies, and to fight,   27
  I should do thus.   *Flourish.*

CAESAR Welcome to Rome.

ANTONY Thank you.

CAESAR Sit.

ANTONY Sit, sir.

CAESAR Nay, then.   *[They sit.]*

ANTONY
  I learn you take things ill which are not so,
  Or being, concern you not.

CAESAR   I must be laughed at   35
  If, or for nothing or a little, I   36
  Should say myself offended, and with you
  Chiefly i'th' world; more laughed at that I should   38
  Once name you derogately, when to sound your name   39
  It not concerned me.   40

ANTONY
  My being in Egypt, Caesar, what was't to you?

CAESAR
  No more than my residing here at Rome
  Might be to you in Egypt. Yet if you there
  Did practice on my state, your being in Egypt   44
  Might be my question.

ANTONY   How intend you "practiced"?   45

CAESAR
  You may be pleased to catch at mine intent   46
  By what did here befall me. Your wife and brother
  Made wars upon me, and their contestation
  Was theme for you. You were the word of war.   49

ANTONY
  You do mistake your business. My brother never
  Did urge me in his act. I did inquire it,   51
  And have my learning from some true reports   52

  That drew their swords with you. Did he not rather   53
  Discredit my authority with yours,   54
  And make the wars alike against my stomach,   55
  Having alike your cause? Of this my letters   56
  Before did satisfy you. If you'll patch a quarrel,   57
  As matter whole you have to make it with,   58
  It must not be with this.

CAESAR   You praise yourself   59
  By laying defects of judgment to me, but
  You patched up your excuses.

ANTONY   Not so, not so.
  I know you could not lack—I am certain on't—   62
  Very necessity of this thought, that I,   63
  Your partner in the cause 'gainst which he fought,   64
  Could not with graceful eyes attend those wars   65
  Which fronted mine own peace. As for my wife,   66
  I would you had her spirit in such another.   67
  The third o'th' world is yours, which with a snaffle   68
  You may pace easy, but not such a wife.   69

ENOBARBUS Would we had all such wives, that the men
  might go to wars with the women!

ANTONY
  So much uncurbable, her garboils, Caesar,   72
  Made out of her impatience—which not wanted   73
  Shrewdness of policy too—I grieving grant   74
  Did you too much disquiet. For that you must   75
  But say I could not help it.

CAESAR   I wrote to you   76
  When rioting in Alexandria; you   77
  Did pocket up my letters and with taunts
  Did gibe my missive out of audience.

ANTONY   Sir,   79
  He fell upon me ere admitted, then.   80
  Three kings I had newly feasted, and did want   81
  Of what I was i'th' morning. But next day   82
  I told him of myself, which was as much   83
  As to have asked him pardon. Let this fellow
  Be nothing of our strife; if we contend,   85
  Out of our question wipe him.

CAESAR   You have broken   86
  The article of your oath, which you shall never   87
  Have tongue to charge me with.

LEPIDUS Soft, Caesar!   89

ANTONY No, Lepidus, let him speak.

---

15 **compose** come to an agreement   20 **leaner** lesser, more trivial. **rend** divide.   **What's** Whatever is   23 **healing** i.e., attempting to heal   24 **The rather for** all the more because   26 **Nor . . . grow** nor let ill humor be added   27 **to** about to   35 **being** being so, i.e., even if they are amiss   36 **or . . . or** either . . . or   38 **i'th' world** of all people   39 **Once** under any circumstances.   **derogately** disparagingly   39–40 **when . . . concerned me** i.e., if, as you say, it were none of my business.   44 **practice on my state** plot against my position   45 **question** business.   **How intend you** What do you mean   46 **catch at** infer   49 **Was . . . war** had you for its theme. They made war in your name. (*Word* here means "watchword.")   51 **urge . . . act** claim that he was fighting in my behalf.   **inquire** inquire into   52 **reports** reporters

53 **That . . . you** that fought in your army.   54 **Discredit** injure.   **with** along with   55 **stomach** desire   56 **Having . . . cause** i.e., I having just as much reason as you to deplore Lucius's action.   57–9 **If . . . this** If you insist on manufacturing a quarrel out of shreds and patches, as if you had substantial material to make it with, you've chosen a weak matter to use.   62–3 **I know . . . thought** I'm certain you must have realized   64 **he** i.e., Lucius   65 **with . . . attend** regard favorably   66 **fronted** confronted, opposed   67 **her . . . another** i.e., a wife such as she was.   68 **snaffle** bridle bit   69 **pace** put through its paces, manage   72–5 **So . . . disquiet** I unhappily concede that her unmanageable commotions, caused by her impatience (at my being in Egypt) but not lacking in keenness of stratagem, did much to disquiet you, Caesar.   76 **But say** concede that   77 **When** while you were   79 **Did . . . audience** taunted my messenger out of your presence.   80 **fell** burst in   81–2 **did want . . . morning** was not at my best as I had been earlier in the day.   83 **of myself** i.e., of my having had a lot to drink   85 **Be . . . of** have no part in   86 **question** contention   87 **article** terms   89 **Soft** Gently, go easy

The honor is sacred which he talks on now,
Supposing that I lacked it. But, on, Caesar: 92
The article of my oath—

CAESAR
To lend me arms and aid when I required them, 94
The which you both denied.

ANTONY   Neglected, rather;
And then when poisoned hours had bound me up
From mine own knowledge. As nearly as I may 97
I'll play the penitent to you, but mine honesty 98
Shall not make poor my greatness, nor my power 99
Work without it. Truth is that Fulvia, 100
To have me out of Egypt, made wars here,
For which myself, the ignorant motive, do 102
So far ask pardon as befits mine honor
To stoop in such a case.

LEPIDUS   'Tis noble spoken. 104

MAECENAS
If it might please you to enforce no further
The griefs between ye; to forget them quite 106
Were to remember that the present need
Speaks to atone you.

LEPIDUS   Worthily spoken, Maecenas. 108

ENOBARBUS   Or, if you borrow one another's love for the
instant, you may, when you hear no more words of
Pompey, return it again. You shall have time to wrangle in when you have nothing else to do.

ANTONY
Thou art a soldier only. Speak no more.

ENOBARBUS   That truth should be silent I had almost
forgot.

ANTONY
You wrong this presence. Therefore speak no more. 116

ENOBARBUS   Go to, then; your considerate stone. 117

CAESAR
I do not much dislike the matter, but
The manner of his speech; for't cannot be
We shall remain in friendship, our conditions 120
So diff'ring in their acts. Yet, if I knew
What hoop should hold us staunch, from edge to edge 122
O'th' world I would pursue it.

AGRIPPA   Give me leave, Caesar.

CAESAR   Speak, Agrippa.

AGRIPPA
Thou hast a sister by the mother's side,
Admired Octavia. Great Mark Antony
Is now a widower.

CAESAR   Say not so, Agrippa.
If Cleopatra heard you, your reproof
Were well deserved of rashness. 130

ANTONY
I am not married, Caesar. Let me hear
Agrippa further speak.

AGRIPPA
To hold you in perpetual amity,
To make you brothers, and to knit your hearts
With an unslipping knot, take Antony
Octavia to his wife, whose beauty claims
No worse a husband than the best of men,
Whose virtue and whose general graces speak 138
That which none else can utter. By this marriage 139
All little jealousies, which now seem great, 140
And all great fears, which now import their dangers, 141
Would then be nothing. Truths would be tales, 142
Where now half tales be truths. Her love to both 143
Would each to other and all loves to both
Draw after her. Pardon what I have spoke,
For 'tis a studied, not a present thought,
By duty ruminated.

ANTONY   Will Caesar speak?

CAESAR
Not till he hears how Antony is touched 148
With what is spoke already. 149

ANTONY   What power is in Agrippa
If I would say, "Agrippa, be it so,"
To make this good?

CAESAR   The power of Caesar and
His power unto Octavia.

ANTONY   May I never 153
To this good purpose, that so fairly shows, 154
Dream of impediment! Let me have thy hand
Further this act of grace, and from this hour 156
The heart of brothers govern in our loves
And sway our great designs!

CAESAR   There's my hand.
                              [They clasp hands.]
A sister I bequeath you whom no brother
Did ever love so dearly. Let her live
To join our kingdoms and our hearts; and never 161
Fly off our loves again!

LEPIDUS   Happily, amen! 162

ANTONY
I did not think to draw my sword 'gainst Pompey,
For he hath laid strange courtesies and great 164
Of late upon me. I must thank him only, 165
Lest my remembrance suffer ill report; 166
At heel of that, defy him.

LEPIDUS   Time calls upon 's. 167
Of us must Pompey presently be sought, 168
Or else he seeks out us.

---

92 **Supposing** implying   94 **required** requested   97 **From . . .
knowledge** from knowing myself.   98–100 **mine . . . it** my honesty
(in admitting my overindulgence) will not go so far as to dishonor
my greatness, nor, conversely, will my authority be used in a dishonorable way.   102 **motive** moving or inciting cause   104 **noble** nobly
106 **griefs** grievances   108 **atone** reconcile   116 **presence** company.
117 **Go . . . stone** i.e., All right, all right. I'll keep my thoughts to
myself.   120 **conditions** temperaments, dispositions   122 **hoop** barrel hoop.   **staunch** firm, watertight   130 **Were . . . rashness** would
richly deserve the rebuke it would get for such rashness.

138–9 **Whose . . . utter** whose virtues declare themselves better than
any words about them could do.   140 **jealousies** misunderstandings,
suspicions   141 **import** imply; carry with them   142–3 **Truths . . .
truths** True reports (no matter how distressing) would then be dis-
counted as mere rumors, whereas at present half-true reports are
taken for the whole truth.   148–9 **touched With** affected by
153 **unto** over   154 **so fairly shows** looks so promising   156 **Further**
in furtherance of   161–2 **never . . . again** may our amity never desert
us again.   164 **strange** remarkable   165 **only** at least   166 **Lest . . .
report** lest I be accused of ingratitude   167 **At heel of** immediately
after   168 **Of** By.   **presently** at once

ANTONY   Where lies he?

CAESAR
  About the mount Misena.

ANTONY   What is his strength   171
  By land?

CAESAR   Great and increasing; but by sea
  He is an absolute master.

ANTONY   So is the fame.   173
  Would we had spoke together! Haste we for it.   174
  Yet, ere we put ourselves in arms, dispatch we
  The business we have talked of.

CAESAR   With most gladness,   176
  And do invite you to my sister's view,   177
  Whither straight I'll lead you.   178

ANTONY
  Let us, Lepidus, not lack your company.

LEPIDUS
  Noble Antony, not sickness should detain me.   180

            Flourish. Exeunt. Manent Enobarbus, Agrippa,
                                          Maecenas.

MAECENAS   Welcome from Egypt, sir.

ENOBARBUS   Half the heart of Caesar, worthy Maecenas!   182
  My honorable friend, Agrippa!

AGRIPPA   Good Enobarbus!

MAECENAS   We have cause to be glad that matters are so
  well digested. You stayed well by't in Egypt.   186

ENOBARBUS   Ay, sir, we did sleep day out of counte-   187
  nance and made the night light with drinking.   188

MAECENAS   Eight wild boars roasted whole at a breakfast, and but twelve persons there; is this true?

ENOBARBUS   This was but as a fly by an eagle. We had   191
  much more monstrous matter of feast, which worthily
  deserved noting.

MAECENAS   She's a most triumphant lady, if report be   194
  square to her.   195

ENOBARBUS   When she first met Mark Antony, she
  pursed up his heart upon the river of Cydnus.   197

AGRIPPA   There she appeared indeed, or my reporter de-   198
  vised well for her.   199

ENOBARBUS   I will tell you.
  The barge she sat in, like a burnished throne   201
  Burnt on the water. The poop was beaten gold;   202
  Purple the sails, and so perfumèd that
  The winds were lovesick with them. The oars were
        silver,
  Which to the tune of flutes kept stroke, and made
  The water which they beat to follow faster,

As amorous of their strokes. For her own person,   207
  It beggared all description: she did lie
  In her pavilion—cloth-of-gold of tissue—   209
  O'erpicturing that Venus where we see
  The fancy outwork nature. On each side her   211
  Stood pretty dimpled boys, like smiling Cupids,
  With divers-colored fans, whose wind did seem   213
  To glow the delicate cheeks which they did cool,   214
  And what they undid did.

AGRIPPA   Oh, rare for Antony!

ENOBARBUS
  Her gentlewomen, like the Nereides,   216
  So many mermaids, tended her i'th'eyes   217
  And made their bends adornings. At the helm   218
  A seeming mermaid steers. The silken tackle
  Swell with the touches of those flower-soft hands,
  That yarely frame the office. From the barge   221
  A strange invisible perfume hits the sense
  Of the adjacent wharfs. The city cast   223
  Her people out upon her; and Antony,
  Enthroned i'th' marketplace, did sit alone,
  Whistling to th'air, which, but for vacancy,   226
  Had gone to gaze on Cleopatra too,
  And made a gap in nature.

AGRIPPA   Rare Egyptian!

ENOBARBUS
  Upon her landing, Antony sent to her,
  Invited her to supper. She replied
  It should be better he became her guest,
  Which she entreated. Our courteous Antony,
  Whom ne'er the word of "No" woman heard speak,
  Being barbered ten times o'er, goes to the feast,
  And for his ordinary pays his heart   235
  For what his eyes eat only.

AGRIPPA   Royal wench!   236
  She made great Caesar lay his sword to bed;   237
  He plowed her, and she cropped.

ENOBARBUS   I saw her once   238
  Hop forty paces through the public street,
  And having lost her breath, she spoke and panted,
  That she did make defect perfection,   241
  And, breathless, power breathe forth.

MAECENAS
  Now Antony must leave her utterly.

ENOBARBUS   Never. He will not.
  Age cannot wither her, nor custom stale   245
  Her infinite variety. Other women cloy
  The appetites they feed, but she makes hungry

---

171 **Misena** i.e., Misenum, in southern Italy. (Not in Sicily, where 2.1 perhaps takes place.)   173 **So is the fame** So it is reported.
174 **Would . . . together!** Would that we had had a chance to parley before battle!   176 **most** the greatest   177 **to my sister's view** to see my sister   178 **straight** straightway   180.1 *Manent* They remain onstage   182 **Half . . . Caesar** You who are very close to Caesar, one of his closest advisers   186 **digested** disposed.   **stayed well by't** kept at it   187–8 **we . . . countenance** we insulted day by sleeping right through it   188 **light** (1) brightly lit (2) debauched and giddy
191 **This . . . eagle** i.e., This was nothing compared with greater feasting.   194 **triumphant** magnificent   195 **square** just   197 **pursed up** pocketed up, put in her purse   198–9 **devised** invented   201 **burnished** lustrous, shiny   202 **poop** a short deck built over the main deck at the stern of the vessel

207 **As** As if.   **For** As for   209 **cloth-of-gold of tissue** cloth made of gold thread and silk woven together   211 **fancy** imagination   213 **divers-colored** multicolored   214 **glow** cause to glow
216 **Nereides** sea nymphs   217 **So . . . i'th'eyes** as if they were so many mermaids, attended to her every glance or nod   218 **made . . . adornings** made their graceful bowings beautiful.   221 **yarely . . . office** nimbly perform their function.   223 **wharfs** banks.   226 **but for vacancy** except that it would have created a vacuum   235 **ordinary** meal, supper (such as one might obtain at a public table in a tavern)   236 **eat** ate. (Pronounced *et.*)   237 **Caesar** i.e., Julius Caesar, by whom Cleopatra had a son named Caesarion   238 **cropped** bore fruit (a son).   241 **That** so that   245 **custom stale** repeated experience make stale

Where most she satisfies; for vilest things
Become themselves in her, that the holy priests   249
Bless her when she is riggish.   250

MAECENAS
If beauty, wisdom, modesty can settle
The heart of Antony, Octavia is
A blessèd lottery to him.

AGRIPPA   Let us go.   253
Good Enobarbus, make yourself my guest
Whilst you abide here.

ENOBARBUS   Humbly, sir, I thank you.
                                              Exeunt.

❧

[2.3]

Enter Antony, Caesar, Octavia between them.

ANTONY
The world and my great office will sometimes
Divide me from your bosom.

OCTAVIA   All which time
Before the gods my knee shall bow my prayers
To them for you.

ANTONY   Good night, sir. My Octavia,
Read not my blemishes in the world's report.   5
I have not kept my square, but that to come   6
Shall all be done by th' rule. Good night, dear lady.
Good night, sir.

CAESAR   Good night.   *Exit [with Octavia].*

Enter Soothsayer.

ANTONY
Now, sirrah: you do wish yourself in Egypt?   10

SOOTHSAYER   Would I had never come from thence,
nor you thither!   12

ANTONY   If you can, your reason?

SOOTHSAYER   I see it in in my motion, have it not in my   14
tongue; but yet hie you to Egypt again.   15

ANTONY
Say to me, whose fortunes shall rise higher,
Caesar's or mine?

SOOTHSAYER   Caesar's.
Therefore, O Antony, stay not by his side.
Thy daemon—that thy spirit which keeps thee—is   20
Noble, courageous, high unmatchable,   21
Where Caesar's is not; but near him thy angel   22
Becomes afeard, as being o'erpowered. Therefore
Make space enough between you.

ANTONY   Speak this no more.

SOOTHSAYER
To none but thee; no more but when to thee.   25
If thou dost play with him at any game,
Thou art sure to lose; and of that natural luck   27
He beats thee 'gainst the odds. Thy luster thickens   28
When he shines by. I say again, thy spirit   29
Is all afraid to govern thee near him;
But, he away, 'tis noble.

ANTONY   Get thee gone.
Say to Ventidius I would speak with him.
                              Exit [Soothsayer].
He shall to Parthia.—Be it art or hap,   33
He hath spoken true. The very dice obey him,
And in our sports my better cunning faints   35
Under his chance. If we draw lots, he speeds;   36
His cocks do win the battle still of mine   37
When it is all to naught, and his quails ever   38
Beat mine, inhooped, at odds. I will to Egypt;   39
And though I make this marriage for my peace,
I'th'East my pleasure lies.

Enter Ventidius.

                    Oh, come, Ventidius.
You must to Parthia. Your commission's ready;
Follow me, and receive't.   *Exeunt.*

❧

[2.4]

Enter Lepidus, Maecenas, and Agrippa.

LEPIDUS
Trouble yourselves no further. Pray you, hasten
Your generals after.

AGRIPPA   Sir, Mark Antony   2
Will e'en but kiss Octavia, and we'll follow.   3

LEPIDUS
Till I shall see you in your soldier's dress,   4
Which will become you both, farewell.

MAECENAS   We shall,   5
As I conceive the journey, be at th' Mount   6
Before you, Lepidus.

LEPIDUS   Your way is shorter;
My purposes do draw me much about.   8
You'll win two days upon me.

MAECENAS, AGRIPPA   Sir, good success!

LEPIDUS   Farewell.   *Exeunt.*

❧

[2.5]

Enter Cleopatra, Charmian, Iras, and Alexas.

CLEOPATRA
Give me some music; music, moody food
Of us that trade in love.
ALL   The music, ho!

Enter Mardian the eunuch.

CLEOPATRA
Let it alone. Let's to billiards. Come, Charmian.
CHARMIAN
My arm is sore. Best play with Mardian.
CLEOPATRA
As well a woman with an eunuch played
As with a woman. Come, you'll play with me, sir?
MARDIAN   As well as I can, madam.
CLEOPATRA
And when good will is showed, though't come too
      short,   8
The actor may plead pardon. I'll none now.   9
Give me mine angle; we'll to th' river. There,   10
My music playing far off, I will betray
Tawny-finned fishes. My bended hook shall pierce
Their slimy jaws, and as I draw them up
I'll think them every one an Antony,
And say, "Aha! You're caught."
CHARMIAN   'Twas merry when
You wagered on your angling, when your diver
Did hang a salt fish on his hook, which he   17
With fervency drew up.
CLEOPATRA   That time—oh, times!—
I laughed him out of patience; and that night
I laughed him into patience. And next morn,
Ere the ninth hour, I drunk him to his bed,   21
Then put my tires and mantles on him, whilst   22
I wore his sword Philippan.

Enter a Messenger.

                          Oh, from Italy!   23
Ram thou thy fruitful tidings in mine ears,
That long time have been barren.
MESSENGER   Madam, madam—
CLEOPATRA
Antonio's dead! If thou say so, villain,
Thou kill'st thy mistress; but well and free,
If thou so yield him, there is gold, and here
My bluest veins to kiss—a hand that kings   28
Have lipped, and trembled kissing.
                [She offers him gold, and her hand to kiss.]
MESSENGER   First, madam, he is well.

CLEOPATRA
Why, there's more gold. But, sirrah, mark, we use
To say the dead are well. Bring it to that,   33
The gold I give thee will I melt and pour
Down thy ill-uttering throat.
MESSENGER   Good madam, hear me.
CLEOPATRA   Well, go to, I will.   37
But there's no goodness in thy face, if Antony
Be free and healthful—so tart a favor   39
To trumpet such good tidings! If not well,
Thou shouldst come like a Fury crowned with snakes, 41
Not like a formal man.
MESSENGER   Will't please you hear me?   42
CLEOPATRA
I have a mind to strike thee ere thou speak'st.
Yet, if thou say Antony lives, is well,
Or friends with Caesar, or not captive to him,
I'll set thee in a shower of gold and hail
Rich pearls upon thee.
MESSENGER   Madam, he's well.
CLEOPATRA   Well said.
MESSENGER
And friends with Caesar.
CLEOPATRA   Thou'rt an honest man.   48
MESSENGER
Caesar and he are greater friends than ever.
CLEOPATRA
Make thee a fortune from me.
MESSENGER   But yet, madam—
CLEOPATRA
I do not like "But yet"; it does allay   51
The good precedence. Fie upon "But yet"!   52
"But yet" is as a jailer to bring forth
Some monstrous malefactor. Prithee, friend,
Pour out the pack of matter to mine ear,   55
The good and bad together. He's friends with Caesar,
In state of health, thou say'st, and, thou say'st, free.
MESSENGER
Free, madam? No, I made no such report.
He's bound unto Octavia.
CLEOPATRA   For what good turn?   59
MESSENGER
For the best turn i'th' bed.
CLEOPATRA   I am pale, Charmian.
MESSENGER
Madam, he's married to Octavia.
CLEOPATRA
The most infectious pestilence upon thee!
                              Strikes him down.
MESSENGER
Good madam, patience.
CLEOPATRA   What say you?   *Strikes him.*
                              Hence,

2.5 **Location:** Alexandria. Cleopatra's palace.
8 **too short** (A bawdy joke on Mardian's being castrated; *will* suggests
"sexual desire"; *come* suggests "reach orgasm.")   9 **I'll none now** i.e.,
I won't play billiards after all.   10 **angle** rod and line   17 **salt** dried,
preserved in salt   21 **ninth hour** i.e., 9 A.M.   **drunk** drank   22 **tires**
headdresses, or perhaps attire.   **mantles** garments   23 **Philippan**
(Named for Antony's victory over Brutus and Cassius at Philippi.)
28 **yield** (1) grant (2) report

33 **well** i.e., well out of it, in heaven.   **Bring it to that** If that is your
meaning   37 **go to** i.e., all right, then. (Said remonstratingly.)   39 **tart
a favor** sour a face   41 **Fury** avenging goddess of classical mythology
42 **like . . . man** in ordinary human form.   48 **honest** worthy
51–2 **allay . . . precedence** annul the good news that preceded it.
55 **pack of matter** entire contents (as of a peddler's pack)   59 **turn**
favor, purpose. (But the Messenger replies in the sense of "feat, bout,"
with sexual suggestion.)

Horrible villain, or I'll spurn thine eyes   64
Like balls before me! I'll unhair thy head!   65
                              She hales him up and down.
Thou shalt be whipped with wire and stewed in brine,
Smarting in ling'ring pickle!

MESSENGER   Gracious madam,   67
I that do bring the news made not the match.

CLEOPATRA
Say 'tis not so, a province I will give thee
And make thy fortunes proud. The blow thou hadst
Shall make thy peace for moving me to rage,   71
And I will boot thee with what gift beside   72
Thy modesty can beg.

MESSENGER   He's married, madam.   73

CLEOPATRA
Rogue, thou hast lived too long!   *Draw a knife.*

MESSENGER   Nay then, I'll run.
What mean you, madam? I have made no fault.   *Exit.*

CHARMIAN
Good madam, keep yourself within yourself.   76
The man is innocent.

CLEOPATRA
Some innocents scape not the thunderbolt.
Melt Egypt into Nile, and kindly creatures   79
Turn all to serpents! Call the slave again.
Though I am mad, I will not bite him. Call!   81

CHARMIAN
He is afeard to come.

CLEOPATRA   I will not hurt him.
                        [The Messenger is sent for.]
These hands do lack nobility, that they strike
A meaner than myself, since I myself   84
Have given myself the cause.

            Enter the Messenger again.

                              Come hither, sir.   85
Though it be honest, it is never good
To bring bad news. Give to a gracious message
An host of tongues, but let ill tidings tell   88
Themselves when they be felt.   89

MESSENGER   I have done my duty.

CLEOPATRA   Is he married?
I cannot hate thee worser than I do
If thou again say "Yes."

MESSENGER   He's married, madam.

CLEOPATRA
The gods confound thee! Dost thou hold there still?   94

MESSENGER
Should I lie, madam?

CLEOPATRA   Oh, I would thou didst,

So half my Egypt were submerged and made   96
A cistern for scaled snakes! Go, get thee hence.   97
Hadst thou Narcissus in thy face, to me   98
Thou wouldst appear most ugly. He is married?

MESSENGER
I crave Your Highness' pardon.

CLEOPATRA   He is married?

MESSENGER
Take no offense that I would not offend you.   101
To punish me for what you make me do
Seems much unequal. He's married to Octavia.   103

CLEOPATRA
Oh, that his fault should make a knave of thee,   104
That art not what thou'rt sure of! Get thee hence.   105
The merchandise which thou hast brought from
    Rome
Are all too dear for me. Lie they upon thy hand,   107
And be undone by 'em!   *[Exit Messenger.]*

CHARMIAN   Good Your Highness, patience. 108

CLEOPATRA
In praising Antony, I have dispraised Caesar.

CHARMIAN   Many times, madam.

CLEOPATRA
I am paid for't now. Lead me from hence;
I faint. Oh, Iras, Charmian! 'Tis no matter.
Go to the fellow, good Alexas. Bid him
Report the feature of Octavia: her years,
Her inclination. Let him not leave out   115
The color of her hair. Bring me word quickly.
                              [Exit Alexas.]
Let him forever go!—Let him not, Charmian.   117
Though he be painted one way like a Gorgon,   118
The other way's a Mars. *[To Mardian]* Bid you Alexas 119
Bring me word how tall she is.—Pity me, Charmian,
But do not speak to me. Lead me to my chamber.
                              Exeunt.

❖

[2.6]

Flourish. Enter Pompey [and] Menas at one door, with drum and trumpet; at another, Caesar, Lepidus, Antony, Enobarbus, Maecenas, Agrippa, with soldiers marching.

---

64 **spurn** kick   65.1 *hales* drags   67 **pickle** pickling solution.
71 **make thy peace** compensate, mollify me   72 **boot thee with** give
you into the bargain, or, make amends with.   **what** whatever
73 **Thy modesty** one of your modest expectations   76 **keep . . .
yourself** i.e., control yourself.   79 **kindly** endowed with innately
good qualities   81 **mad** (1) angry (2) insane, and so apt to bite
84 **A meaner** one of lower social station   84–5 **since . . . cause** since I
am the one I ought to blame.   85 **the cause** i.e., by loving Antony.
88 **host** multitude   89 **when . . . felt** i.e., by being felt rather than spoken aloud. Let bad tidings announce themselves.   94 **confound**
destroy.   **hold there still** stick to your story.

96 **So** even if   97 **cistern** tank.   **scaled** scaly   98 **Narcissus** beautiful
youth of Greek mythology who fell in love with his own reflected
image   101 **Take . . . offend you** Don't be offended that I hesitate to
offend you (by telling bad news), or, don't interpret as offense what is
not meant to offend.   103 **much unequal** most unjust.   104–5 **Oh,
that . . . sure of!** How regrettable that Antony's fault puts you in the
wrong, you who are not yourself hateful even if you have had to
report hateful news as a certain fact!   107 **dear** (1) expensive (2) emotionally precious   107–8 **Lie . . . by 'em** May they remain in your possession unsold, and may you be bankrupt, financially ruined! (i.e.,
May you never profit from your bad tidings!)   115 **inclination** disposition.   117 **him** Antony   118–19 **Though . . . Mars** (Alludes to a
type of picture known as a perspective, which shows different images
when looked at from different angles of vision. A *Gorgon* is a female
monster with serpents in her hair, capable of turning to stone anything that meets her gaze.)
2.6. Location: Near Misenum, in southern Italy near modern
Naples. (But 2.1 perhaps took place in Messina, Sicily.)

POMPEY
Your hostages I have, so have you mine,
And we shall talk before we fight.
CAESAR   Most meet 2
That first we come to words; and therefore have we
Our written purposes before us sent, 4
Which if thou hast considered, let us know
If 'twill tie up thy discontented sword 6
And carry back to Sicily much tall youth 7
That else must perish here.
POMPEY   To you all three,
The senators alone of this great world, 9
Chief factors for the gods: I do not know 10
Wherefore my father should revengers want, 11
Having a son and friends, since Julius Caesar, 12
Who at Philippi the good Brutus ghosted, 13
There saw you laboring for him. What was't 14
That moved pale Cassius to conspire? And what
Made th'all-honored, honest Roman Brutus, 16
With the armed rest, courtiers of beauteous freedom, 17
To drench the Capitol, but that they would 18
Have one man but a man? And that is it 19
Hath made me rig my navy, at whose burden
The angered ocean foams, with which I meant
To scourge th'ingratitude that despiteful Rome
Cast on my noble father.
CAESAR   Take your time.
ANTONY
Thou canst not fear us, Pompey, with thy sails; 24
We'll speak with thee at sea. At land thou know'st 25
How much we do o'ercount thee.
POMPEY   At land indeed 26
Thou dost o'ercount me of my father's house;
But since the cuckoo builds not for himself, 28
Remain in't as thou mayst.
LEPIDUS   Be pleased to tell us— 29
For this is from the present—how you take 30
The offers we have sent you.
CAESAR   There's the point.

ANTONY
Which do not be entreated to, but weigh 32
What it is worth embraced.
CAESAR   And what may follow, 33
To try a larger fortune.
POMPEY   You have made me offer 34
Of Sicily, Sardinia; and I must
Rid all the sea of pirates; then, to send 36
Measures of wheat to Rome. This 'greed upon,
To part with unhacked edges and bear back 38
Our targes undinted.
CAESAR, ANTONY, LEPIDUS   That's our offer.
POMPEY   Know then 39
I came before you here a man prepared
To take this offer, but Mark Antony
Put me to some impatience. Though I lose 42
The praise of it by telling, you must know, 43
When Caesar and your brother were at blows,
Your mother came to Sicily and did find
Her welcome friendly.
ANTONY   I have heard it, Pompey,
And am well studied for a liberal thanks 47
Which I do owe you.
POMPEY   Let me have your hand.
                              [*They shake hands.*]
I did not think, sir, to have met you here.
ANTONY
The beds i'th'East are soft; and thanks to you,
That called me timelier than my purpose hither, 51
For I have gained by't.
CAESAR   Since I saw you last
There's a change upon you.
POMPEY   Well, I know not
What counts harsh Fortune casts upon my face, 54
But in my bosom shall she never come
To make my heart her vassal.
LEPIDUS   Well met here.
POMPEY
I hope so, Lepidus. Thus we are agreed.
I crave our composition may be written 58
And sealed between us.
CAESAR   That's the next to do. 59
POMPEY
We'll feast each other ere we part, and let's
Draw lots who shall begin.
ANTONY   That will I, Pompey. 61
POMPEY
No, Antony, take the lot. But, first or last, 62

2 meet fitting   **4 purposes** propositions   **6 tie . . . sword** i.e., satisfy your concerns and allow you to forgo a fight   **7 tall** brave   **9 senators alone** i.e., sole rulers of the state (who have thus supplanted the Senate)   **10 factors** agents   **10–14 I do . . . for him** (Julius Caesar defeated Pompey's father, Pompey the Great, and was subsequently assassinated by Brutus and Cassius, among others. Caesar's ghost appeared to Brutus at Philippi, where the combined forces of Antony, Octavius, and Lepidus defeated Brutus and Cassius. [See *Julius Caesar.*] Since Antony, Octavius, and Lepidus thus defeated the avengers of Pompey the Great's death, Pompey the Great's sons and friends should become his avengers by continuing to war on Antony, Octavius, and Lepidus.)   **11 want** lack   **13 ghosted** haunted   **16 honest** honorable   **17 the armed rest** i.e., the rest of those who were armed.   **courtiers . . . freedom** those who serve freedom only   **18 drench** bathe in blood   **19 Have . . . a man** (The republican conspirators acted to keep Julius Caesar from accepting the crown.)   **24 fear** frighten   **25 speak with** confront   **26 o'ercount** outnumber. (But Pompey's use of the word in the next line implies that Antony has cheated him. Plutarch informs us that Antony bought the elder Pompey's house at auction and later refused to pay for it.)   **28 cuckoo** a bird that builds no nest for itself but lays its eggs in other birds' nests.   **29 as thou mayst** as long as you can, or, since you can.   **30 from the present** digressing from the business at hand

32 do . . . to i.e., do not accept merely because we ask   **33 embraced** if accepted by you.   **34 To . . . fortune** i.e., if you decide to risk war with the triumvirs, or, if you join with us to share a greater fortune.   **36 to send** I am to send   **38 To part** we are to part company.   **edges** swords   **39 targes** shields   **42–3 Though . . . telling** i.e., Though I forfeit praise from others by praising myself   **47 well studied for** well prepared to deliver   **51 timelier** earlier   **54 counts** tally marks. (From the practice of casting accounts or reckonings by means of marks or notches on tallies.)   **casts** calculates   **58 composition** agreement   **59 sealed between us** stamped with the official seal of each co-signer.   **61 That will I** I will begin   **62 take the lot** draw lots with the rest of us, accept the results of the lottery.   **first or last** whether you win the lottery to go first or last

Your fine Egyptian cookery shall have
The fame. I have heard that Julius Caesar
Grew fat with feasting there.

ANTONY   You have heard much.

POMPEY   I have fair meanings, sir.   67

ANTONY   And fair words to them.   68

POMPEY   Then so much have I heard.   69
And I have heard Apollodorus carried—   70

ENOBARBUS
No more of that. He did so.

POMPEY   What, I pray you?   71

ENOBARBUS
A certain queen to Caesar in a mattress.   72

POMPEY
I know thee now. How far'st thou, soldier?

ENOBARBUS   Well,
And well am like to do, for I perceive   74
Four feasts are toward.

POMPEY   Let me shake thy hand.   75
                        [*They shake hands.*]
I never hated thee. I have seen thee fight
When I have envied thy behavior.

ENOBARBUS   Sir,
I never loved you much, but I ha' praised ye
When you have well deserved ten times as much
As I have said you did.

POMPEY   Enjoy thy plainness;   80
It nothing ill becomes thee.   81
Aboard my galley I invite you all.
Will you lead, lords?

CAESAR, ANTONY, LEPIDUS   Show 's the way, sir.

POMPEY   Come.   83
                Exeunt. Manent Enobarbus and Menas.

MENAS [*aside*]   Thy father, Pompey, would ne'er have
made this treaty.—You and I have known, sir.   85

ENOBARBUS   At sea, I think.

MENAS   We have, sir.

ENOBARBUS   You have done well by water.

MENAS   And you by land.

ENOBARBUS   I will praise any man that will praise me,
though it cannot be denied what I have done by land.

MENAS   Nor what I have done by water.

ENOBARBUS   Yes, something you can deny for your own
safety: you have been a great thief by sea.

MENAS   And you by land.

ENOBARBUS   There I deny my land service. But give me   96
your hand, Menas. [*They shake hands.*] If our eyes had
authority, here they might take two thieves kissing.   98

MENAS   All men's faces are true, whatsome'er their hands
are.

ENOBARBUS   But there is never a fair woman has a true   101
face.

MENAS   No slander; they steal hearts.   103

ENOBARBUS   We came hither to fight with you.

MENAS   For my part, I am sorry it is turned to a drinking.   105
Pompey doth this day laugh away his fortune.

ENOBARBUS   If he do, sure he cannot weep't back
again.

MENAS   You've said, sir. We looked not for Mark   109
Antony here. Pray you, is he married to Cleopatra?

ENOBARBUS   Caesar's sister is called Octavia.

MENAS   True, sir. She was the wife of Caius Marcellus.

ENOBARBUS   But she is now the wife of Marcus Antonius.

MENAS   Pray ye, sir?   115

ENOBARBUS   'Tis true.

MENAS   Then is Caesar and he forever knit together.

ENOBARBUS   If I were bound to divine of this unity, I   118
would not prophesy so.

MENAS   I think the policy of that purpose made more in   120
the marriage than the love of the parties.

ENOBARBUS   I think so too. But you shall find the band
that seems to tie their friendship together will be
the very strangler of their amity. Octavia is of a holy, cold,
and still conversation.   125

MENAS   Who would not have his wife so?

ENOBARBUS   Not he that himself is not so, which is
Mark Antony. He will to his Egyptian dish again.
Then shall the sighs of Octavia blow the fire up in
Caesar, and, as I said before, that which is the strength
of their amity shall prove the immediate author of   131
their variance. Antony will use his affection where it   132
is; he married but his occasion here.   133

MENAS   And thus it may be. Come, sir, will you
aboard? I have a health for you.   135

ENOBARBUS   I shall take it, sir. We have used our
throats in Egypt.

MENAS   Come, let's away.   *Exeunt.*

❖

[2.7]

*Music plays. Enter two or three Servants with a
banquet.*

FIRST SERVANT   Here they'll be, man. Some o' their
plants are ill-rooted already; the least wind i'th' world   2
will blow them down.

---

67 fair i.e., friendly   **68 fair** i.e., well-chosen   **69 Then . . . heard** i.e.,
I am not implying more about Antony in Egypt than my words hon-
estly mean.   **70–2 Apollodorus . . . mattress** (Alludes to a tale told by
Plutarch according to which Cleopatra had herself rolled up in a mattress and carried secretly by Apollodorus to meet Julius Caesar.)
74 like likely   **75 toward** coming up.   **80 Enjoy thy plainness** Give
free rein to your bluntness   **81 nothing . . . thee** suits you not at all
badly.   **83.1 Manent** They remain onstage   **85 known** known each
other   **96 There** In respect to that   **98 authority** i.e., to make arrests,
like a constable.   **take** arrest.   **two thieves kissing** (1) our two thiev-
ing hands shaking (2) two thieves greeting each other.

101 true honest (because women use cosmetic art to conceal defects)
103 No . . . hearts i.e., You speak true, since women in their own way are
thieves, stealing men's affections.   **105 a drinking** an occasion for drinking.   **109 You've said** You've spoken truly   **115 Pray ye, sir?** Are you in
earnest?   **118 divine of** prophesy about   **120 made more** played more
of a role   **125 conversation** demeanor.   **131–2 author . . . variance** cause
of their falling out.   **132–3 use . . . it is** i.e., satisfy his passion in Egypt
133 his occasion what his interests demanded   **135 health** toast
2.7. Location: On board Pompey's galley, off Misenum in southern
Italy. A table and stools are brought on.
0.2 banquet a course of the feast, probably dessert.   **2 plants**
(1) planted trees (2) soles of the feet

SECOND SERVANT   Lepidus is high-colored.   4

FIRST SERVANT   They have made him drink alms-drink.   5

SECOND SERVANT   As they pinch one another by the   6
disposition, he cries out, "No more," reconciles them   7
to his entreaty, and himself to th' drink.   8

FIRST SERVANT   But it raises the greater war between
him and his discretion.

SECOND SERVANT   Why, this it is to have a name in   11
great men's fellowship. I had as lief have a reed that   12
will do me no service as a partisan I could not heave.   13

FIRST SERVANT   To be called into a huge sphere,   14
and not to be seen to move in't, are the holes where   15
eyes should be, which pitifully disaster the cheeks.   16

A sennet sounded. Enter Caesar, Antony,
Pompey, Lepidus, Agrippa, Maecenas, Enobarbus,
Menas, with other captains [and a Boy].

ANTONY
Thus do they, sir: they take the flow o'th' Nile   17
By certain scales i'th' pyramid. They know   18
By th' height, the lowness, or the mean if dearth   19
Or foison follow. The higher Nilus swells   20
The more it promises; as it ebbs, the seedsman
Upon the slime and ooze scatters his grain,
And shortly comes to harvest.

LEPIDUS   You've strange serpents there.

ANTONY   Ay, Lepidus.

LEPIDUS   Your serpent of Egypt is bred now of your   26
mud by the operation of your sun; so is your crocodile.

ANTONY   They are so.

POMPEY   Sit—and some wine. A health to Lepidus!   29
[They sit and drink.]

LEPIDUS   I am not so well as I should be, but I'll   30
ne'er out.   31

ENOBARBUS   Not till you have slept; I fear me you'll be
in till then.   33

LEPIDUS   Nay, certainly, I have heard the Ptolemies'
pyramises are very goodly things; without contradic-   35
tion I have heard that.

MENAS *[aside to Pompey]*   Pompey, a word.

POMPEY *[to Menas]*   Say in mine ear. What is't?

MENAS *(whispers in 's ear)*
Forsake thy seat, I do beseech thee, captain,
And hear me speak a word.

POMPEY *[to Menas]*
Forbear me till anon.—This wine for Lepidus!   41

LEPIDUS   What manner o' thing is your crocodile?

ANTONY   It is shaped, sir, like itself, and it is as broad as
it hath breadth. It is just so high as it is, and moves
with it own organs. It lives by that which nourisheth   45
it, and, the elements once out of it, it transmigrates.   46

LEPIDUS   What color is it of?

ANTONY   Of it own color too.

LEPIDUS   'Tis a strange serpent.

ANTONY   'Tis so. And the tears of it are wet.   50

CAESAR   Will this description satisfy him?

ANTONY   With the health that Pompey gives him, else
he is a very epicure.   *[Menas whispers again.]*   53

POMPEY *[aside to Menas]*
Go hang, sir, hang! Tell me of that? Away!
Do as I bid you.—Where's this cup I called for?

MENAS *[aside to Pompey]*
If for the sake of merit thou wilt hear me,   56
Rise from thy stool.

POMPEY *[rising]*   I think thou'rt mad. The matter?
[They walk aside.]

MENAS
I have ever held my cap off to thy fortunes.   58

POMPEY
Thou hast served me with much faith. What's else to
say?—   59
Be jolly, lords.

ANTONY   These quicksands, Lepidus,
Keep off them, for you sink.
[Menas and Pompey speak aside.]

MENAS
Wilt thou be lord of all the world?

POMPEY   What say'st thou?

MENAS
Wilt thou be lord of the whole world? That's twice.

POMPEY
How should that be?

MENAS   But entertain it,   64
And, though thou think me poor, I am the man
Will give thee all the world.

POMPEY   Hast thou drunk well?

MENAS
No, Pompey, I have kept me from the cup.
Thou art, if thou dar'st be, the earthly Jove.

---

4 **high-colored** flushed.   5 **alms-drink** i.e., drink charitably consumed in the furtherance of reconciliation. (See next speech and
note.)   6–8 **As . . . drink** As they chafe one another, prompted by
their various temperaments, Lepidus entreats them to stop quarreling, and reconciles himself to the peacemaking business of downing
one drink after another in response to their toasts.   11 **a name** a
name only   12 **had as lief** would just as soon   13 **partisan** long-
bladed spear. (Here, metaphorically, too large a weapon for Lepidus
to wield.)   14–16 **To . . . cheeks** To be summoned by fortune to greatness and yet not be able to fulfill the role greatly is like having eye
sockets with no eyes in them, a defect that will disfigure (*disaster*) the
cheeks. (The underlying image is of a heavenly body that cannot
move properly in its sphere, causing *disaster*, meaning both disfigurement and the evil effects of unfavorable aspect of a planet.)
16.1 *sennet* trumpet call signaling the approach of a procession
17 **sir** (Usually thought to refer to Caesar, but the matter is uncertain.)
take measure   18 **scales** graduated markings   19 **mean** middle
20 **foison** plenty   26 **Your serpent** i.e., This serpent that people talk
about. (The colloquial indefinite *your*.)   29 **health** toast. (Lepidus is
obliged to drink up every time a toast is proposed to him.)   30–1 **I'll
ne'er out** i.e., I'll never refuse a toast, never quit.   33 **in** drink, in
your cups. (With a play of antitheses between *in* and *out* in line 31.)
35 **pyramises** (Lepidus's drunken error for *pyramides*, plural of
pyramis or *pyramid*.)

41 **Forbear . . . anon** Excuse me for a moment.   45 **it own** its own.
(Also in line 48.)   46 **elements** vital elements   50 **tears** (Alludes to
the ancient belief that the crocodile wept insincere "crocodile tears"
over its victim before devouring it.)   53 **epicure** (1) glutton (2) atheist. (The Epicureans did not believe in an afterlife. Antony's jesting
point is that only an atheist or epicure would be skeptical of such a
satisfying description as Antony has just given of the crocodile.)
56 **merit** i.e., my merits as a loyal follower, or, the merit of my ideas
58 **held . . . off** i.e., been a respectful and faithful servant   59 **faith**
faithfulness.   64 **But entertain it** Only accept the possibility

Whate'er the ocean pales or sky inclips   69
Is thine, if thou wilt ha 't.
POMPEY   Show me which way.
MENAS
These three world-sharers, these competitors,   71
Are in thy vessel. Let me cut the cable,
And, when we are put off, fall to their throats.   73
All there is thine.
POMPEY   Ah, this thou shouldst have done
And not have spoke on't! In me 'tis villainy;   75
In thee 't had been good service. Thou must know, 76
'Tis not my profit that does lead mine honor;
Mine honor, it. Repent that e'er thy tongue   78
Hath so betrayed thine act. Being done unknown,   79
I should have found it afterwards well done,
But must condemn it now. Desist, and drink.
                        [*He returns to the feast.*]
MENAS [*aside*]   For this,
I'll never follow thy palled fortunes more.   83
Who seeks and will not take when once 'tis offered 84
Shall never find it more.
POMPEY   This health to Lepidus!
ANTONY
Bear him ashore. I'll pledge it for him, Pompey.   86
ENOBARBUS
Here's to thee, Menas!   [*They drink.*]
MENAS   Enobarbus, welcome!
POMPEY   Fill till the cup be hid.
ENOBARBUS   There's a strong fellow, Menas.
            [*Pointing to one who carries off Lepidus.*]
MENAS   Why?
ENOBARBUS   'A bears the third part of the world, man; 91
see'st not?
MENAS
The third part, then, is drunk. Would it were all,
That it might go on wheels!   94
ENOBARBUS   Drink thou; increase the reels.   95
MENAS   Come.
POMPEY
This is not yet an Alexandrian feast.
ANTONY
It ripens towards it. Strike the vessels, ho!   98
Here's to Caesar!
CAESAR   I could well forbear 't.
It's monstrous labor when I wash my brain
And it grows fouler.
ANTONY   Be a child o'th' time.
CAESAR   Possess it, I'll make answer.   102
But I had rather fast from all four days   103

Than drink so much in one.
ENOBARBUS [*to Antony*]   Ha, my brave emperor! 104
Shall we dance now the Egyptian Bacchanals   105
And celebrate our drink?   106
POMPEY   Let's ha 't, good soldier.
ANTONY   Come, let's all take hands
Till that the conquering wine hath steeped our sense 109
In soft and delicate Lethe.
ENOBARBUS   All take hands.   110
Make battery to our ears with the loud music,   111
The while I'll place you; then the boy shall sing.
The holding every man shall bear as loud   113
As his strong sides can volley.   114
     Music plays. Enobarbus places them hand in hand.

               The Song.

BOY [*sings*]
Come, thou monarch of the vine,
Plumpy Bacchus with pink eyne!   116
In thy fats our cares be drowned,   117
With thy grapes our hairs be crowned.
ALL   Cup us till the world go round,   119
Cup us till the world go round!
CAESAR
What would you more? Pompey, good night.—Good
   brother,
Let me request you off. Our graver business   122
Frowns at this levity. Gentle lords, let's part;
You see we have burnt our cheeks. Strong Enobarb   124
Is weaker than the wine, and mine own tongue
Splits what it speaks. The wild disguise hath almost 126
Anticked us all. What needs more words? Good night. 127
Good Antony, your hand.
POMPEY   I'll try you on the shore. 128
ANTONY
And shall, sir. Give 's your hand.
POMPEY   Oh, Antony,
You have my father's house. But what? We are
   friends.
Come down into the boat.
ENOBARBUS   Take heed you fall not. 131
          [*Exeunt all but Enobarbus and Menas.*]
Menas, I'll not on shore.
MENAS   No, to my cabin.
These drums, these trumpets, flutes! What!
Let Neptune hear we bid a loud farewell
To these great fellows. Sound and be hanged, sound
   out!   *Sound a flourish, with drums.*

---

69 **pales** impales, fences in.   **inclips** embraces   71 **competitors** partners. (With secondary sense of "rivals.")   73 **are put off** have put to
sea   75 **on't** of it.   76 **Thou must know** I must inform you that
78 **Mine honor, it** i.e., my honor comes before my personal profit.
Repent Regret   79 **unknown** i.e., without my knowledge   83 **palled**
decayed, darkened   84 **Who** He who   86 **pledge it** i.e., drink the
toast (since Lepidus is too far gone to drink)   91 **'A** He   94 **go on
wheels** go fast or easily. (Proverbial.)   95 **reels** (1) revels (2) reeling
and whirling of drunkenness.   98 **Strike the vessels** Broach or
tap the casks   102 **Possess . . . answer** My answer is, be master of
the time; or, possibly, Drink it off, I'll drink in return.   103 **all** all
nourishment

104 **brave** splendid   105 **Bacchanals** drunken dance to Bacchus, god
of wine   106 **celebrate** consecrate with observances   109 **Till that**
until   110 **Lethe** i.e., forgetfulness. (Literally, the river of oblivion in
Hades.)   111 **Make battery to** Assault   113 **holding** refrain.   **bear**
carry, sing   114 **volley** sing in return, answering the stanza with the
refrain.   116 **pink eyne** i.e., eyes half-shut, from drinking.   117 **fats**
vats, vessels   119 **Cup** Intoxicate   122 **off** to disembark.   124 **we . . .
cheeks** our complexions are flushed with drinking.   126 **disguise**
(1) masque (2) transforming drunkenness   127 **Anticked us** (1) made
dancers of us in a masque (2) made buffoons or fools of us   128 **try
you** i.e., take you on in a drinking contest   131 **boat** small boat for
taking the party ashore.

ENOBARBUS　　Hoo! says 'a. There's my cap.
　　　　　　　　　　　　　　　　　　[*He flings it in the air.*]
MENAS　　Hoo! Noble captain, come.　　　　　　*Exeunt.*

❖

[3.1]

Enter Ventidius as it were in triumph [with Silius, and other Romans, officers, and soldiers], the dead body of Pacorus borne before him.

VENTIDIUS
　Now, darting Parthia, art thou struck, and now　　1
　Pleased fortune does of Marcus Crassus' death　　2
　Make me revenger. Bear the King's son's body
　Before our army. Thy Pacorus, Orodes,　　4
　Pays this for Marcus Crassus.
SILIUS　　　　　　　　　　　Noble Ventidius,
　Whilst yet with Parthian blood thy sword is warm,
　The fugitive Parthians follow. Spur through Media,　　7
　Mesopotamia, and the shelters whither
　The routed fly. So thy grand captain, Antony,
　Shall set thee on triumphant chariots and　　10
　Put garlands on thy head.
VENTIDIUS　　　　　　　Oh, Silius, Silius,
　I have done enough. A lower place, note well,　　12
　May make too great an act. For learn this, Silius:
　Better to leave undone than by our deed
　Acquire too high a fame when him we serve's away.
　Caesar and Antony have ever won
　More in their officer than person. Sossius,　　17
　One of my place in Syria, his lieutenant,　　18
　For quick accumulation of renown,
　Which he achieved by th' minute, lost his favor.　　20
　Who does i'th' wars more than his captain can　　21
　Becomes his captain's captain; and ambition,
　The soldier's virtue, rather makes choice of loss　　23
　Than gain which darkens him.　　24
　I could do more to do Antonius good,
　But 'twould offend him, and in his offense　　26
　Should my performance perish.
SILIUS　　Thou hast, Ventidius, that　　28
　Without the which a soldier and his sword　　29
　Grants scarce distinction. Thou wilt write to Antony?　　30
VENTIDIUS
　I'll humbly signify what in his name,

That magical word of war, we have effected:　　32
How with his banners and his well-paid ranks
The ne'er-yet-beaten horse of Parthia　　34
We have jaded out o'th' field.
SILIUS　　　　　　　　　Where is he now?　　35
VENTIDIUS
He purposeth to Athens, whither, with what haste
The weight we must convey with 's will permit,　　37
We shall appear before him.—On, there. Pass along!
　　　　　　　　　　　　　　　　Exeunt.

❖

[3.2]

Enter Agrippa at one door, Enobarbus at another.

AGRIPPA　　What, are the brothers parted?　　1
ENOBARBUS
　They have dispatched with Pompey; he is gone.　　2
　The other three are sealing. Octavia weeps　　3
　To part from Rome; Caesar is sad; and Lepidus,　　4
　Since Pompey's feast, as Menas says, is troubled
　With the greensickness.
AGRIPPA　　　　　　　　'Tis a noble Lepidus.　　6
ENOBARBUS
　A very fine one. Oh, how he loves Caesar!　　7
AGRIPPA
　Nay, but how dearly he adores Mark Antony!
ENOBARBUS
　Caesar? Why, he's the Jupiter of men.
AGRIPPA
　What's Antony? The god of Jupiter.
ENOBARBUS
　Spake you of Caesar? How, the nonpareil!
AGRIPPA
　O Antony, O thou Arabian bird!　　12
ENOBARBUS
　Would you praise Caesar, say "Caesar"; go no further.
AGRIPPA
　Indeed, he plied them both with excellent praises.
ENOBARBUS
　But he loves Caesar best; yet he loves Antony.
　Hoo! Hearts, tongues, figures, scribes, bards, poets,
　　cannot　　16
　Think, speak, cast, write, sing, number, hoo!　　17
　His love to Antony. But as for Caesar,
　Kneel down, kneel down, and wonder.
AGRIPPA　　　　　　　　　　　Both he loves.

3.1. Location: The Middle East.
1 darting (The Parthians were famous for archery and for the Parthian dart which they discharged as they fled.)　**Parthia** i.e., Orodes, King of Parthia　**2 Crassus' death** (Crassus, member of the first triumvirate with Pompey the Great and Julius Caesar, was overthrown and treacherously murdered by Orodes in 53 B.C.)　**4 Pacorus, Orodes** (Pacorus was the son of Orodes.)　**7 The . . . follow** follow the fleeing Parthians.　**10 triumphant** triumphal　**12 A lower place** One of lower rank　**17 More . . . person** more through the actions of their lieutenants than by their own efforts.　**18 of my place** of the same rank as I.　**his lieutenant** i.e., the commanding officer acting for Antony　**20 by th' minute** minute by minute, continually　**21 Who** He who　**23–4 rather . . . him** prefers to lose rather than gain in such a way as to darken his reputation.　**26 offense** taking offense　**28–30 that . . . distinction** i.e., discretion, without the which a soldier can scarcely be distinguished from the sword he uses.

32 word watchword.　**effected** achieved　**34 horse** cavalry　**35 jaded** driven exhausted like jades, inferior horses　**37 with 's** with us
3.2. Location: Rome.
1 brothers parted brothers-in-law departed.　**2 dispatched** concluded the business　**3 sealing** affixing seals to their agreements, settling matters.　**4 sad** sober　**6 greensickness** a kind of anemia supposed to affect young women, especially those afflicted with love-longing. (Used ironically here to refer to Lepidus's hangover and to his love for Antony and Caesar.)　**7 fine** (*Lepidus* in Latin means "fine," "elegant.")　**12 Arabian bird** i.e., the fabled phoenix. (Only one existed at a time; it re-created itself by arising from its ashes.)　**16 figures** figures of speech　**17 cast** calculate.　**number** write verses

ENOBARBUS
They are his shards, and he their beetle. [*Trumpets
    within.*] So;   20
This is to horse. Adieu, noble Agrippa.   21

AGRIPPA
Good fortune, worthy soldier, and farewell.

Enter Caesar, Antony, Lepidus, and Octavia.

ANTONY   No further, sir.   23

CAESAR
You take from me a great part of myself;
Use me well in't.—Sister, prove such a wife
As my thoughts make thee, and as my farthest bond   26
Shall pass on thy approof.—Most noble Antony,   27
Let not the piece of virtue which is set   28
Betwixt us as the cement of our love
To keep it builded be the ram to batter
The fortress of it; for better might we
Have loved without this mean, if on both parts   32
This be not cherished.

ANTONY   Make me not offended
In your distrust.

CAESAR   I have said.

ANTONY   You shall not find,   34
Though you be therein curious, the least cause   35
For what you seem to fear. So the gods keep you,
And make the hearts of Romans serve your ends!
We will here part.

CAESAR
Farewell, my dearest sister, fare thee well.
The elements be kind to thee, and make   40
Thy spirits all of comfort! Fare thee well.

OCTAVIA [*weeping*]   My noble brother!

ANTONY
The April's in her eyes; it is love's spring,
And these the showers to bring it on.—Be cheerful.

OCTAVIA [*to Caesar*]
Sir, look well to my husband's house; and—   45

CAESAR
What, Octavia?

OCTAVIA   I'll tell you in your ear.
                              [*She whisper to Caesar.*]

ANTONY
Her tongue will not obey her heart, nor can   47
Her heart inform her tongue—the swan's down
    feather,   48
That stands upon the swell at full of tide,   49
And neither way inclines.   50

ENOBARBUS [*aside to Agrippa*]   Will Caesar weep?
AGRIPPA [*aside to Enobarbus*]   He has a cloud in 's face.
ENOBARBUS [*aside to Agrippa*]
He were the worse for that, were he a horse;   53
So is he, being a man.

AGRIPPA [*aside to Enobarbus*]   Why, Enobarbus,
When Antony found Julius Caesar dead,
He cried almost to roaring; and he wept
When at Philippi he found Brutus slain.

ENOBARBUS [*aside to Agrippa*]
That year indeed he was troubled with a rheum.   58
What willingly he did confound he wailed,   59
Believe't, till I wept too.

CAESAR   No, sweet Octavia,
You shall hear from me still. The time shall not   61
Outgo my thinking on you.

ANTONY   Come, sir, come,   62
I'll wrestle with you in my strength of love.
Look, here I have you [*embracing him*]; thus I let you
    go,
And give you to the gods.

CAESAR   Adieu. Be happy!

LEPIDUS
Let all the number of the stars give light
To thy fair way!

CAESAR   Farewell, farewell!   *Kisses Octavia.*

ANTONY   Farewell!
        Trumpets sound. Exeunt [in separate groups].

❖

[3.3]

Enter Cleopatra, Charmian, Iras, and Alexas.

CLEOPATRA
Where is the fellow?

ALEXAS   Half afeard to come.

CLEOPATRA
Go to, go to.

Enter the Messenger as before.

              Come hither, sir.

ALEXAS   Good Majesty,   2
Herod of Jewry dare not look upon you   3
But when you are well pleased.

CLEOPATRA   That Herod's head
I'll have; but how, when Antony is gone,
Through whom I might command it?—Come thou
    near.

MESSENGER   Most gracious Majesty!

CLEOPATRA   Didst thou behold Octavia?

---

20 shards patches of dung, or, perhaps, wings or wing-cases, i.e., pro-
tectors, patrons   **21 This is to horse** i.e., The trumpet call gives the
signal to depart.   **23 No further** i.e., You need not go on urging your
point, or, you need accompany me no further   **26–7 as . . . approof**
such that my utmost bond shall be justified in certifying what you
will prove to be.   **28 piece** masterpiece   **32 mean** intermediary, or
means   **34 In** by.   **I have said** i.e., I stand by what I've said.
35 curious overly inquisitive or touchy   **40 elements** heavens
45 husband's house i.e., Antony's house, as at 2.7.130, though
Octavia is also a widow; see 3.3.29   **47–50 Her . . . inclines** i.e., Her
conflicting emotions make her unable to speak aloud, like a swan's
down feather floating at full tide, moving neither up nor down
stream.

53 He . . . horse (Alludes to the belief that a horse with a dark spot on
its face was apt to be bad-tempered.)   **58 rheum** i.e., running at the
eyes. (Said of any discharge of secretion from the head.)   **59 What . . .
bewailed** He bewailed what he intentionally destroyed   **61 still** regularly.   **61–2 The time . . . you** Time itself will not outlast my thinking of you.
3.3. Location: Alexandria. Cleopatra's palace.
2 Go to (An expression of impatience.)   **3 Herod of Jewry** i.e., Even
the famous tyrant who slaughtered the children. (See 1.2.29–30.)

MESSENGER
Ay, dread Queen.
CLEOPATRA   Where?
MESSENGER   Madam, in Rome.
I looked her in the face, and saw her led
Between her brother and Mark Antony.
CLEOPATRA
Is she as tall as me?
MESSENGER   She is not, madam.
CLEOPATRA
Didst hear her speak? Is she shrill-tongued or low?
MESSENGER
Madam, I heard her speak. She is low-voiced.
CLEOPATRA
That's not so good. He cannot like her long.   15
CHARMIAN
Like her! Oh, Isis, 'tis impossible.
CLEOPATRA
I think so, Charmian. Dull of tongue, and dwarfish.—
What majesty is in her gait? Remember,
If e'er thou looked'st on majesty.
MESSENGER   She creeps:
Her motion and her station are as one.   20
She shows a body rather than a life,   21
A statue than a breather.
CLEOPATRA   Is this certain?   22
MESSENGER
Or I have no observance.
CHARMIAN   Three in Egypt   23
Cannot make better note.
CLEOPATRA   He's very knowing,   24
I do perceive't. There's nothing in her yet.
The fellow has good judgment.
CHARMIAN   Excellent.
CLEOPATRA   Guess at her years, I prithee.
MESSENGER   Madam,
She was a widow—
CLEOPATRA   Widow? Charmian, hark.
MESSENGER   And I do think she's thirty.
CLEOPATRA
Bear'st thou her face in mind? Is't long or round?
MESSENGER   Round, even to faultiness.
CLEOPATRA
For the most part, too, they are foolish that are so.—
Her hair, what color?
MESSENGER   Brown, madam; and her forehead
As low as she would wish it.   36
CLEOPATRA [giving money]   There's gold for thee.
Thou must not take my former sharpness ill.
I will employ thee back again; I find thee   39
Most fit for business. Go make thee ready;

Our letters are prepared.   [Exit Messenger.]
CHARMIAN   A proper man.   41
CLEOPATRA
Indeed, he is so. I repent me much
That so I harried him. Why, methinks, by him,   43
This creature's no such thing.
CHARMIAN   Nothing, madam.   44
CLEOPATRA
The man hath seen some majesty, and should know.
CHARMIAN
Hath he seen majesty? Isis else defend,   46
And serving you so long!   47
CLEOPATRA
I have one thing more to ask him yet, good
    Charmian—
But 'tis no matter; thou shalt bring him to me
Where I will write. All may be well enough
CHARMIAN   I warrant you, madam.   Exeunt.   51

❖

[3.4]

Enter Antony and Octavia.

ANTONY
Nay, nay, Octavia, not only that—
That were excusable, that and thousands more
Of semblable import—but he hath waged   3
New wars 'gainst Pompey; made his will, and read it 4
To public ear;
Spoke scantly of me; when perforce he could not   6
But pay me terms of honor, cold and sickly
He vented them, most narrow measure lent me;   8
When the best hint was given him, he not took't,   9
Or did it from his teeth.
OCTAVIA   Oh, my good lord,   10
Believe not all, or, if you must believe,
Stomach not all. A more unhappy lady,   12
If this division chance, ne'er stood between,   13
Praying for both parts.
The good gods will mock me presently
When I shall pray, "Oh, bless my lord and husband!"
Undo that prayer by crying out as loud,   17
"Oh, bless my brother!" Husband win, win brother,
Prays and destroys the prayer; no midway
Twixt these extremes at all.
ANTONY   Gentle Octavia,
Let your best love draw to that point which seeks   21
Best to preserve it. If I lose mine honor,   22

---

15 **not so good** i.e., not so good for her.   20 **Her . . . one** i.e., she
moves with so little animation that it's all the same whether she's
moving or standing.   21 **shows** appears as   22 **breather** living
being.   23–4 **Three . . . note** There are not three people in Egypt who
are better observers.   36 **As . . . it** i.e., such that she wouldn't wish it
to be any lower. (A colloquial way of suggesting she is ugly; high
foreheads were thought more beautiful.)   39 **employ . . . again** send
you back with a message

41 **proper** good   43 **harried** maltreated.   **by** according to   44 **no such
thing** nothing much.   46 **else defend** forbid that it be otherwise. (An
interjection.)   47 **serving** i.e., he having served   51 **warrant** assure
3.4. Location: Athens.
3 **semblable** similar   4 **read it** (In order to win the populace by
showing them what benefits they might expect from him.)   6 **scantly**
slightly   8 **vented** gave vent to, expressed.   **narrow measure lent
me** gave me minimal praise   9 **hint** occasion (to praise Antony)
10 **from his teeth** i.e., between clenched teeth, not from the heart.
12 **Stomach** resent   13 **chance** occur   17 **Undo** i.e., and then undo,
or, I shall undo   21–2 **Let . . . it** let your warmest love be given to that
one of us who seeks to preserve it (your love) best.

I lose myself; better I were not yours
Than yours so branchless. But, as you requested, 24
Yourself shall go between 's. The meantime, lady, 25
I'll raise the preparation of a war 26
Shall stain your brother. Make your soonest haste; 27
So your desires are yours.

OCTAVIA   Thanks to my lord. 28
The Jove of power make me, most weak, most weak,
Your reconciler! Wars twixt you twain would be
As if the world should cleave, and that slain men 31
Should solder up the rift. 32

ANTONY
When it appears to you where this begins, 33
Turn your displeasure that way, for our faults 34
Can never be so equal that your love 35
Can equally move with them. Provide your going; 36
Choose your own company and command what cost
Your heart has mind to.   Exeunt.

❧

[3.5]

Enter Enobarbus and Eros, [meeting].

ENOBARBUS How now, friend Eros?
EROS There's strange news come, sir.
ENOBARBUS What, man?
EROS Caesar and Lepidus have made wars upon Pompey.
ENOBARBUS This is old. What is the success? 6
EROS Caesar, having made use of him in the wars 7
'gainst Pompey, presently denied him rivality, would 8
not let him partake in the glory of the action; and, not
resting here, accuses him of letters he had formerly 10
wrote to Pompey; upon his own appeal seizes him. 11
So the poor third is up, till death enlarge his confine. 12
ENOBARBUS
Then, world, thou hast a pair of chops, no more; 13
And throw between them all the food thou hast,
They'll grind the one the other. Where's Antony? 15
EROS
He's walking in the garden—thus, and spurns 16
The rush that lies before him; cries, "Fool Lepidus!" 17

And threats the throat of that his officer 18
That murdered Pompey.
ENOBARBUS   Our great navy's rigged. 19
EROS
For Italy and Caesar. More, Domitius: 20
My lord desires you presently. My news 21
I might have told hereafter.
ENOBARBUS   'Twill be naught,
But let it be. Bring me to Antony.
EROS   Come, sir. *Exeunt.*

❧

[3.6]

Enter Agrippa, Maecenas, and Caesar.

CAESAR
Contemning Rome, he has done all this and more 1
In Alexandria. Here's the manner of 't:
I'th' marketplace, on a tribunal silvered, 3
Cleopatra and himself in chairs of gold
Were publicly enthroned. At the feet sat
Caesarion, whom they call my father's son, 6
And all the unlawful issue that their lust
Since then hath made between them. Unto her
He gave the stablishment of Egypt, made her 9
Of lower Syria, Cyprus, Lydia,
Absolute queen.
MAECENAS   This in the public eye?
CAESAR
I'th' common showplace, where they exercise. 12
His sons he there proclaimed the kings of kings:
Great Media, Parthia, and Armenia
He gave to Alexander; to Ptolemy he assigned
Syria, Cilicia, and Phoenicia. She
In th' habiliments of the goddess Isis 17
That day appeared, and oft before gave audience,
As 'tis reported, so.
MAECENAS   Let Rome be thus informed.
AGRIPPA   Who, queasy with his insolence already, 21
Will their good thoughts call from him. 22
CAESAR
The people knows it, and have now received
His accusations.
AGRIPPA   Who does he accuse?
CAESAR
Caesar, and that, having in Sicily
Sextus Pompeius spoiled, we had not rated him 26
His part o'th'isle. Then does he say he lent me 27

---

24 **branchless** pruned (of honor). 25 **The meantime** In the meantime 26–7 **I'll . . . brother** I'll raise an army that will deprive your brother of his luster. 28 **So . . . yours** i.e., thus you have obtained your desire (to go). (Or, *so* may mean "as long as.") 31 **cleave** split 32 **Should** would be needed to 33 **where this begins** who started this quarrel 34 **our** i.e., Caesar's and mine 34–6 **our faults . . . them** i.e., you will have to judge between our faults and choose. 36 **Provide** Make arrangements for
3.5. Location: Athens.
6 **success** outcome, result. 7 **him** i.e., Lepidus 8 **presently** immediately. **rivality** rights of a partner. (Caesar and Lepidus have newly gone to war against Pompey and have defeated him.) 10 **resting here** stopping with this insult 11 **his own appeal** Caesar's own accusation 12 **up** shut up (in prison). **enlarge his confine** set him free. 13 **a pair . . . more** a single pair of jaws, with no third partner 15 **They'll . . . other** the jaws will still grind against each other, grind each other down. 16 **thus** (Eros imitates Antony's angry walk.) **spurns** kicks 17 **rush** strewn rushes

18 **And . . . officer** and threatens the life of the officer of his
19 **Pompey** (After his defeat by Caesar and Lepidus, Pompey was murdered—perhaps, according to history, on Antony's orders, but here Antony blames his officer.) 20 **More** I have more to say
21 **presently** immediately.
3.6. Location: Rome.
1 **Contemning** Disdaining 3 **tribunal** seat of state, dais 6 **my father's** i.e., Julius Caesar's. (Julius Caesar had adopted his grandnephew Octavius as his son.) 9 **stablishment** settled possession 12 **exercise** put on entertainments and sports. 17 **habiliments** attire 21 **queasy** nauseated, "fed up." (Refers to the Roman people.) 22 **call** withdraw 26 **spoiled** despoiled, plundered. **rated him** allotted to Antony 27 **th'isle** i.e., Sicily.

Some shipping, unrestored. Lastly, he frets   28
That Lepidus of the triumvirate   29
Should be deposed, and, being, that we detain   30
All his revenue.
AGRIPPA   Sir, this should be answered.
CAESAR
'Tis done already, and the messenger gone.
I have told him Lepidus was grown too cruel,
That he his high authority abused
And did deserve his change. For what I have
    conquered,   35
I grant him part; but then in his Armenia,
And other of his conquered kingdoms, I
Demand the like.
MAECENAS   He'll never yield to that.
CAESAR
Nor must not then be yielded to in this.

Enter Octavia with her train.

OCTAVIA
Hail, Caesar, and my lord! Hail, most dear Caesar!
CAESAR
That ever I should call thee castaway!
OCTAVIA
You have not called me so, nor have you cause.
CAESAR
Why have you stol'n upon us thus? You come not
Like Caesar's sister. The wife of Antony
Should have an army for an usher and
The neighs of horse to tell of her approach   46
Long ere she did appear. The trees by th' way   47
Should have borne men, and expectation fainted,
Longing for what it had not. Nay, the dust
Should have ascended to the roof of heaven,
Raised by your populous troops. But you are come
A market maid to Rome, and have prevented   52
The ostentation of our love, which, left unshown,   53
Is often left unloved. We should have met you   54
By sea and land, supplying every stage   55
With an augmented greeting.
OCTAVIA   Good my lord,
To come thus was I not constrained, but did it
On my free will. My lord, Mark Antony,
Hearing that you prepared for war, acquainted
My grievèd ear withal, whereon I begged
His pardon for return.
CAESAR   Which soon he granted,   61
Being an obstruct 'tween his lust and him.   62
OCTAVIA
Do not say so, my lord.
CAESAR   I have eyes upon him,
And his affairs come to me on the wind.
Where is he now?

OCTAVIA   My lord, in Athens.
CAESAR
No, my most wrongèd sister. Cleopatra
Hath nodded him to her. He hath given his empire
Up to a whore; who now are levying   69
The kings o'th'earth for war. He hath assembled
Bocchus, the King of Libya; Archelaus,
Of Cappadocia; Philadelphos, King
Of Paphlagonia; the Thracian king, Adallas;
King Manchus of Arabia; King of Pont;
Herod of Jewry; Mithridates, King
Of Comagene; Polemon and Amyntas,
The Kings of Mede and Lycaonia,
With a more larger list of scepters.   78
OCTAVIA   Ay me, most wretched,
That have my heart parted betwixt two friends
That does afflict each other!
CAESAR   Welcome hither.
Your letters did withhold our breaking forth   82
Till we perceived both how you were wrong led   83
And we in negligent danger. Cheer your heart.   84
Be you not troubled with the time, which drives   85
O'er your content these strong necessities,   86
But let determined things to destiny   87
Hold unbewailed their way. Welcome to Rome,   88
Nothing more dear to me. You are abused   89
Beyond the mark of thought, and the high gods,   90
To do you justice, makes his ministers   91
Of us and those that love you. Best of comfort,   92
And ever welcome to us.
AGRIPPA   Welcome, lady.
MAECENAS   Welcome, dear madam.
Each heart in Rome does love and pity you.
Only th'adulterous Antony, most large   97
In his abominations, turns you off   98
And gives his potent regiment to a trull   99
That noises it against us.
OCTAVIA   Is it so, sir?   100
CAESAR
Most certain. Sister, welcome. Pray you
Be ever known to patience. My dear'st sister! *Exeunt.* 102

❖

[3.7]

Enter Cleopatra and Enobarbus.

---

28 **unrestored** that I did not return to him.   29 **of** from   30 **being** having been deposed   35 **For** As for   46 **horse** horses   47 **by** along   52 **prevented** forestalled (by your unannounced arrival)   53 **ostentation** ceremonial display   53–4 **which . . . unloved** which, if not made manifest through ceremonious display, often remains unappreciated or ceases to exist.   55 **stage** stage of your journey   61 **pardon** permission   62 **Being . . . him** i.e., since your return to Rome removed the obstacle between him and the gratification of his desires.

69 **who** i.e., and they   78 **a more larger** an even longer   82 **withhold . . . forth** restrain my advancing to battle   83 **wrong led** wronged, abused   84 **negligent danger** danger through neglect of taking necessary action.   85 **the time** the present state of affairs   85–6 **which . . . necessities** i.e., which tramples your happiness underfoot like a team of animals pulling a wagon   87–8 **let . . . way** allow inevitable events to go unbewailed to their destined conclusion.   89 **Nothing . . . me** i.e., you who are more dear to me than anything.   90 **mark** reach   90–2 **the high . . . you** i.e., the high gods (here treated as a singular subject of the verb "makes," and referred to as "his" in line 91) make us and those that love you their ministers of justice in your cause.   97 **large** unrestrained   98 **turns you off** rejects you   99 **regiment** government, rule.   **trull** prostitute   100 **noises it** is clamorous   102 **Be . . . patience** be patient.
3.7. Location: Near Actium, on the northwestern coast of Greece. Antony's camp.

CLEOPATRA
I will be even with thee, doubt it not.
ENOBARBUS   But why, why, why?
CLEOPATRA
Thou hast forspoke my being in these wars,   3
And say'st it is not fit.
ENOBARBUS   Well, is it, is it?   4
CLEOPATRA
If not denounced against us, why should not we   5
Be there in person?
ENOBARBUS [aside]   Well, I could reply.
If we should serve with horse and mares together,   7
The horse were merely lost; the mares would bear   8
A soldier and his horse.
CLEOPATRA   What is't you say?   9
ENOBARBUS
Your presence needs must puzzle Antony,   10
Take from his heart, take from his brain, from's time
What should not then be spared. He is already
Traduced for levity, and 'tis said in Rome   13
That Photinus, an eunuch, and your maids   14
Manage this war.
CLEOPATRA   Sink Rome, and their tongues rot
That speak against us! A charge we bear i'th' war,   16
And as the president of my kingdom will   17
Appear there for a man. Speak not against it.   18
I will not stay behind.

Enter Antony and Canidius.

ENOBARBUS   Nay, I have done.
Here comes the Emperor.
ANTONY   Is it not strange, Canidius,
That from Tarentum and Brundusium
He could so quickly cut the Ionian sea   22
And take in Toryne?—You have heard on't, sweet?   23
CLEOPATRA
Celerity is never more admired   24
Than by the negligent.
ANTONY   A good rebuke,
Which might have well becomed the best of men,   26
To taunt at slackness. Canidius, we
Will fight with him by sea.
CLEOPATRA   By sea, what else?
CANIDIUS   Why will my lord do so?
ANTONY   For that he dares us to't.   30
ENOBARBUS
So hath my lord dared him to single fight.

CANIDIUS
Ay, and to wage this battle at Pharsalia,
Where Caesar fought with Pompey. But these offers,
Which serve not for his vantage, he shakes off,
And so should you.
ENOBARBUS   Your ships are not well manned;
Your mariners are muleteers, reapers, people   36
Engrossed by swift impress. In Caesar's fleet   37
Are those that often have 'gainst Pompey fought;
Their ships are yare, yours heavy. No disgrace   39
Shall fall you for refusing him at sea,   40
Being prepared for land.
ANTONY   By sea, by sea.
ENOBARBUS
Most worthy sir, you therein throw away
The absolute soldiership you have by land,
Distract your army, which doth most consist   44
Of war-marked footmen, leave unexecuted   45
Your own renownèd knowledge, quite forgo
The way which promises assurance, and
Give up yourself merely to chance and hazard   48
From firm security.
ANTONY   I'll fight at sea.
CLEOPATRA
I have sixty sails, Caesar none better.
ANTONY
Our overplus of shipping will we burn,
And with the rest full-manned, from th' head of
    Actium   52
Beat th'approaching Caesar. But if we fail,
We then can do't at land.

Enter a Messenger.

    Thy business?
MESSENGER
The news is true, my lord; he is descried.   55
Caesar has taken Toryne.
ANTONY
Can he be there in person? 'Tis impossible;
Strange that his power should be. Canidius,   58
Our nineteen legions thou shalt hold by land,
And our twelve thousand horse. We'll to our ship.
Away, my Thetis!

Enter a Soldier.

    How now, worthy soldier?   61
SOLDIER
O noble Emperor, do not fight by sea;
Trust not to rotten planks. Do you misdoubt
This sword and these my wounds? Let th'Egyptians
And the Phoenicians go a-ducking; we   65

---

3 forspoke spoken against   **4 fit** appropriate.   **5 If . . . us** i.e., Even if the war were not declared against me (which it is)   **7 horse** stallions **8 merely** utterly   **8–9 bear . . . horse** be mounted by a rider and a stallion.   **10 puzzle** bewilder   **13 Traduced** criticized, censured **14 an eunuch** (Probably Mardian. In North's Plutarch, Caesar complains that "Mardian the eunuch, Photinus, and Iras . . . and Charmian . . . ruled the affairs of Antonius' empire." But Photinus [or Pothinus] was a eunuch, too.)   **16 charge** responsibility, cost **17 president** ruler   **18 for** in the capacity of   **22 Ionian** (Often applied to the Aegean, but here the Adriatic. Tarentum and Brundusium or Brundisium are in the "heel" of Italy, across the Adriatic from Actium and Toryne.)   **23 take in** conquer   **24 Celerity** Swiftness.   **admired** wondered at   **26 becomed** become, suited   **30 For that** Because

36 muleteers mule-drivers, peasants   **37 Engrossed** collected wholesale.   **impress** impressment, conscription.   **39 yare** quick, maneuverable   **40 fall** befall   **44 Distract** divide, divert.   **most** for the most part   **45 footmen** foot soldiers.   **unexecuted** unused **48 merely** entirely   **52 head** promontory   **55 he is descried** he has been sighted.   **58 his power** i.e., his army, let alone himself **61 Thetis** sea goddess, the mother of Achilles.   **65 go a-ducking** (1) get drenched (2) cringe

Have used to conquer standing on the earth　　　66
And fighting foot to foot.

ANTONY　　　　　　　　　　Well, well, away!

Exeunt Antony, Cleopatra, and Enobarbus.

SOLDIER
By Hercules, I think I am i'th' right.

CANIDIUS
Soldier, thou art; but his whole action grows　　69
Not in the power on't. So our leader's led,　　70
And we are women's men.

SOLDIER　　　　　　　　　You keep by land　　71
The legions and the horse whole, do you not?　　72

CANIDIUS
Marcus Octavius, Marcus Justeius,
Publicola, and Caelius are for sea;
But we keep whole by land. This speed of Caesar's
Carries beyond belief.　　　　　　　　　　　76

SOLDIER　　While he was yet in Rome
His power went out in such distractions as　　78
Beguiled all spies.

CANIDIUS　　　　　　Who's his lieutenant, hear you?

SOLDIER
They say, one Taurus.

CANIDIUS　　　　　　　Well I know the man.

Enter a Messenger.

MESSENGER　　The Emperor calls Canidius.

CANIDIUS
With news the time's in labor, and throws forth　　82
Each minute some.　　　　　　　　*Exeunt.*　　83

❧

[3.8]

Enter Caesar [and Taurus] with his army, marching.

CAESAR　Taurus!

TAURUS　My lord?

CAESAR
Strike not by land; keep whole. Provoke not battle
Till we have done at sea. Do not exceed
The prescript of this scroll. [*He gives a scroll.*] Our
　　fortune lies　　　　　　　　　　　　　5
Upon this jump.　　　　　　　　　*Exeunt.*　　6

❧

[3.9]

Enter Antony and Enobarbus.

ANTONY
Set we our squadrons on yond side o'th' hill,
In eye of Caesar's battle, from which place　　　2
We may the number of the ships behold
And so proceed accordingly.　　　　　*Exeunt.*

❧

[3.10]

Canidius marcheth with his land army one way over the stage, and Taurus, the lieutenant of Caesar, the other way. After their going in is heard the noise of a sea fight.

Alarum. Enter Enobarbus.

ENOBARBUS
Naught, naught, all naught! I can behold no longer.　1
Th'*Antoniad*, the Egyptian admiral,　　　　　2
With all their sixty, fly and turn the rudder.
To see't mine eyes are blasted.

Enter Scarus.

SCARUS　　　　　　　　　　Gods and goddesses,
All the whole synod of them!

ENOBARBUS　　　　　　　　What's thy passion?　　5

SCARUS
The greater cantle of the world is lost　　　6
With very ignorance; we have kissed away　　7
Kingdoms and provinces.

ENOBARBUS　　　　　　　How appears the fight?

SCARUS
On our side like the tokened pestilence,　　　9
Where death is sure. Yon ribaudred nag of Egypt—　10
Whom leprosy o'ertake!—i'th' midst o'th' fight,
When vantage like a pair of twins appeared　　12
Both as the same, or rather ours the elder,　　13
The breeze upon her, like a cow in June,　　14
Hoists sails and flies.

ENOBARBUS　　　　　　That I beheld.
Mine eyes did sicken at the sight, and could not
Endure a further view.

SCARUS　　　　　　　　She once being loofed,　　18
The noble ruin of her magic, Antony,　　　19
Claps on his sea wing and, like a doting mallard,　20
Leaving the fight in height, flies after her.　　21
I never saw an action of such shame.
Experience, manhood, honor, ne'er before

---

66 **Have used** are accustomed.　**standing on the earth** (1) fighting on land (2) standing upright, not *ducking,* or "cringing"　**69–70 his . . . on't** his whole strategy has been developed without regard to where his power really lies.　**71 men** servingmen.　**72 horse** cavalry. **whole** undivided, held in reserve　**76 Carries** surpasses (like an arrow in archery)　**78 distractions** detachments, divisions **82–3 With . . . some** More news is born each minute. (*Throws forth* means "gives birth.")
3.8. Location: A field near Actium, as before.
5 prescript orders　**6 jump** chance, hazard.
3.9. Location: A field near Actium, as before.

2 **eye** sight.　**battle** battle line
3.10 Location: A field near Actium, as before.
1 **Naught** All has come to naught　2 **admiral** flagship　5 **synod** assembly　6 **cantle** corner; hence, piece or part　7 **With very ignorance** through utter stupidity　9 **tokened pestilence** (Certain red spots appeared on the bodies of the plague-smitten, called tokens.) 10 **ribaudred** foul, obscene　**12–13 When . . . same** i.e., when the advantage was equal on either side　13 **elder** i.e., more advanced, more likely to inherit　14 **breeze** (1) gadfly (2) light wind　18 **loofed** luffed, with ship's head brought close to the wind. (With a pun on *aloofed,* "becoming distant.")　19 **ruin of** object ruined by　20 **Claps . . . sea wing** i.e., hoists sail, preparing for flight like a water bird. **mallard** drake　21 **in** at its

Did violate so itself.

ENOBARBUS   Alack, alack!

Enter Canidius.

CANIDIUS
Our fortune on the sea is out of breath,
And sinks most lamentably. Had our general
Been what he knew himself, it had gone well.
Oh, he has given example for our flight
Most grossly by his own!

ENOBARBUS
Ay, are you thereabouts? Why then, good night
    indeed.   30

CANIDIUS
Toward Peloponnesus are they fled.   31

SCARUS
'Tis easy to't, and there I will attend   32
What further comes.

CANIDIUS   To Caesar will I render   33
My legions and my horse. Six kings already   34
Show me the way of yielding.

ENOBARBUS   I'll yet follow
The wounded chance of Antony, though my reason   36
Sits in the wind against me.   [*Exeunt separately.*] 37

❖

[3.11]

Enter Antony with attendants.

ANTONY
Hark! The land bids me tread no more upon't;
It is ashamed to bear me. Friends, come hither.
I am so lated in the world that I   3
Have lost my way forever. I have a ship
Laden with gold. Take that, divide it; fly,   5
And make your peace with Caesar.

ALL   Fly? Not we.

ANTONY
I have fled myself, and have instructed cowards
To run and show their shoulders. Friends, begone.   8
I have myself resolved upon a course
Which has no need of you. Begone.
My treasure's in the harbor. Take it. Oh,
I followed that I blush to look upon!   12
My very hairs do mutiny, for the white   13
Reprove the brown for rashness, and they them   14

For fear and doting. Friends, begone. You shall
Have letters from me to some friends that will
Sweep your way for you. Pray you, look not sad,   17
Nor make replies of loathness. Take the hint   18
Which my despair proclaims. Let that be left   19
Which leaves itself. To the seaside straightway!   20
I will possess you of that ship and treasure.
Leave me, I pray, a little. Pray you now,
Nay, do so, for indeed I have lost command.   23
Therefore I pray you. I'll see you by and by.   24

[*Exeunt attendants. Antony*] *sits down.*

Enter Cleopatra led by Charmian, [Iras,] and Eros.

EROS
Nay, gentle madam, to him, comfort him.

IRAS   Do, most dear Queen.

CHARMIAN   Do; why, what else?

CLEOPATRA   Let me sit down. O Juno!

ANTONY   No, no, no, no, no.

EROS   See you here, sir?

ANTONY   Oh, fie, fie, fie!

CHARMIAN   Madam!

IRAS   Madam, O good Empress!

EROS   Sir, sir!

ANTONY
Yes, my lord, yes. He at Philippi kept   35
His sword e'en like a dancer, while I struck   36
The lean and wrinkled Cassius, and 'twas I
That the mad Brutus ended. He alone   38
Dealt on lieutenantry, and no practice had   39
In the brave squares of war; yet now—no matter.   40

CLEOPATRA
Ah, stand by.

EROS   The Queen, my lord, the Queen.   41

IRAS
Go to him, madam, speak to him.
He's unqualitied with very shame.   43

CLEOPATRA   Well then, sustain me. Oh!

EROS
Most noble sir, arise. The Queen approaches.
Her head's declined, and death will seize her but   46
Your comfort makes the rescue.

ANTONY
I have offended reputation,
A most unnoble swerving.

EROS   Sir, the Queen.   49

30 thereabouts i.e., of that mind, thinking of desertion. good night indeed i.e., it's all over. 31 Peloponnesus southern Greece (from which Antony then crosses the Mediterranean to Egypt) 32 to't to get to it. attend await 33 render surrender 34 horse cavalry. 36 wounded chance broken fortunes 37 Sits . . . me i.e., is on my downwind side, tracking me and hunting me down. 3.11. Location: Historically, events such as dispatching the Schoolmaster to Caesar took place in Egypt; however, the dramatic impression of this scene is that it occurs soon after the battle. 3 lated belated, like a traveler still journeying when night falls 5 fly flee 8 shoulders i.e., backs. 12 that that which 13 mutiny contend among themselves 14 they them i.e., the brown hairs reprove the white

17 Sweep your way clear your way (to Caesar) 18 loathness unwillingness. hint opportunity 19 that i.e., Antony and his cause 20 leaves is untrue to, deserts 23 lost command i.e., of myself and of my authority. 24 pray entreat (as opposed to "command") 35 Yes . . . yes (Antony is absorbed in his own bitter thoughts, as also in lines 29 and 31.) He i.e., Octavius. kept kept in its sheath 36 e'en . . . dancer i.e., as though for ornament only, in a dance 38 ended i.e., defeated. (Not killed; Brutus and Cassius committed suicide.) He alone Caesar merely 39 Dealt on lieutenantry let his subordinates do the fighting 40 brave squares splendid squadrons, bodies of troops drawn up in square formation 41 stand by (Cleopatra indicates she is about to faint and needs assistance.) 43 unqualitied dispossessed of his own nature, i.e., not himself 46 but unless 49 swerving lapse, transgression.

ANTONY
　Oh, whither hast thou led me, Egypt? See　　　　　50
　How I convey my shame out of thine eyes　　　　　51
　By looking back what I have left behind　　　　　52
　'Stroyed in dishonor.
CLEOPATRA　　　　　Oh, my lord, my lord,　　　53
　Forgive my fearful sails! I little thought　　　　54
　You would have followed.
ANTONY　　　　　Egypt, thou knew'st too well
　My heart was to thy rudder tied by th' strings,　　　56
　And thou shouldst tow me after. O'er my spirit
　Thy full supremacy thou knew'st, and that
　Thy beck might from the bidding of the gods　　　59
　Command me.
CLEOPATRA　　　Oh, my pardon!
ANTONY　　　　　Now I must　　　　　60
　To the young man send humble treaties, dodge　　　61
　And palter in the shifts of lowness, who　　　　62
　With half the bulk o'th' world played as I pleased,
　Making and marring fortunes. You did know
　How much you were my conqueror, and that
　My sword, made weak by my affection, would　　　66
　Obey it on all cause.
CLEOPATRA　　　Pardon, pardon!　　　67
ANTONY
　Fall not a tear, I say; one of them rates　　　　68
　All that is won and lost. Give me a kiss.　　[*They kiss.*]
　Even this repays me.—We sent our schoolmaster;　　70
　Is 'a come back?—Love, I am full of lead.—
　Some wine, within there, and our viands! Fortune
　　knows　　　　　72
　We scorn her most when most she offers blows.
　　　　　　　　　　　　　　　　　Exeunt.

❧

[3.12]

Enter Caesar, Agrippa, [Thidias,] and Dolabella,
with others.

CAESAR
　Let him appear that's come from Antony.
　Know you him?
DOLABELLA　　　Caesar, 'tis his schoolmaster—
　An argument that he is plucked, when hither　　　3
　He sends so poor a pinion of his wing,　　　　4
　Which had superfluous kings for messengers　　　5

Not many moons gone by.

　　　Enter Ambassador from Antony.

CAESAR　　　　　Approach and speak.
AMBASSADOR
　Such as I am, I come from Antony.
　I was of late as petty to his ends　　　　　8
　As is the morn-dew on the myrtle leaf
　To his grand sea.
CAESAR　　　　Be't so. Declare thine office.　　10
AMBASSADOR
　Lord of his fortunes he salutes thee, and
　Requires to live in Egypt; which not granted,　　12
　He lessens his requests, and to thee sues　　　13
　To let him breathe between the heavens and earth　14
　A private man in Athens. This for him.
　Next, Cleopatra does confess thy greatness,
　Submits her to thy might, and of thee craves
　The circle of the Ptolemies for her heirs,　　　18
　Now hazarded to thy grace.
CAESAR　　　　　For Antony,　　19
　I have no ears to his request. The Queen
　Of audience nor desire shall fail, so she　　　21
　From Egypt drive her all-disgracèd friend
　Or take his life there. This if she perform
　She shall not sue unheard. So to them both.
AMBASSADOR
　Fortune pursue thee!
CAESAR　　　　Bring him through the bands.　25
　　　　　　　　　[*Exit Ambassador, attended.*]
　[*To Thidias*] To try thy eloquence now 'tis time.
　　Dispatch.
　From Antony win Cleopatra. Promise,
　And in our name, what she requires; add more,　28
　From thine invention, offers. Women are not　29
　In their best fortunes strong, but want will perjure　30
　The ne'er-touched vestal. Try thy cunning, Thidias.　31
　Make thine own edict for thy pains, which we　32
　Will answer as a law.
THIDIAS　　　　Caesar, I go.　　33
CAESAR
　Observe how Antony becomes his flaw,　　　34
　And what thou think'st his very action speaks　　35
　In every power that moves.
THIDIAS　　　　Caesar, I shall.　　*Exeunt.*　36

❧

50–3 **See . . . dishonor** i.e., See how ashamed I am to have you see me
like this, looking back on what I have left behind dishonorably
destroyed.　**54 fearful** timorous　**56 th' strings** (1) the heartstrings
(2) towing cable　**59–60 Thy . . . Command me** your mere beckoning
would command me away from doing the bidding of the gods themselves.　**61 treaties** entreaties, propositions for settlement.　**dodge**
shuffle, cringe　**62 palter** use trickery, prevaricate, equivocate.
shifts of lowness pitiful evasions used by those lacking power
66 affection passion　**67 on all cause** whatever the reason.　**68 Fall**
Let fall.　**rates** equals　**70 Even this** This by itself.　**schoolmaster**
(Identified in Plutarch as Euphronius, tutor to Antony's children by
Cleopatra.)　**72 viands** food.
3.12 Location: Egypt. Caesar's camp.
3 An argument an indication　**4 pinion** i.e., pinion-feather, outer
feather　**5 Which** who

8 petty to insignificant in terms of　**10 To . . . sea** compared to its, the
dewdrop's, great source, the sea.　**thine office** your official business.
12 Requires asks.　**which not granted** and if that request is not
granted　**13 sues** petitions　**14 breathe** i.e., live　**18 circle** crown
19 hazarded . . . grace dependent on your favor.　**For** As for　**21 Of**
audience neither of hearing.　**so** provided that　**25 Bring** Escort.
bands troops on guard, military lines.　**28 requires** asks　**28–9 add . . .**
offers add ideas of your own.　**29–31 Women . . . vestal** Women are
not strong even at the height of their good fortune, but need will
cause even an untouched vestal virgin to break her vows.
31 cunning skill　**32 Make . . . edict** Decree your own reward
33 answer as a law confirm as if it were a law.　**34 becomes his flaw**
bears his misfortune and disgrace　**35–6 And . . . moves** and what
you think his gestures signify in every move he makes.

[3.13]

Enter Cleopatra, Enobarbus, Charmian, and Iras.

CLEOPATRA
  What shall we do, Enobarbus?
ENOBARBUS   Think, and die.   1
CLEOPATRA
  Is Antony or we in fault for this?   2
ENOBARBUS
  Antony only, that would make his will   3
  Lord of his reason. What though you fled
  From that great face of war, whose several ranges   5
  Frighted each other? Why should he follow?
  The itch of his affection should not then   7
  Have nicked his captainship, at such a point,   8
  When half to half the world opposed, he being   9
  The merèd question. 'Twas a shame no less   10
  Than was his loss, to course your flying flags   11
  And leave his navy gazing.
CLEOPATRA   Prithee, peace.

Enter the Ambassador with Antony.

ANTONY   Is that his answer?
AMBASSADOR   Ay, my lord.
ANTONY
  The Queen shall then have courtesy, so she   15
  Will yield us up.
AMBASSADOR   He says so.
ANTONY   Let her know't.—
  To the boy Caesar send this grizzled head,
  And he will fill thy wishes to the brim
  With principalities.
CLEOPATRA   That head, my lord?
ANTONY [*to the Ambassador*]
  To him again. Tell him he wears the rose
  Of youth upon him, from which the world should
    note
  Something particular. His coin, ships, legions,   22
  May be a coward's, whose ministers would prevail   23
  Under the service of a child as soon
  As i'th' command of Caesar. I dare him therefore
  To lay his gay caparisons apart   26
  And answer me declined, sword against sword,   27
  Ourselves alone. I'll write it. Follow me.
            [Exeunt Antony and Ambassador.]
ENOBARBUS [*aside*]
  Yes, like enough, high-battled Caesar will   29

Unstate his happiness and be staged to th' show   30
Against a sworder! I see men's judgments are   31
A parcel of their fortunes, and things outward   32
Do draw the inward quality after them   33
To suffer all alike. That he should dream,   34
Knowing all measures, the full Caesar will   35
Answer his emptiness! Caesar, thou hast subdued   36
His judgment too.

Enter a Servant.

SERVANT   A messenger from Caesar.
CLEOPATRA
  What, no more ceremony? See, my women,
  Against the blown rose may they stop their nose   39
  That kneeled unto the buds.—Admit him, sir.
            [Exit Servant.]
ENOBARBUS [*aside*]
  Mine honesty and I begin to square.   41
  The loyalty well held to fools does make   42
  Our faith mere folly; yet he that can endure   43
  To follow with allegiance a fall'n lord
  Does conquer him that did his master conquer   45
  And earns a place i'th' story.

Enter Thidias.

CLEOPATRA   Caesar's will?
THIDIAS
  Hear it apart.
CLEOPATRA   None but friends. Say boldly.   47
THIDIAS
  So haply are they friends to Antony.   48
ENOBARBUS
  He needs as many, sir, as Caesar has,
  Or needs not us. If Caesar please, our master   50
  Will leap to be his friend. For us, you know   51
  Whose he is we are, and that is Caesar's.
THIDIAS   So.   52
  Thus then, thou most renowned: Caesar entreats
  Not to consider in what case thou stand'st   54
  Further than he is Caesar.
CLEOPATRA   Go on: right royal.   55

3.13. Location: Alexandria. Cleopatra's palace.
1 Think, and die Think despondently, and die of melancholy or by suicide. **2 we** I **3 will** desire (especially sexual) **5 ranges** ranks, lines (of ships) **7 affection** sexual passion **8 nicked** cut short or maimed, or got the better of. **point** crisis **9–10 When . . . question** when the two halves of the world found themselves in conflict, Antony being the sole ground of the quarrel. **11 course** pursue (as in hunting) **15 so** provided that **22 Something particular** some exceptional exploit. **23 May be** could as well be. **ministers** agents, subordinates **26 gay caparisons** resplendent trappings **27 answer me declined** meet me as I am, lowered in fortune and advanced in years **29 like** likely. **high-battled** provided with a mighty army

30–1 Unstate . . . sworder set aside his advantageous fortune and be exhibited publicly in a sword-fight contest with a mere gladiator. **31–4 I see . . . alike** I see that men's judgments are inextricably linked to their fortunes, whereby outward circumstances draw after them inward qualities of character in such a way that both suffer at the same time. **35 Knowing all measures** i.e., having experienced every degree of fortune. **full** at full fortune **36 Answer** (1) meet man to man with (2) correspond with **39 blown** overblown, starting to decay **41 honesty** (With meaning also of "honor.") **square** quarrel. **42–3 The . . . folly** A stubborn loyalty bestowed on fools is folly itself **45 Does . . . conquer** i.e., achieves a moral victory over the very fortune or the person that subdued one's own master **47 apart** in private. **48 haply** perhaps **50 Or . . . us** i.e., or else he doesn't need even us, his case being hopeless. **51 For** As for **52 Whose . . . Caesar's** i.e., we are Antony's friends, and he is Caesar's, so that we, too, are Caesar's. **54–5 Not . . . Caesar** i.e., not to worry about your situation other than to consider that you are dealing with Caesar, the embodiment of magnanimity. **55 right royal** i.e., that is very magnanimous.

THIDIAS
    He knows that you embrace not Antony
    As you did love, but as you feared him.
CLEOPATRA   Oh!
THIDIAS
    The scars upon your honor therefore he
    Does pity as constrainèd blemishes,
    Not as deserved.
CLEOPATRA   He is a god and knows
    What is most right. Mine honor was not yielded,   61
    But conquered merely.
ENOBARBUS [aside]   To be sure of that,   62
    I will ask Antony. Sir, sir, thou art so leaky
    That we must leave thee to thy sinking, for
    Thy dearest quit thee.   Exit Enobarbus.
THIDIAS   Shall I say to Caesar
    What you require of him? For he partly begs   66
    To be desired to give. It much would please him
    That of his fortunes you should make a staff
    To lean upon; but it would warm his spirits
    To hear from me you had left Antony
    And put yourself under his shroud,   71
    The universal landlord.
CLEOPATRA   What's your name?
THIDIAS
    My name is Thidias.
CLEOPATRA   Most kind messenger,
    Say to great Caesar this in deputation: 74
    I kiss his conquering hand. Tell him I am prompt 75
    To lay my crown at 's feet, and there to kneel
    Till from his all-obeying breath I hear   77
    The doom of Egypt.
THIDIAS   'Tis your noblest course.   78
    Wisdom and fortune combating together,   79
    If that the former dare but what it can,   80
    No chance may shake it. Give me grace to lay   81
    My duty on your hand.   [He kisses her hand.]
CLEOPATRA   Your Caesar's father oft,   83
    When he hath mused of taking kingdoms in,   84
    Bestowed his lips on that unworthy place,
    As it rained kisses.

       Enter Antony and Enobarbus.

ANTONY   Favors? By Jove that thunders!   86
    What art thou, fellow?
THIDIAS   One that but performs
    The bidding of the fullest man, and worthiest   88
    To have command obeyed.
ENOBARBUS [aside]   You will be whipped.

ANTONY [calling for Servants]
    Approach, there!—Ah, you kite!—Now, gods and
      devils!   90
    Authority melts from me of late. When I cried "Ho!",
    Like boys unto a muss kings would start forth   92
    And cry, "Your will?"—Have you no ears? I am
    Antony yet.

       Enter a Servant [followed by others].

       Take hence this jack and whip him.   94
ENOBARBUS [aside]
    'Tis better playing with a lion's whelp   95
    Than with an old one dying.
ANTONY   Moon and stars!
    Whip him. Were't twenty of the greatest tributaries   97
    That do acknowledge Caesar, should I find them
    So saucy with the hand of she here—what's her name
    Since she was Cleopatra? Whip him, fellows,
    Till like a boy you see him cringe his face   101
    And whine aloud for mercy. Take him hence.
THIDIAS
    Mark Antony—
ANTONY   Tug him away! Being whipped,
    Bring him again. This jack of Caesar's shall
    Bear us an errand to him.
       Exeunt [Servants] with Thidias.
    [To Cleopatra] You were half blasted ere I knew you.
      Ha?   106
    Have I my pillow left unpressed in Rome,
    Forborne the getting of a lawful race,   108
    And by a gem of women, to be abused   109
    By one that looks on feeders?   110
CLEOPATRA   Good my lord—
ANTONY   You have been a boggler ever.   112
    But when we in our viciousness grow hard—
    Oh, misery on't!—the wise gods seel our eyes,   114
    In our own filth drop our clear judgments, make us
    Adore our errors, laugh at 's while we strut
    To our confusion.
CLEOPATRA   Oh, is't come to this?   117
ANTONY
    I found you as a morsel cold upon
    Dead Caesar's trencher; nay, you were a fragment   119
    Of Gnaeus Pompey's, besides what hotter hours,   120
    Unregistered in vulgar fame, you have   121
    Luxuriously picked out. For I am sure,   122
    Though you can guess what temperance should be,

---

61 right true.   **62 merely** utterly.   **66 require** ask.   **partly** i.e., as commensurate with his dignity   **71 shroud** shelter. (With suggestion too of a burial cloth.)   **74 in deputation** by you as deputy   **75 prompt** ready   **77 all-obeying** obeyed by all   **78 The doom of Egypt** i.e., my fate.   **79–81 Wisdom . . . shake it** When wisdom and fortune are at odds, if the wise person will have the resolution to desire only what what fortune will allow, then fortune cannot shake that wisdom.   **83 Your Caesar's father** i.e., Julius Caesar, actually Octavius' great-uncle. (See note at 3.6.6.)   **84 mused . . . in** thought about conquering kingdoms   **86 As** as if   **88 fullest** most fortunate, best

90 kite a rapacious bird of prey that feeds on ignoble objects, and a slang word for "whore." (Said of Cleopatra.)   **92 muss** game in which small objects are thrown down to be scrambled for   **94 jack** fellow. (Contemptuous.)   **95 whelp** cub   **97 tributaries** rulers paying tribute   **101 cringe** contract in pain   **106 blasted** withered, blighted   **108 getting** begetting.   **lawful** legitimate   **109 abused** deceived, betrayed   **110 feeders** servants.   **112 boggler** waverer, shifty person. (Often used of shying horses.)   **114 seel** blind. (A term in falconry for sewing shut the eyes of wild hawks in order to tame them.)   **117 confusion** destruction.   **119 trencher** wooden plate.   **fragment** leftover   **120 Gnaeus Pompey's** (See 1.5.32 and note.)   **121 vulgar fame** common gossip   **122 Luxuriously** lustfully

You know not what it is.

CLEOPATRA   Wherefore is this?   124

ANTONY
To let a fellow that will take rewards
And say "God quit you!" be familiar with   126
My playfellow, your hand, this kingly seal
And plighter of high hearts! Oh, that I were   128
Upon the hill of Basan, to outroar   129
The hornèd herd! For I have savage cause,   130
And to proclaim it civilly were like
A haltered neck which does the hangman thank
For being yare about him.

Enter a Servant with Thidias.

                              Is he whipped?   133

SERVANT   Soundly, my lord.
ANTONY   Cried he? And begged 'a pardon?
SERVANT   He did ask favor.
ANTONY [*to Thidias*]
If that thy father live, let him repent
Thou wast not made his daughter; and be thou sorry
To follow Caesar in his triumph, since
Thou hast been whipped for following him.
    Henceforth
The white hand of a lady fever thee;   141
Shake thou to look on't. Get thee back to Caesar.
Tell him thy entertainment. Look thou say   143
He makes me angry with him; for he seems
Proud and disdainful, harping on what I am,
Not what he knew I was. He makes me angry,
And at this time most easy 'tis to do't,
When my good stars, that were my former guides,
Have empty left their orbs and shot their fires   149
Into th'abysm of hell. If he mislike   150
My speech and what is done, tell him he has
Hipparchus, my enfranchèd bondman, whom   152
He may at pleasure whip, or hang, or torture,
As he shall like, to quit me. Urge it thou.   154
Hence with thy stripes, begone!
                    Exit [Servant with] Thidias.
CLEOPATRA   Have you done yet?
ANTONY
Alack, our terrene moon is now eclipsed,   156
And it portends alone the fall of Antony.
CLEOPATRA   I must stay his time.   158
ANTONY
To flatter Caesar, would you mingle eyes

With one that ties his points?

CLEOPATRA   Not know me yet?   160

ANTONY
Coldhearted toward me?

CLEOPATRA   Ah, dear, if I be so,
From my cold heart let heaven engender hail,
And poison it in the source, and the first stone
Drop in my neck; as it determines, so   164
Dissolve my life! The next Caesarion smite,
Till by degrees the memory of my womb,   166
Together with my brave Egyptians all,   167
By the discandying of this pelleted storm   168
Lie graveless till the flies and gnats of Nile
Have buried them for prey!

ANTONY   I am satisfied.   170
Caesar sits down in Alexandria, where   171
I will oppose his fate. Our force by land   172
Hath nobly held; our severed navy too
Have knit again, and fleet, threat'ning most sealike. 174
Where hast thou been, my heart? Dost thou hear,
    lady?   175
If from the field I shall return once more
To kiss these lips, I will appear in blood;   177
I and my sword will earn our chronicle.   178
There's hope in't yet.
CLEOPATRA   That's my brave lord!
ANTONY
I will be treble-sinewed, hearted, breathed,   181
And fight maliciously. For when mine hours   182
Were nice and lucky, men did ransom lives   183
Of me for jests; but now I'll set my teeth   184
And send to darkness all that stop me. Come,   185
Let's have one other gaudy night. Call to me   186
All my sad captains. Fill our bowls once more;
Let's mock the midnight bell.
CLEOPATRA   It is my birthday.
I had thought t'have held it poor; but since my lord 189
Is Antony again, I will be Cleopatra.
ANTONY   We will yet do well.
CLEOPATRA [*to attendants*]
Call all his noble captains to my lord.
ANTONY
Do so. We'll speak to them, and tonight I'll force
The wine peep through their scars. Come on, my
    queen,
There's sap in't yet. The next time I do fight   195

---

124 Wherefore is this? i.e., What brought this on?   **126 quit** reward. (*God quit you* is said obsequiously to acknowledge a tip.)   **128 plighter** pledger   **129–30 hill of Basan . . . The hornèd herd** (Allusion to the strong bulls of Bashan, Psalms 22:12 and 68:15. Antony imagines himself as the greatest horned beast, i.e., cuckold, of that herd.)   **133 yare** deft, quick   **141 fever thee** make you shiver   **143 entertainment** reception.   **Look** Be sure that   **149 orbs** spheres   **150 th'abysm** the abyss   **152 Hipparchus** (According to Plutarch, the man was a deserter to Caesar's side.)   **enfranchèd** enfranchised, freed   **154 quit** requite, pay back   **156 our . . . eclipsed** i.e., (1) the moon in eclipse portends disaster (2) the waning of the love of Cleopatra (equated with Isis, the moon goddess) spells the end for me   **158 stay his time** i.e., be patient until his fury has subsided.

160 ties his points i.e., helps Caesar as a valet with the metal-tipped laces used to fasten articles of clothing.   **164 neck** throat or head.   **determines** comes to an end, dissolves. (See line 168.)   **166 memory of my womb** i.e., my offspring   **167 brave** splendid. (Also in line 180.)   **168 discandying** melting.   **pelleted** falling in pellets   **170 for prey** i.e., by eating them.   **171 sits down in** lays siege to   **172 oppose his fate** confront his (seemingly irresistible) fortune.   **174 fleet** float   **175 heart** courage.   **177 in blood** (1) bloody from battle (2) full-spirited.   **178 chronicle** place in history.   **181 treble-sinewed . . . breathed** thrice myself in strength, courage, and endurance   **182 maliciously** violently, fiercely.   **183 nice** delicate, refined   **183–4 men . . . jests** I allowed enemies to be ransomed for trifles or as a magnanimous gesture   **185 to darkness** i.e., to death, the underworld   **186 gaudy** festive   **189 held it poor** celebrated it simply   **195 sap in't** i.e., life in our enterprise

I'll make Death love me, for I will contend   196
Even with his pestilent scythe.
                        Exeunt [all but Enobarbus].

ENOBARBUS
Now he'll outstare the lightning. To be furious   198
Is to be frighted out of fear, and in that mood
The dove will peck the estridge; and I see still   200
A diminution in our captain's brain
Restores his heart. When valor preys on reason,   202
It eats the sword it fights with. I will seek   203
Some way to leave him.   *Exit.*

❖

[4.1]

*Enter Caesar, Agrippa, and Maecenas, with his
army, Caesar reading a letter.*

CAESAR
He calls me boy, and chides as he had power   1
To beat me out of Egypt. My messenger
He hath whipped with rods, dares me to personal
   combat,
Caesar to Antony. Let the old ruffian know
I have many other ways to die, meantime
Laugh at his challenge.
MAECENAS   Caesar must think,
When one so great begins to rage, he's hunted   8
Even to falling. Give him no breath, but now   9
Make boot of his distraction. Never anger   10
Made good guard for itself.
CAESAR   Let our best heads   11
Know that tomorrow the last of many battles
We mean to fight. Within our files there are,   13
Of those that served Mark Antony but late,   14
Enough to fetch him in. See it done,   15
And feast the army; we have store to do't,   16
And they have earned the waste. Poor Antony!   17
                              Exeunt.

♣

[4.2]

*Enter Antony, Cleopatra, Enobarbus,
Charmian, Iras, Alexas, with others.*

ANTONY
He will not fight with me, Domitius?

ENOBARBUS   No.
ANTONY   Why should he not?
ENOBARBUS
He thinks, being twenty times of better fortune,
He is twenty men to one.
ANTONY   Tomorrow, soldier,
By sea and land I'll fight. Or I will live   6
Or bathe my dying honor in the blood
Shall make it live again. Woo't thou fight well?   8
ENOBARBUS
I'll strike, and cry, "Take all."
ANTONY   Well said. Come on!   9
Call forth my household servants. Let's tonight   10

Enter three or four servitors.

Be bounteous at our meal.—Give me thy hand.
Thou hast been rightly honest—so hast thou—   12
Thou—and thou—and thou. You have served me
   well,
And kings have been your fellows.
CLEOPATRA [*aside to Enobarbus*]   What means this?   14
ENOBARBUS [*aside to Cleopatra*]
'Tis one of those odd tricks which sorrow shoots
Out of the mind.
ANTONY   And thou art honest too.
I wish I could be made so many men,   17
And all of you clapped up together in   18
An Antony, that I might do you service
So good as you have done.
ALL   The gods forbid!
ANTONY
Well, my good fellows, wait on me tonight:
Scant not my cups, and make as much of me   22
As when mine empire was your fellow too,   23
And suffered my command.
CLEOPATRA [*aside to Enobarbus*]   What does he mean?   24
ENOBARBUS [*aside to Cleopatra*]
To make his followers weep.
ANTONY   Tend me tonight;
May be it is the period of your duty.   26
Haply you shall not see me more, or if,   27
A mangled shadow. Perchance tomorrow   28
You'll serve another master. I look on you
As one that takes his leave. Mine honest friends,
I turn you not away, but, like a master
Married to your good service, stay till death.
Tend me tonight two hours, I ask no more,
And the gods yield you for't!
ENOBARBUS   What mean you, sir,   34
To give them this discomfort? Look, they weep,

196–7 I will . . . scythe i.e., I will outdo even Death himself and his
scythe of *pestilence* or plague.   **198 outstare** stare down.   **furious**
frenzied   **200 estridge** ostrich, or, a kind of hawk.   **still** constantly
202–3 When . . . with When valor turns to unreasonable fury, it
destroys the very quality of reasonableness that valor depends on in
battle.
4.1 Location: Before Alexandria. Caesar's camp.
1 as as if   **8 rage** rave   **9 breath** breathing space   **10 boot** advantage.
distraction frenzy.   **11 best heads** commanding officers   **13 files** (As
in "rank and file.")   **14 late** lately   **15 fetch him in** surround, capture him.   **16 store** provisions   **17 waste** lavish expenditure.
4.2 Location: Alexandria. Cleopatra's palace.

6 Or Either   **8 Shall** that will.   **Woo't** Wilt   **9 strike . . . Take all**
(1) fight to the finish, crying, "Winner take all" (2) strike sail and surrender.   **10.1 *servitors*** attendants.   **12 honest** true, loyal   **14 fellows** i.e., fellow servants of me.   **17 made . . . men** divided into as
many men as you are   **18 clapped up** combined   **22 Scant not my
cups** i.e., Provide generously   **23 fellow** i.e., fellow servant   **24 suffered** acknowledged, submitted to   **26 period** end   **27 Haply** Perhaps.   **if** if you do   **28 shadow** ghost.   **34 yield** reward

And I, an ass, am onion-eyed. For shame,
Transform us not to women.
ANTONY   Ho, ho, ho!
Now the witch take me if I meant it thus!   38
Grace grow where those drops fall! My hearty friends,   39
You take me in too dolorous a sense,
For I spake to you for your comfort, did desire you
To burn this night with torches. Know, my hearts,   42
I hope well of tomorrow, and will lead you
Where rather I'll expect victorious life
Than death and honor. Let's to supper, come,
And drown consideration.   Exeunt.   46

❧

[4.3]

Enter a company of Soldiers.

FIRST SOLDIER
Brother, good night. Tomorrow is the day.
SECOND SOLDIER
It will determine one way. Fare you well.   2
Heard you of nothing strange about the streets?   3
FIRST SOLDIER   Nothing. What news?
SECOND SOLDIER
Belike 'tis but a rumor. Good night to you.   5
FIRST SOLDIER   Well, sir, good night.

They meet other Soldiers.

SECOND SOLDIER   Soldiers, have careful watch.
THIRD SOLDIER   And you. Good night, good night.
                They place themselves in every corner of the stage.
SECOND SOLDIER   Here we. And if tomorrow   9
Our navy thrive, I have an absolute hope
Our landmen will stand up.
FIRST SOLDIER   'Tis a brave army, and full of purpose.   12
                Music of the hautboys is under the stage.
SECOND SOLDIER   Peace! What noise?
FIRST SOLDIER   List, list!   14
SECOND SOLDIER   Hark!
FIRST SOLDIER   Music i'th'air.
THIRD SOLDIER   Under the earth.
FOURTH SOLDIER   It signs well, does it not?   18
THIRD SOLDIER   No.
FIRST SOLDIER   Peace, I say! What should this mean?
SECOND SOLDIER
'Tis the god Hercules, whom Antony loved,
Now leaves him.
FIRST SOLDIER   Walk; let's see if other watchmen
Do hear what we do.
                [*They advance toward their fellow watchmen.*]
SECOND SOLDIER   How now, masters?   24

ALL [*speak together*]   How now? How now? Do you
   hear this?
FIRST SOLDIER   Ay. Is't not strange?
THIRD SOLDIER   Do you hear, masters? Do you hear?
FIRST SOLDIER
Follow the noise so far as we have quarter;   29
Let's see how it will give off.   30
ALL   Content. 'Tis strange.   *Exeunt.*

❧

[4.4]

*Enter Antony and Cleopatra, with [Charmian and]
others [attending].*

ANTONY
Eros! Mine armor, Eros!
CLEOPATRA   Sleep a little.
ANTONY
No, my chuck.—Eros, come, mine armor, Eros!   2

Enter Eros [with armor].

Come, good fellow, put thine iron on.   3
If fortune be not ours today, it is
Because we brave her. Come.
CLEOPATRA   Nay, I'll help too.   5
What's this for?   [*She helps to arm him.*]
ANTONY   Ah, let be, let be! Thou art
The armorer of my heart. False, false; this, this.   7
CLEOPATRA
Sooth, la, I'll help. Thus it must be.
ANTONY   Well, well,   8
We shall thrive now. See'st thou, my good fellow?
Go, put on thy defenses.
EROS   Briefly, sir.   10
CLEOPATRA
Is not this buckled well?
ANTONY   Rarely, rarely.   11
He that unbuckles this, till we do please   12
To doff't for our repose, shall hear a storm.   13
Thou fumblest, Eros, and my queen's a squire   14
More tight at this than thou. Dispatch. O love,   15
That thou couldst see my wars today, and knew'st   16
The royal occupation! Thou shouldst see   17
A workman in't.

Enter an armed Soldier.

                        Good morrow to thee. Welcome.   18
Thou look'st like him that knows a warlike charge. 19

---

29 **as we have quarter** as our watch post extends.   30 **give off** cease.
4.4. Location: Alexandria. The palace.
2 **chuck** (A term of endearment.)   3 **thine iron** i.e., my armor that
you have there. (Or perhaps he is telling Eros to arm.)   5 **brave** defy
7 **False** You're putting it on wrong   8 **Sooth** In truth   10 **defenses**
armor.   **Briefly** In a moment   11 **Rarely** Excellently   12–13 **He . . .
storm** i.e., Anyone who attempts to burst my armor in the fight,
before I choose myself to unarm and rest, will be greeted by a storm
of blows.   14 **squire** armor-bearer of a knight   15 **tight** deft, skillful.
Dispatch Finish up.   16–17 **knew'st . . . occupation** (would that) you
could appreciate how excellently I carry out the royal art of warfare.
18 **workman** craftsman, professional   19 **charge** duty, responsibility.

---

38 **the witch take me** may I be bewitched   39 **Grace grow** (1) May
rue or herb of grace grow (2) May gracious fortune flourish.   **hearty**
loving   42 **burn . . . torches** i.e., revel through the night.   46 **drown
consideration** drown brooding thought in our winecups.
4.3 Location: Alexandria. Before the palace.
2 **determine one way** be decided, come to an end one way or the
other.   3 **about** in   5 **Belike** Probably   9 **Here we** Here's our station.   12 **brave** splendid, gallant   12.1 **hautboys** oboelike instruments   14 **List** Listen   18 **signs well** is a good sign   24 **masters**
good sirs. (Also in line 28.)

To business that we love we rise betimes 20
And go to't with delight.

SOLDIER   A thousand, sir,
Early though 't be, have on their riveted trim 22
And at the port expect you.   *Shout. Trumpets flourish.* 23

Enter Captains and soldiers.

CAPTAIN
The morn is fair. Good morrow, General.

ALL
Good morrow, General.

ANTONY   'Tis well blown, lads. 25
This morning, like the spirit of a youth
That means to be of note, begins betimes.
So, so. Come, give me that. This way. Well said. 28
Fare thee well, dame. Whate'er becomes of me,
This is a soldier's kiss. [*He kisses her.*] Rebukable,
And worthy shameful check it were, to stand 31
On more mechanic compliment. I'll leave thee 32
Now like a man of steel.—You that will fight,
Follow me close. I'll bring you to't. Adieu.
                Exeunt [Antony, Eros, Captains, and soldiers].

CHARMIAN
Please you, retire to your chamber?

CLEOPATRA   Lead me.
He goes forth gallantly. That he and Caesar might
Determine this great war in single fight!
Then Antony—but now—Well, on.   *Exeunt.*

❖

[4.5]

*Trumpets sound. Enter Antony and Eros; [a
Soldier meeting them].*

SOLDIER
The gods make this a happy day to Antony! 1

ANTONY
Would thou and those thy scars had once prevailed 2
To make me fight at land!

SOLDIER   Hadst thou done so,
The kings that have revolted, and the soldier 4
That has this morning left thee, would have still
Followed thy heels.

ANTONY   Who's gone this morning?

SOLDIER   Who?
One ever near thee. Call for Enobarbus,
He shall not hear thee, or from Caesar's camp
Say, "I am none of thine."

ANTONY   What sayest thou?

SOLDIER   Sir,
He is with Caesar.

EROS   Sir, his chests and treasure

He has not with him.

ANTONY   Is he gone?

SOLDIER   Most certain.

ANTONY
Go, Eros, send his treasure after. Do it.
Detain no jot, I charge thee. Write to him—
I will subscribe—gentle adieus and greetings. 14
Say that I wish he never find more cause
To change a master. Oh, my fortunes have
Corrupted honest men! Dispatch.—Enobarbus! 17
                                        Exeunt.

❖

[4.6]

*Flourish. Enter Agrippa, Caesar, with Enobarbus,
and Dolabella.*

CAESAR
Go forth, Agrippa, and begin the fight.
Our will is Antony be took alive;
Make it so known.

AGRIPPA   Caesar, I shall.   [*Exit.*]

CAESAR
The time of universal peace is near. 5
Prove this a prosp'rous day, the three-nooked world 6
Shall bear the olive freely.

Enter a Messenger.

MESSENGER   Antony 7
Is come into the field.

CAESAR   Go charge Agrippa 8
Plant those that have revolted in the van, 9
That Antony may seem to spend his fury
Upon himself.   *Exeunt [all but Enobarbus].*

ENOBARBUS
Alexas did revolt and went to Jewry on 12
Affairs of Antony, there did dissuade 13
Great Herod to incline himself to Caesar
And leave his master Antony. For this pains,
Caesar hath hanged him. Canidius and the rest
That fell away have entertainment but 17
No honorable trust. I have done ill,
Of which I do accuse myself so sorely 19
That I will joy no more.

Enter a Soldier of Caesar's.

SOLDIER   Enobarbus, Antony
Hath after thee sent all thy treasure, with
His bounty overplus. The messenger 22

---

20 **betimes** early   22 **riveted trim** i.e., armor riveted into place
23 **port** gate   25 **'Tis well blown** i.e., The morning begins well. (Or,
refers to trumpets in line 23 s.d.)   28 **Well said** Well done.   31 **check**
reproof   31–2 **stand . . . compliment** insist on vulgar and routine ceremonies of leavetaking.
4.5. Location: Before Alexandria. Antony's camp.
1 **happy** fortunate   2 **once** formerly   4 **revolted** deserted

14 **subscribe** sign   17 **Dispatch** Make haste, get on with it.
4.6. Location: Before Alexandria. Caesar's camp.
5 **The . . . near** (The Renaissance identified Octavius Caesar, or the
Emperor Augustus as he was subsequently titled, with this *Pax
Romana*, peace under the Roman Empire.)   6 **Prove this** If this prove
to be.   **three-nooked** three-cornered. (Refers to Asia, Europe, and
Africa.)   7 **bear** (1) bring forth (2) wear as a triumphal garland.
olive symbol of peace   8 **charge Agrippa** order Agrippa to   9 **van**
vanguard, front lines   12 **Jewry** Judaea   13 **dissuade** i.e., from following Antony   17 **entertainment** employment, maintenance
19 **sorely** heavily   22 **overplus** in addition.

Came on my guard, and at thy tent is now   23
Unloading of his mules.
ENOBARBUS   I give it you.
SOLDIER   Mock not, Enobarbus,
I tell you true. Best you safed the bringer   27
Out of the host. I must attend mine office,   28
Or would have done't myself. Your emperor
Continues still a Jove.   *Exit.*
ENOBARBUS
I am alone the villain of the earth,   31
And feel I am so most. O Antony,   32
Thou mine of bounty, how wouldst thou have paid   33
My better service, when my turpitude
Thou dost so crown with gold! This blows my heart. 35
If swift thought break it not, a swifter mean   36
Shall outstrike thought; but thought will do't, I feel. 37
I fight against thee? No, I will go seek
Some ditch wherein to die. The foul'st best fits
My latter part of life.   *Exit.*

❧

[4.7]

*Alarum. Drums and trumpets. Enter Agrippa
[and others].*

AGRIPPA
Retire! We have engaged ourselves too far.
Caesar himself has work, and our oppression   2
Exceeds what we expected.   *Exeunt.*   3

Alarums. Enter Antony, and Scarus wounded.

SCARUS
O my brave Emperor, this is fought indeed!
Had we done so at first, we had droven them home   5
With clouts about their heads.
ANTONY   Thou bleed'st apace.   6
SCARUS
I had a wound here that was like a T,
But now 'tis made an H.   *[Sound retreat] far off.*
ANTONY   They do retire.   8
SCARUS
We'll beat 'em into bench holes. I have yet   9
Room for six scotches more.   10

Enter Eros.

EROS
They are beaten, sir, and our advantage serves   11
For a fair victory.
SCARUS   Let us score their backs   12
And snatch 'em up, as we take hares, behind!
'Tis sport to maul a runner.
ANTONY   I will reward thee   14
Once for thy spritely comfort and tenfold
For thy good valor. Come thee on.
SCARUS   I'll halt after.   *Exeunt.*   17

❧

[4.8]

*Alarum. Enter Antony again in a march; Scarus,
with others.*

ANTONY
We have beat him to his camp. Run one before   1
And let the Queen know of our gests. *[Exit a Soldier.]*
                        Tomorrow,   2
Before the sun shall see 's, we'll spill the blood
That has today escaped. I thank you all,
For doughty-handed are you, and have fought   5
Not as you served the cause, but as't had been   6
Each man's like mine; you have shown all Hectors.   7
Enter the city, clip your wives, your friends,   8
Tell them your feats, whilst they with joyful tears
Wash the congealment from your wounds and kiss
The honored gashes whole.

Enter Cleopatra [attended].

                    [To Scarus] Give me thy hand;
To this great fairy I'll commend thy acts,   12
Make her thanks bless thee. *[To Cleopatra]* O thou day
o'th' world,   13
Chain mine armed neck; leap thou, attire and all,   14
Through proof of harness to my heart, and there   15
Ride on the pants triumphing!   *[They embrace.]*
CLEOPATRA   Lord of lords,   16
O infinite virtue, com'st thou smiling from   17
The world's great snare uncaught?
ANTONY   My nightingale,
We have beat them to their beds. What, girl, though
gray
Do something mingle with our younger brown, yet
ha' we   20
A brain that nourishes our nerves and can   21

---

23 **on my guard** while I was standing guard   27 **Best you safed** You
would do well to provide safe-conduct for   28 **host** army.   **attend
mine office** see to my duties   31 **alone** the the only, the greatest
32 **And . . . most** and am the one who feels it most.   33 **mine** abundant store   35 **blows** causes to swell to the bursting point   36 **mean**
i.e., suicide   37 **thought** melancholy.   **do't** i.e., break my heart
4.7. Location: Field of battle between the camps.
2 has work is hard pressed.   **our oppression** the heavy attacks
against us   **3 s.d. Exeunt** (The cleared stage technically marks a new
scene, although the alarums provide a sense of continuous action.)
5 droven driven   **6 clouts** (1) bandages (2) blows and knocks
8 H i.e., the bottom of the T has been cut across to make an H lying
on its side. (There is a pun on *ache*, pronounced *aitch*.)   **9 bench
holes** the holes of privies, i.e., any desperate place to hide.
10 scotches cuts

11–12 our . . . victory i.e., we are in such a favorable position that a
complete victory seems in prospect.   **12 score** mark by cuts from a
whip   **14 a runner** one in retreat.   **17 halt** limp
4.8. Location: Before Alexandria. The action is virtually continuous.
1 beat driven.   **Run one** Let someone run   **2 gests** deeds.
5 doughty-handed valiant   **6–7 Not . . . mine** not as if you were
merely serving the general cause, but as if it were your cause personally   **7 shown** shown yourselves   **8 clip** embrace   **12 fairy**
enchantress, dispenser of good fortune   **13 day** light   **14 Chain . . .
neck** hang around my neck in an embrace like a medal on a chain
15 proof of harness proof-armor, tested armor   **16 pants** heartbeats
17 virtue valor   **20 something** somewhat   **21 nerves** sinews, tendons

Get goal for goal of youth. Behold this man;   22
Commend unto his lips thy favoring hand.—   23
Kiss it, my warrior. [*Scarus kisses Cleopatra's hand.*] He
    hath fought today
As if a god, in hate of mankind, had
Destroyed in such a shape.

CLEOPATRA   I'll give thee, friend,
An armor all of gold; it was a king's.

ANTONY
He has deserved it, were it carbuncled   28
Like holy Phoebus' car. Give me thy hand.   29
Through Alexandria make a jolly march;
Bear our hacked targets like the men that owe them.   31
Had our great palace the capacity
To camp this host, we all would sup together   33
And drink carouses to the next day's fate,   34
Which promises royal peril. Trumpeters,   35
With brazen din blast you the city's ear;
Make mingle with our rattling taborins,   37
That heaven and earth may strike their sounds
    together,   38
Applauding our approach. [*Trumpets sound.*] *Exeunt.*

❖

[4.9]

*Enter a Sentry and his company. Enobarbus
follows.*

SENTRY
If we be not relieved within this hour,
We must return to th' court of guard. The night   2
Is shiny, and they say we shall embattle   3
By the second hour i'th' morn.
FIRST WATCH   This last day was a shrewd one to 's.   5
ENOBARBUS   Oh, bear me witness, night—
SECOND WATCH
What man is this?
FIRST WATCH   Stand close, and list him.   8
                    [*They stand aside.*]

ENOBARBUS
Be witness to me, O thou blessèd moon,
When men revolted shall upon record   10
Bear hateful memory: poor Enobarbus did
Before thy face repent.
SENTRY   Enobarbus?
SECOND WATCH   Peace! Hark further.

ENOBARBUS
O sovereign mistress of true melancholy,   15
The poisonous damp of night dispunge upon me,   16
That life, a very rebel to my will,
May hang no longer on me. Throw my heart
Against the flint and hardness of my fault,
Which, being dried with grief, will break to powder   20
And finish all foul thoughts. O Antony,
Nobler than my revolt is infamous,
Forgive me in thine own particular,   23
But let the world rank me in register   24
A master-leaver and a fugitive.   25
O Antony! O Antony!   [*He dies.*]
FIRST WATCH   Let's speak to him.
SENTRY
Let's hear him, for the things he speaks
May concern Caesar.
SECOND WATCH   Let's do so. But he sleeps.
SENTRY
Swoons rather, for so bad a prayer as his
Was never yet for sleep.
FIRST WATCH   Go we to him.   31
                    [*They approach Enobarbus.*]
SECOND WATCH   Awake, sir, awake. Speak to us.
FIRST WATCH   Hear you, sir?
SENTRY   The hand of death hath raught him.   34
                        Drums afar off.
Hark, the drums demurely wake the sleepers.   35
Let us bear him to th' court of guard;
He is of note. Our hour is fully out.   37
SECOND WATCH
Come on, then. He may recover yet.
                    Exeunt [*with the body*].

❖

[4.10]

Enter Antony and Scarus, with their army.

ANTONY
Their preparation is today by sea;
We please them not by land.
SCARUS   For both, my lord.
ANTONY
I would they'd fight i'th' fire or i'th' air;   3
We'd fight there too. But this it is: our foot   4
Upon the hills adjoining to the city
Shall stay with us—order for sea is given;   6

---

22 **Get . . . of** i.e., stay competitively equal with. **this man** i.e., Scarus
23 **Commend** Entrust, commit 28 **carbuncled** set with jewels
29 **Phoebus' car** the chariot of the sun. 31 **Bear . . . them** bear our
hacked shields, well suited to the warriors who, like their shields,
have sustained blows. (*Owe* means "own.") 33 **camp this host**
accommodate this army 34 **carouses** toasts 35 **royal peril** i.e., war,
the sport of monarchs. 37 **taborins** drums 38 **That . . . together** i.e.,
that the heavens may echo and augment the loud noise of the drums
4.9 Location: Caesar's camp.
2 **court of guard** guardroom. 3 **shiny** bright, moonlit. **embattle**
assemble for the combat 5 **shrewd** unlucky 8 **close** concealed.
list listen to 10 **revolted** who have broken their allegiance. **upon
record** in the record of history

15 **mistress . . . melancholy** i.e., the moon, so addressed because of
her supposed influence in causing lunacy 16 **dispunge** pour down
(as from a squeezed sponge) 20 **Which** i.e., the heart. **dried with
grief** (Cold and melancholy blood was thought to strangle and dry
up the heart.) 23 **in . . . particular** in your own person 24 **rank me
in register** put me down in its records 25 **master-leaver** (1) one who
deserts his master (2) nonpareil of deserters. **fugitive** deserter.
31 **for** a prelude to 34 **raught** reached 35 **demurely** with solemn
sound 37 **of note** of rank.
4.10 Location: The field of battle.
3 **fire . . . air** (Along with earth and water, where Antony is already
prepared, fire and air make up the traditional four elements of all
matter.) 4 **foot** foot soldiers 6 **for sea** to fight at sea

They have put forth the haven—   7
Where their appointment we may best discover   8
And look on their endeavor.   *Exeunt.*

[4.11]

Enter Caesar and his army.

CAESAR
But being charged, we will be still by land,   1
Which, as I take't, we shall; for his best force   2
Is forth to man his galleys. To the vales,   3
And hold our best advantage.   *Exeunt.*   4

[4.12]

Enter Antony and Scarus.

ANTONY
Yet they are not joined. Where yond pine does stand,
I shall discover all. I'll bring thee word
Straight how 'tis like to go.   *Exit.*
          Alarum afar off, as at a sea fight.
SCARUS   Swallows have built   3
In Cleopatra's sails their nests. The augurers   4
Say they know not, they cannot tell, look grimly,
And dare not speak their knowledge. Antony
Is valiant, and dejected, and by starts
His fretted fortunes give him hope and fear   8
Of what he has and has not.

Enter Antony.

ANTONY   All is lost!
This foul Egyptian hath betrayèd me.
My fleet hath yielded to the foe, and yonder
They cast their caps up and carouse together
Like friends long lost. Triple-turned whore! 'Tis thou   13
Hast sold me to this novice, and my heart
Makes only wars on thee. Bid them all fly;
For when I am revenged upon my charm,   16
I have done all. Bid them all fly. Begone!
                              [Exit Scarus.]
O sun, thy uprise shall I see no more.
Fortune and Antony part here; even here
Do we shake hands. All come to this? The hearts   20
That spanieled me at heels, to whom I gave   21
Their wishes, do discandy, melt their sweets   22

On blossoming Caesar; and this pine is barked   23
That overtopped them all. Betrayed I am.
Oh, this false soul of Egypt! This grave charm,   25
Whose eye becked forth my wars and called them
     home,   26
Whose bosom was my crownet, my chief end,   27
Like a right gypsy hath at fast and loose   28
Beguiled me to the very heart of loss.   29
[*Calling*] What, Eros, Eros!

Enter Cleopatra.

                    Ah, thou spell! Avaunt!   30
CLEOPATRA
Why is my lord enraged against his love?
ANTONY
Vanish, or I shall give thee thy deserving
And blemish Caesar's triumph. Let him take thee   33
And hoist thee up to the shouting plebeians!
Follow his chariot, like the greatest spot   35
Of all thy sex; most monsterlike be shown   36
For poor'st diminutives, for dolts, and let   37
Patient Octavia plow thy visage up
With her preparèd nails!   *Exit Cleopatra.*
                    'Tis well thou'rt gone,
If it be well to live; but better 'twere
Thou fell'st into my fury, for one death   41
Might have prevented many.—Eros, ho!—   42
The shirt of Nessus is upon me. Teach me,   43
Alcides, thou mine ancestor, thy rage.   44
Let me lodge Lichas on the horns o'th' moon,   45
And with those hands, that grasped the heaviest club,
Subdue my worthiest self. The witch shall die.
To the young Roman boy she hath sold me, and I fall
Under this plot. She dies for't.—Eros, ho!   *Exit.*

[4.13]

Enter Cleopatra, Charmian, Iras, [and] Mardian.

CLEOPATRA
Help me, my women! Oh, he's more mad

---

7 forth forth from   **8 appointment** disposition of forces, equipment.
discover descry
4.11. Location: The field of battle.
1 But being Unless we are.   **still** inactive   **2 we shall** i.e., we will be
left undisturbed   **3 Is forth** has gone forth.   **vales** valleys   **4 hold . . .
advantage** take the most advantageous position.
**4.12 Location: The field of battle at first, though by scene's end the
action appears to be located in Alexandria.**
3 Straight immediately.   **like** likely   **4 augurers** augurs, soothsayers
8 fretted worn away, vexed, checkered   **13 Triple-turned** Three times
faithless (to Julius Caesar, Gnaeus Pompey, and now Antony)
16 charm practicer of charms or spells   **20 shake hands** i.e., in parting.   **hearts** good fellows   **21 spanieled** fawned upon like a spaniel
22 Their wishes whatever they wished.   **discandy** melt, dissolve

23 this pine i.e., Antony.   **barked** stripped of its bark and thus killed
25 This grave charm i.e., This sorceress who casts fatal spells
26 becked beckoned   **27 Whose . . . end** whose embraces were the
crown of my achievement and my goal   **28 right** veritable.   **fast and
loose** a cheating game in which the victim bets that he can make fast
a knot in an ingeniously coiled rope, whereupon the knot is pulled
loose   **29 loss** ruin.   **30 spell** enchantment.   **Avaunt!** Begone!
33 blemish Caesar's triumph i.e., mutilate you and thereby frustrate
Caesar's plan to display you in his triumphal procession into Rome.
35 spot blemish, disgrace   **36 shown** exhibited   **37 diminutives**
underlings, i.e., the populace   **41 Thou fell'st into** you had fallen a
victim to   **42 many** i.e., many other deaths resulting from my rage.
43–5 Nessus . . . Lichas (When Hercules or *Alcides* had fatally
wounded the centaur *Nessus* for trying to rape Hercules's wife
Deianira, Nessus vengefully gave his blood-soaked shirt to Deianira
as a supposed love charm for her husband. The poison gave Hercules
such agony that he cast his page *Lichas* into the air.)
**4.13 Location: Alexandria. This scene appears to follow scene 12
closely. The sense of location is very fluid, and it is not clear where
the end of scene 12 takes place.**

Than Telamon for his shield; the boar of Thessaly   2
Was never so embossed.
CHARMIAN   To th' monument!   3
There lock yourself and send him word you are dead.
The soul and body rive not more in parting   5
Than greatness going off.
CLEOPATRA   To th' monument!   6
Mardian, go tell him I have slain myself.
Say that the last I spoke was "Antony,"
And word it, prithee, piteously. Hence, Mardian,
And bring me how he takes my death. To th'
     monument!   *Exeunt.*

❖

[4.14]

Enter Antony and Eros.

ANTONY
Eros, thou yet behold'st me?
EROS   Ay, noble lord.
ANTONY
Sometime we see a cloud that's dragonish,   2
A vapor sometime like a bear or lion,
A towered citadel, a pendant rock,   4
A forkèd mountain, or blue promontory
With trees upon't that nod unto the world
And mock our eyes with air. Thou hast seen these
     signs;
They are black vesper's pageants.
EROS   Ay, my lord.   8
ANTONY
That which is now a horse, even with a thought
The rack dislimns and makes it indistinct   10
As water is in water.
EROS   It does, my lord.
ANTONY
My good knave Eros, now thy captain is   12
Even such a body. Here I am Antony,
Yet cannot hold this visible shape, my knave.
I made these wars for Egypt, and the Queen,
Whose heart I thought I had, for she had mine—
Which whilst it was mine had annexed unto't
A million more, now lost—she, Eros, has
Packed cards with Caesar and false-played my glory   19
Unto an enemy's triumph.   20

Nay, weep not, gentle Eros. There is left us
Ourselves to end ourselves.

Enter Mardian.

                          Oh, thy vile lady!
She has robbed me of my sword.
MARDIAN   No, Antony,   23
My mistress loved thee, and her fortunes mingled
With thine entirely.
ANTONY   Hence, saucy eunuch, peace!
She hath betrayed me and shall die the death.   26
MARDIAN
Death of one person can be paid but once,   27
And that she has discharged. What thou wouldst do   28
Is done unto thy hand. The last she spake   29
Was, "Antony, most noble Antony!"
Then in the midst a tearing groan did break
The name of Antony; it was divided   32
Between her heart and lips. She rendered life   33
Thy name so buried in her.
ANTONY   Dead, then?
MARDIAN   Dead.   34
ANTONY
Unarm, Eros. The long day's task is done,
And we must sleep. [*To Mardian*] That thou depart'st
     hence safe
Does pay thy labor richly; go.   *Exit Mardian.*
               Off, pluck off! [*Eros unarms him.*]
The sevenfold shield of Ajax cannot keep   38
The battery from my heart. Oh, cleave, my sides!   39
Heart, once be stronger than thy continent;   40
Crack thy frail case! Apace, Eros, apace.   41
No more a soldier. Bruisèd pieces, go;
You have been nobly borne.—From me awhile.   43
                                   Exit Eros.
I will o'ertake thee, Cleopatra, and
Weep for my pardon. So it must be, for now
All length is torture; since the torch is out,   46
Lie down, and stray no farther. Now all labor
Mars what it does; yea, very force entangles   48
Itself with strength. Seal then, and all is done.   49
Eros!—I come, my queen.—Eros!—Stay for me.   50
Where souls do couch on flowers, we'll hand in hand,   51
And with our sprightly port make the ghosts gaze.   52

---

2 **Telamon** Ajax Telamon, who after the capture of Troy went mad and slew himself when he was not awarded the shield and armor of Achilles.   **the boar of Thessaly** the boar sent by Diana or Artemis to ravage the fields of Calydon, slain by Meleager   3 **embossed** foaming at the mouth from rage and exhaustion.   **monument** tomb presumably built to house Cleopatra's royal remains after her death, like the pyramids.   5 **rive** split, sever   6 **going off** i.e., bidding farewell to its glory.
4.14 Location: Alexandria. (See location of scene 13; again, the sense of time is immediate and the place is fluid.)
2 **dragonish** shaped like a dragon   4 **pendant** overhanging   8 **black . . . pageants** i.e., the evanescent splendor of a sunset heralding the approach of night.   10 **The rack dislimns** the mass of cloud changes its shape   12 **knave** lad   19 **Packed cards** i.e., stacked the deck.   **false-played** falsely played away   20 **triumph** (1) victory (2) trump card.

23 **sword** i.e., prowess as a soldier, masculinity.   26 **die the death** be put to death.   27 **of** by   28 **discharged** paid.   29 **unto thy hand** for you, without your having to lift a finger.   32–3 **it . . . lips** i.e., she groaned out half of Antony's name and then died with the unspoken part in her heart only.   33–4 **She . . . in her** She gave back to Nature that part of your name thus buried in her heart.   38 **sevenfold** with seven thicknesses. (The shield of Ajax was of brass reinforced with seven thicknesses of oxhide.)   39 **battery** battering   40 **thy continent** that which contains you   41 **Apace** Quickly   43 **From** Go from   46 **length** prolongation of life.   **the torch** i.e., the life of Cleopatra   48 **very force** any resolute action   49 **with strength** i.e., with its own strength.   **Seal** Finish the business (as in sealing a letter)   50 **Eros** (The meaning of Eros's name, erotic love, is especially apt here.)   51 **couch** lie (here, in the Elysian fields)   52 **sprightly** (1) high-spirited (2) spiritlike, ghostly.   **port** bearing

Dido and her Aeneas shall want troops,   53
And all the haunt be ours.—Come, Eros, Eros!   54

Enter Eros.

EROS
What would my lord?

ANTONY   Since Cleopatra died
I have lived in such dishonor that the gods
Detest my baseness. I, that with my sword
Quartered the world, and o'er green Neptune's back   58
With ships made cities, condemn myself to lack   59
The courage of a woman—less noble mind
Than she which by her death our Caesar tells
"I am conqueror of myself." Thou art sworn, Eros,
That when the exigent should come which now   63
Is come indeed, when I should see behind me
Th'inevitable prosecution of   65
Disgrace and horror, that on my command
Thou then wouldst kill me. Do't. The time is come.
Thou strik'st not me, 'tis Caesar thou defeat'st.
Put color in thy cheek.

EROS   The gods withhold me!   69
Shall I do that which all the Parthian darts,
Though enemy, lost aim and could not?

ANTONY   Eros,
Wouldst thou be windowed in great Rome and see   72
Thy master thus with pleached arms, bending down   73
His corrigible neck, his face subdued   74
To penetrative shame, whilst the wheeled seat   75
Of fortunate Caesar, drawn before him, branded   76
His baseness that ensued?

EROS   I would not see't. 77

ANTONY
Come, then, for with a wound I must be cured.
Draw that thy honest sword, which thou hast worn   79
Most useful for thy country.

EROS   Oh, sir, pardon me!   80

ANTONY
When I did make thee free, swor'st thou not then
To do this when I bade thee? Do it at once,
Or thy precedent services are all   83
But accidents unpurposed. Draw, and come.   84

EROS
Turn from me then that noble countenance

Wherein the worship of the whole world lies.   86

ANTONY   Lo thee!   [*He turns away.*]
EROS [*drawing his sword*]
My sword is drawn.

ANTONY   Then let it do at once
That thing why thou hast drawn it.

EROS   My dear master,
My captain, and my emperor, let me say,
Before I strike this bloody stroke, farewell.

ANTONY   'Tis said, man, and farewell.

EROS
Farewell, great chief. Shall I strike now?

ANTONY   Now, Eros.

EROS (*kills himself*)
Why, there then! Thus I do escape the sorrow
Of Antony's death.   [*He dies.*]

ANTONY   Thrice nobler than myself!
Thou teachest me, O valiant Eros, what
I should, and thou couldst not. My queen and Eros   97
Have by their brave instruction got upon me   98
A nobleness in record. But I will be   99
A bridegroom in my death, and run into't
As to a lover's bed. Come, then, and Eros,
Thy master dies thy scholar. To do thus
I learned of thee.   [*He falls on his sword.*]
How, not dead? Not dead?
The guard, ho! Oh, dispatch me!   104

Enter [Dercetus and others of] a Guard.

FIRST GUARD   What's the noise?

ANTONY   I have done my work ill, friends.
Oh, make an end of what I have begun!

SECOND GUARD   The star is fallen.

FIRST GUARD   And time is at his period.   109

ALL   Alas, and woe!

ANTONY   Let him that loves me strike me dead.

FIRST GUARD   Not I.

SECOND GUARD   Nor I.

THIRD GUARD   Nor anyone.   *Exeunt [Guard].*

DERCETUS
Thy death and fortunes bid thy followers fly.
This sword but shown to Caesar, with this tidings,
Shall enter me with him. [*He takes up Antony's sword.*] 117

Enter Diomedes.

DIOMEDES   Where's Antony?

DERCETUS   There, Diomed, there.

DIOMEDES
Lives he? Wilt thou not answer, man? [*Exit Dercetus.*]

ANTONY
Art thou there, Diomed? Draw thy sword and give me
Suffing strokes for death.

DIOMEDES   Most absolute lord,
My mistress Cleopatra sent me to thee.

---

53 **Dido . . . troops** We will be the most distinguished lovers in the Elysian fields, outshining even the Queen of Carthage and her famous lover. (In the *Aeneid*, Aeneas deserts Dido in order to found Rome, putting public good ahead of private passion as Antony does not. Dido scorns Aeneas when they meet in the underworld; Antony here imagines himself and Cleopatra in the Elysian fields.)   **want troops** lack followers   54 **all . . . ours** i.e., we shall be the objects of everyone's attention.   58–9 **Quartered . . . cities** divided and conquered the world, and at sea assembled flotillas as dense and populous as cities   59 **to lack** for lacking   63 **exigent** exigency, time of compelling trial   65 **prosecution** consequence   69 **The gods withhold me!** i.e., God forbid!   72 **windowed** placed as in a window   73 **pleached** folded or bound   74 **corrigible** submissive to correction   75 **penetrative** penetrating.   **wheeled seat** chariot   76–7 **branded . . . ensued** stigmatized, as by a brand, the shame of him that followed.   79 **honest** honorable   80 **pardon me!** excuse me from doing this!   83 **precedent** former   84 **accidents unpurposed** events leading to no purpose.

86 **worship** honor, worth   97 **I should . . . not** I should have done for myself and you couldn't do for me.   98–9 **got . . . record** won a noble place in history before I have.   104 **dispatch** finish   109 **his period** its end.   117 **enter . . . him** admit me to his service, put me in his good graces.

ANTONY
When did she send thee?

DIOMEDES   Now, my lord.

ANTONY   Where is she?

DIOMEDES
Locked in her monument. She had a prophesying fear
Of what hath come to pass. For when she saw—
Which never shall be found—you did suspect   127
She had disposed with Caesar, and that your rage   128
Would not be purged, she sent you word she was
    dead;
But, fearing since how it might work, hath sent
Me to proclaim the truth, and I am come,
I dread, too late.

ANTONY
Too late, good Diomed. Call my guard, I prithee.

DIOMEDES [calling]
What ho, the Emperor's guard! The guard, what ho!
Come, your lord calls.

Enter four or five of the Guard of Antony.

ANTONY
Bear me, good friends, where Cleopatra bides.   136
'Tis the last service that I shall command you.

FIRST GUARD
Woe, woe are we, sir, you may not live to wear   138
All your true followers out.

ALL   Most heavy day!   139

ANTONY
Nay, good my fellows, do not please sharp fate
To grace it with your sorrows. Bid that welcome   141
Which comes to punish us, and we punish it,
Seeming to bear it lightly. Take me up.
I have led you oft; carry me now, good friends,
And have my thanks for all.

Exeunt, bearing Antony [and Eros].

[4.15]

*Enter Cleopatra and her maids aloft, with
Charmian and Iras.*

CLEOPATRA
Oh, Charmian, I will never go from hence.

CHARMIAN
Be comforted, dear madam.

CLEOPATRA   No, I will not.
All strange and terrible events are welcome,
But comforts we despise. Our size of sorrow,
Proportioned to our cause, must be as great
As that which makes it.

Enter [below] Diomedes.

                                How now? Is he dead?

DIOMEDES
His death's upon him, but not dead.
Look out o'th'other side your monument;
His guard have brought him thither.

*Enter [below] Antony, and the Guard
[bearing him].*

CLEOPATRA   O sun,
Burn the great sphere thou mov'st in; darkling stand   11
The varying shore o'th' world! O Antony,
Antony, Antony! Help, Charmian, help, Iras, help!
Help, friends below! Let's draw him hither.

ANTONY   Peace!
Not Caesar's valor hath o'erthrown Antony,
But Antony's hath triumphed on itself.

CLEOPATRA
So it should be, that none but Antony
Should conquer Antony; but woe 'tis so!

ANTONY
I am dying, Egypt, dying. Only
I here importune death awhile, until   20
Of many thousand kisses the poor last
I lay upon thy lips.

CLEOPATRA   I dare not, dear—   22
Dear my lord, pardon—I dare not,
Lest I be taken. Not th'imperious show   24
Of the full-fortuned Caesar ever shall
Be brooched with me. If knife, drugs, serpents, have   26
Edge, sting, or operation, I am safe.   27
Your wife Octavia, with her modest eyes
And still conclusion, shall acquire no honor   29
Demuring upon me. But come, come, Antony—   30
Help me, my women—we must draw thee up.
Assist, good friends.

ANTONY   Oh, quick, or I am gone.

[They begin lifting.]

CLEOPATRA
Here's sport indeed! How heavy weighs my lord!
Our strength is all gone into heaviness,   34
That makes the weight. Had I great Juno's power,
The strong-winged Mercury should fetch thee up
And set thee by Jove's side. Yet come a little;
Wishers were ever fools. Oh, come, come, come!   38

They heave Antony aloft to Cleopatra.

And welcome, welcome! Die when thou hast lived;   39
Quicken with kissing. Had my lips that power,   40
Thus would I wear them out.   [She kisses him.]

ALL   A heavy sight!   42

ANTONY   I am dying, Egypt, dying.
Give me some wine, and let me speak a little.

---

11 sphere concentric sphere in which, according to Ptolemaic astronomy, the sun moved about the earth as did the planets and stars. **darkling** in darkness   **20 importune** i.e., beg a delay of   **22 I dare not** i.e., I dare not come down   **24 th'imperious show** the imperial triumphal procession   **26 brooched** adorned (as with a brooch) **27 operation** power, efficacy   **29 still conclusion** silent judgment **30 Demuring** looking demurely   **34 heaviness** (1) sadness (2) weight **38 Wishers . . . fools** Those who wish for things are always fools. **39 Die . . . lived** i.e., Die after living intensely. (With a pun on *die* suggesting sexual consummation; hence *Quicken* in line 40.)   **40 Quicken** revive   **42 heavy** doleful

---

127 found found true   **128 disposed with** come to terms with **136 bides** abides, dwells.   **138–9 live . . . out** outlive those that serve you.   **141 To grace** by gracing or honoring **4.15. Location: Alexandria. Cleopatra's monument.** **0.1 *aloft*** in the gallery above the main stage

CLEOPATRA

No, let me speak, and let me rail so high
That the false huswife Fortune break her wheel, 46
Provoked by my offense.

ANTONY   One word, sweet Queen: 47
Of Caesar seek your honor, with your safety. Oh! 48

CLEOPATRA

They do not go together.

ANTONY   Gentle, hear me.
None about Caesar trust but Proculeius.

CLEOPATRA

My resolution and my hands I'll trust,
None about Caesar.

ANTONY

The miserable change now at my end
Lament nor sorrow at, but please your thoughts 54
In feeding them with those my former fortunes,
Wherein I lived the greatest prince o'th' world,
The noblest; and do now not basely die,
Not cowardly put off my helmet to
My countryman—a Roman by a Roman
Valiantly vanquished. Now my spirit is going;
I can no more.

CLEOPATRA   Noblest of men, woo't die? 61
Hast thou no care of me? Shall I abide
In this dull world, which in thy absence is
No better than a sty? [Antony dies.] Oh, see, my
     women,
The crown o'th'earth doth melt. My lord!
Oh, withered is the garland of the war;
The soldier's pole is fall'n! Young boys and girls 67
Are level now with men. The odds is gone, 68
And there is nothing left remarkable
Beneath the visiting moon.   [She faints.]

CHARMIAN   Oh, quietness, lady!

IRAS   She's dead too, our sovereign.

CHARMIAN   Lady!

IRAS   Madam!

CHARMIAN   Oh, madam, madam, madam!

IRAS   Royal Egypt, Empress!   [Cleopatra stirs.]

CHARMIAN   Peace, peace, Iras.

CLEOPATRA

No more but e'en a woman, and commanded
By such poor passion as the maid that milks
And does the meanest chares. It were for me 80
To throw my scepter at the injurious gods,
To tell them that this world did equal theirs
Till they had stol'n our jewel. All's but naught;
Patience is sottish, and impatience does 84
Become a dog that's mad. Then is it sin 85
To rush into the secret house of death
Ere death dare come to us? How do you, women?

What, what, good cheer! Why, how now, Charmian?
My noble girls! Ah, women, women! Look,
Our lamp is spent, it's out. Good sirs, take heart. 90
We'll bury him; and then, what's brave, what's noble, 91
Let's do't after the high Roman fashion
And make death proud to take us. Come, away.
This case of that huge spirit now is cold.
Ah, women, women! Come. We have no friend
But resolution, and the briefest end. 96
     Exeunt, [those above] bearing off Antony's body.

❖

[5.1]

Enter Caesar, Agrippa, Dolabella, Maecenas,
[Gallus, Proculeius,] with his council of war.

CAESAR

Go to him, Dolabella, bid him yield;
Being so frustrate, tell him, he mocks 2
The pauses that he makes.

DOLABELLA   Caesar, I shall.   [Exit.] 3

Enter Dercetus, with the sword of Antony.

CAESAR

Wherefore is that? And what art thou that dar'st
Appear thus to us?

DERCETUS   I am called Dercetus.
Mark Antony I served, who best was worthy
Best to be served. Whilst he stood up and spoke
He was my master, and I wore my life
To spend upon his haters. If thou please 9
To take me to thee, as I was to him
I'll be to Caesar; if thou pleasest not,
I yield thee up my life.

CAESAR   What is't thou say'st?

DERCETUS

I say, O Caesar, Antony is dead.

CAESAR

The breaking of so great a thing should make 14
A greater crack. The round world 15
Should have shook lions into civil streets 16
And citizens to their dens. The death of Antony 17
Is not a single doom; in the name lay 18
A moiety of the world.

DERCETUS   He is dead, Caesar, 19
Not by a public minister of justice,
Nor by a hirèd knife; but that self hand 21
Which writ his honor in the acts it did
Hath, with the courage which the heart did lend it,

---

90 Good sirs (Addressed to the women.)   91 brave fine   96 briefest swiftest
5.1. Location: Alexandria. Caesar's camp.
2 frustrate helpless, baffled   2–3 mocks . . . makes makes himself ridiculous by his delays (in yielding).   9 spend expend   14 breaking (1) destruction (2) disclosure   15 crack (1) cracking apart (2) loud report.   16 civil city   17 their i.e., the lions', or else, the citizens scurry to safety indoors, in their own "dens." (In either case, nature is inverted in a kind of disorder that earlier accompanied the death of Julius Caesar.)   18 Is . . . doom i.e., signifies the death and destruction of much more than a single man   19 moiety half   21 self same

46 false huswife treacherous hussy   47 offense offensive speech.
48 Of from   54 Lament i.e., neither lament   61 woo't wilt thou
67 pole polestar or battle standard. (Probably with a suggestion of a sexual potency now withered and fallen through death.)   68 The odds is gone The distinction between great and small has disappeared   80 chares chores, drudgery.   were would be fitting
84–5 Patience . . . mad i.e., Patience is for fools, and impatience is for the mad; both are useless here.

Splitted the heart. This is his sword.

[*He offers the sword.*]

I robbed his wound of it. Behold it stained
With his most noble blood.

CAESAR   Look you sad, friends?
The gods rebuke me, but it is tidings   27
To wash the eyes of kings.

AGRIPPA   And strange it is
That nature must compel us to lament
Our most persisted deeds.

MAECENAS   His taints and honors   30
Waged equal with him.

AGRIPPA   A rarer spirit never   31
Did steer humanity; but you gods will give us   32
Some faults to make us men. Caesar is touched.

MAECENAS
When such a spacious mirror's set before him,
He needs must see himself.

CAESAR   O Antony,
I have followed thee to this; but we do launch   36
Diseases in our bodies. I must perforce   37
Have shown to thee such a declining day,   38
Or look on thine; we could not stall together   39
In the whole world. But yet let me lament
With tears as sovereign as the blood of hearts   41
That thou, my brother, my competitor   42
In top of all design, my mate in empire,   43
Friend and companion in the front of war,   44
The arm of mine own body, and the heart   45
Where mine his thoughts did kindle—that our stars,   46
Unreconciliable, should divide   47
Our equalness to this. Hear me, good friends—   48

Enter an Egyptian.

But I will tell you at some meeter season.   49
The business of this man looks out of him;   50
We'll hear him what he says.—Whence are you?   51

EGYPTIAN
A poor Egyptian yet, the Queen my mistress,   52
Confined in all she has, her monument,
Of thy intents desires instruction,
That she preparedly may frame herself   55
To th' way she's forced to.

CAESAR   Bid her have good heart.
She soon shall know of us, by some of ours,   57

How honorable and how kindly we
Determine for her; for Caesar cannot live
To be ungentle.

EGYPTIAN   So the gods preserve thee!   *Exit.*

CAESAR
Come hither, Proculeius. Go and say
We purpose her no shame. Give her what comforts   62
The quality of her passion shall require,   63
Lest, in her greatness, by some mortal stroke   64
She do defeat us; for her life in Rome   65
Would be eternal in our triumph. Go,   66
And with your speediest bring us what she says   67
And how you find of her.

PROCULEIUS   Caesar, I shall.   68

Exit Proculeius.

CAESAR   Gallus, go you along.   [*Exit Gallus.*]
                    Where's Dolabella,
To second Proculeius?

ALL   Dolabella!

CAESAR
Let him alone, for I remember now   71
How he's employed. He shall in time be ready.
Go with me to my tent, where you shall see
How hardly I was drawn into this war,   74
How calm and gentle I proceeded still   75
In all my writings. Go with me and see   76
What I can show in this.   *Exeunt.*

❧

[5.2]

Enter Cleopatra, Charmian, Iras, and Mardian.

CLEOPATRA
My desolation does begin to make
A better life. 'Tis paltry to be Caesar;   2
Not being Fortune, he's but Fortune's knave,   3
A minister of her will. And it is great
To do that thing that ends all other deeds,   5
Which shackles accidents and bolts up change,   6
Which sleeps and never palates more the dung,   7
The beggar's nurse and Caesar's.   8

Enter [to the gates of the monument] Proculeius.

PROCULEIUS
Caesar sends greeting to the Queen of Egypt,
And bids thee study on what fair demands   10
Thou mean'st to have him grant thee.

CLEOPATRA   What's thy name?

27 **but it is** if it is not   30 **persisted** persistently desired or pursued
31 **Waged equal with** battled equally in   32 **steer humanity** govern
any individual.   **will give** insist on giving   36 **followed** pursued
36–7 **but . . . bodies** i.e., I have hurt you to cure myself, as men lance
diseases in their own bodies   37 **perforce** necessarily   38 **shown to
thee** i.e., suffered myself at your hands   39 **stall** dwell   41 **as sovereign . . . hearts** as precious or efficacious as heart's blood   42 **competitor** associate, partner (and rival)   43 **In . . . design** at the head of
every grand enterprise   44 **front** forehead, face   45–6 **the heart . . .
kindle** the brave heart where my heart kindled its (*his*) thoughts of
courage   47–8 **should . . . this** should divide our equal partnership to
this extreme.   49 **meeter season** more suitable time.   50 **looks . . .
him** reveals itself in his expression   51 **Whence are you?** Where do
you come from?   52 **A . . . yet** i.e., Egyptian Cleopatra, still reduced
in circumstance (and awaiting your will), or, I am a poor Egyptian
still, though subject to Rome's authority   55 **frame herself** shape her
course of action   57 **ours** my people

62 **purpose** intend   63 **passion** grief   64 **greatness** greatness of spirit
65 **life in Rome** presence in Rome alive   66 **eternal in our triumph**
an eternal glory in my triumphal procession.   67 **with your speediest** as quickly as you can   68 **of** concerning   71 **Let him alone** Don't
bother about him now   74 **hardly** reluctantly   75 **still** always
76 **writings** i.e., letters to Antony.
5.2. Location: Alexandria. Cleopatra's monument.
2 **better** i.e., rising above the vicissitudes of fortune   3 **knave** servant
5–8 **To do . . . Caesar's** i.e., to commit suicide, a sleep that arrests accident and change, and in which the sleeper relishes no more the
dungy earth that sustains both Caesar and the beggar.   10 **study on**
consider carefully

PROCULEIUS
 My name is Proculeius.
CLEOPATRA   Antony
 Did tell me of you, bade me trust you; but
 I do not greatly care to be deceived,   14
 That have no use for trusting. If your master 15
 Would have a queen his beggar, you must tell him
 That majesty, to keep decorum, must
 No less beg than a kingdom. If he please
 To give me conquered Egypt for my son,
 He gives me so much of mine own as I   20
 Will kneel to him with thanks.
PROCULEIUS   Be of good cheer;
 You're fall'n into a princely hand. Fear nothing.
 Make your full reference freely to my lord, 23
 Who is so full of grace that it flows over
 On all that need. Let me report to him
 Your sweet dependency, and you shall find 26
 A conqueror that will pray in aid for kindness 27
 Where he for grace is kneeled to.
CLEOPATRA   Pray you, tell him
 I am his fortune's vassal, and I send him 29
 The greatness he has got. I hourly learn 30
 A doctrine of obedience, and would gladly
 Look him i'th' face.
PROCULEIUS   This I'll report, dear lady.
 Have comfort, for I know your plight is pitied
 Of him that caused it.   34
      [*Roman soldiers enter from*
     behind Cleopatra and take her prisoner.]
 You see how easily she may be surprised.
 [*To the soldiers*] Guard her till Caesar come.
IRAS   Royal Queen!
CHARMIAN
 Oh, Cleopatra! Thou art taken, Queen.
CLEOPATRA [*drawing a dagger*]
 Quick, quick, good hands.
PROCULEIUS   Hold, worthy lady, hold!
         [*He disarms her.*]
 Do not yourself such wrong, who are in this
 Relieved, but not betrayed.
CLEOPATRA   What, of death too, 40
 That rids our dogs of languish?
PROCULEIUS   Cleopatra, 41
 Do not abuse my master's bounty by
 Th'undoing of yourself. Let the world see
 His nobleness well acted, which your death 44
 Will never let come forth.
CLEOPATRA   Where art thou, Death? 45
 Come hither, come! Come, come, and take a queen

 Worth many babes and beggars!
PROCULEIUS   Oh, temperance, lady! 47
CLEOPATRA
 Sir, I will eat no meat, I'll not drink, sir;
 If idle talk will once be necessary,   49
 I'll not sleep, neither. This mortal house I'll ruin,
 Do Caesar what he can. Know, sir, that I
 Will not wait pinioned at your master's court, 52
 Nor once be chastised with the sober eye
 Of dull Octavia. Shall they hoist me up
 And show me to the shouting varletry 55
 Of censuring Rome? Rather a ditch in Egypt
 Be gentle grave unto me! Rather on Nilus' mud
 Lay me stark nak'd and let the waterflies
 Blow me into abhorring! Rather make 59
 My country's high pyramides my gibbet 60
 And hang me up in chains!
PROCULEIUS   You do extend
 These thoughts of horror further than you shall
 Find cause in Caesar.

     Enter Dolabella.

DOLABELLA   Proculeius,
 What thou hast done thy master Caesar knows,
 And he hath sent for thee. For the Queen, 65
 I'll take her to my guard.
PROCULEIUS   So, Dolabella,
 It shall content me best. Be gentle to her.
 [*To Cleopatra*] To Caesar I will speak what you shall
  please,   68
 If you'll employ me to him.
CLEOPATRA   Say I would die.
     Exit Proculeius [*with soldiers*].
DOLABELLA
 Most noble Empress, you have heard of me?
CLEOPATRA
 I cannot tell.
DOLABELLA Assuredly you know me.
CLEOPATRA
 No matter, sir, what I have heard or known.
 You laugh when boys or women tell their dreams;
 Is't not your trick?
DOLABELLA   I understand not, madam. 74
CLEOPATRA
 I dreamt there was an emperor Antony.
 Oh, such another sleep, that I might see
 But such another man!
DOLABELLA   If it might please ye—
CLEOPATRA
 His face was as the heavens, and therein stuck 78
 A sun and moon, which kept their course and lighted

---

14 **do . . . to be** am wary of being 15 **That** since I 20 **as that**
23 **Make . . . reference** Refer your case 26 **dependency** submissive-
ness 27 **pray . . . kindness** beg your assistance to ensure that he may
omit no kindness 29–30 **I send . . . got** i.e., I acknowledge his superiority over all he has won, including myself. 34 **Of** by. 0.1 *Roman
soldiers* (Perhaps led by Gallus; see 5.1.69. Possibly some speech for
him has been omitted.) 40 **Relieved** rescued. **of death too** i.e.,
(1) am I *relieved* or deprived even of death (2) am I *betrayed* even of the
right to die. 41 **our dogs of languish** even our dogs of lingering disease. 44 **acted** accomplished 45 **let come forth** allow to be displayed.

47 **babes and beggars** i.e., those whom death takes easily and often.
49 **If . . . necessary** even if on occasion I must resort to idle talk (to
keep myself awake) 52 **wait pinioned** wait in attendance, like a bird
with clipped wings, unable to fly 55 **varletry** rabble 59 **Blow . . .
abhorring** cause me to swell abhorrently with maggots, or, deposit
their eggs on me until I become abhorrent. 60 **gibbet** gallows
65 **For** As for 68 **what** whatever 74 **trick** manner, way. 78 **stuck**
were set

The little O, the earth.

DOLABELLA   Most sovereign creature—

CLEOPATRA   His legs bestrid the ocean; his reared arm   81
Crested the world; his voice was propertied   82
As all the tunèd spheres, and that to friends;   83
But when he meant to quail and shake the orb,   84
He was as rattling thunder. For his bounty,   85
There was no winter in't; an autumn 'twas
That grew the more by reaping. His delights   87
Were dolphinlike; they showed his back above   88
The element they lived in. In his livery   89
Walked crowns and crownets; realms and islands
were   90
As plates dropped from his pocket.

DOLABELLA   Cleopatra—   91

CLEOPATRA
Think you there was or might be such a man
As this I dreamt of?

DOLABELLA   Gentle madam, no.

CLEOPATRA
You lie, up to the hearing of the gods.
But if there be nor ever were one such,   95
It's past the size of dreaming. Nature wants stuff   96
To vie strange forms with fancy; yet t'imagine   97
An Antony were nature's piece 'gainst fancy,   98
Condemning shadows quite.

DOLABELLA   Hear me, good madam: 99
Your loss is as yourself, great; and you bear it
As answering to the weight. Would I might never   101
O'ertake pursued success but I do feel,   102
By the rebound of yours, a grief that smites
My very heart at root.

CLEOPATRA   I thank you, sir.
Know you what Caesar means to do with me?

DOLABELLA
I am loath to tell you what I would you knew.

CLEOPATRA
Nay, pray you, sir.

DOLABELLA   Though he be honorable—

CLEOPATRA   He'll lead me, then, in triumph.

DOLABELLA   Madam, he will, I know't.   *Flourish.*

*Enter Proculeius, Caesar, Gallus, Maecenas,
and others of his train.*

ALL   Make way there! Caesar!

CAESAR   Which is the Queen of Egypt?

DOLABELLA   It is the Emperor, madam.

                                   Cleopatra kneels.

CAESAR   Arise, you shall not kneel. I pray you, rise.
Rise, Egypt.

CLEOPATRA   [*rising*]   Sir, the gods will have it thus;
My master and my lord I must obey.

CAESAR   Take to you no hard thoughts.   116
The record of what injuries you did us,
Though written in our flesh, we shall remember
As things but done by chance.

CLEOPATRA   Sole sir o'th' world,   119
I cannot project mine own cause so well   120
To make it clear, but do confess I have   121
Been laden with like frailties which before
Have often shamed our sex.

CAESAR   Cleopatra, know
We will extenuate rather than enforce.   124
If you apply yourself to our intents,   125
Which towards you are most gentle, you shall find
A benefit in this change; but if you seek
To lay on me a cruelty by taking   128
Antony's course, you shall bereave yourself   129
Of my good purposes and put your children
To that destruction which I'll guard them from
If thereon you rely. I'll take my leave.

CLEOPATRA
And may, through all the world! 'Tis yours, and we,   133
Your scutcheons and your signs of conquest, shall   134
Hang in what place you please. Here, my good lord.   135
                          [*She gives him a scroll.*]

CAESAR
You shall advise me in all for Cleopatra.   136

CLEOPATRA
This is the brief of money, plate, and jewels   137
I am possessed of. 'Tis exactly valued,
Not petty things admitted. Where's Seleucus?   139

          [*Enter Seleucus.*]

SELEUCUS   Here, madam.

CLEOPATRA
This is my treasurer. Let him speak, my lord,
Upon his peril, that I have reserved
To myself nothing.—Speak the truth, Seleucus.

SELEUCUS
Madam, I had rather seal my lips
Than to my peril speak that which is not.

CLEOPATRA   What have I kept back?

SELEUCUS
Enough to purchase what you have made known.

---

81 bestrid straddled (like the Colossus of Rhodes)   **82 Crested** surmounted   **82–3 propertied . . . friends** endowed with qualities which, when he spoke to friends, recalled the harmony of the heavenly bodies in their spheres   **84 quail** make quail, overawe.   **orb** world   **85 For** As for   **87–9 His . . . in** i.e., Like the dolphin sportfully rising up out of the sea, his pleasures arose out of the element in which he lived, both glorying in and transcending that element.   **89–90 In . . . crownets** i.e., Among his retainers (those who would wear his livery) were kings and princes   **91 plates** coins   **95 nor ever were** or if there never existed   **96 It's . . . dreaming** no dream can come up to it, my image of him.   **96–9 Nature . . . quite** Nature lacks material to equal the remarkable forms produced by fancy or imagination; yet an Antony such as I have pictured forth would himself be a work of nature, in fact would be Nature's masterpiece in competition with the imagination.   **101 As . . . weight** commensurate with the weightiness of the loss.   **101–2 Would . . . feel** May I never succeed at what I desire if I do not feel

116 Take . . . thoughts Don't torment yourself with reproaches.   **119 sir** master   **120 project** set forth   **121 clear** free of blame   **124 enforce** press home.   **125 If . . . intents** If you comply with my plans   **128 lay . . . cruelty** force me to be cruel   **129 bereave** rob   **133 And may** i.e., (1) You may leave when you choose (2) You may have your will in anything   **134 scutcheons** shields showing armorial bearings; hence, shields hung up as monuments of victory   **135 Hang** be hung up in display as your trophies. (But with a hidden suggestion of "be hanged as your captives.")   **136 in all for Cleopatra** i.e., in all matters pertaining to yourself.   **137 brief** list   **139 Not . . . admitted** petty things omitted.

CAESAR
Nay, blush not, Cleopatra. I approve
Your wisdom in the deed.

CLEOPATRA   See, Caesar! Oh, behold
How pomp is followed! Mine will now be yours,   150
And, should we shift estates, yours would be mine.   151
The ingratitude of this Seleucus does
Even make me wild.—Oh, slave, of no more trust
Than love that's hired! [*Seleucus retreats from her.*]
         What, goest thou back? Thou shalt   154
Go back, I warrant thee! But I'll catch thine eyes,
Though they had wings. Slave, soulless villain, dog!
Oh, rarely base!

CAESAR   Good Queen, let us entreat you.   157

CLEOPATRA
Oh, Caesar, what a wounding shame is this,
That thou vouchsafing here to visit me,   159
Doing the honor of thy lordliness
To one so meek, that mine own servant should
Parcel the sum of my disgraces by   162
Addition of his envy! Say, good Caesar,   163
That I some lady trifles have reserved,   164
Immoment toys, things of such dignity   165
As we greet modern friends withal, and say   166
Some nobler token I have kept apart
For Livia and Octavia, to induce   168
Their mediation; must I be unfolded   169
With one that I have bred? The gods! It smites me 170
Beneath the fall I have. [*To Seleucus*] Prithee, go hence,
Or I shall show the cinders of my spirits   172
Through th'ashes of my chance. Wert thou a man,   173
Thou wouldst have mercy on me.

CAESAR   Forbear, Seleucus.   [*Exit Seleucus.*] 175

CLEOPATRA
Be it known that we, the greatest, are misthought 176
For things that others do; and when we fall
We answer others' merits in our name,   178
Are therefore to be pitied.

CAESAR   Cleopatra,
Not what you have reserved nor what acknowledged
Put we i'th' roll of conquest. Still be't yours;
Bestow it at your pleasure, and believe   182
Caesar's no merchant, to make prize with you   183
Of things that merchants sold. Therefore be cheered.
Make not your thoughts your prisons. No, dear
    Queen,   185
For we intend so to dispose you as   186

Yourself shall give us counsel. Feed and sleep.
Our care and pity is so much upon you
That we remain your friend; and so adieu.

CLEOPATRA
My master, and my lord!

CAESAR   Not so. Adieu.
         Flourish. Exeunt Caesar and his train.

CLEOPATRA
He words me, girls, he words me, that I should not 191
Be noble to myself. But hark thee, Charmian.   192
              [*She whispers to Charmian.*]

IRAS
Finish, good lady. The bright day is done,
And we are for the dark.

CLEOPATRA [*to Charmian*]   Hie thee again.   194
I have spoke already, and it is provided;   195
Go put it to the haste.

CHARMIAN   Madam, I will.

         Enter Dolabella.

DOLABELLA
Where's the Queen?

CHARMIAN   Behold, sir.   [*Exit.*]

CLEOPATRA   Dolabella!

DOLABELLA
Madam, as thereto sworn by your command,
Which my love makes religion to obey,
I tell you this: Caesar through Syria
Intends his journey, and within three days
You with your children will he send before.
Make your best use of this. I have performed
Your pleasure and my promise.

CLEOPATRA   Dolabella,
I shall remain your debtor.

DOLABELLA   I your servant.
Adieu, good Queen. I must attend on Caesar.

CLEOPATRA
Farewell, and thanks.   *Exit* [*Dolabella*].
              Now, Iras, what think'st thou?
Thou an Egyptian puppet shall be shown
In Rome as well as I. Mechanic slaves   209
With greasy aprons, rules, and hammers shall   210
Uplift us to the view. In their thick breaths,
Rank of gross diet, shall we be enclouded   212
And forced to drink their vapor.

IRAS   The gods forbid!   213

CLEOPATRA
Nay, 'tis most certain, Iras. Saucy lictors   214
Will catch at us like strumpets, and scald rhymers 215
Ballad us out o' tune. The quick comedians   216
Extemporally will stage us and present   217

150 How . . . followed! how greatness is served!   **Mine** All the pomp and following that attends me   **151 shift estates** reverse fortunes, exchange places   **154 hired** paid for.   **157 rarely** exceptionally **159 vouchsafing** deigning to come   **162 Parcel** particularize **163 envy** malice.   **164 lady** ladylike, feminine   **165 Immoment toys** trifles of no moment or importance   **166 modern** common.   **withal** with   **168 Livia** Octavius Caesar's wife   **169–70 unfolded . . . bred** exposed by one of my household.   **172 cinders** smoldering hot coals **173 chance** (fallen) fortune.   **175 Forbear** Withdraw   **176 misthought** misjudged   **178 We . . . name** we are accountable for the deeds of others done in our name   **182 Bestow** Use   **183 make prize** haggle   **185 Make . . . prisons** i.e., Don't imprison yourself in your thoughts by misconceiving of your situation.   **186 dispose** dispose of

191–2 he words . . . myself he tries to deceive me with mere words to keep me from suicide.   **194 Hie thee again** Return quickly.   **195 spoke** given orders (for the means of suicide)   **209 Mechanic slaves** Common laborers   **210 rules** straight-edged measuring sticks **212 Rank . . . diet** reeking of coarse food   **213 drink** drink in, breathe deeply   **214 lictors** minor officials in attendance on Roman magistrates   **215 scald** scurvy   **216 Ballad us** sing ballads about us. **quick** quick-witted   **217 Extemporally** in improvised performance

Our Alexandrian revels; Antony
Shall be brought drunken forth, and I shall see
Some squeaking Cleopatra boy my greatness   220
I'th' posture of a whore.

IRAS   O the good gods!

CLEOPATRA   Nay, that's certain.

IRAS

I'll never see't! For I am sure my nails
Are stronger than mine eyes.

CLEOPATRA   Why, that's the way
To fool their preparation and to conquer
Their most absurd intents.

       Enter Charmian.

                 Now, Charmian!
Show me, my women, like a queen. Go fetch   227
My best attires. I am again for Cydnus,
To meet Mark Antony. Sirrah Iras, go—   229
Now, noble Charmian, we'll dispatch indeed—   230
And when thou hast done this chare I'll give thee
   leave   231
To play till doomsday. Bring our crown and all.   232
              [Exit Iras.] A noise within.
Wherefore's this noise?

       Enter a Guardsman.

GUARDSMAN   Here is a rural fellow
That will not be denied Your Highness' presence.
He brings you figs.

CLEOPATRA

Let him come in.   *Exit Guardsman.*
           What poor an instrument   236
May do a noble deed! He brings me liberty.
My resolution's placed, and I have nothing   238
Of woman in me. Now from head to foot
I am marble-constant; now the fleeting moon   240
No planet is of mine.

       *Enter Guardsman, and Clown [bringing in a
       basket].*

GUARDSMAN   This is the man.   241

CLEOPATRA   Avoid, and leave him.   *Exit Guardsman.*   242
Hast thou the pretty worm of Nilus there,   243
That kills and pains not?

CLOWN   Truly, I have him, but I would not be the party
that should desire you to touch him, for his biting is
immortal. Those that do die of it do seldom or never   247
recover.

CLEOPATRA   Remember'st thou any that have died on't?

CLOWN   Very many, men and women too. I heard of   250
one of them no longer than yesterday—a very honest
woman, but something given to lie, as a woman   252
should not do but in the way of honesty—how she
died of the biting of it, what pain she felt. Truly, she
makes a very good report o'th' worm. But he that will
believe all that they say shall never be saved by half   256
that they do. But this is most falliable, the worm's an   257
odd worm.

CLEOPATRA   Get thee hence, farewell.

CLOWN   I wish you all joy of the worm.
                   [He sets down his basket.]

CLEOPATRA   Farewell.

CLOWN   You must think this, look you, that the worm
will do his kind.   263

CLEOPATRA   Ay, ay; farewell.

CLOWN   Look you, the worm is not to be trusted but in
the keeping of wise people, for indeed there is no
goodness in the worm.

CLEOPATRA   Take thou no care; it shall be heeded.   268

CLOWN   Very good. Give it nothing, I pray you, for it is
not worth the feeding.

CLEOPATRA   Will it eat me?

CLOWN   You must not think I am so simple but I know
the devil himself will not eat a woman. I know that a
woman is a dish for the gods, if the devil dress her   274
not. But truly, these same whoreson devils do the   275
gods great harm in their women, for in every ten that
they make, the devils mar five.

CLEOPATRA   Well, get thee gone. Farewell.

CLOWN   Yes, forsooth. I wish you joy o'th' worm.
                           Exit.

       [Enter Iras with royal attire.]

CLEOPATRA

Give me my robe. Put on my crown. I have
Immortal longings in me. Now no more   281
The juice of Egypt's grape shall moist this lip.
              [The women dress her.]
Yare, yare, good Iras; quick. Methinks I hear   283
Antony call; I see him rouse himself
To praise my noble act. I hear him mock
The luck of Caesar, which the gods give men   286
To excuse their after wrath. Husband, I come!   287
Now to that name my courage prove my title!   288
I am fire and air; my other elements   289

---

220 **boy** (Allusion to the practice of having women's parts acted by boys on the Elizabethan stage.)   227 **Show** Display   229 **Sirrah** (Compare *sirs*, addressed to the women, in 4.15.90.)   230 **dispatch** (1) finish (2) hasten   231 **chare** task, chore   232.1 *Exit Iras* (It is possible that Charmian leaves, too.)   236 **What** How   238 **placed** fixed 240 **fleeting** inconstant, changing   241 **s.d.** *Clown* rustic   242 **Avoid** Withdraw   243 **worm** snake, serpent. (But elsewhere in this scene with the added connotation of "the male sexual organ" and "earthworm.")   247 **immortal** (Blunder for "mortal.")

250 **heard of** heard from   252 **to lie** (With sexual second meaning hinted at also in *honest*, i.e., "chaste," *die*, i.e., "reach orgasm," and *worm*.)   256 **all . . . half** (The Clown comically reverses the sensible order of these two words.)   257 **falliable** (Blunder for "infallible.") 263 **his kind** its natural function.   268 **Take thou no care** Don't worry   274 **dress** prepare, as in cooking. (With a suggestion also of dressing in alluring clothes.)   275 **whoreson** i.e., rascally, abominable. (A slang expression.)   281 **Immortal longings** longings for immortality   283 **Yare** Quickly   286–7 **which . . . wrath** the luck that the gods give men when they intend to mock and punish them subsequently for their hubris.   288 **to . . . title!** may my courage prove my right to call myself Antony's wife!   289 **other elements** i.e., earth and water, the heavier elements

I give to baser life. So, have you done?
Come then, and take the last warmth of my lips.
Farewell, kind Charmian. Iras, long farewell.
                          [*She kisses them. Iras falls and dies.*]
Have I the aspic in my lips? Dost fall?   293
If thou and nature can so gently part,
The stroke of death is as a lover's pinch,
Which hurts, and is desired. Dost thou lie still?
If thus thou vanishest, thou tell'st the world
It is not worth leave-taking.   298
CHARMIAN
Dissolve, thick cloud, and rain, that I may say
The gods themselves do weep!
CLEOPATRA   This proves me base.
If she first meet the curlèd Antony,   301
He'll make demand of her, and spend that kiss   302
Which is my heaven to have. [*To an asp*] Come, thou
mortal wretch,   303
With thy sharp teeth this knot intrinsicate   304
Of life at once untie. Poor venomous fool,
Be angry, and dispatch. Oh, couldst thou speak,
That I might hear thee call great Caesar ass
Unpolicied!
CHARMIAN   O eastern star!
CLEOPATRA   Peace, peace!   308
Dost thou not see my baby at my breast,
That sucks the nurse asleep?
CHARMIAN   Oh, break! Oh, break!
CLEOPATRA
As sweet as balm, as soft as air, as gentle—
O Antony!—Nay, I will take thee too.
                    [*Applying another asp to her arm.*]
What should I stay—   *Dies.* 313
CHARMIAN
In this wild world? So, fare thee well.   314
Now boast thee, Death, in thy possession lies
A lass unparalleled. Downy windows, close;   316
And golden Phoebus never be beheld
Of eyes again so royal! Your crown's awry;   318
I'll mend it, and then play—   319

          Enter the Guard, rustling in.

FIRST GUARD
Where's the Queen?
CHARMIAN   Speak softly. Wake her not.
FIRST GUARD
Caesar hath sent—
CHARMIAN   Too slow a messenger.
                    [*She applies an asp to herself.*]

Oh, come apace, dispatch! I partly feel thee.
FIRST GUARD
Approach, ho! All's not well. Caesar's beguiled.   323
SECOND GUARD
There's Dolabella sent from Caesar. Call him.
                                       [*Exit a guard.*]
FIRST GUARD
What work is here, Charmian? Is this well done?
CHARMIAN
It is well done, and fitting for a princess
Descended of so many royal kings.
Ah, soldier!   *Charmian dies.*

          Enter Dolabella.

DOLABELLA
How goes it here?
SECOND GUARD   All dead.
DOLABELLA   Caesar, thy thoughts
Touch their effects in this. Thyself art coming   330
To see performed the dreaded act which thou
So sought'st to hinder.

          Enter Caesar and all his train, marching.

ALL   A way there, a way for Caesar!   333
DOLABELLA
Oh, sir, you are too sure an augurer;
That you did fear is done.
CAESAR   Bravest at the last,   335
She leveled at our purposes and, being royal,   336
Took her own way. The manner of their deaths?
I do not see them bleed.
DOLABELLA   Who was last with them?
FIRST GUARD
A simple countryman, that brought her figs.   339
This was his basket.
CAESAR   Poisoned, then.
FIRST GUARD   Oh, Caesar,
This Charmian lived but now; she stood and spake.
I found her trimming up the diadem
On her dead mistress; tremblingly she stood,
And on the sudden dropped.
CAESAR   Oh, noble weakness!
If they had swallowed poison, 'twould appear
By external swelling; but she looks like sleep,   346
As she would catch another Antony   347
In her strong toil of grace.
DOLABELLA   Here on her breast   348
There is a vent of blood and something blown;   349
The like is on her arm.

---

293 **aspic** asp   298 **is . . . leave-taking** does not deserve a ceremonious farewell.   301 **curlèd** with curled hair   302 **make demand** (1) ask questions (2) ask pleasure.   **spend that kiss** expend his desire on her   303 **mortal** deadly.   **wretch** (An affectionate term of abuse, like *fool* in line 305.)   304 **intrinsicate** intricate   308 **Unpolicied** outwitted.   **eastern star** i.e., Venus, the morning star.   313 **What** Why   314 **wild** savage. (Sometimes emended to *vild*, "vile.")   316 **Downy windows** i.e., Soft eyelids   318 **Of** by   319 **mend** fix, straighten

323 **beguiled** cheated, tricked.   330 **Touch their effects** meet with realization   333 **A way** Make a path   335 **That** that which   336 **leveled at** aimed at, guessed   339 **simple** humbly born   346 **like sleep** as if asleep   347 **As** as if   348 **toil** net   349 **vent** discharge.   **blown** deposited, or, swollen

FIRST GUARD
   This is an aspic's trail, and these fig leaves
   Have slime upon them, such as th'aspic leaves
   Upon the caves of Nile.
CAESAR   Most probable
   That so she died; for her physician tells me
   She hath pursued conclusions infinite   355
   Of easy ways to die. Take up her bed,
   And bear her women from the monument.
   She shall be buried by her Antony.
   No grave upon the earth shall clip in it   359

355 conclusions experiments   **359 clip** embrace, clasp

   A pair so famous. High events as these
   Strike those that make them; and their story is   361
   No less in pity than his glory which   362
   Brought them to be lamented. Our army shall   363
   In solemn show attend this funeral,
   And then to Rome. Come, Dolabella, see
   High order in this great solemnity.   366
          Exeunt omnes, [bearing the dead bodies].

361 Strike . . . them touch with sorrow those who brought about these deeds   **361–3 their story . . . lamented** the story of these famous lovers is no less pitiable than the fame of him who brought them low is glorious.   **366.1** *omnes* all

Coriolanus

Coriolanus may be Shakespeare's last tragedy. Even though external evidence is scarce as to its actual date, the style suggests a time around 1608. If so, Shakespeare's final statement on humanity's tragic destiny is disillusioned, wry, almost anticlimactic, in the vein of his Roman and classical tragedies rather than of his tragedies of evil (*Hamlet, Othello, King Lear, Macbeth*). Shakespeare based *Coriolanus* on Plutarch's *Lives of the Noble Grecians and Romans*, in the translation by Sir Thomas North. As in the presumably earlier Plutarchan plays, *Julius Caesar, Timon of Athens*, and *Antony and Cleopatra*, and in the non-Plutarchan *Titus Andronicus* and *Troilus and Cressida*, Shakespeare's ancient political world is one of constant upheaval. In the clash of ideologies, the plebeian mob turns giddily from one idol to the next, and strong men rise briefly, only to be supplanted by rivals. The result of unceasing change is political stalemate. The great men of the ancient world seem fascinatingly alive to us, but they also seem blind to their own limitations, fatally proud, and hemmed in by circumstance. Their virtues and their defects are inseparable and indeed often identical, for private virtues serve these tragic heroes poorly in the amoral and pitiless arena of politics. Their natures cannot easily be moved from a predilection for catastrophe, and so their downfall proceeds inexorably from what Aristotle, writing of Greek tragedy, termed a tragic flaw, or hamartia, in their characters. The ending, ironic rather than cathartic in its effect, leaves us with an impression of tragic waste.

Coriolanus admirably captures this conflict dividing personal nobility from political reality. The play returns to a political problem that has been studied before in *Julius Caesar:* the rivalry in ancient Rome between republican and absolutist forms of government. *Coriolanus*, although written later than *Julius Caesar*, analyzes an earlier period of Roman history when the tribunes chosen to represent the interests of Rome's common people succeeded in blocking the attempts of the aristocratic party to install a military leader of their own persuasion (Caius Marcius, given the honorific name of Coriolanus for his triumphal success over Corioles) as consul with an absolute power that could suppress the political and economic demands of the populace. In *Coriolanus*, we thus witness the birth of republicanism in its distinctively Roman form, a blend of aristocratic and democratic elements; in *Julius Caesar*, we see the demise of this delicately balanced regime. Shakespeare views both events with ironic detachment.

Republicanism was potentially a matter of controversy on the Jacobean stage, insofar as spectators might draw analogies between it and parliamentary efforts to curb the power of the English throne. The differences are real, of course, especially in *Julius Caesar*, in which Caesar's claim to absolute rule has no sanction of divine right and Brutus' republicanism is ineffably genteel rather than populist. *Coriolanus*, however, hits closer to home. Here the plebeians are profoundly dissatisfied with aristocratic rule. Popular unrest over famine and high prices leads to rioting and the expression of democratic sentiments such as were heard and feared by the authorities in England. Riots over scarcity of grain occurred in Northamptonshire, Warwickshire, and Leicestershire during the summer of 1607. King James I, who had come to the throne in 1603, adopted a hostile stance toward Puritan efforts to democratize Church government and of corresponding challenges in Parliament on behalf of the common law. From the vantage point of ancient Rome, distant in time and place, *Coriolanus* appraises the conflict in terms that bear no precise relation to Jacobean England but yet have a timeless relevance. Without taking sides, the play dwells on the ambiguity of the struggle and on the indecisive, self-defeating results achieved by both parties.

As in *Julius Caesar*, men on both sides are passionately sincere but driven to shortsighted extremism. The tribunes insist on behalf of the mob that the people's voice is to be the ultimate law of Rome. Coriolanus, in angry response, sees the mob and its elected tribunes as the enemies of hierarchical prerogative, threatening the very existence of the state. Which view is correct? Is the people's voice a brave force of resistance against aristocratic hauteur and class privilege, as exemplified by Coriolanus, or is the tribunes' program a grab for power by demagogues willing to risk anarchy and to weaken Rome's military might? Shakespeare, like Plutarch, explores the weaknesses and strengths of both parties. He uses a dramatic structure, as in *Julius Caesar*, of sustained ambiguity. If any conclusion emerges, it is that violent political struggle leads only to an undoing of those civilized institutions that the few persons of moderation like Menenius, caught in the middle, strive vainly to preserve.

The citizens play a dominant role in *Coriolanus*. The action begins, as in *Julius Caesar*, with a mob scene, setting a tone of ominous instability. The mob is too easily swayed. Lacking any consistent political philosophy of its own, it will follow whatever charismatic orator catches its fancy. It despises Coriolanus one moment and adulates him the next. Its own members agree that the mob is a "many-headed multitude," directionless and irresponsible (2.3.10–17). Other characters besides Coriolanus protest the offensive stench of the crowd, "stinking" breaths, "reechy" necks, "stinking greasy caps," and unclean teeth (2.1.208, 235; 4.6.138). The Roman citizens are a "herd," "apronmen," "garlic eaters," curs, hares, foxes, geese, a "cockle of rebellion, insolence, sedition" (3.1.35, 73; 4.6.101–3). This deliberately repulsive portrayal, part of an excremental motif that runs throughout the play, merely intensifies what is true in the other Roman plays and in the English history plays as well. Nowhere in Shakespeare does mob action lead to anything constructive or even politically acceptable. At the same time, the mob does not bear chief responsibility for disaster either, in *Coriolanus* or elsewhere in Shakespeare. Individually, its members are good-natured, slow to be aroused, quick to forget injury, too credulous indeed for their own good. In *Coriolanus*, they have to be prompted again and again by the tribunes to press forward with their resentment. Many citizens, left to themselves, are wise and patient. They are a neutral force, dangerous only when whipped up to collective frenzy by demagogic persuasion.

Much blame would seem to fall then on the tribunes, and indeed even the more moderate patricians, such as Menenius, are deeply mistrustful of Junius Brutus and Sicinius Velutus. These tribunes are willing to risk mob violence to achieve their ends, especially when they urge the "rabble of plebeians" to "bustle about Coriolanus" (3.1.183–8). Ignoring Menenius's pleas that "This is the way to kindle, not to quench," and that "Confusion's near" (lines 193, 200), the tribunes deliberately goad Coriolanus to anger. Their strategy is to foment clamor, and "with a din confused / Enforce the present execution," shouting down reason with hysteria (3.3.21–2). They care-

fully stage each confrontation with Coriolanus, rehearsing the citizens in what they are to do, cannily timing their provocations. They talk like conspirators. The metadramatic dimension of this emphasis on staging a political campaign suggests that politics can too easily become a theatrical spectacle of manipulating appearances. Shakespeare's audience, accustomed to governmental warnings against mob violence, would probably have understood the menace posed by the tribunes and would have savored the irony that Rome is weakened rather than strengthened by their machinations.

Still, Shakespeare's portrayal of the tribunes is remarkably sympathetic. They honestly fear that Coriolanus seeks "one sole throne, without assistance" (4.6.34), and that as consul he will do everything he can to suppress the people's liberties. This is no idle fear; Coriolanus's own friends merely counsel him to attack the tribunes after he has achieved power, not before. Although the tribunes do arouse the people to actions they would not otherwise take, the tribunes believe they are doing so in the people's best interests, providing leadership for a constituency that has hitherto lacked a voice. They believe in a government "by the consent of all" that can hold aristocratic insolence in check through the "lawful censure" of the common people. "What is the city but the people?" (3.1.202–4; 3.3.50). Moreover, they are not revolutionaries by temperament and do abandon mob tactics once they have made their point. Their achievements mock them when Rome proves defenseless against the return of Coriolanus, but even here they can argue with some reason that Rome would have achieved peace had it not been for Coriolanus's lawless vengeance.

Perhaps, then, Coriolanus must bear the responsibility for provoking democratic extremism through his contempt of the citizenry. From his first appearance, he antagonizes us, as well as the populace, with his curt, insulting manner. He addresses the people as "dissentious rogues," itching with scabby diseases, and dismisses them as "curs" who are "beneath abhorring" (1.1.163–7). His hatred amounts to revulsion, and we fear he is all too ready to employ his sword on "thousands of these quartered slaves" (line 198). He responds to the tribunes' calculated staging of political opposition by demonstrating that he is no actor. Constitutionally unwilling to prostrate himself to the mob by playing the humble role they ask of him in return for their votes ("It is a part / That I shall blush in acting," he tells his friends at 2.2.145–6), Coriolanus prefers to lose on principle rather than to win through catering to popular demand as an actor might do. "You have put me now to such a part which never / I shall discharge to th' life," he insists to his mother (3.2.107–8). The politician's role is one that belies Coriolanus's true nature in the most fundamentally dishonest way. "Away, my disposition, and possess me / Some harlot's spirit!" Reluctantly he consents to "mountebank their loves, / Cog their hearts from them" (3.2.113–35). Small wonder that the commoners are scarcely impressed by any sincerity in his wooing of their votes. When denied the consulship by the tribunes, in fact, he draws his sword in the marketplace, relishing the opportunity for a military solution. His tendency to forget names betrays a coldness and a self-centeredness that is at times nearly babylike in its narcissism. Although he professes not to speak merely in anger, he is too easily baited by the tribunes and too quick to speak his mind. Even those who admire his virtues concede that "to seem to affect the malice and displeasure of the people is as bad as that which he dislikes, to flatter them for their love" (2.2.21–3). Coriolanus is glad to hear of the impending Volscian attack on Rome, for he prefers war to peace and sees conscription as a way of channeling revolutionary energies against an outward foe. He professes love of his country, but, because his attachment is to an exclusively patrician order, he is ready to turn traitor against a Rome that gives a political voice to the plebeians he so abhors.

Nevertheless, the portrayal of Coriolanus, as of the tribunes, is delicately balanced. We admire Coriolanus's hatred of hypocrisy. He is scrupulously honest, refusing all spoils of war except those to which his fellow soldiers are entitled. Despite his pride in family and name, he genuinely dislikes to hear himself praised. Though he disdains to lead cowardly citizen-soldiers and shines most in single deeds of valor rather than in generalship, he is inspiring and even popular among valiant soldiers like himself. He is generous in praising the achievements of his colleagues. Even in matters of state, he shows resoluteness and integrity. He has a consistent political philosophy, bolstered by Menenius's comparison of the state to a body in which the members must harmoniously interact (1.1.94 ff). Jacobean spectators would recognize in this analogy the orthodox appeal to order and degree they heard regularly from pulpit and throne, even though they might also recognize that it is being self-interestedly applied by one who enjoys the perquisites of noble birth. Coriolanus, at any rate, firmly believes that the established prerogatives of the aristocracy are Rome's only safe bulwark against chaos. By granting power to the tribunes, in his view, the Senate has sealed its doom. He sees the people as their own worst enemies, insatiable and irrational in their demands, unable to comprehend the subtleties of government, instinctively envious of their betters. Such base mortals require subjection to their masters, though they cannot be expected to realize this themselves. Coriolanus knows that his views are out of fashion and that the current trend is to appease popular demands with compromise, but he can see no end to the compromises that will be needed once the tribunes have established their prerogatives. He prefers a battle to the death and welcomes the danger to himself. If his courage and consistency are "too absolute," if he is "too noble for the world" (3.2.41; 3.1.261), he would prefer to believe that the fault lies in that world rather than in him.

Between the extremes of democratic and aristocratic rule, the middle position of compromise offers many attractions. Menenius sanely desires to see "On both sides more respect" and pleads with those who would be "truly your country's friend" to "temperately proceed to what you would / Thus violently redress" (3.1.184; 222–4). Although his sympathies are patrician, he acknowledges the tribunes' power as a political reality which must be dealt with. He finds fault with Coriolanus for not having "temporized" (4.6.17). Menenius is a bluff, honest fellow who directs our sympathies, like the equally outspoken Enobarbus in *Antony and Cleopatra*. Yet compromise always has its ridiculous aspect. Menenius increasingly assumes the self-contradictory role of the appeaser, like York of *Richard II*, urging actions that are repugnant to him personally. His seemingly sage advice to the plebeians in his fable of the belly is in part at least a rhetorical strategy calculated to quiet plebeian restiveness without addressing their real demands. At the last, after having denounced the tribunes for betraying Rome, Menenius must go as their ambassador to beg mercy of Coriolanus. When Aufidius's guardsmen scoff at him for having been turned away by Coriolanus, Menenius is beyond caring for their taunts. He does, in fact, hold to a consistent principle—the survival of his beloved city at whatever cost to his pride. He and Rome pragmatically blunder through, though not without loss of dignity.

Coriolanus's mother, Volumnia, is caught in an even more ironic dilemma. She, of course, shares her son's aristocratic pride, having taught him a code of death before dishonor. The bond between mother and son is extraordinarily, even distressingly, close. Emotionally, it takes the place of Coriolanus's bloodless marriage to the chaste and retiring Virgilia. Volumnia, in fact, speaks of Coriolanus metaphorically as her husband and of his warlike prowess as a vicarious substitute for "the embracements of his bed" (1.3.4–5). Throughout, Coriolanus's deeds of war are love offerings to his mother. Every citizen of Rome knows that whatever Coriolanus has done for his country he also did "to please his mother" (1.1.37). Yet, because Volumnia has not been a properly nourishing mother, Coriolanus is poised between two irreconcilable cravings: to please a mother whose demands can never be satisfied and to fashion an identity that is entirely self-made. He needs her approval but also wishes to be beholden to no one, least of all to her. His rigid masculinity in war, we realize, is in part an attempt to escape from his sense of vulnerability to his mother and to the plebeians whom he must beg for votes—indeed, to Rome itself, the city that has banished him like a rejecting mother and that he finally cannot bring himself to destroy. Even Coriolanus's soldiership collapses into an attempt to please his mother.

The conflict reaches its crisis when Volumnia's oppressive demands take the form of insisting that her son achieve fame not only in war but also in politics. Here she must, like Menenius, encourage the compromise and "policy" that they all hate. She and Menenius stage Coriolanus' public appearances with as much care as the tribunes rehearse their plebeians. They "prompt" Coriolanus to "perform a part" for which he has no aptitude (3.2.108–11); as he later says, capitulating to his mother for the last time, "Like a dull actor now, / I have forgot my part, and I am out" (5.3.40–1). This integrity has its admirable side but brings disaster to Volumnia's plans. She is defeated by the very pride she has engendered in him, and he is defeated by her overriding ambition for him. To win her praise, he must put away his true disposition, becoming effeminate and emasculated like a "harlot" or "an eunuch" (3.2.114–16). To satisfy her quest for fame, he must give up his attack on Rome, perjure himself to Aufidius, and die a condemned traitor to the Volscian state. Volumnia's crushing and engulfing love for her son proves ironically fatal to everything they have cherished.

Coriolanus's relationship to Aufidius is one of love as well as hate, and it, too, poses a fatal conflict. Despite their rivalry to the death, these two military heroes are singularly attracted to one another. Coriolanus confesses "I sin in envying his nobility," and considers Aufidius "a lion / That I am proud to hunt" (1.1.231–7). Coriolanus's fate is to love his enemy and hate his birthplace. Aufidius, in turn, greets Coriolanus with more joy "Than when I first my wedded mistress saw / Bestride my threshold" (4.5.122–3). The homoerotic resonances of this metaphor need not be read literally, but they do recall similar images of emotional bonding among men who are enemies in battle such as Hector and Achilles in *Troilus and Cressida*. The animosity of rivalry persists; Aufidius has always resented Coriolanus's superiority in battle and has planned to overcome him by fair means or foul. In their brief military alliance, Coriolanus proves too attractive a rival, overshadowing the achievements of Aufidius. For these reasons, Aufidius secretly exults in Coriolanus's fatal dilemma, since the Volscian general prefers vengeance to victory over Rome. In a final disillusioning scene, he stages one more public outcry against Coriolanus, goading him into a proud rage, and then with his fellow conspirators ingloriously performs an execution "whereat valor will weep" (5.6.139). Aufidius's virtues, like those of Coriolanus, have been betrayed by his worst instincts. Throughout, the Volscians have been cunning enemies, lying in wait for Rome to tear herself apart. The laws governing the relations between states are brutally competitive, characterized by the "slippery turns" (4.4.12) of fortune that ironically bring together former enemies as allies and then turn them against one another. In this world of sudden reversals, Coriolanus's last act is something he could never have foreseen: saving the Roman state and its tribunes from a destruction he himself had wished on it. As Coriolanus wryly observes of his own destiny (5.3.184–5), "The gods look down, and this unnatural scene / They laugh at."

Onstage today, *Coriolanus* works well as a play of disillusionment and psychological diagnosis of charismatic leadership that is easily attuned to our modern-day mistrust of political infighting and machination. Peter Hall's production at Stratford-upon-Avon in 1959, with Lawrence Olivier as Coriolanus, put mordant stress on the cravenness of the mob and presented Coriolanus's hatred of courtly flattery with genuine sympathy while at the same time stressing his emotional and even neurotic dependency on his mother. In death at the play's end, caught by the ankles as he dangled upside down from an upper platform, Olivier reminded viewers of the grisly end of Mussolini. Tyrone Guthrie's 1963 production for the Nottingham Playhouse, in the decor of the French Empire, explored hysterical and homosexual psychological dimensions in the title figure. In John Barton's 1967 production for the Royal Shakespeare Company and that of Terry Hands in 1977, Coriolanus and Aufidius were costumed in identical armor and other matching effects to underscore the narcissism and sibling-rivalry aspects of their competitive love-hate relationship. Politically, the play has lent itself to Marxist readings, as in Prague in 1959 and especially in Bertolt Brecht's adaptation of 1951–1952, for whom the proletarians were heroic and the tribunes honorable. Brecht's collaborators at the Berliner Ensemble in East Berlin continued in this partisan vein in 1964. For Giorgio Strehler in Milan in 1947, the play was about the Marxist dialectic of history, with its emphasis on material causes and the inevitability of historical change. Other directors have seen in Coriolanus a kind of Napoleon. More apolitical presentions have emphasized the ironic and disillusioning aspects of the play, as in Terry Hands's 1977 production, featuring Alan Howard as Coriolanus, a man doomed by his failure to enact his own heroic myths. An especially splendid production is available on long-playing records, in audio only, with Richard Burton as the eponymous hero—surely a role to which Burton's sardonic and intellectually brilliant acting style is singularly well attuned.

Coriolanus

[Dramatis Personae

CAIUS MARCIUS, *afterward* CAIUS MARCIUS CORIOLANUS

TITUS LARTIUS,
COMINIUS, } *Roman generals*
MENENIUS AGRIPPA, *friend of Coriolanus*
SICINIUS VELUTUS,
JUNIUS BRUTUS, } *Roman tribunes*
NICANOR, *a Roman traitor*
Two Roman PATRICIANS
Two Roman SENATORS
An AEDILE
Two Roman OFFICERS
A Roman LIEUTENANT
Roman SOLDIERS
A Roman HERALD
Seven Roman CITIZENS
MESSENGERS

VOLUMNIA, *Coriolanus's mother*
VIRGILIA, *Coriolanus's wife*

Young MARCIUS, *son of Coriolanus and Virgilia*
VALERIA, *friend of Virgilia*
A GENTLEWOMAN, *attending Virgilia*

TULLUS AUFIDIUS, *Volscian general*
Two SENATORS *of Corioles*
Three Volscian LORDS
A Volscian LIEUTENANT
A Volscian SOLDIER
Three CONSPIRATORS
ADRIAN, *a Volscian*
A CITIZEN *of Antium*
Two Volscian WATCHMEN
Three SERVINGMEN *of Aufidius*

Roman and Volscian Senators, Patricians, Aediles, Lictors, Captains, Soldiers, Citizens, Messengers, Servingmen, an Usher attending Valeria, and Attendants

SCENE: *Rome and the neighborhood; Corioles and the neighborhood; Antium]*

1.1

Enter a company of mutinous Citizens, with staves, clubs, and other weapons.

FIRST CITIZEN   Before we proceed any further, hear me speak.

ALL   Speak, speak.

FIRST CITIZEN   You are all resolved rather to die than to famish?   5

ALL   Resolved, resolved.

FIRST CITIZEN   First, you know Caius Marcius is chief enemy to the people.

ALL   We know't, we know't.

FIRST CITIZEN   Let us kill him, and we'll have corn at   10
our own price. Is't a verdict?   11

ALL   No more talking on't. Let it be done. Away, away!   12

SECOND CITIZEN   One word, good citizens.

FIRST CITIZEN   We are accounted poor citizens, the patricians good. What authority surfeits on would relieve   15
us. If they would yield us but the superfluity while it   16
were wholesome, we might guess they relieved us hu-   17
manely. But they think we are too dear. The leanness   18

1.1. Location: Rome. A street
5 famish starve.

10 corn grain, such as wheat or barley   **11 Is't a verdict?** Are we agreed?   **12 on't** of it, about it.   **15 good** i.e., noble, well-to-do. **authority** those in authority, the nobility   **16 but the superfluity** merely the excess   **17 wholesome** good to eat   **18 too dear** costing more than we are worth (but also, paradoxically, *a gain;* see line 21).

that afflicts us, the object of our misery, is as an inven- 19
tory to particularize their abundance. Our sufferance is 20
a gain to them. Let us revenge this with our pikes ere 21
we become rakes; for the gods know I speak this in 22
hunger for bread, not in thirst for revenge.

SECOND CITIZEN   Would you proceed especially against
Caius Marcius?

ALL   Against him first. He's a very dog to the common- 26
alty. 27

SECOND CITIZEN   Consider you what services he has
done for his country?

FIRST CITIZEN   Very well, and could be content to give
him good report for't, but that he pays himself with
being proud.

SECOND CITIZEN   Nay, but speak not maliciously.

FIRST CITIZEN   I say unto you, what he hath done fa- 34
mously he did it to that end. Though soft-conscienced 35
men can be content to say it was for his country, he
did it to please his mother and to be partly proud, 37
which he is, even to the altitude of his virtue. 38

SECOND CITIZEN   What he cannot help in his nature you
account a vice in him. You must in no way say he is
covetous.

FIRST CITIZEN   If I must not, I need not be barren of ac- 42
cusations. He hath faults, with surplus, to tire in repe- 43
tition. (*Shouts within.*) What shouts are these? The 44
other side o'th' city is risen. Why stay we prating 45
here? To th' Capitol! 46

ALL   Come, come.

FIRST CITIZEN   Soft, who comes here? 48

Enter Menenius Agrippa.

SECOND CITIZEN   Worthy Menenius Agrippa, one that
hath always loved the people.

FIRST CITIZEN   He's one honest enough. Would all the
rest were so!

MENENIUS
What work's, my countrymen, in hand? Where go you
With bats and clubs? The matter? Speak, I pray you. 54

FIRST CITIZEN   Our business is not unknown to the
Senate. They have had inkling this fortnight what we
intend to do, which now we'll show 'em in deeds.
They say poor suitors have strong breaths; they shall 58
know we have strong arms too.

MENENIUS
Why, masters, my good friends, mine honest
neighbors, 60
Will you undo yourselves? 61

FIRST CITIZEN
We cannot, sir. We are undone already.

MENENIUS
I tell you, friends, most charitable care
Have the patricians of you. For your wants, 64
Your suffering in this dearth, you may as well 65
Strike at the heaven with your staves as lift them
Against the Roman state, whose course will on 67
The way it takes, cracking ten thousand curbs 68
Of more strong link asunder than can ever
Appear in your impediment. For the dearth, 70
The gods, not the patricians, make it, and
Your knees to them, not arms, must help. Alack, 72
You are transported by calamity 73
Thither where more attends you, and you slander 74
The helms o'th' state, who care for you like fathers, 75
When you curse them as enemies.

FIRST CITIZEN   Care for us? True indeed! They ne'er
cared for us yet: suffer us to famish, and their storehouses crammed with grain; make edicts for usury to 79
support usurers; repeal daily any wholesome act established against the rich; and provide more piercing 81
statutes daily to chain up and restrain the poor. If the
wars eat us not up, they will; and there's all the love
they bear us.

MENENIUS   Either you must
Confess yourselves wondrous malicious,
Or be accused of folly. I shall tell you
A pretty tale. It may be you have heard it,
But, since it serves my purpose, I will venture
To stale't a little more. 90

FIRST CITIZEN   Well, I'll hear it, sir; yet you must not
think to fob off our disgrace with a tale. But, an't 92
please you, deliver. 93

MENENIUS
There was a time when all the body's members
Rebelled against the belly, thus accused it:
That only like a gulf it did remain 96
I'th' midst o'th' body, idle and unactive,
Still cupboarding the viand, never bearing 98
Like labor with the rest, where th'other instruments 99
Did see and hear, devise, instruct, walk, feel, 100
And, mutually participate, did minister 101

---

19 object spectacle   **19–20 is as . . . abundance** serves as a catalogue
or inventory to point out in detail (by means of contrast) how rich
they are.   **20 sufferance** suffering   **21 pikes** spears, lances; pitch-
forks. (Playing on *rakes,* line 22.)   **22 rakes** i.e., as lean as rakes
26 a very dog i.e., inhumanly cruel   **26–7 commonalty** common people.   **34–5 famously** achieving fame   **35 to that end** i.e., in order to
become famous and as an upshot of his pride.   **soft-conscienced**
weak-minded, lacking real conviction   **37 to be partly proud** partly
out of pride   **38 even . . . virtue** i.e., he is as proud as he is brave.
42 If Even if   **43–4 to tire in repetition** to tire out the speaker in
reporting them.   **45 prating** talking idly   **46 Capitol** Temple of
Jupiter on Capitoline Hill; used here to stand for the Senate building.
48 Soft Stay, stop   **54 bats** cudgels   **58 suitors** petitioners.   **strong**
strong-smelling. (With a play in the next line on *strong,* "mighty.")

60 masters i.e., good sirs. (A term appropriate to ordinary citizens.)
61 undo ruin   **64 For** As for. (Also in line 70.)   **65 dearth** famine
67 on continue on   **68 curbs** restraints. (A term from horsemanship;
the curb is attached to the bit.)   **70 in your impediment** in any hin-
drance you may be able to offer.   **72 knees** i.e., prayers. (With a play
on *arms* as parts of the body and as weapons.)   **73 transported** carried away   **74 attends** awaits   **75 helms** helmsmen   **79 for** permitting   **81 piercing** severe   **90 stale't** make it stale by repeating it
92 fob . . . disgrace set aside by a trick our feeling of suffering hardship.   **an't** if it   **93 deliver** tell your tale.   **96 gulf** open pit,
whirlpool   **98 Still . . . viand** always stowing away the food
99 Like equal.   **where** whereas.   **instruments** organs   **100 devise**
deliberate, think   **101 participate** participating, taking part

Unto the appetite and affection common   102
Of the whole body. The belly answered—

FIRST CITIZEN   Well, sir, what answer made the belly?

MENENIUS
Sir, I shall tell you. With a kind of smile,
Which ne'er came from the lungs, but even thus—   106
For, look you, I may make the belly smile
As well as speak—it tauntingly replied
To th' discontented members, the mutinous parts
That envied his receipt; even so most fitly   110
As you malign our senators for that   111
They are not such as you.

FIRST CITIZEN   Your belly's answer—What?
The kingly-crownèd head, the vigilant eye,
The counselor heart, the arm our soldier,
Our steed the leg, the tongue our trumpeter,
With other muniments and petty helps   117
In this our fabric, if that they—

MENENIUS   What then?   118
'Fore me, this fellow speaks! What then? What then? 119

FIRST CITIZEN
Should by the cormorant belly be restrained,   120
Who is the sink o'th' body—

MENENIUS   Well, what then?   121

FIRST CITIZEN
The former agents, if they did complain,   122
What could the belly answer?

MENENIUS   I will tell you.
If you'll bestow a small—of what you have little—   124
Patience awhile, you'st hear the belly's answer.   125

FIRST CITIZEN
You're long about it.

MENENIUS   Note me this, good friend;
Your most grave belly was deliberate,   127
Not rash like his accusers, and thus answered:
"True is it, my incorporate friends," quoth he,   129
"That I receive the general food at first
Which you do live upon; and fit it is,
Because I am the storehouse and the shop
Of the whole body. But, if you do remember,
I send it through the rivers of your blood
Even to the court, the heart, to the seat o'th' brain; 135
And, through the cranks and offices of man,   136
The strongest nerves and small inferior veins   137
From me receive that natural competency   138

Whereby they live. And though that all at once"—
You, my good friends, this says the belly, mark me—

FIRST CITIZEN
Ay, sir, well, well.

MENENIUS   "Though all at once cannot
See what I do deliver out to each,
Yet I can make my audit up, that all   143
From me do back receive the flour of all,   144
And leave me but the bran." What say you to't?   145

FIRST CITIZEN
It was an answer. How apply you this?

MENENIUS
The senators of Rome are this good belly,
And you the mutinous members. For examine
Their counsels and their cares, digest things rightly 149
Touching the weal o'th' common, you shall find   150
No public benefit which you receive
But it proceeds or comes from them to you
And no way from yourselves. What do you think,
You, the great toe of this assembly?

FIRST CITIZEN   I the great toe? Why the great toe?

MENENIUS
For that, being one o'th' lowest, basest, poorest,
Of this most wise rebellion, thou goest foremost.
Thou rascal, that art worst in blood to run,   158
Lead'st first to win some vantage.   159
But make you ready your stiff bats and clubs.   160
Rome and her rats are at the point of battle;
The one side must have bale.

        Enter Caius Marcius.

                          Hail, noble Marcius!   162

MARCIUS
Thanks.—What's the matter, you dissentious rogues,   163
That, rubbing the poor itch of your opinion,
Make yourselves scabs?

FIRST CITIZEN   We have ever your good word. 165

MARCIUS
He that will give good words to thee will flatter   166
Beneath abhorring. What would you have, you curs,   167
That like nor peace nor war? The one affrights you, 168
The other makes you proud. He that trusts to you,   169
Where he should find you lions, finds you hares;

---

102 affection inclination **106 lungs** i.e., supposed organ of laughter **110 his receipt** what it received. **fitly** fittingly, justly. (Said ironically.) **111 for that** because **117 muniments** furnishings, or defenses **118 fabric** body formed by the conjunction of various parts. **if that** if **119 'Fore me** (An oath.) **120 cormorant** ravenous, rapacious (like the voracious seabird known by that name) **121 sink** cesspool **122 former** just-named **124 small** small quantity **125 you'st** you shall **127 Your** i.e., this **129 incorporate** belonging to one body **135 to the court . . . brain** i.e., to the heart, which is the court and vital center, and to the brain, which is the throne **136 cranks** winding passages. **offices** service rooms of a household; kitchen, etc. **137 nerves** sinews **138 natural competency** sufficiency for the purposes of nature

143 audit balance sheet **144 the flour** i.e., the nourishing part. (With a play on *the flower*, "the pick"; spelled "Flowre" in the Folio.) **145 bran** chaff. **149 digest** analyze, interpret. (With a play on the gastronomic sense.) **150 weal o'th' common** public welfare **158–9 Thou . . . vantage** You inferior specimen of mongrel dog, in the worst of vigor and condition to be leading the pack, are doing so for some tawdry personal advantage. (*Rascal* can also mean "lean deer, not worth the hunting.") **160 stiff bats** sturdy cudgels **162 The one . . . bale** one side or the other must get the worst of it, receive injury. **163 dissentious** rebellious **165 scabs** (1) scurvy fellows, rascals (2) sores. **ever** always **166 give good words to** praise **167 abhorring** contempt. **168 nor . . . nor** neither . . . nor. **The one** War **169 The other** peace. **proud** arrogant and demanding.

Where foxes, geese. You are no surer, no, 171
Than is the coal of fire upon the ice, 172
Or hailstone in the sun. Your virtue is 173
To make him worthy whose offense subdues him, 174
And curse that justice did it. Who deserves greatness 175
Deserves your hate; and your affections are 176
A sick man's appetite, who desires most that
Which would increase his evil. He that depends 178
Upon your favors swims with fins of lead
And hews down oaks with rushes. Hang ye! Trust ye? 180
With every minute you do change a mind
And call him noble that was now your hate, 182
Him vile that was your garland. What's the matter, 183
That in these several places of the city 184
You cry against the noble Senate, who,
Under the gods, keep you in awe, which else 186
Would feed on one another?—What's their seeking? 187

MENENIUS
For corn at their own rates, whereof, they say, 188
The city is well stored.

MARCIUS   Hang 'em! They say?
They'll sit by th' fire and presume to know
What's done i'th' Capitol, who's like to rise, 191
Who thrives and who declines; side factions and
give out 192
Conjectural marriages, making parties strong 193
And feebling such as stand not in their liking 194
Below their cobbled shoes. They say there's grain
enough? 195
Would the nobility lay aside their ruth 196
And let me use my sword, I'd make a quarry 197
With thousands of these quartered slaves as high 198
As I could pick my lance. 199

MENENIUS
Nay, these are almost thoroughly persuaded,
For though abundantly they lack discretion,
Yet are they passing cowardly. But I beseech you, 202
What says the other troop?

MARCIUS   They are dissolved. Hang 'em!
They said they were an-hungry; sighed forth
proverbs, 205
That hunger broke stone walls, that dogs must eat, 206

That meat was made for mouths, that the gods sent
not 207
Corn for the rich men only. With these shreds 208
They vented their complainings, which being
answered 209
And a petition granted them—a strange one,
To break the heart of generosity 211
And make bold power look pale—they threw their
caps
As they would hang them on the horns o'th' moon, 213
Shouting their emulation.

MENENIUS   What is granted them? 214

MARCIUS
Five tribunes to defend their vulgar wisdoms, 215
Of their own choice. One's Junius Brutus,
Sicinius Velutus, and I know not—'Sdeath! 217
The rabble should have first unroofed the city
Ere so prevailed with me. It will in time
Win upon power and throw forth greater themes 220
For insurrection's arguing. 221

MENENIUS   This is strange.

MARCIUS   Go get you home, you fragments! 223

Enter a Messenger, hastily.

MESSENGER
Where's Caius Marcius?

MARCIUS   Here. What's the matter?

MESSENGER
The news is, sir, the Volsces are in arms.

MARCIUS
I am glad on't. Then we shall ha' means to vent 226
Our musty superfluity.—See, our best elders. 227

*Enter Sicinius Velutus, Junius Brutus,
Cominius, Titus Lartius, with other Senators.*

FIRST SENATOR
Marcius, 'tis true that you have lately told us: 228
The Volsces are in arms.

MARCIUS   They have a leader,
Tullus Aufidius, that will put you to't. 230
I sin in envying his nobility,
And were I anything but what I am
I would wish me only he.

COMINIUS   You have fought together? 233

MARCIUS
Were half to half the world by th' ears and he 234
Upon my party, I'd revolt, to make 235

171–3 **You . . . sun** You are no more dependable than a pan of burning coals set down on solid ice or hailstones lying in the sun (both short-lived).   173–5 **Your . . . it** Your distinguishing quality is to glorify the person whose wrongdoing deserves punishment and to curse the justice that punishes him.   175 **Who** Whoever   176 **Deserves** incurs. **affections** desires, propensities   178 **evil** malady.   180 **rushes** slender reeds.   182 **now** just now   183 **garland** object of highest honor and praise.   184 **several** different, various   186 **which else** who otherwise   187 **seeking** demand.   188 **corn** grain.   **rates** prices   191 **like** likely   192–5 **side . . . shoes** (they) take sides in factional disputes and gossip about conjectural alliances among the ruling classes, supporting certain factions while working to destroy others whom they regard as contemptible.   196 **Would the nobility** If only the nobility would.   **ruth** tenderheartedness   197 **quarry** heap of slain men (literally, deer)   198 **quartered** cut into quarters, slaughtered like criminals   199 **pick** pitch   202 **passing** exceedingly   205 **an-hungry** hungry. (The prefix *an* is an archaic intensifier.)   206 **dogs** i.e., even dogs

207 **meat** food   208 **shreds** bits, scraps (of wisdom)   209 **vented** discharged, excreted or farted   211 **generosity** the nobles   213 **As** as if   214 **emulation** rivalry of one another in shouting, or, envy of superiors.   215 **tribunes** official representatives of the people's interests   217 **'Sdeath!** i.e., By God's death! (An oath.)   220 **Win upon** gain advantage over   221 **For insurrection's arguing** to be urged by uprisings.   223 **fragments** scraps. (A term of contempt.)   226 **on't** of it.   **vent** discharge, cast out   227 **musty superfluity** moldy excess.   228 **that** what   230 **to't** i.e., to the test.   233 **together** against one another.   234 **by th' ears** at variance (with the other half)   235 **Upon my party** on my side

Only my wars with him. He is a lion   236
That I am proud to hunt.

FIRST SENATOR   Then, worthy Marcius,
Attend upon Cominius to these wars.   238

COMINIUS
It is your former promise.

MARCIUS   Sir, it is,
And I am constant. Titus Lartius, thou   240
Shalt see me once more strike at Tullus' face.
What, art thou stiff? Stand'st out?

LARTIUS   No, Caius Marcius,   242
I'll lean upon one crutch and fight with t'other
Ere stay behind this business.

MENENIUS   Oh, true bred!

FIRST SENATOR
Your company to th' Capitol, where, I know,   245
Our greatest friends attend us.

LARTIUS [to Cominius]   Lead you on.
[To Marcius] Follow Cominius. We must follow you;
Right worthy you priority.

COMINIUS   Noble Marcius!   248

FIRST SENATOR [to the Citizens]
Hence to your homes, begone!

MARCIUS   Nay, let them follow.
The Volsces have much corn; take these rats thither
To gnaw their garners.—Worshipful mutineers,   251
Your valor puts well forth. Pray follow.   252
                Exeunt. Citizens steal away.
                Manent Sicinius and Brutus.

SICINIUS
Was ever man so proud as is this Marcius?

BRUTUS   He has no equal.

SICINIUS
When we were chosen tribunes for the people—

BRUTUS
Marked you his lip and eyes?

SICINIUS   Nay, but his taunts.

BRUTUS
Being moved, he will not spare to gird the gods.   257

SICINIUS   Bemock the modest moon.   258

BRUTUS
The present wars devour him! He is grown   259
Too proud to be so valiant.

SICINIUS   Such a nature,   260
Tickled with good success, disdains the shadow   261
Which he treads on at noon. But I do wonder

His insolence can brook to be commanded   263
Under Cominius.

BRUTUS   Fame, at the which he aims,   264
In whom already he's well graced, cannot   265
Better be held nor more attained than by
A place below the first; for what miscarries   267
Shall be the general's fault, though he perform
To th'utmost of a man, and giddy censure   269
Will then cry out of Marcius, "Oh, if he
Had borne the business!"

SICINIUS   Besides, if things go well,
Opinion that so sticks on Marcius shall   272
Of his demerits rob Cominius.

BRUTUS   Come.   273
Half all Cominius' honors are to Marcius,   274
Though Marcius earned them not, and all his faults   275
To Marcius shall be honors, though indeed   276
In aught he merit not.

SICINIUS   Let's hence and hear   277
How the dispatch is made, and in what fashion,   278
More than his singularity, he goes   279
Upon this present action.

BRUTUS   Let's along.   Exeunt. 280

❧

[1.2]

Enter Tullus Aufidius with Senators of Corioles.

FIRST SENATOR
So, your opinion is, Aufidius,
That they of Rome are entered in our counsels   2
And know how we proceed.

AUFIDIUS   Is it not yours?
What ever have been thought on in this state   4
That could be brought to bodily act ere Rome
Had circumvention? 'Tis not four days gone   6
Since I heard thence. These are the words—I think   7
I have the letter here. Yes, here it is. [*Finding a letter.*]
[*He reads*] "They have pressed a power, but it is not
    known   9
Whether for east or west. The dearth is great,   10
The people mutinous; and, it is rumored,
Cominius, Marcius your old enemy,
Who is of Rome worse hated than of you,   13
And Titus Lartius, a most valiant Roman,
These three lead on this preparation

---

236 **with** against   238 **Attend upon** serve under   240 **constant** true
to my promise.   242 **stiff** resistant, reluctant. (But Lartius answers as
though the word had meant "stiff with age.")   **Stand'st out?** Do you
refuse to engage?   245 **Your company** Let me request your company
248 **Right . . . priority** you well deserve to take precedence.   251 **garners** granaries, storehouses.   **Worshipful mutineers** Worthy mutineers. (Said with mock politeness.)   252 **puts well forth** begins to
bud, shows a fair promise. (Said ironically.)   252.2 *Manent* They
remain onstage   257 **moved** angered.   **spare to gird** refrain from
scoffing at   258 **modest** i.e., as representing Diana, goddess of
chastity   259 **The present** i.e., May the present   260 **to be** of being.
(Or, Brutus may mean that Marcius's excessive pride makes his valor
dangerous.)   261 **Tickled with** flattered by, greatly excited by

263–4 **can . . . Cominius** can endure to be under the command of
Cominius.   265 **whom** which   267 **miscarries** goes wrong
269 **giddy censure** thoughtless popular opinion   272–3 **Opinion . . .
Cominius** the good reputation that adheres to Marcius will rob
Cominius of his deserts   274 **are to** are given to   275–7 **all his . . .
merit not** all Cominius' failings will redound to Marcius' honor, even
though Marcius doesn't deserve it.   278 **dispatch** execution of the
business   279 **More . . . singularity** i.e., with even more than his
usual share of arrogance and idiosyncrasy   280 **along** go, go join.
1.2. **Location: Corioles (or Corioli), southeast of Rome.**
2 **entered in** acquainted with   4 **What** What things   6 **circumvention** i.e., warning enabling them to circumvent.   **gone** ago   7 **thence**
from there.   9 **pressed a power** raised an army   10 **dearth** famine
13 **of** by

Whither 'tis bent. Most likely 'tis for you.   16
Consider of it."
FIRST SENATOR   Our army's in the field.
We never yet made doubt but Rome was ready
To answer us.
AUFIDIUS   Nor did you think it folly
To keep your great pretenses veiled till when   20
They needs must show themselves, which in the
   hatching,   21
It seemed, appeared to Rome. By the discovery   22
We shall be shortened in our aim, which was   23
To take in many towns ere almost Rome   24
Should know we were afoot.
SECOND SENATOR   Noble Aufidius,
Take your commission; hie you to your bands.   26
Let us alone to guard Corioles.
If they set down before 's, for the remove   28
Bring up your army; but I think you'll find
They've not prepared for us.
AUFIDIUS   Oh, doubt not that;   30
I speak from certainties. Nay, more,
Some parcels of their power are forth already,   32
And only hitherward. I leave Your Honors.   33
If we and Caius Marcius chance to meet,
'Tis sworn between us we shall ever strike   35
Till one can do no more.
ALL   The gods assist you!
AUFIDIUS   And keep your honors safe!
FIRST SENATOR   Farewell.
SECOND SENATOR   Farewell.
ALL   Farewell.   *Exeunt omnes.*   41

♣

[1.3]

*Enter Volumnia and Virgilia, mother and wife to
Marcius. They set them down on two low stools
and sew.*

VOLUMNIA   I pray you, daughter, sing, or express
yourself in a more comfortable sort. If my son were   2
my husband, I should freelier rejoice in that absence   3
wherein he won honor than in the embracements of
his bed where he would show most love. When yet
he was but tender-bodied and the only son of my   6
womb, when youth with comeliness plucked all gaze   7
his way, when for a day of kings' entreaties a mother   8

should not sell him an hour from her beholding, I, con-   9
sidering how honor would become such a person—   10
that it was no better than picturelike to hang by the
wall, if renown made it not stir—was pleased to let   12
him seek danger where he was like to find fame. To a   13
cruel war I sent him, from whence he returned, his
brows bound with oak. I tell thee, daughter, I sprang   15
not more in joy at first hearing he was a man-child than
now in first seeing he had proved himself a man.   17
VIRGILIA   But had he died in the business, madam,
how then?
VOLUMNIA   Then his good report should have been my
son; I therein would have found issue. Hear me pro-   21
fess sincerely: had I a dozen sons, each in my love alike
and none less dear than thine and my good Marcius,
I had rather had eleven die nobly for their country
than one voluptuously surfeit out of action.   25

Enter a Gentlewoman.

GENTLEWOMAN   Madam, the Lady Valeria is come to
visit you.
VIRGILIA
Beseech you, give me leave to retire myself.   28
VOLUMNIA   Indeed, you shall not.
Methinks I hear hither your husband's drum,   30
See him pluck Aufidius down by th' hair;   31
As children from a bear, the Volsces shunning him.   32
Methinks I see him stamp thus, and call thus: 33
"Come on, you cowards! You were got in fear,   34
Though you were born in Rome." His bloody brow
With his mailed hand then wiping, forth he goes   36
Like to a harvestman that's tasked to mow   37
Or all or lose his hire.   38
VIRGILIA
His bloody brow? O Jupiter, no blood!
VOLUMNIA
Away, you fool! It more becomes a man
Than gilt his trophy. The breasts of Hecuba,   41
When she did suckle Hector, looked not lovelier
Than Hector's forehead when it spit forth blood
At Grecian sword, contemning.—Tell Valeria   44
We are fit to bid her welcome.   *Exit Gentlewoman.*   45
VIRGILIA
Heavens bless my lord from fell Aufidius!   46

---

16 Whither 'tis bent wherever it is going.   **20 pretenses** intentions
21 needs necessarily   **22 appeared** became evident.   **discovery** disclosure   **23 be shortened in** fall short of   **24 take in** capture.   **ere
almost** even before   **26 hie** hasten.   **bands** companies of soldiers.
28 set down before 's lay siege to us.   **remove** raising of the siege
30 prepared for us i.e., laid plans to besiege us.   **32 parcels** parts.
forth marching forward   **33 only hitherward** i.e., marching toward
this place and this alone.   **Your Honors** i.e., you. (Plural and honorific.)   **35 ever strike** keep on exchanging blows   **41 s.d. omnes** all.
1.3. Location: Rome. Marcius's house, which may be (as indicated in
Plutarch) his mother's house; see 2.1.194.
2 comfortable sort cheerful manner.   **3 freelier** more readily   **6 tender-bodied** i.e., young   **7 comeliness** beauty.   **all gaze** the gaze of
all   **8 for** even for

9 should . . . beholding i.e., would not let her son out of her sight
even for an hour at any price   **10 such a person** such a fine figure of
a youth   **12 if renown . . . stir** if desire for fame did not stir it to
action   **13 like** likely   **15 bound with oak** i.e., as a badge to signify
that he had saved the life of a Roman citizen. (The *cruel war* was that
against the Latins and Tarquin the Proud; see 2.1.148–9 and note.)
17 now i.e., at that time, when he returned from war   **21 issue** offspring.   **25 voluptuously surfeit** live extravagantly for pleasure
28 retire myself go in.   **30 hither** coming this way   **31 See** i.e.,
methinks I see   **32 As . . . him** (methinks I see) the Volsces avoiding
him as children flee from a bear.   **33 stamp thus** (Volumnia gestures.)
call i.e., exhort his own troops   **34 got** begotten   **36 mailed** protected by mail, armored   **37 tasked** set the task   **38 Or** either.   **hire**
wages.   **41 Than . . . trophy** i.e., than gilding adorns his monument.
Hecuba Queen of Troy, mother of Hector and many other sons
44 contemning scorning the Grecian sword, as if spitting on it.
45 fit ready   **46 bless** protect.   **fell** cruel

VOLUMNIA
He'll beat Aufidius' head below his knee
And tread upon his neck.   48

Enter Valeria, with an usher and a Gentlewoman.

VALERIA   My ladies both, good day to you.
VOLUMNIA   Sweet madam!
VIRGILIA   I am glad to see Your Ladyship.
VALERIA   How do you both? You are manifest house-   52
keepers. What are you sewing here? A fine spot, in   53
good faith. How does your little son?
VIRGILIA   I thank Your Ladyship; well, good madam.
VOLUMNIA   He had rather see the swords and hear a
drum than look upon his schoolmaster.
VALERIA   O' my word, the father's son. I'll swear 'tis a   58
very pretty boy. O' my troth, I looked upon him
o'Wednesday half an hour together. H'as such a con-   60
firmed countenance! I saw him run after a gilded but-   61
terfly, and when he caught it, he let it go again, and
after it again, and over and over he comes and up   63
again, catched it again. Or whether his fall enraged   64
him, or how 'twas, he did so set his teeth and tear   65
it! Oh, I warrant, how he mammocked it!   66
VOLUMNIA   One on 's father's moods.   67
VALERIA   Indeed, la, 'tis a noble child.
VIRGILIA   A crack, madam.   69
VALERIA   Come, lay aside your stitchery. I must have
you play the idle huswife with me this afternoon.   71
VIRGILIA   No, good madam, I will not out of doors.   72
VALERIA   Not out of doors?
VOLUMNIA   She shall, she shall.
VIRGILIA   Indeed, no, by your patience. I'll not over the   75
threshold till my lord return from the wars.
VALERIA   Fie, you confine yourself most unreasonably.
Come, you must go visit the good lady that lies in.   78
VIRGILIA   I will wish her speedy strength and visit her
with my prayers, but I cannot go thither.
VOLUMNIA   Why, I pray you?
VIRGILIA   'Tis not to save labor, nor that I want love.   82
VALERIA   You would be another Penelope. Yet they   83
say all the yarn she spun in Ulysses' absence did but
fill Ithaca full of moths. Come, I would your cambric   85
were sensible as your finger, that you might leave   86
pricking it for pity. Come, you shall go with us.
VIRGILIA   No, good madam, pardon me; indeed, I will
not forth.

VALERIA   In truth, la, go with me, and I'll tell you
excellent news of your husband.
VIRGILIA   Oh, good madam, there can be none yet.
VALERIA   Verily, I do not jest with you. There came
news from him last night.
VIRGILIA   Indeed, madam?
VALERIA   In earnest, it's true; I heard a senator speak it.
Thus it is: the Volsces have an army forth, against
whom Cominius the general is gone with one part of
our Roman power. Your lord and Titus Lartius are set
down before their city Corioles. They nothing doubt   100
prevailing, and to make it brief wars. This is true, on   101
mine honor, and so, I pray, go with us.
VIRGILIA   Give me excuse, good madam. I will obey
you in everything hereafter.
VOLUMNIA   Let her alone, lady. As she is now, she will
but disease our better mirth.   106
VALERIA   In troth, I think she would. Fare you well,   107
then. Come, good sweet lady. Prithee, Virgilia, turn
thy solemness out o' door and go along with us.
VIRGILIA   No, at a word, madam. Indeed, I must not. I   110
wish you much mirth.
VALERIA   Well, then, farewell.   *Exeunt ladies.*

[1.4]

Enter Marcius, Titus Lartius, with drum and
colors, with captains and soldiers, as before the city
[of] Corioles. To them a Messenger.

MARCIUS
Yonder comes news. A wager they have met.
LARTIUS
My horse to yours, no.
MARCIUS   'Tis done.
LARTIUS   Agreed.   2
MARCIUS [*to the Messenger*]
Say, has our general met the enemy?
MESSENGER
They lie in view, but have not spoke as yet.   4
LARTIUS
So, the good horse is mine.
MARCIUS   I'll buy him of you.   5
LARTIUS
No, I'll nor sell nor give him. Lend you him I will   6
For half a hundred years.—Summon the town.   7
MARCIUS   How far off lie these armies?
MESSENGER   Within this mile and half.
MARCIUS
Then shall we hear their 'larum and they ours.   10

48.1 *an usher* a lady's male attendant   52–3 **manifest housekeepers**
out-and-out stay-at-homes.   53 **sewing** embroidering.   **spot** pattern,
figure   58 **O' my** On my   60 **H'as** He has   60–1 **confirmed** resolute
61 **gilded** brilliantly colored   63 **over and over** head over heels
64 **Or whether** Whether   65 **set** clench   66 **mammocked** tore into
fragments   67 **on 's** of his   69 **crack** pert little fellow   71 **huswife**
housewife   72 **out** go out.   75 **over** step over   78 **lies in** is expecting
a child.   82 **want** am deficient in   83 **You would be** i.e., One might
take you for.   **Penelope** faithful wife of Ulysses in Homer's *Odyssey*,
who delayed her suitors by insisting she must finish the weaving
which she then unraveled every night.   85 **moths** (1) insects eating
the cloth (2) idle courtiers parasitically consuming her wealth.
85–6 **I . . . sensible** I wish your fine white linen cambric cloth were as
sensitive   86 **leave** cease

100–1 **nothing doubt prevailing** have no doubt at all that they will
prevail   106 **disease . . . mirth** trouble our good cheer.   107 **troth**
truth, faith   110 **at a word** once for all
1.4. Location: Before Corioles.
2 **My horse . . . no** i.e., I'll bet my horse against yours that they,
Cominius's Roman force and the Volscian army under Aufidius, one
and one half miles away, have not met in battle.   4 **in view** i.e., in
view of one another.   **spoke** i.e., encountered   5 **of** (back) from
6 **nor sell** neither sell   7 **Summon** i.e., Summon by trumpet, to parley   10 **'larum** call to arms

Now, Mars, I prithee, make us quick in work, 11
That we with smoking swords may march from hence 12
To help our fielded friends! Come, blow thy blast. 13

*They sound a parley. Enter two Senators, with
others, on the walls of Corioles.*

Tullus Aufidius, is he within your walls?

FIRST SENATOR
No, nor a man that fears you less than he: 15
That's lesser than a little. (*Drum afar off.*) Hark! Our
drums 16
Are bringing forth our youth. We'll break our walls 17
Rather than they shall pound us up. Our gates, 18
Which yet seem shut, we have but pinned with
rushes; 19
They'll open of themselves. (*Alarum far off.*) Hark you,
far off!
There is Aufidius. List what work he makes 21
Amongst your cloven army.
                        [*Exeunt Volscians from the walls.*]
MARCIUS   Oh, they are at it! 22
LARTIUS
Their noise be our instruction. Ladders, ho! 23

Enter the army of the Volsces [from the city].

MARCIUS
They fear us not, but issue forth their city. 24
Now put your shields before your hearts, and fight
With hearts more proof than shields. Advance, brave
Titus! 26
They do disdain us much beyond our thoughts, 27
Which makes me sweat with wrath. Come on, my
fellows!
He that retires, I'll take him for a Volsce,
And he shall feel mine edge. 30

*Alarum. The Romans are beat back to their
trenches [and thus exeunt].
Enter Marcius, cursing, [with Soldiers].*

MARCIUS
All the contagion of the south light on you, 31
You shames of Rome! You herd of—Boils and plagues
Plaster you o'er, that you may be abhorred 33
Farther than seen, and one infect another 34
Against the wind a mile! You souls of geese, 35
That bear the shapes of men, how have you run

From slaves that apes would beat! Pluto and hell! 37
All hurt behind! Backs red, and faces pale 38
With flight and agued fear! Mend and charge home, 39
Or, by the fires of heaven, I'll leave the foe
And make my wars on you. Look to't. Come on!
If you'll stand fast, we'll beat them to their wives,
As they us to our trenches. Follow 's!

*Another alarum; [the Volsces fly back into the
city,] and Marcius follows them to [the] gates.*

So, now the gates are ope. Now prove good seconds! 44
'Tis for the followers fortune widens them, 45
Not for the fliers. Mark me, and do the like. 46
                Enter the gates and is shut in.
FIRST SOLDIER   Foolhardiness. Not I.
SECOND SOLDIER   Nor I.
FIRST SOLDIER   See, they have shut him in.
ALL   To th' pot, I warrant him. 50
                        Alarum continues.

Enter Titus Lartius.

LARTIUS
What is become of Marcius?
ALL   Slain, sir, doubtless.
FIRST SOLDIER
Following the fliers at the very heels,
With them he enters, who upon the sudden
Clapped to their gates. He is himself alone, 54
To answer all the city.
LARTIUS   Oh, noble fellow! 55
Who sensibly outdares his senseless sword, 56
And, when it bows, stand'st up. Thou art left, Marcius. 57
A carbuncle entire, as big as thou art, 58
Were not so rich a jewel. Thou wast a soldier
Even to Cato's wish, not fierce and terrible 60
Only in strokes, but, with thy grim looks and
The thunderlike percussion of thy sounds,
Thou mad'st thine enemies shake, as if the world
Were feverous and did tremble.

*Enter Marcius, bleeding, [from the city], assaulted
by the enemy.*

FIRST SOLDIER   Look, sir.
LARTIUS   Oh, 'tis Marcius!
Let's fetch him off, or make remain alike. 67
                They fight, and all enter the city.

❧

11 **Mars** Roman god of war   12 **smoking** steaming   13 **fielded** in
the field of battle.   **13.2 on the walls** i.e., in the gallery backstage.
(Throughout this scene, the tiring-house facade represents the *walls* of
Corioles, and a door in that facade represents the *gates*.)   **15–16 nor . . .
little** i.e., Aufidius fears you scarcely at all, and others fear even less
so, if that were possible.   **17 break** break out of   **18 pound us up**
shut us up as in a pound.   **19 rushes** hollow-stemmed reeds   **21 List**
Listen to   **22 cloven** split in two, divided, cut to pieces   **23 Their . . .
instruction** Let the sound of their battle be an example to us to begin.
24 issue forth pour forth from   **26 proof** impenetrable   **27 beyond
our thoughts** more than we thought possible   **30 edge** sword edge.
31 south south wind (as a supposed source of contagion)
33–4 abhorred . . . seen loathed (because of your foul smell) before
you are even seen   **35 Against . . . mile** so greatly that it will carry a
mile against the wind.

37 **Pluto** Roman god of the underworld   38 **hurt behind** wounded in
the back (i.e., in cowardly fashion).   39 **agued** trembling as though
with an ague or fever.   **Mend** (1) Do better, reform your battle ranks
(2) Recover from this fever of cowardice.   **home** to the heart of the
enemy's defenses   **44 seconds** supporters.   **45 followers** pursuers
46 the fliers those pursued.   **50 To th' pot** To the cooking pot (i.e., to
certain destruction)   **54 Clapped to** shut   **55 answer** stand up to,
confront   **56–7 Who . . . up** Who, though sensitive to pain, dares
more than his insensible sword; it might bend to fear, he would not.
57 left left alone (in the city); unique   **58 carbuncle entire** flawless
brilliant, red gemstone   **60 Cato** Marcus Cato the Censor (234–149
B.C.), celebrated in Plutarch as a staunch soldier and exponent of
Roman ethics   **67 fetch him off** rescue him.   **make remain alike**
remain to share his fate.

[1.5]

Enter certain Romans, with spoils.

FIRST ROMAN   This will I carry to Rome.
SECOND ROMAN   And I this.
THIRD ROMAN   A murrain on't! I took this for silver.   3
Exeunt. Alarum continues still afar off.

Enter Marcius and Titus [Lartius] with a trumpet.
Exeunt [Romans with spoils].

MARCIUS
See here these movers that do prize their hours   4
At a cracked drachma! Cushions, leaden spoons,   5
Irons of a doit, doublets that hangmen would   6
Bury with those that wore them, these base slaves,   7
Ere yet the fight be done, pack up. Down with them!
And hark, what noise the General makes! To him!   9
There is the man of my soul's hate, Aufidius,
Piercing our Romans. Then, valiant Titus, take
Convenient numbers to make good the city,   12
Whilst I, with those that have the spirit, will haste
To help Cominius.
LARTIUS   Worthy sir, thou bleed'st.
Thy exercise hath been too violent
For a second course of fight.
MARCIUS   Sir, praise me not.   16
My work hath yet not warmed me. Fare you well.
The blood I drop is rather physical   18
Than dangerous to me. To Aufidius thus
I will appear, and fight.
LARTIUS   Now the fair goddess Fortune
Fall deep in love with thee, and her great charms   22
Misguide thy opposers' swords! Bold gentleman,
Prosperity be thy page!
MARCIUS   Thy friend no less   24
Than those she placeth highest! So, farewell.   25
LARTIUS   Thou worthiest Marcius!   [*Exit Marcius.*]
Go sound thy trumpet in the marketplace.
Call thither all the officers o'th' town,
Where they shall know our mind. Away!   *Exeunt.*

1.5. **Location: The siege of Corioles continues.**
0.1 *Enter* i.e., Enter from the city, through the stage door in the facade;
see 1.4.13.2 note. Also at line 3.2.   **3 murrain** plague.   **3.2** *trumpet*
trumpeter.   **4–5 See . . . drachma!** i.e., (scornfully) Look at these busy
soldiers that cherish the precious time they should be fighting as
though it were a cracked (and therefore valueless) coin of small
denomination!   **6 Irons of a doit** weapons worth a coin of small
value.   **doublets** tight-fitting coats, usually quilted and decorated
6–7 hangmen . . . them i.e., hangmen, entitled to the clothes of persons they put to death, would not have these   **9 the General** i.e.,
Cominius, fighting Aufidius nearby   **12 Convenient numbers**
appropriate or effective numbers.   **make good** hold, secure
16 course bout, engagement.   **praise me not** (Coriolanus answers
ironically, as though Lartius were praising him for bleeding instead of
cautioning him.)   **18 physical** healthful. (Through bloodletting, a
standard treatment.)   **22 charms** spells   **24 Prosperity be thy page!**
i.e., may success attend on you!   **Thy . . . less** i.e., May prosperity be
no less your friend

[1.6]

Enter Cominius, as it were in retire, with soldiers.

COMINIUS
Breathe you, my friends. Well fought! We are come off   1
Like Romans, neither foolish in our stands   2
Nor cowardly in retire. Believe me, sirs,
We shall be charged again. Whiles we have struck,   4
By interims and conveying gusts we have heard   5
The charges of our friends. The Roman gods   6
Lead their successes as we wish our own,   7
That both our powers, with smiling fronts
encount'ring,   8
May give you thankful sacrifice!

Enter a Messenger.

Thy news?
MESSENGER
The citizens of Corioles have issued   10
And given to Lartius and to Marcius battle.
I saw our party to their trenches driven,
And then I came away.
COMINIUS   Though thou speakest truth,
Methinks thou speak'st not well. How long is't since?
MESSENGER   Above an hour, my lord.
COMINIUS
'Tis not a mile; briefly we heard their drums.   16
How couldst thou in a mile confound an hour   17
And bring thy news so late?
MESSENGER   Spies of the Volsces   18
Held me in chase, that I was forced to wheel   19
Three or four miles about; else had I, sir,   20
Half an hour since brought my report.   [*Exit.*]

Enter Marcius, [bloody].

COMINIUS   Who's yonder,   21
That does appear as he were flayed? O gods!   22
He has the stamp of Marcius, and I have   23
Before-time seen him thus.
MARCIUS   Come I too late?   24
COMINIUS
The shepherd knows not thunder from a tabor   25
More than I know the sound of Marcius' tongue
From every meaner man.
MARCIUS   Come I too late?   27

1.6. **Location: Near the camp of Cominius. The fighting near Corioles, heard until now at a short distance, is at a lull.**
0.1 *in retire* disengaged from the fighting. (Also in line 3.)   **1 Breathe
you** Catch your breath.   **are come off** have left the field of battle
2 foolish foolhardy   **4 struck** fought, been striking blows   **5 By . . .
gusts** at intervals and borne to us on the wind   **6 friends** i.e., the
besiegers of Corioles.   **The Roman** May the Roman   **7 their successes** the fortunes of our friends (i.e., Lartius and Marcius)   **8 powers** armies.   **fronts** (1) foreheads, brows (2) front lines   **10 issued**
issued forth   **16 briefly** a short time ago (and at short distance)
17 confound consume   **18 Spies** Scouts   **19 that** so that
19–20 wheel . . . about make a detour of three or four miles   **20 else**
otherwise   **21 since** ago   **22 as** as if   **23 stamp** bearing, form
24 Before-time formerly   **25 knows** distinguishes. (Also in line 26.)
tabor small drum   **27 meaner** less noble

COMINIUS
      Ay, if you come not in the blood of others,   28
      But mantled in your own.
MARCIUS   Oh, let me clip ye   29
      In arms as sound as when I wooed, in heart
      As merry as when our nuptial day was done,
      And tapers burnt to bedward!   [*They embrace.*]   32
COMINIUS
      Flower of warriors, how is't with Titus Lartius?
MARCIUS
      As with a man busied about decrees: 34
      Condemning some to death, and some to exile;
      Ransoming him, or pitying, threat'ning th'other;   36
      Holding Corioles in the name of Rome,
      Even like a fawning greyhound in the leash,
      To let him slip at will.
COMINIUS   Where is that slave   39
      Which told me they had beat you to your trenches?
      Where is he? Call him hither.
MARCIUS   Let him alone;
      He did inform the truth. But for our gentlemen,   42
      The common file—a plague! Tribunes for them!—   43
      The mouse ne'er shunned the cat as they did budge   44
      From rascals worse than they.
COMINIUS   But how prevailed you?
MARCIUS
      Will the time serve to tell? I do not think.
      Where is the enemy? Are you lords o'th' field?
      If not, why cease you till you are so?
COMINIUS
      Marcius, we have at disadvantage fought
      And did retire to win our purpose.   50
MARCIUS
      How lies their battle? Know you on which side   51
      They have placed their men of trust?
COMINIUS   As I guess, Marcius,
      Their bands i'th' vaward are the Antiates,   53
      Of their best trust; o'er them Aufidius,   54
      Their very heart of hope.
MARCIUS   I do beseech you,   55
      By all the battles wherein we have fought,
      By th' blood we have shed together, by th' vows we
            have made
      To endure friends, that you directly set me   58
      Against Aufidius and his Antiates,
      And that you not delay the present, but,   60

      Filling the air with swords advanced and darts,   61
      We prove this very hour.
COMINIUS   Though I could wish   62
      You were conducted to a gentle bath
      And balms applied to you, yet dare I never   64
      Deny your asking. Take your choice of those
      That best can aid your action.
MARCIUS   Those are they
      That most are willing. If any such be here—
      As it were sin to doubt—that love this painting   68
      Wherein you see me smeared; if any fear
      Lesser his person than an ill report;   70
      If any think brave death outweighs bad life,
      And that his country's dearer than himself,
      Let him alone, or so many so minded,   73
      Wave thus [*waving his sword*] to express his
            disposition,
      And follow Marcius.
            They all shout and wave their swords,
            take him up in their arms, and cast up their caps.
      Oh, me alone! Make you a sword of me?   76
      If these shows be not outward, which of you   77
      But is four Volsces? None of you but is   78
      Able to bear against the great Aufidius
      A shield as hard as his. A certain number,
      Though thanks to all, must I select from all;
      The rest shall bear the business in some other fight,
      As cause will be obeyed. Please you to march,   83
      And I shall quickly draw out my command,   84
      Which men are best inclined.
COMINIUS   March on, my fellows.
      Make good this ostentation, and you shall   86
      Divide in all with us.   *Exeunt.*   87

❖

[1.7]

Titus Lartius, having set a guard upon Corioles,
going with drum and trumpet toward Cominius
and Caius Marcius, enters [from the city] with a
Lieutenant, other soldiers, and a scout.

LARTIUS
      So, let the ports be guarded. Keep your duties   1
      As I have set them down. If I do send, dispatch
      Those centuries to our aid; the rest will serve   3
      For a short holding. If we lose the field,   4
      We cannot keep the town.
LIEUTENANT   Fear not our care, sir.   5

28–9 Ay . . . own i.e., If you yourself are bleeding all that blood, you are presumably too weak to help, but if it is enemies' blood, you are in time to shed more.   **29 clip** embrace   **32 tapers . . . bedward** i.e., candles burned low, indicating the approach of bedtime or showing the way to bed.   **34 busied about decrees** busy with judicial decisions   **36 Ransoming . . . th'other** releasing one man for ransom money, mercifully releasing another without ransom, threatening still another   **39 let him slip** unleash him   **42 inform** report. **gentlemen** (Said sarcastically of the ordinary soldiers.)   **43 common file** ordinary soldiers, plebeians   **44 budge** flinch   **50 to . . . purpose** i.e., to regroup.   **51 battle** army, battle line.   **53–4 Their bands . . . trust** the troops in the vanguard are from Antium, their most trustworthy   **55 Their . . . hope** the leader on whom their hopes depend. **58 endure** continue.   **directly** (1) at once (2) face to face   **60 not delay the present** do not delay now

61 advanced raised.   **darts** lances   **62 prove** try the fortunes of **64 balms** healing ointments   **68 painting** i.e., blood   **70 Lesser . . . report** less for his safety than for his reputation   **73 Let . . . minded** let that individual by himself, or as many as are so minded   **76 Oh . . . of me?** Do you make a sword of me alone, choose me as your weapon? (Some editors assign this line to the soldiers.)   **77 outward** external, deceptive   **78 But is** is not the equal of   **83 As . . . obeyed** as necessity shall require.   **84 draw . . . command** pick out my chosen troop   **86 ostentation** show of zeal   **87 Divide** share **1.7. Location:** Before the gates of Corioles. The military action near Corioles continues.
1 ports gates   **3 centuries** companies of a hundred   **4 short holding** i.e., brief occupation of the city.   **5 Fear not** Don't worry about

LARTIUS   Hence, and shut your gates upon 's.   6
[*To the scout*] Our guider, come; to th' Roman camp
    conduct us.
                    Exeunt [separately, the Lieutenant returning
                                    into the city].

[1.8]

> *Alarum as in battle. Enter Marcius and Aufidius*
> *at several doors.*

MARCIUS
I'll fight with none but thee, for I do hate thee
Worse than a promise-breaker.
AUFIDIUS   We hate alike.
Not Afric owns a serpent I abhor   3
More than thy fame and envy. Fix thy foot.   4
MARCIUS
Let the first budger die the other's slave,   5
And the gods doom him after!
AUFIDIUS
If I fly, Marcius, hollo me like a hare.   7
MARCIUS   Within these three hours, Tullus,
Alone I fought in your Corioles' walls,
And made what work I pleased. 'Tis not my blood
Wherein thou see'st me masked. For thy revenge
Wrench up thy power to th' highest.
AUFIDIUS   Wert thou the Hector   12
That was the whip of your bragged progeny,   13
Thou shouldst not scape me here.   *Here they fight,*
                and certain Volsces come in the aid of Aufidius.
                Marcius fights till they be driven in breathless.
Officious, and not valiant, you have shamed me
In your condemnèd seconds.   [*Exeunt.*]   16

[1.9]

> *Flourish. Alarum. A retreat is sounded. Enter, at*
> *one door, Cominius with the Romans; at another*
> *door Marcius, with his arm in a scarf.*

COMINIUS
If I should tell thee o'er this thy day's work,   1
Thou't not believe thy deeds. But I'll report it   2
Where senators shall mingle tears with smiles,

Where great patricians shall attend and shrug,   4
I' th' end admire; where ladies shall be frighted   5
And, gladly quaked, hear more; where the dull
    tribunes,   6
That with the fusty plebeians hate thine honors,   7
Shall say against their hearts, "We thank the gods   8
Our Rome hath such a soldier."
Yet cam'st thou to a morsel of this feast,   10
Having fully dined before.

> *Enter Titus [Lartius] with his power, from the*
> *pursuit.*

LARTIUS   Oh, General,   11
Here is the steed, we the caparison.   12
Hadst thou beheld—
MARCIUS   Pray now, no more. My mother,
Who has a charter to extol her blood,   14
When she does praise me grieves me. I have done
As you have done—that's what I can;
Induced as you have been—that's for my country.
He that has but effected his good will   18
Hath overta'en mine act.
COMINIUS   You shall not be   19
The grave of your deserving. Rome must know   20
The value of her own. 'Twere a concealment
Worse than a theft, no less than a traducement,   22
To hide your doings and to silence that
Which, to the spire and top of praises vouched,   24
Would seem but modest. Therefore, I beseech you—   25
In sign of what you are, not to reward   26
What you have done—before our army hear me.
MARCIUS
I have some wounds upon me, and they smart
To hear themselves remembered.
COMINIUS   Should they not,   29
Well might they fester 'gainst ingratitude   30
And tent themselves with death. Of all the horses,   31
Whereof we have ta'en good and good store, of all   32
The treasure in this field achieved and city,
We render you the tenth, to be ta'en forth   34
Before the common distribution
At your only choice.
MARCIUS   I thank you, General,   36
But cannot make my heart consent to take

---

6 Hence Get a move on
1.8. Location: A field of battle near the Roman camp. The military action near Corioles continues.
0.2 *several* separate   **3 Not . . . serpent** There is no serpent in Africa
4 fame and envy envied reputation.   **Fix thy foot** Stand and fight.
5 budger one who flinches   **7 hollo** cry in pursuit of   **12 Wrench up** strain, wrest, pull   **13 That . . . progeny** who was foremost among your boasted Trojan ancestors in scourging the Greeks. (Marcius, as a Roman, could claim descent from the Trojan prince, Aeneas, legendary founder of Rome.)   **16 condemnèd seconds** futile and despised efforts at assistance.
1.9. Location: Scene continues. The Roman camp. The military action near Corioles continues.
0.1 *retreat* trumpet signal to call off pursuit   **0.3** *scarf* sling.
1–2 If . . . deeds If I recounted to you this day's work of yours, you'd not believe it.

4–5 attend . . . admire listen and shrug their shoulders at first but finally marvel   **6 gladly quaked** thrilling to the *frisson* of danger.
dull sullen   **7 fusty** moldy, ill-smelling   **8 against their hearts** unwillingly   **10–11 Yet cam'st . . . before** i.e., This battle was just a small skirmish in comparison with the major battle you had already fought.   **11 s.d.** *power* army   **12 steed** i.e., Marcius.   **caparison** mere trappings of a steed.   **14 charter . . . blood** right to praise her child   **18 He** Anyone.   **effected** manifested in action   **19 overta'en** surpassed   **19–20 You . . . deserving** You shall not conceal your merit (by your modesty).   **22 traducement** calumny, slander, deceptive hoodwinking   **24 to . . . vouched** proclaimed in the highest possible terms of praise   **25 modest** moderate, barely sufficient (in relation to all you did).   **26 sign** token merely   **29 not** i.e., not hear themselves praised. (A smarting, open wound is less likely to fester.)   **30 'gainst** in the face of   **31 tent . . . death** i.e., find no remedy short of death. (To *tent* a wound is to probe and keep it open with a rolled bandage, to prevent festering.)   **32 good and good store** excellent ones and plenty of them   **34 the tenth** one tenth   **36 At . . . choice** exactly as you choose.

A bribe to pay my sword. I do refuse it,
And stand upon my common part with those   39
That have beheld the doing.   *A long flourish.*   40
       They all cry "Marcius! Marcius!",
         cast up their caps and lances.
         Cominius and Lartius stand bare.
May these same instruments, which you profane,
Never sound more! When drums and trumpets shall
I'th' field prove flatterers, let courts and cities be
Made all of false-faced soothing! When steel grows   44
Soft as the parasite's silk, let him be made   45
An overture for th' wars. No more, I say!   46
For that I have not washed my nose that bled,   47
Or foiled some debile wretch—which without note   48
Here's many else have done—you shout me forth   49
In acclamations hyperbolical,
As if I loved my little should be dieted   51
In praises sauced with lies.
COMINIUS   Too modest are you,   52
More cruel to your good report than grateful
To us that give you truly. By your patience,   54
If 'gainst yourself you be incensed, we'll put you,
Like one that means his proper harm, in manacles,   56
Then reason safely with you. Therefore be it known,
As to us, to all the world, that Caius Marcius
Wears this war's garland, in token of the which   59
My noble steed, known to the camp, I give him,
With all his trim belonging; and from this time,   61
For what he did before Corioles, call him,
With all th'applause and clamor of the host,
Caius Marcius Coriolanus! Bear
Th'addition nobly ever!   65
       Flourish. Trumpets sound, and drums.
ALL   Caius Marcius Coriolanus!
CORIOLANUS   I will go wash,
And when my face is fair you shall perceive   68
Whether I blush or no. Howbeit, I thank you.
I mean to stride your steed, and at all times   70
To undercrest your good addition   71
To th' fairness of my power.
COMINIUS   So, to our tent,   72
Where, ere we do repose us, we will write
To Rome of our success. You, Titus Lartius,
Must to Corioles back. Send us to Rome

The best, with whom we may articulate   76
For their own good and ours.
LARTIUS   I shall, my lord.
CORIOLANUS
The gods begin to mock me. I, that now
Refused most princely gifts, am bound to beg   79
Of my lord general.
COMINIUS   Take't, 'tis yours. What is't?
CORIOLANUS
I sometime lay here in Corioles   81
At a poor man's house; he used me kindly.   82
He cried to me; I saw him prisoner;   83
But then Aufidius was within my view,
And wrath o'erwhelmed my pity. I request you
To give my poor host freedom.
COMINIUS   Oh, well begged!
Were he the butcher of my son, he should
Be free as is the wind. Deliver him, Titus.   88
LARTIUS
Marcius, his name?
CORIOLANUS   By Jupiter, forgot!
I am weary; yea, my memory is tired.
Have we no wine here?
COMINIUS   Go we to our tent.
The blood upon your visage dries; 'tis time
It should be looked to. Come.
       A flourish. Cornets. Exeunt.

❧

[1.10]

Enter Tullus Aufidius, bloody, with two or three Soldiers.

AUFIDIUS   The town is ta'en.
A SOLDIER
'Twill be delivered back on good condition.   2
AUFIDIUS   Condition?
I would I were a Roman, for I cannot,
Being a Volsce, be that I am. Condition?   5
What good condition can a treaty find   6
I'th' part that is at mercy? Five times, Marcius,   7
I have fought with thee; so often hast thou beat me,   8
And wouldst do so, I think, should we encounter
As often as we eat. By th'elements,
If e'er again I meet him beard to beard,
He's mine or I am his. Mine emulation   12
Hath not that honor in't it had; for where   13
I thought to crush him in an equal force,   14
True sword to sword, I'll potch at him some way   15

39 stand . . . part insist on having only my regular share   **40 beheld the doing** seen the action.   **40.3** *bare* bareheaded.   **44 Made . . . soothing** given over utterly to hypocritical flattery.   **44–6 When . . . wars** When steel armor grows as soft as the silk of courtly parasites, let the parasite be made an overture—an excuse or prompting—for us to fight on his behalf. (Marcius implies that Romans would never fight on such conditions, just as cities will never be entirely false, because drums and trumpets, as touchstones of truth, would not permit it.) (A difficult passage to which various emendations have been proposed.)   **47 For that** Because   **48 foiled** have overthrown. **debile** weak.   **note** notice taken   **49 else** others   **51 my little** that the little I have done.   **dieted** fed   **52 In** on, by.   **sauced** seasoned   **54 give** report   **56 means . . . harm** intends to injure himself   **59 garland** (An emblem of victory.)   **61 his trim belonging** the equipment that goes with it   **65 Th'addition** the title   **68 fair** clean   **70 stride** bestride   **71–2 To . . . power** to bear and support the title you have given me to the best of my ability, as if it were a heraldic crest.

76 best i.e., best in blood among the Volscians.   **articulate** come to terms (about the return of Corioles to the Volscians)   **79 bound** obliged   **81 sometime lay** once lodged   **82 used** treated   **83 cried** cried out (at the time of the battle just ended)   **88 Deliver** Release **1.10. Location: Outside of Corioles, after the battle.**
2 condition terms.   **5 be . . . am** i.e., be honorable, proud.   **6 good condition** state of well-being. (With a play on "favorable terms," as in line 2.)   **7 I' . . . mercy** for the side that lies at the mercy of the winner.   **8 so** just so   **12 emulation** rivalry   **13 where** whereas   **14 in an equal force** on equal terms   **15 potch** thrust, poke

Or wrath or craft may get him.

A SOLDIER   He's the devil.   16

AUFIDIUS
Bolder, though not so subtle. My valor's poisoned
With only suff'ring stain by him; for him   18
Shall fly out of itself. Nor sleep nor sanctuary,   19
Being naked, sick, nor fane nor Capitol,   20
The prayers of priests nor times of sacrifice,   21
Embarquements all of fury, shall lift up   22
Their rotten privilege and custom 'gainst   23
My hate to Marcius. Where I find him, were it   24
At home, upon my brother's guard, even there,   25
Against the hospitable canon, would I   26
Wash my fierce hand in 's heart. Go you to th' city;
Learn how 'tis held, and what they are that must   28
Be hostages for Rome.

A SOLDIER   Will not you go?   29

AUFIDIUS
I am attended at the cyprus grove. I pray you—   30
'Tis south the city mills—bring me word thither   31
How the world goes, that to the pace of it   32
I may spur on my journey.

A SOLDIER   I shall, sir.
                                    [*Exeunt separately.*]

2.1

*Enter Menenius with the two tribunes of the
people, Sicinius and Brutus.*

MENENIUS   The augurer tells me we shall have news   1
tonight.

BRUTUS   Good or bad?

MENENIUS   Not according to the prayer of the people,   4
for they love not Marcius.

SICINIUS   Nature teaches beasts to know their friends.   6

MENENIUS   Pray you, who does the wolf love?

SICINIUS   The lamb.

MENENIUS   Ay, to devour him, as the hungry plebeians
would the noble Marcius.

BRUTUS   He's a lamb indeed, that baas like a bear.   11

MENENIUS   He's a bear indeed, that lives like a lamb.   12
You two are old men; tell me one thing that I shall
ask you.

BOTH   Well, sir?

MENENIUS   In what enormity is Marcius poor in, that   16
you two have not in abundance?

BRUTUS   He's poor in no one fault, but stored with all.   18

SICINIUS   Especially in pride.

BRUTUS   And topping all others in boasting.

MENENIUS   This is strange now. Do you two know how
you are censured here in the city, I mean of us o' th'   22
right-hand file? Do you?   23

BOTH   Why, how are we censured?

MENENIUS   Because you talk of pride now—will you
not be angry?

BOTH   Well, well, sir, well?

MENENIUS   Why, 'tis no great matter; for a very little   28
thief of occasion will rob you of a great deal of   29
patience. Give your dispositions the reins and be   30
angry at your pleasures—at the least, if you take it as
a pleasure to you in being so. You blame Marcius for
being proud?

BRUTUS   We do it not alone, sir.

MENENIUS   I know you can do very little alone, for your
helps are many, or else your actions would grow
wondrous single. Your abilities are too infantlike for   37
doing much alone. You talk of pride. Oh, that you
could turn your eyes toward the napes of your necks   39
and make but an interior survey of your good selves!
Oh, that you could!

BOTH   What then, sir?

MENENIUS   Why, then you should discover a brace of   43
unmeriting, proud, violent, testy magistrates, alias   44
fools, as any in Rome.

SICINIUS   Menenius, you are known well enough too.

MENENIUS   I am known to be a humorous patrician, and   47
one that loves a cup of hot wine with not a drop of
allaying Tiber in't; said to be something imperfect in   49
favoring the first complaint, hasty and tinderlike   50
upon too trivial motion; one that converses more with   51
the buttock of the night than with the forehead of the   52
morning. What I think I utter, and spend my malice in   53
my breath. Meeting two such wealsmen as you are—   54

---

16 Or . . . craft in which either wrath or craftiness   **18 stain** disgrace, eclipse   **19 Shall . . . itself** (my valor) shall deviate from its own natural course.   **19–24 Nor . . . Marcius** Neither his being asleep nor protected by sanctuary (as, for example, in *fane* or temple, or at the Capitol, guarded by priests when they offer sacrifices to the gods), nor his being unarmed or ill, nor any restraints (*embarquements*) laid on my fury, will be able to impose the outmoded sanctions of civilized custom against my hatred for Marcius.   **25 At . . . guard** in my own house, under my brother's protection   **26 hospitable canon** law of hospitality   **28–9 what . . . Rome** i.e., who they are that are to be taken to Rome as hostages during the negotiations about the return of Corioles to the Volscians. (See 1.9.76.)   **30 attended** waited for   **31 south** south of.   **mills** i.e., grain mills   **32 to the pace of it** in accordance with the speed of events

2.1. Location: Rome. The ovation prepared for Coriolanus is probably to be imagined as beginning outside the city and moving toward the Capitol (see line 203).

1 augurer auger, Roman religious figure charged with reading signs to predict the future   **4 Not . . . people** Not what the people would wish   **6 beasts** i.e., even beasts

11–12 He's a lamb . . . a lamb i.e., Some lamb! Have you heard his growl?—How can you accuse him of being a bear when he acts so unthreateningly?   **16 enormity** wickedness   **18 stored** well stocked   **22 censured** judged   **23 right-hand file** i.e., party of aristocrats (who took the honorable right-hand position in battle).   **28–30 a very . . . patience** any slight pretext will rob you of your patience.   **37 single** poor, feeble.   **39 turn . . . necks** i.e., turn your gaze in order to see within   **43 brace** pair   **44 testy** headstrong   **47 humorous** whimsical, governed by humors   **49 allaying Tiber** water used to dilute   **49–50 something . . . complaint** somewhat at fault for deciding in favor of the complainant before hearing the other side of the case   **50 tinderlike** quick-tempered   **51 motion** cause   **51–3 one . . . morning** one who is better acquainted with the late hours of the night than with the early hours of the morning.   **53 spend** expend   **54 breath** words.   **wealsmen** statesmen

I cannot call you Lycurguses—if the drink you give 55
me touch my palate adversely, I make a crooked face 56
at it. I cannot say Your Worships have delivered the 57
matter well, when I find the ass in compound with the 58
major part of your syllables; and though I must be con- 59
tent to bear with those that say you are reverend grave
men, yet they lie deadly that tell you you have good 61
faces. If you see this in the map of my microcosm, 62
follows it that I am known well enough too? What 63
harm can your bisson conspectuities glean out of this 64
character, if I be known well enough too? 65

BRUTUS   Come, sir, come, we know you well enough.
MENENIUS   You know neither me, yourselves, nor anything. You are ambitious for poor knaves' caps and 68
legs. You wear out a good wholesome forenoon in 69
hearing a cause between an orange-wife and a faucet- 70
seller, and then rejourn the controversy of threepence 71
to a second day of audience. When you are hearing a 72
matter between party and party, if you chance to be 73
pinched with the colic, you make faces like mummers, 74
set up the bloody flag against all patience, and, in roar- 75
ing for a chamber pot, dismiss the controversy bleed- 76
ing, the more entangled by your hearing. All the peace 77
you make in their cause is calling both the parties 78
knaves. You are a pair of strange ones. 79

BRUTUS   Come, come, you are well understood to be a 80
perfecter giber for the table than a necessary bencher 81
in the Capitol. 82

MENENIUS   Our very priests must become mockers if
they shall encounter such ridiculous subjects as you 84
are. When you speak best unto the purpose, it is not 85
worth the wagging of your beards, and your beards
deserve not so honorable a grave as to stuff a botcher's 87
cushion or to be entombed in an ass's packsaddle.
Yet you must be saying Marcius is proud; who, in a 89
cheap estimation, is worth all your predecessors since 90
Deucalion, though peradventure some of the best of 91

'em were hereditary hangmen. Good e'en to Your Wor- 92
ships. More of your conversation would infect my 93
brain, being the herdsmen of the beastly plebeians. I 94
will be bold to take my leave of you.

Brutus and Sicinius [stand] aside.

Enter Volumnia, Virgilia, and Valeria.

How now, my as fair as noble ladies—and the moon, 96
were she earthly, no nobler—whither do you follow 97
your eyes so fast? 98

VOLUMNIA   Honorable Menenius, my boy Marcius approaches. For the love of Juno, let's go. 100
MENENIUS   Ha? Marcius coming home?
VOLUMNIA   Ay, worthy Menenius, and with most pros- 102
perous approbation. 103
MENENIUS   Take my cap, Jupiter, and I thank thee. [*He
tosses his cap.*] Hoo! Marcius coming home?
VALERIA, VIRGILIA   Nay, 'tis true.
VOLUMNIA   Look, here's a letter from him. [*Showing a
letter.*] The state hath another, his wife another, and I
think there's one at home for you.
MENENIUS   I will make my very house reel tonight. A
letter for me?
VIRGILIA   Yes, certain, there's a letter for you; I saw't.
MENENIUS   A letter for me! It gives me an estate of seven 113
years' health, in which time I will make a lip at the 114
physician. The most sovereign prescription in Galen 115
is but empiricutic and, to this preservative, of no bet- 116
ter report than a horse drench. Is he not wounded? He 117
was wont to come home wounded. 118
VIRGILIA   Oh, no, no, no.
VOLUMNIA   Oh, he is wounded, I thank the gods for't.
MENENIUS   So do I too, if it be not too much. Brings 'a 121
victory in his pocket, the wounds become him.
VOLUMNIA   On 's brows, Menenius. He comes the 123
third time home with the oaken garland.
MENENIUS   Has he disciplined Aufidius soundly? 125
VOLUMNIA   Titus Lartius writes they fought together,
but Aufidius got off.
MENENIUS   And 'twas time for him too, I'll warrant him
that. An he had stayed by him, I would not have been 129
so fidiused for all the chests in Corioles and the gold 130
that's in them. Is the Senate possessed of this? 131
VOLUMNIA   Good ladies, let's go.—Yes, yes, yes; the
Senate has letters from the General, wherein he gives

---

55 **Lycurguses** (Said ironically; Lycurgus was the famous Spartan lawgiver.)   **55–7 if the drink . . . at it** i.e., if I don't like the things you say,
I show it in my expression.   **57 delivered** reported   **58–9 I find . . .
syllables** i.e., I find asininity in nearly everything you say. (With a pun
on *ass in compound*, meaning legal phrases ending in *-as*, like *whereas*.)
61 deadly excessively   **62 this** i.e., all that I have freely admitted.
the map of my microcosm my face, or chart of my little world (as
opposed to the macrocosm or great world)   **63 known . . . too** (Menenius mocks their phrase, line 46, and its implication that they "see
through" him.)   **64 bisson conspectuities** blind understandings
65 character character sketch   **68–9 caps and legs** doffing caps and
making obeisances to indicate respect.   **69–72 You . . . audience** You
wear out a morning that might be put to better use in hearing a case
between a woman fruit-seller and one who sells taps for drawing
liquor from barrels, and then adjourn the silly three-penny dispute
until another hearing.   **73 party and party** the two parties in a dispute
74 pinched with the colic afflicted with griping pains in the belly.
mummers masqueraders, performers in dumb shows   **75 set . . . flag**
i.e., declare violent war   **76–7 bleeding** unhealed, unsettled
77–9 All . . . knaves i.e., All you manage to do is to insult both parties.
(Perhaps a reference to the song "Hold thy peace, thou knave"; see
Twelfth Night, 2.3.63–70.)   **80–2 a perfecter . . . Capitol** i.e., better at din-
ner-table jesting than at sitting in the Senate as a counselor.   **84 subjects**
(1) topics (2) citizens   **85 When** i.e., Even when   **87 botcher** one who
patches old clothes or boots   **89–90 in a cheap estimation** even at the
lowest estimation of his worth   **91 Deucalion** the Noah of classical
story, survivor of a great flood.   **peradventure** perhaps

92 hereditary hangmen men serving as executioners (a very ignoble
occupation) generation after generation.   **Good e'en** Good evening
(used for any time after noon)   **93 conversation** society, company
94 being you being   **96 the moon** i.e., Diana, goddess of chastity
97–8 whither . . . fast? where are you going so eagerly in hopes of
some sight?   **100 Juno** wife of Jupiter and Queen of the gods
102–3 prosperous approbation success and acclaim.   **113 It . . . estate
of** It endows me with   **114 make a lip** make a contemptuous face,
mock   **115 sovereign** efficacious.   **Galen** Greek physician and
authority on medicine (born considerably after the time of Coriolanus)
116 empiricutic quacklike.   **to** compared with   **117 report** reputation,
standing.   **horse drench** dose of medicine for horses.   **118 wont**
accustomed   **121 Brings 'a** If he brings   **123 On 's brows** i.e., The
victory is *on his brows* (in the form of a garland) rather than *in his pocket*,
as Menenius suggests. (Said as a pleasantry.)   **125 disciplined** beaten
129 An If   **130 fidiused** (Menenius's coined word, meaning "treated
as Aufidius deserves, beaten.")   **131 possessed** informed

my son the whole name of the war. He hath in this 134
action outdone his former deeds doubly.

VALERIA   In troth, there's wondrous things spoke of
him.

MENENIUS   Wondrous? Ay, I warrant you, and not
without his true purchasing.   139

VIRGILIA   The gods grant them true!

VOLUMNIA   True? Pow waw.   141

MENENIUS   True? I'll be sworn they are true. Where is
he wounded? [*To the tribunes*] God save Your good
Worships! Marcius is coming home. He has more
cause to be proud.—Where is he wounded?

VOLUMNIA   I'th' shoulder and i'th' left arm. There will
be large cicatrices to show the people, when he shall 147
stand for his place. He received in the repulse of 148
Tarquin seven hurts i'th' body.   149

MENENIUS   One i'th' neck and two i'th' thigh—there's
nine that I know.

VOLUMNIA   He had, before this last expedition, twenty-
five wounds upon him.

MENENIUS   Now it's twenty-seven. Every gash was an
enemy's grave. (*A shout and flourish.*) Hark, the trumpets.

VOLUMNIA   These are the ushers of Marcius. Before him
he carries noise, and behind him he leaves tears.
Death, that dark spirit, in 's nervy arm doth lie, 159
Which, being advanced, declines, and then men die. 160

> *A sennet. Trumpets sound. Enter Cominius the*
> *general, and Titus Lartius; between them,*
> *Coriolanus, crowned with an oaken garland; with*
> *captains and soldiers, and a Herald.*

HERALD
Know, Rome, that all alone Marcius did fight
Within Corioles gates, where he hath won,
With fame, a name to Caius Marcius; these   163
In honor follows "Coriolanus."
Welcome to Rome, renownèd Coriolanus!
                                Sound flourish.

ALL
Welcome to Rome, renownèd Coriolanus!

CORIOLANUS
No more of this. It does offend my heart.
Pray now, no more.

COMINIUS   Look, sir, your mother.

CORIOLANUS   Oh,
You have, I know, petitioned all the gods
For my prosperity!   *Kneels.*

VOLUMNIA   Nay, my good soldier, up, 170
My gentle Marcius, worthy Caius, and
By deed-achieving honor newly named—   172

What is it? Coriolanus must I call thee?—
But, oh, thy wife!

CORIOLANUS [*rising*]   My gracious silence, hail!
Wouldst thou have laughed had I come coffined
   home,
That weep'st to see me triumph? Ah, my dear,
Such eyes the widows in Corioles wear,
And mothers that lack sons.

MENENIUS   Now, the gods crown thee!

CORIOLANUS [*to Menenius*]
And live you yet? [*To Valeria*] Oh my sweet lady,
   pardon.

VOLUMNIA
I know not where to turn. Oh, welcome home!
[*To Cominius*] And welcome, General! And you're
   welcome all.

MENENIUS
A hundred thousand welcomes! I could weep
And I could laugh; I am light and heavy. Welcome. 183
A curse begin at very root on 's heart   184
That is not glad to see thee! You are three
That Rome should dote on; yet, by the faith of men,
We have some old crab trees here at home that will not 187
Be grafted to your relish. Yet welcome, warriors! 188
We call a nettle but a nettle, and   189
The faults of fools but folly.   190

COMINIUS   Ever right.

CORIOLANUS   Menenius ever, ever.   192

HERALD
Give way there, and go on!

CORIOLANUS [*to Volumnia and Virgilia*]
                        Your hand, and yours.
Ere in our own house I do shade my head,   194
The good patricians must be visited,
From whom I have received not only greetings,
But with them change of honors.

VOLUMNIA   I have lived   197
To see inherited my very wishes   198
And the buildings of my fancy. Only   199
There's one thing wanting, which I doubt not but 200
Our Rome will cast upon thee.

CORIOLANUS   Know, good mother,   201
I had rather be their servant in my way
Than sway with them in theirs.

COMINIUS   On, to the Capitol!   203
        Flourish. Cornets. Exeunt in state, as before.
                Brutus and Sicinius [remain].

BRUTUS
All tongues speak of him, and the blearèd sights 204
Are spectacled to see him. Your prattling nurse   205

---

134 name credit, reputation   **139 his true purchasing** deserving on
his part.   **141 Pow waw** i.e., Pish.   **147 cicatrices** scars   **148 stand
for his place** i.e., seek the consulship.   **148–9 repulse of Tarquin**
(Plutarch reports that Marcius fought his first battle against King Tarquin the Proud in about 496 B.C. on the occasion of Tarquin's last
attempt to regain the kingdom; see 1.3.13–15 and note, and 2.2.88 ff.)
159 in 's nervy in his sinewy   **160 being . . . declines** being raised,
descends   **160.1 A sennet** a trumpet call accompanying an entrance
163 With in addition to.   **to** added to   **170 prosperity** success.
172 deed-achieving achieved by deeds

183 light and heavy merry and sad.   **184 on 's** of his   **187 old crab
trees** old crab apple trees, i.e., sour-natured old men (such as the tribunes)   **188 grafted to your relish** implanted with a liking for you
(something that would sweeten the sourness).   **189–90 We . . . folly**
i.e., Some unpleasant and foolish things cannot be changed and must
be acknowledged for what they are.   **192 Menenius ever** Same old
Menenius   **194 shade** rest   **197 change of honors** promotion, fresh
honors.   **198 inherited** realized, possessed   **199 fancy** imagination.
200 wanting lacking   **201 cast upon** offer   **203 sway with** rule over
204–5 bearèd . . . spectacled people with dimmed vision put on spectacles   **205 Your prattling nurse** The typical chattering nurse

Into a rapture lets her baby cry 206
While she chats him. The kitchen malkin pins 207
Her richest lockram 'bout her reechy neck, 208
Clamb'ring the walls to eye him. Stalls, bulks,
   windows 209
Are smothered up, leads filled and ridges horsed 210
With variable complexions, all agreeing 211
In earnestness to see him. Seld-shown flamens 212
Do press among the popular throngs and puff 213
To win a vulgar station. Our veiled dames 214
Commit the war of white and damask in 215
Their nicely-gauded cheeks to th' wanton spoil 216
Of Phoebus' burning kisses—such a pother 217
As if that whatsoever god who leads him 218
Were slyly crept into his human powers 219
And gave him graceful posture.
SICINIUS   On the sudden 220
I warrant him consul.
BRUTUS   Then our office may, 221
During his power, go sleep. 222
SICINIUS
He cannot temperately transport his honors 223
From where he should begin and end, but will 224
Lose those he hath won.
BRUTUS   In that there's comfort.
SICINIUS   Doubt not 225
The commoners, for whom we stand, but they 226
Upon their ancient malice will forget 227
With the least cause these his new honors—which 228
That he will give them make I as little question 229
As he is proud to do't.
BRUTUS   I heard him swear, 230
Were he to stand for consul, never would he
Appear i'th' marketplace nor on him put
The napless vesture of humility, 233
Nor, showing, as the manner is, his wounds
To th' people, beg their stinking breaths.
SICINIUS   'Tis right. 235
BRUTUS
It was his word. Oh, he would miss it rather 236
Than carry it but by the suit of the gentry to him 237

And the desire of the nobles.
SICINIUS   I wish no better
Than have him hold that purpose and to put it
In execution.
BRUTUS   'Tis most like he will. 240
SICINIUS
It shall be to him then as our good wills, 241
A sure destruction.
BRUTUS   So it must fall out
To him, or our authority's for an end. 243
We must suggest the people in what hatred 244
He still hath held them; that to 's power he would 245
Have made them mules, silenced their pleaders, and 246
Dispropertied their freedoms, holding them 247
In human action and capacity
Of no more soul nor fitness for the world
Than camels in their war, who have their provand 250
Only for bearing burdens, and sore blows
For sinking under them.
SICINIUS   This—as you say, suggested
At some time when his soaring insolence
Shall touch the people, which time shall not want 254
If he be put upon't, and that's as easy 255
As to set dogs on sheep—will be his fire 256
To kindle their dry stubble; and their blaze 257
Shall darken him forever.

Enter a Messenger.

BRUTUS   What's the matter? 258
MESSENGER
You are sent for to the Capitol. 'Tis thought
That Marcius shall be consul. I have seen
The dumb men throng to see him, and the blind
To hear him speak. Matrons flung gloves,
Ladies and maids their scarves and handkerchiefs,
Upon him as he passed. The nobles bended
As to Jove's statue, and the commons made
A shower and thunder with their caps and shouts.
I never saw the like.
BRUTUS   Let's to the Capitol,
And carry with us ears and eyes for th' time, 268
But hearts for the event.
SICINIUS   Have with you. *Exeunt.* 269

❖

[2.2]

*Enter two Officers, to lay cushions, as it were in
the Capitol.*

---

206 **rapture** fit   207 **chats him** gossips about Coriolanus.   **malkin** untidy servantmaid   208 **lockram** coarse linen fabric.   **reechy** dirty, filthy   209 **Stalls** Benches in front of shops displaying wares.   **bulks** structures projecting from the front of a shop   210 **leads** leaded roofs   210–11 **ridges . . . complexions** the roof-ridges bestridden by people of all sorts   211 **agreeing** alike   212 **Seld-shown flamens** Priests (of ancient Rome) who rarely appear in public   213 **popular** plebeian, vulgar.   **puff** pant, exert themselves   214 **vulgar station** place in the crowd.   215–17 **Commit . . . kisses** commit their handsomely made-up complexions, in which white and damask pink contend with each other, to the amorous despoiling of the sun's burning kisses   217 **pother** hubbub   218 **him** Coriolanus   219 **his human powers** Coriolanus's body   220 **graceful posture** godlike bearing.   220–1 **On . . . consul** I predict with confidence that he will quickly be elected consul.   222 **power** term of authority   223 **temperately transport** carry in a temperate and self-controlled way   224 **and end** i.e., to a proper conclusion   225–7 **Doubt not . . . forget** Do not doubt that the commoners, whom we represent, will, because of their long-standing hostility, forget   228 **which** i.e., which provocation   229 **make . . . question** I have as little doubt   230 **As** as that   233 **napless vesture** threadbare garment   235 **breaths** i.e., voices, votes.   236 **miss it** i.e., go without the consulship   237 **carry it but** win it otherwise than

240 **like** likely   241 **as . . . wills** as our interest demands   243 **for an end** doomed.   244 **suggest** insinuate to   245 **still** always.   **to 's power** to the extent of his power   246 **mules** i.e., beasts of burden.   **pleaders** i.e., the tribunes   247 **Dispropertied** dispossessed, deprived (them) of   250 **provand** provender, food   254 **want** be lacking   255 **put upon't** urged, incited to it   256 **his fire** i.e., the spark that kindles his hatred   257 **To kindle . . . stubble** (Coriolanus's fiery wrath will, in turn, kindle the inflammable emotions of the plebeians.)   258 **darken** eclipse, deprive of authority or renown   268 **time** present situation   269 **hearts . . . event** deeper desires and purposes for what is to follow.   **Have with you** I'm with you, let's go.
2.2. Location: Rome. The Capitol.

FIRST OFFICER   Come, come, they are almost here. How
many stand for consulships?

SECOND OFFICER   Three, they say; but 'tis thought of   3
everyone Coriolanus will carry it.

FIRST OFFICER   That's a brave fellow, but he's vengeance   5
proud and loves not the common people.

SECOND OFFICER   Faith, there hath been many great men
that have flattered the people who ne'er loved them;   8
and there be many that they have loved, they know   9
not wherefore; so that, if they love they know not   10
why, they hate upon no better a ground. Therefore,
for Coriolanus neither to care whether they love or
hate him manifests the true knowledge he has in their   13
disposition, and out of his noble carelessness lets them   14
plainly see't.

FIRST OFFICER   If he did not care whether he had their
love or no, he waved indifferently twixt doing them   17
neither good nor harm; but he seeks their hate with
greater devotion than they can render it him, and
leaves nothing undone that may fully discover him   20
their opposite. Now, to seem to affect the malice and   21
displeasure of the people is as bad as that which he
dislikes, to flatter them for their love.

SECOND OFFICER   He hath deserved worthily of his country, and his ascent is not by such easy degrees as those   25
who, having been supple and courteous to the people,
bonneted, without any further deed to have them at   27
all into their estimation and report. But he hath so   28
planted his honors in their eyes and his actions in
their hearts that for their tongues to be silent and not
confess so much were a kind of ingrateful injury. To
report otherwise were a malice that, giving itself the   32
lie, would pluck reproof and rebuke from every ear   33
that heard it.

FIRST OFFICER   No more of him; he's a worthy man.
Make way, they are coming.   36

*A sennet. Enter the patricians and the tribunes of
the people, lictors before them; Coriolanus,
Menenius, Cominius the consul. Sicinius and
Brutus take their places by themselves. Coriolanus
stands.*

MENENIUS
Having determined of the Volsces and   37
To send for Titus Lartius, it remains,
As the main point of this our after-meeting,   39
To gratify his noble service that   40
Hath thus stood for his country. Therefore please you,   41

Most reverend and grave elders, to desire
The present consul and last general   43
In our well-found successes to report   44
A little of that worthy work performed
By Caius Marcius Coriolanus, whom
We met here both to thank and to remember
With honors like himself.   [*Coriolanus sits.*]

FIRST SENATOR   Speak, good Cominius.   48
Leave nothing out for length, and make us think
Rather our state's defective for requital   50
Than we to stretch it out. [*To the tribunes*] Masters
o'th' people,   51
We do request your kindest ears and, after,   52
Your loving motion toward the common body   53
To yield what passes here.

SICINIUS   We are convented   54
Upon a pleasing treaty, and have hearts   55
Inclinable to honor and advance
The theme of our assembly.

BRUTUS   Which the rather   57
We shall be blest to do if he remember   58
A kinder value of the people than   59
He hath hereto prized them at.

MENENIUS   That's off, that's off!   60
I would you rather had been silent. Please you
To hear Cominius speak?

BRUTUS   Most willingly;
But yet my caution was more pertinent   63
Than the rebuke you give it.

MENENIUS   He loves your people;
But tie him not to be their bedfellow.   65
Worthy Cominius, speak.

          Coriolanus rises and offers to go away.
          Nay, keep your place.   66

FIRST SENATOR
Sit, Coriolanus. Never shame to hear
What you have nobly done.

CORIOLANUS   Your Honors' pardon.
I had rather have my wounds to heal again
Than hear say how I got them.

BRUTUS   Sir, I hope
My words disbenched you not?

CORIOLANUS   No, sir. Yet oft,   71
When blows have made me stay, I fled from words.
You soothed not, therefore hurt not. But your people,   73
I love them as they weigh—

MENENIUS   Pray now, sit down.   74

---

3 of by   **5 brave** excellent.   **vengeance** terribly   **8 who . . . them**
(1) (aristocrats) who never loved the people, or (2) (people) who never
loved the aristocrats   **9 they** the people   **10 wherefore** why   **13 in**
of   **14 noble carelessness** patrician indifference to public opinion
17 waved indifferently would waver impartially   **20–1 discover . . .
opposite** reveal him to be their adversary.   **21 affect** seek out, desire
25 degrees steps   **27 bonneted** took their hats off.   **have them** gain
their way   **28 estimation and report** esteem and good opinion.
32–3 giving . . . lie manifesting its own falsehood   **36.2 lictors** officials attendant upon Roman magistrates   **37 determined of** i.e.,
reached a decision concerning (the terms for returning Corioles, etc.)
39 after-meeting follow-up meeting   **40 gratify** reward, requite
41 stood for fought for, defended

43 last late, recent   **44 well-found** fortunately met with, found to be
good   **48 like himself** i.e., worthy of his greatness.   **50–1 Rather . . .
out** that our state lacks means to reward adequately rather than that
we are defective in intention to extend what reward we have at our
disposal.   **52 after** in addition to that   **53 loving . . . body** friendly
intervention with the common people   **54 yield** assent to, grant.
passes is voted.   **convented** summoned, convened   **55 Upon** in
order to consider.   **treaty** proposal   **57 theme** business.   **rather**
sooner   **58 blest** happy   **59 kinder value** more favorable estimation
60 off jarring, not pertinent   **63 pertinent** appropriate   **65 tie** oblige
66 s.d. offers starts   **71 disbenched you not** did not make you leave
your seat.   **73 soothed** flattered   **74 as they weigh** according to
their deserts

CORIOLANUS
 I had rather have one scratch my head i'th' sun   75
 When the alarum were struck than idly sit   76
 To hear my nothings monstered.   *Exit Coriolanus.*
MENENIUS   Masters of the people, 77
 Your multiplying spawn how can he flatter—   78
 That's thousand to one good one—when you now see   79
 He had rather venture all his limbs for honor
 Than one on 's ears to hear it?—Proceed, Cominius.   81
COMINIUS
 I shall lack voice. The deeds of Coriolanus
 Should not be uttered feebly. It is held
 That valor is the chiefest virtue and
 Most dignifies the haver; if it be,
 The man I speak of cannot in the world
 Be singly counterpoised. At sixteen years,   87
 When Tarquin made a head for Rome, he fought   88
 Beyond the mark of others. Our then dictator,   89
 Whom with all praise I point at, saw him fight,   90
 When with his Amazonian chin he drove   91
 The bristled lips before him. He bestrid   92
 An o'erpressed Roman, and i'th' Consul's view   93
 Slew three opposers. Tarquin's self he met,
 And struck him on his knee. In that day's feats,   95
 When he might act the woman in the scene,   96
 He proved best man i'th' field, and for his meed   97
 Was brow-bound with the oak. His pupil age   98
 Man-entered thus, he waxèd like a sea,   99
 And in the brunt of seventeen battles since   100
 He lurched all swords of the garland. For this last,   101
 Before and in Corioles, let me say,
 I cannot speak him home. He stopped the fliers,   103
 And by his rare example made the coward   104
 Turn terror into sport. As weeds before
 A vessel under sail, so men obeyed
 And fell below his stem. His sword, death's stamp,   107
 Where it did mark, it took; from face to foot   108
 He was a thing of blood, whose every motion
 Was timed with dying cries. Alone he entered   110

 The mortal gate o'th' city, which he painted   111
 With shunless destiny; aidless came off,   112
 And with a sudden reinforcement struck   113
 Corioles like a planet. Now all's his,   114
 When by and by the din of war 'gan pierce   115
 His ready sense; then straight his doubled spirit   116
 Requickened what in flesh was fatigate,   117
 And to the battle came he, where he did
 Run reeking o'er the lives of men as if   119
 'Twere a perpetual spoil; and till we called   120
 Both field and city ours, he never stood   121
 To ease his breast with panting.
MENENIUS   Worthy man!
FIRST SENATOR
 He cannot but with measure fit the honors   123
 Which we devise him.
COMINIUS   Our spoils he kicked at, 124
 And looked upon things precious as they were   125
 The common muck of the world. He covets less
 Than misery itself would give, rewards   127
 His deeds with doing them, and is content   128
 To spend the time to end it.
MENENIUS   He's right noble.   129
 Let him be called for.
FIRST SENATOR   Call Coriolanus.
OFFICER   He doth appear.

          Enter Coriolanus.

MENENIUS
 The Senate, Coriolanus, are well pleased
 To make thee consul.
CORIOLANUS   I do owe them still   134
 My life and services.
MENENIUS   It then remains
 That you do speak to the people.
CORIOLANUS   I do beseech you,
 Let me o'erleap that custom, for I cannot
 Put on the gown, stand naked, and entreat them   138
 For my wounds' sake to give their suffrage. Please
     you
 That I may pass this doing.
SICINIUS   Sir, the people   140
 Must have their voices; neither will they bate   141
 One jot of ceremony.
MENENIUS [*to Coriolanus*]   Put them not to't.   142
 Pray you, go fit you to the custom and

75–6 have . . . struck i.e., engage in idle pleasure when the battle signal is sounded.   **77 monstered** made into unnatural marvels.
78 multiplying spawn fast-breeding commoners   **79 That's . . . one** in which there are a thousand bad ones to one good one, or, a thousand bad ones contrasted to the noble Coriolanus   **81 on 's** of his. **it** i.e., praise of his honor.   **87 singly counterpoised** equaled by any other individual.   **88 made . . . for** raised a force to attack (and reconquer)   **89 mark** ability, reach.   **dictator** leader constitutionally given absolute authority to deal with a specific emergency, such as a war   **90 point at** i.e., refer to. (The unnamed dictator of those earlier times, probably Aulus Posthumus Regillensis, is not present.)   **91 Amazonian** i.e., beardless (like the female warriors, the Amazons)   **92 bristled lips** i.e., bearded warriors.   **bestrid** stood over in battle, protected   **93 o'erpressed** overwhelmed   **95 on his knee** to his knees.   **96 he . . . scene** i.e., he was young enough not to have been blamed for cowardice. (With an allusion to boys playing women's roles in the theater.)   **97 meed** reward   **98 brow-bound** i.e., presented with a garland as an emblem of victory   **99 Man-entered** initiated into manhood   **100 brunt** violence, shock   **101 lurched** robbed, cheated.   **For** As for   **103 speak him home** praise him adequately.   **the fliers** those who tried to flee the battle   **104 the coward** even the coward   **107 stem** main timber of the prow of a ship. **stamp** tool for imprinting a design or pattern   **108 took** made an impression, slew   **110 Was timed** kept time, was accompanied

111 mortal deadly.   **111–12 which . . . destiny** i.e., which city he stained with the blood of those who could not escape his doom   **113 reinforcement** fresh assault   **114 like a planet** (Refers to the power of striking or blasting, believed in astrology to belong to the planets.)   **114–17 Now . . . fatigate** No sooner had he conquered there than at once the noise of battle began to pierce his alert hearing; then at once his renewed or redoubled spirit revivified his fatigued flesh   **119 reeking** steaming (with enemies' blood)   **120 perpetual spoil** endless slaughter   **121 stood** stopped   **123 He . . . fit** He can't help but measure up to   **124 devise** devise for.   **kicked at** spurned   **125 as** as if   **127 misery** poverty   **127–8 rewards . . . doing them** finds reward for his actions in the satisfaction that comes from having acted well   **128–9 is content . . . end it** is satisfied to be repaid for his time spent with the pleasure of having spent his time thus.   **134 still** ever   **138 naked** exposed   **140 pass** disregard, omit   **141 voices** votes. **bate** abate, do without   **142 Put . . . to't** i.e., Do not force the issue.

Take to you, as your predecessors have,
Your honor with your form.
CORIOLANUS   It is a part   145
That I shall blush in acting, and might well
Be taken from the people.
BRUTUS [*to Sicinius*]   Mark you that?
CORIOLANUS
To brag unto them, "Thus I did, and thus!"
Show them th'unaching scars which I should hide,
As if I had received them for the hire   150
Of their breath only!
MENENIUS   Do not stand upon't.—   151
We recommend to you, tribunes of the people,   152
Our purpose to them, and to our noble consul   153
Wish we all joy and honor.
SENATORS
To Coriolanus come all joy and honor!   155
Flourish cornets. Then exeunt. Manent Sicinius
and Brutus.

BRUTUS
You see how he intends to use the people.
SICINIUS
May they perceive 's intent! He will require them   157
As if he did contemn what he requested   158
Should be in them to give.
BRUTUS   Come, we'll inform them   159
Of our proceedings here. On th' marketplace   160
I know they do attend us.   [*Exeunt.*]   161

❖

[2.3]

Enter seven or eight Citizens.

FIRST CITIZEN   Once if he do require our voices, we   1
ought not to deny him.
SECOND CITIZEN   We may, sir, if we will.
THIRD CITIZEN   We have power in ourselves to do it,
but it is a power that we have no power to do; for if he   5
show us his wounds and tell us his deeds, we are to
put our tongues into those wounds and speak for   7
them; so, if he tell us his noble deeds, we must also tell
him our noble acceptance of them. Ingratitude is
monstrous, and for the multitude to be ingrateful were
to make a monster of the multitude; of the which we,
being members, should bring ourselves to be monstrous members.
FIRST CITIZEN   And to make us no better thought of, a   14
little help will serve; for once we stood up about the   15
corn, he himself stuck not to call us the many-headed   16
multitude.

THIRD CITIZEN   We have been called so of many; not that   18
our heads are some brown, some black, some abram,   19
some bald, but that our wits are so diversely colored;
and truly I think if all our wits were to issue out of one
skull, they would fly east, west, north, south, and their
consent of one direct way should be at once to all the   23
points o'th' compass.
SECOND CITIZEN   Think you so? Which way do you
judge my wit would fly?
THIRD CITIZEN   Nay, your wit will not so soon out as   27
another man's will; 'tis strongly wedged up in a blockhead. But if it were at liberty, 'twould, sure, south-   29
ward.   30
SECOND CITIZEN   Why that way?
THIRD CITIZEN   To lose itself in a fog where, being three
parts melted away with rotten dews, the fourth would   33
return for conscience' sake, to help to get thee a wife.
SECOND CITIZEN   You are never without your tricks. You   35
may, you may.   36
THIRD CITIZEN   Are you all resolved to give your
voices? But that's no matter, the greater part carries it.   38
I say, if he would incline to the people, there was   39
never a worthier man.

Enter Coriolanus in a gown of humility, with
Menenius.

Here he comes, and in the gown of humility. Mark his
behavior. We are not to stay all together, but to come
by him where he stands by ones, by twos, and by
threes. He's to make his requests by particulars,   44
wherein every one of us has a single honor in giving him   45
our own voices with our own tongues. Therefore fol-
low me, and I'll direct you how you shall go by him.
ALL   Content, content.   [*Exeunt Citizens.*]
MENENIUS
Oh, sir, you are not right. Have you not known
The worthiest men have done't?
CORIOLANUS   What must I say?
"I pray, sir"—Plague upon't! I cannot bring
My tongue to such a pace. "Look, sir, my wounds!
I got them in my country's service, when
Some certain of your brethren roared and ran
From th' noise of our own drums."
MENENIUS   Oh, me, the gods!
You must not speak of that. You must desire them
To think upon you.
CORIOLANUS   Think upon me? Hang 'em!
I would they would forget me, like the virtues   58
Which our divines lose by 'em.
MENENIUS   You'll mar all.   59
I'll leave you. Pray you speak to 'em, I pray you,

---

145 with your form with the ceremony that custom prescribes to you.
150 hire wages   **151 breath** i.e., votes.   **stand upon't** make a point of
it.   **152 recommend** commit, consign   **153 purpose to them** proposal
to the people   **155.1 *Manent*** They remain onstage   **157 require** ask,
solicit   **158 condemn what** scorn that what   **159 in them** theirs
160 On In   **161 attend** wait for
2.3. Location: Rome. The Forum, or marketplace.
1 Once if When once, as soon as   **5 no power to do** i.e., no moral
right to exercise   **7 put . . . wounds** i.e., let the wounds inspire our
tongues   **14–15 And . . . serve** And only a small effort on our part
would be needed to convince the patricians not to think well of us
15 once when   **16 stuck not** did not hesitate

18 of by.   **that** because   **19 abram** auburn   **23 consent of** agreement
upon   **27 out** come out, issue forth   **29–30 southward** (The south
wind was believed to bring pestilence.)   **33 rotten** unwholesome
35–6 You may i.e., Go on, say what you like   **38 greater part** majority
39 incline to sympathize with   **44 by particulars** to individuals, one
by one   **45 single** separate, individual   **58 I would** I wish
58–9 like . . . 'em like the virtuous lessons which our priests vainly
seek to instill in them.

In wholesome manner.   *Exit.*

Enter three of the Citizens.

CORIOLANUS   Bid them wash their faces   61
And keep their teeth clean. So, here comes a brace.—   62
You know the cause, sir, of my standing here.

THIRD CITIZEN
We do, sir. Tell us what hath brought you to't.

CORIOLANUS   Mine own desert.

SECOND CITIZEN   Your own desert?

CORIOLANUS   Ay, but not mine own desire.

THIRD CITIZEN   How, not your own desire?

CORIOLANUS   No, sir, 'twas never my desire yet to
trouble the poor with begging.

THIRD CITIZEN   You must think, if we give you anything, we hope to gain by you.

CORIOLANUS   Well then, I pray, your price o'th' consulship?

FIRST CITIZEN   The price is to ask it kindly.

CORIOLANUS   Kindly, sir, I pray, let me ha 't. I have
wounds to show you, which shall be yours in   77
private.—Your good voice, sir. What say you?

SECOND CITIZEN   You shall ha 't, worthy sir.

CORIOLANUS   A match, sir. There's in all two worthy   80
voices begged. I have your alms. Adieu.

THIRD CITIZEN   But this is something odd.   82

SECOND CITIZEN   An 'twere to give again—but 'tis no   83
matter.   *Exeunt [the three Citizens].*

Enter two other Citizens.

CORIOLANUS   Pray you now, if it may stand with the   85
tune of your voices that I may be consul, I have here
the customary gown.

FOURTH CITIZEN   You have deserved nobly of your
country, and you have not deserved nobly.

CORIOLANUS   Your enigma?   90

FOURTH CITIZEN   You have been a scourge to her   91
enemies; you have been a rod to her friends. You have   92
not indeed loved the common people.

CORIOLANUS   You should account me the more virtuous
that I have not been common in my love. I will, sir,   95
flatter my sworn brother, the people, to earn a dearer   96
estimation of them; 'tis a condition they account gen-   97
tle. And since the wisdom of their choice is rather to   98
have my hat than my heart, I will practice the insin-   99
uating nod and be off to them most counterfeitly. That   100

is, sir, I will counterfeit the bewitchment of some pop-   101
ular man and give it bountiful to the desirers. There-   102
fore, beseech you I may be consul.

FIFTH CITIZEN   We hope to find you our friend, and
therefore give you our voices heartily.

FOURTH CITIZEN   You have received many wounds for
your country.

CORIOLANUS   I will not seal your knowledge with show-   108
ing them. I will make much of your voices and so
trouble you no farther.

BOTH CITIZENS   The gods give you joy, sir, heartily!
                                    [Exeunt Citizens.]

CORIOLANUS   Most sweet voices!
Better it is to die, better to starve,
Than crave the hire which first we do deserve.   114
Why in this woolvish toge should I stand here   115
To beg of Hob and Dick that does appear   116
Their needless vouches? Custom calls me to't.   117
What custom wills, in all things should we do't,   118
The dust on antique time would lie unswept   119
And mountainous error be too highly heaped
For truth to o'erpeer. Rather than fool it so,   121
Let the high office and the honor go
To one that would do thus. I am half through;   123
The one part suffered, the other will I do.

Enter three Citizens more.

Here come more voices.—   125
Your voices! For your voices I have fought;
Watched for your voices; for your voices bear   127
Of wounds two dozen odd. Battles thrice six
I have seen and heard of; for your voices have   129
Done many things, some less, some more. Your
    voices!
Indeed, I would be consul.

SIXTH CITIZEN   He has done nobly, and cannot go
without any honest man's voice.

SEVENTH CITIZEN   Therefore let him be consul. The gods
give him joy, and make him good friend to the
people!

ALL   Amen, amen. God save thee, noble Consul!
                                    [Exeunt Citizens.]

CORIOLANUS   Worthy voices!

Enter Menenius, with Brutus and Sicinius.

MENENIUS
You have stood your limitation, and the tribunes   139

---

61 wholesome calculated to do good. (But Coriolanus answers sarcastically to the sense of "healthful.")   **62 brace** pair. (Used contemptuously here.)   **77 yours** available for your inspection   **80 match**
deal, bargain   **82 something** somewhat   **83 An 'twere** If it were
85 stand with be consistent with   **90 enigma** riddle.   **91 scourge**
instrument of punishment   **92 rod** stick or whip used to inflict punishment   **95 common** vulgar, promiscuous. (Playing on *common* in
line 93.)   **96 sworn brother** one of two friends bound by oath to each
other   **96–7 dearer . . . them** higher esteem on their part   **97–8 'tis . . .
gentle** i.e., they think it genteel to be flattered by an aristocrat and
view flattery as noble.   **99 my hat** i.e., my hat in my hand as a gesture of courtesy   **99–100 insinuating** ingratiating   **100 be off** doff
my hat.   **counterfeitly** hypocritically.

101 bewitchment sorcery, bewitching powers   **101–2 popular man**
demagogue   **102 bountiful** bountifully   **108 seal** confirm
114 crave . . . deserve beg the reward or wages we have already
earned.   **115 woolvish toge** wolf's toga (making me look like a wolf
in sheep's clothing)   **116 Hob and Dick** (Typical names for rustics.)
that does appear who make their appearance   **117 needless vouches**
unnecessary confirmations of approval. (To Coriolanus, only the Senate's appointment is necessary.)   **118 in . . . do't** if we should obey
custom indiscriminately   **119 antique time** old-fashioned traditions
121 o'erpeer overtop, be visible over or be able to see over.   **fool it so**
be so foolhardy (as to challenge ancient custom in its huge accumulation of error)   **123 do thus** i.e., go through with this meaningless ritual.   **125 voices** votes.   **127 Watched** kept watch (in camp)
129 heard of heard, i.e., been present at   **139 limitation** allotted time

Endue you with the people's voice. Remains   140
That, in th'official marks invested, you   141
Anon do meet the Senate.
CORIOLANUS   Is this done?   142
SICINIUS
The custom of request you have discharged.   143
The people do admit you, and are summoned
To meet anon, upon your approbation.   145
CORIOLANUS
Where? At the Senate House?
SICINIUS   There, Coriolanus.
CORIOLANUS
May I change these garments?
SICINIUS   You may, sir.
CORIOLANUS
That I'll straight do and, knowing myself again,
Repair to th' Senate House.   149
MENENIUS
I'll keep you company.—Will you along?
BRUTUS
We stay here for the people.
SICINIUS   Fare you well.
                    Exeunt Coriolanus and Menenius.
He has it now, and by his looks methinks
'Tis warm at 's heart.
BRUTUS   With a proud heart he wore
His humble weeds. Will you dismiss the people?

                    Enter the Plebeians.

SICINIUS
How now, my masters, have you chose this man?   155
FIRST CITIZEN   He has our voices, sir.
BRUTUS
We pray the gods he may deserve your loves.
SECOND CITIZEN
Amen, sir. To my poor unworthy notice,   158
He mocked us when he begged our voices.
THIRD CITIZEN
Certainly he flouted us downright.
FIRST CITIZEN
No, 'tis his kind of speech. He did not mock us.
SECOND CITIZEN
Not one amongst us, save yourself, but says
He used us scornfully. He should have showed us
His marks of merit, wounds received for 's country.
SICINIUS   Why, so he did, I am sure.
ALL   No, no. No man saw 'em.
THIRD CITIZEN
He said he had wounds, which he could show in
    private,
And with his hat, thus waving it in scorn,
"I would be consul," says he. "Agèd custom,
But by your voices, will not so permit me;
Your voices therefore." When we granted that,
Here was "I thank you for your voices. Thank you.

Your most sweet voices! Now you have left your
    voices,
I have no further with you." Was not this mockery?   174
SICINIUS
Why either were you ignorant to see't,   175
Or, seeing it, of such childish friendliness
To yield your voices?
BRUTUS   Could you not have told him
As you were lessoned? When he had no power,   178
But was a petty servant to the state,
He was your enemy, ever spake against   180
Your liberties and the charters that you bear
I'th' body of the weal; and now, arriving   182
A place of potency and sway o'th' state,
If he should still malignantly remain
Fast foe to th' plebii, your voices might   185
Be curses to yourselves. You should have said
That as his worthy deeds did claim no less
Than what he stood for, so his gracious nature   188
Would think upon you for your voices and   189
Translate his malice towards you into love,   190
Standing your friendly lord.
SICINIUS   Thus to have said,   191
As you were fore-advised, had touched his spirit   192
And tried his inclination; from him plucked
Either his gracious promise, which you might,
As cause had called you up, have held him to;   195
Or else it would have galled his surly nature,   196
Which easily endures not article   197
Tying him to aught. So putting him to rage,
You should have ta'en th'advantage of his choler   199
And passed him unelected.
BRUTUS   Did you perceive
He did solicit you in free contempt   201
When he did need your loves, and do you think
That his contempt shall not be bruising to you
When he hath power to crush? Why, had your bodies
No heart among you? Or had you tongues to cry   205
Against the rectorship of judgment?
SICINIUS   Have you   206
Ere now denied the asker? And now   207
Again, of him that did not ask but mock,   208
Bestow your sued-for tongues?
THIRD CITIZEN   He's not confirmed.
We may deny him yet.
SECOND CITIZEN   And will deny him.
I'll have five hundred voices of that sound.

---

140 Endue endow.   **Remains** It remains   **141 in . . . invested** dressed in the insignia of office   **142 Anon** immediately   **143 The custom . . . discharged** You have performed the custom of asking the people's voices. **145 upon your approbation** to confirm your having been elected. **149 Repair** go   **155 masters** good sirs   **158 notice** observation

174 further with further use for   **175 ignorant** too dull **178 lessoned** instructed.   **180 ever** always   **182 body of the weal** commonwealth.   **arriving** attaining   **185 plebii** plebeians **188 what . . . for** the office he was seeking   **189 Would think upon** should esteem   **190 Translate** transform   **191 Standing . . . lord** acting on your behalf.   **192 had touched** would have tested (as gold and silver were tested with the touchstone)   **195 As . . . up** if occasion aroused you   **196 galled** irritated, rubbed sore   **197 article** stipulated condition   **199 choler** anger   **201 free** frank   **205 heart** i.e., as a seat of courage and wisdom.   **to cry** only to rebel   **206 rectorship of judgment** guidance of common sense.   **206–7 Have . . . asker?** Haven't you on previous occasions denied one asking for your support?   **208 of** upon

FIRST CITIZEN
    I twice five hundred, and their friends to piece 'em.   212
BRUTUS
    Get you hence instantly, and tell those friends
    They have chose a consul that will from them take
    Their liberties, make them of no more voice
    Than dogs that are as often beat for barking
    As therefor kept to do so.
SICINIUS   Let them assemble,   217
    And on a safer judgment all revoke   218
    Your ignorant election. Enforce his pride   219
    And his old hate unto you. Besides, forget not   220
    With what contempt he wore the humble weed,   221
    How in his suit he scorned you; but your loves,   222
    Thinking upon his services, took from you
    Th'apprehension of his present portance,   224
    Which most gibingly, ungravely, he did fashion   225
    After the inveterate hate he bears you.
BRUTUS   Lay   226
    A fault on us, your tribunes, that we labored,   227
    No impediment between, but that you must   228
    Cast your election on him.
SICINIUS   Say you chose him
    More after our commandment than as guided
    By your own true affections, and that your minds,
    Preoccupied with what you rather must do
    Than what you should, made you against the grain   233
    To voice him consul. Lay the fault on us.
BRUTUS
    Ay, spare us not. Say we read lectures to you,   235
    How youngly he began to serve his country,   236
    How long continued, and what stock he springs of,
    The noble house o'th' Marcians, from whence came
    That Ancus Marcius, Numa's daughter's son,   239
    Who after great Hostilius here was king;
    Of the same house Publius and Quintus were,
    That our best water brought by conduits hither;   242
      243
    And nobly namèd so, twice being censor,   244
    Was his great ancestor.
SICINIUS   One thus descended,
    That hath beside well in his person wrought   246
    To be set high in place, we did commend
    To your remembrances; but you have found,
    Scaling his present bearing with his past,   249

---

212 **piece** add to, reinforce   217 **therefor** for that purpose   218 **safer** sounder   219 **Enforce** Lay stress upon   220 **forget not** don't forget to mention   221 **weed** garment   222 **suit** petition. (With a pun on "garment.")   224 **Th'apprehension** the perceiving, comprehending. **portance** behavior   225 **gibingly, ungravely** jeeringly, mockingly   226 **After** in accord with   227 **A fault** the blame   228 **No impediment between** allowing nothing to stand in the way   233 **against the grain** i.e., against your natural inclination   235 **read lectures to** instructed   236 **youngly** early (in his life)   239 **Numa** legendary successor of Romulus as King of Rome; Tullus Hostilius (line 240) was traditionally the third king; Ancus Martius, the fourth   242 **conduits** aqueducts   243 (A line is evidently missing here. From Plutarch, editors guess that the line may have read something like "And Censorinus, that was so surnamed.")   244 **censor** Roman magistrate charged also with the supervision of the census   246 **That . . . wrought** who in addition has well deserved by his own actions   249 **Scaling** estimating, weighing

---

    That he's your fixèd enemy, and revoke
    Your sudden approbation.
BRUTUS   Say you ne'er had done't—   251
    Harp on that still—but by our putting on.   252
    And presently, when you have drawn your number,   253
    Repair to th' Capitol.
ALL   We will so. Almost all   254
    Repent in their election.   *Exeunt Plebeians.*
BRUTUS   Let them go on.
    This mutiny were better put in hazard   256
    Than stay, past doubt, for greater.   257
    If, as his nature is, he fall in rage
    With their refusal, both observe and answer   259
    The vantage of his anger.
SICINIUS   To th' Capitol, come.   260
    We will be there before the stream o'th' people;
    And this shall seem, as partly 'tis, their own,
    Which we have goaded onward.   *Exeunt.*

❦

[3.1]

Cornets. Enter Coriolanus, Menenius, all the gentry, Cominius, Titus Lartius, and other Senators.

CORIOLANUS
    Tullus Aufidius then had made new head?   1
LARTIUS
    He had, my lord; and that it was which caused
    Our swifter composition.   3
CORIOLANUS
    So then the Volsces stand but as at first,
    Ready, when time shall prompt them, to make road   5
    Upon 's again.
COMINIUS   They are worn, Lord Consul, so,   6
    That we shall hardly in our ages see   7
    Their banners wave again.
CORIOLANUS [*to Lartius*]   Saw you Aufidius?
LARTIUS
    On safeguard he came to me, and did curse   9
    Against the Volsces for they had so vilely   10
    Yielded the town. He is retired to Antium.   11
CORIOLANUS
    Spoke he of me?
LARTIUS   He did, my lord.
CORIOLANUS   How? What?
LARTIUS
    How often he had met you, sword to sword;
    That of all things upon the earth he hated

---

251 **sudden** hasty   252 **putting on** urging.   253 **presently** immediately.   **drawn your number** assembled your supporters   254 **Repair** go, proceed   256 **put in hazard** risked   257 **Than . . . greater** than wait for the chance of a greater uprising that would certainly occur.   259–60 **answer The vantage of** take advantage of
3.1. Location: Rome. A street. The procession is on its way to the marketplace; see line 33.
1 **made new head** raised another army.   3 **composition** coming to terms (about the return of Corioles to the Volscians).   5 **road** inroad, attack   6 **worn** i.e., militarily weakened   7 **ages** lifetimes   9 **On safeguard** Under safe-conduct   10 **for** because   11 **is retired** has returned

Your person most; that he would pawn his fortunes
To hopeless restitution, so he might   16
Be called your vanquisher.
CORIOLANUS   At Antium lives he?
LARTIUS   At Antium.
CORIOLANUS
I wish I had a cause to seek him there,
To oppose his hatred fully. Welcome home.

Enter Sicinius and Brutus.

Behold, these are the tribunes of the people,
The tongues o'th' common mouth. I do despise them,
For they do prank them in authority   24
Against all noble sufferance.   25
SICINIUS [*advancing*]   Pass no further.
CORIOLANUS   Ha? What is that?
BRUTUS
It will be dangerous to go on. No further.
CORIOLANUS   What makes this change?
MENENIUS   The matter?
COMINIUS
Hath he not passed the noble and the common?   31
BRUTUS
Cominius, no.
CORIOLANUS   Have I had children's voices?
FIRST SENATOR
Tribunes, give way. He shall to th' marketplace.
BRUTUS
The people are incensed against him.
SICINIUS   Stop,
Or all will fall in broil.
CORIOLANUS   Are these your herd?   35
Must these have voices, that can yield them now   36
And straight disclaim their tongues? What are your
offices?   37
You being their mouths, why rule you not their teeth?
Have you not set them on?
MENENIUS   Be calm, be calm.
CORIOLANUS
It is a purposed thing, and grows by plot,   40
To curb the will of the nobility.
Suffer't, and live with such as cannot rule   42
Nor ever will be ruled.
BRUTUS   Call't not a plot.
The people cry you mocked them; and of late,   44
When corn was given them gratis, you repined,   45
Scandaled the suppliants for the people, called them   46
Timepleasers, flatterers, foes to nobleness.
CORIOLANUS
Why, this was known before.
BRUTUS   Not to them all.

CORIOLANUS
Have you informed them sithence?
BRUTUS   How? I inform them?   49
COMINIUS
You are like to do such business.   50
BRUTUS
Not unlike, each way, to better yours.   51
CORIOLANUS
Why then should I be consul? By yond clouds,
Let me deserve so ill as you, and make me
Your fellow tribune.
SICINIUS   You show too much of that   54
For which the people stir. If you will pass   55
To where you are bound, you must inquire your way, 56
Which you are out of, with a gentler spirit,   57
Or never be so noble as a consul,
Nor yoke with him for tribune.
MENENIUS   Let's be calm.   59
COMINIUS
The people are abused, set on. This palt'ring   60
Becomes not Rome, nor has Coriolanus   61
Deserved this so dishonored rub, laid falsely   62
I'th' plain way of his merit.
CORIOLANUS   Tell me of corn?   63
This was my speech, and I will speak't again.
MENENIUS   Not now, not now.
FIRST SENATOR   Not in this heat, sir, now.
CORIOLANUS   Now, as I live, I will.
My nobler friends, I crave their pardons. For   68
The mutable, rank-scented meiny, let them   69
Regard me as I do not flatter, and   70
Therein behold themselves. I say again,   71
In soothing them, we nourish 'gainst our Senate
The cockle of rebellion, insolence, sedition,   73
Which we ourselves have plowed for, sowed, and
scattered
By mingling them with us, the honored number,   75
Who lack not virtue, no, nor power, but that
Which they have given to beggars.
MENENIUS   Well, no more.
FIRST SENATOR
No more words, we beseech you.
CORIOLANUS   How? No more?
As for my country I have shed my blood,
Not fearing outward force, so shall my lungs

16 To . . . restitution beyond hope of recovery.   so provided that
24 prank them dress themselves up   25 Against . . . sufferance
beyond the power of nobility to tolerate.   31 passed . . . common
been approved by the nobility and the common people.   35 broil
tumult.   36 yield grant, bestow.   now one instant   37 straight
immediately afterward.   offices duties.   40 purposed premeditated
42 live i.e., you will have to live   44 of late lately   45 repined
demurred   46 Scandaled defamed

49 sithence since.   50 like likely   51 Not . . . yours Not unlikely to
prove, in any case, a better way (of providing for the welfare of the
state) than yours.   54 that that quality   55 stir are aroused, angry.
55–6 If . . . bound i.e., If you wish to get to the marketplace and attain
the consulship   57 are out of have strayed from   59 yoke be joined.
(Sicinius insults Coriolanus by treating his sarcastic offer to be a tribune, lines 52–4, as though it were serious.)   60–1 The people . . .
Rome The commoners are being misled and incited by their tribunes.
Rome does not deserve this equivocating trickery   62–3 this . . .
merit this dishonoring obstacle treacherously placed (as in the game
of bowls) in the clear path of his deserving.   68–71 For . . . themselves As for the changeable, foul-smelling multitude, let them see
themselves in the unflattering truth I show to them.   73 cockle weed
75 honored honorable

Coin words till their decay against those measles   81
Which we disdain should tetter us, yet sought   82
The very way to catch them.

BRUTUS   You speak o'th' people   83
As if you were a god to punish, not
A man of their infirmity.

SICINIUS   'Twere well   85
We let the people know't.

MENENIUS   What, what? His choler?

CORIOLANUS   Choler?
Were I as patient as the midnight sleep,
By Jove, 'twould be my mind.

SICINIUS   It is a mind   89
That shall remain a poison where it is,
Not poison any further.

CORIOLANUS   "Shall remain"?
Hear you this Triton of the minnows? Mark you   92
His absolute "shall"?

COMINIUS   'Twas from the canon.

CORIOLANUS   "Shall"?   93
O good but most unwise patricians! Why,
You grave but reckless senators, have you thus
Given Hydra here to choose an officer,   96
That with his peremptory "shall," being but   97
The horn and noise o'th' monster's, wants not spirit   98
To say he'll turn your current in a ditch   99
And make your channel his? If he have power,   100
Then vail your ignorance; if none, awake   101
Your dangerous lenity. If you are learned,   102
Be not as common fools; if you are not,
Let them have cushions by you. You are plebeians   104
If they be senators; and they are no less   105
When, both your voices blended, the great'st taste   106
Most palates theirs. They choose their magistrate,   107
And such a one as he, who puts his "shall,"
His popular "shall," against a graver bench   109
Than ever frowned in Greece. By Jove himself,   110
It makes the consuls base! And my soul aches
To know, when two authorities are up,   112
Neither supreme, how soon confusion   113

May enter twixt the gap of both and take   114
The one by th'other.

COMINIUS   Well, on to th' marketplace.   115

CORIOLANUS
Whoever gave that counsel to give forth
The corn o'th' storehouse gratis, as 'twas used   117
Sometime in Greece—

MENENIUS   Well, well, no more of that.   118

CORIOLANUS
Though there the people had more absolute power,
I say they nourished disobedience, fed
The ruin of the state.

BRUTUS   Why shall the people give
One that speaks thus their voice?

CORIOLANUS   I'll give my reasons,
More worthier than their voices. They know the corn
Was not our recompense, resting well assured   124
They ne'er did service for't. Being pressed to the war, 125
Even when the navel of the state was touched,   126
They would not thread the gates. This kind of service   127
Did not deserve corn gratis. Being i'th' war,
Their mutinies and revolts, wherein they showed
Most valor, spoke not for them. Th'accusation   130
Which they have often made against the Senate,
All cause unborn, could never be the native   132
Of our so frank donation. Well, what then?   133
How shall this bosom multiplied digest   134
The Senate's courtesy? Let deeds express
What's like to be their words: "We did request it;   136
We are the greater poll, and in true fear   137
They gave us our demands." Thus we debase
The nature of our seats and make the rabble
Call our cares fears, which will in time   140
Break ope the locks o'th' Senate and bring in
The crows to peck the eagles.

MENENIUS   Come, enough.

BRUTUS
Enough, with overmeasure.

CORIOLANUS   No, take more!
What may be sworn by, both divine and human,   144
Seal what I end withal! This double worship—   145
Where one part does disdain with cause, the other
Insult without all reason, where gentry, title, wisdom   147
Cannot conclude but by the yea and no   148
Of general ignorance—it must omit   149
Real necessities, and give way the while   150

81–3 till . . . them till my lungs can utter no more against those loathsome diseases (i.e., the common people), which, though we disdain to be infected by them, we have nonetheless left ourselves open to infection by discoursing with them. **85 of their infirmity** sharing their human imperfections. **89 mind** opinion. **92 Triton of the minnows** i.e., god of the little fish. (Triton was Neptune's son and trumpeter.) **93 from the canon** i.e., out of order, exceeding the authority granted the tribunes. **96 Given** permitted. **Hydra** many-headed monster slain by Hercules; here, the mob **97 his peremptory "shall"** his use of the command form of the verb (*shall*) **98 horn and noise** noisy horn. (See allusion to Triton above.) **wants** lacks **99–100 he'll . . . his** he'll divert the current of your power into a ditch and preempt for himself your channel of authority. **101 vail your ignorance** bow down to him in your ignorant yielding **101–2 awake . . . lenity** arouse yourselves from your dangerous mildness. **102 learned** wise **104 cushions** i.e., seats in the Senate **105–7 and . . . theirs** and they are to all intents and purposes senators if, when their voices are mingled with yours, the resulting action savors of them more than of you. **109 popular** on behalf of the populace. **graver bench** more august deliberative body **110 frowned** looked austere in judgment. **Greece** (Famous for its law-giving institutions.) **112 up** established, in action **113 confusion** chaos

114 gap of both space between the two. **take** destroy **115 by** by means of **117 used** practiced, customary **118 Sometime** formerly **124 our recompense** reward from us **125 pressed** conscripted, enlisted **126 navel** vital center. **touched** threatened **127 thread** pass through **130 spoke not** did not speak well **132 All cause unborn** unjustifiably. **native** natural source or origin **133 frank** freely granted and generous **134 bosom multiplied** multiple stomach. **digest** i.e., consider, regard. (With also the literal sense of eating the grain.) **136 like** likely **137 greater poll** majority, greater number of heads **140 cares** concern (for them and for the state). **which** i.e., which insubordination **144 What** May whatever **145 Seal** confirm. **withal** with. **double worship** divided authority **147 Insult without** behave insolently beyond. **gentry** noble birth **148 conclude** come to a final decision **149 general** popular, common. **omit** neglect **150 the while** in the meanwhile

To unstable slightness. Purpose so barred, it follows   151
Nothing is done to purpose. Therefore, beseech you—   152
You that will be less fearful than discreet,   153
That love the fundamental part of state   154
More than you doubt the change on't, that prefer   155
A noble life before a long, and wish
To jump a body with a dangerous physic   157
That's sure of death without it—at once pluck out
The multitudinous tongue; let them not lick   159
The sweet which is their poison. Your dishonor   160
Mangles true judgment and bereaves the state   161
Of that integrity which should become't,   162
Not having the power to do the good it would
For th'ill which doth control't.

BRUTUS   He's said enough.   164
SICINIUS
He's spoken like a traitor and shall answer   165
As traitors do.
CORIOLANUS   Thou wretch, despite o'erwhelm thee!   166
What should the people do with these bald tribunes,   167
On whom depending, their obedience fails
To th' greater bench? In a rebellion,   169
When what's not meet, but what must be, was law,   170
Then were they chosen. In a better hour,
Let what is meet be said it must be meet,   172
And throw their power i'th' dust.
BRUTUS   Manifest treason!
SICINIUS   This a consul? No!
BRUTUS
The aediles, ho!

    Enter an Aedile.

                Let him be apprehended.   176
SICINIUS   Go, call the people,   [*Exit an Aedile.*]
                        in whose name myself
Attach thee as a traitorous innovator,   178
A foe to th' public weal. Obey, I charge thee,   179
And follow to thine answer.
CORIOLANUS   Hence, old goat!   180
ALL PATRICIANS
We'll surety him.
COMINIUS [*to Sicinius*]   Aged sir, hands off.   181

CORIOLANUS [*to Sicinius*]
Hence, rotten thing! Or I shall shake thy bones
Out of thy garments.
SICINIUS   Help, ye citizens!

    Enter a rabble of plebeians, with the aediles.

MENENIUS   On both sides more respect.   184
SICINIUS
Here's he that would take from you all your power.
BRUTUS   Seize him, aediles!
ALL PLEBEIANS   Down with him! Down with him!
SECOND SENATOR   Weapons, weapons, weapons!
                    They all bustle about Coriolanus.
ALL
Tribunes!—Patricians!—Citizens!—What, ho!—
Sicinius!—Brutus!—Coriolanus!—Citizens!—
Peace, peace, peace!—Stay, hold, peace!
MENENIUS
What is about to be? I am out of breath.
Confusion's near; I cannot speak. You, tribunes
To th' people! Coriolanus, patience!
Speak, good Sicinius.
SICINIUS   Hear me, people. Peace!
ALL PLEBEIANS
Let's hear our tribune. Peace! Speak, speak, speak.
SICINIUS
You are at point to lose your liberties.   197
Marcius would have all from you—Marcius,   198
Whom late you have named for consul.
MENENIUS   Fie, fie, fie!   199
This is the way to kindle, not to quench.
FIRST SENATOR
To unbuild the city and to lay all flat.
SICINIUS
What is the city but the people?
ALL PLEBEIANS   True,
The people are the city.
BRUTUS
By the consent of all, we were established
The people's magistrates.
ALL PLEBEIANS   You so remain.
MENENIUS   And so are like to do.   207
COMINIUS
That is the way to lay the city flat,
To bring the roof to the foundation,
And bury all which yet distinctly ranges   210
In heaps and piles of ruin.
SICINIUS   This deserves death.   211
BRUTUS
Or let us stand to our authority   212
Or let us lose it. We do here pronounce,
Upon the part o'th' people, in whose power
We were elected theirs, Marcius is worthy
Of present death.
SICINIUS   Therefore lay hold of him!   216

151 **slightness** vacillation, trifling. **Purpose so barred** Sound policy and planning being thus obstructed   152 **purpose** any effect.   153 **less . . . discreet** actuated less by fear than by foresight   154–5 **That . . . on't** i.e., you that love the essentials of our government more than you fear changes in it (such as getting rid of the tribunes)   157 **jump** risk (treating). **physic** cure   159 **The multitudinous tongue** the voice of the multitude, i.e., the tribunes   160 **sweet . . . poison** i.e., power which in their hands will undo them as well as Rome. **dishonor** present dishonorable state   161 **bereaves** deprives   162 **become't** adorn it   164 **For . . . control't** because of the dangerous tribunal power that overmasters it.   165 **answer** answer for it   166 **despite** scorn   167 **bald** petty, barren (literally and figuratively)   169 **greater bench** i.e., senators collectively.   170 **When . . . was law** when "might makes right" prevailed   172 **Let . . . be meet** i.e., let us openly say that what is right is what should be done   176 **aediles** officers attached to the tribunes   178 **Attach** arrest. **innovator** revolutionary   179 **weal** welfare.   180 **answer** defense, answer to a charge.   181 **surety** go bail for

184 **more** let there be more   197 **at point to lose** on the verge of losing   198 **Marcius** (Sicinius pointedly omits the title "Coriolanus.")   199 **late** recently   207 **like** likely   210 **distinctly ranges** stretches out in proper order   211 **This** i.e., Coriolanus's defiance of the tribunes   212 **Or** Either. **stand to** maintain   216 **present** immediate

Bear him to th' rock Tarpeian, and from thence   217
Into destruction cast him.

BRUTUS   Aediles, seize him!

ALL PLEBEIANS
Yield, Marcius, yield!

MENENIUS   Hear me one word.
Beseech you, tribunes, hear me but a word.

AEDILES   Peace, peace!

MENENIUS [to the tribunes]
Be that you seem, truly your country's friend,   222
And temperately proceed to what you would
Thus violently redress.

BRUTUS   Sir, those cold ways,
That seem like prudent helps, are very poisonous
Where the disease is violent.—Lay hands upon him
And bear him to the rock.
                    Coriolanus draws his sword.

CORIOLANUS   No, I'll die here.
There's some among you have beheld me fighting.
Come, try upon yourselves what you have seen me.

MENENIUS
Down with that sword! Tribunes, withdraw awhile.

BRUTUS
Lay hands upon him.

MENENIUS   Help Marcius, help!
You that be noble, help him, young and old!

ALL PLEBEIANS   Down with him, down with him!   233
            In this mutiny, the tribunes, the aediles,
                    and the people are beat in.

MENENIUS [to Coriolanus]
Go, get you to your house. Begone, away!
All will be naught else.

SECOND SENATOR   Get you gone.

CORIOLANUS   Stand fast!   235
We have as many friends as enemies.

MENENIUS
Shall it be put to that?

FIRST SENATOR   The gods forbid!
I prithee, noble friend, home to thy house;
Leave us to cure this cause.   239

MENENIUS   For 'tis a sore upon us
You cannot tent yourself. Begone, beseech you.   241

COMINIUS   Come, sir, along with us.

CORIOLANUS
I would they were barbarians, as they are,
Though in Rome littered; not Romans, as they are not,
Though calved i'th' porch o'th' Capitol.

MENENIUS   Begone!
Put not your worthy rage into your tongue.
One time will owe another.

CORIOLANUS   On fair ground   247
I could beat forty of them.

MENENIUS   I could myself

Take up a brace o'th' best of them; yea, the two
    tribunes.   249

COMINIUS
But now 'tis odds beyond arithmetic,   250
And manhood is called foolery when it stands   251
Against a falling fabric. Will you hence   252
Before the tag return, whose rage doth rend   253
Like interrupted waters and o'erbear   254
What they are used to bear?

MENENIUS   Pray you, begone.   255
I'll try whether my old wit be in request   256
With those that have but little. This must be patched   257
With cloth of any color.   258

COMINIUS   Nay, come away.
        Exeunt Coriolanus and Cominius [with others].

A PATRICIAN   This man has marred his fortune.

MENENIUS
His nature is too noble for the world.
He would not flatter Neptune for his trident   262
Or Jove for 's power to thunder. His heart's his mouth.   263
What his breast forges, that his tongue must vent,   264
And, being angry, does forget that ever
He heard the name of death.   A noise within.
                    Here's goodly work!

A PATRICIAN   I would they were abed!

MENENIUS
I would they were in Tiber! What the vengeance!   268
Could he not speak 'em fair?

    Enter Brutus and Sicinius, with the rabble again.

SICINIUS   Where is this viper   269
That would depopulate the city and
Be every man himself?

MENENIUS   You worthy tribunes—

SICINIUS
He shall be thrown down the Tarpeian rock
With rigorous hands. He hath resisted law,   273
And therefore law shall scorn him further trial   274
Than the severity of the public power
Which he so sets at naught.

FIRST CITIZEN   He shall well know   276
The noble tribunes are the people's mouths,
And we their hands.

ALL PLEBEIANS   He shall, sure on't.   279

MENENIUS   Sir, sir—

SICINIUS   Peace!

---

217 **rock Tarpeian** famous precipice on the Capitoline Hill in ancient
Rome from which persons condemned for offenses against the state
were thrown down   222 **that** what   233.2 **beat in** i.e., driven offstage.
235 **naught else** ruined otherwise.   239 **cause** disease.   241 **tent** treat
(by probing a wound), cure   247 **One . . . another** Another time will
compensate for this setback.

249 **Take . . . brace** take on a pair   250 **'tis . . . arithmetic** i.e., we are
thoroughly outnumbered   251 **manhood** manliness.   **foolery** folly
252 **fabric** building.   **hence** leave   253 **tag** rabble   253–5 **doth
rend . . . bear** breaks and overflows, like dammed-up waters, the
banks that normally contain them.   256 **request** demand
257–8 **patched . . . color** i.e., mended in any way possible.
262 **trident** three-pronged spear, the symbol of Neptune, Roman
god of the sea   263 **His . . . mouth** i.e., What he feels is exactly what
he speaks.   264 **vent** express   268 **What the vengeance!** (An oath.)
269 **speak 'em fair** speak to them courteously.   273 **rigorous** severe
274 **scorn** refuse.   **further** any further   276 **sets at naught** views as
worthless.   279 **sure on't** be sure of it.

MENENIUS
Do not cry havoc, where you should but hunt 282
With modest warrant.

SICINIUS   Sir, how comes 't that you 283
Have holp to make this rescue?

MENENIUS   Hear me speak. 284
As I do know the Consul's worthiness,
So can I name his faults.

SICINIUS   Consul? What consul?

MENENIUS   The Consul Coriolanus.

BRUTUS   He consul?

ALL PLEBEIANS   No, no, no, no, no.

MENENIUS
If, by the tribunes' leave and yours, good people, 291
I may be heard, I would crave a word or two,
The which shall turn you to no further harm
Than so much loss of time.

SICINIUS   Speak briefly then,
For we are peremptory to dispatch 295
This viperous traitor. To eject him hence 296
Were but one danger, and to keep him here
Our certain death; therefore it is decreed
He dies tonight.

MENENIUS   Now the good gods forbid
That our renownèd Rome, whose gratitude
Towards her deservèd children is enrolled 301
In Jove's own book, like an unnatural dam 302
Should now eat up her own!

SICINIUS
He's a disease that must be cut away.

MENENIUS
Oh, he's a limb that has but a disease—
Mortal to cut it off; to cure it easy.
What has he done to Rome that's worthy death? 306
Killing our enemies, the blood he hath lost—
Which I dare vouch is more than that he hath
By many an ounce—he dropped it for his country;
And what is left, to lose it by his country 311
Were to us all that do't and suffer it
A brand to th'end o'th' world.

SICINIUS   This is clean kam. 313

BRUTUS
Merely awry. When he did love his country, 314
It honored him.

SICINIUS   The service of the foot,
Being once gangrened, is not then respected
For what before it was.

BRUTUS   We'll hear no more.
Pursue him to his house and pluck him thence,
Lest his infection, being of catching nature,
Spread further.

MENENIUS   One word more, one word.
This tiger-footed rage, when it shall find

The harm of unscanned swiftness, will too late 323
Tie leaden pounds to 's heels. Proceed by process, 324
Lest parties—as he is beloved—break out 325
And sack great Rome with Romans.

BRUTUS   If it were so— 326

SICINIUS   What do ye talk? 327
Have we not had a taste of his obedience?
Our aediles smote? Ourselves resisted? Come.

MENENIUS
Consider this: he has been bred i'th' wars
Since 'a could draw a sword, and is ill schooled 331
In bolted language; meal and bran together 332
He throws without distinction. Give me leave, 333
I'll go to him and undertake to bring him
Where he shall answer, by a lawful form, 335
In peace, to his utmost peril.

FIRST SENATOR   Noble tribunes, 336
It is the humane way. The other course
Will prove too bloody, and the end of it
Unknown to the beginning.

SICINIUS   Noble Menenius,
Be you then as the people's officer.—
Masters, lay down your weapons.

BRUTUS   Go not home.

SICINIUS
Meet on the marketplace.—We'll attend you there, 342
Where, if you bring not Marcius, we'll proceed
In our first way.

MENENIUS   I'll bring him to you.
[To the Senators] Let me desire your company. He must
   come,
Or what is worst will follow.

FIRST SENATOR   Pray you, let's to him. 347
         Exeunt omnes.

❖

[3.2]

Enter Coriolanus, with Nobles.

CORIOLANUS
Let them pull all about mine ears, present me 1
Death on the wheel or at wild horses' heels, 2
Or pile ten hills on the Tarpeian rock,
That the precipitation might down stretch 4
Below the beam of sight, yet will I still 5
Be thus to them.

A PATRICIAN   You do the nobler.

CORIOLANUS   I muse my mother 8
Does not approve me further, who was wont 9

323 **unscanned** unconsidered   324 **Tie . . . heels** tie leaden weights to his heels.   **process** legal method   325 **parties** factions   326 **with** by means of; along with   327 **What** Why   331 **'a** he   332 **bolted** sifted, refined   332–3 **meal . . . throws** he throws flour and husks together   333 **Give** If you give   335–6 **answer . . . peril** stand trial peacefully even though his life is at stake.   342 **attend** await   347.1 *omnes* all. **3.2. Location: Rome. Coriolanus's house.**
1 **pull . . . ears** pull everything down on top of me, crush me. **present me** i.e., sentence me to   2 **wheel** instrument of torture and death by which the victim's limbs were broken   4 **precipitation** precipitousness   5 **Below . . . sight** further than the eye can see   8 **muse** wonder that   9 **further** to a greater degree.   **was wont** used

282 **cry havoc** give the order for general slaughter (as in *Julius Caesar*, 3.1.275)   283 **modest warrant** limited license.   284 **holp . . . rescue** helped to remove this prisoner from custody by force.   291 **leave** permission   295 **peremptory** determined   296 **eject him hence** exile him   301 **deservèd** deserving   302 **dam** mother   306 **Mortal** fatal   311 **by** at the hands of   313 **brand** i.e., brand of infamy, stigma. **clean kam** quite beside the point.   314 **Merely** Completely

To call them woolen vassals, things created 10
To buy and sell with groats, to show bare heads 11
In congregations, to yawn, be still, and wonder 12
When one but of my ordinance stood up 13
To speak of peace or war.

Enter Volumnia.

                              I talk of you.
Why did you wish me milder? Would you have me
False to my nature? Rather say I play
The man I am.
VOLUMNIA   Oh, sir, sir, sir,
I would have had you put your power well on 18
Before you had worn it out.
CORIOLANUS   Let go. 20
VOLUMNIA
You might have been enough the man you are
With striving less to be so. Lesser had been
The thwartings of your dispositions if
You had not showed them how ye were disposed
Ere they lacked power to cross you.
CORIOLANUS   Let them hang! 25
VOLUMNIA   Ay, and burn too.

Enter Menenius with the Senators.

MENENIUS
Come, come, you have been too rough, something too
     rough; 27
You must return and mend it.
FIRST SENATOR   There's no remedy,
Unless, by not so doing, our good city
Cleave in the midst and perish.
VOLUMNIA   Pray be counseled.
I have a heart as little apt as yours, 31
But yet a brain that leads my use of anger
To better vantage.
MENENIUS   Well said, noble woman!
Before he should thus stoop to th' herd, but that 34
The violent fit o'th' time craves it as physic 35
For the whole state, I would put mine armor on,
Which I can scarcely bear.
CORIOLANUS   What must I do? 37
MENENIUS
Return to th' tribunes.
CORIOLANUS   Well, what then? What then?
MENENIUS   Repent what you have spoke.
CORIOLANUS
For them? I cannot do it to the gods.
Must I then do't to them?
VOLUMNIA   You are too absolute, 41

Though therein you can never be too noble, 42
But when extremities speak. I have heard you say 43
Honor and policy, like unsevered friends, 44
I'th' war do grow together. Grant that, and tell me
In peace what each of them by th'other lose
That they combine not there.
CORIOLANUS   Tush, tush!
MENENIUS   A good demand. 47
VOLUMNIA
If it be honor in your wars to seem
The same you are not, which for your best ends
You adopt your policy, how is it less or worse 50
That it shall hold companionship in peace
With honor as in war, since that to both
It stands in like request?
CORIOLANUS   Why force you this? 53
VOLUMNIA
Because that now it lies you on to speak 54
To th' people, not by your own instruction, 55
Nor by th' matter which your heart prompts you,
But with such words that are but roted in 57
Your tongue, though but bastards and syllables
Of no allowance to your bosom's truth. 59
Now, this no more dishonors you at all
Than to take in a town with gentle words, 61
Which else would put you to your fortune and 62
The hazard of much blood.
I would dissemble with my nature where 64
My fortunes and my friends at stake required
I should do so in honor. I am in this 66
Your wife, your son, these senators, the nobles; 67
And you will rather show our general louts 68
How you can frown than spend a fawn upon 'em 69
For the inheritance of their loves and safeguard 70
Of what that want might ruin.
MENENIUS   Noble lady!— 71
Come, go with us; speak fair. You may salve so, 72
Not what is dangerous present, but the loss 73
Of what is past.
VOLUMNIA   I prithee now, my son, 74
Go to them, with this bonnet in thy hand, 75
And thus far having stretched it—here be with them— 76
Thy knee bussing the stones—for in such business 77
Action is eloquence, and the eyes of th'ignorant

---

10 woolen coarsely clad   **11 To . . . groats** i.e., to be nothing more than petty traders. (*Groats* are fourpenny pieces.)   **12 congregations** assemblies.   **yawn** i.e., gape with amazement   **13 ordinance** rank   **18 I would . . . well on** I would have preferred that you had learned to achieve and use your authority well   **20 Let go** Enough.   **25 Ere . . . you** before they lost the power to thwart your attempt to become consul.   **27 something** somewhat   **31 apt** compliant   **34–5 but that . . . physic** were it not that the feverish convulsions of the time need it as medicine   **37 Which . . . bear** i.e., which I am nearly too old for.   **41 absolute** uncompromising

42–3 therein . . . speak i.e., being uncompromising in your nobility is a fine thing, except when the situation is critically extreme.   **44 policy** the proper consideration of stratagem and craft.   **unsevered** inseparable   **47 demand** question.   **50 adopt** adopt as   **53 It . . . request** it is equally needed.   **force** urge   **54 lies you on** is your duty   **55 instruction** i.e., conviction, inner prompting   **57 are but roted in** have been learned merely by rote in   **59 Of . . . to** unacknowledged by   **61 take in** capture   **62 else . . . fortune** otherwise would force you to take your chance (in battle)   **64 dissemble . . . nature** pretend to be other than I was   **66 in honor** in compliance with the requirements of honor.   **66–7 I am . . . wife** In this I represent your wife   **68 And . . . louts** and yet you'd rather show our vulgar commoners   **69 fawn** flattering appeal   **70 inheritance** obtaining   **71 that want** i.e., the lack of their loves   **72 salve** remedy   **73–4 Not . . . past** not only the present danger but what has been lost already.   **75 bonnet** cap   **76 And . . . them** and go to them holding your hat out thus—do this to please them. (She gestures.)   **77 bussing** kissing

More learnèd than the ears—waving thy head, 79
With often thus correcting thy stout heart, 80
Now humble as the ripest mulberry 81
That will not hold the handling. Or say to them 82
Thou art their soldier, and being bred in broils 83
Hast not the soft way which, thou dost confess,
Were fit for thee to use as they to claim, 85
In asking their good loves; but thou wilt frame 86
Thyself, forsooth, hereafter theirs, so far 87
As thou hast power and person.

MENENIUS   This but done 88
Even as she speaks, why, their hearts were yours; 89
For they have pardons, being asked, as free 90
As words to little purpose.

VOLUMNIA   Prithee now,
Go, and be ruled; although I know thou hadst rather
Follow thine enemy in a fiery gulf 93
Than flatter him in a bower.

        Enter Cominius.

                    Here is Cominius. 94

COMINIUS
I have been i'th' marketplace; and, sir, 'tis fit 95
You make strong party, or defend yourself 96
By calmness or by absence. All's in anger.

MENENIUS
Only fair speech.

COMINIUS   I think 'twill serve, if he
Can thereto frame his spirit.

VOLUMNIA   He must, and will.
Prithee, now, say you will, and go about it.

CORIOLANUS
Must I go show them my unbarbed sconce? Must I 101
With my base tongue give to my noble heart
A lie that it must bear? Well, I will do't.
Yet, were there but this single plot to lose, 104
This mold of Marcius, they to dust should grind it 105
And throw't against the wind. To th' marketplace!
You have put me now to such a part which never
I shall discharge to th' life.

COMINIUS   Come, come, we'll prompt you. 108

VOLUMNIA
I prithee now, sweet son, as thou hast said
My praises made thee first a soldier, so,
To have my praise for this, perform a part
Thou hast not done before.

CORIOLANUS   Well, I must do't.

Away, my disposition, and possess me
Some harlot's spirit! My throat of war be turned, 114
Which choirèd with my drum, into a pipe 115
Small as an eunuch or the virgin voice 116
That babies lulls asleep! The smiles of knaves 117
Tent in my cheeks, and schoolboys' tears take up 118
The glasses of my sight! A beggar's tongue 119
Make motion through my lips, and my armed knees,
Who bowed but in my stirrup, bend like his
That hath received an alms! I will not do't, 122
Lest I surcease to honor mine own truth 123
And by my body's action teach my mind
A most inherent baseness.

VOLUMNIA   At thy choice, then. 125
To beg of thee, it is my more dishonor
Than thou of them. Come all to ruin. Let 127
Thy mother rather feel thy pride than fear 128
Thy dangerous stoutness, for I mock at death 129
With as big heart as thou. Do as thou list. 130
Thy valiantness was mine, thou suck'st it from me,
But owe thy pride thyself.

CORIOLANUS   Pray, be content. 132
Mother, I am going to the marketplace.
Chide me no more. I'll mountebank their loves, 134
Cog their hearts from them, and come home beloved 135
Of all the trades in Rome. Look, I am going.
Commend me to my wife. I'll return consul,
Or never trust to what my tongue can do
I'th' way of flattery further.

VOLUMNIA   Do your will.

                    Exit Volumnia.

COMINIUS
Away! The tribunes do attend you. Arm yourself 140
To answer mildly; for they are prepared
With accusations, as I hear, more strong
Than are upon you yet.

CORIOLANUS
The word is "mildly." Pray you, let us go. 144
Let them accuse me by invention; I 145
Will answer in mine honor.

MENENIUS   Ay, but mildly. 146

CORIOLANUS
Well, mildly be it then. Mildly!   *Exeunt.*

                    ❦

[3.3]

        Enter Sicinius and Brutus.

---

79 learnèd i.e., receptive. **waving** bowing up and down **80 stout** proud **81 Now . . . mulberry** now as soft and malleable as overripe fruit. (Or *humble* may mean "abase, let droop.") **82 hold** bear, tolerate **83 broils** battles **85 fit** as fit. **as they** as for them **86 In asking** in your asking for. **frame** conform **87 forsooth** truly, indeed. **theirs** to suit their wish **87–8 so far . . . person** to the full extent of your ability and authority. **89 were** would be, will be **90 as free** i.e., which they will grant as freely **93 in** into **94 bower** (1) arbor (2) lady's private chamber. **95 fit** appropriate **96 make strong party** support your side strongly, or gather a strong faction around you **101 unbarbed sconce** unhelmeted head. **104 this single plot** this piece of earth only (i.e., my own person) **105 mold** (1) bodily form (2) earth **108 discharge to th' life** perform convincingly.

114 harlot's (1) rascal's (2) whore's. **throat of war** i.e., soldier's voice **115 choirèd** harmonized, sang in tune **116 Small** high-pitched **117 babies lulls** lulls babies **118 Tent** lodge, set up camp **118–19 take up . . . sight** occupy my eyeballs. **122 an alms** a gift of charity. **123 surcease** cease **125 inherent** irremovable, fixed **127–9 Let . . . stoutness** Let me rather suffer the worst your pride can do for us than fear to confront your dangerous obstinacy **130 big heart** noble courage. **list** please. **132 owe** own **134 mountebank** win over as with the tricks of a quack medicine salesman **135 Cog** cheat, beguile **140 attend** await. **Arm** Prepare **144 word** watchword **145 accuse . . . invention** invent charges against me all they like **146 in** in accordance with
3.3. Location: Rome. The Forum or marketplace.

BRUTUS
In this point charge him home, that he affects　　　　1
Tyrannical power. If he evade us there,
Enforce him with his envy to the people,　　　　　　　3
And that the spoil got on the Antiates　　　　　　　　4
Was ne'er distributed.

　　　　　　　Enter an Aedile.

　　　　　　　　　　　What, will he come?　　　　5
AEDILE　He's coming.
BRUTUS　How accompanied?
AEDILE
With old Menenius, and those senators
That always favored him.
SICINIUS　　　　　　　　Have you a catalogue
Of all the voices that we have procured
Set down by th' poll?
AEDILE　　　　　　　　I have; 'tis ready.　　　11
SICINIUS
Have you collected them by tribes?
AEDILE　　　　　　　　　　　I have.　　　12
SICINIUS
Assemble presently the people hither;　　　　　　　13
And when they hear me say "It shall be so
I'th' right and strength o'th' commons," be it either
For death, for fine, or banishment, then let them,
If I say "Fine," cry "Fine!", if "Death," cry "Death!",
Insisting on the old prerogative　　　　　　　　　　18
And power i'th' truth o'th' cause.
AEDILE　　　　　　　　　I shall inform them.　　19
BRUTUS
And when such time they have begun to cry,　　　　20
Let them not cease, but with a din confused
Enforce the present execution　　　　　　　　　　　22
Of what we chance to sentence.
AEDILE　　　　　　　　　　Very well.
SICINIUS
Make them be strong, and ready for this hint
When we shall hap to give't them.
BRUTUS　　　　　　　　　　Go about it.　　　25
　　　　　　　　　　　　[*Exit Aedile.*]
Put him to choler straight. He hath been used　　　26
Ever to conquer and to have his worth　　　　　　　27
Of contradiction. Being once chafed, he cannot　　　28
Be reined again to temperance; then he speaks
What's in his heart, and that is there which looks　30
With us to break his neck.　　　　　　　　　　　　31

　　　　　　　Enter Coriolanus, Menenius, and Cominius, with
　　　　　　　others [*Senators and patricians*].

SICINIUS　Well, here he comes.
MENENIUS　Calmly, I do beseech you.
CORIOLANUS
Ay, as an hostler, that for th' poorest piece　　　　34
Will bear the knave by th' volume.—Th' honored gods　35
Keep Rome in safety and the chairs of justice
Supplied with worthy men! Plant love among 's!
Throng our large temples with the shows of peace,　38
And not our streets with war!
FIRST SENATOR　Amen, amen.
MENENIUS　A noble wish.

　　　　　　　Enter the Aedile, with the plebeians.

SICINIUS　Draw near, ye people.
AEDILE
List to your tribunes. Audience! Peace, I say!　　　43
CORIOLANUS　First, hear me speak.
BOTH TRIBUNES　Well, say.—Peace, ho!
CORIOLANUS
Shall I be charged no further than this present?　　46
Must all determine here?
SICINIUS　　　　　　　　　I do demand　　　47
If you submit you to the people's voices,　　　　　　48
Allow their officers, and are content　　　　　　　　49
To suffer lawful censure for such faults　　　　　　　50
As shall be proved upon you?
CORIOLANUS　　　　　　　I am content.
MENENIUS
Lo, citizens, he says he is content.
The warlike service he has done, consider. Think
Upon the wounds his body bears, which show
Like graves i'th' holy churchyard.
CORIOLANUS　　　　　　　Scratches with briers,
Scars to move laughter only.
MENENIUS　　　　　　　　Consider further,
That when he speaks not like a citizen,
You find him like a soldier. Do not take
His rougher accents for malicious sounds,
But, as I say, such as become a soldier
Rather than envy you.
COMINIUS　　　　　　　Well, well, no more.　　61
CORIOLANUS　What is the matter
That, being passed for consul with full voice,
I am so dishonored that the very hour
You take it off again?
SICINIUS　Answer to us.　　　　　　　　　　　　66
CORIOLANUS　Say, then. 'Tis true, I ought so.　　67
SICINIUS
We charge you that you have contrived to take
From Rome all seasoned office and to wind　　　　69
Yourself into a power tyrannical,

---

1 **charge him home** press home your charges.　**affects** aspires to, desires　3 **Enforce . . . to** confront him with his inveterate malice toward　4 **spoil got on** property taken from　5 s.d. *Aedile* (See note at 3.1.176.)　11 **by th' poll** by individual names, by head count　12 **tribes** divisions of the Roman populace.　13 **presently** immediately　18 **old prerogative** traditional privilege or position　19 **truth** justice.　**cause** case.　20 **cry** cry out, shout　22 **Enforce . . . execution** insist on immediate carrying out　25 **hap** happen　26 **Put . . . straight** Incense him to anger straightway.　**used** accustomed　27–8 **his worth . . . contradiction** plenty of opportunity to answer back, giving as good as he gets.　30–1 **looks With us** promises, with our help

34–5 **an hostler . . . volume** a horse-groom, who for a measly coin will put up with being called knave any number of times.　35 **Th' honored** May the honored　38 **shows** ceremonies　43 **List** Listen. **Audience!** Listen, give heed!　46 **this present** this present occasion, the matter in hand.　47 **determine** come to an end, be concluded. **demand** ask　48 **If** whether　49 **Allow** acknowledge the authority of　50 **censure** judgment　61 **Rather . . . you** rather than such as show malice toward you.　66 **Answer to us** i.e., We'll do the asking, not you.　67 **so** to do so.　69 **seasoned** established.　**wind** insinuate

For which you are a traitor to the people.

CORIOLANUS
How? Traitor?

MENENIUS   Nay, temperately! Your promise.

CORIOLANUS
The fires i'th' lowest hell fold in the people!   73
Call me their traitor? Thou injurious tribune!   74
Within thine eyes sat twenty thousand deaths,   75
In thy hands clutched as many millions, in   76
Thy lying tongue both numbers, I would say   77
"Thou liest" unto thee with a voice as free
As I do pray the gods.

SICINIUS   Mark you this, people?

ALL PLEBEIANS   To th' rock, to th' rock with him!

SICINIUS   Peace!
We need not put new matter to his charge.   83
What you have seen him do and heard him speak,
Beating your officers, cursing yourselves,
Opposing laws with strokes, and here defying   86
Those whose great power must try him—even this,
So criminal and in such capital kind,   88
Deserves th'extremest death.

BRUTUS   But since he hath
Served well for Rome—

CORIOLANUS   What do you prate of service?   90

BRUTUS   I talk of that that know it.

CORIOLANUS   You?

MENENIUS
Is this the promise that you made your mother?

COMINIUS   Know, I pray you—

CORIOLANUS   I'll know no further.
Let them pronounce the steep Tarpeian death,
Vagabond exile, flaying, pent to linger   97
But with a grain a day, I would not buy   98
Their mercy at the price of one fair word,
Nor check my courage for what they can give,   100
To have't with saying "Good morrow."

SICINIUS   For that he has, 101
As much as in him lies, from time to time   102
Envied against the people, seeking means   103
To pluck away their power, as now at last   104
Given hostile strokes, and that not in the presence   105
Of dreaded justice, but on the ministers
That doth distribute it: in the name o'th' people
And in the power of us the tribunes, we,
Ev'n from this instant, banish him our city,
In peril of precipitation   110
From off the rock Tarpeian, never more
To enter our Rome gates. I'th' people's name,
I say it shall be so.

ALL PLEBEIANS
It shall be so, it shall be so! Let him away!

He's banished, and it shall be so!

COMINIUS
Hear me, my masters, and my common friends—

SICINIUS
He's sentenced. No more hearing.

COMINIUS   Let me speak.
I have been consul, and can show for Rome
Her enemies' marks upon me. I do love
My country's good with a respect more tender,   120
More holy and profound, than mine own life,
My dear wife's estimate, her womb's increase,   122
And treasure of my loins. Then if I would
Speak that—

SICINIUS   We know your drift. Speak what?

BRUTUS
There's no more to be said, but he is banished   126
As enemy to the people and his country.
It shall be so.

ALL PLEBEIANS   It shall be so, it shall be so!

CORIOLANUS
You common cry of curs, whose breath I hate   130
As reek o'th' rotten fens, whose loves I prize   131
As the dead carcasses of unburied men
That do corrupt my air, I banish you!
And here remain with your uncertainty!   134
Let every feeble rumor shake your hearts!
Your enemies, with nodding of their plumes,   136
Fan you into despair! Have the power still   137
To banish your defenders, till at length
Your ignorance—which finds not till it feels,   139
Making but reservation of yourselves,   140
Still your own foes—deliver you   141
As most abated captives to some nation   142
That won you without blows! Despising
For you the city, thus I turn my back.   144
There is a world elsewhere.

       Exeunt Coriolanus, Cominius,
       [*Menenius, Senators, and patricians*].

AEDILE   The people's enemy is gone, is gone!

ALL PLEBEIANS
Our enemy is banished! He is gone! Hoo! Hoo!
       They all shout and throw up their caps.

SICINIUS
Go see him out at gates, and follow him,
As he hath followed you, with all despite;   149
Give him deserved vexation. Let a guard   150
Attend us through the city.

ALL PLEBEIANS
Come, come, let's see him out at gates! Come.
The gods preserve our noble tribunes! Come.
       Exeunt.

♣

---

73 fold in enfold, envelop   **74 their traitor** a traitor to them.   **injurious** insulting   **75–7 Within . . . numbers** (Understand "although" before each of the three clauses.)   **83 put new matter** add new particulars **86 strokes** blows   **88 capital** death-deserving   **90 prate** talk idly **97–8 pent . . . day** imprisoned to starve with but a small particle of food a day   **100 check** restrain   **101 To have't with saying** if I might have it merely by saying.   **For that** Because   **102 in him lies** he could **103 Envied against** showed malice toward   **104 as** i.e., and inasmuch as (he has)   **105 not** not merely   **110 precipitation** being thrown

120 respect regard, feeling   **122 estimate** reputation   **126 but** but that   **130 cry** pack   **131 reek** vapor   **134 remain** may you remain. **uncertainty** inconstancy, fickleness; also, insecurity (as explained in the following lines).   **136 Your** May your.   **with** merely with **137 Have** May you have   **139–41 which . . . foes** which learns only through experience, seeking only to preserve yourselves (or, leaving no one unbanished except yourselves), you being always your own worst enemies   **142 abated** humbled   **144 For** because of **149 despite** disdain, contempt   **150 vexation** torment.

4.1

*Enter Coriolanus, Volumnia, Virgilia, Menenius,
Cominius, with the young nobility of Rome.*

CORIOLANUS
Come, leave your tears. A brief farewell. The beast   1
With many heads butts me away. Nay, mother,
Where is your ancient courage? You were used   3
To say extremities was the trier of spirits;   4
That common chances common men could bear;
That when the sea was calm all boats alike
Showed mastership in floating; fortune's blows   7
When most struck home, being gentle wounded
    craves   8
A noble cunning. You were used to load me   9
With precepts that would make invincible
The heart that conned them.   11

VIRGILIA
O heavens! O heavens!

CORIOLANUS   Nay, I prithee, woman—

VOLUMNIA
Now the red pestilence strike all trades in Rome,   13
And occupations perish!

CORIOLANUS   What, what, what!   14
I shall be loved when I am lacked. Nay, mother,   15
Resume that spirit when you were wont to say,   16
If you had been the wife of Hercules,
Six of his labors you'd have done and saved   18
Your husband so much sweat. Cominius,
Droop not. Adieu. Farewell, my wife, my mother.
I'll do well yet. Thou old and true Menenius,
Thy tears are salter than a younger man's,
And venomous to thine eyes.—My sometime general,   23
I have seen thee stern, and thou hast oft beheld
Heart-hard'ning spectacles; tell these sad women
'Tis fond to wail inevitable strokes   26
As 'tis to laugh at 'em. My mother, you wot well   27
My hazards still have been your solace, and—   28
Believe't not lightly—though I go alone,
Like to a lonely dragon that his fen   30
Makes feared and talked of more than seen, your son
Will or exceed the common or be caught   32
With cautelous baits and practice.

VOLUMNIA   My first son,   33
Whither wilt thou go? Take good Cominius
With thee awhile. Determine on some course
More than a wild exposture to each chance   36

That starts i'th' way before thee.

VIRGILIA   O the gods!   37

COMINIUS
I'll follow thee a month, devise with thee   38
Where thou shalt rest, that thou mayst hear of us
And we of thee; so if the time thrust forth
A cause for thy repeal, we shall not send   41
O'er the vast world to seek a single man,
And lose advantage, which doth ever cool   43
I'th'absence of the needer.

CORIOLANUS   Fare ye well.   44
Thou hast years upon thee, and thou art too full
Of the wars' surfeits to go rove with one   46
That's yet unbruised. Bring me but out at gate.   47
Come, my sweet wife, my dearest mother, and
My friends of noble touch; when I am forth,   49
Bid me farewell, and smile. I pray you, come.
While I remain above the ground, you shall
Hear from me still, and never of me aught
But what is like me formerly.

MENENIUS   That's worthily
As any ear can hear. Come, let's not weep.
If I could shake off but one seven years
From these old arms and legs, by the good gods,
I'd with thee every foot.

CORIOLANUS   Give me thy hand.
Come.   *Exeunt.*

❖

[4.2]

*Enter the two tribunes, Sicinius and Brutus, with
the Aedile.*

SICINIUS [*to the Aedile*]
Bid them all home. He's gone, and we'll no further.   1
The nobility are vexed, whom we see have sided
In his behalf.

BRUTUS   Now we have shown our power,
Let us seem humbler after it is done
Than when it was a-doing.

SICINIUS   Bid them home.
Say their great enemy is gone, and they
Stand in their ancient strength.

BRUTUS   Dismiss them home.   7
                [*Exit Aedile.*]
Here comes his mother.

Enter Volumnia, Virgilia, and Menenius.

SICINIUS   Let's not meet her.
BRUTUS   Why?
SICINIUS   They say she's mad.

BRUTUS
They have ta'en note of us. Keep on your way.
[*They start to leave.*]

VOLUMNIA
Oh, you're well met. Th' hoarded plague o'th' gods   13
Requite your love!

MENENIUS   Peace, peace! Be not so loud.   14

VOLUMNIA
If that I could for weeping, you should hear—   15
Nay, and you shall hear some. Will you be gone?

VIRGILIA
You shall stay too. I would I had the power   17
To say so to my husband.

SICINIUS   Are you mankind?   18

VOLUMNIA
Ay, fool, is that a shame?—Note but this fool.—   19
Was not a man my father? Hadst thou foxship   20
To banish him that struck more blows for Rome
Than thou hast spoken words?

SICINIUS   O blessèd heavens!

VOLUMNIA
More noble blows than ever thou wise words,
And for Rome's good. I'll tell thee what—yet go.
Nay, but thou shalt stay too. I would my son   25
Were in Arabia, and thy tribe before him,   26
His good sword in his hand.

SICINIUS   What then?

VIRGILIA   What then?
He'd make an end of thy posterity.   28

VOLUMNIA   Bastards and all.
Good man, the wounds that he does bear for Rome!

MENENIUS   Come, come, peace.

SICINIUS
I would he had continued to his country
As he began, and not unknit himself   33
The noble knot he made.

BRUTUS   I would he had.   34

VOLUMNIA
"I would he had"? 'Twas you incensed the rabble—
Cats, that can judge as fitly of his worth   36
As I can of those mysteries which heaven
Will not have earth to know!

BRUTUS
Pray, let's go.

VOLUMNIA   Now, pray, sir, get you gone.
You have done a brave deed. Ere you go, hear this:
As far as doth the Capitol exceed
The meanest house in Rome, so far my son—   42
This lady's husband here, this, do you see?—
Whom you have banished, does exceed you all.

BRUTUS
Well, well, we'll leave you.

SICINIUS   Why stay we to be baited   45
With one that wants her wits?   *Exeunt tribunes.*

VOLUMNIA   Take my prayers with you.   46
I would the gods had nothing else to do
But to confirm my curses! Could I meet 'em   48
But once a day, it would unclog my heart   49
Of what lies heavy to't.

MENENIUS   You have told them home,   50
And, by my troth, you have cause. You'll sup with me?   51

VOLUMNIA
Anger's my meat. I sup upon myself,
And so shall starve with feeding. [*To Virgilia*] Come,
let's go.
Leave this faint puling and lament as I do,   54
In anger, Juno-like. Come, come, come.   55

MENENIUS   Fie, fie, fie!   *Exeunt.*

❦

4.3

*Enter [Nicanor,] a Roman, and [Adrian,] a
Volsce.*

ROMAN   I know you well, sir, and you know me. Your
name, I think, is Adrian.

VOLSCE   It is so, sir. Truly, I have forgot you.

ROMAN   I am a Roman; and my services are, as you are,
against 'em. Know you me yet?   5

VOLSCE   Nicanor, no?

ROMAN   The same, sir.

VOLSCE   You had more beard when I last saw you, but
your favor is well approved by your tongue. What's the   9
news in Rome? I have a note from the Volscian state   10
to find you out there. You have well saved me a day's
journey.

ROMAN   There hath been in Rome strange insurrections:
the people against the senators, patricians, and nobles.

VOLSCE   Hath been? Is it ended, then? Our state thinks
not so. They are in a most warlike preparation, and
hope to come upon them in the heat of their division.

ROMAN   The main blaze of it is past, but a small thing
would make it flame again; for the nobles receive so to
heart the banishment of that worthy Coriolanus that
they are in a ripe aptness to take all power from the
people and to pluck from them their tribunes forever.
This lies glowing, I can tell you, and is almost mature   23
for the violent breaking out.

VOLSCE   Coriolanus banished?

ROMAN   Banished, sir.

VOLSCE   You will be welcome with this intelligence,
Nicanor.

---

13 hoarded stored up   **14 Requite** repay   **15 If that** If   **17 You shall stay too** (Sometimes read as if addressed to the second of the two tribunes, but it may mean "you shall too stay," i.e., whether you want to or not. See line 25.)   **18 mankind** masculine (i.e., railing like a man), or, infuriated. (Volumnia responds as though it meant "of the human race.")   **19 Note but this fool** (The line could read, "Note but this, fool," addressed to Sicinius.)   **20 foxship** craftiness   **25 would** wish   **26 Arabia** i.e., a deserted spot, with no place to hide.   **tribe** family, clan, set   **28 posterity** descendants.   **33–4 unknit . . . made** i.e., untied the knot of service and gratitude binding him and Rome together.   **36 Cats** (A term of contempt.)   **42 meanest** poorest

45–6 baited With harassed by   **48 'em** i.e., the tribunes   **49 unclog** unburden   **50 to't** upon it.   **told them home** berated them thoroughly   **51 sup** dine   **54 puling** whimpering   **55 Juno-like** resembling Juno, chief goddess of the Romans (whose unforgiving anger is mentioned by Virgil in *Aeneid* 1.4).   **4.3. Location: A road between Rome and Antium.**   **5 against 'em** i.e., on behalf of the Volsces against Rome.   **9 your . . . tongue** your face and appearance are well confirmed by your voice.   **10 note** instruction   **23 glowing** smoldering

ROMAN   The day serves well for them now. I have heard   29
it said the fittest time to corrupt a man's wife is when
she's fall'n out with her husband. Your noble Tullus
Aufidius will appear well in these wars, his great
opposer Coriolanus being now in no request of his   33
country.

VOLSCE   He cannot choose. I am most fortunate thus   35
accidentally to encounter you. You have ended my
business, and I will merrily accompany you home.

ROMAN   I shall, between this and supper, tell you most   38
strange things from Rome, all tending to the good of
their adversaries. Have you an army ready, say you?

VOLSCE   A most royal one: the centurions and their   41
charges, distinctly billeted, already in th'entertain-   42
ment, and to be on foot at an hour's warning.   43

ROMAN   I am joyful to hear of their readiness, and am
the man, I think, that shall set them in present action.   45
So, sir, heartily well met, and most glad of your
company.

VOLSCE   You take my part from me, sir; I have the most   48
cause to be glad of yours.

ROMAN   Well, let us go together.   *Exeunt.*

[4.4]

*Enter Coriolanus in mean apparel, disguised
and muffled.*

CORIOLANUS
A goodly city is this Antium. City,
'Tis I that made thy widows. Many an heir
Of these fair edifices 'fore my wars   3
Have I heard groan and drop. Then know me not,
Lest that thy wives with spits and boys with stones
In puny battle slay me.

Enter a Citizen.

Save you, sir.   6

CITIZEN
And you.

CORIOLANUS   Direct me, if it be your will,
Where great Aufidius lies. Is he in Antium?   8

CITIZEN
He is, and feasts the nobles of the state
At his house this night.

CORIOLANUS   Which is his house, beseech you?

CITIZEN
This here before you.

CORIOLANUS   Thank you, sir. Farewell.
                            Exit Citizen.

O world, thy slippery turns! Friends now fast sworn,   12
Whose double bosoms seems to wear one heart,
Whose hours, whose bed, whose meal and exercise
Are still together, who twin, as 'twere, in love   15
Unseparable, shall within this hour,   16
On a dissension of a doit, break out   17
To bitterest enmity; so fellest foes,   18
Whose passions and whose plots have broke their
sleep   19
To take the one the other, by some chance,   20
Some trick not worth an egg, shall grow dear friends   21
And interjoin their issues. So with me: 22
My birthplace hate I, and my love's upon
This enemy town. I'll enter. If he slay me,
He does fair justice; if he give me way,   25
I'll do his country service.   *Exit.*

❖

[4.5]

Music plays. Enter a Servingman.

FIRST SERVINGMAN   Wine, wine, wine! What service is
here? I think our fellows are asleep.   [*Exit.*]   2

Enter another Servingman.

SECOND SERVINGMAN   Where's Cotus? My master calls
for him. Cotus!   *Exit.*

Enter Coriolanus.

CORIOLANUS
A goodly house. The feast smells well, but I
Appear not like a guest.

Enter the First Servingman.

FIRST SERVINGMAN   What would you have, friend?
Whence are you? Here's no place for you. Pray go to   8
the door.   *Exit.*   9

CORIOLANUS
I have deserved no better entertainment   10
In being Coriolanus.

Enter Second Servingman.

SECOND SERVINGMAN   Whence are you, sir? Has the
porter his eyes in his head, that he gives entrance
to such companions? Pray, get you out.   14

CORIOLANUS   Away!

SECOND SERVINGMAN   Away? Get you away.

---

29 **them** i.e., the Volsces   33 **of** by   35 **choose** do otherwise (than
appear well).   38 **this** this present time   41 **centurions** officers each
in command of a hundred men or "century"   41–2 **their charges** the
men under their command   42 **distinctly billeted** separately enrolled
42–3 **in th'entertainment** mobilized, on the payroll   45 **present**
immediate   48 **my part** i.e., the words I should say
4.4. Location: Antium. Before Aufidius's house.
3 **'fore my wars** in the face of my onslaught   6 **puny** petty.   **Save**
God save   8 **lies** dwells.

12 **slippery turns** fickle shifts of fortune.   **fast** firmly   15 **still** ever
16 **this hour** an hour   17 **dissension of a doit** i.e., paltry dispute. (A
doit is a small coin.)   18 **so fellest** similarly fiercest   19–20 **Whose . . .
other** whose passionate plotting to undo each other have kept them
awake at night   21 **trick** trifle   22 **interjoin . . . issues** (1) bind
together their fortunes and affairs (2) link themselves by marriage of
their children.   25 **give me way** let me have my will and do what I
want, accede to my request
**4.5. Location: Antium. The house of Aufidius. The sense of time
here is virtually continuous; the stage is imaginatively transformed
from the outside to the inside of Aufidius's house.**
2 **fellows** fellow servants   8–9 **go to the door** get out.   10 **entertainment** reception.   14 **companions** rascals, base persons.

CORIOLANUS   Now thou'rt troublesome.

SECOND SERVINGMAN   Are you so brave? I'll have you 18
talked with anon. 19

*Enter Third Servingman. The First, [entering,]
meets him.*

THIRD SERVINGMAN   What fellow's this?

FIRST SERVINGMAN   A strange one as ever I looked on.
I cannot get him out o'th' house. Prithee, call my
master to him.

THIRD SERVINGMAN   What have you to do here, fellow?
Pray you, avoid the house. 25

CORIOLANUS   Let me but stand. I will not hurt your
hearth.

THIRD SERVINGMAN   What are you?

CORIOLANUS   A gentleman.

THIRD SERVINGMAN   A marvelous poor one.

CORIOLANUS   True, so I am.

THIRD SERVINGMAN   Pray you, poor gentleman, take
up some other station; here's no place for you. Pray 33
you, avoid. Come.

CORIOLANUS   Follow your function, go, and batten on 35
cold bits.   *Pushes him away from him.*

THIRD SERVINGMAN   What, you will not?—Prithee, tell
my master what a strange guest he has here.

SECOND SERVINGMAN   And I shall.
Exit Second Servingman.

THIRD SERVINGMAN   Where dwell'st thou?

CORIOLANUS   Under the canopy. 41

THIRD SERVINGMAN   Under the canopy?

CORIOLANUS   Ay.

THIRD SERVINGMAN   Where's that?

CORIOLANUS   I'th' city of kites and crows. 45

THIRD SERVINGMAN   I'th' city of kites and crows?
What an ass it is! Then thou dwell'st with daws too? 47

CORIOLANUS   No, I serve not thy master.

THIRD SERVINGMAN   How, sir? Do you meddle with 49
my master?

CORIOLANUS   Ay, 'tis an honester service than to meddle
with thy mistress. Thou prat'st and prat'st. Serve
with thy trencher. Hence! 53
Beats him away. [Exit Third Servingman.]

Enter Aufidius with the [Second] Servingman.

AUFIDIUS   Where is this fellow?

SECOND SERVINGMAN   Here, sir. I'd have beaten him
like a dog, but for disturbing the lords within. 56
[He and First Servingman stand aside.]

AUFIDIUS *[to Coriolanus]*
Whence com'st thou? What wouldst thou? Thy name?
Why speak'st not? Speak, man. What's thy name?

CORIOLANUS *[unmuffling]*   If, Tullus,
Not yet thou know'st me, and, seeing me, dost not
Think me for the man I am, necessity
Commands me name myself.

AUFIDIUS   What is thy name?

CORIOLANUS
A name unmusical to the Volscians' ears,
And harsh in sound to thine.

AUFIDIUS   Say, what's thy name?
Thou hast a grim appearance, and thy face
Bears a command in't; though thy tackle's torn, 66
Thou show'st a noble vessel. What's thy name? 67

CORIOLANUS
Prepare thy brow to frown. Know'st thou me yet?

AUFIDIUS   I know thee not. Thy name?

CORIOLANUS
My name is Caius Marcius, who hath done
To thee particularly and to all the Volsces 71
Great hurt and mischief; thereto witness may 72
My surname, Coriolanus. The painful service, 73
The extreme dangers, and the drops of blood
Shed for my thankless country are requited
But with that surname—a good memory, 76
And witness of the malice and displeasure
Which thou shouldst bear me. Only that name
    remains.
The cruelty and envy of the people,
Permitted by our dastard nobles, who
Have all forsook me, hath devoured the rest,
And suffered me by th' voice of slaves to be
Whooped out of Rome. Now this extremity 83
Hath brought me to thy hearth; not out of hope—
Mistake me not—to save my life, for if
I had feared death, of all the men i'th' world
I would have 'voided thee, but in mere spite, 87
To be full quit of those my banishers, 88
Stand I before thee here. Then if thou hast
A heart of wreak in thee, that wilt revenge 90
Thine own particular wrongs and stop those maims 91
Of shame seen through thy country, speed thee
    straight 92
And make my misery serve thy turn. So use it
That my revengeful services may prove
As benefits to thee, for I will fight
Against my cankered country with the spleen 96
Of all the under fiends. But if so be 97
Thou dar'st not this, and that to prove more fortunes 98
Thou'rt tired, then, in a word, I also am
Longer to live most weary, and present
My throat to thee and to thy ancient malice; 101
Which not to cut would show thee but a fool,

Since I have ever followed thee with hate,
Drawn tuns of blood out of thy country's breast,   104
And cannot live but to thy shame, unless
It be to do thee service.
AUFIDIUS   Oh, Marcius, Marcius!
Each word thou hast spoke hath weeded from my
  heart
A root of ancient envy. If Jupiter
Should from yond cloud speak divine things
And say "'Tis true," I'd not believe them more
Than thee, all-noble Marcius. Let me twine
Mine arms about that body, whereagainst
My grainèd ash an hundred times hath broke   113
And scarred the moon with splinters. [*They embrace.*]
    Here I clip   114
The anvil of my sword, and do contest   115
As hotly and as nobly with thy love
As ever in ambitious strength I did
Contend against thy valor. Know thou first,
I loved the maid I married; never man
Sighed truer breath. But that I see thee here,
Thou noble thing, more dances my rapt heart   121
Than when I first my wedded mistress saw
Bestride my threshold. Why, thou Mars, I tell thee   123
We have a power on foot, and I had purpose   124
Once more to hew thy target from thy brawn,   125
Or lose mine arm for't. Thou hast beat me out   126
Twelve several times, and I have nightly since   127
Dreamt of encounters twixt thyself and me—
We have been down together in my sleep,   129
Unbuckling helms, fisting each other's throat—   130
And waked half dead with nothing. Worthy Marcius,   131
Had we no other quarrel else to Rome but that
Thou art thence banished, we would muster all   133
From twelve to seventy and, pouring war   134
Into the bowels of ungrateful Rome,
Like a bold flood o'erbear't. Oh, come, go in,   136
And take our friendly senators by th' hands,
Who now are here, taking their leaves of me,
Who am prepared against your territories,   139
Though not for Rome itself.
CORIOLANUS   You bless me, gods!
AUFIDIUS
Therefore, most absolute sir, if thou wilt have   141
The leading of thine own revenges, take
Th'one half of my commission; and set down—   143
As best thou art experienced, since thou know'st

Thy country's strength and weakness—thine own
  ways,
Whether to knock against the gates of Rome
Or rudely visit them in parts remote
To fright them ere destroy. But come in.
Let me commend thee first to those that shall   149
Say yea to thy desires. A thousand welcomes!
And more a friend than e'er an enemy;
Yet, Marcius, that was much. Your hand. Most
  welcome!   *Exeunt [Coriolanus and Aufidius].*
                        Two of the Servingmen [come forward].
FIRST SERVINGMAN   Here's a strange alteration!
SECOND SERVINGMAN   By my hand, I had thought to
  have strucken him with a cudgel; and yet my mind
  gave me his clothes made a false report of him.   156
FIRST SERVINGMAN   What an arm he has! He turned me
  about with his finger and his thumb as one would
  set up a top.   159
SECOND SERVINGMAN   Nay, I knew by his face that there
  was something in him. He had, sir, a kind of face,
  methought—I cannot tell how to term it.
FIRST SERVINGMAN   He had so, looking as it were—
  Would I were hanged but I thought there was more   164
  in him than I could think.
SECOND SERVINGMAN   So did I, I'll be sworn. He is
  simply the rarest man i'th' world.   167
FIRST SERVINGMAN   I think he is. But a greater soldier
  than he you wot on.   169
SECOND SERVINGMAN   Who, my master?
FIRST SERVINGMAN   Nay, it's no matter for that.   171
SECOND SERVINGMAN   Worth six on him.   172
FIRST SERVINGMAN   Nay, not so neither. But I take him 173
  to be the greater soldier.
SECOND SERVINGMAN   Faith, look you, one cannot tell
  how to say that. For the defense of a town our general
  is excellent.
FIRST SERVINGMAN   Ay, and for an assault too.

              Enter the Third Servingman.

THIRD SERVINGMAN   Oh, slaves, I can tell you news—
  news, you rascals!
FIRST AND SECOND SERVINGMEN   What, what, what?
  Let's partake.
THIRD SERVINGMAN   I would not be a Roman, of all
  nations; I had as lief be a condemned man.   184
FIRST AND SECOND SEVINGMEN   Wherefore? Wherefore?   185
THIRD SERVINGMAN   Why, here's he that was wont to   186
  thwack our general, Caius Marcius.
FIRST SERVINGMAN   Why do you say "thwack our general"?
THIRD SERVINGMAN   I do not say "thwack our general,"
  but he was always good enough for him.

104 **tuns** large barrels   113 **grainèd ash** spear with long-grained
ashen shaft   114 **clip** embrace   115 **anvil** i.e., Coriolanus, in fighting
against whom Aufidius has formed and shaped his martial prowess
121 **dances** makes to dance.   **rapt** enraptured   123 **Bestride** step
across   124 **power on foot** force in the field   125 **hew . . . brawn** cut
your shield from your muscular arm   126 **out** thoroughly   127 **several** distinct, separate   129 **down together** fighting on the ground.
sleep i.e., dreams   130 **helms** helmets.   **fisting** clutching   131 **And
. . . nothing** and I have awakened exhausted from sleeplessness for
no reason, spent but alone.   133 **muster all** enlist everyone
134 **twelve** i.e., aged twelve   136 **o'erbear't** overflow, surge over,
beat down Rome.   139 **am prepared** i.e., have forces ready to move
141 **absolute** perfect   143 **commission** command.   **set down** determine upon

149 **commend** present   156 **gave** told   159 **set up** set going   164 **but
I thought** if I didn't think   167 **rarest** most remarkable   169 **you wot
on** you know of, know who I mean—i.e., Aufidius.   171 **Nay . . . that**
i.e., Never mind about names.   172 **on** of   173 **him** i.e., Aufidius.
(Some commentators argue that *him* is Coriolanus; the servingmen
tend to contradict themselves in their newfound admiration for Coriolanus and their loyalty toward their own general.)   184 **as lief** as
soon   185 **Wherefore?** Why?   186 **was wont** used

SECOND SERVINGMAN   Come, we are fellows and friends. He was ever too hard for him; I have heard him say so himself.

FIRST SERVINGMAN   He was too hard for him, directly to say the truth on't, before Corioles; he scotched him 195 and notched him like a carbonado. 196

SECOND SERVINGMAN   An he had been cannibally 197 given, he might have boiled and eaten him too.

FIRST SERVINGMAN   But, more of thy news.

THIRD SERVINGMAN   Why, he is so made on here within 200 as if he were son and heir to Mars; set at upper end o'th' 201 table; no question asked him by any of the senators but they stand bald before him. Our general himself 203 makes a mistress of him, sanctifies himself 204 with 's hand, and turns up the white o'th' eye to his 205 discourse. But the bottom of the news is, our general is 206 cut i'th' middle and but one half of what he was yesterday, for the other has half by the entreaty and grant of the whole table. He'll go, he says, and sowl 209 the porter of Rome gates by th'ears. He will mow all down before him, and leave his passage polled. 211

SECOND SERVINGMAN   And he's as like to do't as any man I can imagine.

THIRD SERVINGMAN   Do't? He will do't! For look you, sir, he has as many friends as enemies; which friends, sir, as it were, durst not, look you, sir, show themselves, as we term it, his friends whilst he's in directitude. 217

FIRST SERVINGMAN   Directitude? What's that?

THIRD SERVINGMAN   But when they shall see, sir, his crest up again, and the man in blood, they will out of their 220 burrows like coneys after rain, and revel all with him. 221

FIRST SERVINGMAN   But when goes this forward?

THIRD SERVINGMAN   Tomorrow, today, presently. You 223 shall have the drum struck up this afternoon. 'Tis, as it were, a parcel of their feast, and to be executed 225 ere they wipe their lips.

SECOND SERVINGMAN   Why, then we shall have a stirring 227 world again. This peace is nothing but to rust iron, increase tailors, and breed ballad makers.

FIRST SERVINGMAN   Let me have war, say I. It exceeds peace as far as day does night. It's spritely walking, 231 audible, and full of vent. Peace is a very apoplexy, 232 lethargy; mulled, deaf, sleepy, insensible; a getter of 233 more bastard children than war's a destroyer of men.

SECOND SERVINGMAN   'Tis so. And as wars in some sort may be said to be a ravisher, so it cannot be denied but peace is a great maker of cuckolds.

FIRST SERVINGMAN   Ay, and it makes men hate one another.

THIRD SERVINGMAN   Reason: because they then less need one another. The wars for my money! I hope to see Romans as cheap as Volscians.—They are rising, 242 they are rising.

FIRST AND SECOND SERVINGMEN   In, in, in, in!

Exeunt.

❖

[4.6]

Enter the two tribunes, Sicinius and Brutus.

SICINIUS
We hear not of him, neither need we fear him.
His remedies are tame: the present peace 2
And quietness of the people, which before
Were in wild hurry. Here do we make his friends 4
Blush that the world goes well, who rather had,
Though they themselves did suffer by't, behold
Dissentious numbers pest'ring streets than see 7
Our tradesmen singing in their shops and going
About their functions friendly.

BRUTUS
We stood to't in good time.

Enter Menenius.

                                    Is this Menenius? 10

SICINIUS
'Tis he, 'tis he. Oh, he is grown most kind
Of late.—Hail, sir!

MENENIUS   Hail to you both!

SICINIUS
Your Coriolanus is not much missed
But with his friends. The commonwealth doth stand, 14
And so would do were he more angry at it. 15

MENENIUS
All's well, and might have been much better if
He could have temporized. 17

SICINIUS   Where is he, hear you?

MENENIUS   Nay, I hear nothing.
His mother and his wife hear nothing from him.

Enter three or four Citizens.

ALL CITIZENS
The gods preserve you both!

SICINIUS   Good e'en, our neighbors.

BRUTUS
Good e'en to you all, good e'en to you all.

FIRST CITIZEN
Ourselves, our wives, and children, on our knees

---

195 on't of it.   **scotched** scored, gashed   **196 carbonado** meat scored across for broiling.   **197 An** If   **200 made on** made much of   **201 at upper end** i.e., at the place of honor   **203 but** unless.   **bald** bareheaded   **204–5 sanctifies . . . hand** touches his (Coriolanus's) hand as though it were a holy relic or that of his mistress   **206 bottom** last item, gist   **209 sowl** drag   **211 polled** stripped (as one would strip branches or foliage).   **217 directitude** (A blunder for something like *discretitude* or *discredit*.)   **220 in blood** in full vigor. (Usually said of hounds.)   **will out** will come out   **221 coneys** rabbits   **223 presently** immediately.   **225 parcel** part   **227 stirring** active   **231–2 It's . . . vent** (War is like a hunting hound: lively, audible in full cry, and quick to pick up the scent.)   **232 apoplexy** paralysis   **233 mulled** insipid, drowsy.   **getter** begetter

242 rising i.e., rising from table
4.6. Location: Rome. A public place.
2 His . . . tame (Sicinius argues that the quietness of the populace affords no opportunity for those who hope to foment further trouble and thereby bring about Coriolanus's return.)   **4 hurry** commotion.
7 pest'ring crowding, blocking   **10 stood to't** i.e., stood up against Coriolanus   **14 But with** except among   **15 were** even were
17 temporized compromised.

Are bound to pray for you both.

SICINIUS   Live and thrive!

BRUTUS

Farewell, kind neighbors. We wished Coriolanus
Had loved you as we did.

ALL CITIZENS   Now the gods keep you!

BOTH TRIBUNES   Farewell, farewell.   *Exeunt Citizens.*

SICINIUS

This is a happier and more comely time   28
Than when these fellows ran about the streets
Crying confusion.

BRUTUS   Caius Marcius was
A worthy officer i'th' war, but insolent,
O'ercome with pride, ambitious, past all thinking
Self-loving.

SICINIUS

And affecting one sole throne, without assistance.   34

MENENIUS   I think not so.

SICINIUS

We should by this, to all our lamentation,   36
If he had gone forth consul, found it so.   37

BRUTUS

The gods have well prevented it, and Rome
Sits safe and still without him.

Enter an Aedile.

AEDILE   Worthy tribunes,
There is a slave, whom we have put in prison,
Reports the Volsces with two several powers   41
Are entered in the Roman territories,
And with the deepest malice of the war
Destroy what lies before 'em.

MENENIUS   'Tis Aufidius,
Who, hearing of our Marcius' banishment,
Thrusts forth his horns again into the world,   46
Which were inshelled when Marcius stood for Rome,   47
And durst not once peep out.

SICINIUS   Come, what talk you of Marcius?   49

BRUTUS

Go see this rumorer whipped. It cannot be
The Volsces dare break with us.

MENENIUS   Cannot be?   51
We have record that very well it can,
And three examples of the like hath been
Within my age. But reason with the fellow   54
Before you punish him, where he heard this,
Lest you shall chance to whip your information   56
And beat the messenger who bids beware
Of what is to be dreaded.

SICINIUS   Tell not me.
I know this cannot be.

BRUTUS   Not possible.

Enter a Messenger.

MESSENGER

The nobles in great earnestness are going
All to the Senate House. Some news is come
That turns their countenances.

SICINIUS   'Tis this slave—   62
Go whip him 'fore the people's eyes—his raising,   63
Nothing but his report.

MESSENGER   Yes, worthy sir,
The slave's report is seconded, and more,   65
More fearful, is delivered.

SICINIUS   What more fearful?   66

MESSENGER

It is spoke freely out of many mouths—
How probable I do not know—that Marcius,
Joined with Aufidius, leads a power 'gainst Rome,
And vows revenge as spacious as between   70
The young'st and oldest thing.

SICINIUS   This is most likely!   71

BRUTUS

Raised only that the weaker sort may wish   72
Good Marcius home again.

SICINIUS   The very trick on't.   74

MENENIUS   This is unlikely.
He and Aufidius can no more atone   76
Than violent'st contrariety.   77

Enter [a Second] Messenger.

SECOND MESSENGER

You are sent for to the Senate.
A fearful army, led by Caius Marcius   79
Associated with Aufidius, rages
Upon our territories, and have already
O'erborne their way, consumed with fire, and took   82
What lay before them.

Enter Cominius.

COMINIUS   Oh, you have made good work!

MENENIUS   What news? What news?

COMINIUS

You have holp to ravish your own daughters and   86
To melt the city leads upon your pates,   87
To see your wives dishonored to your noses—   88

MENENIUS   What's the news? What's the news?

COMINIUS

Your temples burnèd in their cement, and   90
Your franchises, whereon you stood, confined   91
Into an auger's bore.

MENENIUS   Pray now, your news?—   92
You have made fair work, I fear me.—Pray, your
    news?

---

28 **comely** gracious   34 **affecting . . . assistance** desiring to rule alone, without any help or partnership in rule.   36 **this** this time   37 **found** have found   41 **several powers** separate armed forces   46 **Thrusts . . . again** (i.e., like a snail)   47 **inshelled** i.e., drawn in the shell like a snail's horns.   **stood** fought   49 **what** why   51 **break** break their treaty   54 **age** lifetime.   56 **information** source of information

62 **turns** changes   62–3 **'Tis . . . raising** It is this slave's rumor-raising, for which let him be publicly whipped   65 **seconded** confirmed   66 **delivered** reported.   70–1 **as spacious . . . thing** comprehensive enough to embrace every living person.   72 **Raised** Invented, stirred up. (See *raising*, line 63 above.)   74 **trick on't** stratagem of it.   76 **atone** come to a reconciliation   77 **violent'st contrariety** most extreme opposites.   79 **fearful** frightening   82 **O'erborne their way** carried all before them   86 **holp** helped   87 **leads** roofs of lead.   **pates** heads   88 **to** before   90 **in their cement** i.e., to their foundations   91 **franchises** political rights.   **stood** insisted   92 **auger's bore** hole drilled by an auger, i.e., narrow space.

If Marcius should be joined wi'th' Volscians—
COMINIUS   If?
He is their god. He leads them like a thing
Made by some other deity than Nature,
That shapes man better; and they follow him
Against us brats with no less confidence   98
Than boys pursuing summer butterflies
Or butchers killing flies.
MENENIUS   You have made good work,
You and your apron-men, you that stood so much   101
Upon the voice of occupation and   102
The breath of garlic eaters!
COMINIUS   He'll shake your Rome about your ears.
MENENIUS
As Hercules did shake down mellow fruit.   105
You have made fair work!
BRUTUS   But is this true, sir?
COMINIUS   Ay, and you'll look pale
Before you find it other. All the regions   109
Do smilingly revolt, and who resists   110
Are mocked for valiant ignorance   111
And perish constant fools. Who is't can blame him?   112
Your enemies and his find something in him.   113
MENENIUS   We are all undone, unless
The noble man have mercy.
COMINIUS   Who shall ask it?
The tribunes cannot do't for shame; the people
Deserve such pity of him as the wolf
Does of the shepherds. For his best friends, if they   118
Should say "Be good to Rome," they charged him
    even   119
As those should do that had deserved his hate   120
And therein showed like enemies.
MENENIUS   'Tis true.   121
If he were putting to my house the brand   122
That should consume it, I have not the face
To say "Beseech you, cease." You have made fair
    hands,   124
You and your crafts! You have crafted fair!
COMINIUS   You have brought   125
A trembling upon Rome, such as was never
S' incapable of help.
BOTH TRIBUNES   Say not we brought it.
MENENIUS
How? Was't we? We loved him, but, like beasts
And cowardly nobles, gave way unto your clusters,   129

Who did hoot him out o'th' city.
COMINIUS   But I fear
They'll roar him in again. Tullus Aufidius,   131
The second name of men, obeys his points   132
As if he were his officer. Desperation
Is all the policy, strength, and defense
That Rome can make against them.

Enter a troop of Citizens.

MENENIUS   Here come the clusters.—
And is Audifius with him? You are they
That made the air unwholesome when you cast
Your stinking greasy caps in hooting at
Coriolanus' exile. Now he's coming,
And not a hair upon a soldier's head
Which will not prove a whip. As many coxcombs   141
As you threw caps up will he tumble down,
And pay you for your voices. 'Tis no matter;
If he could burn us all into one coal,   144
We have deserved it.
ALL CITIZENS   Faith, we hear fearful news.
FIRST CITIZEN   For mine own part,
When I said, banish him, I said, 'twas pity.
SECOND CITIZEN   And so did I.
THIRD CITIZEN   And so did I; and, to say the truth, so
did very many of us. That we did, we did for the best;   151
and though we willingly consented to his banishment,
yet it was against our will.
COMINIUS   You're goodly things, you voices!
MENENIUS   You have made good work,
You and your cry!—Shall 's to the Capitol?   156
COMINIUS   Oh, ay, what else?
                      Exeunt both [Cominius and Menenius].
SICINIUS
Go, masters, get you home, be not dismayed.
These are a side that would be glad to have   159
This true which they so seem to fear. Go home,
And show no sign of fear.
FIRST CITIZEN   The gods be good to us! Come, masters,
let 's home. I ever said we were i'th' wrong when we
banished him.
SECOND CITIZEN   So did we all. But, come, let 's home.
                                        Exeunt Citizens.
BRUTUS   I do not like this news.
SICINIUS   Nor I.
BRUTUS
Let 's to the Capitol. Would half my wealth   168
Would buy this for a lie!
SICINIUS   Pray, let 's go.   169
                                        Exeunt tribunes.

❧

98 **brats** mere children   101 **apron-men** artisans (who wore aprons)
102 **voice of occupation** votes of the laboring men   105 **Hercules . . .
fruit** (Hercules's eleventh labor was to carry off the golden apples of
the Hesperides.)   109 **other** otherwise.   110 **smilingly** gladly.
who whoever   111 **valiant ignorance** foolish valor   112 **constant**
loyal   113 **Your . . . him** i.e., Both your enemies, the patricians, and
his enemies, the Volscians, find cause to ally themselves with him, or,
all find him irresistible.   118 **For** As for   119–21 **they charged . . .
enemies** they would be urging him with the same language that
those who deserved his hate (the tribunes and plebeians) would use
and in that respect would be behaving as his enemies would behave.
122 **brand** torch   124 **made fair hands** done fine work. (Said ironically.)   125 **crafted fair** (1) cleverly advanced the interests of the
crafts or occupations (2) shown your expert craft or cunning.
129 **clusters** mobs

131 **roar . . . again** i.e., roar with pain when he returns.   132 **second . . .
men** second greatest name among men.   **his points** Coriolanus's
instructions   141 **coxcombs** i.e., fools' heads   144 **into one coal** into
one cindery mass   151 **That** What   156 **cry** pack.   **Shall 's** Shall we
go   159 **side** party, faction   168–9 **Would . . . lie!** I would give half of
my fortune if this could be proven a lie!

[4.7]

Enter Aufidius with his Lieutenant.

AUFIDIUS   Do they still fly to th' Roman?

LIEUTENANT
I do not know what witchcraft's in him, but
Your soldiers use him as the grace 'fore meat,
Their talk at table, and their thanks at end;
And you are darkened in this action, sir,   5
Even by your own.

AUFIDIUS   I cannot help it now,   6
Unless by using means I lame the foot   7
Of our design. He bears himself more proudlier,   8
Even to my person, than I thought he would
When first I did embrace him. Yet his nature
In that's no changeling, and I must excuse   11
What cannot be amended.

LIEUTENANT   Yet I wish, sir—
I mean for your particular—you had not   13
Joined in commission with him, but either
Have borne the action of yourself or else   15
To him had left it solely.

AUFIDIUS
I understand thee well, and be thou sure,
When he shall come to his account, he knows not   18
What I can urge against him. Although it seems—   19
And so he thinks, and is no less apparent
To th' vulgar eye—that he bears all things fairly   21
And shows good husbandry for the Volscian state,   22
Fights dragonlike, and does achieve as soon   23
As draw his sword, yet he hath left undone   24
That which shall break his neck or hazard mine
Whene'er we come to our account.

LIEUTENANT
Sir, I beseech you, think you he'll carry Rome?   27

AUFIDIUS
All places yields to him ere he sits down,   28
And the nobility of Rome are his;
The senators and patricians love him too.
The tribunes are no soldiers, and their people
Will be as rash in the repeal as hasty   32
To expel him thence. I think he'll be to Rome
As is the osprey to the fish, who takes it   34
By sovereignty of nature. First he was
A noble servant to them, but he could not
Carry his honors even. Whether 'twas pride,   37

Which out of daily fortune ever taints   38
The happy man; whether defect of judgment,   39
To fail in the disposing of those chances   40
Which he was lord of; or whether nature,   41
Not to be other than one thing, not moving   42
From th' casque to th' cushion, but commanding
    peace   43
Even with the same austerity and garb   44
As he controlled the war; but one of these—
As he hath spices of them all—not all,   46
For I dare so far free him—made him feared,   47
So hated, and so banished. But he has a merit   48
To choke it in the utt'rance. So our virtues   49
Lie in th'interpretation of the time;   50
And power, unto itself most commendable,   51
Hath not a tomb so evident as a chair   52
T'extol what it hath done.   53
One fire drives out one fire; one nail, one nail;
Rights by rights falter, strengths by strengths do fail.   55
Come, let 's away. When, Caius, Rome is thine,
Thou art poor'st of all; then shortly art thou mine.

                                                    Exeunt.

❧

[5.1]

*Enter Menenius, Cominius; Sicinius, Brutus,
the two tribunes; with others.*

MENENIUS
No, I'll not go. You hear what he hath said   1
Which was sometime his general, who loved him   2
In a most dear particular. He called me father;   3
But what o' that? Go you that banished him;
A mile before his tent fall down and knee   5
The way into his mercy. Nay, if he coyed   6
To hear Cominius speak, I'll keep at home.

COMINIUS
He would not seem to know me.

MENENIUS   Do you hear?   8

COMINIUS
Yet one time he did call me by my name.
I urged our old acquaintance, and the drops

4.7. Location: A camp, at a small distance from Rome.
5 you . . . action your glory is dimmed in this undertaking   **6 your
own** i.e., your followers, or, your own action (in making Coriolanus
your fellow general).   **7–8 means . . . design** i.e., such means as
would cripple our assault on Rome.   **11 changeling** i.e., fickle thing
13 for your particular regarding your self-interest   **15 Have . . . yourself** had led the campaign yourself   **18 account** day of reckoning
19 urge against him accuse him of.   **21 vulgar** common.   **bears** carries out   **22 husbandry for** management on behalf of   **23 achieve**
accomplish his goals   **24 As draw** as he does draw   **27 carry** capture
28 sits down besieges   **32 repeal** recall from exile   **34 osprey** fish
hawk, said to have had the power to fascinate fishes so by its kingly
sovereignty (line 35) that they would turn belly up and allow themselves to be taken without a struggle   **37 Carry . . . even** bear his
honors temperately.

38–9 out of . . . man as a result of continuous success always corrupts
the fortunate man   **40 disposing** clever using   **41 whether nature**
whether it was his nature   **42 Not . . . thing** i.e., always rigidly the
same, in peace as in war   **43 casque** helmet (as symbolic of the warrior).   **cushion** i.e., seat for a senator   **44 austerity and garb** austere
behavior   **46 spices** tastes, traces.   **not all** not all in full measure
47 free free from blame   **48 So . . . banished** because he was feared
he was hated, and because he was hated he was banished.   **48–9 he . . .
utt'rance** i.e., his merit is of the perverse sort that undoes the praise it
should receive; it *chokes* itself by its very *utt'rance*. (Also interpreted as
meaning, "He has so many counterbalancing good points that the
words stick in my throat.")   **50 the time** contemporary opinion
51–3 power . . . done i.e., power, however worthy in itself, is quickly
forgotten even while it is being commemorated from the public rostrum.   **55 Rights . . . fail** i.e., great deeds, eclipsed by the subsequent
deeds of others, are soon forgotten.
5.1. Location: Rome. A public place.
1 he i.e., Cominius   **2 Which** who.   **sometime** formerly   **3 In . . .
particular** with warmest personal affection.   **He** i.e., Coriolanus
5 knee crawl on your knees   **6 coyed** showed reluctance, disdained
8 would not seem pretended not

That we have bled together. "Coriolanus"
He would not answer to; forbade all names.
He was a kind of nothing, titleless,
Till he had forged himself a name o'th' fire
Of burning Rome.

MENENIUS   Why, so; you have made good work!
A pair of tribunes that have wracked for Rome   16
To make coals cheap! A noble memory!   17

COMINIUS
I minded him how royal 'twas to pardon   18
When it was less expected. He replied,
It was a bare petition of a state   20
To one whom they had punished.

MENENIUS   Very well.
Could he say less?

COMINIUS
I offered to awaken his regard   23
For 's private friends. His answer to me was,
He could not stay to pick them in a pile   25
Of noisome musty chaff. He said 'twas folly,   26
For one poor grain or two, to leave unburnt
And still to nose th'offense.   28

MENENIUS   For one poor grain or two!
I am one of those! His mother, wife, his child,
And this brave fellow too, we are the grains;
You are the musty chaff, and you are smelt
Above the moon. We must be burnt for you.

SICINIUS
Nay, pray, be patient. If you refuse your aid
In this so-never-needed help, yet do not
Upbraid 's with our distress. But sure, if you
Would be your country's pleader, your good tongue,
More than the instant army we can make,   38
Might stop our countryman.

MENENIUS   No, I'll not meddle.

SICINIUS
Pray you, go to him.

MENENIUS   What should I do?

BRUTUS
Only make trial what your love can do
For Rome, towards Marcius.

MENENIUS
Well, and say that Marcius return me,
As Cominius is returned, unheard—what then?
But as a discontented friend, grief-shot   45
With his unkindness? Say't be so?

SICINIUS   Yet your good will
Must have that thanks from Rome after the measure   48
As you intended well.

MENENIUS   I'll undertake't.   49
I think he'll hear me. Yet, to bite his lip   50

And hum at good Cominius much unhearts me.   51
He was not taken well; he had not dined.   52
The veins unfilled, our blood is cold, and then
We pout upon the morning, are unapt   54
To give or to forgive; but when we have stuffed
These pipes and these conveyances of our blood   56
With wine and feeding, we have suppler souls
Than in our priestlike fasts. Therefore I'll watch him
Till he be dieted to my request,   59
And then I'll set upon him.

BRUTUS
You know the very road into his kindness,
And cannot lose your way.

MENENIUS   Good faith, I'll prove him,   62
Speed how it will. I shall ere long have knowledge   63
Of my success.   *Exit.*

COMINIUS   He'll never hear him.

SICINIUS   Not?   64

COMINIUS
I tell you, he does sit in gold, his eye   65
Red as 'twould burn Rome; and his injury   66
The jailer to his pity. I kneeled before him;
'Twas very faintly he said "Rise"; dismissed me   68
Thus, with his speechless hand. What he would do
He sent in writing after me; what he would not,   70
Bound with an oath to yield to his conditions;   71
So that all hope is vain
Unless his noble mother and his wife,   73
Who, as I hear, mean to solicit him
For mercy to his country. Therefore, let 's hence
And with our fair entreaties haste them on.   *Exeunt.*

[5.2]

Enter Menenius to the Watch, or Guard.

FIRST WATCH   Stay! Whence are you?

SECOND WATCH   Stand, and go back.   2

MENENIUS
You guard like men; 'tis well. But, by your leave,
I am an officer of state, and come
To speak with Coriolanus.

FIRST WATCH   From whence?

MENENIUS   From Rome.

FIRST WATCH
You may not pass; you must return. Our general
Will no more hear from thence.

---

16 wracked for brought ruin to. (With a play on "striven for.")
17 coals charcoal (which will be cheap because Rome will be burnt to cinders; see 4.6.144). **memory** memorial. **18 minded** reminded
20 bare barefaced, paltry   **23 offered** attempted   **25 stay . . . them** take time to pick them out   **26 noisome** evil-smelling   **28 nose th' offense** smell the offensive stuff.   **38 instant army** army we can raise at this instant   **45 But as** i.e., What if he send me back only as. **grief-shot** grief-stricken   **48–9 after . . . As** in proportion that **50 to bite his lip** (An expression of anger, like humming in line 51; see below, 5.4.21.)

51 unhearts disheartens, discourages   **52 taken well** approached at the right time   **54 pout upon** are out of temper with   **56 conveyances** channels   **59 dieted to** fed properly so as to be in a mood for   **62 prove** attempt   **63 Speed** turn out, succeed   **64 success** outcome.   **65 in gold** in a golden chair   **66 Red** i.e., with anger; also the color normally used to describe gold.   **his injury** his sense of having been wronged   **68 faintly** coldly, indifferently   **70–1 what . . . conditions** i.e., what terrible actions he would not take against Rome if he bound ourselves under oath to agree to his terms. (See 5.3.14.) Or Cominius may mean that Coriolanus is bound by his own oath not to relent.   **73 Unless** if it were not for, except for
5.2. Location: The Volscian camp before Rome.
2 Stand Stop

SECOND WATCH

You'll see your Rome embraced with fire before
You'll speak with Coriolanus.

MENENIUS   Good my friends,
If you have heard your general talk of Rome
And of his friends there, it is lots to blanks   13
My name hath touched your ears. It is Menenius.

FIRST WATCH

Be it so; go back. The virtue of your name   15
Is not here passable.

MENENIUS   I tell thee, fellow,   16
Thy general is my lover. I have been   17
The book of his good acts, whence men have read
His fame unparalleled happily amplified;   19
For I have ever verified my friends—   20
Of whom he's chief—with all the size that verity   21
Would without lapsing suffer. Nay, sometimes,   22
Like to a bowl upon a subtle ground,   23
I have tumbled past the throw, and in his praise   24
Have almost stamped the leasing. Therefore, fellow,   25
I must have leave to pass.

FIRST WATCH   Faith, sir, if you had told as many lies in   27
his behalf as you have uttered words in your own, you
should not pass here; no, though it were as virtuous
to lie as to live chastely. Therefore go back.   30

MENENIUS   Prithee, fellow, remember my name is
Menenius, always factionary on the party of your   32
general.

SECOND WATCH   Howsoever you have been his liar, as
you say you have, I am one that, telling true under   35
him, must say you cannot pass. Therefore go back.   36

MENENIUS   Has he dined, canst thou tell? For I would
not speak with him till after dinner.

FIRST WATCH   You are a Roman, are you?

MENENIUS   I am, as thy general is.

FIRST WATCH   Then you should hate Rome, as he does.
Can you, when you have pushed out your gates the   42
very defender of them, and, in a violent popular ig-   43
norance, given your enemy your shield, think to front   44
his revenges with the easy groans of old women, the   45
virginal palms of your daughters, or with the palsied   46
intercession of such a decayed dotant as you seem to   47
be? Can you think to blow out the intended fire your
city is ready to flame in with such weak breath as
this? No, you are deceived; therefore, back to Rome

and prepare for your execution. You are condemned;
our general has sworn you out of reprieve and pardon.   52

MENENIUS   Sirrah, if thy captain knew I were here, he   53
would use me with estimation.   54

FIRST WATCH   Come, my captain knows you not.

MENENIUS   I mean thy general.

FIRST WATCH   My general cares not for you. Back, I say,
go, lest I let forth your half-pint of blood. Back! That's
the utmost of your having. Back!   59

MENENIUS   Nay, but, fellow, fellow—

Enter Coriolanus with Aufidius.

CORIOLANUS   What's the matter?

MENENIUS   Now, you companion, I'll say an errand for   62
you. You shall know now that I am in estimation; you   63
shall perceive that a Jack guardant cannot office me   64
from my son Coriolanus. Guess but by my entertain-   65
ment with him if thou stand'st not i'th' state of hang-   66
ing or of some death more long in spectatorship and   67
crueller in suffering; behold now presently, and   68
swoon for what's to come upon thee. [*To Coriolanus*]
The glorious gods sit in hourly synod about thy partic-   70
ular prosperity and love thee no worse than thy old
father Menenius does! O my son, my son! Thou art
preparing fire for us; look thee, here's water to quench   73
it. I was hardly moved to come to thee; but being as-   74
sured none but myself could move thee, I have been
blown out of our gates with sighs, and conjure thee
to pardon Rome and thy petitionary countrymen. The   77
good gods assuage thy wrath, and turn the dregs of it
upon this varlet here—this, who, like a block, hath   79
denied my access to thee.

CORIOLANUS   Away!

MENENIUS   How? Away?

CORIOLANUS

Wife, mother, child, I know not. My affairs
Are servanted to others. Though I owe   84
My revenge properly, my remission lies   85
In Volscian breasts. That we have been familiar,   86
Ingrate forgetfulness shall poison rather   87
Than pity note how much. Therefore, begone.   88
Mine ears against your suits are stronger than
Your gates against my force. Yet, for I loved thee,   90
Take this along; I writ it for thy sake, [*giving a letter*]
And would have sent it. Another word, Menenius,
I will not hear thee speak.—This man, Aufidius,
Was my beloved in Rome; yet thou behold'st!

---

13 lots to blanks i.e., a thousand to one. (Literally, prize-winning tick-
ets compared with valueless ones.)   **15 virtue** strength   **16 passable**
current (like a coin), and able to provide passage.   **17 lover** friend.
19 happily aptly, felicitously   **20–2 For . . . suffer** for I have always
expatiated on the good name of my friends—of whom he is chief—to
the fullest extent possible without distorting the facts.   **23 bowl** ball
used in bowls.   **subtle** deceptively irregular   **24 tumbled . . . throw**
overshot the mark   **25 stamped the leasing** given the stamp of truth
to lying (i.e., overstated praise of him).   **27 if** even if   **30 chastely**
honestly. (But with a sexual quibble, taking *lie* in a sexual sense.)
32 factionary active as a partisan   **35–6 telling . . . him** telling the
truth in his service   **42 out** out at; out of   **43–4 violent popular igno-**
rance folly of mob violence   **44 shield** defender, i.e., Coriolanus.
front confront, oppose   **45 easy groans** i.e., groans that are easily
provoked   **46 virginal . . . daughters** uplifted hands of your virgin
daughters   **47 dotant** dotard, old fool

52 out of beyond the reach of   **53 Sirrah** (Term of address to inferiors.)   **54 use** treat.   **estimation** esteem.   **59 the utmost of your hav-**
ing all you are going to get.   **62 companion** fellow.   **say an errand**
deliver a message   **63 in estimation** well regarded   **64 Jack**
guardant knave on guard duty.   **office** officiously keep   **65–6 enter-**
tainment with reception by   **66 stand'st . . . state** are not at risk
67 spectatorship watching   **68 presently** immediately   **70 synod**
council, assembly   **73 water** i.e., tears   **74 hardly moved** with difficulty persuaded   **77 petitionary** suppliant, petitioning   **79 block**
(1) impediment (2) blockhead   **84 servanted** subjected.   **owe** own,
possess   **85 properly** as my own.   **remission** power to forgive
86–8 That . . . much i.e., Close as we have been, I will allow ungrateful forgetfulness (prompted by Rome's ingratitude) to poison the
memory of our friendship rather than allow my pity to recall how
much we meant to each other.   **90 for** because

AUFIDIUS   You keep a constant temper.   95
                    Exeunt. Manent the Guard and Menenius.
FIRST WATCH   Now, sir, is your name Menenius?
SECOND WATCH   'Tis a spell, you see, of much power.
    You know the way home again.
FIRST WATCH   Do you hear how we are shent for keep-   99
    ing your greatness back?
SECOND WATCH   What cause, do you think, I have to
    swoon?
MENENIUS   I neither care for the world nor your general.
    For such things as you, I can scarce think there's any,   104
    you're so slight. He that hath a will to die by himself   105
    fears it not from another. Let your general do his
    worst. For you, be that you are, long; and your misery   107
    increase with your age! I say to you, as I was said to,
    Away!   *Exit.*
FIRST WATCH   A noble fellow, I warrant him.
SECOND WATCH   The worthy fellow is our general. He's
    the rock, the oak not to be wind-shaken.   *Exit Watch.*

[5.3]

                    *Enter Coriolanus and Aufidius [with Volscian
                    soldiers. Coriolanus and Aufidius sit.]*

CORIOLANUS
    We will before the walls of Rome tomorrow
    Set down our host. My partner in this action,   2
    You must report to th' Volscian lords how plainly   3
    I have borne this business.
AUFIDIUS   Only their ends   4
    You have respected, stopped your ears against
    The general suit of Rome, never admitted
    A private whisper, no, not with such friends
    That thought them sure of you.
CORIOLANUS   This last old man,
    Whom with a cracked heart I have sent to Rome,
    Loved me above the measure of a father,
    Nay, godded me indeed. Their latest refuge   11
    Was to send him, for whose old love I have—
    Though I showed sourly to him—once more offered   13
    The first conditions, which they did refuse
    And cannot now accept. To grace him only   15
    That thought he could do more, a very little   16
    I have yielded to. Fresh embassies and suits,   17
    Nor from the state nor private friends, hereafter   18
    Will I lend ear to. (*Shout within.*) Ha? What shout is
    this?

Shall I be tempted to infringe my vow
In the same time 'tis made? I will not.

            *Enter Virgilia, Volumnia, Valeria, young
            Marcius, with attendants.*

My wife comes foremost; then the honored mold   22
Wherein this trunk was framed, and in her hand   23
The grandchild to her blood. But, out, affection!
All bond and privilege of nature, break!   25
Let it be virtuous to be obstinate.   [*The women bow.*] 26
What is that curtsy worth? Or those doves' eyes,   27
Which can make gods forsworn? I melt, and am not
Of stronger earth than others. My mother bows,
As if Olympus to a molehill should
In supplication nod, and my young boy
Hath an aspect of intercession which   32
Great Nature cries "Deny not." Let the Volsces   33
Plow Rome and harrow Italy, I'll never
Be such a gosling to obey instinct, but stand   35
As if a man were author of himself
And knew no other kin.
VIRGILIA   My lord and husband!
CORIOLANUS
    These eyes are not the same I wore in Rome.   38
VIRGILIA
    The sorrow that delivers us thus changed   39
    Makes you think so.
CORIOLANUS   Like a dull actor now,   40
    I have forgot my part, and I am out,   41
    Even to a full disgrace. Best of my flesh,
    Forgive my tyranny, but do not say   43
    For that, "Forgive our Romans." Oh, a kiss
    Long as my exile, sweet as my revenge!   [*They kiss.*]
    Now, by the jealous queen of heaven, that kiss   46
    I carried from thee, dear, and my true lip
    Hath virgined it e'er since. You gods! I prate,   48
    And the most noble mother of the world
    Leave unsaluted. Sink, my knee, i'th' earth.   *Kneels.*
    Of thy deep duty more impression show   51
    Than that of common sons.
VOLUMNIA   Oh, stand up blest!
                                        [*He rises.*]
    Whilst with no softer cushion than the flint
    I kneel before thee, and unproperly   54
    Show duty, as mistaken all this while
    Between the child and parent.   [*She kneels.*]
CORIOLANUS   What's this?

---

95 constant temper firm mind.   **95.1** *Manent* They remain onstage   **99 shent** rebuked   **104 For** As for. (Also in line 107.)   **105 slight** insignificant.   **by himself** by his own hand   **107 that** what.   **long** through a long (and tedious) lifetime
5.3. Location: The Volscian camp, as in scene 2. The tent of Coriolanus.
2 Set down our host lay siege with our army.   **3 plainly** openly, straightforwardly   **4 their ends** i.e., the Volscians' purposes   **11 godded** deified.   **latest refuge** last resource   **13 showed** acted   **15 grace** gratify   **16–17 a very . . . yielded to** I have conceded a little, but almost nothing.   **18 Nor** neither

22 mold form, body (of my mother)   **23 this trunk** my body   **25 bond . . . nature** natural ties and claims of love   **26 obstinate** hard-hearted.   **27 curtsy** (1) bow (2) courtesy.   **doves' eyes** i.e., beautiful and seductive eyes. (See Song of Solomon 1:15.)   **32 aspect of intercession** pleading look   **33 Let** Even should   **35 gosling** baby goose (i.e., foolish, inexperienced person).   **to** as to   **38–40 These . . . so** (Coriolanus says, "I see differently now that I am not in Rome." Virgilia replies, taking his words literally, "Our sorrow has so changed us that you cannot recognize us." *Delivers* means "presents.")   **41 I am out** I have forgotten my lines, I am at a loss for words   **43 tyranny** cruelty   **46 jealous . . . heaven** i.e., Juno, patroness of marriage   **48 virgined it** remained untouched.   **prate** talk idly   **51 more impression** (1) a deeper mark (in the earth) (2) a clearer sign (of filial obedience)   **54 unproperly** unfittingly, violating due propriety

Your knees to me? To your corrected son?   57
                              [*He raises her.*]
Then let the pebbles on the hungry beach   58
Fillip the stars! Then let the mutinous winds   59
Strike the proud cedars 'gainst the fiery sun,   60
Murd'ring impossibility, to make   61
What cannot be slight work.
VOLUMNIA   Thou art my warrior;   62
I holp to frame thee. Do you know this lady?   63
CORIOLANUS
The noble sister of Publicola,
The moon of Rome, chaste as the icicle   65
That's curded by the frost from purest snow   66
And hangs on Dian's temple—dear Valeria!
VOLUMNIA [*indicating young Marcius*]
This is a poor epitome of yours,   68
Which by th'interpretation of full time   69
May show like all yourself.
CORIOLANUS [*to his son*]   The god of soldiers,   70
With the consent of supreme Jove, inform   71
Thy thoughts with nobleness, that thou mayst prove
To shame unvulnerable, and stick i'th' wars   73
Like a great seamark, standing every flaw   74
And saving those that eye thee!
VOLUMNIA [*to young Marcius*]   Your knee, sirrah.   75
                    [*Young Marcius kneels.*]
CORIOLANUS   That's my brave boy!
VOLUMNIA
Even he, your wife, this lady, and myself
Are suitors to you.
CORIOLANUS   I beseech you, peace.
Or, if you'd ask, remember this before:
The thing I have forsworn to grant may never   80
Be held by you denials. Do not bid me   81
Dismiss my soldiers or capitulate   82
Again with Rome's mechanics. Tell me not   83
Wherein I seem unnatural; desire not
T'allay my rages and revenges with
Your colder reasons.
VOLUMNIA   Oh, no more, no more!
You have said you will not grant us anything;
For we have nothing else to ask but that
Which you deny already. Yet we will ask,
That, if you fail in our request, the blame   90
May hang upon your hardness. Therefore hear us.

CORIOLANUS
Aufidius, and you Volsces, mark; for we'll
Hear naught from Rome in private. [*He sits.*] Your
   request?
VOLUMNIA
Should we be silent and not speak, our raiment   94
And state of bodies would bewray what life   95
We have led since thy exile. Think with thyself   96
How more unfortunate than all living women
Are we come hither; since that thy sight, which
   should   98
Make our eyes flow with joy, hearts dance with
   comforts,
Constrains them weep and shake with fear and
   sorrow,
Making the mother, wife, and child to see
The son, the husband, and the father tearing
His country's bowels out. And to poor we
Thine enmity's most capital. Thou barr'st us   104
Our prayers to the gods, which is a comfort
That all but we enjoy; for how can we,
Alas, how can we for our country pray,
Whereto we are bound, together with thy victory,
Whereto we are bound? Alack, or we must lose   109
The country, our dear nurse, or else thy person,
Our comfort in the country. We must find
An evident calamity, though we had   112
Our wish, which side should win; for either thou   113
Must as a foreign recreant be led   114
With manacles through our streets, or else
Triumphantly tread on thy country's ruin,
And bear the palm for having bravely shed   117
Thy wife and children's blood. For myself, son,
I purpose not to wait on fortune till   119
These wars determine. If I cannot persuade thee   120
Rather to show a noble grace to both parts   121
Than seek the end of one, thou shalt no sooner
March to assault thy country than to tread—
Trust to't, thou shalt not—on thy mother's womb   124
That brought thee to this world.
VIRGILIA   Ay, and mine,
That brought you forth this boy to keep your name
Living to time.
YOUNG MARCIUS   'A shall not tread on me;   127
I'll run away till I am bigger, but then I'll fight.
CORIOLANUS
Not of a woman's tenderness to be   129
Requires nor child nor woman's face to see.   130
I have sat too long.   [*He rises.*]
VOLUMNIA   Nay, go not from us thus.   131
If it were so that our request did tend

---

57 corrected chastised   **58 hungry** unfertile, barren   **59 Fillip** strike **60 Strike . . . sun** uproot huge cedar trees and throw them against the sun   **61 Murd'ring** negating the very concept of   **62 What . . . slight work** an easy task of what cannot be, is impossible.   **63 holp** helped **65 moon of Rome** (Allusion to Diana, goddess of chastity and associated with the moon.)   **66 curded** congealed   **68 epitome** abridgement   **69 by . . . time** when time shall have revealed and fulfilled all. (Time will expand the *epitome*, giving *interpretation* to its full meaning.)   **70 show** look.   **The god of soldiers** i.e., Mars   **71 inform** inspire   **73 To . . . unvulnerable** (1) incapable of shameful deeds (2) proof against being shamed.   **stick** stand out   **74 seamark** reference object used by mariners in navigating.   **standing . . . flaw** withstanding every gust   **75 eye thee** i.e., guide themselves by you, use you as a *seamark*.   **80–1 The thing . . . denials** i.e., it would be unjust to regard me as refusing to grant what I have sworn not to grant and hence no longer have the power of granting.   **82 capitulate** come to terms   **83 mechanics** tradesmen.   **90 fail in** do not grant

94 Should we Even if we should.   **raiment** clothes   **95 bewray** reveal   **96 Think with thyself** Reflect   **98 thy sight** the sight of you **104 capital** fatal.   **109 or** either   **112 evident** certain   **113 which** whichever   **114 recreant** traitor   **117 palm** i.e., emblem of victory **119 purpose** propose   **120 determine** come to an end, settle matters. **121 grace** favor, mercy.   **parts** sides   **124 Trust . . . not** (Read this parenthetical phrase after *sooner* in line 122.)   **127 'A** He **129–30 Not . . . see** If a man is not to yield to a womanly tenderness, he must not look upon any child's or woman's face.   **131 sat** i.e., stayed here listening

To save the Romans, thereby to destroy
The Volsces whom you serve, you might condemn us
As poisonous of your honor. No, our suit
Is that you reconcile them, while the Volsces   136
May say, "This mercy we have showed," the Romans,
"This we received," and each in either side   138
Give the all-hail to thee and cry, "Be blest   139
For making up this peace!" Thou know'st, great son,
The end of war's uncertain, but this certain,
That, if thou conquer Rome, the benefit
Which thou shalt thereby reap is such a name
Whose repetition will be dogged with curses,
Whose chronicle thus writ: "The man was noble,
But with his last attempt he wiped it out,   146
Destroyed his country, and his name remains
To th'ensuing age abhorred." Speak to me, son.
Thou hast affected the fine strains of honor,   149
To imitate the graces of the gods,
To tear with thunder the wide cheeks o'th' air,   151
And yet to charge thy sulfur with a bolt   152
That should but rive an oak. Why dost not speak?   153
Think'st thou it honorable for a nobleman
Still to remember wrongs? Daughter, speak you;   155
He cares not for your weeping. Speak thou, boy;   156
Perhaps thy childishness will move him more
Than can our reasons. There's no man in the world
More bound to 's mother, yet here he lets me prate   159
Like one i'th' stocks.—Thou hast never in thy life   160
Showed thy dear mother any courtesy,
When she, poor hen, fond of no second brood,   162
Has clucked thee to the wars and safely home,   163
Loaden with honor. Say my request's unjust,
And spurn me back; but if it be not so,
Thou art not honest, and the gods will plague thee   166
That thou restrain'st from me the duty which   167
To a mother's part belongs.—He turns away.
Down, ladies! Let us shame him with our knees.
To his surname Coriolanus 'longs more pride   170
Than pity to our prayers. Down! [They kneel.] An end;
This is the last. So we will home to Rome,
And die among our neighbors.—Nay, behold 's!
This boy, that cannot tell what he would have,   174
But kneels and holds up hands for fellowship,   175
Does reason our petition with more strength   176
Than thou hast to deny't.—Come, let us go.

                                              [They rise.]

This fellow had a Volscian to his mother;   178
His wife is in Corioles, and his child   179
Like him by chance.—Yet give us our dispatch.   180
I am hushed until our city be afire,
And then I'll speak a little.
                          [He] holds her by the hand, silent.
CORIOLANUS   Oh, mother, mother!
What have you done? Behold, the heavens do ope,
The gods look down, and this unnatural scene
They laugh at. Oh, my mother, mother! Oh!
You have won a happy victory to Rome;
But for your son—believe it, oh, believe it!—
Most dangerously you have with him prevailed,
If not most mortal to him. But let it come.—   189
Aufidius, though I cannot make true wars,   190
I'll frame convenient peace. Now, good Aufidius,   191
Were you in my stead, would you have heard
A mother less? Or granted less, Aufidius?
AUFIDIUS
I was moved withal.
CORIOLANUS   I dare be sworn you were.   194
And, sir, it is no little thing to make
Mine eyes to sweat compassion. But, good sir,   196
What peace you'll make, advise me. For my part,
I'll not to Rome. I'll back with you; and pray you,   198
Stand to me in this cause.—Oh, mother! Wife!   199
AUFIDIUS [aside]
I am glad thou hast set thy mercy and thy honor
At difference in thee. Out of that I'll work
Myself a former fortune.
                  [The ladies make signs to Coriolanus.]
CORIOLANUS [to the ladies]   Ay, by and by;   202
But we will drink together; and you shall bear
A better witness back than words, which we,   204
On like conditions, will have countersealed.   205
Come, enter with us. Ladies, you deserve
To have a temple built you. All the swords
In Italy, and her confederate arms,   208
Could not have made this peace.   Exeunt.

                          ❖

[5.4]

            Enter Menenius and Sicinius.

MENENIUS   See you yond coign o'th' Capitol, yond cor-   1
nerstone?
SICINIUS   Why, what of that?

---

136 while so that at the same time   138 each everyone.   in on
139 all-hail general acclaim   146 attempt undertaking.   it i.e., his
nobility   149 affected sought, cherished   151 cheeks (On Renaissance maps, the winds were often portrayed as issuing from the
cheeks of Aeolus, Greek god of the winds.)   152–3 And . . . oak and
yet to load your lightning with a thunderbolt that should only split
an oak. (Volumnia cautions against the unwise use of such power.)
155 Still always   156 cares not for is unmoved by   159–60 prate . . .
stocks i.e., talk uselessly like a prisoner who has been publicly humil-
iated.   162 When whereas.   fond desirous   163 clucked marshaled
as a hen her brood   166 honest honorable, just   167 thou restrain'st
you withhold   170 'longs belongs   174 This . . . have This boy, Coriolanus's son, who does not understand what he is asking for   175 for
fellowship merely to keep us company   176 reason argue for

178 to for   179 his child this boy, supposed his son   180 dispatch
dismissal, leave to go. (With implication also of "demise.")   189 mortal fatally   190 true i.e., as I vowed to do   191 convenient fitting,
proper   194 withal by it.   196 sweat compassion i.e., weep with
pity.   198 back go back   199 Stand to stand by   202 former fortune
fortune great as formerly.   204 better witness i.e., formal document
of peace   205 On . . . countersealed having agreed to the same conditions, will both have sealed and guaranteed.   208 her confederate
arms the weapons of her allies
5.4. Location: Rome. A public place.
1 coign corner

MENENIUS   If it be possible for you to displace it with your little finger, there is some hope the ladies of Rome, especially his mother, may prevail with him. But I say there is no hope in't; our throats are sentenced, and stay upon execution.   8

SICINIUS   Is't possible that so short a time can alter the condition of a man?   10

MENENIUS   There is differency between a grub and a butterfly, yet your butterfly was a grub. This Marcius is grown from man to dragon. He has wings; he's more than a creeping thing.

SICINIUS   He loved his mother dearly.

MENENIUS   So did he me; and he no more remembers his mother now than an eight-year-old horse. The tartness of his face sours ripe grapes. When he walks, he moves like an engine, and the ground shrinks before   19
his treading. He is able to pierce a corslet with his eye,   20
talks like a knell, and his hum is a battery. He sits in   21
his state as a thing made for Alexander. What he bids   22
be done is finished with his bidding. He wants noth-   23
ing of a god but eternity and a heaven to throne in.   24

SICINIUS   Yes, mercy, if you report him truly.   25

MENENIUS   I paint him in the character. Mark what   26
mercy his mother shall bring from him. There is no more mercy in him than there is milk in a male tiger; that shall our poor city find. And all this is long of you.   29

SICINIUS   The gods be good unto us!

MENENIUS   No, in such a case the gods will not be good unto us. When we banished him, we respected not them; and, he returning to break our necks, they respect not us.

Enter a Messenger.

MESSENGER [*to Sicinius*]
Sir, if you'd save your life, fly to your house!
The plebeians have got your fellow tribune
And hale him up and down, all swearing, if   37
The Roman ladies bring not comfort home,
They'll give him death by inches.

Enter another Messenger.

SICINIUS   What's the news?   39

SECOND MESSENGER
Good news, good news! The ladies have prevailed,
The Volscians are dislodged, and Marcius gone.   41
A merrier day did never yet greet Rome,
No, not th'expulsion of the Tarquins.   43

SICINIUS
Friend, art thou certain this is true?
Is't most certain?

SECOND MESSENGER
As certain as I know the sun is fire.
Where have you lurked, that you make doubt of it?
Ne'er through an arch so hurried the blown tide   48
As the recomforted through th' gates. Why, hark you!   49
      Trumpets, hautboys, drums beat, all together.
The trumpets, sackbuts, psalteries, and fifes,   50
Tabors and cymbals, and the shouting Romans,   51
Make the sun dance. Hark you!   *A shout within.*

MENENIUS   This is good news.
I will go meet the ladies. This Volumnia
Is worth of consuls, senators, patricians,
A city full; of tribunes, such as you,
A sea and land full. You have prayed well today.
This morning for ten thousand of your throats
I'd not have given a doit. Hark, how they joy!   58
      Sound still, with the shouts.

SICINIUS
First, the gods bless you for your tidings!
Next, accept my thankfulness.

SECOND MESSENGER
Sir, we have all great cause to give great thanks.

SICINIUS   They are near the city?

SECOND MESSENGER   Almost at point to enter.   63

SICINIUS   We'll meet them, and help the joy.   *Exeunt.*

[5.5]

Enter two Senators with ladies [Volumnia, Virgilia, Valeria] passing over the stage, with other lords.

FIRST SENATOR
Behold our patroness, the life of Rome!
Call all your tribes together, praise the gods,
And make triumphant fires! Strew flowers before them!
Unshout the noise that banished Marcius;   4
Repeal him with the welcome of his mother.   5
Cry, "Welcome, ladies, welcome!"

ALL   Welcome, ladies, welcome!
      A flourish with drums and trumpets. [Exeunt.]

8 **stay upon** await   **10 condition** nature   **19 engine** heavy instrument of war, such as a battering ram   **20 corslet** body armor   **21 a knell** the tolling of a bell announcing a death.   **hum** (An expression of anger.)   **battery** artillery assault.   **22 state** chair of state. **as . . . Alexander** as though he were a statue of Alexander the Great (who lived after Coriolanus).   **23 finished . . . bidding** i.e., as good as done once he orders it.   **23–4 wants nothing** lacks no attribute   **24 throne** be enthroned   **25 mercy** i.e., he lacks mercy   **26 in the character** to the life.   **29 long of** owing to   **37 hale** drag   **39 death by inches** slow and lingering death.   **41 dislodged** gone from their camp   **43 th'expulsion of the Tarquins** i.e., the expulsion of Rome's last kings and beginning of the Republic.

48 **arch** i.e., arch of a bridge, such as London Bridge.   **blown** swollen, driven by the wind   **49.1** *hautboys* oboelike instruments   **50 sackbuts** early trombones.   **psalteries** stringed instruments played by plucking the strings   **51 Tabors** small drums   **58 doit** very small coin.   **63 at point** ready
5.5. Location: Rome. A street near the gate, seemingly continuous from the previous scene; the time is virtually continuous.
4 **Unshout** Recall, or, cancel by more shouting   **5 Repeal** recall

[5.6]

Enter Tullus Aufidius, with attendants.

AUFIDIUS
Go tell the lords o'th' city I am here.
Deliver them this paper. [*He gives a paper.*] Having read
    it,
Bid them repair to th' marketplace, where I,   3
Even in theirs and in the commons' ears,
Will vouch the truth of it. Him I accuse   5
The city ports by this hath entered and   6
Intends t'appear before the people, hoping
To purge himself with words. Dispatch.
                                    [*Exeunt attendants.*]

*Enter three or four Conspirators of Aufidius's
    faction.*

                                        Most welcome!

FIRST CONSPIRATOR
How is it with our general?
AUFIDIUS   Even so
As with a man by his own alms empoisoned
And with his charity slain.
SECOND CONSPIRATOR   Most noble sir,   11
If you do hold the same intent wherein
You wished us parties, we'll deliver you   13
Of your great danger.
AUFIDIUS   Sir, I cannot tell.   14
We must proceed as we do find the people.
THIRD CONSPIRATOR
The people will remain uncertain whilst
Twixt you there's difference, but the fall of either   17
Makes the survivor heir of all.
AUFIDIUS   I know it,
And my pretext to strike at him admits   19
A good construction. I raised him, and I pawned   20
Mine honor for his truth; who, being so heightened,   21
He watered his new plants with dews of flattery,   22
Seducing so my friends; and to this end
He bowed his nature, never known before
But to be rough, unswayable, and free.   25
THIRD CONSPIRATOR   Sir, his stoutness   26
When he did stand for consul, which he lost
By lack of stooping—
AUFIDIUS   That I would have spoke of.   28
Being banished for 't, he came unto my hearth,
Presented to my knife his throat. I took him,

Made him joint servant with me, gave him way   31
In all his own desires; nay, let him choose
Out of my files, his projects to accomplish,   33
My best and freshest men; served his designments   34
In mine own person; holp to reap the fame
Which he did end all his; and took some pride   36
To do myself this wrong—till at the last
I seemed his follower, not partner, and
He waged me with his countenance, as if   39
I had been mercenary.
FIRST CONSPIRATOR   So he did, my lord.   40
The army marveled at it, and, in the last,   41
When he had carried Rome and that we looked   42
For no less spoil than glory—
AUFIDIUS   There was it   43
For which my sinews shall be stretched upon him.   44
At a few drops of women's rheum, which are   45
As cheap as lies, he sold the blood and labor
Of our great action. Therefore shall he die,
And I'll renew me in his fall. But hark!   48
            *Drums and trumpets sounds,
            with great shouts of the people.*
FIRST CONSPIRATOR
Your native town you entered like a post,   49
And had no welcomes home; but he returns,
Splitting the air with noise.
SECOND CONSPIRATOR   And patient fools,
Whose children he hath slain, their base throats tear
With giving him glory.
THIRD CONSPIRATOR   Therefore, at your vantage,   53
Ere he express himself or move the people
With what he would say, let him feel your sword,
Which we will second. When he lies along,   56
After your way his tale pronounced shall bury   57
His reasons with his body.
AUFIDIUS   Say no more.   58
Here come the lords.

            Enter the Lords of the city.

ALL LORDS
You are most welcome home.
AUFIDIUS   I have not deserved it.
But, worthy lords, have you with heed perused   61
What I have written to you?
ALL LORDS   We have.
FIRST LORD   And grieve to hear 't.
What faults he made before the last, I think   65

5.6. Location: Corioles. A Volscian city. (Plutarch sets this action in
Antium, Aufidius's "native town" [in line 49], but in line 94 and
following, the place is Corioles.)
3 repair go   **5 vouch** affirm.   **Him** He whom   **6 ports** gates.   **by
this** by this time   **11 with his** by his own   **13 parties** as allies, partners   **14 Of** from   **17 difference** disagreement   **19 pretext** intention,
motive   **20 construction** interpretation.   **pawned** pledged   **21 truth**
loyalty.   **heightened** raised to power   **22 He . . . flattery** i.e., he
bestowed flattering honors on those who now depended on him for
patronage   **25 free** plainspoken.   **26 stoutness** obstinacy   **28 That . . .
of** I was about to mention that.

31 joint servant partner   **33 files** ranks, troops   **34 designments**
designs, enterprises   **36 end all his** gather in as all his own
39 waged remunerated.   **countenance** patronage, favor   **40 mercenary** a hired soldier.   **41 last** end   **42 had carried** had virtually overcome, or, might have overcome   **43 There was it** That was the thing
44 my . . . upon I shall exert all my strength against   **45 rheum** i.e.,
tears   **48 renew me** restore my reputation   **49 post** messenger
53 at your vantage seizing your opportune moment   **56 along**
prostrate   **57 After . . . pronounced** telling your own version of the
story   **58 reasons** justifications   **61 with heed** carefully   **65 made**
committed

Might have found easy fines; but there to end   66
Where he was to begin, and give away   67
The benefit of our levies, answering us   68
With our own charge, making a treaty where   69
There was a yielding—this admits no excuse.   70

AUFIDIUS   He approaches. You shall hear him.

Enter Coriolanus, marching with drum and colors;
the commoners being with him.

CORIOLANUS

Hail, lords! I am returned your soldier,
No more infected with my country's love   73
Than when I parted hence, but still subsisting   74
Under your great command. You are to know
That prosperously I have attempted, and   76
With bloody passage led your wars even to
The gates of Rome. Our spoils we have brought home
Doth more than counterpoise a full third part   79
The charges of the action. We have made peace   80
With no less honor to the Antiates
Than shame to th' Romans; and we here deliver,
Subscribed by th' consuls and patricians,   83
Together with the seal o'th' Senate, what
We have compounded on.   [*He offers a document.*]   85

AUFIDIUS   Read it not, noble lords,
But tell the traitor, in the highest degree
He hath abused your powers.

CORIOLANUS   "Traitor"? How now?

AUFIDIUS   Ay, traitor, Marcius.

CORIOLANUS   "Marcius"?

AUFIDIUS

Ay, Marcius, Caius Marcius. Dost thou think
I'll grace thee with that robbery, thy stol'n name
Coriolanus, in Corioles?
You lords and heads o'th' state, perfidiously
He has betrayed your business and given up,
For certain drops of salt, your city Rome—   97
I say your city—to his wife and mother,
Breaking his oath and resolution like
A twist of rotten silk, never admitting   100
Counsel o'th' war, but at his nurse's tears   101
He whined and roared away your victory,
That pages blushed at him and men of heart   103
Looked wond'ring each at other.

CORIOLANUS   Hear'st thou, Mars?

AUFIDIUS   Name not the god, thou boy of tears!

CORIOLANUS   Ha?

AUFIDIUS   No more.   107

CORIOLANUS

Measureless liar, thou hast made my heart
Too great for what contains it. "Boy"? O slave!   109
Pardon me, lords, 'tis the first time that ever
I was forced to scold. Your judgments, my grave lords,
Must give this cur the lie; and his own notion—   112
Who wears my stripes impressed upon him, that
Must bear my beating to his grave—shall join
To thrust the lie unto him.

FIRST LORD   Peace, both, and hear me speak.

CORIOLANUS

Cut me to pieces, Volsces. Men and lads,
Stain all your edges on me. "Boy"? False hound!   118
If you have writ your annals true, 'tis there   119
That, like an eagle in a dovecote, I   120
Fluttered your Volscians in Corioles.
Alone I did it. "Boy"!

AUFIDIUS   Why, noble lords,
Will you be put in mind of his blind fortune,   123
Which was your shame, by this unholy braggart,
'Fore your own eyes and ears?

ALL CONSPIRATORS   Let him die for't.

ALL PEOPLE   Tear him to pieces!—Do it presently!—   126
He killed my son!—My daughter!—He killed my
cousin Marcus!—He killed my father!

SECOND LORD   Peace, ho! No outrage! Peace!
The man is noble, and his fame folds in   130
This orb o'th' earth. His last offenses to us
Shall have judicious hearing. Stand, Aufidius,   132
And trouble not the peace.

CORIOLANUS   Oh, that I had him,
With six Aufidiuses, or more, his tribe,
To use my lawful sword!

AUFIDIUS   Insolent villain!

ALL CONSPIRATORS   Kill, kill, kill, kill, kill him!
                    Draw the Conspirators, and kill Marcius,
                          who falls. Aufidius stands on him.

LORDS   Hold, hold, hold, hold!

AUFIDIUS

My noble masters, hear me speak.

FIRST LORD   Oh, Tullus!

SECOND LORD

Thou hast done a deed whereat valor will weep.   139

THIRD LORD

Tread not upon him, masters. All be quiet;
Put up your swords.

AUFIDIUS

My lords, when you shall know—as in this rage,
Provoked by him, you cannot—the great danger

---

66 easy fines light penalties   **66–7 there . . . begin** to give up right at the threshold of his potentially greatest victory   **68 levies** expenses incurred in raising an army   **68–9 answering . . . charge** rewarding us with our own expenses, or, answering our protests with the claim that he acted with the authority we had given him in charge   **70 yielding** surrender   **73 infected with** influenced by. (But with the suggestion of contamination.)   **74 hence** i.e., from Antium. **subsisting** continuing   **76 prosperously . . . attempted** my warlike enterprise has been prosperous   **79 Doth . . . part** outweigh by a full third   **80 charges** costs   **83 Subscribed** signed   **85 compounded** agreed   **97 certain . . . salt** some particular tears (i.e., those of Volumnia and Virgilia)   **100 twist** twisted thread   **100–1 never . . . war** never taking counsel from other officers   **103 heart** courage

107 No more i.e., (1) No more than a boy (2) Do not dare to ally yourself with Mars.   **109 Too . . . it** swollen with rage so that my breast cannot contain it.   **112 notion** understanding, sense of the truth   **118 edges** swords   **119 there** recorded there   **120 dovecote** pigeon house   **123 blind fortune** gift of Fortune, the blind goddess; mere good luck   **126 presently** immediately.   **130 folds in** overspreads, enwraps   **132 judicious** judicial.   **Stand** Stop   **139 whereat** at which

Which this man's life did owe you, you'll rejoice
That he is thus cut off. Please it Your Honors
To call me to your Senate, I'll deliver
Myself your loyal servant, or endure
Your heaviest censure.

FIRST LORD   Bear from hence his body,
And mourn you for him. Let him be regarded
As the most noble corpse that ever herald
Did follow to his urn.

SECOND LORD   His own impatience
Takes from Aufidius a great part of blame.

144

146

151

Let's make the best of it.

AUFIDIUS   My rage is gone,
And I am struck with sorrow. Take him up.
Help, three o'th' chiefest soldiers; I'll be one.
Beat thou the drum that it speak mournfully;
Trail your steel pikes. Though in this city he
Hath widowed and unchilded many a one,
Which to this hour bewail the injury,
Yet he shall have a noble memory.
Assist.   *Exeunt, bearing the body of Marcius.*
                              A dead march sounded.

155

157

160

---

144 did owe you had for you, held in store for you   **146 deliver** show, demonstrate   **151 impatience** rage

155 be one i.e., be the fourth.   **157 Trail . . . pikes** Carry your lances reversed with the point trailing along the ground (as a sign of mourning).   **160 memory** memorial.

Appendix 1

Canon, Dates,
and Early Texts

By "canon" we mean a listing of plays that can be ascribed to Shakespeare on the basis of reliable evidence. Such evidence is either "internal," derived from matters of style or poetics in the plays themselves (see General Introduction), or "external," derived from outside the play. The latter includes any reference by Shakespeare's contemporaries to his plays, any allusions in the plays themselves to contemporary events, the entering of Shakespeare's plays for publication in the Stationers' Register (S. R.), actual publication of the plays, and records of early performances. These matters of external evidence are also essential in attempting to date the plays.

The greatest single source of information is the First Folio text of Shakespeare's plays, sponsored by Shakespeare's fellow actors John Heminges and Henry Condell and published in 1623. It contains all the plays included in this present edition of Shakespeare except *Pericles* and *The Two Noble Kinsmen* and offers strong presumptive evidence of being a complete and accurate compilation of Shakespeare's work by men who knew him and cherished his memory. It provides the only texts we have for these eighteen plays: *The Comedy of Errors, The Two Gentlemen of Verona, The Taming of the Shrew, 1 Henry VI, King John, As You Like It, Twelfth Night, Julius Caesar, All's Well That Ends Well, Measure for Measure, Timon of Athens, Macbeth, Antony and Cleopatra, Coriolanus, Cymbeline, The Winter's Tale, The Tempest,* and *Henry VIII.* This includes nearly half the known canon of Shakespeare's plays. Our debt to the First Folio is incalculable and confirms our impression of its reliability.

The information of the First Folio is further confirmed by contemporary references. In 1598, a cleric and minor writer of the period named Francis Meres wrote in his *Palladis Tamia, Wit's Treasury*:

As the soul of Euphorbus was thought to live in Pythagoras, so the sweet, witty soul of Ovid lives in mellifluous and honey-tongued Shakespeare: witness his *Venus and Adonis,* his *Lucrece,* his sugared sonnets among his private friends, etc.

As Plautus and Seneca are accounted the best for comedy and tragedy among the Latins, so Shakespeare among the English is the most excellent in both kinds for the stage; for comedy, witness his *Gentlemen of Verona,* his *Errors,* his *Love's Labor's Lost,* his *Love's Labor's Won,* his *Midsummer's Night Dream,* and his *Merchant of Venice*; for tragedy his *Richard the II, Richard the III, Henry the IV, King John, Titus Andronicus* and his *Romeo and Juliet.*

Though this list was meant to offer praise, not to be an exhaustive catalogue, it is remarkably full. If the tantalizing *Love's Labor's Won* refers to *The Taming of the Shrew,* Meres's list of comedies is substantially complete down almost to 1598. It does not include the comedies that Shakespeare appears to have written around that date or soon afterward: *Much Ado About Nothing, The Merry Wives of Windsor, As You Like It,* and *Twelfth Night.* Meres correctly names all of Shakespeare's history plays except the *Henry VI* trilogy and of course the later histories, *Henry V* (1599) and *Henry VIII* (1613). He names both of Shakespeare's early tragedies that are not based on English history: *Titus Andronicus* and *Romeo and Juliet.* He tells us about the important nondramatic poems, which did not appear in the First Folio, since that volume is devoted exclusively to plays. Not much can be made of the order in which Meres names the plays, however, for we learn from other sources that *Richard III* clearly precedes *Richard II* in date of composition and that *King John* precedes the *Henry IV* plays.

Other writers of the 1590s add further confirming evidence. John Weever, in an epigram "*Ad Gulielmum Shakespeare,*" published in 1599, refers to "Rose-cheeked Adonis" and "Fair fire-hot Venus," to "Chaste Lucretia" and "Proud lust-stung Tarquin," and to "*Romeo, Richard—* more whose names I know not." Richard Barnfield, in

Poems in Divers Humors (1598), praises Shakespeare for "*Venus*" and "*Lucrece.*" Both Thomas Nashe and Robert Greene seemingly refer to the *Henry VI* plays, missing from Meres's list. Nashe, in his *Pierce Penniless* (1592), speculates how it would "have joyed brave Talbot (the terror of the French) to think that after he had lain two hundred years in his tomb, he should triumph again on the stage." Talbot is the hero of *1 Henry VI*, and we know of no other play on the subject. Greene, in his *Greene's Groats-worth of Wit* (1592), lashes out at an "upstart crow, beautified with our feathers, that with his '*Tiger's heart wrapped in a player's hide*' supposes he is as well able to bombast out a blank verse as the best of you, and, being an absolute *Johannes Factotum*, is in his own conceit the only Shake-scene in a country." The line about "Tiger's heart" is deliberately misquoted from *3 Henry VI*, 1.4.137. (It is possible that this famous attack on Shakespeare was actually written not by Greene himself but by Henry Chettle, his literary executor.)

Titus Andronicus (c. 1589–1592)

On February 6, 1594, "a Noble Roman Historye of Tytus Andronicus" was entered in the Stationers' Register, the official record book of the London Company of Stationers (booksellers and printers), to John Danter, along with "the ballad thereof." The entry probably, though not certainly, refers to Shakespeare's play. Later in that same year, at any rate, Danter published a Quarto volume with the following title:

THE MOST LAMentable Romaine Tragedie of Titus Andronicus: As it was Plaide by the Right Honourable the Earle of *Darbie*, Earle of *Pembrooke*, and Earle of *Sussex* their Seruants. LONDON, Printed by Iohn Danter, and are to be sold by *Edward White* & *Thomas Millington*, at the little North doore of Paules at the signe of the Gunne. 1594.

This text seems to have been set from Shakespeare's manuscript in an unpolished state. A Second Quarto appeared in 1600, adding the name of the Lord Chamberlain's company to those who had acted the play. It was set up from a slightly damaged copy of the First Quarto. Although the Second Quarto made some improvements, these were probably by the compositor and not the author, or may have been made in a press-corrected Q1 no longer extant (since we have only one copy today). A Third Quarto (1611), set up from the second, contributed new errors. The First Folio text of 1623 was derived from the Third Quarto, but with an authentic added scene (3.2) from a manuscript source and with additional stage directions that suggest a playhouse playbook. One theory is that the copy used by the Folio printers, the Third Quarto, had been corrected from an annotated copy of the

Second Quarto that had been used as a playbook, or perhaps directly from the playbook. Despite these improvements, the First Quarto clearly remains the authoritative text except for 3.2.

The date of *Titus* must be prior to 1594. Philip Henslowe's *Diary* records a performance of a "Titus & Ondronicus" by the Earl of Sussex's men on January 24, 1594, and indicates it was "ne" or new. This could certainly mean a new play, but it could also mean it was newly revised or newly acquired. Since the players on this occasion, Sussex's men, were listed third on the 1594 title page after Derby's and Pembroke's men, they may just have acquired *Titus*. Two allusions may point to an earlier date: *A Knack to Know a Knave* (performed in 1592) and *The Troublesome Reign of King John* (published 1591) may contain echoes of *Titus*, though the text of the former is memorially reconstructed and could therefore contain a remembered reference up to the date of publication in 1594. Stylistic considerations favor a date around 1589–1592 or even earlier.

The authorship of *Titus* would appear at first glance to belong entirely to Shakespeare. Although the 1594 Quarto does not mention Shakespeare's name (a common omission in such early texts, especially since the author was as yet relatively unknown), Francis Meres in his *Palladis Tamia*, 1598, assigns the play to Shakespeare, and the Folio editors include it in the 1623 edition. Doubts began to arise, however, when Edward Ravenscroft observed in 1687 that he had been "told by some anciently conversant with the stage that it was not originally his, but brought by a private author to be acted, and he only gave some master touches to one or two of the principal parts or characters." This remark touched off a controversy that continues today; for example, J. Dover Wilson in his New Cambridge Shakespeare (1948), J. C. Maxwell in his Arden edition (1953), and Jonathan Bate in his Arden 3 edition (1995). Plausible arguments have been brought forward that George Peele may have contributed scenes 1 through 3 of Act 1, scenes 1 and 2 of Act 2, and scene 1 of Act 4. Ravenscroft's testimonial is suspect, to be sure, both because it came one hundred years after the fact and because Ravenscroft himself was embarked on an adaptation of *Titus* and so might have wished to denigrate the original. The efforts at assigning portions of the play to Shakespeare's contemporaries have sometimes been motivated by a wish to rescue Shakespeare's reputation from the violent and garish effects of this play. Most recent criticism prefers to regard the play as an interesting experiment in revenge tragedy by a young artist, with many shrewdly characteristic Shakespearean touches. Even so, joint authorship remains a lively possibility. See the Introduction to the play in this volume.

Henslowe's *Diary* records the performance of a "Tittus & Vespacia" on April 11, 1592, a "ne" play by Strange's men. Despite the similarity of the title, this play was probably on an independent subject.

Romeo and Juliet (1594–1596)

A corrupt and unregistered Quarto of *Romeo and Juliet* appeared in 1597 with the following title:

AN excellent conceited Tragedie OF Romeo and Iuliet, As it hath been often (with great applause) plaid publiquely, by the right Honourable the L. of *Hunsdon* his Seruants. LONDON, Printed by Iohn Danter. 1597.

This edition, intended no doubt to capitalize on the play's great popularity, seems to have been memorially reconstructed by two or more actors (probably those playing Romeo and Paris), and possibly thereafter to have been used as a playbook. Its appearance seems to have caused the issuance two years later of a clearly authoritative version:

THE MOST EXcellent and lamentable Tragedie, of Romeo and *Iuliet. Newly corrected, augmented, and amended*: As it hath bene sundry times publiquely acted, by the right Honourable the Lord Chamberlaine his Seruants. LONDON Printed by Thomas Creede, for Cuthbert Burby, and are to be sold at his shop neare the Exchange. 1599.

This text is some 800 lines longer than the first and corrects errors in that earlier version. It seems at one point, however, to have been contaminated by the First Quarto, as though the manuscript source for the Second Quarto (probably the author's rough draft) was defective at some point. A passage from 1.2.53 to 1.3.34 was apparently set directly from the First Quarto. (On this matter, see George W. Williams's old-spelling edition of the play, Duke Univ. Press, 1964.) Q1 may also have influenced Q2 in some other isolated instances. Despite this contamination, however, the Second Quarto is the authoritative text, except for the passage of direct indebtedness to Q1. Q2 served as the basis for the Third Quarto (1609), which in turn served as copy for the Fourth Quarto (undated, but placed in 1622) and the First Folio of 1623. A Fifth Quarto appeared in 1637. The Folio text may embody a few authoritative readings of its own, perhaps by way of reference to a theatrical manuscript.

Francis Meres, in his *Palladis Tamia*, 1598, assigns the play to Shakespeare. So does John Weever in his *Epigrams* of 1599. Internal evidence on dating is not reliable. The Nurse observes that "'Tis since the earthquake now eleven years" (1.3.24); however, it has been discovered that suitable earthquakes occurred in 1580, 1583, 1584, and 1585, giving us a wide choice of dates even if we accept the dubious proposition that the Nurse is speaking accurately. Astronomical reckoning of the position of the moon at the time the play purportedly takes place ("A fortnight and odd days" before Lammastide, August 1, 1.3.16) indicates the year 1596; again, however, we have no reason to assume Shakespeare cared about this sort of internal accuracy. More suggestive perhaps is the argument that Danter's unauthorized publication in 1597 was seeking to exploit a popular new play—one the acting company certainly did not yet wish to see published, since it was a moneymaker. Danter assigns the play to Lord Hunsdon's servants, a name that Shakespeare's company could have used only from July 22, 1596 (when the old Lord Chamberlain, Henry Carey, first Lord Hunsdon, died) to March 17, 1597 (when George Carey, second Lord Hunsdon, was appointed to his father's erstwhile position as Lord Chamberlain). Danter could simply have been using the name of the company at the time he obtained the play, but he may also have indicated performance in late 1596. Danter printed only the first four sheets, but he must have done so by February–March 1597, when his presses were seized. Stylistically, the play is clearly of the "lyric" period of *A Midsummer Night's Dream* and *Richard II*. There are also stylistic affinities to the sonnets and to the narrative poems of 1593–1594. A date between 1594 and 1596 is likely, especially toward the latter end of this period. Whether the play comes before or after *A Midsummer Night's Dream* is, however, a matter of conjecture.

Julius Caesar (1599)

Julius Caesar was first published in the First Folio of 1623. The text is an excellent one, based evidently on a theater playbook or a transcript of it; some theatrical features, such as a provision for the doubling of Cassius and Caius Ligarius, appear to represent a staging configuration that Shakespeare had not anticipated. On the other hand, some stage directions sound authorial, as though Shakespeare's own words had survived into the playbook. Some confusions have survived as well, notably in the handling of Lucilius, Lucius, Titinius, and Pindarus in 4.2. In the Folio, the play is included among the tragedies and entitled *The Tragedy of Julius Caesar*, although the table of contents lists it as *The Life and death of Julius Caesar*.

The play's first performance must have occurred in 1599 or slightly earlier. On September 21, 1599, a Swiss visitor named Thomas Platter crossed the River Thames after lunch with a company of spectators to see "the tragedy of the first Emperor Julius Caesar" performed in a thatched-roofed building. The description fits the Globe, the Rose, and the Swan theaters, but the last of these was not in regular use. The Admiral's men at the Rose are not known to have had a Caesar play, whereas the Chamberlain's men certainly had Shakespeare's play about this time. They had only recently moved from their Theatre in the northeast suburbs of London to the Globe south of the river, and *Julius Caesar* was probably a new play for the occasion.

John Weever, in *The Mirror ofMartyrs* (1601), is surely referring to Shakespeare's play when he describes "the many-headed multitude" listening first to "Brutus' speech, that Caesar was ambitious" and then to "eloquent Mark Antony." (The dedication to Weever's book claims he wrote it "some two years ago," in 1599; however, since this book has been shown to be heavily indebted to a work that first appeared in 1600, Weever's allusion is not as helpful in limiting the date as was once thought.) Ben Jonson's *Every Man in His Humor*, acted in 1599, may also contain allusions to Shakespeare's play. Francis Meres does not mention it in 1598 in his *Palladis Tamia*.

Hamlet (c. 1599–1601)

Like everything else about *Hamlet*, the textual problem is complicated. On July 26, 1602, James Roberts entered in the Stationers' Register, the official record book of the London Company of Stationers (booksellers and printers), "A booke called the Revenge of Hamlett Prince Denmarke as yt was latelie Acted by the Lord Chamberleyne his servantes." For some reason, however, Roberts did not print his copy of *Hamlet* until 1604, by which time the following unauthorized edition had appeared:

THE Tragicall Historie of HAMLET *Prince of Denmarke* By William Shake-speare. As it hath beene diuerse times acted by his Highnesse seruants in the Cittie of London: as also in the two Vniuersities of Cambridge and Oxford, and else-where. At London printed for N. L. [Nicholas Ling] and Iohn Trundell. 1603.

This edition, the First Quarto of *Hamlet*, seems to have been memorially reconstructed by actors who toured the provinces (note the references to Cambridge, Oxford, and so on), with some recollection of an earlier *Hamlet* play (the *Ur-Hamlet*) written before 1589 and acted during the 1590s. The actors seemingly had no recourse to an authoritative manuscript. One of these actors may have played Marcellus and possibly Lucianus and Volti-mand. Their version appears to have been based on an adaptation of the company's original playbook, which itself stood once removed from Shakespeare's working papers by way of an intermediate manuscript. The resulting text is very corrupt, and yet it seems to have affected the more authentic text, because the compositors

of the Second Quarto made use of it, especially when they typeset the first act.

The authorized Quarto of *Hamlet* appeared in 1604. Roberts, the printer, seems to have reached some agreement with Ling, one of the publishers of the First Quarto, for their initials are now paired on the title page:

THE Tragicall Historie of HAMLET, *Prince of Denmarke*. By William Shakespeare. Newly imprinted and enlarged to almost as much againe as it was, according to the true and perfect Coppie. AT LONDON, Printed by I. R. [James Roberts] for N. L. [Nicholas Ling] and are to be sold at his shoppe vnder Saint Dunstons Church in Fleetstreet. 1604.

Some copies of this edition are dated 1605. This text was based seemingly on Shakespeare's own papers, with the bookkeeper's annotations, but is marred by printing errors and is at times contaminated by the First Quarto—presumably, when the printers found Shakespeare's manuscript unreadable. This Second Quarto served as copy for a Third Quarto in 1611, Ling having meanwhile transferred his rights in the play to John Smethwick. A Fourth Quarto, undated but before 1623, was based on the Third.

The First Folio text of 1623 omits more than two hundred lines found in the Second Quarto, yet it supplies some clearly authentic passages. It seems to derive from a transcript of Shakespeare's draft, in which cuts made by the author were observed—cuts made by Shakespeare quite possibly because he knew the draft to be too long for performance and which had either not been marked in the Second Quarto copy or had been ignored there by the compositors. The Folio also incorporates other alterations seemingly made for clarity or in anticipation of performance. To this theatrically motivated transcript, Shakespeare apparently contributed some revisions. Subsequently, this version evidently was copied again by a careless scribe who took many liberties with the text. Typesetting from this inferior manuscript, the Folio compositors occasionally consulted the Fourth Quarto, but not often enough. Thus, even though the Folio supplies some genuine readings, as does the First Quarto when both the Folio and the Second Quarto are wrong, the Second Quarto remains the most authentic version of the text.

Since the text of the Second Quarto is too long to be accommodated in the two hours' traffic of the stage and since it becomes even longer when the words found only in the Folio are added, Shakespeare must have known it would have to be cut for performance and probably marked at least some omissions himself. Since he may have consented to such cuts primarily because of the constraints of time, however, this present edition holds to the view that the passages in question should not be excised from the text we read. The *Hamlet* presented here is doubtless longer than any version ever acted in Shakespeare's day and thus does not represent a script for any actual performance, but it may well represent the play as

Shakespeare wrote it and then expanded it somewhat while also including passages that he may reluctantly have consented to cut for performance. It is also possible that some cuts were artistically intended, but, in the face of real uncertainty in this matter, an editorial policy of inclusion gives to the reader those passages that would otherwise have to be excised or put in an appendix on questionable grounds of authorial "intent."

Hamlet must have been produced before the Stationers' Register entry of July 26, 1602. Francis Meres does not mention the play in 1598 in his *Palladis Tamia*. Gabriel Harvey attributes the "tragedy of Hamlet, Prince of Denmark" to Shakespeare in a marginal note in Harvey's copy of Speght's Chaucer; Harvey acquired the book in 1598, but he could have written the note any time between then and 1601, or even 1603. More helpful in dating is *Hamlet*'s clear reference to the so-called War of the Theaters, the rivalry between the adult actors and the boy actors whose companies had newly revived in 1598–1599 after nearly a decade of inactivity (see 2.2.337–62). The Children of the Chapel Royal began acting at Blackfriars in 1598 and provided such keen competition in 1599–1601 that the adult actors were at times forced to tour the provinces (see *Hamlet*, 2.2.332–62). *Hamlet*'s reference to the rivalry appears, however, only in the Folio text and could represent a late addition. The reference to an "inhibition" imposed on acting companies "by the means of the late innovation" (2.2.332–3), printed in the 1604 Quarto, may possibly refer to the abortive uprising of the Earl of Essex on February 8, 1601, or to a decree issued by the Privy Council on June 22, 1600, restricting London companies to two performances a week in each of two playhouses. Revenge tragedy was also in fashion during these years: John Marston's *Antonio's Revenge*, for example, dates from 1599–1601, and *The Malcontent* is from about the same time or slightly later, though it is hard to tell who influenced whom. *Hamlet*'s apparent indebtedness to John Florio's translation of Montaigne suggests that Shakespeare had access to that work in manuscript before its publication in 1603; the Florio had been registered for publication in 1595 and 1600.

Othello (c. 1603–1604)

On October 6, 1621, Thomas Walkley entered in the Stationers' Register, the official record book of the London Company of Stationers (booksellers and printers), "The Tragedie of Othello, the moore of Venice," and published the play in the following year:

THE Tragoedy of Othello, The Moore of Venice. *As it hath beene diuerse times acted at the* Globe, and at the Black-Friers, by *his Maiesties Seruants. Written by* VVilliam Shakespeare. LONDON, Printed by N. O. [Nicholas Okes] for *Thomas Walkley*, and are to be sold at his shop, at the Eagle and Child, in Brittans Bursse. 1622.

This text of this Quarto is a good one, based probably on a scribal transcript of Shakespeare's working manuscript, although it is some one hundred and sixty lines shorter than the Folio text of 1623, mostly in scattered small omissions. The Folio text may have been derived (via an intermediate transcript) from a revision of the original authorial manuscript, in which Shakespeare himself copied over his work and made a large number of synonymous or nearly synonymous changes as he did so. These papers, edited by someone else to remove profanity as required by law and introducing other stylistic changes in the process, seemingly became the basis of the playbook and also of the Folio text. E. A. J. Honigmann (*The Texts of "Othello" and Shakespearian Revision*, 1996) proposes that Ralph Crane prepared a transcript to serve as copy for the Folio text, though not all scholars have agreed.

The textual situation is thus complex. The Folio text appears to contain a significant number of authorial changes, but it was also worked on by one or more sophisticating scribes and by compositors whose changes are sometimes hard to distinguish from those of Shakespeare. The Quarto text was printed by a printing establishment that was not known for careful work but does stand close in some ways to a Shakespearean original. Editorially, then, the Folio is the copy text, and its readings are to be preferred when the Quarto is not clearly correct and especially when the Folio gives us genuinely new words, but the Quarto's readings demand careful consideration when the Folio text may be suspected of mechanical error (e.g., the shortening of words in full lines) or compositorial substitution of alternative forms, normalizations, and easy adjustments of meter. There are times when the Folio's compositor may have been misled by nearby words or letters in his copy. And, because the Folio's stage directions are probably scribal, attention should be paid to those in the Quarto.

According to a Revels account that was suspected of being a forgery soon after its publication in 1842 but is now generally accepted, the earliest mention of the play is on "Hallamas Day, being the first of Nouembar," 1604, when "the Kings Maiesties plaiers" performed "A Play in the Banketinge house att Whit Hall Called The Moor of Venis." Possible echoes of *Othello* in *The Honest Whore, Part I*, by Thomas Dekker and Thomas Middleton (1604) and in Richard Knolles's *History of the Turks* (1603) help fix a forward date of composition. Francis Meres does not list the play in 1598. On stylistic grounds, the play is usually dated in 1603 or 1604, although arguments are sometimes presented for a date as early as 1601 or 1602.

King Lear (c. 1605–1606)

On November 26, 1607, Nathaniel Butter and John Busby entered in the Stationers' Register, the official record book of the London Company of Stationers (booksellers and printers), "A booke called. Master William Shakespeare his historye of Kinge Lear, as yt was played before the Kinges maiestie at Whitehall vppon Sainct Stephens night at Christmas Last, by his maiesties servantes playinge vsually at the Globe on the Banksyde." Next year appeared the following Quarto:

M. William Shak-speare: HIS True Chronicle Historie of the life and death of King LEAR and his three Daughters. *With the vnfortunate life* of Edgar, *sonne* and heire to the Earle of Gloster, and his sullen and assumed humor of Tom of Bedlam: *As it was played before the Kings Maiestie at Whitehall vpon S.* Stephans *night in Christmas Hollidayes.* By his Maiesties seruants playing vsually at the Gloabe on the Bancke-side. LONDON, Printed for *Nathaniel Butter*, and are to be sold at his shop in *Pauls* Church-yard at the signe of the Pide Bull neere St. *Austins* Gate. 1608.

This Quarto is often called the "Pied Bull" Quarto in reference to its place of sale. Twelve copies exist today, in ten different "states," because proofreading was being carried on while the sheets were being run off in the press; the copies variously combine corrected and uncorrected sheets. A Second Quarto, printed in 1619 by William Jaggard for Thomas Pavier with the fraudulent date of 1608, was based on a copy of the First Quarto, combining corrected and uncorrected sheets.

The First Folio text of 1623 may have been typeset from a playbook cut for performance or from a transcript of such a manuscript, and the playbook in its turn appears to have been based on Shakespeare's fair copy (with revisions) of his first draft. The Folio compositors also almost certainly consulted a copy of the Second Quarto from time to time or may have typeset directly from this Quarto as annotated with reference to Shakespeare's fair copy. In writing the fair copy, Shakespeare may have marked some three hundred lines for deletion, but it is possible that he did so chiefly to shorten the time of performance. He also seems to have added some one hundred lines, an apparent contradiction in view of the need for cutting, but possibly dictated by Shakespeare's developing sense of his play. It is also possible that the cuts were carried out by someone else in the preparation of the playbook.

The First Quarto, on the other hand, appears to have been printed from Shakespeare's unrevised and evidently untidy working papers. It is often corrupt, owing in part to type shortages, compositorial uncertainties with the manuscript, and other difficulties in Nicholas Okes's shop. Still, in some matters—especially variants indifferent in meaning (such as *an/if* or *thine/thy*)— the First Quarto may be closer to Shakespeare's preferences than the Folio, behind which are several stages of transmission.

This edition agrees with most recent students of the *Lear* text that the Folio represents a theatrical revision, in which the cuts were devised for performance by Shakespeare's company and quite possibly by Shakespeare himself as a member of that company. The case for artistic preference in the making of those cuts, on the other hand, is less certain and may have been overstated. Many of the cuts have the effect of shortening scenes, especially in the latter half of the play. Some scenes, like 3.6, show open gaps as a result of the cutting: Lear's "Then let them anatomize Regan" (line 75) implies the trial of Goneril as it is dramatized in the First Quarto but cut from the Folio. Other omissions also read like expedients, although they can also be explained by a hypothesis of literary and theatrical rewriting; if Shakespeare himself undertook the cutting, he would presumably do so as expertly as possible. The fact that the Folio text gives almost no rewritten speeches may suggest that the large cuts were motivated by the need for shortening. This edition holds to the principle that it is unwise to omit the material cut from the Folio text, since we cannot be sure that Shakespeare would have shortened the text had there been no external constraints. At the same time, the added material in the Folio is clearly his and belongs in his conception of the play. The resulting text is a conflation, but one that avoids cutting material that Shakespeare may well have regretted having to excise.

The Stationers' Register entry for November 26, 1607, describes a performance at court on the previous St. Stephen's night, December 26, 1606. The title page of the First Quarto confirms this performance on St. Stephen's night. Such a performance at court was not likely to have been the first, however. Shakespeare's repeated use of Samuel Harsnett's *Declaration of Egregious Popish Impostures*, registered on March 16, 1603, sets an early limit for composition of the play. Other circumstances point to composition of the Quarto text in 1605 or 1606. In May 1605, an old play called *The True Chronicle History of King Leir* was entered in the Stationers' Register as a "Tragecall historie," a phrase possibly suggesting the influence of Shakespeare's play, since the old *King Leir* does not end tragically. Moreover, the title page of the old *King Leir*, issued in 1605, proclaims the text to be "as it hath bene diuers and sundry times lately acted." In view of the unlikelihood that such an old play (written before 1594) would be revived in 1605, scholars have suggested that the title page was the publisher's way of trying to capitalize on the recent popularity of Shakespeare's play. In this case, the likeliest date for the composition of Shakespeare's *King Lear* would be in the winter of 1604–1605. Shakespeare certainly used the old *King Leir* as a chief source, but he need not have waited for its publication in 1605 if, as seems perfectly plausible, his company owned the playbook. This hypothesis of the publication of the old *King Leir* after performances of Shakespeare's play must do battle, however, with indications that Shakespeare did not write *King Lear* until late 1605 or 1606. Gloucester's mentioning of "These late eclipses in the sun and moon" (1.2.106) seems to refer to an eclipse of the moon in September and of the sun in October 1605.

There may be echoes in the First Quarto of *King Lear* of *Eastward Ho!* by George Chapman, Ben Jonson, and John Marston, written in early 1605, and *Miseries of Enforced Marriage*, written by mid-1605. *King Lear* may allude to concerns at court about the King's frequent absences for hunting, about monopolies, the giving away of knighthoods, the King's need of money, and the like, all of which would have seemed pertinent in 1605–1606. The Folio revisions may date from some time around 1610, according to the editors of the Oxford Shakespeare.

Macbeth (c. 1606–1607)

Macbeth was first printed in the First Folio of 1623. It was set up from a playbook or a transcript of one. The text is unusually short and seems to have been cut for reasons of censorship or for some special performance. Moreover, all of 3.5 and parts of 4.1 (39–43, 125–32) appear to be interpolations, containing songs from Thomas Middleton's *The Witch* (c.1609–1616). Middleton may have been responsible for other alterations and additions.

Simon Forman, in his manuscript *The Book of Plays and Notes thereof per Formans for Common Policy*, records the first known performance of *Macbeth* on April 20, 1611, at the Globe Theatre. The play must have been in existence by 1607, however, for allusions to it seemingly occur in *Lingua* and *The Puritan* (both published in 1607) and in *The Knight of the Burning Pestle* (probably acted in 1607). On the other hand, the play itself seemingly alludes to James I's royal succession in 1603, to his touching for "the king's evil" (see 4.3.147), and to the trial of the notorious Gunpowder Plot conspirators in March 1606. The interpolations from Middleton's *The Witch* are probably from a later date, perhaps after 1613.

Timon of Athens (c. 1605–1608)

Timon of Athens first appeared in the First Folio of 1623. The text seems to have been based on an unusually early draft of the author's papers, with manifest inconsistencies still present that would have been straightened out in a final draft. If Thomas Middleton was coauthor of the play with Shakespeare, as seems very likely (see play Introduction), the collaboration might have contributed to the discrepancies about the value of money and the like. The play seems to have been a last-minute substitution in the Folio, to replace *Troilus and Cressida* when, for some reason (probably copyright difficulties), that play had to be removed from its original position following *Romeo and Juliet*. The Folio editors possibly had not intended to use *Timon* at all. The manuscript used by the printers seems to have been copied over in places by a second hand, as though the manuscript was too illegible for the printer to use. H. J. Oliver's suggestion (in his Arden edition of 1959, reprinted 1977) that Ralph Crane acted as transcriber has not found general acceptance.

Dating of the play is unusually difficult. No records of performances exist from the early seventeenth century; nor is there any trace of the play until it was registered for publication on November 8, 1623. Stylistically, it seems close to the late tragedies. Its pessimism reminds us of *King Lear,* and its use of Plutarch suggests *Antony and Cleopatra.*

Antony and Cleopatra (1606–1607)

On May 20, 1608, Edward Blount entered in the Stationers' Register, the official record book of the London Company of Stationers (booksellers and printers), "A booke Called. Anthony. and Cleopatra," along with "A booke called. The booke of Pericles prynce of Tyre." Blount was friendly with Shakespeare's company, and his entry may have been a "staying entry" designed to forestall unauthorized publication of these texts. If so, the tactic did not succeed with *Pericles,* issued in 1609 by another publisher, but it did succeed with *Antony and Cleopatra.* The play was first printed in the First Folio of 1623. It is a good text, set evidently from Shakespeare's own draft in a more finished state than most of his working papers, or possibly from a transcript of those papers, though not yet prepared to be a playbook.

The year 1608 is thus the latest possible date for *Antony and Cleopatra.* Evidently, it was written in 1606–1607, however, for a "newly altered" edition in 1607 of Samuel Daniel's play *Cleopatra* seems to have been influenced by Shakespeare's play. Shakespeare himself had probably consulted the original edition of *Cleopatra,* published in 1594, or the slightly revised edition of 1599, but Daniel's more thorough revision in 1607 shows signs of his having seen Shakespeare's play in the interim. Also, a play by Barnabe Barnes called *The Devil's Charter* (1607) may contain a parody of Cleopatra's death by asps. Although the printed text of this play advertises corrections and augmentations that could postdate a court performance in February 1607, recent scholarship favors the likelihood that Barnes saw *Antony and Cleopatra* before that—perhaps in late 1606.

Coriolanus (c. 1608)

Coriolanus was first printed in the First Folio of 1623. Its text was perhaps set from a transcript of the playbook that clarified Shakespeare's stage directions while also preserving some authorial flavor in them and some Shakespearean spellings. Although printing errors are numerous, they are, for the most part, easy to correct. Dating of the play is uncertain. No early performance is on record. The late style and some possible allusions point to sometime around 1608. Menenius's fable of the belly (1.1.94 ff.) is probably indebted to William Camden's *Remains*, published 1605. The demonstrations of the plebeians about distribution of grain may allude to the Midland riots of 1607–1608. Echoes of the play may appear in Robert Armin's *The Italian Taylor and His Boy* and in Ben Jonson's *Epicene*, both from 1609. Thus, a date in 1608 is plausible but only approximate.

Appendix 2

Sources

Titus Andronicus

We do not possess today any work that Shakespeare and (probably) his collaborator could have used for their immediate source in writing *Titus Andronicus.* An eighteenth-century chapbook called *The History of Titus Andronicus,* once thought to provide a reliable account of a prose original to which the dramatists had access, has now been shown to be an expansion of the story based on a ballad of 1594 which in turn was modeled on the extant play. Some scholars once argued that the Stationers' Register entry in 1594 by the printer John Danter for his publication of "a Noble Roman Historye of Tytus Andronicus" with "the ballad thereof" refers to a lost prose account. This hypothesis seems no longer tenable. Danter did, after all, publish Shakespeare's play in that same year, and the ballad appears to owe some of its details to the play. The existence of a prose *History of Titus* when the play was written remains nothing more than a tantalizing possibility. (A ballad of "Titus Andronicus's Complaint," published in 1620 in Richard Johnson's *The Golden Garland of Princely Pleasures*, attests to the continued currency of the story in the early seventeenth century.)

The prose *History* is a fictitious medley of revenge stories inspired by Seneca and Ovid. It is set in the last days of the Roman Empire but contains no recognizable historical characters or events. Titus Andronicus is a Roman senator who defends Rome against the Goths in a protracted ten-year struggle, losing twenty-two of his own sons in the conflict. He slays the Gothic King Tottilius in battle and captures the Queen, Attava. When Tottilius's two sons Alaricus and Abonus continue the assault on Rome, the Roman Emperor wearies of the conflict and resolves to marry Attava against the advice of his general, Andronicus. The Queen, naturally regarding Titus as an enemy, proceeds to obtain powerful positions for her own kinsmen. She succeeds in having Titus banished, but he is recalled by popular insistence. Attava has an affair with her nameless Moorish servant and has a black child by him. Discovery of the child leads to the Moor's banishment, but he, too, is later recalled. Attava opposes the marriage of Titus's daughter Lavinia to the Emperor's only son (by a former marriage), since she desires the possession of the empire for her own sons. The remainder of the story proceeds much as in the play, except that we do not learn what happens to Rome after Titus's death. Shakespeare's chief additions include Titus's candidacy for, and rejection of, the throne, the struggle between Saturninus and Bassianus, the sacrifice of Tamora's son Alarbus, and a greatly magnified role for Aaron the Moor.

Although the prose version itself made use of Ovid and Seneca, Shakespeare evidently consulted these authors directly as well. The play contains many explicit references to classical authors, most notably when Lavinia turns the pages of Ovid's *Metamorphoses* to the story of Philomela's rape (4.1). In Ovid's famous account (Book 6, 526 ff.), King Tereus of Thrace rapes Philomela, cuts out her tongue (but not her hands) to prevent her from revealing the crime, and keeps her prisoner. She nevertheless manages to weave her story into a tapestry and send it to her sister, Procne, who liberates Philomela and plots with her to serve Tereus's and Procne's son Itys to him at a banquet.

A similar grisly feast takes place in Seneca's *Thyestes*, from which Shakespeare may well have drawn some particulars. Atreus, the wronged avenger, murders the two sons of Thyestes and serves them to him. As in Shakespeare's play, there are two sons rather than one. Of these two sons, one is guilty of ambition, whereas Ovid's Itys is an innocent victim. The slayer is a male avenger, not (as in Ovid's account) the mother of the slain victim. Senecan conventions of underworld spirits of revenge and the like are also present in the play, though they may have reached Shakespeare by way of Thomas Kyd's *The Spanish Tragedy* and other plays of the late 1580s. The works of both Ovid and Seneca were commonly taught in Elizabethan grammar schools, though they were also available in English translation: Ovid by Arthur Golding (1567) and Seneca by Jasper Heywood (1560). Christopher Marlowe's *Tamburlaine* and *The Jew of Malta* certainly had an influence, especially on Shakespeare's conception of Aaron the Moor.

Two continental plays about Titus, the German *Tragaedia von Tito Andronico* (1620) and the Dutch *Aran en Titus* by Jan Vos (1641), were once thought to have been derived from an English play before 1594, which might then have served as a source for Shakespeare. In the German play, the name of Titus's son Lucius is Vespasian, and this fact has caused scholars to wonder if the "Tittus & Vespasia" acted in April 1592 by the acting company known as Lord Strange's men (as mentioned in Philip Henslowe's *Diary*) was about Titus Andronicus. Lucius's part is small for such prominence in a title, however, and the prevailing opinion today is that Henslowe's play was on an independent subject.

Romeo and Juliet

Shakespeare's chief source for *Romeo and Juliet* was a long narrative poem by Arthur Brooke called *The Tragical History of Romeus and Juliet, written first in Italian by Bandell and now in English by Ar. Br.* (1562). Other English versions of this popular legend were available to Shakespeare, in particular William Painter's *The Palace of Pleasure* (1566), but Shakespeare shows only a passing indebtedness to it. Brooke mentions having seen (prior to 1562) a play about the two lovers, but such an old play is not likely to have been of much service to Shakespeare. Nor does he appear to have extensively consulted the various continental versions that lay behind Brooke's poem. Still, these versions help explain the genesis of the story.

The use of a sleeping potion to escape an unwelcome marriage goes back at least to the *Ephesiaca* of Xenophon of Ephesus (by the fifth century A.D.). Masuccio of Salemo, in his *Il Novellino* (1476), seems to have been the first to combine this sleeping potion story with an ironic aftermath of misunderstanding and suicide (as found in the Pyramus and Thisbe story of Ovid's *Metamorphoses*). In Masuccio's account, the lovers Mariotto and Giannozza of Siena are secretly married by a friar. When Mariotto kills a prominent citizen of Siena in a quarrel, he is banished to Alexandria. Giannozza, to avoid marriage with a suitor of her father's choosing, takes a sleeping potion

given her by the friar and is buried as though dead. She is thereupon taken from the tomb by the friar and sent on her way to Alexandria. Mariotto, however, having failed to hear from her because the messenger is intercepted by pirates, returns in disguise to her tomb where he is discovered and executed. Giannozza, hearing this sad news, retires to a Sienese convent and dies of a broken heart.

In Luigi da Porto's *Historia novellamente ritrovata di due Nobili Amanti* (published c. 1530), based on Masuccio's account, the scene shifts to Verona. Despite the feuding of their two families, the Montecchi and the Cappelletti, Romeo and Guilietta meet and fall in love at a carnival ball. Romeo at once forgets his unrequited passion for a scornful lady. Friar Lorenzo, an experimenter in magic, secretly marries the lovers. Romeo tries to avoid brawling with the Cappelletti, but when some of his own kinsmen suffer defeat, he kills Theobaldo Cappelletti. After Romeo's departure for Mantua, Guilietta's family arranges a match for her with the Count of Lodrone. Friar Lorenzo gives Guilietta a sleeping potion and sends a letter to Romeo by a fellow friar, but this messenger is unable to find Romeo in Mantua. Romeo, hearing of Guilietta's supposed death from her servant Peter, returns to Verona with a poison he already possesses. Guilietta awakens in time to converse with Romeo before he dies. Then, refusing the Friar's advice to retire to a convent, she dies by stopping her own breath. This story provides no equivalents for Mercutio and the Nurse, although a young man named Marcuccio appears briefly at the Cappellettis's ball.

Da Porto's version inspired that of Matteo Bandello in his *Novelle* of 1554. Some details are added: Romeo goes to the ball in a vizard (mask), he has a servant named Pietro, a rope ladder is given to the Nurse enabling Romeo to visit Julietta's chamber before their marriage, Romeo obtains a poison from one Spolentino, and so on. The young man at the ball, Marcuccio, is now named Mercutio but is still a minor figure. This Bandello version was translated into French by Pierre Boaistuau in his *Histoires Tragiques* (1559); Boaistuau adds the Apothecary (who is racked and hanged for his part in the tragedy) and has Romeo die before Juliet awakens and slays herself with Romeo's dagger.

Despite Arthur Brooke's implication on the title page that his version is based on Bandello, the narrative poem *Romeus and Juliet* is taken from Boaistuau. Brooke's poem is a severely pious work written in "Poulter's Measure," couplets with alternating lines of six and seven feet. Brooke openly disapproves of the lovers' carnality and haste, although fortunately the story itself remains sympathetic to Romeus and Juliet. Brooke stresses star-crossed fortune and the antithesis of love and hate. He reduces Juliet's age from eighteen (as in Bandello) to sixteen. (Shakespeare further reduces her age to less than fourteen.) Brooke's narrative is generally close to Shakespeare's, though with important exceptions. Shakespeare compresses time from some nine months to a few days. In Brooke, for example, some two weeks elapse between the masked ball and Romeus's encounter with Juliet in her garden, and about two months elapse between the marriage and Tybalt's death. Shakespeare also unifies his play by such devices as introducing Tybalt and Paris early in the story; in Brooke's poem, Tybalt appears only at the time he is slain, and Juliet's proposed marriage to Count Paris emerges as a threat only after Romeus's banishment. Shakespeare's greatest transformation is of the characters. Brooke's Juliet is scheming. His Mercutio remains a shadowy figure, as in Bandello *et al.* Brooke's Nurse is unattractive, although she does occasionally hint at comic greatness: for example, she garrulously confides to Romeus the details of Juliet's infancy and then keeps Juliet on tenterhooks while she prates about Romeus's fine qualities (lines 631–714). Even if Shakespeare's play is incomparably superior to Brooke's drably versified poem, the indebtedness is extensive.

Julius Caesar

Julius Caesar represents Shakespeare's first extensive use of the work of the first-century Greek biographer Plutarch, in Thomas North's translation (based on the French of Jacques Amyot) of *The Lives of the Noble Grecians and Romans* (1579 and 1595). Plutarch was to become Shakespeare's most often-used source in the 1600s; prior to 1599 he had consulted it briefly on a number of other occasions. In *Julius Caesar*, he borrows details from three lives: Caesar, Brutus, and Antonius. He uses particular traits of character, such as Caesar's belief that it is "better to die once than always to be afraid of death," Brutus's determination to "frame his manners of life by the rules of virtue and study of philosophy," Cassius's choleric disposition and his "hating Caesar privately more than he did the tyranny openly," and Antonius's inclination to "rioting and banqueting."

The events of the play are substantially present in Plutarch, especially in "The Life of Julius Caesar." Antonius runs the course on the Feast of Lupercal to cure barrenness and offers the diadem to Caesar. Flavius and Marullus despoil the images of Caesar. Caesar observes that he mistrusts pale and lean men such as Brutus and Cassius. Papers are thrown by the conspirators where Brutus can find them, proclaiming "Thou sleepest, Brutus, and art not Brutus indeed." Caesar's death is preceded by prodigies: a slave's hand burns but is unconsumed, a sacrificial beast is found to contain no heart. When Caesar encounters the soothsayer who previously had warned him of his fate and boasts that "the ides of March be come," the soothsayer has the last word: "So they be, but yet are they not past." Brutus's wife Portia complains to him of being treated "like a harlot," not like

a partner. Brutus commits what Plutarch calls two serious errors when he forbids his fellow conspirators to kill Antonius and when he permits Antonius to speak at Caesar's funeral. Cinna the Poet is slain by an angry crowd mistaking him for Cinna the conspirator. A ghost appears to Brutus shortly before the last battle saying, "I am thy ill angel, Brutus, and thou shalt see me by the city of Phillippes," to which Brutus replies, "Well, I shall see thee then." Antonius says of the vanquished conspirators that "there was none but Brutus only that was moved to do it, as thinking the act commendable of itself: but that all the other conspirators did conspire his death for some private malice or envy." Shakespeare's debt to Plutarch is greater than these few examples can indicate.

Of course, Shakespeare reshapes and selects, as in his history plays. He compresses into one day Caesar's triumphant procession, the disrobing of the images, and the offer of the crown to Caesar on the Lupercal, when, in fact, these events were chronologically separate. Casca is by and large an invented character, and Octavius's role is considerably enlarged. Brutus's servant Lucius is a minor but effective addition, illustrating Brutus's capacity for warmth and humanity. Brutus's two speeches after the assassination (as mentioned by Plutarch) become one, and Antonius's speech is made to follow immediately after. (In Plutarch, Antonius speaks the following day, after the reading of the will.) Shakespeare accentuates the irrationality and vacillation of the mob, for in Plutarch the people are never much swayed by Brutus's rhetoric, even though they respectfully allow him to speak. The unforgettable speeches of both Brutus and Antonius are not set down at all in Plutarch. More compression of time occurs after the assassination: in Plutarch, Octavius does not arrive in Rome until some six weeks afterward and does not agree to the formation of the Triumvirate until more than a year of quarreling has taken place. The inexorable buildup of tension in Shakespeare's play is the result of careful selection from a vast amount of material. Shakespeare's borrowing from "The Life of Marcus Brutus" is no less extensive and is at the same time reshaped and given new emphasis.

Although Shakespeare depended heavily on Plutarch, he was also aware of later and conflicting traditions about Caesar. On the one hand, Dante's *Divine Comedy* (c. 1310–1321) consigns Brutus and Cassius to the lowest circle of hell, along with Judas Iscariot and other betrayers of their masters. Geoffrey Chaucer's "The Monk's Tale," from the *Canterbury Tales*, similarly portrays Caesar as the manly and uncorruptible victim of envious attackers. On the other hand, Montainge stresses the hubris of Caesar in aspiring to divinity. (Shakespeare could have read Montaigne in the French original or, if he had access to a manuscript, in John Florio's English translation, published in 1603.) A pro-Brutus view could also be found in the Latin *Julius Caesar* of

Marc-Antoine Muret (1553) and the French *César* of Jacques Grévin (1561). That Shakespeare knew these works is unlikely, but they kept alive a tradition with which he was certainly familiar. Possibly he knew such Roman works as Lucan's account of Caesar in the *Pharsalia* and Cicero's letters and orations, which were republican in tenor. Other possible sources include the *Chronicle of the Romans' Wars* by Appian of Alexandria (translated 1578), the anonymous play *Caesar's Revenge* (published 1606–1607, performed in the early 1590s at Oxford), and Thomas Kyd's *Cornelia* (translated from the French Senecan tragedy by Garnier). *Il Cesare* by Orlando Pescetti (1594) is now almost universally rejected as a possible source. The result of Shakespeare's acquaintance with both pro- and anti-Caesar traditions is that he subordinates his own political vision to a balanced presentation of history, showing the significant strengths and disabling weaknesses in both Caesar and the conspirators.

Hamlet

The ultimate source of the *Hamlet* story is Saxo Grammaticus's *Historia Danica* (1180–1208), the saga of one Amlothi or (as Saxo calls him) Amlethus. The outline of the story is essentially that of Shakespeare's play, even though the emphasis of the Danish saga is overwhelmingly on cunning, brutality, and bloody revenge. Amlethus's father is Horwendil, a Governor of Jutland, who bravely kills the King of Norway in single combat and thereby wins the hand in marriage of Gerutha, daughter of the King of Denmark. This good fortune goads the envious Feng into slaying his brother Horwendil and marrying Gerutha, "capping unnatural murder with incest." Though the deed is known to everyone, Feng invents excuses and soon wins the approbation of the fawning courtiers. Young Amlethus vows revenge but, perceiving his uncle's cunning, feigns madness. His mingled words of craft and candor awaken suspicions that he may be playing a game of deception.

Two attempts are made to lure Amlethus into revealing that he is actually sane. The first plan is to tempt him into lechery, on the theory that one who lusts for women cannot be truly insane. Feng causes an attractive woman to be placed in a forest where Amlethus will meet her as though by chance; but Amlethus, secretly warned of the trap by a kindly foster brother, spirits the young lady off to a hideaway where they can make love unobserved by Feng's agents. She confesses the plot to Amlethus. In a second stratagem, a courtier who is reported to be "gifted with more assurance than judgment" hides himself under some straw in the Queen's chamber in order to overhear her private conversations with Amlethus. The hero, suspecting just such a trap, feigns madness and begins crowing like a noisy rooster, bouncing up and down on the straw until he finds the eavesdropper. Amlethus stabs the man to death, drags him forth, cuts the body into morsels, boils them, and flings the bits "through the mouth of an open sewer for the swine to eat." Thereupon he returns to his mother to accuse her of being an infamous harlot. He wins her over to repentant virtue and even cooperation. When Feng, returning from a journey, looks around for his counselor, Amlethus jestingly (but in part truly) suggests that the man went to the sewer and fell in.

Feng now sends Amlethus to the King of Britain with secret orders for his execution. However, Amlethus finds the letter to the British King in the coffers of the two unnamed retainers accompanying him on the journey and substitutes a new letter ordering their execution instead. The new letter, purportedly written and signed by Feng, goes on to urge that the King of Britain marry his daughter to a young Dane being sent from the Danish court. By this means, Amlethus gains an English wife and rids himself of the escorts. A year later Amlethus returns to Jutland, gets the entire court drunk, flings a tapestry (knitted for him by his mother) over the prostrate courtiers, secures the tapestry with stakes, and then sets fire to the palace. Feng escapes this holocaust, but Amlethus cuts him down with the King's own sword. (Amlethus exchanges swords because his own has been nailed fast into its scabbard by his enemies.) Subsequently, Amlethus convinces the people of the justice of his cause and is chosen King of Jutland. After ruling for several years, he returns to Britain, bigamously marries a Scottish Queen, fights a battle with his first father-in-law, is betrayed by his second wife, and is finally killed in battle.

In Saxo's account, we thus find the prototypes of Hamlet, Claudius, Gertrude, Polonius, Ophelia, Rosencrantz, and Guildenstern. Several episodes are close in narrative detail to Shakespeare's play: the original murder and incestuous marriage, the feigned madness, the woman used as a decoy, the eavesdropping counselor, and especially the trip to England. A translation of Saxo into French by François de Belleforest, in *Histoires Tragiques* (1576 edition), adds a few details, such as Gertrude's adultery before the murder and Hamlet's melancholy. Belleforest's version is longer than Saxo's, with more psychological and moral observation and more dialogue. Shakespeare probably consulted it.

Shakespeare need not have depended extensively on these older versions of his story, however. His main source was almost certainly an old play of *Hamlet*. Much evidence testifies to the existence of such a play. The *Diary* of Philip Henslowe, a theater owner and manager, records a performance, not marked as "new," of a *Hamlet* at Newington Butts on June 11, 1594, by "my Lord Admiral's men" or "my Lord Chamberlain's men," probably the latter. Thomas Lodge's pamphlet,

Wit's Misery, and the World's Madness (1596), refers to "the visard of the ghost which cried so miserably at the theater, like an oyster wife, 'Hamlet, revenge!' " And Thomas Nashe, in his *Epistle* prefixed to Robert Greene's romance *Menaphon* (1589), offers the following observation:

It is a common practice nowadays amongst a sort of shifting companions, that run through every art and thrive by none, to leave the trade of noverint, whereto they were born, and busy themselves with the endeavors of art, that could scarcely Latinize their neck verse if they should have need; yet English Seneca read by candlelight yields many good sentences, as "Blood is a beggar," and so forth; and if you entreat him fair in a frosty morning, he will afford you whole *Hamlets*, I should say handfuls, of tragical speeches. But O grief! *Tempus edax rerum*, what's that will last always? The sea exhaled by drops will in continuance be dry, and Seneca, let blood line by line and page by page, at length must needs die to our stage; which makes his farnished followers to imitate the Kid in Aesop, who, enamored with the Fox's newfangles, forsook all hopes of life to leap into a new occupation; and these men, renouncing all possibilities of credit or estimation, to intermeddle with Italian translations . . .

Nashe's testimonial describes a *Hamlet* play, written in the Senecan style by some person born to the trade of "noverint," or scrivener, who has turned to hack writing and translation. The description has often been fitted to Thomas Kyd, though this identification is not certain. (Nashe could be punning on Kyd's name when he refers to "the Kid in Aesop.") Certainly Thomas Kyd's *The Spanish Tragedy* (c. 1587) shows many affinities with Shakespeare's play and provides many Senecan ingredients missing from Saxo and Belleforest: the ghost, the difficulty in ascertaining whether the ghost's words are believable, the resulting need for delay and a feigning of madness, the moral perplexities afflicting a sensitive man called upon to revenge, the play within the play, the clever reversals and ironically caused deaths in the catastrophe, the rhetoric of tragic passion. Whether or not Kyd, in fact, wrote the *Ur-Hamlet*, his extant play enables us to see more clearly what that lost play must have contained. The unauthorized First Quarto of *Hamlet* (1603) also offers a few seemingly authentic details that are not found in the authoritative Second Quarto but are found in the earlier sources and may have been a part of the *Ur-Hamlet*. For example, after Hamlet has killed Corambis (corresponding to Polonius), the Queen vows to assist Hamlet in his strategies against the King; later, when Hamlet has returned to England, the Queen sends him a message by Horatio warning him to be careful.

One last document sheds light on the *Ur-Hamlet*. A German play, *Der bestrafte Brudermord (Fratricide Punished)*, from a now-lost manuscript dated 1710, seems to have been based on a text used by English actors traveling in Germany in 1586 and afterward. Though changed by translation and manuscript transmission, and too

entirely different from Shakespeare's play to have been based on it, this German version may well have been based on Shakespeare's source-play. Polonius's name in this text, Corambus, is the Corambis of the First Quarto of 1603. (The name may mean "cabbage cooked twice," from *coramblebis*, a proverbially dull dish.)

Der bestrafte Brudermord begins with a prologue in the Senecan manner, followed by the appearance of the ghost to Francisco, Horatio, and sentinels of the watch. Within the palace, meanwhile, the King carouses. Hamlet joins the watch, confiding to Horatio that he is "sick at heart" over his father's death and his mother's hasty remarriage. The ghost appears to Hamlet, tells him how the juice of hebona was poured into his ear, and urges revenge. When Hamlet swears Horatio and Francisco to silence, the ghost (now invisible) says several times "We swear," his voice following the men as they move from place to place. Hamlet reveals to Horatio the entire circumstance of the murder. Later, in a formal session of the court, the new King speaks hypocritically of his brother's death and explains the reasons for his marriage to the Queen. Hamlet is forbidden to return to Wittenberg, though Corambus's son Leonhardus has already set out for France.

Some time afterward, Corambus reports the news of Hamlet's madness to the King and Queen, and presumes on the basis of his own youthful passions to diagnose Hamlet's malady as lovesickness. Concealed, he and the King overhear Hamlet tell Ophelia to "go to a nunnery." When players arrive from Germany, Hamlet instructs them in the natural style of acting and then requests them to perform a play before the King about the murder of King Pyrrus by his brother. (Death is again inflicted by hebona poured in the ear.) After the King's guilty reaction to the play, Hamlet finds him alone at prayers but postpones the killing lest the King's soul be sent to heaven. Hamlet kills Corambus behind the tapestry in the Queen's chamber and is visited again by the ghost (who says nothing, however). Ophelia, her mind deranged, thinks herself in love with a court butterfly named Phantasmo. (This creature is also involved in a comic action to help the clown Jens with a tax problem.)

The King sends Hamlet to England with two unnamed courtiers who are instructed to kill Hamlet after their arrival. A contrary wind takes them instead to an island near Dover, where Hamlet foils his two enemies by kneeling between them and asking them to shoot him on signal; at the proper moment, he ducks and they shoot one another. He finishes them off with their own swords and discovers letter on their persons ordering Hamlet's execution by the English King if the original plot should fail. When Hamlet returns to Denmark, the King arranges a duel between him and Corambus's son Leonhardus. If Leonhardus's poisoned dagger misses its mark, a beaker of wine containing finely ground oriental diamond dust is to do the rest. Hamlet is informed of the impending duel by Phantasmo (compare Osric), whom Hamlet taunts condescendingly and calls "Signora Phantasmo." Shortly before the duel takes place, Ophelia is reported to have thrown herself off a hill to her death. The other deaths occur much as in Shakespeare's play. The dying Hamlet bids that the crown be conveyed to his cousin, Duke Fortempras of Norway, of whom we have not heard earlier.

From the extensive similarities between *Hamlet* and this German play, we can see that Shakespeare inherited his narrative material almost intact, though in a jumble and so pitifully mangled that the modern reader can only laugh at the contrast. No source study in Shakespeare reveals so clearly the extent of Shakespeare's wholesale borrowing of plot and the incredible transformation he achieved in reordering his materials.

Othello

Shakespeare's main source for *Othello* was the seventh story from the third decade of G. B. Giraldi Cinthio's *Hecatommithi* (1565). Cinthio was available in French but not in English translation during Shakespeare's lifetime. The verbal echoes in Shakespeare's play are usually closer to the Italian original than to Gabriel Chappuys's French version of 1584. Cinthio's account may have been based on an actual incident occurring in Venice around 1508.

Shakespeare is considerably indebted to Cinthio's story for the essentials of the narrative: the marriage of a Moorish captain to a Venetian lady, Disdemona, whose relatives wish her to marry someone else, the mutual attraction to noble qualities of mind in both husband and wife, their happiness together at first, the dispatching of the Moor to Cyprus to take charge of the garrison there, Disdemona's insistence on accompanying her husband through whatever dangers may occur (though the sea voyage, as it turns out, is a very calm one), the ensign's treachery and resolve to destroy the Moor's happiness with Disdemona, her begging her husband to reinstate the squadron leader whom the Moor has demoted for fighting on guard duty (although no mention is made of drunkenness or of the ensign's role in starting the trouble), the ensign's insinuations to the Moor that his wife is cuckolding him because she is becoming weary of her marriage with a black man, the ensign's difficulty in providing ocular proof, his planting of Disdemona's handkerchief in the squadron leader's quarters and his showing the Moor that the handkerchief is now in the squadron leader's possession, his arranging for the Moor to witness at a distance a conversation between the ensign and squadron leader that is, in fact, not about Disdemona, Disdemona's confusion when she is asked to produce the handkerchief, the attack on the squadron leader in the dark, the murder of Disdemona in her bed, the Moor's

deep regret at the loss of his wife, the eventual punishment of both the Moor and and the ensign, and the telling of the story publicly by the ensign's wife, who has heretofore kept silent because of her fear of her husband.

Although these correspondences in the story are many, Shakespeare has changed a great deal. He provides Desdemona with a caring and saddened father, Brabantio, out of Cinthio's brief suggestion of family opposition to her marriage, and adds the entire opening scene in which Iago arouses the prejudices of Brabantio. Roderigo is a brilliantly invented character used to reveal Iago's skill in manipulation. Cinthio's ensign, though thoroughly wicked, never expresses a resentment for the squadron leader's promotion and favored treatment by the Moor; instead, the ensign lusts for Disdemona and turns against her and the Moor only when his passion is unrequited. In his complex portrayal of a consuming and irrational jealousy in Iago, Shakespeare goes far beyond his source, making use as well of the inventive villainy of the Vice in the English late medieval morality play. In Cinthio's account, the ensign filches the handkerchief from Disdemona while she is hugging the ensign's three-year-old daughter; the ensign's wife is uninvolved in this mischief, though she does unwillingly learn of her husband's villainy (since he has an idea of using her in his plot) and later feels constrained to hold her tongue when Disdemona asks her if she knows why the Moor is behaving so strangely. (As is usual in prose narrative, the passage of time is much more extended than in Shakespeare's play.)

In the later portions of the story, the changes are more marked. Cinthio relates an episode in which the squadron leader, finding the handkerchief in his room, takes it back to Disdemona while the Moor is out but is interrupted by the Moor's unexpected return home; Shakespeare instead has Cassio approach Desdemona (earlier in the story) to beg her assistance in persuading Othello to reinstate him. Cinthio tells of a woman in the squadron leader's household who copies the embroidery of the handkerchief before it is returned and is seen with it at a window by the Moor; here, Shakespeare finds a suggestion for Bianca, but her role is considerably augmented, partly with the help of a passing remark in Cinthio's account that the squadron leader is attacked and wounded as he leaves the house of a courtesan with whom he occasionally takes his pleasure. In the absence of any character corresponding to Roderigo, the Cinthio narrative assigns to the ensign himself the role of wounding the squadron leader. The manner in which Disdemona is murdered is strikingly different. Cinthio has nothing equivalent to the tender scene between Desdemona and Emilia as Desdemona prepares to go to bed. Cinthio's Moor hides the ensign in a dressing room next to his bedroom and commissions the ensign to bludgeon her to death with a sand-filled stocking, after which the two murderers cause the ceiling of the room to collapse on her and create the impression that a rafter has smashed her skull.

Cinthio also treats the aftermath of the murder in a very different way. The Moor, distracted with grief, turns on the ensign and demotes him, whereupon the ensign persuades the squadron commander to take vengeance on the Moor as his attacker (according to the lying ensign) and killer of Disdemona. When the squadron commander accuses the Moor before the Seigniory, the Moor keeps silent but is banished and eventually killed by Disdemona's relatives. The ensign, returning to his own country, gets in trouble by making a false accusation and dies as the result of torture. Cinthio sees this as God's retribution. The ensign's wife lives to tell her story, unlike Shakespeare's Emilia.

The changed ending is essential to Shakespeare's play. Emilia becomes a more complex figure than the ensign's wife: Shakespeare implicates her in the stealing of the handkerchief but also accentuates her love for Desdemona and her brave denunciation of her husband when at last she knows the full truth. Othello's ritual slaying of Desdemona avoids the appalling butchery of the source story. Shakespeare's ending is more unified, and brings both Othello and Iago to account for the deeds they have committed in this play. Most important, Shakespeare transforms a sensational murder story into a moving tragedy of love.

King Lear

The story of Lear goes back into ancient legend. The motif of two wicked sisters and a virtuous youngest sister reminds us of Cinderella. Lear himself appears to come from Celtic mythology. Geoffrey of Monmouth, a Welshman in close contact with Celtic legend, included a Lear or Leir as one of the pseudo-historical Kings in his *Historia Regum Britanniae* (c. 1136). This fanciful mixture of history and legend traces a supposed line of descent from Brut, great-grandson of Aeneas of Troy, through Locrine, Bladud, Leir, Gorboduc, Ferrex and Porrex, Lud, Cymbeline, Bonduca, Vortigern, Arthur, and so forth, to the historical Kings of England. The Tudor monarchs made much of their purported claim to such an ancient dynasty, and in Shakespeare's day this mythology had a quasi-official status demanding a certain reverential suspension of disbelief.

King Leir, according to Geoffrey, is the father of three daughters, Gonorilla, Regan, and Cordeilla, among whom he intends to divide his kingdom. To determine who deserves most, he asks them who loves him most. The two eldest sisters protest undying devotion, but Cordeilla, perceiving how the others flatter and deceive him, renounces hyperbole and promises only to love him as a daughter should love a father. Furious, the King denies Cordeilla her third of the kingdom but permits her to marry Aganippus, King of the Franks, without dowry. Thereafter, Leir bestows his two eldest daughters on the Dukes of Albania and Cornubia (Albany and Cornwall), together with half the island during his lifetime and the possession of the remainder after his death. In due course, his two sons-in-law rebel against Leir and seize his power. Thereafter Maglaunus, Duke of Albania, agrees to maintain Leir with sixty retainers, but, after two years of chafing at this arrangement, Gonorilla insists that the number be reduced to thirty. Angrily, the King goes to Henvin, Duke of Cornubia, where all goes well for a time; within a year, however, Regan demands that Leir reduce his retinue to five knights. When Gonorilla refuses to take him back with more than one retainer, Leir crosses into France and is generously received by Cordeilla and Aganippus. An invasion restores Leir to his throne. Three years later, he and Aganippus die, after which Cordeilla rules successfully for five years until overthrown by the sons of Maglaunus and Henvin. In prison she commits suicide.

This story, as part of England's mythic genealogy, was repeated in various Tudor versions, such as *The First Part of the Mirror for Magistrates* (1574), William Warner's *Albion's England* (1586), and Raphael Holinshed's *Chronicles* (second edition, 1587). Warner refers to the King's sons-in-law as "the Prince of Albany" and "the Cornish prince"; Holinshed refers to them as "the Duke of Albania" and "the Duke of Cornwall" but reports that it is Cornwall who marries the eldest daughter Gonorilla. *The Mirror*, closer to Shakespeare in these details, speaks of "Gonerell" as married to "Albany" and of "Cordila" as married to "the King of France." Edmund Spenser's *The Faerie Queene* (2.10.27–32) reports that "Cordeill" or "Cordelia" ends her life by hanging herself. Other retellings appear in Gerard Legh's *Accidence of Armory* and William Camden's *Remains*. All of these accounts leave the story virtually unchanged.

Shakespeare's immediate source for *King Lear* was an old play called *The True Chronicle History of King Leir*. It was published in 1605 but plainly is much earlier in style. The Stationers' Register, the official record of the London Company of Stationers (booksellers and printers), for May 14, 1594, lists "A booke called the Tragecall historie of Kinge Leir and his Three Daughters &c.," and a short time earlier Philip Henslowe's *Diary* records the performance of a "Kinge Leare" at the Rose Theatre on April 6 and 8, 1594. The actors were either the Queen's or the Earl of Sussex's men (two acting companies), though probably the Queen's. The play may have been written as early as 1588. George Peele, Robert Greene, Thomas Lodge, and Thomas Kyd have all been suggested as possible authors. Shakespeare probably knew the play before its publication in 1605.

This play of *Leir* ends happily, with the restoration of Leir to his throne. Essentially, the play is a legendary history with a strong element of romance. The two wicked sisters are warned of the King's plans for dividing his kingdom by an obsequious courtier named Skalliger (compare Oswald). It is Skalliger, in fact, who proposes the idea of apportioning the Kingdom in accord with the lovingness of the daughters' responses. Cordella receives the ineffectual support of an honest courtier, Perillus (compare Kent) but is disinherited by her angry father. Trusting herself to God's mercy and setting forth alone to live by her own labor, Cordella is found by the Gallian King and his bluff companion Mumford, who have come to England disguised as palmers to see if the English King's daughters are as beautiful as reported. The King hears Cordella's sad story, falls in love with her, and woos her (still wearing his disguise) in the name of the Gallian King. When she virtuously suggests the palmer woo for himself, he throws off his disguise and marries her forthwith.

Meanwhile the other sons-in-law, Cornwall and Combria (compare Albany), draw lots for their shares of the kingdom. Leir announces that he will sojourn with Cornwall and Gonorill first. Cornwall treats the King with genuine solicitude, but Gonorill, abetted by Skalliger, tauntingly drives her father away. The King acknowledges to his loyal companion Perillus that he has wronged Cordella. Regan, who rules her mild husband as she pleases, receives the King with seeming tenderness but secretly hires an assassin to end his life. (Gonorill is partner in this plot.) The suborned agent, frightened into remorse by a providentially sent thunderstorm, shows his intended victim the letter ordering the assassination.

The Gallian King and Cordella, who have previously sent ambassadors to Leir urging him to come to France, now decide to journey with Mumford into Britain disguised as countryfolk. Before they can do so, however, Leir and Perillus arrive in France, in mariners' garb, where they encounter Cordella and her party dressed as country folk. Cordella recognizes Leir's voice, and father and daughter are tearfully reunited. The Gallian King invades England and restores Leir to his throne.

Shakespeare has changed much in the narrative of his source. He discards not only the happy ending but also the attempted assassination and the numerous romance-like uses of disguise (although Tom o' Bedlam, in an added plot, repeatedly uses disguise). Shakespeare eliminates the humorous Mumford and replaces Perillus with both Kent and the Fool. He turns Cornwall into a villain and Albany into a belated champion of justice. He creates the storm scene out of a mere suggestion of such an event, serving a very different purpose, in his source.

Most of all, he adds the parallel plot of Gloucester, Edgar, and Edmund. Here Shakespeare derived some of his material from Sir Philip Sidney's *Arcadia* (1590). In Book 2, chapter 10 of this greatest of Elizabethan prose romances, the two heroes, Pyrocles and Musidorus, encounter a son leading his blind old father. The old man

tells his pitiful tale. He is the deposed King of Paphlagonia, father of a bastard son named Plexirtus who, he now bitterly realizes, turned the King against his true son Leonatus—the very son who is now his guide and guardian. The true son, having managed to escape his father's order of execution, has been forced to live poorly as a soldier, while the bastard son has proceeded to usurp his father's throne. In his wretchedness, the King has been succored by his forgiving true son and has been prevented from casting himself off the top of a hill. At the conclusion of this narrative, the villain Plexirtus arrives and attacks Leonatus; reinforcements arrive on both sides, but eventually Plexirtus is driven off, enabling the King to return to his court and bestow the crown on Leonatus. The old King thereupon dies, his heart having been stretched beyond the limits of endurance.

Other parts of the *Arcadia* may have given Shakespeare further suggestions; for example, the disguises adopted by Kent and Edgar are like those of Zelmane and Pyrocles in Sidney's prose work, and Albany's speeches about anarchy and the monstrosity that results from assaults on the rule of law recall one of Sidney's deepest concerns. Edmund is decidedly indebted to the allegorical Vice figure of the late medieval morality play tradition. For Tom o' Bedlam's mad language, Shakespeare consulted Samuel Harsnett's *Declaration of Egregious Popish Impostures*, 1603. (See Kenneth Muir's Arden edition of *King Lear*, pp. 253–6, for an extensive comparison.)

Macbeth

Shakespeare's chief source for *Macbeth* was Raphael Holinshed's *Chronicles* (1587 edition). Holinshed had gone for most of his material to Hector Boece, *Scotorum Historiae* (1526–1527), who in turn was indebted to a fourteenth-century priest named John of Fordun and to a fifteenth-century chronicler, Andrew of Wyntoun. By the time Holinshed found it, the story of Macbeth had become more fiction than fact. The historical Macbeth, who ruled from 1040 to 1057, did take the throne by killing Duncan, but in a civil conflict between two clans contending for the kingship. Contemporary observers credit him with having been a good ruler. Although he was defeated by the Earl of Northumbria (the Siward of Shakespeare's play) at Birnam Wood in 1054, the Earl was forced by his own losses to retire, and Macbeth ruled three years longer before being slain by Duncan's son Malcolm. Banquo and Fleance are fictional characters apparently invented by Boece.

In Holinshed's telling of the story, Duncan is a King with a soft and gentle nature, negligent in punishing his enemies and thereby an unwitting encourager of sedition. It falls to his cousin, Macbeth, a critic of this soft line, and to Banquo, the Thane of Lochaber, to defend Scotland against her enemies: first against Macdowald (Macdonwald in Shakespeare), with his Irish kerns and gallow-glasses, and then against Sueno, King of Norway. (Shakespeare fuses these battles into one.) Shortly thereafter, Macbeth and Banquo encounter "three women in strange and wild apparel, resembling creatures of elder world," who predict their futures as in the play. Although Macbeth and Banquo jest about the matter, common opinion later maintains that "these women were either the Weird Sisters, that is (as ye would say), the goddesses of destiny, or else some nymphs or fairies, endued with knowledge of prophecy." Certainly Macbeth soon becomes the Thane of Cawdor, whereupon, jestingly reminded of the three sisters' promise by Banquo, he resolves to seek the throne. His way is blocked, however, by Duncan's naming of his eldest but still underage son Malcolm to be Prince of Cumberland and heir to the throne. Macbeth's resentment at this is understandable, since Scottish law provides that, until the King's son is of age, the "next of blood unto him"—that is, Macbeth himself, as Duncan's cousin—should reign. Accordingly, Macbeth begins to plot with his associates how to usurp the kingdom by force. His "very ambitious" wife urges him on because of her "unquenchable desire" to be Queen. Banquo is one among many trusted friends with whose support Macbeth slays the King at Inverness or at Bothgowanan. (No mention is made of a visit to Macbeth's castle.) Malcolm and Donald Bane, the dead King's sons, fly for their safety to Cumberland, where Malcolm is well received by Edward the Confessor of England; Donald Bane proceeds on to Ireland.

Holinshed's Macbeth is at first no brutal tyrant, as in Shakespeare. For some ten years he rules well, using great liberality and correcting the laxity of his predecessor's reign. (Holinshed does suggest, to be sure, that his justice is only contrived to court popularity among his subjects.) Inevitably, however, the Weird Sisters' promise of a posterity to Banquo goads Macbeth into ordering the murder of his onetime companion. Fleance escapes Macbeth's henchmen in the dark and afterward founds the lineage of the Stuart Kings. (This genealogy is fictitious.) Macbeth's vain quest for absolute power further causes him to build Dunsinane fortress. When Macduff refuses to help, the King turns against him and would kill him except that "a certain witch, whom he had in great trust," tells the King he need never fear a man born of woman nor any vanquishment till Birnam Wood come to Dunsinane. Macduff flees for his safety into England and joins Malcolm, whereupon Macbeth's agents slaughter Macduff's wife and children at Fife. Malcolm, fearing that Macduff may be an agent of Macbeth, dissemblingly professes to be a voluptuary, miser, and tyrant, but, when Macduff responds as he should in righteous sorrow at Scotland's evil condition, Malcolm reveals his steadfast commitment to the cause of right. These leaders return to Scotland and defeat Macbeth at Birnam Wood, with their soldiers carrying branches before them. Macduff, pro-

claiming that he is a man born of no woman since he was "ripped out" of his mother's womb, slays Macbeth.

Despite extensive similarities, Shakespeare has made some significant changes. Duncan is no longer an ineffectual king. Macbeth can no longer justify his claim to the throne. Most important, Banquo is no longer partner in a broadly based though secret conspiracy against Duncan. Banquo is, after all, ancestor of James I (at least according to this legendary history), and so his hands must be kept scrupulously clean; King James disapproved of all tyrannicides, whatever the circumstances. Macbeth is no longer a just lawgiver. The return of Banquo's ghost to Macbeth's banqueting table is an added scene. Macbeth hears the prophecy about Birnam Wood and Macduff from the Weird Sisters, not, as in Holinshed, from some witch. Lady Macbeth's role is considerably enhanced, and her sleepwalking scene is original. Shakespeare compresses time, as he usually does.

In making some of these alterations, Shakespeare turned to another story in Holinshed's chronicle of Scotland: the murder of King Duff by Donwald. King Duff, never suspecting any treachery in Donwald, often spends time at the castle of Forres, where Donwald is captain of the castle. On one occasion, Donwald's wife, bearing great malice toward the King, shows Donwald (who already bears a grudge against Duff) "the means whereby he might soonest accomplish" the murder. The husband and wife ply Duff's few chamberlains with much to eat and drink. Donwald abhors the act "greatly in heart" but perseveres "through instigation of his wife." Four of Donwald's servants actually commit the murder under his instruction. Next morning, Donwald breaks into the King's chamber and slays the chamberlains, as though believing them guilty. Donwald is so overzealous in his investigation of the murder that many lords begin to suspect him of having done it. For six months afterward, the sun refuses to appear by day and the moon by night.

The chronicle accounts in Holinshed of Malcolm and Edward the Confessor supplied Shakespeare with further details. A more important supplementary source may have been George Buchanan's *Rerum Scoticarum Historia* (1582), a Latin history not translated in Shakespeare's lifetime, presenting a more complex psychological portrait of the protagonist than in Holinshed. Finally, Shakespeare may have used King James I's *Daemonology* (1597), John Studley's early seventeenth-century version of Seneca's *Medea*, Samuel Harsnett's *Declaration of Egregious Popish Impostures* (1603), and accounts of the Scottish witch trials published around 1590.

Timon of Athens

Shakespeare certainly made use of a brief passage from "The Life of Marcus Antonius" in Thomas North's English translation (from the French of Jacques Amyot) of the first-century Greek biographer Plutarch's *Lives of the Noble Grecians and Romans* (1579). This passage is a digression used to illustrate Antonius's embittered withdrawal to an Egyptian island after his defeat at Actium, in which he compares himself to the famous misanthrope of Athens, Timon. As Plutarch reports Timon's story, citing Plato and Aristophanes as his sources, Timon is a hater of mankind because he has been victimized by deception and ingratitude. Timon shuns all company but that of young Alcibiades and occasionally that of Apemantus. When asked by Apemantus why he favors Alcibiades, Timon replies that he knows Alcibiades will some day do great mischief to the Athenians. On another occasion, Timon mounts a public rostrum and invites his Athenian listeners to come hang themselves on a fig tree growing in his yard before he cuts it down (see 5.1.204–11). When Timon dies, he is buried upon the seashore (5.1.213–17). Plutarch transcribes two epitaphs—one by the poet Callimachus and one by Timon himself—both of which appear virtually word for word in Shakespeare's play (5.4.70–3). (Shakespeare probably meant to cancel one, for dramatically they are inconsistent with each other.) Plutarch thus provides Shakespeare not only with several incidents in the life of Timon but also with the link connecting Timon, Alcibiades, and Apemantus. The twenty-eighth novel in William Painter's *The Palace of Pleasure* (1566) retells the events narrated by Plutarch but without adding any new information.

Oddly, Shakespeare seems to have absorbed little from Plutarch's "Life of Alcibiades," though that account does tell how the general leaves Athens in disgrace and sides with Athens's enemies but ultimately relents when he sees that the Athenians are sorry for the injury they have done him. Alcibiades is a handsome young man and is fond of women; his concubine Timandra buries him. Despite these scattered hints, however, Plutarch's "Life of Alcibiades" provides no basis for Shakespeare's plot.

The comedy of Timon by Aristophanes, to which Plutarch alludes, has not survived. Nor has Plato's description. Apparently, these accounts were based on a historical figure of fifth-century Athens, Timon the son of Echecratides. Allusions to him in classical literature are common enough to suggest that his name had become synonymous with misanthropy. The fullest surviving classical record of this tradition is a dialogue by Lucian of Samosata (c. A.D. 125–180) called *Timon, or The Misanthrope*. No English translation was available in Shakespeare's lifetime, but he could have read Lucian in Italian, Latin, or French translation.

The dialogue begins as Timon, impoverished and abandoned by his fair-weather friends, calls upon Zeus to punish such injustice. Zeus hears this diatribe and learns from Hermes the sad tale of Timon's victimization by his ungrateful fellow mortals. Aware that he has been neglectful of this case, Zeus orders Hermes to descend with Plutus (Riches) and restore Timon to prosperity. Although Plutus fears he will be treated improvidently as before, Zeus is insistent. Plutus (personifying Riches) confesses to Hermes, as they descend, how he (i.e., wealth) deceives people. Hermes and Plutus find Timon digging, accompanied by Poverty, Toil, Endurance, and other such allegorical companions. Poverty and his fellows are reluctant to leave Timon, for they know he has been happier with them than in his former days; Timon, too, protests that he wants nothing to do with prosperity. Still, the will of the gods must be obeyed, and Timon discovers treasure where he is digging.

Just as he mordantly predicts, opportunists now seek him out. One is Gnathonides the flatterer, a former recipient of Timon's hospitality who only recently has repaid that kindness by offering Timon a noose. Another, Philiades, once received from Timon a farm as a dowry for his daughters but has spurned Timon in his poverty; now he makes a pretense of offering money, knowing Timon not to be in need. A third petitioner is the orator Demea, whose debt Timon once paid to obtain his release from jail; now, having insulted Timon in his poverty, Demea comes with a fulsome and patently fictitious decree that he has composed in Timon's honor. Fourth is Thrasicles, a hypocritical philosopher who preaches self-denial but drinks to excess and who professes to come now, not for his own benefit, but for those to whom he will gladly distribute Timon's new wealth. Timon drives them off one by one and then resorts to throwing stones at the ever increasing crowd of flatterers. (This parade of villains, and their satirical discomfiture, bear an interesting resemblance to Aristophanes's *The Birds*.)

Many details here are suggestive of Shakespeare's play and are not in Plutarch: Timon's generosity to friends (including the payment of a debt and the providing of a marriage dowry), his friends' ungrateful response when he is in need, the finding of gold in the ground followed by the reappearance of his former friends, the insincere offer of money, the flattering composition in praise of Timon. The personified abstractions are parablelike, as in Shakespeare's play. Yet verbal parallels between Shakespeare and Lucian are tenuous at best. Probably, Shakespeare knew some later version based on Lucian. Renaissance works inspired by Lucian are not hard to find, but none seems to be the direct source for Shakespeare. He is not likely to have known an Italian play called *Timone* by Matteo Maria Boiardo (c. 1487).

More suggestive of Shakespeare's play is an English academic play written at Cambridge (c. 1581–1600, or perhaps c. 1609–1610?) and preserved in the Dyce manuscript. (The editor Alexander Dyce first published this Elizabethan manuscript in 1842.) In this version, Timon's servant Laches warns against the effects of prodigality. When one friend, Eutrapelus, experiences financial trouble, Timon gives him five talents. Laches is driven out by

Timon but returns disguised as a soldier to serve his master. At a final banquet, Timon mocks his guests with stones painted to resemble artichokes. When he finds gold, Timon's false mistress shows her readiness to take it. Even a farcical comic subplot reminds us that Shakespeare's *Timon* contains an unrelated and perhaps vestigial Fool scene. Yet this academic play may have been written after Shakespeare's play, though surely not based on it (since *Timon* was not published until 1623 and apparently was never acted), and the likeliest explanation for the similarities is a common source. Perhaps Shakespeare knew and used a play that is now lost.

Apemantus does not have a prominent role in any of the versions here discussed, though he is mentioned in Plutarch. Apemantus bears a resemblance to many satirical railers and crabbed philosophers in Renaissance literature, such as Diogenes in John Lyly's play of *Campaspe* (1584) and Jaques in Shakespeare's *As You Like It*.

Antony and Cleopatra

In writing *Antony* and *Cleopatra*, Shakespeare relied to an unusual extent on his chief source, "The Life of Marcus Antonius" in the first-century Greek biographer Plutarch's *The Lives of the Noble Grecians and Romans* (in an English version by Sir Thomas North, 1579). Perhaps the best-known example in all Shakespeare of his skillful use of source material is in 2.2.201–36, when Enobarbus describes the first meeting of Antony and Cleopatra on the river Cydnus. Putarch reports the event as follows:

She disdained to set forward otherwise but to take her barge in the river of Cydnus, the poop whereof was of gold, the sails of purple, and the oars of silver, which kept stroke in rowing after the sound of the music of flutes, hautboys, citterns, viols, and such other instruments as they played upon in the barge. And now for the person of herself: she was laid under a pavilion of cloth of gold of tissue, appareled and attired like the goddess Venus, commonly drawn in picture; and hard by her, on either hand of her, pretty fair boys appareled as painters do set forth god Cupid, with little fans in their hands with the which they fanned wind upon her. Her ladies and gentlewomen also, the fairest of them, were appareled like the nymphs Nereides (which are the mermaids of the waters) and like the Graces, some steering the helm, others tending the tackle and ropes of the barge, out of the which there came a wonderful passing sweet savor of perfumes that perfumed the wharf's side, pestered with innumerable multitudes of people. Some of them followed the barge all alongst the river's side; others also ran out of the city to see her coming in. So that in the end, there ran such multitudes of people one after another to see her that Antonius was left post alone in the marketplace, in his imperial seat, to give audience.

Shakespeare retains virtually every detail describing Cleopatra's barge: the poop of gold, the sails of purple, the oars of silver, the flutes, the boys with fans, the gentlewomen like the Nereides, and so on. He borrows phrases and images virtually intact from North, as in the account of Cleopatra's own person. Yet Shakespeare also transforms this scene by putting the description in the mouth of Enobarbus, a largely invented character. Enobarbus's sardonic view derived from military experience, his wry but genuine admiration for Cleopatra, and the prurient curiosity of his Roman listeners—all combine to produce the paradox of cloying appetite and insatiable hunger that helps to define the unforgettable greatness of Cleopatra as a character.

Shakespeare turns to Plutarch for other fabulous stories as well: eight wild boars roasted whole for only twelve guests (2.2.189–90), Cleopatra teasing Antony by causing an old dried salt fish to be placed on his fishing line (2.5.15–18), Menas the pirate suggesting to Pompey that they cut the anchor cable with all their noble guests still aboard (2.7.62–85), Cleopatra's sudden changes from weeping to laughing, and her willingness to be flattered by those who tell her Antony has married Octavia solely out of necessity (3.3), Octavius's tenderness for his sister, the ill-omened nesting of swallows in Cleopatra's sails (4.12.3–4), Antony's disregarding the advice of a valiant captain not to fight at sea (3.7.62–71), Cleopatra's study of swift means of death (5.2.353–6), Antony's jealous reaction to the embassy of the young Thyreus, or Thidias (3.13.86–170), the suicide of Antony's servant Eros (4.14.85–97), Cleopatra's difficulty in lifting Antony up to her tomb or monument (4.15.30–8), his warning that she should trust none but Proculeius (4.15.50), Cleopatra's deception of Caesar through persuading him that she desires to live (5.2.110–90), the countryman with the basket of figs (5.2.233–5), Cleopatra's death "attired and arrayed in her royal robes" attended by Charmian and Iras, and much more.

Despite these extensive and detailed borrowings, Shakespeare is highly innovative in his use of his sources. He compresses time in order to give a sense of dramatic momentum to the events of many years. He creates vibrant characters like Enobarbus, Charmian, Iras, Mardian, the Soothsayer, Menas, Thidias, Dollabella, and many others for whom the historical sources provide only a sketchy impression or no information at all. In his characterization of the main figures as well, Shakespeare is not content to rely on Plutarch's estimate. To Plutarch, Antony is the tragic victim of infatuation. For all Cleopatra's cultivation and fascination—she knows several languages and rules her country with royal bearing—she is the source of Antony's downfall. Plutarch's attitude is, like Enobarbus's, admiring but ironic. "In the end," he writes, "the horse of the mind, as Plato termeth it, that is so hard of rein (I mean the unreined lust of concupiscence) did put out of Antonius's head all honest and commendable thoughts." This "Roman" view is present in *Antony and Cleopatra*, to be sure, but is counterbalanced by the "Egyptian" view that finds greatness in Antony and Cleopatra's capacity for love. Shakespeare's play sets up a debate among conflicting traditions, as found in various medieval and Renaissance treatments of this famous story. The moralistic perspective condemning vice was popular in medieval texts, such as *De Casibus Virorum Illustrium* and its continuation, John Lydgate's *The Fall of Princes*. The interpretation of Cleopatra as love's martyr was to be found in Geoffrey Chaucer's *The Legend of Good Women*. And, finally, the view of Antony and Cleopatra as heroic protagonists rising above their guilt found expression in several neo-Senecan dramas of the later sixteenth century. Most important for Shakespeare were *The Tragedy of Antony*, translated from Robert Garnier's *Marc Antoine* by Mary Herbert, Countess of Pembroke, in about 1590 (published 1592 and 1595), and *The Tragedy of Cleopatra* by Samuel Daniel (1594), a companion play dealing mainly with the end of Cleopatra's life. Garnier's play had been based on Étienne Jodelle's *Cléopâtre Captive* (1552), the first regular French tragedy. Shakespeare certainly gained from such works as these a sense of tragic greatness in his protagonists. He seems also to have been aware of favorable and unfavorable historical appraisals of Octavius Caesar as both a great ruler and a ruthless and even treacherous politician. One influential work on the more critical side may have been the *Chronicle of the Romans' Wars* by Appian of Alexandria (translated 1578). Virgil's *Aeneid* gave Shakespeare a model for a drama of passion set in the context of Roman history.

Coriolanus

Coriolanus probably represents Shakespeare's last use of the first-century Greek biographer Plutarch's *The Lives of the Noble Grecians and Romans*, as translated by Sir Thomas North (1579) from a French version by Jacques Amyot. "The Life of Caius Marcius Coriolanus" provided most of the material for Shakespeare's play, just as "The Life of Marcus Antonius" had provided most of the material for *Antony and Cleopatra*. Plutarch's Coriolanus is a man of exceeding nobility but also of excessive impatience and churlish incivility. In war he practices *virtus*, or "valiantness" as North translates it. He wins his title of Coriolanus by storming the city of Corioles (Corioli) almost single-handed. He is the son of a widow whose good opinion he cherishes; as Plutarch reports, "he thought nothing made him so happy and honorable as that his mother might hear everybody praise and commend him, that she might always see him return with a crown upon his head, and that she might still embrace him with tears running down her cheeks for joy." Coriolanus vehemently disapproves of leniency toward the populace, believing it to be an invitation to anarchy. He is, natural-

ly, an enemy of the people's first tribunes, Junius Brutus and Sicinius Velutus, who, in Plutarch's estimation, "had only been the causers and procurers of this sedition."

Plutarch informs us that, when Coriolanus stands for consul and follows the custom of appearing in the marketplace clad only in a poor gown, the people remember his martial prowess; on the day of the election itself, however, they recall their old hate of him and refuse his candidacy. Coriolanus, in his typically choleric and intemperate fashion, makes no attempt to conceal his outrage at this insult. (Plutarch comments editorially on his behavior as "the fruits of self-will and obstinacy.") When he is banished, Coriolanus goes in disguise to Antium, to the house of Tullus Aufidius, his great rival, knowing perfectly well that "Tullus did more malice and envy him than he did all the Romans besides." Coriolanus and Tullus have long been admiring rivals: "they were ever at the encounter one against another, like lusty courageous youths striving in all emulation of honor, and had encountered many times together." Returning vengefully to Rome, Coriolanus is "determined at the first to persist in his obstinate and inflexible rancor," but finally relents through "natural affection," and receives his wife and mother. Volumnia's oration to him, reported in full by Plutarch, causes Coriolanus to cry out: "you have won a happy victory for your country, but mortal and unhappy for your son."

Shakespeare's changes simultaneously enhance the haughtiness of Coriolanus and the volatility of the commoners, thereby increasing the distance between the two sides. Shakespeare's Coriolanus is revolted by the custom of wearing a robe and showing his wounds to the people, and shows his contempt more snarlingly than in Plutarch's *Lives*. He is, unlike Plutarch's protagonist, reluctant to seek office and has to be persuaded to it by his mother and friends. Shakespeare minimizes the legitimate griefs of the Roman people—Plutarch makes it plain that the Senate does favor the rich and that the people are oppressed by usurers—and accentuates their political instability. Shakespeare shows them as being manipulated against Coriolanus by the scheming tribunes, whereas in Plutarch the people make up their own minds to oppose Coriolanus for the consulship. Shakespeare also magnifies the roles of Volumnia and of Menenius. Volumnia, though she is mentioned by Plutarch, takes no active part in the story until Coriolanus attacks Rome; Menenius's chief function in Plutarch is to relate the fable of the belly. Shakespeare compresses and rearranges events as he usually does: for example, in Plutarch the people actually leave Rome to demonstrate their grievances and agree to return only when granted the election of tribunes to represent their interests, whereas in Shakespeare the tribunes have already been elected when the play begins. In Shakespeare, Coriolanus is banished as the result of a dispute over his consulship, not (as in Plutarch) as the result of an insurrection over scarcity of grain.

Shakespeare probably also knew the story of Coriolanus in another classical source, Livy's *Roman History*, Book 2, as translated by Philemon Holland (1600). Other versions of the story were available to him, including an outline of Roman history by L. Annaeus Florus (also called Publius Annius Florus), written in the second century A.D., based chiefly on Livy. Plutarch, however, seems to have provided Shakespeare with virtually everything he needed. Even Shakespeare's alterations of Plutarch tend to enhance rather than revise Plutarch's overall thesis and appraisal of the characters in his history.

Appendix 3

Shakespeare in Performance

Lois Potter, University of Delaware

Although we know a good deal about the conditions of performance at the time Shakespeare's plays were first produced, much of this information (summarized in the Introduction, pp. xliv–xlvii) raises as many questions as it answers. We know, for example, that Shakespeare wrote most of his plays for the Lord Chamberlain's men, first formed in 1594 after a period of plague and theater closures, and that the company (officially servants of the courtier whose duties included supervising court entertainments) was honored with the title of the King's men at the accession of James I. Elizabethan acting companies were all male, with boys or young men playing women's roles, but we know almost nothing about how they acted, or who played which parts. We know that the stages of the public, partially roofed playhouses jutted into the yard where the audience stood on three sides, looking up at the actors; the rest of the spectators sat in covered galleries looking down on them. But we are not sure whether the gallery above the stage, pictured in the contemporary illustration of the Swan Theatre interior shown on page xlvi, was meant for musicians, spectators, or both. (And of course we do not know how much the Globe's interior resembled the Swan's.) If, as appears from the illustrations of theater interiors on pages xlvi and lxiv, some spectators normally watched the action from behind the stage, the actors would have had to move a great deal during a scene, as in modern theater-in-the-round productions, to make sure that they were visible and audible to all parts of their audience.

However much information we have, we still cannot know if aspects of the theater that were common then but unusual in our eyes were taken for granted by the spectators who watched the plays in the reigns of Elizabeth and James I. Did they think of the boy actresses as boys or believe in them as women? Those who had traveled to France and Italy would have known that women played women's parts in those countries and were often as famous as the male actors. What was the acting style for love scenes between a man and a cross-dressed boy, and what was the range of responses to it? The players in the open theaters performed by day (normally beginning at 2 P.M.), but used torches and candles to indicate when the action was supposed to be taking place at night. Did audiences find it difficult to accept a convention by which actors, fully visible to the audience, declare that they are unable to see anything? There is probably no single answer. It is likely that then, as always, audience members differed in the extent to which they preferred to believe in the performance or feel superior to it.

To the audiences of Shakespeare's time, the theaters were sumptuous and impressive buildings. Their wooden interiors were painted to look like marble, and the ceiling of the Globe was apparently decorated with the signs of the zodiac (perhaps, when Hamlet and Othello addressed the heavens, they looked at both a real and an artificial sky). Visitors from abroad were taken to see plays; actors traveled with them as far as Prague; versions of them were being translated into German as early as 1618. All this indicates how much English plays and players were respected. By about 1597, the company for which Shakespeare wrote was the one most frequently invited to perform at court, evidence that it was considered the best in London.

The theater in fact offered a great deal of visual and musical pleasure even for those who could not understand the language. Vast sums of money were spent on costumes. The most valuable surviving evidence, an account book of Philip Henslowe, manager of the Rose playhouse, shows that their bright or striking colors (often red and black, with silver and gold) allowed them to stand out on a stage that depended on daylight for most of its illumination. These were not "costumes" but clothes, sometimes bought in secondhand shops and sometimes donated or sold by gentlemen patrons. Characters normally wore contemporary dress, but with some indications of historical costume, like togas for classical characters (see the contemporary drawing, usually taken to be an illustration of *Titus Andronicus*, on p. lxi). Costumes and wigs, as well as false beards, were obviously important for a theater in which twelve to fourteen actors frequently doubled in as many as thirty roles. Music was frequently used in productions and a number of writers, including Shakespeare, incorporated popular contemporary songs into their plays. Robert Johnson, who is credited with the songs to a number of Jacobean plays, may have been the company's in-house composer. Some plays may have had as much music as a modern musical comedy, though very little of it has been identified.

Shakespeare's plays were designed to show off the actors' talents: singing, playing an instrument, dancing, and fencing. Most of his most popular plays end with either a dance or a fight, and nearly all of his tragic heroes (with the interesting exceptions of Othello and Antony) have at least one heroic fight scene. Since memorization and oratory were part of every grammar school education, audiences could recognize the superior memories of the actors who learned the long and complicated speeches that Shakespeare wrote for them. The combination of great actors and a dramatist who wrote great roles for them was attractive to other playwrights, and helped to ensure the company's continuing preeminence.

Shakespeare's practice of writing plays dominated by one very large starring role probably followed Richard Burbage's rise to stardom. Many contemporary references identify him with Richard III (see the anecdote on pp. lix–lx), and he is also known to have played Romeo, Hamlet, Othello, and Lear. John Lowin, who joined the company in 1602–1603, seems to have partnered Burbage in plays with two substantial roles. Shakespeare was unusual in that he wrote equally well for tragic and comic actors, and for the company clown, a type of performer traditionally famous for his ad-libs. Will Kemp, the most famous comedian of his day, certainly created the role of Dogberry—his name accidentally replaces the character's in one quarto of the play. It is not absolutely certain that he played Falstaff, but his departure from the Lord Chamberlain's men in 1599 is often linked with Shakespeare's writing the character out of *Henry V* after having apparently promised (at the end of *2 Henry IV*) to include him in the sequel. Those who think that Shakespeare was in agreement with Hamlet's advice to the players ("Let those that play your clowns speak no more than is set down for them") wonder whether Kemp's inability to refrain from "speaking" led to friction with his leading playwright.

Kemp's successor was Robert Armin, and it is often said that the more literary quality of Shakespeare's later fools resulted from their being tailored for the new actor.

Little is known about the other chief sharers in the company, though attempts have been made to identify them with, for example, references to exceptionally thin or exceptionally fat actors. It is not known whether any particular young actor inspired Shakespeare to write his best female roles, but many boys seem to have been good enough to have a personal following. A spectator who saw *Othello* in Oxford in 1610 mentions how moved the spectators were at the sight of Desdemona after her death.

It has often been suggested that Hamlet's insistence on naturalness, and the First Player's modest claim to have "reformed" the practice of overacting at least to some extent, reflect a perceived difference between the actors for whom Shakespeare wrote and the more melodramatic ones in the company led by Philip Henslowe and its leading actor Edward Alleyn. Yet Alleyn, who created the major Marlowe roles, was no less intelligent and talented than Burbage. It was Alleyn who retired early to live the life of a gentleman (in 1597, when he was only 31), with one brief comeback in 1601–1604. Burbage, on the other hand, went on acting up to his death at the age of 46, a fact that suggests a more theatrical personality than Alleyn's. If there was a movement toward greater naturalism in the 1590s, it probably resulted from greater professionalization and better training of actors, along with greater sophistication of the audiences themselves.

As the Lord Chamberlain's men grew more successful, they looked for a more select location. In 1597 James Burbage, Richard's father, purchased part of the disused monastic site of Blackfriars in the City of London. Protests from the local residents forced him to rent out the building to boys' companies (which performed less frequently) until, early in the reign of James I, times became more favorable. Finally moving into the new premises some time after 1607, the company was able to restrict its public to those who could afford the higher admission prices. In the indoor theaters, all the spectators were seated. Comfortable spectators cause less trouble than uncomfortable ones. The smaller size may have allowed for a more "realistic" style of playing. At the same time, the company continued to use the Globe throughout the period, as well as acting at court and elsewhere, so the actors must have been able to adapt their style to circumstances. In many ways, Shakespeare's last plays are his least "realistic," since they often involve magic, but the technology available in the Blackfriars playhouse may have made the magic convincing.

Besides, if realistic acting means acting that makes one forget that one is watching a play, it is unlikely that the drama was ever truly realistic. Other dramatists' allusions to Shakespeare are obviously meant to break the dramatic illusion: "What, Hamlet, are you mad?" asks a character in *Eastward Ho!* (1605), speaking to a servant who is named Hamlet only so that someone can ask him that question. Shakespeare himself also refers to his own plays. It is likely that the lovers' suicides in "Pyramus and This-be," performed at the end of *A Midsummer Night's Dream*, are meant as an absurd version of the end of *Romeo and Juliet*; Malvolio's madness, in *Twelfth Night*, probably parodies Hamlet's. Perhaps a comedy can make jokes about a tragedy without destroying the atmosphere, but *Hamlet* does the same thing. When Polonius tells Hamlet about playing Julius Caesar "at the university," and being killed by Brutus, many of their audience would remember that, not long before, the two actors speaking these lines had played Caesar and Brutus, respectively, in *Julius Caesar*.

The deaths of Shakespeare in 1616 and of Burbage in 1619 may have temporarily affected Shakespeare's theatrical popularity. Burbage was so much identified with the major roles that, according to one elegy, these characters seemed to have died with him. The Earl of Pembroke may have been typical when, in a letter, he expresses reluctance to go to the theater again. John Taylor, who replaced Burbage in 1619, inherited a number of his roles. He and Lowin led the company for the next twenty years, with first John Fletcher and then Philip Massinger as their leading dramatist. The company had been called the King's men since 1603, but the name was even more appropriate under Charles I than under his father, since the actors were much closer to the court. Taylor even served as acting coach to Queen Henrietta Maria and her ladies when they put on a pastoral tragicomedy in 1633.

Though not all Puritans or parliamentarians were hostile to the theater, and not all of Charles I's courtiers approved of it, the English civil war created a further association between theater and crown. Parliament closed the theaters at the start of the war in 1642, refusing to reopen them even when hostilities had ended. Performances continued nevertheless: professionals acted illegally in the theater buildings that were still usable, or, like amateurs, legally in private houses and inns. Some also went abroad and acted for English royalists in exile. Since the prohibition applied only to plays, scenes involving popular characters (Hamlet and the gravediggers, Falstaff, Bottom) were adapted and disguised as "drolls"—comic sketches—that could be performed in a mixed program of music, dance, and drama. The 1662 frontispiece to a collection of these drolls (p. lxiv) shows how Falstaff and Mrs. Quickly were probably costumed in this period.

The Restoration and the Eighteenth Century (1660–1776)

At the Restoration of 1660, one of Charles II's first acts was to establish two licensed acting companies, one patronized by him, the other by his brother the Duke of York. Each company was assigned a selection of plays from the prewar period. Shakespeare's were among the first to be revived; indeed, actors were already playing them in London before the new theaters had opened. Although one of the speakers in Dryden's dialogue on drama (*An Essay of Dramatic Poesy*, 1665) says that Beaumont and Fletcher's plays were more popular than Shakespeare's or Jonson's, the evidence indicates that Shakespeare went on being a frequently acted dramatist throughout this period. Since the King's company seems to have received preferential treatment, it is likely that the plays awarded to them—*1 Henry IV*, *The Merry Wives of Windsor*, and Othello—were the most popular of Shakespeare's works in 1660.

It was natural that Shakespeare's works would need updating; nearly fifty years after their author's death, their language, grammar, and jokes were already becoming obsolete. Audiences saw themselves as too refined for plays with clowns and devils. Both theater managers (Thomas Killigrew and William Davenant) had been playwrights before the war, and both produced the prewar drama with extensive alterations. *The Taming of the Shrew*, as produced in 1667 by the King's company under Killigrew, was called, improbably, *Sauny the Scot*, after the new comic servant who replaced Grumio; the actor John Lacy wrote the title role for himself, exploiting the anti-Scots feeling that had been exacerbated by the Civil War. "Scenes," or scenery, the norm in the theaters of France and Italy, had already been used in prewar masques, and in the 1630s Davenant had already been planning to open a theater equipped to use it for plays. As manager of the Duke's company, he set about revising old plays to create more possibilities for spectacle. His *The Law Against Lovers* (1662) conflated *Measure for Measure* and *Much Ado About Nothing*, neither of which was well known at the period. The result was an emphasis on the romantic part of both plays, as opposed to their low comedy. He added more music and scenery in his adaptations of *Macbeth* (1664) and *The Tempest* (1667); in later revivals, these two works became almost operatic. The new theaters were rather small, and actors still played at the front of the stage, with the wings and backdrop of the new scenery stretching away behind them. Scene changes could be made quickly by rolling away one sliding backdrop to reveal another one behind it, sometimes with a new set of characters already in place. The same painted wings and backdrop were expected to serve for a number of plays, acting as a kind of shorthand to distinguish indoor from outdoor settings. The idea that each play belonged to its own particular visual world did not gain currency until well into the nineteenth century.

Charles II had insisted, in his patent for the new theaters, that the custom of boy actors—unique to England—must end. Most of the women who became actresses during the early years of the Restoration were, inevitably, untrained. The famous Nell Gwyn, mistress of Charles II, was a star of the King's company. She was considered delightful in contemporary comedies, some of which were written especially for her; however, Pepys always insisted that she was disastrous in serious roles, and there is no record of her playing Shakespeare. The new actresses could exploit their natural gifts, their beauty, and their novelty, but no one wanted to see them in character parts, especially those of elderly women. As a result, roles like the witches in *Macbeth* were taken by men, often the company's low comedians, a practice that continued for centuries. The small number of parts for attractive young women in Shakespeare now became a problem. Davenant was skillful at multiplying them. He expanded the part of Lady Macduff; Miranda, no longer the only woman in *The Tempest*, acquired a naïve younger sister, while Caliban and Ariel were likewise paired off with a female monster and spirit respectively.

Some of these changes also had a moral purpose. Davenant balanced the wickedness of Macbeth and his Lady by developing the virtuous Macduffs as foils to them. He also gave Macbeth a death speech (only one line long) to show that the dying man recognized the vanity of his ambition. Later adaptations were still more concerned with "poetic justice." This term meant simply that art ought to reward virtue and punish vice, not because this is what happens in the real world, but because art's duty is to offer virtuous models whenever possible. John Dryden, who had worked with Davenant on *The Tempest*, later wrote free adaptations of both *Antony and Cleopatra* and *Troilus and Cressida*, in which the lovers, far from being unfaithful, are only sympathetic victims of misunderstanding. His version of *Antony and Cleopatra*, called *All for Love, or, the World Well Lost* (1675–1677), largely replaced its model for much of the next century, and was often played under Shakespeare's title. Though Dryden claimed that he had made Antony's wife Octavia a virtuous foil to Cleopatra, the play's success was due less to its superior morality (indeed, its most popular scene was one in which the two women insult each other) than to its simplification of the structure, which subordinated political history to the love story. Shadwell's *Timon of Athens* (1678) provided a faithful woman as well as a faithful steward, to contrast with the mercenary friends and mistress who desert the hero. Thomas Otway's *Caius Marius* (1679) made the suicides of Romeo and Juliet more acceptable by locating them in a classical world. One of Otway's other innovations—letting the heroine revive in time to converse with the hero before they die—was to outlast the adaptation itself. Nahum Tate's *King Lear* (1681) made the virtuous Cordelia a large and dramatic role, worthy of a star actress. He also added a love interest between her and Edgar, and provided a happy ending in which Lear is restored to his throne. The adaptation remained in the repertory for 150 years, and Samuel Johnson defended it in 1765 on the grounds that,

although the unjust tragic ending might be more true to life, "all reasonable beings naturally love justice." Tate's omission of the Fool, a character associated with old-fashioned theater, was not even noticed.

After 1679, the Popish Plot and uncertainty over the royal succession led to Shakespearean adaptations designed to score political points. In 1680, John Crowne wrote *The Misery of Civil War* (1680), the first of two adaptations based on the *Henry VI* plays, while Tate's *The Sicilian Usurper*, adapted from *Richard II*, fell foul of the censor, even though its deposed ruler was more sympathetic than Shakespeare's. In the following year, Tate reversed the order of scenes in *King Lear*, beginning with Edmund's first soliloquy: a bastard son claiming his right to inherit was bound to be topical in the reign of a king who had no legitimate children and whose next heir was a Roman Catholic brother. The turbulent political climate kept audiences away, and the two companies amalgamated in 1682. Very few plays of any kind survive from the last years of Charles II's reign and the three years of James II's leading to the revolution of 1688. In the reign of William and Mary (James's daughter), *King Lear* was once again so topical that it could not be staged. Mary and her sister Anne looked all too much like Lear's daughters, especially since Tate's version ends with the king's abdication in favor of his daughter and son-in-law.

Colley Cibber's *Richard III* (1699), the most successful of all adaptations, benefited from the fact that a number of Shakespeare's history plays had dropped out of the repertory by the end of the century, thus providing a quarry from which the adapter could borrow. Feeling that he had a free hand, Cibber removed Queen Margaret and, since he intended to play Richard himself, gave him some good lines from other histories, including (from *2 Henry IV*) the death speech that Shakespeare had neglected to write for his hero. This Richard, literally an actor's dream, was more theatrically popular than Shakespeare's had been, a fact that kept the version alive well into the twentieth century (the Olivier film, which also cut Margaret's role, used two recognizable Cibber lines). Cibber had some difficulties with the licenser just before the first performance because it was feared that his opening scene, showing the deposed Henry VI in the Tower, would remind its audiences of the deposed James II. He made sure to show his loyalty in his next adaptation— *King John*, under the title *Papal Tyranny*, coincided with the threatened invasion, in 1715, of James II's exiled Catholic son. As one of the managers of Drury Lane, and as poet laureate (from 1730), Cibber became a popular target for satire, and he is best remembered for Pope's attacks on him in *The Dunciad* (1743). But his entertaining autobiography, *An Apology for the Life of Colley Cibber, Comedian* (1740), is still the best source of information on the early eighteenth-century theater.

Indeed, without Cibber's book, it would be difficult to say much about Shakespearean acting at the turn of the eighteenth century. Though Thomas Betterton was recognized as the greatest actor of his age from the first years of the Restoration, those, like Samuel Pepys, who saw him at this time, praised him highly but in vague terms. Because of the division of the theatrical repertory, Betterton acquired some major Shakespearean roles, like Othello, only after the unification of the two companies in 1682, when senior actors of the King's company took the opportunity to retire. After this, he had virtually a monopoly, and went on playing a much-acclaimed Hamlet until he was seventy, as well as taking the role of Falstaff in what seems to have been his own adaptation of the *Henry IV* plays. Cibber's description of Betterton's Hamlet reacting to the first sight of his father's ghost became a point of comparison for later Hamlets well into the nineteenth century. It is clear that his effects had to do with "presence" rather than with movement—though, of course, Cibber was describing him in his last years, when he was presumably less active.

The early female performers are still more shadowy figures. Women had appeared on stage as singers, or singing actresses, in "operas" performed in the 1650s, and one of these, perhaps Margaret Hughes, may have been the first to play a Shakespearean role (probably Desdemona). Mary Sanderson, who became Mrs. Betterton, was the first Lady Macbeth. Her successor, Elizabeth Barry, was primarily a tragic actress. She is said to have owed her initial success to careful instruction by her lover, the Earl of Rochester, who recognized the importance of constant repetition and, like a modern director, insisted that she should rehearse in the dress that she was going to wear in performance. The best-loved comic actress of Cibber's youth, Anne Bracegirdle, played several Shakespearean comedy heroines alongside the Congreve roles for which she was famous. The popularity of *The Merry Wives of Windsor* may have been due not only to Betterton's playing of Falstaff but also to its two excellent roles for actresses past their first youth, probably the only women in the company experienced enough to do justice to Shakespearean comedy.

Though the history of Shakespeare editing begins in the early eighteenth century, the plays still belonged essentially to the theater; hence, the publication of acting editions, which allowed audiences to read what they were actually going to see in the theater, usually heavily cut and partially modernized. Even so, the first half of the century saw a steady return to original versions, as one role after another was suddenly revealed to be a superb vehicle for a particular actor. Shylock, for instance, had been a not-very-interesting comic miser in a not-very-interesting romantic comedy, often replaced by George Granville's adaptation, *The Jew of Venice* (1701). When Shakespeare's original was revived in 1741, Charles Macklin astonished his fellow-actors as much as the audience by emphasizing Shylock's terrifying malevolence.

Although later actors would play the character more sympathetically, Macklin made him what he has been ever since: a disturbing character who cannot be assimilated into a comic structure. Something of a theorist on acting, Macklin, in teaching other actors, insisted on clear and intelligent diction. Perhaps for that reason, his Iago was the most convincing of the period.

Richard III, in Cibber's version, was the role in which David Garrick made his London debut in 1741. The actor became famous almost instantly and went on to manage the Drury Lane Theatre from 1747 to 1776. Garrick was a self-proclaimed idolater of Shakespeare whose "Jubilee" at Stratford-upon-Avon in 1769 not only inaugurated the practice of celebrations and festivals but also led contemporaries to regard him as almost equal in importance with his author. Despite his reputation for restoring Shakespeare, Garrick was as much of an adapter as his famous predecessors, turning *The Taming of the Shrew* and the last part of *The Winter's Tale* into short three-act plays and making operas out of *A Midsummer Night's Dream* and *The Tempest*. His *Macbeth* had a death speech, much more dramatic and pathetic than the one-line moral that Davenant had given him. His *Romeo and Juliet* had a pathetic farewell scene based on the one in Otway's *Caius Marius*. In response to French criticisms, he even directed a *Hamlet* in 1771 with the low comedy of the gravediggers omitted. Yet he also revived many plays not seen in their Shakespearean form since the Restoration, showing by his acting what superb roles they contained. He was equally gifted at comedy and tragedy. Two of his most popular roles were Benedick and (Tate's) King Lear. *Julius Caesar* and *Othello*, plays in which Betterton had been particularly successful, were better acted by Garrick's chief rival, Spranger Barry, a tall and handsome actor with a beautiful voice. Garrick, shorter and less romantic in appearance, was famous for his mobile and expressive features that allowed him to delineate the transitions between the "passions." It was this grasp of human psychology that he praised in Shakespeare and that others praised in him. His most significant leading lady, Hannah Pritchard, must have been equally versatile, since she was famous both as Rosalind and as Lady Macbeth. It was, however, characteristic of Garrick that he was able to form an excellent company around himself, including a number of fine actresses and low comedians. Without these conditions, it would have been impossible to revive so many of the comedies.

The Romantic Period (1776–1850)

Between Garrick's retirement in 1776 and the end of the century, the theaters changed to the point where a rapid, subtle style like Garrick's was becoming almost impossible. The Licensing Act of 1737 had limited spoken drama to Drury Lane and Covent Garden, the descendents of the two London theaters licensed in 1660 by Charles II. The late eighteenth century saw the rapid growth of a London population in search of entertainment. The two theaters responded by increasing their audience capacity until, at the end of the century, Covent Garden held over 3,000 spectators, and Drury Lane 3,600. When much of the audience was too far from the stage to see facial expressions or hear the softer tones of an actor's voice, the most successful performers were those who could establish themselves through their volume or through visual effects. Two tall and statuesque actors, John Philip Kemble and his more gifted sister, Sarah Siddons, dominated the theater of this period. Siddons's Lady Macbeth was probably the finest performance of the age: when she said that she could smell blood, at least one contemporary spectator declared that he could smell it too. Her other finest Shakespearean roles were Isabella in *Measure for Measure* and Hermione in *The Winter's Tale*, both of them strong women whose sublime moral grandeur dwarfed everyone else. Kemble's attempt to impose greater discipline and unity on theatrical productions, with more historically "correct" sets and costumes, resulted in what must have been the most genuinely classical theater yet seen in Britain. *Coriolanus*, with Kemble in the title role and Siddons as a heroically obsessed Volumnia, was the triumph of their approach. It was ironic that it should have come in an age dominated by the spirit of revolution and of the complex attitudes that are summed up as Romanticism.

It was to this spirit that Edmund Kean appealed. Those who saw him make his famous London debut as Shylock in 1814, wearing a black wig instead of the traditional red one, would have realized at once that he was going to play, not a tragic villain, but a tragic victim. He had been a singer, dancer, and Harlequin before taking London by storm, and his acting benefited from these other skills. Unlike Kemble, who expressed authority and aristocratic dignity, he excelled as Shakespeare's outsiders and outlaws: the hunchbacked Richard III (still in Cibber's softened version), the Moor Othello, and the melancholy Hamlet. Knowing his gift for pathos, he starred in an adaptation of *3 Henry VI* (where York sobs over his murdered son) and attempted to bring back the original ending of *King Lear* (where Lear grieves over the dead Cordelia), but audiences were not yet ready for either. Those who saw him at his best never forgot his haunting delivery of Richard III's forebodings before Bosworth and Othello's farewell to arms, which provided the kind of appreciative, poetic commentary on Shakespeare that characterized the best contemporary criticism.

Kean's career was short, wrecked by drink and scandal. In 1833, just as he had reached his miserable end, another actor, using the stage name of Keane, made his Covent Garden debut in the role of Othello. Ira Aldridge, a black American, may have hoped to announce himself as Kean's successor, but racial prejudice in England prevented him from being accepted as a leading tragedian. He would, however, play Othello all over Europe, and especially in Russia, in bilingual productions with local casts. Like Kean, he sought out the roles of victims and social outcasts: Aaron in his own adaptation of *Titus Andronicus*, as well as (in white make-up) Macbeth, Shylock, and King Lear; like Kean, he was also capable of singing songs in dialect or even a Russian folksong. The excitement that German and Russian spectators felt at the sight of a black actor playing a black character would become an important part of theatrical experience a century later; at this point, it was a novelty. In the 1860s Aldridge finally acted in major London theaters and might have returned to the United States after the Civil War if he had not died unexpectedly while on tour in Poland.

Meanwhile, both of the unruly London theaters were managed, in turn, by William Macready, who, as his diary makes clear, took seriously his responsibility to a dramatist he worshipped. Still more than Kemble, he behaved like a modern director, with a vision of the production as a whole. His revivals of the history plays showed the possibilities of historical reconstruction. He is best known for restoring the Fool to *King Lear* in 1838, though he gave the role to a young woman to ensure that it would be played for pathos rather than low comic effects that might distract from his own scenes. A number of fine actresses played opposite him: Helen Faucit, young, fragile, refined, who would later write a perceptive if sentimental account of her approach to acting some of Shakespeare's female characters; Fanny Kemble, a member of the famous Kemble family, whose memoirs indicate the struggle involved for women in a star-dominated theater; Charlotte Cushman, a powerful visitor from America who sometimes played male roles. The plays were still heavily cut and showed the influence of earlier adaptations, but by the end of his career, Macready could fairly claim to have restored a good deal of Shakespeare's text and to have made the theater more respectable. The repeal of the Licensing Act in 1843, which allowed smaller theaters to cater to different publics, also encouraged gentrification. Samuel Phelps, who managed the working-class Sadler's Wells Theatre from 1844 to 1869, did even more than Macready had, performing thirty-four of Shakespeare's plays; he even restored the original *Richard III*, though other actors continued to prefer the Cibber version. Charles Kean (son of Edmund), at the Princess's Theatre from 1850 to 1859, carried the historicizing process still further; his "archaeological" productions were likely to be accompanied by notes explaining the reason for the choice of period, costumes, and props.

Still, it was only rarely that anyone had the opportunity to impose a concept of Shakespearean production on an acting company in his own theater. Star actors tended to spend much of their time on tour, both in England and America, performing their favorite roles after perhaps one rehearsal with the resident company. Far from seeking new ways to interpret a play, these actors had to rely on standardized stage business (when Mr. Wopsle plays Hamlet in Dickens's *Great Expectations*, an unsympathetic audience comments loudly on each theatrical cliché as it occurs). They naturally tended to conceive of their characters in isolation and to favor tragedy over comedy, which requires ensemble playing. (Similarly, nineteenth-century critics usually focus on the analysis of individual characters.) A common practice was the pitting of one actor against another in a famous role, arguing over which one was the "true" Hamlet or Lear. In one case, the rivalry developed a nationalistic dimension. Macready's visit to America, in 1849, is notorious for the riot at Astor Place in New York, when soldiers fired on and killed some of the crowd outside the theater. The rioters had been trying to drown out Macready's performance of *Macbeth* out of a mistaken loyalty to the American tragedian, Edwin Forrest. On a visit to Britain, Forrest had hissed Macready for some foppish business with a handkerchief that the actor, as Hamlet, had used to illustrate the phrase "I must be idle." Now his personal hostility became a quarrel about effete English acting versus the manly American tradition. In fact, the distinction was largely meaningless: many well-known American actors had begun their careers in England or Ireland. While some American Shakespeareans might have seen themselves as part of the Forrest tradition, and some (like the touring performers depicted by Mark Twain in *Huckleberry Finn*) were of no tradition at all, most American actors continued to look to Europe for models.

The Victorian Era and the Early Twentieth Century (1850–1912)

The greatest American actor of the next generation, Edwin Booth, was a refined and melancholy figure whose readings of the great Shakespearean roles were psychological and poetic. Booth was the son of Junius Brutus Booth, who had acted in London opposite Edmund Kean, and the brother of John Wilkes Booth, the assassin of Abraham Lincoln. (Ironically, all three members of this acting family had once performed together in the great assassination play, *Julius Caesar*.) Though Booth briefly attempted theater management, he spent much of his time in the exhausting business of touring. He clearly thought deeply about his own roles, and about the moments when other characters interacted with him. His correspondence with the New Variorum Shakespeare

editor, H.H. Furness, is quoted in many notes of that edition—an early example of successful communication between the theater and the scholarly world. Yet when Booth was alternating the two leading roles of *Othello* with Henry Irving in 1881, he sent his servant to take notes at rehearsal for him. Nothing in his experience had prepared him for a theater in which the actor-manager expected everyone to fit into a total artistic conception.

It was Irving, the first actor to be knighted, who dominated English Shakespearean acting in the late Victorian era. His pictorial sense was even stronger than that of the actor-managers who preceded him, and the technical means at his disposal in the Lyceum Theatre, which he began to manage in 1878, were much better. The old system of sliding screens in grooves, flanked by a series of wings, had been replaced by the "box set," which was built like a piece of architecture, creating a complete environment. Electric lighting, introduced in the 1880s, provided new, subtle visual effects. The elaborate and beautiful sets often required interminable scene changes and, sometimes, rearrangement of the plays to accommodate them. Irving's own performances were usually controversial. His Malvolio, like his Shylock, was a tragic figure, while his Iago was so witty and likeable that, playing opposite Booth's Othello, he stole all the sympathy from the hero. His theater offered a beautiful dream for the spectator to share: if it also disturbed the spectator, it was through its revelation of the psychological depths of character, never through its comments on social and political issues. Irving's leading lady, Ellen Terry, was both beautiful and brilliant; in most productions she was allowed to be only the former. Bernard Shaw, longing for her to appear in plays about "grownup" topics, by himself or Henrik Ibsen, resented her imprisonment in Irving's world. For Shaw and other modern thinkers, Shakespeare was becoming synonymous with nostalgia and with the moralistic and idealistic thinking that the new drama regarded as a vice. The early twentieth-century theater was finally affected by these critical attempts to reform it, but two kinds of production coexisted for some time. At His Majesty's Theatre, Herbert Beerbohm Tree, like Irving, offered psychologically based character acting in a beautiful scenic environment, recreating Cleopatra's Egypt and Henry VIII's England; having seen his lavish production of *Macbeth*, one critic commented that "Nature put up a pretty feeble imitation of what several barrels of stones and a few sheets of tin could do in His Majesty's." At the Savoy, on the other hand, Harley Granville Barker, a disciple of Bernard Shaw, developed a decorative visual style that was not tied to a specific historical period.

Meanwhile, a more experimental approach to acting was being developed in Germany. The country's unusual political structure, with small dukedoms and cities sponsoring their own theaters, made it possible for the

Duke of Saxe-Meiningen to sponsor his own company of players, sixty-six in all. His leading actors were unremarkable but, when he took them on tour in the 1880s, audiences were impressed by his handling of large groups. The Duke insisted that those who played major roles in one production should be walk-ons in another, so that crowds could be properly rehearsed instead of being assembled from those gathered around the stage door and drilled by the stage manager immediately before each performance.

Frank Benson, a young Oxford graduate, saw the Saxe-Meiningen company at Drury Lane in 1881, and was inspired to develop his own touring company—though, unlike the Duke, he acted in his own productions and consequently shaped them from a star's point of view. From 1886 on, the Bensonians became regular visitors at Stratford-upon-Avon. Shakespeare's birthplace had been briefly famous in 1769, the year of Garrick's Jubilee, but it was only in 1879, when the first Memorial Theatre was built, that tourists had any reason to visit for more than a few hours. Benson essentially created the first Stratford company, though it used the theater only during a short "Festival" season. Having a regular venue and a devoted audience enabled him to revive unusual works, if often drastically cut. In 1901 he inaugurated the new century with a "Grand Cycle" of Shakespeare's histories—the first English production of the plays as a group.

The desire to return to fuller texts and something like the original conditions of Shakespearean performance was initially associated with Germany and then with outsiders like William Poel, who founded the English Stage Society in 1894. Previously, Poel had given an experimental matinee of the First Quarto Hamlet at St. George's Hall in 1881. More surprisingly (though his friendship with Bernard Shaw in part explains it), the popular London actor Johnston Forbes-Robertson played an unusually full text of Hamlet in 1897, with characters like Reynaldo and Fortinbras appearing for the first time in centuries. Then Benson's company played an uncut Hamlet in 1899 and 1900. Poel, who often worked with amateurs, using all-purpose curtains rather than scenery on what was meant to be an Elizabethan stage, revived works previously considered unperformable, by Shakespeare's contemporaries as well as by Shakespeare. For example, he gave the first important Troilus and Cressida to be seen in London since 1734, dressing it in Elizabethan rather than classical costume. It was 1912. He had discovered the play's antiwar potential.

The Twentieth Century

World War I drastically curtailed many Shakespearean projects, including those for a gigantic celebration of the anniversary of his death in 1916, which at one point was intended to include the opening of a National Theatre. Although this theater did not come into existence until nearly 100 years after Irving had first suggested it, other developments were creating the conditions that would make Shakespeare plays, with their large casts, commercially viable.

One was the rise of repertory theaters, which could support a large company and a varied range of plays. The most famous of these was London's Royal Victoria, or "Old Vic," founded in 1914. Under a number of gifted directors (notably Robert Atkins, who had directed all the plays in the 1623 Folio by 1923, Harcourt Williams, and Tyrone Guthrie), it was the home to many legendary productions, including John Gielgud's first Hamlet (1929) and Olivier's first Hamlet (1937). At the Birmingham Repertory Theatre, Barry Jackson had already directed a modern-dress Hamlet in 1925. Modern dress had been common practice until the nineteenth century; it now seemed eccentric, but would by the end of the century become almost the norm. The Memorial Theatre at Stratford, after struggling to find its identity, saw some brilliant productions by Peter Brook in the 1940s and 1950s, including three plays traditionally considered minor: Love's Labor's Lost (1946), Measure for Measure (1948), and a Titus Andronicus (1955), starring Olivier, at which audience members regularly fainted at what was then unusual stage violence: the amputation of the hero's hand and the cutting of the villains' throats. Stratford and the Old Vic were becoming rival Shakespeare companies and in the 1960s each achieved a new status. The Memorial Theatre was renamed the Royal Shakespeare Theatre in 1960, with Peter Hall as director, whereas the Old Vic was designated the National Theatre in 1963. Olivier directed its opening production of Hamlet, with Peter O'Toole in the title role, and played a famous Othello in 1964. The National Theatre eventually moved into new premises in an arts complex, with three stages, on the South Bank of the Thames.

In the United States, the most exciting Shakespeare productions also occurred during a period of government subsidy: it was depression-era financing that enabled Orson Welles to direct Shakespeare on radio, and, for the Mercury Theatre, his "voodoo" Macbeth (1938) with an all-black cast, his anti-Fascist Julius Caesar (1937), and his condensation of the major history plays, Five Kings, which, although unsuccessful, later influenced his Falstaff film, Chimes at Midnight (1966). The other significant development in North America was the growth of summer Shakespeare festivals at outdoor Elizabethan-style theaters, beginning with the Elizabethan Stage at Ashland, Oregon (founded 1935), and the Guthrie-designed Festival Theatre at Stratford, Ontario (1953). Festival seasons allowed juxtapositions of related plays and the yearly performance of successive plays in a history cycle.

It was the English Stratford-upon-Avon, however, that fully seized on the history plays, performing the *Richard II–Henry V* group in 1951, during the Festival of Britain that celebrated the country's emergence from wartime and postwar rationing. For the rest of the century, the "cycle" of history plays would be recognized as a national epic, to be performed for special occasions. For the new Royal Shakespeare Company, Peter Hall and John Barton produced the *Henry VI–Richard III* group of plays— rewritten, reduced to three plays, and called *The Wars of the Roses*. They revived these, along with the other *Henry* plays, for the Shakespeare quatercentenary in 1964. The histories were produced again in 1975 by Terry Hands, with Alan Howard playing all the kings except Henry IV; in 1982 the *Henry IV* plays opened the company's new London theater at the Barbican under Trevor Nunn; and the company, now under Adrian Noble, marked the arrival of the millennium with a freshly conceived production of the *Richard II–Richard III* sequence. Just as the 1951 production showed the influence of Tillyard's essays on the histories as a unified cycle, the plays of the year 2000, deliberately disparate in style and even venue, were the product of a critical movement that emphasized discontinuity and diversity.

Contemporary Critical Approaches

By now, productions might require as much interpretation as plays. In the last half of the twentieth century, the spread of school and university education had created a substantial population that had studied at least one Shakespeare play and a smaller population, including some theater practitioners, that had read not only the plays but also the criticism. Stratford's John Barton, a former Cambridge don, directed *Twelfth Night* (1969) as if it were by Chekhov, encouraging the audience to imagine the unspoken feelings of the characters—not only Viola (Judi Dench), smiling through heartbreak, but Maria, in her apparently hopeless love for Sir Toby, and Sir Andrew in his even more hopeless love for Olivia. This attention to character, often created out of masses of tiny realistic details, informed some of the theater's most highly praised productions. Barton's *Richard II* (1973) worked very differently, externalizing the play's images in ways that were clearly independent of the characters' awareness: for instance, a glimpse of a melting snowman echoed Richard's wish that he were "a mockery king of snow" and linked the fall and rise of kings to a natural cycle of dissolution and renewal.

Other major critical approaches, easier to categorize, quickly found their way onto the stage. Political readings, often influenced by a Brechtian production style, dominated the 1960s and 1970s. These were usually Marxist and anti-authority: lines in which characters expressed high moral sentiments might be juxtaposed (legitimately) with those in which they showed themselves less noble, or (illegitimately) by setting them in a context that undermined them, as when, in Peter Zadek's *Held Henry* (Hero Henry), Henry V delivers the St. Crispin's Day speech to his bored mistress. Even before its first English publication in 1964, *Shakespeare Our Contemporary*, by the Polish critic Jan Kott, had powerfully influenced theater with his comparison of *Hamlet* and the histories to life under a totalitarian regime, *King Lear* to Theater of the Absurd, and the comedies to a Freudian nightmare. Both Brecht and Kott could be recognized behind Peter Brook's *King Lear* (1962), which, in place of the traditional sympathy with the king (a frighteningly harsh Paul Scofield), emphasized his and his followers' brutality toward Goneril's servants, and ruthlessly cut anything that might be cathartic; the Dover cliff meeting between Lear and Gloucester frankly drew on the stage imagery of Samuel Beckett's *Waiting for Godot*. Brook's *A Midsummer Night's Dream* (1970), which based its erotic treatment of Titania and Bottom on Kott's work, found a purely theatrical language for the critical commonplaces about the play's metatheatricality. Without makeup, under bright light, in a white-walled gymnasium that replaced the traditional moonlit forest, Oberon and Puck sat on trapezes and passed the aphrodisiac "flower," a metal plate, from one spinning metallic wand to another. The fact that this operation could, and occasionally did, go wrong was the point: it reminded the audience that the real magic lay in its own willingness to trust the actors. Even the "Pyramus and Thisbe" actors in the final scene were treated as serious artists, representatives of working-class culture who deserved respect. For many of his later productions, Peter Brook went abroad in search of a multilingual, multiethnic cast, searching for ways of escaping the "easy" assumptions about Shakespeare.

It was in fact race and gender rather than class that dominated Shakespeare production in the last quarter of the century. The concern with race began with the great American theatrical event of the 1940s, Margaret Webster's production of *Othello* with the charismatic Paul Robeson in the title role. After the longest run of any Shakespeare play on Broadway, it was taken on tour all over America in 1945, playing only in desegregated theaters. Although Robeson had already played Othello in London (1930), and would do so again at Stratford-upon-Avon, England, in 1959, his long period of disgrace in the politically polarized United States of the 1950s delayed the movement toward race-based casting as a norm. After initial embarrassment about racist language in Shakespeare, the theater began deliberately to explore its implications, as race became a subject for academic study. The range of *Othello* videos available by the 1990s indicates the play's performance history: besides Orson

Welles's film from 1952, these include the National Theatre production of 1964 starring Laurence Olivier and the BBC one with Antony Hopkins (1981), both with white actors in the title role; Trevor Nunn's Chekhovian version originally staged in 1989; the historic South African production by Janet Suzman, a political act at a time when apartheid still existed; and Oliver Parker's 1994 version, with Laurence Fishburne (opposite Kenneth Branagh's convincingly ordinary Iago), consciously conveying the concentrated power and sensuality associated with blackness. Confusion between "color-blind casting" (when the audience is supposed to ignore the race of both actor and character) and "race-based casting" (when the audience is being told something about race through the casting) was deliberately cultivated in Jude Kelly's *Othello* (Washington, D.C., 1997). This production enabled Patrick Stewart to achieve his otherwise unrealizable ambition of playing the title role by surrounding a white Othello with African American and Hispanic actors, yet with the play's racial references unaltered.

Just as some critics of racism felt that *Othello* and *The Merchant of Venice* had become theatrically unacceptable, some feminist responses to Shakespeare argued the same about *The Taming of the Shrew*, in which a female character is made to acquiesce in her humiliation by a husband who uses patriarchal arguments to justify his behavior. The play had usually been directed to soften its final moral, either by making it clear that the protagonists have fallen in love at first sight or by emphasizing its nature as a play within a play, safely distant from real life. A famous production by Michael Bogdanov (Royal Shakespeare Theatre, 1978) doubled the drunken tinker Sly with Petruchio and showed Kate being brutalized into a dazed submission that horrified even her husband. Obviously, the play in this version was no longer a comedy. A less obvious effect of feminism has been the increasing attention paid to Shakespeare's female characters. They tend now to be on stage more than the text directs, as when Ophelia stands appalled while her father reads Hamlet's love letters to the court or Gertrude enters in time to hear Claudius and Laertes plan to poison Hamlet, so that her decision to drink from the cup is recognized as a heroic device to save her son's life. The young Elizabeth of York, who does not appear in the text of *Richard III* although she is important to its plot, has frequently been seen and even heard in stage versions, as in the 1995 film by Richard Loncraine. The fact that women are often denied speech at crucial moments can be turned to an advantage, as when John Barton and a number of subsequent directors of *Measure for Measure* in the 1980s made Isabella silently refuse the Duke's proposal, which earlier actors and directors had assumed she would eagerly accept.

Still more important, in a theater in which women are far more likely than men to be underemployed, were devices that increased the number of Shakespearean roles for women. Cross-dressed performances, parallel to the productions focused on race, hovered between gender based and gender blind. Deborah Warner's *Richard II* in 1995, with Fiona Shaw as the title character (National Theatre, London), suggested a troubled and potentially erotic relationship between Richard and Bolingbroke without defining it further. In the all-male Cheek-by-Jowl production of *As You Like It* (1995), the audience was never certain whether it was meant to be thinking of Rosalind (Adrian Lester) as male or female. A similar confusion was exploited when Michael Kahn's *King Lear* (Washington, D.C., 1999) cast Cordelia as a deaf-mute, signing her lines, which were then interpreted by the Fool. This decision, which would have been meaningless if the audience had not known that the actress (Monique Holt) really was a deaf-mute, might be seen either as a return to the self-conscious theatricality of the Renaissance stage or as an example of identity politics.

Shakespeare on Film

Of course, the sense of identity between actor and role is strongest in the cinema, where physical appearance matters more and where audiences are particularly likely to bring with them recollections of an actor's previous roles. Films of Shakespeare plays are as old as film itself. Their transfer to videotape and then laserdisc and DVD, a process that began in the 1970s, has given them a much wider circulation and canonized some performances: Olivier's Richard III, for instance, now has much the same iconic status that Cibber gave to Betterton's Hamlet. Orson Welles's film versions of *Macbeth* (1947) and *Othello* (1952), visually remarkable as they were, have benefited from remastering to make their soundtracks more intelligible. The BBC made-for-TV versions of Shakespeare, 1979–1985, often disappointed both film and Shakespeare enthusiasts, though for different reasons, but have been widely used in schools. Kenneth Branagh's films, including a remarkable four-hour uncut *Hamlet* (1996), have been surprisingly successful in making the plays accessible to a popular audience. His *Henry V* (1989) was unfairly praised for being more "real" than Olivier's; both films were star-centered, with Olivier playing a more controlled king, Branagh a more vulnerable one. Whereas Olivier began his film with a view of an idealized Elizabethan London, then of a playhouse viewed from a superior perspective as old-fashioned and in some ways comic, Branagh introduced his Chorus (Derek Jacobi) in a room full of movie cameras, though he later allowed him to move among the actors in the film. As often in films, the moments most remembered were visual: Henry's (Branagh's) grief when, in order to enforce proper discipline, he is obliged to order the hanging of Bardolph, or the long shot, after the Battle of Agincourt, that shows Henry carrying the dead boy in a procession of English soldiers singing *Non nobis Domine*.

Branagh's youth was an asset in bringing Shakespeare to a young audience. Later filmmakers have aimed at a still younger group. *William Shakespeare's Romeo and Juliet* (directed by Baz Luhrmann, 1996), filled as it was with icons of contemporary youth culture, is perhaps the first of these, though it retains Shakespeare's language, juxtaposing it with contradictory images, so that it can be understood either as a complex visual-verbal experience or as a rather simple visual one. The *Hamlet* directed by Michael Almereyda (2000) represents its young characters as college students obsessed with modern technology: Hamlet (Ethan Hawke) is an amateur filmmaker and Ophelia is a photographer; "To be or not to be" is spoken in a video store against a background of videos labeled "Action." For students of the new field of Shakespeare in Popular Culture, Teenage Shakespeare, with the stories rewritten in contemporary language and settings, is becoming a genre in its own right. *Ten Things I Hate About You* (directed by Gil Junger, 1999) and *O* (directed by Tim Blake Nelson, 2001) retell *The Taming of the Shrew* and *Othello* in American high school settings. *The Children's Midsummer Night's Dream* (directed by Christine Edzard, 2001) has a cast of primary school children.

International Contexts and Contemporary Adaptations

Not only have the plays been adapted for every age group, they have turned out to speak an international language. This had not always been true, though English and French actors had visited each other's countries since the seventeenth century: in 1629 French actresses were booed by English audiences, still accustomed to an all-male stage; one group of English actors was booed in the Paris of 1818, but another visiting company in 1827 inspired French writers and actors to try to understand Shakespeare. English and American audiences saw *Othello* with new eyes when the Italian actor Tommaso Salvini, followed by several other famous Italians, performed on tour in the late nineteenth century. Along with the visit of the Berliner Ensemble to London in 1956, the most important influences in the late twentieth century came from Asian, especially Japanese, theater and from central and eastern Europe. Kurosawa's films, *Throne of Blood* (*Macbeth*, 1957) and *Ran* (*King Lear*, 1986), transpose Shakespearean plots into Japanese culture and images. Successful Russian films have ranged from the visually stunning colors of Yan Fried's *Twelfth Night* and Sergei Yutkevitch's *Othello* (both 1955) to Grigori Kozintsev's black-and-white *Hamlet* (1964) and *King Lear* (1971).

The opening up of contacts with central and eastern Europe after 1989 has resulted in visits from theater companies of the former eastern bloc countries. When London audiences in 1990 saw *Hamlet* by the Bulandra Theatre of Romania (directed by Alexander Tocilescu), they discovered that plays often regarded in Britain and America as "conservative" tools of the "establishment" had elsewhere been a powerful vehicle for the expression of political dissent. When first produced in 1985, Tocilescu's *Hamlet* was clearly understood to be equating the rottenness of Elsinore with the world created by Nicolae Ceaucescu, the dictator executed in 1989; Ion Caramitru, the actor who played Hamlet, had been one of the leaders of the revolution. In Czech productions of Shakespeare, similarly, actors and audience had gathered in a deliberate act of misreading directed at the occupying Russians: in *Love's Labor's Lost*, of all plays, the princess's suggestion that the courtiers disguised as Muscovites should "be gone" was the high point of the evening.

Western directors have sometimes attempted to deal with a difficult text by interpreting it as "Other," particularly as Japanese: the samurai warrior culture was the background to Barry Kyle's *The Two Noble Kinsmen* (Swan Theatre, Stratford, 1986) and to David Farr's *Coriolanus* (Royal Shakespeare Theatre, 2002), whereas Ron Daniels's *Timon of Athens* (The Other Place, Stratford, 1980) drew on the concept of a society based on gift-giving. Conversely, Yukio Ninagawa's Japanese Shakespeare productions have combined Japanese costumes with a soundtrack of European music (*Macbeth*) and interpreted *The Tempest* through the story of the famous Japanese exile, Shunkan. Such cross-cultural borrowings have sometimes been denigrated as "cultural tourism," by which critics seem to mean that it is illegitimate to appropriate the merely visual aspects of a culture to which one does not belong.

Similarly, the reconstructed "Shakespeare's Globe" in London, which opened in 1997, was accused of attempting to appropriate the emotions of another historical period. Perhaps because the opening production was *Henry V*, the "groundlings" who stood in the yard for only £5 apiece seemed to be modeling themselves on their counterparts in the Globe sequence of Olivier's film, who boo when they hear that Falstaff has been banished. Their willingness to boo the French (and, in the next season, Shylock) at first shocked the critics, and it was suggested that this theater might be suited only to comedies and histories demanding a presentational style, but productions of *Hamlet* (2000) and *King Lear* (2001) showed that it was possible to control audience response to the tragedies. Mark Rylance's *Hamlet* skillfully played his line about groundlings "capable of nothing but inexplicable dumbshow," so that he could respond to their laughter by adding "*and* noise." Whether or not the theater can really tell anyone anything about Elizabethan stage conventions and audience response, it has given considerable pleasure. Other Globes, more and less historically based, now can be found in several countries (the United States, Japan, Poland, and the Czech Republic, among others), while the open stage of Stratford, Canada, remains one of the most successful modifications of the Elizabethan model. In a reversal of the search for authenticity, the Shakespeare Theatre in Washington, D.C., has abandoned its home in the reconstructed Fortune Theatre at the Folger Shakespeare Library for a purpose-built modern auditorium. In fact, the two kinds of theater can coexist. The well-established Shakespeare festivals of Stratford, Ontario; Ashland, Oregon; and Santa Cruz, California, have added well-equipped indoor theaters to their outdoor acting spaces, and an indoor auditorium is projected as an addition to Shakespeare's Globe in London. A reconstruction of the Blackfriars Playhouse opened in Staunton, Virginia, in 2001.

Although it has been impossible to discuss the theatrical fortunes of every Shakespeare play, it may be interesting to end by reflecting how greatly these have fluctuated. If some plays, like *Hamlet* and *Macbeth*, have always been popular, the history of others is more checkered. Some of the comedies most popular today, such as *As You Like It* and *Twelfth Night*, were regarded as insipid in the eighteenth century, redeemed only by their scenes of low comedy and occasional sententious speeches. *The Merry Wives of Windsor* was the most popular comedy during the Restoration; *King John* and *Henry VIII* were more popular in the nineteenth century than *Richard II* or *2 Henry IV*. *Othello* was acted without the "willow scene" (4.3) for most of the eighteenth and nineteenth centuries, and *Troilus and Cressida* and *Titus Andronicus* were performed, if at all, only in heavily adapted versions. It is arguable that the attitude to Shakespeare that Bernard Shaw ridiculed as "Bardolatry" reached its height, not in the Victorian age, but at the end of the twentieth century, a time when any Shakespeare play, however minor, was likely to find a director and an audience. One reason might be that the subsidized theaters had been giving fewer controversial productions since 1980, emphasizing instead what the plays have in common with musical comedies and films. An important American contribution to Shakespeare in performance has taken the form of musicals like *The Boys from Syracuse* (1938), *Kiss Me Kate* (1948), and *West Side Story* (1957), based respectively on *The Comedy of Errors*, *The Taming of the Shrew*, and *Romeo and Juliet*; now, many productions of the comedies followed the Restoration practice of filling them with popular music. What was new was not the practice of adaptation but the attitude toward it. In the mid century, the plays were taken to be fixed quantities: the job of the theater director, as of the critic, was to uncover the "real" work, whether through more authentic staging, a more accurate text, or a better understanding of its meaning. By the end of the millennium, when some theorists were insisting that the text itself was unknowable, it is not surprising to find a much greater tolerance for re-creations and explorations of the plays in other forms.

Bibliography

Abbreviations Used

English Literary History	*ELH*
Publications of the Modern Language Association of America	*PMLA*
Shakespeare Quarterly	*SQ*
Shakespeare Studies	*ShakS*
Shakespeare Survey	*ShS*

Works of Reference

Abbott, E. A. *A Shakespearian Grammar*. New ed., London, 1870.

Allen, Michael J. B., and Kenneth Muir, eds. *Shakespeare's Plays in Quarto*. Berkeley, 1981.

Bentley, G. E. *The Jacobean and Caroline Stage*. 7 vols. Oxford, 1941–1968.

Bergeron, David M. *Shakespeare: A Study and Research Guide*. New York, 1975; 2nd ed., rev. David Bergeron and Geraldo de Sousa. Lawrence, Kans., 1987.

Bullough, Geoffrey, ed. *Narrative and Dramatic Sources of Shakespeare*. 8 vols. London, 1957–1975.

Chambers, E.K. *The Elizabethan Stage*. 4 vols. Oxford, 1923; rev., 1945.

———. *The Mediaeval Stage*. 2 vols. Oxford, 1903.

———. *William Shakespeare: A Study of Facts and Problems*. 2 vols. Oxford, 1930.

Dent, R. W. *Shakespeare's Proverbial Language: An Index*. Berkeley, 1981.

Garland Shakespeare Bibliographies, gen. ed. William Godshalk. Published in separate volumes for various plays, at varying dates. Garland: New York.

Greg, W. W. *A Bibliography of the English Printed Drama to the Restoration*. 4 vols. London, 1939–1959.

———, ed. *Shakespeare Quarto Facsimiles*. London, 1939–. (An incomplete set; Greg's work has been supplemented by Charlton Hinman.)

Harbage, Alfred. *Annals of English Drama, 975–1700*. Rev. S. Schoenbaum.

Philadelphia, 1964; 3rd ed., Sylvia Stoler Wagonheim, 1989.

Hinman, Charlton, ed. *The Norton Facsimile: The First Folio of Shakespeare*. New York, 1968.

Hosley, Richard, ed. *Shakespeare's Holinshed*. New York, 1968.

Kökeritz, Helge. *Shakespeare's Names*. New Haven, 1959.

———. *Shakespeare's Pronunciation*. New Haven, 1953.

Long, John. *Shakespeare's Use of Music: Comedies*. Gainesville, Fla., 1955. *Final Comedies*, 1961; *Histories and Tragedies*, 1971.

McDonald, Russ. *The Bedford Companion to Shakespeare: An Introduction with Documents*. Boston, 1996; 2nd ed., 2001.

McManaway, James G., and Jeanne Addison Roberts, compilers. *A Selective Bibliography of Shakespeare*. Charlottesville, Va., 1975.

Muir, Kenneth. *Shakespeare's Sources*. 2 vols. London, 1957.

———, and S. Schoenbaum, eds. *A New Companion to Shakespeare Studies*. London and New York, 1971.

Munro, John, ed. *The Shakespeare Allusion Book*. 2 vols. London and New York, 1909; reissued 1932.

Naylor, Edward W. *Shakespeare and Music*. New ed., London, 1931.

Noble, Richmond. *Shakespeare's Biblical Knowledge*. London, 1935.

———. *Shakespeare's Use of Song*. London, 1923.

Onions, C. T. *A Shakespeare Glossary*. Rev. and enlgd. R. D. Eagleson. Oxford, 1986.

Pegasus Shakespeare Bibliographies. Annotated bibliographies of Shakespeare studies in a 12-volume series, gen. ed. Richard L. Nochimson, including *Love's Labor's Lost, A Midsummer Night's Dream*, and *The Merchant of Venice* (Clifford Chalmers Huffman), *Richard II, Henry IV, I and II*, and *Henry V* (Joseph Candido), *Hamlet* (Michael E. Mooney), *The Rape of Lucrece, Titus Andronicus, Julius Caesar*,

Antony and Cleopatra, and *Coriolanus* (Clifford Chalmers Huffman and John W. Velz), *King Lear* and *Macbeth* (Rebecca W. Bushnell), and *Shakespeare and the Renaissance Stage to 1616* and *Shakespearean Stage History 1616 to 1998* (Hugh Macrae Richmond). Binghamton, N.Y. (1995) and Asheville, N.C., 1996—.

Publications of the Modern Language Association of America (PMLA). Annual Bibliography.

Rothwell, Kenneth S., and Annabelle Henkin Melzer. *Shakespeare on Screen: An International Filmography and Videography*. New York and London, 1990.

Schmidt, Alexander. *Shakespeare-Lexicon*. 5th ed. Berlin, 1962.

Seager, H. W. *Natural History in Shakespeare's Time*. London, 1896.

Seng, Peter J. *The Vocal Songs in the Plays of Shakespeare*. Cambridge, Mass., 1967.

Shakespeare Bulletin.

Shakespeare-Jahrbuch.

Shakespeare Newsletter.

Shakespeare Quarterly. Annual Bibliography.

Shakespeare Studies.

Shakespeare Survey.

Spencer, T. J. B., ed. *Shakespeare's Plutarch*. Harmondsworth, Eng., 1964.

Spevack, Marvin. *The Harvard Concordance to Shakespeare*. Cambridge, Mass., 1973.

Sternfeld, Frederick W. *Music in Shakespearean Tragedy*. London, 1963, 1967.

Thomson, J. A. K. *Shakespeare and the Classics*. London, 1952.

Wells, Stanley, ed. *Shakespeare: Select Bibliographical Guides*. London, 1973.

———, ed. *The Cambridge Companion to Shakespeare Studies*. Cambridge, Eng., 1986.

Life in Shakespeare's England

Allen, Don Cameron. *The Star-Crossed Renaissance*. Durham, N.C., 1941.

Baker, Herschel. *The Image of Man: A Study of the Idea of Human Dignity in Classical Antiquity, the Middle Ages, and the Renaissance*. Cambridge, Mass., 1961. (First published in 1947 as *The Dignity of Man*.)

———. *The Wars of Truth: Studies in the Decay of Christian Humanism in the Earlier Seventeenth Century*. Cambridge, Mass., 1952.

Bakhtin, Mikhail M. *Rabelais and His World*, trans. H. Iswolsky. Cambridge, Mass., 1968.

Barkan, Leonard. *Nature's Work of Art: The Human Body as Image of the World*. New Haven, 1975.

———. *The Gods Made Flesh: Metamorphosis and the Pursuit of Paganism*. New Haven, 1986.

Barroll, J. Leeds. *Politics, Plague, and Shakespeare's Theater: The Stuart Years*. Ithaca, N.Y., 1991.

Bindoff, S. T., et al., eds. *Elizabethan Government and Society*. Essays presented to Sir John Neale. London, 1961.

Bush, Douglas. *The Renaissance and English Humanism*. Toronto, 1939.

Buxton, John. *Elizabethan Taste*. London, 1963.

Byrne, Muriel St. Clare. *Elizabethan Life in Town and Country*. 8th ed. London, 1970.

Camden, Carroll. *The Elizabethan Woman*. Houston, 1952.

Caspari, Fritz. *Humanism and the Social Order in Tudor England*. Chicago, 1954.

Cassirer, Ernst. *The Platonic Renaissance in England*, trans. J. E. Pettegrove. Austin, Tex., 1953.

De Grazia, Margreta, Maureen Quilligan, and Peter Stallybrass, eds. *Subject and Object in Renaissance Culture*. Cambridge, Eng., 1996.

Einstein, Lewis. *Tudor Ideals*. New York, 1921.

Elizabeth I. *Collected Works*, eds. Leah S. Marcus, Janel Mueller, and Mary Beth Rose. Chicago, 2000.

Elton, G. R. *The Tudor Revolution in Government*. Cambridge, Eng., 1959.

Fumerton, Patricia, and Simon Hunt, eds. *Renaissance Culture and the Everyday*. Philadelphia, 1999.

Gallagher, Lowell. *Medusa's Gaze: Casuistry and Conscience in the Renaissance*. Stanford, 1991.

Harrison, G. B. *An Elizabethan Journal*. London, 1928; supplements.

———. *A Jacobean Journal . . . 1603–1606*. London, 1941.

———. *A Second Jacobean Journal . . . 1607 to 1610*. Ann Arbor, Mich., 1958.

Haydn, Hiram. *The Counter-Renaissance*. New York, 1950.

Helgerson, Richard. *Forms of Nationhood: The Elizbethan Writing of England*. Chicago, 1992.

Heninger, S. K., Jr. *A Handbook of Renaissance Meteorology*. Durham, N.C., 1960.

Hirst, Derek. *Authority and Conflict: England, 1603–1658*. Cambridge, Mass., 1986.

Huizinga, Johan. *The Waning of the Middle Ages*. London, 1924; Baltimore, 1955.

Hurstfield, Joel. *Elizabeth I and the Unity of England*. London, 1960.

Jones, Ann Rosalind, and Peter Stallybrass. *Renaissance Clothing and the Materials of Memory*. Cambridge, Eng., 2000.

Jordan, Constance. *Renaissance Feminism: Literary Texts and Political Models*. Ithaca, N.Y., 1990.

Judges, A. V., ed. *The Elizabethan Underworld*. London and New York, 1930. Rpt., London, 1965.

Kewes, Paulina, ed. *Plagiarism in Early Modern England*. Basingstoke, Hampshire, Eng., 2003.

Knights, L. C. *Drama and Society in the Age of Jonson*. London, 1937.

Kocher, Paul. *Science and Religion in Elizabethan England*. San Marino, Calif., 1953.

Lee, Morris. *Great Britain's Solomon: James VI and I in His Three Kingdoms*. Urbana, Ill., 1990.

Lovejoy, A. O. *The Great Chain of Being*. Cambridge, Mass., 1936.

MacCaffrey, Wallace T. *The Shaping of the Elizabethan Regime*. Princeton, 1968.

Marotti, Arthur F., ed. *Catholicism and Anti-Catholicism in Early Modern English Texts*. Basingstoke, Hampshire, Eng., 1999.

Matar, Nabil. *Turks, Moors, and Englishmen in the Age of Discovery*. New York, 1999.

Mattingly, Garrett. *The Armada*. Boston, 1959.

McEachern, Claire, and Debora Shuger, eds. *Religion and Culture in Renaissance England*. Cambridge, Eng., 1997.

McElwee, W. *The Wisest Fool in Christendom*. [About James VI and I.] New York, 1958.

McPeek, James A. S. *The Black Book of Knaves and Unthrifts in Shakespeare and Other Renaissance Authors*. Storrs, Conn., 1969.

Neale, John E. *Elizabeth I and Her Parliaments*. 2 vols. London and New York, 1953–1958.

———. *The Elizabethan House of Commons*. London, 1949.

———. *Queen Elizabeth I*. London, 1934; New York, 1957.

Nichols, John, ed. *The Progresses and Public Processions of Queen Elizabeth*. 3 vols. London, 1823.

Patterson, Annabel M. *Reading Holinshed's Chronicles*. Chicago, 1994.

Peck, Linda Levy. *Court Patronage and Corruption in Early Stuart England*. Boston, 1990.

Penrose, Boies. *Travel and Discovery in the Renaissance, 1420–1620*. Cambridge, Mass., 1955.

Quinones, Ricardo J. *The Renaissance Discovery of Time*. Cambridge, Mass., 1972.

Rowse, A. L. *The England of Elizabeth: The Structure of Society*. London, 1951.

Stallybrass, Peter, and Allon White. *The Politics and Poetics of Transgression*. Ithaca, N.Y., and London, 1986.

Stone, Lawrence. *The Crisis of the Aristocracy, 1558–1641*. Oxford, 1965.

———. *The Family, Sex and Marriage in England, 1500–1800*. London, 1977.

Stow, John. *Survey of London*, ed. C. L. Kingsford. Oxford, 1971.

Targoff, Ramie. *Common Prayer: The Language of Public Devotion in Early Modern England*. Chicago, 2001.

Tawney, R. H. *Religion and the Rise of Capitalism*. New York, 1926, 1962.

Tillyard, E. M. W. *The Elizabethan World Picture*. London, 1943, 1967.

Underdown, David. *Revel, Riot, and Rebellion: Popular Politics and Culture in England, 1603–1660*. Oxford, 1985.

Whigham, Frank. *Ambition and Privilege: The Social Tropes of Elizabethan Courtesy Theory*. Berkeley, 1984.

Willson, David Harris. *King James VI & I*. New York, 1956.

Wilson, F. P. *Elizabethan and Jacobean*. Oxford, 1945.

Wilson, J. Dover, ed. *Life in Shakespeare's England*. Cambridge, Eng., 1911; 2nd ed., 1926.

Woodbridge, Linda. *Women and the English Renaissance*. Urbana, Ill., 1984.

Wright, Louis B. *Middle-Class Culture in Elizabethan England*. Chapel Hill, N.C., 1935.

Wrightson, Keith. *English Society, 1580–1680*. New Brunswick, N.J., 1982.

Zeeveld, W. Gordon. *Foundations of Tudor Policy*. Cambridge, Mass., 1948.

Shakespeare's Predecessors and Contemporaries

See also, under *Works of Reference*, Bentley, Chambers, Greg, and Harbage; under *London Theaters and Dramatic Companies*, McMillin and MacLean; under *Shakespeare Criticism Since 1980*, Dollimore, Garber (*Cannibals*), Goldberg, Greenblatt, Jardine, Loomba, Mullaney, Newman, and Skura; and under *The Tragedies*, Bushnell.

Altman, Joel B. *The Tudor Play of Mind: Rhetorical Inquiry and the Development of Elizabethan Drama*. Berkeley, 1978.

Bamford, Karen. *Sexual Violence on the Jacobean Stage*. New York, 2000.

Barber, C. L. *Creating Elizabethan Tragedy: The Theater of Kyd and Marlowe*. Chicago, 1988.

Bartels, Emily C. *Spectacles of Strangeness: Imperialism, Alienation, and Marlowe*. Philadelphia, 1993.

Bednarz, James P. *Shakespeare and the Poets' War*. New York, 2001.

Belsey, Catherine. *The Subject of Tragedy: Identity and Difference in Renaissance Drama*. London, 1985.

Berry, Philippa. *Of Chastity and Power: Elizabethan Literature and the Unmarried Queen*. London and New York, 1989.

Bevington, David. *From "Mankind" to Marlowe: Growth of Structure in the Popular Drama of Tudor England*. Cambridge, Mass., 1962.

———. *Tudor Drama and Politics*. Cambridge, Mass., 1968.

———, and Peter Holbrook, eds. *The Politics of the Stuart Court Masque*. Cambridge, Eng., 1991.

Bowers, Fredson T. *Elizabethan Revenge Tragedy, 1587–1642*. Princeton, 1940.

Braden, Gordon. *Renaissance Tragedy and the Senecan Tradition*. New Haven, 1985.

Braunmuller, A. R., and Michael Hattaway, eds. *The Cambridge Companion to English Renaissance Drama*. Cambridge, Eng., 1990.

Bristol, Michael D. *Carnival and Theater: Plebeian Culture and the Structure of Authority in Renaissance England.* London, 1985.

Brooke, C. F. Tucker, ed. *The Shakespeare Apocrypha.* Oxford, 1908.

Brooks, Douglas A. *From Playhouse to Printing House: Drama and Authorship in Early Modern England.* Cambridge, Eng., 2000.

Bruster, Douglas. *Drama and the Market in the Age of Shakespeare.* Cambridge, Eng., 1992.

Burt, Richard. *Licensed by Authority: Ben Jonson and the Discourses of Censorship.* Ithaca, N.Y., 1993.

Bushnell, Rebecca W. *Tragedies of Tyrants: Political Thought and Theater in the English Renaissance.* Ithaca, N.Y., 1990.

Butterworth, Philip. *Theatre of Fire: Special Effects in Early English and Scottish Theatre.* London, 1998.

Caputi, Anthony. *John Marston, Satirist.* Ithaca, N.Y., 1961.

Cohen, Walter. *Drama of a Nation: Public Theater in Renaissance England and Spain.* Ithaca, N.Y., 1985.

Comensoli, Viviana, and Anna Russell, eds. *Enacting Gender on the English Renaissance Stage.* Urbana, Ill., 1999.

Cox, John D., and David Scott Kastan, eds. *A New History of Early English Drama.* New York, 1997.

Craik, T. W. *The Tudor Interlude.* Leicester, 1958, 1962.

Dawson, Anthony B., and Paul Yachnin. *The Culture of Playgoing in Shakespeare's England: A Collaborative Debate.* Cambridge, Eng., 2001.

Deats, Sara Munson. *Sex, Gender, and Desire in the Plays of Christopher Marlowe.* Newark, Del., 1997.

Dessen, Alan C. *Elizabethan Drama and the Viewer's Eye.* Chapel Hill, N.C., 1977.

Diehl, Huston. *Staging Reform, Reforming the Stage: Protestantism and Popular Theater in Early Modern England.* Ithaca, N.Y., 1997.

Dillon, Janette. *Theatre, Court and City, 1595–1610: Drama and Social Space in London.* Cambridge, Eng., 2000.

DiGangi, Mario. *The Homoerotics of Early Modern Drama.* Cambridge, Eng., 1997.

Dolan, Frances E. *Dangerous Familiars: Representations of Domestic Crime in England, 1550–1700.* Ithaca, N.Y., 1994.

Doran, Madeleine. *Endeavors of Art: A Study of Form in Elizabethan Drama.* Madison, Wis., 1954, 1972.

Farley-Hills, David. *Shakespeare and the Rival Playwrights, 1600–1606.* London, 1990.

Findlay, Alison. *A Feminist Perspective on Renaissance Drama.* Oxford, 1999.

——. *Illegitimate Power: Bastards in Renaissance Drama.* Manchester, Eng., 1994.

Finkelpearl, Philip. *John Marston of the Middle Temple.* Cambridge, Mass., 1969.

Freer, Coburn. *The Poetics of Jacobean Drama.* Baltimore, 1981.

Gardiner, H. C. *Mysteries' End.* New Haven, 1946.

Gibbons, Brian. *Jacobean City Comedy.* London, 1968.

Hall, Kim F. *Things of Darkness: Economies of Race and Gender in Early Modern England.* Ithaca, N.Y., 1995.

Hardison, O. B., Jr. *Christian Rite and Christian Drama in the Middle Ages.* Baltimore, 1965.

Hassel, R. Chris. *Renaissance Drama and the English Church Year.* Lincoln, Neb., 1979.

Hattaway, Michael. *Elizabethan Popular Theatre: Plays in Performance.* London, 1982.

Hawkins, Harriett. *Likenesses of Truth in Elizabethan and Restoration Drama.* Oxford, 1972.

Helgerson, Richard. *Adulterous Alliances: Home, State, and History in Early Modern European Drama and Painting.* Chicago, 2000.

Hendricks, Margo, and Patricia Parker, eds. *Women, "Race," and Writing in the Early Modern Period.* London and New York, 1994.

Holbrook, Peter. *Literature and Degree in Renaissance England: Nashe, Bourgeois Tragedy, Shakespeare.* Newark, Del., 1994.

Howard, Jean. *The Stage and Social Struggle in Early Modern England.* London and New York, 1994.

Hunter, G. K. *John Lyly: The Humanist as Courtier.* Cambridge, Mass., 1962.

Kastan, David Scott, and Peter Stallybrass, eds. *Staging the Renaissance: Reinterpretations of Elizabethan and Jacobean Drama.* New York and London, 1991.

Kernan, Alvin. *The Cankered Muse: Satire of the English Renaissance.* New Haven, 1959.

Kiefer, Frederick. *Writing on the Renaissance Stage: Written Words, Printed Pages, Metaphoric Books.* Newark, Del., 1996.

Kirsch, Arthur C. *Jacobean Dramatic Perspectives.* Charlottesville, Va., 1972.

Kolve, V. A. *The Play Called Corpus Christi.* Palo Alto and London, 1966.

Leggatt, Alexander. *Citizen Comedy in the Age of Shakespeare.* Toronto, 1973.

——. *Jacobean Public Theatre.* London, 1992.

Leishman, J. B., ed. *The Three Parnassus Plays (1598–1601).* London, 1949.

Levin, Harry. *The Overreacher: A Study of Christopher Marlowe.* Cambridge, Mass., 1952, 1964.

Levin, Richard. *The Multiple Plot in English Renaissance Drama.* Chicago, 1971.

Margeson, J. M. R. *The Origins of English Tragedy.* Oxford, 1967.

Marrapodi, Michele, ed., with A. J. Hoenselaars. *The Italian World of English Renaissance Drama: Cultural Exchange and Intertextuality.* Newark, Del., 1998.

Maus, Katharine Eisaman. *Inwardness and Theater in the English Renaissance Drama.* Chicago, 1995.

McAlindon, T. *English Renaissance Tragedy.* London, 1986.

McLuskie, Kathleen. *Renaissance Dramatists.* (Feminist Readings.) Atlantic Highlands, N.J., 1989.

Orgel, Stephen. *The Illusion of Power: Political Theater in the English Renaissance.* Berkeley, 1975.

——. *Impersonations: The Performance of Gender in Shakespeare's England.* Cambridge, Eng., 1996.

Orgel, Stephen, and Roy Strong. *Inigo Jones: The Theatre of the Stuart Court.* 2 vols. London and Berkeley, 1973.

Ornstein, Robert. *The Moral Vision of Jacobean Tragedy.* Madison, Wis., 1960.

Rabkin, Norman, ed: *Reinterpretations of Elizabethan Drama.* New York, 1969.

Rasmussen, Mark David, ed. *Renaissance Literature and Its Formal Engagements.* Basingstoke, Hampshire, 2002.

Rose, Mary Beth. *The Expense of Spirit: Love and Sexuality in English Renaissance Drama.* Ithaca, N.Y., 1988.

——. *Gender and Heroism in Early Modern English Literature.* Chicago, 2002.

——. ed. *Renaissance Drama as Cultural History.* Evanston, Ill., 1990.

Sanders, Wilbur. *The Dramatist and the Received Idea: Studies in the Plays of Marlowe and Shakespeare.* Cambridge, Eng., 1968.

Shannon, Laurie. *Sovereign Amity: Figures of Friendship in Shakespearean Contexts.* Chicago, 2002.

Shapiro, James. *Rival Playwrights: Marlowe, Jonson, Shakespeare.* New York, 1991.

Smith, Bruce R. *The Acoustic World of Early Modern England.* Chicago, 1999.

Smith, David L., Richard Strier, and David Bevington, eds. *The Theatrical City: Culture, Theatre and Politics in London, 1567–1649.* Cambridge, Eng., 1995.

Southern, Richard. *The Medieval Theatre in the Round.* London, 1957.

Spivack, Bernard. *Shakespeare and the Allegory of Evil.* New York, 1958.

Traub, Valerie, M. Lindsay Kaplan, and Dympna C. Callaghan, eds. *Feminist Readings of Early Modern Culture: Emerging Subjects.* Cambridge, Eng., 1996.

Vickers, Brian. *"Counterfeiting" Shakespeare: Evidence, Authorship, and John Ford's "Funerall Elegye."* Cambridge, Eng., 2002.

Waith, Eugene M. *The Herculean Hero in Marlowe, Chapman, Shakespeare, and Dryden.* New York, 1962.

Whigham, Frank. *Seizures of the Will in Early Modern English Drama.* Cambridge, Eng., 1996.

White, Paul Whitfield. *Marlowe, History, and Sexuality: New Critical Essays on Christopher Marlowe.* New York, 1998.

——. *Theatre and Reformation: Protestantism, Patronage and Playing in Tudor England.* Cambridge, Eng., 1993.

Wickham, Glynne. *Early English Stages, 1300 to 1660.* 3 vols. London, 1959–1972.

Wilson, F. P. *Marlowe and the Early Shakespeare.* Oxford, 1953.

Woodbridge, Linda. *Women and the English Renaissance: Literature and the Nature of Womankind, 1540–1620.* Urbana, Ill., 1984.

Woolf, Rosemary. *The English Mystery Plays.* Berkeley and Los Angeles, 1972.

Yachnin, Paul. *Stage-Wrights: Shakespeare, Jonson, Middleton, and the Making of Theatrical Value*. Philadelphia, 1997.

Zimmerman, Susan, ed. *Erotic Politics: Desire on the Renaissance Stage*. London and New York, 1992.

London Theaters and Dramatic Companies

See also, under *Works of Reference*, Bentley, and Chambers (*Elizabethan Stage*).

Astington, John H., ed. *The Development of Shakespeare's Theater*. New York, 1992.

Beckerman, Bernard. *Shakespeare at the Globe, 1599–1609*. New York, 1962, 1967.

Bentley, Gerald Eades. *The Profession of Dramatist in Shakespeare's Time, 1590–1642*. Princeton, 1971.

———. *The Profession of Player in Shakespeare's Time, 1590–1642*. Princeton, 1984.

Berry, Herbert. *Shakespeare's Playhouses*. New York, 1987.

Bradley, David. *From Text to Performance in the Elizabethan Theatre: Preparing the Play for the Stage*. Cambridge, Eng., 1992.

Clare, Janet. *"Art Made Tongue-Tied by Authority": Elizabethan and Jacobean Dramatic Censorship*. Manchester, Eng., 1990.

Cook, Ann Jennalie. *The Privileged Playgoers of Shakespeare's London, 1576–1642*. Princeton, 1981.

Dutton, Richard. *Mastering the Revels: The Regulation and Censorship of English Renaissance Drama*. Iowa City, 1991.

Feuillerat, Albert, ed. *Documents Relating to the Office of the Revels in the Time of Queen Elizabeth*. Louvain (Louven), Belgium, 1908.

Foakes, R. A., ed. *The Henslowe Papers: The Diary, Theatre Papers, and Bear Garden Papers*. In full and in facsimile. 3 vols. in 2. London, 1976.

Foakes, R. A., and R. T. Rickert, eds. *Henslowe's Diary*. London, 1961.

Gair, W. Reavley. *The Children of Paul's*. Cambridge, Eng., 1982.

Greg, W. W., ed. *Dramatic Documents from the Elizabethan Playhouses: Stage Plots; Actors' Parts; Prompt Books*. 2 vols. Oxford, 1931.

Gurr, Andrew. *Playgoing in Shakespeare's London*. Cambridge, Eng., 1987; 2nd ed., 1996.

———. *The Shakespearian Playing Companies*. Oxford, 1996.

——— *The Shakespearean Stage, 1574–1642*. Cambridge, Eng., 1970; 2nd ed., 1980.

Gurr, Andrew, and John Orrell. *Rebuilding Shakespeare's Globe*. London and New York, 1989.

Harbage, Alfred. *Shakespeare's Audience*. New York, 1941.

Hodges, C. Walter. *The Globe Restored*. London, 1953; 2nd ed., New York, 1968.

Hosley, Richard. "Was There a Music-room in Shakespeare's Globe?" *ShS* 13 (1960), 113–23.

Ingram, William. *The Business of Playing: The Beginnings of the Adult Professional Theater in Elizabethan London*. Ithaca, N.Y., 1992.

King, T. J. *Casting Shakespeare's Plays: London Actors and Their Roles, 1590–1642*. Cambridge, Eng., 1992.

———. *Shakespearean Staging, 1599–1642*. Cambridge, Mass., 1971.

Knutson, Roslyn Lander. *The Repertory of Shakespeare's Company, 1594–1613*. Fayetteville, Ark., 1991.

———. *Playing Companies and Commerce in Shakespeare's Time*. Cambridge, Eng., 2001.

Linthicum, Marie C. *Costume in the Drama of Shakespeare and His Contemporaries*. Oxford, 1936.

Mann, David. *The Elizabethan Player: Contemporary Stage Representation*. London, 1991.

McMillin, Scott. *The Elizabethan Theatre and "The Book of Sir Thomas More."* Ithaca, N.Y., 1987.

McMillin, Scott, and Sally-Beth MacLean. *The Queen's Men and Their Plays*. Cambridge, Eng., 1998.

Nelson, Alan H. *Early Cambridge Theatres: College, University, and Town Stages, 1464–1720*. Cambridge, Eng., 1994.

Nungezer, Edwin. *A Dictionary of Actors*. London and New Haven, 1929.

Shapiro, Michael. *Children of the Revels: The Boys' Companies of Shakespeare's Time and Their Plays*. New York, 1977.

Wickham, Glynne. *Early English Stages, 1300 to 1660*. 3 vols. London, 1959–1972.

Shakespeare's Life and Work

Alexander, Peter. *Shakespeare's Life and Art*. New ed., New York, 1961.

Baldwin, T. W. *William Shakspere's Small Latine and Lesse Greeke*. 2 vols. Urbana, Ill., 1944.

Chambers, E. K. *William Shakespeare: A Study of Facts and Problems*. 2 vols. Oxford, 1930.

Eccles, Mark. *Shakespeare in Warwickshire*. Madison, Wis., 1961.

Honan, Park. *Shakespeare: A Life*. Oxford, 1998.

Matus, Irvin Leigh, *Shakespeare, In Fact*. New York, 1994.

Schoenbaum, S. *Shakespeare's Lives*. Oxford and New York, 1970.

———. *William Shakespeare: A Documentary Life*. Oxford, 1975. Also published with fewer illustrations and a slightly revised text as *A Compact Documentary Life*. 1977.

———. *William Shakespeare: Records and Images*. Oxford, 1981.

Wells, Stanley. *Shakespeare: A Life in Drama*. New York and London, 1995.

Wheeler, Richard P. "Deaths in the Family: The Loss of a Son and the Rise of Shakespearean Comedy," *SQ* 51 (2000), 127–53.

Shakespeare's Language: His Development as Poet and Dramatist

See also, under *Works of Reference*, Abbott, Onions, and Schmidt.

Byrne, Muriel St. Clare. "The Foundations of Elizabethan Language," *ShS* 17 (1964), 223–39.

Cercignani, Fausto. *Shakespeare's Works and Elizabethan Pronunciation*. Oxford, 1981.

Charney, Maurice. *Shakespeare's Roman Plays: The Function of Imagery in the Drama*. Cambridge, Mass., 1961.

———. *Style in Hamlet*. Princeton, 1969.

Clemen, Wolfgang H. *The Development of Shakespeare's Imagery*. Cambridge, Mass., 1951.

Cruttwell, Patrick. *The Shakespearean Moment and Its Place in the Poetry of the Seventeenth Century*. London, 1954.

Desmet, Christy. *Reading Shakespeare's Characters: Rhetoric, Ethics, and Identity*. Amherst, Mass., 1992.

Dobson, E. J. *English Pronunciation, 1500–1700*. 2 vols. 2nd ed. Oxford, 1968.

Donawerth, Jane. *Shakespeare and the Sixteenth-Century Study of Language*. Urbana, Ill., 1984.

Doran, Madeleine. *Shakespeare's Dramatic Language*. Madison, Wis., 1976.

Empson, William. *The Structure of Complex Words*. London, 1951; 3rd ed., 1977.

Hulme, Hilda M. *Explorations in Shakespeare's Language*. London, 1962.

Kermode, Frank. *Shakespeare's Language*. New York, 2000.

Kökeritz, Helge. *Shakespeare's Names*. New Haven, 1959.

———. *Shakespeare's Pronunciation*. New Haven, 1953.

Lanham, Richard A. *The Motives of Eloquence: Literary Rhetoric in the Renaissance*. New Haven, 1976.

Magnussen, Lynne. *Shakespeare and Social Dialogue: Dramatic Language and Elizabethan Letters*. Cambridge, Eng., 1999.

Mahood, M. M. *Shakespeare's Wordplay*. London, 1957.

Miriam Joseph, Sister. *Shakespeare's Use of the Arts of Language*. New York, 1947. Rpt. in part as *Rhetoric in Shakespeare's Time*. 1962.

Nares, Robert. *A Glossary . . . of Shakespeare and His Contemporaries*. New ed. J. O. Halliwell and Thomas Wright. 2 vols. London, 1859, 1905, Rpt. Detroit, 1966.

Partridge, Eric. *Shakespeare's Bawdy*. London, 1947, 1955.

Spurgeon, Caroline. *Shakespeare's Imagery and What it Tells Us*. Cambridge, Eng., 1935.

Thompson, Ann and John O. *Shakespeare: Meaning and Metaphor*. Iowa City, 1987.

Thorne, Alison. *Vision and Rhetoric in Shakespeare: Looking Through Language*. Basingstoke and New York, 2000.

Vickers, Brian. *The Artistry of Shakespeare's Prose*. London, 1968.

Willbern, David. *Poetic Will: Shakespeare and the Play of Language*. Philadelphia, 1997.

Willcock, Gladys D. "Shakespeare and Elizabethan English," *ShS* 7 (1954), 12–24.

Wright, George T. *Shakespeare's Metrical Art*. Berkeley, 1988.

Shakespeare Criticism to the 1930s

Badawi, M. M. *Coleridge: Critic of Shakespeare*. Cambridge, Eng., 1973.

Bradby, Anne, ed. *Shakespeare Criticism, 1919–35*. London, 1936.

Coleridge, S. T. *Coleridge on Shakespeare: The Text of the Lectures of 1811–12*, ed. R. A. Foakes. Charlottesville, Va., 1971.

———. *Coleridge's Writings on Shakespeare*, ed. Terence Hawkes. New York, 1959.

Evans, G. Blakemore, ed. *Shakespeare: Aspects of Influence*. Cambridge, Mass., 1976.

Hazlitt, William. *Characters of Shakespear's Plays*. London, 1817.

Johnson, Samuel. *Johnson on Shakespeare*, ed. Arthur Sherbo. Vol. 7 of *The Yale Edition of the Works of Samuel Johnson*. New Haven, 1968.

Kermode, Frank, ed. *Four Centuries of Shakespearean Criticism*. New York, 1965.

Knight, G. Wilson. *The Shakespearian Tempest*. London, 1932, 1953.

Muir, Kenneth. "Fifty Years of Shakespearian Criticism: 1900–1950," *ShS* 4 (1951), 1–25.

Rabkin, Norman, ed. *Approaches to Shakespeare*. New York, 1964.

Ralli, Augustus. *A History of Shakespearian Criticism*. 2 vols. London, 1932.

Raysor, T. M., ed. *Samuel Taylor Coleridge: Shakespearean Criticism*. 2 vols. 2nd ed. London, 1960.

Schlegel, August Wilhelm. *Lectures on Dramatic Art and Literature*, trans. John Black, 1846. Rpt., New York, 1965.

Schücking, Levin L. *Character Problems in Shakespeare's Plays*. London, 1917; trans., 1922.

Shaw, G. B. *Shaw on Shakespeare*, ed. Edwin Wilson. New York, 1961.

Sherbo, Arthur. *Samuel Johnson, Editor of Shakespeare*. Urbana, Ill., 1956.

Smith, David Nichol, ed. *Shakespeare Criticism: A Selection*. World's Classics, Oxford, 1916.

———, ed. *Eighteenth Century Essays on Shakespeare*. 2nd ed. Oxford, 1963.

Stoll, E. E. *Art and Artifice in Shakespeare*. Cambridge, Eng., 1933, 1962.

Vickers, Brian, ed. *Shakespeare: The Critical Heritage*. Several volumes. London and Boston, 1974—.

Welsford, Enid. *The Fool: His Social and Literary History*. London, 1935; rpt. 1966.

Westfall, A. V. *American Shakespearean Criticism, 1607–1865*. New York, 1939.

Shakespeare Criticism from the 1940s to the 1970s

Armstrong, Edward A. *Shakespeare's Imagination: A Study of the Psychology of Association and Inspiration*. London, 1946.

Bethell, S. L. *Shakespeare and the Popular Dramatic Tradition*. London and Durham, N.C., 1944.

Bevington, David, and Jay L. Halio, eds. *Shakespeare: Pattern of Excelling Nature*. Newark, Del., 1978.

Bloom, Allan, with Harry V. Jaffa. *Shakespeare's Politics*. New York and London, 1964.

Brown, John Russell. *Shakespeare's Plays in Performance*. London, 1966.

Bryant, J. A., Jr. *Hippolyta's View: Some Christian Aspects of Shakespeare's Plays*. Lexington, Ky., 1961.

Burckhardt, Sigurd. *Shakespearean Meanings*. Princeton, 1968.

Burke, Kenneth. *Language as Symbolic Action*. Berkeley, 1966.

Calderwood, James L. *Shakespearean Metadrama*. Minneapolis, 1971.

Coghill, Neville. *Shakespeare's Professional Skills*. Cambridge, Eng., 1964.

Colie, Rosalie L. *Shakespeare's Living Art*. Princeton, 1974.

Council, Norman. *When Honour's at the Stake: Ideas of Honour in Shakespeare's Plays*. London, 1973.

Danby, John F. *Poets on Fortune's Hill: Studies in Sidney, Shakespeare, and Beaumont and Fletcher*. London, 1952.

Dean, Leonard F., ed. *Shakespeare: Modern Essays in Criticism*. New York, 1967.

Driver, Tom F. *The Sense of History in Greek and Shakespearean Drama*. New York, 1960.

Dusinberre, Juliet. *Shakespeare and the Nature of Women*. New York, 1975. 2nd ed., 1996.

Eagleton, Terence. *Shakespeare and Society*. New York and London, 1967.

Edwards, Philip. *Shakespeare and the Confines of Art*. London and New York, 1968.

Empson, William. *The Structure of Complex Words*. London, 1951.

Fiedler, Leslie A. *The Stranger in Shakespeare*. New York, 1972.

Fly, Richard. *Shakespeare's Mediated World*. Amherst, Mass., 1976.

Frye, Roland M. *Shakespeare and Christian Doctrine*. Princeton, 1963.

Garber, Marjorie B. *Dream in Shakespeare: From Metaphor to Metamorphosis*. New Haven and London, 1974.

Goddard, Harold C. *The Meaning of Shakespeare*. Chicago, 1951.

Goldman, Michael. *Shakespeare and the Energies of Drama*. Princeton, 1972.

Granville-Barker, Harley. *Prefaces to Shakespeare*. 2 vols. Princeton, 1946–1947.

Harbage, Alfred. *As They Liked it*. New York, 1947.

———. *Shakespeare and the Rival Traditions*. New York, 1952.

Hawkes, Terence. *Shakespeare's Talking Animals: Language and Drama in Society*. London, 1973.

Hawkins, Harriett. *Poetic Freedom and Poetic Truth: Chaucer, Shakespeare, Marlowe, Milton*. Oxford, 1976.

Holland, Norman. *Psychoanalysis and Shakespeare*. New York, 1966.

———. *The Shakespearean Imagination*. New York, 1964.

Jones, Emrys. *The Origins of Shakespeare*. Oxford, 1977.

Jorgensen, Paul A. *Shakespeare's Military World*. Berkeley and Los Angeles, 1956.

Kernan, Alvin B. *The Playwright as Magician: Shakespeare's Image of the Poet in the English Public Theater*. New Haven, 1979.

———, ed. *Modern Shakespearean Criticism*. New York, 1970.

Kettle, Arnold, ed. *Shakespeare in a Changing World*. London and New York, 1964.

Knights, L. C. *Some Shakespearean Themes*. London, 1959.

Kott, Jan. *Shakespeare Our Contemporary*. New York, 1964.

Leavis, F. R. *The Common Pursuit*. London, 1952.

Levin, Richard. *New Readings vs. Old Plays: Recent Trends in the Reinterpretation of English Renaissance Drama*. Chicago, 1979.

McAlindon, T. *Shakespeare and Decorum*. London and New York, 1973.

Rabkin, Norman. *Shakespeare and the Common Understanding*. New York, 1967.

Righter, Anne. *Shakespeare and the Idea of the Play*. London, 1962.

Rossiter, A. P. *Angel with Horns*. London, 1961.

Sanders, Wilbur. *The Dramatist and the Received Idea: Studies in the Plays of Marlowe and Shakespeare*. Cambridge, Eng., 1968.

Sewell, Arthur. *Character and Society in Shakespeare*. London, 1951.

Soellner, Rolf. *Shakespeare's Patterns of Self-Knowledge*. Columbus, Ohio, 1972.

Spencer, Theodore. *Shakespeare and the Nature of Man*. New York, 1942.

Spivack, Bernard. *Shakespeare and the Allegory of Evil*. New York, 1958.

Stewart, J. I. M. *Character and Motive in Shakespeare*. London, 1949.

Stirling, Brents. *The Populace in Shakespeare*. New York, 1949.

Traversi, Derek. *An Approach to Shakespeare*. 2 vols. Rev. ed. London, 1968.

Van Laan, Thomas F. *Role-Playing in Shakespeare*. Toronto, 1978.

Watson, Curtis Brown. *Shakespeare and the Renaissance Concept of Honor*. Princeton, 1960.

Weimann, Robert. *Shakespeare and the Popular Tradition in the Theater*, ed. Robert Schwartz. Baltimore, 1978.

Whitaker, Virgil K. *Shakespeare's Use of Learning*. San Marino, Calif., 1953.

Zeeveld, W. Gordon. *The Temper of Shakespeare's Thought*. New Haven and London, 1974.

Shakespeare Criticism Since 1980, including New Historicism, Gender Studies, and Poststructuralism

See also, under *Shakespeare's Predecessors and Contemporaries*, Bednarz, Belsey, Braden, Bristol, Bruster, Cohen, Dolan, Farley-Hills, Findlay (two items), Freer, McLuskie, Orgel, Rasmussen, Rose, Shannon, and Vickers; and under *Shakespeare Criticism from the 1940s to the 1970s*, Weimann.

Adelman, Janet. *Suffocating Mothers: Fantasies of Maternal Origin in Shakespeare's Plays, "Hamlet" to "The Tempest."* Chicago, 1992.

Alexander, Catherine M. S., and Stanley Wells, eds. *Shakespeare and Race.* Cambridge, Eng., 2000.

Auden, W. H. *Lectures on Shakespeare*, ed. Arthur Kirsch. Princeton, 2000.

Bamber, Linda. *Comic Women, Tragic Men: A Study of Gender and Genre in Shakespeare.* Stanford, 1982.

Barber, C. L. *The Whole Journey: Shakespeare's Power of Development.* Berkeley, 1986.

Bate, Jonathan. *The Genius of Shakespeare.* Oxford, 1997.

Belsey, Catherine. *Shakespeare and the Loss of Eden: The Construction of Family Values in Early Modern Culture.* New Brunswick, N.J., 1999.

Berger, Harry, Jr. *Making Trifles of Terrors: Redistributing Complicities in Shakespeare.* ed. Peter Erickson. Stanford, 1997.

Bergeron, David, ed. *Pageantry in the Shakespearean Theater.* Athens, Ga., 1985.

Bevington, David. *Shakespeare.* Oxford, 2002.

Boose, Lynda E. "The Father and the Bride in Shakespeare," *PMLA* 97 (1982), 325–47.

Bristol, Michael. *Shakespeare's America, America's Shakespeare.* London and New York, 1990.

Bulman, James C., ed. *Shakespeare, Theory, and Performance.* London and New York, 1996.

Calderwood, James. *Shakespeare and the Denial of Death.* Amherst, Mass., 1987.

Callaghan, Dympna C. *Shakespeare Without Women: Representing Gender and Race on the Renaissance Stage.* London and New York, 2000.

———, ed. *A Feminist Companion to Shakespeare.* Oxford, 2000.

Callaghan, Dympna, Lorraine Helms, and Jyotsna Singh. *The Weyward Sisters: Shakespeare and Feminist Politics.* Cambridge, Eng., 1994.

Carey, John, ed. *English Renaissance Studies.* Oxford, 1980.

Cartelli, Thomas. *Repositioning Shakespeare: National Formations, Postcolonial Appropriations.* London and New York, 1999.

Cavell, Stanley. *Disowning Knowledge in Six Plays of Shakespeare.* Cambridge, Eng., 1987.

Charnes, Linda. *Notorious Identity: Materializing the Subject in Shakespeare.* Cambridge, Mass., 1993.

Cook, Ann Jennalie. *Making a Match: Courtship in Shakespeare and His Society.* Princeton, 1991.

Cox, John D. *Shakespeare and the Dramaturgy of Power.* Princeton, 1989.

Daileder, Celia R. *Eroticism on the Renaissance Stage: Transcendence, Desire, and the Limits of the Visible.* Cambridge, Eng., 1998.

Danson, Lawrence. *Shakespeare's Dramatic Genres.* Oxford, 2000.

Dawson, Anthony B. *Indirections: Shakespeare and the Art of Illusion.* Toronto, 1984.

De Grazia, Margreta, Maureen Quilligan, and Peter Stallybrass, eds. *Subject and Object in Renaissance Culture.* Cambridge, Eng., 1996.

Desmet, Christy. *Reading Shakespeare's Characters: Rhetoric, Ethics, and Identity.* Amherst, Mass., 1992.

Desmet, Christy, and Robert Sawyer, eds. *Shakespeare and Appropriation.* London and New York, 1999.

Dobson, Michael. *The Making of the National Poet: Shakespeare, Adaptation, and Authorship, 1660–1769.* Oxford, 1992.

Dolan, Frances E. *Dangerous Familiars: Representations of Domestic Crime in England, 1550–1700.* Ithaca, N.Y., 1994.

Dollimore, Jonathan. *Radical Tragedy: Religion, Ideology and Power in the Drama of Shakespeare and His Contemporaries.* Chicago, 1984; New York, 1989.

Dollimore, Jonathan, and Alan Sinfield. *Political Shakespeare: New Essays in Cultural Materialism.* Manchester, Eng., 1985.

Drakakis, John, ed. *Alternative Shakespeares.* London, 1985.

Dubrow, Heather, and Richard Strier, eds. *The Historical Renaissance: New Essays on Tudor and Stuart Literature and Culture.* Chicago, 1988.

Eagleton, Terence. *William Shakespeare.* Oxford, 1986.

Edwards, Philip, et al., eds. *Shakespeare's Styles.* Cambridge, Eng., 1980.

Engle, Lars. *Shakespearean Pragmatism: Market of His Time.* Chicago, 1993.

Erickson, Peter. *Patriarchal Structures in Shakespeare's Drama.* Berkeley, 1985.

Erickson, Peter, and Coppélia Kahn, eds. *Shakespeare's Rough Magic: Essays in Honor of C. L. Barber.* Newark, Del., 1985.

French, Marilyn. *Shakespeare's Division of Experience.* New York, 1981.

Frye, Northrop. *Northrop Frye on Shakespeare*, ed. Robert Sandler. New Haven, 1986.

Fumerton, Patricia, and Simon Hunt, eds. *Renaissance Culture and the Everyday.* Philadelphia, 1999.

Garber, Marjorie. *Coming of Age in Shakespeare.* London, 1981.

———. *Shakespeare's Ghost Writers: Literature as Uncanny Causality.* London and New York, 1987.

———, ed. *Cannibals, Witches, and Divorce: Estranging the Renaissance.* Baltimore, 1987.

Gibbons, Brian. *Shakespeare and Multiplicity.* Cambridge, Eng., 1993.

Gillies, John. *Shakespeare and the Geography of Difference.* Cambridge, Eng., 1994.

Goldberg, Jonathan. *James I and the Politics of Literature: Jonson, Shakespeare, Donne, and Their Contemporaries.* Baltimore, 1983.

———. *Sodometries: Renaissance Texts, Modern Sexualities.* Stanford, 1992.

Grady, Hugh, ed. *Shakespeare and Modernity: Early Modern to Millennium.* London and New York, 2000.

Greenblatt, Stephen. *Learning to Curse: Essays in Early Modern Culture.* London and New York, 1990.

———. *Marvelous Possessions: The Wonder of the New World.* Chicago, 1991.

———. *Renaissance Self-Fashioning: From More to Shakespeare.* Chicago, 1980.

———. *Shakespearean Negotiations: The Circulation of Social Energy in Renaissance England.* Berkeley, 1988.

Habib, Imtiaz. *Shakespeare and Race: Postcolonial Praxis in the Early Modern Period.* Lanham and Oxford, 2000.

Hall, Kim F. *Things of Darkness: Economies of Race and Gender in Early Modern England.* Ithaca, N.Y., 1994.

Hamilton, Donna B. *Shakespeare and the Politics of Protestant England.* Lexington, Ky., 1992.

Hamlin, William M. *The Image of America in Montaigne, Spenser, and Shakespeare: Renaissance Ethnography and Literary Tradition.* New York, 1995.

Hawkes, Terence. *Meaning by Shakespeare.* London and New York, 1992.

———, ed. *Alternative Shakespeares.* Vol. 2. London and New York, 1996.

Holland, Norman, et al., eds. *Shakespeare's Personality.* Berkeley, 1989.

Howard, Jean E. *Shakespeare's Art of Orchestration: Stage Technique and Audience Response.* Urbana, Ill., 1984.

———. *The Stage and Social Struggle in Early Modern England.* London, 1994.

———, and Marion F. O'Connor, eds. *Shakespeare Reproduced: The Text in History and Ideology.* London and New York, 1987.

———, and Scott Cutler Shershow, eds. *Marxist Shakespeares.* London and New York, 2000.

James, Heather. *Shakespeare's Troy: Drama, Politics, and the Translation of Empire.* Cambridge, Eng., 1997.

Jardine, Lisa. *Reading Shakespeare Historically.* London and New York, 1996.

———. *Still Harping on Daughters: Women and Drama in the Age of Shakespeare.* Sussex and Totowa, N.J., 1983; New York, 1989.

Kahn, Coppélia. *Man's Estate: Masculine Identity in Shakespeare.* Berkeley, 1981.

———. *Roman Shakespeare: Warriors, Wounds, and Women.* London and New York, 1997.

Kamps, Ivo, ed. *Materialist Shakespeare: A History.* London, 1995.

———, ed. *Shakespeare Left and Right.* New York and London, 1991.

Kastan, David Scott. *Shakespeare After Theory.* London, 1999.

———. *Shakespeare and the Book.* Cambridge, Eng., 2001.

———. *Shakespeare and the Shapes of Time.* Hanover, N.H., 1982.

———, ed. *A Companion to Shakespeare.* Oxford, 1999.

Kernan, Alvin. *Shakespeare, the King's Playwright: Theater in the Stuart Court, 1603–1613.* New Haven, 1995.

Kerrigan, William. *Shakespeare's Promises.* Baltimore, 1999.

Kirsch, Arthur. *Shakespeare and the Experience of Love.* Cambridge, Eng., 1981.

Knapp, Robert S. *Shakespeare—The Theater and the Book.* Princeton, 1989.

Knowles, Richard, ed. *Shakespeare and Carnival: After Bakhtin.* London and New York, 1998.

Lenz, Carolyn, et al., eds. *The Woman's Part: Feminist Criticism of Shakespeare.* Urbana, Ill., 1980.

Little, Arthur L., Jr. *Shakespeare Jungle Fever: National-Imperial Re-Visions of Race, Rape, and Sacrifice.* Stanford, 2000.

Loomba, Ania. *Gender, Race, Renaissance Drama.* Manchester, Eng., 1989.

Loomba, Ania, and Martin Orkin, eds. *Post-colonial Shakespeares.* London and New York, 1998.

Mahon, John W., and Thomas A. Pendleton, eds. *"Fanned and Winnowed Opinion": Shakespearean Essays Presented to Harold Jenkins.* London, 1987.

Mallin, Eric. *Inscribing the Time: Shakespeare and the End of Elizabethan England.* Berkeley, 1995.

Marcus, Leah. *Puzzling Shakespeare: Local Reading and its Discontents.* Berkeley, 1988.

Mazzio, Carla, and Douglas Trevor, eds. *Historicism, Psychoanalysis, and Early Modern Culture.* London and New York, 2000.

McDonald, Russ, ed. *Shakespeare Reread: The Texts in New Contexts.* Ithaca, N.Y., 1994.

McMullan, Gordon, and Jonathan Hope, eds. *The Politics of Tragicomedy: Shakespeare and After.* London and New York, 1992.

Melchiori, Giorgio. *Shakespeare's Garter Plays: "Edward III" to "Merry Wives of Windsor."* Newark, Del., 1994.

Miola, Robert S. *Shakespeare's Reading.* Oxford and New York, 2000.

———. *Shakespeare's Rome.* Cambridge, Eng., 1983.

Montrose, Louis. *The Purpose of Playing: Shakespeare and Cultural Politics of the Elizabethan Theatre.* Chicago, 1996.

Mullaney, Steven. *The Place of the Stage: License, Play, and Power in Renaissance England.* Chicago, 1988.

Neely, Carol Thomas. *Broken Nuptials in Shakespeare's Plays.* New Haven, 1985.

Newman, Karen. *Fashioning Femininity and the English Renaissance Drama.* Chicago, 1991.

Novy, Marianne. *Love's Argument: Gender Relations in Shakespeare.* Chapel Hill, N.C., 1984.

———, ed. *Women's Re-Visions of Shakespeare.* Urbana, Ill., 1990.

Nuttall, A. D. *A New Mimesis: Shakespeare and the Representation of Reality.* London, 1983.

Orgel, Stephen. *The Authentic Shakespeare and Other Problems of the Early Modern Stage.* London and New York, 2002.

Orgel, Stephen, and Sean Keilen, eds. *Shakespeare and History; Post-modern Shakespeare; Shakespeare and the Interpretive Tradition; Shakespeare and the Literary Tradition; Shakespeare and Gender; Political Shakespeare.* In separate volumes, New York, 1999.

Parker, Patricia. *Shakespeare from the Margins: Language, Culture, Context.* Chicago, 1996.

———, and Geoffrey Hartman, eds. *Shakespeare and the Question of Theory.* London, 1985.

Paster, Gail Kern. *The Body Embarrassed: Drama and the Disciplines of Shame in Early Modern England.* Ithaca, N.Y., 1993.

Patterson, Annabel. *Shakespeare and the Popular Voice.* Oxford, 1989.

Rabkin, Norman. *Shakespeare and the Problem of Meaning.* Chicago, 1981.

Salingar, Leo. *Dramatic Form in Shakespeare and the Jacobeans.* Cambridge, Eng., 1986.

Schwartz, Murray, and Coppélia Kahn, eds. *Representing Shakespeare: New Psychoanalytic Essays.* Baltimore, 1980.

Siemon, James R. *Shakespearean Iconoclasm.* Berkeley, 1985.

Sinfield, Alan. *Faultlines: Cultural Materialism and the Politics of Dissident Reading.* Berkeley, 1992.

Skura, Meredith Anne. *The Literary Use of the Psychoanalytic Process.* New Haven, 1981.

———. *Shakespeare the Actor and the Purposes of Playing.* Chicago, 1993.

Smith, Bruce R. *Homosexual Desire in Shakespeare's England.* Chicago, 1991.

———. *Shakespeare and Masculinity.* Oxford, 2000.

Stockholder, Kay. *Dream Works: Lovers and Families in Shakespeare's Plays.* Toronto, 1987.

Taylor, Gary. *Reinventing Shakespeare: A Cultural History from the Restoration to the Present.* New York, 1989.

Traub, Valerie. *Desire and Anxiety: Circulations of Sexuality in Shakespearean Drama.* London, 1992.

Vickers, Brian. *Appropriating Shakespeare: Contemporary Critical Quarrels.* New Haven, 1993.

Watson, Robert N. *The Rest is Silence: Death as Annihilation in the English Renaissance.* Berkeley, 1994.

———. *Shakespeare and the Hazards of Ambition.* Cambridge, Mass., 1984.

Wayne, Valerie, ed. *The Matter of Difference: Materialist Feminist Criticism of Shakespeare.* Ithaca, N.Y., 1991.

Weimann, Robert. *Author's Pen and Actor's Voice: Playing and Writing in Shakespeare's Theatre.* Cambridge, Eng., 2000.

Wells, Robin Headlam. *Shakespeare on Masculinity.* Cambridge, Eng., 2000.

———. *Shakespeare, Politics, and the State.* London, 1986.

Wheeler, Richard P. *Shakespeare's Development and the Problem Comedies: Turn and Counter-Turn.* Berkeley, 1981.

White, Paul Whitfield, and Suzanne R. Westfall, eds. *Shakespeare and Theatrical Patronage in Early Modern England.* Cambridge, Eng., 2002.

Williams, Gordon. *Shakespeare, Sex, and the Print Revolution.* London and Atlantic Highlands, N.J., 1996.

Woodbridge, Linda. *The Scythe of Saturn: Shakespeare's Magical Thinking.* Urbana, Ill., 1994.

Woodbridge, Linda, and Edward Berry, eds. *True Rites and Maimed Rites: Ritual and Anti-Ritual in Shakespeare and His Age.* Urbana, Ill., 1992.

Ziegler, Georgianna, ed. *Shakespeare's Unruly Women.* Washington, D.C., 1997.

Shakespeare in Performance; Dramaturgy

See also, under *Shakespeare Criticism from the 1940s to the 1970s,* Goldman and Granville-Barker.

Bartholomeusz, Dennis. *Macbeth and the Players.* Cambridge, Eng., 1969.

Barton, John. *Playing Shakespeare.* London, 1984.

Bevington, David. *Action is Eloquence: Shakespeare's Language of Gesture.* Cambridge, Mass., 1984.

Brockbank, Philip, ed. *Players of Shakespeare.* Cambridge, Eng., 1985.

Brown, Ivor. *Shakespeare and the Actors.* London, 1970.

Brown, John Russell. *Shakespeare's Plays in Performance.* London, 1966.

———. *Shakespeare's Dramatic Style.* London, 1970.

Bulman, J. C., and H. R. Coursen, eds. *Shakespeare on Television.* Hanover, N.H., 1988.

Carlisle, Carol Jones. *Shakespeare from the Greenroom: Actors' Criticisms of Four Major Tragedies.* Chapel Hill, N.C., 1969.

Cohn, Ruby. *Modern Shakespeare Offshoots.* Princeton, 1976.

Cook, Judith. *Shakespeare's Players.* London, 1983.

Davies, Anthony, and Stanley Wells, eds. *Shakespeare and the Moving Image: The Plays on Film and Television.* Cambridge, Eng., 1994.

Dessen, Alan C. *Recovering Shakespeare's Theatrical Vocabulary.* Cambridge, Eng., 1995.

———. *Rescripting Shakespeare: The Text, the Director, and Modern Productions.* Cambridge, Eng., 2002.

———, and Leslie Thomson. *A Dictionary of Stage Directions in English Drama, 1580–1642.* Cambridge, Eng., 1999.

Donohue, Joseph W., Jr. *Dramatic Character in the English Romantic Age.* Princeton, 1970.

Downer, Alan S. *The Eminent Tragedian, William Charles Macready.* Cambridge, Mass., 1966.

Edelman, Charles. *Brawl Ridiculous: Swordfighting in Shakespeare's Plays.* Manchester, Eng., 1992.

Hodgdon, Barbara. *The Shakespeare Trade: Performances and Appropriations.* Philadelphia, 1998.

Hogan, Charles B. *Shakespeare in the Theatre, 1701–1800.* 2 vols. Oxford, 1952–1957.

Jackson, Russell, and Robert Smallwood, eds. *Players of Shakespeare 2.* Cambridge, Eng., 1988. Followed by Vols. 3 (1993); and 4, ed. Smallwood (1998).

Jones, Emrys. *Scenic Form in Shakespeare.* Oxford, 1971.

Jorgens, Jack L. *Shakespeare on Film.* Bloomington, Ind., 1977.

Manvell, Roger. *Shakespeare and the Film.* London and New York, 1971.

McGuire, Philip C. *Speechless Dialect: Shakespeare's Open Silences.* Berkeley, 1985.

McGuire, Philip C., and David A. Samuelson. *Shakespeare: The Theatrical Dimension.* New York, 1979.

Odell, George C. D. *Shakespeare from Betterton to Irving.* 2 vols. New York, 1920, 1966.

Poel, William. *Shakespeare in the Theatre.* London, 1913, 1968.

Price, Joseph G., ed. *The Triple Bond: Plays, Mainly Shakespearean, in Performance.* University Park, Pa., 1975.

Rutter, Carol Chillington, ed. *Documents of the Rose Playhouse*. Manchester, Eng., 1999.

Rutter, Carol, et al. *Clamorous Voices: Shakespeare's Women Today.* New York, 1989.

Shapiro, Michael. *Gender in Play on the Shakespearean Stage: Boy Heroines and Female Pages.* Ann Arbor, Mich., 1994.

Shattuck, Charles H. *The Shakespeare Promptbooks: A Descriptive Catalogue.* Urbana, Ill., 1965.

———. *Shakespeare on the American Stage from the Hallams to Edwin Booth.* Washington, D.C., 1976; *from Booth and Barrett to Sothern and Marlowe,* Washington, D.C., 1987.

Slater, Ann Pasternak. *Shakespeare the Director.* Brighton, Sussex, and Totowa, N.J., 1982.

Speaight, Robert. *William Poel and the Elizabethan Revival.* London, 1954.

Sprague, Arthur Colby. *Shakespeare and the Actors.* Cambridge, Mass., 1944.

———. *Shakespearian Players and Performances.* Cambridge, Mass., 1953.

Styan, J. L. *Shakespeare's Stagecraft.* Cambridge, Eng., 1967.

Wells, Stanley. *Royal Shakespeare: Four Major Productions at Stratford-upon-Avon.* Manchester, Eng., 1977.

The Tragedies

See also, under *Shakespeare's Predecessors and Contemporaries,* Belsey.

Armstrong, Philip. *Shakespeare's Visual Regime: Tragedy, Psychoanalysis, and the Gaze.* Basingstoke and New York, 2000.

Baldo, Jonathan. *The Unmasking of Drama: Contested Representation in Shakespeare's Tragedies.* Detroit, 1996.

Barker, Francis, ed. *The Culture of Violence: Essays on Tragedy and History.* Chicago, 1993.

Barroll, J. Leeds. *Artificial Persons: The Formation of Character in the Tragedies of Shakespeare.* Columbia, S. C., 1974.

Bayley, John. *Shakespeare and Tragedy.* London, 1981.

Bell, Millicent. *Shakespeare's Tragic Skepticism.* New Haven, 2002.

Berry, Philippa. *Shakespeare's Feminine Endings: Disfiguring Death in the Tragedies.* London and New York, 1999.

Berry, Ralph. *Tragic Instance: The Sequence of Shakespeare's Tragedies.* Newark, Del., 1999.

Bradley, A. C. *Shakespearean Tragedy.* London, 1904. *(Hamlet, Othello, King Lear, Macbeth.)*

Brooke, Nicholas. *Shakespeare's Early Tragedies.* London and New York, 1968.

Brown, John Russell, and Bernard Harris, eds. *Early Shakespeare.* London, 1961.

Bulman, James C. *The Heroic Idiom of Shakespearean Tragedy.* Newark, Del., 1985.

Bushnell, Rebecca. *Tragedies of Tyrants: Political Thought and Theater in the English Renaissance.* Ithaca, N.Y., 1990.

Campbell, Lily B. *Shakespeare's Tragic Heroes: Slaves of Passion.* Cambridge, Eng., 1930.

Champion, Larry S. *Shakespeare's Tragic Perspective.* Athens, Ga., 1976.

Charlton, H. B. *Shakespearian Tragedy.* Cambridge, Eng., 1948.

Cunningham, I. V. *Woe or Wonder: The Emotional Effect of Shakespearean Tragedy.* Denver, 1951. Rpt. in *Tradition and Poetic Structure.* Denver, 1960.

Danson, Lawrence. *Tragic Alphabet: Shakespeare's Drama of Language.* New Haven and London, 1974.

Dickey, Franklin M. *Not Wisely But Too Well: Shakespeare's Love Tragedies.* San Marino, Calif., 1957.

Eliot, T. S. "Shakespeare and the Stoicism of Seneca," *Selected Essays, 1917–1932.* London, 1932.

Everett, Barbara. *Young Hamlet: Essays on Shakespeare's Tragedies.* Oxford, 1989.

Falco, Raphael. *Charismatic Authority in Early Modern English Tragedy.* Baltimore, 2000.

Farnham, Willard. *Shakespeare's Tragic Frontier.* Berkeley, 1950.

Frye, Northrop. *Fools of Time: Studies in Shakespearean Tragedy.* Toronto, 1967.

Gajowski, Evelyn. *The Art of Loving: Female Subjectivity and Male Discursive Traditions in Shakespeare's Tragedies.* Newark, Del., 1992.

Garner, Shirley Nelson, and Madelon Sprengnether, eds. *Shakespearean Tragedy and Gender.* Bloomington, Ind., 1996.

Goldman, Michael. *Acting and Action in Shakespearean Tragedy.* Princeton, 1985.

Grene, Nicholas. *Shakespeare's Tragic Imagination.* New York, 1992.

Hawkes, Terence. *Shakespeare and the Reason: A Study of the Tragedies and the Problem Plays.* London, 1964.

Held, George F. *The Good That Lives After Them: A Pattern in Shakespeare's Tragedies.* Heidelberg, 1995.

Holloway, John. *The Story of the Night: Studies in Shakespeare's Major Tragedies.* London and Lincoln, Neb., 1961.

Honigmann, E. A. J. *Myriad-Minded Shakespeare: Essays, Chiefly on the Tragedies and Problem Comedies.* New York, 1989.

———. *Shakespeare: Seven Tragedies Revisited: The Dramatist's Manipulation of Response.* London and New York, 1976. 2nd ed., 2002.

Hunter, Robert Grams. *Shakespeare and the Mystery of God's Judgments.* Athens, Ga., 1976.

Ide, Richard S. *Possessed with Greatness: The Heroic Tragedies of Chapman and Shakespeare.* Chapel Hill, N.C., 1980.

Kiefer, Frederick. *Fortune and Elizabethan Tragedy.* San Marino, Calif., 1983.

Kirsch, Arthur. *The Passions of Shakespeare's Tragic Heroes.* Charlottesville, Va., 1990.

Knight, G. Wilson. *The Wheel of Fire.* London, 1930, 1965.

Lawlor, John. *The Tragic Sense in Shakespeare.* London, 1960.

Leech, Clifford. *Shakespeare's Tragedies and Other Studies in Seventeenth-Century Drama.* London, 1950.

———, ed. *Shakespeare: The Tragedies.* Chicago, 1965.

Liebler, Naomi Conn. *Shakespeare's Festive Tragedy: The Ritual Foundations of Genre.* London and New York, 1995.

Mack, Maynard. *Everybody's Shakespeare: Reflections Chiefly on the Tragedies.* Lincoln, Neb., 1993.

———. "The Jacobean Shakespeare: Some Observations on the Construction of the Tragedies," *Jacobean Theatre,* ed. John Russell Brown and Bernard Harris. Stratford-upon-Avon Studies 1. London, 1960.

Mack, Maynard, Jr. *Killing the King: Three Studies in Shakespeare's Tragic Structure.* New Haven and London, 1973.

Margolies, David. *Monsters of the Deep: Social Dissolution in Shakespeare's Tragedies.* Manchester, Eng., 1992.

McAlindon, T. *Shakespeare's Tragic Cosmos.* Cambridge, Eng., 1991.

Miola, Robert S. *Shakespeare and Classical Tragedy: The Influence of Seneca.* Oxford, 1992.

Neill, Michael. *Issues of Death: Mortality and Identity in English Renaissance Tragedy.* Oxford, 1997.

Nevo, Ruth. *Tragic Form in Shakespeare.* Princeton, 1972.

Proser, Matthew N. *The Heroic Image in Five Shakespearean Tragedies.* Princeton, 1965.

Rackin, Phyllis. *Shakespeare's Tragedies.* New York, 1978.

Reid, Robert Lanier. *Shakespeare's Tragic Form: Spirit in the Wheel.* Newark, Del., 2000.

Ribner, Irving, *Patterns in Shakespearean Tragedy.* New York, 1960.

Rosen, William. *Shakespeare and the Craft of Tragedy.* Cambridge, Mass., 1960.

Sanders, Wilbur, and Howard Jacobson. *Shakespeare's Magnanimity: Four Tragic Heroes, Their Friends and Families.* Oxford, 1978.

Shaheen, Naseeb. *Biblical References in Shakespeare's Tragedies.* Newark, Del., 1987.

Smith, Molly. *The Darker World Within: Evil in the Tragedies of Shakespeare and His Successors.* Newark, Del., 1991.

Snyder, Susan. *The Comic Matrix of Shakespeare's Tragedies.* Princeton, 1979.

Spivack, Bernard. *Shakespeare and the Allegory of Evil.* New York, 1958.

Whitaker, Virgil. *The Mirror up to Nature.* San Marino, Calif., 1965.

Wilson, Harold S. *On the Design of Shakespearian Tragedy.* Toronto, 1957.

Young, David. *The Action to the Word: Structure and Style in Shakespearean Tragedy.* New Haven, 1990.

The Greek and Roman Tragedies

See also, under *Shakespeare Criticism Since 1980,* Paster (Chapter 3).

Brower, Reuben A. *Hero and Saint: Shakespeare and the Graeco-Roman Heroic Tradition.* New York and Oxford, 1971.

Cantor, Paul A. *Shakespeare's Rome: Republic and Empire.* Ithaca, N.Y., 1976.

Charney, Maurice, ed. *Discussions of Shakespeare's Roman Plays.* Boston, 1964.

———. *Shakespeare's Roman Plays: The Function of Imagery in the Drama.* Cambridge, Mass., 1961.

Knight, G. Wilson. *The Imperial Theme: Further Interpretations of Shakespeare's Tragedies Including the Roman Plays.* London, 1931, 1953.

Leggatt, Alexander. *Shakespeare's Political Drama: The History Plays and the Roman Plays.* London and New York, 1988.

MacCallum, M. W. *Shakespeare's Roman Plays and Their Background.* London, 1910.

Maxwell, J. C. "Shakespeare's Roman Plays: 1900–1956," *ShS* 10 (1957), 1–11.

Miles, Geoffrey. *Shakespeare and the Constant Romans.* Oxford, 1996.

Miola, Robert S. *Shakespeare's Rome.* Cambridge, Eng., 1983.

Nicoll, Allardyce, ed. *Shakespeare Survey 10* (1957).

Paris, Bernard J. *Character as a Subversive Force in Shakespeare: The History and Roman Plays.* Rutherford, N.J., and London, 1991.

Phillips, James E., Jr. *The State in Shakespeare's Greek and Roman Plays.* New York, 1940.

Simmons, J. L. *Shakespeare's Pagan World: The Roman Tragedies.* Charlottesville, Va., 1973.

Thomas, Vivian. *Shakespeare's Roman Worlds.* London, 1989.

Thomson, J. A. K. *Shakespeare and the Classics.* London, 1952.

Traversi, Derek. *Shakespeare: The Roman Plays.* Palo Alto, Calif., 1963.

Velz, John W. "The Ancient World in Shakespeare: Authenticity or Anachronism? A Retrospect," *ShS* 31 (1978), 1–12.

———. *Shakespeare and the Classical Tradition: A Critical Guide to Commentary, 1660–1960.* Minneapolis, 1968.

Titus Andronicus

See also, under *The Tragedies,* Brooke, Brown and Harris, Danson, Garner and Sprengnether (essay by Eaton), and Spivack; under *The Greek and Roman Tragedies,* Brower (Chapter 4), Maxwell, Miola, and Thomson; under *Shakespeare's Predecessors and Contemporaries,* Bowers, and Hattaway (Chapter 8); under *Shakespeare Criticism from the 1940s to the 1970s,* Calderwood; and under *Shakespeare Criticism Since 1980,* Wayne (essay by Wynne-Davies).

Barroll, J. Leeds. "Shakespeare and Roman History," *Modern Language Review* 53 (1958), 327–43.

Bartels, Emily C. "Making More of the Moor: Aaron, Othello, and Renaissance Refashionings of Race," *SQ* 41 (1990), 433–54.

Bradbrook, M. C. "Moral Heraldry: *Titus Andronicus, Rape of Lucrece, Romeo and Juliet,*" in *Shakespeare and Elizabethan Poetry.* London, 1951.

Dessen, Alan C. *Titus Andronicus.* Shakespeare in Performance. Manchester, Eng., 1989.

Green, Douglas E. "Interpreting 'her martyr'd signs': Gender and Tragedy in *Titus Andronicus,*" *SQ* 40 (1989), 317–26.

Liebler, Naomi Conn. "Getting It All Right: *Titus Andronicus* and Roman History," *SQ* 45 (1994), 263–78.

Lindroth, Mary. " 'Some Devise of Further Misery': Taymor's *Titus* Brings Shakespeare to Film Audience with a Twist," *Literature and Film Quarterly* 29 (2002), 107–15.

Metz, G. Harold. "Stage History of *Titus Andronicus,*" *SQ* 28 (1977), 154–69.

———. *Shakespeare's Earliest Tragedy: Studies in "Titus Andronicus."* Madison, N.J., London, 1996.

Nevo, Ruth. "Tragic Form in *Titus Andronicus,*" *Further Studies in English Language and Literature,* ed. A. A. Mendilow. Jerusalem, 1973.

Palmer, D. J. "The Unspeakable in Pursuit of the Uneatable: Language and Action in *Titus Andronicus,*" *Critical Quarterly* 14 (1972), 320–39.

Ray, Sid. " 'Rape, I Fear, was Root of Thy Annoy': The Politics of Consent in *Titus Andronicus,*" *SQ* 49 (1998), 22–39.

Rowe, Katharine A. "Dismembering and Forgetting in *Titus Andronicus,*" *SQ* 45 (1994), 279–303.

Royster, Francesca. "White-limed Walls: Whiteness and Gothic Extremism in Shakespeare's *Titus Andronicus,*" *SQ* 51 (2000), 432–55.

Sommers, Alan. " 'Wilderness of Tigers': Structure and Symbolism in *Titus Andronicus,*" *Essays in Criticism* 10 (1960), 275–89.

Tricomi, Albert H. "The Aesthetics of Mutilation in *Titus Andronicus,*" *ShS* 27 (1974), 11–19.

———. "The Mutilated Garden in *Titus Andronicus,*" *ShakS* 9 (1976), 89–105.

Waith, Eugene M. "The Metamorphosis of Violence in *Titus Andronicus,*" *ShS* 10 (1957), 39–49.

Willbern, David. "Rape and Revenge in *Titus Andronicus,*" *English Literary Renaissance* 8 (1978), 159–82.

Willis, Deborah. " 'The gnawing vulture': Revenge, Trauma Theory, and *Titus Andronicus,*" *SQ* 53 (2002), 1–21.

Wilson, J. Dover. "*Titus Andronicus* on the Stage in 1595," *ShS* 1 (1948), 17–22.

Romeo and Juliet

See also, under *The Tragedies,* Brooke, Brown and Harris (essay by Lawlor), Charlton, Dickey, Nevo, Ribner, and Snyder; under *Shakespeare's Language,* Mahood; under *Shakespeare Criticism to the 1930s,* Hazlitt; under *Shakespeare Criticism from the 1940s to the 1970s,* Calderwood, Granville-Barker, and Rabkin (pp. 162–84); under *Shakespeare Criticism Since 1980,* Callaghan (*A Feminist Companion,* essay by Berry), Daileader, Edwards et al. (essay by Wells), Erickson and Kahn (essay by Snow), Lenz et al. (essay by Kahn), and Novy (*Love's Argument*); and under *Shakespeare in Performance,* Brockbank (essay by Brenda Bruce).

Appelbaum, Robert. " 'Standing to the wall': The Pressures of Masculinity in *Romeo and Juliet,*" *SQ* 48 (1997), 251–72.

Auden, W. H. "Commentary on the Poetry and Tragedy of *Romeo and Juliet.*" The Laurel Shakespeare, gen. ed. Francis Fergusson. New York, 1958.

Evans, Bertrand. "The Brevity of Friar Lawrence," *PMLA* 65 (1950), 841–65.

Evans, Robert O. *The Osier Cage: Rhetorical Devices in "Romeo and Juliet."* Lexington, Ky., 1966.

Everett, Barbara. "*Romeo and Juliet:* The Nurse's Story," *Critical Quarterly* 14 (1972), 129–39.

Halio, Jay, ed. *"Romeo and Juliet": Texts, Contexts, and Interpretation.* Newark, Del., 1995.

Hosley, Richard. "The Use of the Upper Stage in *Romeo and Juliet,*" *SQ* 5 (1954), 371–9.

Levenson, Jill L. *Shakespeare in Performance: "Romeo and Juliet."* Manchester, Eng., 1987.

Melchiori, Giorgio. "Peter, Balthasar, and Shakespeare's Art of Doubling," *Modern Language Review* 78 (1983), 777–92.

Williams, George W., ed. *The Most Excellent and Lamentable Tragedie of Romeo and Juliet.* Durham, N.C., 1964.

Julius Caesar

See also, under *The Greek and Roman Tragedies,* Brower, Charney (both titles), Knight, Miola, and Traversi; under *Shakespeare's Language,* Doran; under *Shakespeare Criticism to the 1930s,* Shaw; under *Shakespeare Criticism from the 1940s to the 1970s,* Burckhardt, Council, Goldman (Chapter 4), Granville-Barker, Kernan (essay by Mack), Rabkin (pp. 105–19), and Stirling; and under *Shakespeare Criticism Since 1980,* Kahn.

Blits, Jan H. *The End of the Ancient Republic: Essays on "Julius Caesar."* Durham, N.C., 1982.

Burke, Kenneth. "Antony in Behalf of the Play," *Southern Review* 1 (1935), 308–19. Rpt. in *The Philosophy of Literary Form.* Baton Rouge, La., 1941.

Knights, L. C. "Shakespeare and Political Wisdom: A Note on the Personalism of *Julius Caesar* and *Coriolanus,*" *Sewanee Review* 61 (1953), 43–55.

Liebler, Naomi Conn. " 'Thou Bleeding Piece of Earth': The Ritual Ground of *Julius Caesar,*" *ShakS* 14 (1981), 175–96.

Miola, Robert S. "*Julius Caesar* and the Tyrannicide Debate," *Renaissance Quarterly* 38 (1985), 271–89.

Ornstein, Robert. "Seneca and the Political Drama of *Julius Caesar,*" *Journal of English and Germanic Philology* 57 (1958), 51–6.

Parker, Barbara L. " 'A Thing Unfirm': Plato's *Republic* and Shakespeare's *Julius Caesar,*" *SQ* 44 (1993), 30–43.

Paster, Gail Kern. " 'In the spirit of men there is no blood': Blood as Trope of Gender in *Julius Caesar,*" *SQ* 40 (1989), 284–98.

Ribner, Irving. "Political Issues in *Julius Caesar,*" *Journal of English and Germanic Philology* 56 (1957), 10–22.

Ripley, John. *"Julius Caesar" on Stage in England and America, 1599–1973.* Cambridge, Eng., 1980.

Rose, Mark. "Conjuring Caesar: Ceremony, History, and Authority in 1599," *English Literary Renaissance* 19 (1989), 291–304.

Velz, John W. "Clemency, Will, and Just Cause in *Julius Caesar,*" *ShS* 22 (1969), 109–18.

———. " 'If I Were Brutus Now . . . ': Role-Playing in *Julius Caesar,*" *ShakS* 4 (1968), 149–59.

———. "Undular Structure in *Julius Caesar,*" *Modern Language Review* 66 (1971), 21–30.

Hamlet

See also, under *Shakespeare's Language,* Donawerth; under *The Tragedies,* Barker, Bradley, Brooke, Goldman, Holloway, Kirsch, Mack, Mack Jr., Rosen, and Whitaker; under *The Greek and Roman Tragedies,* Brower; under *Shakespeare's Predecessors and Contemporaries,* Bowers, and Rabkin (essay by Booth); under *Shakespeare Criticism to the 1930s,* Coleridge (*Coleridge's Writings*); under *Shakespeare Criticism from the 1940s to the 1970s,* Granville-Barker, Hawkes, and Righter; under *Shakespeare Criticism Since 1980,* Cavell (Chapter 5), Drakakis (essay by Rose), Erickson, Garber (*Shakespeare's Ghost Writers,* Chapter 6), Loomba and Orkin (essay by Bertoldi), Mazzio and Trevor (essays by De Grazia and Guillory), McDonald (essay by Parker), Parker and Hartman (essays by Weimann, Ferguson, and Hawkes), Patterson (Chapters 1 and 5), and Schwartz and Kahn (essays by Fineman and Leverenz); and under *Shakespeare in Performance,* Bevington.

Bertram, Paul, and Bernice W. Kliman, eds. *The Three-Text "Hamlet": Parallel Texts of the First and Second Quartos and First Folio.* New York, 1991.

Bowers, Fredson T. "Hamlet as Minister and Scourge," *PMLA* 70 (1955), 740–9.

Calderwood, James L. *To Be and Not to Be: Negation and Metadrama in "Hamlet."* New York, 1983.

Charney, Maurice. *Style in "Hamlet."* Princeton, 1969.

Clayton, Thomas, ed. *The "Hamlet" First Published (Q1, 1603): Origin, Form, Intertextualities.* Newark, Del., 1992.

Dawson, Anthony B. *Hamlet.* Shakespeare in Performance. Manchester, Eng., 1995.

Eliot, T. S. "Hamlet and His Problems," *Selected Essays, 1917–1932.* London and New York, 1932.

Erlich, Avi. *Hamlet's Absent Father.* Princeton, 1977.

Ewbank, Inga-Stina. "*Hamlet* and the Power of Words," *ShS* 30 (1977), 85–102.

Fergusson, Francis. *The Idea of a Theater.* Princeton, 1949.

Foakes, R. A. *"Hamlet" versus "Lear": Cultural Politics and Shakespeare's Art.* Cambridge, Eng., 1993.

Frye, Roland Mushat. *The Renaissance "Hamlet": Issues and Responses in 1600.* Princeton, 1984.

Greenblatt, Stephen. *Hamlet in Purgatory.* Princeton, 2001.

Heilbrun, Carolyn G. *Hamlet's Mother and Other Women.* New York, 1990.

James, D. G. *The Dream of Learning.* Oxford, 1951.

Jones, Ernest. *Hamlet and Oedipus.* Rev. ed. New York, 1949, 1954.

Joseph, Bertram. *Conscience and the King.* London, 1953.

Kerrigan, William. *Hamlet's Perfection.* Baltimore, 1994.

Kitto, H. D. F. *Form and Meaning in Drama.* London, 1956.

Knights, L. C. *An Approach to Hamlet.* London, 1960.

Lacan, Jacques. "Desire and the Interpretation of Desire in *Hamlet,*" *Yale French Studies* 55/56 (1977), 11–52.

Lee, John. *Shakespeare's "Hamlet" and the Controversies of Self.* Oxford, 2000.

Levin, Harry. *The Question of Hamlet.* New York and London, 1959.

Lewis, C. S. "Hamlet: The Prince or the Poem?" *Proceedings of the British Academy* 28 (1942), 139–54.

Mack, Maynard. "The World of *Hamlet,*" *Yale Review* 41 (1952), 502–23.

McCoy, Richard C. "A Wedding and Four Funerals: Conjunction and Commemoration in *Hamlet,*" *ShS* 54 (2001), 122–39.

McGee, Arthur. *The Elizabethan Hamlet.* New Haven, 1987.

Muir, Kenneth, and Stanley Wells, eds., *Aspects of "Hamlet": Articles Reprinted from "Shakespeare Survey."* Cambridge, Eng., 1979. (Especially essay by Inga-Stina Ewbank.)

Murray, Gilbert. *Hamlet and Orestes.* Annual Shakespeare Lecture for the British Academy, 1914. London, 1919.

Nicoll, Allardyce, ed. *Shakespeare Survey 9* (1956).

Nietzsche, Friedrich. "The Birth of Tragedy or: Hellenism and Pessimism" (1872), *The Birth of Tragedy and The Case of Wagner,* trans. Walter Kaufmann. New York, 1967.

Rose, Mark. "*Hamlet* and the Shape of Revenge," *English Literary Renaissance* 1 (1971), 132–43.

Rosenberg, Marvin. *The Masks of "Hamlet."* Newark, Del., 1992.

Skulsky, Harold. " 'I Know My Course': Hamlet's Confidence," *PMLA* 89 (1974), 477–86.

States, Bert O. *"Hamlet" and the Concept of Character.* Baltimore, 1992.

Tronch-Pérez, Jesús. *A Synoptic "Hamlet": A Critical-Synoptic Edition of the Second Quarto and First Folio Texts of "Hamlet."* Valencia, Spain, 2002.

Wilson, J. Dover. *What Happens in "Hamlet."* London and New York, 1935, 1951.

Wright, George T. "Hendiadys and *Hamlet,*" *PMLA* 96 (1981), 168–93.

Young, David. "Hamlet, Son of Hamlet," *Perspectives on "Hamlet,"* eds. William G.

Holzberger and Peter B. Waldock. Lewisburg, Pa., and London, 1975.

Othello

See also, under *The Tragedies,* Philippa Berry, Bradley, Dickey, Garner and Sprengnether (essays by Orlin, Hendricks, and Rose), Goldman, Hawkes, Holloway, Knight, Snyder, and Spivack; under *Shakespeare's Language,* Doran; under *Shakespeare's Predecessors and Contemporaries,* Hendricks and Parker (essays by Boose and Parker); under *Shakespeare Criticism to the 1930s,* Coleridge (*Coleridge's Writings*) and Johnson; under *Shakespeare Criticism from the 1940s to the 1970s,* Empson, Fiedler, Granville-Barker, and Sewell; and under *Shakespeare Criticism Since 1980,* Cavell (Chapter 3), Daileder, Erickson, Erickson and Kahn (essay by Wheeler), Greenblatt (*Renaissance Self-Fashioning,* Chapter 6), Howard and O'Connor (essay by Newman), Kirsch, Lenz et al. (essay by Neely), Loomba and Orkin (essay by Burton), McDonald (essay by Parker), Novy (*Love's Argument,* Chapter 7), and Parker and Hartman (essays by Parker and Showalter).

Adamson, Jane. *"Othello" as Tragedy: Some Problems of Judgment and Feeling.* Cambridge, Eng., 1980.

Altman, Joel B. " 'Preposterous Conclusions': Eros, *Enargeia,* and the Composition of *Othello,*" *Representations* 18 (1987), 129–57.

Bartels, Emily C. "Making More of the Moor: Aaron, Othello, and Renaissance Refashionings of Race," *SQ* 41 (1990), 433–54.

Bates, Catherine. "Weaving and Writing in *Othello,*" *SQ* 46 (1995), 51–60.

Bayley, John. *The Characters of Love.* London, 1960.

Boose, Lynda E. "Othello's Handkerchief: 'The Recognizance and Pledge of Love'," *English Literary Renaissance* 5 (1975), 360–74.

Calderwood, James L. *The Properties of "Othello."* Amherst, Mass., 1989.

Dean, Leonard F., ed. *A Casebook on "Othello."* New York, 1961.

Evans, Robert C. "Friendship in Shakespeare's *Othello,*" *Ben Jonson Journal* 6 (1999), 109–46.

Everett, Barbara. "Inside *Othello.*" *ShS* 53 (2000), 184–95.

———. "Reflections on the Sentimentalist's *Othello,*" *Critical Quarterly* 3 (1961), 127–39. (A comment on the Leavis article below.)

Garner, S. N. "Shakespeare's Desdemona," *ShakS* 9 (1976), 233–52.

Hankey, Julie, ed. *Plays in Performance: "Othello."* Bristol, 1987.

Heilman, Robert B. *Magic in the Web: Action and Language in "Othello."* Lexington, Ky., 1956.

Honigmann, E. A. J. *The Texts of "Othello" and Shakespearian Revision.* London, 1996.

Hyman, Stanley Edgar. *Iago: Some Approaches to the Illusion of His Motivation.* New York, 1970.

Jones, Eldred. *Othello's Countrymen: The African in English Renaissance Drama.* London, 1965.

Korda, Natasha. *Shakespeare's Domestic Economies: Gender and Property in Early Modern England.* Philadelphia, 2002 (Chapter 4).

Leavis, F. R. "Diabolic Intellect and the Noble Hero: Or The Sentimentalist's Othello," *The Common Pursuit.* London, 1952.

Muir, Kenneth, ed. *Shakespeare Survey 21* (1968).

Nowottny, Winifred M. T. "Justice and Love in *Othello*," *University of Toronto Quarterly* 21 (1952), 330–44.

Orkin, Martin. "Othello and the 'plain face' of Racism," *SQ* 38 (1987), 166–88.

Orlin, Lena Cowen. *Private Matters and Public Culture in Post-Reformation England.* Ithaca, N.Y., 1994.

Rosenberg, Marvin. *The Masks of "Othello."* Berkeley, 1961.

Seltzer, Daniel. "Elizabethan Acting in *Othello*," *SQ* 10 (1959), 201–10.

Snyder, Susan, ed. *"Othello": Critical Essays.* New York, 1988.

Stoll, E. E. *"Othello": An Historical and Comparative Study.* Minneapolis, 1915. Rpt. New York, 1964.

Wine, Martin L. *"Othello": Text and Performance.* London, 1984.

King Lear

See also, under *Life in Shakespeare's England*, De Grazia, Quilligan, and Stallybrass (essay by De Grazia); under *The Tragedies*, Bradley, Cunningham, Frye, Goldman, Holloway, Hunter, Kirsch, Knight, and Rosen; under *The Greek and Roman Tragedies*, Brower; under *Textual Criticism and Bibliography*, Blayney, and Taylor and Warren; under *Shakespeare's Language*, Doran; under *Shakespeare Criticism to the 1930s*, Hazlitt, Johnson, and Stoll; under *Shakespeare Criticism from the 1940s to the 1970s*, Bloom (essay by Jaffa), Burckhardt, Empson, Fly, Granville-Barker, Knights, Kott, and Sewell; and under *Shakespeare Criticism Since 1980*, Auden, Boose, Cavell (Chapter 2, identical with the Cavell entry below), Dollimore, Dollimore and Sinfield (essay by McLuskie), Dubrow and Strier (essay by Strier), Erickson, Erickson and Kahn (essay by Berger), Garber (*Shakespeare's Ghost Writers*, Chapter 5), Greenblatt (*Shakespearean Negotiations*, Chapter 4), Loomba and Orkin (essay by Visser), Novy (*Love's Argument*), Patterson (Chapter 5), and Wayne (essay by Thompson).

Alpers, Paul J. "*King Lear* and the Theory of the 'Sight Pattern'," *In Defense of Reading*, ed. Reuben A. Brower and Richard Poirier. New York, 1962.

Berger, Harry, Jr. *"King Lear"*: The Lear Family Romance," *Centennial Review* 23 (1979), 348–76.

Booth, Stephen. *"King Lear," "Macbeth," Indefinition, and Tragedy,* New Haven, 1983.

Brownlow, F. W. *Shakespeare, Harsnett, and the Devils of Denham.* Newark, Del., 1993.

Cavell, Stanley. "The Avoidance of Love: A Reading of *King Lear*," *Must We Mean What We Say?* New York, 1969. Rpt. in *Disowning Knowledge in Six Plays of Shakespeare.* Cambridge, Eng., 1987.

Colie, Rosalie L., and F. T. Flahiff, eds. *Some Facets of "King Lear."* Toronto, 1974.

Danby, John F. *Shakespeare's Doctrine of Nature: A Study of "King Lear."* London, 1949.

Delany, Paul. *"King Lear"* and the Decline of Feudalism," *PMLA* 92 (1977), 429–40.

Elton, William R. *King Lear and the Gods.* San Marino, Calif., 1966. Rpt. Lexington, Ky., 1988.

Everett, Barbara. "The New *King Lear*," *Critical Quarterly* 2 (1960), 325–39.

Foakes, R. A. *"Hamlet" Versus "Lear": Cultural Politics and Shakespeare's Art.* Cambridge, Eng., 1993.

Freud, Sigmund. "The Theme of the Three Caskets," *Complete Psychological Works of Sigmund Freud* 12 (1911–1913), pp. 291–301. London, 1958.

Goldberg, S. L. *An Essay on "King Lear."* Cambridge, Eng., 1974.

Graham, Kenneth J. E. " 'Without the form of justice': Plainness and the Performance of Love in *King Lear*," *SQ* 42 (1991), 438–61.

Hardison, O. B., Jr. "Myth and History in *King Lear*," *SQ* 26 (1975), 227–42.

Heilman, Robert B. *This Great Stage: Image and Structure in "King Lear."* Baton Rouge, La., 1948. Rpt. Seattle, 1963.

Heinemann, Margot. " 'Demystifying the Mystery of State': *King Lear* and the World Upside Down," *ShS* 44 (1992), 75–83.

James, D. G. *The Dream of Learning.* Oxford, 1951.

Jorgensen, Paul A. *Lear's Self-Discovery,* Berkeley, 1967.

Kahn, Coppélia. "The Absent Mother in *King Lear*," *Rewriting the Renaissance: The Discourses of Sexual Difference in Early Modern Europe*, eds. Margaret W. Ferguson et al. Chicago, 1986.

Kernan, Alvin. "Formalism and Realism in Elizabethan Drama: The Miracles in *King Lear*," *Renaissance Drama* 9 (1966), 59–66.

Kirsch, Arthur. "The Emotional Landscape of *King Lear*," *SQ* 39 (1988), 154–70.

Kronenfeld, Judy. *King Lear and the Naked Truth: Rethinking the Language of Religion and Resistance.* Durham, N.C., 1998.

Leggatt, Alexander. *King Lear.* Shakespeare in Performance. Manchester, Eng., 1991.

Lothian, J. M. *"King Lear": A Tragic Reading of Life.* Toronto, 1949.

Lusardi, James P., and June Schlueter. *Reading Shakespeare in Performance: "King Lear."* Rutherford, N.J., 1991.

Mack, Maynard. *King Lear in Our Time.* Berkeley, 1965.

Maclean, Norman. "Episode, Scene, Speech, and Word: The Madness of Lear," *Critics and Criticism*, ed. R. S. Crane. Chicago, 1952.

Michie, Donald M., ed. *A Critical Edition of "The True Chronicle History of King Leir and His Three Daughters, Gonorill, Ragan and Cordella."* New York, 1991.

Murphy, John L. *Darkness and Devils: Exorcism and "King Lear."* Athens, Ohio, 1984.

Reibetanz, John. *The "Lear" World: A Study of "King Lear" in Its Dramatic Context.* Toronto, 1977.

Rosenberg, Marvin. *The Masks of "King Lear."* Berkeley, 1972.

Scott, William O. "Contracts of Love and Affection: Lear, Old Age, and Kingship," *ShS* 55 (2002), 36–42.

Sewall, Richard B. *The Vision of Tragedy.* New Haven, 1959.

Snyder, Susan. "*King Lear* and the Psychology of Dying," *SQ* 33 (1982), 449–60.

Soellner, Rolf. "*King Lear* and the Magic of the Wheel," *SQ* 35 (1984), 274–89.

Tate, Nahum. *The History of King Lear* (1681), ed. James Black. Lincoln, Neb. 1975.

Taylor, Gary, and Michael Warren, eds. *The Division of the Kingdoms: Shakespeare's Two Versions of "King Lear."* Oxford, 1983.

Urkowitz, Steven. *Shakespeare's Revision of "King Lear."* Princeton, 1980.

Warren, Michael, preparer. *The Parallel "King Lear," 1608–1623: Parallel Texts of the First Quarto (1608) and the First Folio (1623).* Berkeley, 1989.

Wittreich, Joseph. *"Image of that Horror": History, Prophecy, and Apocalypse in "King Lear."* San Marino, Calif., 1984.

Macbeth

See also, under *The Tragedies*, Berry, Bradley, Garner and Sprengnether (essay by Adelman), Goldman, Holloway, Hunter, Kirsch, Mack, Mack Jr., and Rosen; under *Shakespeare Criticism to the 1930s*, Smith (essay by De Quincey); under *Shakespeare Criticism from the 1940s to the 1970s*, Sanders and Sewell; and under *Shakespeare Criticism Since 1980*, Garber (*Cannibals*, essay by Adelman), Howard and O'Connor (essay by Goldberg), Mullaney (Chapter 5), Schwartz and Kahn (essay by Gohlke), Watson, and Woodbridge and Berry (essay by Willis).

Bartholomeusz, Dennis. *"Macbeth" and the Players.* Cambridge, Eng., 1969.

Booth, Stephen. *"King Lear," "Macbeth," Indefinition, and Tragedy.* New Haven, 1983.

Brooks, Cleanth. "The Naked Babe and the Cloak of Manliness," *The Well Wrought Urn.* New York, 1947.

Calderwood, James L. *If It Were Done: "Macbeth" and Tragic Action.* Amherst, 1986.

Driver, Tom. *The Sense of History in Greek and Shakespearean Drama.* New York, 1960.

Elliott, G. R. *Dramatic Providence in "Macbeth."* Princeton, 1958.

Fergusson, Francis. "*Macbeth* as the Imitation of an Action," *English Institute Essays 1951* (1952), 31–43.

Freud, Sigmund. "Some Character-Types Met with in Psycho-Analytic Work," trans. E. Cobern Mayne, *Collected Papers.* Vol. 4, pp. 326–32. London, 1925.

Gardner, Helen. "Milton's 'Satan' and the Theme of Damnation in Elizabethan Tragedy," *English Association Essays and Studies* n.s. 1 (1948), 46–66.

Jorgensen, Paul A. *Our Naked Frailties: Sensational Art and Meaning in "Macbeth."* Berkeley, 1971.

Kliman, Bernice W. *Macbeth*. Shakespeare in Performance. Manchester, Eng., 1992.

Knights, L. C. "How Many Children Had Lady Macbeth? An Essay in the Theory and Practice of Shakespeare Criticism," *Explorations*. London, 1946. Rpt. Westport, Conn., 1975.

Norbrook, David. "*Macbeth* and the Politics of Historiography," *Politics of Discourse: The Literature and History of Seventeenth-Century England*, eds. Kevin Sharpe and Steven Zwicker, pp. 78–116. Berkeley, 1987.

Orgel, Stephen. "Macbeth and the Antic Round," *ShS 52* (1999), 143–53. Rpt. in Orgel, under *Shakespeare Criticism Since 1980*.

Paul, Henry N. *The Royal Play of Macbeth*. New York, 1950.

Purkiss, Diane. *The Witch in History: Early Modern and Twentieth-Century Representations*. London and New York, 1996.

Rosenberg, Marvin. *The Masks of "Macbeth."* Berkeley, 1978.

Sinfield, Alan. "*Macbeth*: History, Ideology and Intellectuals," *Critical Quarterly* 28 (1986), 63–77.

Spender, Stephen. "Time, Violence, and *Macbeth*," *Penguin New Writing*, 3. London, 1940–1941.

Williams, Raymond. "Monologue in *Macbeth*," *Teaching the Text*, eds. Susanne Kappeler and Norman Bryson. London, 1983.

Wills, Garry. *Witches and Jesuits: Shakespeare's "Macbeth."* Oxford, 1995.

Timon of Athens

See also, under *The Tragedies*, Knight; under *The Greek and Roman Tragedies*, generally; under *Shakespeare's Predecessors and Contemporaries*, Kernan; under *Shakespeare Criticism to the 1930s*, Hazlitt and Johnson; under *Shakespeare Criticism from the 1940s to the 1970s*, Burke, Empson, and Fly; and under *Shakespeare Criticism Since 1980*, Paster (Chapter 4).

Baldo, Jonathan. "The Shadow of Levelling in *Timon of Athens*," *Criticism* 35 (1993), 559–88.

Bevington, David, and David L. Smith. "James I and *Timon of Athens*," *Comparative Drama* 33 (1999), 56–87.

Cohen, Derek. "The Politics of Wealth: *Timon of Athens*," *Neophilologus* 77 (1993), 149–60.

Davidson, Clifford. "*Timon of Athens*: The Iconography of False Friendship," *Huntington Library Quarterly* 43 (1980), 181–200.

Fulton, Robert. "Timon, Cupid, and the Amazons," *ShakS* 9 (1976), 283–99.

Greene, Jody. " 'You must eat men': The Sodomistic Economy of Renaissance Patronage," *GLQ: A Journal of Lesbian and Gay Studies* 1 (1994), 163–87.

Kahn, Coppélia. " 'Magic of Bounty': *Timon of Athens*, Jacobean Patronage, and Maternal Power," *SQ* 38 (1987), 34–57.

Knights, L. C. "*Timon of Athens*," *The Morality of Art: Essays Presented to G. Wilson Knight*, ed. D. W. Jefferson. London, 1969.

Lancashire, Anne. "*Timon of Athens*: Shakespeare's *Dr. Faustus*," *SQ* 21 (1970), 35–44.

Miola, Robert S. "Timon in Shakespeare's Athens," *SQ* 31 (1980), 21–30.

O'Dair, Sharon. "The Statue of Class in Shakespeare: Or, Why Critics Love to Hate Capitalism," *Discontinuities: New Essays on Renaissance Literature and Criticism*, eds. Viviana Comensoli and Paul Stevens, pp. 201–23. Toronto, 1998.

Scott, William O. "The Paradox of Timon's Self-Cursing," *SQ* 35 (1984), 290–304.

Soellner, Rolf. *Timon of Athens: Shakespeare's Pessimistic Tragedy*. With a Stage History by Gary Jay Williams. Columbus, Ohio, 1979.

Walker, Lewis. "Fortune and Friendship in *Timon of Athens*," *Texas Studies in Literature and Language* 18 (1977), 577–600.

Waters, D. Douglas. "Shakespeare's *Timon of Athens* and Catharsis," *Upstart Crow* 8 (1988), 93–105.

Antony and Cleopatra

See also, under *The Tragedies*, Frye, Garner and Sprengnether (essays by Cook and Charnes), Goldman, Holloway, Mack, and Rosen; under *The Greek and Roman Tragedies*, Brower, Cantor, Charney, Miola, and Traversi; under *Shakespeare's Predecessors and Contemporaries*, Comensoli and Russell (essay by Adelman), and Waith; under *Shakespeare's Language*, Doran; under *Shakespeare Criticism to the 1930s*, Coleridge (*Coleridge's Writings*); under *Shakespeare Criticism from the 1940s to the 1970s*, Bethell, Burke, Colie, Granville-Barker, Kettle (essay by Nandy), McAlindon, and Van Laan; and under *Shakespeare Criticism Since 1980*, Auden, Bamber, Cavell (pp. 18–37), Charnes, Dollimore (*Radical Tragedy*), Edwards et al. (essay by Hibbard), Erickson (Chapter 4), Holland et al. (essay by Sprengnether), and Neely.

Adelman, Janet. *The Common Liar: An Essay on "Antony and Cleopatra."* New Haven, 1973.

Barroll, J. Leeds. *Shakespearean Tragedy: Genre, Tradition, and Change in "Antony and Cleopatra."* Washington, D.C., 1984.

Bono, Barbara J. "The Shakespearean Synthesis: *Antony and Cleopatra*," *Literary Transvaluation: From Vergilian Epic to Shakespearean Tragicomedy*. Berkeley, 1984.

Bradley, A. C. *Oxford Lectures on Poetry*. London, 1909, 1961.

Drakakis, John, ed. "*Antony and Cleopatra*." Basingstoke, 1994.

Kaula, David. "The Time Sense of *Antony and Cleopatra*," *SQ* 15:3 (1964), 211–23.

Knights, L. C. *Some Shakespearean Themes*. London, 1959.

Lamb, Margaret. "*Antony and Cleopatra*" on the English Stage. Rutherford, N.J., and London, 1980.

Leavis, F. R. "*Antony and Cleopatra* and *All for Love*: A Critical Exercise," *Scrutiny* 5 (1936–1937), 158–69.

Levine, Laura. *Men in Women's Clothing: Anti-Theatricality and Effeminization, 1579–1642*. Cambridge, Eng., 1994.

Lloyd, Michael. "Cleopatra as Isis," *ShS 12* (1959), 88–94.

Mack, Maynard. "*Antony and Cleopatra*: The Stillness and the Dance," *Shakespeare's Art: Seven Essays*, ed. Milton Crane. Chicago, 1973.

Madelaine, Richard, ed. *Antony and Cleopatra*. Shakespeare in Production. Cambridge, Eng., 1998.

Markels, Julian. *The Pillar of the World: "Antony and Cleopatra" in Shakespeare's Development*. Columbus, Ohio, 1968.

Mayer, Jean-Christophe, ed. *Lectures de Shakespeare: "Antony and Cleopatra."* Rennes, France, 2000.

Rackin, Phyllis. "Shakespeare's Boy Cleopatra, the Decorum of Nature, and the Golden World of Poetry," *PMLA* 87 (1972), 201–12.

Reimer, A. P. *A Reading of Shakespeare's "Antony and Cleopatra."* Sydney, 1968.

Scott, Michael. *Antony and Cleopatra*. Text and Peformance. London, 1983.

Steppat, Michael. *The Critical Reception of Shakespeare's "Antony and Cleopatra" from 1607 to 1905*. Amsterdam, 1980.

Williamson, Marilyn L. *Infinite Variety: "Antony and Cleopatra" in Renaissance Drama and Earlier Tradition*. Mystic, Conn., 1974.

Wood, Nigel, ed. "*Antony and Cleopatra*." Theory in Practice. Buckingham and Philadelphia, 1996.

Yachnin, Paul. "Shakespeare's Politics of Loyalty: Sovereignty and Subjectivity in *Antony and Cleopatra*," *Studies in English Literature* 33 (1993), 343–63.

Coriolanus

See also, under *The Tragedies*, Brown and Harris (essays by Hunter and Wickham), Danson, Holloway, and Rosen; under *The Greek and Roman Tragedies*, Brower, Cantor, Charney, Miola, and Phillips; under *Shakespeare's Predecessors and Contemporaries*, Waith; under *Shakespeare Criticism to the 1930s*, Hazlitt; under *Shakespeare Criticism from the 1940s to the 1970s*, Burke, Granville-Barker, Knights, Kott, and Rossiter; and under *Shakespeare Criticism Since 1980*, Cavell (Chapter 4), Dollimore, Goldberg (Chapter 4), Howard and O'Connor (essays by Bristol and Sorge), Kahn, Marcus (Chapter 4), Mazzio and Trevor (essay by Goldberg), Parker and

Hartman (essay by Cavell), Patterson (Chapter 6), and Watson.

Adelman, Janet. "'Anger's My Meat': Feeding, Dependency, and Aggression in *Coriolanus*," *Shakespeare, Pattern of Excelling Nature*, eds. David Bevington and Jay L. Halio. Newark, Del., 1978.

Barton, Anne. "Livy, Machiavelli, and Shakespeare's *Coriolanus*," *ShS 38* (1985), 115–29.

Berry, Ralph. "The Metamorphoses of *Coriolanus*," *SQ* 26 (1975), 172–83.

———. "Sexual Imagery in *Coriolanus*," *Studies in English Literature* 13 (1973), 301–16.

Bloom, Harold, ed. *William Shakespeare's "Coriolanus."* New York, 1988. (Including an essay by Burke.)

Bradley, A. C. *A Miscellany*. London, 1929.

Brecht, Bertolt. *Coriolanus*, trans. Ralph Manheim, *Bertolt Brecht: Collected Plays*, Vol. 9, eds. Ralph Manheim and John Willett. New York, 1972.

Brockman, B. A., ed. *Shakespeare's "Coriolanus,": A Casebook*. London, 1977.

Browning, I. R. "*Coriolanus*: 'Boy of Tears'": *Essays in Criticism* 5 (1955), 18–31.

Calderwood, James L. "*Coriolanus:* Wordless Meanings and Meaningless Words," *Studies in English Literature* 6 (1966), 211–24.

Fish, Stanley. "How to Do Things with Austin and Searle: Speech-Act Theory and Literary Criticism," *Is There a Text In This Class?* Cambridge, Mass., 1980.

Jagendorf, Zvi. "*Coriolanus*: Body Politic and Private Parts," *SQ* 41 (1990), 455–69.

MacLure, Millar. "Shakespeare and the Lonely Dragon," *University of Toronto Quarterly* 24 (1955), 109–20.

Rabkin, Norman. "*Coriolanus*: The Tragedy of Politics," *SQ* 17 (1966), 195–212.

Ripley, John. *"Coriolanus" on Stage in England and America, 1609–1994*. Madison, N.J., and London, 1998.

Smith, Bruce R. "Rape, rap, rupture, rapture": R-rated futures on the global market," *Textual Practice 9* (1995), 421–43.

Stockholder, Katherine. "The Other Coriolanus," *PMLA* 85 (1970), 228–36.

Vickers, Brian. *Shakespeare: "Coriolanus."* London, 1976.

Textual Notes

These textual notes do not offer an historical collation, either of the early quartos and folios or of more recent editions; they are simply a record of departures in this edition from the copy text. For most plays the notes give the adopted reading of this edition in bold face, followed by the rejected reading in the relevant copy text. Where two substantive early texts are involved, or where a reading from some other earlier edition has been adopted, the notes provide information on the source of the reading in square brackets. In a few texts, adopted readings of editions more recent than the First Folio are indicated by [eds.]. Alterations in lineation are not indicated, nor are some minor and obvious typographical errors; changes in punctuation are indicated when the resulting change in meaning is substantive.

Abbreviations used:
F The First Folio
Q Quarto
O Octavo
s.d. stage direction
s.p. speech prefix

Titus Andronicus

Copy text: the First Quarto of 1594, except for 3.2, based on F. Act and scene divisions are missing from the Quarto; act divisions alone are marked in the Folio.

1.1. 14 seat, to virtue consecrate, seate to vertue, consecrate. [The punctuation variations from the edited text are considerable in this play and are generally not recorded in these notes.] **18 MARCUS** [not in Q] **35 the field** [Q follows with a half line and three more lines: "and at this day, / To the Monument of that *Andronicy* / Done sacrifice of expiation, / And slaine the Noblest prisoner of the *Gothes*."] **55.1 *Exeunt* Exit 64 CAPTAIN** [not in Q] **69.6 *three sons* two sonnes 78 rites** rights [also at line 143] **98 *manes* manus 129.1 *Exeunt* Exit 157 LAVINIA** [not in Q] **164 Rome's** Roomes **193 Rome** Roome **227 Titan's** [F] Tytus **243 Pantheon** Pathan **265 chance** [F] change **281 *cuique* cuiqum 300 [and elsewhere] SATURNINUS** *Emperour* **317 Phoebe** *Thebe* **318 gallant'st** [F] gallanst **334 queen, Pantheon. Lords,** Queene: Panthean Lords **359 MARTIUS** *Titus two sonnes speakes* **QUINTUS** [not in Q] **361 MARTIUS** *Titus sonne speakes* **369 QUINTUS** *3. Sonne* **370 MARTIUS** *2. Sonne* [also at line 372] **389.1 *They all kneel* they all kneele and say 390 ALL** [not in Q] **391.1 *Exeunt* Exit 392 dreary** dririe [Q] sudden [F] **399** [F; not in Q] **475 LUCIUS** [F; not in Q] **476 mildly** mi'd ie

2.1. 37 [and elsewhere] AARON *Moore* **110 than** this

2.2. 1 morn [F] Moone **11** [Q provides a s.p.: *Titus*] **24 run** runnes

2.3. 13 snake [F] snakes **33 and** ann **43 lose** loose **69 try** [F] trie thy **72 swart** F (swarth) swartie [Q] **85 note** notice **88 [and elsewhere] TAMORA** *Queene* **131 ye desire** we desire **150 heard** hard **153 Some** So me **158 thee! For** thee for **160 ears** [F] yeares **175 their** there **180 satisfy** satisfice **192 AARON** [not in Q] **208.1 *Exit* [at line 207 in Q] 210 unhallowed** [F] vnhollow **222 berayed in blood** bereaud in blood [Q, with marginal correction in contemporary handwriting: "heere reau'd of lyfe"] **231 Pyramus** [F] Priamus **236 Cocytus'** *Ocitus* **260 [and elsewhere] SATURNINUS** *King* **260 gripped** griude **276** [Q provides a s.p.: *King*] **291 fault** faults

2.4. 5 scrawl scrowle **11 MARCUS** [not in Q] **27 him** them **30 three** their

3.1. 0.1 *over on* 17 urns ruines **21 on thy** [F] out hy **67 handless** handles **146 his** her **225 blow** flow **281 employed:** imployde in these Armes [Q] employd in these things [F]

3.2 [the entire scene is missing in Q; copy text is F] **0.1 *banquet* Bnaket** [F] **1 [and throughout scene] TITUS** *An.* **13 with outrageous** without ragious **38 mashed** mesh'd **39 complainer** complaynet **52 thy knife** knife **53 fly** Flys **54 thee, murderer!** the murderour: **55 are cloyed** cloi'd **72 myself** my selfes

4.1. 1 [and throughout] BOY [F] *Puer* **10 MARCUS** [not in Q] **19 griefs** greeues **42 *Metamorphoses* Metamorphosis 46 s.d. *Help her*** [as dialogue in Q] **51 quotes** coats **54 Forced** Frocd **79 TITUS** [not in Q] **89 hope** hop (?) I op (?)

4.2. 15 Lordships, that Lordships **51 Good** God **96 Alcides** *Alciades* **125 that** [F] your **154 Muly lives** *Muliteus*

4.3. 56 Saturn *Saturnine*, to **66 Jupiter** *Iubiter* [also at 79, 83, 84] **77 News . . . come** [assigned in Q to Clown] **96 from you** [Q follows with four lines: *Titus.* Tell mee, can you deliuer an Oration to the Em- / perour with a grace. / *Clowne.* Nay truelie sir, I could neuer say grace in all / my life.]

4.4. 5 know, as know know **43 good e'en** Godden **48 By 'r** be **93 feed** seede **98 ears** [F] yeares **105 on** [F] in

5.1. 9 A GOTH *Goth* [also at lines 121, 152, and 162] **17 ALL THE GOTHS** [not in Q] **20 ANOTHER GOTH** *Goth* **23 building, suddenly** building suddainely **43 here's** [F] her's **53 Get me a ladder** [assigned in Q to Aaron] **113 extreme** extreanie **133 haystacks** haystalks

5.2. 18 it action [F] that accord **38 them out** the mout **49 globe** Globes **52 murderers** murder **caves** cares **56 Hyperion's** *Epeons* **61 Are they** Are them **65 worldly** wordlie **121.1 *Enter Marcus* [after line 120 in Q] 140 Yield** Yee'd **144 dam** Dame **196** [after line 203 in Q]

5.3. 3 A GOTH *Got.* **15.2 *Sound trumpets* [after line 16 in Q] 26 gracious lord** [F] Lord **36 Virginius** *Viginius* **124 witness, this is**

true. witnes this is true,   125 cause course   141 ALL *Marcus*
142 MARCUS [no s.p. here in Q; see previous note]   144 adjudged [F]
adiudge   146 ALL [not in Q]   154 bloodstained blood slaine
163 Sung Song   172 BOY [F] *Puer*

Romeo and Juliet

Copy text: the Second Quarto of 1599, except for 1.2.53–1.3.34, for which
Q1 (the First Quarto) is the prior authority. Act and scene divisions are
absent from the Second Quarto and the Folio.

1.1. 27 it in [Q1] it   38 side sides   73 CITIZENS *Offi.*   76 CAPULET'S
WIFE *Wife*   92 Verona's *Neronas*   120 drave driue   147 his is
153 sun same   177 create [Q1] created   179 well-seeming [Q1]
welseeing   189 grief to [Q1] grief, too   192 lovers' louing   202 Bid
a [Q1] A   make [Q1] makes   206 markman mark man
211 unharmed [Q1] vncharmd   218 makes make

1.2. 14 The earth Earth   32 on one   38–9 written here written. Here
46 One [Q1] on   56 Good e'en Goddess   57 God gi' good e'en
Godgigoden   70 and Livia [Q1] Liuia [Q2]   79 thee [Q1] you [Q2]
91 fires fier [Q1]

1.3. 12 an [Q2] a [Q1]   18 shall [Q1] *stal* [Q2]   33 wi' th' [Q1: *with*]
with the [Q2]   50 [and elsewhere] WIFE *Old La.*   66 disposition [F]
dispositions   67, 68 honor [Q1] houre   100 it fly [Q1] flie
105 [and elsewhere] WIFE *Mo.*

1.4. 7–8 [Q1; not in Q2]   23 MERCUTIO *Horatio*   31 quote cote
39 done [Q1] dum   42 Of Or   45 like lamps [Q1] lights lights
47 five fine   57 atomi [Q1] ottamie   59–61 [these lines follow line 69
in Q2]   66 film Philome   69 maid [Q1] man   72 O'er [Q1] On
74 on one   76 breaths [Q1] breath   80 parson's Persons   81 dreams
he [Q1] he dreams   90 elflocks Elklocks   111 forfeit [Q1] fofreit

1.5. 0.1 [Q2 adds: "*Enter* Romeo"]   1 FIRST SERVINGMAN *Ser.* [also at
lines 6 and 12]   3 SECOND SERVINGMAN 1   7 court cupboard
Courtcubbert   11 THIRD SERVINGMAN 2   14 FOURTH SERVINGMAN 3
15 longest longer   17 CAPULET 1. *Capu.* [also at lines 35 and 40]
18 a bout about   57 antic anticque   96 ready [Q1] did readie

2.0. Chorus 1 CHORUS [not in Q2]   4 matched match

2.1. 7 Nay . . . too [assigned in Q2 to Benvolio]   10 one [Q1] on
11 Pronounce [Q1] prouaunt   dove [Q1] day   13 heir [Q1] her
14 trim [Q1] true   39 open-arse, and open, or   pop'ring Poprin

2.2. 16 do [Q1] to   20 eyes [Q1] eye   41–2 nor any . . . name ô be some
other name / Belonging to a man   45 were [Q1] wene   82 pilot Pylat
83 washed [Q1] washeth   92–3 false . . . They false at louers periuries.
/ They   99 havior behaiuour   101 more cunning coying   110 circled
[Q1] circle   146 [and elsewhere] rite right   149, 151 NURSE [not in Q2]
150, 151 JULIET [not in Q2]   163 than mine then   168 nyas Neece
180 gyves giues   187 Sleep . . . breast [Q1; assigned in Q2 to Juliet]
189–90 [preceded in Q2 by an earlier version of lines 1–4 of the next
scene, in which "fleckled darkness" reads "darknesse fleckted" and "and
Titan's fiery wheels" reads "made by *Tytans* wheels"]

2.3. 2 Check'ring [Q1] Checking   22 sometime's sometime   50 me
me: 51 wounded. Both our wounded both, our   85 not. She
whom [Q1] me not, her

2.4. 18 BENVOLIO [Q1] *Ro.*   28 antic antique   28–9 phantasimes
phantacies   33 pardon-me's pardons mees   40 but a a   68 Switch
. . . switch Swits . . . swits   113–14 for himself [Q1] himself
205 dog's dog   212 s.d. *Exeunt* Exit

2.5. 11 three there   15 And M. And   26 I had [Q1] I

2.6. 18 gossamer gossamours   27 music's musicke

3.1. 2 Capels are *Capels*   67 injured iniuried   73 *stoccada* stucatho
90 your houses houses   107 soundly too. Your soundly, to your
121 Alive He gan   123 fire-eyed [Q1] fier end   136 FIRST CITIZEN
Citti.   138 FIRST CITIZEN *Citi.*   141 all all: 165 agile [Q1] aged
183 MONTAGUE *Capu.*   187 hate's heart's   191 I [Q1] it
196.1 *Exeunt* Exit

3.2. 1 JULIET [not in Q2]   9 By And by   12 [and elsewhere] lose loose
15 grown grow   47 darting arting   49 shut shot   51 Brief sounds
Briefe, sounds,   of my my   54 [and elsewhere] corpse coarse

60 one on   72 It . . . day it did [assigned in Q2 to Juliet]   73 O . . .
face [assigned in Q2 to Nurse]   76 Dove-feathered Rauenous
doue-featherd   79 damnèd dimme   143.1 *Exeunt Exit*

3.3. 0.1 [Q2 has "*Enter Friar and Romeo*"]   39 [Q2 follows with a line:
"This may flyes do, when I from this must flie"]   43 [printed in Q2
before line 40]   52 Thou [Q1] Then   61 madmen [Q1] mad man
70.1 *Knock Enter Nurse, and knocke*   73 s.d. *Knock They knocke*
74 Who's whose   75.1 *Knock Slud knock*   80.1 *Enter Nurse* [below
line 78 in Q2]   110 denote [Q1] deuote   117 lives [Q1] lies
144 pout'st upon puts vp   168 disguised disguise

3.4. 10 [and elsewhere] WIFE *La.*   13 be [Q1] me   23 We'll keep Well,
keepe

3.5. 13 exhaled exhale   19 the the the   31 changed change   36.1 *Enter
Nurse Enter Madame and Nurse*   54 JULIET *Ro.*   67.1 [bracketed s.d.
from Q1]   82 pardon him padon   130–1 body . . . a bark body? /
Thou counterfeits. A Barke   133–4 is, . . . flood; is: . . . floud,
139 gives giue   142 How? Will How will   151–2 proud . . . Thank
proud mistresse minion you? / Thanke   160 [and elsewhere] CAPULET
Fa.   172 CAPULET Oh, God-i'-good-e'en Father, Godigeden
173 NURSE [not in Q2]   181 liened liand

4.1. 7 talked [Q1] talke   45 cure [Q1] care   46 Ah [Q1] O   72 slay
[Q1] stay   78 off [Q1] of   83 chopless [Q1] chapels   85 his tomb
his   98 breath [Q1] breast   100 To wanny Too many   110 In Is [Q2
follows with a line: "Be borne to buriall in thy kindreds graue"]
111 shalt shall   115 and he an he   116 waking walking
126 s.d. *Exeunt Exit*

4.2. 3, 6 SERVINGMAN *Ser.*   14 willed wield   26 becomèd becomd
38 [and elsewhere] WIFE *Mo.*   47.1 *Exeunt Exit*

4.3. 20 vial Violl   49 wake walke

4.4. 1 [and elsewhere] WIFE *La.*   12.1 *Exeunt Exit*   13.1–2 [after line 14
in Q2]   15 FIRST SERVINGMAN *Fel.*   18 SECOND SERVINGMAN *Fel.*
21 Thou Twou   faith father   23 s.d. [after line 21 in Q2]

4.5. 40 all; life all life   41 long [Q1] loue   51 behold bedold   65 cure
care   65–6 not . . . Heaven not, / In these confusions heauen
82 fond some   96 FIRST MUSICIAN *Musi.*   98 s.d. *Exit* Exit omnes
[below line 99]   99, 103 FIRST MUSICIAN *Fid.*   99 by [Q1] my
99.1 *Enter Peter Enter Will Kemp*   107 FIRST MUSICIAN Minstrels [and
subsequently in this scene indicated by *Minst.* or *Minstrel*]   123 Then
. . . wit [assigned in Q2 to 2 *M*]   127 And . . . oppress [Q1; not in
Q2]   133, 136 Pretty [Q1] Prates   145 s.d. *Exeunt Exit*

5.1. 15 fares my [Q1] doth my Lady   17, 27, 32 BALTHASAR *Man*
24 e'en in   defy [Q1] denie   33.1 [at line 32, after "good lord," in
Q2]   76 pay [Q1] pray   86 s.d. *Exit Exeunt*

5.3. 3 yew [Q1] young   21.2 [*Balthasar*] [Q1] Peter   25 light. Upon
light vpon   40, 43 BALTHASAR *Pet.*   68 conjuration commiration
71 PAGE *Boy* [Q1; s.p. missing in Q2 and line treated as a s.d.]
102 fair faire? I will beleeue   107 palace pallat   108 [Q2 has four
undeleted lines here: "Depart againe, come lye thou in my arme, /
Heer's to thy health, where ere thou tumblest in. / O true Appothecarie!
/ Thy drugs are quicke. Thus with a kisse I die."]   123 [and elsewhere]
BALTHASAR *Man*   137 yew yong   168 FIRST WATCH *Watch* [also at
lines 172, 195, 199]   171 PAGE *Watch boy*   182 SECOND WATCH *Watch*
183, 187 FIRST WATCH *Chief. watch*   187 too too too   190 shrieked
shrike   194 our your   199 slaughtered Slaughter   201 [Q2 has a s.d.
here: "*Enter Capulet and his wife*"]   209 more early [Q1] now earling
232 that thats   274–5 place . . . This place. To this same monument /
This   281 PAGE *Boy*   299 raise raie

Julius Caesar

Copy text: the First Folio. Act divisions are marked in the Folio; scene
divisions are editorially supplied.

1.1. 0.1 [and elsewhere] *Marullus Murellus*   37 Pompey? . . . oft
Pompey many a time and oft?   61 [and elsewhere] whe'er where

1.2. 0.1 [and elsewhere] *Calpurnia Calphurnia*   24.1 *Manent Manet*
124 [and elsewhere] lose loose   254 like. He like he   301 digest
digest

1.3. 129 In favor's like Is Fauors, like
2.1. 28 [and elsewhere] lest least   40 ides first   67 of of a   83 put path   122 women, then, women. Then   136 oath, when Oath. When   214 eighth eight   268 his hit   281 the tho   310.1 *Enter Lucius and Ligarius* [after "with haste" in line 310 in F]   314 [and through line 322] LIGARIUS *Cai.*
2.2. 23 did neigh do neigh   46 are heare   81 Of And
2.3. 1 ARTEMIDORUS [not in F]   120 to blame too blame
3.1. 40 law lane   114 states State   116 lies lye   201 [and elsewhere] corpse Coarse [also Course and Corpes]   256 ANTONY [not in F]   277.1 *Octavius' Octauio's* [also at 5.2.4]   285 for from
3.2. 106 art are   205 ALL [not in F]   222 wit writ   260 s.d. *Exeunt Exit*   262 s.d. *Enter Servant* [after "fellow" in F]
3.3. 6 Whither Whether
4.2. 34–6 FIRST, SECOND, THIRD SOLDIER [not in F]   50 Lucius *Lucillius*   52 Lucilius *Lucius*   52.1 *Manent Manet*
4.3. 209–10 off / If off. / If   230 s.d. *Enter Lucius* [before line 230 in F]   244, 246 [and throughout] Claudius *Claudio*   246 [and throughout] Varro *Varrus*   252 will will it   303, 307 VARRO, CLAUDIUS *Both*
5.1. 42 teeth teethes   67.1 *Exeunt Exit*   70 [F has s.d.: "*Lucillius and Messala stand forth*"]   71 LUCILIUS (stands forth) *Luc.*   73 MESSALA (stands forth) *Messa.*   99 rest rests
5.3. 99 fare far   104 Thasos *Tharsus*   108 Flavius *Flauio*
5.4. 7 LUCILIUS [not in F]   9 O *Luc.* O   12, 15 FIRST SOLDIER *Sold.*   16.1 *Enter Antony* [before line 16 in F]   17 the news thee newes
5.5. 33 too, Strato to *Strato*   77 With all Withall

Hamlet

Copy text: the Second Quarto of 1604–1605 [Q2]. The First Folio text also represents an independently authoritative text; although seemingly not the correct choice for copy text, the Folio text is considerably less marred by typographical errors than is Q2. The adopted readings in these notes are from F unless otherwise indicated; [eds.] means that the adopted reading was first proposed by some editor since the time of F. Some readings also are supplied from the First Quarto of 1603 [Q1]. Act and scene divisions are missing in Qq 1–2; the Folio provides such markings only through 1.3 and at Act 2.

1.1. 1 Who's Whose   19 soldier [F, Q1] souldiers   44 off [Q1] of   48 harrows horrowes   67 sledded Polacks [eds.] sleaded pollax   77 why [F, Q1] with   cast cost   91 heraldry [F, Q1] heraldy   92 those [F, Q1] these   95 returned returne   97 cov'nant comart   98 designed [eds.] desseigne   112 e'en so [eds.] enso   116 mote [eds.] moth   119 tenantless tennatlesse   125 feared [eds.] feare   142 you [F, Q1] your   144 at it it   181 conveniently [F, Q1] conueuient
1.2. 0.2 [and elsewhere] Gertrude Gertrad   1 KING *Claud.*   67 so so much   77 good coold   82 shapes [Q3] chapes   83 denote deuote   96 a or   105 corpse [eds.] course   112 you. For you for   114 retrograde retrogard   129 sullied [eds.] sallied [Q2] solid [F]   132 self seale   133 weary wary   137 to this thus   140 satyr [F4] satire   143 would [F, Q1] should   149 even she [F; not in Q2]   175 to drink deep [F, Q1] for to drinke   178 to see [F, Q1] to   199 waste [F2] wast [Q2, F]   206 jelly with . . . fear, gelly, with . . . feare   210 Where, as [Q5] Whereas   225 Indeed, indeed [F, Q1] Indeede   241 Very like, very like [F, Q1] Very like   242 hundred hundreth   243 MARCELLUS, BERNARDO [eds.] *Both*   247 tonight to nigh   256 fare farre   257 eleven a leauen   259.1 *Exeunt* [at line 258 in Q2]   262 Foul [F, Q1] fonde
1.3. 3 convoy is conuay, in   12 bulk bulkes   18 [F; not in Q2]   29 weigh way   49 like a a   74 Are Or   75 be boy   76 loan loue   110 Running [eds.] Wrong [Q2] Roaming [F]   116 springes springs   126 tether tider   130 implorators imploratotors   131 bawds [eds.] bonds   132 beguile beguide
1.4. 2 is a is   6.1 *go off* [eds.] *goes of*   17 revel [Q3] reueale   19 clepe clip   36 evil [eds.] eale [Q2] ease [Q3]   37 often dout [eds.] of a doubt   49 inurned interr'd [Q2, Q1]   61, 79 wafts waues   80 off of   82 artery arture   86.1 *Exeunt Exit*   87 imagination [F, Q1] imagion

1.5. 1 Whither [eds.] Whether   20 on [eds.] an   21 fretful porcupine [F, Q1] fearfull Porpentine   44 wit [eds.] wits   48 what a what   56 lust [F, Q1] but   angel Angle   57 sate [F] sort   59 scent [eds.] sent   68 alleys [eds.] allies   69 posset possesse   96 stiffly swiftly   119 bird and   128 HORATIO, MARCELLUS *Booth* [also at line 151]   heaven, my lord heauen   138 Look you, I'll I will   157 s.d. cries *Ghost cries*   179 some'er so mere   185 Well well, well [Q1, Q2]
2.1 0.1 man [eds.] *man or two*   3 marvelous meruiles   29 Faith, no Fayth   41 warrant wit   42 sullies sallies   43 wi' th' with   60 o'ertook or tooke   64 takes take   76 s.d. *Exit Reynaldo. Enter Ophelia* [after line 75 in Q2]   107 passion passions   114 quoted [eds.] coted
2.2. 0.1 [and elsewhere] *Rosencrantz Rosencraus*   57 o'erhasty hastie   73 three [F, Q1] threescore   90 since brevity breuitie   125 This [Q2 has a speech prefix: *Pol.* This]   126 above about   137 winking working   143 his her   148 watch wath   149 to a to   151 'tis [F, Q1; not in Q2]   170.1 [at line 169 in Q2] *Exeunt* [eds.] *Exit*   210 sanity sanctity   212–13 and suddenly . . . him [F; not in Q2]   213 honorable lord Lord   214 most humbly take take   215 cannot, sir cannot   216 more not more   224 excellent extent   228–9 overhappy. / On euer happy on   229 cap lap   240–70 Let . . . attended [F; not in Q2]   267 ROSENCRANTZ, GUILDENSTERN *Both* [F]   273 even euer   288 could can   292 off of   304 What a What   306–7 admirable, in action how . . . angel, in [F, subst.] admirable in action, how . . . Angell in   310 no, nor nor   314 you yee   321 of on   324–5 the clown . . . sear [F; not in Q2]   tickle [eds.] tickled [F]   326 blank black   337–62 How . . . too [F; not in Q2]   342 berattle [eds.] be-ratled [F]   349 most like [eds.] like most [F]   373 lest my let me   381 too to   398–9 tragical-historical, tragical-comical-historical-pastoral [F; not in Q2]   401 light . . . these [eds.] light for the lawe of writ, and the liberty: these   425 By 'r by   429 e'en to 't ento't   French falconers friendly Fankners   433 [and elsewhere] FIRST PLAYER *Player*   436–7 caviare cauiary   443 affectation affection   446 tale [F, Q1] talke   456 heraldry [F, Q1] heraldy   dismal. Head dismall head   474 Then senseless Ilium [F; not in Q2]   481 And, like Like   495 fellies [F4] follies [Q2] Fallies [F]   504 "Moblèd queen" is good [F; not in Q2; F reads "Inobled"]   506 bisson Bison   514 husband's [F, Q1] husband   519 whe'er where   540 a [F; not in Q2]   541 or [F, Q1] lines, or   546 s.d. *Exeunt players* [see textual note at line 548.1]   547 till tell   548.1 *Exeunt* [F; Q2 has "*Exeunt Pol. and Players*" after line 547]   554 his the   556 and an   559 to Hecuba [F, Q1] to her   561 the cue that   582 Oh, vengeance [F; not in Q2]   584 father [Q1, Q3, Q4; not in Q2, F]   588 scullion [F] stallyon [Q2] scalion [Q1]   600 the devil a deale the devil the deale
3.1. 1 And An   28 too two   32 lawful espials [F; not in Q2]   33 Will Wee'le   46 loneliness lowlines   to too   56 Let's withdraw with-draw   56.2 *Enter Hamlet* [after line 55 in Q2]   65 wished. To wisht to   73 disprized despiz'd   84 of us all [F, Q1; not in Q2]   86 sicklied sickled   93 well, well, well well   100 the these   108 your honesty you   119 inoculate euocutat   122 to a a   130 knaves all knaues   144 paintings too [Q1] paintings   146 jig, you amble gig & amble   147 lisp list   148 your ignorance [F, Q1] ignorance   155 Th'expectancy Th'expectation   159 music musickt   160 that what   161 tune time   162 feature stature   164 [Q2 has "*Exit*" at the end of this line]   191 unwatched vnmatcht
3.2. 10 tatters totters   split [F, Q1] spleet   27 of the of   29 praise praysd   37 sir [F; not in Q2]   45.1 *Enter . . . Rosencrantz* [after line 47 in Q2]   88 detecting detected   96 now. My lord, now my Lord.   107 [and elsewhere] QUEEN *Ger.*   108 metal mettle   112–13 [F; not in Q2]   127 devil deule [Q2] Diuel [F]   133.1 sound [eds.] *sounds*   133.7 *Anon comes anon come*   135 miching [F, Q1] munching   140 keep counsel [F, Q1] keepe   153 [and throughout scene] PLAYER KING *King*   154 orbèd orb'd the   159 [and throughout scene] PLAYER QUEEN *Quee.*   162 your our   164 [Q2 follows here with an extraneous unrhymed line: "For women feare too much, euen as they loue"]   165 For And   166 In Eyther none, in   167 love Lord   179 Wormwood, wormwood That's wormwood   180 PLAYER QUEEN [not in Q2]   188 like the   197 joys joy   217 An And   221 a widow [F,

Q1] I be a widow **be** [F] be a **226.1** *Exit* [F, Q1] *Exeunt* **240 wince** [Q1] winch [Q2, F] **241.1** [after line 242 in Q2] **254 Confederate** [F, Q1] Considerat **256 infected** [F, Q1, Q4] inuected **258 usurp** vsurps **264** [F; not in Q2] **274 with two** with **288.1** [F; after line 293 in Q2] **308 start** stare **317 of my** of **343.1** [after line 341 in Q2] **357 thumb** the vmber **366 to the top of** to **370 can fret me** [F] fret me not [Q2] can fret me, yet [Q1] **371.1** [after line 372 in Q2] **385 POLONIUS** [F; not in Q2] **386 Leave me, friends** [so F; Q2 places before "I will say so," and assigns both to Hamlet] **388 breathes** breakes **390 bitter . . . day** business as the bitter day **395 daggers** [F, Q1] dagger

3.3. 19 huge hough **22 ruin** raine **23 but with** but **35.1** *Exit* [after "I know" in F] **50 pardoned** pardon **58 Offense's** [eds.] Offences **shove** showe **73 pat . . . a-praying** but now a is a praying **75 revenged** reuendge **79 hire and salary** base and silly **81 With all** Withall

3.4. 5–6 with him . . . Mother, Mother, Mother [F; not in Q2] **7 warrant** wait **8.1** *Enter Hamlet* [at line 5 in Q2] **21 inmost** most **23 Help, ho!** Helpe how **43 off** of **51 tristful** heated **53** [assigned in Q2 to Hamlet] **60 heaven-kissing** heaue, a kissing **89 panders** pardons **91 mine . . . soul** my very eyes into my soule **92 grainèd** greeued **93 not leave** leaue there **100 tithe** kyth **146 Ecstasy** [F; not in Q2] **150 I the** the **165 live** leaue **172 Refrain tonight** to refraine night **193 ravel** rouell **205 to breathe** [eds.] to breath **222 a** [F, Q1] a most **224.1** *Exeunt* [eds.] *Exit*

4.1. 32.1 [at 31 in Q2]

4.2. 0.1 [Q2: "*Enter Hamlet, Rosencraus, and others.*"] **2–3** [F; not in Q2; the s.p. in F is "*Gentlemen*"] **4 HAMLET** [not in Q2] **5.1** [F; not in Q2] **7 Compounded** Compound **18–19 an ape** [not in Q2] **31–2 Hide . . . after** [F; not in Q2]

4.3. 44 With fiery quickness [F; not in Q2] **56 and so** so **72 were** will **begun** begin

4.4. 20–1 name. To name To

4.5. 16 Let . . . in [assigned in Q2 to Horatio] **20.1** [after line 16 in Q2] **38 with** all with **52 clothes** close **57 Indeed, la** Indeede **62 to** too **83 in their** in **98** [F; not in Q2] **100.1** [below line 97 in Q2] **103 impetuous** [Q3, F2] impitious [Q2] impittious [F] **109 They** The **146 swoopstake** [eds.] soapstake [Q1 reads "Swoop-stake-like"] **158 Let her come in** [assigned in Q2 to Laertes and placed before "How now, what noyse is that?"] **s.d.** *Enter Ophelia* [after line 157 in Q2] **162 Till** Tell **165 an old** [F, Q1] a poore **166–8, 170** [F; not in Q2] **186 must** [F, Q1] may **191 affliction** [F, Q1] afflictions **199 All flaxen** Flaxen **203 Christian** [F] Christians **souls, I pray God** [F, Q1] soules **204 you see** you **217 trophy, sword** trophe sword

4.6. 7, 9 FIRST SAILOR *Say.* **9 an't** and **22 good turn** turne **26 bore** bord **30 He** *So* **31 will give** will

4.7. 6 proceeded proceede **7 crimeful** criminall **15 conjunctive** concliue **22 gyves** Giues **23 loud a wind** loued Arm'd **25 had** haue **37 How . . . Hamlet** [F; not in Q2] **38 This** These **46–7 your pardon** you pardon **48 and more strange** [F; not in Q2] **Hamlet** [F; not in Q2] **59 shall live** [F, Q1] liue **62 checking** the King **78 ribbon** [eds.] ribaud **89 my** me **101 escrimers** [eds.] Scrimures **116 wick** [eds.] weeke **123 spendthrift** [Q5] spend thirfts **135 on** ore **139 pass** pace **141 for that** for **151 shape. If** shape if **157 ha 't** hate **160 prepared** prefard **168 hoar** horry **172 cold** cull-cold **192 douts** [F "doubts"] drownes

5.1. 1 [and throughout] **FIRST CLOWN** *Clowne* **3** [and throughout] **SECOND CLOWN** *Other* **9** *se offendendo* so offended **12 and to** to **Argal** or all **34–7 SECOND CLOWN: Why . . . arms?** [F; not in Q2] **43 that frame** that **55.1** [before line 65 in Q2] **60 stoup** soope **70 daintier** dintier **85 meant** [F, Q1, Q3] went **89 mazard** massene **106–7 Is . . . recoveries** [F; not in Q2] **107–8 Will his** will **109 double ones too** doubles **120 Oh** or **121** [F; not in Q2] **143 Of all** Of **165 nowadays** [F; not in Q2] **183 Let me see** [F; not in Q1] **192 chamber** [F, Q1] table **208–9 As thus** [F; not in Q2] **216 winter's** waters **226, 235 PRIEST** *Doct.* **231 Shards, flints** Flints

246 t' have haue **247 treble** double **262 and rash** rash **288 thus** this **296.1** [*Exit*] *Horatio and Horatio* **301 shortly** thereby **302 Till** Tell

5.2. 5 Methought my thought **6 bilboes** bilbo **9 pall** fall **17 unseal** vnfold **19 Ah,** [eds.] A **29 villainies** villaines **30 Ere** Or **43 "as"es** as sir **52 Subscribed** Subscribe **57, 68–80** [F; not in Q2] **73 interim is** [eds.] *interim's* [F] **78 court** [eds.] count [F] **81** [and throughout] **OSRIC** *Cour.* **82 humbly** humble **93 Put your** your **98 sultry** sully **for** or **107 gentleman** [eds.] gentlemen **109 feelingly** [Q4] fellingly **114 dozy** [eds.] dazzie **yaw** [eds.] raw **141 his** [eds.] this **142 him by them,** him, by them **149 hangers** hanger **156 carriages** carriage **159 might be** be might **162 impawned, as** [eds.] all [Q2] impon'd, as [F] **174 purpose, I** purpose; I **181–2 Yours, yours. 'A does** Yours doo's **186 comply** so sir **190 yeasty** histy **191 fanned** [eds.] prophane [Q2] fond [F] **winnowed** trennowed **210 But thou** [eds.] thou **218 be now** be **220 will come** well come **238** [F; not in Q2] **248 To keep** To **till all** **252 foils. Come on** foiles. **255 off** of **261 bettered** better **270 union** Vnice ["Onixe" in some copies] **288 A touch, a touch, I** I **302 afeard** sure **316 Hamlet. Hamlet** *Hamlet* **319 thy** [F, Q1] my **327 murderous** [F; not in Q2] **328 off** of **thy union** [F, Q1] the Onixe **345 ha 't** [eds.] hate [Q2] have 't [F] **366 proud** prou'd **369 FIRST AMBASSADOR** *Embas.* **381 th' yet** yet **385 forced** for no **394 on** no

Passages contained only in F and omitted from Q2 are noted in the textual notes above. Listed below are the more important instances in which Q2 contains words, lines, and passages omitted in F.

1.1. 112–29 BERNARDO I think . . . countrymen
1.2. 58–60 wrung . . . consent
1.3. 9 perfume due
1.4. 17–38 This heavy-headed . . . scandal **75–8** The very . . . beneath
2.1. 122 Come
2.2. 17 Whether . . . thus **217** except my life **363** very **366** 'Sblood (and some other profanity passim) **371** then **444–5** as wholesome . . . fine **521–2** of this **589** Hum
3.2. 169–70 Where . . . there **216–17** To . . . scope
3.4. 72–7 Sense . . . difference **79–82** Eyes . . . mope **168–72** That monster . . . put on **174–7** the next . . . potency **187** One word . . . lady **209–17** There's . . . meet
4.1. 4 Bestow . . . while **41–4** Whose . . . air
4.2. 4 But soft
4.3. 26–9 KING Alas . . . worm
4.4. 9–67 *Enter Hamlet . . . worth*
4.5. 33 Oho
4.7. 68–82 LAERTES My lord . . . graveness **101–3** Th' escrimers . . . them **115–24** There . . . ulcer
5.1. 154 There
5.2. 106–42 here is . . . unfellowed (replaced in F by "you are not ignorant of what excellence Laertes is at his weapon") **154–5 HORATIO** [*to Hamlet*] I knew . . . done **193–207** *Enter a Lord . . .* lose, my lord (replaced in F by "You will lose this wager, my lord") **222** Let be

Othello

Copy text: the First Folio. The adopted readings are from the Quarto of 1622 [Q1], unless otherwise indicated; [eds.] means that the adopted reading was first proposed by some editor subsequent to the First Folio. Act and scene divisions are marked in the Folio with the exception of 2.3.

1.1. 1 Tush, never Neuer **4 'Sblood, but** But **16 And, in conclusion** [Q1; not in F] **26 togaed** Tongued **30 other** others **34 God bless** blesse **68 full** fall **thick-lips** Thicks-lips **74 changes** chances **75** [and elsewhere] **lose** [eds.] loose **81 Thieves, thieves, thieves** Theeues, Theeues **83.1** *Brabantio above* [in F, printed as a speech prefix to line 84] **88 Zounds, sir** Sir [also at line 111] **103 bravery** knauerie **119 are now** are **158 pains** apines **161 sign. That** [eds.] signe) that **186 night** might

1.2. 34 Duke Dukes   **50 carrack** Carract   **64 her!** [eds.] her   **69 darlings** Dearelinge   **89 I do** do

1.3. 1 There is There's   **these** this   **61 DUKE AND SENATORS** [*All* Q1] *Sen.*   **101 maimed** main'd   **108 upon** vp on   DUKE [Q1; not in F]   **109 overt** ouer   **112 [and elsewhere] FIRST SENATOR** *Sen.*   **124 till** tell   **132 battles** Battaile   **fortunes** Fortune   **141 travels'** Trauellours   **143 rocks, and** Rocks   **heads** head   **145 other** others   **146 Anthropophagi** *Antropophague*   **147 Do grow** Grew   **149 thence** hence   **157 intentively** instinctiuely   **161 sighs** kisses   **203 grece** grise   **204 Into your favor** [Q1; not in F]   **222 piercèd** pierc'd   **ear** eares   **227 sovereign** more soueraigne   **233 couch** [eds.] Coach [F] Cooch [Q1]   **237 These** [eds.] This   **244 Nor I. I would not** Nor would I   **251 did love** loue   **267 me** [eds.] my   **273 instruments** Instrument   **281 DESDEMONA Tonight, my lord?** DUKE This night [Q1; not in F]   **285 With** And   **294 FIRST SENATOR** *Sen.*   **296.1** *Exeunt Exit*   **302 matters** matter   **303 the** the the   **329 beam** [eds.] braine [F] ballance [Q1]   **333–4 our unbitted** or vnbitted   **335 scion** [eds.] Seyen [F] syen [Q1]   **353 error** errors   **354 She . . . she must** [Q1; not in F]   **358 a supersubtle** super-subtle   **378–82 RODERIGO What . . . purse** [Q1; not in F]   **386 a snipe** Snpe   **389 He's** [Ha's Q1] She ha's   **396 ear** eares

2.1. 35 prays praye   **36 heaven** Heauens   **42 THIRD GENTLEMAN** *Gent.*   **44 arrivance** Arriuancie   **45 this** the   **58 SECOND GENTLEMAN** *Gent.* [also at lines 61, 68, and 95]   **72 clog** enclogge   **84 And . . . comfort** [Q1; not in F]   **90 tell me** tell   **94 the sea** Sea   **96 their** this   **107 list** leaue   **111 doors** doore   **156 [and elsewhere] ne'er** *neu'r*   **158 such wight** *such wightes*   **170 gyve** [eds.] giue   **174 An** and   **175 courtesy** Curtsie   **176 clyster pipes** Cluster-pipes   **214.1** *Exeunt* [eds.] *Exit*   **216 hither** thither   **229 again** a game   **239 fortune** Forune   **241–2 compassing** compasse   **243–4 finder out** finder   **244 occasions** occasion   **has** he's   **263 mutualities** mutabilities   **300 for wife** for wift   **307 rank** right   **308 nightcap** Night-Cape

2.2. 6 addiction [eds.] addition   **10 Heaven bless** Blesse

2.3. 27 stoup [eds.] stope   **38 unfortunate** infortunate   **52 lads** else   **57 to put** put to   **61, 71 God** heauen   **76 Englishman** Englishmen   **91 Then . . . auld** [*Then . . . owd* Q1] *And take thy awl'd*   **93 'Fore God** Why   **97 God's** heau'ns   **106 God forgive** Forgiue   **110 speak** I speake   **123 the** his   **138 s.d.** *Cry within*: Help! Help! [from Q1: "Helpe, helpe, within"]   **139 Zounds, you** You   **152 God's will** Alas   **153 Montano—sir** *Montano*   **156 God's will, Lieutenant, hold** Fie, fie Lieutenant   **158 Zounds, I** I   **161 sense of place** [eds.] place of sense   **184 wont be** wont to be   **201 Zounds, if I** If I once   **212 leagued** league   **218 Thus** This   **227 the** then   **246 well now** well   **250 vile** vil'd   **255 God** Heauen   **260 thought** had thought   **283 Oh, God** Oh   **308 I'll** I   **311 denotement** [eds.] deuotement   **325–6 me here** me   **337 were't** were   **356 s.d.** *Enter Roderigo* [after line 356 in F]   **369 hast** hath   **372 By the Mass** Introth   **378 on;** [on Q1] on   **379 the while** [eds.] a while

3.1. 1 *Musicians* [eds.] *Musicians, and Clowne*   **5 [and at lines 7, 9, and 15]** A MUSICIAN *Mus.*   **21 s.d.** *Exeunt* [eds.] *Exit*   **22 hear** heare me   **26 General's wife** Generall   **31 CASSIO Do, good my friend** [Q1; not in F]   **42 s.d.** *Exit* [at line 41 in F]   **52 To . . . front** [Q1; not in F]

3.3. 16 circumstance Circumstances   **41 you** your   **55 Yes, faith** I sooth   **66 or** on   **80 By'r Lady** Trust me   **103 you** he   **118 By heaven** Alas   **124 In** Of   **148 that all** that: All   **free to free** free   **152 But some** Wherein   **160 oft** of   **161 wisdom then** wisdome   **175 By heaven, I'll** Ile   **183 fondly** [eds.] soundly [F] strongly [Q1]   **188 God** Heauen   **194 Is once** Is   **196 blown** blow'd   **199 dances well** Dances   **216 God** Heauen   **218 keep't** [eds.] keepe [Q1] kept [F]   **225 [and elsewhere] to** too   **230 I'faith** Trust me   **232 my** your   **249 disproportion** disproportions   **264 to hold** to   **275 qualities** Quantities   **276 human** humane   **289 of** to   **294 oh, then heaven mocks** Heauen mock'd   **301 Faith** Why   **305.1** *Exit* [at line 304 in F]   **328 faith** but   **345 s.d.** *Enter Othello* [after "I did say so" in F]   **354 of her** in her   **385 remorse;** [remorce. Q1] remorse   **407 see, sir** see   **411 supervisor** super-vision   **439 then laid** laid   **440 Over** ore   **sighed** sigh   **kissed** kisse   **441 Cried** cry   **455 any that was** [eds.] any, it was   **468 mind perhaps** minde   **471 Ne'er feels** [eds.] Neu'r keepes

3.4. 23 that the   **37 It yet** It   **56 faith** indeed   **77 I'faith** Indeed   **79 God** Heauen   **83 Heaven bless** Blesse   **88 can, sir** can   **94–5 DESDEMONA I pray . . . Cassio. OTHELLO The handkerchief!** [Q1; not in F]   **99 I'faith** Insooth   **100 Zounds** Away   **142 s.d.** *Exit* [after line 141 in F]   **164 that** the   **169.1** *Exit* [after line 168 in F]   **172 I'faith** Indeed   **182 friend.** [eds.] Friend,   **183 absence** [eds.] absence, [Q1] Absence: [F]   **188 by my faith** in good troth

4.1. 32 Faith Why   **36 Zounds, that's** that's   **45 work** workes   **52 No, forbear** [Q1; not in F]   **72 couch** [Coach Q1] Cowch;   **79 unsuiting** [Q1 corrected] vnfitting [Q1 uncorrected] resulting [F]   **81 'scuse** scuses   **97 clothes** Cloath   **103 conster** conserue   **105 you now** you   **109 power** dowre   **113 a woman** woman   **114 i'faith** indeed   **121 Do you triumph, Roman?** Do ye triumph, Romaine?   **122 marry her** marry   **125 win** [eds.] winnes   **126 Faith** Why   **shall marry** marry   **133 beckons** becomes   **138 by this hand, she** [Q1; not in F]   **165 Faith, I** I   **167 Faith** Yes   **214.1** [after line 212 in F]   **217 God save** Saue   **240 By my troth** Trust me   **253 Truly, an** Truely   **286 denote** deonte [F uncorrected] deuote [F corrected]

4.2. 32 Nay May   **33 knees** knee   **35 But not the words** [Q1; not in F]   **51 kinds** kind   **56 A** The   **66 Ay, there** [eds.] I heere   **71 ne'er** neuer   **83 Impudent strumpet** [Q1; not in F]   **96 keep** keepes   **s.d.** *Enter Emilia* [after line 94 in F]   **155 O God** Alas   **162 them in** [eds.] them: or   **174 And . . . you** [Q1; not in F]   **177 you to** to   **190 Faith, I** I   **for** and   **201 By this hand** Nay   **232 takes** taketh   **236 of** [Q1; not in F]

4.3. 10.1 *Exit* [after line 9 in F]   **22 favor in them** fauour   **25 faith** Father   **26 before thee** before   **35 Barbary** *Braberie*   **43 sighing** [eds.] *singing* [F corrected] *sining* [F uncorrected]   **73 Good troth** Introth   **74 By my troth** Introth   **78 Uds pity** why   **107 God** Heauen

5.1. 1 bulk Barke   **22 Be't** But   **hear** heard   **36 Forth** For   **50 Did** Do   **91 Oh, heaven** Yes, 'tis   **106 out o'** o'   **113 'Las, what's . . .** What's Alas, what is . . . What is   **116 dead** quite dead   **126 Faugh!** Fie Fie

5.2. 34 heaven Heauens   **37 say so** say   **56 Yes, presently** Presently   **61 Then Lord** O Heauen   **96 here** high   **104 Should** Did   **108 s.d.** *Enter Emilia* [after line 108 in F]   **121 Oh, Lord** Alas   **131 heard** heare   **148 Nay, had** had   **225 Oh, God! Oh, heavenly God** Oh Heauen! oh heauenly Powres   **226 Zounds** Come   **248 have here** haue   **317 not. Here** [not: here Q1] not) heere   **357 Indian** Iudean

King Lear

Copy text: the First Folio, except for those 300 or so lines found only in the First Quarto of 1608 [Q1]. Unless otherwise indicated, adopted readings are from the corrected state (Qb) of Q1. A few readings are supplied from the Second Quarto of 1619 [Q2]. All readings subsequent to 1619 are marked as supplied by "eds." Act and scene divisions are as marked in F, except that F docs not mark 2.3 and 2.4, and omits 4.3 entirely, so that 4.4 is marked "*Scena Tertia*" and similarly with 4.5 and 4.6 (though 4.7 is marked "*Scena Septima*").

1.1. 5 equalities qualities   **20–2 account . . . yet** [eds.] account, though . . . for: yet   **35 liege** Lord   **55 words** word   **66 issue** issues   **68 Speak** [Q1; not in F]   **74 possesses** professes   **85 interessed** [eds.] interest   **104** [Q1; not in F]   **110 mysteries** [eds.] miseries [F] mistresse [Q1]   **135 turns** turne   **156 as a** as   **157 nor** nere   **161 LEAR** *Kear*   **162 KENT** *Lent*   **165 CORNWALL** [eds.] *Cor.*   **166 the** thy   **173 sentence** sentences   **191 GLOUCESTER** *Cor.*   **217 best object** obiect   **229 well** will   **252 respects of fortune** respect and Fortunes   **272 Ye** [eds.] The   **285 shame them** with shame   **286.1** *Exeunt* [eds.] *Exit*   **293 hath not** hath   **306 hit** sit

1.2. 1 [and elsewhere] EDMUND *Bast.*   **21 top** [eds.] to'   **56 waked wake** 97–9 EDMUND Nor . . . earth [Q1; not in F]   **134 Fut, I** I   **136 Edgar** [Q1; not in F]   **137 and pat** [eds.] Pat [F] and out [Q1]   **147–55 as . . . come,** [Q1; not in F]   **182 s.d.** [at line 181 in F]

1.3. 3 [and elsewhere] OSWALD [eds.] *Ste.*   **17–21** [Q1; not in F]   **26–7 I would . . . speak** [Q1; not in F]   **28 very** [Q1; not in F]

1.4. 1 well will   **31 canst** canst thou   **43.1 *Enter steward*** [eds.; after line 44 in F]   **50 daughter** Daughters   **76.1 *Enter steward*** [eds.; after line 77 in F]   **96 KENT** *Lear*   **Fool** my Boy   **135 Dost** Do'st thou   **138–53 That . . . snatching** [Q1; not in F]   **158 crown** Crownes   **175 fools** Foole   **195 nor crumb** not crum   **214 it had** it's had   **229–32** [Q1; not in F]   **255 Oh . . . come** [Q1; not in F]   **303 Yea . . . this** [Q1; not in F]   **343 You're** Your are   **attasked** at task

1.5. 0.1 Kent Kent, Gentleman   **51 s.d. *Exit*** Exeunt

2.1. 2 you your   **19.1** [after line 18 in F]   **39 stand 's** stand   **69 I should** should I   **70 ay, though** though   **78 I never got him** [Q1; not in F]   **78 s.d.** [at line 76 in F, after "seeke it"]   **79 why** wher   **87 strange news** strangenesse   **100 spoil** wast   **122 poise** prize   **125 least thought** best though   **132 *Flourish. Exeunt*** [eds.] *Exeunt. Flourish*

2.2. 22 clamorous clamours   **45 an** if   **52 What's** What is   **66 you'll** you will   **78 Bring . . . their** Being . . . the   **79 Renege** Reuenge   **80 gale** gall   **83 Smile** Smoile   **84 an** if   **101 take't** take it   **109 flickering** flicking   **124 dread** dead   **127 their** there   **132 respect** respects   **142.1** [at line 140 in F]   **144–8 His . . . with** [Q1; not in F]   **146 contemned'st** [eds.] temnest [Q1]   **148 King** King his Master, needs   **153** [Q1; not in F]   **154 Come . . . away** [assigned in F to Cornwall]   **good** [Q1; not in F]   **154.1 *Exeunt*** Exit   **155 Duke's** Duke

2.3. 18 sheepcotes Sheeps-Coates

2.4. 2 messenger Messengers   **9 man's** man   **18–19** [Q1; not in F]   **30 panting** painting   **33 whose** those   **56 *Hysterica*** [eds.] *Historica*   **62 the** the the   **74 have** hause   **128 you** your   **130 mother's** Mother   **183 s.d.** [after line 182 in F]   **185.1** [at line 183 in F, after "Stockes"]   **187 fickle** fickly   **190 s.d.** [after line 188 in F]   **213 hot-blooded** hot-bloodied   **285 s.d.** [after "weeping" in line 286 in F]   **297 s.d.** [after line 296 in F]   **298 Whither** Whether [also in line 299]   **302 bleak** high

3.1. 7–15 tears . . . all [Q1; not in F]   **10 outstorm** [eds.] outscorne [Q1]   **30–42** [Q1; not in F]

3.2. 3 drowned drown   **38.1** [after line 36 in F]   **50 pother** pudder   **85–6** [these lines follow line 92 in F]

3.3. 17 for 't for it

3.4. 7 skin. So 'tis skinso: 'tis   **10 thy** they   **12 This** the   **27 s.d.** [at line 26 in F]   **31 looped** lop'd   **38.1 *Enter Fool*** [F, after line 36: "*Enter Edgar, and Foole*"]   **44.1** [after line 36 in F]   **46 blows the cold wind** blow the windes   **51 through fire** though Fire   **52 ford** Sword   **57, 58 Bless** Blisse   **90 deeply** deerely   **99 sessa** [eds.] *Sesey*   **112.1** [after line 108 in F]   **114 fiend** [Q1; not in F]   **115 till the** at   **116 squinnies** [eds.] squints [F] squemes [Q1]   **134 stock-punished** stockt, punish'd   **hath had** hath   **173 in th'** into th'

3.5. 11 he which hee   **26 dearer** deere

3.6. 5.1 *Exit* [at line 3 in F]   **17–55** [Q1; not in F]   **21 justicer** [eds.] Iustice [Q1]   **22 Now** [Q2] no [Q1]   **24 eyes at trial, madam?** eyes, at tral madam   **25 burn** [eds.] broome [Q1]   **34 cushions** [eds.] cushings [Q1]   **36 robèd** robbed   **51 joint** [eds.] ioyne [Q1]   **53 on** [eds.] an [Q1]   **67 mongrel grim** Mongrill, Grim   **68 lym** [eds.] Hym   **69 Bobtail tike or trundle-tail** Or Bobtaile tight, or Troudle taile   **73 Sessa** sese   **76 makes** make   **85.1** [after line 80 in F]   **97–101 KENT** Oppressèd . . . behind [Q1; not in F]   **101 GLOUCESTER** [not in F]   **102–15** [Q1; not in F]

3.7. 10 festinate [eds.] festiuate   **18 lord's dependents** Lords, dependents   **23 s.d. *Exeunt*** [eds.] *Exit* [at line 22 in F]   **61 rash** sticke   **66 dern** sterne   **75 FIRST SERVANT** *Seru.* [also *Seru.* or *Ser.* at lines 79, 82, 84]   **83** [F provides a stage direction: "*Killes him*"]   **102–10** [Q1; not in F]   **102 SECOND SERVANT** *Seruant* [and called "1 *Ser*" at line 106 in Q1]   **103 THIRD SERVANT** 2 *Seruant* [Q1]   **107 Roguish** [Qa; not in Qb]   **109 THIRD SERVANT** 2 *Ser.*   **110.1 *Exeunt*** Exit

4.1. 2 flattered. To be worst flattered to be worst,   **41 Then . . . gone** Get thee away   **57–62 Five . . . master** [Q1; not in F]   **60 Flibbertigibbet** [eds.] *Stiberdigebit* [Q1]   **60–1 mopping and mowing** [eds.] Mobing, & Mohing [Q1]

4.2. 0.1 Bastard Bastard, and Steward   **2 s.d. steward** [Q1; placed at scene beginning in F]   **30 whistling** whistle   **32–51 I fear . . . deep** [Q1; not in F]   **33 its** [eds.] ith [Q1]   **48 these** [eds.] this [Q1]   **54–60 that . . . so** [Q1; not in F]   **58 to threat** threat [Q1 corrected]

61 shows seemes   **63–9, 70** [Q1; not in F]   **76 thereat enraged** threat-enrag'd   **80 justicers** [Q1 corrected] Iustices

4.3. 1–57 [scene omitted in F]   **11 sir** [eds.] say [Q1]   **16 strove** [eds.] streme [Q1]   **20 seemed** [eds.] seeme [Q1]   **22 dropped. In** dropt in   **32 then** her, then   **44 benediction, turned her** benediction turnd her,   **57 s.d. *Exeunt*** [eds.] *Exit* [Q1]

4.4 [F reads "*Scena Tertia*"]   **3 fumiter** [eds.] femiter [Q1] Fenitar [F]   **6 century** Centery   **18 distress** desires   **28 right** Rite

4.5 [F reads "*Scena Quarta*"]   **8 letters** Letter   **23 Something** Some things   **27 oeillades** [eds.] Eliads   **41 meet him** meet

4.6 [F reads "*Scena Quinta*"]   **17 walk** walk'd   **57 summit** Somnet   **66–7 strangeness. / Upon . . . cliff what** [eds.] strangenesse, / Vpon . . . Cliffe. What   **71 enridgèd** enraged   **83 coining** crying   **97 white** the white   **124 they're** they are   **161 thine** thy   **164 Through** Thorough   **small** great   **165 Plate sin** [eds.] Place sinnes   **197 Ay . . . dust** [Q1; not in F]   **205 one** a   **218.1 *Exit*** [after "moved on" in line 218 in F]   **235 Durst** Dar'st   **238 'cagion** 'casion   **263–4 not. / To** not / To   **269 done if . . . conqueror. Then** [eds.] done. If . . . Conqueror then   **274 and . . . venture** [Q1; not in F]   **275 indistinguished** indinguish'd   **288 s.d. *Drum afar off*** [after line 286 in F]

4.7. 25 doubt not doubt   **25–6 CORDELIA Very . . . there** [Q1; not in F]   **33 warring** iarring   **34–7 To stand . . . helm** [Q1; not in F]   **59 hands** hand   **60 No, sir** [Q1; not in F]   **83–4 and . . . lost** [Q1; not in F]   **91–103** [Q1; not in F]

5.1. 12–14 [Q1; not in F]   **18 me not** not   **19–20** [Q1; not in F]   **24–9 Where . . . nobly** [Q1; not in F]   **35** [Q1; not in F]   **41 s.d. *Exeunt . . . armies*** [after line 39 in F]   **48 love** loues

5.3. 13 and hear poor rogues and heare (poore Rogues)   **39–40** [Q1; not in F]   **49 and appointed guard** [Q1 corrected; not in F]   **56–61 At . . . place** [Q1; not in F]   **57 We** [Q1 corrected] mee [Q1 uncorrected]   **59 sharpness** [Q1 corrected] sharpes [Q1 uncorrected]   **72 GONERIL** *Alb.*   **85 attaint** arrest   **86 sister** Sisters   **87 bar** [eds.] bare   **100 he is** hes   **105 EDMUND A herald, ho, a herald** [Q1; not in F]   **105.1 *Enter a Herald*** [after line 104 in F]   **106 ALBANY** [not in F]   **112 CAPTAIN Sound, trumpet** [Q1; not in F]   **118 EDMUND Sound** [Q1; not in F]   **124–5 lost, / By . . . canker-bit.** lost / By Treasons tooth: bare-gnawne, and Canker-bit,   **132 the** my priuiledge, The   **135 Despite** Despise   **146 tongue some say of** tongue (some say) of   **149 those** these   **151 scarcely** scarely   **153.1 *Fight*** [eds.] *Fights*. ["*Alarums. Fights*" is opposite "Saue him, saue him," in line 154 in F.]   **155 arms** Warre   **158 stopple** stop   **163 GONERIL** *Bast.*   **163 s.d. *Exit*** [at line 162 after "for 't" in F]   **208–25 This . . . slave** [Q1; not in F]   **217 him** [eds.] me [Q1]   **241.1** [after line 234 in F]   **255 The captain** [Q1; not in F]   **262 you** your   **280 CAPTAIN** *Gent.*   **282 them** him   **294 You are** [eds.] Your are [F] You'r [Q1]   **299.1** [after "to him" in line 299 in F]   **320 rack** wracke

The above textual notes list all instances in which material not in F is included from Q1. To enable the reader to compare further the F and Q1 texts, a list is provided here of material not in Q1 that is to be found in F. There are some 100 lines in all.

1.1. 40–5 while . . . now   **49–50** Since . . . state   **64–5** and . . . rivers   **83–5** to whose . . . interested   **88–9** LEAR Nothing? CORDELIA Nothing   **165** ALBANY, CORNWALL Dear sir, forbear.

1.2. 112–17 This . . . graves   **169–75** I pray . . . brother

1.4. 260 ALBANY Pray . . . patient   **273** Of . . . you   **321–33** This . . . unfitness

2.4. 6 KENT No, my lord   **21** KENT By Juno . . . ay   **45–54** FOOL Winter's . . . year   **96–7** GLOUCESTER Well . . . man   **101–2** Are they . . . Fiery? The   **139–44** LEAR Say . . . blame   **298–9** CORNWALL Whither . . . horse

3.1. 22–9 Who . . . furnishings

3.2. 79–96 FOOL This . . . time. *Exit*

3.4. 17–18 In . . . endure   **26–7** In . . . sleep   **37–8** Fathom . . . Tom

3.6. 12–14 FOOL No . . . him   **85** FOOL And . . . noon

4.1. 6–9 Welcome . . . blasts

4.2. 26 Oh, the . . . man

4.6. 165–70 Plate . . . lips

5.2. 11 GLOUCESTER And . . . too

5.3. 78 Dispose . . . thine 91 GONERIL An interlude 147 What . . . delay 226 ALBANY Speak, man 316–17 Do you . . . look there

Macbeth

Copy text: the First Folio. Act and scene divisions follow the Folio text, except that 5.8 is not marked in the Folio.

1.1. 9 SECOND WITCH All 10 THIRD WITCH [not in F] 11 ALL [at line 9 in F]
1.2. 1 [and elsewhere] DUNCAN King 13 gallowglasses Gallowgrosses 14 quarrel Quarry 21 ne'er neu'r 26 thunders break Thunders
1.3. 32 Weird weyward [elsewhere in F spelled "weyard"] 39 Forres Soris 97 death. As death, as 98 Came Can 111 lose loose
1.4. 1 Are Or
1.5. 1 [and elsewhere] LADY MACBETH Lady 12 lose loose 47 it hit
1.6. 4 martlet Barlet 9 most must
1.7. 6 shoal Schoole 48 do no
2.1. 56 strides sides 57 sure sowre 58 way they they may
2.2. 13.1 [at line 8 in F, after "die"]
2.3. 41.1 [after line 40 in F] 142 nea'er neere
3.1. 76 MURDERERS Murth. 116 BOTH MURDERERS Murth. [also at line 141] 142.1 Exeunt [at line 144 in F]
3.3. 7 and end
3.4. 79 time times 122.1 Exeunt Exit
3.6. 24 son Sonnes 38 the their
4.1. 34 cauldron Cawdron 38.1 to and 59 germens Germaine 93 Dunsinane Dunsmane 94 s.d. Descends Descend 98 Birnam Byrnan [also spelled "Byrnam" at line 93 and "Birnan," "Byrnane," and "Birnane" in Act 5] 119 eighth eight
4.2. 1 [and throughout] LADY MACDUFF Wife 22 none moue 70–1 ones . . . methinks, ones / To fright you thus. Me thinks 80 s.d. Enter Murderers [after "What are these faces" in F] 81 [and throughout scene] FIRST MURDERER Mur. 84 shag-haired shagge-ear'd
4.3. 4 downfall'n downfall 15 deserve discerne 35 Fare Far 108 accurst accust 124 detraction, here detraction. Heere 134 thy they 144 essay assay 146.1 [after "amend" in F] 161 not nor 237 tune time
5.1. 38 fear who feare? who
5.3. 41 Cure her Cure 54 pristine pristiue 57 senna Cyme 62.1 Exeunt [at line 64 in F]
5.4. 16 SIWARD Sey.

Timon of Athens

Copy text: the First Folio. Act and scene divisions, missing in the Folio, are editorially supplied.

The Actors' Names [Supplied at the end of the play. F also lists Lucius as one of the "Seruants to Vsurers," and the order of names has been changed for Apemantus and Ventidius and some others.]

1.1. 0.1 and Merchant Merchant, and Mercer 23 gum Gowne oozes vses 27 chafes chases 43 man men 50 tax wax 77 conceived to scope. conceyu'd, to scope 92 hands hand slip sit 116 [and subsequently] OLD ATHENIAN Oldm. 160.1 Exeunt Exit 184.1 Enter Apemantus Enter Apermantus [at line 182 in F] 222 cost cast 227 APEMANTUS pe. 234 feigned fegin'd 259 there! their 286 Come Comes 287 taste raste 296 FIRST LORD [not in F]
1.2. 0.2 [and elsewhere] Ventidius Ventigius 30 ever verie 41 their there 91 thousands, did thousands? Did 98 'em, and 'em? And 105 Oh, joy's e'en Oh ioyes, e'ne 107 To forget their faults, to forget their Faults. 113 s.d. Sound tucket [F continues: "Enter the Maskers of Amazons with Lutes in their hands, dauncing and playing"] 114 s.d. Enter Servant [after "How now?" in F] 120.1 Enter Cupid [F continues: "with the Maske of Ladies"] 124 Th'ear There 125 and smell all 129 FIRST LORD Luc. 129.1–2 [see notes at lines 113 and 120 above] 144.2 singles single 151 FIRST LADY 1 Lord 167 s.d. Enter Flavius [at line 176, after "welcome," in F] 181 SECOND SERVANT Ser. 211 rode rod 213 THIRD LORD 1. L.

2.1. 34 Ay, go, sir. I go sir? 35 in compt in. Come
2.2. 1 [and elsewhere] FLAVIUS Stew. 4 resumes resume 11 [and elsewhere] VARRO'S SERVANT Var. 13 [and elsewhere] ISIDORE'S SERVANT Isid. 41 broken debt, broken 64 [and elsewhere] ALL THE SERVANTS Al. [or All] 75, 104 mistress' Masters 81 PAGE Boy 96 Ay. Would I would 132 proposed propose 139 found sound 160 of or 191 Flaminius Flauius 211 treasure, cannot Treature cannot
3.1. 0.2 Enter enters 1 [and elsewhere] LUCULLUS'S SERVANT Ser.
3.2. 27 [and elsewhere] LUCIUS Lucil. 35 [and elsewhere] He's Has 61.1 [at line 60 in F]
3.3. 5 Owe Owes 23 I 'mongst 'mong'st 25 He'd Had
3.4. 0.1 Men man 1 [and elsewhere] VARRO'S FIRST SERVANT Var. man 2 [and elsewhere] TITUS'S SERVANT Tit. [and elsewhere] HORTENSIUS'S SERVANT Hort. 3 [and elsewhere] LUCIUS'S SERVANT Luci. 6 [and elsewhere] PHILOTUS'S SERVANT Phil. 14 recoverable. I fear recouerable, I feare: 15–16 purse; / That is, purse, that is: 45 [and elsewhere] VARRO'S SECOND SERVANT 2. Varro 59 If If't 78 an answer answer 88 HORTENSIUS'S Servant 1. Var. 89 BOTH VARRO'S SERVANTS 2. Var. 112 Sempronius Sempronius Vllorxa
3.5. 18 An And 23 behave behooue 51 lion, Lyon? felon fellow 52 judge, Iudge? 53 suffering. suffering, 66 Why, I Why 70 'em him 85 honors Honour
3.6. 1 FIRST LORD 1 [and so throughout scene] 19 here's heares 54 FIRST AND SECOND LORDS Both 80 tag legge 87 OTHERS other 91 with your you with 115 THIRD LORD 2 116 SECOND LORD 3
4.1. 6 steads! To general filths steeds, to generall Filthes. 8 fast; fast 9 back, backe; 13 Son Some
4.3. 10 senator Senators 12 pasture Pastour 13 lean leaue 16 grece grize 41 at, this at. This 88 tub-fast Fubfast 119 bars Barne 124 thy the 135 [and throughout scene] PHRYNIA AND TIMANDRA Both 158 scolds scold'st 187 thy human the humane 206 fortune future 225 mossed moyst 246 Outlives Out-liues: 254 clasped claspt: 255 swathe, proceeded swath proceeded, 257 drudges drugges 258 command, command'st: 287 my thy 314 meddlers Medlers 368–9 thee. I'd beat thee, but thee, Ile beate thee; But 387 son and sire Sunne and fire 401.1 [after line 402 in F] 402 them then 414 [and throughout scene] BANDITTI All 439 villainy Villaine 439–40 do 't, Like workmen. doo't. Like Workemen, 458 us, not vs not 462.1 Exeunt Exit 479 grant'st grunt'st, man, I man. / I 482 I; all I all 497 mild wilde 514 A If not a
5.1. 5–6 Phrynia and Timandra Phrinica and Timandylo 50 worship worshipt 66 go naked; men go, / Naked men 70 men 115 in vain vaine 125 chance chanc'd 132 cauterizing Cantherizing 146 sense since 147 its own fail it owne fall 181 reverend'st reuerends 194 through thorow
5.2. 1 [and throughout scene] THIRD SENATOR 1 5 [and throughout scene] FOURTH SENATOR 2 14 FIRST SENATOR 3
5.3. 2 Who's Whose
5.4. 27 out. out, 28 Shame . . . excess (Shame that they wanted, cunning in excesse) 55 Descend Defend 65 SOLDIER Mes.

Antony and Cleopatra

Copy text: the First Folio. Act and scene divisions, missing in the Folio, are editorially supplied.

1.1. 41 On One 52 whose who
1.2. 4 charge change 41 fertile fore-tell 64–5 Alexas [printed in F as s.p.] 83 Saw Saue 90 Alexas Alexias 93 [and through line 118] FIRST MESSENGER Messen. (or Mess.) 116 minds windes 119 ho how 120 SECOND MESSENGER 1. Mes. 121 THIRD MESSENGER 2. Mes. 124 FOURTH MESSENGER 3. Mes. 126 FOURTH MESSENGER Mes. 137.1 Enter Enobarbus [after "hatch," line 137, in F] 144 occasion an occasion 162 travel Trauaile 186 leave loue 191 Hath Haue 200 hair heire 202 place is places requires require
1.3. 2 who's Whose 20 What, says What sayes 43 services Seruicles 63 vials Violles 80 blood. No more. blood no more? 82 by my by

1.4. 3 Our One   **8 Vouchsafed** vouchsafe   **9 abstract** abstracts
34 FIRST MESSENGER *Mes.*   **44 deared** fear'd   **46 lackeying** lacking
48 SECOND MESSENGER *Mes.*   **57 wassails** Vassailes   **58 Modena**
Medena   **59 Pansa** *Pausa*   **77 we** me
1.5. 3 mandragora *Mandragoru*   **5 time** time: **35.1 Alexas** *Alexas from*
Caesar   **52 dumbed** dumbe   **53, What, was** What was
64 man mans
2.1. 2 [and throughout scene] MENAS *Mene.*   **22 joined** ioyne
39 ne'er neere   **42 warred** wan'd   **44–5 greater. . . . all,** greater, . . . all:
2.2. 77 Alexandria; you Alexandria you   **113 soldier only. Speak**
Souldier, onely speak   **128 so say** say   **129 reproof** proofe
180.1 Exeunt *Exit* omnes   *Manent* Manet   **204 lovesick . . . The**
Loue-sicke. With them the   **214 glow** gloue   **216 gentlewomen**
Gentlewoman   **233 heard** hard
2.3. 23 afeard a feare   **25 thee; . . . to thee.** thee no more but: when to
thee,   **31 away** alway   **32 [and elsewhere] Ventidius** *Ventigius*
41 s.d. Enter Ventidius [after "Ventigius," line 41, in F]
2.4. 6 th' Mount Mount   **9 MAECENAS, AGRIPPA** *Both*
2.5. 2 ALL *Omnes*   **10 river. There** Riuer there   **11 off, I** off. I
12 finned fine   **23 s.d. Enter a Messenger** [after "Italy," line 23, in F]
28 him, there him. / There   **44 is** 'tis   **85 s.d. Enter . . . again** [after
"sir" line 85, in F]
2.6. 0.1 Menas [listed after *Agrippa* in F]   **16 th'all-honored** all-honor'd
19 is his   **39 CAESAR, ANTONY, LEPIDUS** *Omnes*   **42–3 impatience.**
Though . . . telling, impatience: though . . . telling.   **58 compostion**
composion   **67 meanings** meaning   **71 more of** more   **83 CAESAR,**
ANTONY, LEPIDUS *All*   **83.1 Manent** *Manet*
2.7. 1 their th'their   **4 colored** Conlord   **39 s.d. whispers in 's ear** [at
line 41 in F]   **93 is** he is   **101 grows** grow   **113 bear** beate   **115 BOY**
[not in F]   **119 ALL** [not in F]   **122 off. Our** of our   **126 Splits**
Spleet's   **130 father's** Father   **132 MENAS** [not in F]
3.1. 5 [and throughout scene] SILIUS *Romaine*   **8 [and elsewhere]**
whither whether
3.2. 10 AGRIPPA *Ant.*   **16 figures** Figure   **49 full** the full   **60 wept**
weepe
3.3. 2 s.d. Enter . . . before [after "sir," line 2, in F]   **19 looked'st** look'st
3.4. 8 them, then   **9 took't** look't   **24 yours** your   **30 Your** You
38 has he's
3.5. 13 world would   **hast** hadst   **chops** chaps   **15 grind** the one
grind
3.6. 13 he there hither   **the kings** the King   **30 being, that** being that,
62 obstruct abstract   **73 Adallas** *Adullas*   **74 Manchus** *Mauchus*
76 Comagene Comageat   **Polemon** *Polemen*   **77 Lycaonia** Licoania
3.7. 4 it is it it   **14 Photinus, an** *Photinus* an   **19 s.d. Canidius**
Camidias [also spelled "*Camidius*" in this scene and elsewhere]
21 Brundusium Brandusium   **23 Toryne** Troine   **29 [and else-**
where] CANIDIUS *Cam.*   **36 muleteers** Militers   **52 Actium** Action
57 impossible; impossible   **67.1 Exeunt** exit   **70 leader's** led
Leaders leade   **73 CANIDIUS** *Ven.*   **80 Well I** Well, I   **82 in** with
3.8. 6 s.d. Exeunt exit
3.9. 4 s.d. Exeunt exit
3.10. 0.5. Enobarbus *Enobarbus and Scarus*   **14 June** Inne   **28 he** his
3.11. 6 ALL *Omnes*   **19 that** them   **46 seize** cease   **50 led** lead   **57 tow**
stowe   **58 Thy** The
3.12. 0.1. Dolabella *Dollabello*   **13 lessens** Lessons
3.13. 26 caparisons Comparisons   **34 alike. That** alike, that   **55 Cae-**
sar *Caesars*   **74 deputation** disputation   **76 kneel / Till** kneele. / Tell
him,   **94 s.d. Enter a Servant** [after "him," in line 94, in F]   **104 This**
the   **114–15 eyes, / In . . . filth** eyes / In . . . filth,   **133 s.d. Enter . . .**
Thidias [after "whipped," in line 133, in F]   **140 whipped . . . Hence-**
forth whipt. For following him, henceforth   **165 smite** smile
168 discandying discandering   **171 sits** sets   **202 on** in
204 s.d. Exeunt *Exit Exeunt*
4.2. 1 Domitius *Domitian*   **20 ALL** *Omnes*
4.3. 8 THIRD 1   **25, 31 ALL** *Omnes*
4.4. 5 too too, *Anthony*   **6 ANTONY** [not in F, or mistakenly placed in
line 5 as part of Cleopatra's speech]   **8 CLEOPATRA** [not in F]

24 CAPTAIN *Alex.*   **32–3 compliment . . . Now** Complement, Ile leaue
thee. / Now
4.5. 1, 3, 6 SOLDIER *Eros*   **17 Dispatch.—Enobarbus** Dispatch
Enobarbus   **17.1 Exeunt** Exit
4.6. 37–8 do 't . . . I do o't. I feele / I
4.7 3 s.d. Exeunt Exit   **8 s.d.** [after "heads," line 6, in F]
4.8. 2 gests guests   **18 My** Mine   **23 favoring** sauouring
4.12. 3 s.d. Alarum . . . fight [at 0.1 in F]   **4 augurers** Auguries
21 spanieled pannelled
4.13. 10 death. To death to'
4.14. 4 towered toward   **10 dislimns** dislimes   **19 Caesar** *Caesars*
104 ho how   **119 DERCETUS** *Decre.*   **145.1 Exeunt** Exit
4.15. 26–7 me. If . . . operation, me, if . . . operation.   **56 lived** the
liued. The   **78 e'en** in   **96.1 off** *of*
5.1. 0.1 Maecenas *Menas*   **3.1 DERCETUS** *Decretas*   **5, 13, 19 DERCETUS**
Dec.   **5 Dercetus** *Decretas*   **26 you sad, friends?** you sad Friends,
28, 31 AGRIPPA *Dol.*   **48.1** [after "says," line 51, in F]   **54 intents**
desires intents, desires,   **59 live** leaue
5.2. 26 dependency dependacie   **35** [F repeats s.p. *Pro.*]   **55 varletry**
Varlotarie   **69.1** [after "to him" in F]   **80 O, the** o'th'   **86 autumn**
'twas *Antony* it was   **102 success but** successe: But   **103 smites**
suites   **144 seal** seele   **156 soulless villain** Soule-lesse, Villain
178 merits in our name, merits, in our name   **207 s.d. Exit** [at line
206 in F]   **216 Ballad** Ballads   **223 my** mine   **228 Cydnus** *Cidrus*
318 awry away   **319.1 in** in, and Dolabella   **342–3 diadem . . . mis-**
tress; Diadem; . . . Mistris

Coriolanus

Copy text: the First Folio. Act divisions are from the Folio; scene divisions are from subsequent editorial tradition.

1.1. 7 [and throughout play] Marcius *Martius*   **15 on** one
33 SECOND CITIZEN *All*   **42–3 accusations. He** Accusations he
55 FIRST CITIZEN 2 *Cit.* [and so throughout scene]   **64 you. For your**
wants, you for your wants.   **90 stale's** scale's   **105 you. With** you
with   **108 tauntingly** taintingly   **123 you.** you,   **125 awhile,** awhile;
171 geese. You are no Geese you are: No   **214 Shouting** Shooting
218 unroofed vnroo'st   **227.1 Junius Annius**   **240 Lartius** *Lucius*
242 [and at 1.1.246 and 1.5.21] LARTIUS *Tit.*   **245, 249 [and else-**
where] FIRST SENATOR *Sen.*   **252.2 Manent** Manet
1.2. 0.1 Corioles *Coriolus*   **4 on** one   **16 Whither** Whether
27–8 Corioles / . . . before's *Corioles* / If . . . before's:
1.3. 37 that's that   **44 sword, contemning.—Tell** sword. *Contenning,*
tell   **82 VIRGILIA** *Vlug.*   **84 yarn** yearne   **85 Ithaca** *Athica*
105 lady. . . . now, Ladie, as she is now:
1.4. 0.3, 13.2 Corioles *Coriolus*   **18 up. Our** vp our   **20 s.d. Alarum far**
off [after line 20 in F]   **32 herd of—Boils** Heard of Byles   **43 trench-**
es. Follow 's Trenches followes   **46.1 gates** *Gati*   *and is shut in* [in
F, this is part of the s.d. at line 43.2]   **57 left, Marcius.** left *Martius,*
58 entire, intire;   **59 Were** Weare   **60 Cato's** *Calues*
1.5. 3.3 Exeunt [before "*Alarum*" in line 3.1 in F]   **7 them,** them.   **8 up.**
vp,   **9 him!** him
1.6. 9 s.d. [after line 9 in F]   **21 Who's** Whose   **22 flayed** Flead
30 wooed, in heart woo'd in heart;   **53 Antiates** Antients   **70 Lesser**
Lessen   **73 alone, or** alone: Or   **84 I** foure
1.7. 7.1 Exeunt Exit
1.8. 11 masked. For maskt, for   **12 Wert** Wer't
1.9. 32 good . . . all good, and good store of all,   **41 May** [F provides a
s.p., "*Mar.*"]   **49 shout** shoot   **64, 66 [and elsewhere] Caius Mar-**
cius *Marcus Caius*   **66 ALL** *Omnes*   **67, 78, 81, 89 CORIOLANUS**
Martius   **93.1 A flourish. Cornets.** [at the beginning of scene 10 in F]
1.10. 19 itself. Nor it selfe, nor
2.1. 18 with all withall   **24 how are** ho ware   **51 upon too** vppon, to
57 cannot can   **61 you you** you   **62 faces. If** faces, if   **64 bisson**
beesome   **70–1 faucet-seller** Forcet-seller   **85 are. When . . . pur-**
pose, are, when . . . purpose.   **106 VALERIA, VIRGILIA** 2. *Ladies*
123 brows, Menenius. Browes: *Menenius,*   **156 s.d.** [after line 156 in

F]   160.2 **[and elsewhere]** *Lartius Latius*   164 **"Coriolanus"**
Martius Caius Coriolanus   177 **wear** were   179 CORIOLANUS *Com.*
185 **You** Yon   203.2 *Brutus Enter Brutus*   **Sicinius** *Scicinius* [and
sometimes elsewhere]   233 **napless** Naples   254 **touch** teach
2.2. 25 **ascent** assent   67 **[and elsewhere]** FIRST SENATOR *Senat.*
81 **one on 's** on ones   91 **chin** Shinne   **bristled** brizled   108 **took;
from face to foot** tooke from face to foot: 155 *Manent Manet*
160 **here. On the marketplace** heere on th' Market place,
2.3. 28 **wedged** wadg'd   38–9 **it. I say, if** it, I say. If   52 **tongue** tougne
67 **but not** but   88, 91, 106 FOURTH CITIZEN 1   104 FIFTH CITIZEN 2
111 BOTH CITIZENS *Both*   114 **hire** higher   115 **toge** tongue
118 **do't,** doo't?   132 SIXTH CITIZEN 1. *Cit.*   134 SEVENTH CITIZEN
2. *Cit.*
3.1. 46 **suppliants for** Suppliants: for   60 **abused, set on. This** abus'd:
set on, this   94 **good** God!   129 **Their** There   137 **poll** pole
146 **Where one** Whereon   164 **He's** Has [also at line 165]
169 **bench? In a rebellion,** Bench, in a rebellion: 176 **s.d.** *Enter an
Aedile* [after line 175 in F]   181 ALL PATRICIANS *All*   187 **[and else-
where]** ALL PLEBEIANS *All*   189 ALL [at line 191 in F]   219 ALL PLE-
BEIANS *All Ple.*   233.1–2 [preceded in F by *"Exeunt"*]   234 **your** our
235 CORIOLANUS *Com.*   242 COMINIUS *Corio.*   243 CORIOLANUS
Mene.   245 MENENIUS [not in F]   283 **comes 't** com'st   315 SICINIUS
Menen.   334 **bring him** bring him in peace
3.2. 7 A PATRICIAN *Noble*   14 **s.d.** *Enter Volumnia* [after line 6 in F]
23 **thwartings** things   34 **herd** heart   67 **son, these . . . nobles;**
Sonne: These . . . Nobles,   80 **With** Which   103 **bear? Well, I** beare
well? I   104 **plot to lose,** Plot, to loose   115 **drum, into a pipe**
Drumme into a Pipe,   117 **lulls** lull
3.3. 5 **s.d.** [after line 5 in F]   34 **for th'** fourth   38 **Throng** Through
59 **accents** Actions   73 **hell fold** hell. Fould   76 **clutched** clutcht:
77 **numbers,** numbers.   107 **it; in** it. In   118 **for** from   143–4
blows! Despising . . . city, thus blowes, despising . . . City. Thus

145.1 *Cominius Cominius, with Cumalijs*   147 **Hoo! Hoo!** Hoo, oo
147.1 [after line 145.1 in F]
4.1. 5 **chances** chances.   24 **thee** the   34 **wilt** will   37 VIRGILIA *Corio.*
4.2. 23 **words,** words.   46 **s.d.** *Exeunt Exit*   55 [F has s.d. *"Exeunt"*]
56 **s.d.** *Exeunt* Exit
4.3. 9 **approved** appear'd   32 **will** well
4.4. 6 **s.d.** [after line 6 in F]   23 **hate** haue
4.5. 75 **requited** requitted: 83 **Whooped** Hoop'd   136 **o'erbear't**
o're-beate   152.2 *Two Enter two*   169 **on** one   181, 185 FIRST AND
SECOND SERVINGMEN *Both*   194 **him, directly** him directly,   195 **Cor-
loles;** Corioles,   209 **sowl** sole   211 **polled** poul'd   233 **sleepy** sleepe
4.6. 10 **s.d.** [after line 9 in F]   21 **[and elsewhere]** ALL CITIZENS *All*
36 **lamentation** Lamention   61 **come** comming   78 SECOND MES-
SENGER *Mes.*   127 BOTH TRIBUNES *Tri.*   144 **one** oue   146 ALL CITI-
ZENS *Omnes*   151 **us. That** vs, that   165.1 *Exeunt* Exit
4.7. 19 **him. Although** him, although   21 **fairly** fairely: 34 **osprey**
Aspray   37 **'twas** 'was   39 **defect** detect   49 **virtues** Vertue,
55 **falter** fouler
5.2. 65 **by my** my   76 **our** your   88 **pity note how much.** pitty: Note
how much,   95.1 *Manent Manet*
5.3. 15 **accept. To** accept, to   16 **more, a** more: A   48 **prate** pray
63 **holp** hope   66 **curded** curdied   127 YOUNG MARCIUS *Boy*
149 **fine** fiue   152 **charge** change   163 **clucked** clock'd   169 **with
our** with him with our   192 **stead** steed
5.4. 40 **[and throughout scene]** SECOND MESSENGER *Mess.*   49.1 *all
together* altogether   51 **cymbals** Symboles
5.5. 4 **Unshout** Vnshoot
5.6. 33 **projects to accomplish,** projects, to accomplish   43–4 **it /
For . . . him.** it: / For . . . him,   46 **lies, he** Lies; he   56 **second. When**
second, when   57 **way his** way. His   63 ALL LORDS *All*   104 **other**
others   117 **pieces, Volsces. Men** peeces Volces men   121 **Fluttered**
Flatter'd   136.1 *Draw Draw both*

Glossary

Shakespearean Words and Meanings of Frequent Occurrence

A

'A: he (unaccented form).

Abate: lessen, diminish; blunt, reduce; deprive; bar, leave out of account, except; depreciate; humble.

Abuse (N): insult, error, misdeed, offense, crime; imposture, deception; also the modern sense.

Abuse (V): deceive, misapply, put to a bad use; maltreat; frequently the modern sense.

Addition: something added to one's name to denote rank; mark of distinction; title.

Admiration: wonder; object of wonder.

Admire: wonder at.

Advantage (N): profit, convenience, benefit; opportunity, favorable opportunity; pecuniary profit; often shades toward the modern sense.

Advantage (V): profit, be of benefit to, benefit; augment.

Advice: reflection, consideration, deliberation, consultation.

Affect: aim at, aspire to, incline toward; be fond of, be inclined; love; act upon contagiously (as a disease). (PAST PART.) **Affected**: disposed, inclined, in love, loved.

Affection: passion, love; emotion, feeling, mental tendency, disposition; wish, inclination; affectation.

Alarum: signal calling soldiers to arms (in stage directions).

An: if; but; **an if:** if, though, even if.

Anon: at once, soon; presently, by and by.

Answer: return, requite; atone for; render an account of, account for; obey, agree with; also the modern sense.

Apparent: evident, plain; seeming.

Argument: subject, theme, reason, cause; story; excuse.

As: according as; as far as; namely; as if; in the capacity of; that; so that; that is, that they.

Assay: try, attempt; accost, address; challenge.

Atone: reconcile; set at one.

Attach: arrest, seize.

Aweful, awful: commanding reverential fear or respect; profoundly respectful or reverential.

B

Band: bond, fetters, manacle (leash for a dog). **Band** and **bond** are etymologically the same word; **band** was formerly used in both senses.

Basilisk: fabulous reptile said to kill by its look. The basilisk of popular superstition was a creature with legs, wings, a serpentine and winding tail, and a crest or comb somewhat like a cock. It was the offspring of a cock's egg hatched under a toad or serpent.

Bate: blunt, abate, reduce; deduct, except.

Battle: army; division of an army.

Beshrew: curse, blame; used as a mild curse, "Bad or ill luck to."

Bias: tendency, bent, inclination, swaying influence; term in bowling applied to the form of the bowl, the oblique line in which it runs, and the kind of impetus given to cause it to run obliquely.

Blood: nature, vigor; supposed source of emotion; passion; spirit, animation; one of the four humors (see **humor**).

Boot (N): advantage, profit; something given in addition to the bargain; booty, plunder.

Boot (V): profit, avail.

Brave (ADJ.): fine, gallant; splendid, finely arrayed, showy; ostentatiously defiant.

Brave (V): challenge, defy; make splendid.

Brook: tolerate, endure.

C

Can: can do; know; be skilled; sometimes used for *did*.

Capable: comprehensive; sensible, impressible, susceptible; capable of; gifted, intelligent.

Careful: anxious, full of care; provident; attentive.

Carry: manage, execute; be successful, win; conquer; sustain; endure.

Censure (N): judgment, opinion; critical opinion, unfavorable opinion.

Censure (V): judge, estimate; pass sentence or judgment.

Character (N): writing, printing, record; handwriting; cipher; face, features (bespeaking inward qualities).

Character (V): write, engrave, inscribe.

Check (N): reproof; restraint.

Check (V): reprove, restrain, keep from; control.

Circumstance: condition, state of affairs, particulars; adjunct details; detailed narration, argument, or discourse; formality, ceremony.

Clip: embrace; surround.

Close: secret, private; concealed; uncommunicative; enclosed.

Cog: cheat.

Coil: noise, disturbance, turmoil; fuss, to-do, bustle.

Color: appearance; pretext, pretense; excuse.

Companion: fellow (used contemptuously).

Complete: accomplished, fully endowed; perfect, perfect in quality; also frequently the modern sense.

Complexion: external appearance; temperament, disposition; the four complexions—sanguine, choleric, phlegmatic, and melancholy—corresponding to the four humors (see **humor**); also the modern sense.

Composition: compact, agreement, constitution.

Compound: settle, agree.

Conceit: conception, idea, thought; mental faculty, wit; fancy, imagination; opinion, estimate; device, invention, design.

Condition: temperament, disposition; characteristic, property, quality; social or official position, rank or status; covenant, treaty, contract.

Confound: waste, spend, invalidate, destroy; undo, ruin; mingle indistinguishably, mix, blend.

Confusion: destruction, overthrow, ruin; mental agitation.

Continent: that which contains or encloses; earth, globe; sum, summary.

Contrive: plot; plan; spend or pass (time).

Conversation: conduct, deportment; social intercourse, association.

Converse: hold intercourse; associate with, have to do with.

Cope: encounter, meet; have to do with.

Copy: model, pattern; example; minutes or memoranda.

Cousin: any relative not belonging to one's immediate family.

Cry you mercy: beg your pardon.

Cuckold: husband whose wife is unfaithful.

Curious: careful, fastidious; anxious, concerned; made with care, skillfully, intricately, or daintily wrought; particular.

Cursed, curst: shrewish, perverse, spiteful.

D

Dainty: minute; scrupulous, particular; particular about (with **of**); refined, elegant; also the modern sense.

Date: duration, termination, term of existence; limit or end of a term or period, term.

Dear: precious; best; costly; important; affectionate; hearty; grievous, dire; also the modern sense.

Debate: discuss; fight.

Decay (N): downfall, ruin; cause of ruin.

Decay (V): perish, be destroyed; destroy.

Defeat (N): destruction, ruin.

Defeat (V): destroy, disfigure, ruin.

Defy: challenge, challenge to a fight; reject; despise.

Demand (N): inquiry; request.

Demand (V): inquire, question; request.

Deny: refuse (to do something); refuse permission; refuse to accept; refuse admittance; disown.

Depart (N): departure.

Depart (V): part; go away from, leave, quit; take leave (of one another); **depart with, withal:** part with, give up.

Derive: gain, obtain; draw upon, direct (to); descend; pass by descent, be descended or inherited; trace the origin of.

Difference: diversity of opinion, disagreement, dissension, dispute; characteristic or distinguishing feature; alteration or addition to a coat of arms to distinguish a younger or lateral branch of a family.

Digest: arrange, perfect; assimilate, amalgamate; disperse, dissipate; comprehend, understand; put up with (FIG. from the physical sense of digesting food).

Discourse (N): reasoning, reflection; talk, act of conversing, conversation; faculty of conversing; familiar intercourse; relating (as by speech).

Discourse (V): speak, talk, converse; pass (the time) in talk; say, utter, tell, give forth; narrate, relate.

Discover: uncover, expose to view; divulge, reveal, make known; spy out, reconnoiter; betray; distinguish, discern; also the modern sense.

Dispose (N): disposal; temperament, bent of mind, disposition; external manner.

Dispose (V): distribute, manage, make use of; deposit, put or stow away; regulate, order, direct; come to terms. (PAST PART.) **Disposed:** in a good frame of mind; inclined to be merry.

Dispute: discuss, reason; strive against, resist.

Distemper (V): disturb; (N): disorder, ill humor; illness.

Doit: old Dutch coin, one-half an English farthing.

Doubt (N): suspicion, apprehension; fear, danger, risk; also the modern sense.

Doubt (V): suspect, apprehend; fear; also the modern sense.

Doubtful: inclined to suspect, suspicious, apprehensive; not to be relied on; almost certain.

Duty: reverence, respect, expression of respect; submission to authority, obedience; due.

E

Earnest: money paid as an installment to secure a bargain; partial payment; often used with *quibble* in the modern sense.

Ease: comfort, assistance, leisure; idleness, sloth, inactivity; also the modern sense.

Ecstasy: frenzy, madness, state of being beside oneself, excitement, bewilderment; swoon; rapture.

Element: used to refer to the simple substances of which all material bodies were thought to be composed; specifically earth, air, fire, and water, corresponding to the four humors (see **humor**); atmosphere, sky; atmospheric agencies or powers; that one of the four elements which is the natural abode of a creature; hence, natural surroundings, sphere.

Engage: pledge, pawn, mortgage; bind by a promise, swear to; entangle, involve; enlist; embark on an enterprise.

Engine: mechanical contrivance; artifice, device, plot.

Enlarge: give free scope to; set at liberty, release.

Entertain: keep up, maintain, accept; take into one's service; treat; engage (someone's) attention or thought; occupy, while or pass away pleasurably; engage (as an enemy); receive.

Envious: malicious, spiteful, malignant.

Envy: ill-will, malice; hate; also the modern sense.

Even: uniform; direct, straightforward; exact, precise; equable, smooth, comfortable; equal, equally balanced.

Event: outcome; affair, business; also frequently the modern sense.

Exclaim: protest, rail; accuse, blame (with **on**), reproach.

Excursion: stage battle or skirmish (in stage directions).

Excuse: seek to extenuate (a fault); maintain the innocence of; clear oneself, justify or vindicate oneself; decline.

F

Fact: deed, act; crime.

Faction: party, class, group, set (of persons); party strife, dissension; factious quarrel, intrigue.

Fail: die, die out; err, be at fault; omit, leave undone.

Fair (N): fair thing; one of the fair sex; someone beloved; beauty (the abstract concept).

Fair (ADJ.): just; clear, distinct; beautiful; of light complexion or color of hair.

Fair (ADV): fairly.

Fairly: beautifully, handsomely; courteously, civilly; properly, honorably, honestly; becomingly, appropriately; favorably, fortunately; softly, gently, kindly.

Fall: let fall, drop; happen, come to pass; befall; shades frequently toward the modern senses.

Falsely: wrongly; treacherously; improperly.

Fame: report; rumor; reputation.

Familiar (N): intimate friend; familiar or attendant spirit, demon associated with, and obedient to, a person.

Familiar (ADJ.): intimate, friendly; belonging to household or family, domestic; well-known; habitual, ordinary, trivial; plain, easily understood.

Fancy: fantasticalness; imaginative conception, flight of imagination; amorous inclination or passion, love; liking, taste.

Fantasy: fancy, imagination; caprice, whim.

Favor: countenance, face; complexion; aspect, appearance; leave, permission, pardon; attraction, charm, good will; **in favor:** benevolently.

Fear (N): dread, apprehension; dreadfulness; object of dread or fear.

Fear (V): be apprehensive or concerned about, mistrust, doubt; frighten, make afraid.

Fearful: exciting or inspiring fear, terrible, dreadful; timorous, apprehensive, full of fear.

Feature: shape or form of body, figure; shapeliness, comeliness.

Fellow: companion; partaker, sharer (of); equal, match; customary form of address to a servant or an inferior (sometimes used contemptuously or condescendingly).

Fine (N): end, conclusion; **in fine:** finally.

Fine (ADJ.): highly accomplished or skillful; exquisitely fashioned, delicate; refined, subtle; frequently the modern sense.

Flaw: fragment; crack, fissure; tempest, squall, gust of wind; outburst of passion.

Flesh (V): reward a hawk or hound with a piece of flesh of the game killed to excite its eagerness of the chase; hence, to inflame by a foretaste of success; initiate or inure to bloodshed (used for a first time in battle); harden, train.

Flourish: fanfare of trumpets (in stage directions).

Fond: foolish, doting; **fond of:** eager for; also the modern sense.

Fool: term of endearment and pity; frequently the modern sense.

For that, for why: because.

Forfend: forbid, avert.

Free: generous, magnanimous; candid, open; guiltless, innocent.

Front: forehead, face; foremost line of battle; beginning.

Furnish: equip, fit out (furnish forth); endow; dress, decorate, embellish.

G

Gear: apparel, dress; stuff, substance, thing, article; discourse, talk; matter, business, affair.

Get: beget.

Gloss: specious fair appearance; lustrous surface.

Go to: expression of remonstrance, impatience, disapprobation, or derision.

Grace (N): kindness, favor, charm, divine favor; fortune, luck; beneficent virtue; sense of duty or propriety; mercy, pardon; embellish; **do grace:** reflect credit on, do honor to, do a favor for.

Grace (V): gratify, delight; honor, favor.

Groat: coin equal to four pence.

H

Habit: dress, garb, costume; bearing, demeanor, manner; occasionally in the modern sense.

Happily: haply, perchance, perhaps; fortunately.

Hardly: with difficulty.

Have at: I shall come at (you) (i.e., listen to me), I shall attack (a person or thing); let me at.

Have with: I shall go along with; let me go along with; come along.

Having: possession, property, wealth, estate; endowments, accomplishments.

Head: armed force.

Hind: servant, slave; rustic, boor, clown.

His: its. **His** was historically the possessive form of both the masculine and neuter pronouns. **Its,** although not common in Shakespeare's time, occurs in the plays occasionally.

Holp: helped (archaic past tense).

Home: fully, satisfactorily, thoroughly, plainly, effectually; to the quick.

Honest: holding an honorable position, honorable, respectable; decent, kind, seemly, befitting, proper; chaste; genuine; loosely used as an epithet of approbation.

Humor: mood, temper, cast of mind, temperament, disposition; vagary, fancy, whim; moisture (the literal sense); a physiological and, by transference, a psychological term applied to the four chief fluids of the human body—phlegm, blood, bile or choler, and black bile or melancholy. A person's disposition and temporary state of mind were determined according to the relative proportions of these fluids in the body; consequently, a person was said to be phlegmatic, sanguine, choleric, or melancholy.

I

Image: likeness; visible form; representation; embodiment, type; mental picture, creation of the imagination.

Influence: supposed flowing from the stars or heavens of an ethereal fluid, acting upon the characters and destinies of men (used metaphorically).

Inform: take shape, give form to, imbue, inspire; instruct, teach; charge (against).

Instance: evidence, proof, sign, confirmation; motive, cause.

Invention: power of mental creation, the creative faculty; work of the imagination, artistic creation, premeditated design; device, plan, scheme.

J

Jar (N): discord in music; quarrel, discord.

Jar (V): be out of tune; be discordant, quarrel.

Jump: agree, tally, coincide, fit exactly; risk, hazard.

K

Keep: continue, carry on; dwell, lodge, guard, defend, care for, employ, be with; restrain, control; confine in prison.

Kind (N): nature, established order of things; manner, fashion, respect; race, class, kindred, family; **by kind:** naturally.

Kind (ADJ.): natural; favorable; affectionate.

Kindly (ADJ.): natural, appropriate; agreeable; innate; benign.

Kindly (ADV): naturally; gently, courteously.

L

Large: liberal, bounteous, lavish; free, unrestrained; **at large:** at length, in full; in full detail, as a whole, in general.

Late: lately.

Learn: teach; inform (someone of something); also the modern sense.

Let: hinder.

Level: aim; also shades toward the modern sense.

Liberal: possessed of the characteristics and qualities of wellborn persons; genteel, becoming, refined; free in speech; unrestrained by prudence or decorum; licentious.

Lie: be in bed; be still; be confined, be kept in prison; dwell, sojourn, reside, lodge.

Like: please, feel affection; liken, compare.

List (N): strip of cloth, selvedge; limit, boundary; desire.

List (V): choose, desire, please; listen to.

Liver: the seat of love and of violent passions generally (see also **spleen**).

'Long of: owing to, on account of.

Look: power to see; take care, see to it; expect; seek, search for.

M

Make: do; have to do (with); consider; go; be effective, make up, complete; also the modern sense.

Manage: management, conduct, administration; action and paces to which a horse is trained; short gallop at full speed.

Marry: mild interjection equivalent to "Indeed!" Originally, an oath by the Virgin Mary.

May: can; also frequently the modern sense to denote probability; **might** has corresponding meanings and uses.

Mean, means (N): instrument, agency, method; effort; opportunity (for doing something); something interposed or intervening; money, wealth (frequently in the plural form); middle position, medium; tenor or alto part in singing (usually in the singular form).

Mean (ADJ.): average, moderate, middle; of low degree, station, or position; undignified, base.

Measure (N): grave or stately dance, graceful motion; tune, melody, musical accompaniment; treatment meted out; moderation, proportion; limit; distance, reach.

Measure (V): judge, estimate; traverse.

Mere: absolute, sheer; pure, unmixed; downright, sincere.

Mew (up): coop up (as used of a hawk), shut up, imprison, confine.

Mind (N): thoughts, judgment, opinion, message; purpose, intention, desire; disposition; also the modern sense of the mental faculty.

Mind (V): remind; perceive, notice, attend; intend.

Minion: saucy woman, hussy; follower; favorite, favored person, darling (often used contemptuously).

Misdoubt (N): suspicion.

Misdoubt (V): mistrust, suspect.

Model: pattern, replica, likeness.

Modern: ordinary, commonplace, everyday.

Modest: moderate, marked by moderation, becoming; characterized by decency and propriety; chaste.

Moiety: half; share; small part, lesser share; portion, part of.

Mortal: fatal; deadly, of or for death; belonging to mankind; human, pertaining to human affairs.

Motion: power of movement; suggestion, proposal; movement of the soul; impulse, prompting; also the modern sense.

Move: make angry; urge, incite, instigate, arouse, prompt; propose, make a proposal to, apply to, appeal to, suggest; also the modern sense.

Muse: wonder, marvel; grumble, complain.

N

Napkin: handkerchief.

Natural: related by blood; having natural or kindly feeling; also the modern sense.

Naught: useless, worthless; wicked, naughty.

Naughty: wicked; good for nothing, worthless.

Nerves: sinews.

Nice: delicate; fastidious, dainty, particular, scrupulous; minute, subtle; shy, coy; reluctant, unwilling; unimportant, insignificant, trivial; accurate, precise; wanton, lascivious.

Nothing (ADJ.): not at all.

O

Of: from, away from; during; on; by; as regards; instead of; **out of:** compelled by; made from.

Offer: make an attack; menace; venture, dare, presume.

Opinion: censure; reputation or credit; favorable estimate of oneself; self-conceit, arrogance; self-confidence; public opinion, reputation; also the modern sense.

Or: before; also used conjunctively where no alternative is implied; **or . . . or:** either . . . or; whether . . . or.

Out (ADV): without, outside; abroad; fully, quite; at an end, finished; at variance, aligned the wrong way.

Out (INTERJ.): an expression of reproach, impatience, indignation, or anger.

Owe: own; also the modern sense.

P

Pack (V): load; depart, begone; conspire.

Pageant: show, spectacle, spectacular entertainment; device on a moving carriage.

Pain: punishment, penalty; labor, trouble, effort; also frequently the modern sense.

Painted: specious, unreal, counterfeit.

Parle (N): parley, conference, talk; bugle call for parley.

Part (V): depart, part from; divide.

Particular (N): detail; personal interest or concern; details of a private nature; single person.

Party: faction, side, part, cause; partner, ally.

Pass (V): pass through, traverse; exceed; surpass; pledge.

Passing (ADJ. and ADV.): surpassing, surpassingly, exceedingly.

Passion (N): powerful or violent feeling, violent sorrow or grief; painful affection or disorder of the body; sorrow; feelings or desires of love; passionate speech or outburst.

Passion (v): sorrow, grieve.

Peevish: silly, senseless, childish; perverse, obstinate, stubborn; sullen.

Perforce: by violence or compulsion; forcibly; necessarily.

Phoenix: mythical Arabian bird believed to be the only one of its kind; it lived five or six hundred years, after which it burned itself to ashes and reemerged to live through another cycle.

Physic: medical faculty; healing art, medical treatment; remedy, medicine, healing property.

Pitch: height; specifically, the height to which a falcon soars before swooping on its prey (often used figuratively); tarlike substance.

Policy: conduct of affairs (especially public affairs); prudent management; stratagem, trick; contrivance; craft, cunning.

Port: bearing, demeanor; state, style of living, social station; gate.

Possess: have or give possession or command (of something); inform, acquaint; also the modern sense.

Post (N): courier, messenger; post-horse; haste.

Post (v): convey swiftly; hasten, ignore through haste (with **over** or **off**).

Practice (N): execution; exercise (especially for instruction); stratagem, intrigue; conspiracy, plot, treachery.

Practice (v): perform, take part in; use stratagem, craft, or artifice; scheme, plot; play a joke on.

Pregnant: resourceful; disposed, inclined; clear, obvious.

Present (ADJ.): ready, immediate, prompt, instant.

Present (v): represent.

Presently: immediately, at once.

Prevent: forestall, anticipate, foresee; also the modern sense.

Process: drift, tenor, gist; narrative, story; formal command, mandate.

Proof: test, trial, experiment; experience; issue, result; proved or tested strength of armor or arms; also the modern sense.

Proper: (one's or its) own; peculiar, exclusive; excellent; honest, respectable; handsome, elegant, fine, good-looking.

Proportion: symmetry; size; form, carriage, appearance, shape; portion, allotment; rhythm.

Prove: make trial of; put to test; show or find out by experience.

Purchase (N): acquisition; spoil, booty.

Purchase (v): acquire, gain, obtain; strive, exert oneself; redeem, exempt.

Q

Quaint: skilled, clever; pretty, fine, dainty; handsome, elegant; carefully or ingeniously wrought or elaborated.

Quality: that which constitutes (something); essential being; good natural gifts; accomplishment, attainment, property; art, skill; rank, position; profession, occupation, business; party, side; manner, style; cause, occasion.

Quick: living (used substantively to mean "living flesh"); alive; lively, sharp, piercing; hasty, impatient; with child.

Quillets: verbal niceties, subtle distinctions.

Quit: requite, reward; set at liberty; acquit, remit; pay for, clear off.

R

Rack (v): stretch or strain beyond normal extent or capacity to endure; strain oneself; distort.

Rage (N): madness, insanity; vehement pain; angry disposition; violent passion or appetite; poetic enthusiasm; warlike ardor or fury.

Rage (v): behave wantonly or riotously; act with fury or violence; enrage; pursue furiously.

Range: extend or lie in the same plane (with); occupy a position; rove, roam; be inconstant; traverse.

Rank (ADJ.): coarsely luxuriant; puffed up, swollen, fat, abundant; full, copious; rancid; lustful; corrupt, foul.

Rate (N): estimate; value or worth; estimation, consideration; standard, style.

Rate (v): allot; calculate, estimate, compute; reckon, consider; be of equal value (with); chide, scold, berate; drive away by chiding or scolding.

Recreant (N): traitor, coward, cowardly wretch (also as ADJ.).

Remorse: pity, compassion; also the modern sense.

Remove: removal, absence; period of absence; change.

Require: ask, inquire of, request.

Resolve: dissolve, melt, dissipate; answer; free from doubt or uncertainty, convince; inform; decide; also the modern sense.

Respect (N): consideration, reflection, act of seeing, view; attention, notice; decency, modest deportment; also the modern sense.

Respect (v): esteem, value, prize; regard, consider; heed, pay attention to; also the modern sense.

Round: spherical; plain, direct, brusque; fair; honest.

Roundly: plainly, unceremoniously.

Rub: obstacle (a term in the game of bowls); unevenness; inequality.

S

Sack: generic term for Spanish and Canary wines; sweet white wine.

Sad: grave, serious; also the modern sense.

Sadness: seriousness; also the modern sense.

Sans: without (French preposition).

Scope: object, aim, limit; freedom, license; free play.

Seal: bring to completion or conclusion; conclude, confirm, ratify, stamp; also the modern sense.

Sennet: a series of notes sounded on a trumpet to herald the approach or departure of a procession (used in stage directions).

Sense: mental faculty, mind; mental perception, import, rational meaning; physical perception; sensual nature; **common sense:** ordinary or untutored perception, observation or knowledge.

Sensible: capable of physical feeling or perception, sensitive; capable of or exhibiting emotion; rational; capable of being perceived.

Serve: be sufficient; be favorable; succeed; satisfy the need for; serve a turn; answer the purpose.

Several: separate, distinct, different; particular, private; various.

Shadow: shade, shelter; reflection; likeness, image; ghost; representation, picture of the imagination, phantom; also the modern sense.

Shift: change; stratagem, strategy, trick, contrivance, device to serve a purpose; **make shift:** manage.

Shrewd: malicious, mischievous, ill-natured; shrewish; bad, of evil import, grievous; severe.

Sirrah: ordinary or customary form of address to inferiors or servants; disrespectful form of address.

Sith: since.

Smock: woman's undergarment; used typically for "a woman."

Something: somewhat.

Sometime: sometimes, from time to time; once, formerly; at times, at one time.

Speed (N): fortune, success; protecting and assisting power; also the modern sense.

Speed (v): fare (well or ill); succeed; be successful; assist, guard, favor.

Spleen: the seat of emotions and passions; violent passion; fiery temper; malice; anger, rage; impulse, fit of passion; caprice; impetuosity (see also **liver**).

Spoil: destruction, ruin; plunder; slaughter, massacre.

Starve: die of cold or hunger; be benumbed with cold; paralyze, disable; allow or cause to die.

State: degree, rank; social position, station; pomp, splendor, outward display, clothes; court, household of a great person; shades into the modern sense.

Stay: wait, wait for; sustain; stand; withhold, withstand; stop.

Stead: assist; be of use to, benefit, help.

Still: always, ever, continuously or continually, constant or constantly; silent, mute; also modern senses.

Stomach: appetite, inclination, disposition; resentment; angry temper, resentful feeling; proud spirit, courage.

Straight: immediately.

Strange: belonging to another country or person, foreign, unfriendly; new, fresh; ignorant; estranged.

Success: issue, outcome (good or bad); sequel, succession, descent (as from father to son).

Suggest: tempt; prompt; seduce.

Suggestion: temptation.

T

Table: memorandum, tablet; surface on which something is written or drawn.

Take: strike; bewitch; charm; infect; destroy; repair to for refuge; modern senses.

Tall: goodly, fine; strong in fight, valiant.

Target: shield.

Tax: censure, blame, accuse.

Tell: count; relate.

Thorough: through.

Throughly: thoroughly.

Toward: in preparation; forthcoming, about to take place; modern senses.

Toy: trifle, idle fancy; folly.

Train: lure, entice, allure, attract.

Trencher: wooden dish or plate.

Trow: think, suppose, believe; know.

U

Undergo: undertake, perform; modern sense.

Undo: ruin.

Unfold: disclose, tell, make known, reveal; communicate.

Unhappy: evil, mischievous; fatal, ill-fated; miserable.

Unjust: untrue, dishonest; unjustified, groundless; faithless, false.

Unkind: unnatural, cruel, faulty; compare **kind.**

Use (n): custom, habit; interest paid.

Use (v): make practice of; be accustomed; put out at interest.

V

Vail: lower, let fall.

Vantage: advantage; opportunity; benefit, profit; superiority.

Virtue: general excellence; valor, bravery; merit, goodness, honor; good accomplishment, excellence in culture; power; essence, essential part.

W

Want: lack; be in need of; be without.

Watch: be awake, lie awake, sit up at night, lose sleep; keep from sleep (TRANS.).

Weed: garment, clothes.

Welkin: sky, heavens.

Wink: close the eyes; close the eyes in sleep; have the eyes closed; seem not to see.

Withal: with; with it, this, or these; together with this; at the same time.

Wot: know.

Index